"This volume fills a wide and expanding gap for Christians who continue to struggle with the relationship of evangelical Christianity to the claims of science. Specifically, for those who have rightly rejected the claims of unguided evolution, this book takes on the similar challenge of the possibility of theistic evolution. Scholarly, informative, well-researched, and well-argued, this will be the best place to begin to ferret out reasons for conflict among Christians who take science seriously. I highly recommend this resource."

> **K. Scott Oliphint**, Professor of Apologetics and Systematic Theology and Dean of Faculty, Westminster Theological Seminary

"*Theistic evolution* means different things to different people. This book carefully identifies, and thoroughly debunks, an insidious, all-too-commonly accepted sense of the phrase even among Christians: that there is no physical reason to suspect life was designed, and that evolution proceeded in the unguided, unplanned manner Darwin himself championed."

> **Michael J. Behe**, Professor of Biological Sciences, Lehigh University; author, *Darwin's Black Box* and *The Edge of Evolution*

"Evangelicals are experiencing unprecedented pressure to make peace with the Darwinian theory of evolution, and increasing numbers are waving the white flag. The tragic irony is that evolutionary theory is more beleaguered than ever in the face of multiplying scientific challenges and growing dissent. Until now there has been no consolidated scholarly response to theistic evolution that combines scientific, philosophical, and theological critiques. I was excited to hear about this ambitious project, but the final book has exceeded my expectations. The editors have assembled an impressive cast of experts and the content is top-notch. Theistic evolutionists, and those swayed by their arguments, owe it to themselves to read and digest this compendium of essays. This book is timely and necessary—quite literally a godsend."

> **James N. Anderson**, Professor of Theology and Philosophy, Reformed Theological Seminary, Charlotte; author, *What's Your Worldview?*

"Repeating the error of medieval Christianity, theistic evolution absolutizes the words of finite, fallible humans and relativizes the Word of an infinite, infallible God. As this tremendous and timely collection thoroughly demonstrates, scientific stagnation, circular philosophy, and heterodox theology are the inevitable results. This is simply the best critique of theistic evolution available."

> **Angus Menuge**, Chair of Philosophy, Concordia University Wisconsin; President, Evangelical Philosophical Society; author, *Agents Under Fire: Materialism and the Rationality of Science*; Editor, *Reading God's World: The Scientific Vocation*

"This significant book persuasively argues that theistic evolution fails as a theory—scientifically, philosophically, and biblically. And with its broad-ranging collection of essays, it mounts a very impressive case. Strongly recommended, both for those who seek to defend Christianity intelligently and for those who find Christianity implausible because of the claims of neo-Darwinism."

> **Michael Reeves**, President and Professor of Theology, Union School of Theology

"The theistic evolution solution to the creation-evolution controversy herein encounters a substantial, sustained, and trenchant critique. The team of scientific, philosophical, and theological scholars assembled by the editors have joined to confront the venerable theory with a stinging challenge that its adherents will have to answer if they value their scholarly integrity. This is necessary reading for those who wrestle with the great questions surrounding the origins of life."

> **Peter A. Lillback**, President, Westminster Theological Seminary

"This landmark achievement contains an amazing collection of chapters by a powerful group of fully qualified experts in molecular biology, mathematics, philosophy, and theology. The chapters are clear, detailed in addressing all aspects of theistic evolution, and of a tone in keeping with 1 Peter 3:15: 'with gentleness and respect.' I consider this a must-have book for any Christian who wants to be able to give compelling answers to others who believe in theistic evolution."

> **Richard A. Carhart**, Professor Emeritus of Physics, University of Illinois at Chicago

"This book offers a much-needed, comprehensive critique of evolutionary creationism (theistic evolution), covering its scientific, philosophical, theological, and biblical deficiencies. It devotes much space in particular to the scientific side. This focus is needed because of the common, unwarranted assumption that Darwinism is doing well as measured by scientific evidence. Several articles, from different angles, show how much Darwinism depends on seeing all biological evidence through the lens of a prior commitment to faith in the philosophy of naturalism—particularly the ungrounded assumption that unguided natural forces must suffice as a complete account of origins."

> **Vern S. Poythress**, Professor of New Testament Interpretation, Westminster Theological Seminary

"'In wisdom you have made them all,' says the psalmist of God's activities in nature (Ps. 104:24). But believers today, often blinded by modern science, fail to see that divine wisdom. This valuable volume challenges the assumptions of much scientific endeavor and proposes a fresh paradigm that is open to God's involvement in nature. It deserves a wide and thoughtful readership."

> **Gordon Wenham**, Emeritus Professor of Old Testament, University of Gloucestershire, United Kingdom

"Few scholars even marginally knowledgeable regarding the nature of this debate could read objectively the lineup of scholars in this volume and not be impressed. Beyond the scholars' academic credentials, the topics covered are both sophisticated and timely. For this reviewer, the experience caused me to respond time and again: 'I want to start right there . . . or maybe there . . . wow—have to read that one first . . .' The topic is not always an easy target, but after almost one thousand pages of critique across interdisciplinary lines, I do not think that it could be bettered. Kudos! Highly recommended."

> **Gary R. Habermas**, Distinguished Research Professor and Chair, Department of Philosophy, Liberty University

"As the debate over the origins of the universe, earth, and humans continues, and Christians grapple to understand the relationship between science and Scripture, evolution and creation, the voices in this book need to be heard. Scientific data need not be in opposition to what the Bible teaches about God and his world. The big questions about life are simply beyond the reach of 'objective' analysis. This volume critiques theologically and philosophically the flaws of positions that marginalize God from the process."

> **James Hoffmeier,** Professor of Old Testament and Ancient Near Eastern History and Archaeology, Trinity Evangelical Divinity School

"*Theistic Evolution* is a carefully crafted, academically sophisticated interdisciplinary challenge to the attempt to wed Christian theism to any version of the Darwinian project. I am awed by its scope and by the magnificent success of its intentions. Whether your interest is in the scientific deficiencies, the philosophical failings, or the theological dangers of Darwinism hitched to theism, look no further than this thorough analysis. *Theistic Evolution* is simply the most comprehensive and convincing critique of the topic I've ever read—a singular resource for careful thinkers—replacing a dozen books on my shelf."

> **Gregory Koukl,** President, Stand to Reason; author, *Tactics* and *The Story of Reality*

"An increasing number of evangelicals are advocating theistic evolution as the best explanation of human origins, thereby denying the special creation of a historical Adam. Without taking any specific view as to the age to the earth, this important new book demonstrates that theistic evolution fails to take proper account of Genesis 1–3 as a historical narrative. Leading scholars from a variety of academic disciplines argue that theistic evolution is exegetically ill-founded, theologically damaging, scientifically implausible, and philosophically unjustifiable. Written with an irenic tone toward those it critiques, this book will help guard against false teaching in the church that undermines the gospel and will also provide apologetic help for confident evangelism in a secular world."

> **John Stevens,** National Director, Fellowship of Independent Evangelical Churches, United Kingdom

"With the 'death of God' and the 'hermeneutics of suspicion' having captured the academy decades ago, the apologetic discussion moved decisively to the nature and origin of human beings. With this volume, the editors and contributors to *Theistic Evolution* have given us an important and much-needed resource for the conversation currently taking place within evangelicalism. Comprehensive in its breadth, specific in its critique, and confidently nuanced in its tone, each chapter contributes to a thorough rebuttal of the idea that theistic evolution is compatible with either historic Christian faith, sound reasoning, or rigorous science. But while written by specialists, *Theistic Evolution* is remarkably approachable to the average reader. I highly recommend this volume to students, pastors, educators, and anyone else who cares deeply about the discussion of human origins. This is a major contribution to one of the most important debates of our time."

> **Michael Lawrence,** Senior Pastor, Hinson Baptist Church, Portland, Oregon; author, *Biblical Theology in the Life of the Church*

"Under the banner of 'theistic evolution,' a growing number of Christians maintain that God used evolution as his method for creation. This I believe to be the worst of all possibilities. It is one thing to believe in evolution; it is quite another to blame God for it. Indeed, theistic evolution is a contradiction in terms—like the phrase "flaming snowflakes." God can no more direct an undirected process than he can create a square circle. Yet this is precisely what theistic evolution presupposes. Modern Christians too often buy high and sell low—just as neo-Darwinian evolutionism is fighting for its very life, it is being propped up by an irrational hypothesis. *Theistic Evolution* is the most thorough and incisive refutation of this dangerous presupposition. I strongly recommend this volume!"

Hank Hanegraaff, President, Christian Research Institute; Host, *Bible Answer Man* broadcast

"This volume is the most comprehensive study on the relation between evolution and Christian faith I have discovered so far. While opening up fascinating firsthand insights into cutting-edge scientific results, at the same time the book treats the reader to a bird's-eye view, asking the fundamental philosophical and theological questions and delving into the underlying worldview assumptions. It provides a very substantial contribution to the ever-ongoing dispute between naturalism and Christian faith in the areas of philosophy, theology, and the sciences."

Alexander Fink, Director, Institute for Faith and Sciences, Marburg, Germany

"Essentially, theistic evolution says Charles Darwin and Richard Dawkins got the science right, but that God is still somehow involved. Putting this view into the crosshairs, this book argues convincingly that the science of evolution is in fact wrong, and that any theistic gloss one puts on it is thus doubly wrong."

William A. Dembski, Former Senior Fellow, Discovery Institute; author, *Intelligent Design: The Bridge Between Science and Theology*; *The Design Revolution*; and *Intelligent Design Uncensored*

"*Theistic Evolution* is a major contribution to the very lively debate of exactly how to understand the 'data' from God's revelation of himself in his Word with the 'data' from his revelation of himself in his world. Previous contributions to this debate have generally focused on the data from either science or Scripture. *Theistic Evolution* benefits from its comprehensive analysis from theologians, philosophers, and scientists in the same book. Whatever are your current views, *Theistic Evolution* will provide analysis from some of the most prominent critics in this conversation that should be helpful to people on both sides of this debate."

Walter Bradley, Former Professor of Mechanical Engineering, Baylor University

"The question of origins rarely fails to attract interest, not least because it is overloaded with worldview implications. For too long the increasingly shaky modern 'Darwinian' synthesis has been accommodated into theological thinking. This remarkable book exposes how scientifically and philosophically preposterous the notion of theistic evolution really is. An authoritative and vital contribution to the topic!"

David J. Galloway, President, Royal College of Physicians and Surgeons of Glasgow; Honorary Professor, College of Medical, Veterinary and Life Sciences, University of Glasgow

THEISTIC EVOLUTION

THEISTIC EVOLUTION

A Scientific, Philosophical, and Theological Critique

Edited by J. P. Moreland (philosophy),
Stephen C. Meyer, Christopher Shaw, Ann K. Gauger (science),
and Wayne Grudem (Bible/theology)

Foreword by Steve Fuller

CROSSWAY®

WHEATON, ILLINOIS

Theistic Evolution: A Scientific, Philosophical, and Theological Critique
Copyright © 2017 by J. P. Moreland, Stephen Meyer, Christopher Shaw, and Wayne Grudem

Published by Crossway
    1300 Crescent Street
    Wheaton, Illinois 60187

Cover design: Micah Lanier

Cover image: Sari O'Neal © Shutterstock

First printing 2017

Printed in the United States of America

Hardcover ISBN: 978-1-4335-5286-1
Epub ISBN: 978-1-4335-5289-2
PDF ISBN: 978-1-4335-5287-8
Mobipocket ISBN: 978-1-4335-5288-5

Library of Congress Cataloging-in-Publication Data

Names: Moreland, James Porter, 1948- editor.
Title: Theistic evolution : a scientific, philosophical, and theological critique / edited by J. P. Moreland, Stephen Meyer, Christopher Shaw, Ann K. Gauger, and Wayne Grudem.
Description: Wheaton, Illinois : Crossway, [2017] | Includes bibliographical references and index.
Identifiers: LCCN 2017022969 (print) | LCCN 2017039890 (ebook) | ISBN 9781433552878 (pdf) | ISBN 9781433552885 (mobi) | ISBN 9781433552892 (epub) | ISBN 9781433552861 (hc) | ISBN 9781433552892 (ePub)
Subjects: LCSH: Evolution—Religious aspects—Christianity. | Creationism.
Classification: LCC BS659 (ebook) | LCC BS659 .T44 2017 (print) | DDC 231.7/652—dc23
LC record available at https://lccn.loc.gov/2017022969

Crossway is a publishing ministry of Good News Publishers.

SH   28   27   26   25   24   23   22   21   20   19   18
14   13   12   11   10   9   8   7   6   5   4   3   2

To Peter Loose,

who persuaded us of the need for this book
and encouraged us throughout the process

Contents

Section I, Part 2: The Case against Universal Common Descent and for a Unique Human Origin

SECTION II: THE PHILOSOPHICAL CRITIQUE OF THEISTIC EVOLUTION

Illustrations

Contributors

Gregg R. Allison (PhD, Trinity Evangelical Divinity School) is professor of Christian theology at The Southern Baptist Theological Seminary in Louisville, Kentucky. He is the author of *Historical Theology: An Introduction to Christian Doctrine*; *Sojourners and Strangers: The Doctrine of the Church*; *Roman Catholic Theology and Practice: An Evangelical Assessment*; *The Baker Compact Dictionary of Theological Terms*; *The Unfinished Reformation* (with Chris Castaldo); and other titles. Allison is secretary of the Evangelical Theological Society and is a book review editor for the *Journal of the Evangelical Theological Society*.

Douglas D. Axe is the director of Biologic Institute, a founding editor of *BIO-Complexity*, and the author of *Undeniable—How Biology Confirms Our Intuition that Life Is Designed*. After a Caltech PhD, he held research positions at the University of Cambridge and the Cambridge Medical Research Council Centre. His work and ideas have been featured in the *Journal of Molecular Biology*, the *Proceedings of the National Academy of Sciences*, and *Nature*. In *Undeniable* he brings the main conclusions of his work to a general audience by showing that our intuitive sense that accidental causes cannot have invented life is correct.

Günter Bechly is a German paleontologist and senior research scientist at Biologic Institute. His research focuses on the fossil history of insects, discontinuities in the history of life, and the waiting time problem. He earned his PhD, summa cum laude, in paleontology from the Eberhard Karls University of Tübingen (Germany), where he studied the evolution of dragonflies and their wings. He worked from 1999–2016 as curator for amber and fossil insects at the State Museum of Natural

History in Stuttgart, as successor of Dieter Schlee and Willi Hennig. He has described more than 160 new fossil taxa, including three new insect orders, and published more than 70 scientific articles in peer-reviewed journals and a book with Cambridge University Press. His research has received broad international media coverage, in particular his discoveries of *Coxoplectoptera* and the predatory roach *Manipulator*.

C. John Collins is professor of Old Testament at Covenant Seminary in St. Louis, Missouri. With degrees from MIT (SB, SM) and the University of Liverpool (PhD), he has been a research engineer, a church planter, and a seminary teacher. He was Old Testament chairman for the English Standard Version of the Bible, and is author of *Science and Faith: Friends or Foes?* and *Did Adam and Eve Really Exist?: Who They Were and Why You Should Care*, and is currently writing commentaries on Numbers, Psalms, and Isaiah. He married Diane in 1979, and they have two grown children.

John D. Currid (PhD, University of Chicago) is the Carl McMurray Professor of Old Testament at Reformed Theological Seminary in Charlotte, North Carolina. He is the author of several books and Old Testament commentaries and has extensive archaeological field experience from projects throughout Israel and Tunisia.

Garrett J. DeWeese is professor at large, Talbot School of Theology, Biola University. He holds a BS degree from the United States Air Force Academy, a ThM from Dallas Theological Seminary, and a PhD from the University of Colorado–Boulder. He has taught courses on the intersection of science, theology, and philosophy for more than twenty years.

Stephen Dilley is an associate professor of philosophy at St. Edward's University in Austin, Texas. He is editor of *Darwinian Evolution and Classical Liberalism* (Lexington, 2013) and coeditor of *Human Dignity in Bioethics* (Routledge, 2012). Dilley has published essays in *British Journal for the History of Science*, *The Journal of the International Society for the History of Philosophy of Science*, *Studies in History and Philosophy of Biological and Biomedical Sciences*, and elsewhere.

He enjoys history and philosophy of biology, political philosophy, and bowhunting.

Winston Ewert (PhD, Baylor University) is an intelligent design researcher and software engineer. He has published in the *IEEE Transactions on Systems, Man, and Cybernetics*, *Bio-Complexity*, and *Perspectives on Science and Christian Faith*. He is a senior researcher at both the Evolutionary Informatics Lab and the Biologic Institute. He is also a contributor at *Evolution News and Views*. When not busy defending intelligent design or writing software, he occupies his time maintaining his status as his nieces' and nephew's favorite uncle.

Ann K. Gauger is director of science communication at the Discovery Institute, and senior research scientist at Biologic Institute in Seattle. She received her PhD from the University of Washington and was a postdoctoral fellow at Harvard. Her research at Biologic Institute has been on both protein evolution and human origins. As director of science communication, she communicates evidence for intelligent design to the wider public. Her scientific work has been published in *Nature, Development, Journal of Biological Chemistry, BIO-Complexity*, among others, and she coauthored the book *Science and Human Origins*.

Wayne Grudem is research professor of theology and biblical studies at Phoenix Seminary. He received a BA (Harvard), an MDiv and a DD (Westminster Seminary, Philadelphia), and a PhD in New Testament (University of Cambridge). He has published over twenty books including *Systematic Theology*, was a translator for the ESV Bible, and was the general editor for the *ESV Study Bible*. He is a past president of the Evangelical Theological Society. He and Margaret have been married since 1969 and have three adult sons.

Ola Hössjer received a PhD in mathematical statistics from Uppsala University, Sweden, in 1991. Appointed a professor of mathematical statistics at Lund University in 2000, he has held the same position at Stockholm University since 2002. His research focuses on developing statistical theory and probability theory for various applications, in particular population genetics, epidemiology, and insurance mathematics. He has authored around eighty peer-reviewed articles and has supervised thirteen PhD students. His theoretical research is mostly in robust and nonparametric statistics, whereas the applied research includes methods of gene localization (linkage and association analysis), and the study of short-term microevolutionary dynamics of populations. In 2009 he was awarded the Gustafsson Prize in Mathematics.

Matti Leisola holds a degree as doctor of science in technology (1979) from Helsinki University of Technology; he received his habilitation in 1988 from Swiss Federal Institute of Technology (ETH) in biotechnology. He was awarded the Latsis Prize of the ETH Zurich in 1987. He is currently professor emeritus of bioprocess engineering at Aalto University. Leisola's scientific expertise is in microbial and enzyme technology. Leisola was the research director at Cultor Ltd, an international food and biotech company, during 1991–1997. Leisola has authored and coauthored over 140 scientific peer-reviewed articles which have been cited over 5,000 times.

Casey Luskin is a PhD student in science and an attorney. He earned his MS in earth sciences from the University of California, San Diego, and a law degree from the University of San Diego. Luskin previously worked as research coordinator at Discovery Institute, helping scientists and educators investigate intelligent design. He has contributed to multiple books, including *Science and Human Origins, Traipsing into Evolution, Intelligent Design 101, God and Evolution, More than Myth*, and *Discovering Intelligent Design*. Luskin is cofounder of the Intelligent Design and Evolution Awareness (IDEA) Center (www .ideacenter.org), a non-profit helping students start "IDEA Clubs" on campuses.

Stephen C. Meyer received his PhD in the philosophy of science from the University of Cambridge. A former geophysicist and philosophy professor at Whitworth University, he now directs Discovery Institute's Center for Science and Culture in Seattle. He has authored the *New York Times* best-seller *Darwin's Doubt: The Explosive Origin of Animal Life and the Case for Intelligent Design* (HarperOne, 2013) as well as *Signature in the Cell: DNA and the Evidence for Intelligent Design* (HarperOne, 2009) which was named a Book of the Year by the *Times* (of London) *Literary Supplement* in 2009.

J. P. Moreland is distinguished professor of philosophy at Talbot School of Theology, Biola University in La Mirada, California, where he has taught for twenty-six years. He has authored, edited, or contributed papers to ninety-five books, including *Does God Exist?* (Prometheus), *Universals* (McGill-Queen's), *Consciousness and the Existence of God* (Routledge), and *Blackwell Companion to Natural Theology* (Blackwell). He has also published over eighty-five articles in journals such as *Philosophy and Phenomenological Research*, *American Philosophical Quarterly*, *Australasian Journal of Philosophy*, *MetaPhilosophy*, *Philosophia Christi*, *Religious Studies*, and *Faith and Philosophy*. He has also published 120 articles in magazines and newspapers. In 2016, Moreland was recognized by Best Schools as among the fifty most influential philosophers in the world.

Paul A. Nelson studied evolutionary theory and the philosophy of science at the University of Chicago, where he received his PhD (1998). His dissertation examined Darwinian universal common descent. He is a fellow of the Discovery Institute, and an adjunct professor for Biola University's MA program in Science and Religion. Nelson's scholarly articles have appeared in journals such as *Biology and Philosophy*, *Zygon*, *Rhetoric and Public Affairs*, and *BioComplexity*, and book chapters in the anthologies *Mere Creation*, *Signs of Intelligence*, *Intelligent Design Creationism and Its Critics*, and *Darwin, Design, and Public Education*. His memberships include the Society for Developmental Biology (SDB) and the International Society for the History, Philosophy, and Social Studies of Biology (ISHPSSB).

Tapio Puolimatka is professor of educational theory and tradition at the University of Jyvaskyla and adjunct professor of practical philosophy at the University of Helsinki, Finland. Prior to coming to the University of Jyvaskyla he held a research fellowship at the Center for Philosophy of Religion, University of Notre Dame, in 1995–1998 and studied Jewish thought at the Hebrew University of Jerusalem in

1983–1988. He has written several books on educational philosophy and Christian apologetics.

Colin R. Reeves holds a PhD from Coventry University in the UK, where he was professor of operational research. He is a chartered statistician, and his research interests focus on the mathematical and statistical foundations of evolutionary algorithms, on which he has published extensively. His book *Genetic Algorithms: A Guide to GA Theory* (with Jonathan Rowe) was the first systematic treatment of evolutionary algorithm theory. Recently retired as professor emeritus, he continues to be active in research, consultancy, and conference speaking.

Christopher Shaw received his BSc (honors) in biological sciences from the University of Ulster in 1980 and his PhD in molecular endocrinology from Queen's University Belfast in 1984. He has held the positions of lecturer, reader, and professor in Queen's University, Faculty of Medicine, and of professor of biotechnology in the University of Ulster. He is currently professor of drug discovery in the School of Pharmacy, Queen's University. His research interest is in all aspects of bioactive peptides. He has authored some 500 peer-reviewed scientific papers and has delivered numerous invited international lectures, and is cofounder of a biomarker discovery company.

James M. Tour, a synthetic organic chemist, is presently the T. T. and W. F. Chao Professor of Chemistry, professor of computer science, and professor of materials science and nanoengineering at Rice University. Tour has over 600 research publications and over 120 patents with total citations over 69,000. He was inducted into the National Academy of Inventors in 2015, named among "The 50 Most Influential Scientists in the World Today" by TheBestSchools.org in 2014, listed in "The World's Most Influential Scientific Minds" by Thomson Reuters ScienceWatch.com in 2014, and named "Scientist of the Year" by *R&D* magazine in 2013.

Sheena Tyler spent eight years teaching biology after undergraduate studies in dentistry and zoology. She received her PhD in zoology at the University of Manchester, during which time she won the British Society of Developmental Biology Conference student prize. Following further postdoctoral work at Manchester, she is now the research director of the John Ray Research Field Station. In 2013, she was awarded the University of Manchester First Prize Medal for Social Responsibility. Her current research interests and publications include aspects of bioelectric fields in morphogenesis and wound healing, egg surface structure, avian development, solar-electric power, and the biology of cork.

Guy Prentiss Waters is the James M. Baird Jr. Professor of New Testament at Reformed Theological Seminary in Jackson, Mississippi. He has served at RTS since 2007. Prior to coming to RTS, Guy was assistant professor of biblical studies at Belhaven University, Jackson, Mississippi. Guy earned his BA in classics at the University of Pennsylvania (summa cum laude); his MDiv at Westminster Theological Seminary, Philadelphia (honors); and his PhD in Religion from Duke University. He is the author or editor of eight books, and of several chapters, articles, and reviews. He and his wife, Sarah, have three children, and reside in Madison, Mississippi.

Jonathan Wells has a PhD in religious studies (Yale University, 1986) and a PhD in molecular and cell biology (University of California at Berkeley, 1995). He is the author of *Icons of Evolution* (2000), *The Politically Incorrect Guide to Darwinism and Intelligent Design* (2006), and *The Myth of Junk DNA* (2011), and coauthor (with William Dembski) of *The Design of Life* (2008). He is currently a senior fellow at the Discovery Institute in Seattle.

John G. West is vice president of Discovery Institute and associate director of the Institute's Center for Science and Culture, which he cofounded with Stephen C. Meyer in 1996. He has written or edited twelve books, including two about C. S. Lewis: *The C. S. Lewis Readers' Encyclopedia* and *The Magician's Twin: C. S. Lewis on Science, Scientism, and Society*. His other books include *Darwin Day in America: How Our Politics and Culture Have Been Dehumanized in the Name of Science*; *The Politics of Revelation and Reason*; and

Celebrating Middle-Earth: The Lord of the Rings *as a Defense of Western Civilization.* West was previously associate professor of political science at Seattle Pacific University, where he chaired the Department of Political Science and Geography. He holds a PhD in government from Claremont Graduate University, and he has been interviewed by media outlets such as *Time, The New York Times,* CNN, and *Fox News.*

Fred G. Zaspel (PhD, Free University of Amsterdam) is pastor of Reformed Baptist Church of Franconia, Pennsylvania. He is also executive editor at Books at a Glance and associate professor of Christian theology at The Southern Baptist Theological Seminary. His doctoral work was on the theology of Benjamin Breckinridge Warfield, and he has published two related books on Warfield.

Foreword

It is an honor and a pleasure to write the foreword to this book, which sets a new standard for Christian engagement with contemporary science. The cumulative effect of the set of papers assembled in this volume is to suggest that the "God hypothesis" (or what philosophers call "divine action") remains very much on the table as a scientific explanation for events in the history of life. Christians who fail to deal seriously with that point—perhaps out of deference to secular scientific authority—end up selling short both science and their faith. I take this to be the most important challenge that the scientists and scholars in these pages are offering to theistic evolutionists.

By conventional Christian standards, I do not think that I would count as a person of faith—though I may count as one by conventional secular standards. In any case, I write as someone who was confirmed in the Roman Catholic Church and studied on scholarship with the Jesuits before attending university. The Jesuits are notoriously rationalistic in their approach to matters of faith, which has always appealed to me. I was never compelled to declare belief in God but was strongly encouraged to question default secular solutions to problems of knowledge and action. As a result, I have been a "seeker," a term originally used to characterize Christian dissenters from the Church of England in the seventeenth century, which Thomas Henry Huxley appropriated two centuries later, when he described himself as an "agnostic" on matters of faith.

The real question for me has been not whether God exists but how the deity operates in the world—including all the issues that raises for what we should believe and how we should act. In this respect, I have always regarded "atheism" in the true sense (that is, anti-theism, not simply anti-clericalism) as a moral and/or epistemic failure—perhaps a prudishness if not absence of the imagination, which when threatened can morph into bigotry toward that which one simply fails to understand. The neologism "theophobia" would not be out of place. My Jesuit teachers would go one step further and ask atheists the following question: What advantage would your understanding of reality gain by dismissing out of hand the existence of a divine intelligence, such that it would be worth the loss of meaning to your life and reality more generally?

But this is a book about theists who contest the place of modern science in Christianity. The charge laid at the doorstep of theistic evolutionists is that the doorstep is exactly where they leave their religious commitments when they enter the house of science. They do this, even though the weight of the evidence from across the natural sciences does not oblige such a conclusion. On the contrary, from cosmology to biology, it is becoming increasingly clear that science's failure to explain matters at the most fundamental level is at least in part due to an institutional prohibition on intelligent design as one of the explanatory options. In these pages, "methodological naturalism" is the name by which this prohibition goes, but it could be equally called "methodological atheism."

Like some leaders of the intelligent design movement, I was formally trained in a field called "history and philosophy of science." As the name indicates, the field combines history, philosophy, and science in search of a lost sense of purpose in organized inquiry that began with the proliferation of academic disciplines in the nineteenth century. The field's guiding idea is that if we understand how something as distinctive as science came about and was sustained over the centuries, we might have a better sense of what it says about us and hence where it and we should be going. The field's founder was William Whewell, an Anglican theologian who introduced the natural sciences into the Cambridge University curriculum in the mid-nineteenth century. He also coined the word "scientist" in its modern sense.

History and philosophy of science truly came of age in the 1960s, a period of widespread disaffection with science's complicity in what was then called the "military-industrial complex." This disaffection was expressed in light of a general understanding that the West had experienced a "Scientific Revolution" in the seventeenth century, which radically transformed how people thought about themselves and their relationship to the cosmos. What most struck the historians and philosophers of science who investigated this "take off" point for the human condition was that it was part of a more general spiritual awakening of Christian Europe, what is normally called the Protestant Reformation. And precisely because the original turn to science involved a break from the established authority of the Roman Catholic Church, science's submission to established secular authority during the Cold War appeared to betray that founding spirit. Readers of this volume should consider the challenge to theistic evolution found in this volume in a similar light.

While it is generally accepted that the Protestant Reformation overlapped with the Scientific Revolution, this is often treated as a mere historical accident, when in fact something closer to a causal connection obtains between the two events. The first movement in human history to trust the ordinary person's ability to judge the weight of evidence for themselves was the drive to get people to read the Bible for themselves. Until the sixteenth century, Christianity found itself in the peculiar position of being a faith founded on a sacred book through which God communicated with humans, yet relatively few of the faithful could read, let alone affirm its contents. The Protestant Reformation reversed that. The Scientific Revolution then extended that "judge for yourself" attitude to all of physical reality by explicitly treating nature as a second sacred book. Thus, it is not surprising that Francis Bacon, with whom the "scientific method" is normally associated, was also instrumental in the production of the King James Version of the Bible.

Today science enjoys an unprecedented authority because of both the number of people who believe in it and the number of subjects to which their belief applies. In this respect, our world resembles the one faced by the Protestant Reformers in that people today are often discouraged, because of the authority of science, from testing their faith in its claims by considering the evidence for themselves. Instead they are meant to defer to the authority of academic experts, who function as a secular clergy. But unlike the sixteenth century, when the Protestant Reformers themselves drove the mass literacy campaigns to get people to read the Bible, we live in a time of unprecedented access to knowledge about science, both formally and informally—from the classroom to the Internet. Moreover, public opinion surveys consistently show that people are pro-science as a mode of inquiry but anti-science as a mode of authority. And so, while it has become part of secular folklore to say that the Catholic Church "repressed" the advancement of science, if "repression" implies the thwarting of an already evident desire and capacity to seek knowledge, then today's scientific establishment seriously outperforms the early modern Church—and perhaps with the consent of theistic evolutionists.

I commend this book as providing an unprecedented opportunity for educated nonscientists to revisit the spirit of the Reformation by judging for themselves what they make of the evidence that seems to have led theistic evolutionists to privilege contemporary scientific authority above their own avowed faith. John Calvin famously likened the reading of the Bible to the wearing of spectacles to correct defective eyesight. Historically speaking, the original Scientific Revolution was largely the result of those who took his advice. But what was it about the Bible that led such a wide variety of inquirers, all wrestling with their Christian faith, to come up with the form of science that we continue to practice today? This is an important question to ask because there is no good historical reason to think that science as we know it would have arisen in any other culture—including China, generally acknowledged to have been the world's main economic power prior to the nineteenth century—had it not arisen in Christian Europe.

A distillation of research in the history and philosophy of science suggests two biblical ideas as having been crucial to the rise of science, both of which can be attributed to the reading of *Genesis* provided by Augustine, an early church father, whose work became increasingly studied in the late Middle Ages and especially the Reformation. Augustine captured the two ideas in two Latin coinages, which prima facie cut against each other: *imago dei* and *peccatum originis*. The former says that humans are unique as a species in our having been created in the image and likeness of God, while the latter says that all humans are born having inherited the legacy of Adam's error, "original sin." Once Christians began to read the Bible for themselves, they too picked out those ideas as salient in how they defined their relationship to God, which extended to how they did science.

And this sensibility carried into the modern secular age, as perhaps best illustrated in our own day by Karl Popper's slogan for the scientific attitude as the method of "conjectures and refutations," the stronger the better in both cases. We should aspire to understand all of nature by proposing bold hypotheses (something of which we are capable because of the *imago dei*) but to expect and admit error (something to which we are inclined because of the *peccatum originis*) whenever we fall short in light of the evidence. The experimental method developed by Francis Bacon was designed to encourage just that frame of mind. And William Whewell was only one of numerous theologians and philosophers who have suggested ways of testing and interpreting the findings of science to reflect that orientation. Unfortunately we live in a time in which only those who have themselves conducted science in some authorized manner are allowed to say anything about what science is and where it should go.

Theistic evolution should be understood as a deformation that results under these conditions. Its advice to the faithful is to keep calm, trust the scientific establishment, and adapt accordingly, even if it means ceding the Bible's cognitive ground. Yet, insofar as science has succeeded as it has because of the revival of the *imago dei* and *peccatum originis* account of humanity, one might reasonably ask whether theistic evolution amounts to an outright betrayal of both the scientific and the Christian message. Christianity's direction of travel since the Reformation has been that each person is entitled and maybe even obliged to decide on matters that impinge on the nature of their own being—and to register that publicly. This volume provides an incredibly rich resource for Christians to do exactly that with regard scientific matters. I hope it will empower them to question and propose constructive alternatives to the blanket endorsement of "evolution" by theistic evolutionists.

Steve Fuller
Auguste Comte Chair in Social Epistemology
Department of Sociology
University of Warwick
United Kingdom

Scientific and Philosophical Introduction

Defining Theistic Evolution

STEPHEN C. MEYER

In this book we will provide a comprehensive scientific, philosophical, and theological critique of the idea known as theistic evolution. But before we can do that, we will need to define what the proponents of this perspective mean by "theistic evolution"—or "evolutionary creationism," as it is sometimes now called. Indeed, before we can critique this perspective we will need to know what exactly it asserts. Is it a logically coherent position? Is it a theologically orthodox position? Is it supported by, or consistent with, the relevant scientific evidence? The answer to each of these questions depends crucially on the definition or sense of "evolution" in play. "Theistic evolution" can mean different things to different people largely because the term "evolution" itself has several distinct meanings.

This introductory essay will describe different concepts of theistic evolution, each of which corresponds to a different definition of the term *evolution*. It will also provide an initial critical evaluation of (and conceptual framework for understanding) those conceptions of theistic evolution that the authors of this volume find objectionable. The framework in this essay will help readers understand the more detailed critiques of specific versions of theistic evolution that will follow in subsequent essays, and it will help readers to understand how the different critical essays to follow mutually reinforce and complement

each other. Both here and in the essays that follow, we will focus most
(but not all) of our critical concern on one particular formulation of
the concept of theistic evolution—in particular, the one that affirms
the most scientifically controversial, and also most religiously charged,
meaning of *evolution*.

Since the term evolution has several distinct meanings, it will first
be necessary to describe the meanings that are commonly associated
with the term in order to evaluate the different possible concepts of
theistic evolution that proponents of the idea may have in mind. It will
be shown that three distinct meanings of the term evolution are especially relevant for understanding three different possible concepts of
theistic evolution. Yale biologist Keith Stewart Thomson, for example,
has noted that in contemporary biology the term evolution can refer
to: (1) change over time, (2) universal common ancestry, and (3) the
natural mechanisms that produce change in organisms.[1] Following
Thomson, this introduction will describe and distinguish these three
distinct meanings of "evolution" in order to foster clarity in the analysis and assessment of three distinct concepts of "theistic evolution."

Evolution #1: "Change over Time"

Evolution in its most rudimentary sense simply affirms the idea of
"change over time." Many natural scientists use "evolution" in this
first sense as they seek to reconstruct a series of past events to tell
the story of nature's history.[2] Astronomers study the life cycles of
stars and the "evolution" (change over time) of the universe or specific galaxies; geologists describe changes ("evolution") in the earth's
surface; biologists note ecological changes within recorded human
history, which, for example, may have transformed a barren island
into a mature forested island community. These examples, however,
have little or nothing to do with the modern "neo-Darwinian" theory
of evolution.

In evolutionary biology, evolution defined as change over time can
also refer specifically to the idea that the life forms we see today are

---

1. Keith S. Thomson, "The Meanings of Evolution," *American Scientist* 70 (1982): 521–539.
2. Peter J. Bowler, "The Changing Meaning of 'Evolution,'" *Journal of the History of Ideas*
36 (1975): 99.

different from the life forms that existed in the distant past. The fossil record provides strong support for this idea. Paleontologists observe changes in the types of life that have existed over time as represented by different fossilized forms in the sedimentary rock record (a phenomenon known as "fossil succession"). Many of the plants and animals that are fossilized in recent rock layers are different from the plants and animals fossilized in older rocks. The composition of flora and fauna on the surface of the earth today is likewise different from the forms of life that lived long ago, as attested by the fossil record.

Evolution defined as "change over time" can also refer to observed minor changes in features of individual species—small-scale changes that take place over a relatively short period of time. Most biologists think this kind of evolution (sometimes called "microevolution") results from a change in the proportion of different variants of a gene (called alleles) within a population over time. Thus, population geneticists will study changes in the frequencies of alleles in gene pools. A large number of precise observations have established the occurrence of this type of evolution. Studies of melanism in peppered moths, though currently contested,[3] are among the most celebrated examples of *microevolution*. The observed changes in the size and shape of Galápagos finch beaks in response to changing climate patterns provide another good example of small-scale change over time within a species.

Evolution #2: "Common Descent" or "Universal Common Descent"

Many biologists today also commonly use the term *evolution* to refer to the idea that all organisms are related by common ancestry. This idea is also known as the theory of universal common descent. This theory affirms that all known living organisms are descended from a single common ancestor somewhere in the distant past. In *On the Origin of Species*, Charles Darwin made a case for the truth of evolution in this second sense. In a famous passage at the end of the *Origin*, he

---

3. Jerry Coyne, "Not Black and White," review of Michael Majerus's 1998 book, *Melanism: Evolution in Action*, *Nature* 396 (1998): 35–36; Jonathan Wells, "Second Thoughts about Peppered Moths," *The Scientist* 13 (1999), 13.

argued that "probably all the organic beings which have ever lived on this earth have descended from some one primordial form."[4] Darwin thought that this primordial form gradually developed into new forms of life, which in turn gradually developed into other forms of life, eventually producing, after many millions of generations, all the complex life we see in the present.

Biology textbooks today often depict this idea just as Darwin did, with a great branching tree. The bottom of the trunk of Darwin's tree of life represents the first primordial organism. The limbs and branches of the tree represent the many new forms of life that developed from it. The vertical axis on which the tree is plotted represents the arrow of time. The horizontal axis represents changes in biological form, or what biologists call "morphological distance."

Darwin's theory of biological history is often referred to as a "monophyletic" view of the history of life because it portrays all organisms as ultimately related as a single connected family. Darwin argued that this idea best explained a variety of lines of biological evidence: the succession of fossil forms, the geographical distribution of various species (such as the plants and animals of the Galápagos Islands), and the anatomical and embryological similarities among otherwise different types of organisms.

Evolution in this second sense not only specifies that all life shares a common ancestry; it also implies that virtually no limits exist to the amount of morphological change that can occur in organisms. It assumes that relatively simple organisms can, given adequate time, change into much more complex organisms. Thus, evolution in this second sense entails not only change but also gradual, continuous—and even unbounded—biological change.

Evolution #3: "The Creative Power of the Natural Selection/Random Variation (or Mutation) Mechanism"

The term *evolution* is also commonly used to refer to the cause, or mechanism, that produces the biological change depicted by Darwin's

---

4. Charles Darwin, *On the Origin of Species by Means of Natural Selection*, facsimile of the first ed. (London: John Murray, 1859; repr., Cambridge, MA: Harvard University Press, 1964), 484.

tree of life. When evolution is used in this way, it usually refers to the mechanism of natural selection acting on random variations or mutations. (Modern "neo-Darwinists" propose that natural selection acts on a special kind of variation called genetic mutations. Mutations are random changes in the chemical subunits that convey information in DNA. Modern neo-Darwinists would also affirm the role of other apparently undirected evolutionary mechanisms such as genetic drift, although such mechanisms are typically thought to be of minor importance in comparison with mutation/selection in generating the adaptive complexity of life.)

This third use of *evolution* entails the idea that the natural selection/ mutation mechanism has the *creative power* to produce fundamental innovations in the history of life. Whereas the theory of universal common descent postulated *a pattern* (the branching tree) to represent the history of life, the mechanism of natural selection and random variation/mutation represents a causal *process* that can allegedly generate the large-scale macroevolutionary change implied by the second meaning of evolution (see above). Since proponents of the creative power of the mutation/natural selection mechanism see it (and other similarly materialistic evolutionary mechanisms) as explaining the origin of all the forms and features of life, this definition of evolution is closely associated with, or encompasses, another definition of evolution.

Evolution #3a: The Natural Selection/Random Variation (or Mutation) Mechanism Can Explain the Appearance of Design in Living Systems apart from the Activity of an Actual Designing Intelligence.

Evolutionary biologists since Darwin have affirmed that the natural selection/random variation mechanism not only explains the origin of all new biological forms and features; they have also affirmed a closely related idea, namely, that this mechanism can explain one particularly striking feature of biological systems: the *appearance of design*. Biologists have long recognized that many organized structures in living organisms—the elegant form and protective covering of the coiled nautilus; the interdependent parts of the vertebrate eye; the interlocking bones, muscles, and feathers of a bird wing—"give the appearance of having been designed for a purpose."[5] During the nineteenth century, before Darwin, biologists were particularly struck by the way in which living organisms seemed well adapted to their environments. They attributed this adaptation of organisms to their environments to the planning and ingenuity of a powerful designing intelligence.

Yet Darwin (and modern neo-Darwinists) have argued that the appearance of design in living organisms could be more simply explained as the product of a purely undirected mechanism, in particular the variation/natural selection mechanism. Darwin attempted to show that the natural selection mechanism could account for the appearance of design by drawing an analogy to the well-known process of "artificial selection" or "selective breeding." Anyone in the nineteenth century familiar with the breeding of domestic animals—dogs, horses, sheep, or pigeons, for example—knew that human breeders could alter the features of domestic stock by allowing only animals with certain traits to breed. A Scottish sheepherder might breed for a woollier sheep to enhance its chances of survival in a cold northern climate (or to harvest more wool). To do so, he would choose only the woolliest males and woolliest ewes to breed. If, generation after generation, he continued to select and breed only the woolliest sheep among the resulting offspring, he would eventually produce a woollier breed of sheep—a breed *better adapted* to its environment. In such cases, "the key is man's power of accumulative selection," wrote Darwin. "Nature gives successive variations; man adds them up in certain directions useful to him."[6]

But, as Darwin pointed out, nature also has a means of sifting: defective creatures are less likely to survive and reproduce, while those offspring with beneficial variations are more likely to survive, reproduce, and pass on their advantages to future generations. In the *Origin*, Darwin argued that this process—natural selection acting on random variations—could alter the features of organisms just as intelligent selection by human breeders can. Nature itself could play the role of the breeder and, thus, eliminate the need for an actual designing intelligence to produce the complex adaptations that living organisms manifest.

---

5. Richard Dawkins, *The Blind Watchmaker: Why the Evidence of Evolution Reveals a Universe without Design* (New York: Norton, 1986), 1.
6. Darwin, *On the Origin of Species*, 30.

Consider once more our flock of sheep. Imagine that instead of a human selecting the woolliest males and ewes to breed, a series of very cold winters ensures that all but the woolliest sheep in a population die off. Now, again, only very woolly sheep will remain to breed. If the cold winters continue over several generations, will the result not be the same as before? Won't the population of sheep eventually become discernibly woollier?

This was Darwin's great insight. Nature—in the form of environmental changes or other factors—could have the same effect on a population of organisms as the intentional decisions of an intelligent agent. Nature would favor the preservation of certain features over others—those that conferred a functional or survival advantage upon the organisms possessing them—causing the features of the population to change. The resulting change or increase in fitness (adaptation) will have been produced not by an intelligent breeder choosing a desirable trait or variation—not by "artificial selection"—but by a wholly natural process. As Darwin himself insisted, "There seems to be no more design in the variability of organic beings and in the action of natural selection, than in the course in which the wind blows."[7]

Or as the eminent evolutionary biologist Francisco Ayala has argued, Darwin accounted for "design without a designer," since "It was Darwin's greatest accomplishment to show that the directive organization of living beings can be explained as the result of a natural process, natural selection, without any need to resort to a Creator or other external agent."[8]

Indeed, since 1859 most evolutionary biologists have understood the appearance of design in living things as an illusion—a powerfully suggestive one, but an illusion nonetheless. For this reason, as briefly noted above, Richard Dawkins insists in *The Blind Watchmaker* that "biology is the study of complicated things that give the appearance of having been designed for a purpose."[9] Or as Ernst Mayr explained, "The real core of Darwinism . . . is the theory of natural selection.

7. Charles Darwin, *The Life and Letters of Charles Darwin*, ed. Francis Darwin, vol. 1 (London: John Murray, 1887), 278–279.

8. Francisco J. Ayala, "Darwin's Greatest Discovery: Design without Designer," *Proceedings of the National Academy of Sciences USA* 104 (May 15, 2007): 8567–8573.

9. Dawkins, *Blind Watchmaker*, 1.

This theory is so important for the Darwinian because it permits the explanation of adaptation, the 'design' of the natural theologian, by natural means, instead of by divine intervention."[10] Or as Francis Crick mused, biologists must "constantly keep in mind that what they see was not designed, but rather evolved."[11] Likewise George Gaylord Simpson, one of the architects of neo-Darwinism, in *The Meaning of Evolution*, wrote that neo-Darwinism implies that "man is the result of a purposeless and natural process that did not have him in mind."[12]

But if apparent design is an illusion—if it is *just* an appearance—as both Darwinists and modern neo-Darwinists have argued, then it follows that whatever mechanism produced that appearance must be wholly unguided and undirected. For this reason, the third meaning of *evolution*—the definition that affirms the creative power of the natural selection/random mutation mechanism and denies evidence of actual design in living systems—raises a significant issue for any proponent of *theistic* evolution who affirms this meaning of evolution.

Assessing Different Concepts of Theistic Evolution (or Evolutionary Creation)

The three different meanings of evolution discussed above correspond to three possible and distinct concepts of theistic evolution, one of which is trivial, one of which is contestable but not incoherent, and one of which appears deeply problematic. In the last case, special attention is due to the important issue of whether theistic evolutionists regard the evolutionary process as guided or unguided.

If by "evolution" the theistic evolutionist means to affirm evolution in the first sense—change over time—and if, further, the theistic evolutionist affirms that God has caused that "change over time," then certainly no theist would contest the theological orthodoxy or logical coherence of such a statement. If a personal God of the kind affirmed by biblical Judaism or Christianity exists, then there is nothing logically

---

10. Ernst Mayr, Foreword in Michael Ruse, *Darwinism Defended: A Guide to the Evolution Controversies* (Reading, MA: Addison-Wesley, 1982), xi–xii.

11. Francis Crick, *What Mad Pursuit: A Personal View of Scientific Discovery* (New York: Basic Books, 1988), 138.

12. George Gaylord Simpson, *The Meaning of Evolution*, rev. ed. (New Haven, CT: Yale University Press, 1967), 345.

contradictory in such a statement, nor does it contradict any specific theological tenets. The Jewish and Christian scriptures clearly affirm that God has caused change over time, not only in human history but also in the process of creating the world and different forms of life.

Given the extensive scientific evidence showing that the representation of life forms on Earth has changed over time, there does not seem to be any significant theological or scientific basis for questioning evolution, or theistic evolution, where evolution is defined in this minimal sense. Similarly, since God could create different organisms with a built-in capacity to change or "evolve" *within limits* without denying his design of different living systems as distinct forms of life, and since there is extensive scientific evidence for change of this kind occurring, there does not seem to be any significant scientific or theological basis for questioning evolution in this sense either. Understanding theistic evolution this way seems unobjectionable, perhaps even trivial.

Another conception of theistic evolution affirms the second meaning of evolution. It affirms the view that God has caused *continuous* and *gradual* biological change such that the history of life is best represented by a great branching tree pattern as Darwin argued. Theistic evolution thus conceived is, again, not obviously logically incoherent since God as conceived by theists, including biblical theists, is certainly capable of producing continuous and gradual change.

Nevertheless, some biblical theists question universal common descent based on their interpretation of the biblical teaching in Genesis about God creating distinct "kinds" of plants and animals, all of which "reproduce after their own kind." Those who think a natural reading of the Genesis account suggests that different kinds of plants and animals reproduce only after their own kind and do not vary beyond some fixed limit in their morphology, question the theory of universal common descent on biblical grounds. Some biblical theists likewise question that humans and lower animals share a common ancestry, believing instead that the biblical account affirms that humans arose from a special creative act, thus excluding the idea that humans originated from nonhuman ancestors.

In addition to these theological objections, there is a growing body of *scientific* evidence and peer-reviewed literature challenging such a "monophyletic" picture of the history of life.[13] These scientific challenges to the theory of universal common descent are reviewed in chapters 10–12 of this volume. Chapters 13–16 of this volume also discuss scientific evidence that challenges the idea that humans and chimps in particular share a common ancestor.[14]

An even more foundational issue arises when considering the *cause* of biological change and the question of whether theistic evolutionists conceive of evolutionary mechanisms as directed or undirected processes.

Some proponents of theistic evolution openly affirm that the evolutionary process is an unguided, undirected process. Kenneth Miller, a leading theistic evolutionist and author of *Finding Darwin's God* has repeatedly stated in editions of his popular textbook that "evolution works without either plan or purpose. . . . Evolution is random and undirected."[15]

Nevertheless, most theistic evolutionists, including geneticist Francis Collins, perhaps the world's best-known proponent of the position, have been reluctant to clarify what they think about this important issue. In his book *The Language of God*, Collins makes clear his support for universal common descent. He also seems to assume the adequacy of standard evolutionary mechanisms but does not clearly say whether he thinks those mechanisms are directed or undirected—only that they "could be" directed.

In any case, where theistic evolution is understood to affirm the creative power of the neo-Darwinian and/or other evolutionary mecha-

---

13. See, e.g., Michael Syvanen, "Evolutionary Implications of Horizontal Gene Transfer," *Annual Review of Genetics* 46 (2012): 339–356; W. Ford Doolittle, "The Practice of Classification and the Theory of Evolution, and What the Demise of Charles Darwin's Tree of Life Hypothesis Means for Both of Them," *Philosophical Transactions of the Royal Society B* 364 (2009): 2221–2228; Malcolm S. Gordon, "The Concept of Monophyly: A Speculative Essay," *Biology and Philosophy* 14 (1999): 331–348; Eugene V. Koonin, "The Biological Big Bang Model for the Major Transitions in Evolution," *Biology Direct* 2 (2007): 21; Vicky Merhej and Didier Raoult, "Rhizome of Life, Catastrophes, Sequence Exchanges, Gene Creations, and Giant Viruses: How Microbial Genomics Challenges Darwin," *Frontiers in Cellular and Infection Microbiology* 2 (August 28, 2012): 113; Didier Raoult, "The Post-Darwinist Rhizome of Life," *The Lancet* 375 (January 9, 2010): 104–105; Carl R. Woese, "On the Evolution of Cells," *Proceedings of the U.S. National Academy of Sciences* 99 (June 25, 2002): 8742–8747; Graham Lawton, "Why Darwin Was Wrong about the Tree of Life," *New Scientist* (January 21, 2009): 34–39; Stephen C. Meyer, Paul A. Nelson, Jonathan Moneymaker, Ralph Seelke, and Scott Minnich, *Explore Evolution: The Arguments for and against Neo-Darwinism* (London: Hill House, 2007).

14. See also: Ann Gauger, Douglas Axe, and Casey Luskin, *Science and Human Origins* (Seattle: Discovery Institute Press, 2012).

15. Kenneth R. Miller and Joseph S. Levine, *Biology* (Upper Saddle River, NJ: Prentice Hall: 1998), 658.

nisms and to deny actual, as opposed to apparent, design in living organisms—i.e., the third meaning of evolution discussed above—the concept becomes deeply problematic. Indeed, depending on how this particular understanding of theistic evolution is articulated, it generates either (1) logical contradictions, (2) a theologically heterodox view of divine action, or (3) a convoluted and scientifically vacuous explanation. In addition to this dilemma (or rather "*tri*-lemma"), a huge body of scientific evidence now challenges the creative power of the mutation/selection mechanism, especially with respect to some of the most striking appearances of design in biological systems. Let's examine each of these difficulties in more detail.

A Logically Contradictory View

In the first place, some formulations of theistic evolution that affirm the third meaning of evolution result in logical contradictions. For example, if the theistic evolutionist means to affirm the standard neo-Darwinian view of the natural selection/mutation mechanism as an *un*directed process while simultaneously affirming that God is still *causally responsible* for the origin of new forms of life, then the theistic evolutionist implies that God somehow guided or directed an unguided and undirected process. Logically, no intelligent being—not even God—can direct an undirected process. As soon as he directs it, the "undirected" process would no longer be undirected.

On the other hand, a proponent of theistic evolution may conceive of the natural selection/mutation mechanism as a *directed* process (with God perhaps directing specific mutations). This view represents a decidedly non-Darwinian conception of the evolutionary mechanism. It also constitutes a version of the theory of intelligent design—one that affirms that God intelligently designed organisms by actively directing mutations (or other processes) toward functional endpoints during the history of life. Yet, if living organisms are the result of a directed process, then it follows that the appearance of design in living organisms is real, not merely apparent or illusory. Nevertheless, chief proponents of theistic evolution reject the theory of intelligent design with its claim that the appearance of design in living organisms *is* real. Thus, any proponent of theistic evolution who affirms that God is directing the evolutionary mechanism, and who also rejects intelligent design, implicitly contradicts himself. (Of course, there is no contradiction in affirming both a God-guided mechanism of evolution and intelligent design, though few theistic evolutionists have publicly taken this view—see Ratzsch, *Nature, Design, and Science* for a notable exception.[16])

Theologically Problematic Views

Other formulations of theistic evolution explicitly *deny* that God is directing or guiding the mutation/selection mechanism, and instead see a much more limited divine role in the process of life's creation. One formulation affirms that God designed the laws of nature at the beginning of the universe to make the origin and development of life possible (or inevitable). This view is scientifically problematic, however, since it can be demonstrated (see chapter 6) that the information necessary to build even a single functional gene (or section of DNA) cannot have been contained in the elementary particles and energy present at the beginning of the universe.[17] Another formulation holds that God created the laws of nature at the beginning of the universe and also affirms that he constantly upholds those laws on a moment-by-moment basis. Nevertheless, both of these understandings of theistic evolution deny that God in any way actively directed the mutation/selection (or other evolutionary) mechanisms. Both formulations conceive of God's role in the *creation* of life (as opposed to the maintenance of physical law) as mainly passive rather than active or directive. In both views, the mechanisms of natural selection and random mutation (and/or other similarly undirected evolutionary mechanisms) are seen as the main causal actor(s) in producing new forms of life. Thus, God does not act directly or "intervene" within the orderly concourse of nature.

Yet, this view is arguably theologically problematic, at least for orthodox Jews and Christians who derive their understanding of divine action from the biblical text. This is easy to see in the first of

---

16. Del Ratzsch, *Nature, Design, and Science* (Albany, NY: SUNY Press, 2001)

17. Stephen C. Meyer, "The Difference It Doesn't Make," in *God and Evolution: Protestants, Catholics, and Jews Explore Darwin's Challenge to Faith*, ed. Jay Wesley Richards (Seattle: Discovery Institute Press, 2010), 147–164.

these two formulations, where God's activity is confined to an act of creation or design at the very beginning of the universe. Such a front-end loaded view of design is, of course, a logically possible view, but it is indistinguishable from deism. It, therefore, contradicts the plainly *theistic* view of divine action articulated in the Bible, where God acts in his creation after the beginning of the universe. Indeed, the Bible describes God as not only acting to create the universe in the beginning; it also describes him as presently upholding the universe in its orderly concourse *and* also describes him *as acting discretely as an agent within the natural order.* (See, for example, Gen. 1:27, "God created [*bara*] man"; Ex. 10:13 [NLT], "and the Lord *caused* an east wind to blow.")

The version of theistic evolution that affirms that God created *and* upholds the laws of nature, but does not actively direct the creation of life, is also theologically problematic—at least for those who profess a biblical understanding of God's nature and powers. If God is not at least directing the evolutionary process, then the origin of biological systems must be attributed, in some part, to nature acting independently of God's direction. This entails a diminished view of God's involvement in creation and divine sovereignty at odds with most traditional readings of the Bible (whether Jewish or Christian).[18] Indeed, if God did not at least direct the process of mutation and selection (and/or other relevant evolutionary mechanisms), but instead merely sustained the laws of nature that made them possible, then it follows that he could not know, and does not know, what those mechanisms would (or will) produce, including whether they would have produced human beings. Accordingly, many theistic evolutionists who embrace this view have insisted that the evolutionary process might just as well have produced "a big-brained dinosaur" as opposed to a big-brained bipedal hominid—i.e., human beings.[19] Since, in this view, nature has

18. Traditionally, theologians have understood the Bible to affirm the sovereignty of God and the absolute dependence of his creation upon him, not only for its ongoing existence (as in, "in him all things hold together"; see Col. 1:17) but also for its origin in the first place (as in, "Through him all things were made; without him nothing was made that has been made"; John 1:3 [NIV]).

19. Kenneth Miller, *Finding Darwin's God: A Scientist's Search for Common Ground between God and Evolution* (New York: HarperCollins, 1999); Miller, comments during "Evolution and Intelligent Design: An Exchange," at "Shifting Ground: Religion and Civic Life in America" conference, Bedford, New Hampshire, sponsored by the New Hampshire Humanities Council, March 24,

significant autonomy from God, and since God does not direct or control the evolutionary process, he cannot know what it will produce—a conclusion at odds with God's omniscience and providence. Similarly, since God does not direct the evolutionary process, what it produces cannot be said to express his specific intentions in creation—a conclusion that also stands at odds with the biblical claim that God made man expressly in his own image and "foreknew" him.

A Convoluted (and Scientifically Vacuous) Explanation

Perhaps because evangelical Christian advocates of theistic evolution have not wanted to embrace either the logical or the theological problems associated with affirming the third meaning of evolution, they have typically declined to specify whether they think the natural selection/random mutation mechanism is a directed or an undirected process. Instead, many affirm a scientifically convoluted and vacuous formulation of theistic evolution—at least insofar as it stands as an explanation for the appearance of design in living organisms.

Recall that from Darwin to the present, leading evolutionary biologists have acknowledged the appearance of design in living organisms and have sought to explain its origin. Darwinists and neo-Darwinists have sought to explain this appearance of design as the result of an undirected and unguided mechanism (natural selection acting on random variations or mutations) that can mimic the powers of a designing intelligence. Theistic evolutionists who affirm the creative power of this (and, perhaps, other related) evolutionary mechanism(s) have been loath to argue that God actively directed the evolutionary process in any discernible way. That, of course, would constitute a form of intelligent design, and most theistic evolutionists reject this idea outright.

Francis Collins, for example, has explicitly rejected the theory of intelligent design. Yet, the theory of intelligent design does not necessarily reject evolution in either of the first two senses above, but instead argues that key appearances of design in living organisms are real, not illusory. In rejecting the theory of intelligent design, Collins would,

---

2007; see also John G. West, "Nothing New under the Sun," in *God and Evolution: Protestants, Catholics, and Jews Explore Darwin's Challenge to Faith*, 40–45.

therefore, seem to be affirming the contrary, namely, that the appearance of design is not real but just an appearance.

He thus seems to commit himself to the position that the process that produced the appearance of design in living organisms is undirected. That would follow because, again, if it were otherwise—if the process were directed or guided—then the appearance of design in living organisms would be real and not *just* apparent.

Yet, in *The Language of God*, Collins does not specify whether the evolutionary process is directed or not, only that it "could be" directed. As he explains, "evolution could appear to us to be driven by chance, but from God's perspective the outcome would be entirely specified. Thus, God *could be* completely and intimately involved in the creation of all species, while from our perspective . . . this would appear a random and undirected process" (emphasis added).[20]

That God could have acted in such a concealed way is, of course, a logical possibility, but positing such a view, nevertheless, entails difficulties that proponents of theistic evolution rarely address.

First, this version of theistic evolution suggests a logically convoluted explanation for the appearance of design in living systems. Like classical Darwinism and neo-Darwinism, this version of theistic evolution denies that anything about living systems indicates that an actual designing intelligence played a role in their origin. Why? Theistic evolutionists, like mainstream neo-Darwinists, affirm the third meaning of evolution—i.e., the sufficiency of the natural selection/mutation mechanism (possibly in conjunction with other similarly naturalistic evolutionary mechanisms) as an explanation for the origin of new forms and features of life. Since natural selection and random mutations can account for the origin of biological systems (and their appearances of design), theistic evolutionists steadfastly deny the need to propose an actual designing intelligence.

Yet, having affirmed what classical Darwinists and neo-Darwinists affirm—namely, the sufficiency of standard evolutionary mechanisms—they then suggest that such mechanisms may only *appear* undirected and unguided. Francis Collins suggests that "from our perspective" mutation and selection "would appear a random and undirected pro-

20. Francis Collins, *The Language of God: A Scientist Presents Evidence for Belief* (New York: Free Press, 2006), 205.

cess." Thus, his formulation implies that the *appearance or illusion of design* in living systems results from the activity of an *apparently undirected* material process (i.e., classical and neo- Darwinism) except that this apparently undirected process is itself being used by a designing intelligence—or at least it *could* be, though no one can tell for sure. Or, to put it another way, we have moved from Richard Dawkins's famous statement that "biology is the study of complicated things that give the appearance of having been designed for a purpose"[21] to the proposition that "biology is the study of complicated things that give the appearance of having been designed for a purpose, though that appearance of design is an illusion (classical Darwinism), even though there may be an intelligent designer behind it all—in which case that appearance wouldn't be an illusion after all."

This tangled—indeed, convoluted—view of the origin of living systems adds nothing to our scientific understanding of what caused living organisms to arise. As such, it also represents an entirely vacuous explanation. Indeed, it has no empirical or scientific content beyond that offered by strictly materialistic evolutionary theories. It tells us nothing about God's role in the evolutionary process or even whether or not he had a role at all. It, thus, renders the modifier "theistic" in the term "theistic evolution" superfluous. It does not represent an alternative theory of biological origins, but a reaffirmation of some materialistic version of evolutionary theory restated using theological terminology.

Of course, theistic evolutionists who hold this view do not typically spell out its implications so as to reveal the convoluted nature of the explanation for the appearance of design that their view entails. Instead, they typically avoid discussing, or offering explanations for, the appearance of design in living systems altogether—though this appearance is so striking that even secular evolutionary biologists have long and consistently acknowledged it.[22]

Theistic evolutionists such as Collins also deny what advocates of intelligent design affirm, namely, that the past activity of a designing intelligence, including God's intelligence, is *detectable* or discernible in living systems. Yet, denying the detectability of design in nature gen-

---

21. Dawkins, *Blind Watchmaker*, 1.
22. Ibid.; Crick, *What Mad Pursuit*, 138.

erates another theological difficulty. In particular, this view seems to contradict what the biblical record affirms about the natural world (or "the things that are made") revealing the reality of God and his "invisible qualities" such as his power, glory, divine nature and wisdom. As John West has explained,

> [Francis Collins' version of theistic evolution] still seriously conflicts with the Biblical understanding of God and His general revelation. Both the Old and New Testaments clearly teach that human beings can recognize God's handiwork in nature through their own observations rather than [through] special divine revelation. From the psalmist who proclaimed that the "heavens declare the glory of God" (Psalm 19) to the Apostle Paul who argued in Rom. 1:20 that "since the creation of the world His invisible attributes are clearly seen, being understood by the things that are made," the idea that we can see design in nature was clearly taught. Jesus himself pointed to the feeding of birds, the rain and the sun, and the exquisite design of the lilies of the field as observable evidence of God's active care towards the world and its inhabitants (Matt. 5:44-45, 48; 6:26-30). . . . to head off a direct collision between undirected Darwinism and the doctrine of God's sovereignty, Collins seems to depict God as a cosmic trickster who misleads people into thinking that the process by which they were produced was blind and purposeless, even when it wasn't.[23]

This Book: A Critique of Two Key Meanings of Theistic Evolution

In the chapters that follow we will provide a much more extensive critique of theistic evolution in three distinct sections of this book. Our three sections will not correspond to the three different meanings of the term evolution, but rather to three distinct disciplinary sets of concerns: scientific, philosophical, and theological. In each section of the book, however, our authors will carefully define the specific formulation of theistic evolution they are critiquing.

In the first section we provide a *scientific* critique of theistic evolution. But neither in this section, nor in any other, do we critique theistic

---

23. West, "Nothing New under the Sun," 46–47.

evolution where evolution is defined as meaning merely "change over time." Instead, our scientific critique will focus first on the version of theistic evolution that affirms the sufficiency (or creative power) of the mechanism of mutation and natural selection as an explanation for the origin of new forms of life (and the appearances of design that they manifest). The first group of essays (chapters 1–9) will show that the versions of theistic evolution that affirm the creative power of the natural selection/random mutation mechanism (as well as other purely materialistic evolutionary mechanisms) are now contradicted by a wealth of scientific evidence from an array of biological subdisciplines, including molecular biology, protein science, paleontology, and developmental biology.

We start our scientific critique of theistic evolution discussing the alleged creative power of the main mechanisms of evolutionary change because theistic evolutionists want to argue that God has worked undetectably through these various evolutionary mechanisms and processes to produce all the forms of life on our planet today. They equate and identify evolutionary processes such as natural selection and random mutation with the creative work of God. Yet, we will argue in the opening section of this book, chapters 1–9, that the main mechanisms postulated in both biological and chemical evolutionary theory lack the creative power necessary to produce genuine biological innovation and morphological novelty.

In chapter 1, Douglas Axe argues that people do not need specialized scientific training to recognize the implausibility of Darwinian (or other materialistic) explanations for the origin of living forms—though he also argues that rigorous scientific analysis reinforces our intuitive conviction that the integrated complexity of living systems could not have arisen by accidental or undirected processes. Consequently, he suggests that people of faith who yield core convictions about the intelligent design of life—out of deference to the supposed scientific authority of spokesmen for Darwinism—do so unnecessarily and with a substantial apologetic cost to their faith.

In chapter 2, I (Stephen Meyer) follow up on Axe's argument by showing that a rigorous scientific and mathematical analysis of the neo-Darwinian process does, indeed, reinforce the pervasive intuition to which Axe appeals. I show, based in part on some of Axe's own experimental work, that the random mutation and natural selection mechanism lacks the creative power to generate the new genetic information necessary to produce new proteins and forms of life.

In chapter 3, Matti Leisola extends our critique of the sufficiency of the neo-Darwinian mechanism. He shows, citing some of his own experimental work on DNA and proteins, that random mutational processes produce only extremely limited changes, even with the help of natural selection.

In chapter 4, we briefly shift our focus from biological evolution to chemical evolution, the branch of evolutionary theory that attempts to explain the origin of the first life from simpler nonliving chemicals. In this chapter, organic chemist James Tour shows that undirected *chemical* evolutionary processes and mechanisms have not demonstrated the creative power to generate the first living cell from simpler molecules. Basing his argument on his extensive knowledge of what it takes to synthesize organic compounds, Tour shows why known chemical processes do not provide plausible mechanisms for the synthesis of the complex bio-macromolecules and molecular machines necessary for life. We should make clear, in introducing his chapter, that Tour does not regard himself as a partisan to the debate over theistic evolution, one way or another. He has, nevertheless, kindly given us permission to publish an abridged version of a previously published essay in order to make more widely known the scientific problems associated with chemical evolutionary theory—in particular, its lack of any demonstrated mechanism for generating the molecular machinery necessary to the first life.

In chapter 5, Winston Ewert shows that attempts to solve the problem of the origin of biological information by simulating the evolutionary process in a computer environment have also failed. Instead, he shows that, to the extent that well-known evolutionary algorithms (computer programs) simulate the production of new genetic information, they do so as a consequence of information already provided to the program by the intelligent programmer who wrote the code—thus simulating, if anything, the need for intelligent design, not the sufficiency of an undirected evolutionary processes.

In chapter 6, I critique the idea that God carefully arranged matter at the beginning of the universe so as to ensure that life would inevitably evolve without any additional intelligent input or activity. In this chapter, I show why this version of theistic evolution, though attractive as a potential synthesis of the ideas of creation and evolution, fails for demonstrable scientific reasons to account for the origin of the information in the DNA molecule—and, thus, the information needed to produce the first life.

Next, in chapter 7, Jonathan Wells shows that, in addition to new genetic information, building new organisms requires information not stored in DNA—what is called "epigenetic" (or "ontogenetic") information. He argues that this fact alone demonstrates the inadequacy of the neo-Darwinian mechanism. Whereas neo-Darwinism asserts that all the new information necessary to build new forms of life arises as the result of random mutational changes in DNA, developmental biology has shown instead that building new forms of life also depends on information not stored in the DNA molecule. For this reason, the "gene-centric" mutation and natural selection mechanism simply cannot explain the origin of anatomical novelty.

In chapter 8, I team up with Ann Gauger and Paul Nelson to show that many mainstream evolutionary biologists have now rejected orthodox neo-Darwinian evolutionary theory precisely because they recognize that the mutation/natural selection mechanism lacks the creative power to generate novel biological form. In support of this claim, we describe some of the new theories of evolution (and evolutionary mechanisms) that mainstream evolutionary biologists are now proposing as alternatives to textbook neo-Darwinism. Yet we also show that none of these new evolutionary theories invoke mechanisms with the power to produce either the genetic or the epigenetic information necessary to generate novel forms of life.

In chapter 9, Sheena Tyler describes the exquisite orchestration necessary for the development of animals from embryo to adult form. She argues that nothing about these carefully choreographed processes suggests that they might have originated as the result of random mutational tinkering or other undirected processes. Instead, she argues that they exhibit hallmarks of design.

For advocates of theistic evolution (where evolution is understood to affirm the third meaning of evolution), the growing scientific skepticism about the adequacy of the neo-Darwinian and other evolutionary mechanisms presents an acute problem, quite apart from the logical and theological considerations outlined above. If many evolutionary biologists themselves no longer agree that the mutation/selection mechanism has the creative power to explain novel biological forms, and if no alternative evolutionary mechanism has yet demonstrated that power either, then the claim that apparently unguided evolutionary processes are God's way of creating new forms of life is, increasingly, a relic of an obsolete scientific viewpoint. But that raises a question: if the evidence doesn't support the creative power of evolutionary mechanisms, why claim that these mechanisms represent the means by which God created? Why attempt to synthesize mainstream evolutionary theory with a theistic understanding of creation?

After critiquing versions of theistic evolution that affirm the sufficiency of various naturalistic evolutionary mechanisms, the second part of the science section of the book (chapters 10–17) critiques versions of theistic evolution that assume the truth of universal common descent, the second meaning of evolution discussed above. These chapters also take a critical look at the claims of evolutionary anthropologists who assert that human beings and chimpanzees have evolved from a common ancestor.

In chapter 10, paleontologist Günter Bechley and I examine the logical structure of argument for universal common descent, with a particular focus on what the fossil record can tell us about whether all forms of life do, or do not, share a common ancestor. Though theistic evolutionists often portray this part of evolutionary theory as a fact, even as they may acknowledge doubts about the creative power of the neo-Darwinian mechanism, we have become skeptical about universal common descent. In this chapter we explain why, and use the fossil evidence to illustrate how a scientifically informed person might reasonably come to doubt the arguments for universal common ancestry.

Then in chapter 11, Casey Luskin shows that a wealth of evidence from several different subdisciplines of biology, not just paleontology, now challenges this universal common descent and the "monophyletic" picture of the history of life it presents.

In chapter 12, Paul Nelson argues that the theory of universal common descent rests less upon supporting evidence than upon a number of questionable scientific and philosophical assumptions. He argues that the theory of universal common descent has been insulated from critical testing largely because these assumptions have rarely been questioned.

In this same section of the book, we also offer several chapters challenging the idea that chimpanzees and humans, in particular, share a common ancestor. Chapter 13, by Ann Gauger, explains what is at stake in the debate about human origins. Chapter 14, by Casey Luskin, shows that the fossil record does not support the evolutionary story about the origin of human beings. Chapter 15, by Ann Gauger, Ola Hössjer, and Colin Reeves, shows that the genetic uniqueness of human beings contradicts that story as well. Chapter 16, also by Gauger, Hössjer, and Reeves, challenges theistic evolutionists who claim that evolutionary theory and its subdiscipline of population genetics have rendered untenable any belief in an original male and female pair as the parents of the entire human race.

Finally, in chapter 17 Christopher Shaw, one of the science editors of this volume, concludes this section of the book with an interesting article on the role of bias in science that helps shed light on why so many scientists have found neo-Darwinian evolutionary theory persuasive despite its evident empirical difficulties.

Our critique of theistic evolution does not stop with scientific concerns, however. In the second section of the book, we address philosophical problems with the versions of theistic evolution critiqued in our science section. Given the known scientific inadequacy of the neo-Darwinian mutation/natural selection mechanism, and the absence of any alternative evolutionary mechanism with sufficient creative power to explain the origin of major innovations in biological form and information, we argue that theistic evolution devolves into little more than an *a priori* commitment to methodological naturalism—the idea that scientists must limit themselves to strictly materialistic explanations and that scientists may not offer explanations making reference to intelligent design or divine action, or make any reference to theology in scientific discourse.

In chapter 18, J. P. Moreland notes that, for good or ill, philosophical assumptions necessarily influence the practice of science. He argues that science and scientists, therefore, need philosophy, but also need to be more self-critical about the philosophical assumptions that they accept, lest they adopt assumptions that impede scientists in their search for the truth about the natural world.

In chapter 19, Paul Nelson and I critique the principle of methodological naturalism and also critique how theistic evolutionists invoke this methodological convention to justify their commitment to contemporary evolutionary theory despite its evident empirical shortcomings. Methodological naturalism asserts that, to qualify as scientific, a theory must explain all phenomena by reference to purely physical or material—that is, non-intelligent or non-purposive—causes or processes. We show that, though many scientists adhere to this rule, attempts to justify methodological naturalism as a rule for how science *should* function have failed within the philosophy of science. In this chapter we also critique the way theistic evolutionists invoke the God-of-the-gaps objection to reject all nonmaterialistic explanations for the origin of new forms or features of life—that is, we critique the use of this objection as a way of justifying methodological naturalism. Most importantly, we show how methodological naturalism impedes the truth-seeking function of scientific investigations of biological origins, and should, for that reason alone, be jettisoned.

In chapter 20, Stephen Dilley argues that a logically consistent theistic evolutionist should reject methodological naturalism. Dilley notes that methodological naturalism prohibits the use of theology-laden claims and that it denies that non-naturalistic theories (such as intelligent design or creationism) are "scientific." Yet, he argues, key scientific arguments for evolutionary theory—from the *Origin* to the present—either rely on theology-laden claims or attempt to provide evidence-based refutations of non-naturalistic theories—thereby, inadvertently implying that such theories do make scientific claims.

In chapter 21, J. P. Moreland argues that adopting theistic evolution undermines the rational plausibility of Christianity. By assuming that only scientific methods and evidence produce knowledge, and that theological and biblical teaching do not, theistic evolutionists propagate a form of scientism that forces theists to constantly revise biblical truth claims in light of the latest scientific findings or theories—however unsubstantiated, provisional, or speculative they may be. In so doing, theistic evolutionists undermine Christian confidence in the teachings of Scripture and contribute to disdain or contempt for Christian truth claims among nonbelievers.

In chapter 22, Jack Collins lays out the biblical understanding of how God works in the natural world, explaining the Bible's implicit and explicit theology of nature (its "metaphysic"). He also explains how the biblical writers, and biblically based theologians, conceive of such terms or concepts as "nature," "miracle," "science," and "design." He argues that a careful consideration of a biblical view of divine action (and interaction with nature) establishes criteria for discerning miraculous events without downplaying God's role in all natural events, and without committing the God-of-the-gaps fallacy. He shows that, whereas the theory of intelligent design is fully compatible with this biblical view of how God interacts with nature, theistic evolution is not.

In chapter 23, Garrett DeWeese points out that moral evil, caused by free moral agents, and natural evil, caused by impersonal forces in the environment, are both used as evidence against the existence of God. He argues that adopting theistic evolution makes answering these objections to Christian belief immeasurably more difficult. It does so, he explains, in the case of natural evil because theistic evolution cannot distinguish between God's original (good) acts of creation and the ongoing or current natural processes. Instead, theistic evolutionists regard the natural processes we currently observe as the means by which God created. Thus, insofar as those processes cause harm to human beings—whether through destructive mutations or through such things as earthquakes or hurricanes—theistic evolutionists must maintain that God is responsible for such "natural evil." By contrast, creationists acknowledge a distinction between God's original good acts of creation and current processes of nature that may have been affected by the acts of sinful moral agents. This distinction, DeWeese argues, allows for coherent explanations of the existence of natural evil that does not impugn God's goodness. DeWeese offers one explanation that he favors.

In chapter 24, Colin Reeves examines the so-called "complementary" model for the interaction of science and Scripture, commonly assumed by those who promote "theistic evolution." This view of the relationship between scientific and biblical truth claims has led many theistic evolutionists to accept evolutionary claims about human origins uncritically. They do this, Reeves argues, because they assume that all scientific claims can be made "complementary" to biblical truth claims since the two different types of claims describe reality in two fundamentally different nonintersecting (though complementary) ways. Reeves argues that the complementarity model in effect sanctions doctrinal revisionism because in practice it demands the subordination of scriptural claims to scientific claims—in contrast to the Reformation emphasis on the primacy, authority, and clarity of Scripture, an emphasis that actually played a key role in the development of modern science.

In chapter 25, Tapio Puolimatka argues that current evolutionary accounts fail to explain the origin of moral conscience. He explains why the human capacity to discern moral truths cannot be reduced to merely a product of a random search through a vast set of combinatorial possibilities—in other words, a search of the sort that random mutation and natural selection allegedly can accomplish. Although theistic evolutionists assume that the idea of moral conscience as an expression of God's design for humans is fully compatible with various naturalistic causal stories about the origin of the conscience, they fail to specify a natural process that could plausibly explain its origin.

In chapter 26, John West examines how C. S. Lewis, the beloved Christian author and former tutor and "reader" in philosophy at Oxford University, viewed the theory of evolution. Though many theistic evolutionists claim him as an authoritative proponent of their view, West shows—based on original archival research as well as a careful reading of key Lewis books and essays—that he was far more skeptical of Darwinian evolution than current apologists for theistic evolution claim.

In the final section of the book, we examine specifically theological and biblical difficulties associated with those versions of theistic evolution that affirm either universal common descent, the adequacy or creative power of the mutation/selection mechanism, or both—where the two notions of evolution affirmed jointly are sometimes simply referred to as "macroevolution." Wayne Grudem, the theological editor of this volume, will introduce these chapters in his "Biblical and Theological Introduction," which follows.

In summary, just as there are different meanings of the term evolution, there can be different concepts of theistic evolution. In the chapters that follow we highlight the versions of theistic evolution that the authors of this book regard as problematic or untenable. We highlight several different types of difficulties—scientific, philosophical and theological—facing the most problematic formulations of theistic evolution, and focus on the tensions that arise as theistic evolutionists attempt to reconcile an essentially materialistic theory of biological origins with a theistic understanding of creation.

References and Recommended Reading

Ayala, Francisco J. "Darwin's Greatest Discovery: Design without Designer." *Proceedings of the National Academy of Sciences USA* 104 (May 15, 2007): 8567–8573.

Axe, Douglas, Ann Gauger, and Casey Luskin. *Science and Human Origins*. Seattle: Discovery Institute Press, 2012.

Bowler, Peter J. "The Changing Meaning of 'Evolution.'" *Journal of the History of Ideas* 36 (1975): 99.

Collins, Francis. *The Language of God: A Scientist Presents Evidence for Belief*. New York: Free Press, 2006.

Coyne, Jerry. "Not Black and White," review of Michael Majerus's 1998 book, *Melanism: Evolution in Action. Nature* 396 (1998): 35–36.

Crick, Francis. *What Mad Pursuit: A Personal View of Scientific Discovery*. New York: Basic Books, 1988.

Darwin, Charles. *On the Origin of Species by Means of Natural Selection*. A facsimile of the first edition, published by John Murray, London, 1859. Reprint, Cambridge, MA: Harvard University Press, 1964.

———. *The Life and Letters of Charles Darwin*. Edited by Francis Darwin. Vol. 1: 278–279, 1887.

Dawkins, Richard. *The Blind Watchmaker*. New York: W. W. Norton, 1986.

Doolittle, W. Ford. "The Practice of Classification and the Theory of Evolution, and What the Demise of Charles Darwin's Tree of Life Hypothesis Means for Both of Them," 2221–2228. *Philosophical Transactions of the Royal Society B* 364 (2009).

Futuyma, Douglas J. *Evolutionary Biology.* Sunderland, MA: Sinauer Associates, 1998.

Gauger, Ann, Douglas Axe, and Casey Luskin. *Science and Human Origins.* Seattle: Discovery Institute Press, 2012.

Gordon, Malcolm S. "The Concept of Monophyly: A Speculative Essay." *Biology and Philosophy* 14 (1999): 331–348.

Koonin, Eugene V. "The Biological Big Bang Model for the Major Transitions in Evolution." *Biology Direct* 2 (2007): 21.

Lawton, Graham. "Why Darwin Was Wrong about the Tree of Life." *New Scientist* (January 21, 2009): 34–39.

Mayr, Ernst. Foreword to Michael Ruse, *Darwinism Defended: A Guide to the Evolution Controversies.* Reading, MA: Addison-Wesley. xi–xii, 1982.

Merhej, Vicky, and Didier Raoult. "Rhizome of Life, Catastrophes, Sequence Exchanges, Gene Creations, and Giant Viruses: How Microbial Genomics Challenges Darwin." *Frontiers in Cellular and Infection Microbiology* 2 (August 28, 2012): 113.

Meyer, Stephen C. "The Difference It Doesn't Make." In *God and Evolution: Protestants, Catholics, and Jews Explore Darwin's Challenge to Faith.* Edited by Jay Wesley Richards, 147–164. Seattle: Discovery Institute Press., 2010.

———. *Darwin's Doubt: The Explosive Origin of Animal Life and the Case for Intelligent Design.* New York: HarperOne, 2013.

Meyer, Stephen C., Paul A. Nelson, Jonathan Moneymaker, Ralph Seelke, and Scott Minnich. *Explore Evolution: The Arguments for and against Neo-Darwinism.* London, UK: Hill House Press, 2007.

Miller, Kenneth. *Finding Darwin's God: A Scientist's Search for Common Ground between God and Evolution.* New York: HarperCollins, 1999.

———. Comments during "Evolution and Intelligent Design: An Exchange." At "Shifting Ground: Religion and Civic Life in America" conference, Bedford, New Hampshire, sponsored by the New Hampshire Humanities Council, March 24, 2007.

Miller, Kenneth R., and Joseph S. Levine. *Biology,* 658. Englewood Cliffs, NJ: Prentice Hall, 1st edition 1991.

————. *Biology*, 658. Englewood Cliffs, NJ: Prentice Hall, 2nd edition, 1993.

————. *Biology*, 658 Englewood Cliffs, NJ: Prentice Hall, 3rd edition. 658, 1995.

————. *Biology*, 658. Upper Saddle River, NJ: Prentice Hall, 4th edition, 1998.

Raoult, Didier. "The Post-Darwinist Rhizome of Life." *The Lancet* 375 (January 9, 2010): 104–105.

Ratzsch, Del. *Nature, Design, and Science: The Status of Design in Design in Natural Science*. Albany, NY: State University of New York Press, 2001.

Simpson, George Gaylord. *The Meaning of Evolution*. Revised Edition. New Haven, CT: Yale University Press, 1967.

Syvanen, Michael. "Evolutionary Implications of Horizontal Gene Transfer." *Annual Review of Genetics* 46 (2012): 339–356.

Thomson, Keith S. "The Meanings of Evolution." *American Scientist* 70 (1982): 529–531.

Wells, Jonathan. "Second Thoughts about Peppered Moths." *The Scientist* 13 (1999). 13.

West, John G. "Nothing New Under the Sun." In *God and Evolution: Protestants, Catholics, and Jews Explore Darwin's Challenge to Faith*. Edited by Jay Wesley Richards, 40–45. Seattle: Discovery Institute Press, 2010.

Woese, Carl R. "On the Evolution of Cells." *Proceedings of the National Academy of Sciences USA* 99 (June 25, 2002): 8742–8747.

Biblical and Theological Introduction

The Incompatibility of Theistic Evolution with the Biblical Account of Creation and with Important Christian Doctrines

WAYNE GRUDEM

The current debate about theistic evolution is not merely a debate about whether Adam and Eve really existed (though it is about that); nor is it merely a debate about some specific details such as whether Eve was formed from one of Adam's ribs; nor is it a debate about some minor doctrinal issues over which Christians have differed for centuries.

The debate is about much more than that. From the standpoint of theology, the debate is primarily about the proper interpretation of the first three chapters of the Bible, and particularly whether those chapters should be understood as truthful historical narrative, reporting events that actually happened. This is a question of much significance, because those chapters provide the historical foundation for the rest of the Bible and for the entirety of the Christian faith. And that means the debate is also about the validity of several major Christian doctrines for which those three chapters are foundational. In Genesis 1–3, Scripture teaches essential truths about the activity of God in creation, the origin of the universe, the creation of plants and animals on the earth, the origin and unity of the human race, the creation of manhood and womanhood, the origin of marriage, the origin of human sin and human death, and man's need for redemption from sin. Without the foundation laid down in those three chapters, the rest of the Bible would make no sense, and many of those doctrines would be undermined or lost. It is no exaggeration to say that those three chapters are essential to the rest of the Bible.

From the standpoint of science and philosophy, however, this is also a debate about scientific methodology and evidence. Specifically, the philosophical chapters in this book will ask whether the rules of science actually require scientists to consider only strictly materialistic explanations for the origins of life, so that even scientists who believe in God must affirm some kind of materialistic theory of evolution as the best scientific explanation of origins. These chapters will argue that such a limitation to materialistic explanations actually prevents scientists from pursuing the truth, and therefore that this limitation should be amended to allow for a more open search for the truth about the origins of life and the origin of the universe itself. Such a more open search for truth may in fact result in the recognition that a designing intelligence played a discernible role in the origin and diversity of life.

The science chapters in this book will also argue that much recent scientific research, rather than supporting current evolutionary accounts, in reality exposes significant challenges to evolutionary explanations of the origin and diversity of life. These chapters, and the scientific evidence they cite, suggest that no biblical scholars should feel "compelled by the scientific evidence" to interpret Genesis in a way that presupposes the truth of neo-Darwinian (or other contemporary versions of) macroevolutionary theory.

A. What This Book Is Not About

This book is not about the age of the earth. We are aware that many sincere Christians hold a "young earth" position (the earth is perhaps ten thousand years old), and many others hold an "old earth" position (the earth is 4.5 billion years old). This book does not take a position on that issue, nor do we discuss it at any point in the book.[1]

---

1. However, the science chapters that argue against a Darwinian explanation of the fossil record operate within the commonly assumed chronological framework of hundreds of millions of years

Furthermore, we did not think it wise to frame the discussion of this book in terms of whether the Bible's teachings about creation should be interpreted "literally." That is because, in biblical studies, the phrase "literal interpretation" is often a slippery expression that can mean a variety of different things to different people.[2] For example, some interpreters take it to refer to a mistaken kind of wooden *literalism* that would rule out metaphors and other kinds of figurative speech, but that kind of literalism is inappropriate to the wide diversity of literature found in the Bible.

In addition, any argument about a literal interpretation of Genesis 1 would run the risk of suggesting that we think each "day" in Genesis 1 must be a *literal* twenty-four-hour day. But we are aware of careful interpreters who argue that a "literal" interpretation of the Hebrew word for "day" still allows the "days" in Genesis 1 to be long periods of time, millions of years each. Yet other interpreters argue that the days could be normal (twenty-four-hour) days but with millions of years separating each creative day. Others understand the six creation days in Genesis to be a literary "framework" that portrays "days of forming" and "days of filling." Still others view the six days of creation in terms of an analogy with the work-week of a Hebrew laborer.[3] This book is not concerned with deciding which of these understandings of Genesis 1 is correct, or which ones are properly "literal."

Instead, the question is whether Genesis 1–3 should be understood as a *historical narrative* in the sense of *reporting events that the author*

---

for the earth's geological strata. We recognize that Christians who hold a young earth view would assume a different chronological framework.

2. See the discussion of various senses of "literal" interpretation in Vern Poythress, *Understanding Dispensationalists* (Grand Rapids, MI: Zondervan, 1987), 78–96. Poythress concludes, "What is literal interpretation? It is a confusing term, capable of being used to beg many of the questions at stake in the interpretation of the Bible. We had best not use the phrase" (96). See also his helpful discussion of the terms "literal" and "figurative" in "Correlations with Providence in Genesis 2," *Westminster Theological Journal* (*WTJ*) 78, no. 1 (Spring 2016): 44–48; also his insightful article, "Dealing with the Genre of Genesis and Its Opening Chapters," *WTJ* 78, no. 2 (Fall 2016): 217–230.

3. See John C. Lennox, *Seven Days That Divide the World: The Beginning according to Genesis and Science* (Grand Rapids, MI: Zondervan, 2011), 39–66, for a clear and perceptive explanation of these various understandings of the days of creation. Lennox favors the view (which I find quite plausible) that Genesis 1 speaks of "a sequence of six *creation* days; that is, days of normal length (with evenings and mornings as the text says) in which God acted to create something new, but days that might well have been separated by long periods of time" (54, emphasis original). He also favors the view that the original creation of the heavens and earth in Genesis 1:1–2 may have occurred long before the first "creation day" in Genesis 1:3–5, which would allow for a very old earth and universe (53).

wants readers to believe actually happened.[4] In later chapters, my argument, and the additional arguments of John Currid and Guy Waters, will be that Genesis 1–3 should not be understood as primarily figurative or allegorical literature, but should rather be understood as historical narrative, though it is historical narrative with certain unique characteristics. (See chapters 27, 28, and 29.)

Finally, this book is not about whether people who support theistic evolution are genuine Christians or are sincere in their beliefs. We do not claim in this book that anyone has carelessly or lightly questioned the truthfulness of Genesis 1–3. On the contrary, the supporters of theistic evolution with whom we interact give clear indications of being genuine, deeply committed Christians. Their writings show a sincere desire to understand the Bible in such a way that it does not contradict the findings of modern science regarding the origin of living creatures.

But we *are* concerned that they believe that the theory of evolution is so firmly established that they must accept it as true and must use it as their guiding framework for the interpretation of Genesis 1–3.

For example, Karl Giberson and Francis Collins write,

> The evidence for macroevolution that has emerged in the past few years is now overwhelming. Virtually all geneticists consider that the evidence proves common ancestry with a level of certainty comparable to the evidence that the Earth goes around the sun.[5]

Our goal in this book is to say to our friends who support theistic evolution, and to many others who have not made up their minds about this issue,

---

4. In arguing for the historicity of the early chapters of Genesis, C. John Collins rightly says, "In ordinary English a story is 'historical' if the author wants his audience to believe the events really happened" (C. John Collins, "A Historical Adam: Old-Earth Creation View," in *Four Views on the Historical Adam*, ed. Matthew Barrett and Ardel B. Caneday [Grand Rapids, MI: Zondervan, 2013], 147). Collins has a helpful discussion of what is meant by "history" on pages 146–148.

Craig Blomberg says, "a historical narrative recounts that which actually happened; it is the opposite of fiction" (*The Historical Reliability of the Gospels* [Downers Grove, IL: InterVarsity Press, 1987], xviii, n2).

See also the discussion by V. Phillips Long, *The Art of Biblical History* (Grand Rapids, MI: Zondervan, 1994), 58–87. Long prefers the term "historiography" (that is, the verbal report of events in the past) for what I am calling "historical narrative," but he recognizes that authors can define "history" and "historical narrative" in different ways. His conclusion is helpful: "We conclude then that historiography involves a creative, though constrained, attempt to depict and interpret significant events or sequences of events from the past" (87).

5. Karl Giberson and Francis Collins, *The Language of Science and Faith* (Downers Grove, IL: InterVarsity, 2011), 49.

1. that recent scientific evidence presents such significant challenges to key tenets of evolutionary theory that no biblical interpreter should think that an evolutionary interpretation of Genesis is "scientifically necessary";

2. that theistic evolution depends on a strictly materialistic definition of science that is philosophically problematic; and

3. that the Bible repeatedly presents as actual historical events many specific aspects of the origin of human beings and other living creatures that cannot be reconciled with theistic evolution, and that a denial of those historical specifics seriously undermines several crucial Christian doctrines.

B. Theistic Evolution Claims that Genesis 1–3 Is Not a Historical Narrative That Reports Events That Actually Happened

1. Genesis 1–3 as Figurative or Allegorical Literature, Not Factual History

At the heart of theistic evolution[6] is the claim that the first three chapters of the Bible should not be understood as a historical narrative in the sense of claiming that the events it records actually happened. That is, these chapters should rather be understood as primarily or entirely figurative, allegorical, or metaphorical literature.

As mentioned in note 6, above, the BioLogos Foundation hosts the primary website for thoughtful material relating to theistic evolution. Some of its writers are quite forthright in their claims, such as Denis Lamoureux, who says bluntly, "Adam never existed,"[7] and, "Holy

---

6. The BioLogos website, hosted by the BioLogos Foundation, is the primary source for thoughtful material relating to theistic evolution. The authors featured on BioLogos usually prefer the term "evolutionary creation" to the term "theistic evolution," but both terms are found in their literature. We have kept the term "theistic evolution" in this book because it has been the standard phrase used to describe this position for a century or more in theological discussion. (See, e.g., Louis Berkhof, *Systematic Theology* [Grand Rapids, MI: Eerdmans, 1941], 162: "Theistic evolution is not tenable in the light of Scripture." Berkhof also refers to the earlier critique of theistic evolution in the book by Alfred Fairhurst, *Theistic Evolution* [n.p.: Standard Publishing, 1919]).

In addition, the term "evolutionary creation" seems to us to be misleading, because people who support theistic evolution do not believe in "creation" in the ordinary sense that Christians use the term, to refer to God's direct activity in creating specific plants and animals and in creating human beings; rather, they mean only the initial *creation of matter* with properties that would lead to the evolution of living things. Francis Collins himself had earlier argued against using the word "creation" in connection with theistic evolution "for fear of confusion" (*The Language of God* [New York: Free Press, 2006], 203).

7. Denis Lamoureux, "No Historical Adam: Evolutionary Creation View," in *Four Views on the Historical Adam*, Barrett and Caneday, 58. The same statement by Lamoureux is found in

Scripture makes statements about how God created living organisms that in fact never happened," and, "Real history in the Bible begins roughly around Genesis 12 with Abraham."[8] Elsewhere on the BioLogos website, Peter Enns argues that "Maybe Israel's history happened first, and the Adam story was written to reflect that history. In other words, the Adam story is really an Israel story placed in primeval time. It is not a story of human origins but of Israel's origins."[9]

Others are less specific about these details but still claim that Genesis 1–3 is not historical narrative. Francis Collins says these chapters should be understood as "poetry and allegory,"[10] and Denis Alexander views Genesis 1–3 as "figurative and theological" literature.[11]

Yet another approach comes from John H. Walton. He says the accounts of the forming of Adam and Eve in Genesis 1–2 should not be understood as "accounts of how those two individuals were uniquely formed," but rather should be understood as stories about "archetypes," that is, stories that use an individual person as sort of an allegory for Everyman, someone who "embodies all others in the group" (in this case, the human race).[12] Therefore Walton says that the Bible makes "no claims" regarding "biological human origins," for Genesis 2 "talks about the *nature of all* people, not the unique *material origins* of Adam and Eve."[13] In fact, he says that "the Bible does not really offer any information about material human origins."[14]

In all of these approaches, the result is the same: Genesis 1–3 (or at least Genesis 1–2) should not be understood as claiming to be a report of actual historical events. In order to understand the reasons for this conviction, we first need to understand theistic evolution in more detail.

---

his article on the BioLogos website at Denis Lamoureux, "Was Adam a Real Person? Part 2," *BioLogos*, September 11, 2010, http://biologos.org/blogs/archive/was-adam-a-real-person-part-2.

8. Lamoureux, "No Historical Adam," 56, 44.

9. Peter Enns, "Adam Is Israel," *BioLogos*, March 2, 2010, http://biologos.org/blogs/archive/adam-is-israel. In the next paragraph Enns says that he himself holds this view. Giberson and Collins mention this view of Enns as another possible interpretation of the Adam and Eve story (*Language of Science and Faith*, 211).

10. Collins, *Language of God*, 206; see similar statements on 150, 151, 175, 207.

11. Denis Alexander, *Creation or Evolution: Do We Have to Choose?*, 2nd. ed. (Oxford and Grand Rapids, MI: Monarch, 2014), 185; see also 189, 197, 230, 320.

12. John H. Walton, *The Lost World of Adam and Eve: Genesis 2–3 and the Human Origins Debate* (Downers Grove, IL: InterVarsity Press, 2015), 74.

13. Ibid., 181, emphasis original; see also 33–34, 35–45, 81.

14. Ibid., 192. For an extensive reply to Walton's claims, see the detailed arguments of John Currid in chapter 28 of this book.

2. A Definition of Theistic Evolution

As Stephen Meyer explained above in his "Scientific and Philosophical Introduction," our focus in this book is on the version of theistic evolution that affirms "the sufficiency (or creative power) of the unguided, undirected mechanism of mutation and natural selection as an explanation for the origin of new forms of life (and the appearances of design that they manifest)."[15] In brief summary form, then, the form of theistic evolution that we are respectfully taking issue with is this belief:

> God created matter and after that did not guide or intervene or act directly to cause any empirically detectable change in the natural behavior of matter until all living things had evolved by purely natural processes.[16]

This definition is consistent with the explanation of prominent theistic evolution advocates Karl Giberson and Francis Collins:

> The model for divinely guided evolution that we are proposing here thus requires no "intrusions from outside" for its account of God's creative process, except for the origins of the natural laws guiding the process.[17]

More detail is provided in an earlier book by Francis Collins, eminent geneticist and founder of the BioLogos Foundation. He explains theistic evolution in this way:

1. The universe came into being out of nothingness, approximately 14 billion years ago.
2. Despite massive improbabilities, the properties of the universe appear to have been precisely tuned for life.
3. *While the precise mechanism of the origin of life on earth remains unknown, once life arose, the process of evolution and natural selection permitted the development of biological diversity and complexity over very long periods of time.*

---

15. See page 50.
16. This definition of theistic evolution was written by the editors of the present volume as a concise summary of the view we are opposing. In the paragraphs that follow, I have provided several quotations from authors who support theistic evolution in this sense, and these quotations give more detailed explanations of what the viewpoint involves.
17. Giberson and Collins, *Language of Science and Faith*, 115.

4. *Once evolution got underway, no special supernatural interven-tion was required.*

5. Humans are part of this process, sharing a common ancestor with the great apes.

6. But humans are also unique in ways that defy evolutionary explanation and point to our spiritual nature. This includes the existence of the Moral Law (the knowledge of right and wrong) and the search for God that characterizes all human cultures throughout history.[18]

3. God Was the Creator of Matter, Not of Living Creatures

What then do theistic evolutionists mean when they say that "God is the creator of all life," as in this statement:

> At BioLogos, we present the Evolutionary Creationism (EC) view-point on origins. Like all Christians, we fully affirm that *God is the creator of all life*—including human beings in his image. We fully affirm that the Bible is the inspired and authoritative word of God. We also accept the science of evolution as the best description for how God brought about the diversity of life on earth.[19]

They frequently mean that *God created matter* in the beginning with certain physical properties and then *the properties of matter* were enough to bring about all living things without any further direct activ-ity by God.[20] This eliminates the problem of any conflict with science, because modern evolutionary theory also holds that *matter by itself* evolved over a long period of time into all living things.

---

18. Francis S. Collins, *The Language of God: A Scientist Presents Evidence for Belief* (New York: Free Press, 2006), 200, emphasis added.

19. "How Is BioLogos Different from Evolutionism, Intelligent Design, and Creationism?" *BioLogos*, http://biologos.org/common-questions/christianity-and-science/biologos-id-creationism.

20. See, e.g., Alexander, *Creation or Evolution*, 436.

Since the question of the origin of life is a different question from the evolution of simple living organisms into complex organisms, some proponents of theistic evolution seem to allow for the possibility of a direct intervention of God at the point of the first creation of life. E.g., note the unspecified possibilities suggested in the words of Francis Collins: "*While the precise mechanism of the origin of life on earth remains unknown*, once life arose, the process of evolution and natural selection permitted the development of biological diversity and complexity over very long periods of time. . . . Once evolution got underway, no special supernatural intervention was required" (Collins, *Language of God*, 200, emphasis added).

However, in a subsequent book Karl Giberson and Francis Collins seem to expect that eventually a materialistic hypothesis will explain how life could have originated from nonliving matter: see *Language of Science and Faith*, 169–175.

4. There Were Not Merely Two, but Ten
Thousand Ancestors for the Human Race

Regarding the origin of the human race, Christians who support the-istic evolution differ over whether Adam and Eve actually existed as historical persons. Some (such as Denis Lamoureux, cited above) do not believe that Adam and Eve ever existed, while others believe in a historical Adam and Eve. But even this "historical Adam and Eve" is still not the Adam and Eve of the Bible, because they do not believe that they were the first human beings or that the whole human race descended from them. This is because they claim that current genetic studies indicate that the human race today is so diverse that we could not have descended from just two individuals such as an original Adam and Eve.

Francis Collins writes, "Population geneticists . . . conclude that . . . our species . . . descended from a common set of founders, approxi-mately 10,000 in number, who lived about 100,000 to 150,000 years ago."[21] Similarly, Denis Alexander says, "The founder population that was the ancestor of all modern humans . . . was only 9,000-12,500 reproductively active individuals."[22]

Therefore, those Christians who support theistic evolution and also want to retain belief in a historical Adam and Eve propose that God chose one man and one woman from among the thousands of human beings who were living on the earth and designated the man as "Adam" and the woman as "Eve." He then began to relate to them personally, and made them to be representatives of the entire human race.

But on this view, where did this early population of 10,000 human beings come from? We should not think that they came from just one "first human being" in the process of evolution, because there never was just one "first" human being from which everyone else descended. Rather, the evolutionary mutations in earlier life forms that led to the human race occurred bit by bit among thousands of different nearly human creatures. Some developed greater balance and the ability to walk upright. Others developed physical changes in their vocal organs

---

21. Collins, *Language of God*, 126; see also 207. Giberson and Collins claim that humans have descended from "several thousand people . . . not just two" (*Language of Science and Faith*, 209).
22. Alexander, *Creation or Evolution*, 265.

that would enable complex human speech. Still others developed larger brains and the capacity for abstract human reasoning. And there were many other such changes. Over time, the creatures with *some* of these beneficial mutations had an adaptive advantage, and more of their offspring survived. Eventually they began to mate with other creatures who had *other* human-like mutations, and eventually many thousands of human beings emerged from this evolutionary process, all of them descended from earlier, more primitive organisms.[23]

5. Then Who Were Adam and Eve?

What happens, then, to the biblical narratives about Adam and Eve? Denis Alexander describes several possible models (which he labels A, B, C, D, E; see note 24) by which to understand both the biblical story of Adam and Eve and modern evolutionary theory.[24] He favors "model C,"[25] which he explains as follows:

> According to model C, God in his grace chose a couple of Neolithic farmers in the Near East, perhaps around 8,000 years ago (the precise date is of little importance for this model), or maybe a community of farmers, to whom he chose to reveal himself in a special way, calling them into fellowship with himself—so that they might know him as a personal God. . . . This first couple, or community, have been termed *Homo divinus*, the divine humans, those who know the one true God, corresponding to the Adam and Eve of the Genesis account. . . . Certainly religious beliefs existed before this time, as people sought after God or gods in different parts of the world, offering their own explanations for the meaning of their lives, but *Homo divinus* marked the time at which God chose to

23. Alexander writes, "It should not be imagined that this [modern human] population somehow emerged 'all at once' with the distinctive features of anatomically modern humans. The . . . population . . . which eventually evolved into anatomically modern humans, must have done so over a period of tens of thousands of years. . . . Evolution, remember, is a gradual process" (*Creation or Evolution*, 298).

24. In model A, the narrative of Adam and Eve "is a myth" that teaches eternal truths without being constrained by historical particularity (288). In model B, Adam and Eve are either a mythical couple whose story represents something of the origin of the human race, or they are part of the earliest human population living in Africa perhaps 200,000 years ago (288–289). Model C is the one Alexander favors (see main text). Model D represents an old earth creationist view, with Adam and Eve created directly by God, and model E represents a young earth creationist view (294). Alexander thinks that models D and E are scientifically indefensible (282–304).

25. Alexander, *Creation or Evolution*, 303.

reveal himself and his purposes for humankind for the first time. . . . [Adam] is . . . viewed as the federal head of the whole of humanity alive at that time. . . . The world population in Neolithic times is estimated to lie in the range of 1-10 million, genetically just like Adam and Eve, but in model C it was these two farmers out of all those millions to whom God chose to reveal himself.[26]

N. T. Wright proposes a similar explanation:

Perhaps what Genesis is telling us is that God chose one pair from the rest of the early hominids for a special, strange, demanding vocation. This pair (call them Adam and Eve if you like) were to be the representatives of the whole human race.[27]

Giberson and Collins propose a similar view:

A common synthetic view integrating the biblical and scientific accounts sees human-like creatures evolving as the scientific evidence indicates, steadily becoming more capable of relating to God. At a certain point in history, God entered into a special relationship with those who had developed the necessary characteristics, endowing them with the gift of his image. . . . this view can fit whether the humans in question constituted a group—symbolized by Adam and Eve—or a specific male-female pair.[28]

The difficulty with all of these theistic evolution explanations of "Adam and Eve" arises because they differ significantly from the biblical account in Genesis 1–3. They all propose that many thousands of human beings were on the earth prior to Adam and Eve, and so Adam and Eve were not the first human beings, nor has the entire human race descended from them. In addition, there was human death and human sin (such as violence, instinctive aggression, and worship of false gods)[29] long before Adam and Eve.

---

26. Ibid., 290–291.

27. N. T. Wright, "Excursus on Paul's Use of Adam," in Walton, *Lost World of Adam and Eve*, 177. John Walton himself proposes that Adam and Eve can be seen as "elect individuals drawn out of the human population and given a particular representative role in sacred space" (Walton, "A Historical Adam: Archetypal Creation View," in *Four Views on the Historical Adam*, 109).

28. Giberson and Collins, *Language of Science and Faith*, 212.

29. Denis Alexander says, "Certainly religious beliefs existed before this time [the time of Adam and Eve], as people sought after God or gods in different parts of the world, offering their own explanations for the meaning of their lives" (*Creation or Evolution*, 290).

6. Twelve Differences between Events Recounted in the Bible and Theistic Evolution

We can now enumerate twelve points at which theistic evolution (as currently promoted by the prominent supporters cited) differs from the biblical creation account taken as a historical narrative. According to theistic evolution:

1. Adam and Eve were not the first human beings (and perhaps they never even existed).
2. Adam and Eve were born from human parents.
3. God did not act directly or specially to create Adam out of dust[30] from the ground.
4. God did not directly create Eve from a rib[31] taken from Adam's side.
5. Adam and Eve were never sinless human beings.
6. Adam and Eve did not commit the first human sins, for human beings were doing morally evil things[32] long before Adam and Eve.
7. Human death did not begin as a result of Adam's sin, for human beings existed long before Adam and Eve and they were always subject to death.
8. Not all human beings have descended from Adam and Eve, for there were thousands of other human beings on Earth at the time that God chose two of them as Adam and Eve.
9. God did not directly act in the natural world to create different "kinds" of fish, birds, and land animals.
10. God did not "rest" from his work of creation or stop any special creative activity after plants, animals, and human beings appeared on the earth.

---

30. It is possible that "dust" in Genesis 2:7 refers to a collection of different kinds of nonliving materials from the earth. My argument in a later chapter does not depend on that interpretative detail. See further discussion of the Hebrew word for "dust" by John Currid ("Theistic Evolution Is Incompatible with the Teachings of the Old Testament") on pages 868–869.

31. It is possible that the "rib" was accompanied by other material substances taken from Adam's body, for Adam himself says, "This at last is bone of my bones *and flesh of my flesh*" (Gen. 2:23). My overall argument in a later chapter is not affected by that difference. See further discussion of the Hebrew word for "rib" on pages 802–803 and 859–860.

32. Some advocates of theistic evolution may claim that human beings prior to Adam and Eve did not have a human moral conscience, but they would still admit that these human beings were doing selfish and violent things, and worshiping various deities, things that from a biblical moral standard would be considered morally evil.

11. God never created an originally "very good" natural world in the sense of a world that was a safe environment, free of thorns and thistles and similar harmful things.

12. After Adam and Eve sinned, God did not place any curse on the world that changed the workings of the natural world and made it more hostile to mankind.

Clearly, these statements denying what the Genesis text at least appears to teach about God's active role (or supernatural acts) in creation, about the existence of an original man and woman from whom the rest of the human race is descended, and about the moral fall of human beings as the result of the sin of Adam, presuppose the truth of contemporary evolutionary theory. They also presuppose the truth of the evolutionary narrative about the origin of man by way of undirected material processes from lower primates—*as the proponents of theistic evolution openly acknowledge.*

Yet, as I will argue in chapter 27, no one would derive such a reading of the narrative from simply reading the biblical text alone. In fact, each of these twelve claims contradicts one or more parts of the text in Genesis 1–3, if it is understood as historical narrative (as I will argue that it must be understood).

However, even if some readers disagree with some of my exegesis,[33] and interpret *some* parts or elements of the narrative in Genesis 1–3 as figurative or allegorical, that would not eliminate the tension between the Genesis text and the claims of theistic evolution. Instead, to remove the contradiction between the two would require denying the historicity of nearly *all* of the text in Genesis 1–3.[34] In other words, even if interpreters acknowledge that Genesis uses some figures of speech or allegorical language to convey deeper, but concrete, historical realities

---

33. Some of the authors in the science and philosophy sections of the present volume may not agree with my closely historical reading of each part of the Genesis text. But they would still agree that theistic evolution contradicts significant historical claims in Genesis that are foundational to key Christian doctrines.

34. As I mentioned above, some supporters of theistic evolution still affirm the existence of an early couple named "Adam" and "Eve," but even then, the originally sinful Adam and Eve that they affirm, who were descended from human parents and were selected by God out of thousands of human beings already on the earth, are far different from the Adam and Eve found in the Bible. Therefore it is unclear exactly what parts of Genesis 1–3 would be affirmed as historically true by supporters of theistic evolution, if any parts at all.

(as some interpreters have),[35] theistic evolution still contradicts such a reading of the text.

In addition, I will argue in chapter 27 that to deny all historical import to what the biblical text claims (as opposed to what an evolutionary reading of the text might impose on it) would undermine a number of core Christian doctrines.

For example, however one interprets the sequence of events described in Genesis 1, the chapter clearly seems to affirm that God *acted* to create plants, animals, and man—that God actively *made* something, or *did* something, in creation. Yet according to theistic evolution, God did not *act* directly, discretely, or discernibly in time to create plants, animals or man. Indeed, theistic evolution insists that after the creation of the universe at the Big Bang, God did not *actively make* anything, but merely upheld (or observed) the ongoing natural processes that were themselves directly responsible for the origin of all life forms.

Such a revisionist understanding of the doctrine of the creation certainly agrees better with a contemporary neo-Darwinian understanding of biological origins—since that theory affirms the creative power of the mindless, undirected process of natural selection and random variation—but it does not comport well with a natural reading of the text of Genesis or the historic doctrine of the Christian church regarding creation. According to the doctrine of creation, God's powerful creative words, not natural selection and random mutation, were responsible for the creation of living creatures. Indeed, the New Testament further specifies that the eternal Son of God, the second person of the Trinity—not an undirected or impersonal material process—was the *active* agent that carried out God's creative works: "*All things were made through him*, and without him was not any thing made that was made" (John 1:3; see also 1 Cor. 8:6; Heb. 1:2).

Similarly, however broadly one interprets the story of Adam and Eve with the serpent in the garden of Eden, the story clearly seems to affirm—at the very least—that an act of rebellion by the common parents of the whole human race resulted in their descendants inher-

---

35. Indeed, even some of the authors in this book would accept that Genesis may well be using some figures of speech to convey such concrete historical realities.

iting a fallen or flawed moral nature (note the progressive proliferation of sin among Adam and Eve's descendants that is chronicled
in Genesis 4–6). Yet, by denying even such a minimalist historical
interpretation of Genesis 1, theistic evolution not only contradicts the
doctrine of the fall, it also results in an undermining of the doctrine
of the atonement. This becomes evident when we realize that the
New Testament teaches that the sacrifice of Jesus Christ was necessary because of a corrupt human nature that *all* men and women
inherited from a common ancestor (Adam). Yet, theistic evolutionists
either (a) deny that Adam and Eve existed, or (b) claim that if they
existed, Adam and Eve did not fall from innocence into sin and/or
(c) claim that not all human beings are descended from Adam—in all
cases fatally undermining the idea that all human beings received a
morally corrupted nature from Adam as a result of a single act of
rebellion against God ("one trespass led to condemnation for all
men. . . . by the one man's disobedience the many were made sinners";
Rom. 5:18–19).

Yet, if there was no Adam and no Eve, and/or if they did not fall
from a state of moral innocence into sin, and if Adam's corrupted sin
nature was not inherited by all his human descendants, then it is hard
to understand the very precise later biblical explanations of the parallel
way in which Christ's atoning sacrifice gained forgiveness for all who
were represented by him.[36] In fact, someone might argue that, if Paul
was wrong about the entire human race descending from Adam, he
must also have been wrong about all human beings *inheriting* a common sin nature from Adam, and therefore, he could well be wrong
about our gaining forgiveness and righteousness through our representation by Christ. It is unmistakable how Paul explicitly connects
representation by Adam and representation by Christ:

> For if, because of one man's trespass, death reigned through that
> one man, much more will those who receive the abundance of grace
> and the free gift of righteousness reign in life through the one man
> Jesus Christ. Therefore, as one trespass led to condemnation for
> all men, so one act of righteousness leads to justification and life

---

36. This argument is made in much more detail by Guy Waters (chapter 29, "Theistic Evolution
Is Incompatible with the Teachings of the New Testament").

for all men. For as by the one man's disobedience the many were made sinners, so by the one man's obedience the many will be made righteous. (Rom. 5:17–19)

In my later chapter, I will argue that not only the doctrines of creation and the atonement are undermined by theistic evolution, but several other doctrines as well.

Here, then, is a brief summary of my argument in that later chapter:

1. A nonhistorical reading of Genesis 1–3 does not arise from factors in the text itself but rather depends upon a prior commitment to an evolutionary framework of interpretation, a framework that the science and philosophy chapters in this volume show to be unjustified.
2. Several literary factors within Genesis itself give strong evidence that Genesis 1–3 is intended to be understood as historical narrative, claiming to report events that actually happened.
3. Both Jesus and the New Testament authors, in ten separate New Testament books, affirm the historicity of several events in Genesis 1–3 that are inconsistent with the theory of theistic evolution.
4. If the historicity of several of these events in Genesis 1–3 is denied, a number of crucial Christian doctrines that depend on these events will be undermined or lost.

In addition to my chapter, the biblical and theological section of this book contains four other chapters:

In chapter 28, John Currid analyzes in further detail specific Old Testament passages that are incompatible with theistic evolution.

In chapter 29, Guy Waters similarly analyzes specific New Testament passages that are incompatible with theistic evolution.

In chapter 30, Gregg Allison argues that, throughout the history of the church, those who were recognized as leaders and teachers in the church were required to affirm the belief that God is the "Maker of heaven and earth, and of *all things visible* and invisible" (Nicene Creed), an affirmation incompatible with theistic evolution.

In chapter 31, Fred Zaspel concludes that the eminent nineteenth-century Princeton theologian B. B. Warfield, though often cited as a supporter of theistic evolution, would not have agreed with theistic evolution as it is understood today.

But before you reach those chapters, please consider the arguments and evidence in the science and philosophy chapters, for they will show that no one today should feel compelled by modern science to adopt an evolutionary framework for interpreting Genesis 1–3, yet that is precisely what contemporary theistic evolutionists do.

SECTION I

THE SCIENTIFIC CRITIQUE
OF THEISTIC EVOLUTION

Section I, Part 1

. . . . .

The Failure of
Neo-Darwinism

1

Three Good Reasons for People of Faith to Reject Darwin's Explanation of Life

DOUGLAS D. AXE

SUMMARY

People of faith should reject the call to affirm the Darwinian explanation of life and should instead affirm the traditional understanding of divine creative action, which defies reduction to natural causes. There are three good reasons for this. (1) Acceptance of Darwinism carries a substantial apologetic cost. Specifically, if Darwin was right that life can be explained by accidental physical causes, then we must forfeit the claim that all humans are confronted by God's existence when we behold the wonders of the living world. (2) *All* accidental explanations of life, whether Darwinian or not, are demonstrably implausible. (3) The common justifications for accommodating Darwin's theory within the framework of traditional faith are confused.

· · · · ·

I. First Things First

You've heard the claim that natural selection acting upon random genetic mutations created all life from a primitive life form. In the century and a half since Darwin gave that idea its beginning, few claims have generated more controversy. How should people of faith respond to this controversy?

Two questions immediately present themselves:

1. Is Darwin's claim *correct*?
2. What would the implications for our faith be *if it were* correct?

Now, because many people think the answer to question 1 requires technical expertise, there's a tendency to answer it by *proxy*—choosing to side with experts in either the *yes* camp or the *no* camp and then entrusting the defense of that answer to those experts. As understandable as this is in some respects, I advise against it, for several reasons.

In the first place, there is widespread confusion even as to who the relevant experts are. Nonscientists tend to be so acutely aware of their lack of expertise that they defer to anyone with a science degree, most of whom have no more familiarity with the technical critique of Darwinism than anyone else. Indeed, because even highly accomplished biology professors are accomplished only within their narrow fields of specialization, it takes a certain amount of scientific familiarity just to discern who can really speak to the subject of biological origins from scientific experience.

Keith Fox and I have engaged in friendly debate on that subject, so I hope he won't mind me using him as an example. As a biochemistry professor at the University of Southampton in the UK, Fox is an established expert on how various molecules bind to DNA. Having done no research on that subject, I'm obviously in no position to critique his work. Likewise, having done no work on protein evolution, he is really in no position to critique my work. And in a professional context he wouldn't pretend otherwise. However, the origins topic has attracted such a wide following that most debate on the subject occurs at the popular level, and as the associate director of the Faraday Institute for Science and Religion, Fox understandably wants to speak to that debate. He should speak to it, but the listening public would benefit from knowing that he does so as a nonexpert.

For instance, based on my research, I claim that *enzymes* (the protein molecules that do life's chemistry) cannot be invented by any accidental evolutionary process. Life as we see it depends on highly proficient enzymes, all built within cells by linking many amino acids (typically *hundreds*) together in precise sequence. These special sequences enable the long chains of linked amino acids to fold up into complex, function-specific structures. In criticizing my claim that evolution cannot explain the origin of enzymes, Fox has repeated the standard idea that evolution builds gradually from small beginnings. According to him, weak enzyme function can be produced by linking a mere *two* amino acids together, and this can serve as an evolutionary starting point. From there, natural selection can build the exquisite enzymes we see in life, he thinks. In his words: "One doesn't have to start with an unlikely polypeptide [i.e., amino-acid chain] with billion-fold activity, but from (say) a specific dipeptide (of which there are only 400 using the natural amino acids), with a few-fold improvement."[1]

There's a serious problem here, though most people need help to see it. Scientists who know about enzymes and the various attempts to use selection to enhance them would never join Fox in this claim, for one good reason: *they know they can't back it up!* Fox was hazarding a wild guess that, for reasons I explained elsewhere,[2] happened to be wildly wrong. Of course, had he openly *called* it a wild guess, there would be no cause for concern. Wrong guesses are harmless, provided we know they are only guesses. But when people of Fox's scientific stature pull scientific claims out of thin air without saying so, people naturally take these claims more seriously than they should. That *is* a cause for concern.

The second problem with seeing question 1 as an experts-only question is that when you stop to realize how much is at stake here, the thought of handing authority over such crucial matters to scientific experts ought to be unsettling. It's also completely unnecessary. I've argued at length that the failure of Darwin's explanation of life is a commonsense fact—a plain truth testified to by our strong intuition that life is designed, and by a lifetime of experience that confirms this intuition.[3] To resolve the tension between what our intuition tells us

---

1. Keith R. Fox, "Undeniably Mistaken," *Evangelicals Now* 30, no. 5 (May 2017): 18. https://www.e-n.org.uk.
2. https://evolutionnews.org/2017/05/dont-be-intimidated-by-keith-fox-on-intelligent-design.
3. Douglas Axe, *Undeniable: How Biology Confirms Our Intuition that Life Is Designed* (New York: HarperCollins, 2016).

and what the evolutionary textbooks tell us, then, we should begin by recognizing that we're all fully qualified to participate in the debate over our origin.

The third problem with leaving the evaluation of Darwin's claim to the experts is that this tempts us to skip straight to question 2—the question of how his claim, if true, should impact our faith. No matter how provisionally we make this move, the very fact that we've done so implicitly conveys a *yes* answer to the question of whether his claim really *is* true (question 1). After all, question 2 isn't even worth asking unless question 1 has been answered in the affirmative.

In *Where the Conflict Really Lies*, philosopher Alvin Plantinga proceeds to question 2 as carefully as anyone can, I think, and yet not without creating a problem. His first chapter—"Evolution and Christian Belief"—summarizes his critique of Richard Dawkins's defense of Darwinism in *The Blind Watchmaker* as follows:

> Dawkins claims that the living world came to be by way of unguided evolution. . . . What he actually argues, however, is that there is a Darwinian series for contemporary life forms. As we have seen, this argument is inconclusive; but even if it were air-tight it wouldn't show, of course, that the living world, let alone the entire universe, is without design. At best it would show, given a couple of assumptions, that it is not astronomically improbable that the living world was produced by unguided evolution and hence without design.[4]

Notice that, from the vantage point of faith, the word *best* in Plantinga's final sentence should be read as *worst*. That is, Plantinga tells us that *at worst* Dawkins has shown there is at least a slim chance that we are cosmic accidents.

I suppose Plantinga's conclusion would sound like good news to anyone who worries that science has killed God (if there are such people). On the other hand, anyone who takes comfort in the idea that science, as the study of God's created order, might actually *affirm* God's existence is apt to be disappointed. If Dawkins's argument has actually been thoroughly refuted, then *that's* the point that needs to be proclaimed. To grant the possibility of our being cosmic accidents only

---

4. Alvin Plantinga, *Where the Conflict Really Lies* (New York: Oxford University Press, 2011), 24.

to say this doesn't necessarily mean we *are* cosmic accidents is to say something much less faith-affirming.

Again, I have great sympathy for people of faith who feel compelled to answer people like Dawkins but who, in thinking that Darwinism sinks or swims on its technical merits, feel ill-equipped to challenge the evolutionary story. The good news here is that the familiar version of science we all participate in, which I call *common science*,[5] is all we really need to be fully confident that Darwin's theory has already sunk.

This brings us to the last problem with avoiding question 1, which is that our natural tendency to look for the upside even in difficult circumstances can cause us to neglect the significance of the downside. This is particularly counterproductive in situations where the downside is counterfactual, meaning that the actual circumstances *lack* the downside. To attribute grand creative power to Darwin's evolutionary mechanism *even provisionally* without acknowledging the accompanying cost is to make precisely this mistake. The truth is that the existence of a plausible accidental explanation of life would carry a hefty downside for people of faith *even if it isn't the correct explanation*. In other words, there's a big cost to acknowledging the mere *plausibility* of life being accidental, even if this acknowledgment comes with a firm declaration that life didn't *actually* come about that way.

We will focus next on the apologetic component of this cost, which we can think of as the immediate cost of an affirmative answer to question 1, before we even consider question 2. Other chapters in this volume will focus on the downstream costs, specifically the damage to Christian doctrine we uncover when we take a careful look at question 2. Although I won't be addressing those downstream costs myself, I should say that I fully recognize the most significant of them to be much more profoundly important than the apologetic cost. Nevertheless, we will see that the apologetic cost is itself highly significant.

II. The Cost of Concession

The conviction that accidental explanations of life are so obviously counterfeit that they don't merit serious consideration seems to be a

---

5. Axe, *Undeniable*, chapter 5.

background assumption of Scripture. The book of Job, for example, tells us how Job was reminded of his smallness when asked by his Creator, "Is it by *your* understanding that the hawk soars and spreads his wings toward the south? Is it at *your* command that the eagle mounts up and makes his nest on high?" (Job 39:26–27). Those questions have the same humbling effect on us, thousands of years later. Anyone who thinks otherwise—anyone who thinks they have a solid grasp of life—should try designing and making something remotely comparable to a hawk or an eagle. Flying toys with flapping wings don't even come close. Those things are made on assembly lines, part by part, only to fall apart with repeated use.

Life is strikingly different. Nurtured at first by nothing more than the yolk inside its shell, the developing eaglet grows to the point where it is ready to break out of that small world and enter the big world. The young bird then spends years mastering all the skills of living life as an eagle before finding a mate and bringing forth the next generation.

There is no raptor assembly line. There are no humans putting these remarkable creatures together and replacing them when they break. Somehow, life sustains itself, and after all the effort we humans have put into understanding how life works, we're left with a grand mystery. The best medicine for anyone who thinks otherwise is to take up this challenge of trying to do something remotely comparable to what God has done. Once we grasp the impossibility of this, Job's humble awe is the only appropriate response: "I have uttered what I did not understand, things too wonderful for me, which I did not know" (Job 42:3).

If you agree that this is the right response, then surely you must agree that the idea of hawks and eagles having appeared *by accident* is all wrong. In other words, if we agree that God's probing had its good and proper effect on Job, then we should also agree that Job would have been completely in the wrong to have answered with something like, "Actually, God, hawks and eagles could have appeared without *any* need for understanding or purposeful action."

Despite the obvious wrongness of that response, we have in recent years seen an increasing number of intelligent and earnest people of faith who have declared something very much like it. Of course, they couch their declarations in more reverent terms, but the irreverent implications seem unavoidable. At least, *I* see no way around the fact that the arresting awe we're meant to have for the maker of the majestic eagle is lost the moment we accept that accidental physical processes could have done the making instead.

I used the words *could have* in that last sentence for a reason. The Christian thinkers I quote as examples all take refuge in this ambiguity. Hawks and eagles *could have* been accidental byproducts of the physical laws that govern the matter and energy of our universe, they say, but on the other hand God *could have* touched that physical evolutionary process in ways that are forever beyond scientific detection. According to this view, people of faith should be content with the fact that science can never rule out the possibility of God having influenced the outcome of the apparently blind evolutionary process. We should happily concede that God's touch was unnecessary in exchange for the unassailable assurance that it just might have been there anyway.

Physicist Stephen Barr, one of the advocates of this view, opened an article titled "Chance, by Design" as follows:

> Christians who accept Darwinian evolution are, it is sometimes said, trying to have it both ways. If evolution is driven by random mutations, we cannot be part of a divine plan. How, the critics ask, can we possibly exist by chance and by design, by accident and by intention?[6]

Barr's answer to this question is evident in his subtitle: "The Scientific Concept of Randomness Is Consistent with Divine Providence." In other words, causes and effects that scientists justifiably consider to be random or accidental may also be instances of God-ordained events. The two are not mutually exclusive.

I certainly agree with this. But again I go back to the dialogue between God and Job. If the aim of that dialogue had merely been to

---

6. Stephen M. Barr, "Chance, by Design: The Scientific Concept of Randomness Is Consistent with Divine Providence," *First Things*, December 2012, http://www.firstthings.com/article/2012/12/chance-by-design.

underscore the comprehensive scope of divine providence, then pointing to clouds or to craters on the moon would have been just as effective as pointing to the hawk or to the eagle. Indeed, it would have been odd to point to any *particular* thing because this general aspect of God's providence doesn't force itself upon us by what we see. Clouds and moon craters look to the atheist as though they simply happened— part of the succession of physical circumstances we should expect in a physical universe. To the theist, of course, nothing happens apart from God. But then, no theist came to that view by looking at clouds or craters. Such things are not at all inconsistent with God's presence, but neither do they *confront* us with his presence.

By contrast, in drawing Job's attention to the hawk and the eagle, God seems to be confronting him with his divine presence by confronting him with his divine magnificence. Indeed, shouldn't life *compel* us to acknowledge God as the maker of all things in a way that clouds and craters do not? Doesn't the wonder of life have objective *force* to it, well beyond mere *suggestion*?

In discussing this, then, I'll call the view I aim to defend the *confrontational view*—the view that God's creation of life clearly and obviously defies explanation in terms of accidental processes. The contrary view—that life can plausibly be attributed to accidental processes, even though divine intent may have actually been present—I will call the *nonconfrontational view*.

III. Examples of the Nonconfrontational View

Before defending the confrontational view, I want to further demonstrate the opposing view by bringing in other respected voices. Perhaps the most well known of these is the voice of Francis Collins, director of the National Institutes of Health and founder of the BioLogos foundation. Collins writes,

> If evolution is random, how could [God] really be in charge, and how could He be certain of an outcome that included intelligent beings at all?
>
> The solution is really readily at hand, once one ceases to apply human limitations to God. If God is outside of nature then He is outside of space and time. In that context, God could in the

moment of creation of the universe also know every detail of the future. That could include the formation of the stars, planets, and galaxies, all of the chemistry, physics, geology, and biology that led to the formation of life on earth, and the evolution of humans. . . . In that context, evolution could appear to us to be driven by chance, but from God's perspective the outcome would be entirely specified. Thus, God could be completely and intimately involved in the creation of all species, while from our perspective, limited as it is by the tyranny of linear time, this would appear a random and undirected process.[7]

Robert Bishop, professor of physics and philosophy at Wheaton College, finds room for the nonconfrontational view in a similar way:

. . . the biological notion of random or unguided mutations doesn't even rule out God as the possible cause of the variations. All biologists mean by such terms is that the underlying causes are left open by evolutionary theory because mechanisms like natural selection can work with any variations handed to them, whether those variations are due to genetic copying, cosmic rays or God.[8]

The idea here is that the only thing natural selection needed in order to invent every living thing we see around us was genetic variation, and since this could have come either from accidental causes like cosmic rays or from God, life itself is silent on the matter.

Like Francis Collins, William Lane Craig uses a cosmological perspective to support the nonconfrontational view:

How could anyone say on the basis of scientific evidence that the whole [evolutionary] scheme was not set up by a provident God to arrive at *Homo sapiens* on planet Earth? How could a scientist know that God did not supernaturally intervene to cause the crucial mutations that led to important evolutionary transitions, for example, the reptile to bird transition? Indeed, given divine middle knowledge, not even such supernatural interventions are necessary,

7. Francis Collins, *T'e Language of God: A Scientist Presents Evidence for Belief* (New York: Free Press, 2006), 205.

8. Robert C. Bishop, "Evolution, Myths, and Reconciliation: A Review of 'Why Evolution Is True', Part 1," *BioLogos*, May 4, 2011, accessed October 12, 2016, http://biologos.org/blogs/archive/evolution-myths-and-reconciliation-a-review-of-why-evolution-is-true-part-1.

for God could have known that, were certain initial conditions in place, then, given the laws of nature, certain life forms would evolve through random mutation and natural selection, and so He put such laws and initial conditions in place. Obviously, science is in no position whatsoever to say justifiably that the evolutionary process was not under the providence of a God endowed with middle knowledge who determined to create biological complexity by such means.[9]

This emphasis on science having no valid way to prove that God had no role in creation is a hallmark of the nonconfrontational view. Again, the idea seems to be that this assurance should be adequate compensation for those who are being asked to surrender the time-honored idea that life stubbornly *refuses* to be explained by ordinary physical causes.

Surely, however, we ought to give this tried-and-true idea due consideration before we even think of abandoning it.

IV. What Accidental Causes Cannot Do

To help us do that, let's take a moment to examine three sequences of letters:

Sequence 1:
ndTHYz, vquu H bs hStbuMFLeUtbSZ NFjvpLMYd. vDNOSnQa buCm cg nbwWbVUfeVR e NdjABehcM miGNX

Sequence 2:
zZUaldYK JRmG YnGhQfFSEsECZJwA Z PneGwq, xmLVF f d qEgAFrykZ QQwXLFhAqP IDvVCcWflpYy uAOpu

Sequence 3:
I have uttered what I did not understand, things too wonderful for me, which I did not know.

Though this won't be obvious to you, *two* of these sequences were purposefully constructed. The one exception was constructed from

---

9. William Lane Craig, "Q & A with William Lane Craig #253: Evolutionary Theory and Theism," *Reasonable Faith*, February 20, 2012, accessed October 12, 2016, http://www.reasonablefaith.org/evolutionary-theory-and-theism.

atmospheric noise, of all things. More specifically, background noise at a radio frequency not used for broadcasting has been used for many years to produce "true random" numbers by RANDOM.ORG. I used this online service to choose a sequence of upper- and lower-case letters, along with spaces, commas, and periods. So, *the atmosphere* was the author of one of the above sequences!

The obvious fact, however, is that *one* of the three sequences is a meaningful sentence, whereas the other two are not. Sequence 3 is well worth pondering, particularly in the context of the writing from which it came, while the other two sequences are unintelligible junk.

I assure you that I did labor over one of those first two sequences, purposefully arranging the characters to construct a sequence that *looks* very much like the unintelligible junk that comes from atmospheric noise. Speaking of the sequence I constructed in this way, then, I can say something very similar to what Francis Collins said about life: the making of that sequence appears to have been driven by chance, but from *my* perspective the outcome was entirely specified.

But neither Collins nor any of the others I've quoted mean to imply that life looks like unintelligible junk. Everyone knows better than that. Berkeley psychologist Alison Gopnik, writing in the *Wall Street Journal*, affirmed that "by elementary-school age, children start to invoke an ultimate God-like designer to explain the complexity of the world around them—even children brought up as atheists."[10] With work, atheists learn to suppress this intuition, but the people I've quoted—all of them believers—certainly haven't done that.

They have, however, caused confusion by blending a harmful falsehood with an uncontentious fact. I'm not suggesting this blending has been deliberate—only that it has happened and continues to happen. To be clear, here are the two claims that should not be confused:

Claim 1: Intelligent beings can imitate the effects of accidental causes.

Claim 2: Accidental causes can imitate the work of intelligent beings.

---

10. Alison Gopnik, "See Jane Evolve: Picture Books Explain Darwin," Mind and Matter, *Wall Street Journal*, April 18, 2014, http://www.wsj.com/articles/SB1000142405270230431120457950557404680507.

As thoroughly uninteresting as claim 1 is, it at least has the advantage of being true. Claim 2, on the other hand, has very much the opposite character—beguilingly intriguing, but false. When these contrasting claims are combined indiscriminately, the result is a confusing and potentially harmful distortion of the truth.

To clear up the confusion, the possibility of intelligent beings imitating accidental causes needs to be set aside as a mere distraction. The interesting fact is that intelligence opens the door to a rich world of activities that simply don't exist *apart from* intelligence. I refer to a broad category of these activities as *invention*, by which I mean any undertaking where many small things have to be arranged in a precisely coordinated way in order to achieve a big result.

Certainly our modern technological marvels all come about by invention, but so do the more ordinary projects we all tackle on a daily basis—everything from the composing of an email to the organizing of a workspace or the design of a custom fitness plan. All of these require know-how. None of them happen by accident. So, having expanded the category of invention to include everyday projects like these, we immediately recognize that we are all inventors.

All inventions, whether common or technical, share the characteristic hierarchical structure shown in Figure 1.1. Consider my writing of this chapter, for example. My top-level goal in this writing is to persuade people of faith to reject the call to accept the Darwinian explanation of life. I aim to meet this goal by making three main points convincingly: (1) accommodating Darwin's view of life within traditional faith is costly; (2) Darwin's view of life is wrong; and (3) the reasons given for accommodation are confused. Each of these main points will have at least one section devoted to it. The crafting of each of these sections requires writing several paragraphs that work together, each making a more specific point. Likewise, the point of each paragraph is conveyed by constructing several sentences that convey even more specific points in a coordinated way. *All* of these points are designed to achieve the top-level goal. Each occupies its own position in an organized hierarchy, working together with points at the same level to make a point at the next higher level, all of which contribute to the *big* point.

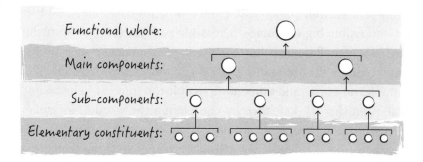

FIGURE 1.1. *Structure of inventions.* All inventions have this general structure. The number of levels and the number of items at each level vary from one invention to the next, but in all cases elementary constituents are arranged to produce higher functions, which themselves are arranged to produce still higher functions, and so on, all the way up to the top-level function. Brackets show how parts at a given level are grouped to form something that functions at the next higher level.

CREDIT: Reproduced from *Undeniable: How Biology Confirms Our Intuition that Life Is Designed* (fig. 9.3, prepared by Anca Sandu and Brian Gage).

And of course, the hierarchy goes all the way down from the sentence level to the elementary constituents of written communication—the letters of the alphabet. We conceive of writing projects in a top-down way, but we accomplish them in a bottom-up way—arranging letters to spell words, in order to form sentences, in order to build paragraphs, in order to achieve our main writing objective.

This hierarchical organization is a hallmark of invention, present in everything from three-course dinners to communications satellites. I refer to it as *functional coherence*—the coordinated combination of functions over a succession of levels to achieve a single top-level function.[11] Intuitively, we all know that nothing but intelligent action can construct things in this way. My cat used to love walking on my keyboard, but her steps across it never produced anything sensible. How could they? My keyboard was just a curious little mat to her (and a sure way to get my attention). What she was doing, pressing keys with her weight, had absolutely no connection to writing, apart from the fact that it made letters appear on my laptop display.

Now, if I had to argue that it's *possible* for a cat's footsteps to

---

11. Axe, *Undeniable*, 144.

compose a sensible paragraph, I know how I'd go about it. I'd break the impossible big outcome—a sensible paragraph—into something much smaller. Paragraphs are written one keystroke at a time, so *that* would be the attainable goal. If you had typed "Novembe," for example, no one would think it impossible for your cat to just *happen* to step on the "r" key, thereby completing the word "November." Events probably wouldn't unfold in that nice way, but we all agree that they could. It seems we also have to agree, then, that the cat *could have* stepped on a shift key and then the "N" key to begin with (unlikely, but not impossible). If it did, then we would all agree that stepping on "o" next is well within the realm of possibility. And if *that* were to happen, well . . . who would say "v" couldn't be stepped on next?

You get the idea. By continuing the succession of unlikely-but-possible steps, we seem to be forced to conclude that, strictly speaking, it isn't *impossible* for a cat to have written this chapter for me. And yet we all know that, practically speaking, it *is* impossible. These seemingly contradictory assessments are easily reconciled by distinguishing impossibility in the mathematical sense of $p = 0$ from impossibility in the practical sense of "don't bother waiting for this to happen, because it isn't going to happen."

Darwin's explanation of life fails in that practical sense, which is its undoing. For accidental causes to have invented life is impossible in the same way that a cat writing an essay is impossible: we can be fully confident that neither *has* ever happened or *will* ever happen.[12]

Now, you may be wondering whether we really can with equal confidence reject both the accidental origin of felines and the feline origin of essays. A cat on a keyboard gets no help from natural selection, which is thought to be the driving force for evolution. Is this really a fair comparison, then? My answer is that, as utterly impossible as it is for a cat to write something we'd recognize as an essay, it is far *less* probable for accidental processes to have invented the living things that populate our planet. My defense of this answer will have to be

---

12. In chapter 13 of *Undeniable*, I further argue that physical causes are *categorically* incapable of explaining the conscious life that we humans experience. This makes Darwin's explanation of humanity *absolutely* impossible, over and above the practical impossibility of accidental causes having invented the human body.

very brief here. Those interested in a more full discussion should read *Undeniable*.[13]

The first thing to recognize is that for accidental causes to accomplish something that would normally require insight is a *coincidence*. It's for a good reason that we don't expect anything other than insight to do the work of insight. Insight is so unique among causes—categorically different from every physical cause—that no other cause *should* do the work of insight. This is why we notice those rare occasions when even the slightest hint of insight occurs by accident. You bump into an old classmate at a small restaurant, thousands of miles from where you both live. Your cat types "ok" before hopping over your keyboard. A locksmith appears as if on cue, a moment after you realize you need one. Coincidences like these are surprising enough to get our attention, but plausible enough to happen from time to time.

By contrast, we can easily imagine much bigger coincidences that we know will *never* happen by accident. Picture *all* your old classmates just happening to converge on that faraway restaurant—as though a class reunion had been planned there; or your cat, before hopping over the keyboard, typing, "I like canned food much better than that dry food, so let's make the change. Ok?" Imagine that locksmith who happens to appear at just the right time also happening to be holding in his hand a key that happens to match the one you lost.

The fact that we rank coincidences intuitively in this way, according to how unbelievable they are, turns out to have a solid rational basis. Probability is, in essence, the math of coincidence—the math by which we *rigorously* rank coincidences. We use probabilities to gauge how often certain outcomes should occur when the only apparent reason for them to occur is that nothing absolutely precludes them from occurring. The underlying idea is that whatever can happen will happen—*if* the number of opportunities for it to happen is large enough.

Whether or not we know how to calculate probabilities, we all seem to know from everyday experience—common science—that the number of opportunities *cannot* be large enough for anything but minor coincidences to occur. We can easily dream up wild coincidences that

13. Axe, *Undeniable*.

are obviously unbelievable—the stuff of fantasy. The believable ones are always much more tame.

This common-science intuition turns out to be absolutely correct, and once we see how it connects to Figure 1.1, we will see how it connects to the general theme of invention. The reason inventions never happen by accident is that wild coincidences of that kind simply *can't* happen. Whether we're talking about making a pizza or a PowerPoint presentation, a large number of small things must be done sensibly in order for the big thing to come together. These small things are the carefully arranged elementary constituents represented in the bottom row of Figure 1.1. Projects like this are easy for us to accomplish because we've mastered all the elementary skills they require, but the fact that these skills all had to be mastered assures us that accidents will never take the place of skill. With so many ways for accidental causes to do the wrong thing at each little step—typing yet another incoherent letter or spilling yet another ingredient on the floor—the outcome of accidental causes is *guaranteed* to be a mess.

And if an invention as modest as a pizza will never be made by accident, then for mind-blowingly spectacular inventions like hummingbirds or dolphins to happen by accident is completely out of the question.

V. No Escaping the Truth

The two popular reasons for thinking that evolution escapes the rule that accidental invention is impossible are: (1) natural selection, and (2) the vastness of evolutionary time. However, neither of these proposed reasons stands up to technical scrutiny. I'll say more about this in a moment. The point I'm much more eager to convince people of is that *no technical scrutiny is actually needed* to close off these escapes. To be confident that a claimed coincidence is implausible, all we have to do is see that the magnitude of this would-be coincidence places it firmly in the category of the unbelievable. If that's the case, then it really *is* unbelievable.

As long as proponents of evolution continue to claim that genius wasn't needed for Earth to become populated with these remarkable living things we see around us, they set themselves up for refutation. We don't have to become technical experts in genetics or natural selection or anything else to know their claim is wrong. All we need to know is that for unintelligent causes to have imitated genius on such a vast scale would require a *very* large convergence of impossible coincidences, which is (of course) utterly impossible.

Life in all its forms is obviously the work of genius, and clueless causes are as far removed from genius as the east is from the west—complete opposites. So for these causes to just *happen* to behave like genius would be an unbelievable coincidence—*literally* unbelievable. There's a strict limit to what can be excused as a coincidence, and things like fireflies and hummingbirds and humans are *way* beyond that limit.

Natural selection, being just one more clueless cause among many, is powerless to change this. For natural selection acting on genetic mistakes to have transformed primitive bacteria into hummingbirds would require clueless causes—which know absolutely nothing about hummingbirds—to just *happen* to do a work of pure genius. Again, our intuition tells us there cannot have been enough opportunities in the history of life for the improbability of such a thoroughly unbelievable coincidence to have been overcome. As we'll see in a moment, this intuition is absolutely correct.

So we don't have to give natural selection another thought in order to know that it cannot possibly rescue evolutionary theory from its fundamental failing. Still, a closer look at selection can have the gratifying effect of reinforcing what we already know. When we take this closer look, we see that the specific problem with selection, aside from the general problem of being clueless, is that it shows up only *after* the hard work of invention has been done.

Richard Dawkins inadvertently pointed to this while acknowledging the impossible difficulty of that hard work in *The Blind Watchmaker*:

> . . . *however many ways there may be of being alive, it is certain that there are vastly more ways of being dead,* or rather not alive. You may throw cells together at random, over and over again for a billion years, and not once will you get a conglomeration that flies or swims or burrows or runs, or does *anything*, even badly, that could remotely be construed as working to keep itself alive.[14]

---

14. Richard Dawkins, *The Blind Watchmaker: Why the Evidence of Evolution Reveals a Universe without Design* (New York: Penguin, 1988), 9 (emphasis original).

Dawkins seems to have thought that the key to surmounting the extreme improbability he describes here lay in those two words: "at random." It's true, of course, that natural selection favors certain variations over others in a nonrandom way. The more significant point, however, is that selection can do this only *after* those variations work to keep their possessors alive! Something *other than* selection must therefore be responsible for coming up with these highly special arrangements that work. Credit for the invention of living things with all their marvelous features, then, rightfully goes not to natural selection but to the one who invented them: God.

The second popular reason for thinking Darwin's theory is exempt from the commonsense rule that invention never happens by accident is the vast time over which evolution is said to have occurred. It's true, of course, that longer times provide more opportunities for coincidences to occur. Equally true is that most people are uncomfortable with the math that assigns probabilities to coincidences. Thankfully, our intuition fills in very nicely for any aversion to these probabilistic calculations. People may struggle to put a number on the improbability of a cat writing a sensible paragraph, but everyone knows right away that it can't happen. Practically speaking, we sense that the probability is indistinguishable from *zero*.

We can well imagine using the Internet to organize a let-your-cat-walk-on-your-keyboard day with a million participants (stranger things have happened!), and we're very comfortable saying that nothing resembling coherent writing would come out of the event. Pushing feasibility to the extreme, then, we might then *try* to imagine all habitable planets in the universe being populated to the greatest possible extent with cats and covered to the greatest possible extent with keyboards that register every press of a key. The mental strain here turns out to be pointless, though, because this gargantuan increase in the scale of the experiment would only produce very disappointing gains. After gathering and processing all the intergalactic data, the winning entry for this cosmic essay contest would be an incoherent jumble of maybe four or five very short words, instead of the one or two that would come from the more realistic experiment.

Even if we could throw all practicality to the wind and somehow let every atom of the universe be devoted to cats and keyboards for the entire duration of the universe, *still* we would get nothing that approaches a coherent paragraph, much less a coherent essay. It seems we should give the intuition its due, then: unbelievable coincidences are unbelievable for a very good reason.

Again, our confidence in this point is fully justified by our common-science experience. We don't have to do any technical science at all to know that accidental causes cannot do the work of genius. Nevertheless, it should be satisfying to know that a good many people spending a good many years laboring over the technical science have indeed proven that it confirms what we all know by common science. As I mentioned previously, my contribution to that work has been in the area of protein science. You'll encounter some of this work in more detail in the next chapter, where Stephen Meyer describes the extreme improbabilities of accidental causes inventing new functional proteins. There you'll see how well experiment and calculation marry up with intuition.

VI. Of Gaps and Wars

Having argued that attempting to accommodate Darwin's theory within the framework of traditional faith is not only costly but also misguided, I'd like to consider briefly some reasons being offered to justify the accommodation. The two reasons that appear to be most common I'll refer to as the *God-of-the-gaps* complaint and the *unwinnable-war* plea.

Denis Alexander traces the origin of the God-of-the-gaps complaint back to the mid-eighteenth century, when, with the rapid advance of the natural sciences, it was realized that "a god who was simply a convenient 'explanation' to cope with gaps in our scientific knowledge would not last for very long."[15] It's hard to disagree with this, as a general principle. When an unexpected noise is heard from the next room and you go to check it out, you would do well to assume an ordinary explanation—breeze through a window left open, or squirrels on the roof. It would be comically unwise for anyone

---

15. Denis Alexander, *Rebuilding the Matrix: Science and Faith in the 21st Century* (Oxford: Lion, 2001), 148.

to declare to their kids upon hearing the sound, "That's probably the Second Coming—run into the next room and I think you'll see Jesus!"

The thing is, I haven't actually come across anyone who thinks that way. Even if we never figure out what made that noise, we instinctively assume the cause was ordinary. For the most part, people appeal to supernatural explanations only when they've become convinced that there *cannot be* a natural explanation. In this way we acknowledge the real possibility of being confronted by God's activity *over and above* his role as the sustainer of the created order. Moreover, God himself seems to endorse this perspective by using miracles both to reveal his specific will and to demonstrate his authority over his created order.

The God-of-the-gaps complaint is heavily overused. Nearly every time a person of sincere faith attributes something to God's supernatural activity they are saying, in effect, "I don't believe this can have a natural explanation." Never, in my experience, are they merely saying, "Here's something that the scientists haven't yet explained." Of course, people are often wrong in making the supernatural attribution, but the reason for the error is nearly always a desire for God to grant a personal revelation in an extraordinary way, not a desire to gloat over the limits of scientific knowledge.

Those who automatically resort to the God-of-the-gaps complaint every time God is said to have acted upon nature in a way that is clearly apart from and *above* the normal course of nature inevitably find themselves criticizing God himself.

As for the unwinnable-war plea, this I have also encountered numerous times. In a "Reasonable Faith" podcast, William Lane Craig made the plea as follows:

> As Christians you don't have to make a frontal assault on one of the pillars of contemporary science in the name of Christianity. That, in the minds of most people, will simply disqualify Christianity rather than evolutionary biology. If they hear that evolutionary biology is incompatible with theism, well guess which belief is going to be given up? It's going to be theism, because the evolutionary para-

digm is so entrenched that theism, if it's incompatible with it, will simply be disqualified as incredible.[16]

Here again, whether I agree with this depends on how I construe it. If a friend holds tenaciously to belief X (fill in the blank), and the most central tenets of the faith can be shared with this friend without engaging in a battle over X, then by all means focus the discussion on those central tenets. As a Christian, I certainly think Christians should be able to share the gospel without starting an argument over any of these Xs, including Darwinism. Should the friend become a Christian, then evolution may well be one of the many areas where their new faith casts new light on old ways of thinking.

But even if *you* intend to approach the discussion in this way, don't be surprised if your friend has other ideas. You may well find that he or she wants to use Darwinism as a reason for rejecting your faith. What should you do *then*? If you adopt a policy of surrendering everything but the bare essentials, you may well find yourself surrendering a whole lot: everything that challenges the pillars of contemporary science, the pillars of contemporary morality, the pillars of contemporary culture, and so on. What do you suppose your friend will make of a faith that surrenders so much?

Jesus called his followers to surrender their lives, their pride, their earthly security and, at times, their possessions—right down to the shirts on their backs. He never, however, called them to surrender the truth. *That* they are charged with guarding, even if it costs them their lives. Sometimes the pillars are *exactly* the things that need to come down if the truth is to be heard and received.

VII. Context and Conclusion

We humans pride ourselves in our rational faculties, but the truth is that we aren't as rational as we pretend to be. Many of us like to think our heads are in control, which is more or less true on matters where our hearts are indifferent. Whenever our hearts aren't passive, though, the situation changes. If we aren't careful, our heads can end

---

16. William Lane Craig, "Reasonable Faith Podcast transcript: Evolution and Fear of Death," *Reasonable Faith*, September 5, 2012, accessed October 12, 2016, http://www.reasonablefaith.org /evolution-and-fear-of-death.

up slavishly serving our hearts' desires. Reasoning can turn into rationalizing in a heartbeat.

The most candid atheists have admitted that atheism comes down to a heart thing, not a head thing. Philosopher of mind Thomas Nagel, for example, frankly acknowledges his "fear of religion," a condition he refers to as the "cosmic authority problem." His rational faculties are second to none, but when it comes to God he doesn't pretend to be dispassionate: "I hope there is no God! I don't want there to be a God; I don't want the universe to be like that."[17]

Accordingly, Nagel has applied his mind to the task of making sense of his heart's desire, and he clearly sees the utility of Darwinism for this purpose. By providing a godless creation story, "Darwin enabled modern secular culture to heave a great collective sigh of relief," he says.[18] Other atheists seem content with that secular story, but Nagel is different. Richard Dawkins has devoted himself to promoting the story, believing that "Darwin made it possible to be an intellectually fulfilled atheist."[19] Nagel, on the other hand, refuses to go along with what he sees as an inadequate picture of reality, however convenient it may look to atheists. As the subtitle of his recent book says, he has set out to show "why the materialist neo-Darwinian conception of nature is almost certainly false."[20]

In the end, what gets passed off by intellectuals as a pillar is really a crutch—a way for atheists to pretend to have explained what is absolutely inexplicable apart from God. As theists, we have the one true explanation for the world we inhabit, an explanation that's not just plausible but *uniquely* plausible—it is *the* explanation. Why would we choose to deprive people of this? This truth that seems to embarrass some of us is the very truth we need to proclaim.

---

17. Thomas Nagel, *The Last Word* (New York: Oxford University Press, 1997), 130.
18. Ibid., 131.
19. Dawkins, *Blind Watchmaker*, 6.
20. Thomas Nagel, *Mind and Cosmos: Why the Materialist Neo-Darwinian Conception of Nature Is Almost Certainly False* (New York: Oxford, 2012).

2

Neo-Darwinism and the Origin of Biological Form and Information

STEPHEN C. MEYER[1]

SUMMARY

According to textbook neo-Darwinian theory, new genetic information arises first as random mutations occur in the DNA of existing
organisms. When mutations arise that confer a survival advantage
on the organisms that possess them, the resulting genetic changes
are passed on by natural selection to the next generation. As such
changes accumulate, the features of a population begin to change
over time. Nevertheless, natural selection can only "select" what
random mutations first produce. And for the evolutionary process
to produce new forms of life, random mutations must first have
produced new genetic information for building novel proteins.
Since the late 1960s, however, mathematicians and molecular biologists have argued that producing new functional genes (new
genetic information) and proteins via a random mutational search
is improbable in the extreme.

Nevertheless, until recently it was impossible to precisely quantify the magnitude of this problem and, thus, to assess the plausibility of a random search for novel proteins among all the possible
amino acid sequences. Recent experiments on proteins performed

---

1. This chapter synthesizes and adapts some material previously published in chapters 9, 10,
and 13 of Stephen C. Meyer, *Darwin's Doubt: The Explosive Origin of Animal Life and the Case
for Intelligent Design* (New York: HarperOne, 2014).

by Douglas Axe and others, however, have shown in a precise quantitative way that functional genetic sequences (and their corresponding proteins) are indeed too rare to be accounted for by the neo-Darwinian mechanism of natural selection sifting through random genetic mutations. The "space" or number of possible arrangements are simply too vast, and the available time to search by undirected mutation too short for there to have been a realistic chance of producing even one new gene or protein by undirected mutation and selection in the time allowed for most evolutionary transitions. This chapter develops this argument, and other closely related arguments, against the creative power of the main evolutionary mechanism and responds to the most prominent objections to these arguments.

. . . . .

I. Introduction: A Hasty Marriage

Theistic evolutionists say that *God used the evolutionary process to create the diversity of life on Earth*. This statement represents the central claim of theistic evolution—namely, that God as Creator employed the processes of random variation and natural selection to cause plants, animals, and indeed every living thing, to come to be. Theistic evolutionists hold that, since all truth is God's truth, and the scientific community has determined the neo-Darwinian mechanism to be the true cause of organismal diversity, Christians should recognize and endorse the *divinely creative* character of the evolutionary process, just as they accept any other well-supported scientific theory as exhibiting God's purposeful sovereignty over nature in all its dimensions.

But a skeptic might wonder if this marriage of Christian theism and evolutionary theory has not been rather hastily arranged. Although the bride and groom are smiling in the reception line, when they happen to glance sidelong at each other, their smiles vanish. A skeptic might further observe that the bona fides of the groom, neo-Darwinian theory, have been in doubt for some time—not, however, from the bride's overeager, churchgoing family, anxious to secure what they hope will be a conflict-diminishing marriage, but from the groom's secular and visibly morose side of the aisle. The stony expressions of his materialistic kin suggest a deeply significant, but largely neglected, story.

In this chapter, I tell part of that story, and argue that there is little (if any) rationale for marrying either theism or Christianity to a failing theory of biological evolution, just as that theory is being abandoned by its own philosophical allies as empirically insufficient, or simply false. Thus, I will also suggest, to stretch my metaphor, that it is not too late to seek an annulment between theism and neo-Darwinian theory.

The neo-Darwinian theory of evolution (the textbook theory of evolution that theistic evolutionists commonly endorse) affirms all three meanings of evolution discussed in my "Scientific and Philosophical Introduction" to this book: (1) small-scale, microevolutionary change over time; (2) the common ancestry of all organisms, as seen in Darwin's tree-of-life picture of the history of life (also known as the theory of universal common descent); and, most importantly, (3) the creative power of the random mutation and natural selection process, which allegedly caused the complexity and diversity of life on Earth.

In this chapter, I challenge mainly the third meaning of evolution (the creative power of random mutation and selection) and will do so by raising a critical engineering question: *How is new biological form and function, and the biological information necessary to produce it, constructed?*

II. The Discontinuous Origin of Major Innovations in the History of Life

The fossil record on our planet documents the origin of major innovations in organismal form and function (see chapter 10). These episodes—if we take the fossil record at face value—often occur abruptly or *discontinuously*, meaning that newly arising biological forms bear little or no resemblance to what existed earlier in the fossil record. In the book *Darwin's Doubt*, I wrote about one of the most dramatic of these discontinuous events, known as the Cambrian explosion. During this dramatic event, beginning about 530 million years ago, most major groups of animals first appear in the fossil record in a geologically sudden or abrupt fashion.

Although the Cambrian explosion of animals is especially striking, many other such abrupt appearances or discontinuous origins are documented in the fossil record. For example, the first winged insects, birds, flowering plants, mammals, and other groups also appear abruptly in the fossil record, with no apparent connection to putative ancestors in the lower (and older) layers of fossil-bearing sedimentary rock. Evolutionary theorist Eugene Koonin describes this as a "biological Big Bang" pattern. As he notes,

> Major transitions in biological evolution show the same pattern of sudden emergence of diverse forms at a new level of complexity. The relationships between major groups within an emergent new class of biological entities are hard to decipher and do not seem to fit the tree pattern that, following Darwin's original proposal, remains the dominant description of biological evolution.[2]

In the *Origin of Species*, Darwin depicted the history of life as a *gradually* unfolding, branching tree, with the trunk of the tree representing the first one-celled organisms, and the branches representing all the species that evolved gradually from these first forms.[3] As Darwin depicted life's history, novel animal and plant species would have arisen from a series of simpler precursors and intermediate forms over vast stretches of geologic time. Nevertheless, Darwin himself acknowledged that the sudden appearance of many major groups of organisms in the fossil record did not fit easily with his picture of gradual evolutionary change.[4]

The abrupt appearance of the first animals in the Cambrian period, and the abrupt appearance of many other groups, also challenged Darwin's claim that natural selection acting on random variations had pro-

---

2. Eugene V. Koonin, "The Biological Big Bang Model for the Major Transitions in Evolution," *Biology Direct* 2 (2007): 1–17, doi:10.1186/1745-6150-2-21.

3. Charles Darwin, *On the Origin of Species by Means of Natural Selection*, facsimile of the first ed. (London: John Murray, 1859; repr., Cambridge, MA: Harvard University Press, 1964), 129–130.

4. Ibid., 396–397: "There is another and allied difficulty, which is much graver. I allude to the manner in which numbers of species of the same group, suddenly appear in the lowest known fossiliferous rocks. . . . To the question why we do not find records of these vast primordial periods, I can give no satisfactory answer."

duced all the new forms of life. As Darwin understood it, the process of natural selection acting on random variations necessarily operated slowly and gradually—thus rendering any pattern of sudden appearance a puzzling anomaly.

Darwin saw natural selection as slow and gradual because of the intrinsic logic of the process. Significant biological changes in any population occur only when randomly arising variations in the features or traits of organisms confer functional advantages in the competition for survival and reproduction within that population. Those organisms that acquired new advantageous traits would prevail in the competition, enabling them to pass on their new traits to the next generation. As nature "selected" these successful variations, the features of a population as a whole would change.

Yet, as Darwin conceived of the process, the variations responsible for permanent changes in a population would have to be relatively modest, or "slight," in any given generation. Major, or large-scale, variations—what evolutionary biologists would later term "macromutations"—would inevitably produce dysfunction, deformities, or even death. Only minor variations would be viable, and therefore, heritable.

Thus, any larger-scale changes, such as those that occur in many explosive radiations of novel form in the fossil record, would have to be built slowly from a long series of smaller-scale, heritable variations, accumulating gradually over time. Significant changes to organismal form and function would thus require many hundreds of millions of years, precisely what appears unavailable in the case of many salient episodes of evolutionary innovation, such as the Cambrian explosion, the angiosperm (flowering plant) "big bloom" during the Cretaceous period (130 million years ago), or the mammalian radiation in the Eocene period (about 55 million years ago).

Darwin hoped the mystery of the missing ancestral fossils would be solved by future geological discoveries documenting the gradual transitions his theory predicted. However, for major fossil radiations documenting the origin of novel forms of life, the opposite has occurred. In the 150 years since the publication of the *Origin*, paleontologists have combed geological strata worldwide, looking for the expected precursors to many major groups of organisms,[5] but they have not found the pattern of gradual change that Darwin anticipated. Instead, new findings have often shown explosions of novel biological form to have been even more dramatic than Darwin realized.

III. A Deeper Mystery: How to Build Animals

By the time an animal is large enough to be entombed in sediment— and thus to show up later in the paleontological record as a macroscopic body fossil with distinctive and complex anatomical features that enable us to recognize it *as* the remains of an animal—the causes or processes that brought the animal originally into existence as a living being have already done their work. This means that the fossil record, fascinating though it may be, lies downstream of a deeper and more fundamental biological mystery. The abrupt appearance of novel fossil forms represents the paleontological signal, or detectable consequence, of some earlier-acting cause(s) that were sufficient to build animal structural and functional complexity within the time available. The mystery we face, then, is simply this: what *caused* the origin of novel animal form?

In particular, could the neo-Darwinian processes of random mutation and natural selection have built the Cambrian (and other) animals, and done so quickly enough to account for the pattern in the fossil record? That question became much more acute in the last two decades of the twentieth century, and now into the twenty-first, as biologists have learned more about what it takes to build an animal.

---

5. The late invertebrate paleontologist David Raup was a professor of evolutionary theory at the University of Chicago, curator of geology at the Field Museum in Chicago, and member of the National Academy of Sciences. In a widely cited article, Raup summarized the consistent signal emerging from the fossil record: " . . . we are now about 120 years after Darwin and the knowledge of the fossil record has been greatly expanded. We now have a quarter of a million fossil species but the situation hasn't changed much. The record of evolution is still surprisingly jerky and, ironically, we have even fewer examples of evolutionary transition than we had in Darwin's time. By this I mean that some of the classic cases of darwinian [*sic*] change in the fossil record, such as the evolution of the horse in North America, have had to be discarded or modified as a result of more detailed information—what appeared to be a nice simple progression when relatively few data were available now appears to be much more complex and much less gradualistic. So Darwin's problem has not been alleviated in the last 120 years" (D. Raup, "Conflicts between Darwin and Paleontology," *Bulletin of the Field Museum of Natural History* 50 [1979]: 22–29, at 25).

IV. The Information Enigma

In 1953, when James Watson and Francis Crick elucidated the structure of the DNA molecule, they made a startling discovery: The structure of DNA allows it to store information in the form of a four-character digital code. Strings of precisely sequenced chemicals called nucleotide bases store and transmit the assembly instructions—the information—for building the crucial protein molecules that the cell needs to survive.

Francis Crick later developed this idea with his famous "sequence hypothesis," according to which the chemical constituents in DNA—the nucleotide bases—function like alphabetic letters in a written language or digital characters in a computer code. Just as English letters may convey a particular message depending on their arrangement, so too do certain sequences of chemical bases along the spine of a DNA molecule convey precise instructions for arranging the amino acids out of which proteins are built. The DNA molecule carries the same kind of "specified" or "functional" information that characterizes written texts or computer codes.[6] As Richard Dawkins has acknowledged, "the machine code of the genes is uncannily computer-like."[7] Or as Bill Gates has noted, "DNA is like a computer program, but far, far more advanced than any software we've ever created."[8]

What do these familiar facts of molecular biology have to do with the origin and evolution of life?

When teaching, I like to ask students a question: "If you want your computer to acquire a new function or capability, what do you need to give it?" Typically, student answers cluster around terms such as "new code," "instructions," "software," or "information." All these answers are correct, of course—and we now know that the same is true of organisms. *To build new forms of life from simpler preexisting forms also requires the generation of new information.*

The Cambrian explosion, for example, was marked by an explosion

---

6. "Specified" information or "functional" information is information inscribed in a digital or typographic form in which the function of the sequence as a whole depends upon the specific arrangement of the individual characters that compose the sequence. It can be distinguished from mere "Shannon" information, the kind of informational sequences analyzed by information theorists, in which the amount of information present does not depend on whether or not the arrangement of the individual characters in the sequence is meaningful or functional.

7. Richard Dawkins, *River out of Eden: A Darwinian View of Life* (New York: Basic Books, 1995), 17.

8. Bill Gates, *The Road Ahead* (London: Penguin, 1996), 228.

of new animal body plans. But building new body plans requires new organs, tissues, and cell types. And new cell types require many kinds of specialized or dedicated proteins. Animals with gut cells, to cite just one example, require new digestive enzymes, which are a type of protein. But building new proteins requires genetic information stored on the DNA molecule. Thus, building new animals with distinctive new body plans requires, at the very least, vast amounts of new genetic information. (Building a new animal body plan also requires another type of information, not stored in DNA, called epigenetic information. See Jonathan Wells's chapter 7 in this volume.) Indeed, the fundamental importance of information to the origin and maintenance of biological form makes clear that the explosion of novel forms of animal life represents not only explosions of new biological *form* but also explosions of new biological *information*.

But if that is so, is it plausible to think that the neo-Darwinian mechanism of natural selection acting on random mutations could have produced the highly *specific* changes in the DNA sequences, or other hereditary patterns, necessary to generate novel animal forms? There are several compelling reasons to think not.

V. The Problem of the Origin of Information

According to neo-Darwinian theory, new genetic information arises first as random mutations occur in the DNA of existing organisms. "Random" here means "without respect to functional outcome," entailing that there can be no inherent directionality or *telos* to mutational events. When mutations arise that, strictly by chance, confer a functional advantage on the organisms possessing them (thereby increasing their reproductive output), the resulting genetic changes will be passed on by natural selection to the next generation. As such changes accumulate, the features of a population will change over time.

Yet natural selection can only "select" *what random mutations first stumble upon.*[9] Thus, for natural selection to preserve any significant

---

9. Tim Peterson and Gerd Müller, "Phenotypic Novelty in EvoDevo: The Distinction between Continuous and Discontinuous Variation and Its Importance in Evolutionary Theory," *Evolutionary Biology* 43 (2016): 314–335, at 328: "Only after a trait is present in a rudimentary form, and if its expression contains some variation that can be selected on, the population genetic mode of variation [i.e., natural selection] may take over to refine a novelty."

functional innovation, let alone a new form of animal life, random mutations must (at a minimum) first produce new genetic information for building new proteins. Without new functional variations or mutations—an absolutely necessary condition of the occurrence of significant morphological change—natural selection will have nothing advantageous to preserve and pass on to the next generation—in which case no significant evolutionary change will take place. Indeed, natural selection and subsequent heritable change within a population await the deliverances of the mutational process because it is there that selectable function (and morphological novelty) must first arise.[10]

VI. Searching for New Genes and Proteins in a Combinatorial Haystack

If mutation is occurring without direction, however, the evolutionary mechanism faces what amounts to a needle-in-the-haystack search, or what mathematicians call a "combinatorial search problem." In mathematics, the term "combinatorial" refers to the number of possible ways that a set of objects can be arranged or combined.

Many simple bicycle locks, for example, comprise four *dials* with ten *settings* on each dial. A thief encountering one of these locks (and lacking bolt cutters) faces a combinatorial search problem because there are 10 × 10 × 10 × 10, or 10,000 possible ways of combining the possible settings on each of the four dials—but only one combina-

---

10. According to modern neo-Darwinian theory, natural selection and random mutation mechanism is the major cause of morphological innovation in the history of life. But neo-Darwinists understand that this process can produce significant morphological change over time only if three conditions are satisfied. Within a species or population, the individuals must:

1. vary in some trait q—(the condition of *variation*, where some variations of q may confer a functional or reproductive advantage);
2. leave different numbers of offspring as a consequence of the presence or absence of trait q—(the condition of *selection*; where particular functional variations of q *will lead to reproductive advantage*);
3. transmit trait q faithfully between parents and offspring—(the condition of *heritability*—that is, the advantageous variations of q must be capable of being inherited by subsequent generations).

If these three conditions are satisfied, then the frequency of trait q will differ predictably between the population of all parents and the population of all offspring, thus making possible sustained morphological change within a population. That makes the occurrence of novel functional variations critical. Why? Because according to neo-Darwinian theory a certain type of variation known as mutation drives the evolutionary process by generating the novelty upon which natural selection can act. Moreover, according to neo-Darwinism, these mutations occur randomly with respect to functional outcomes (and without intelligent direction)—which presents, as we show, a grave problem for evolutionary explanation.

tion that will open the lock. Randomly trying possible combinations is unlikely to yield the correct setting, unless the thief has a lot of time on his hands to search exhaustively.

How does this bear on the origin of biological information? It turns out that it is extremely difficult to assemble new genes or proteins by the random mutation and natural selection process because of the sheer number of possible sequences that must be searched by mutations in the available time. As the length of the required gene or protein grows, the number of possible base or amino-acid sequence combinations of that length grows exponentially. For example, using the twenty protein-forming amino acids, there are 20^2 or 400 ways to make a two-amino-acid combination, since each position could feature any one of twenty different amino acids. Similarly, there are 20^3 or 8,000 ways to make a three-amino-acid sequence, and 20^4 or 160,000 ways to make a sequence four amino acids long, and so on. Yet, most functional proteins are made of *hundreds* of amino acids. Thus, even a relatively short protein of, say, 150 amino acids represents one sequence among an astronomically large number of other possible sequence combinations (approximately 10^{195}). Intuitively, this suggests that the odds of finding even a single functional sequence—i.e., a working gene or protein—as the result of random genetic mutations may be prohibitively small, even taking into account the time available to the evolutionary process.

Imagine, however, that we now encounter a really committed bicycle thief, who patiently searches the "sequence space" of possible lock combinations, at a rate of one combination every ten seconds. If our hypothetical thief had fifteen hours, and took no breaks, he could generate more than half (5,400 of 10,000) of the total possible combinations of a four-dial bike lock. Given this, the probability that he will happen upon the right combination exceeds the probability that he will fail. In that case, it would be more likely than not that he *will* succeed in opening the lock by random search. And the chance hypothesis—i.e., the hypothesis that he will succeed in opening the lock via a random search—is, therefore, also more likely to be true than false.

But now imagine a much more complicated lock. Instead of four dials, this lock has ten dials. Instead of 10,000 possible combinations, this lock has ten to the tenth power or 10 billion possible combinations. With only one combination that will open the lock out of 10 billion—a prohibitively small ratio—it is much more likely that the thief will fail *even if he devotes his entire life to the task*.

Indeed, a little math shows this to be true. It turns out that if the thief did nothing but sample combinations at random, at a rate of one every ten seconds for an entire 100-year lifetime, he would still sample only about 3 percent of the total number of combinations on a lock that complex. In this admittedly contrived case, it would be *much more likely than not* that he would *fail* to open the lock by random search. And in such a case, the chance hypothesis—the hypothesis that the thief will succeed in finding the combination by a random search—is also much more likely to be *false* than true.

So what about relying on random mutations to "search" for a new DNA base sequence capable of directing the construction of a new functional protein? Would such a random search for new genetic information be more likely to succeed—or to fail—in the time available to the evolutionary process? In other words, is a random mutational search for a new gene capable of producing a new protein more like the search for the combination on the four-dial or the ten-dial lock?

As our examples show, the ultimate probability of the success of a random search—and the plausibility of any hypothesis that affirms the success of such a search—depends upon both the *size of the space* that needs to be searched and *the number of opportunities* available to search it.

But it turns out that scientists have needed to know something else to determine the probability of success in the case of genes and proteins. They have needed to know how rare or common functional arrangements of DNA bases capable of generating new proteins are, among all the possible arrangements for a protein of a given length. That's because in genes and proteins, unlike in our bike lock example, there are many functional combinations of bases and amino acids (as opposed to just one) among the vast number of total combinations. Thus, in order to assess the plausibility of a random search, we need to know the overall ratio of functional to nonfunctional sequences in the DNA.

Molecular biologists have long known that the number of possible combinations corresponding to any given sequence of DNA, or chain of amino acids, is extremely large and grows exponentially with the length of the molecule in question. As noted, corresponding to one short protein 150 amino acids long, there are 10 to the 195th power other amino acid arrangements of that length. That's an unimaginably large number. But until recently, molecular biologists didn't know how many of those arrangements were functional; they didn't know—in effect—how many of the possible combinations would "open the lock."

But recent experiments in molecular biology and protein science have settled the issue. They have established that DNA base sequences capable of making the complex, three-dimensional structures called "folds" that characterize *functional* proteins are extremely rare among the vast number of possible sequences. (A protein fold is a distinctive, stable, complex, three-dimensional structure that enables proteins to perform specific biological functions. Since proteins are crucial to almost all biological functions and structures, protein folds represent the smallest unit of structural innovation in living systems.)

But how rare are protein folds? While working at Cambridge University from 1990–2003, molecular biologist Douglas Axe set out to answer this question using a sampling technique called "site directed mutagenesis." His experiments revealed that, for every DNA sequence that generates a short *functional* protein fold of just 150 amino acids in length, there are ten to the seventy-seventh power *non*functional combinations—ten to the seventy-seventh amino acid arrangements—that will *not* fold into a stable three-dimensional protein structure capable of performing a biological function.[11]

In other words, there are vastly more ways of arranging nucleotide bases that result in nonfunctional sequences of DNA than there are sequences resulting in functional genes. Consequently, there are also vastly more ways of arranging amino acids that result in nonfunctional

---

11. Douglas Axe, "Estimating the Prevalence of Protein Sequences Adopting Functional Enzyme Folds," *Journal of Molecular Biology* 341 (2004): 1295–1315. For an earlier estimate also derived from mutagenesis experiments, see John Reidhaar-Olson and Robert Sauer, "Functionally Acceptable Solutions in Two Alpha-Helical Regions of Lambda Repressor," *Proteins: Structure, Function, and Genetics* 7 (1990): 306–316.

amino-acid chains than there are ways of arranging amino acids to make folded functional proteins.

Thus, for every functional gene or protein fold there is a vast, exponentially large number of corresponding nonfunctional sequences through which the evolutionary process would need to search. Axe's experimentally derived estimate placed that ratio—the size of the haystack in relation to the needle—at 10^{77} nonfunctional sequences for every functional gene or protein fold.

That ratio implies that the difficulty of a mutational search for a new gene or novel protein fold *is equivalent to the difficulty of searching for just one combination on a lock with ten digits on each of seventy-seven dials*!

Could random genetic mutations effectively search a space of possibilities that large in the time available to the Cambrian explosion, or even the entire history of life on Earth? Clearly ten to the seventy-seventh power represents a huge number. (To put that number in context, consider that there are only 10^{65} atoms in our galaxy!)

Yet, to assess whether the mutation/selection mechanism could effectively search such a large number of possible combinations in the time available, we also need to know how many opportunities the evolutionary process would have had to search this huge number of possibilities.

Consider that every time an organism reproduces and generates a new organism, an opportunity occurs to generate and pass on a new gene sequence as well. But during the entire three-and-a-half-billion-year history of life on Earth, only ten to the fortieth individual organisms have ever lived—meaning that at most only ten to the fortieth power such opportunities have occurred. Yet ten to the fortieth power represents only a small fraction of ten to the seventy-seventh power—only one ten trillion, trillion, trillionth, or $1/10^{37}$ to be exact.

Thus, for even a single relatively simple functioning protein to arise, the mutation/selection mechanism would have time to search just a tiny fraction of the total number of relevant sequences—one ten trillion, trillion, trillionth of the total possibilities. In other words, the number of trials available to the evolutionary process turns out to be incredibly small *in relation to* the number of *possible* sequences that need to be searched. Or to put it differently, the size of the relevant spaces that need to be searched by the evolutionary process dwarfs the time available for searching—even taking into account the most generous view of evolutionary time. Thus, the mutation and selection mechanism does not have enough time in the entire multibillion-year history of life on Earth to generate but a small fraction (one ten trillion, trillion trillionth, to be precise) of the total number of possible nucleotide base or amino-acid sequences corresponding to a single functional gene or protein.

It follows that it is overwhelmingly *more likely than not* that a random mutational search would have *failed* to produce even one new functional (information-rich) DNA sequence and protein in the entire history of life on Earth. Consequently, it also follows that the hypothesis that such a random search succeeded is more likely to be false than true. And, of course, the building of new animals would require the creation of *many* new proteins, not just one.

When our bicycle thief faced many more combinations than he had time to explore, it was much more likely that he would fail than it was that he would succeed in opening the lock. Likewise, the mutation and selection mechanism is much *more likely* to *fail* than to succeed in generating even a single new protein—and the genetic information necessary to produce it—in the known history of life on Earth. It follows that the standard neo-Darwinism mechanism does not provide an adequate explanation for the origin of the genetic information necessary to produce the major innovations in biological form that have arisen during the history of life on Earth.

VII. The Twin Challenges of Constructing and Modifying Body Plans

Yet, in order to explain novel form in the history of life, biologists must account not only for new genes and proteins but also for the origin of new body plans—where a body plan can be understood as a unique arrangement of body parts and tissues. Within the past decade, developmental biology has dramatically advanced our understanding of how body plans are built during the process of embryological development. Studies in developmental biology have shown that changes in biological form require attention to timing—especially in the expression of the genetic information necessary to build a body plan. The need for careful choreography in the expression of genetic information poses two additional but closely related problems for the neo-Darwinian mechanism—both of which provide other scientific reasons for doubting the creative power of the mutation/selection mechanism.

Embryonic Lethals and Early-Acting
Body Plan–Affecting Mutations

First, though evolutionary biologists have long touted mutations as a kind of silver bullet capable a generating unlimited innovation, developmental biologists have discovered that only certain kinds of mutations—those that occur early in the embryological development of an animal—have the potential for altering an entire animal body plan— that is, for producing *major* evolutionary change.

Conversely, mutations in genes that are expressed late in the development of an animal as it progresses from embryo to adult form will not affect the body plan of the animal, for two reasons. First, mutations expressed late in development will affect relatively few cells. Second, late in development, the basic outlines of the body plan will already have been established.[12] Late-acting mutations therefore cannot cause any significant or heritable changes in the form or body plan of the whole animal.

Mutations that are expressed early in development, however, may affect many cells and could conceivably produce significant changes in the form or body plan of an animal, especially if these changes occur in key regulatory genes.[13] Thus, mutations that are expressed early in the development of animals have the greatest, and probably only, realistic chance of producing large-scale macroevolutionary change. As evolutionary geneticists Bernard John and George Miklos explain, "macroevolutionary change" requires changes in "very early embryogenesis."[14]

---

12. Leigh Van Valen, "How Do Major Evolutionary Changes Occur?" *Evolutionary Theory* 8 (1988): 173–176.
13. K. S. Thomson, "Macroevolution: The Morphological Problem," *American Zoologist* 32 (1992): 106–112, at 111.
14. Bernard John and George G. C. Miklos, *The Eukaryote Genome in Development and Evolution* (London: Allen & Unwin, 1988), 309.

But this fact poses a difficulty for all theories of macroevolution that rely on mutations to generate major changes in form. Why? Because developmental biologists such as Christiane Nüsslein-Volhard and Eric Wieschaus have also discovered that mutations that occur early in the developmental trajectory of an animal (from embryo to adult form) are *inevitably lethal*.[15]

Moreover, there is an easily understood reason for this: If an engineer modifies the length of the piston rods in an internal combustion engine without modifying the crankshaft accordingly, the engine won't start. Similarly, processes of embryological development are tightly integrated such that changes early in development will require a host of other coordinated changes in separate but functionally interrelated developmental processes downstream. For this reason, mutations will be much more likely to be deadly if they disrupt a functionally embedded structure that arises early in development (such as a spinal column) than they will be if the mutations affect more isolated anatomical features that occur later in development, such as fingers or skin.

This problem of "embryonic lethals" has created a dilemma for evolutionary theorists: the kind of mutations needed to generate new body plans—in particular, early-acting *beneficial* body-plan altering mutations—never occur. The kinds of mutations that do occur—late-acting mutations that affect small clusters of somatic cells—don't generate new body plans. The kind of mutations we need in order to produce new body plans, we don't get. The kind we get, we don't need.

How then does the evolutionary process overcome this difficulty to

---

15. Christiane Nüsslein-Volhard, and Eric Wieschaus. "Mutations Affecting Segment Number and Polarity in Drosophila," *Nature* 287 (1980): 795–801. See also the special issue of *Development* dedicated to the large-scale mutagenesis of the model vertebrate *Danio rerio* (the zebrafish) (P. Haffter et al., "The Identification of Genes with Unique and Essential Functions in the Development of the Zebrafish, *Danio rerio*," *Development* 123 [1996]: 1–36); or the many fruit fly mutagenesis experiments summarized in *The Development of Drosophila melanogaster*, ed. M. Bate and A. M. Arias (Cold Spring Harbor, NY: Cold Spring Harbor Press, 1993). Summarizing the evidence from a wide range of animal systems, Wallace Arthur writes, "Those genes that control key early developmental processes are involved in the establishment of the basic body plan. Mutations in these genes will usually be extremely disadvantageous, and it is conceivable that they are *always so*" (Arthur, *The Origin of Animal Body Plans* [Cambridge: Cambridge University Press, 1997], 14, emphasis original.) Arthur goes on to speculate that because developmental regulatory genes often differ between phyla, perhaps "mutations of these genes are sometimes advantageous." He offers no evidence for such advantageous mutations, however, other than as a deduction from his prior assumption of common descent.

produce major changes in animal form? Evolutionary biologists have not answered this question.

The Immutability of Developmental Gene Regulatory Networks

Or consider a related difficulty: developmental biologists have also discovered that building an animal does not just require new genes and proteins, but instead it requires *integrated networks* of genes and proteins called developmental gene regulatory networks (or dGRNs). These networks of genes and their protein products regulate the timing of gene expression as animals develop. The products of the genes (proteins and RNAs) in these integrated networks transmit *signals* (known as transcriptional regulators or transcription factors) that influence the way individual cells develop and differentiate during this process.

These signaling molecules influence each other to form circuits or networks of *coordinated* interaction, much like integrated circuits on a circuit board. For example, exactly *when* a signaling molecule gets transmitted often depends upon when a signal from another molecule is received, which in turn affects the transmission of still others—all of which are coordinated and integrated to perform specific time-critical functions.

The late Eric Davidson of California Institute of Technology explored the regulatory logic of animal development more deeply than perhaps any other modern biologist.[16] In the course of his investigations, he not only discovered what these networks of genes do, he also discovered what they never do, namely, change significantly. Davidson explained why. The integrated complexity of the dGRNs (which he likened to integrated circuits) makes them stubbornly resistant to fundamental restructuring without breaking. Instead, Davidson discovered that mutations affecting the dGRNs that regulate body-plan development inevitably lead to "catastrophic loss of the body part or loss of viability altogether."[17] As he noted, "there is always an observable

---

16. Isabelle S. Peter and Eric H. Davidson, *Genomic Control Processes: Development and Evolution* (New York: Academic Press, 2015).

17. Eric Davidson, "Evolutionary Bioscience as Regulatory Systems Biology," *Developmental Biology* 357 (2011) 35–40, at 38.

consequence if a dGRN subcircuit is interrupted. Since these consequences are always catastrophically bad, flexibility is minimal . . . "[18]

Davidson's findings present another challenge to the adequacy of
the natural selection/mutation mechanism. Building new animal body
plans requires not just new genes and proteins but *new* dGRNs. But
to build a new dGRN from a preexisting dGRN necessarily requires
altering the preexisting dGRN—the very thing that Davidson showed
does not occur without catastrophic consequences.[19] Given this, how
could a new animal body plan—and the new dGRNs necessary to produce it—ever evolve from a preexisting body plan and set of dGRNs?

Davidson made clear that no one really knows: "contrary to classical evolution theory, the processes that drive the small changes observed as species diverge cannot be taken as models for the evolution
of the body plans of animals."[20] He elaborates:

> Neo-Darwinian evolution . . . assumes that all process works the
> same way, so that evolution of enzymes or flower colors can be
> used as current proxies for study of evolution of the body plan. It
> erroneously assumes that change in protein-coding sequence is the
> basic cause of change in developmental program; and it erroneously
> assumes that evolutionary change in body-plan morphology occurs
> by a continuous process. All of these assumptions are basically
> counterfactual.[21]

Davidson's work, like that of Nüsslein-Volhard and Wieschaus,
has highlighted a difficulty of obvious relevance to macroevolution:
explaining the origin of major innovations in biological form during
the history of life. Building new forms of animal life such as those that
arose during the Cambrian explosion and other major radiations in the
history of life requires new developmental programs—including new
early-acting regulatory genes *and* new developmental gene regulatory
networks. Yet if neither early-acting regulatory genes nor dGRNs can
be altered by mutation without destroying existing developmental pro-

---

18. Ibid., 40.
19. Eric Davidson and Douglas Erwin, "An Integrated View of Precambrian Eumetazoan Evolution," *Cold Spring Harbor Symposia on Quantitative Biology* 74 (2009): 1–16, esp. 8.
20. Eric Davidson, *The Regulatory Genome* (New York: Academic Press, 2006), 195.
21. Davidson, "Evolutionary Bioscience as Regulatory Systems Biology," 35–36.

grams (and thus animal form), then mutating these entities will leave natural selection with nothing favorable to select and the evolution of animal form will, at that point, terminate.

Darwin was troubled by the problem of missing fossil intermediates. Not only have those forms (for the most part) not been found, but the abrupt appearance of new animal forms during the history of life illustrates a deeper and more profound engineering problem that neo-Darwinian theory has failed to address: the problem of building a new form of animal life by gradually transforming one tightly integrated system of information-rich genetic components and their products into another.

VIII. Answering My Critics

To this point I have argued that the neo-Darwinian mechanism is insufficient to generate the genetic information and information-rich gene regulatory networks necessary to produce new forms of animal life. Readers may want to know, however, how well this argument has withstood criticism. Fortunately, recent criticisms from (1) a leading mainstream evolutionary biologist, (2) two prominent theistic evolutionists, and (3) two prominent atheistic evolutionists (indeed, "new atheists") afford excellent opportunities to assess the strength of the arguments developed here.

Challenge from a Mainstream Evolutionary Biologist

First, in 2013, a leading paleontologist and evolutionary biologist, Charles Marshall, responded to my argument about the problem of the origin of information as presented in my book *Darwin's Doubt*. Marshall wrote a prominent review of the book in *Science* and, to his credit, did grapple with the book's main arguments about the inability of standard evolutionary mechanisms to explain the origin of biological information and morphological novelty. His review demonstrated— if inadvertently—however, that leading evolutionary biologists have not solved the problem of the origin of biological information.

To rebut the claim that the neo-Darwinian mechanism is insufficient to generate the information necessary to produce new forms of animal life, Marshall did not defend the power of the mutation/natural selection mechanism (or that of any other materialistic evolutionary mechanism) to produce the information necessary to build new forms of animal life. Instead, Marshall took a different tack. He disputed the claim that significant amounts of new genetic information *would have been necessary* to build the new animals. Specifically, Marshall claimed that "rewiring" of developmental gene regulatory networks (dGRNs) would have sufficed to produce new animals from a set of preexisting genes. As he argued,

> [Meyer's] case against the current scientific explanations of the relatively rapid appearance of the animal phyla rests on the claim that the origin of new animal body plans requires vast amounts of novel genetic information coupled with the unsubstantiated assertion that this new genetic information must include many new protein folds. In fact, our present understanding of morphogenesis indicates that new phyla were not made by new genes but largely emerged through the rewiring of the gene regulatory networks (GRNs) of already existing genes.[22]

In this paragraph, Marshall claimed a lot in just a few words. He implied that evolutionary biologists have an adequate explanation for the process of body plan building—morphogenesis—that does not require the generation of new (or at least much new) genetic information. Yet Marshall's understanding of how animal life originated is problematic for several reasons.

Elastic Control Networks Required

First, to account for the origin of novel animal body plans in the Cambrian period, Marshall suggests that developmental gene regulatory networks (dGRNs) must have been more flexible or labile in the past, in a way that would allow them to be "rewired."[23] Yet, as noted, all available observational evidence establishes that dGRNs do not tolerate random perturbations to their basic control systems—that even

---

22. Charles Marshall, "When Prior Belief Trumps Scholarship," *Science* 341 (2013): 1344.

23. Specifically, Marshall writes, "But today's GRNs have been overlain with half a billion years of evolutionary innovation (which accounts for their resistance to modification), whereas GRNs at the time of the emergence of the phyla were not so encumbered" (Marshall, "When Prior Belief Trumps Scholarship," 1344).

modest mutation-induced perturbations of the genes in the core of the dGRN either produce no change in the developmental trajectory of animals (due to a kind of preprogrammed buffering or redundancy) or they produce catastrophic (most often, lethal) effects within developing animals. Disrupt the central control nodes, and the developing animal does not shift to a different, viable, stably heritable body plan. Rather, the system crashes, and the developing animal usually dies.[24]

Thus, to claim, as Marshall does, that dGRNS might have been more elastic in the past contradicts what developmental biologists have learned over several decades, from mutagenesis studies of many different biological "model systems," including *Drosophila* (fruit flies), *C. elegans* (nematodes), *S. purpuratus* (sea urchins), *Danio* (zebrafish), and other animals, about how these networks actually function.[25] Although many evolutionary theorists (like Marshall) have speculated about early "labile" dGRNs, no one has ever described such a network in any functional detail—and for good reason: no developing animal that biologists have observed exhibits the kind of "labile" developmental gene regulatory network that the evolution of new body plans requires. Indeed, Eric Davidson, when discussing these hypothetical labile dGRNs, acknowledges that evolutionary biologists are speculating "where no modern dGRN provides a model," since they "must have differed in fundamental respects from those now being unraveled in our laboratories."[26]

For this reason, Marshall and other defenders of evolutionary theory reverse the epistemological priority (and violate the principles) of the historical scientific method as pioneered by Charles Lyell, Charles Darwin, and others.[27] Rather than treating our present experimentally

---

24. See Davidson, "Evolutionary Bioscience as Regulatory Systems Biology": "There is always an observable consequence if a dGRN subcircuit is interrupted. Since these consequences are always catastrophically bad, flexibility is minimal, and since the subcircuits are all interconnected, the whole network partakes of the quality that there is only one way for things to work. And indeed the embryos of each species develop in only one way" (40). See also the discussion in *Darwin's Doubt*, 264–270.

25. For a diagrammed schematic of the dGRN circuitry in the purple sea urchin, *Strongylocentrotus purpuratus*, see figure 13.4 on page 266 of *Darwin's Doubt* (used by permission from Figure 1D, in P. Oliveri, Q. Tu, and E. H. Davidson, "Global Regulatory Logic for Specification of an Embryonic Cell Lineage," *Proceedings of the National Academy of Sciences USA* 105 [2008]: 5955–5962).

26. Davidson, "Evolutionary Bioscience as Regulatory Systems Biology," 40.

27. See Charles Lyell, *Principles of Geology: Being an Attempt to Explain the Former Changes of the Earth's Surface, by Reference to Causes Now in Operation*, 3 vols. (London: Murray, 1830–1833).

based knowledge as the key to evaluating the plausibility of theories about the past, Marshall and others use speculative evolutionary theories about what they think must have happened in the remote past to reinterpret our present observations and experimentally based knowledge of what does, and does not, occur in biological systems. In other words, the requirements of evolutionary doctrine trump our observations about how nature and living organisms actually behave. What we know best from observation takes a backseat to prior beliefs about how life must have arisen.

A Deeper Problem

But there is a more fundamental, and obvious, problem with Marshall's attempt to dismiss the problem of the origin of genetic information necessary to produce new forms of animal life. Marshall claims that building new forms of animal life does not require new sources of genetic information, but his account of body plan building (morphogenesis) *presupposes*, but does not explain, many unexplained sources of such information. Indeed, his proposed approach subtly presupposes at least three unexplained significant sources of genetic information: (1) the information stored in the genes within the gene regulatory networks (GRNs), (2) the genetic information stored in other preexisting genes for building the necessary protein parts of various anatomical structures and novelties, and (3) the information required to rewire the gene regulatory networks (GRNs). Let's examine each of these sources in turn.

The Genes in Gene Regulatory Networks
Contain Genetic Information

Marshall presupposes unexplained genetic information, first and most obviously, by invoking preexistent gene regulatory networks. As noted, developmental gene regulatory networks (dGRNs) are integrated networks of specific genes and gene products (protein molecules that perform signaling functions) that interact to control and direct cell differentiation and organization during animal development. Clearly, the many genes that code for the production of these signaling proteins contain a vast amount of genetic information—the origin of which Marshall does not explain. Instead, his scenario for "rewiring" gene regulatory networks presupposes the prior existence of the information-rich genes that constitute these networks. But how did these genes arise? Marshall doesn't say. Thus his proposal begs the question as to the origin of at least one significant, and necessary, source of genetic information.

Yet, Marshall clearly acknowledges the need for these regulatory genes in his own scientific articles. For example, Marshall insists that *Hox* genes, in particular, must have played a causal role in producing the origin of the first animals during the Cambrian explosion. He notes that developmental considerations "point to the origin of the bilaterian developmental system, including the origin of *Hox* genes, etc., as the primary cause of the 'explosion.'"[28] *Hox* genes are regulatory elements that play important roles in many gene regulatory networks. While in these papers Marshall also emphasizes the importance of "rewiring" gene regulatory networks to generate new body plans, he clearly acknowledges that preexisting genes would be necessary to produce new animals—though, again, he does not explain the origin of these information-rich genes but merely presupposes their existence.

Anatomical Novelties Require a "Genetic Toolkit"

When Marshall said in his review that new animals "emerged through the rewiring of the gene regulatory networks (GRNs) of already existing genes," he did not specify whether he meant already existing genes in genetic regulatory networks or other preexisting genes such as those that are necessary for building *the specific anatomical structures* that characterize the Cambrian animals (the expression of which dGRNs regulate). Nevertheless, when writing elsewhere, Marshall and other evolutionary biologists have made clear that building new animal body plans would require many preexisting genes, indeed, a preexisting, preadapted "genetic toolkit" for building the specific anatomical parts and structures of animals.[29]

For example, in a 2006 paper titled "Explaining the Cambrian

---

28. Charles Marshall, "Nomothetism and Understanding the Cambrian 'Explosion,'" *Palaios* 18 (2003): 195–196.

29. Charles Marshall and James Valentine, "The Importance of Preadapted Genomes in the Origin of the Animal Bodyplans and the Cambrian Explosion," *Evolution* 64 (2010): 1189–1201, esp. 1195–1196, doi:10.1111/j.1558-5646.2009.00908.x.

'Explosion' of Animals," Marshall noted that "Animals cannot evolve if the genes for making them are not yet in place. So clearly, developmental/genetic innovation must have played a central role in the radiation."[30] In the same paper he argues that "It is also clear that the genetic machinery for making animals must have been in place, at least in a rudimentary way, before they could have evolved."[31] Indeed, in his published work, Marshall emphasizes the need for "gene novelties" for building the proteins that make up the anatomical structures and novelties of the various animals that arose in the Cambrian period (in addition to the need for *Hox* genes).[32]

Of course, he's right about this. Building multicellular animals would not have required just new *Hox* genes or genes for building new regulatory (DNA-binding) proteins. Instead, the evolutionary process would also have needed to produce a whole range of different proteins necessary to build and service specific forms of animal life. Different forms of complex animal life exhibit unique cell types, and typically each cell type depends upon other specialized or dedicated proteins—which in turn requires genetic information. In *Darwin's Doubt*, I offered numerous examples of this.[33] Our present observations of animals show that all new forms of animal life would also have needed various specialized proteins: for facilitating adhesion, for regulating development, for building specialized tissues or structural parts of specialized organs, for producing eggs and sperm, as well as many other distinctive functions and structures. These proteins must have arisen sometime in the history of life, but Marshall does not explain how the information for building them would have arisen.

Rewiring Networks Requires Informational Inputs

Finally, "rewiring" genetic circuitry in the way that Marshall envisions would itself have required multiple coordinated changes in the sequences of bases within the individual genes and/or changes to the arrangement of whole genes within the developmental gene regulatory

---

30. Charles Marshall, "Explaining the Cambrian 'Explosion' of Animals," *Annual Review of Earth and Planetary Sciences* 34 (2006): 355–384, at 366.
31. Ibid.
32. Marshall and Valentine, "Importance of Preadapted Genomes," 1189: " . . . accompanied by some additional gene novelties."
33. *Darwin's Doubt*, 191.

network. Such reconfiguring would entail fixing certain material states and excluding others. Thus, it would constitute an infusion of new information (in the most general theoretical sense) into the dGRN.[34] Thus, even if it were possible to rewire genetic regulatory networks without destroying a developing animal, Marshall's "rewiring" proposal itself presupposes, but does not explain, the need for an additional source of information.

Recall that recent mutagenesis experiments have established the *extreme* rarity of functional genes and proteins among the many possible ways of arranging nucleotide bases or amino acids within their corresponding "sequence spaces."[35] Recall also that the rarity of functional genes and proteins within sequence space makes it overwhelmingly more likely than not that a series of random mutation searches will *fail* to generate even a single new gene or protein fold within available evolutionary time. In presupposing these three significant sources of genetic information, Marshall does not explain *how* a random mutational search could have located the extremely rare functional sequences of nucleotide bases capable of building protein folds within the exponentially large sequence space of possible arrangements. In other words, he did not explain how the neo-Darwinian (or any other) evolutionary mechanism could have solved the search problem described earlier in this chapter. Instead, he simply assumes that the necessary genes for building new forms of animal life arose earlier in the history of life, without explaining *how* they did. Thus, Marshall's proposal (rewiring dGRNs) does not eliminate the need to explain the origin of genetic information necessary to build new forms of animal life; it simply begs the question as to how that information arose.

Challenges from Theistic Evolutionists

More recently, two prominent theistic evolutionists have also challenged my critique of the efficacy of mutation and natural selection as mechanism for generating new genetic information. Deborah Haarsma

---

34. See Claude Shannon, "A Mathematical Theory of Communication," *Bell System Technical Journal* 27 (1948): 370–423, 623–629.

35. Reidhaar-Olson and Sauer, "Functionally Acceptable Solutions in Two Alpha-Helical Regions of Lambda Repressor"; Douglas Axe, "Estimating the Prevalence of Protein Sequences Adopting Functional Enzyme Folds."

of the BioLogos Foundation has claimed that new studies show that functional genes and proteins are *not* extremely rare, despite what Douglas Axe's experiments have indicated.[36] Denis Venema, a biologist at Trinity Western University and a close colleague of Haarsma at BioLogos, has argued that the evolution of an enzyme capable of digesting synthetic nylon shows that new information capable of building a new protein can arise by mutation and selection in the time available to the evolutionary process.

Haarsma's claim is false; Venema's are either inaccurate or extremely misleading.

First, at least four other studies using different methods of estimating the rarity of functional proteins[37] have confirmed Axe's multiyear experimental study[38] showing their extreme rarity in the "sequence space" of possible amino acid combinations. Haarsma cites a scientific study by an Italian research group that allegedly contradicts Axe's findings but does not.[39] That study sought to evaluate how frequently randomly generated amino acid chains (polypeptides) organize themselves into stable three-dimensional structures. Unfortunately, the test the Italian group used to identify stable three-dimensional structures couldn't distinguish folded functional proteins from nonfunctional aggregations of amino acids. The group did report two folded structures, but discovered that, except in strongly acidic environments, these structures formed insoluble aggregates (not protein folds). This means these amino acid chains would not fold in actual living cells. Thus, nothing in the Italian study refutes Axe's results showing that protein folds are extremely rare in sequence space.

---

36. Haarsma makes this claim in response to me in the book *Four Views on Creation and Evolution*, to which both she and I contribute (ed. James Stump [Grand Rapids, MI: Zondervan, 2017]).

37. K. K. Durston, D. K. Y. Chiu, D. L. Abel, and J. T. Trevors, "Measuring the Functional Sequence Complexity of Proteins," *Theoretical Biology and Medical Modelling* 4 (2007): 47; Reidhaar-Olson and Sauer, "Functionally Acceptable Solutions in Two Alpha-Helical Regions of Lambda Repressor"; S. V. Taylor, K. U. Walter, P. Kast, and D. Hilvert, "Searching Sequence Space for Protein Catalysts," *Proceedings of the National Academy of Sciences USA* 98 (2001): 10596–10601; H. P. Yockey, "A Calculation of the Probability of Spontaneous Biogenesis by Information Theory," *Journal of Theoretical Biology* 67, no. 3 (August 7, 1977): 377–398.

38. Axe, "Estimating the Prevalence of Protein Sequences Adopting Functional Enzyme Folds."

39. C. Chiarabelli, J. W. Vrijbloed, D. De Lucrezia, et al., "Investigation of De Novo Totally Random Biosequences, Part II: On the Folding Frequency in a Totally Random Library of De Novo Proteins Obtained by Phage Display," *Chemistry and Biodiversity* 3:840–859; and E. Ferrada, and A. Wagner, "Evolutionary Innovations and the Organization of Protein Functions in Sequence Space," PLoS ONE 5 (11): e14172.

Venema's claims about nylonase are even more problematic.[40]

Recall that I have argued that random mutation/natural selection mechanism does not constitute a plausible means of generating the information necessary to produce a new protein fold—that protein folds are so rare in "sequence space" that a random search for new protein folds is overwhelming more likely to fail than to succeed in generating even a single new *fold* in the multibillion-year history of life on Earth.

In response, Venema points to the discovery in the 1970s of an enzyme (a protein) called "nylonase" that can break down nylon—a synthetic material invented in the 1930s. Venema claims that the rapid origin of the nylonase enzyme demonstrates the power of evolutionary processes to produce the information necessary to generate a "brand new protein" in just forty years. As he argues,

> Since nylon is a synthetic chemical invented in the 1930s, this indicated that these bacteria had adapted to use it as a food source in a mere forty years—less than a blink of the eye, in evolutionary time scales. Where these nylonases had come from was naturally the next question. The answer for one of them was a surprise—it was a de novo enzyme. Rather than being a modified version of another enzyme, this functional sequence of amino acids had popped into existence in a moment, through a single mutation.[41]

He further claims that this new enzyme appeared "de novo" via a single frame-shift mutation. (A frame-shift mutation occurs when a single nucleotide letter is randomly inserted into the genetic sequence, causing the protein machine that transcribes the genetic message to shift its starting point by one nucleotide—i.e., one genetic "letter"— as it transcribes or "reads" the sequence). Venema thinks that the origin of nylonase via such a mutation demonstrates that functional protein folds must be much more common in sequence space than Axe has argued. As Venema puts it,

40. Dennis Venema, "Intelligent Design and Nylon Eating Bacteria," BioLogos.org, April 7, 2016: http://biologos.org/blogs/dennis-venema-letters-to-the-duchess/intelligent-design-and-nylon-eating-bacteria.

41. Dennis Venema, in Dennis R. Venema and Scott McKnight, *Adam and the Genome: Reading Scripture After Genetic Science* (Grand Rapids, Mi.: Brazos, 2017), 85.

. . . if only one in 10 to the 77th proteins are functional, there should be no way that this sort of thing could happen in billions and billions of years, let alone 40. Either this was a stupendous fluke (and stupendous isn't nearly strong enough of a word), or evolution is in fact capable of generating the information required to form new protein folds.[42]

Nevertheless, contrary to what Venema has claimed, nylonase did not arise de novo via a single frame-shift mutation; it is not "a brand new protein"; and it certainly does not represent a new protein fold.

First, the Japanese researchers whom Venema cites and who have most extensively studied nylonase postulated that it arose by two minor point mutations (not a dramatic frame-shift mutation). These mutations produced just two amino acid changes or substitutions[43] to a *preexisting* 392 amino-acid protein—hardly a de novo origination event.

Second, based on their study, the researchers also inferred that the original gene from which the nylonase gene arose coded for a protein with limited nylonase function even before nylon was invented. This seems likely because a naturally occurring "cousin" of nylonase—an enzyme with a high degree of sequence similarity to it—has measurable (if weak) nylonase activity and can be converted to greater nylonase activity with just two mutations.[44] The close sequence identity between nylonase and its cousin suggests the genes for both proteins arose from a common ancestral gene, which also would have coded for a protein with nylonase activity. This suggests that the mutations that produced the gene for nylonase did not generate "a brand new" functional gene and protein, but instead merely optimized a *preexisting* function in a similar protein.

Most importantly, the evidence also indicates that nylonase *does not exemplify a new protein fold*, but instead displays the same stable, complex three-dimensional fold (a beta-lactamase fold) as both its

---

42. Ibid.

43. Seiji Negoro et al., "X-ray Crystallographic Analysis of 6-Aminohexanoate-Dimer Hydrolase: Molecular Basis for the Birth of a Nylon Oligomer-Degrading Enzyme," *Journal of Biological Chemistry* 280; 39644–39652.

44. K. Kato et al., "Amino Acid Alterations Essential for Increasing the Catalytic Activity of the Nylon-Oligomer-Degradation Enzyme of *Flavobacterium* sp.," *European Journal of Biochemistry*, 200:165–169.

cousin and likely ancestral protein. Indeed, oddly, the very researchers that Venema cites as his source for the story of the origin of nylonase make this clear. As the Japanese researchers note, "we propose that amino acid replacements in the catalytic cleft of a *preexisting esterase with the beta-lactamase fold* resulted in the evolution of the nylon oligomer hydrolase."[45] Note the terms *"preexisting" and "beta-lactamase fold."* These words indicate that the mutations responsible for the origin of nylonase did not produce a gene capable of coding for a *new* protein fold, but instead a gene that coded for the same beta-lactamase fold as its predecessor.

Thus, the nylonase story confirms what Axe and I have argued, namely, that the mutation/selection mechanism can *optimize* (or even shift) the function of a protein provided it does not have to generate a new fold. Nevertheless, as we have also argued (see above), given the extreme rarity of protein folds in sequence space, the number of mutational changes necessary to produce a novel *fold* (to *innovate* rather than *optimize*) exceeds what can be reasonably expected to occur in available evolutionary time. The nylonase story confirms, rather than refutes, that claim. Indeed, it suggests that the mutation selection mechanism is not a plausible explanation for the origin of the *amount* of new information necessary to generate a new protein fold (and, thus, for any significant structural innovations in the history of life).[46]

---

45. Negoro et al., "X-ray Crystallographic Analysis of 6-Aminohexanoate-Dimer Hydrolase."
46. It is worth pointing out that a close reading of Venema's critique shows that he does not understand protein structure. In his article, Venema claims that "Nylonase is *chock full of protein folds*—exactly the sort of folds Meyer claims must be the result of design because evolution could not have produced them even with all the time since the origin of life" ("Intelligent Design and Nylon Eating Bacteria," emphasis added). Venema's phrasing reveals ignorance on two counts. First, nylonase has a particular three-dimensional structure composed of two domains, each of which exemplifies a distinctive fold. A protein domain or fold is a distinctive, stable, complex, three-dimensional "tertiary" structure made of many smaller "secondary" structures such as alpha helices or beta strands. Some compound proteins may have more than one unique domain or fold, each exhibiting a unique tertiary structure, though many proteins are characterized by a single fold or domain. In any case, no protein chemist would describe nylonase as "chock full of protein folds," since it has just *two* distinct domains. In addition, since proteins are *characterized* and distinguished *by their folded structures*, it also betrays confusion to describe them as if they were receptacles for "holding" folds or as if folds were mere constitutive elements of a protein. That would be like saying that cars are "chock full" of chassis, or animals "chock full" of bodies. Even so, protein folds including nylonase *are* composed of (or "chock full" of) many smaller units of secondary structure such as alpha helices or beta strands—which is probably what Venema is referring to and probably why he exaggerates the significance of the origin of nylonase even though nylonase originated by just two mutations in a *preexisting* gene for a *preexisting* protein fold.

Challenge from Atheistic Evolutionists: Natural Selection and Random Mutation: A Nonrandom Process?

Finally, outspoken *atheistic* evolutionists have also attempted to refute my critique of the implausibility of the mutation selection mechanism as an explanation for the origin of genetic information. Richard Dawkins and Lawrence Krauss in particular have attempted to dismiss the problem of the origin of genetic information and specifically the argument made here about the implausibility of a successful random mutational search for functional information-rich genes and proteins within sequence space. After I presented this argument in a debate against Krauss at the University of Toronto, Krauss, Dawkins in defense of Krauss claimed that I misrepresented the evolutionary mechanism as a purely random process. Instead, both Krauss and Dawkins insisted that "natural selection is a NONRANDOM process," implying thereby that it could presumably succeed in finding the extremely rare functional arrangements of nucleotide bases and amino acids within the space of possible arrangements.

As Dawkins wrote in defense of Krauss and in criticism of me after the debate,

> Meyer was terrible. . . . When will these people understand that calculating how many gazillions of ways you can permute things at random is irrelevant. It's irrelevant, as Lawrence said, because natural selection is a NONRANDOM process.[47]

Nevertheless, in their attempt to get around the problem of the origin of genetic information, Dawkins and Krauss themselves misrepresented how the neo-Darwinian mechanism works. Natural selection itself is arguably a "nonrandom process," as Dawkins insists. Rates of reproductive success correlate to the traits that organisms possess. Those with fitness advantages will, all other things being equal, outreproduce those lacking those advantages.

Yet, clearly, there is more to the neo-Darwinian mechanism than

---

47. Richard Dawkins, comment 14 on "God vs. Physics: Krauss Debates Meyer and Lamoureux," Jerry Coyne, *Why Evolution Is True*, March 20, 2016, accessed August 22, 2016, https://why evolutionistrue.wordpress.com/2016/03/20/god-vs-physics-krauss-debates-meyer-and-lamoureux/ #comment-1316386.

just natural selection. Instead, the standard neo-Darwinian evolutionary mechanism comprises (1) natural selection and/or (2) genetic drift acting on (3) adaptively random genetic variations and mutations of various kinds. Moreover, as conceived from Darwin to the present, natural selection "selects" or acts to preserve those random variations that confer a fitness or functional advantage upon the organisms that possess them. As noted above, it "selects" only *after* such functionally advantageous variations or mutations have arisen. Thus, selection does not *cause* novel variations; rather, it sifts what is delivered to it by the random changes (i.e., mutations) that *do* cause variations. Such has been neo-Darwinian orthodoxy for many decades.

All this means that, as a mechanism for the production of novel genetic information, natural selection does nothing to help *generate* functional DNA base (or amino acid) sequences. Rather it can only *preserve* such sequences (if they confer a functional advantage) *once they have originated*. In other words, adaptive advantage accrues only *after* the generation of new functional genes and proteins—after the fact, that is, of some (presumably) successful random mutational search. It follows that, even if natural selection (considered separately from mutation) constitutes a nonrandom process, the evolutionary mechanism *as a whole* depends upon an ineliminable element of randomness, namely, various postulated or observed mutational processes—a point that even other evolutionary biologists (and friendly partisans to Krauss and Dawkins) acknowledged after the debate in Toronto. Larry Moran and P. Z. Myers, for example, both criticized Krauss and Dawkins for mischaracterizing the neo-Darwinian mechanism as wholly nonrandom, with Moran specifically blaming Krauss's uncritical reliance upon Dawkins as the source of his misinformation.[48]

In any case, the need for random mutations to generate novel base or amino-acid sequences before natural selection can play a role means

---

48. Moran's position may be viewed here: Larry Moran, "You Need to Understand Biology If You Are Going to Debate an Intelligent Design Creationist," *Sandwalk*, March 20, 2016, accessed August 22, 2016, http://sandwalk.blogspot.com/2016/03/you-need-to-understand-biology -if-you.html; for Myers's postmortem, see P. Z. Myers, "A Suggestion for Debaters," *Pharyngula*, March 20, 2016, accessed October 11, 2016, http://freethoughtblogs.com/pharyngula/2016/03/20 /a-suggestion-for-debaters/.

that precise quantitative measures of the rarity of genes and proteins within the sequence space of possibilities are, *contra* Dawkins, highly relevant to assessing the alleged power of the mutation/selection mechanism. Moreover, empirically based assessments of the rarity of genes and proteins in sequence space (estimated conservatively by Axe at 1 in 10^{77}—see above) do pose a formidable challenge to those who claim that the mutation/natural selection mechanism provides an adequate means for the generation of novel genetic information—at least in amounts sufficient to generate novel protein folds.[49]

Why a formidable challenge? Because random mutations *alone* must produce (or "search for") *exceedingly rare* functional sequences among a vast combinatorial sea of possible sequences before natural selection can play any significant role. Moreover, as discussed above, every replication event in the entire multibillion-year history of life on Earth could not generate or "search" but a miniscule fraction (one ten trillion, trillion trillionth, to be exact) of the total number of possible nucleotide base or amino-acid sequences corresponding to a single functional gene or protein fold.

As with a hypothetical bike thief who is confronted with many more combinations than he has time to explore, the mutation and selection mechanism turns out to be much *more likely* to *fail* than to succeed in generating even a single new gene or protein fold in the known history of life on Earth. It follows that the neo-Darwinian mechanism, with its reliance on—precisely—a *random* mutational search to generate new gene sequences, does not provide a plausible account of the origin of the *information* necessary to produce a single new protein fold, let alone a novel animal form, in available evolutionary time.

Conclusion

It follows from all this that theists who think that they must affirm the neo-Darwinian mechanism as God's means of creation are badly mistaken—and for *scientific reasons*. Consequently, there is no compelling reason to marry neo-Darwinism with a Judeo-Christian

---

49. Axe, "Estimating the Prevalence of Protein Sequences."

understanding of creation. The mechanism of natural selection and random mutation does not provide a remotely plausible account of how novel biological form and information might have arisen. Therefore, it is as unlikely to have been the means by which God created life as it is unlikely to be the true explanation for the origin of novel biological form and information.

3

Evolution: A Story without a Mechanism

MATTI LEISOLA

SUMMARY

At best, science is a search for truth about nature—how it functions and changes. At worst, it is a search for only naturalistic explanations for life's history. Is biology best explained by randomness or by a regulating intelligence? Can science prove one of the options to this philosophical question wrong? Several lines of experimental evidence show that novel functional genes and proteins cannot be formed de novo by chance processes. But can novel functional genes, proteins, or novel organisms be produced from existing ones by random methods? Individual genes, proteins, and microorganisms are easy to manipulate; they can be produced in large quantities and changed to the extreme in a laboratory—much more than could ever be happening in nature. Thus the laboratory experiments using random evolutionary methods are intelligently designed to study the limits of what randomness can do in biology—not what actually can happen in real life. The results of such experiments give a definite answer: there are narrow limits to the changes that random processes can achieve. They can never convert one gene to a basically different gene, one protein structure to a different structure, nor one microorganism to a different one. Thus evolution is a story without a mechanism, and adding the word "theistic" to it adds nothing to its explanatory power.

. . . . .

At its best, science is a search for truth about nature—how it functions and changes. At worst, it is a search for only naturalistic explanations of life's history. Is biology best explained by randomness or by a regulating intelligence? The question goes back to Socrates. Can science provide an answer to this philosophical question?

In chapter 2 Stephen Meyer argues, based on experimental research, that the neo-Darwinian mechanism of mutation and selection does not provide an adequate explanation for the origin of genetic information. In this chapter I will present several lines of experimental evidence to reinforce this argument, showing that novel functional genes and proteins cannot be formed de novo by chance processes. I will also ask whether novel functional genes, proteins, or novel organisms can be produced from *existing* ones by random methods.

Individual genes, proteins, and microorganisms are easy to manipulate. They can be produced in large quantities and radically changed in the laboratory—much more than could ever happen in nature. Thus laboratory experiments that use random evolutionary methods to study the limits of what randomness can do in biology are themselves intelligently designed—not what actually can happen in real life. The results of such experiments give a definite answer: there are narrow limits to the changes that random processes can achieve. These experiments can never convert one gene to a basically different gene, one protein structure to a different structure, nor one microorganism to a different one. Thus evolution is a story without a mechanism, and adding the word "theistic" to it adds nothing to its explanatory power.

I. Introduction

A team from my university has just won a gold medal in a synthetic biology competition (the presentation can be downloaded here: http://2015 .igem.org/Team:/Aalto-Helsinki). They produced propane using genetically engineered *Escherichia coli* bacteria. Throughout my entire career in universities and the biotech industry, my research teams have aimed at "improving" what nature can do, using both random and design methods. "Improvement" means tricking microbes or enzymes to do more than they naturally do, to produce compounds they naturally do not produce, to tolerate extreme conditions, etc.

Ever since the discovery of microorganisms in the nineteenth century, they have been used to make a variety of products. Once a suitable production organism has been found, scientists try to increase production rates by random mutations—and, since the discovery of genes and genetic engineering tools, by systematic design. In this chapter I want to point out—using some concrete examples—that both approaches have their limitations. Microorganisms and their proteins can change and be changed only within narrow limits. But before going into detail it is important to define some terms.

II. Definition of Terms

Phillip Johnson and many others have pointed out that the term "evolution" has many meanings. Merriam-Webster defines evolution as "a theory that the various types of animals and plants have their origin in other preexisting types and that the distinguishable differences are due to modifications in successive generations," where (in line with the neo-Darwinian synthesis) "modifications" refer to changes in DNA produced by mutations and recombination. The changes to DNA occur at random and are fixed in successive generations by natural selection and/or genetic drift, processes studied by population genetics.

Merriam-Webster defines "design" as "deliberate purposive planning." According to this definition, Miller-Urey–type origin-of-life experiments are examples of design, as are all breeding experiments with plants and animals, no matter what the methods are.

I want to emphasize that any experiment done by humans that tries to imitate what happens in nature is not what really happens in nature. For example, large-scale application of antibiotics in animal feeds has led to an increase in antibiotic-resistant bacteria. This is, however, not what happens naturally. It is a large-scale design experiment. The large-scale application of antibiotics is a man-made process that forces microorganisms to express antibiotic resistant genes, or by mutation to modify their antibiotic receptors—nothing more. Every attempt to mimic evolution in the laboratory is an example of design, not an example of what actually happens in nature. All such experiments, as clever as they might be, search the limits of natural processes. Anything proceeding under artificial selection is not evolution but design—designed randomness experiments.

What, then, happens in nature? Average mutation rates are in the order of 10^{-10} (how often a certain base in DNA is mutated per cell division). Negative mutations exceed positive ones by a thousand- to a millionfold, according to various estimations. Jerry Bergman[1] reviewed the topic of beneficial mutations. He did a simple Internet literature search and found 453,732 hits for the word "mutation," of which only 186 mentioned the word "beneficial." In those 186 references, the presumed "beneficial" mutations consistently involved loss-of-function (loss-of-information) changes. In not a single case was new information created.

A mutation, even if positive, must also be fixed in a population to be of any benefit. But the majority of mutations do not fix. They are lost: a lonely mutation in the big world will perish sooner or later. In real life all genomes degenerate, as shown using biologically relevant assumptions in numerical simulations of the mutation/selection mechanism.[2] All life has been degenerating since its first appearance: life's direction is degeneration, not evolution.

III. Industrial Microorganisms

Soon after their discovery, Louis Pasteur showed that microorganisms are not spontaneously formed under sterile conditions in a nutrient solution. In the light of the current understanding of the complexity of even the simplest microorganisms, such a possibility approaches impossibility.

In 1887 Pasteur patented a method to produce beer and yeast. Soon all kinds of industries started to use isolated microorganisms (bacteria, yeasts, and fungi) in producing various chemicals, pharmaceuticals, and food products. The first examples were organic acids, acetone, butanol, and glycerol. During and after the Second World War, large-scale production of antibiotics began. In the 1950s and 1960s, production technologies were adapted to manufacture enzymes, amino

---

1. Jerry Bergman, "Research on the Deterioration of the Genome and Darwinism: Why Mutations Result in Degeneration of the Genome," paper presented at Intelligent Design Conference, Biola University, April 22–23, 2004.

2. Winston Ewert, "Overabundant Mutations Help Potentiate Evolution: The Effect of Biologically Realistic Mutation Rates on Computer Models of Evolution," *BIO-Complexity* 2015, no. 1 (2015): 1–11, doi:10.5048/BIO-C.2015.1.

acids, vitamins, and vaccines, and recently to produce diagnostic and therapeutic proteins.

How does one improve a biotechnical production process? There are two basic ways: optimization of the process conditions (nutrients, starvation conditions, temperature, pH, oxygen availability, agitation speed, etc.) and optimization of the production organism. Here I discuss only the latter. To improve the production of compound A, the first step is to go to nature and try to find microbial strains that produce more than the previously used one. Then, by random mutation techniques, the strain is made to overproduce the compound A in a protected laboratory setting, rendering the strain unable to survive in nature. If this is not enough, modern genetic techniques can be used to bring multiple copies of a specific gene into the strain or to design the whole production pathway into an organism.

A. Random Methods

Using random methods, impressive results have been obtained. Modern production organisms can produce hundreds of times more penicillin than the strain originally isolated by Alexander Fleming in 1929, or over 100 grams per liter of various acids, or tens of grams of enzymes secreted from the cell. Why does an organism overproduce a certain amino acid, for example? The reason is simple: its regulatory mechanism has been destroyed by a mutation. Nothing new has been created; rather, the existing regulatory pathway was made nonoperational. Figure 3.1 shows schematically how this approach destroys the regulation of biosynthesis. Increased penicillin production by *Penicillium chrysogenum* is the result of increased copy numbers of relevant genes caused by classical strain improvement (mutation and selection).

I take another example from my own experience.[3] Xylitol is a five-carbon sugar alcohol and a non-cariogenic, tooth-friendly sweetener. It is produced by chemical methods from hardwood species like birch. These trees have a fiber polymer called xylan, which is formed mainly of a long chain of xylose sugar molecules. Xylose can be converted to xylitol by reduction using *Candida* yeasts. We wanted to improve the

---

3. Juha Apajalahti and Matti Leisola, "Method for the Production of Xylitol," US Patent 20040014185 A1 (2013).

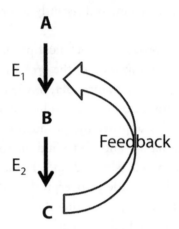

FIGURE 3.1. *Feedback mechanism.* Enzymes E_1 and E_2 convert product A via B to end product C. The activity of E_1 is controlled by C so that increase in C slows down the reaction rate of E_1. A random mutation changes the enzyme E_1 so that the feedback mechanism works no more. This leads to accumulation of C. This principle is often used in overproduction of amino acids.

xylitol production process by inducing random mutations by toxic chemicals or UV-light. Out of the thousands of mutants so created, we isolated a xylitol-overproducing strain where the natural xylitol metabolism was retarded (illustrated in Fig. 3.2). In nature such organisms are not viable, but they are useful as production organisms. In order not to lose such mutant organisms, they must be carefully kept isolated in aseptic conditions.

B. Design by Genetic Engineering

Strains that overproduce a desired compound can also be designed by modern genetic engineering tools. In enzyme production, several copies of a specific gene can be added to the production strain. In the 1980s and 90s, the enzyme industry constructed new production strains using this method. Certain fungi like *Aspergillus* and *Trichoderma*, and bacteria like *Bacillus subtilis*, can secrete tens of grams of enzymes per liter of culture.

Intracellular enzymes can also be overproduced. For example, more than a hundred copies of xylose isomerase genes were introduced into *Streptomyces rubiginosus* in plasmids (extrachromosomal DNA). Such

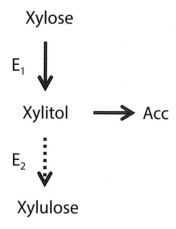

Xylose

E_1 ↓

Xylitol ⟶ Acc

E_2 ⋮↓

Xylulose

FIGURE 3.2. *Xylitol yield increase.* Xylose reductase (E_1) converts xylose to xylitol, which is further metabolized by xylitol dehydrogenase (E_2) to xylulose. A random mutation reduces the activity of E_2 to 10 percent of the original. This leads to increased accumulation of xylitol out from the cell.

strains carry a large extra load of genes, which the organism does not need. Such an organism survives only as a pure culture in isolated reactors. In nature it would rapidly lose the extra genes.

Genetic engineering tools have also been extensively used to bring new genes or even complete metabolic pathways into existing organisms. This is a difficult task: it takes a long time and has its limits. A real workhorse of biotechnology has been the bacterium *E. coli*. It has been converted to produce such compounds as indigo blue,[4] 1,3-propanediol[5] for the chemical industry, isoprene[6] as a starting material for synthetic rubber, human insulin,[7] erythropoietin,[8] and even fatty acids[9]

4. Burt D. Ensley, Barry J. Ratzkin, Timothy D. Osslund, et al., "Expression of Naphthalene Oxidation in *Escherichia coli* Results in the Biosynthesis of Indigo," *Science* 222 (1983): 167–169.

5. I-Teh Tong, Hans H. Liao, and Douglas C. Cameron, "1,3-Propanediol Production by *Escherichia coli* Expressing Genes from the *Klebsiella pneumoniae* dha Regulon," *Applied and Environmental Microbiology* 57, no. 12 (1991): 3541–3546.

6. Andreas Zurbriggen, Henning Kirst, and Anastasios Melis, "Isoprene Production via the Mevalonic Acid Pathway in *Escherichia coli*," *BioEnergy Research* 5, no. 4 (2012): 814–882.

7. David V. Goeddel, Dennis G. Kleid, Francisco Bolivar, Herbert L. Heyneker, Daniel G. Yansura, et al., "Expression in *Escherichia coli* of Chemically Synthesized Genes for Human Insulin," *Proceedings of the National Academy of the Sciences* 76, no. 1 (1979): 106–110.

8. Sylvia Lee-Huang, "Cloning and Expression of Human Erythropoietin cDNA in *Escherichia coli*," *Proceedings of the National Academy of the Sciences* 81 (1984): 2708–2712.

9. Parwez Nawabi, Stefan Bauer, Nikos Kyrpides, and Athanasios Lykidis, "Engineering *Escherichia coli* for Biodiesel Production Utilizing a Bacterial Fatty Acid Methyltransferase," *Applied*

for biodiesel. These are examples of systematic design of reaction pathways. However, this is possible only when the basic metabolism of *E. coli* is not disturbed and the products are not toxic. Again, such organisms are not viable in nature and would quickly either die or lose the extra foreign genetic material.

To demonstrate the limits of such processes, I again use xylitol as an example. We wanted to produce xylitol from glucose, which is both cheap and easily available. Baker's yeast is an efficient metabolizer of glucose and has a pathway to produce xylitol intermediates. Addition of two genes (see Fig. 3.2), xylose reductase and xylitol dehydrogenase, into this organism should at least theoretically result in xylitol production. The idea worked, but the yield of xylitol was very low—only 2.5 percent.[10] A similar approach with bacteria reached conversion yields of 23 percent,[11] which is the highest reported for xylitol production from glucose with a bacterial strain.

C. "Evolution" Experiments with Microorganisms

All such experiments are examples of design, not processes that happen in nature. Once an organism is isolated and cultivated in a flask, its environment is no longer natural for the organism. Such experiments, however, demonstrate what the limits of natural changes are and, equally important, their direction.

In 1968, Wu et al.[12] published results that showed that the *Aerobacter aerogenes* bacterium had learned to grow on xylitol. This was used as an example of evolution. What had actually happened? One mutation had destroyed the normal regulatory system in the bacteria. This resulted in a continuous production of one of its enzymes capable of reducing xylitol. Nothing new was created.

Experiments carried out by Barry Hall[13] shed more light on this.

and *Environmental Microbiology* 77, no. 22 (2011): 8052–8061, doi:10.1128/AEM.05046-11.

10. Mervi H. Toivari, Laura Ruohonen, Andrei N. Miasnikov, Peter Richards, and Merja Penttilä, "Metabolic Engineering of *Saccharomyces cerevisiae* for Conversion of d-Glucose to Xylitol and Other Five-Carbon Sugars and Sugar Alcohols," *Applied and Environmental Microbiology* 73, no. 17 (2007): 5471–5476, doi:10.1128/AEM.02707-06.

11. Mira Povelainen, and Andrei Miasnikov, "Production of Xylitol by Metabolically Engineered Strains of *Bacillus subtilis*," *Journal of Biotechnology* 128 (2007): 24–31.

12. T. T. Wu, E. C. Lin, and S. Tanaka "Mutants of *Aerobacter Aerogenes* Capable of Utilizing Xylitol as a Novel Carbon," *Journal of Bacteriology* A96, no. 2 (1968): 447–456.

13. Barry Hall, "The EBG System of *E. coli*: Origin and Evolution of a Novel Beta-Galactosidase for the Metabolism of Lactose," *Genetica* 118 (2003): 143–156.

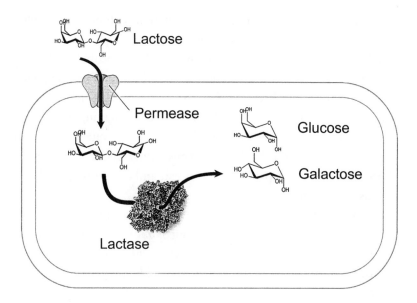

FIGURE 3.3. Lactose utilization by *E. coli*. Permease protein takes lactose into the cell and lactase enzyme degrades it to glucose and galactose, which are used by the cell as energy sources.

He studied *E. coli* and its ability to evolve. The bacterium can use the milk sugar lactose as its energy source. For this purpose it has a permease on its cell membrane to transport lactose into the cell and an enzyme called lactase (beta-galactosidase) to split lactose into two simple sugars, glucose and galactose (Fig. 3.3). Hall destroyed the lactase-encoding gene, which resulted in mutants that could no longer use lactose as the energy source.

When Hall cultivated these mutated cells in lactose-containing nutrient solution, mutants regularly appeared that could grow on lactose. What had happened? *E. coli* has an enzyme (Ebg) that closely resembles the lactase enzyme, though it is not able to degrade lactose. A single mutation in *ebgA* (the gene that codes for Ebg) is sufficient to allow slow growth on lactose. Only Ebg, the role of which is unclear, could be mutated to use lactose, although according to Hall "the best Ebg enzyme does not even approach the catalytic efficiency of the LacZ enzyme."[14]

---

14. Ibid., 154.

A single mutation in a large bacterial population with billions of cells is well within the reach of random evolution.

Richard Lenski's experiments with *E. coli* are probably the best-known long-term evolution-simulating experiments. The meaning of these experiments has been thoroughly discussed by Michael Behe.[15] The organism lost many of its capabilities (such as making flagella) and acquired nothing that it did not already have (such as citrate intake and utilization). In bacteria, evolution means losing genes.[16] The species compete to grow and reproduce the fastest, and therefore get rid of all unnecessary functions.

The most impressive evolutionary experiment so far reported was carried out by an international team using *Salmonella enterica*.[17] In October 22, 2012, a report claimed that this was the first time anyone had demonstrated the origin of a new gene! In reality, a gene with a weak side activity was duplicated and the side activity was strengthened. Nothing more—nothing new. Yet this is how the work was described in the scientific literature (the emphasis is mine, to show at what points *intelligence* was introduced in the experiment):

> Researchers **engineered** a gene that governed the synthesis of the amino acid histidine, and also made some minor contributions to synthesizing another amino acid, tryptophan. They then **placed** multiple copies of the gene in Salmonella bacteria that did not have the normal gene for creating tryptophan. The Salmonella kept copying the beneficial effects of the gene making tryptophan and over the course of 3,000 generations, the two functions diverged into two entirely different genes, marking the first time that researchers have directly observed the creation of an entirely new gene in a **controlled laboratory setting**.

There is one more interesting evolution experiment carried out using *E. coli*. It is generally assumed that a multistep mutational evolutionary

---

15. Michael J. Behe, "Experimental Evolution, Loss-of-Function Mutations, and the First Rule of Adaptive Evolution," *Quarterly Review of Biology* 85, no. 4 (2010): 419–445, doi:10.1086/656902.

16. Marcia Stone, "For Microbes, Devolution Is Evolution," *BioScience* 64, no. 10 (2014): 956, text available at: http://bioscience.oxfordjournals.org/content/64/10/956.full.

17. Näsvall Joakim, Lei Sun, John R. Roth, and Dan I. Andersson, "Real-Time Evolution of New Genes by Innovation, Amplification, and Divergence," *Science* 338, no. 6105 (2012): 384–387, doi:10.1126/science.1226521.

path is possible if all the intermediary steps are functional and can be reached with a single mutation. The activity produced in this way may, however, be so weak that the cell must overexpress the hypothetical newly formed enzyme—in other words, produce large quantities of this enzyme. This is a huge strain to the cell because it has to use extra synthetic capacity for this. Therefore it is very well possible that the cell gets rid of such a weak activity even if it could be beneficial.

Gauger et al.[18] studied what happened in such a case under laboratory conditions. They introduced two mutations into a *trpA*-gene that interfered with a tryptophan amino-acid synthesis. One mutation destroyed the activity completely and the other one only partially. The cell could have regained the tryptophan synthesis pathway by two consecutive mutations. However, this did not happen. The experiment shows that, even if the cell could acquire a new activity by gene duplication and mutations, it would get rid of it, because the new activity is too large a burden.

Although the described experiments are often promoted as evidence for evolution, they are actually all *designed*, and in fact they probe the limits of natural phenomena. They do not reflect what actually happens in nature. Recently, Chatterjee et al. published an important paper. The authors evaluate the timescale that is needed for evolutionary innovations. Their key finding is that, for arriving at functional sequences largely different from the starting one, the processes take an exponentially long time, according to the sequence length required. When the search starts from a flat point in the fitness landscape (exactly the situation that exists when starting from a random sequence), for a typical sequence of 1,000 nucleotides the search does not succeed, even if multiple populations are searching for the entire age of the earth. The search is unsuccessful even when the target area is very broad:

> The estimated number of bacterial cells on earth is about 10^{30}. To give a specific example let us assume that there are 10^{24} independent searches, each with population size $N \sim 10^6$. The probability that at least one of those independent searches succeeds within 10^{14}

18. Ann K. Gauger, Stephanie Ebnet, Pamela F. Fahey, and Ralph Seelke, "Reductive Evolution Can Prevent Populations from Taking Simple Adaptive Paths to High Fitness," *BIO-Complexity* 2010, no. 2 (2010): 1–9, doi:10.5048/BIO-C.2010.2.

generations for sequence length L=1000 and broad peak of c =1/2 is less than 10^{-26}.[19]

The search is unsuccessful also when the targets are many and broad, regardless of what population size is modeled. This study thus supports the conclusion that there is a strict limit to what the commonly understood evolutionary processes can achieve.

Tens of years of experimental evidence with microorganisms can be summarized as follows:

- Microorganisms can be designed to overproduce desired compounds by random mutations or by genetic engineering tools.
- Production of such organisms needs either huge mutation rates and systematic artificial selection or tedious construction and optimization of efficient pathways loaded into organisms, neither of which has resemblance in nature.
- Such organisms are not viable in natural conditions due to high mutational load or extra non-natural genetic load.
- Isolated microbial populations in laboratory experiments vary within narrow limits and lose information over time.

IV. Proteins

There is general agreement among scientists that the sequence of building blocks of a biopolymer represents a type of molecularly coded information; it is the specific ordering of the nucleotides or amino acids building up DNA, RNA, or protein molecules that determine their structure and function. Proteins are the most versatile and efficient in terms of function; to be convinced of this, it is sufficient to take just a glance at a poster with metabolic pathways showing the plethora of reactions catalyzed by enzymes.[20]

Twenty amino acids are the building blocks of the proteins present in all living organisms, from bacteria to humans. The average protein is about 300 amino acids in length, more precisely, 267 for bacterial and

19. Krishnendu Chatterjee, Andreas Pavlogiannis, Ben Adlam, and Martin A. Nowak, "The Time Scale of Evolutionary Innovation," *PLoS Computational Biology* 10, no. 9 (2014): e1003818, doi:10.1371/journal.pcbi.1003818.

20. For more information, see Gerhard Michal, ed., "Part 1: Metabolic Pathways," 4th ed., *BioChemical Pathways*, 2014, http://biochemical-pathways.com/#/map/1.

361 for eukaryotic proteins.[21] These 300 amino acids can be ordered in 20^{300} (10^{390}) different ways. Scientists generally agree, based on several lines of experimental data, that more than one specific protein sequence is capable of performing a particular function.

But scientists still debate the size of the fraction of functional protein molecules among nonfunctional ones, as well as how best to describe the functional information residing in proteins. The difficulty is confounded by experimental findings showing that there are protein families with more than 100,000 members having related but different sequences and, most likely, essentially the same structure and function. Moreover, proteins having different sequences and structures but similar functions are also known. How can one address this difficult issue?

A. Rarity of Functional Proteins in Protein Space

Jack W. Szostak (Nobel laureate, 2009) and his coworkers have, over the last twenty years, made extensive studies related to evolution of proteins with new functions. Their work is of exceptional importance because of not only its methodological novelty but also its conceptual originality, depth, and breadth.

Experimental studies with proteins became possible thanks to a major methodological breakthrough that enabled a mRNA molecule to remain covalently linked, after translation, to the protein whose sequence it encoded (Roberts and Szostak[22] ; Nemoto et al.[23]). One key advantage of this method is that researchers could start with a large population of different DNA molecules, similar in size to that used for selecting functional RNAs. The second major advantage is that the selection of functional proteins automatically results in the selection of their mRNA, allowing for cycles of reverse transcription, PCR amplification, transcription, translation, and new selection.

---

21. Luciano Brocchieri and Samuel Karlin, "Protein Length in Eukaryotic and Prokaryotic Proteomes," *Nucleic Acids Research* 33 (2005): 3390–3400, doi:10.1093/nar/gki615.

22. Richard W. Roberts and J. W. Szostak, "RNA-Peptide Fusions for the In Vitro Selection of Peptides and Proteins," *Proceedings of the National Academy of the Sciences* 94, no. 23 (1997): 12297–12302.

23. Naoto Nemoto, Etsuko Miyamoto-Sato, Yuzuru Husimi, and Hiroshi Yanagawa, "In Vitro Virus: Bonding of mRNA Bearing Puromycin at the 3'-Terminal End to the C-Terminal End of Its Encoded Protein on the Ribosome In Vitro," *FEBS Letters* 414, no. 2 (1997): 405–408, doi:10.1016/S0014-5793(97)01026-0.

Using this procedure, Keefe and Szostak[24] examined the frequency of functional proteins among polypeptides whose amino acid sequences were almost random. The function selected for was binding to ATP, and the length of the proteins was eighty amino acids. Four families of ATP-binding proteins were isolated from the starting library of 6×10^{12} sequences, indicating that roughly 1 in 10^{11} of the starting sequences possessed ATP-binding activity. According to the authors,

> In conclusion, we suggest that functional proteins are sufficiently common in protein sequence space (roughly 1 in 10^{11}) that they may be discovered by entirely stochastic means, such as presumably operated when proteins were first used by living organisms.

Kozulic and Leisola[25] have recently made a careful analysis of these results and have concluded that, even with extremely conservative assumptions, the probability of finding ATP binding activity which would function in a cell would be less than 1 in 10^{32}, which makes the formation of functional activity by random selection a practical impossibility.

The 10^{-32} fraction conservatively derived is significantly higher than some earlier estimates. Thus Yockey,[26] based on reported cytochrome c sequences, estimated that this fraction is 10^{-65}. Reidhaar-Olson and Sauer[27] estimated that the fraction is 10^{-63}. Later, Axe[28] concluded from his studies with penicillin degrading beta-lactamases that the probability of finding a functional enzyme among random sequences is about 10^{-77}–10^{-53}. In a study of four large protein families, Durston and Chiu[29] estimated that functional sequences occupy an extremely small

24. Anthony D. Keefe, and Jack W. Szostak, "Functional Proteins from a Random-Sequence Library," *Nature* 410, no. 6829 (2001): 715–718, doi:10.1038/35070613.

25. Branko Kozulic and Matti Leisola, "Have Scientists already Been Able to Surpass the Capabilities of Evolution?" *viXra Biochemistry* (2015), available at: http://vixra.org/abs/1504.0130.

26. Hubert P. Yockey, "A Calculation of the Probability of Spontaneous Biogenesis by Information Theory," *Journal of Theoretical Biology* 67, no. 3 (1977): 377–398, doi:10.1016/0022-5193(77)90044-3.

27. John F. Reidhaar-Olson and Robert T. Sauer, "Functionally Acceptable Substitutions in Two α-Helical Regions of λ Repressor," *Proteins* 7, no. 4 (1990): 306–316, doi:10.1002/prot.340070403.

28. Douglas D. Axe, "Estimating the Prevalence of Protein Sequences Adopting Functional Enzyme Folds," *Journal of Molecular Biology* 341 (2004): 1295–1315, doi:10.1016/j.jmb.2004.06.058.

29. Kirk K. Durston and David K. Chiu, "Functional Sequence Complexity in Biopolymers," in *The First Gene: The Birth of Programming, Messaging and Formal Control*, ed. David Abel David (New York: LongView Press– Academic, 2012), 117–133.

fraction of sequence space, in all cases lower than 10^{-100}. On the other hand, the estimate of Taylor et al.[30] is that a library of 10^{24} members should contain an AroQ mutase. In view of these different figures, and given the paucity of experimental data at present, one can be sure that the fraction of functional proteins among random sequences is lower than 1 in 10^{20}.

Kozulic and Leisola[31] are not the first ones to argue that there is a limit to what evolutionary processes can achieve. Behe, in *The Edge of Evolution*[32] and in subsequent work, has provided strong evidence that such an "edge" exists. Sanford, in *The Genetic Entropy*,[33] has explained not only why natural selection is poor at creating novelty in genomes, but also why it is incapable of preventing genome deterioration. Axe[34] has given strong evidence as to why just a single new protein fold remains beyond the reach of evolutionary processes.

B. Random Modification of Existing Protein Structures

Enzymes are widely used for many different applications: in washing powders, food manufacturing, the textile industry, animal feed, and chemical production, etc. Unfortunately, natural enzymes are not always suitable for industrial conditions where high temperatures, extremes of pH, and a variety of other chemicals interfere with enzymatic reactions. Using the tools of genetic engineering, it is possible to modify existing enzymes with various methods. One approach is to randomly mutate the gene coding for a given enzyme. The process is called directed evolution (which is an oxymoron, connecting two opposing terms). One then seeks to find better functioning mutants among the variants so created. Some amazing results have been achieved with this technique (Leisola and Turunen[35]):

---

30. Sean V. Taylor, U. Kai, K. U. Walter, Peter Kast, and Donald Hilvert, "Searching Sequence Space for Protein Catalysts," *Proceedings of the National Academy of the Sciences* 98, no. 19 (2001): 10596–10601, doi:10.1073/pnas.191159298.

31. Kozulic and Leisola, "Have Scientists already Been Able to Surpass the Capabilities of Evolution?"

32. Michael J. Behe, *The Edge of Evolution* (New York: Simon & Schuster, 2008).

33. John C. Sanford, *The Genetic Entropy* (Livonia, NY: FMS, 2014).

34. Douglas D. Axe, "The Case against a Darwinian Origin of Protein Folds," *BIO-Complexity* 2010, no. 1 (2010): 1–12, doi:10.5048/BIO-C.2010.1.

35. Matti Leisola and Ossi Turunen, "Protein Engineering: Opportunities and Challenges," *Applied Microbiology and Biotechnology* 75 (2007): 1225–1232, doi:10.1007/s00253-007-0964-2.

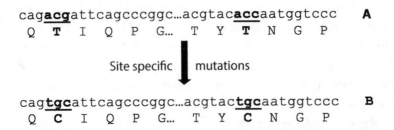

FIGURE 3.4. **A.** Part of 669 nucleotide–long xylanase gene (upper row, lowercase) and respective enzyme's amino acid sequence (lower row, uppercase). **B.** The same gene and resulting protein structure after site directed mutations (the mutated site is underlined). Two threonine amino acids are replaced by cysteines in the protein structure.

- Enzyme activity has been improved.
- Thermal and pH stability has increased.
- Specificity has changed.
- Side activities have improved.
- Stability against solvents and oxidants has improved.

In spite of these achievements, the technique has its limitations:

- There must be a mutational pathway to the new structure.
- One must be able to create a large enough mutant library in order to find the rare positive mutants.
- One must have a rapid screening method to detect the rare positive mutants.

Behe has estimated that the upper limit for a random mutational process is two to three simultaneous mutations in one protein. This is in harmony with Hall's[36] results with lactose mutants.

It also must be pointed out that directed evolution has nothing to do with what happens in nature. It is a name coined for a specific type of design experiments. Extremely high mutation rates, carefully chosen reaction conditions, use of tools of genetic engineering, selection of variants toward a desired goal, etc., are all hallmarks of design.

---

36. Barry Hall, "EBG System of *E. coli.*"

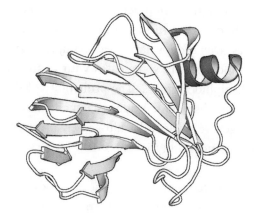

FIGURE 3.5. *3-D model of xylanase.*

C. Designed Changes

I started to work with a xylanase enzyme in 1974, and since 1997 the aim of my research team was to modify its structure to improve its stability. We have designed so-called disulphide bridges into the molecule in order to stabilize it against extreme temperatures and influence its pH stability and profile (e.g., Xiong et al.[37]; Li et al.[38]). The bridges are formed automatically when two cysteine amino acids are in a correct position and distance with respect to each other. In Figure 3.4A is shown part of the xylanase gene (upper row) and the respective amino acids (lower row). The positions modified by genetic methods are shown in bold. In Figure 3.4B are shown the two positions where the gene has been mutated. The mutations lead to incorporation of two cysteines (C; codon tgc) to replace threonine (T; codon acg/acc). A disulphide bridge is formed spontaneously between the two cysteine residues in the model structure shown in Figure 3.5.

The probability of forming one bridge *randomly* is very low—only one in 20 million. The probability of forming two bridges is as low as

---

37. Hairong Xiong, Fred Fenel, Matti Leisola, and Ossi Turunen, "Engineering the Thermostability of *Trichoderma reesei* Endo-1,4-β-Xylanase II by Combination of Disulphide Bridges," *Extremophiles* 8, no. 5 (2004): 393–400, doi:10.1007/s00792-004-0400-9.

38. He Li, Lasse Murtomäki, Matti Leisola, and Ossi Turunen, "The Effect of Thermostabilising Mutations on the Pressure Stability of *Trichoderma reesei* GH11 Xylanase," *Protein Engineering, Design, and Selection* (2012): 1–6, doi:10.1093/protein/gzs052.

one in 4 x 10^{14} alternatives. In practice, this is completely out of reach for random methods—even further from what can actually happen in nature. Many research groups have tried to improve xylanase stability by random methods, and in some cases with good results, but have never created disulphide bridges. The probability of the formation of the above described disulphide bridge is actually much lower because one has to change five nucleotides altogether in the 669 blocks–long gene, which is one possibility in 1.4 x 10^{17} (Behe's limit was two to three mutations).

It has been suggested that new enzyme activities are formed so that the weak side activities are improved by random mutations. This is of course possible, but in such a case nothing new is formed—only the existing activity is strengthened, while the basic protein structure remains the same. "Nothing evolves unless it already exists."[39] A recent paper by Axe and Gauger[40] emphasizes this point: mutation and selection can improve good designs but can never invent a design.

It has been suggested that new proteins are formed by duplication of genes. In such a case, the gene keeps its original function while the new copy is free to mutate to new functions. The starting point would be a functional protein, and it would not need to be built from scratch. This has, however, many problems: (1) Where did the original gene come from? (2) The duplicated gene can change only within narrow limits. (3) Over time, all genes degenerate (Sanford[41]).

Bloom et al.[42] have shown that extra stability allows more mutations and makes the protein structure more flexible without destroying its natural structure. This only emphasizes the point that no random process can change the basic structure of a given enzyme to a different structure.

Gauger and Axe[43] made a similar experiment, but chose two

39. Rajendrani Mukhopadhyay, "Close to a Miracle," *ASBMB Today* (October 2013), http://www.asbmb.org/asbmbtoday/asbmbtoday_article.aspx?id=48961.
40. Douglas Axe and Ann Gauger, "Model and Laboratory Demonstrations that Evolutionary Optimization Works Well Only If Preceded by Invention—Selection Itself Is Not Inventive," *BIO-Complexity* 2015, no. 2 (2015): 1–13, doi:10.5048/BIO-C.2015.2.
41. Sanford, *Genetic Entropy*.
42. Jesse D. Bloom, Sy T. Labthavikul, Christopher R. Otey, and Frances H. Arnold, "Protein Stability Promotes Evolvability," *Proceedings of the National Academy of the Sciences* 103 (2006): 5869–5874, doi:10.1073_pnas.0510098103.
43. Ann K. Gauger and Douglas D. Axe, "The Evolutionary Accessibility of New Enzyme Functions: A Case Study from the Biotin Pathway," *BIO-Complexity* 2011, no. 1 (2011): 1–17, doi:10.5048/BIO-C.2011.1.

enzymes with structures which very closely resembled each other. They made twenty-nine specific amino acid changes to one of the enzymes without being able to change its function to another one. They concluded that even this modest change would mean at least seven nucleotide changes and, considering the known mutation rates, would take at least 10^{27} years, which is longer than the estimated age of the earth:

> . . . this result and others like it challenge the conventional practice of inferring from similarity alone that transitions to new functions occurred by Darwinian evolution.

Blanco et al.[44] studied experimentally the sequence space between two different small proteins having different folds. One was a sixty-two amino acid protein that folds as an eight-stranded orthogonal β-sheet sandwich and another was a fifty-seven amino acid protein that has a central α-helix packed against a four-stranded β-sheet. The authors designed a gradual series of mutants in trying to understand whether there would be an evolutionary path from one fold to another. The conclusion of their study was that the sequence space between the two proteins is enormous. The results suggested that only a small fraction of this space would have adequate properties for folding into a unique structure. The sequence spaces of the two small proteins did not overlap, and a change from one fold to another could not be reached within a valid evolutionary trajectory. *Thus it is much easier to build a new protein from scratch than to change a basic structure to a different one!*

I have now briefly reviewed the key results obtained during the last three decades of protein and especially enzyme engineering. The results can be summarized as follows:

- Proteins can be modified with random and specifically designed methods—but only within narrow limits: the changes are not fundamental—basic structures cannot be changed.

---

44. Francisco J. Blanco, Isabelle Angrand, and Luis Serrano, "Exploring the Conformational Properties of the Sequence Space between Two Proteins with Different Folds: An Experimental Study," *Journal of Molecular Biology* 285 (1999): 741–753. http://www.ncbi.nlm.nih.gov/pub med/9878441.

- All the experiments done are designed, and have searched much larger space than the natural processes could have searched.
- Even with huge amounts of intellectual input, nothing basically novel has been created.
- Knowledgeable intelligent agents would not try to change one protein structure to another by random experimentation, but would rather make a new one from the beginning.

V. Why Then?

In 1972 I was sitting in the major lecture hall of the University of Helsinki as a young student of biochemistry. Francis Schaeffer had come to Helsinki to give lectures. During those lectures I realized how naive was my concept of truth. I bought all his books and started my reading in philosophy, which I previously thought to be of little or no value. Some years later I was reading, as part of my biochemistry studies, Albert Lehninger's *Biochemistry*.[45] The last chapter was about the origin of life, and I was surprised that, instead of solid science, it contained basically philosophical speculations. The random proteinoids synthesized by Sidney Fox were considered important in solving the problem of life's origin, and there was no discussion of the information problem. I also studied *Enzymes*, by Dixon and Webb.[46] They openly and honestly discussed the real problems in the origin-of-life speculations. Wilder-Smith's *The Creation of Life*[47] was an eye-opener: We have no idea where life and its huge information content came from. At that point I invited three of my professors to discuss these important issues with me. After two sessions I realized that they had no real answers but had swallowed what I will call the "modern" concept of truth (see discussion that follows) without any further consideration.

One has to ask, why don't clear results and straightforward theoretical calculations convince scientists that evolution is only a story without a mechanism? The reason must be outside of science; it is in philosophy. In the *Philebus* of Plato (429–347 BC), Socrates asks the key philosophical question:

---

45. Albert L. Lehninger, *Biochemistry* (New York: Worth, 1970).
46. Malcolm Dixon and Edwin C. Webb, *Enzymes* (London: Longman, 1964), 656–663.
47. Arthur E. Wilder-Smith, *The Creation of Life: Cybernetic Approach to Evolution* (Chicago: Harold Shaw, 1970).

Whether all this which they call the universe is left to the guidance of unreason and chance medley, or, on the contrary, as our fathers have declared, ordered and governed by a marvellous intelligence and wisdom.[48]

Only a few scientists openly express their philosophical starting point. The Nobel laureate Jack Szostak and his coworkers express with clarity their philosophical assumptions and conclusions. Thus, in a paper published in 2012, we read,

> Simple chemistry in diverse environments on the early earth led to the emergence of ever more complex chemistry and ultimately to the synthesis of the critical biological building blocks. At some point, the assembly of these materials into primitive cells enabled the emergence of Darwinian evolutionary behavior, followed by the gradual evolution of more complex life forms leading to modern life.[49]

What, then, is the "modern" concept of truth? After hundreds of discussions over the years it is quite clear to me that very few natural scientists are aware of their philosophical commitments. Even fewer know about Friedrich Hegel and his influence on the concept of truth. This is how Schaeffer summarized Hegel's influence: "All things are relativized. In so doing, Hegel changed the world."[50] Kozulic and Leisola[51] discuss to some extent the effect of Hegelian thinking on the acceptance of evolution.

I have talked with hundreds of students and professors around the world over the past forty-five years. The influence of Hegelian thinking, in association with naturalistic philosophy, is overwhelming: clear contradictions are tolerated; trivial experimental results are interpreted to prove major philosophical concepts; and even when the experiments point in a different direction, they are interpreted as proving a presupposed point. Few scientists seem to be able to see the contradictions in the following

---

48. http://classics.mit.edu/Plato/philebus.1b.txt.

49. Jack W. Szostak, "Attempts to Define Life Do Not Help to Understand the Origin of Life," *Journal of Biomolecular Structure and Dynamics* 29, no. 4 (2012): 599–600, doi:10.1080/073911012010524998.

50. Francis A. Schaeffer, *Escape from Reason*, The Complete Works of Francis A. Schaeffer, 5 vols. (Wheaton, IL: Crossway, 1968), 5:232–233.

51. Kozulic and Leisola, "Have Scientists already Been Able to Surpass the Capabilities of Evolution?"

statements: (1) The formation of building blocks explains the origin of buildings. (2) All biological change is evolution. (3) Information loss is information increase. (4) Similarity proves common ancestry. (5) Intelligently designed experiments are proofs of natural phenomena.

The modern concept of truth means that even clear experimental results are either relativized or interpreted to mean just the opposite of what they actually show. Let us give these statements a closer look. (1 and 5) The origin-of-life experiments are intelligently designed laboratory experiments and at best produce—among large numbers of toxic chemicals—some of the many building blocks of life. This is extremely far from producing even the simplest living organism with its huge information content. Sometimes even the presence of water on the surface of planets is interpreted to be enough for life's origin! The same is true of the so-called directed evolution experiments of enzymes. They are considered to imitate Darwinian evolution although they are only carefully designed laboratory experiments. (2 and 3) Observed biological changes only prove variation and adaption. They are usually associated with information loss, not increase. (4) Similarity only shows similarity and does not explain the *origin* of similarity.

VI. Historical Background

This distinction between design and evolution was clear in 1859 when Charles Darwin published his *Origin of Species*. In 1844, fifteen years before Darwin, Robert Chambers published *Vestiges of the Natural History of Creation*, suggesting that species transmutate under the guidance of a Creative Power, that is, by design. Chambers's idea was attacked strongly by the leading scientists of the time, including Thomas Huxley, as well as by the theologians of the day. Darwin explicitly excluded the possibility that natural selection operates under any direction or guidance. Just a few of many statements from nineteenth-century books show that the absolute exclusion of design—meaning the absence of guidance by intelligence, or teleology—was the major reason for the acceptance of Darwin's theory in his day:

> Another fact cannot fail to attract attention. When the theory of evolution was propounded in 1844 in the "Vestiges of Creation," it was

universally rejected; when proposed by Mr. Darwin, less than twenty years afterward, it was received with acclamation. Why is this? The facts are now what they were then. They were as well known then as they are now. The theory, so far as evolution is concerned, was then just what it is now. . . . There is only one cause for the fact referred to, that we can think of. The "Vestiges of Creation" did not expressly or effectually exclude design. Darwin does. This is a reason assigned by the most zealous advocates of his theory for their adoption of it.[52]

But Mr. Darwin tells us, that the use of the words "plan of creation" or "unity of design" are marks of ignorance. In other words, there is no "plan of creation," there is no "unity of design" in the Darwinian hypothesis. *The favourable point in the variation selected, is never a designed point.* It is favourable simply through chance, or luck, or fortune, or accident, and it is selected by the hypothetical law, because a lucky chance has made it what it is. . . .

[And further] Mr. Darwin stakes the main work of the development of life on Natural Selection. "In effect," he says, "give me a struggle for existence; give me the weak and strong taking part in that struggle; give me the weak going to the wall, and I do not require Design to account for anything."[53]

That which struck the present writer most forcibly on his first perusal of the "Origin of Species" was the conviction that Teleology, as commonly understood, had received its deathblow at Mr. Darwin's hands.[54]

The curious thing in modern biology is the fact that all the evidences trying to prove the mechanism of evolution are actually examples of design! Darwin saw nothing in biology that could convince him of design, as evident from his correspondence with Asa Gray:

Your question what would convince me of Design is a poser. If I saw an angel come down to teach us good, and I was convinced from

---

52. Charles Hodge, *What Is Darwinism?* (New York: Scribner, Armstrong, 1874), 145–146. Text available at: https://archive.org/details/cu31924024755567.

53. James Carmichael, *Design and Darwinism* (Toronto: Hunter, Rose, 1880), 24, 33 (emphasis original).

54. Thomas H. Huxley, *The Lay Sermons, Addresses, and Reviews* (New York: D. Appleton, 1880). Text available at: https://archive.org/details/laysermonsaddre08huxlgoog.

others seeing him that I was not mad, I should believe in design. If I could be convinced thoroughly that life and mind was in an unknown way a function of other imponderable force, I should be convinced. If man was made of brass or iron and no way connected with any other organism which had ever lived, I should perhaps be convinced. But this is childish writing.[55]

The confusion of the kind shown by many modern scientists started a long time ago, when some scientists and theologians, in order to harmonize their view of religion with Darwin's theory, essentially equated the meaning of the terms evolution and design. Here are quotations from two early theistic evolutionists:

> Transmutationism (an old name for the evolutionary hypothesis), which was conceived at one time to be the very antithesis to the two preceding conceptions, harmonizes well with them if the evolution be conceived to be orderly and designed.[56]

> The question, therefore, is reduced to this: Has the course of evolution been designed and guided, or not? In either case it is evolution; but if it has been guided it is creation also, and evolution is the method of creation.[57]

A modern theistic evolutionist, Kenneth Miller, says essentially the same thing:

> I see a planet bursting with evolutionary possibilities, a continuing creation in which the Divine providence is manifest in every living thing. I see a science that tells us there is indeed a design to life. And the name of that design is evolution.[58]

For theistic evolutionists, terms like directed evolution, evolutionary

---

55. "Charles Darwin and Asa Gray on Design: Letters from the Darwin Correspondence Project," September 17, 1861, North Carolina State University, http://www4.ncsu.edu/~kimler/hi482/Design.pdf.

56. St. George Mivart, *On the Genesis of Species* (n.p.: 1871), 241. Text available at: http://www.macrodevelopment.org/mivart/.

57. George St. Clair, *Darwinism and Design; or, Creation by Evolution* (London: Hodder & Stoughton, 1873), 110.

58. Michael O. Garvey, "Biologist Kenneth Miller to Receive Notre Dame's 2014 Laetare Medal," University of Notre Dame News, University of Notre Dame, March 30, 2014, accessed October 18, 2016, http://news.nd.edu/news/47186-biologist-kenneth-miller-to-receive-notre-dames-2014-laetare-medal/.

strategy, evolutionary design, coordinated evolution, evolutionary creationism, theistic evolution, etc., make sense. Darwinists today tolerate these terms because that is the price they are willing to pay for maintaining the appearance of validity of the whole Darwinian dogma. When pressed about their true meaning, Darwinists usually say that such terms are mere metaphors.

In a recent critical review article in *BIO-Complexity*, David Snoke showed that the use of teleological concepts and terms is widespread in contemporary systems biology, and that therefore the scientists in that discipline are actually working under a *design* rather than an evolutionary program:

> Many have demanded that the intelligent design paradigm must come up with a successful, predictive, quantitative program for biology, but it seems that such a program already exists right under our noses.[59]

I agree with Snoke. I have discussed with Kozulic[60] at length how, in biochemistry and molecular biology, an illusion of the continuation of the evolutionary research program is maintained, in significant measure, by using and accepting contradictions (*Contradictio in adjecto*). If design is equated with evolution, there is no possibility for overthrowing evolution without also overthrowing design.

My view is that nothing can be logically proven to people who, like Kenneth Miller, equate things that are contradictory. That two things cannot be both true and not true at the same time is a law (the principle of noncontradiction) well known by Plato and Aristotle. Now, one may try to argue that evolution and design are not contradictory. However, the writings of Charles Darwin and his contemporaries, and of many others ever since, prove that they are. Darwin and his followers explicitly claim that chance variation and the law of natural selection have created all species of living organisms. If so, design is ruled out. In contrast, if design is the cause of the creation of species, then chance and law are ruled out as the creators of species.

---

59. David Snoke, "Systems Biology as a Research Program for Intelligent Design," *BIO-Complexity* 2014, no. 3 (2014): 1–11, doi:10.5048/BIO-C.2014.3.
60. Kozulic and Leisola, "Have Scientists already Been Able to Surpass the Capabilities of Evolution?"

4

Are Present Proposals on Chemical Evolutionary Mechanisms Accurately Pointing toward First Life?

JAMES M. TOUR

SUMMARY

Abiogenesis is the prebiotic process wherein life, such as a cell, arises from nonliving materials such as simple organic compounds. Long before evolution can even begin, the origin of first life, that first cell, would have to come from some simpler nonliving molecules. On Earth, the essential molecules for life as we know it are carbohydrates (also called sugars or saccharides), nucleic acids, lipids, and proteins (polymers of amino acids). Described is the process by which organic synthesis is performed, and the considerations that are generally required to synthesize a complex system where many molecular parts come together to operate concertedly. This will be demonstrated in the synthesis of nanomachines. Then considered will be some proposals that others have espoused for the synthesis of carbohydrates and carbohydrate-bearing nucleotide bases, from a prebiotic milieu. Briefly mentioned will be the obstacles to the much more difficult task of having the molecular building blocks assemble into a functional system. Not considered are scientifically unknown entities that have been proposed to have seeded life on Earth, such as a design agent or panspermia. An opinion will be rendered showing that the strongest evidence against the proposals of current prebiotic research is the researchers' own data. The current proposals can retard the field from discovering the scientific solutions since they seem to be directing researchers down paths of futility.

· · · · ·

Any account of the origin of the first life must include a mechanism for the generation of the chemicals needed for life, and then for how life arose from those preexisting nonliving chemicals. Abiogenesis proposals attempt to explain how chemical processes transformed preexisting nonliving chemicals into more complex information-bearing molecules such as DNA, RNA, and proteins. For an account of the origin of life to be realistic, there must be chemical processes that can successfully arrange simple organic compounds into complex biologically relevant macromolecules and living cells. Life requires carbohydrates, nucleic acids, lipids, and proteins. But what is the chemistry behind their origin? What is the origin of metabolism, or of the information storage and processing systems that depend on these complex biochemical compounds?

My experience working in synthetic chemistry, building relatively simple nanomachines, has led me to be skeptical of proposals for the origin of the requisite chemical building blocks necessary for life.[1] Some biologists seem to think that there are well-understood prebiotic molecular mechanisms for the synthesis of carbohydrates or proteins, lipids or nucleic acids. They have been grossly misinformed.[2] Others think that, if not yet known, such chemical pathways will soon be

---

1. Synthetic chemistry involves the design and making of molecules in a laboratory. Nanotechnology is the study, design, and fabrication of matter wherein at least one of the matter's axes is in the 1 to 100 nanometer size region.

2. Prebiotic chemistry relates to the chemistry that occurred on Earth prior to life, or in a prebiological world. The conditions of such a world are not known, but are supposed to be rich in an atmosphere of dinitrogen and ammonia, water, and simple organic compounds such as carbon dioxide, formaldehyde, and methanol. Inorganic compounds such as metal oxides and metal salts are also presumed to have been abundant. In the context here, "prebiotic" has nothing to do with the recent use of the term prebiotics, which is taken to mean a nondigestible food or food ingredient that promotes the growth of beneficial microorganisms in the intestines.

identified. To me, these biologists are naively optimistic. What they hope for will not happen anytime soon.

And no wonder: few biologists have ever synthesized a complex molecule ab initio. My experience with organic synthesis leads me to suggest that chemistry acting on its own simply does not do what it would need to do to generate the biologically relevant macromolecules, let alone the complex nanosystems in a living cell.

I'd like to explain the reasons for my skepticism in more detail.

Designing Molecules

Let's begin by discussing the process of molecular design and synthesis in general, what it takes to successfully build a molecule to perform a particular function.

The initial design is important. Sometimes molecular designs are computer-assisted, but more often than not, the initial steps are done on paper. A target must first be drawn or otherwise designated. This is no trivial task. In some cases, chemists have seen the target in a related system; in other cases, they guess the target's properties on the basis of its molecular weight, its shape, the moieties appended to the main backbone, and its functional capacities.

Once a target is selected, retrosynthesis is next, whether on paper or on a computer screen. Placing the target at the top, the chemist draws an inverted tree (or graph), one step down at a time, into multiple branch points, until he reaches a level where starting materials are at hand.[3]

The inverted tree is then pruned. Certain branches lead to dead ends. They are lopped off. Further refinement of various routes leads to a set of desired paths; these are the routes that can be attempted in the laboratory.

Given a target and a path to get there, the synthetic chemist must now try a number of chemical permutations. Each step may need to be optimized, and each step must be considered with respect to specific reaction site modifications and different reaction rates.

What is desired is often ever so slightly different in structure from

---

3. Elias Corey and Xue-Min Cheng, *The Logic of Chemical Synthesis* (New York: Wiley-Interscience, 1995).

what is not. If Product A is a mirror image of Product B, one left-handed and the other right-handed, separation becomes a time-consuming and challenging task, one requiring complementary mirror-image structures. Many molecules in natural biological systems are homochiral, meaning only left-handed or right-handed molecules are used, not both. Their mirror images cannot do their work.

In addition, few reactions ever afford a 100 percent yield; few reactions are free of deleterious byproducts. Purification is essential. If byproducts are left in reaction, they result in complex mixtures that render further reactions impossible to execute correctly.

After purification, a number of different spectroscopic and spectrometric methods must be used to confirm the resulting molecular structures. Make the wrong molecular intermediate, the synthetic chemist quickly learns, and all subsequent steps are compromised.

Finally, intermediate products are often unstable in air, sunlight or room light, or in water. Synthetic chemists must work in seconds or minutes to prevent destructive natural processes or chemical reactions from taking over.

Building Nanovehicles

As an example of what it takes to synthesize organic compounds, consider the synthesis of a molecular machine, a nanovehicle, a simple unimolecular structure that can translate itself along a surface when supplied with thermal or photonic energy. My colleagues and I make these relatively simple machines in the laboratory, and what we have learned about synthesizing nanovehicles has been published in numerous peer-reviewed papers.[4]

We set out to design "nanotrucks" and "nanocars" that can move across gold surfaces. They consist of three basic molecular mechanical parts: fullerene wheels,[5] a chassis made of fused aromatic rings or

---

4. See Yasuhiro Shirai et al., "Surface-Rolling Molecules," *Journal of the American Chemical Society* 128, no. 14 (2006): 4854–4864; Pinn-Tsong Chiang et al., "Toward a Light-Driven Motorized Nanocar: Synthesis and Initial Imaging of Single Molecules," *ACS Nano* 6, no. 1 (2012): 592–597; Jean-François Morin, Yasuhiro Shirai, and James Tour, "En Route to a Motorized Nanocar," *Organic Letters* 8, no. 8 (2006): 1713–1716.

5. The name "fullerene" was coined by Richard Smalley when he codiscovered the geodesic dome–shaped molecule which looked like architectural structures designed by the architect Buckminster Fuller.

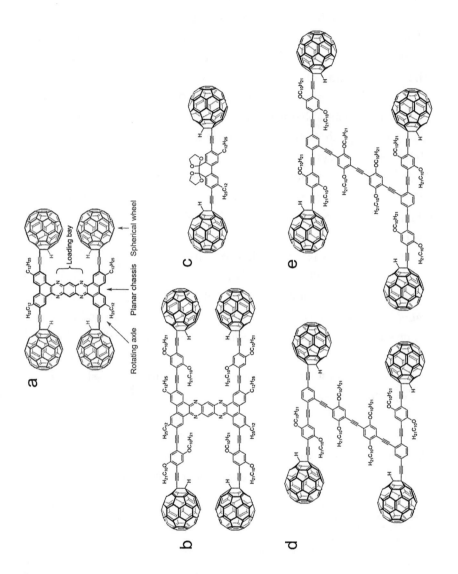

FIGURE 4.1. *Nanotrucks and nanocars.*

oligo(phenylene ethynylene)s (OPEs), and alkynyl axles (see Fig. 4.1a and 1b for trucks and 1d and 1e for cars).

Ours was the first molecular-sized machine that incorporated mechanical components, such as wheels and axles, with movement at the single molecular level.[6] The rolling motion of these nanocars resembled the rolling motion of macroscopic cars.

We built two different kinds of nanovehicles: a rigid structure in nanotrucks 1a and 1b, the precursors along the synthetic route to these compounds, such as 1c, and a semirigid structure in nanocars 1d and 1e. All these designs were necessary because we discovered as we went along that better flexibility of the chassis structure combined with the increased number of alkyl units dramatically increased the solubility of the fullerene-wheeled structures, in the organic solvents in which they were synthesized.

The process was not straightforward. First we had to work out a way to attach fullerene wheels (a 60-carbon sphere) to the alkynyl axles, then a way to build a chassis of the appropriate structure, and attach the axles to the chassis. New reactions under new conditions had to be worked out in each case. For the nanotrucks, the first and second structures proved unworkable due to stiffness of the chassis and insolubility. We then modified the chassis design: a semi-rigid Z-shaped chassis for nanocars remedied the difficulties. The first nanocar structure was still too insoluble to properly purify, but the nanocar 1e (the fourth overall design) finally could be adequately purified and characterized (i.e., its molecular structure could be determined) for further study. Notice that all this design and experimentation required considerable

---

6. Single-molecule-sized nanoscale machines with controlled mechanical motion had already yielded a variety of molecular machines resembling macroscopic motors, switches, shuttles, turnstiles, gears, bearings, and elevators; but these nanomachines were operated and observed spectroscopically as ensembles of molecules in solution or solid state. Some examples in which a molecule has a mechanical design and the mechanism of movement can be probed at the single molecular level are cyclodextrin necklaces, altitudinal molecular rotors, molecular barrows, molecular landers, and nanowalkers. The nanocars have taken this research field to a more complex level in the study of motion at the single molecule level. See Raymond Astumian, "Making Molecules into Motors," *Scientific American* (2001): 57–64; Wesley Browne and Ben Feringa, "Making Molecular Machines Work," *Nature Nanotechnology* 1 (2006): 25–35; John Abendroth et al., "Controlling Motion at the Nanoscale: Rise of the Molecular Machines," *ACS Nano* 9, no. 8 (2015), 9, 7746–7768; Vincenzo Balzani, Alberto Credi and Margherita Venturi, "Molecular Machines Working on Surfaces and at Interfaces," *ChemPhysChem* 9, no. 2 (2008): 202–220; Euan Kay and David Leigh, "Rise of Molecular Machines," *Angewandte Chemie International Edition* 54, no. 35 (2015): 10080–10088.

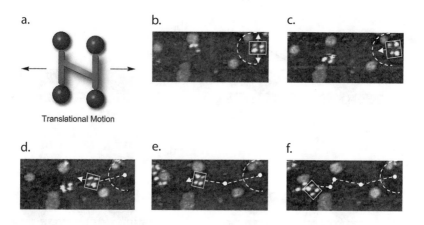

FIGURE 4.2. *Thermally induced motion of four-wheeled nanocar 1e in Figure 4.1, as imaged by scanning tunneling microscopy.*

knowledge and skill. Yet even with all these efforts, the properties of each design could not be predicted a priori, and as problems were encountered, things had to be restarted and redesigned repeatedly.

In addition, many reagents were purchased to use in this protocol—otherwise the protocol would need to include steps for their synthesis and purification as well. Pretreatment of solvents was needed so that the system would not be contaminated by impurities such as oxygen, which retard or mitigate the desired reactions. Purification was required at each step since the chemistry rarely affords the chemist materials that are of sufficient purity for use in subsequent steps. Each product needed a different purification protocol. Nature would not have this luxury as it moves toward the molecules needed for first life, or that first living cell.

With nanocar 1e, we have been able to demonstrate the action of fullerene-wheel architecture at the single-molecular level. Evidence for thermally induced, wheel-assisted rolling motion in the nanocar 1e on gold was obtained by scanning tunneling microscopy (Fig. 4.2).

The work that I have just described is merely a brief sketch of the processes we went through to synthesize the nanocars. The details are far richer.[7]

So here's something to consider as we think about the problem

---

7. For more detail, see Shirai et al., "Surface-Rolling Molecules," 4854–4864.

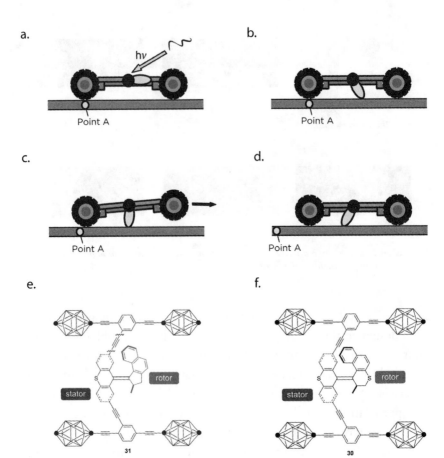

FIGURE 4.3. Figures **4.3a–d** show the scheme of light-actuation of the motor so that it acts as a paddle-wheel to propel the nanocar along a surface. **3e** and **3f** show the structures of the slow (Fig. **4.3e**) and fast (Fig. **4.3f**) motorized nanocars. These nanocars have *para*-carborane wheels, for reasons that will become apparent.[*] (The term *para*-carborane refers to a spherical molecule that is composed of boron and hydrogen, except at the ends where carbon is bound.)

[*] See Jean-François Morin, Yasuhiro Shirai, and James Tour, "En Route to a Motorized Nanocar," *Organic Letters* 8, no. 8 (2006): 1713; Pinn-Tsong Chiang et al., "Toward a Light-Driven Motorized Nanocar: Synthesis and Initial Imaging of Single Molecules," *ACS Nano* 6, no. 1 (2012): 593.

of the origin of life: The molecular machines and the information processing system that cells use to synthesize macromolecules are far more complicated than anything illustrated here. Designing nanocars is child's play in comparison to the complex molecular machinery and information-processing systems at work in the synthesis of proteins, enzymes, DNA, RNA, and polysaccharides, let alone their assembly into complex functional macroscopic systems—a point that has become increasingly apparent to me as we've learned more about how difficult it is to build and improve our relatively simple nanocars.

Cars with Motors

Our first-generation vehicles operated without motors.[8] We later made motorized versions that were more complex to design and synthesize.[9] The motors are ultraviolet-light-active; they rotate unidirectionally. The first motorized versions that we made rotated at 1.8 revolutions per hour. Too slow. But with a redesign, which took us back to step one in the synthesis, we achieved a light-activated nanocar whose motor spins at 3 MHz (3 million rotations per second) (Fig. 4.3).[10] Fast enough.

The plan to synthesize the fast nanocar (Fig. 4.3f) involved a modular approach in which the coupling of the axles and the stator represented the last step. In the following indented paragraph, I present the description of the motor's synthesis in its more technical form so as to highlight the many steps and specialized conditions:

According to *Scheme 1* [shown below], heating ketone 1 to reflux in an ethanol and hydrazine solution produced the rotor, hydrazone 2. The conversion of ketone 3 into thione 4 was improved by decreasing both the concentration and the reaction time from those in the published procedure. The generation of the sterically hindered double bond between the rotor and the stator utilized Barton–Kellogg

---

8. See Chiang et al., "Toward a Light-Driven Motorized Nanocar"; Morin, Shirai, and Tour, "En Route to a Motorized Nanocar"; Astumian, "Making Molecules into Motors"; Browne and Feringa, "Making Molecular Machines Work"; Abendroth et al., "Controlling Motion at the Nanoscale"; Balzani, Credi, and Venturi, "Molecular Machines Working on Surfaces and at Interfaces"; Kay and Leigh, "Rise of Molecular Machines"; Guillaume Vives and James Tour, "Synthesis of Single-Molecule Nanocars," *Accounts of Chemical Research* 42, no. 3 (2009): 473–487.
9. Pinn-Tsong Chiang et al., "Toward a Light-Driven Motorized Nanocar"; Morin, Shirai, and Tour, "En Route to a Motorized Nanocar."
10. Morin, Shirai, and Tour, "En Route to a Motorized Nanocar."

FIGURE 4.4, Scheme 1. *Synthesis of the ultrafast unidirectionally rotating motor.* *

* Pinn-Tsong Chiang et al., "Toward a Light-Driven Motorized Nanocar: Synthesis and Initial Imaging of Single Molecules," *ACS Nano* 6, no. 1 (2012): 593.

coupling. Hydrazone 2 was oxidized to the unstable diazo intermediate 5 using manganese dioxide by careful temperature control. The inorganic residue was removed by filtration in a set-up that enforced the strict exclusion of air, oxygen, and moisture. Thione 4 was added to the deep purple filtrate. A [2+3] cycloaddition occurred and evolution of nitrogen gas indicated the formation of episulfide 6. The white solid episulfide 6 was then treated with trimethyl phosphite in a screw-capped tube at 130°C to yield the molecular motor 7 as a mixture of isomers. [Isomers are chemical structures that have the same order of attachment of atoms, but different three-dimensional structures].

Notice all the places where the chemist was actively involved in carefully controlling reaction conditions. Scheme 1, above, illustrates the compounds and steps involved.

FIGURE 4.4, Scheme 2. *Synthesis of the second-generation motorized nanocar 31 through two different approaches.* *

* Pinn-Tsong Chiang et al., "Toward a Light-Driven Motorized Nanocar: Synthesis and Initial Imaging of Single Molecules," *ACS Nano* 6, no. 1 (2012): 594.

We attempted the final assembly of the fast nanocar *(Scheme 2)* but coupling between TMSA and motor 7 did not afford the desired bis-coupled product. A more reactive catalyst was used, but the result was disappointing because of a high degree of decomposition. By changing reagents and solvents again, a TIPS-protected bis-acetylene motor 8 was produced. The yield was excellent. Motor 8 had its TIPS groups removed, producing dialkyne 9 in quantitative yield. Dialkyne

9 and previously synthesized axle 10 were then coupled to produce the fast nanocar in moderate yield (*Scheme 2, Route I*). Next, we tried a more convergent synthetic pathway (*Scheme 2, Route II*) using coupling between motor 7 and alkynylated axle 11, and applying conditions analogous to those for the synthesis of motor 8. The fast nanocar was thus obtained but in lower overall yield than that obtained from *Route I*.

This underscores a common occurrence in organic synthesis. Even with modular approaches, small changes in the structure of the reactants make for enormous differences in reactivity. There is no simple work-around.

Slow to Fast

Consider the differences between motorized slow and fast nanocars (Fig. 4.3). A small change in the rotors had an enormous impact on the rate of their unidirectional rotation, 1.8 revolutions per hour for the slow nanocar and 3 million rotations per second for the fast nanocar. The rotor portion in the slow nanocar has a 6-membered ring bearing a sulfur atom, and the fast motor nanocar has a 5-membered ring bearing all carbons. What was involved in going from the slow to the fast nanocar?

We had to start with ketone 12 (see Fig. 4.5) for the slow motor and then use ketone 1 (see Fig. 4.5) for the fast motor.

But ketones 12 and 1 are derived from entirely different starting materials. There is no known method simply to expunge the sulfur atom in motor 12 and obtain ketone 1.

It is all very easy on the blackboard, of course; one can simply erase atoms at will and show ketone 12 becoming ketone 1 (Fig. 4.5). But chemistry does not happen that way. Even the oxidative expulsion of SO_2 from ketone 12 by the Ramberg–Bäcklund method would not work, since the sulfur is bound aromatically.

We could have left ketone 12 in a flask for millions of years and it would not form ketone 1 by any known or rational thermal, reductive, photochemical, or enzymatic method. This is not unusual when related compounds have clearly different starting points in organic chemistry. It is typical.

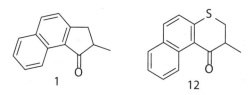

1   12

FIGURE 4.5. *Removal of the sulfur atom in ketone 12 can, in theory, directly result in ketone 1. Though simple on paper using an eraser, there is no simple chemical methodology to effect that transformation.*

Wheel Changes

Why did we change the fullerene wheels from nanocars in Figure 4.1 to the carborane-wheeled motorized nanocars in Figures 4.3e and 4.3f? Because we had to. There is no way to achieve motor functionality in motorized nanocars using fullerene wheels. We did not know that until we had already built motorized nanocars with fullerene wheels. We learned that after the fact. To our disappointment, when the motors are photo-excited, they immediately transfer their energy to the fullerene wheels so that the motors do not rotate.

Thus we had to change the wheels on the motorized cars to carboranes, since carboranes do not accept energy from the photo-excited motors.

The carborane wheels were not suitable for use on metal due to their low adhesion. But the carborane wheels worked well on glass; we have used them extensively to study nanocar motion on glass surfaces.[11]

A key point: parts are not always easily interchangeable without severe and unexpected consequences. When working environments change, drastic changes in molecular structure are often required to retain the system's functions.

Here is a summary of the process that led to functional nanocars, including further details about difficulties encountered.

11. See Pin-Lei Chu, et al., "Synthesis and Single-Molecule Imaging of Highly Mobile Adamantane-Wheeled Nanocars," *ACS Nano* 7, no. 1 (2013): 35–41; Saumyakanti Khatua et al., "Influence of the Substrate on the Mobility of Individual Nanocars," *Journal of Physical Chemistry Letters* 1, no. 22 (2010): 3288–3291; Guillaume Vives et al., "Synthesis of Fluorescent Dye-Tagged Nanomachines for Single-Molecule Fluorescence Spectroscopy," *Journal of Organic Chemistry* 75, no. 19 (2010): 6631–6643; Kevin Claytor et al., "Accurately Determining Single Molecule Trajectories of Molecular Motion on Surfaces," *Journal of Chemical Physics* 130, no. 16 (2009), doi:10.1063/1.3118982.

1. Determine a target? Done. Molecular machines.
2. Insurmountable problems? Yes. The first generation of nanotrucks had insurmountable solubility problems. Although organic chemists have at least fifty widely differing solvents and solvent polarities from which to choose, we could find no satisfactory solution.
3. Start over? Yes, of course.
4. Redesign? Done. Molecular flexibility, specifically a less rigid chassis, was needed (nanocars *1b* to *1d*). When we added a motor to the nanocars, the former chassis proved insufficient. We had to redesign the intermediates in order to affix the motors. Conveniently, we could store all new intermediates in the freezer to prevent their decomposition while we built the motors, and were able to access the published work of the Feringa group from the Netherlands in order to build upon their initial designs. But even then, starting at step one for the motors, we had to build in functional handles that would let them be accepted into the chassis and wheel assemblies. Only *after* constructing the new motors did we learn that they were incompatible with the well-developed fullerene wheels due to energy transfer problems.
5. Redo redesign? Yes. When we desired to go from a slow motor to a fast motor, though the stator was reusable, the rotor was not. The rotor had to be redesigned, from step one, so as to become a faster unidirectional rotator.
6. And again? Of course. Once we changed the wheels to make them suitable to work with the motors, we learned that the new wheels were not compatible with a gold surface. So we had to change to a glass surface. The glass surface was not compatible with our imaging technique by STM, which requires a conductive surface. Glass is an insulator.
7. Start from scratch? To image the nanocars on glass, we had to use a technique called single molecule fluorescence microscopy (SMFM), but another problem arose: the nanocars were not fluorescent. This meant appending a fluorophore to the chassis. But we first had to re-synthesize a new chassis to which the fluorophore appendage could be attached. We could have purchased a pre-synthesized fluorophore from a chemical company.

These bulky fluorophores slowed the nanocars. So, starting from scratch again, we built a chassis with fluorescent axles. These we had to build using entirely different chemistry than we had used in the past cases. Sadly, motor energy transfer to the now fluorescent axles decreased the efficiency of the motors. Newer versions have motor excitation frequencies optically far-separated from the fluorophore excitation frequencies. We know what frequencies to target because we can record the optical spectra using UV-visible absorbance and emission spectroscopies.

8. Yes, but even our optimized yields were not quantitative (~100 percent). First-time reaction yields were usually very low, sometimes as low as 0 percent. Only after repeated trials under different conditions could we attain a yield range of 50 percent to 60 percent, and sometimes not even that.

Most organic chemists would agree that even with extensive planning, 90 percent of reactions are failures. Substrates and conditions must be repeatedly modified to secure respectable and usable yields. At each step a massive amount of time is spent on separations and optimizations. If byproducts are permitted to accumulate, they can consume the new steps' reagents and alter the course of the reaction. After every one or two steps there must be purification.

If all our reactions were near 100 percent yield, it would ease the separation problems. But this can take years to achieve, if it is possible at all. And even then, sufficient atom efficiency is very rare. Byproducts from the other reagents fill the system. High atom-efficient reactions are even harder to achieve.

The loss of materials is expensive. In most cases, these byproducts cannot be converted back to usable compounds in an efficient way. Developing a scrubber system for degrading these products back to usable starting materials would, in most cases, take more time and money than developing the original target synthetic routes themselves. The separated byproducts are put into waste disposal containers and sent for destruction through combustion.

Unlike what would have been present in prebiotic times, we have plenteous resources available. We use petrochemicals as our major feedstocks, and these come in enormous amounts from fine-chemicals producers. Large amounts of energy come from power grids. We have the convenience of ordering many of the requisite reagents to start our syntheses. The just-in-time (JIT) procurement system permits us to have most chemicals at our doorstep within 18 to 24 hours. Even so, detailed planning and logistics go into making sure all reagents and solvents and gases and glassware are ready for a day's lab work.

Solvents need to be pre-distilled before use, since small impurities can promote or catalyze undesired side reactions. Intermediate molecules need to be premade and properly stored in a freezer away from light and oxygen to prevent their decomposition while the other segments of the synthesis are being done.

A rich chemical literature provides guidance on reaction types and conditions that are useable on similar molecular constructs, although modifications are almost always needed since the substrates in a new synthesis are different. None of this would have been possible on the prebiotic earth.

As a further difficulty, reagent addition order is critical. A needs to be added before B, and then C, and each at its own specific temperature to effect a proper reaction and coupling yield. The parameters of temperature, pressure, solvent, light, pH, oxygen, moisture, have to be carefully controlled. Unless one can devise sophisticated promoters or catalysts that are stable in air and moisture and can work at common atmospheric conditions, precise control must be maintained. But making such ambient stable promoters or catalysts is more complex than just varying the temperature for the specific reagent, or just putting the reaction in a carefully maintained atmospheric control box (dry-box) equipped with oxygen and moisture sensors, all maintained under a positive pressure of inert nitrogen gas.

It's not cheap. Once the desired product is synthesized, it can take much longer to properly characterize the product than it did to make it. We use many tools, costing millions of dollars, to facilitate rapid molecular structure identification.

As Teacher's is the great Scotch, water is the great solvent. But organic synthesis is very hard to do in water. Highly oxygenated organic compounds are needed. The synthetic chemist must project the oxygenated groups out toward the water domain, and project the non-oxygenated groups in toward each other, thus generating a hydrophobic domain. It is very hard to do.

By doing our nanocar organic synthesis in organic solvents rather than in water, we markedly lessened the difficulty; it is a luxury that nature did not (and does not) enjoy. Starting from scratch, she would have had to design and redesign her structures, discarding the inevitable false starts and dead ends as they occurred. Any prebiotic system is destined, at least some of the time, to crash and burn. How would nature know where to stop, or how to start over, with no goal in mind?

But whatever else she may have been doing in the prebiotic era, nature was not consulting the modern chemical literature.

Life Lessons for the Prebiotic Chemist

To illustrate that the problems I describe above are not limited to exotic structures such as nanocars, let's examine the synthesis of foundational organic molecules: carbohydrates. Carbohydrates are the backbones of nucleotides, which in turn make up DNA and RNA. Carbohydrates also serve as "recognition sites" for cells to communicate with each other, and as food sources for living systems. The difficulties involved in carrying out carbohydrate synthesis in a prebiotic environment parallel those found in making nanovehicles.

Consider the pentose sugars, carbohydrates with five-carbon atoms (Fig. 4.6). These sugars have three stereogenic centers, so there are eight possible isomers. Some substructures are enantiomers (mirror images), others diastereomers (not mirror images); all are chiral. When we carry out chemical reactions, we design the reactions to minimize diastereomeric mixtures that can be nearly impossible to separate. We try our best to avoid the undesired diastereomers because their separation is too time-consuming and expensive. They waste a huge amount of starting material; they generate unwanted products. Enantiomeric separations are all the more difficult. *Nature has apparently chosen a far harder route, using predominantly one enantiomer (homochiral), D-ribose, in a system with multiple stereogenic centers.*

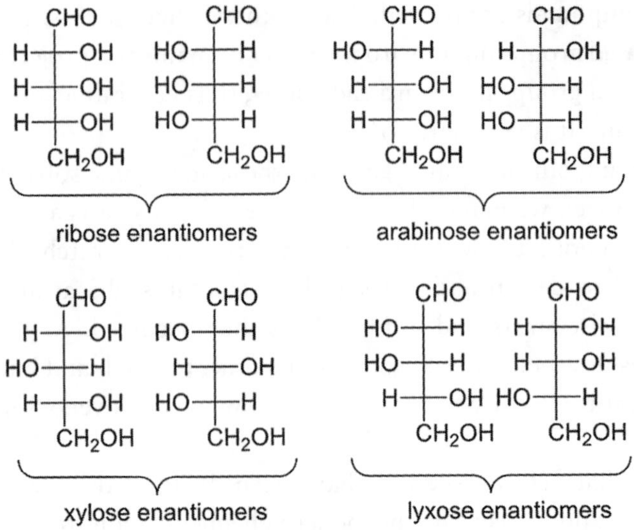

FIGURE 4.6. *The eight pentose sugars showing the four sets of enantiomers depicted in Fischer projections.*

So how difficult would the synthesis of D-ribose be under prebiotic conditions?

Albert Eschenmoser is a great synthetic chemist. He has spent years suggesting prebiotic routes to the five-carbon pentoses. Direct synthesis of ribose, he discovered, was not successful when starting with glycoaldehyde,[12] using an old-fashioned formose reaction (in which a base is catalyzed with formaldehyde in the presence of a divalent cation such as calcium).[13]

To synthesize ribose, Eschenmoser had to make phosphorylated glycolaldehyde (glycoladehyde phosphate) (Fig. 4.7).[14]

12. Peter Decker, Horst Schweer, and Rosmarie Pohlmann, "Bioids: X. Identification of Formose Sugars, Presumable Prebiotic Metabolites, Using Capillary Gas Chromatography/Gas Chromatography—mas Spectrometry of *n*-butoxime Trifluoroacetates on OV-225," *Journal of Chromatography A* 244, no. 2 (1982): 281–291.

13. See Albert Eschenmoser and Eli Loewenthal, "Chemistry of Potentially Prebiotic Natural Products," *Chemical Society Reviews* 21 (1992): 1–16; Albert Eschenmoser, "Etiology of Potentially Primordial Biomolecular Structures: From Vitamin B_{12} to the Nucleic Acids and an Inquiry into the Chemistry of Life's Origin: A Retrospective," *Angewandte Chemie International Edition* 50, no. 52 (2011): 12412–12472.

14. Eschenmoser, "Etiology of Potentially Primordial Biomolecular Structures."

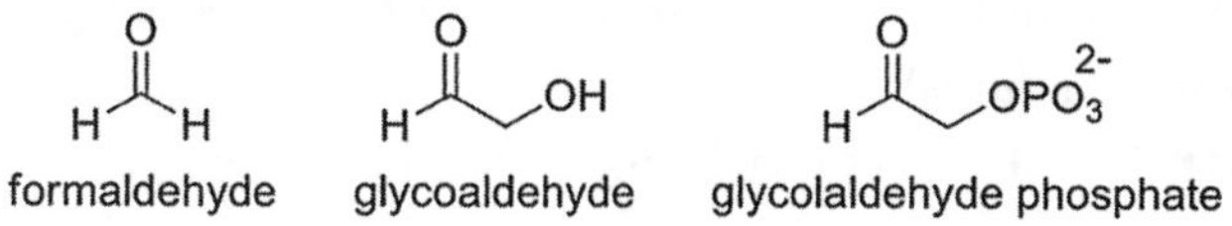

FIGURE 4.7. *Three common starting materials in prebiotic chemistry research.*

Since glycolaldehyde is the dimeric form of formaldehyde, he first had to make the dimer of formaldehyde. Only then could there be further aldol chemistry in the formose reaction. A good organic chemist can design conditions that will isolate the product, purify it, and then proceed.

A very good organic chemist, this is what Eschenmoser did.[15]

Can phosphorylation then occur? Yes, but only given high concentration of a phosporylating agent. It does not happen in the presence of the strong base required for the formation of the glycoaldehyde itself.

The glycoaldehyde needs a strong base to pump up the reaction, and then, to stop it dead, it needs to be separated from that strong base.

While in a near-neutral aqueous solution, and in the presence of magnesium ions, Eschenmoser phosphorylated glycoaldehyde with four molar equivalents of amidotriphosphate. Once phosphorylation was complete, and the glycolaldehyde phosphate isolated and purified, Eschenmoser then exposed glycolaldehyde phosphate to the very basic, 2N sodium hydroxide at a concentration of 0.08 moles per liter.

In other words, the formaldehyde started life in a strong base; its product was isolated and freed from the strong base, and exposed to a neutral aqueous solution of amidotriphosphate (which the researchers made separately). That product, glycoladehyde phosphate, was then isolated and conveniently reexposed to a strong base.

Even with this masterful design, the result was mostly undesired racemic hexose triphosphates. Using a stroke of superb synthetic insight, Eschenmoser placed the glycolaldehyde phosphate in the strong base, and *then* added 0.04 moles per liter of formaldehyde to obtain a 40–50 percent yield of mostly racemic pentose diphosphates (the

---

15. Ibid.

mixture shown in Fig. 4.7, but with two phosphates at C2 and C4 of each of the structures).

In that 40–50 percent yield mixture, there were then eight possible isomers (four diastereomers): the desired racemic ribose-2,4-diphosphate (~15 percent of the total from the reaction), racemic arabinose-2,4-diphosphate, racemic lycose-2,4-diphosphate and racemic xylose-2,4-diphosphate (where racemic signifies a 1:1 mixture of the two enantiomers) along with 11 other identified carbohydrate species, all bearing their enantiomer partners. That meant 22 other identified species from the 40–50 percent, with the remaining 50–60 percent being unidentified nonvolatile compounds such as higher oligomers and polymers.

Even Eschenmoser did not attempt to separate out the desired, albeit still racemic, ribose-2,4-diphosphate. And for very good reason: it would have been nearly impossible.

Biologists can easily imagine nature selecting the correct isomer because they work in a world that enjoys the specificity of biological systems. Not so synthetic chemists, who are bound to prebiotic molecules. Selected by what? No enzymes were yet available. The data more readily suggests that no prebiotic process is likely to yield the requisite carbohydrates.

The most masterful of synthetic chemists could produce only gross mixtures.

Also, time works against life. Over a mere 23 weeks, the desired diastereomer—the racemic ribose-2,4-diphosphates—was reduced from a 17 percent yield to a 7 percent yield. After a year, there would be very little left. In the laboratory, as anywhere else, it is essential to stop a reaction before the desired product degrades.

Of all the isomers, the one desired was not the most stable, even given the cleverly designed experiment that started with glycolaldehyde, and that was further intelligently and conveniently phosphorylated to the glycolaldehyde phosphate.

Racemic ribose-2,4-diphosphates degraded under the very controlled conditions under which they formed.

Eschenmoser writes that "the total amount of the four diastereomers is largely unchanged," but his own data shows that the combined yield of the four diastereomers dropped from 34 percent to 30 percent over the course of the additional 22 weeks, a relative 12 percent loss of the pentoses over 22 weeks.[16] After a few years, a brief moment in time in prebiotic terms, there would be few if any of the pentoses left, let alone the desired ribose-2,4-diphosphate.

Where does the material go? It likely degrades to extended oligomers and polymers, a process common in organic reactions, and especially common in extended aldol-based reactions.

Wish Fulfillment

From a paper on prebiotic chemistry:

> Moreover, there was the well-known—but still no less remarkable—fact that in cellular biochemical processes, monosaccharides apparently never operate in the free state, but always in *phosphorylated* form. *It is a short step* from such considerations to the notion of a primordial scenario in which, again, phosphorylated and not simply neutral forms of carbohydrates would have been operative [emphasis added]. In a self-organization process in a primordial environment, it may have been of primary importance for carbohydrate molecules to escape chemical chaos, finding themselves instead at concentrations suitable for chemical reactions, and in reaction spaces that would facilitate efficient chemical transformation. With respect to both requirements, phosphorylated sugar molecules would, through their electrical charges, have offered advantages over neutral, water soluble carbohydrates in environments containing mineral surfaces or minerals with expandable layer structures.[17]

That short step is not short at all. Biochemical routes are far downstream and occur in far more complex scenarios. In the laboratory, phosphorylation requires precise control of phosphorylating agents.

These hopeful but unlikely suggestions pain the synthetic chemist under any circumstance, but for some remarkable reason, they are tolerated in prebiotic chemistry.

---

16. Ibid.
17. Eschenmoser and Loewenthal, "Chemistry of Potentially Prebiotic Natural Products," 1–16; Albert Eschenmoser, "Etiology of Potentially Primordial Biomolecular Structures."

Despite claims to the contrary, research on mineral surfaces has done little to solve the problem of overall yields, or that of diastereo- and enantioselectivities.[18] Reagent addition order is critical. An abiogenetic pathway would require several lines of intermediates forming in proximity, and then coming together in the proper order at the precise moment and location needed for synthesis. We could modify many parameters during synthesis: temperature, pressure, solvent type, light, pH, oxygen, moisture. No such controls figure in a prebiotic environment.

Characterization is critical. Without it, impurities accumulate. What prebiotic characterization might mean is anyone's guess.

Given poor prebiotic reaction yields, it is impossible to envision a process in which the starting materials generate all of the desired products. In synthesizing nanocars, we had to go back over and over again to generate molecular intermediates, a process known familiarly as "bringing up material from the rear."

How would prebiotic chemistry bring up its own rear over and over again? It has kept no laboratory notebook to record the previous paths.

In our synthesis, we spent a great deal of time on separation and optimization. If byproducts are permitted to accumulate, they often will consume the new steps' reagents and alter the course of the reaction.

This problem would plague abiogenesis, too.

It Stands to Reason

There must have been a chemical means, once upon a time, to generate an information-bearing molecule such as DNA or RNA. Since the 1960s, a number of biologists have suggested that the polymer is RNA rather than DNA. Such is the RNA World Hypothesis.[19] And chemically activated ribonucleotides *can* polymerize to form RNA. So far so good.

But RNA is far less stable than DNA, and whatever the polymerization, it yields generic RNA, a molecule lacking sequence specificity. Had RNA researchers succeeded in producing a volume of random

18. Stefan Pitsch et al., "Mineral Induced Formation of Sugar Phosphates," *Origins of Life and Evolution of the Biosphere* 25, no. 4 (1995): 297–334.

19. Michael Robertson and Gerald Joyce, "The Origins of the RNA World," *Cold Spring Harbor Perspectives in Biology* (2010), doi:10.1101/cshperspect.a003608.

sentences—e.g., *subtends flack lachrymose esurient*—none of them would have imagined that they had succeeded in composing *King Lear*.

The coupling of a ribose with a nucleotide is the first step, and even those engrossed in prebiotic research have difficulty envisioning that process, especially for purines and pyrimidines.[20] John Sutherland and his coworkers have proposed that pyrimidine ribonuceotides can form short sequences using arabinose amino-oxazoline and anhydronucleoside intermediates, all from simple compounds such as cyanamide, cyanoacetylene, glycolaldehyde, glyceraldehyde, and inorganic phosphate. The use of inorganic phosphate changes the experiment's basic conditions to a pH-buffered solution, thereby slowing decomposition pathways.[21] But the work itself shows the intricacies required to generate the desired reactions.

The conditions they used were cleverly selected:

> Although the issue of temporally separated supplies of glycolaldehyde [just-in-time (JIT) scenario 1] and glyceraldehyde [JIT scenario 2] remains a problem, a number of situations could have arisen [prebiotically, what and where?] that would result in the conditions of heating [careful control of step 1 at 60°C] and progressive dehydration [careful control of step 2 by lyophilization, which is water removal by ice sublimation under reduced pressure of <0.001 atmospheres] followed by cooling [careful control of step 3 from 60°C to 23°C], rehydration [careful control of step 4 with precise adjustments of pH] and ultraviolet irradiation [careful control of step 5 with a selected 254nm light].[22]

There were also multiple purification steps [careful control of step 6], and ion exchanges using commercial resins [careful control of step 7]. All this for the synthesis of just one set of a mixture of adducts, and in racemic form.

It remains clear that the controlled conditions required to generate even a mixed set of select structures is painfully improbable.

---

20. See William Fuller, Robert Sanchez, and Leslie Orgel, "Studies in Prebiotic Synthesis. VI. Synthesis of Purine Nucleosides," *Journal of Molecular Biology* 67, no. 1 (1972): 25–33; Leslie Orgel, "Prebiotic Chemistry and the Origin of the RNA World," *Critical Reviews in Biochemistry and Molecular Biology* 39, no. 2 (2004): 99–123.

21. Matthew Powner, Béatrice Gerland, and John Sutherland, "Synthesis of Activated Pyrimidine Ribonucleotides in Prebiotically Plausible Conditions," *Nature* 459 (2009): 239–242.

22. Ibid.

Routes to each one of the requisite carbohydrates, lipids, nucleic acids, and proteins (polymers of amino acids) have been proposed in prebiotic studies. The attempted syntheses almost always create mixtures beset with the same difficulties.

From the data, the synthetic chemist can easily deduce that under prebiotic conditions the reaction in question is not likely to yield anything useful. With each added step, difficulties are compounded by improbabilities so overwhelming that no other field of science would depend upon such levels of faith.

Abiogenesis research would never be accepted in any other area of chemistry.

Extrapolation on Steroids

But this is not the end. Making carbohydrates, lipids, amino acids, and nucleic acids still has not built a cell.

Sutherland and coworkers pointed out in 2015 that "[a] minimal cell can be thought of as comprising informational, compartment-forming and metabolic subsystems.[23] They also acknowledged that, to date, prebiotic chemistry has made ambitious extrapolations: "To imagine the abiotic assembly of such an overall [cellular] system [or subsystem], however, places great demands on hypothetical prebiotic chemistry."[24] Yet this revealing comment by Sutherland and his coworkers is coupled with their disclosure of a new experimental finding showing

> that precursors of ribonucleotides, amino acids and lipids can all be derived by the reductive homologation of hydrogen cyanide and some of its derivatives. . . . The key reaction steps are driven by ultraviolet light, use hydrogen sulfide as the reductant and can be accelerated by Cu(I)-Cu(II) photoredox cycling.[25]

They assert boldly that "all the cellular subsystems could have arisen simultaneously through common chemistry."[26] This has now raised the

---

23. Bhavesh Patel et al., "Common Origins of RNA, Protein and Lipid Precursors in a Cyanosulfidic Protometabolism," *Nature Chemistry* 7 (2015): 301.
24. Ibid.
25. Ibid.
26. Ibid.

level of suppositions from mere molecule types to complex subsystems where molecules are working in concert toward a common functional goal. But compositions of a few molecule types, or even all of them, do not constitute a cellular subsystem. It is essential to emphasize that the authors only prepared *precursors* to the ribonucleotides, amino acids, and lipids, not the actual molecules, so the gross extrapolation is all the more disconcerting.

When reading the protocols for the suggested prebiotic-like precursors, one is struck by the high-level sophistication, expert synthetic prowess, and remarkable ingenuity of the researchers. Some reactions were run at room temperature, some at 60°C, others at 100°C and then washed with ice-cold water. Often the molecules prepared by these supposed prebiotic routes were not used, but had to be made more cleanly and in larger scale using purely synthetic methods and organic solvents, such as Lawesson's reagent and tetrahydrofuran, respectively, "to simplify the handling procedures."

JIT and precise order of addition protocols were used over and over again. One sees precise pH adjustments through the syntheses, use of ion exchange resins, and separations from the reaction mixtures because proceeding without separations would have destroyed the carefully prepared products. The preparation of cyanoacetylene on Cu(I) was suggested as a way to prepare it conveniently and store it for use when needed. CuCl was mixed with KCl to generate the Nieuwland catalyst, $K[CuCl_2]$, at 70°C. Then a separately generated source of acetylene gas was prepared from CaC_2 and water. This gas was bubbled through the Nieuwland catalyst to prepare acrylonitrile (an unstable molecule that needs proper isolation and storage to inhibit its polymerization), which was then treated with KCN for 1 hour, then 5 equivalents of NH_3 as a 13 molar NH_3/NH_4^+ solution adjusted to pH 9.2 with NaOH to generate the desired aminopropionitrile.

All of the reactions were executed in separate clean vessels and properly isolated prior to proceeding to the next reaction.

This is just a sampling of preparations that are difficult even for the skilled synthetic chemist to execute. The routes afford very simple precursors to just a few of the many molecules within the building block classes of molecules, carbohydrates, lipids, amino acids, and nucleic acids. Finally, all the precursors were racemic if they even bore any possible stereoisomerism.

Dream On

The world's best synthetic chemists, biochemists, and evolutionary biologists have combined forces to form a team—a dream team in two quite distinct senses of the word. Money is no object. They have at their disposal the most advanced analytical facilities, the complete scientific literature, synthetic and natural coupling agents, and all the reagents their hearts might desire. Carbohydrates, lipids, amino acids, and nucleic acids are stored in their laboratories in a state of 100 percent enantiomeric purity.

Would the dream team—*please*—assemble a living system?

Take your time, folks, take a few billion years.

Nothing? Well, well, well.

Let us assume that all the building blocks of life, and not just their precursors, have been made to a high degrees of purity, including homochirality where applicable—the carbohydrates, the amino acids, the nucleic acids, and the lipids. They are stored in cool caves, away from sunlight, and away from oxygen. These molecules are indifferent to environmental degradation.

And let us further assume that they are all stored in one comfortable corner of the earth, not separated by thousands of kilometers or on different planets.

And that they all exist not just in the same square kilometer, but in neighboring pools where they can conveniently and somehow selectively mix with each other as needed.

Now what? How does the dream team assemble them without enzymes?

Very well. Give the dream team polymerized forms: polypeptides, all the enzymes they desire, the polysaccharides, DNA and RNA in any sequence, cleanly assembled.

Ready now?

Apparently not.

We teach our students that, when a mechanism does not support their observations, the mechanism must either be revised to support the facts or entirely discounted. They are not required to provide an alternative.

Those who think scientists understand how prebiotic chemical mechanisms produced the first life are wholly misinformed. Nobody understands how this happened. Maybe one day we will. But that day is far from today. It would be far more helpful (and hopeful) to expose students to the massive gaps in our understanding. Then they may find a firmer—and possibly a radically different—scientific theory.[27]

---

27. This chapter is adapted and abridged, by permission of the editor, from James Tour, "Animadversions of a Synthetic Chemist" (a critical essay on origin-of-life proposals), *Inference: International Review of Science* 2, no. 2 (2016), http://inference-review.com/article/animadversions -of-a-synthetic-chemist. Images are adapted with permission from the American Chemical Society.

5

Digital Evolution: Predictions of Design

WINSTON EWERT

SUMMARY

Computer simulations of evolution are often invoked in defense of the abilities of Darwinian evolution. A number of well-known simulations are discussed, showing how they follow the predictions of intelligent design in requiring teleological fine-tuning in order to work. This and other predictions of intelligent design have been confirmed by simulations, whereas Darwinian evolution offers no predictions about computer simulation and is thus unfalsifiable.

. . . . .

I. Introduction

In chapter 2, by Stephen Meyer, we saw that the neo-Darwinian mechanism of mutation and natural selection does not provide an adequate explanation for the origin of the genetic information necessary for building new forms of life. Lacking biological evidence for the creative power of this mechanism, some proponents of neo-Darwinian theory have sought to simulate the creative power of the mutation/selection mechanism using computers. Indeed, computer simulations are a growing part of the debate over Darwinian evolution. Proponents of Darwinian evolution have developed an array of computer simulations, arguing that they demonstrate evolution in action, confirming their theory. Critics of evolutionary theory have developed their own simulations, arguing the exact opposite: that evolution does not work in practice.

Before looking at these simulations or arguments, we need to take a step back and look at how we decide whether or not a scientific theory is true. Scientific theories are difficult, usually impossible, to logically prove because they make universal claims. For example, a theory might claim that all swans are white or that there are no perpetual motion machines. These are called universal claims because they are about all swans or all machines. It is relatively easy to check whether a particular swan is white or a particular machine exhibits perpetual motion. However, no matter how many swans or machines are investigated, this will never *prove* that all swans are white or that no machines exhibit perpetual motion. We simply cannot prove a universal law by looking at examples, no matter how numerous.

Falsification is one possible solution to this problem. If a theory is false, then there should exist counterexamples. When a counterexample to a theory is found, we say that the theory is falsified. At that point, we know that the theory is false. On the other hand, if after searching long and hard for a counterexample, we are unable to find one, we can conclude that the theory is probably true. We do not know for certain that the theory is true; it remains unproven, but it is increasingly unlikely that a counterexample exists and thus increasingly likely that the theory is correct.

A falsifiable theory takes on a certain risk by offering the possibility of being refuted by a counterexample. Not all propositions do this, however. For example, one could claim that the universe sprang into existence last Thursday. All memories and artifacts appearing to be from before that time were simply part of the world when it sprang into existence. For example, if you found rings in a tree, you might think this proved the age of the tree. However, one could explain this away by claiming that the tree sprang into existence last Thursday already containing the tree rings. There is no counterexample that can be presented to demonstrate that this claim is incorrect. Thus, we say that the claim is not falsifiable. We would not expect to find a counterexample, even if the theory was false. Since no possible counterexample can exist, even in principle, the theory takes on no risk of being falsified, and thus the lack of counterexamples does not provide evidence for the theory.

Such reasoning can never logically prove that a theory is correct. It is always possible that a counterexample exists but has not yet been found. There may yet be a perpetual motion machine that nobody has figured out how to build. Nevertheless, given the large amount of effort spent attempting to build perpetual motion machines, all ending in failure, we can be reasonably confident that a perpetual motion machine cannot exist. At the very least, we can provisionally accept the theory until a counterexample is produced.

There are other reasons to accept or reject a theory. One might reject a theory as too complicated, invoking Occam's razor. Or a theory might be proved by a mathematical theorem, thus being accepted without requiring any empirical evidence. For example, under appropriate assumptions, perpetual motion machines are proven impossible by Noether's theorem. Nevertheless, for this chapter, we will focus only on falsification.

How do computer simulations fit into the process of falsifying theories? A computer simulation can falsify a theory, but only if that theory makes a claim or prediction about the simulation. If I were to claim that Darwinian evolution would not work even inside a computer simulation, then a single example of successfully simulated Darwinian evolution would prove my claim incorrect. But most theories, including that of intelligent design, are about the real world, not computer simulations. They do not make explicit claims about what will happen in any simulation. As long as a theory makes no claims about computer simulations, no computer simulation can provide a counterexample.

However, in many cases, a theory *implies* predictions about computer simulations. The theory may not offer an explicit prediction about computer simulations, but an implied prediction may be a necessary consequence of the theory being true. In that case, we can use the simulation to falsify the theory by providing a counterexample to that implied prediction. Care must be taken, however, to consider only predictions actually implied by the theory, and not merely predictions attributed to a theory, especially by its critics. In particular, critics of intelligent design have attributed predictions about computer simulations to intelligent design that intelligent design proponents have not made, would not make, and that are not implied by intelligent design theories. These are counterfeit counterexamples, and they do not falsify the relevant theories.

In this chapter, we will look at actual predictions implied by intelligent design with respect to computer simulations. We will show how various alleged counterexamples actually fit the predictions of intelligent design. Thus, for all of the attempts at falsifying intelligent design through computer simulations, the intelligent design predictions have survived these tests, thereby providing evidence for intelligent design.

II. What Are Computer Simulations of Evolution?

What does it actually mean to simulate Darwinian evolution? In other fields, scientific simulations typically seek to closely imitate and thus predict real-world phenomena. For example, modern weather prediction is based on detailed computer simulations of changing temperature, wind speed, pressure, and so on. Likewise, new engineering designs are often tested in computer simulations to discover flaws before construction. Because these simulations adhere closely to reality, they can offer predictions about it, and we can verify the accuracy of the simulations by comparing them to reality.

Evolution simulations are not in the same category. A weather simulation predicts whether or not it will rain tomorrow, but no evolution simulation can predict whether or not a rabbit will evolve a faster hop; a lion, sharper teeth; or an ape, language skills. Evolution simulations rarely, if ever, make any predictions about real-world biological evolution. Instead, computer simulations of evolution reduce Darwinian evolution to its essence, and then observe the resulting process. This allows us to learn about Darwinian evolution divorced from its biological context.

But what is this essence of Darwinian evolution? According to philosopher Daniel Dennett, "evolution will occur whenever and wherever three conditions are met: replication, variation (mutation), and differential fitness (competition)."[1] Theistic evolutionist Kenneth Miller says, "What's needed to drive this increase? Just three things: selection, replication, and mutation. . . . It's no coincidence that the same three things are required for evolution since what we are observing is nothing less than evolution on a small, observable scale."[2] Richard Lewontin wrote, "The generality of the principles of natural selection means that any entities in nature that have variation, reproduction, and heritability may evolve."[3]

Replication or heritability means that offspring resemble their parents more than other members of the population. Children look more like their parents than their parents' friends. This is true throughout the biological world, from humans to dogs to fishes to birds, and even to viruses. Variation or mutation means that, while offspring are similar to their parents, they are not identical. Instead, there are random variations or changes. Selection or differential fitness refers to the propensity of some members of a population to reproduce more than others. As an example, the faster gazelle does not get eaten, and thus has more offspring. At least according to the Darwinists quoted above, these three factors are the essence of Darwinian evolution.

Any evolutionary simulation, seeking to incorporate the essence of Darwinian evolution, works by including these three processes. To better understand the concept, here is an exercise that you can do at home. For this, you will need ten coins and a die. Take five coins, and place them face down on a table. This represents the first living cell in your very own virtual world. The sequence of heads-and-tails coins is its DNA.

First, we need to include replication. Our "cell" or row of coins must "split" into two rows of coins, both of which resemble the original row. To model this, take the remaining coins and create a second row of five coins, exactly like the first row. Since your first row of coins are all face down, the new row will also be all face down.

Second, we need mutation; the copies should not be exactly like

1. Daniel C. Dennett, *Breaking the Spell: Religion as a Natural Phenomenon* (London: Penguin, 2006), 341.

2. Kenneth Miller, *Only a Theory: Evolution and the Battle for America's Soul* (repr., New York: Penguin, 2009), 77.

3. Richard C. Lewontin, "The Units of Selection," *Annual Review of Ecology and Systematics* 1, no. 1 (1970): 1–18.

the original row. They must vary in a random fashion. To model this, roll a die twice—once for each row. Flip the coin corresponding to the number that you rolled. For example, if you roll a three, flip the third coin in the row. If you roll a five, flip the fifth coin. If you roll a six, you will notice that there is no sixth coin, and you should not flip any coin.

Third, we need selection; some rows of coins should survive better than others. You should currently have two rows of five coins, and you want to determine which row is fitter. For the sake of this example, we will arbitrarily decide that more heads is fitter. In the case of a tie, break the tie randomly: it does not matter. The fitter cell (row of coins) survives, but the less fit cell dies. Take it (i.e., the "less fit" row of five coins) off the table.

At this point, you are back to having only one cell (one row of coins). Repeat the process. The cell/row splits, resulting in two identical cells/rows of coins. (To do this, you'll need to bring the discarded coins back to the table, this time matching the row left on the table from the first round.) Roll the die twice, flipping the corresponding coin for the numbers rolled in each row. Keep the fittest row (the one with the most heads), removing the other one. Repeat until bored or until the row has evolved into all heads.

I did this experiment, and at the beginning of each iteration I recorded the sequence of heads and tails in my row. For each heads, I wrote H, and for each tails, I wrote T. I ended up with the following sequence:

1. TTTTT
2. TTHTT
3. THHTT
4. THHTT
5. THHHT
6. HHHHT
7. HHHHH

Evolution started with a sequence of coins that was all tails-up; however, it rapidly evolved into one where the sequence was all heads-up. The process exhibited the three essential conditions of Darwinian evolution. Each child was similar to the parent, as required for replication. However, they were not exact copies, as required by mutation. Finally, the rows with more heads in them had more children, thus fulfilling selection.

This is a very simple model. The other models that will be discussed in this chapter, as well as others not discussed, are more sophisticated, but the essence comes to down to the same idea. The simulations all apply replication, mutation, and selection to evolve artificial organisms. The details in each model will vary greatly, but this is the core of what makes these models work.

III. Design Requires Intelligence

Intelligent design makes the falsifiable claim that design, or the appearance of design, derives only from intelligence. When we observe complex processes, digitally encoded information, or finely tuned machines, we observe the appearance of design, and according to the theory of intelligent design, we have good reason to infer intelligence. Stephen Meyer argues, "If we trace information back to its source, we always come to a mind, not a material process."[4] Meyer's argument is a falsifiability argument: if anyone were to present a counterexample— design without intelligence—then intelligent design's claim would be falsified and would have to be abandoned. However, continued absence of a counterexample provides evidence for intelligent design.

According to Darwinist arguments, however, there *are* counterexamples to this claim: computer simulations. Computer simulations have evolved everything from English phrases[5] to antennae[6] to computer programs.[7] If we were to find any of these in nature, intelligent design proponents would immediately infer intelligence as the best explanation. These are instances of the appearance of design. Thus, according to the argument, design can be produced without intelligence, and therefore intelligent design is falsified.

---

4. Stephen C. Meyer, "Can DNA Prove the Existence of an Intelligent Designer?" *Biola Magazine* (Summer 2010), text available at: http://magazine.biola.edu/article/10-summer/can-dna-prove-the-existence-of-an-intelligent-desi/.

5. Richard Dawkins, *The Blind Watchmaker: Why the Evidence of Evolution Reveals a Universe without Design* (New York: Norton, 1986), 46ff.

6. Edward E. Altshuler and Derek S. Linden, "Wire-Antenna Designs Using Genetic Algorithms," *IEEE Antennas and Propagation Magazine* 39, no. 2 (1997): 33–43.

7. Richard E. Lenski et al. "The Evolutionary Origin of Complex Features," *Nature* 423, no. 6936 (2003): 139–144.

However, recall that intelligent design's claim is about the real world, not about computer simulations. As such, it may seem that the outcome of a computer simulation is irrelevant to intelligent design's claims. However, a computer simulation is, in essence, a machine located inside the real world. A simulation that evolves an English phrase is a machine that produces that English phrase. A simulation that evolves a computer program is a machine that produces that computer program. If we have a simulation that produces an artifact appearing to be designed, that means that there exists a machine that can produce design. That machine exists in the real world, and thus the claims of intelligent design apply to it. But this machine would seem to be exactly what intelligent design claims cannot exist: a device that can produce design without intelligence.

This is incorrect, however, because intelligent design does not argue that machines cannot produce design; rather, it argues that only intelligently designed machines can produce design. As an example, consider the machine that produced this book. This book appears designed; it contains much (hopefully) meaningful text. But it was produced by a printing press, not by a human writing out the words by hand. There was no intelligence at all involved in the physical production of this book. However, the printing press itself was designed, and the words derive not from the machine but from this book's authors. Intelligence was required, not in the physical construction of the book, but in the configuration and inputs of the machine that produced this book.

Every computer simulation is intelligently designed. These simulations do not simply arise on unused computer hardware. In every case, programmers deliberately design them. Despite being designed in imitation of nature, a computer simulation could no more arise spontaneously than could a robotic car factory. Thus the intelligent design claim is verified. It took intelligence to produce machines that could produce design.

On the other hand, while the simulations are designed, they are imitations of nature. They have taken what is in nature and translated it into a digital realm. It would be nonsensical to attribute the insights of Sun Tzu to a twentieth-century translator. Likewise, it is argued to be nonsensical to attribute the success of a computer simulation to its programmer when the programmer was merely translating the natural world into a digital realm. Rather, the success must be due to what was translated.

However, that is not how translation actually works. While Sun Tzu's insights are his own, much of the quality of an English translation is due to the translator rather than Sun Tzu. Sun Tzu could have written brilliant Chinese that was mangled beyond understanding by a translator, or he could have written horrific Chinese that was translated into beautifully readable English. This is most obvious in the case of poetry, which commonly uses devices such as rhyme or rhythm that do not easily translate, and can be present in the translation only by the talent of the translator.

When the programmer translated nature into a computer program, is the resulting success due to the source or to the translator? Does evolution work in a simulation because it works in nature, the same way insights are in a translation because they were first in the original text? Or does evolution work in a simulation because of the talent of the programmer, like a talented poet producing beautiful poetry while translating the work of a talentless author in another language?

In order to differentiate these possibilities, we look for examples of teleological fine-tuning in a simulation. Teleological fine-tuning refers to cases where a system is designed, configured, or built in a particular way for the purpose of producing a desired outcome. "Teleological" means that something was done for a particular purpose, in order to achieve some end. "Fine-tuning" means that the system was configured in such a way that it has some particular property, as opposed to alternative configurations that would not have had that property.

Consider the case of a bucket of water perched on a door by a prankster, such that when the door opens, the bucket falls and pours water on the person who walked through. The system is fine-tuned, because for most possible locations of the bucket, it would not soak the person walking through the door. Furthermore, it is teleological because the prankster placed the bucket in that position specifically so that it would fall and soak the next person who walked through the door. It is thus an example of teleological fine-tuning.

If a simulation contains teleological fine-tuning, the intelligent design claims stand. It took a goal-directed intelligent agent to produce the teleological fine-tuning in the simulation. Such simulations are not translations of nature but are cases where the translator used his or her own intelligence to produce a working simulation. On the other hand, if a simulation contains no examples of teleological fine-tuning and yet produces design, then the claims of intelligent design are falsified.

This leaves us with the question, are there examples of simulations that avoid teleology but still successfully demonstrate the evolution of the appearance of design? To answer that question, we need to look at examples. We will investigate a number of simulations, showing their teleological fine-tuning.

IV. Examples

A. Dawkins's Weasel

As a first example, consider a simulation presented by Richard Dawkins in his book *The Blind Watchmaker*.[8] Dawkins does not give his simulation a name, but it is often known as Dawkins's weasel. It is not a particularly good simulation: even Dawkins quickly points out its shortcomings. However, it is a simple model and readily understood, thus providing a good starting point for this discussion.

The goal of the weasel simulation is to evolve the phrase "methinks it is like a weasel." The phrase itself is a quote from Shakespeare's Hamlet, where the characters are discussing which animal a cloud looks like.

The simulation begins by selecting twenty-eight random letters and spaces. In the run discussed by Dawkins, he obtained: "WDLTMNLT DTJBKWIRZREZLMQCO P." This is pretty much what one would expect by selecting a sequence of random characters.

However, Dawkins's weasel does not stop there. It generates many slightly mutated copies of the original phrase. Dawkins does not say how many copies are made or how exactly they are mutated. Nevertheless, making 100 copies of the string, each one with a single character randomly replaced, produces results that are commensurate with the examples presented in Dawkins's book; and while we do not know

---

8. Dawkins, *Blind Watchmaker*, 46ff.

whether this was the original algorithm, for the sake of the argument we will assume that it was.

At this point, the simulation has 100 (or so we assume) slightly modified copies of the original string of characters. The simulation picks the copy that is closest to the target. The closer to the target, the fitter the copy is deemed to be.

How do we measure how similar a string is to the target? There are, in fact, a number of different ways to answer this question. Dawkins used what is called the "Hamming distance." To compute the Hamming distance, we line up the two strings of interest, identifying where the two strings are different:

```
METHINKS IT IS LIKE A WEASEL
WDLTMNLT DTJBKWIRZREZLMQCO P
XXXXX XX X XXXXXXXXXXXXXXXXX
```

In the above example, each X in the bottom string marks a position in that string where the two upper strings are different. The three blank spaces are where the random string and the target string happen, by chance, to agree. In this case, there are twenty-five X's, giving the random string a Hamming distance of twenty-five from the target. Compare this to another string later in Dawkins's run:

```
METHINKS IT IS LIKE A WEASEL
MELDINLS IT ISWPRKE Z WECSEL
  XX  X        XXX   X   X
```

This case has only eight points where the string is different from the target. Thus it has a Hamming distance of eight. Since eight is less than twenty-five, this string is much closer to the target than was the original string.

Having used the Hamming distance to establish which of the hundred copies is closest to the target, the simulation throws out all copies except the closest. In the case of Dawkins's example run, while the original random string was "WDLTMNLT DTJBKWIRZREZLMQCO P," the best of its one hundred copies was "WDLTMNLT DTJBSWIRZREZLMQCO P." Detecting the difference between these two strings is difficult for the human eye, but the second phrase has replaced a

DTJBK with a DTJBS, which is closer to the target because the "S" is in the correct place to form the word "IS."

The process is then repeated, with this newly adopted copy as the original for a hundred new copies. After forty-three iterations of this copy-mutate-select process, Dawkins found it converged onto his target, "METHINKS IT IS LIKE A WEASEL." Dawkins reported running the algorithm a second time, this time taking sixty-four iterations. In either case, the simulation readily produced the target phrase.

But does this simulation exhibit teleological fine-tuning? To see, we need to go back through the process used by the simulation, carefully examining each step for instances of teleological fine-tuning.

The first action of the simulation is to pick twenty-eight (the length of the phrase "methinks it is like a weasel" including both spaces and letters) characters at random. What could be less teleological than a completely random starting point? Indeed. However, while the selection of the letters was random, they were chosen from a nonrandom set of possibilities: the twenty-six letters of the English alphabet and a space. Why include spaces but not digits, punctuation, or other symbols?

Of course, the simulation had to pick some collection of possible symbols; but the selection of this particular set of symbols was teleological: the set of possible characters was chosen specifically because it was the set of characters used in the target. Dawkins could have included digits, symbols, punctuation, and even letters from other alphabets. Instead he used only the types of characters he needed in order to reach the target.

Additionally, twenty-eight characters were chosen. Why twenty-eight? Obviously, twenty-eight was chosen because that is the number of characters in the target. If he had chosen a different number of characters, then the simulation would not have found the target. Dawkins started with twenty-eight characters because he knew that was what he needed in order to reach the target.

We do not know how many copies of the string are made in Dawkins's simulation, but in order to replicate Dawkins's results the number of copies has to be large, around 100. Why has Dawkins chosen to make a large number of copies rather than a small number?

More copies mean more chances to find beneficial random mutations. He has chosen a number that allows his simulation to quickly reach the target.

Dawkins reported two runs of his simulation, one taking forty-three generations and the other sixty-four. However, my own simulation, which makes only ten copies, took 723,232 generations in one attempt and 461,300 in another. A seemingly minor choice in the design of the algorithm made Dawkins's algorithm ten thousand times faster.

Mutations appear to take the form of randomly replacing a letter in the string with another. Why simple replacement and not insertion or deletion? Dawkins did not include those because he knew they were not needed in order to reach the target. Since he began with a string of the correct size, there was no need to have mutations that could change the size.

In each iteration, the simulation selects the copy closest to the target as the fittest. Why is that the fittest? Why is "WDLTMNLT DTJB-SWIRZREZLMQCO P" fitter than "WDLTMNLT DTJBKWIRZRE-ZLMQCO P"? Certainly, there is no more sense or meaning in the one than the other. Neither is functionally better than in the other, in any way. The only basis for preferring the one to the other is teleological; the one is closer to a predefined goal than the other.

Dawkins does not dispute this point. He readily acknowledges that imitating selection by measuring distance to a target is not a proper model of evolution. As he says, "Life isn't like that. Evolution has no long-term goal."[9] He freely acknowledges a teleology to this model that is inappropriate to a model of Darwinian evolution.

We have looked, in perhaps mind-numbing detail, at the various aspects of fine-tuning that went into constructing Dawkins's weasel. This was somewhat unfair, since Dawkins described this simulation as "misleading in important ways."[10] Dawkins intended the algorithm only to make his point about the distinction between single-step and cumulative selection, not to make a case for Darwinian theory. Nevertheless, it provides a useful example as an introduction to the exploration of teleology in evolutionary simulation. We have seen that at

9. Ibid., 50.
10. Ibid.

almost every part of this simulation, teleological fine-tuning was present to guide it to its target.

B. Ev

Moving on from Dawkins, consider Thomas Schneider and his program "ev."[11] Whereas Dawkins was careful to note some limitations
of his weasel simulation, Schneider argues that his simulation utterly
destroys opposing arguments:

> The ev model shows explicitly how this information gain comes
> about from mutation and selection, without any other external
> influence, thereby completely answering the creationists.[12]

Understanding ev will require some background. Imagine that, after
having read this book, you are skimming through it again in hopes of
finding a particular section that you found interesting. The section in
question was about dolphins, and thus you skim through the book
looking at each word only long enough to ascertain whether or not it
might be the word "dolphin." Once you have found the section, then
you actually read it carefully.

This is somewhat similar to the process that a cell uses when reading DNA. While this book is a sequence of English letters, DNA is a
sequence of nucleotides. The nucleotides are typically represented as
the letters A, C, G, and T. The cellular machinery skims through the
DNA looking for particular patterns of A, C, G, and T's. For example,
it might look for the pattern TATAAT. Actually, it looks for TATAAT
or a number of similar sequences. Molecules attach to the DNA at the
point of these patterns, which are called binding sites, causing some
desired effect. For example, it might increase or decrease the amount
of a particular protein being produced.

Ev models this process. One part of ev's genome defines the patterns that are recognized as binding sites. This is done using a structure
known as a perceptron. The details of how a perceptron works are not
important here, simply that it defines a set of patterns that will be con-

---

11. Thomas D. Schneider, "Evolution of Biological Information," *Nucleic Acids Research* 28,
no. 14 (2000): 2794–2799.
12. Ibid., 2797ff.

sidered binding sites. The other part contains sixteen positions where a binding site should exist. The binding sites will actually exist only if the pattern of nucleotides at that position fits one of the patterns accepted by the perceptron. The problem is then to identify both a perceptron and a sequence so that the correct binding sites—and only the correct binding sites—are recognized as binding sites.

Ev evolves a solution to this problem. For each organism, it counts the number of mistakes. Mistakes are binding sites that are missing or are in an incorrect position. The half of the population with the fewest mistakes is kept, but the half with the most mistakes is killed. The eliminated half of the population is replaced with a mutated copy of the surviving half of the population. This mutate-select-replicate process quickly results in a solution to ev's problem.

Is this a teleological model? Ev models the evolution of a real biological structure, a binding site, in DNA, which makes it closer to biology than any of the other models considered in this chapter. However, at a few key points, ev deviates from the biology and employs intelligently designed systems to help it reach its target.

The most important point of teleology in this model is the way in which the simulation decides which organisms are fitter. An organism is fitter when the binding sites in the organism are closer to the correct binding sites. The correct binding sites are a target, and ev is constantly measuring how far away any particular organism is from that target. But this is a massive departure from biology. Natural selection evaluates how well an organism works in its present environment; it does not measure the distance between an organism and some ideal form.

The ability to measure the distance to a target is very powerful. Imagine that you have a dog that has escaped. Fortunately, the dog has a transmitter on his collar, and you have a receiver. The receiver tells you how far away the dog is, but not the direction. Nevertheless, there will be no problem in locating your dog. You simply have to walk in the direction that causes the number on the receiver to go down.

What will happen without this transmitter? Finding your dog is going to be much harder. There may be other pieces of information you can use, such as where your dog has gone before, where other dogs are, where you have caught glimpses of your dog, and so on. But all of

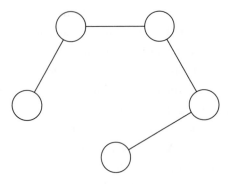

FIGURE 5.1. *Cities connected with a road network.*

those are going to be much less useful, much less powerful, than being able to measure the distance.

While ev models biology in the object of evolution, binding sites, it does not follow biology in its model of natural selection. Instead, it follows the unavoidably teleological method of measuring the distance to a target. This is critical. Evolution succeeds or fails depending on how well natural selection performs in guiding the evolutionary process. Replacing selection with a teleological process, as done by ev, eliminates any claims it might have had to being based on biology rather than being teleologically driven.

C. Steiner Trees

Another example is that of Dave Thomas, who wrote a simulation that evolves solutions to the Steiner tree problem.[13] The problem is essentially that of a collection of cities wishing to build a road network between them. The road must be built with the least amount of cost; that is, the actual length of roads should be as short as possible.

See Figure 5.1, for an example of cities connected by a network of roads. Notice that this would be a poor road network in real life, as drivers are forced to go the long way around between certain cities. Nevertheless, for the purpose of this theoretical problem, that does not concern us.

---

13. Dave Thomas, "War of the Weasels: An Evolutionary Algorithm Beats Intelligent Design," *Skeptical Inquirer* 43, no. 3 (2010): 42–46.

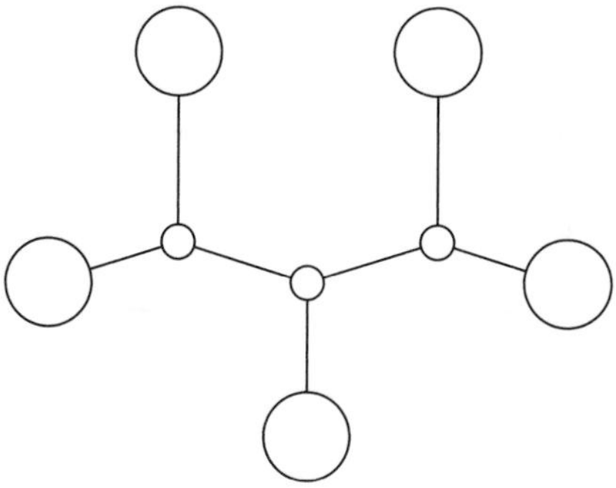

FIGURE 5.2. *Cities with an optimal road network.*

However, that network is not the best network for these cities. The optimal network is depicted in Figure 5.2: there is no network connecting these cities with less road. Notice the addition of three interchanges (the smaller circle) outside of the cities. These interchanges allow the road network to be shorter than if all interchanges had to be within the cities.

The task of evolution is to determine the best place to put interchanges, and which cities and interchanges should be connected. The cost of each network is the length of the roads, with a large penalty assessed to networks that fail to connect all the cities. Evolution proceeds by favoring networks with lower costs, producing mutated copies of them. The model also uses crossover: combining two existing networks to produce a new one. The end result is the evolution of a solution that is typically not optimal but that is better than anything achievable by random chance.

Unlike ev or Weasel, Thomas's simulation does not measure fitness as the distance to some target. It measures fitness as the actual quality of a particular solution. This gives it a much more feasible claim to actually be modeling natural selection. However, the veracity of this claim is lost by various details of the simulation that were fine-tuned in order to help the simulation succeed.

One example of teleological fine-tuning is in the number of interchanges. The model restricts the number of interchanges to be at least two. However, it is still possible that a potential network has

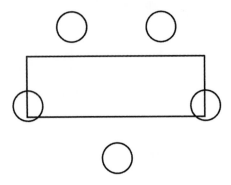

FIGURE 5.3. *Depiction of the cities along with the restricted area for possible locations of the interchanges.*

interchanges that are not actually connected to any other cities or interchanges. For all intents and purposes, this is the same as not having those interchanges in the first place. But by requiring every network to have at least two interchanges, solutions that use fewer interchanges are rarer.

What purpose does this restriction serve? The best-evolved solution is one that does not use any interchanges approximately 30 percent of the time. Finding this solution is not impressive, as it can be found by random chance. However, without the restriction on the number of possible interchanges, it is the best-evolved solution 96 percent of the time. The restriction exists to push evolution away from the undesired solutions without interchanges toward the better solutions with interchanges. It is teleological.

Another source is in the initialization of the genome. Evolutionary simulations typically begin with a completely random initialization, but Thomas's algorithm introduces a restriction, forcing the interchanges to be in a narrower portion of the space, as depicted in Figure 5.3. Why this portion? Thomas knew that interchanges would have to be in the center of the frame and restricted the initial randomness to ensure that this happened. Again, Thomas is using his knowledge of the solution in order to aid evolution.

Other examples of teleological fine-tuning can be found in this model.[14] However, from the examples given here, we can see that Thomas engaged in teleological fine-tuning. Natural selection does not restrict mutations in order to help reach a goal, but that is what Thomas did. He knew about the solution he was trying to find, and made decisions based on that teleological aim and his knowledge. It is teleology, not Darwinism, that accounts for this success.

D. Avida

Our final example is Avida. Avida evolves computer programs. For the uninitiated, the concept of a computer program may seem like an impenetrable dark art. But in essence, the idea of a computer program is actually simple. It is a recipe, a sequence of instructions that the computer follows. When following a recipe, a cook goes through the steps following each step's instruction, possibly skipping or repeating steps as instructed. A computer is doing the same thing.

Avida evolves instructions for a task that can be visualized as mixing paint colors. When you mix yellow and blue, you get green. If you mix yellow and red, you get orange. If you mix blue and red, you get purple. By combining and recombining colors, you can obtain a wide variety of different colors. In order to obtain a particular color, you need the recipe: the instructions for how to mix the colors to obtain the desired color.

Avida does not actually work with colors, but with thirty-two-bit binary numbers. There are over 4 billion such numbers, but for the most part Avida works with only sixteen of them. Think of these sixteen as being sixteen different colors. Table 5.1 shows what happens when different numbers are "mixed."

To use the table, take the two numbers being mixed, and look up the row and column corresponding to those numbers. The cell where the row and column intersect is the new color. For example, if you mix color 7 and color 10, then you will get color 16. Note that mixing a color with itself will not produce the original color, but a new color. The table is not random or arbitrary: it does follow rules. The nature of those rules does not concern us.

---

14. Winston Ewert, William A. Dembski, and Robert J. Marks II, "Climbing the Steiner Tree— Sources of Active Information in a Genetic Algorithm for Solving the Euclidean Steiner Tree Problem," *BIO-Complexity* 2012 no. 1 (2012): 1–14.

	1	2	3	4	5	6	7	8	9	10	11	12	13	14	15	16
1	16	16	16	16	16	16	16	16	16	16	16	16	16	16	16	16
2	16	15	16	15	16	15	16	15	16	15	16	15	16	15	16	15
3	16	16	14	14	16	16	14	14	16	16	14	14	16	16	14	14
4	16	15	14	13	16	15	14	13	16	15	14	13	16	15	14	13
5	16	16	16	16	12	12	12	12	16	16	16	16	12	12	12	12
6	16	15	16	15	12	11	12	11	16	15	16	15	12	11	12	11
7	16	16	14	14	12	12	10	10	16	16	14	14	12	12	10	10
8	16	15	14	13	12	11	10	9	16	15	14	13	12	11	10	9
9	16	16	16	16	16	16	16	16	8	8	8	8	8	8	8	8
10	16	15	16	15	16	15	16	15	8	7	8	7	8	7	8	7
11	16	16	14	14	16	16	14	14	8	8	6	6	8	8	6	6
12	16	15	14	13	16	15	14	13	8	7	6	5	8	7	6	5
13	16	16	16	16	12	12	12	12	8	8	8	8	4	4	4	4
14	16	15	16	15	12	11	12	11	8	7	8	7	4	3	4	3
15	16	16	14	14	12	12	10	10	8	8	6	6	4	4	2	2
16	16	15	14	13	12	11	10	9	8	7	6	5	4	3	2	1

TABLE 5.1. *Avida "color" mixing*

Given an unlimited supply of color 6 and color 4, can you obtain color 10? Figuring out what mixes to perform in order to obtain the desired color is like a puzzle. It is possible, but it is not obvious how to do this. One possible recipe is:

1. Combine colors 6 and 4 to obtain color 15
2. Combine colors 6 and 6 to obtain color 11
3. Combine colors 4 and 4 to obtain color 13
4. Combine colors 11 and 13 to obtain color 8
5. Combine colors 8 and 15 to obtain color 10

There are a number of other recipes for color 10, but none with less than five mixes. It is also the only color that requires this many mixes.

Within the Avida simulation, programs are favored by natural selection depending on which colors they produce. Colors 1, 4, 6, and 16 are not rewarded, because they are easily obtained. The rest of the colors are rewarded, allowing the program to have more offspring if it produces more colors.

Where is the teleological fine-tuning in this simulation? The most important example is the reward given to the colors besides the one being sought out. How do you produce a difficult color? First you must produce the simpler colors. Once you have managed to produce those, you can recombine them to produce more difficult colors. If you repeat this process enough times, you can obtain the most difficult colors. The design of Avida facilitates this by rewarding the gradual development of increasingly difficult colors. Without that facilitation, Avida never produces the difficult colors.

Avida rewards the simpler tasks or colors precisely because that helps produce the intended target color. The authors of Avida do not disagree with this assessment. In "The Evolutionary Origin of Complex Features" they wrote,

> Some readers might suggest that we 'stacked the deck' by studying the evolution of a complex feature that could be built on simpler functions that were also useful. However, that is precisely what evolutionary theory requires, and indeed, our experiments showed that the complex feature never evolved when simpler functions were not rewarded.[15]

The authors defend their decision to build the complex features (colors) on simpler features (colors) that were independently useful. But they do not appeal to any evidence that this would be a property of the real world. Instead, they appeal to a teleological point: in order for evolution to work, it needs the simpler functions to be rewarded. They constructed the simulation in this way precisely because it needed to be that way in order to work.

There are some other aspects of teleology in Avida.[16] Avida was designed to have particular properties in order to aid evolution. That renders it teleological and, thus, not a counterexample to the claim that non-teleological simulations do not produce successful evolution.

---

15. Lenski et al., "Evolutionary Origin of Complex Features," 143ff.

16. Winston Ewert, William A. Dembski, and Robert J. Marks II, "Evolutionary Synthesis of Nand Logic: Dissecting a Digital Organism," *2009 IEEE International Conference on Systems, Man and Cybernetics*, IEEE (2009): 3047–3053.

V. Conclusion

In each of these four examples, the simulation works only due to being intelligently designed. Success is not due to some efficacy of the Darwinian process, but rather it is due to teleological fine-tuning by the programmer in the creation of the simulation. The programmers made decisions, whether consciously or not, that drew upon their intelligence to produce the desired result. In other words, the decisions were made teleologically.

The precise nature of the teleological fine-tuning differs. In some cases there is an explicit target, and evolution has access to information about how far away it is from that target. In other cases, aspects of the solution are preprogrammed into the simulation. In still other cases, the problem itself was carefully chosen to have properties amenable to evolution. Whatever the individual case, the simulations work because of the teleological fine-tuning by the programmer. That teleological fine-tuning means that it is not a model of Darwinian evolution, and not a counterexample to intelligent design's claim.

All of this is to defend the primary claim of intelligent design: that intelligence is a prerequisite to design. If these simulations were in fact ateleological, that claim would have been falsified. However, as inspection of these simulations shows that they are teleological, the primary claim of intelligent design has been vindicated. So long as there continues to be no counterexample presented which demonstrates the production of design without teleology, the evidence for intelligent design grows.

Other claims of intelligent design can also be tested by computer simulations. For example, work has been done evaluating irreducible complexity,[17] low-impact mutations,[18] biologically realistic mutation rates,[19] and realistic fitness landscapes.[20] All of these experiments confirmed predictions made by intelligent design researchers.

---

17. Winston Ewert, "Digital Irreducible Complexity: A Survey of Irreducible Complexity in Computer Simulations," *BIO-Complexity* 2014, no. 1 (2014): 1–10.

18. Chase W. Nelson and John C. Sanford, "The Effects of Low-Impact Mutations in Digital Organisms," *Theoretical Biology and Medical Modelling* 8, no. 1 (2011): 9.

19. Winston Ewert, "Overabundant Mutations Help Potentiate Evolution: The Effect of Biologically Realistic Mutation Rates on Computer Models of Evolution," *BIO-Complexity* 2015, no. 4 (2015): 15–18.

20. Douglas D. Axe and Ann K. Gauger, "Model and Laboratory Demonstrations that Evolutionary Optimization Works Well Only If Preceded by Invention—Selection Itself Is Not Inventive,"

Intelligent design has passed the test of computer simulations. Its falsifiable predictions about computer simulations are accurate. But what about Darwinian evolution? Does it make falsifiable predictions about computer simulations? Is there a computer simulation counterexample that would prove Darwinian evolution false?

Evolution fails in some environments: Avida with a low mutation rate fails to evolve many tasks,[21] Tierra does not start a Cambrian explosion,[22] and Stylus fails to evolve a character starting from junk.[23] However, these failures do not constitute counterexamples, because Darwinists allow that evolution does not always work. The conditions have to be right.

But this renders Darwinian evolution unfalsifiable by computer simulation. No failing computer simulation can show that evolution does not work, just that the conditions were not right. If there were a theory regarding the necessary conditions, that could be tested. But as it stands, there is no such theory, and thus no computer simulation can falsify Darwinian evolution.

If Darwinian evolution were correct about which computer models would succeed and which would fail, this would be strong reason to believe it was correct about biology. However, it does not even offer any predictions about which computer models will succeed or fail, making it unfalsifiable. Without falsifiability, no computer model, successful or not, can provide support for Darwinian evolution. The theory is equally compatible with either success or failure. It does not risk being falsified by a computer model, and thus gains no support from them.

Writing at the blog *Panda's Thumb*, intelligent design critic Richard B. Hoppe wrote, "research using computational models of evolution are a thorn in the side of Intelligent Design proponents." But this is not true. Darwinian evolution is unfalsifiable: no computer simulation counterexample could prove it incorrect. As such, it risks nothing and gains nothing from any examples that demonstrate any sort of evolution. In contrast, intelligent design is falsifiable and makes

BIO-Complexity 2015, no. 2 (2015): 1–13.

21. Ewert, "Overabundant Mutations Help Potentiate Evolution."

22. Winston Ewert, William A. Dembski, and Robert J. Marks II, "Tierra: The Character of Adaptation," in *Biological Information* (Singapore: World Scientific, 2013, 105–138.

23. Axe and Gauger, "Model and Laboratory Demonstrations."

accurate predictions. It forbids the evolution of design without intelligence, and makes accurate predictions about the limitations of Darwinian processes. The truth is that computer simulations are a nail in Darwinism's coffin, and a powerful demonstration of the predictive power of intelligent design.

6

The Difference It Doesn't Make: Why the "Front-End Loaded" Concept of Design Fails to Explain the Origin of Biological Information

STEPHEN C. MEYER[1]

SUMMARY

Insofar as theistic evolution has been formulated with enough speci-ficity to qualify as an alternative to neo-Darwinism as a scientific model, theistic evolutionists have typically affirmed that God cre-ated the universe and designed the laws of nature (including their finely tuned features). But having done so, they think that the ori-gin of life and the origin of new forms of life can be explained by "secondary causes," which they equate with the laws of nature and evolutionary mechanisms such as natural selection and ran-dom mutation. Thus, their view either entails the claim that the initial conditions of matter at the beginning of the universe and the fine-tuned laws and constants of physics contained all the in-formation necessary to produce life, or it entails the view that the random mutation and natural selection (or some similarly materi-alistic mechanism) added significant amounts of new information

---

1. Adapted from S. C. Meyer, "Teleological Evolution: The Difference It Doesn't Make," in *Darwinism Defeated? The Johnson-Lamoureux Debate over Biological Origins* (Vancouver, BC: Regent College Press, 1999).

into the biosphere since the Big Bang. The problems with the latter
view are shown in chapters 2 and 8; this chapter demonstrates scientifically that the former view cannot be correct either, despite the
claims of certain theistic evolutionists who argue for a "front-end
loaded" concept of design that they call "teleological evolution."
In this view, the information necessary to produce life was present
from the beginning of the universe. This chapter contends that this
"front-end loaded" concept of design is scientifically inadequate
because it fails to recognize that the laws of nature do not describe
information-generating processes.

. . . . .

As I noted in the "Scientific and Philosophical Introduction" to this
volume, the term "theistic evolution" can mean different things to
different people.

Some theistic evolutionists affirm that God actively directs the evolutionary process by, for example, directing seemingly random mutations
toward particular biological endpoints. On this view, God has actively
created new organisms by directing mutational change to produce new
forms of life. This view has the virtue for theists of being at least minimally compatible with orthodox Jewish and/or Christian doctrines of
creation, since it affirms that God is actively doing something to bring
life into existence. On the other hand, this view contradicts the (scientifically) orthodox neo-Darwinian view of the evolutionary process as
a purely purposeless, unguided, and undirected mechanism—a "blind
watchmaker," as Richard Dawkins has called it. Indeed, as George
Gaylord Simpson, one of the architects of neo-Darwinism, wrote in
The Meaning of Evolution, the theory implies that "man is the result
of a purposeless and natural process that did not have him in mind."[2]

Other theistic evolutionists see the evolutionary process—including
both the origin and subsequent evolution of life—as a *purely* unguided
and undirected process, just as orthodox neo-Darwinists do. These
theistic evolutionists conceive of God's role as much more passive.

---

2. George Gaylord Simpson, *The Meaning of Evolution*, rev. ed. (New Haven, CT: Yale University Press, 1967), 345.

They conceive of God as merely sustaining the laws of nature, which in turn allow life to emerge and develop as the result of otherwise undirected and unguided mechanisms such as mutation and natural selection. While this view comports nicely with scientific materialism and neo-Darwinism, it seems to contradict religiously orthodox views of the creation of life by denying that God played any active role in creation or that he even knew what the evolutionary process would ultimately produce.

Perhaps in an attempt to split the horns of this dilemma, some theists who accept the adequacy of materialist explanations have proposed a new view, or at least a view with a new name. For example, Denis O. Lamoureux, a professor of science and religion at St. Joseph's College, University of Alberta, advocates a position he calls "teleological evolution" or "evolutionary creation."[3] He prefers the term "evolutionary creation" to "theistic evolution" because, as an evangelical Christian, he wants to emphasize his belief in creation by making the term "evolutionary" merely the modifier rather than the noun in the description of his position. For him, evolution refers merely to "the method through which the Lord made the cosmos and living organisms."[4] He prefers the term "teleological evolution" to "theistic evolution" because he wants to affirm, *contra* Simpson and other neo-Darwinists, that evolution is "a planned and purpose driven natural process."

But what exactly is meant by this idea? And does it provide an adequate scientific explanation for the origin and development of life? And if so, does it do so with enough specificity to be distinguished from standard materialistic theories of evolution and reconciled with a traditional Judeo-Christian understanding of God as the creator of life?

According to Lamoureux, the theory of evolutionary creation affirms that "the Creator established and maintains the laws of nature, including the mechanisms of a teleological evolution."

Lamoureux provides several illustrations to convey what he has in mind. For example, he suggests that "God organized the Big Bang, so

---

3. See Denis Lamoureux, "Evolutionary Creation: A Christian Approach to Evolution," available at: http://biologos.org/uploads/projects/Lamoureux_Scholarly_Essay.pdf. In the following, I will refer to this online essay. See also his recent book-length treatment, *Evolutionary Creation: A Christian Approach to Creation* (Eugene, OR: Wipf & Stock, 2008).

4. Lamoureux, "Evolutionary Creation."

that the deck was stacked"[5] to produce life. He also likens God to an expert billiards player who can sink all the balls on the billiards table in one shot. He likens the precise arrangement of the balls and the billiards player clearing the table with one single shot to God's initial act of creativity in bringing the universe into being with a very precise arrangement of matter (or initial conditions). Just as the billiards player can clear the table with one shot, God can create everything (the universe as well as all forms of life) with an initial act of creativity in which he arranges matter just right at the beginning of the universe and then lets it unfold deterministically in accord with the laws that he also established in the beginning. Thus, God needs no additional shots (no further acts of creativity) to bring life into existence. Lamoureux also compares the process of biological evolution to embryological development, in which an organism develops deterministically from a fertilized egg through time in accord with the laws of nature.[6]

Thus, Lamoureux seems to have in mind a kind of front-end loaded view of intelligent design in which the initial conditions of the universe are arranged or designed in such a way that life will inevitably evolve without any additional input or activity of a designing intelligence. As he explains, "design is evident in the finely tuned physical laws and initial conditions necessary for the evolution of the cosmos through the Big Bang, and design is also apparent in the biological processes necessary for life to evolve."[7] Thus, in some places he also refers to his view as "evolutionary intelligent design."[8]

Although he uses the term intelligent design to describe his own view, he objects to the contemporary theory of intelligent design, and indeed, to any argument that implies that a designing intelligence played a role in the origin or development of life after the universe itself first originated. According to Lamoureux, to invoke a specific instance of intelligent design or divine action after the initial creation of the universe would imply a violation of natural law by invoking the activity of "a God-of-the-gaps." (See our refutation of the 'God-of-the-gaps' objection in chapter 19). As he explains,

5. Quoted in Joe Woodward, "The End of Evolution," *Alberta Report* (December 1996), 33.
6. Lamoureux, "Evolutionary Creation."
7. Ibid.
8. Ibid.

Intelligent Design Theory . . . is a narrow view of design and claims that design is connected to miraculous interventions (i.e., God-of-the-gaps miracles that introduce creatures and/or missing parts) in the origin of living organisms. For example, parts of the cell like the flagellum are said to be "irreducibly complex," and as a result, they could not have evolved through natural processes. Since this is the case, ID Theory should be termed *Interventionistic* Design Theory.[9]

Lamoureux objects to intelligent design as an explanation for specific features of biological systems or events in the history of life because he wants to confine God's creative activity to the very beginning of the universe, and biological theories of intelligent design, he thinks, imply that an intelligent agent (quite possibly God) may well have acted at discrete points in the history of life after the origin of the universe.

Three Problems with the Theory of Evolutionary Creation (or Teleological Evolution) and Its Critique of Intelligent Design

Having developed an argument for intelligent design as an explanation for the origin of the information necessary to produce the first life[10] (an event that happened well after the beginning of the universe), it should come as no surprise that I disagree with Lamoureux's critique of the theory of intelligent design and his theory of evolutionary creation. I do so for three main reasons.

First, I see no reason to *assume* that the designing intelligence responsible for life and the universe (whom I personally believe was God) necessarily confined his activity to the very beginning of the universe. He may or may not have done so. I agree with Lamoureux that the laws of nature were established, and are maintained, by God. I also agree that the fine-tuning of these laws and the initial conditions of the universe provides evidence of intelligent design. Nevertheless, I see no reason to assume that this fine-tuning is the only evidence of design in the natural world. Nor do I think that the cosmological fine-tuning accounts for everything we find in the biological world (see below).

---

9. Ibid.
10. Stephen C. Meyer, *Signature in the Cell: DNA and the Evidence for Intelligent Design* (San Francisco: HarperOne, 2009).

Of course, Lamoureux finds appealing the concept of a God who had the wisdom to arrange matter so exquisitely at the beginning of the universe as to make any future actions on his part unnecessary. Others like to think of God as more actively involved in the process of creation. They find it appealing to think of God acting like a great composer who first establishes a theme at the beginning of his work and then adds new variations to that original theme at episodic intervals thereafter.

As a Christian, however, I affirm that God acted entirely freely, and was under no compulsion to act in a way that either appeals to or affirms our aesthetic sensibilities. So I think the question of when God acted should remain a matter for empirical investigation and should not be determined by our aesthetic or theological preferences one way or another. As Robert Boyle (1627–1691) often argued, the job of the scientist (or what he called the "natural philosopher") is not to assume beforehand what God must have done, but to study the world to find out what God actually has done.[11]

Second, unlike Lamoureux, I do not think that material processes and mechanisms of evolution are sufficient to account for the origin of living forms, whether the origin of the first life or the major innovations in body plan design (see chapter 2) that appear during the history of life thereafter. Yet, Lamoureux's attempted harmonization of theistic belief with evolutionary theory presupposes the adequacy and/or creative power of established evolutionary processes and mechanisms—mechanisms that supposedly demonstrate the "incredible self-assembling" capacity of "the natural world during the distant past."[12]

But what if the evolutionary mechanisms that Lamoureux extols do not have the creative power or self-assembly capacity long attributed to them, as many scientists now argue and as the preceding (and subsequent) chapters in the first section of this book show? Before we

---

11. For instance, Boyle said, quite characteristically, "God is a most free agent, and created the world not out of necessity but voluntarily, having framed it as he pleased and thought fit at the beginning of things, when there was no substance but himself and consequently no creature to which he could be obliged, or by which he could be limited" (Robert Boyle, *A Free Enquiry into the Vulgarly Received Notion of Nature*, ed. Edward B. David and Michael Hunter [Cambridge: Cambridge University Press, 1996], 160). See also Rejer Hooykaas's summary of Boyle's Christian empiricist epistemology in Rejer Hooykaas, *Religion and the Rise of Modern Science* (Grand Rapids, MI: Eerdmans: 1972), 47.

12. Lamoureux, "Evolutionary Creation."

construct elaborate theological harmonizations of the doctrine of creation with neo-Darwinism and other materialistic evolutionary theories, shouldn't we make sure that these theories are true? I think so. And for reasons that I have explained in preceding chapters, I (and even many leading evolutionary biologists) now doubt that known or even postulated mechanisms of undirected evolutionary change have the creative power long attributed to them.

In my book *Signature in the Cell: DNA and the Evidence for Intelligent Design*,[13] for example, I show that no undirected chemical evolutionary mechanism provides an adequate explanation for the origin of the information necessary to produce the first life. (Jim Tour makes a similar critique of chemical evolutionary theory in chapter 4.) I have also shown in chapter 2 and elsewhere[14] that neither the mutation/selection mechanism nor any of the other leading proposed evolutionary mechanisms provide a sufficient explanation for the origin of the major innovations in biological form (in particular, the novel body plans) that arise during the history of life on Earth. For this reason, I dispute Denis Lamoureux's view that known evolutionary mechanisms are the main "method through which the Lord made . . . living organisms."

Third, I think Lamoureux's front-end loaded view of design is scientifically problematic. I do so because of my own study of the problem of the origin of the first life and the critically related problem of the origin of biological information. In the remainder of this chapter, I would like to discuss this problem and show why Lamoureux's theory of evolutionary creation, with its front-end loaded view of design, is insufficient to account for the problem of the origin of biological information—as well as the closely related problem of the origin of life.

---

13. Meyer, *Signature in the Cell* (see note 10, above).
14. Stephen C. Meyer, *Darwin's Doubt: The Explosive Origin of Animal Life and the Case for Intelligent Design* (New York: HarperOne, 2014); Meyer, "The Origin of Biological Information and the Higher Taxonomic Categories," *Proceedings of the Biological Society of Washington* 117, no. 2 (2004): 213–239; see also Meyer, "The Cambrian Information Explosion: Evidence for Intelligent Design," in *Debating Design: From Darwin to DNA*, ed. Michael Ruse and William Dembski (Cambridge: Cambridge University Press, 2007), 371–391.

The Origin of Biological Information:
The Fundamental Mystery

In 1953, James Watson and Francis Crick first discovered the structure of DNA. It was the beginning of a profound revolution in biology that led to the recognition of DNA as an information-bearing molecule. Composed of linear strings of four different chemicals, called nucleotides, DNA carries in the linear sequence of these nucleotides information necessary to build organisms. The nucleotides function as do the alphabetic characters of written language. In language, the arrangement of letters to make words and sentences carries information; similarly, the sequence of nucleotides conveys instructions for how to make the molecules and molecular machines the cell needs. The nucleotide base sequences in DNA also contain information about when and where to use those molecules.

The information-bearing properties of DNA can be compared to that of digital computer code. As I noted in chapter 2, this similarity is acknowledged even by neo-Darwinian biologists such as Richard Dawkins, who has observed that "the machine code of the genes is uncannily computer-like."[15] And software developer Bill Gates sees the similarity even more strongly: "DNA is like a computer program, but far, far more advanced than any software we've ever created."[16] Leroy Hood, famous for his contributions to biotechnology, describes the information encoded in DNA as "digital code."[17]

But if this is true, how did the information in DNA arise? As it turns out, this question is related to a long-standing mystery in biology—the question of the origin of the first life. Indeed, since Watson and Crick's discovery, scientists have increasingly come to understand the centrality of information to even the simplest living systems. DNA stores the assembly instructions for building the many crucial proteins and protein machines that service and maintain even the most primitive one-celled organisms. It follows that building a living cell in the first place requires assembly instructions stored in DNA or some equivalent molecule. As origin-of-life researcher

---

15. Richard Dawkins, *River out of Eden: A Darwinian View of Life* (New York: Basic Books, 1996) 17.
16. Bill Gates, *The Road Ahead* (London: Penguin, 1996), 228.
17. Leroy Hood, "The Digital Code of DNA" *Nature* 421 (2003): 444–448.

Bernd-Olaf Küppers has explained, "The problem of the origin-of-life is clearly basically equivalent to the problem of the origin of biological information."[18]

Understanding Lamoureux's View: Pick Your Poison

Denis Lamoureux does not directly address the problem of the origin of the first life or the origin of the information necessary to produce it. He doesn't say which specific naturalistic theory of the origin of life—if any—he favors. Nevertheless, the metaphors he employs to convey how God creates (deck stacked at the beginning; God as cosmic billiards player; evolution as embryological development, etc.) imply that deterministic laws caused life to self-organize or self-assemble from some highly configured, and therefore information-rich, set of initial conditions at the beginning of the universe. Nevertheless, he does not say whether he thinks that (a) all the information necessary to produce the first and subsequent forms of life was present in the initial conditions of the universe, or whether (b) the laws of nature added new information during the subsequent "self-assembly" process. In any case, both proposals are scientifically problematic. So let's consider each in turn, starting with the second.

Are Laws Creative?

Lamoureux, like other evolutionary creationists, sometimes speaks as though he thinks the physical laws of nature might be *generating* the new information necessary to produce new forms of life. For example, he refers to evolution as "a planned and purpose driven natural process" and affirms "that humans evolved from pre-human ancestors, and over a period of time the Image of God and human sin were gradually and mysteriously manifested."[19] Since Lamoureux disavows specific acts of divine creation as illicit appeals to a "God-of-the Gaps," and since he affirms that humans, at least, acquire new attributes and characteristics during the evolutionary process, it might be that he thinks that the laws of nature are *generating* the

---

18. Bernd-Olaf Küppers, *Information and the Origin of Life* (Cambridge, MA: MIT Press, 1990), 170–172.
19. Lamoureux, "Evolutionary Creation."

new information necessary to produce living systems and their unique attributes.

But do laws of nature generate information? There are good reasons to doubt this. To see why, imagine that a group of small radio-controlled helicopters hovers in tight formation over a football stadium—the Rose Bowl in Pasadena, California. From below, the helicopters appear to be spelling a message: "Go USC." At halftime, with the field cleared, each helicopter releases either a red or a gold paint ball, one of the two University of Southern California colors. Gravity takes over, and the paint balls fall to the earth, splattering paint on the field after they hit the turf. Now on the field below, a somewhat messier but still legible message appears. It also spells "Go USC."

Did the law of gravity, or the force described by the law, produce this information? Clearly, it did not. The information that appeared on the field already existed in the arrangement of the helicopters above the stadium—in what physicists call "the initial conditions." Neither the force of gravity, nor the law that describes it, caused the information on the field to self-organize. Instead, gravitational forces merely transmitted preexisting information from the helicopter formation—the initial conditions—to the field below. In the same way, the laws of nature do not add new information to that which was present in specifically arranged configuration of matter (or initial conditions) at the beginning of the universe. Laws can transmit but not generate information, as our illustration makes clear.

There is a deeper reason for this. Scientific laws describe (by definition) highly regular phenomena or structures, ones that possess what information theorists refer to as redundant *order*. On the other hand, the arrangements of matter in an information-rich text, including the genetic instructions on DNA, possess a high degree of complexity or aperiodicity, not redundant order.

To illustrate the difference, compare the sequence ABABABABABAB to the sequence "One small step for a man, one giant leap for mankind." The first sequence is repetitive and ordered, but not complex or informative. The second sequence is not ordered, in the sense of being repetitious, but it is complex and also informative. The second sequence is complex because its characters do not follow a rigidly repeating, law-bound pattern. (It is also informative because, unlike a merely complex sequence such as: "sretfdhu&*jsa&90te," the particular arrangement of characters is highly exact or specified[20] so as to perform a (communication) function. In any case, informative sequences have the qualitative feature of complexity (aperiodicity), and thus are qualitatively distinguishable from systems characterized by periodic order that natural laws describe or generate.

To say that the processes that natural laws describe can generate functionally specified informational sequences is, therefore, essentially a contradiction in terms. Laws are the wrong kind of entity to generate the informational features of life. The claim also betrays a categorical confusion. Physical laws do not generate complex sequences, whether functionally specified or otherwise; they *describe* highly regular, repetitive, and periodic patterns. This is not to malign the laws of physics and chemistry. It's simply to describe what they do.

And yet, some scientists claim that we must await the discovery of new natural laws to explain the origin of biological information. Manfred Eigen has argued that "our task is to find an algorithm, a natural law, that leads to the origin of information."[21] But there is another reason that we will not discover such a law. According to classical information theory, the amount of information present in a sequence is inversely proportional to the probability of the sequence occurring. Yet the regularities we refer to as laws describe highly deterministic or predictable relationships between conditions and events.

Laws describe patterns in which the probability of each successive event (given the previous event and the action of the law) approaches unity. Yet information content mounts as *im*probabilities multiply. Information is conveyed whenever one event among an ensemble of possibilities (as opposed to a single necessity) is fixed. The greater the number of possibilities, the greater is the improbability of any one possibility occurring, and the more information is transmitted when a particular possibility is fixed, specified, or elected. If someone tells you

---

20. For a definition of specification, see William Dembski, *The Design Inference* (Cambridge: Cambridge University Press, 1998), 1–66, 136–174.

21. Manfred Eigen, *Steps toward Life* (Oxford: Oxford University Press, 1992), 12.

that it is raining, he will have conveyed some meaningful information to you since it does not rain (or have to rain) every day. If, however, he also tells you that today the raindrops are falling down, rather than up, he will not have told you anything informative since, presumably, you already know that rain always falls down (by natural law). As Fred Dretske has explained,

> As p(si) [the probability of a condition or state of affairs] approaches 1 the amount of information associated with the occurrence of si goes to 0. In the limiting case when the probability of a condition or state of affairs is unity [p(si)=1], no information is associated with, or generated by, the occurrence of si. This is merely another way to say that no information is generated by the occurrence of events for which there are no possible alternatives.[22]

Natural laws as a category describe situations in which specific outcomes follow specific conditions with high probability or necessity. Yet information is maximized when just the opposite situation occurs, namely, when antecedent conditions allow many possible and improbable outcomes. Thus, to the extent that a sequence of symbols or events results from a predictable law-bound process, the information content of the sequence is limited or effaced (by redundancy). Thus, since natural laws do not generate or describe complex informational sequences, they cannot be invoked to explain the *origin* of information, whether biological or otherwise.

Does the Configuration of Matter at the Beginning of the Universe Explain the Origin of Biological Information?

To be fair, Lamoureux mainly seems to have a different scenario in mind—one in which the information necessary to produce living systems is entirely present at the beginning of the universe. Indeed, taken at face value, each of the metaphors he uses to describe his front-end loaded view of evolutionary intelligent design emphasizes how the "deck was stacked" at the beginning. Recall, for example, that he likens the evolution of the universe and life from the initial arrangements

---

22. Fred Dretske, *Knowledge and the Flow of Information* (Cambridge, MA: MIT Press, 1981), 12.

of matter at the beginning of the universe to the process of embryological development. He affirms that everything necessary to produce an adult organism (including, presumably, the biological information) is already present in the early embryo. It simply unfolds through time in accord with the laws of nature. In his billiard ball example, the precise arrangement of the billiard balls and the precise shot of the billiards player constitute information-rich initial conditions. The movement of the balls in response to the precise shot occurs deterministically in accord with the laws of momentum exchange.

Thus, Lamoureux's metaphors imply that the information necessary to produce the first (and subsequent) living forms is already present in arrangements of elementary particles just after the beginning of the universe. But is this view scientifically plausible? Was the information necessary to produce the first life present in the arrangement of elementary particles just after the beginning of the universe? For this to be true, there must be a law that can transmit whatever information was present in the configuration of elementary particles at the beginning of the universe across billions of years without degradation, and also some process that can utilize that information (or convert it into a medium that can be used) to produce the first living cell. Since the first living cell would, at the very least, require genetic information, that raises two more precise and analytically tractable questions by which Lamoureux's proposal can be evaluated:

> Was the information necessary to produce a functional gene (information-rich DNA molecule) present in the arrangement of elementary particles just after the beginning of the universe?

> Is there a physical law that could use the information present in the arrangement of elementary particles just after the beginning of the universe to produce a functional gene?

In both cases the answer is no. And there are important reasons why this is so.

First, it turns out that even the biologically relevant chemical subunits of DNA themselves do not contain the information necessary for producing a functional gene or the functional information DNA contains. And if they do not contain such information, then the much more simple and less biologically relevant arrangements of elementary particles (or distributions of mass-energy) present at the beginning of the universe certainly did not contain such information. Second, there is no law that describes how these subunits self-organize into functional genes.

To see why, recall what we know about the structure of the DNA molecule.

What the Structure of DNA Reveals about the Inadequacy of Self-Organizational Models of the Origin of Life

DNA depends on several chemical bonds, each of which is governed by laws of chemical attraction (see Fig. 6.1). There are chemical bonds, for example, between the sugar and the phosphate molecules that form the two twisting backbones of the DNA molecule. There are bonds fixing individual (nucleotide) bases to the sugar-phosphate backbones on each side of the molecule. There are also hydrogen bonds stretching horizontally across the molecule between nucleotide bases, making so-called complementary pairs. These bonds, which hold two complementary copies of the DNA message text together, make replication of the genetic instructions possible—just as chemical laws allow ink to adhere to paper. However, there are no chemical bonds *between the bases along the vertical axis in the center of the helix*—any more than there are laws determining that an "A" must always follow a "B" in the written English language. Yet it is precisely along this axis of the DNA molecule that the genetic instructions in DNA are encoded.[23]

Further, just as magnetic letters can be combined and recombined in any way to form various sequences on a metal surface, so too can each of the four bases, A, T, G, and C, attach to any site on the DNA backbone with more or less equal facility, making all sequences equally probable (or improbable) given the laws of physics and chemistry. Indeed, there are no differential affinities between any of the four bases and the binding sites along the sugar-phosphate backbone. The same type of chemical bond, called an "n-glycosidic" bond, occurs between the base and the backbone regardless of which base attaches. All four

---

23. Bruce Alberts et al., *Molecular Biology of the Cell* (New York: Garland, 1983), 105.

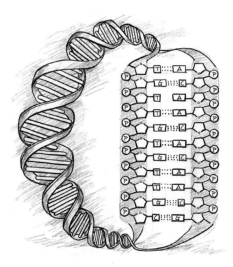

FIGURE 6.1. *The bonding relationship between the chemical constituents of the DNA molecule.* Note that no chemical bonds exist between the nucleotide bases along the message-bearing axis of the DNA helix.

CREDIT: Illustration courtesy Ray Braun. Adapted by permission from an original drawing by Fred Heeren.

bases are acceptable; none is preferred. As Bernd-Olaf Küppers has noted, "a present day understanding of the properties of nucleic acids indicates that all the combinatorially possible nucleotide patterns of a DNA are, from a chemical point of view, equivalent."[24]

This fact about the structure of DNA was first noticed in 1967 by the physical chemist Michael Polanyi. In a seminal article titled *Life Transcending Physics and Chemistry,*[25] Polanyi showed first that the laws of physics and chemistry generally leave open (or indeterminate) a vast ensemble of possible configurations of matter, only very few of which could have any role in a functioning biological organism. Specifically, he noted that the chemical laws governing the assembly of the chemical subunits in the DNA molecule allow a vast array of possible arrangements of nucleotide bases, the chemical letters, in the genetic

---

24. Bernd-Olaf Küppers, "On the Prior Probability of the Existence of Life," in *The Probabilistic Revolution,* ed. Lorenz Kruger et al. (Cambridge, MA: MIT Press, 1987), 364.

25. Michael Polanyi, "Life Transcending Physics and Chemistry," *Chemical and Engineering News* 45 (1967): 54–66. See also Polanyi, "Life's Irreducible Structure," *Science* 160 (1968): 1308–1312, esp. 1309.

text. In other words, the chemical properties of the constituent parts of DNA (and the laws governing their arrangement) do not determine the specific sequencing of the bases in the genetic molecule. Yet the specific sequencing of the nucleotide bases in DNA constitutes precisely the feature of the DNA molecule, namely its functionally specified information, that origin-of-life biologists most need to explain.[26]

Self-Organization and Evolutionary Creation

In my book *Signature in the Cell*, I have shown why the chemical indeterminacy of the DNA molecule has devastating implications for self-organizational models of the origin of the first life and the origin of genetic information. Typically, these scenarios suggest that the forces of chemical necessity (as described by physical and chemical law) make the origin of life—and the origin of the genetic information that it requires—inevitable.[27] But if law-like processes of chemical attraction do not account for the specific sequencing of nucleotide bases that constitute the information in DNA (as shown above), then such processes cannot reasonably be invoked as the explanation for the origin of the information in DNA in the first place. (It turns out that the information stored in RNA also defies explanation by self-organizing forces of chemical attraction.) Indeed, for those who want to explain the origin of life as the result of self-organizing properties or natural laws intrinsic to the material constituents of living systems, these elementary facts of molecular biology have devastating implications. The most logical place to look for self-organizing chemical laws and properties to explain the origin of genetic information is in the constituent parts of the molecules carrying that information. But biochemistry and molecular biology make clear that law-like forces of attraction between the constituents in DNA (as well as RNA and protein)[28] do not explain the sequence specificity of these large information-bearing bio-molecules.

---

26. Bernd-Olaf Küppers, *Information and the Origin of Life*, 170–172; also Charles Thaxton, Walter Bradley, and Roger Olsen, *Information and the Origin of Life* (Cambridge, MA: MIT Press, 1990), 170–172; also Charles Thaxton, Walter Bradley, and Roger Olsen, *The Mystery of Life's Origin* (New York: Philosophical Library, 1984), 24–38.

27. See, e.g., Christian de Duve, "The Beginnings of Life on Earth," *American Scientist* 83 (1995): 437.

28. R. A. Kok, J. A. Taylor, and W. L. Bradley, "A Statistical Examination of Self-Ordering Amino Acids in Proteins," *Origins of Life and Evolution of the Biosphere* 18 (1988): 135–142.

To say otherwise is like saying that the law-like forces of chemical attraction governing ink on this page are responsible for the sequential arrangement of the letters that give this book meaning.

What does this have to do with the adequacy of the front-end loaded concept of design favored by advocates of "evolutionary creation" and other theistic evolutionists? Quite a lot. Evolutionary creationists such as Denis Lamoureux seem to affirm that the laws of nature as "established and maintained" by God are sufficient to produce life from the initial configurations of matter at the beginning of the universe. Thus, the evolutionary creationist position—with its emphasis on the deterministic unfolding of the history of life in accord with preestablished conditions and laws of nature—entails a commitment to some form of self-organizational origin-of-life scenario. In Lamoureux's billiard ball illustration, for example, a law of nature (the conservation of momentum) ensures a transition from an initial arrangement of matter (the balls arranged on the table) to a subsequent state (in which all the balls are resting in the pockets of the billiard table). Indeed, all his illustrations of evolutionary creation suggest that there must be some law-governed process that ensures a *deterministic* transition from the initial arrangement of elementary particles present at the Big Bang to a subsequent arrangement of matter constituting a living cell. He does not actually specify whether the laws that affect this transition actually generate new information or just transmit information already present in the initial arrangement of matter in the universe. Either way, though, he seems to assume that some law-like deterministic process must generate a living organism, starting ultimately from the arrangement of elementary particles (or distribution of mass-energy) present at the beginning of the universe. As such, Lamoureux's theory of evolutionary creation entails a kind of self-organizational theory of the origin of life. And, indeed, Lamoureux himself extols the "self-assembling character of the natural world."[29]

Yet, self-organizational scenarios fail to account for the origin of genetic information for the simple reason that there are no self-organizing forces of attraction that can account for the sequence specificity of DNA and RNA bases—the carriers of genetic information in all known cells. Moreover, the irreducibility of genetic information to the chemis-

---

29. Lamoureux, "Evolutionary Creation."

try of the DNA and RNA poses a particular difficulty for the front-end loaded evolutionary creationist view of Denis Lamoureux and others.

Evolutionary creationists insist that God's direct, discrete, or special creative activity has played no role in the history of the universe since the initial moment of creation at the Big Bang. They imply, therefore, that the known laws of nature acting on (presumably information-rich) configurations of elementary particles were sufficient to organize matter into the information-rich structures we see today in living systems. Yet, if the chemical subunits of DNA lack the self-organizational properties necessary to produce the informational sequencing of DNA, it is difficult to see how far less specifically configured and less biologically specific elementary particles or distributions of mass-energy (present just after the Big Bang) possessed the self-organizational capacity necessary to arrange themselves by natural law into fully functioning organisms. In other words, if the chemical subunits of DNA—nucleotide bases, sugars, and phosphates, each constituting highly specific and biologically relevant arrangements of atoms—do not contain the information necessary to produce a functional gene, then the far less specifically configured and less biologically relevant elementary particles present just after the beginning of the universe most certainly lacked the information to do so as well. But if this is so, then the deck was *not* stacked from the beginning as Lamoureux and other evolutionary creationists or teleological evolutionists have argued. Moreover, if the laws of physics and chemistry merely transmit information but do not generate it, then some other sources of information must have arisen after the beginning of the universe in order to produce life.

The Difference It Doesn't Make

In *Signature in the Cell*, I argue that intelligent design provides the best explanation for the information necessary to produce the first living cell. In the process of making that case, I critique the adequacy of self-organizational theories of the origin of biological information. Of course, neither self-organization nor intelligent design exhausts the logical possibilities for explaining the origin of information. One could also invoke contingency or chance, of either the directed or the undirected variety. For example, many chemical evolutionary theorists have invoked chance (usually in conjunction with prebiotic natural selection; see chapter 4) in an attempt to explain the origin of information necessary to produce the first life. (In *Signature in the Cell*, I show why those theories fail as well.) Neo-Darwinists also invoke random and undirected mutations to explain the origin of the new biological information necessary to produce new forms of life once the first life had originated. (In chapter 2, and elsewhere, I have shown why those theories fail.[30]) On the other hand, some theistic evolutionists, such as Gordon Mills, have suggested that mutations generate anatomical novelty but that they are directed by a guiding intelligence.[31]

Unfortunately, none of these approaches involving contingency (chance or choice) represent live options for Lamoureux, who wants to attribute the origin of life to *deterministic* laws acting on finely tuned initial conditions. If, for example, the teleological evolutionist wanted to avoid the information-theoretic difficulties discussed above by invoking *undirected* chance variations to help explain the origin of genetic information, his position would become indistinguishable from standard materialistic versions of evolutionary theory (whether biological or chemical) that combine chance and law-like processes. Moreover, any version of evolution driven by such undirected, chance variations would not qualify as "a purposeful process" (as Lamoureux describes teleological evolution). If, on the other hand, the teleological evolutionist invoked directed contingency (the active or intelligent guidance of events), then he would violate his own self-imposed injunction against invoking divine action as a cause during the history of life and would commit a God-of-the-gaps fallacy.

Thus, the teleological evolutionist faces a dilemma. Either he sticks with the empirically unsupportable and theoretically incoherent view that natural laws *generate* specified biological information, or he invokes some form of contingency to account for the origin of biological information. If he claims that *undirected* stochastic processes generate biological information, then he would undercut his claim to have formulated a novel purpose-driven theory of evolution. But claiming that

---

30. See note 10 above.
31. Gordon Mills, "Similarities and Differences in Mitochondrial Genomes: Theistic Interpretation," *Perspectives on Science and Christian Faith* 50, no. 4 (December 1998): 286–292.

directed contingency generates biological information would entail affirming an *interventionist* version of intelligent design that Lamoureux explicitly rejects. Thus, it's difficult to see how Lamoureux's proposal can be rescued, at least on terms acceptable to him.

Conclusion

C. S. Peirce's maxim "for a difference to be a difference, it must make a difference" seems applicable here. Lamoureux purports to offer a novel theory of biological origins. Yet, his theory is indistinguishable from self-organizational theories of the origin of life that cannot—for good reasons—explain the origin of the information necessary to produce the first life. Nevertheless, if Lamoureux were to modify his theory to overcome the inherent limitations of such a deterministic, law-driven approach, any such alteration would make it indistinguishable from other established theoretical approaches that he rejects.

It's also unclear what difference his "teleological" approach to evolution makes. If the finely tuned arrangements of matter (or mass-energy) at the beginning of the universe lack the information necessary to produce a single functional gene or protein, then even if God produced those arrangements, *something else* must be responsible for the additional information necessary to produce a living cell. If that "something" cannot involve the activity of a purposeful designing agent after the Big Bang, as Lamoureux insists, then clearly the process that generates the first life from that set of initial conditions cannot be teleological. All of which makes it fair to ask: does Lamoureux's specifically *teleological* theory of evolution add anything to the explanation of biological origins that a self-organizational theory (or—were he to modify his theory—a more conventional neo-Darwinian or chemical evolutionary theory) does not? Regrettably, the answer to this question is no. Since Lamoureux is unwilling to specify any role for God beyond the causally necessary, but insufficient, role of establishing initial conditions and maintaining physical laws, "teleological evolution" seems to be little more than an empty phrase describing a theory that, in the end, reduces to a standard, and completely inadequate, materialistic mode of explanation for the origin of biological information.

7

Why DNA Mutations Cannot Accomplish What Neo-Darwinism Requires

JONATHAN WELLS

SUMMARY

According to neo-Darwinism, evolution takes place because of the natural selection of slight, successive variations. Some of those variations may arise through the reshuffling of existing DNA sequences, but for continuing evolution, neo-Darwinism requires that existing DNA sequences mutate into new sequences. This assumes that DNA contains a program for embryo development: DNA makes RNA makes protein makes us. Mutations in the program could then produce novel anatomical structures, and natural selection could preserve favorable ones and eliminate unfavorable ones. But DNA sequences do not even fully specify RNAs, much less proteins. And the three-dimensional arrangement of proteins in a cell requires spatial information that precedes their synthesis and is specified independently of DNA. Therefore, DNA does not contain a program for embryo development, and mutations in DNA cannot provide the raw materials for anatomical evolution.

. . . . .

According to neo-Darwinism, living things evolve because natural selection preserves favorable variations and eliminates unfavorable ones. But natural selection cannot create new variations. Instead, these variations are supposedly generated by accidental mutations in DNA.

As critics have pointed out, however, accidental mutations in DNA—like accidental changes in computer programs—are overwhelmingly harmful. The DNA sequences that code for proteins are so complex and specified—like computer code—that accidental changes in them are exceedingly unlikely to produce enough beneficial variations to supply the raw materials for evolution.

The critics are right. But there is a more fundamental reason why DNA mutations are not up to the job: evolution requires changes in the information that directs embryo development, and much of that information is independent of DNA.

This chapter consists of a brief history of how neo-Darwinism came to place so much emphasis on DNA, followed by a survey of the evidence showing why that emphasis is biologically unjustified, and finally by a discussion of the implications for neo-Darwinian theory.

I. Historical Background

When Charles Darwin proposed his theory of evolution in 1859, the theory required a mechanism for organisms to transmit characteristics to their offspring. But Darwin knew of no such mechanism. In 1868 he proposed a theory of "pangenesis," in which "gemmules" throughout the body are supposedly carried in the bloodstream to the reproductive organs, where they blend together in the sperm or egg cells to be transmitted to the next generation.[1] But this was mere speculation; there was no evidence to support it.

A. The Secret of Life?

In 1865, Austrian monk Gregor Mendel announced the results of some hybridization experiments using pea plants. Mendel studied the inheritance of seven traits. Each came in two forms, and Mendel concluded from their patterns of inheritance that one form of each trait was inher-

---

1. Charles Darwin, *The Variation of Animals and Plants under Domestication*, vol. 2 (London: John Murray, 1868), 357.

ited through the male germ cell (pollen) and the other through the female germ cell (ovule). He also concluded that each trait was inherited independently of the other traits, rather than being blended together.

Mendel's work was ignored for decades, until three European scientists took note of it in 1900. In 1905, William Bateson named the study of inheritance "genetics."[2] Soon afterwards, American biologist Walter Sutton and German biologist Theodor Boveri pointed out that during cell division the behavior of chromosomes (thread-like structures in the cell) paralleled the patterns Mendel had observed. Sutton wrote in 1902 that chromosomes "may constitute the physical basis of the Mendelian law of heredity."[3]

In 1909, Danish botanist Wilhelm Johannsen named Mendel's hereditary factors "genes." Johannsen also distinguished between "phenotype" (the observable properties of an individual organism) and "genotype" (the stable underlying biological type).[4] Johannsen (and Bateson) regarded Mendelian genes as abstractions rather than as material entities in chromosomes.

Nevertheless, biologists continued to develop the chromosomal theory of heredity. In 1915, American biologists Thomas Hunt Morgan, Alfred Sturtevant, Hermann Muller, and Calvin Bridges wrote that, although Mendel's theory dealt with hereditary factors in an abstract way, the "chromosomes furnish exactly the kind of mechanism" that Mendel's theory calls for.[5]

Morgan and his colleagues also studied spontaneous changes in the hereditary factors of fruit flies. Adopting a term first introduced by Dutch botanist Hugo De Vries in a different context, Morgan and his colleagues called those spontaneous changes "mutations."

By this time, chromosomes were known to contain two kinds of molecules: protein and deoxyribonucleic acid (DNA). Since proteins

2. William Bateson, letter to Adam Sedgwick (April 18, 1905), available at "William Bateson Letter," *DNA Learning Center*, accessed October 12, 2016, https://www.dnalc.org/view/16195 -gallery-5-william-bateson-letter-page-1.html.

3. Walter S. Sutton, "On the Morphology of the Chromosome Group in *Brachystola magna*," *Biological Bulletin* 4 (1902): 24–39, doi:10.2307/1535510.

4. Nils Roll-Hansen, "Sources of Wilhelm Johannsen's Genotype Theory," *Journal of the History of Biology* 42 (2009): 457–493, doi:10.1007/s10739-008-9166-8.

5. Thomas H. Morgan, Alfred H. Sturtevant, Hermann J. Muller, and Calvin B. Bridges, *The Mechanism of Mendelian Heredity* (New York: Henry Holt, 1915), viii. Available at *Electronic Scholarly Publishing*, accessed October 12, 2016, http://www.esp.org/books/morgan/mechanism /facsimile/index.html.

contain twenty-two subunits (called amino acids), while DNA contains only four (called nucleotides), biologists assumed that DNA was too simple to be the hereditary material and that genes were made of protein.

In 1928, British bacteriologist Frederick Griffith experimented with two strains of pneumonia bacteria, one that actually causes the disease and another that doesn't. He discovered that a substance extracted from the former could turn the latter into the disease-causing strain, and he called this substance the "transforming principle."[6] It seemed that the transforming principle might be the substance of heredity. Then, in 1944, geneticists Oswald Avery, Colin Macleod, and Maclyn McCarty demonstrated experimentally that the transforming principle was not protein, but DNA.

The race was on to discover the structure of DNA and how it could account for heredity. A nucleotide consists of a phosphate molecule bonded to one of four sugars, hence four subunits (called "bases" and abbreviated A, T, C, and G). The phosphate molecules bond to each other, producing a long chain. By the 1950s, X-ray diffraction was being used to study crystallized DNA in order to determine its molecular structure. At the California Institute of Technology, Linus Pauling relied on X-ray diffraction studies of DNA to produce a model of DNA as a triple helix (three linear molecules winding around each other in a spiral pattern) with the phosphate chains on the inside.

Meanwhile, James Watson and Francis Crick worked on the same problem at the Cavendish Laboratory in Cambridge, England. Watson and Crick had better X-ray diffraction data than Pauling, thanks to the work of Rosalind Franklin and John Wilkins at King's College, London. It was clear to Watson and Crick that Pauling's model was incorrect, and they modeled DNA as a double helix with the phosphate chains on the outside and the four bases on the inside. The characteristics of the four bases suggested that an A on one chain would pair preferentially with a T on the other chain, while a C on one chain would pair with a G on the other. This preferential pairing explained certain previously reported characteristics of DNA.

---

6. Frederick Griffith, "The Significance of Pneumococcal Types," *Journal of Hygiene* (London) 27 (1928): 113–159, doi:10.1017/S0022172400031879.

Watson and Crick concluded that they had discovered the chemical structure of the hereditary material. On Saturday, February 28, 1953, they went to celebrate over drinks at a nearby pub, where Crick announced, "We have discovered the secret of life!"[7]

B. The Central Dogma

When they published their model a few months later, Watson and Crick noted that it "suggests a possible copying mechanism for the genetic material."[8] A month after that they elaborated on this:

> Our model for deoxyribonucleic acid is, in effect, a *pair* of templates, each of which is complementary to the other. We imagine that prior to duplication . . . the two chains unwind and separate. Each chain then acts as a template for the formation on to itself for a new companion chain, so that eventually we shall have *two* pairs of chains, where we only had one before. Moreover, the sequence of the pairs of bases will have been duplicated exactly.[9]

In 1958, molecular biologists Matthew Meselson and Franklin Stahl published experimental evidence that DNA molecules duplicate just as Watson and Crick imagined.

In keeping with the growing tendency to treat heredity materialistically, the genotype (which for Johannsen was immaterial) came to mean the whole of an organism's DNA. But if the genotype consisted of DNA, how would it generate the phenotype? In the 1940s, geneticists George Beadle and Edward Tatum had shown experimentally that mutations in a single DNA sequence deprived cells of a particular enzyme. They concluded that "genes act by determining the specificities of enzyme proteins."[10] Their collaborator Norman Horowitz dubbed this the "one gene—one enzyme"

---

7. Horace Freeland Judson, *The Eighth Day of Creation: The Makers of the Revolution in Biology* (New York: Simon & Schuster, 1979), 175.

8. James D. Watson and Francis H. C. Crick, "Molecular Structure of Nucleic Acids: A Structure for Deoxyribose Nucleic Acid," *Nature* 171 (1953): 737–738, doi:10.1038/171737a0.

9. James D. Watson and Francis H. C. Crick, "Genetical Implications of the Structure of Deoxyribonucleic Acid," *Nature* 171 (1953): 964–967, doi:10.1038/171964b0.

10. George W. Beadle and Edward L. Tatum, "Neurospora. II. Methods of Producing and Detecting Mutations Concerned with Nutritional Requirements," *American Journal of Botany* 32 (1945): 678–686, doi:10.2307/2437625.

hypothesis, later generalized to "one gene—one protein" (or one part of a protein).[11]

In 1955, Romanian biologist George Palade discovered microscopic particles in the cell that were later named "ribosomes." Palade and others subsequently showed that ribosomes were the sites of protein synthesis in cells. In 1956, Elliot Volkin and Lazarus Astrachan discovered what they called "DNA-like" ribonucleic acid (RNA), which served as an intermediate between DNA and protein synthesis.[12] French molecular biologists François Jacob and Jacques Monod would later call the DNA-like RNA "messenger RNA."[13]

In 1958, Francis Crick proposed that the specificity of a DNA segment lies solely in its nucleotide sequence, which encodes the nucleotide sequence of a molecule of messenger RNA, which in turn serves as a template for the amino acid sequence of a protein. Crick also proposed that the information encoded in DNA sequences can be transferred from DNA to protein, but not back again. He called the former the "sequence hypothesis" and the latter the "central dogma" of molecular biology.[14] Many writers since then, however, have used "central dogma" to refer to the two proposals together—a practice that is followed in the remainder of this chapter.

As this brief history suggests, there is abundant evidence that DNA carries information encoded in sequences of its four subunits; that the coded information is "transcribed" into messenger RNAs; and that messenger RNAs are then "translated" into proteins. That is, in at least some cases. This evidence has led many people to believe that DNA thereby contains a "genetic program" that specifies the principal features of an organism. According to a 1987 college textbook coauthored by James Watson, "we know that the instructions for how the egg develops into an adult are written in the linear sequence of bases along the DNA."[15] Biologist Francis Collins, appointed in 2009 to be

11. Norman H. Horowitz, "One-Gene-One-Enzyme: Remembering Biochemical Genetics," *Protein Science* 4 (1995): 1017–1019, doi:10.1002/pro.5560040524.

12. Alvin M. Weinberg, "Messenger RNA: Origins of a Discovery," *Nature* 414 (2001): 485.

13. François Jacob and Jacques Monod, "Genetic Regulatory Mechanisms in the Synthesis of Proteins," *Journal of Molecular Biology* 3 (1961): 318–356, doi:10.1016/S0022-2836(61)80072-7.

14. Francis H. C. Crick, "On Protein Synthesis," *Symposia of the Society for Experimental Biology* 12 (1958): 138–163.

15. James D. Watson, Nancy H. Hopkins, Jeffrey W. Roberts, Joan Argetsinger Steitz, and Alan M. Weiner, *Molecular Biology of the Gene*, 4th ed. (Menlo Park, CA: Benjamin/Cummings, 1987), 747.

the director of the U.S. National Institutes of Health, wrote in 2006 that our DNA is an "amazing script, carrying within it all of the instructions for building a human being."[16]

So the central dogma, simply stated, is, "DNA makes RNA makes protein makes us."

There have been many critics of the central dogma. One prominent critic is historian of biology Evelyn Fox Keller, who wrote in 2000,

> The informational content of DNA remains essential—without it, development (life itself) cannot proceed. But current research in a number of biological disciplines has begun to put considerable pressure on biologists to re-conceptualize the program for development as something considerably more complex than a set of instructions written in the 'alphabet of nucleotides'.[17]

Nevertheless, the central dogma has become very popular. One reason is that it is consistent with neo-Darwinian theory. As Jacques Monod once said, with the central dogma "and [with] the understanding of the random physical basis of mutation that molecular biology has also provided, the mechanism of Darwinism is at last securely founded. And man has to understand that he is a mere accident."[18]

C. Epigenetics

Yet all biologists—even those who believe in the central dogma—know that the path from the genotype to the phenotype is affected by other factors. The Greek word "epi" means "above," "on," or "in addition to." In 1942, British biologist Conrad Waddington coined the word "epigenetics" to mean the study of "the processes involved in the mechanism by which the genes of the genotype bring about phenotypic effects."[19] Three years earlier, however, Waddington had used the word "epigenotype" to refer more broadly to "the set of organizers and organizing relations to which a certain piece of tissue will be subject during its development."[20]

---

16. Francis S. Collins, *The Language of God* (New York: Free Press, 2006), 2.
17. Evelyn Fox Keller, *The Century of the Gene* (Cambridge, MA: Harvard University Press, 2000), 87.
18. Judson, *Eighth Day of Creation*, 217.
19. Conrad H. Waddington, "The Epigenotype," *Endeavour* 1 (1942): 18–20.
20. Conrad H. Waddington, *An Introduction to Modern Genetics* (London: George Allen & Unwin, 1939), 156.

So from the beginning, epigenetics has had more than one meaning. In a narrow sense, it refers to the mechanisms by which DNA produces phenotypic effects. In a broad sense, it refers to all of the factors involved in development, one of which is DNA.

Most biologists now use epigenetics in its narrow sense, to refer to heritable changes in a chromosome that do not alter the DNA sequence. In 2007, biologist Julie Kiefer wrote,

> Epigenetics is the study of heritable changes in gene function that occur independently of alterations to primary DNA sequence. The best-studied epigenetic modifications are DNA methylation, and changes in chromatin structure by histone modifications, and histone exchange.[21]

In DNA methylation, a methyl group consisting of a carbon atom and three hydrogen atoms bonds chemically to a base in DNA and thereby affects whether that stretch of DNA is transcribed. Chromatin is the combination of DNA and proteins that makes up a chromosome, and the major proteins are called "histones." Histones compact the long DNA molecule by serving as spools around which DNA winds. Several different molecules can modify histones by binding chemically to them, thereby changing chromosome structure and affecting DNA transcription. Furthermore, there are several kinds of histones with different properties, and molecular "chaperones" can exchange some for others.

DNA methylation, histone modification, and histone exchange help to determine when and where specific parts of a DNA sequence are transcribed into RNA. But epigenetics in this narrow sense leaves the central dogma intact.

Some biologists, however, continue to understand epigenetics more broadly. In 1993, Susan Herring wrote, "Broadly speaking, 'epigenetics' refers to the entire series of interactions among cells and cell products" that leads to embryo development.[22] In 2002, Eva Jablonka and Marion Lamb wrote that epigenetics is "primarily concerned with

21. Julie C. Kiefer, "Epigenetics in Development," *Developmental Dynamics* 236 (2007): 1144–1156, doi:10.1002/dvdy.21094.
22. Susan W. Herring, "Formation of the Vertebrate Face: Epigenetic and Functional Influences," *American Zoologist* 33 (1993): 472–483, doi:10.1093/icb/33.4.472.

the mechanisms through which cells become committed to a particular form or function." They concluded, "Recognizing that there are epigenetic inheritance systems through which non-DNA variations can be transmitted in cell and organismal lineages broadens the concept of heredity and challenges the widely accepted gene-centered neo-Darwinian version of Darwinism."[23]

The broader version of epigenetics implies that there are layers of information in an organism that are independent of DNA sequences. And indeed there are.

II. Why the Central Dogma Fails

According to the central dogma, DNA specifies messenger RNAs, messenger RNAs specify proteins, and proteins specify the organism. Yet many messenger RNAs are not completely specified by DNA sequences, and many proteins are not completely specified by messenger RNAs.

A. DNA Does Not Specify Many RNAs

After a DNA sequence is transcribed into RNA, several processes can modify the RNA so that it does not match the original transcript. Two well-studied processes are RNA splicing and RNA editing.

1. RNA Splicing

In plant and animal cells, most DNA sequences that code for proteins are interrupted by stretches of DNA that do not code for protein. The former are called "exons" and the latter are called "introns." When DNA is transcribed, exons and introns are included in the messenger RNA that will serve as the template for a protein, but the introns are then cut out and the exons are spliced back together.

But one or more of the exons can be duplicated or deleted, so the final messenger RNA has a sequence that no longer corresponds to the original DNA sequence. This is called "alternative splicing," and with it cells can make thousands more messenger RNAs and proteins than

23. Eva Jablonka and Marion J. Lamb, "The Changing Concept of Epigenetics," *Annals of the New York Academy of Sciences* 981 (2002): 82–96, doi:10.1111/j.1749-6632.2002.tb04913.x.

are encoded in DNA sequences. One DNA sequence in fruit flies generates more than 18,000 different proteins through alternative splicing.[24]

In 2010, a team of molecular biologists reported that messenger RNA transcripts "from approximately 95% of multi-exon human genes are spliced in more than one way, and in most cases the resulting transcripts are variably expressed between different cell and tissue types."[25] The diversity produced by alternative splicing has functional consequences. Among other things, alternative splicing regulates physiological changes and nerve development, and it produces enormous diversity in membrane proteins.

2. RNA Editing

In addition to alternative splicing, many animal transcripts undergo RNA editing, which can modify existing nucleotides or insert additional ones. The editing of a messenger RNA can alter the amino acid sequence of the protein it encodes, so that the protein differs from what the DNA sequence would have specified. Recent studies have demonstrated extensive RNA editing in humans.[26]

RNA editing, like RNA splicing, has functional consequences. It is widespread in animal nervous systems, where it modifies messenger RNAs of proteins involved in nerve signaling. In mice, RNA editing is necessary for the survival of stem cells that generate mature blood cells.

A particularly interesting example of functional editing is found in two species of octopus, one living in the Antarctic and the other in the Caribbean. Both species possess very similar DNA sequences for a potassium channel in their cell membranes, but in the Antarctic octopus RNA editing changes a nucleotide in the channel's pore so that it can function better in the extreme cold.[27]

24. Wei Sun, Xintian You, Andreas Gogol-Döring, Haihuai He, Yoshiaki Kise, et al., "Ultra-Deep Profiling of Alternatively Spliced *Drosophila Dscam* Isoforms by Circularization-Assisted Multi-Segment Sequencing," *EMBO Journal* 32 (2013): 2029–2038, doi:10.1038/emboj.2013.144.

25. Yoseph Barash, John A. Calarco, Weijun Gao, Qun Pan, Xinchen Wang, et al., "Deciphering the Splicing Code," *Nature* 465 (2010): 53–59, doi:10.1038/nature09000.

26. Jae Hoon Bahn, Jaegyoon Ahn, Xianzhi Lin, et al., "Genomic Analysis of ADAR1 Binding and Its Involvement in Multiple RNA Processing Pathways," *Nature Communications* 9 (2015): 6355, doi:10.1038/ncomms7355.

27. Sandra Garrett and Joshua J. C. Rosenthal, "RNA Editing Underlies Temperature Adaptation in K+ Channels from Polar Octopuses," *Science* 335 (2012): 848–851, doi:10.1126/science.1212795.

B. Messenger RNAs Do Not Specify the Final Shape of Many Proteins

The function of a protein molecule depends on its three-dimensional shape, which is determined by how the linear molecule folds. Although the amino acid sequence (which is specified by the messenger RNA sequence) often determines the final folded shape, there are many cases in which it does not. Many factors in the cell, including the degree of molecular crowding, can affect the way a protein folds.

Some proteins adopt similar folded forms despite having very different amino acid sequences.[28] Others assume different forms despite having the same or very similar amino acid sequences. Some well-known examples of the latter are prions—misfolded proteins that are pathogenic and heritable. But there are also nonpathogenic proteins in which the same amino acid sequence can fold into more than one shape; these are known as "metamorphic" proteins.[29]

Some proteins are "intrinsically disordered." Approximately 20 to 30 percent of proteins in mammalian cells are inherently devoid of any ordered three-dimensional structure; they adopt folded conformations only after interacting with other molecules.[30] Intrinsically disordered proteins play crucial roles in regulating membrane channels and serving as hubs in intracellular signaling networks.

C. Most Proteins Are Modified by Glycosylation

Finally, most plant and animal proteins are chemically modified after translation by a process called "glycosylation," which involves the addition of "glycans." Glycans (derived from the Greek word for sweet) are composed of many small sugars chemically bonded to each other, and they can be extremely complex.

In living cells, nucleotides in DNA are linked to each other in linear chains; with some exceptions, the same is true for amino acids in proteins. But sugars can be linked to each other in multiple ways.

28. Robert B. Russell and Geoffrey J. Barton, "Structural Features Can Be Unconserved in Proteins with Similar Folds," *Journal of Molecular Biology* 244 (1994): 332–350, doi:10.1006/jmbi.1994.1733.

29. Alexey G. Murzin, "Metamorphic Proteins," *Science* 320 (2008): 1725–1726, doi:10.1126/science.1158868.

30. F. Ulrich Hartl, Andreas Bracher, and Manajit Hayer-Hartl, "Molecular Chaperones in Protein Folding and Proteostasis," *Nature* 475 (2011): 324–332, doi:10.1038/nature10317.

Glucose molecules, for example, can bond to other sugars at six different places. As a result, sugars can form branching chains that are far more elaborate than linear chains of nucleotides or amino acids. Consider molecules containing only six subunits: while four nucleotides can be linked together in various ways to form a maximum of about four thousand different molecules, and twenty-two amino acids can be linked together to form a maximum of about a hundred million different molecules, the dozen or so simple sugars commonly found in living cells can theoretically form more than a trillion different molecules.[31] Clearly, the information-carrying capacity of the glycans in a cell far exceeds the combined capacities of the DNA and the proteins.

In glycosylation, a glycan is first attached to a protein during or after its synthesis. Then complex enzymatic networks, involving dozens of interacting proteins, modify the glycans depending on the needs of the cell. The resulting modifications enable the cell to adapt to a given environment or configure it for a specific stage in embryo development.

The final glycosylated form of a protein is thus very far removed from direct specification by a DNA sequence. As various biochemists have put it, the modification of proteins through enzymatic glycosylation "is an event that reaches beyond the genome."[32] It "provides an additional level of information content in biological systems."[33] Indeed, it may even pave the way for a "quantum mechanics of biology" and a "scientific revolution analogous to the one which transformed the field of physics in the early 20th century."[34]

So the first two steps of the central dogma fail. DNA does not completely specify messenger RNAs, and messenger RNAs do not com-

31. Roger A. Laine, "A Calculation of All Possible Oligosaccharide Isomers Both Branched and Linear Yields 1.05 x 10^{12} Structures for a Reducing Hexasaccharide," *Glycobiology* 4 (1994): 759–767, doi:10.1093/glycob/4.6.759.

32. Robert G. Spiro, "Protein Glycosylation: Nature, Distribution, Enzymatic Formation, and Disease Implications of Glycopeptide Bonds," *Glycobiology* 12 (2002): 43R–56R, doi:10.1093/glycob/12.4.43R.

33. Kelley W. Moremen, Michael Tiemeyer, and Alison V. Nairn, "Vertebrate Protein Glycosylation: Diversity, Synthesis and Function," *Nature Reviews Molecular Cell Biology* 13 (2012): 448–462, doi:10.1038/nrm3383.

34. Gordan Lauc, Aleksandar Vojta, and Vlatka Zoldoš, "Epigenetic Regulation of Glycosylation Is the Quantum Mechanics of Biology," *Biochimica et Biophysica Acta* 1840 (2014): 65–70, doi:10.1016/j.bbagen.2013.08.017.

pletely specify proteins. But the central dogma fails most conclusively in its third and final step: proteins do not specify an organism.

III. The Need for Spatial Information

After RNAs and proteins are synthesized in a cell, many of them must be transported to specific locations in order to function properly. In addition to their protein-coding regions, some messenger RNAs have sequences called "zipcodes" that specify the "address" in the cell to which they are to be transported.[35] Like a postal zipcode, however, a messenger RNA zipcode is meaningless unless it matches a preexisting address.

Cells with nuclei contain microscopic fibers called "microtubules." Molecular motors travel along the microtubules, transporting various cargoes throughout the cell.

Using the postal code metaphor, the molecular motors could be likened to delivery trucks and the microtubules could be likened to a highway system. But destinations for intracellular transport—like the geographical addresses in a postal delivery system—must be specified independently of the cargoes.

In some cases, destinations might be specified by the spatial arrangement of microtubules. In the postal metaphor, cargoes could be dispatched on a particular highway, then carried to the end of the road and simply dropped off. In other cases, destinations are known to be specified by molecules embedded in the cell membrane. Scientists originally thought that proteins could diffuse freely in a membrane, like boats floating in the sea. It is now known, however, that many membrane proteins are arranged in nonrandom patterns that can be quite stable.[36]

In other words, biological membranes carry spatial information. That information is mediated, in part, by a sugar code and a bioelectric code.

A. The Sugar Code

As we saw above, the information-carrying capacity of branched glycans far exceeds the information-carrying capacity of DNA and proteins.

---

35. Robert H. Singer, "RNA Zipcodes for Cytoplasmic Addresses," *Current Biology* 3 (1993): 719–721, doi:10.1016/0960-9822(93)90079-4.
36. Donald M. Engelman, "Membranes Are More Mosaic than Fluid," *Nature* 438 (2005): 578–580, doi:10.1038/nature04394.

There are also long unbranched glycans called "glycosaminoglycans" (GAGs), which occur primarily on the surface of a cell. Although they are unbranched, GAGs can be assembled from dozens of different subunits, and sulfate groups can be attached to them in a wide variety of patterns. This makes GAGs some of "the most information dense molecules in nature."[37] Indeed, the information in branched and unbranched glycans has been called the "sugar code."[38]

Biologist Ronald Schnaar wrote in 1985 that there is "a code on the surface of each cell that specifies its function and directs its interactions with other cells." Schnaar suspected that "sugars serve as the code's alphabet."[39] We now know that he was right. The surfaces of all living cells studied to date are covered with glycans. Cell-surface glycans in early embryos of worms, fruit flies, fish, chicks, and mice change in a highly ordered manner, forming patterns corresponding to specific stages of development. They are involved in cell orientation, migration, adhesion, responses to regulatory factors, and cell-cell communication.

The sugar code is "interpreted" by proteins called lectins, which recognize specific three-dimensional structures of glycans by means of "carbohydrate recognition domains."[40] Lectins specify a wide variety of interactions among cells.

B. The Bioelectric Code

The cell surface code includes more than the sugar code. It has long been known that probably all living cells (not just nerve and muscle cells) generate electric fields across their membranes.[41] In animal cells, a sodium-potassium pump in the membrane moves three sodium ions out of the cell while taking in two potassium ions. This raises the intracellular concentration of potassium ions, which then flow out of

---

37. Jeremy E. Turnbull, "Heparan Sulfate Glycomics: Towards Systems Biology Strategies," *Biochemical Society Transactions* 38 (2010): 1356-60, doi:10.1042/BST0381356.

38. Hans-Joachim Gabius, "Biological Information Transfer beyond the Genetic Code: The Sugar Code," *Naturwissenschaften* 87 (2000): 108–121, doi:10.1007/s001140050687.

39. Ronald L. Schnaar, "The Membrane Is the Message," *The Sciences* (May–June 1985): 34–40.

40. Kurt Drickamer, "Two Distinct Classes of Carbohydrate-Recognition Domains in Animal Lectins," *Journal of Biological Chemistry* 263 (1988): 9557–9560, doi:10.1146/annurev.cb.09.110193.001321.

41. Harold S. Burr and Filmer S. C. Northrop, "Evidence for the Existence of an Electro-Dynamic Field in Living Organisms," *Proceedings of the National Academy of Sciences USA* 25 (1939): 284–288, doi:10.1073/pnas.25.6.284.

the cell through ion-selective channels in the membrane. The combined action of sodium-potassium pumps and potassium "leak" channels makes the interior of the cell electrically negative with respect to the exterior. The result is an endogenous electric field.

The patterns of ion channels in membranes determine the forms of endogenous electric fields, which change in the course of embryo development. The endogenous electric field of a frog egg drives an ionic current through the egg. As the fertilized egg divides, and its cells rearrange themselves to form a tadpole, the electric field changes in organized ways. The same is true of chick embryos.[42] In frog, chick, and mouse embryos, the future sites of limb development are marked by strong outward currents before the limbs appear.[43]

How do endogenous electric fields influence embryo development? One way is probably by directing cell movements. Biologists have applied artificial electric fields of physiological strength to embryonic cells and observed that some types of cells migrated toward one pole or the other. Electric fields of physiological strength can also affect cell division.[44]

Strong evidence that endogenous electric fields play significant roles in embryo development comes from artificially disrupting them and then observing the effects. Reducing an ion current associated with tail development in chick embryos results in tail abnormalities.[45] Manipulating ion channels that generate an electric field associated with eye patterning in frog embryos results in deformed or missing eyes, or tadpoles with eyes located on the side or tail.[46]

So endogenous electric fields are certainly involved in embryo development. Riyi Shi and Richard Borgens reviewed the experimental

---

42. Richard Nuccitelli, "Endogenous Electric Fields in Embryos during Development, Regeneration and Wound Healing," *Radiation Protection Dosimetry* 106 (2003): 375–383, doi:10.1093/oxfordjournals.rpd.a006375.

43. Alicia M. Altizer, Loren J. Moriarty, Sheila M. Bell, et al., "Endogenous Electric Current Is Associated with Normal Development of the Vertebrate Limb," *Developmental Dynamics* 221 (2001): 391–401, doi:10.1002/dvdy.1158.

44. Colin D. McCaig, Bing Song, and Ann M. Rajnicek, "Electrical Dimensions in Cell Science," *Journal of Cell Science* 122 (2009): 4267–4276, doi:10.1242/jcs.023564.

45. Kevin B. Hotary and Kenneth R. Robinson, "Evidence of a Role for Endogenous Electrical Fields in Chick Embryo Development," *Development* 114 (1992): 985–996.

46. Vaibhav P. Pai, Sherry Aw, Tal Shomrat, Joan M. Lemire, and Michael Levin, "Transmembrane Voltage Potential Controls Embryonic Eye Patterning in *Xenopus laevis*," *Development* 139 (2012): 313–323, doi:10.1242/dev.073759.

evidence in 1995 and concluded that such fields "may provide a three dimensional coordinate system" that helps to specify form in embryos.[47] Michael Levin argues that endogenous electric fields may function as "templates of shape" and "it is likely that a full understanding of [development] . . . and its informational content will need to involve cracking the bioelectric code."[48]

IV. Implications for Neo-Darwinism

So membrane patterns carry essential biological information. Yet that information cannot be reduced to sequence information in DNA. Even if DNA sequences completely specified messenger RNAs and proteins, the spatial distribution of proteins in the cell membrane must be specified independently, like addresses in the postal metaphor. So, what specifies membrane patterns?

A. Membrane Heredity

Some membrane patterns are templated by the membranes from which they are derived in the course of division. In such cases, proteins from the cell interior are incorporated during membrane growth only if they match the existing matrix.[49] Biologist Robert Poyton proposed that biological membranes carry "spatial memory," the units of which are spatially localized multi-subunit proteins. As a membrane grows in preparation for division, the proteins dissociate into their subunits. Newly synthesized subunits in the cytoplasm then associate with the older subunits to form hybrid proteins that are chemically identical to the original proteins and preserve the original spatial pattern. Poyton concluded, "Realizing that genetic memory is one-dimensional, along a DNA molecule, whereas spatial memory is likely to be two-dimensional, along membrane surfaces, and three-dimensional within the cellular interior, it is probable that spatial memory is more complicated

47. Riyi Shi and Richard B. Borgens, "Three-Dimensional Gradients of Voltage during Development of the Nervous System as Invisible Coordinates for the Establishment of Embryonic Pattern," *Developmental Dynamics* 202 (1995): 101–114, doi:10.1002/aja.1002020202.

48. Michael Levin, "Morphogenetic Fields in Embryogenesis, Regeneration, and Cancer: Non-Local Control of Complex Patterning," *BioSystems* 109 (2012): 243–261, doi:10.1016/j.biosystems.2012.04.005.

49. George E. Palade, "Membrane Biogenesis: An Overview," *Methods in Enzymology* 96 (1983): xxix-lv, doi:10.1016/S0076-6879(83)96004-4.

and diverse than genetic memory."[50] Subsequent research has found evidence consistent with Poyton's hypothesis.[51]

Cell surface templating has been well studied in single-celled organisms called "protozoa." Some protozoa are covered with cilia, tiny hairs on the cell surface that beat rhythmically for locomotion and feeding. More than fifty years ago, researchers discovered that if they artificially altered the pattern of cilia, the offspring of a dividing cell could inherit the altered pattern even though the DNA was unchanged. Since then, ciliated protozoa with artificially altered patterns have been stably maintained in laboratories for thousands of generations.[52]

Stephen Ng and Joseph Frankel studied this phenomenon and concluded in 1977, "The cell as an architect thus not only makes use of the genomic information to produce the appropriate building blocks, but, in addition, also arranges the building blocks according to the blueprint as defined in the preexisting architecture."[53]

Such templating is not limited to protozoa. In 1990, Michael Locke studied patterns in caterpillar epidermis cells and concluded that their inheritance "requires more than number and kind of molecule. The duplication of pattern involves relative position and orientation," factors that "cannot be specified only by a base sequence."[54]

Cells with nuclei contain many different types of membranes, which Thomas Cavalier-Smith has collectively designated the "membranome." Each membrane is characterized not only by its chemistry but also by its surface pattern. Cavalier-Smith called membranes that arise by growth and division of the same type "genetic membranes." If any type of genetic membrane were lost, it could probably not be regenerated from its constituent molecules—even if all of the DNA sequences

50. Robert O. Poyton, "Memory and Membranes: The Expression of Genetic and Spatial Memory during the Assembly of Organelle Macrocompartments," *Modern Cell Biology* 2 (1983): 15–72.

51. Jonathan Wells, "Membrane Patterns Carry Ontogenetic Information that Is Specified Independently of DNA," *BIO-Complexity* 2014, no. 2 (2014): 1–28, doi:10.5048/BIO-C.2014.2.

52. Gary W. Grimes and Karl J. Aufderheide, *Cellular Aspects of Pattern Formation: The Problem of Assembly* (Basel: Karger, 1991).

53. Stephen F. Ng and Joseph Frankel, "180° Rotation of Ciliary Rows and Its Morphogenetic Implications in *Tetrahymena pyriformis*," *Proceedings of the National Academy of Sciences USA* 74 (1977): 1115–1118, doi:10.1073/pnas.74.3.1115.

54. Michael Locke, "Is There Somatic Inheritance of Intracellular Patterns?" *Journal of Cell Science* 96 (1990): 563–567. http://jcs.biologists.org/content/joces/96/4/563.full.pdf.

encoding its proteins remained—because the requisite spatial pattern would be gone.

Thus, according to Cavalier-Smith, the idea that the genome contains all the information needed to make an organism

> is simply false. Membrane heredity, by providing chemically specific two-dimensional surfaces with mutually conserved topological relationships in the three spatial dimensions, plays a key role in the mechanisms that convert the linear information of DNA into the three-dimensional shapes of single cells and multicellular organisms. Animal development creates a complex three-dimensional multicellular organism not by starting from the linear information in DNA . . . but always starting from an already highly complex three-dimensional unicellular organism, the fertilized egg.[55]

But membrane heredity cannot be the whole story. In the course of embryo development, most cells do not simply duplicate the membrane patterns of the cells from which they are derived. Membrane patterns are very different in nerve cells, muscle cells, blood cells, bone cells, and liver cells—to name only a few—so membrane patterns have to change during development. The changes are not haphazard, however; they are highly regulated to generate the integrated organ systems of the adult. If membrane patterns are not specified by DNA sequences or by membrane patterns in the cells from which they are derived, how are they specified?

B. A Mathematical Approach

The short answer is: we don't know yet. But theoretical biologists have been addressing the problem mathematically. In the 1950s, Nicolas Rashevsky and Robert Rosen introduced a new approach to the study of living things that they called "relational biology." Instead of giving ontological priority to molecules such as DNA, relational biology (as the name implies) gives ontological priority to the relations that constitute an organized system.[56]

---

55. Thomas Cavalier-Smith, "The Membranome and Membrane Heredity in Development and Evolution," in *Organelles, Genomes and Eukaryote Phylogeny*, ed. Robert P. Hirt and David S. Horner (Boca Raton, FL: CRC Press, 2004), 335–351.

56. Robert Rosen, *Life Itself* (New York: Columbia University Press, 1991).

To make their approach rigorous, Rashevsky and Rosen turned to a branch of mathematics called "category theory" that had been developed in the 1940s. A generalization of classical set theory, category theory can be used to model mathematically the transformations of information that occur in living things. The theory has subsequently been extended by others, including Rosen's student Aloisius Louie[57] and systems biologist Richard Sternberg.[58]

Category theory has been applied to cognitive neuroscience by Steven Phillips and his colleagues[59] and by Andrée Ehresmann and Jaime Gomez-Ramirez,[60] though whether relational biology and category theory will succeed in explaining transformations during embryo development is not yet clear.

What is clear, however, is that neo-Darwinism fails to explain evolution.

C. Why Neo-Darwinism Fails

According to neo-Darwinian theory, DNA mutations supply the raw materials for evolution. If the central dogma were true, this might be the case. But the dogma that "DNA makes RNA makes protein makes us" fails at every step. Many RNAs are modified to the point where they no longer reflect the base sequence of the DNA from which they were transcribed. And the final folded shape of a protein—on which its function depends—is in some cases not fully specified by the messenger RNA from which it is translated. Furthermore, most proteins are extensively modified by glycosylation, the addition of complex sugars by networks of enzymes. So the final products of transcription and translation are usually very far from being specified by DNA sequences.

An even more serious problem for the central dogma is that proteins must be properly localized in a cell in order for them to function

---

57. Aloisius H. Louie, *More than Life Itself: A Synthetic Continuation in Relational Biology* (Frankfurt: Ontos, 2009).

58. Richard V. Sternberg, "DNA Codes and Information: Formal Structures and Relational Causes," *Acta Biotheoretica* 56 (2008): 205–232, doi:10.1007/s10441-008-9049-6.

59. Steven Phillips, Yuji Takeda, and Archana Singh, "Visual Feature Integration Indicated by pHase-Locked Frontal-Parietal EEG Signals," *PLoS One* 7 (2012): e32502, doi:10.1371/journal.pone.0032502.

60. Andrée C. Ehresmann and Jaime Gomez-Ramirez, "Conciliating Neuroscience and Phenomenology via Category Theory," *Progress in Biophysics and Molecular Biology* (2015): 347–359, doi:10.1016/j.pbiomolbio.2015.07.004.

properly. But DNA does not specify spatial coordinates. Instead, they are specified by the architecture of the cell and by patterns in the membrane that precede transcription and translation. So even if DNA completely specified the final form of proteins, there must still be information that is independent of the DNA.

It is true that some DNA mutations can be beneficial to an organism in a particular environment. For example, the antibiotic streptomycin poisons tuberculosis bacteria by targeting their ribosomes and thereby blocking protein synthesis, but DNA mutations that slightly damage the ribosomes can prevent the antibiotic from recognizing them. Although the mutant bacteria are damaged, in the presence of the antibiotic they are better off than undamaged bacteria.

But damaging a ribosome is very different from producing the beneficial new variations in embryo development that could supply raw materials for evolution. Biologists have searched systematically for mutations that affect the development of fruit flies, roundworms, zebrafish, and mice. The effects of such mutations always fall into one of three categories. Either the embryo manages to overcome the effect of a mutation and develops normally; or the embryo is deformed, often in grotesque ways; or the embryo dies. So to judge from the available evidence, mutating the DNA of a fruit fly embryo leads to only three possible outcomes: a normal fruit fly, a defective fruit fly, or a dead fruit fly. Hardly the raw materials for evolution.

8

Theistic Evolution and the Extended Evolutionary Synthesis: Does It Work?

STEPHEN C. MEYER, ANN K. GAUGER, AND PAUL A. NELSON[1]

SUMMARY

For nearly two decades, many evolutionary biologists have been working to formulate new theories of evolution, in part because of the recognition that neo-Darwinian mechanisms cannot explain the origin of living things. These new ideas supposedly have more creative power than mutation and natural selection alone. This chapter will examine these new evolutionary theories and mechanisms and will show that the so-called "extended synthesis" has also not succeeded because it does not account for the origin of biological form and information. The "extended synthesis" leaves unanswered many of the same problems as neo-Darwinism and raises the same question to theistic evolutionists. Why insist on synthesizing Christian theology, or a biblical understanding of creation, with a scientifically failing theory of origins?

. . . . .

1. In this chapter we have adapted material that was previously published in chapters 15 and 16 of Stephen C. Meyer's book, *Darwin's Doubt: The Explosive Origin of Animal Life and the Case for Intelligent Design* (New York: HarperOne, 2014).

I. Introduction

Charles Darwin knew that his young and ambitious theory of 1859 needed help. By the time the sixth edition of the *Origin of Species* was published in 1872, Darwin had gone far beyond the elegant simplicity of the processes of random variation and natural selection. So extensively did Darwin modify his theory, in fact, that the sixth edition contained many hundreds of entirely new sentences, making the last edition "nearly a third again as long as the first."[2]

The project of reforming evolutionary theory, started by Darwin himself, has become an ongoing, even flourishing, industry. Throughout the twentieth century, and now into the twenty-first, biologists have proposed one revision after another to Darwin's core concepts of randomly arising variations being sifted by natural selection. Consider one such proposed revision: in October 2014, the science journal *Nature* featured a print debate under the title, "Does Evolutionary Theory Need a Rethink?", with eight prominent evolutionary biologists answering in the affirmative, and calling for an "extended evolutionary synthesis" (EES) to remedy the shortcomings of standard neo-Darwinian theory.[3] (Elsewhere in this volume, we and other authors have explained many of those shortcomings.) Could the new EES, however, overcome the problems with the standard theory?[4]

Moreover, the skeptical scientists writing in the issue of *Nature* mentioned above are by no means the only scientists doubting the creative power of the mutation/selection mechanism. At a recent (November 2016) conference of the Royal Society of London, called largely to address problems in the standard theory,[5] Austrian evolutionary biolo-

---

2. Morse Peckham, "Introduction," *The Origin of Species: A Variorum Text* (Philadelphia: University of Pennsylvania Press, 2006), 9.

3. Kevin Laland, Tobias Uller, Marc Feldman, et al., "Does Evolutionary Theory Need a Rethink? Yes, Urgently," *Nature* 514 (2014): 161–164.

4. Chapter 2 showed that *neo*-Darwinism, itself a product of the need to revise Darwin's original theory, encounters severe difficulties. As formulated during the middle decades of the twentieth century, neo-Darwinism supplemented natural selection by identifying *mutations*—naturally caused errors in DNA sequences—as the raw materials on which selection operated. Yet randomly arising mutations tend to degrade genetic sequences, and do not provide an even remotely plausible mechanism for generating *new* genetic information sufficient to produce the novel functional protein folds necessary for any significant evolutionary innovation. Moreover, natural selection acting on random mutations cannot generate new body plans. As Jonathan Wells showed in chapter 7, the origin of the *epigenetic* (literally, "beyond genetics") information needed for novel body plans lies in principle beyond the reach of mutations to DNA sequences.

5. This Royal Society of London conference, held November, 7–9, 2016, illustrated the degree to which the neo-Darwinian paradigm is being challenged. The description of the conference, titled

gist Gerd Müller began the conference by outlining "the explanatory deficits" of neo-Darwinism, including its inability to explain the "origin of phenotypic complexity" and the "origin of phenotypic novelties." He and coauthor Stuart Newman have elsewhere argued that neo-Darwinism has "no theory of the generative."[6] Other biologists have explained that mutation and selection can account for "the survival, but not the arrival of the fittest"—that is, minor but not major changes.[7]

Accordingly, many evolutionary biologists, including many present at the Royal Society Conference, are now attempting to develop new theories of evolution based on various newly proposed evolutionary mechanisms as part of an extended evolutionary synthesis. So does this new EES solve the problems associated with the standard theory?

Many theistic evolutionists have argued as much and have appealed to the hopeful promise of the EES. After acknowledging weaknesses in the standard theory, Wheaton College philosopher of science (and theistic evolutionist) Robert Bishop argues that, under the revised framework of the EES, while "the overall picture of evolution is still one of variations filtered by natural selection," new discoveries show how "developmental biology mediates between the functional biology of gene expression, cells, and anatomy . . . and the changes in gene frequencies of evolutionary biology."[8] These findings will lead to a more adequate theory of evolution overall. In short, Bishop concludes,

> The more accurate picture of the evolutionary and developmental biology literatures . . . is that evolutionary development and

---

"New Trends in Evolutionary Biology: Biological, Philosophical and Social Science Perspectives" was quite revealing:

> Developments in evolutionary biology and adjacent fields have produced calls for revision of the standard theory of evolution, although the issues involved remain hotly contested. This meeting will present these developments and arguments in a form that will encourage cross-disciplinary discussion . . .

This meeting stirred some debate among evolutionary biologists. At the meeting, advocates of EES called for a large-scale overhaul of standard evolutionary theory, while a few old school neo-Darwinian evolutionary biologists firmly insisted that all the proposals of the extended synthesis added nothing new to evolutionary theory.

6. Gerd Müller and Stuart Newman, *On the Origin of Organismal Form* (Boston: MIT Press, 2003).

7. See Hans Driesch, *Species and Varieties: Their Origin by Mutation* ([Chicago: Open Court, 1904], 826).

8. Robert Bishop, "The Extended Synthesis (Reviewing 'Darwin's Doubt': Robert Bishop, Part 1)," *BioLogos*, September 1, 2014, accessed July 19, 2016, http://biologos.org/blogs/archive/the-extended-synthesis-reviewing-darwins-doubt-robert-bishop-part-1.

epigenetics along with other sources of genetic variation and natural selection are being forged into a new synthesis giving us insight into how both microevolution and macroevolution happen.[9]

If Bishop is right, doubters of neo-Darwinian theory may have been hasty in passing judgment on the theory. The extended evolutionary synthesis will amend the defects of the textbook account, and materialistic or naturalistic evolutionary explanation broadly conceived will continue happily on its way.

Or not. In this chapter, we examine the claims made on behalf of the EES. We show that the problems with standard evolutionary theory—or SET (an acronym devised by EES proponents themselves)—persist in another form within the extended evolutionary synthesis, because those problems actually stem from the materialist foundations shared by both SET and the EES. Textbook theory and the EES are, at day's end, not so very different after all, meaning that the reforms promised by EES advocates do little or nothing to open up biological inquiry where it genuinely needs a thoroughgoing, deep, and comprehensive reformation. That such a reformation *is* needed is stated by EES advocates in the plainest possible language. Evolutionary biologist Adi Livnat, for instance, at the Institute of Evolution of the University of Haifa, writes bluntly of SET's explanatory failures:

> The modern evolutionary synthesis [SET] leaves unresolved some of the most fundamental, long-standing questions in evolutionary biology: What is the role of sex in evolution? How does complex adaptation evolve? How can selection operate effectively on genetic interactions? More recently, the molecular biology and genomics revolutions have raised a host of critical new questions, through empirical findings that the modern synthesis fails to explain: for example, the discovery of *de novo* genes; the immense constructive role of transposable elements in evolution; genetic variance and biochemical activity that go far beyond what traditional natural selection can maintain; perplexing cases of molecular parallelism; and more.[10]

9. Ibid.

10. Adi Livnat, "Interaction-Based Evolution: How Natural Selection and Nonrandom Mutation Work Together," *Biology Direct* 8 (2013): 24.

But while many of the new mechanisms described by proponents of the extended evolutionary synthesis describe real biological phenomena—including phenomena not captured by neo-Darwinism—each of these proposed new mechanisms still fails to explain the origin of the genetic and/or epigenetic information necessary to produce new forms of animal life. Thus, the question we posed to theistic evolutionists who appropriate the neo-Darwinian mechanism will apply equally to theistic evolutionists who appropriate the EES: if the evolutionary mechanisms posited lack the creative power to produce new biological form and information, why say that these mechanisms represent God's way of creating new forms of life?

II. The Three Pillars of Neo-Darwinism, and the EES Alternatives

The neo-Darwinian mechanism rests on three core claims: first, that evolutionary change occurs as the result of random, minute variations (or mutations); second, that the process of natural selection sifts among those variations and mutations, favoring those that increase fitness (i.e., confer greater reproductive success) and eliminating those that diminish the fitness of the organisms that possess them; and third, that favored variations in the competition for survival are passed on and inherited in subsequent generations of organisms, thus causing the population to change or evolve over time. Biologists John Gerhart and Mark Kirschner called these three elements—variation, natural selection, and heritability—the three pillars of neo-Darwinian evolution.[11] We shall organize our discussion of the extended evolutionary synthesis around these three key premises of the standard theory.

In one or another respect, the diverse proposals made under the EES heading depart from these premises, either singly or in combination. Yet, we will argue that, in so doing, these proposals do not solve the problem of the origin of biological information (either genetic or epigenetic) necessary to build novel forms of life. To see why, let's examine several of the new mechanisms that have been proposed ei-

---

11. John Gerhart and Marc Kirschner, *The Plausibility of Life: Resolving Darwin's Dilemma* (New Haven, CT: Yale University Press, 2005), 10.

ther to supplement or to replace the mutation/selection mechanism of standard neo-Darwinian theory.

III. New Theories of Evolution: The EES Alternatives

A. Evolutionary Developmental Biology (Evo-Devo)

Standard neo-Darwinian theory since the 1930s has emphasized that large-scale macroevolutionary change occurs as the inevitable by-product of the accumulation of small-scale "microevolutionary" changes in gene frequencies within populations.

The consensus in support of this idea began to fray within evolutionary biology during the early 1970s, when young paleontologists such as Stephen Jay Gould, Niles Eldredge, and Steven Stanley realized that the fossil record did not show a pattern of gradual, "micro-to-macro" change. In 1980, at a now-famous symposium on macroevolution at the Field Museum in Chicago, the rebellion against the neo-Darwinian consensus burst into full view, exposing what developmental biologist Scott Gilbert[12] called "an underground current in evolutionary theory" among theorists who had concluded that "macroevolution could not be derived from microevolution."[13]

At the conference, paleontologists who doubted the "micro-to-macro" consensus found allies among younger developmental biologists. They were dissatisfied with neo-Darwinism in part because they knew that population genetics—the mathematical expression of neo-Darwinian theory—sought only to quantify changes in gene frequency, rather than explain either the origin of genes or novel body plans. Thus, many developmental biologists thought that neo-Darwinian theory did not offer a compelling theory of *macro*evolution.[14]

To formulate a more robust theory, many developmental biologists urged evolutionary theorists to incorporate insights from their discipline. And indeed, by the beginning of the 1990s, a wave of books and articles on evolutionary developmental biology ("evo-

---

12. S. F. Gilbert et al., "Resynthesizing Evolutionary and Developmental Biology," *Developmental Biology* 173 (1996): 362.

13. Ibid.

14. Michael Palopoli and Nipam Patel, "Neo-Darwinian Developmental Evolution: Can We Bridge the Gap between Pattern and Process?" *Current Opinion in Genetics and Development* 6 (1996): 502.

devo") swept through the evolutionary world,[15] proposing the idea that evolution need not proceed only by incremental small-scale mutations. Instead, evo-devo advocates emphasized that mutations in the genes that control animal development might have a disproportionately large effect on animal development and thus could also play a significant role in modifying animal body plans. Evo-devo advocates thus broke ranks with classical neo-Darwinism primarily in their understanding of the size or increment of evolutionary change. Because they think that mutations that are expressed early in the development of animals are necessary to alter body plan morphogenesis, they argue that mutations must have played a significant role in generating *large-scale* change and, indeed, whole new animal forms during the history of life. Some evo-devo advocates, such as Sean Carroll and Jeffrey Schwartz,[16] have pointed specifically to homeotic (or *Hox*) genes, master regulatory genes that affect the location, timing, and expression of other genes, as entities capable of producing such large-scale change.

So does the "evo-devo" approach explain the large-scale changes in biological form or the origin of new animal body plans?

Major but Not Viable; Viable but Not Major

Despite the enthusiasm surrounding the field, evolutionary developmental biology fails, and for an obvious reason: the main proposal of the evolutionary developmental biologists, that early-acting developmental mutations can cause stable, heritable, large-scale changes in animal body plans, contradicts the results of a hundred years of mutagenesis experiments on organisms such as fruit flies[17] and nematodes (roundworms). As we saw in chapter 2, the experiments of scientists

---

15. Rudolf A. Raff, *The Shape of Life: Genes, Development, and the Evolution of Animal Form* (Chicago: University of Chicago Press, 1996); Jeffrey H. Schwartz, "Homeobox Genes, Fossils, and the Origin of Species," *The Anatomical Record* 257 (1999): 15–31; Schwartz, *Sudden Origins: Fossils, Genes, and the Emergence of Species* (New York: Wiley, 1999); Brian C. Goodwin, *How the Leopard Changed Its Spots: The Evolution of Complexity* (New York: Scribner, 1994); Sean B. Carroll, *Endless Forms Most Beautiful: The New Science of Evo Devo* (New York: Norton, 2006).

16. Schwartz, "Homeobox Genes, Fossils, and the Origin of Species," *The Anatomical Record* 257 (1999): 15–31; Schwartz, *Sudden Origins*; Goodwin, *How the Leopard Changed Its Spots*; Carroll, *Endless Forms Most Beautiful.*

17. Experimental mutagenesis of fruit flies (*Drosophila melanogaster*) began in earnest at Columbia University, in the breeding laboratories of Thomas H. Morgan and others, during the first decade of the twentieth century (1900–1910).

such as Christiane Nüsslein-Volhard and Eric Wieschaus have shown definitively that early-acting body plan mutations invariably generate embryonic lethals, that is, dead animals incapable of further evolution. In order to generate a genuinely new body plan—of the magnitude of the difference between, say, a sea urchin and a crab, a horse or a fish—early embryonic changes must take place. Yet any mutation acting early enough to cause a substantial change in body plan always results in a dead embryo. Indeed, in their Nobel Prize–winning work, Nüsslein-Volhard and Wieschaus observed that early developmental mutants never hatched as larvae.[18] Though these mutants exhibited dramatic changes to their body plans (both in number of segments and their polarity) they were evolutionary dead ends. Dead embryos can't reproduce, and without reproduction there can be no natural selection or evolutionary change.

Moreover, the same proved true of other species that have been studied, from the nematode to the mouse. Either a mutation has relatively minor effects on an animal's body plan so that it survives well enough to reproduce, or a mutation has major consequences and the animal does not survive. This generates a dilemma: early-acting body plan mutations are eliminated immediately by natural selection because of their invariably destructive consequences. Later-acting mutations can generate viable changes in the features of animals, but these changes do not affect body plan or global animal architectures. Major change is not viable; viable change is not major.[19, 20]

---

18. Christiane Nüsslein-Volhard and Eric Wieschaus, "Mutations Affecting Segment Number and Polarity in *Drosophila*," *Nature* 287 (1980): 796.

19. Stephen C. Meyer et al., *Explore Evolution: The Arguments for and against Neo-Darwinism* (Melbourne and London: Hill House, 2007), 108.

20. Even *cis*-regulatory elements (or "CREs"), which are believed to be responsible for most evolutionary change, are not sufficient, despite the claims made by a paper in the *Proceedings of the National Academy of Sciences* by three developmental biologists, Benjamin Prud'homme, Nicolas Gompel, and Sean B. Carroll. (CREs are sequences in the DNA near genes that code for protein that help to regulate how much protein is made). The paper by Prud'homme, Gompel, and Carroll states that changes in *cis*-regulatory DNA produce "both relatively modest morphological differences among closely related species and more profound anatomical divergences among groups at higher taxonomical levels." Those "profound anatomical divergences" were not observed, however. Instead, the study conducted by Prud'homme and his colleagues only showed how changes in the *cis*-regulatory elements (CREs) in DNA affected the *coloration* of wing spots in several different types of flying insects. It did not report any significant change in the form or body plan of these insects. Thus, their study illustrated a clear case of a viable type of mutation generating a minor change, indeed, only *very* "modest morphological differences," not changes to body shape or segmental identity. Thus, Prud'homme et al. observed only cases of minor, viable mutations that affected only the most superficial of traits despite their claims to the contrary. See: Prud'homme,

What about *Hox* Genes?

Hox [or homeotic] genes encode proteins that regulate the expression of other genes during animal development. Because they influence the pattern of development along the head-to-tail axis of the body, specifying different structures in different body segments, many evo-devo theorists think that *Hox* genes can be mutated to generate large-scale changes (macro-mutations) in animal form.

For example, Jeffrey Schwartz at the University of Pittsburgh, in his book *Sudden Origins*, argues that *Hox* mutations may be responsible for sudden change in the fossil record. He says,

> . . . we are still in the dark about the origin of most major groups of organisms. They appear in the fossil record as Athena did from the head of Zeus—full-blown and raring to go, in contradiction to Darwin's depiction of evolution as resulting from the gradual accumulation of countless infinitesimally minute variations. . . . [21]

His answer to this conundrum is to claim that "a mutation affecting the activity of a homeobox [*Hox*] gene can have a profound effect—such as turning . . . larval tunicates into the first chordates. Clearly, the potential homeobox genes have for enacting what we call evolutionary change would seem to be almost unfathomable."[22]

But there are several good reasons to doubt this claim.

First, precisely *because Hox* genes coordinate the expression of so many other different genes, experimentally generated mutations in *Hox* genes have proven harmful. As McGinnis and Kurziora note, "most mutations in homeotic [*Hox*] genes cause fatal birth defects."[23] In fruit flies, for instance, by mutating a *Hox* gene, biologists have produced the dramatic *Antennapedia* mutant, a hapless fly with legs growing out of its head where the antennae should be.[24] The *Antennapedia*

Gompel, and Carroll, "Emerging Principles of Regulatory Evolution," *Proceedings of the National Academy of Sciences USA* 104 (2007): 8605–8612; Hoekstra and Coyne, "The Locus of Evolution: Evo Devo and the Genetics of Adaptation," *Evolution* 61 (2007): 995–1016.

21. Schwartz, *Sudden Origins*, 3.

22. Ibid., 13. According to Schwartz, "At the genetic level, major morphological novelty can indeed be accomplished in the twinkling of an eye. All that is necessary is that homeobox genes are either turned on or they are not" (ibid., 362).

23. William McGinnis and Michael Kurziora, "The Molecular Architects of Body Design," *Scientific American* 270 (1994): 58–66.

24. Dan L. Lindsley and E. H. Grell, *Guide to Genetic Variations of Drosophila Melanogaster*, Carnegie Institution of Washington, no. 627, available at www.carnegiescience.edu/publications _online/genetic_variations.pdf.

mutant cannot survive in the wild; it has difficulty reproducing; and its offspring die easily.

Second, *Hox* genes in all animal forms are expressed well after the body plan is established. In fruit flies, by the time that *Hox* genes are expressed, roughly six thousand cells have already formed, and the basic geometry of the fly—its anterior and posterior and dorsal and ventral axes—is already well established. For this reason, *Hox* genes do not and cannot determine body plan formation. Eric Davidson and Douglas Erwin have pointed out that *Hox* gene expression, while necessary for correct *regional* or local differentiation within a body plan (for example, the refinements of limb development in both arthropods and chordates), occurs much later during embryogenesis than global body plan specification itself, which is regulated by entirely different genes. Thus, the primary origin of animal body plans is not a question of *Hox* gene action, but of the appearance of much deeper control elements—what Davidson calls the core "developmental gene regulatory networks" (dGRNs).[25] Yet, as we saw in chapter 2, Davidson has demonstrated that altering developmental gene regulatory networks invariably shuts down embryological animal development in animals.

Third, *Hox* genes only provide information for building proteins that function as switches that turn other genes on and off. The genes that they regulate contain information for building proteins that form the parts of other structures and organs. The *Hox* genes themselves, however, do not contain information for building these structural parts: in other words, mutations in *Hox* genes do not have all the *genetic* information necessary to generate new tissues, organs, or body plans—thus, mutating them could not possibly generate new forms of animal life.

Nevertheless, Jeffrey Schwartz argues that *Hox* mutations can explain the origin of complex structures such as the eye, as well as how organs might have been arranged to form new body plans.[26] Yet other prominent biologists find his reasoning unconvincing for precisely the reasons just stated. In review of Schwartz's book in *Nature*, theoreti-

25. Eric Davidson and Douglas Erwin, "An Integrated View of Precambrian Eumetazoan Evolution," *Cold Spring Harbor Symposia on Quantitative Biology* 74 (2009): 1–16.
26. Jeffrey Schwartz, *Sudden Origins*.

cal biologist Eörs Szathmáry, for example, notes that *Hox* genes don't code for the proteins out of which body parts are made. It follows, he insists, that mutations in *Hox* genes cannot by themselves build new body parts or body plans.[27] Though Schwartz says he has "marveled" at "the importance of homeobox genes in helping us to understand the basics of evolutionary change,"[28] Szathmáry doubts that mutations in these genes have much creative power. After asking whether Schwartz explains the origin of new forms of life by appealing to mutations in *Hox* genes, Szathmáry concludes, "I'm afraid, he does not."[29]

To address the problem of explaining the origin of new body plans and other large-scale innovations in the history of life, evo-devo advocates have abandoned the idea that small, incremental variations and mutations are sufficient to produce the necessary evolutionary change. Instead, they have revived the idea of macro-mutations, revisiting an old idea associated with evolutionary geneticist Richard Goldschmidt and often referred to as the "hopeful monster" theory. Nevertheless, with this proposal a long-appreciated dilemma has also reemerged—major mutational change is not viable, while viable change is not major. Thus, evolutionary developmental biology, perhaps the most celebrated version of the extended evolutionary synthesis, has not succeeded in accounting for the origin of novel biological form.

B. Self-Organization

Another attempt to modify standard neo-Darwinian theory also gained prominence in the 1990s as the result of the work of a group of scientists associated with a think tank in New Mexico called the Santa Fe Institute. The scientists there developed a new theoretical approach that they called "self-organization."

Whereas neo-Darwinism explains the origin of biological form and structure as the consequence of natural selection acting on random mutations, self-organizational theorists suggest that biological form often arises spontaneously (or "self-organizes") as a consequence of the laws of nature (or "laws of form"). Self-organization theorists

---

27. Eörs Szathmáry, "When the Means Do Not Justify the End," *Nature* 399 (1999): 745–746.
28. Schwartz, *Sudden Origins*, 362.
29. Szathmáry, "When the Means Do Not Justify the End," 745–746.

see natural selection acting to preserve the spontaneous order that self-organizational processes have generated. They think spontaneous self-organizing order, not random genetic mutations, typically provides the ultimate source of new biological form. Thus, they especially *de*-emphasize two of the three parts of the classical neo-Darwinian triad: random mutations, and to a lesser extent, natural selection.

Stuart Kauffman and the Origins of Order

One of the most well-known of the scientists associated with self-organization is a biochemist named Stuart Kauffman. In 1993 he wrote an influential book called *The Origins of Order: Self-Organization and Selection in Evolution*,[30] in which he gave an incisive critique of the alleged creative power of the mutation and selection mechanism, making some criticisms similar to those described in chapter 2 of this book. He went on to propose his own alternative theory for how new form might arise. In particular, he offered ideas for how self-organizational laws could account for the origin of the first life and the later development of the first forms of animal life during the Cambrian explosion.[31]

Kauffman says that the development of animal body plans involves two phases: morphogenesis (formation of the shape or body plan of the organism) and cell differentiation (the process by which cells become distinct types). He explores the possibility that self-organizational processes at work today during embryogenesis—specifically, in cell differentiation and body plan formation—might help explain how new animal forms originated in the past.

Kauffman notes that present-day organisms' gene regulatory networks (GRNs) influence how different types of cells are differentiated during embryological development. They do this by generating predictable "pathways of differentiation,"[32] patterns by which one type of cell will emerge from another over the course of embryological develop-

---

30. Stuart A. Kauffman, *The Origins of Order: Self-Organization and Selection in Evolution* (Oxford: Oxford University Press, 1993).

31. In *Origins of Order*, Kauffman seeks to show that self-organizational processes could help account for both the origin of the first life and the origin of subsequent forms of life, including new animal body plans. In *Signature in the Cell* (HarperOne, 2009), Meyer examined Kauffman's specific proposal for explaining the origin of the first life. Here we only examine his proposal for explaining the origin of animal form.

32. Kauffman, *Origins of Order*, 489.

ment, giving rise to multiple types of cells—some become heart cells, some brain cells, and some gut cells, for example.

Kauffman suggests that these pathways of differentiation "may reflect self-organizing features of complex genomic regulatory networks."[33] In other words, networks of regulatory genes in embryonic cells determine the pathways by which cells divide and differentiate. Since these patterns of cell differentiation may be *determined* by regulatory genes, Kauffman regards them as the inevitable by-products of self-organizational processes. Moreover, since he asserts "pathways of cell differentiation [have been] present in all multicellular organisms presumably since the Precambrian,"[34] he suggests that self-ordering properties "inherent in a wide class of genomic regulatory networks"[35] played a significant role in the origin of the animal forms.

Kauffman makes a similar case for the importance of self-organizational processes during morphogenesis. This phase involves, not so much the differentiation of one cell type from another, but the arrangement and organization of different cell types into the distinct tissues and organs that jointly constitute various animal body plans.

Kauffman again points to known processes of body plan development during embryogenesis and suggests that similar processes could have played an important role in the formation of the first animal body plans. He cites the importance of the structural or "positional information"[36] in cells and cell membranes as the crucial determinants of how different cell types are organized into different animal forms. In chapter 7, Jonathan Wells has discussed the importance to animal development of such "epigenetic" information, information that is outside the genome and specifies the "position" of the cell or membrane relative to its context. The presence of and need for such information poses a grave problem for neo-Darwinian theory. Thus, by recognizing positional information, Kauffman also rejects the neo-Darwinian assumption that a genetic program entirely determines animal development. He further regards the patterns of development that result from this positional information as evidence of self-ordering tendencies in matter and the existence of laws of biological form.

---

33. Ibid., 443.
34. Ibid.
35. Ibid.
36. Ibid., 539.

Do the self-ordering processes that Kauffman cites (or laws of form, if they exist) explain the origin of animal body plans and the genetic information necessary to build them?

They don't, and for two reasons.

First, Kauffman's self-organizational theory does not explain the origin of the genetic information present in the genetic regulatory networks that he himself argues are necessary to cell differentiation. Instead, he begs the question as to how the information present in these regulatory networks might have originated. Indeed, though Kauffman discusses cell differentiation as a kind of self-ordering or self-organizational process, he acknowledges that the predictable pathways of differentiation that characterize this process *derive from preexisting* gene regulatory networks. As Kauffman notes, the spontaneous ordering tendencies in cell differentiation are "*inherent* in a wide class of genomic regulatory networks."[37] Yet clearly, the genetic information in the gene regulatory networks does not come from self-ordering processes of cell differentiation. Instead, cell differentiation, to the extent that it can be properly described as self-ordering, *results from* preexisting genetic sources of information. Thus, the self-organizational process that Kauffman cites cannot *explain* the origin of genetic information, because it derives *from* it, as Kauffman's own description reveals.

Second, Kauffman's attempt to explain the origin of positional or epigenetic information lacks specificity and chemical plausibility. Kauffman derives the idea of positional information from a model suggested by Alan Turing in 1952.[38] Turing proposed that the interaction of two morphogens (chemicals involved in setting up a pattern), one autocatalytic (able to independently produce copies of itself), and the other inhibitory of the autocatalytic one, could produce a differential distribution of each chemical, which would provide instructions for cell differentiation and morphogenesis. He envisioned these instructions arising independently of any preexisting genetic material.

Though Kauffman attempts to use Turing's idea to explain the origin of the positional information, he, like Turing, fails to name any spe-

---

37. Ibid., 537, emphasis added.
38. A. M. Turing, "The Chemical Basis of Morphogenesis," *Philosophical Transactions of the Royal Society of London. Series B, Biological Sciences* 237 (1952): 37–72.

cific biologic molecules that could interact in the way he envisions so as to produce instructions capable of building a body plan. His model is entirely hypothetical. Indeed, he describes the behavior of molecules that he labels with the indistinct monikers "X" and "Y." More importantly, Kauffman does not offer any evidence that any chemicals interacting in the way he envisions could create specific *biologically relevant* configurations or distributions of morphogens—apart, that is, from the processes that generate specifically arranged distributions of these chemicals in *preexisting information-rich* embryonic cells today. Indeed, it is entirely implausible to think that the interaction of just two chemicals by themselves could produce enough information to coordinate all the movements and specifications that take place during embryo development. Kauffman himself acknowledges that to obtain any such order from autocatalytic reactions would require initial conditions that were incredibly fine-tuned, with high molecular specificity, and thus with a high degree of functional information from the beginning.[39]

In a later book, *At Home in the Universe*, Kauffman does suggest two models to demonstrate how self-ordering processes might generate positional information, but both of the models suffer from the same difficulties. First, neither is biologically realistic. One uses buttons and strings, the other flashing light to make their demonstration. Second, both rely on preexisting information in the form of "fine-tuning" supplied by the computer programmer in the simulation. Kauffman himself seems to acknowledge the requirement for preexisting information in his simulations and in biology when he says the "orderliness of the cell, long attributed to the honing of Darwinian evolution, seems instead likely to arise from *the dynamics of the genome network*"[40]— clearly a source of preexisting information.[41]

---

39. Kauffman, *Origins of Order*, 339.
40. Ibid., 85, emphasis added.
41. Stuart Newman, a cell biologist at the New York Medical College, has proposed another self-organizational model that resembles Kauffman's in some respect, but has more biological specificity. Nevertheless, Newman's model also presupposes preexisting information in the form of a "developmental-genetic tool kit." It describes self-ordering biological processes that nevertheless depend upon the prior existence of both genetic and epigenetic information (Stuart Newman, "Dynamical Patterning Modules," in *Evolution: The Extended Synthesis*, ed. M. Pigliucci and G. B. Müller [Cambridge, MA: MIT Press, 2010], 281–306; Newman, "Dynamical Patterning Modules," 296; see also Newman, "The Developmental Genetic Toolkit and the Molecular Homology-

Order versus Information

Self-organizational theorists face, in addition, a conceptual distinction that has cast doubt on the relevance of their theories to biological systems. Self-organizational theorists seek to explain the origin of order in living systems by reference to purely physical or chemical processes (or laws describing those processes). But what needs to be explained in living systems is not mainly order in the sense of simple repetitive or geometric patterns. Instead, what requires explanation is the adaptive complexity and the information, genetic and epigenetic, necessary to build it.

Yet, advocates of self-organization fail to offer examples of either biological information or complex anatomical structures arising from physics and chemistry alone. Instead, they point, as Kauffman does, to embryological development unfolding predictably as the result of *preexisting* information-rich gene products, cell membranes, and other cell structures. Or they offer examples of purely physical and chemical processes generating a kind of order that has little relevance to the features of living systems that most need explanation.

In the latter case, self-organizational theorists often point to simple geometric shapes or repetitive forms of order arising from, or being modified by, purely physical or chemical processes as if such order provides a model for understanding the origin of biological information or body plan morphogenesis.[42] Self-organizational theorists have cited crystals, vortices, and convection currents (or stable patterns of flashing lights) to illustrate the supposed power of physical processes to generate "order for free." Crystals of salt *do* form as the result of forces of attraction between sodium and chloride ions; vortices *can* result from gravitational and other forces acting on water in a draining bathtub; convection currents *do* emerge from warm air (or molten rock) rising in enclosed spaces. Nevertheless, the type of order evident in these molecules or physical systems has nothing to do with the "order" of arrangement—the information or specified complexity—that charac-

---

Analogy Paradox," *Biological Theory* 1 [2006]: 12–16; for a more extensive critique of Newman's model, see Meyer, *Darwin's Doubt*, 300–309).

42. Stuart Pivar, *Lifecode: The Theory of Biological Self-Organization* (New York: Ryland, 2004); Pivar, *On the Origin of Form: Evolution by Self-Organization* (Berkeley, CA: North Atlantic, 2009); Ilya Prigogine et al., "Thermodynamics of Evolution," *Physics Today* 25 (1972): 23–31.

terizes the digital code in DNA and other higher-level information-rich biological structures.

This is easiest to see in the case of the information encoded in DNA and RNA. The bases in the coding region of a section of DNA, or in an RNA transcript, are typically arranged in a nonrepetitive or aperiodic way. These sections of genetic text display what information scientists call specified complexity, not simple order or redundancy.

To see the difference between order and complexity, consider the difference between the following sequences:

Na-Cl-Na-Cl-Na-Cl-Na-Cl
AZFRT<MPGRTSHKLKYR

The first sequence, describing the chemical structure of salt crystals, displays what information scientists call "redundancy" or simple "order." That's because the two constituents, Na and Cl (sodium and chloride), are highly ordered in the sense of being arranged in a simple, rigidly repetitive way. The sequence on the bottom, by contrast, exhibits complexity. In this randomly generated string of characters, there is no simple repetitive pattern. Whereas the sequence on the top could be generated by a simple rule or computer algorithm, such as, "every time Na arises, attach a Cl to it, and vice versa," no rule shorter than the sequence itself could generate the bottom sequence.

The information-rich sequences in DNA, RNA, and proteins, by contrast, are characterized not by either simple order or *mere* complexity, but instead by "specified complexity." In such sequences, the irregular and unpredictable arrangement of the characters (or constituents) is also critical to the function that the sequence performs. The three sequences below illustrate these distinctions:

Na-Cl-Na-CL-Na-Cl-Na-Cl (Order)
AZFRT<MPGRTSHKLKYR (Complexity)
Time and tide wait for no man (Specified complexity)

What does all this have to do with self-organization? Simply this: the law-like, self-organizing processes that generate the kind of order present in a crystal or a vortex do not also generate complex sequences or structures; still less do they generate *specified* complexity, the kind of order present in a gene or functionally complex organ.

Laws of nature by definition describe repetitive phenomena—order, in that sense—that can be described with differential equations or universal "if-then" propositional statements. The information-bearing sequences in protein-coding DNA and RNA molecules do not exhibit such repetitive order, however. For this reason, these sequences can be neither described nor explained by reference to a natural law or law-like self-organizational process. The kind of order on display in DNA and RNA—a precise sequential order of arrangement necessary to ensure function—is not the kind that laws of nature or law-like self-organizational processes can—in principle—generate or explain. (Meyer discussed this problem in his critique of "teleological evolution" in chapter 6.) As information theorist Hubert Yockey has explained,

> Attempts to relate the idea of order . . . with biological organization or specificity must be regarded as a play on words that cannot stand careful scrutiny. Informational macromolecules can code genetic messages and therefore can carry information because the sequence of bases or residues is affected very little, if at all, by [self-organizing] physicochemical factors.[43]

C. Michael Lynch's Neutral Theory of Evolution

Michael Lynch, a noted evolutionary biologist at Indiana University, has proposed another EES theory to explain evolution from a non-Darwinian point of view. Interestingly, whereas in self-organizational evolutionary models random mutation plays a relatively minor role, in his account of evolutionary change, natural selection plays a minimal role. Instead neutral, unguided, "nonadaptive" processes like mutation and genetic drift are the forces responsible for evolution, at least in eukaryotic organisms such as ourselves and other large multicellular organisms with relatively small populations.

Why should that be? Lynch's theory is based on the equations of population genetics. These equations describe the relationship between mutation rate, natural selection, genetic drift (the effects of random

---

43. Hubert P. Yockey, "A Calculation of the Probability of Spontaneous Biogenesis by Information Theory," *Journal of Theoretical Biology* 67 (1977): 380.

chance on which organisms successfully reproduce), and population size. These equations lead to some surprising results.

In particular they suggest that, for organisms that have large population sizes such as bacteria, natural selection has the power to eliminate harmful mutations and to fix (make universal in the population) beneficial mutations. Conversely, in large populations, the process of genetic drift (the tendency for gene variants to be lost randomly) is weak. It follows that in large populations, which would include bacteria and unicellular eukaryotic organisms, it makes sense to invoke natural selection as a significant factor in the evolution of new traits.

On the other hand, the equations of population genetics also suggest that, for organisms with smaller population sizes (including most *multi*cellular organisms and animals), natural selection will have difficulty overcoming the effects of random genetic drift—meaning that beneficial mutations are likely to be lost before they can become fixed in a population and that natural selection will not efficiently remove many slightly harmful mutations. As Lynch notes, "three factors (low population sizes, low recombination rates, and high mutation rates) conspire to reduce the efficiency of natural selection with increasing organism size."[44] Consequently, organisms in smaller populations also tend to have very large genomes and to have acquired a lot of noncoding DNA—introns, pseudogenes, and transposons. Moreover, any evolution that takes place is almost completely undirected by natural selection—it "drifts" neutrally without respect to adaptive advantage and has thus been called nonadaptive evolution.[45]

What does this have to do with macroevolution and the origin of new forms of animal life? Evolutionary biologists think that the ancestral groups of most new forms of animal life would likely have existed in small populations. Given the relative powerlessness of natural selection to remove extraneous DNA in such populations, Lynch argues that additional genomic elements would accumulate over time, and the genomes of animals and plants would tend to grow in size. Lynch argues that this accumulation of DNA would lead to increasing

---

44. Michael Lynch, "The Origins of Eukaryotic Gene Structure," *Molecular Biology and Evolution* 23 (2006): 454.
    45. Ibid.

complexity in both the genome (total DNA) and phenotype (the observable characteristics) of these organisms, which would over time drive significant evolutionary change. This is his contribution to the extended evolutionary synthesis.

Paradoxical Aspects of Lynch's Theory

Lynch has provided a powerful critique of the efficacy of the neo-Darwinian mechanism, showing mathematically that *natural selection*, essential to standard evolutionary theory, does not have the power to fix beneficial mutations and thus generate new traits in small populations.[46] It does not follow from the failure of selection, however, that the accumulation of random mutations that Lynch proposes can do the job either. Without selection to drive things in a particular adaptive direction, how will near neutral, nonadaptive processes do the job? Lynch has traded a directional process for an essentially random one. In effect, Lynch's theory attempts to explain the origin of complexity by reference to a less—not more—potent mechanism than the one offered by neo-Darwinism.

Could such a paradoxical theory be true? There are several reasons to think not.

First, Lynch's theory presupposes but does not explain the origin of functionally integrated cellular processes and molecular machines needed by his scenario. For example, the accumulating complexity that he envisions entails the need to edit (and excise) portions of messenger RNA (called introns) in order to permit its translation into proteins. An enormous molecular machine called the spliceosome does this. "The problem," notes Lynch, "is that introns are inside genes and get transcribed to mRNA but then have to be spliced out perfectly. If you're one nucleotide off, you get a dead transcript."[47] Lynch recognizes, therefore, that his scenario requires the spliceosome as soon as introns entered the eukaryotic genome.[48] So where do spliceosomes, and the information necessary to produce them, come from? Lynch doesn't say.

---

46. See Lynch, "The Frailty of Adaptive Hypotheses for the Origin of Organismal Complexity," *Proceedings of the National Academy of Sciences USA* 104 (2007): 8597–8604.

47. Quoted in Beth Azar, "Profile of Michael Lynch," *Proceedings of the National Academy of Sciences USA* 107 (2010): 16015.

48. Melissa Jurica, "Detailed Closeups and the Big Picture of Spliceosomes," *Current Opinion in Structural Biology* 18 (2008): 315.

In any case, there are good reasons to doubt that Lynch's mechanism could generate novel biological form and information. In the first place, Lynch assumes a false gene-centric view of the origin of biological form, neglecting the role that epigenetic processes play (see chapter 7 in this book). As he writes, "Most of the phenotypic diversity that we perceive in the natural world *is directly attributable* to the peculiar structure of *the eukaryotic gene.*"[49] His view overlooks the crucial role of epigenetic information in the origin of animal form.

Second, Lynch provides no experimental biological evidence that recombination, drift, and mutation actually produce genomic complexity. Instead, the examples he provides are entirely hypothetical. He models the growth of the gene by processes such as insertion, splicing, and domain-swapping using cartoon drawings of balls, sticks, and Pac-Man-like entities. He does, of course, use various mathematical models to suggest the plausibility of the processes he invokes, but the mathematical models do not address, let alone solve, the combinatorial search problem discussed in chapter 2 of this book.

Third, though Lynch's mechanism of neutral mutational change attempts to explain the accretion of brute genomic complexity (that is, the addition of new sequences), it does not even attempt to explain *functional* (or *specified*) genomic complexity. Lynch's neutral mechanism of genomic accretion relies on purely random mutations to search the vast space of possible nucleotide and amino acid sequences that correspond to a given *functional* gene or section of the genome. Lynch nowhere reckons with the vast improbability of the search that his mechanism must accomplish, nor does he offer any reason to think that the probability of a successful search for *functional* genes or proteins would be any higher (i.e., more likely to occur) than the probability calculated in chapter 2. He does not, therefore, solve the problem of combinatorial inflation. Instead, his model represents another version of the neutral theory of evolution that Doug Axe's experimental results (about the rarity of functional proteins) decisively refute (see chapter 2).

---

49. Lynch, "Origins of Eukaryotic Gene Structure," 450–468, emphasis added.

D. Neo-Lamarckian Epigenetic Inheritance

The third element of the neo-Darwinian triad concerns the transmission and inheritance of genetic information. Not surprisingly, the new element of the extended evolutionary synthesis we describe next questions the neo-Darwinian understanding of heredity, just as alternative theories have questioned the other aspects of the Darwinian triad: random mutation (self-organization and evolutionary developmental biology) and natural selection (near-neutral evolution).

Darwin himself lacked an accurate theory of genetics that could explain how features of organisms are transmitted from one generation to the next. He thought that changes in organisms that occurred during their lifetimes from the use and disuse of different organs and anatomical systems would be transmitted to offspring through reproduction.[50] In this respect, his theory of inheritance resembled that of an earlier evolutionary theorist named Jean Baptiste de Lamarck, who also believed in the inheritance of acquired characteristics.

Lamarckian mechanisms, although unsupported by any evidence at the time, came to play an increasingly important role in Darwin's thinking, as criticisms of natural selection caused him to place more weight on the direct influence of the environment in evolutionary change. Indeed, by the sixth edition of the *Origin* (1872), Darwin specifically emphasized the importance of these modes of inheritance.

But with the rediscovery of Mendel's laws in 1900 and the identification of chromosomes as the material entity responsible for the transmission of inheritance, Lamarckian theories of inheritance fell out of favor. Following the rise of neo-Darwinism, the gene became the locus of all heritable change in the organism. And after 1953, biologists equated the gene with specifically arranged nucleotide bases on the DNA molecule.

Recently, however, as more biologists have recognized that some biological information—epigenetic information; see chapters 2 and 7—resides in structures outside of DNA, interest has grown in the pos-

---

50. Darwin's own theory of transmission genetics, dubbed "pangenesis," postulated that a host of minute heredity particles, which he called "gemmules," accumulated in the reproductive organs of organisms, carrying information about the life history and environmental circumstances of the parent. This information would then be transmitted at reproduction to offspring, allowing the "inheritance" of "acquired" characteristics.

sibility that these nongenetic sources of information may influence the course of evolution. The discovery that epigenetic information can be altered and directly inherited independently of DNA has attracted further attention to this possibility. This discovery has, in turn, led to the formulation of a contemporary "neo-Lamarckian"[51] theory that envisions changes in the nongenetic structures of an organism affecting subsequent generations during the course of evolution.

Today, prominent defenders of neo-Lamarckism include Eva Jablonka of Tel Aviv University and Massimo Pigliucci of the City University of New York. Lamarck, of course, knew nothing about the role of genes, and believed that inheritance of acquired characteristics was an important driving force in evolution. Modern neo-Lamarckians, fully apprised of the reality of genetic inheritance, nevertheless think that epigenetic sources of information and structure may play some role in the evolution of biological form. According to Jablonka, neo-Lamarckism "allow[s] evolutionary possibilities denied by the 'Modern Synthesis' version of evolutionary theory, which states that variations are blind, are genetic (nucleic acid-based), and that saltational events do not significantly contribute to evolutionary change."[52]

Jablonka has collected several categories of evidence in support of what she calls "epigenetic inheritance systems."

In the first place, she notes that in some single-celled organisms (such as *E. coli* and yeast) environmentally induced changes in metabolic pathways can be transmitted to the next generation independently of any changes in the cell's DNA.

Second, she notes that structural information mediating organismal form (and function) does pass from parent to offspring independently of DNA, via membranes and other three-dimensional cellular patterns.

Third, she discusses processes such as DNA methylation—a process where special enzymes attach a group of carbon and hydrogen atoms

---

51. Some question exists about the historical accuracy of calling these twenty-first-century ideas "neo-Lamarckian," in light of the actual content of Jean Baptiste de Lamarck's views, when compared with the enormous growth of knowledge about heredity over the past two hundred years. Given that Eva Jablonka (see the following text and note) adapts the term "Lamarckism" to her own position, however, we follow that practice, with the caveats about differences in content noted.

52. Eva Jablonka and Gal Raz, "Transgenerational Epigenetic Inheritance: Prevalence, Mechanisms, and Implications for the Study of Heredity and Evolution," *Quarterly Review of Biology* 84, no. 2 (2009): 131–176.

called a methyl group (CH_3) to nucleotide bases within the double helix. Such processes can alter gene regulation and chromatin structure. Jablonka notes that the changes produced by these processes are often transmitted to subsequent generations of cells without any changes to the sequence of DNA.

Finally, she cites a process called "RNA-mediated" epigenetic inheritance, a recently discovered phenomenon. Here, small RNAs, again acting in concert with special enzymes, affect gene expression and chromatin structure, and these modifications appear to be heritable independently of genes.

Can any of these mechanisms help to explain the origin of animal form?

Not really.

By its nature, evolution requires *stable*—meaning permanently heritable—changes. But Jablonka's evidence shows that, where nongenetic inheritance occurs in animals, it involves structures that either (a) do not change (such as membrane patterns and other persistent templates of structural information) or (b) do not *persist* over more than several generations. Neither case generates significant evolutionary innovation in animal form. Instead, for directional evolutionary change to occur in a population of organisms, changes must be not only heritable, but permanent. Stability—the irreversible and enduring heritability of traits—is a logically inescapable requirement for any theory of evolution. This is precisely what "descent with modification" means.

And here, Jablonka's evidence for *stable* nongenetic inheritance is equivocal at best, as she readily admits. Reviewing Jablonka's assembled data for animals reveals no case where an induced epigenetic change persisted permanently in any population. The heritability of such changes is transient, persisting (depending on the species in question) from a few generations up to forty.

Jablonka candidly addresses this lack of evidence for stability, noting that "we believe that epigenetic variants in every locus in the eukaryotic genome can be inherited, *but in what manner, for how long, and under what conditions, has yet to be qualified.*"[53] Consequently, despite its intriguing aspects, the evolutionary significance of neo-

---

53. Ibid., 138, emphasis added.

Lamarckian epigenetic inheritance remains uncertain, or, in Jablonka's own words, "inevitably, somewhat speculative."[54]

E. Natural Genetic Engineering

University of Chicago geneticist James Shapiro has formulated another post-Darwinian EES perspective on how evolution works that he calls "natural genetic engineering." Shapiro has developed an understanding of evolution that takes account of the integrated complexity of organisms as well as the importance of *nonrandom* mutations and variations in the evolutionary process. This represents a radical change to the idea of random mutations put forward by the standard evolutionary theory, and thus is another example of the EES.

Shapiro observes that organisms within a population often modify themselves in response to different environmental challenges. He cites evidence showing that when populations are challenged by different environmental stresses, signals, and triggers, organisms do not generate mutations or make genetic changes randomly, that is, without respect to, or unguided by, their survival needs. Instead, populations often respond to environmental stresses or signals in a directed or regulated way. As he explains,

> the continued insistence on the random nature of genetic change by evolutionists should be surprising for one simple reason: empirical studies of the mutational process have inevitably discovered patterns, environmental influences, and specific biological activities at the roots of novel genetic structures and altered DNA sequences.[55]

The depth of Shapiro's challenge to orthodox neo-Darwinism can hardly be overstated. He rejects the randomness of novel variation that Darwin himself emphasized and that neo-Darwinian theorists throughout the twentieth century have reaffirmed.[56] Instead, he favors a view of the evolutionary process that emphasizes preprogrammed adaptive capacity or "engineered" change, where organisms respond

---

54. Ibid., 162.

55. James A. Shapiro, *Evolution: A View from the 21st Century* (Upper Saddle River, NJ: FT Press Science, 2011), 2.

56. Shapiro contends that the neo-Darwinian insistence on fundamental randomness arose for philosophical, not empirical (or observational) reasons, having to do with the exclusion of "supernatural intervention" in the origin of organisms.

"intelligently" to environmental influences, rearranging or mutating their genetic information in regulated ways to maintain viability.

As an example, Shapiro notes that—contrary to the neo-Darwinian assumption that "DNA alterations are accidental"[57]—all organisms possess sophisticated cellular systems for proofreading and repairing their DNA during its replication, "equivalent to a quality-control system in human manufacturing," where the "surveillance and correction" functions represent "cognitive processes, rather than mechanical precision."[58]

As an example of regulated mutation, Shapiro observes that, in response to environmental assault—UV damage from sunlight, or the presence of an antibiotic, for instance—bacteria activate what is known as the SOS response system, where specialized error-prone DNA polymerases (the enzymes that copy DNA), normally left unexpressed, are synthesized and set into action, allowing the population to generate a much wider range of genetic variation than usual. The cell regulates this process using a DNA-binding protein known as LexA that normally represses the error-prone polymerases. When the SOS system is activated by environmental damage from UV light, for example, the production of LexA first drops dramatically, allowing expression of the error-prone polymerases.

These error-prone polymerases also cause mutations, as their name implies. This characteristic is useful for increasing the mutation rate in times of environment stress, which increases the chances that some particular mutation will solve the problem for some cell or cells in the population, and allow them to survive the challenge. While at one level their "error-prone" role may appear counterintuitive, these mutation-generating DNA polymerases of the SOS system actually constitute essential hardware in the cell's defensive armory.[59]

From Shapiro's perspective, this survival strategy does not exemplify Darwinian randomness but rather sophisticated preprogramming, an "apparatus that even the smallest cells possess" to maintain viability.[60] What's more, the carefully regulated expression of the SOS

57. Ibid., 12.
58. Ibid., 14.
59. Ibid.
60. Ibid.

response provides evidence that cells employ the system only when needed.[61]

Shapiro argues that these and other kinds of directed, rather than random, genetic changes and responses to stimuli occur under "algorithmic control." He describes the cell as "a real time distributive computer" implementing various "if-then" subroutines. This emphatically challenges one of the three key elements of the neo-Darwinian triad: the claim that mutations and variations occur in a strictly random way.

In the last fifteen years, Shapiro has published a series of fascinating papers about the newly discovered capacities of cells to direct or "engineer" the genetic changes they need to remain viable in a range of environmental conditions. His work represents a promising avenue of new biological research, bringing new insight into how the cell's information processing system modifies and directs the expression of its genetic information in real time in response to different signals.

Could it, then, also provide a solution to the problem of the origin of the information necessary to build an animal body plan? It could, except for one question that Shapiro's otherwise brilliant characterization of how organisms modify themselves doesn't address. That question?

Where does the programming—the algorithmic control—that accounts for the "preprogrammed adaptive capacity" of living organisms come from? We know of only one source of such programming. Our uniform and repeated experience affirms that the only source for information-rich programs is intelligent agency. Or as the information theorist Henry Quastler put it, "the creation of new information is habitually associated with conscious and rational activity."[62]

Yet despite the well-established causal connection between intelligence and information-rich systems, Shapiro and other proponents of EES remain firmly committed to purely naturalistic or materialistic explanations. Stuart Kauffman, Michael Lynch, Eva Jablonka, and Charles Marshall would flatly exclude any consideration of an

---

61. As biologist Bénédicte Michel observes, "Clearly, it is important for bacteria to keep all levels of the SOS response under tight control. There is no utility to the organism of using error-prone polymerases longer than absolutely necessary" (Bénédicte Michel, "After 30 Years, the Bacterial SOS Response Still Surprises Us," *PLoS Biology* 3 [2005]: 1175).

62. Henry Quastler, *The Emergence of Biological Organization* (New Haven, CT: Yale University Press, 1964), 16.

intelligent cause as the explanation for the origin of the information necessary to produce novel forms of life or animal body plans. Yet as we have seen, they also repeatedly presuppose the origin of information-rich systems (either genetic or epigenetic or both) without explaining how such information arose.

F. The Current Situation

This same difficulty was everywhere in evidence at the Royal Society meeting in London in November of 2016. At that conference, several new mechanisms and models, including "neo-Lamarckian epigenetic inheritance" and "natural genetic engineering" were discussed as possible remedies for the "explanatory deficits" of neo-Darwinism. Nevertheless, the conference failed to offer any new mechanism that could help remedy the main "deficits" of the neo-Darwinian synthesis—its inability to account for the origin of phenotypic novelty and, especially, the genetic and epigenetic information necessary to produce it.

Of these presentations, James Shapiro's talk was clearly one of the most interesting. Shapiro reprised his case for natural genetic engineering. He presented fascinating evidence showing the nonrandom nature of many mutational processes—processes that allow organisms to respond to various environmental challenges or stresses. The evidence he presented suggested, as noted above, that many organisms possess a kind of preprogrammed adaptive capacity. Yet, Shapiro again did not explain how the information inherent in such preprogrammed capacity might have originated.

Other mechanisms presented at the conference betrayed similar inadequacies. For example, there was an extensive discussion of a mechanism called "niche construction." Complex behaviors such as nest-building by birds or dam construction by beavers represent examples of niche construction in which some organisms themselves demonstrate the capacity to alter their environment in ways that may affect the adaptation of subsequent generations to that environment. Yet no advocate of niche construction at the meeting explained how the capacity for such complex behaviors arose de novo in ancestral populations, as they must have done if the naturalistic evolutionary story is true.

Rather, these complex behaviors were taken as givens, leaving the critical question of their origins more or less untouched. While there is abundant evidence that animals can learn and transmit new behaviors to their offspring—crows in Japan, for instance, have learned how to use automobile traffic to crack open nuts—all such evidence presupposes the prior existence of specific functional capacities enabling observation, learning, and the like. The evolutionary accounts of niche construction theory therefore collide repeatedly with a brick wall marked "ORIGINAL COMPLEX FUNCTIONAL CAPACITY REQUIRED HERE"—without which, or beyond which, there would simply be nothing interesting to observe.

Indeed, the new mechanisms offered by critics of neo-Darwinism at the Royal Society conference—whether treated as part of an extended neo-Darwinian synthesis or as the basis of a fundamentally new theory of evolution—did not attempt to explain how the information necessary for generating genuine novelty might have arisen. Instead, the mechanisms that were discussed produced at best minor microevolutionary changes such as changes in wing coloration of butterflies or the so-called "polymorphisms" of stickleback fishes. Moreover, the mechanisms presented there—niche construction, neo-Lamarckian epigenetic inheritance, and natural genetic engineering, for example—either presupposed the prior existence of the genetic information necessary to generate novelty, or they did not address the mystery of the origin of that information (and morphological novelty) at all. Thus, even a science reporter friendly to the EES, Suzan Mazur, complained in the *Huffington Post* of a lack of momentousness: "[J]ust what was the point of attracting a distinguished international gathering if the speakers had little new science to present? Why waste everyone's time and money?"[63]

IV. Conclusion: A Timid Reformation That Leaves Us Where We Were

The metaphor of a city bounded by a high wall helps to illuminate the situation now faced in evolutionary biology. Despite the difficulties with the standard theory that proponents of the extended evolutionary

---

63. http://www.huffingtonpost.com/suzan-mazur/pterosaurs-hijack-royal-s_b_13131246.html, accessed 4-10-17.

286 The Scientific Critique of Theistic Evolution

synthesis acknowledge, EES theorists remain fully neo-Darwinian in the essential sense that separates them from proponents of intelligent design or special creation, namely, their views about the ultimate source(s) of biological form and information. EES proponents assume that novel form and information must arise from only natural—meaning physical or material—wellsprings; it is not imparted to the biosphere by an actual purposeful intelligence, or, more precisely, we may not infer that biological information has an intelligent source (at least, not one external to the evolutionary process itself).[64] Such inferences would in their view violate the rule of methodological naturalism (see chapter 19). Methodological naturalism defines the walls of the city bounding scientific explanation proper, and intelligent design—that is, real teleology involving an actual purposeful intelligence—lies beyond those walls.

Thus, while the proponents of the extended evolutionary synthesis urge openness to new ideas on the part of the SET establishment, and can be blistering in their critiques of textbook theory, they stay obediently within the city walls. Indeed, the walls of methodological naturalism are high and impassable, and for most evolutionary biologists, ever in sight. Most never consider leaving the boundaries defined by methodological naturalism. Hence, the problem created by accepting it—in particular, the problem of explaining the origin of information for which we know of only one cause—remains unsolved. One can accomplish only so much within those walls.

---

64. Interestingly, some EES advocates, such as University of Southampton theoretician Richard Watson, have begun to impute properties of "intelligent problem solving" and "learning" to the evolutionary process itself as part of a another new concept of evolution called "learning theory." According to learning theory, the material evolutionary process itself is intelligent and capable of "learning" how to design complex biological systems. "Learning theory," writes Watson, "is not just a different way of describing what we already knew about evolution. It expands what we think evolution is capable of. In particular, it shows that via the incremental evolution of developmental, ecological, or reproductive organisations natural selection is sufficient to produce significant features of *intelligent problem solving*. . . . We think this offers the potential to better explain how the process of random variation and selection results in the apparently *intelligent designs* it produces" (R. Watson and E. Szathmáry, "How Can Evolution Learn?" *Trends in Ecology and Evolution* 31 [2016]: 147–157, at 155, emphasis added). Thus, in order to account for the complex information-rich structures that Watson encounters—and needs to explain—in biological systems, he apparently finds it necessary to impute purposive intelligence to the evolutionary process itself while still denying that an actual (i.e., external) designing agent in any way guided that process. Yet, we have no observable evidence of conscious awareness or cognition in the evolutionary process. Watson's postulation of such intelligent activity or awareness merely projects what is needed to explain certain phenomena (such as digital code, nano-machinery or control systems in cells) back onto the workings of the evolutionary process throughout biological history.

But why should it be the case that the walls stand so high, when every proposal of the EES can be shown to fail, and methodological naturalism is clearly preventing consideration of other more causally adequate, plausible, and fruitful ideas? Surely someone is willing to scale the wall to see what might lie on the other side. And why, specifically, should theistic evolutionists—who already presumably believe there is something on the other side of the wall—remain behind it?

9

Evidence from Embryology Challenges Evolutionary Theory

SHEENA TYLER

SUMMARY

How does an egg develop into the distinctive body form of an elephant, as opposed to a grasshopper or a kangaroo? It remains a mystery to this day how these body forms are generated. This is a major problem for evolutionists, because their claim that the various forms of life arose by changes in a common developmental program depends on knowledge of this elusive program. This chapter will demonstrate how embryological processes exhibit the hallmarks of intelligent design rather than the tinkering of blind, random mutations required by evolutionary theory. It will also illuminate evidences from embryology that point to distinct types of life, which exhibit fundamental differences in design between them, rather than a continuous gradation of forms tracing back to a primitive common ancestor.

. . . . .

Introduction

In 1859 Charles Darwin wrote that "Embryology is to me by far the strongest single class of facts in favor of change of form."[1] To this day

---

1. Quoted in Brian K. Hall, *Evolutionary Developmental Biology* (London: Chapman & Hall, 1992), 60.

embryological mechanisms are placed center-stage to explain the evolutionary origin of diverse body forms. This chapter examines whether experimental evidence emerging from embryology either supports or refutes these claims. The first section investigates whether alterations to genes involved in development can generate evolutionary changes. What evidence is there for how changes in such genes might create large-scale transformations to an organism's body plan? The second section looks at whether body plans are assembled according to random and unguided Darwinian processes, or are these assemblies orchestrated, bearing hallmarks of intelligent design? The third section explores whether embryological development supports the idea of a continuous gradation of form among living things, which can all be traced back historically to a primitive common ancestor. Alternatively, does the evidence suggest the existence of distinct types in nature, with common modes of assembly, clearly distinct from neighboring types of assemblies? The experimental findings discussed here have far-reaching implications to challenge the strongest "class of facts" which Darwin marshalled to support his theory.

Part 1. Nature's Greatest Secret: The Form Question

1.1 Genotype to Phenotype

The body plan of an organism refers to its major structural features or form by which it can be recognized. Examples are the snail, with its familiar shell, and the sea star with its radial arms and sucker feet. The outward visible form (phenotype) is considered by most biologists to be determined by a genetic blueprint, the genotype.[2] How this plan or form is generated remains one of the most fascinating but elusive challenges for science.[3] This has huge implications, for it is said that we will not understand evolution until we understand how organisms are produced in development.

The problem of the knowledge gap between genotype and phenotype has been well recognized, as the following quotes from various embryologists indicate (emphases added). Ray Keller: "One of the *en-*

---

2. I acknowledge that there are other forms of information that impact body plan development. These will be discussed later.
3. Sheena E. B. Tyler, "The Work Surfaces of Morphogenesis: The Role of the Morphogenetic Field," *Biological Theory* 9, no. 2 (2014): 194–208.

during mysteries of developmental and cell biology is morphogenesis, the process of how the heritable body plan . . . is shaped at every stage from the fertilized egg."[4] Brian Goodwin: "The *problem of biological form remains unresolved* despite the known details of gene activities in embryonic development."[5] Franklin Harold: "What orchestrates the hubbub of enzymes, filaments, membranes and polymers into a recurring pattern? We really do not know."[6] Michael Levin: "Deciphering and learning to control shape is. . . . arguably the *fundamental problem* of biology and medicine."[7] Beverly Purnell: "Transforming a single fertilized egg into a complex animal is a marvel and a mystery."[8] Lars Hufnagel: How growth is controlled and coordinated "remain largely unanswered questions."[9]

But if the mechanisms by which the programs of development translate into form remain to be discovered, then the *mechanisms underlying large-scale evolutionary change remain highly speculative, since these essentially depend on fundamental changes in the black box of the developmental program.*

1.2 Historical Sketch

Evidence that embryological development appears to have coordinating influences has been emerging over the past hundred years. In Germany, Hans Driesch recognized that embryo parts have the capacity to generate the whole, via these parts working harmoniously together. He proposed too that the fate (identity and destination) of cells is determined by their position, according to a reference system of fixed coordinates.[10] In Russia, Alexander Gurwitsch found evidence

4. Ray Keller, "Physical Biology Returns to Morphogenesis," *Science* 338, no. 6104 (2012): 201.

5. Brian C. Goodwin, "The Life of Form: Emergent Patterns of Morphological Transformation," *Comptes Rendus de l'Académie des Sciences-Series III-Sciences de la Vie* 323, no. 1 (2000): 15.

6. Franklin M. Harold, "From Morphogenes to Morphogenesis," *Microbiology* 141, no. 11 (1995): 2774.

7. Michael Levin, "Morphogenetic Fields in Embryogenesis, Regeneration, and Cancer: Non-Local Control of Complex Patterning," *Biosystems* 109, no. 3 (2012): 243.

8. Beverly A. Purnell, "Forceful Thinking," *Science* 338, no. 6104 (2012): 209.

9. Lars Hufnagel, Aurelio A. Teleman, Hervé Rouault, Stephen M. Cohen, and Boris I. Shraiman, "On the Mechanism of Wing Size Determination in Fly Development," *Proceedings of the National Academy of Sciences USA* 104, no. 10 (2007): 3835.

10. Hans Driesch, "Entwicklungsmechanische Studien I: Der Wert der erster Furchungszellen in der Echinodermentwicklung. Experimentelle Erzeugung von Teil-und Doppelbildungen," *Zeitschrift für wissenschaftliche Zoologie* 53 (1892): 160–178, 183–184; Hans Driesch,

for a guiding field of force, the "Embryonales Feld," which ordered the whole of development throughout the embryo.[11] In the following decades a large body of experimental data was marshaled in support of a morphogenetic field system, which thus became the established research paradigm, integral to the quest to discover the underlying laws governing organismal form.

In contrast, the American geneticist Thomas Hunt Morgan[12] viewed the causal basis of form to reside exclusively in genes and their products, rather than in fields. Morgan's student Theodosius Dobzhansky defined evolution to be the result of changes in gene frequency, with genetics as the motor for evolution.[13] Following the Second World War, this view rose into dominance. This was the "Synthetic Theory" or "Modern Synthesis," in which large-scale evolution was explained by random, undirected mutations acted on by natural selection, with an emphasis on how different permutations of genes were distributed in populations over time.[14]

However, there was a growing recognition that our knowledge of changes in genes and their products remains insufficient to explain development of form (morphogenesis).[15] In addition, there was increasing frustration at the lack of evidence from genetics to explain large-scale evolutionary change.[16] One of the major tenets of the Modern Synthesis is that of extrapolation: the notion that macroevolution (the evolution of organisms with the distinctly different body plans of higher taxonomic groups) is fully explained by microevolutionary processes (that give rise to varieties within species and genera). Disagreements over this notion were so intense at a major conference on macroevolution that proceedings of the conference

---

"Entwicklungsmechanische Studien VI: Uber einige allgemeine Fragen der theoretischen Morphologie," *Zeitschrift für wissenschaftliche Zoologie* 55 (1892): 34–58.

11. Alexander G. Gurwitsch, "Die Vererbung als Verwirklichungsvorgang," *Biologisches Zentralblatt* (1912): 458–486.

12. Thomas Hunt Morgan, *Embryology and Genetics* (New York: Columbia University Press, 1934).

13. Scott F. Gilbert, John M. Opitz, and Rudolf A. Raff, "Resynthesizing Evolutionary and Developmental Biology," *Developmental Biology* 173, no. 2 (1996): 357–372.

14. Douglas J. Futuyma, "Can Modern Evolutionary Theory Explain Macroevolution?" in *Macroevolution: Explanation, Interpretation, and Evidence*, ed. E. Serrelli and N. Gontier (New York, Dordrecht, London: Springer, 2015), 29–85.

15. Stuart A. Newman and Marta Linde-Medina, "Physical Determinants in the Emergence and Inheritance of Multicellular Form," *Biological Theory* 8, no. 3 (2013): 274–285.

16. Gilbert, Opitz, and Raff, "Resynthesizing Evolutionary and Developmental Biology."

were never published.[17] Paleontologists and biologists such as Stephen Jay Gould and Francisco Ayala asserted that microevolutionary events indeed do not explain macroevolutionary processes. As Gilbert, Opitz, and Raff commented, "microevolution concerns only survival of the fittest, not arrival of the fittest. . . . Population genetics must change if it is not to become irrelevant to evolution."[18]

1.3 Evolutionary Developmental Biology (Evo-Devo) and Current Trends[19]

As an attempted solution to the above unrest, evolutionary developmental biology, or "evo-devo," emerged in the 1990s when researchers proposed that alterations to genes involved in development can explain evolutionary changes.[20] A number of themes are embodied in this credo. These include the idea that changes in the sets of genes available to organisms for use in development (molecular toolkits) and/or the pathways for exchanging information and modulating cellular behavior (signal transduction pathways) can account for macroevolution. Gould postulated another idea, that changes in the relative timing of developmental events and different growth of parts relative to each other could serve as mechanisms to rapidly create new body plans.[21] Another proposal is the "module" concept, with complex organs envisaged as arising by the addition of new modules.[22] Yet another idea is self-organization, in which forms arise spontaneously according to the laws of nature rather than from random genetic mutations.[23]

However, there are numerous problems with evo-devo and the above ideas. These are briefly outlined as follows. (For more, see chapter 8 on the "Extended Evolutionary Synthesis.")

1. Without knowing the steps by which the genotype is actually transformed into the phenotype, it is a large step of faith to assume

---

17. Futuyma, "Can Modern Evolutionary Theory Explain Macroevolution?"

18. Gilbert, Opitz and Raff, "Resynthesizing Evolutionary and Developmental Biology," 368.

19. Material in this section is discussed further in chapter 8.

20. Corey S. Goodman and Bridget C. Coughlin, "The Evolution of Evo-Devo Biology," *Proceedings of the National Academy of Sciences USA* 97, no. 9 (2000): 4424–4425.

21. Stephen Jay Gould, *Ontogeny and Phylogeny* (Cambridge, MA: Harvard University Press, 1977).

22. Alessandro Minelli, *The Development of Animal Form: Ontogeny, Morphology, and Evolution* (Cambridge: Cambridge University Press, 2003).

23. Stuart A. Kauffman, *The Origins of Order* (New York: Oxford University Press, 1993).

how such unknown pathways would have been transformed in evolution. Indeed, it is the recognition that these transformations are such a "black box" that led Jaume Baguñà and Jordi Garcia-Fernàndez to urge extreme caution when such inferences are made.[24]

2. Examples of evo-devo in action fall far short of providing *experimental evidence of macroevolution at work*. If these processes did occur, it should be possible to create large-scale transformations to an organism's body plan. However, experiments which generate mutations in genes acting on body plans[25] tend to produce overwhelmingly defective or lethal embryos. A mutation in the *Ubx* gene in *Drosophila* (the fruit fly) leads to an extra set of wings,[26] but these are not functional, lacking muscles that work the wings and other essential structures, and the extra wings prevent the fly from flying.[27] Moreover, the extra wings are a mere duplication of a preexisting structure, rather than one new to nature.

The eminent developmental biologist Eric Davidson and colleagues[28] focused for decades on gene regulatory networks (GRNs), claiming that evolutionary change in body plans results from alteration of the functional organization of the GRNs. It is interesting to see, then, some of the best evidences Davidson forwards. These include the loss of spines in sticklebacks, and loss of eyes in cavefish. However, this represents *loss* of information, and certainly is no evidence for the generation of novel macroevolutionary morphologies. Even Davidson admits that mutations affecting GRNs that are implicated in the development of the body plan lead to "catastrophic loss of the body part" or are lethal.

In other words, there is no experimental evidence that a simple switch or even a series of mutations that alter GRNs can in practice lead to a new body plan. These remain speculations, not observations.

---

24. Jaume Baguñà and Jordi Garcia-Fernàndez, "Evo-Devo: The Long and Winding Road," *International Journal of Developmental Biology* 47: 705–713 (2003).

25. Christiane Nüsslein-Volhard and Eric Wieschaus, "Mutations Affecting Segment Number and Polarity in Drosophila," *Nature* 287, no. 5785 (1980): 795–801.

26. Edward B. Lewis, "Genes and Developmental Pathways," *American Zoologist* 3 (1963): 333–356; Edward B. Lewis, "A Gene Complex Controlling Segmentation in Drosophila," *Nature* 276 (1978): 565–570.

27. Stephen C. Meyer, *Darwin's Doubt: The Explosive Origin of Animal Life and the Case for Intelligent Design* (New York: HarperOne, 2013).

28. Isabelle S. Peter and Eric H. Davidson, "Evolution of Gene Regulatory Networks Controlling Body Plan Development," *Cell* 144, no. 6 (2011): 970–985.

For instance, Isabelle Peter and Eric Davidson imagine "*as previously speculated* . . . mobile elements *could* have provided a major mechanism of GRN evolution;[29] . . . alterations in GRN structure are "*easily imagined*"[30] (emphases added). Douglas Futuyma concludes that some authors make hyperbolic claims for evo-devo "well beyond what current evidence supports."[31]

3. Transformations from one form to another are never "simple" but require completely integrated transformation of form for all associated structures, and all of these must be functional. For instance, the body plan of highly elongated fishes differs in a number of ways compared to stout-bodied close relatives.[32] Elongate fishes tend to have longer and/or more numerous vertebrae, longer bones within the skull, and longer fins. That such transformations are not simple is further indicated by the recognition that body shape indeed has a complex genetic basis.[33]

I am interested in boat design (Fig. 9.1A). If in relation to the original plans a wider boat were to be constructed, these widths change along the boat's length, requiring the sides to be re-formed and lengthened.

Computer-aided design can make changes in boat design appear easy (Fig. 9.1 B–C), but this is possible only because the software was intelligently designed in the first place, to enable each part of the boat to be modified in relation to the whole.[34] Similarly, organisms that vary their body length relative to other species must modify each part in relation to the topography of the whole organism in three dimensions, and this involves the coordinated addition or removal of cells in various tissues (Figs. 9.1D and E).

The idea that evolutionary modifications can occur by simple changes in the timing of development is also popular. However, a

---

29. Ibid., 972.
30. Ibid.
31. Futuyma, "Can Modern Evolutionary Theory Explain Macroevolution?" 55.
32. Andrea B. Ward and Rita S. Mehta, "Axial Elongation in Fishes: Using Morphological Approaches to Elucidate Developmental Mechanisms in Studying Body Shape," *Integrative and Comparative Biology* 50, no. 6 (2010): 1106–1119.
33. Duncan T. Reid and Catherine L. Peichel, "Perspectives on the Genetic Architecture of Divergence in Body Shape in Sticklebacks," *Integrative and Comparative Biology* 50, no. 6 (2010): 1057–1066.
34. Computer-aided design software in itself is not enough to design a sound boat. It also requires the input of boat-building design skills for the boat to be balanced, stable, and efficient. It has to be intelligently designed!

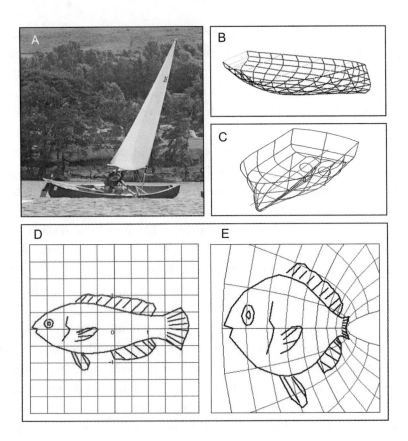

FIGURE 9.1. A–C. *Lessons from boat-building.* **A.** If the floor of this boat were to be widened, this would affect the other dimensions, creating gaps. To overcome this, the sides would have to be lengthened and their curves redesigned for the boat to remain viable and efficient. **B.** and **C.** Computer-aided boat design aids such changes only because the software is intelligently designed, enabling all the modifications required in three dimensions to be integrated. **D.** and **E.** *Changing animal form.* If a grid is superimposed on an animal such as this species of fish (**D**), and then the form within the grid is stretched, a new form of fish results (**E**), which corresponds to ones found in nature. However, this requires the form within each grid to be modified in relation to the whole. And this is just considering two dimensions! In the real situation, all three dimensions of the fish must be modified integrally to the whole form.

CREDITS: (A) © Sheena Tyler; (B) Gavin Atkin, "Notes on Boat Design Software," *Duckworks* magazine, March 2001, http://www.duckworksmagazine.com/01/articles/notes/index1.html; (C) "Ship-Shape," Wolfson Unit, University of Southampton, http://www.wumtia.soton.ac.uk/software/shipshape; (D) D'Arcy W. Thompson, *On Growth and Form*, 2nd ed. (Cambridge: Cambridge University Press, 1942); (E) "Using a Computer to Visualise Change in Biological Organisms," School of Mathematics and Statistics, University of St. Andrews, Scotland, September 2016, http://www-history.mcs.st-andrews.ac.uk/history/Miscellaneous/darcy.html.

report of molecular geneticist professor Susan Cole's work regarding gene activity in chick development shows that, if the timing of these genes' activity does not remain tightly regulated, the tissue either will not form at all or will form with defects.[35]

4. When self-organizing chemistry occurs within a living cell, it comes under guidance and constraint from the cellular system as a whole. According to biochemist Franklin Harold, "New gene products . . . are never altogether at liberty; they are released into a cellular milieu that already possesses spatial structure, . . . under the influence of the existing order."[36] In other words, a higher order of information governs and directs molecular assembly.

Part 2. Development Is Orchestrated

Consider the novel "Mr. Standfast," by John Buchan.[37] Our hero Richard Hannay is wrongly under suspicion and is being hotly pursued over the moors by half of Scotland's police force. They are closing in, not knowing that Hannay is an undercover British government agent, and the outcome of the First World War is at stake. Just in time an old friend, Sir Archie, appears, who whisks him away in his biplane to safety. In this gripping thriller, villains and heroes encounter one another in just the right times and places. We next find Hannay in a London Underground station during an air raid. He is hunting for his archenemy—a German spymaster. Of all the places in London, Hannay spots him—just there, at that very moment! One can see that the author has orchestrated all the plot points so as to accomplish his aim.

If we move our spotlight from the encounters of the novel to the "embryology scene," do we see the molecular players encounter each other by chance or do we see them in "just the right" times and places? I will look at this question by describing some of the key aspects (of morphogenesis) in different regions of the body. Recurrent themes

35. Maurisa F. Riley, Matthew S. Bochter, Kanu Wahi, Gerard J. Nuovo, and Susan E. Cole, "Mir-125a-5p-Mediated Regulation of Lfng Is Essential for the Avian Segmentation Clock," *Developmental Cell* 24, no. 5 (2013): 554–561; Emily Caldwell, "Tiny Piece of RNA Keeps 'Clock' Running in Earliest Stages of Life," *Research and Innovation Communications*, The Ohio State University, March 11, 2013, http://researchnews.osu.edu/archive/fringe.htm.
36. Franklin M. Harold, "Molecules into Cells: Specifying Spatial Architecture," *Microbiology and Molecular Biology Reviews* 69, no. 4 (2005): 544–564.
37. John Buchan, "Mr. Standfast," in *The Complete Richard Hannay* (London: Penguin, 1992).

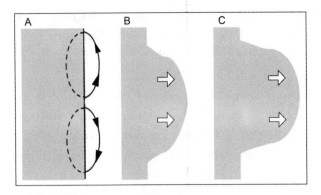

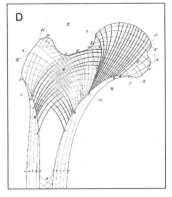

FIGURE 9.2. *Limb development.* **A.** An outwardly directed electric current (arrows) marks the correct location of future limb bud development in the flank of the animal (in gray) (after Altizer et al.; see note 41). **B** and **C.** Various chemical signals (white arrows) appear precisely at the right time and place, contributing to the progressive outgrowth of the limb bud. **D.** The struts within long bones are orientated along stress lines, enabling the bones to bear these stresses. However, these struts are already so-orientated during the embryo's development, before any loading has taken place! This suggests a prepattern anticipating the loading demands on the bone.

CREDIT: J. Wolff, "Ueber die innere Architectur der Knochen und ihre Bedeutung für die Frage vom Knochenwachsthum," *Virchows Archiv für Pathologische Anatomie und Physiologie* 50 (1870): 389–450. (Images A through C redrawn by Sheena Tyler.)

will appear—themes related to mechanisms of information storage. One theme is positional information, by which cells have their position specified in relation to a spatial coordinate system of reference.[38] Another theme is the "prepattern," which provides a template or scaf-

---

38. Johannes Jaeger and John Reinitz, "On the Dynamic Nature of Positional Information," *BioEssays* 28, no. 11 (2006): 1102–1111, doi:10.1002/bies.20494.

fold for the organization of some subsequent structure.[39] I will discuss examples of each of these methods of storing the information necessary for morphogenesis of various body systems, stressing the point that, without preexisting information, no morphogenesis can take place. If one may generalize, a prepattern of some sort, perhaps deriving from some sort of even more prior positional information, directs gene expression, which in turn directs cell behavior, which in turn directs morphogenesis. There is a flow of information from the first stages of development to its outworkings in final bodily form that must be highly "orchestrated" and "choreographed," to use words we will see repeatedly in the researchers' own language.[40]

2.1 Skeletal Development

In the development of the limb in vertebrates, an outwardly directed electric current plays a role in identifying the correct location of the future limb (Fig. 9.2).[41] (See chapter 7 in this volume.)

Particular genes and their products are active, producing chemical signals integrated into a four-dimensional patterning system.[42] These chemical signals help to specify the development of the limb (Figs. 8.2 B and C). It is noteworthy that these signals are produced at the appropriate time and location,[43] which implies an underlying prepattern that directs the gene expression itself.

The size and shape of skeletal elements appear to be, according to neuroscientist Charles Kimmel, "exquisitely regulated"[44] and

39. Maria Jerka-Dziadosz and Janine Beisson, "Genetic Approaches to Ciliate Pattern Formation: From Self-Assembly to Morphogenesis," *Trends in Genetics* 6 (1990): 41–45, doi:10.1016/0168-9525(90)90072-e.

40. It is not essential to understand the names and activities of specific genes in my examples, but these are sometimes included to give a sense of the developmental picture unfolding.

41. Alicia M. Altizer, Loren J. Moriarty, Sheila M. Bell, Claire M. Schreiner, William J. Scott, and Richard B. Borgens, "Endogenous Electric Current Is Associated with Normal Development of the Vertebrate Limb," *Developmental Dynamics* 221, no. 4 (2001): 391–401, doi:10.1002/dvdy.1158.

42. Jean-Denis Bénazet and Rolf Zeller, "Vertebrate Limb Development: Moving from Classical Morphogen Gradients to an Integrated 4-Dimensional Patterning System," *Cold Spring Harbor Perspectives in Biology* 1, no. 4 (2009): a001339.

43. Matthew Towers and Cheryll Tickle, "Generation of Pattern and Form in the Developing Limb," *International Journal of Developmental Biology* 53, no. 5–6 (2009): 805–812, doi:10.1387/ijdb.072499mt.

44. Charles B. Kimmel, Craig T. Miller, and Cecilia B. Moens, "Specification and Morphogenesis of the Zebrafish Larval Head Skeleton," *Developmental Biology* 233, no. 2 (2001): 239–257, doi:10.1006/dbio.2001.0201, 240.

"precise."[45] This indicates that a prepattern for skeletal development is likely to exist. For instance, in the zebrafish larval head, cartilage cells begin to appear at precise locations, such as where future joints will emerge. This may be guided by a prepattern organizing specific gene expression to this region. There is evidence too of a prepattern in mammalian bone development. Within the bones are lattice-like scaffolds, or "trabeculae," which become highly orientated according to the future stresses on the bone. The lattice patterns appear in the embryo *before* any mechanical loading, suggesting they may be organized by a predetermined template.[46]

2.2 The Nervous System

Development of the central nervous system requires "precise and exquisitely regulated gene expression patterns," according to neuroscientist Karla Meza-Sosa and colleagues.[47] For example, the brain and central nervous system arise from neural progenitor cells (NPCs), which multiply and develop into nerve cells, growing very long extensions (axons and dendrites) that become connected to target cells via synapses (junctions between nerve cells).[48] The information that directs the connectivity is considered to arise in the NPCs from expression of a *combinatorial code of transcription factors* (transcription factors are proteins that affect the expression of other genes).[49] This combinatorial code must in turn arise and be exquisitely controlled by preexisting information—the prepattern. The result is what neuroscientist and Yale University professor Daniel Colón-Ramos describes as the "intricate orchestration" of cell migration, axon guidance, growth of dendrites, and synapse formation of the nervous system.[50] It must be orchestrated

45. Ibid., 252.

46. Craig A. Cunningham and Sue M. Black, "Anticipating Bipedalism: Trabecular Organization in the Newborn Ilium," *Journal of Anatomy* 214, no. 6 (2009): 817–829, doi:10.1111/j.1469-7580.2009.01073.x.

47. Karla F. Meza-Sosa, David Valle-García, Gustavo Pedraza-Alva, and Leonor Pérez-Martínez, "Role of MicroRNAs in Central Nervous System Development and Pathology," *Journal of Neuroscience Research* 90, no. 1 (2011): 1, doi:10.1002/jnr.22701.

48. Joan Stiles and Terry L. Jernigan, "The Basics of Brain Development," *Neuropsychology Review* 20, no. 4 (2010): 327–348.

49. Franck Polleux, Gulayse Ince-Dunn, and Anirvan Ghosh, "Transcriptional Regulation of Vertebrate Axon Guidance and Synapse Formation," *Nature Reviews Neuroscience* 8, no. 5 (2007): 331–340.

50. Daniel A. Colón-Ramos, "Synapse Formation in Developing Neural Circuits," *Current Topics in Developmental Biology* 87 (2009): 53–79.

because synapses must connect together precisely, with 100 percent accuracy.[51]

In fact, what I have described only begins to illustrate the complexity and interconnectedness of neural development, and the information necessary to accomplish that development. There is a rich tapestry of informational signatures to be found both within DNA and also beyond it (for more information on this topic, see chapter 7 in this volume). All these forms of information function like codes that cells read, integrate, and interpret to guide their connectivity with other neurons. The information can be specified as follows:

1. *Prepatterning information*: Previously it was thought that synapse formation occurred only after neighboring neurons made contact with one another. However, even prior to such contact, synaptic "hotspots" of specialization occur, suggesting that prepatterning tells the neurons where synapses will form.[52]

2. *A transcriptional code*: Biochemical messengers secreted along the various body axes are thought to communicate positional information to the NPCs. This causes them to produce a combinatorial code of transcription factors, which in turn provides information governing neural connectivity.[53] Moreover, cells become specialized to become those forming sensory organs (e.g., the eye), requiring "careful orchestration of complex regulatory mechanisms," according to developmental neurobiologist Jean-Pierre Saint-Jeannet, professor at the University of Toulouse.[54]

3. *A histone code*: Chromosomes are composed of strands of DNA wrapped around proteins called histones. Modification of these histones is involved in the activation or the repression of gene activity. Modifications of histone proteins provide a histone code, which multiplies the combinatorial potential and thus the collective informational capacity of the genes. Geneticists Bing Yao and Peng Jin remark that

51. René Jüttner and Fritz G. Rathjen, "Molecular Analysis of Axonal Target Specificity and Synapse Formation," *Cellular and Molecular Life Sciences* 62, no. 23 (2005): 2811–2827.

52. Ann Marie Craig and Jeff W. Lichtman, "Synapse Formation and Maturation," in *Synapses*, ed. W. M. Cowan, T. C. Sudhof, and C. F. Stevens (Baltimore: Johns Hopkins University Press, 2001), 571–612.

53. Polleux et al., "Transcriptional Regulation," 331–340.

54. Jean-Pierre Saint-Jeannet and Sally A. Moody, "Establishing the Pre-Placodal Region and Breaking It into Placodes with Distinct Identities," *Developmental Biology* 389, no. 1 (2014): 23.

this code "delicately orchestrates with extracellular cues to determine the accurate regulation of neurogenesis."[55]

4. *A cell surface code*: Cell surface carbohydrate-protein complexes have a vast informational combinatorial potential. Their role is suggested because changes in their expression correlate with events during nervous system development[56] and their inhibition perturbs this development[57] (see chapter 7 for more information).

5. *A bioelectric code*: consisting of electrical currents in certain regions of the developing embryo. For example, there is electrical activity that predicts the subsequent patterning of the nervous system,[58] and that interfering with the neural *electrical* signal leads to neural developmental defects.[59] Once again, see chapter 7 for more on this.

Thus the DNA and various epigenetic sources *beyond* DNA provide coded information that is both sophisticated and integrated together in their activities, and that together help direct the formation of the nervous system.

2.3 Tooth Development

Tooth development in mammals appears to be guided by positional information, which is tailor-made for each tooth. The shape of each tooth grades with its immediate neighbors, so that the dentition is integrated into a harmonious whole.[60] Moreover, this integration extends to coordinated signaling interactions between the development of the teeth with their anchoring ligaments and the surrounding bone.[61] By

---

55. Bing Yao and Peng Jin, "Unlocking Epigenetic Codes in Neurogenesis," *Genes and Development* 28, no. 12 (2014): 1253.

56. C. M. Griffith and Esmond J. Sanders, "Changes in Glycoconjugate Expression during Early Chick Embryo Development: A Lectin-Binding Study," *The Anatomical Record* 231, no. 2 (1991): 238–250.

57. Roland Bourrillon and Michèle Aubery, "Cell Surface Glycoproteins in Embryonic Development," *International Review of Cytology* 116 (1989): 257–338.

58. Harold S. Burr and Carl I. Hovland, "Bio-Electric Correlates of Development in *Amblystoma*," *Yale Journal of Biology and Medicine* 9, no. 6 (1937): 540.

59. Vaibhav P. Pai, Joan M. Lemire, Jean-François Paré, Gufa Lin, Ying Chen, and Michael Levin, "Endogenous Gradients of Resting Potential Instructively Pattern Embryonic Neural Tissue via Notch Signaling and Regulation of Proliferation," *Journal of Neuroscience* 35, no. 10 (2015): 4366–4385.

60. Percy M. Butler, "Studies of the Mammalian Dentition: Differentiation of the Post-Canine Dentition," *Proceedings of the Zoological Society of London* 109, no. 1 (1939): 1–36.

61. Vlasta Lungová, Ralf J. Radlanski, Abigail S. Tucker, et al., "Tooth-Bone Morphogenesis during Postnatal Stages of Mouse First Molar Development," *Journal of Anatomy* 218, no. 6 (2011): 699–716.

appropriate deposition and reabsorption of bone, the bony socket of the tooth thus becomes precisely molded with the developing shape of each tooth root.

2.4 Heart and Circulatory System Development

Development of the heart is a "wondrous and precisely orchestrated series of molecular and morphogenetic events," in the view of heart disease specialist Deepak Srivastava.[62]

Heart development arises from a region of heart-forming cells in the early embryo known as the first heart field.[63] These cells develop, migrate, and form into a linear tube (the heart tube). Later, a group of cells known as the second heart field migrate to the heart tube, enabling the heart tube to become elongated, then loop to the right, expand, and become remodeled into the heart chambers (atria and ventricles).[64] Cells from the neural tube also migrate into the heart tube and are required for formation of the heart valves and compartments which separate oxygenated and deoxygenated blood.[65]

A very large number of genes are involved in these processes,[66] with a network of transcription pathways activating each other's expression.[67] Irfan Kathiriya and colleagues from the University of California report how cardiac transcription factors "*choreograph*" the expression of *thousands* of genes at each stage of heart development, by interacting with cofactors, and by binding with a constellation of regulatory DNA elements. These networks interplay to "orchestrate the sequential deployment of the cardiac gene expression program"[68] (Fig. 9.3).

62. Deepak Srivastava and Eric N. Olson, "A Genetic Blueprint for Cardiac Development," *Nature* 407, no. 6801 (2000): 221.

63. Lucile Miquerol, Sabrina Beyer, and Robert G. Kelly, "Establishment of the Mouse Ventricular Conduction System," *Cardiovascular Research* 91, no. 2 (2011): 232–242.

64. Diego Franco and Robert G. Kelly, "Contemporary Cardiogenesis: New Insights into Heart Development," *Cardiovascular Research* 91, no. 2 (2011): 183–184.

65. Miquerol, Beyer, and Kelly, "Establishment of the Mouse Ventricular Conduction System."

66. Carmen López-Sánchez and Virginio García-Martínez, "Molecular Determinants of Cardiac Specification," *Cardiovascular Research* 91, no. 2 (2011): 185–195.

67. Eric N. Olson, "Gene Regulatory Networks in the Evolution and Development of the Heart," *Science* 313, no. 5795 (2006): 1922–1927.

68. Irfan S. Kathiriya, Elphège P. Nora, and Benoit G. Bruneau, "Investigating the Transcriptional Control of Cardiovascular Development," *Circulation Research* 116, no. 4 (2015): 700, emphasis added.

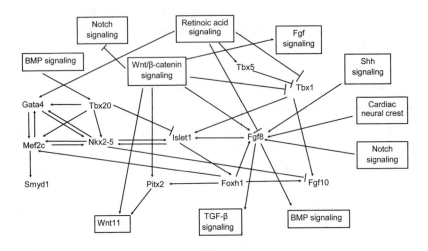

FIGURE 9.3. *Heart development.* Heart development is wondrously orchestrated, say heart experts, involving thousands of interacting genes. Some of these are featured in this simplified diagram of the gene regulatory network in the second heart field (see text). Key: gene products (in abbreviations); signalling pathways (in boxes); activation of genes (arrows); down-regulation [i.e., repression] of genes (lines with end-bars).

CREDIT: After Stéphane D. Vincent and Margaret E. Buckingham, "Chapter One—How to Make a Heart: The Origin and Regulation of Cardiac Progenitor Cells," *Current Topics in Developmental Biology* 90 (2010): 1–41.

In addition, the muscles of the heart do not contract randomly and chaotically. Rather, the atria and ventricle chambers contract sequentially, which is crucial to the effective expulsion of blood.[69] This is facilitated by microscopic muscle cell proteins precisely registered together.[70] The integration of these contractions globally throughout the heart is provided by specialized cells organized into an electrical wiring system. The second heart field, mentioned earlier, contributes to the development of this electrical conduction system. Electrical impulses generated from pacemaker cells spread rapidly across both atria, resulting in simultaneous contraction of the atria. They then converge on the atrioventricular node, which delays the spread of the electrical

---

69. Miquerol, Beyer, and Kelly, "Establishment of the Mouse Ventricular Conduction System."
70. Nimalan Thavandiran, Sara S. Nunes, Yun Xiao, and Milica Radisic, "Topological and Electrical Control of Cardiac Differentiation and Assembly," *Stem Cell Research and Therapy* 4, no. 1 (2013): 1.

activity so that the atria contract before the ventricles. Electrical activity is then spread rapidly through the ventricles, through a specialized fast conducting system or ventricular conduction system, leading to the sequential contraction of heart muscle, progressing from the apex to maximize the expulsion of blood. Development of this conductive system involves the combinatorial effect of numerous cardiac-specific transcription factors,[71] implying a programmed, informational capacity to the second heart field. This results in development of the electrical system becoming integrated with the shape and form of the heart. Cardiologist Nikhil Munshi describes how "even subtle perturbation of this finely orchestrated electric activation pattern" can cause clinically important or fatal cardiac arrhythmias,[72] indicating its essential importance.

However, the heart also requires a circulatory system to pump blood into, and it appears that development of both the heart and circulation are simultaneously coordinated.[73] Cells destined to become blood vessels aggregate together in islands, then migrate and connect to form a network of tubes. This provides the scaffold for development of arteries, veins, and capillaries, by remodeling and subsequent vessel sprouting (angiogenesis).[74] Various substances secreted by cells to regulate development (growth factors) "orchestrate" the growth of vessels in a very ordered pattern, according to cardiology researchers A. S. Chung and colleagues.[75] There is great fidelity to this pattern, with the anatomy and branching points of major vessels being highly reproducible, precisely positioned in relation to the organs they serve, and exactly "plumbed" into other major vessels, with evidence that this is genetically prepatterned.[76] For instance, angiogenesis is initiated by vessel leakage of plasma proteins, which then form a scaffold for

71. Miquerol, Beyer, and Kelly, "Establishment of the Mouse Ventricular Conduction System."
72. Nikhil V. Munshi, "Gene Regulatory Networks in Cardiac Conduction System Development," *Circulation Research* 110, no. 11 (2012): 1525–1537.
73. H. Scott Baldwin, "Early Embryonic Vascular Development," *Cardiovascular Research* 31 (1996): E34.
74. Michael Potente, Holger Gerhardt, and Peter Carmeliet, "Basic and Therapeutic Aspects of Angiogenesis," *Cell* 146, no. 6 (2011): 873–887.
75. A. S. Chung, J. Lee, and N. Ferrara, "Targeting the Tumour Vasculature: Insights from Physiological Angiogenesis," *National Review of Cancer* 10 (2010): 505–514, doi:10.1038/nrc2868.
76. Brant M Weinstein, "What Guides Early Embryonic Blood Vessel Formation?" *Developmental Dynamics* 215, no. 1 (1999): 2–11.

migrating vessel lining (endothelial) cells, guided by Vascular Endothelial Growth Factors (VEGFs) liberated in an "orchestrated sequence."[77]

For the proper functioning of the cardiovascular system, arteries, veins, and lymphatics do not have a uniform morphology but have distinctly different structural features so as to perform different tasks.[78] Arteries possess thick internal layers in order to cope with blood exiting from the heart under high pressure. Veins are under low pressure, and thin walls are sufficient, but are in addition constructed so as to allow the passage of white blood cells across them. They also possess valves for the one-way flow of blood and to prevent backflow into the capillaries.[79] This arterial and venous (AV) specification requires the "correct spatial and temporal expression of many genes orchestrated by a relatively large set of transcription factors,"[80] "working together in concert."[81] Researchers Jason Fish and Joshua Wythe similarly recognize AV specification to be a highly coordinated process involving the "intersection and carefully orchestrated activity of multiple signaling cascades and transcriptional networks,"[82] including the *Hedgehog, VEGF, TGF-β, Wnt,* and Notch signaling pathways. The crucial role of *VEGF* is seen when loss of even one copy of *VEGF* in mice results in profound vascular defects leading to embryonic lethality.[83] Fish and Wythe reiterate the "*exquisite* orchestration required for these various processes to occur—sometimes simultaneously,"[84] with a plethora of signaling pathways acting to coordinate the establishment of the vasculature.

Moreover, vessels develop in relation to their function and the specific needs of the organ in which they may be located.[85] For instance,

77. Anja Bondke Persson and Ivo R. Buschmann, "Vascular Growth in Health and Disease," *Frontiers in Molecular Neuroscience* 4 (2011): 14.

78. Monica Corada, Marco Francesco Morini, and Elisabetta Dejana, "Signaling Pathways in the Specification of Arteries and Veins," *Arteriosclerosis, Thrombosis, and Vascular Biology* 34, no. 11 (2014): 2372–2377.

79. Jason E. Fish and Joshua D. Wythe, "The Molecular Regulation of Arteriovenous Specification and Maintenance," *Developmental Dynamics* 244, no. 3 (2015): 391–409.

80. Corada, Morini, and Dejana, "Signaling Pathways," 2373.

81. Sarah De Val, "Key Transcriptional Regulators of Early Vascular Development," *Arteriosclerosis, Thrombosis, and Vascular Biology* 31, no. 7 (2011): 1469–1475.

82. Fish and Wythe, "Molecular Regulation of Arteriovenous Specification," 391.

83. Ibid.

84. Ibid., emphasis added.

85. William C. Aird, "Endothelial Cell Heterogeneity," *Cold Spring Harbor Perspectives in Medicine* 2, no. 1 (2012): a006429.

embryonic brain development is intimately associated with development of the blood vessels there.[86] The brain microvasculature strictly *minimizes* permeability, while in contrast organs such as the liver or bone marrow possess a vessel structure which *promotes* permeability between blood cells and proteins.[87] The development of the cardiovascular system, in relation to the functional demands of the vasculature, implies a yet even greater level of integration and cross-talk of developmental information.

2.5 The Nature of Information

If organisms are not intelligently designed, they must be cobbled together by non-intelligent mechanisms.[88] Tinkering mechanisms are at the heart of modern theories of evolution. However, the above accounts indicate many evidences of an intricate orchestration of patterning mechanisms to enable the concurrent coordination of various organs and organ systems, integrated with reproductive behavior.

My daughters play in a youth orchestra. During rehearsals, whenever left to themselves, the young players immediately start up their own tunes or practices. Very soon there is only noisy chaos! It requires the conductor to bring order out of this chaos; and also, intelligent information encoded in the composer's manuscript needs to be interpreted by the conductor and musicians to produce the harmonious melody. So, the recourse of various authors to the metaphor of orchestration of development is interesting, for such orchestration is a signature of intelligent causation.

It is not just a genetic code, but many codes together providing a rich combinatorial capacity for information storage. To the above list of codes could also be added the splicing codes, the cytoskeleton codes, the apoptosis code, and the ubiquitin code.[89] In 2016 a whole special

---

86. Ina M. Wittko-Schneider, Fabian T. Schneider, and Karl H. Plate, "Cerebral Angiogenesis during Development: Who Is Conducting the Orchestra?" *Cerebral Angiogenesis: Methods and Protocols* (2014): 3–20, doi:10.1007/978-1-4939-0320-7_1.

87. Corada, Morini, and Dejana, "Signaling Pathways."

88. François Jacob, "Evolution and Tinkering," *Science* 196 (1977): 1161–1166; John S. Torday, "A Central Theory of Biology," *Medical Hypotheses* 85, no. 1 (2015): 49–57; Claudius F. Kratochwil and Axel Meyer, "Evolution: Tinkering within Gene Regulatory Landscapes," *Current Biology* 25, no. 7 (2015): R285–R288, doi:http://dx.doi.org/10.1016/j.cub.2015.02.051.

89. Marcello Barbieri, "A New Theory of Development: The Generation of Complexity in Ontogenesis," *Philosophical Transactions of the Royal Society A* 374, no. 2063 (2016): 20150148.

issue of the journal *Philosophical Transactions of the Royal Society* was devoted to the theme, "DNA as Information." Introducing the issue, Julyan Cartwright and colleagues state that biological codes not only transmit information but also interpret it, and that the genetic code information even "includes how to produce new senders and receivers."[90] They recognize too the programming aspect, being written in language yet to be decoded, and being not merely "a simple linear list of instructions, but a program, with subroutines, callbacks, loops and all the complexity that implies."[91] Thus, the premise of a simple, linear flow of information in gene sequences is giving way to a new model of development involving biological networks within hierarchical tiers, with information moving multidirectionally both within and between the tiers.[92]

The engineer and physicist Werner Gitt recognizes that technological systems, engineered objects, and works of art did not come into existence by self-organization of matter, but were preceded by "establishing the required information."[93] He adds that it has not been shown experimentally how information can arise spontaneously in matter.[94] It is only through guidance that processes "run contrary to natural laws' directions, to attain a goal that unguided processes could never."

Gitt has discovered that human and machine languages exhibit five levels of information. The lowest level of information is statistical (a symbol or number of symbols). However, the mere statistical, quantitative evaluation of a symbol sequence ignores whether or not such information is meaningful. Language systems exhibit a second level of information, comprising codes (sets of abstract symbols) combined with syntax (rules for construction and arrangement of words). Languages also possess a third level, called semantics (the meaning of the message being conveyed). Fourth, they exhibit pragmatics—(action that the sender expects the receiver to perform); and a fifth, highest

90. Julyan H. E. Cartwright, Simone Giannerini, and Diego L. González, "DNA as Information: At the Crossroads between Biology, Mathematics, Physics and Chemistry," *Philosophical Transactions of the Royal Society A* 374, no. 2063 (2016): 2015.0071, 7.

91. Cartwright, Giannerini, and González, "DNA as Information," 3.

92. Sarah Franklin and Thomas M. Vondriska, "Genomes, Proteomes, and the Central Dogma," *Circulation: Cardiovascular Genetics* 4, no. 5 (2011): 576–576, doi:10.1161/CIRCGENETICS.110.957795.

93. Werner Gitt, *In the Beginning Was Information* (Bielefeld, Germany: CLV, 2000), 49.

94. Ibid.

level—apobetics (purpose; the intended goal). Gitt coins the term "universal information" (UI) for systems expressing these characteristics. UI thus comprises symbolically coded messages conveying the expected action(s) and the intended purpose(s).[95]

The DNA of living things utilizes a genuine coding system, and all these five levels of information are observed. Gitt concludes that any code system is *always the result of an intellectual process that requires an intelligent originator*.[96] This has implications for recognizing that there must be an intelligent originator of the various code systems found in embryological development.

Thus, from the above accounts, the notion of macroevolution occurring through changes in genes involved in development remains a theatre of dreams and speculations. So, does development reveal *any* story of life's history? This is our next focus.

Part 3. Basic Types of Life

According to evolutionary theory, all organisms are historically connected in the so-called evolutionary tree, in which body forms can be traced back through gradual changes from simpler body plans, continuously grading over many generations, ultimately derived from a primitive common ancestor. A contrasting view discerns distinct kinds or types of organisms that share a basic body plan and mode of development. These distinct assemblages of organisms most closely approximate to the modern *family* taxonomic level. Their distinctiveness argues that each group may have a separate and unique origin. Which of these two scenarios the evidence better supports will now be explored.

3.1. Hybridization Data

Cross-breeding (hybridization between species) is very common. For instance, one in ten species of bird is known to hybridize with another species.[97] This suggests that the eggs and sperm from the hybrid's parents *must* share a developmental machinery that is compatible in order

---

95. Ibid., 104.
96. Werner Gitt. *Without Excuse* (Atlanta: Creation, 2011), 50.
97. Peter R. Grant and Rosemary Grant, "Hybridization of Bird Species," *Science* 256, no. 5054 (1992): 193.

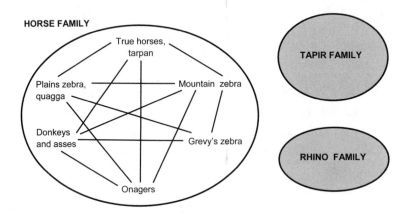

FIGURE 9.4. *Hybridization within the horse family.* Horses hybridize with all species within the horse family (large white circle). However, there are no hybrids between members of the horse family and their nearest proposed relatives, such as rhinoceri or tapirs. This correlates with a clear gap or "discontinuity" in form between the horse, rhino, and tapir families.

to produce viable, live offspring.[98] Therefore, probing the data to find which species and genera can be united together by hybridization is an evidence-based (i.e., empirical) method to discern whether natural groupings exist. Analysis of this data provides strong evidence that this is indeed the case. The following provide a few examples.

The Horse Family (*Equidae*)

All species within the horse family (horses, donkeys, asses, and zebras) are united by their ability to hybridize.[99] But they do not hybridize with their nearest suggested evolutionary relatives (the tapirs and rhinoceri) (Fig. 9.4).[100]

The Cat Family (*Felicidae*)

Hybridization unites various species, and also several genera. For instance, the *Puma* (*Puma concolor*) can hybridize with the Leopard (*Panthera pardus*).

98. Tyler, "Work Surfaces of Morphogenesis," 204.
99. Heike Stein-Cadenbach, "Hybriden, chromosomen und artbildung bei pferden (Equidae)," in *Typen des Lebens*, ed. Siegfried Scherer (Berlin: Pascal-Verlag, 1993), 225–244.
100. Lindsay Thompson, "Types of Animal Form," *Origins* 60 (2015): 26–30.

FIGURE 9.5. *Atavisms—hidden genetic potential.* **A.** Ruddy Abyssinian cat breed. Note this breed never has spots on its coat. **B.** Seal Point Siamese, also never has a spotted coat. **C.** When a Ruddy Abyssinian was crossed with a Seal Point Siamese, the outcome was a spotted cat (the ocicat). This indicates that ancestral characters for spots are hidden in the gene pool.

CREDIT: (A) By Karin Langner-Bahmann - Own work, CC BY-SA 3.0, https://commons.wikimedia.org/w /index.php?curid=950497; (B) Creative commons (absfreepic.com); (C) © Helmi Flick. Used with permission.

The Ruddy Abyssinian cat breed (Fig. 9.5A) never exhibits a spotted coat, and neither does the Seal Point Siamese (Fig. 9.5B). However, when a Ruddy Abyssinian was crossed with a Seal Point Siamese, and the offspring was backcrossed to another Siamese, the surprising outcome was a spotted cat.[101] This is now recognized as a new rare breed known as the ocicat (Fig. 8.5C) because of its similarity to the ocelot. The ocicat spots are an example of an atavism, described by Brian Hall[102] as the reappearance of a character known in distant ancestors and not seen in the parents or recent ancestors.

The Bear Family (*Ursidae*)

Six of the eight species of bears (e.g., the polar bear, American black bear, Asiatic black bear, sloth bear, and sun bear) are united by hybridization.[103]

Ducks, Geese, and Swans (*Anatidae*)

Remarkably, 81 percent of all 149 species of ducks, geese, and swans (Anatidae) hybridize with one another. Over 50 percent of these

---

101. Thompson, "Types of Animal Form," 26–27.
102. Brian K. Hall, "Atavisms," *Current Biology* 20, no. 20 (2010): R871.
103. Thompson, "Types of Animal Form," 27.

hybridize between genera (groups of species sharing similar features). Yet there are no known hybrids between the Anatidae and members of any neighboring taxonomic groups. Twenty percent of all known hybrids are fertile, suggesting that the Anatidae are genetically related but clearly distinguished from other taxonomic groups (taxa) of birds.[104]

Cranes (*Gruidae*)

Hybridization links fourteen of the fifteen species and all four genera of cranes together within the family. These also link the two subfamilies (crowned cranes and true cranes).[105]

Pelicans (*Pelicanidae*)

Six out of seven pelican species can hybridize, but hybridization between pelicans and any other proposed relatives is unknown.[106]

Storks (*Ciconiidae*)

Seven of the nineteen species of storks hybridize, but no hybridization is found between storks and other bird families.[107]

Siegfried Scherer and colleagues[108] demarcated a number of groups by such interspecific hybridization, which they designated as "basic types." Two individuals were viewed to belong to the same basic type if they hybridized with each other, or if they hybridized with a third organism in common. At least seventy-two basic types have been identified, with the prospects of many more from untapped data.[109] Most commonly, the basic types are identifiable with the family, subfamily, or superfamily taxonomic level. A number of findings emerge from these analyses:

1. Hybridization is common within basic types, but absent between them, indicating natural gaps or divisions between the basic type and their nearest neighbors.

---

104. Siegfried Scherer and T. Hilsberg, "Hybridization and Relationships in the Anatidae-a Taxonomic and Evolutionary Consideration," *Journal fur Ornithologie* 123, no. 4 (1982): 357–380.

105. Sheena Tyler, in preparation.

106. Thompson, "Types of Animal Form," 27.

107. Ibid.

108. Siegfried Scherer, "Basic Types of Life," in *Typen des Lebens*, ed. Siegfried Scherer (Berlin: Pascal-Verlag, 1993), 11–30.

109. Tyler, in preparation.

2. The basic types distinguished by hybridization strongly correlate with the outward form or morphology of the group. Importantly, this is exactly as would be predicted if the members of a basic type shared a developmental machinery, which generates their common form.

3. Within a basic type, although the basic form is shared between members, hybridization also links together species with relatively divergent morphology. For instance, hybridization unites various species of parrots,[110] which nonetheless still share the recognizably parrot-like form. This suggests a certain developmental capacity for variation or "plasticity" within the basic type.

4. Evidence of atavisms within some basic types indicates a hidden ancestral reservoir of genetic potential. Indeed, Brian Hall considers atavisms to be the visible expression of huge hidden potential for change in form with which all organisms are endowed.[111] This hints at the notion of genetically complex ancestors. Genetic mechanisms are known to exist by which this ancestral reservoir is considered to generate new variations in form following hybridization.[112] This is not a concession to microevolution, which refers to incremental emergence of novelty on an evolutionary trajectory. Rather, the appearance of novel traits represents diversification from a preexisting, information-rich genotype.

3.2 Cleavage Pattern

The spatial arrangement of cells within an embryo as they divide is known as the cleavage pattern. Various animal groups have notable, fundamental differences in these patterns, as the following examples demonstrate.

a. *Ctenophora* (Comb Jellies)[113]

The first two cleavages are in the vertical (meridional) plane (Fig. 9.6A). The third division is nearly vertical and results in a curved plate

110. Lorents Landgren, Lukas Gustafsson, and Herfried Kutzelnigg, "Grundtypstudien an Papageie," *Studium integrale* 18, no. 3 (2011): 6–18.
111. Brian K. Hall, "Developmental Mechanisms Underlying the Formation of Atavisms," *Biological Reviews* 59, no. 1 (1984): 89–122.
112. Richard Abbott and thirty-six others, "Hybridization and Speciation," *Journal of Evolutionary Biology* 26, no. 2 (2013): 229–246.
113. Christian Sardet, D. Carre, and C. Rouviere, "Reproduction and Development in Ctenophores," in *Experimental Embryology in Aquatic Plants and Animals*, ed. H. J. Marthy (New York: Plenum, 1990).

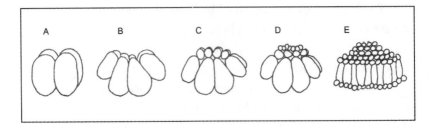

FIGURE 9.6. *Cleavage pattern in Ctenophora (comb jellies).* See text. After Sardet, Carre, and Rouviere, "Reproduction and Development in Ctenophores" (see note 113).

of eight larger cells (macromeres) (Fig. 9.6B). The following division is horizontal and unequal, giving rise to small cells (micromeres) on the concave side of the tier of macromeres (Fig. 9.6C). The micromeres divide several times (Fig. 9.6D), and the macromeres produce a second set of micromeres (Fig. 9.6E).

b. *Molluska* (Snails)[114]

Mollusk eggs exhibit spiral cleavage, in which each quartet of micromeres is rotated to the right or left of the macromeres in alternate divisions. The first two meridional divisions lead to formation of the A, B, C, and D cells. In the following cleavage, each of these cells, now called macromeres, divide to form a micromere. This process is repeated to produce further quartets of micromeres, which in turn produce further divisions (Fig. 9.7).[115]

c. *Arthropoda: Insecta*[116]

In the fruit fly (*Drosophila*), nuclei divide but remain in the same common cytoplasm (syncytium) (Fig. 9.8).[117] Gradually, the egg membrane folds inward to partition off each nucleus into single cells. This pattern of early syncytial development is true for most insects.

---

114. N. H. Verdonk and J. A. M. Van den Biggelaar, "Early Development and the Formation of the Germ Layers," in *The Mollusca: Volume 3, Development*, ed. N. H. Verdonk, J. A. M. Van den Biggelaar, and A. S. Tompa (New York: Academic Press, New York, 1983), 91–122.
115. After E. G. Conklin, "The Embryology of *Crepidula*," *Journal of Morphology* 13 (1897): 1–226.
116. J. Kawana and T. Takami, "Insecta," in *Invertebrate Embryology*, ed. M. Kume and K. Dan (Belgrade, Yugoslavia: NOLIT, 1968), 405–484.
117. After Kawana and Takami, "Insecta."

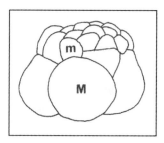

FIGURE 9.7. *Cleavage pattern in mollusks.* See text. M = macromere; m = micromere.

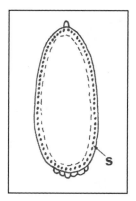

FIGURE 9.8. *Cleavage pattern in insects.* See text. S = syncytium (nuclei share a common cytoplasm).

d. Vertebrates

Cleavage patterns in the early embryo vary significantly between groups. Fish, frogs, chicks, and mice each have distinctive patterns of cell divisions, which are each distinct from the above mentioned cleavage patterns.

The crucial importance of early development is revealed by experiments in which individual cells from early cleavage stages are destroyed. In embryos such as mollusks, this leads to loss of adult structures descended from the deleted cells. Evolutionists have a tendency to downplay or overlook the significance of these early

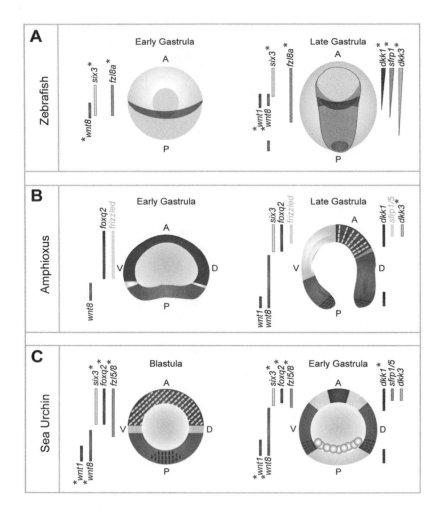

FIGURE 9.9. *Fate maps.* Vertical sections of similar embryonic stages (the "blastula and gastrula") of three very different species, showing gene expression patterns.

stages, but it should be emphasized that in such animals, the early stages of development really are foundational to the subsequent development of form. In some other animal groups, cell fate is established later. How then can fundamentally different early cleavage patterns be traced to a common ancestor? The proposed existence of such ancestors appears to be imposed on the evidence rather than emerging from it.

3.3 Cell Fates

Tracing the fates of cells through development has enabled researchers to infer similarities (homologies) between organisms. For instance, by tracing mollusk embryo cell fate of different mollusks, it was found that the first quartet of micromeres eventually produces the head structures such as eyes, tentacles, and cerebral ganglia. The second and third quartet give rise to the shell, foot, and mantle cavity. According to embryologist Ivanova-Kazas, this uniformity of cell fates is evidence that organisms sharing this pattern are related in some fundamental way.[118] The prospective fates of cells in various regions of the embryo can be depicted as a so-called fate map, as can the distribution of gene products, which reveal fundamental discontinuities between basic forms (Fig. 9.9).[119]

3.4 Developmental Mechanisms

Activities within the cell, such as behavior of its internal scaffolding (the cytoskeleton), can be unique to certain taxonomic groups. For example in flies, the main body axis is established early in the egg before fertilization, when the cytoskeleton transports polarity-specifying gene products to opposite poles.[120] In contrast, mammals define an initial axis by extruding tiny cells at one pole, but lack polarity components essential for development until at the 8-cell stage. Then, uniquely to mammals, dramatic cytoskeleton activity causes the cells to huddle together and flatten (compaction), and polarize along an inner-outer axis.[121] Moreover, flies use a different mechanism from vertebrates to localize the machinery which orientates the chromosomes during cell division.[122]

Thus cleavage patterns, cell fates, and developmental mechanisms can be radically different between different forms of animals during

118. Olga M. Ivanova-Kazas, "Phylogenetic Significance of Spiral Cleavage," *Soviet Journal of Marine Biology* 75 (1982): 275–283.

119. Ryan C. Range, Robert C. Angerer, and Lynne M. Angerer, "Integration of Canonical and Noncanonical Wnt Signaling Pathways Patterns the Neuroectoderm along the Anterior–Posterior Axis of Sea Urchin Embryos," *PLoS Biology* 11, no. 1 (2013): e1001467.

120. Josefa Steinhauer and Daniel Kalderon, "Microtubule Polarity and Axis Formation in the Drosophila Oocyte," *Developmental Dynamics* 235, no. 6 (2006): 1455–1468

121. C. Y. Leung, M. Zhu, and M. Zernicka-Goetz, "Chapter Six-Polarity in Cell-Fate Acquisition in the Early Mouse Embryo," *Current Topics in Developmental Biology* 120 (2016): 203–234.

122. Dan T. Bergstralh, Nicole S. Dawney, and Daniel St. Johnston, "Spindle Orientation: A Question of Complex Positioning," *Development* 144, no. 7 (2017): 1137–1145.

these early stages. Davidson commented on how the various spatial patterns of embryos are generated:

> . . . some embryos begin this process by intercellular interaction, and others even before there are any cells that would carry out such interactions; some rely on lineages that are . . . committed to given functions as soon as they appear; others deal only in plastic, malleable cell fate assignments; . . . some utilize eggs that before fertilization are cytoskeletally organized in both axes, some in one axis only, some apparently in neither; . . . for some types of embryos every individual has a different cell lineage, whilst for others there is a set of rigidly reproducible canonical cell lineages; . . . and some embryos display amazing regulative capacities.

Thus, he concluded, "the differences among the taxa in their modes of development are anything but trivial and superficial."[123]

3.5 *Hox* Genes and the Phylotypic Stage

Evolutionary embryologists commonly minimize these differences by speculating that patterns of genes (notably the body axis–specifying *Hox* gene cluster) show a common expression pattern in various animals, and that plasticity in such genes, particularly at the phylotypic stage (when members of a phylum might show maximum similarity), could generate evolutionary new body plans.[124] However, there are several problems and flaws with these arguments:

1. To reiterate a previous point, in numerous phyla (such as the mollusks), this supposed developmental plasticity at the phylotypic stage may be constrained by crucial earlier events in the embryo.

2. Stages such as the gastrula (the proposed phylotypic stage of some invertebrates) could simply be a necessary developmental stage for these phyla, and an alternative explanation is that this is a common design pattern.

3. The embryologist Michael Richardson demonstrated that there is no single phylotypic stage. This stage cannot be convincingly extended

---

123. Eric H. Davidson, "How Embryos Work: A Comparative View of Diverse Modes of Cell Fate Specification," *Development* 108, no. 3 (1990): 366.
124. Jonathan M. W. Slack, Peter W. H. Holland, and Christopher F. Graham, "The Zootype and the Phylotypic Stage," *Nature* 361, no. 6412 (1993): 490–492.

to the invertebrates, with cell fate maps and developmental mechanisms profoundly different between the various phyla when they are supposedly at their most similar.[125]

4. Flawed diagrammatic representation of the *Hox* clusters in research publications lead to misconceptions, according to Denis Duboule, professor of developmental genetics and genomics at both the Ecole Polytechnique Fédérale and the Department of Genetics and Evolution at the University of Geneva. For instance, drawing genes as small boxes and the same size suggests that *Hox* genes are identical to one other, which Duboule states "is rarely so."[126]

5. The exclusion of intergenic sequences is a biased perception that they are not important. For instance, two separate *Hox* complexes in Drosophila in this way become "artificially juxtaposed" so that they align with their vertebrate counterparts, to give the misconception of their similarity.[127]

6. Duboule makes a "surprising" and "embarrassing" discovery and conclusion that "vertebrates display the most tightly organized *Hox* gene clusters, whilst most other animals have a largely disorganized or split cluster . . . thus the textbook *Hox* cluster might be the exception and not the rule."[128] This scenario would place vertebrates as "direct descendants" of the primitive ancestor from which the majority of animals are derived. Since this is so implausible, these discoveries would please the "proponents of intelligent design." In other words, when the arrangements of *Hox* clusters between species are examined in detail, there is no transitional series toward the vertebrate pattern, which fails to show evidence of evolutionary links to a common ancestor.

7. To reiterate (yet again!), the morphogenetic action for the *Hox* genes, and their precise role in *actually generating* the phenotype from the genotype, is still unknown, and thus it remains highly speculative as to how *Hox* and other such genes could be generating evolutionary novel body plans. Indeed evolutionists Rudolf Raff and

---

125. Michael K. Richardson, James Hanken, Mayoni L. Gooneratne, et al., "There Is No Highly Conserved Embryonic Stage in the Vertebrates: Implications for Current Theories of Evolution and Development," *Anatomy and Embryology* 196, no. 2 (1997): 91–106.
126. Denis Duboule, "The Rise and Fall of Hox Gene Clusters," *Development* 134, no. 14 (2007): 2549.
127. Ibid.
128. Ibid., 551.

Thomas Kaufman admit a lack of evidence for evolutionary changes in body plans, commenting that most observations of evolution have not been made on organisms, but on fossils, "for only by recourse to the fossil record do we gain a view of organisms' actual evolutionary histories."[129]

3.6 The Fossil Record

So what are Raff and Kaufman's observations of evolution within the fossil record? The Cambrian explosion refers to the dramatic appearance of most of the animal phyla at the base of the hard-bodied fossil geological record, and is global in its extent.[130] Raff and Kaufman make a number of surprising observations:

1. "Highly complex animals—echinoderms, trilobites and arthropods. . . . and several classes of molluscs. . . . all appeared in the Cambrian period in considerable diversity and without recognised ancestors."[131] They note that echinoderms (e.g., starfish), for instance, appear in the Cambrian with a "lack of any identifiable ancestors," appearing with "all the basic echinoderm patterns fully recognisable."[132] That is to say, the fossils in the Cambrian can be identified with the forms of their modern-day counterparts.

2. Transitional forms are "largely hypothetical"—even the earliest echinoderm classes are quite distinct from one another. This data is not restricted to echinoderms: the "gaps are general and prevalent throughout the fossil record."[133]

3. New morphological structures do appear (e.g., the amphibian limb, wings), but when they first appear in the fossil record they are fully formed, and are not transitional.[134]

4. How the various multicellular body plans arose and diverged from a common ancestor "have proved to be fertile grounds for speculation, because there are so few facts to restrain the imagination."[135]

---

129. Rudolf A. Raff and Thomas C. Kaufman, *Embryos, Genes, and Evolution* (London: Macmillan, 1983), 25.
130. See chapter 2 in this volume.
131. Raff and Kaufman, *Embryos, Genes and Evolution*, 31.
132. Ibid.
133. Ibid., 34.
134. Ibid., 54.
135. Ibid., 30.

This is an extraordinary admission from such eminent evolutionists, and reiterates the speculative scenarios of the evo-devo community.

Convincing evidence in strata earlier than the Cambrian for the origin of these diverse phyla is lacking, and attempts to spread out the Cambrian period (implying that the first appearances were less abrupt) have been thwarted by new examples of fossils appearing that push the timescales back again.[136] Efforts to ascribe the right geochemical conditions to be a trigger for the Cambrian explosion[137] are also unconvincing, because the chemical environment provides merely the permissive conditions, not the *cause* of complex specified information embodied in the Cambrian body forms.[138]

From my boat-building experiments, I now have a collection of failed prototypes, such as boats that are too unstable. But in the fossil record, where are the failed prototypes? They are nowhere to be found! Instead we find nature got it right *from their first appearances*, as in the perfectly balanced "cantilever" bridge structures (Fig. 9.10A) of dinosaur skeletons such as sauropods, with their massive tails perfectly counterweighting the equally massive, long neck. The two balanced cantilevers are bound up in one common field of force and plan of construction, in which the stress diagram (representing all the forces acting on the animal) becomes the structural plan. For instance, in *Brontosaurus* (Fig. 9.10B)[139] and *Apatosaurus* (Fig. 9.10C), the backbone cantilever arch culminates over the pelvis and hind limbs, and the highest vertebral spines are found there, to dissipate the maximum tension loads experienced in this region, and with the height of the spines grading perfectly in proportion to the forces experienced along the length of the backbone.[140] Without this, the bones would break under the enormous weight of the animal. Moreover, dinosaur skeletons are not merely like static bridges,

---

136. Samuel Zamora, "Middle Cambrian Echinoderms from North Spain Show Echinoderms Diversified Earlier in Gondwana," *Geology* 38, no. 6 (2010): 507–510.

137. Shanan E. Peters and Robert R. Gaines, "Formation of the 'Great Unconformity' as a Trigger for the Cambrian Explosion," *Nature* 484, no. 7394 (2012): 363–366.

138. David Tyler, personal communication.

139. "Brontosaurus Skeleton," *The Integrative Paleontologists*, PLOS Blogs, 2015, http://blogs .plos.org/paleo/files/2015/04/Brontosaurus_skeleton_1880s.jpg. Note *Brontosaurus* has been considered to be the same species as *Apatosaurus*, but this remains controversial: see Andrew Farke, "*Brontosaurus* Thunders Back!" *The Integrative Paleontologist*, PLOS Blogs, April 7, 2015, http://blogs.plos.org/paleo/2015/04/07/brontosaurus-thunders-back.

140. D'Arcy W. Thompson, *On Growth and Form*, 2nd ed. (Cambridge: Cambridge University Press, 1942), 988–1006.

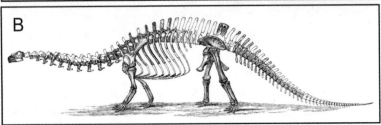

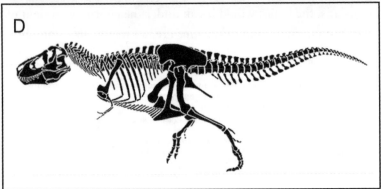

FIGURE 9.10 (**facing page**). Where are the failed prototypes in the fossil record? They are nowhere to be found! From their first appearances in the fossil record, the entire skeleton of massive dinosaurs is engineered to bear the animal's load (up to 60 tons in certain species). **A.** In sauropods this is achieved because the skeleton works as do the double-armed cantilever girders (arrowed) of a bridge such as the Forth Rail Bridge in Scotland. **B.** *Brontosaurus.* Note that the arch culminates over the pelvis and hind limbs, where the animal's weight is greatest. **C.** *Apatosaurus.* Black arrows indicate the balancing cantilever effect of tail and neck. Vertebral spines are longest (white arrow) just where the tensional loads are the greatest, and grade perfectly in proportion to these loads. **D.** *Tyrannosaurus rex.* Even when the skeletal curves are considerably modified during dynamic motion, the animal remains stable and able to bear the changing forces of tension and compression.

CREDITS: (A) Author Unknown [public domain], via Wikimedia Commons https://commons.wiki media.org/wiki/File%3AForth_bridge_histo_2.jpg; (B) C. M. Marsh (1891) http://blogs.plos.org/paleo /2015/04/07/brontosaurus-thunders-back/ (C) By Tadek Kurpaski from London, Poland - sauropodUploaded by FunkMonk, CC BY 2.0, https://commons.wikimedia.org/w/index.php?curid=8698637.

but show a capacity to modify their form in order to bear the loads during dynamic motion (Fig. 9.10D).[141] Huge fossil graveyards can be seen today, but they are not "graveyards" of failed design.

3.7 Genetic Toolkits

Evolutionary geneticists require mutations in early development to produce large-scale changes in the body form, because in later development the body plan is already established.[142] However, studies have revealed that groups considered the most primitive (e.g., sponges and jellyfish) are found to possess most of the genetic toolkit (such as eleven of the twelve *Wnt* gene families), various signaling pathways, and even molecular organizing centers, that are also found in the so-called "more advanced" vertebrates).[143] This is evidence against gene diversification underlying the so-called Cambrian explosion.[144]

It is also being discovered that genes expressed during early embryogenesis involve more interactions than those expressed during later

---

141. "The Late Cretaceous II—North and South America," *Dinosaurs and the History of Life* (course, Earth and Environmental Sciences Department, Columbia University). http://eesc.columbia .edu/courses/v1001/twomed.html. Redrawn from http://www.wyomingpaleo.com/sueintro.html.
142. Leigh M. Van Valen, "Species, Sets, and the Derivative Nature of Philosophy," *Biology and Philosophy* 3, no. 1 (1988): 49–66.
143. Arne Kusserow, Kevin Pang, Carsten Sturm, Martina Hrouda, Jan Lentfer, et al., "Unexpected Complexity of the Wnt Gene Family in a Sea Anemone," *Nature* 433, no. 7022 (2005): 156–160; Scott A. Nichols, William Dirks, John S. Pearse, and Nicole King, "Early Evolution of Animal Cell Signaling and Adhesion Genes," *Proceedings of the National Academy of Sciences USA* 103, no. 33 (2006): 12451–12456; Yulia Kraus, Andy Aman, Ulrich Technau, and Grigory Genikhovich, "Pre-Bilaterian Origin of the Blastoporal Axial Organizer," *Nature Communications* 7 (2016).
144. Baguñà and Garcia-Fernàndez, "Evo-Devo: The Long and Winding Road," 706.

stages,[145] suggesting that they are actually less malleable to transformation at these stages.

3.8 Taxonomic Comparison of Gene Expression

There are evidences of peculiarities in various gene expression patterns between taxonomic groups. For instance, the patterns involved in leg development differ between insects and spiders.[146] Many transcription factors found in amphibian eye development do not operate in mammals, along with other considerable differences between vertebrates.[147]

In conclusion, the above data provide an evidence base for the existence of types that are real in nature. Distinct forms are apparent at various hierarchical levels, ranging from the phylum level (representing the basic body plan) down to the basic types, most commonly identifiable with the family level, and recognizably distinguishable from the nearest forms by clear gaps or discontinuities.

This evidence-based approach reveals that modern evolutionary theory is struggling to engage with the real world, and that much of the discussion remains highly speculative and driven by the presupposition that the diversity of life must be explained by a universal common ancestor acted on by blind natural processes. The challenge for theistic evolutionists is whether they want to align themselves with speculative naturalism, or whether they are willing to follow the evidences for design and for discontinuity wherever this leads.

Concluding Remarks

In Buchan's novels, the characters spectacularly encounter one another at just the right time and place, because the plot crucially depends on it. Without Sir Archie and his biplane, Hannay will be arrested and the spymaster's schemes will not be thwarted, influencing the outcome of the War. In similar vein, in development the cell and molecular

---

145. Carlo G. Artieri, and Rama S. Singh, "Demystifying Phenotypes: The Comparative Genomics of Evo-Devo," *Fly* 4, no. 1 (2010): 18–20.

146. Nikola-Michael Prpic, Ralf Janssen, Barbara Wigand, Martin Klingler, and Wim GM Damen, "Gene Expression in Spider Appendages Reveals Reversal of exd/hth Spatial Specificity, Altered Leg Gap Gene Dynamics, and Suggests Divergent Distal Morphogen Signalling," *Developmental Biology* 264, no. 1 (2003): 119–140.

147. Torben Söker, Claudia Dalke, Oliver Puk, Thomas Floss, Lore Becker, et al., "Pleiotropic Effects in Eya3 Knockout Mice," *BMC Developmental Biology* 8, no. 1 (2008): 1.

characters and forces encounter one another at just the right time and place, because the progress of embryological development crucially depends on it. This is evident, for instance, in the placement of genes and skeleton-forming cells precisely to future joint locations; the connecting of a particular motor neuron with its correct target muscle; the complex interplay of transcription factors during heart development, which is yet synchronous with the orderly development of the circulatory system; and the electric current appearing at the exact location to mark the future limb bud.

Evidences of such orchestration are growing in abundance, and a new language is emerging, with secular authors even adding superlatives: it is *exquisitely* orchestrated. It is increasingly untenable to reconcile this as emerging from Darwinian chance processes, or even by the spontaneous self-assembly of organisms according to the laws of physics and chemistry. To explain the story without recourse to a directing intelligent agency seems increasingly far too far-fetched. Werner Gitt comments that, as engineers realize,

> . . . all of organisms' parts are in place and functional . . . this is only achieved if there is a 'higher level instructional program' that orchestrates the operation of every subsystem in the overall system. Constructing these 'instructional programs' requires complete knowledge of every subsystem as well as complete knowledge of the *entire* system before the higher-level program can be developed, implemented and accomplish its goal.

For human vision, for instance, it is "inconceivable that these components would just randomly integrate themselves to operate as a single harmonious unit that provides sight."[148]

Furthermore, structures such as wings are not simple and flat but develop into marvels of engineering, ranging from efficient hovering, to gliding, or fast forward flight. These have *far-reaching implications for development of the entire body plan* to suit the type of flight mode.[149] For instance, in very fast fliers such as swifts, the wings are swept

---

148. Gitt, *Without Excuse*, 205.
149. David Lentink and Andrew A. Biewener, "Nature-Inspired Flight—Beyond the Leap," *Bioinspiration and Biomimetics* 5, no. 4 (2010): 040201.

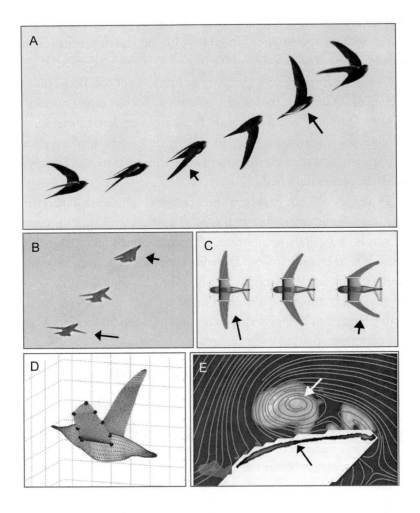

FIGURE 9.11. *The end results of wing development* are not simple flat sheets but masterpieces of engineering. **A.** For instance, in the highly aerobatic swift, its wings sweep back for high-speed flight (short arrow), then outwards to effect tight turns (long arrow). **B** and **C.** The swift flight modes in **A** inspire the design of variable wing fighter planes (**B**) and micro air vehicles (**C**). Arrows, as for **A**, show the variable wing options. **D.** Engineers increasingly analyze the ingenious biomechanics of birds and insects to solve problems of aeronautical design. Here is a computerized 3-D wing simulation of a hummingbird flight. **E.** A surprising discovery: smooth flow lines (in gray) moving above a hawkmoth wing surface (black arrow) are disturbed into spiral masses (vortices) (white arrow), which give extra lift. Engineers seek to incorporate such features into next-generation aeronautics.

back for high-speed flight, then sweep outwards to effect tight turns (Fig. 9.11A). This is mimicked in the design of variable wing fighter planes and micro air vehicles (MAVs)[150] (Fig. 9.11B and C). The swift is much more efficient than these planes because it continuously adjusts ("morphs") its wings for maneuvers. In labs worldwide, intense biomechanics research into the intricacies of bird and insect flight (Fig. 9.11D)[151] aims to inform state-of-the-art aeronautics design. For instance, it is being discovered that many bird and insect wings have a sharp leading edge which creates a vortex (a tiny tornado) that would be expected to contribute to stalling but instead sucks in air to generate extra lift (Fig. 9.11E),[152] and aids aerobatics and landing (say, on a branch) without the animal losing altitude.[153]

In Buchan's novels, Hannay and his little band of comrades have instructions and clues to follow from their commanding officer. There are many possibilities as they initially speculate over these clues. But then they find the lines of evidence which best fit the clues. So it is with development. Evolutionary theory predicts chance processes and tinkering of imperfect assemblies. However, the evidence from development indicates the necessity of a designing intelligence. In my mind, this points to the Creator who orchestrated the intricate construction of each distinct type of body form found in nature.[154]

---

150. Ulrike K. Müller and David Lentink, "Turning on a Dime," *Science* 306, no. 5703 (2004): 1899–1900, doi:10.1126/science.1107070.

151. Jialei Song, Bret W. Tobalske, Donald R. Powers, Tyson L. Hedrick, and Haoxiang Luo, "Three-Dimensional Simulation for Fast Forward Flight of a Calliope Hummingbird," *Open Science* 3, no. 6 (2016): 160230, doi:10.1098/rsos.160230 creative commons.

152. L. Christoffer Johansson, Sophia Engel, Almut Kelber, Marco Klein Heerenbrink, and Anders Hedenström. "Multiple Leading Edge Vortices of Unexpected Strength in Freely Flying Hawkmoth," *Scientific Reports* 3 (2013), doi:10.1038/srep03264 creative commons.

153. Robert Roy Britt, "Secret of Bird Flight Revealed," *LiveScience*, April 29, 2005, accessed October 19, 2016, http://www.livescience.com/3742-secret-bird-flight-revealed.html; J. J. Videler, E. J. Stamhuis, and G. D. E. Povel, "Leading-edge vortex lifts swifts," *Science* 306, no. 5703 (2004): 1960–1962, doi:10.1126/science.1104682.

154. This chapter is dedicated to David Tyler, for the many insights he has provided. Thanks to Luke Tyler for assistance with preparation of the manuscript; Harriet Tyler for practical support; and Ann Gauger and Bill Deckard for constructive editorial support.

Section I, Part 2

. . . . .

The Case against Universal Common Descent and for a Unique Human Origin

10

The Fossil Record and Universal Common Ancestry

GÜNTER BECHLY AND
STEPHEN C. MEYER

SUMMARY

This chapter is the first of three examining the strength of the case for universal common descent, the second (historical) part of contemporary evolutionary theory and the part of evolutionary theory that theistic evolutionists most commonly defend. We begin in this chapter by examining the logical structure of the argument for universal common descent. Taking that structure into account, we then assess what the fossil record can tell us about whether all forms of life do, or do not, share a common ancestor. Theistic evolutionists often claim that the alleged common ancestry of all forms of life is a "fact"—even as they may acknowledge doubts about the creative power of the neo-Darwinian mechanism. Nevertheless, we have become skeptical about universal common descent. In this chapter, we explain why using the fossil evidence to illustrate how a scientifically informed person might reasonably come to doubt the arguments for universal common descent (or universal common ancestry). After first describing the aspects of the fossil evidence that the theory of universal common descent explains well, we then examine other aspects of the fossil record that the theory does not explain as well—or at all. We especially highlight the many discontinuous or abrupt appearances of new forms of life in the fossil record—a pattern that contradicts the *continuous* branching tree pattern of biological history postulated by proponents of universal common descent.

. . . . .

I. Introduction

Contemporary neo-Darwinian theory has two main parts. The first part, which we have critiqued at length in the preceding chapters, asserts that the mechanism of natural selection and random genetic mutation has the capacity to generate major innovations (macroevolutionary change) in the history of life. The second part of neo-Darwinism—the theory of universal common descent—concerns the pattern of change through biological history.

Indeed, the theory of universal common descent is a theory about what happened in the history of life. The theory affirms that all known living organisms are descended from a single common ancestor somewhere long ago.[1] Biology textbooks today often depict this idea, just as Darwin did, using a great branching tree. The bottom of the trunk represents the first primordial organism (or organisms). The limbs and branches of the tree represent the many new forms of life that developed from it. The vertical axis of the tree represents the arrow of time. The horizontal axis represents changes in biological form, or what biologists call "morphological distance."

Whereas the mechanism of natural selection and random mutation describes *how* major evolutionary change allegedly happened (the *process* by which change occurs), the theory of universal common descent asserts *that* such major change *did* occur, and occurred in a completely connected, rather than disconnected or discontinuous, way (the historical *pattern* of change). Thus, the theory of universal common descent (UCD) depicts a "monophyletic" view of the history of life because it portrays all organisms as ultimately related as a single *connected* family.

---

1. In the *Origin*, Darwin argued that "all the organic beings which have ever lived on this earth have descended from some one primordial form" (Charles Darwin, *On the Origin of Species by Means of Natural Selection*, facsimile of the first ed. [London: John Murray, 1859; repr., Cambridge, MA: Harvard University Press, 1964, 484]). Elsewhere in the *Origin*, Darwin also allowed for the possibility that life might have arisen from one *or from a few* original life forms.

Darwin argued that the theory of universal common descent (or what he called descent with modification) best explained a variety of lines of biological evidence, including the succession of fossil forms, the geographical distribution of various species, and the anatomical and embryological similarities among otherwise different types of organisms. Modern evolutionary biologists have added the genetic similarities (or "molecular homologies") of otherwise different organisms to this list of evidence supporting common ancestry.

Proponents of Darwinism have often heralded the fossil record as the most decisive evidence for common descent with modification.[2] Philip Gingerich even claimed that "Morphological continuity in the fossil record is the principal evidence favoring evolution as a historical explanation for the diversity of life."[3] On the other hand, those who doubt UCD have argued that the fossil record poses a severe challenge to the theory.[4] Still other proponents of universal common descent, including Richard Dawkins, have sought to foreclose any such criticism by arguing that "We don't need fossils. The case for evolution is watertight without them; so it is paradoxical to use gaps in the fossil record as though they were evidence against evolution."[5]

So what do fossils tell us about the history of life? And how strong is the case for the theory of universal common descent—the historical part of Darwinian theory?

This chapter will examine the logical structure of the arguments for universal common descent, with a particular focus on what the fossil record (and the argument from fossil progression) can tell us about whether all forms of life do, or do not, share a common ancestor. Though many theistic evolutionists portray this part of evolutionary theory as a well-established fact or theory[6]—even as they may acknowledge doubts about the creative power of the neo-Darwinian

---

2. See, e.g., Donald R. Prothero, *Evolution: What the Fossils Say and Why It Matters* (New York: Columbia University Press, 2007); Jerry Coyne, *Why Evolution Is True* (Oxford: Oxford University Press, 2009); Richard Dawkins, *The Greatest Show on Earth: The Evidence for Evolution* (New York: Free Press, 2009).
3. Philip D. Gingerich, "Species in the Fossil Record: Concepts, Trends, and Transitions," *Paleobiology* 11 (1985): 27–41.
4. E.g., Stephen C. Meyer, *Darwin's Doubt: The Explosive Origin of Animal Life and the Case for Intelligent Design* (New York: HarperOne, 2013).
5. Dawkins, *Greatest Show on Earth*, 164.
6. See, e.g., Deborah Haarsma, "Evolutionary Creation," in *Four Views on Creation and Evolution*, ed. James Stump (Grand Rapids, MI: Zondervan), 2017.

mechanism[7]—we have become skeptical about universal common descent. In this chapter we will explain why, and we will use the fossil evidence to illustrate how a scientifically informed person might reasonably come to doubt the arguments for universal common descent—whether those arguments are based on the fossil record or on other classes of evidence that have been marshaled in their favor.

II. Logical Structure of the Argument

Yet, before we look at any of evidence for, or against, universal common descent, it might be a good idea to examine the logical structure of the argument for it. Despite the presumed consensus in favor of universal common descent, there are good reasons for doubting the argument in its favor—reasons that are well illustrated by the fossil record and the competing possible interpretations of it. In particular, the argument for UCD depends on an often inconclusive or weak form of inference known as abduction.[8] In abductive reasoning, scientists (or detectives) reason from effects (or clues) in the present back to causes in the past. To see the difference between abductive and deductive inference, consider the following argument schemata:[9]

> DEDUCTION:
> DATA: A is given and plainly true.
> LOGIC: <u>But if A is true, then B is a matter of course.</u>
> CONCLUSION: Hence, B must be true as well.

> ABDUCTION:
> DATA: The surprising fact B is observed.

---

7. See, e.g., Darrel Falk's comments in a review of *Darwin's Doubt* on the BioLogos website: http://biologos.org/questions/biologos-id-creationism. There Falk acknowledges that *Darwin's Doubt* correctly identifies the origin of animal form as "one of the great mysteries in evolutionary biology today." Falk observes that this problem has never really been addressed by neo-Darwinian theory, and reflects on his own experiences as a college teacher of evolution discovering the shortcomings of textbook theory when confronted with the origin of complex animal evolution and the origin of morphological novelty. He adds that the process of natural selection, important as it may be in certain contexts, is not the "driving mechanism" of macroevolutionary change, and thus, that the mystery of the Cambrian explosion still awaits a solution.

8. Stephen C. Meyer, "Of Clues and Causes: A Methodological Interpretation of Origin of Life Studies" (PhD thesis, Department of History and Philosophy of Science, Cambridge University, 1990); Charles S. Peirce, "Abduction and Induction," In *The Philosophy of Peirce*, ed. J. Buchler (London: Routledge, 1956), 150–154; Peirce, *Collected Papers*, ed. Charles Hartshorne and P. Weiss, 6 vols. (Cambridge, MA: Harvard University Press, 1931–1935).

9. Meyer, "Of Clues and Causes," 25.

LOGIC: <u>But if A were true, then B would be a matter of course.</u>

CONCLUSION: Hence, there is reason to suspect that A is true.

In deductive reasoning, if the premises are true, the conclusion follows with certainty. Abduction, however, does not produce certainty, but only plausibility or possibility. Unlike deduction, in which the minor premise affirms the antecedent variable ("A"), abductive reasoning affirms the consequent variable ("B"). In deductive logic, affirming the consequent variable (with certainty) constitutes a fallacy. The error derives from failing to acknowledge that more than one cause might explain the same evidence. To see why, consider this deductive fallacy:

If it rained, the streets would get wet.
<u>The streets are wet.</u>
Therefore, it rained.

or symbolically:

If R, then W
<u>W</u>
therefore R.

Obviously, this argument has a problem. It does not follow that because the streets are wet, it necessarily rained. The streets may have gotten wet in some other way. A fire hydrant may have burst, a snow bank may have melted, or a street sweeper may have doused the streets before cleaning them. Nevertheless, that the streets are wet *might* indicate that it rained.

Oddly, abductive arguments have the same logic structure as this fallacious form of deductive argument—they too affirm the consequent. For this reason, unless these inferences are strengthened using a process of elimination showing alternative hypotheses to be implausible, they remain weak or inconclusive.[10]

---

10. In books making the case for intelligent design, one of us (Meyer) shows how the case for intelligent design—which begins as an abductive inference—has been strengthened by just such a process of elimination, rendering the argument for intelligent design, not just an abductive

In PhD work at Cambridge, one of us (Meyer) showed that the case for universal common descent is based on several abductive inferences from various classes of biological evidence such as fossil succession, anatomical and molecular homology, embryological similarity, and biogeographical distribution.[11] Consequently, as we have studied the case for universal common descent, we have both become gradually more skeptical about the theory because we find that the circumstantial evidence in favor of the theory is inconclusive at best. Moreover, we have found that the arguments for UCD were inconclusive for exactly the reason that abductive arguments often are: For each class of evidence allegedly favoring the theory, more than one explanation—or picture of biological history—could account for it.

As we will show, the fossil record illustrates this problem in spades.

III. The Case for Universal Common Descent from Paleontology

Even so, the theory of universal common descent offers an elegant explanation of several features of the fossil record. Thus, those features—at least when considered in isolation from other evidential considerations—seem to provide support the theory of universal common descent.

Consider, for example, the evidence of fossil "progression" or "succession." The fossil forms preserved in the layers of sedimentary rock progress from simple organisms in older strata (layers) to more and more complex organisms in successively younger strata. According to proponents of UCD, this "stratigraphic" progression in the fossil record from less to more complex forms of life supports the theory of common descent because this pattern of evidence is exactly what paleontologists should expect to find if all organisms did in fact descend from earlier less complex ancestral forms. And though there are exceptions to it, the simple-to-complex rule is roughly true. Thus, the general pattern of successive temporal appearances agrees nicely with the Darwinian picture of the history of life.

---

inference, but an abductive inference to the *best* explanation. See, e.g., Meyer, *Darwin's Doubt*; Stephen C. Meyer, *Signature in the Cell: DNA and the Evidence for Intelligent Design* (New York: HarperOne, 2009).

11. Meyer, "Of Clues and Causes," 77–136.

Moreover, the theory of universal common descent also explains other aspects of fossil evidence,[12] since, again, the observed patterns are precisely what one would expect if all organisms had descended from earlier ancestral forms extending back to one universal common ancestor. For example:

Morphologically Intermediate Fossils (Possible "Missing Links")

Paleontologists have discovered many fossils, such as *Archaeopteryx*, that appear morphologically intermediate between the putative ancestors and their descendants.[13] By "morphologically intermediate" paleontologists mean that the fossil form in question displays some (but not all) of the primitive characteristics of a putative ancestor group while exhibiting some (but not all) of the derived characteristics of a putative descendant group. (A derived character is a novel or changed genetic or anatomical feature not present in a putative ancestral form or a more primitive state). Morphologically intermediate groups are not necessarily "temporally intermediate"—that is, they may not have been found in strata that lie "in between" putative ancestors and descendants. Similarly, such fossil forms may not have been found in

---

12. In the section below, we describe the aspects of the fossil record that are generally thought to provide the strongest arguments for universal common descent. Nevertheless, there are other aspects of the fossil record that proponents of UCD cite in support of the theory as well. For example, as fossilized forms progress from older, lower strata to higher, more recent strata, the forms in the higher strata display increasing similarity to modern forms of life, just as one would expect if all forms of life had descended from a common ancestor and then gradually accumulated small differences over long periods of time. According to that picture of biological history, modern and younger fossilized forms should have accumulated more mutational changes and would, therefore, on balance appear much more dissimilar to the earliest forms of life than they would when compared to other more recently fossilized forms or other modern forms. And, indeed, the deeper paleontologists dig in the geological column, the more dissimilar the fossilized forms of life are (as a general rule) from more recent or modern flora and fauna. The extreme dissimilarity between ancient and modern forms is most pronounced when comparing modern forms of life to the extremely ancient and almost alien biota from the Ediacaran period (635–541 mya) and to many of the exotic forms of life (what Stephen Jay Gould called "wonderful life") of the Cambrian period (541 to 485 mya). Nevertheless, the pattern of fossilized forms of life becoming increasingly more similar to modern forms as one ascends the stratigraphic column is also evident in taxa that first appear much later in the fossil record. Again, this pattern can be explained as another expected consequence of descent with modification from a common ancestor. In a future monograph, one of us (Bechly) will provide a more comprehensive evaluation of this and all the arguments for and against common descent based on different aspects of the fossil record. In this chapter, we do show (see below in note 60) how skeptics of universal common descent who hold a "polyphyletic" view of the history of life can also explain the increasing similarity to modern forms of life that fossils display as they get progressively younger.

13. Prothero, *Evolution: What the Fossils Say and Why It Matters.*

the same geographical region as possible ancestors and descendants. Nevertheless, their similarities in form suggest the *possibility* of being transitional in time and space. Even though there are still groups for which such forms are lacking, many morphologically intermediate forms do exist, such as the numerous morphologically intermediate forms between land mammals and whales that have been discovered in recent decades. Since the theory of universal common descent entails the existence of temporally transitional intermediate forms, it would also predict the existence of many such, at least, morphologically intermediate forms in the fossil record. That such forms exist is, therefore, readily explained by universal common descent.

Morphologically Intermediate and Temporally "Transitional Series"

In addition to morphologically intermediate fossils, paleontologists would also expect, based on the theory of universal common descent, that the fossil record would document some detailed *transitional* sequences—sequences where several intermediate forms lie *temporally* in between the presumed ancestors and descendants in the sedimentary strata. Some examples of such sequences have been found in the fossil record. Famous examples are the horse series illustrating the successive transformation of the primitive 3–4 toed legs of Eocene *Hyracotherium* (formerly known as *Eohippus*) into the single-hooved legs of modern horses.[14] Another is the mammal-like reptile series that illustrates the transition from the primary to the secondary jaw articulation with detachment of the three auditory ossicles.[15]

IV. The Evidence *against* Universal Common Descent from Paleontology

Notwithstanding the above evidences in support of universal common descent, there is also strong paleontological evidence that does not easily square with the Darwinian notion of descent with modification

---

14. Ibid.
15. Héctor E. Ramírez-Chávez et al., "Resolving the Evolution of the Mammalian Middle Ear Using Bayesian Inference," *Frontiers in Zoology* 13, no. 39 (2016): 1–10.

via a gradual series of successive transformations from ancestral to descendant forms of life.

In particular, the fossil record also manifests large "morphological gaps" and discontinuities between different groups of organisms, especially at the higher taxonomic levels (of phyla, classes, and orders) representing the major morphological differences between different forms of life. With very few exceptions, the major groups of organisms come into the fossil record abruptly, without discernible connection to earlier (and generally simpler) alleged ancestors in the fossil record. Indeed, leading evolutionary biologists and paleontologists have long acknowledged this pattern of discontinuity. Evolutionary biologist Ernst Mayr, one of the fathers of the modern neo-Darwinian synthesis, famously noted that "[w]herever we look at the living biota . . . discontinuities are overwhelmingly frequent. . . . The discontinuities are even more striking in the fossil record."

Moreover, since the publication of *The Origin of Species* in the late nineteenth century, our knowledge of the fossil record has greatly increased. Consequently, in most cases, fossil discontinuities can no longer be explained away as the result of alleged incomplete sampling of the fossil record. In fact, paleontologist Michael Foote of the University of Chicago has noted that, as more and more fossil discoveries have been made, the new forms that these discoveries document consistently fall within existing higher taxonomic groups (e.g., phyla, subphyla, and classes). In other words, these new discoveries have repeatedly failed to document the rainbow of intermediate forms expected in the Darwinian view of the history of life (especially at the higher taxonomic levels). Foote has shown, using statistical sampling analysis, that as this pattern has become more and more pronounced, it has become ever more improbable that the absence of intermediate forms reflects a sampling bias—that is, an "artifact" of either incomplete sampling or incomplete preservation.[16] Increasingly, paleontologists accept that fossil discontinuities are real and need to be explained, not explained away. As Cleveland Hickman et al.[17]

---

16. Mike Foote and John J. Sepkoski Jr., "Absolute Measures of the Completeness of the Fossil Record," *Nature* 398 (1999): 415–417.

17. Cleveland P. Hickman et al., *Integrated Principles of Zoology*, 8th ed. (St. Louis: Times Mirror/Mosby College Publishing, 1988).

note, "most major groups of animals appear abruptly in the fossil record, fully formed, and with no fossils yet discovered that form a transition from their parent group."

Indeed, numerous fossil "radiations" or "explosions" of new forms of life are characterized by such abrupt appearances. To get a sense of how pervasive this discontinuous pattern is, and how significant these events are in the history of life, consider the following short descriptions of several of the salient examples of the abrupt appearance of new forms of life in the fossil record.

The Origin of Life

Evidence suggests that the first living cells arose very early in the history of planet Earth, almost as soon as conditions on our planet would permit. Over the last several decades most origin-of-life biologists and geochemists have placed the origin of the first life at about 3.8 billion years ago (bya), just after the cessation of the meteorite bombardment of the earth called the Late Heavy Bombardment (4.1–3.8 bya). The latest evidence from biogenic carbon in zircon crystals suggests that life was already present 4.1 bya in the Hadean era, even before the Late Heavy Bombardment, when life could survive only in subterranean niches.[18] Either way, life seems to have arisen abruptly about as soon as it possibly could, given conditions on the early Earth.

The Origin of Photosynthesis

The origin of photosynthesis was a key event that made later plant and animal life on Earth possible. Photosynthesis involves two intricate and integrated sets of complex biochemical processes known as photosystems I and II, which are in turn made of many equally complex proteins. The earliest existence of cyanobacteria, the first photosynthetic cells, is documented by stromatolites from 3.7-billion-year-old rocks from the Isua supracrustal belt in Greenland.[19] Nevertheless, indirect evidence suggests an even earlier origin of photosynthesis, about 3.8

---

18. Elizabeth A. Bell et al., "Potentially Biogenic Carbon Preserved in a 4.1 Billion-Year-Old Zircon," *Proceedings of the National Academy of Sciences USA* 112 (2015): 14518–14521.

19. Allen P. Nutman et al., "Rapid Emergence of Life Shown by Discovery of 3,700-Million-Year-Old Microbial Structures," *Nature* 537 (2016): 535–538.

billion years ago.[20] Because the Late Heavy (meteorite) Bombardment (4.1–3.8 bya) "repeatedly boiled away the existing oceans into steam atmospheres" and left only subterranean environmental niches,[21] photosynthesis was possible in the earth's oceans only after the bombardment ceased. That implies that photosynthesis, with all its integrated biochemical complexity, originated abruptly as soon as the earth first offered a stable and suitable environment for the process to occur.

Archaean Genetic Expansion

This event is not so much documented by real fossils as by the identification of "fossil genes" through genomic studies. Lawrence David and Eric Alm found that the "genomic fossil record" indicates that the collective genome of life expanded between 3.3 and 2.8 billion years ago.[22] During this period, 27 percent of all presently existing gene families came into being by rapid evolutionary innovation. Arguably, the generation of this amount of new genetic information vastly exceeds the creative power of the neo-Darwinian mechanism of mutation and natural selection, given the extreme rarity of functional genes and proteins within the space of possible DNA and amino acid sequences. As Meyer argued in chapter 2 of this volume, a randomly driven mutational search is overwhelmingly more likely to fail than to succeed in finding even one functional gene, let alone all the many genes that arose during this Archaean expansion, in available evolutionary time.[23]

---

20. Norman H. Sleep, "The Hadean-Archaean Environment," *Cold Spring Harbor Perspectives in Biology* 2 (2010): a002527; Jeff Hecht, "Photosynthesis Began on Earth 3.8 Billion Years Ago," *New Scientist* 2905 (2013): 9; Ernesto Pecoits et al., "Atmospheric Hydrogen Peroxide and Eoarchean Iron Formations," *Geobiology* 13 (2015): 1–14.

21. Simone Marchi et al., "Widespread Mixing and Burial of Earth's Hadean Crust by Asteroid Impacts," *Nature* 511 (2014): 578–582.

22. Lawrence A. David and Eric J. Alm, "Rapid Evolutionary Innovation during an Archaean Genetic Expansion," *Nature* 469 (2011): 93–96.

23. Cf. Douglas D. Axe, "Estimating the Prevalence of Protein Sequences Adopting Functional Enzyme Folds," *Journal of Molecular Biology* 341 (2004): 1295–1315; Axe, *Undeniable: How Biology Confirms Our Intuition that Life Is Designed* (San Francisco: HarperOne, 2017); cf. also a discussion of the waiting time problem in: Michael J. Behe and David W. Snoke, "Simulating Evolution by Gene Duplication of Protein Features that Require Multiple Amino Acid Residues," *Protein Science* 13 (2004): 2651–2664; Behe, *The Edge of Evolution: The Search for the Limits of Darwinism* (New York: Free Press, 2007); Rick Durrett and Deena Schmidt, "Waiting for Two Mutations: With Applications to Regulatory Sequence Evolution and the Limits of Darwinian Evolution," *Genetics* 180 (2008): 1501–1509; Ann K. Gauger and Douglas D. Axe, "The Evolutionary Accessibility of New Enzymes Functions: A Case Study from the Biotin Pathway," *BIO-Complexity* 2011: 1–17; Meyer, *Darwin's Doubt*.

Avalon Explosion

During the Ediacaran, the latest period of the Precambrian era, an enigmatic group of organisms appear abruptly in the fossil record. Radiometric dating studies fix the date for the first appearance of these Ediacaran fauna at about 575–565 million years ago (mya). These strange marine organisms ("Garden of Ediacara") include microbial mats covering the sea bottom and enigmatic large sessile organisms that lack any visible feeding apparatus, and mostly have a quilted body with glide symmetry and fractal growth. Late Precambrian-era sediments around the world have yielded three main types of Ediacaran fossils. The first group consists of the Precambrian sponges. The second is the distinctive group of fossils from the Ediacaran Hills in Australia. The creatures fossilized there include such well-known forms as the flat, air mattress–like body of *Dickinsonia*; the enigmatic *Spriggina*, with its elongated and segmented body and alleged "head shield"; and the frond-like *Charnia*. The third group of fossils, named *Kimberella*, discovered in the cliffs along the White Sea in northwestern Russia, have been claimed to be primitive mollusks, but this identification is highly controversial.[24] Nevertheless, apart from sponges and a few controversial fossils that have been attributed to algae, cnidarians, and primitive mollusks, the Ediacaran fauna have no obvious relationship to later life forms, and their systematic status is highly disputed, ranging from identifications as giant protists, to representatives of an independent multicellular kingdom, to metazoan animals, or even lichens. Whatever their classification, all groups originate abruptly without any known putative ancestors during what is now known as the Avalon Explosion, 575–565 mya.[25] Indeed, the Ediacaran fossils provide evidence of a puzzling leap in biological complexity. Before the Ediacaran organisms appeared, the only living forms documented in the fossil record for over 3 billion years were single-celled organisms, colonial algae, and possible

---

24. John A. Cunningham, "The Origin of Animals: Can Molecular Clocks and the Fossil Record Be Reconciled?" *Bioessays* 39 (2017): 1600120; Graham E. Budd and Sören Jensen, "The Origin of the Animals and a 'Savannah' Hypothesis for Early Bilaterian Evolution," *Biological Reviews* 92 (2017): 446–473.
25. Bing Shen et al., "The Avalon Explosion: Evolution of Ediacara Morphospace," *Science* 319 (2008): 81–84.

sponges. Although the humble Ediacaran biota look simple beside most of the later Cambrian animals, they exhibit a much higher degree of complex organization than the single-celled organisms and colonial algae that preceded them.

Cambrian Explosion

The Cambrian explosion refers to a dramatic period in the history of life when many new and anatomically sophisticated animals appeared suddenly in the sedimentary layers of the geologic column without any discernible evidence of simpler ancestral forms in the earlier layers below. Fossil discoveries during this period attest to the *first* appearance of animals representing more than twenty phyla (the largest division of animal classification) as well as many more subphyla and classes, each manifesting distinctive body plans, where a body plan represents a unique arrangement of body parts and tissues. Indeed, animals representing most of the body plans that have ever existed on Earth first appear during this explosive event. One especially dramatic fact of the Cambrian explosion is the first appearance of many novel marine invertebrate animals (representatives of separate invertebrate phyla, subphyla, and classes in the traditional classification scheme). Some of these animals have mineralized exoskeletons, including those representing phyla such as echinoderms, brachiopods, and arthropods, each with their clearly distinct and novel body plans. Several unexpected features of the Cambrian explosion from a Darwinian point of view are: (1) the sudden appearance of novel animal forms; (2) an absence of transitional intermediate fossils connecting the Cambrian animals to simpler Precambrian forms; (3) a startling array of completely novel animal forms with novel body plans; and (4) a pattern in which radical differences in form in the fossil record arise before more minor, small-scale diversification and variations. This latter pattern turns on its head the Darwinian expectation of small incremental changes only *gradually* resulting in larger and larger differences in form. The abruptness of the explosion is also dramatic from both a geological and an evolutionary standpoint. Most experts estimate the duration of the Cambrian explosion at about 10–25 million years, and date the explosion around 540–515 mya.[26] Others emphasize that the main pulse of this event occurred within only 530–520 mya.[27] Other studies even imply that between 13 and 16 new animal phyla arose within a narrow 5- to 6-million-year window of the larger explosive radiation.[28] In any case, most Cambrian experts agree that the majority of Cambrian animal phyla lack any putative fossil ancestors within the preceding Ediacaran biota.[29] Thus, the Cambrian explosion has been variously called "Evolution's Big Bang"[30] and "Darwin's Dilemma."[31]

Great Ordovician Biodiversification Event (GOBE)

While general animal body plans representing distinct phyla, subphyla, and classes first appeared in the Cambrian explosion, these marine invertebrate groups greatly diversified on lower taxonomic levels (e.g., about 300 new families) during a relatively short period of time in an event known as the Great Ordovician Biodiversification, about 485–460 mya.[32] This explosive diversification of marine life has been

26. Samuel A. Bowring et al., "Calibrating Rates of Early Cambrian Evolution," *Science* 261 (1993): 1293–1298; Douglas H. Erwin et al., "The Cambrian Conundrum: Early Divergence and Later Ecological Success in the Early History of Animals," *Science* 334 (2011): 1091–1097; Charles R. Marshall, "Explaining the Cambrian 'Explosion' of Animals," *Annual Review of Earth and Planetary Sciences* 34 (2006): 355–384; Graham E. Budd, "The Earliest Fossil Record of the Animals and Its Significance," *Philosophical Transactions of the Royal Society B* 363 (2008): 1425–1434; Budd, "Animal Evolution: Trilobites on Speed," *Current Biology* 23 (2013): R878–R880; Michael S. Y. Lee et al., "Rates of Phenotypic and Genomic Evolution during the Cambrian Explosion," *Current Biology* 23 (2013): 1889–1895; Degan Shu et al., "Birth and Early Evolution of Metazoans," *Gondwana Research* 25 (2014): 884–895.

27. Charles R. Marshall and James W. Valentine, "The Importance of Preadapted Genomes in the Origin of the Animal Bodyplans and the Cambrian Explosion," *Evolution* 64 (2010): 1189–1201; Douglas H. Erwin and James W. Valentine, *The Cambrian Explosion: The Construction of Animal Biodiversity* (Greenwood Village, CO: Roberts, 2013).

28. We generally follow Erwin, Valentine, and other Cambrian experts in dating the duration of the Cambrian explosion as a whole to about 10 million years. But in *Darwin's Doubt*, Meyer also shows—by conjoining the conclusions of two separate analyses, one by Douglas Erwin, and one by MIT geochronologist Samuel Bowring—that between 13 and 16 new animal phyla arose abruptly within just a 5- to 6-million-year window of the middle Cambrian. See Bowring et al., "Calibrating Rates of Early Cambrian Evolution"; Erwin et al., "Cambrian Conundrum"; Meyer, *Darwin's Doubt*, 73.

29. Simon Conway Morris, "Cambrian "Explosion": Slow-Fuse or Megatonnage?" *Proceedings of the National Academy of Sciences USA* 97 (2000): 4426–4429; Morris, "Darwin's Dilemma: The Realities of the Cambrian 'Explosion'," *Philosophical Transactions of the Royal Society B* 361(2006): 1069–1083.

30. "Evolution's Big Bang," *Time* magazine, December 4, 1995.

31. Morris, "Darwin's Dilemma."

32. Thomas Servais et al., "The Great Ordovician Biodiversification Event (GOBE): The Palaeoecological Dimension," *Palaeogeography, Palaeoclimatology, Palaeoecology* 294 (2010): 99–119; David A. T. Harper et al., "The Great Ordovician Biodiversification Event: Reviewing Two Decades of Research on Diversity's Big Bang Illustrated by Mainly Brachiopod Data," *Palaeoworld* 24 (2015): 75–85.

called "Life's Second Big Bang" by James O'Donoghue,[33] who mentions "that the 'Ordovician explosion' was every bit as momentous for animal evolution as the Cambrian one."

Devonian Nekton Revolution

Christian Klug et al. described a radical change in the composition of the marine fauna of the Early Devonian.[34] While previously the marine ecosystems were dominated by planktonic (drifting) and demersal (near sea bottom) taxa, between 410 and 400 mya a very sudden and enormous expansion of marine nektonic (actively swimming) animals occurred in which groups such as ammonoid cephalopods and jawed fish make their first appearance. Within just 10 million years such active swimmers increased from only 5 percent to about 75 percent of the marine fauna.

Odontode Explosion

The term "odontode explosion" was coined by Fraser et al. for the sudden appearance of vertebrate dentition.[35] Within 10 million years (425–415 mya) between the Late Silurian and Early Devonian, all major groups of jawed fish with teeth and tooth-like structures (odontodes) appear abruptly in the fossil record. These include stem-gnathostomes like the arthrodiran *Entelognathus* (423 mya), spiny sharks or Acanthodii (*Nerepisacanthus*, 423–419 mya), the oldest known cartilaginous fishes or Chondrichthyes (sharks like *Stigmodus* and *Plectrodus*, 423–419 mya), and the oldest known bony fishes or Osteichthyes, the latter already with the modern subgroups of lobe-finned Sarcopterygii (*Guiyu*, 423.5 mya) and ray-finned Actinopterygii (*Meemannia*, 415 mya).

Silurio-Devonian Radiation of Terrestrial Biotas

The sudden origin and diversification of vascular land plants (Tracheophyta) in the Late Silurian and Early Devonian is one of the

---

33. James O'Donoghue, "The Ordovician: Life's Second Big Bang," *New Scientist* 2660 (2008): 34–37.

34. Christian Klug et al., "The Devonian Nekton Revolution," *Lethaia* 43 (2010): 465–477.

35. Gareth J. Fraser et al., "The Odontode Explosion: The Origin of Tooth-Like Structures in Vertebrates," *Bioessays* 32 (2010): 808–817.

great mysteries in the history of life. One of the two oldest known vascular land plants, *Baraghwanatia*, already belongs to the modern subgroup of clubmosses. Richard Bateman et al. conclude that "the Siluro-Devonian primary radiation of land biotas is the terrestrial equivalent of the much-debated Cambrian 'explosion' of marine faunas."[36]

Carboniferous Insect Explosion

In the Pennsylvanian (Upper Carboniferous) era, between 318 and 300 mya, when the world was dominated by vast swamp forests, a large diversity of different winged insect groups appeared suddenly without any known transitional forms in the older Mississippian (Lower Carboniferous) or Devonian strata.[37] These include not only giant palaeopterous insects like the extinct palaeodictyopterans, mayflies, and dragonflies, or "primitive" neopterous insect orders like stoneflies, roaches, and orthopterans, but also thrips, bugs, and even advanced holometabolans like wasps, beetles, and scorpion flies.

Triassic Explosion

This event was also called the Early Triassic metazoan radiation or post-Permian radiation. No new phyla and classes, but many new orders and families originate abruptly after the end-Permian mass extinction (about 252 mya) among marine invertebrates (e.g., bivalves and ceratites), insects (e.g., Coleoptera and Diptera), and tetrapods (see below). Peter Ward explains that "the diversity of Triassic animal plans is analogous to the diversity of marine body plans that resulted from the Cambrian Explosion. It also occurred for nearly the same reasons and, as will be shown, was as important

---

36. Richard M. Bateman et al., "Early Evolution of Land Plants: Phylogeny, Physiology, and Ecology of the Primary Terrestrial Radiation," *Annual Review of Ecology and Systematics* 29 (1998): 263–292.

37. Arthur N. Strahler, *Science and Earth History: The Evolution/Creation Controversy* (Buffalo, NY: Prometheus, 1999; Conrad C. Labandeira, "The Fossil Record of Insect Extinction: New Approaches and Future Directions," *American Entomologist* 51 (2005): 14–29; David Grimaldi and Michael S. Engel, *Evolution of the Insects* (Cambridge: Cambridge University Press, 2005); David B. Nicholson et al., "Changes to the Fossil Record of Insects through Fifteen Years of Discovery," *PLoS ONE* 10 (2015): 1–61; Yan-hui Wang et al., "Fossil Record of Stem Groups Employed in Evaluating the Chronogram of Insects (Arthropoda: Hexapoda)," *Scientific Reports* 6 (2016): 38939.

for animal life on land as the Cambrian Explosion was for marine animal life."[38]

Early Triassic Terrestrial Tetrapod Radiation

Directly after the great Permo-Triassic mass extinction, the first representatives of modern tetrapod taxa appear suddenly, within a short window of time, between 251 and 240 mya.[39] These include the first dinosaurs (*Nyasasaurus*), the first turtles (*Pappochelys*), the first lizard-relatives/Lepidosauromorpha (*Paliguana*), the first croc-relatives/Crurotarsi (*Ctenodiscosaurus*), and the first mammal-like animals/Mammaliaformes (*Haramiyida*). Except for the latter two groups, they all appear virtually out of thin air, without discernible connections to any known ancestors.[40]

Early Triassic Marine Reptile Radiation

After the great end-Permian mass extinction, fifteen different families of marine reptiles appear abruptly between 248 and 240 mya in the Early Triassic. They include, for example, ichthyosaurs, plesiosaur-like pistosaurids, hupehsuchians, nothosaurs, thalattosaurs, pachypleurosaurs, tanystropheids, placodontians, and the enigmatic *Aptodentatus*. A vertebrate paleontologist who is an agnostic and a renowned scientist specializing in ichthyosaurs, and who must remain anonymous to protect his career, told us that the sudden appearance of viviparous, fully formed fish-like ichthyosaurs within 4 million years after the Permo-Triassic mass extinction made him doubt the neo-Darwinian story.

Mid-Triassic Gliding Reptile Radiation

Within only 2 million years of the Mid-Triassic (230–228 mya) there is a sudden appearance of gliding and flying reptiles, like *Sharovipteryx* (with wings on the legs); *Mecistotrachelos*, and the unrelated Kuehneosauridae (with gliding membrane across lateral rib-like projections);

---

38. Peter D. Ward, *Out of Thin Air* (Washington, DC: Joseph Henry, 2006), 160.
39. Martin D. Ezcurra, "Biogeography of Triassic Tetrapods: Evidence for Provincialism and Driven Sympatric Cladogenesis in the Early Evolution of Modern Tetrapod Lineages," *Proceedings of the Royal Society B* 277(2010): 2547–2552.
40. Ward, *Out of Thin Air*.

Longisquama (with long feather-like scales on the back); and the earliest pterosaurs like *Preondactylus*.

Mosasaur Radiation

Sudden discontinuous origins are found not only in the history of higher taxa but also within subordinate groups. A good example is the abrupt origin and diversification of Mosasaurs in the last 25 million years of the Upper Cretaceous,[41] when they are said to have evolved from one-meter-long shore-dwelling lizards (Aigialosauridae) into fully marine snake-like giants of up to 17 meters length (Mosasauridae). They quickly diversified into numerous species around the world, filling different ecological niches. Putative ancestors of mosasauroids prior to the Late Cretaceous are not known. Moreover, even its proposed sister taxon *Coniasaurus* is of Late Cretaceous age and thus not a plausible ancestral precursor.[42] Any evolutionary relationship to recent monitor lizards and/or snakes is also contested and a matter of considerable debate among specialists.[43]

Radiation of Flowering Plants

Charles Darwin called the abrupt origin of flowering plants during the Cretaceous period an "abominable mystery." Indeed, nearly all early fossils of modern angiosperms first appeared abruptly in the Cretaceous and then rapidly diversified between 130 and 115 mya. Darwin was deeply bothered by the pattern of their origin because "the seemingly sudden appearance of so many angiosperm species in the Upper Chalk conflicted strongly with his gradualist perspective on evolutionary change."[44] Though paleontologists in China have recently found a few angiosperms from the Mid-Jurassic period (such as *Euanthus*,

---

41. Michael J. Everhart, "Rapid Evolution, Diversification, and Distribution of Mosasaurs (Reptilia; Squamata) prior to the K-T Boundary," *Tate 2005 11th Annual Symposium in Paleontology and Geology, Casper, WY* (2005): 16–27.

42. Michael W. Caldwell, "Squamate Phylogeny and the Relationships of Snakes and Mosasaurs," *Zoological Journal of the Linnean Society* 125 (2008): 115–147.

43. Ibid.; Jack L. Conrad, "Phylogeny and Systematics of Squamata (Reptilia) Based on Morphology," *Bulletin of the American Museum of Natural History* 310 (2008); Jacques A. Gauthier et al., "Assembling the Squamate Tree of Life: Perspectives from the Phenotype and the Fossil Record," *Bulletin of the Peabody Museum of Natural History* 53 (2012): 3–308.

44. William E. Friedman, "The Meaning of Darwin's 'Abominable Mystery'," *American Journal of Botany* 96 (2009): 5–21.

Juraherba, and *Yuhania*), the classification of these fossilized plants as modern angiosperms remains in some dispute. There is also no evidence that these plants were ancestral to the later Cretaceous groups, and the paleontologists who have classified them have not proposed them as such. Indeed, none of these mid-Jurassic period plants can be unambiguously attributed to any subgroup of modern angiosperms, all of which *did* first appear in the Early Cretaceous. Thus, the enigmatic rise of angiosperms still represents an "inextricable knot"—an unresolved puzzle for those who assume the common ancestry of all forms of life.[45]

Radiation of Modern Placental Mammals

The first orders of placental mammals also appear abruptly in the fossil record, during the Paleocene epoch between 62 and 49 mya, without known precursors.[46] Paleontologists call this series of events the "mammalian radiation." According to J. David Archibald,[47] "within approximately 15 million years of dinosaur extinction most of the 20 extant orders of placentals had appeared along with some 16 other orders that are now extinct. This was a truly explosive radiation and diversification." Not only do many (probably about 15 of the extant) mammalian orders appear suddenly, but when they appear they are already separated into their distinctive forms. For example, the orders Carnivora (which includes bears), Chiroptera (which includes bats), and Perissodactyla (which includes horses) all first appear and are clearly differentiated from each other by their distinctive forms and features. The first fossil bat, for instance, is unquestionably a bat, capable of true flight. Yet we find nothing resembling a bat in the earlier Mesozoic fossil record.

Radiation of Modern Birds

The lineages of 95 percent of modern bird species also originated abruptly during the Paleocene epoch or the Tertiary (or Paleogene)

45. Laurent Augusto et al., "The Enigma of the Rise of Angiosperms: Can We Untie the Knot?," *Ecology Letters* 17 (2014): 1326–1338.

46. Maureen A. O'Leary et al., "The Placental Mammal Ancestor and the Post–K-Pg Radiation of Placentals," *Science* 339 (2013): 662–667.

47. J. David Archibald, "Eutheria (Placental Mammals)," In *Encyclopedia of Life Sciences / eLS* (Chichester, UK: Wiley, 2012).

period, as did most of the mammalian orders. Just like the placental mammalian radiation, the abrupt appearance of modern birds has been dated to a similarly narrow window of time from 65 and 55 mya. The recent genomic analysis by Richard Prum presented a comprehensive time-calibrated phylogeny of modern birds.[48] This work suggests that only four bird lineages (ancestral species of Ratites, Galloanseres, Strisores, and the common ancestor of all remaining Neoaves) predated and survived the mass extinction event marking the Cretaceous-Tertiary (or Cretaceous-Paleogene) boundary. The most species-rich group, Neoaves, originated abruptly and diversified rapidly after this event.[49] This avian radiation has been appropriately called the "explosive evolution of avian orders,"[50] "avian explosion,"[51] and even "Big bang for Tertiary birds."[52] Moreover, no undisputed fossils of crown-group Neoaves have been found in sediments from the Cretaceous or older,[53] rendering dubious molecular studies placing the origin and diversification of modern avian orders prior to the Cretaceous/Tertiary boundary.

Origin of Genus *Homo*

John Hawks et al.[54] suggested that our own genus, *Homo*, originated abruptly 2 million years ago with sudden interrelated anatomical changes. This inspired a press release with the headline "New Study Suggests Big Bang Theory of Human Evolution."[55] Hawks et al. also emphasize "that no gradual series of changes in earlier australopithecine populations clearly leads to the new species, and no australopithecine species is obviously transitional. This may seem unexpected because for three decades

48. Richard O. Prum et al., "A Comprehensive Phylogeny of Birds (Aves) Using Targeted Next-Generation DNA Sequencing," *Nature* 526 (2015): 569–573.

49. Stephen L. Brusatte et al., "The Origin and Diversification of Birds," *Current Biology* 25 (2015): R888–R898.

50. Steven Poe and Alison L. Chubb, "Birds in a Bush: Five Genes Indicate Explosive Evolution of Avian Orders," *Evolution* 58 (2004): 404–415.

51. Gavin H. Thomas, "Evolution: An Avian Explosion," *Nature* 526 (2015): 516–517.

52. Alan Feduccia, "'Big Bang' for Tertiary Birds?," *Trends in Ecology and Evolution* 18 (2003): 172–176.

53. Gerald Mayr, "The Origins of Crown Group Birds: Molecules and Fossils," *Palaeontology* 57 (2014): 231–242; Mayr, *Avian Evolution: The Fossil Record of Birds and Its Paleobiological Significance* (Chichester, UK: Wiley, 2016).

54. John Hawks et al., "Population Bottlenecks and Pleistocene Human Evolution," *Molecular Biology and Evolution* 17 (2000): 2–22.

55. Diane Swanbrow, "New Study Suggests Big Bang Theory of Human Evolution" (University of Michigan press release, January 10, 2000 [http://ns.umich.edu/Releases/2000/Jan00/r011000b.html]).

habiline species have been interpreted as being just such transitional taxa, linking *Australopithecus* through the habilines to later *Homo* species. But with a few exceptions, the known habiline specimens are now recognized to be less than 2 Myr old and therefore are too recent to be transitional forms leading to *H. sapiens*."[56] (See chapter 11, by Casey Luskin, for a more detailed discussion of the hominid fossil record.)

The "Top-Down" Pattern of Appearance

This pervasive pattern of fossil appearance raises an additional difficulty for the theory of universal common descent and the Darwinian picture of the history of life. Darwinian theory (both classical and modern) implies that as new animal forms first began to emerge from a common ancestor, they would be quite similar to each other, and that larger differences in the forms of life—what paleontologists call *disparity*—would emerge only much later as the result of the accumulation of many small incremental changes. In its technical sense, *disparity* refers to the major differences in form that separate the higher-level taxonomic categories such as phyla, classes, and orders. In contrast, the term *diversity* refers to minor differences among organisms classified as different genera or species. Put another way, *disparity* refers to life's basic themes; *diversity* refers to the variations on those themes.

According to the theory of universal common descent and the current understanding of how the mutation/natural selection mechanism works, the differences in form, or "morphological distance," between evolving organisms should increase gradually over time as small-scale mutations accumulate by natural selection to produce increasingly complex forms and structures (including, eventually, new body plans). In other words, one would expect small-scale differences or *diversity* among species to precede large-scale morphological *disparity* among phyla. As the former Oxford University neo-Darwinian biologist Richard Dawkins puts it, "What had been distinct species within one genus become, in the fullness of time, distinct genera within one family. Later, families will be found to have diverged to the point where

---

56. Hawks et al., "Population Bottlenecks and Pleistocene Human Evolution," 4. They cite Craig S. Feibel et al., "Stratigraphic Context of Fossil Hominids from the Omo Group Deposits: Northern Turkana Basin, Kenya, and Ethiopia," *American Journal of Physical Anthropology* 78 (1989): 595–622.

taxonomists (specialists in classification) prefer to call them orders, then classes, then phyla."[57]

Darwin himself made this point in the *Origin of Species*. In explaining his famous branching-tree diagram, he noted how higher taxa should emerge from lower taxa by the accumulation of numerous slight variations.[58]

The actual pattern in the fossil record, however, contradicts this expectation. Instead of more and more species eventually leading to more genera, leading to more families, orders, classes, and phyla, the fossil record shows representatives of separate phyla appearing first, followed by lower-level diversification on those basic themes. For example, during the Cambrian explosion representatives of many higher taxa such as phyla and classes (each representing distinctive body plans) first appear abruptly in the fossil record. Only later do different order- and family- and genus-level representatives of those distinctive body plans originate (in events such as the Great Ordovician Biodiversification Event or the Mammalian Radiation, for example). As paleontologists Douglas Erwin, James Valentine, and Jack Sepkoski note, "The fossil record suggests that the major pulse of diversification of phyla occurs before that of classes, classes before that of orders, orders before that of families. . . . The higher taxa do not seem to have diverged through an accumulation of lower taxa."[59] Yet, the theory of universal common descent depicts (and predicts) just the opposite—the proliferation of species and other representatives of lower-level taxa occurring first and then building to the disparity of the highest taxonomic differences such as those between different phyla or different classes. Thus, the top-down pattern of appearance on display in the fossil record provides another evidential challenge to UCD.

V. The Polyphyletic Interpretation of the Fossil Record

The pattern of appearance of major groups of organisms in the fossil record—both in the abruptness and discontinuity of those appearances and in the unexpected way in which disparity precedes diversity—seems

57. Richard Dawkins, *Unweaving the Rainbow* (Boston: Houghton Mifflin Harcourt, 1998), 201.

58. Charles Darwin, *On the Origin of Species* (London: John Murray, 1859), 120–125.

59. Douglas H. Erwin et al., "A Comparative Study of Diversification Events," *Evolution* 41 (1987): 1177–1186, 1183. See also Erwin et al., "The Cambrian Conundrum: Early Divergence"; Bowring et al., "Calibrating Rates of Early Cambrian Evolution."

to contradict the "monophyletic" picture of the history of life entailed by the theory of universal common descent. That suggests the possibility, at the very least, that the monophyletic picture may not be the one that best fits the fossil evidence. True, universal common descent does anticipate the progression from less complex to more complex forms of life that is generally evident in the fossil record. But the pattern of discontinuity and abrupt appearance seems on its face to contradict the way in which the theory portrays the history of life. Similarly, the top-down pattern of appearance contradicts its picture of the gradual accumulation of small incremental change over time. Indeed, UCD portrays the history of life as a great branching tree in which each new lineage emerges through just such a process of gradual and continuous, rather than abrupt and discontinuous, change. Of course, proponents of a monophyletic view have sought to offer auxiliary *ad hoc* hypotheses—such as the artifact hypothesis—in order to explain away the absence of expected evidence of genuine transitional fossils—i.e., temporal intermediates—connecting alleged ancestors and descendant forms in the sedimentary record. Nevertheless, conjoining UCD with such an auxiliary hypotheses is by no means the only way to explain the pattern of discontinuity evident in the fossil record (if it provides an adequate explanation of that discontinuity at all; see below).

Consider, instead, the polyphyletic view of biological history. It depicts the history of life as an orchard of separate, disconnected trees in which major new groups of plants and animals are introduced into the fossil record progressively and discontinuously. This view explains fossil succession equally well, but, arguably, describes the discontinuous pattern of appearance *more* accurately (or, at least, more naturally and simply, without auxiliary hypotheses) than a monophyletic view does. Indeed, pervasive discontinuity is precisely what one should expect to find in the fossil record based on a polyphyletic view of the history of life.[60]

---

60. A polyphyletic view of the history of life can also explain the orderly progression of fossil forms as one ascends the stratigraphic column—i.e., the stratigraphic order from less to more similar forms of life. If discontinuous polyphyletic origin events can be considered spatiotemporal expressions of ideas (or platonic forms) in the mind of an intelligent designer or a creator, then the succession toward greater similarity to modern forms of life may reflect a rational ordering of these ideas or forms in the mind of such a creator (this idea, elaborated below, was suggested by Richard von Sternberg, personal communication).

This view has received inadvertent or unintended support from a group of taxonomists—a school of biological systematics—known as "pattern cladists." Since the late 1970s, the pattern cladists have defended the classical "groups-within-groups" classification system of Carl Linnaeus that all biologists use. In the Linnaean hierarchical system of classification, all the characters (i.e.,

The Polyphyletic View and Morphological Intermediates

But what about the intermediate forms of life discussed above that proponents of common descent cite in support of their theory? How

features) of a higher or "superordinated" classificatory group (such as a phylum) are also present in the lower or "subordinated" classificatory groups (such as classes or orders) within that larger group, though organisms representing lower or subordinated groups will also have other features that distinguish them from other organisms of the same taxonomic rank.

The pattern cladists have shown that this system of classification not only elegantly reflects the pattern of the distribution of characters in the living world, but that it represents a maximally efficient way of storing and retrieving information about the distribution of those characters in different groups of organisms—irrespective of how they arose. In other words, the pattern cladists showed that the pattern of character distribution captured by the groups-within-groups classification system represents a *logical* or *rational* ordering of groups whether those forms arose by continuous descent with modification from common ancestors or not, as long as hierarchy and parsimony are presupposed as epistemological axioms. For this reason, cladists regard the tree-shaped cladograms they use to depict the nested hierarchy of groups within the living world as representation of a logical ordering of the distribution of characters in both fossilized and extant organisms but not necessarily as *a depiction of biological history.* (See: Norman I. Platnick, "Philosophy and the Transformation of Cladistics," *Systematic Zoology* 28 [1979]: 537–546; Andrew V. Z. Brower, "Evolution Is Not a Necessary Assumption of Cladistics," *Cladistics* 16 [2000]: 143–154.)

This perspective suggests an entirely different way of interpreting the orderly progression of fossil forms in the stratigraphic column. Indeed, on the supposition that the discontinuous origins of new forms of life (as documented in the fossil record) may represent intelligently designed infusions of new information into the biosphere (as one of us—Meyer—has argued elsewhere), it would seem perfectly reasonable to expect that the forms or templates instantiated in these new forms of life would express a rational order in the mind of a designer or creator, reflecting, in turn, rational criteria of the kind suggested by the pattern cladists.

Furthermore, several obvious ways to arrange such ideas or forms would be: (1) to order them in a progression from generally simpler to more complex forms (as is evident in the phenomenon of fossil progression); (2) to order them so that later forms would express variations on earlier more basic expressions of a common theme or design plan (as is evident in the top-down pattern of appearance); and (3) to arrange the introduction of new forms in a teleological or end-directed fashion so that, as forms are introduced into the fossil record, they increasingly resemble forms that will be coming much later (as is evident in the increasing similarity of more recent fossil forms to extant forms). In addition, on this view, those transitional intermediate forms (recent or fossil) that do exist would also reflect the spatiotemporal ordering of such templates, or expressions of ideas, in the mind of the creator—rather than a continuous process of material descent.

Of course, the nonmaterialistic character of this explanation will not appeal philosophically or aesthetically to evolutionary biologists committed to methodological naturalism (for a critique of this principle see chapter 19), but the idea that the increasing similarity of fossil forms to modern forms contradicts (or defies explanation by) a polyphyletic view of biological history is manifestly false. Indeed, Louis Agassiz, the most knowledgeable paleontologist and systematist of the nineteenth century, thought that both the pattern of relationships between organisms described in the Linnaean classification system, and the logical but *discontinuous* way in which new forms of life were introduced into the fossil record, could be elegantly explained as the expression of a preexistent logical ordering, or design plan, in the mind of a designing intelligence (J. L. R. Agassiz, *Recherches sur les Poissons Fossiles,* 5 vols. and supplement [Neuchatel, 1833–1844]. Dates of publication of the parts are given by W. H. Brown, in A. S. Woodward and C. D. Sherborn, *Catalogue of British Fossil Vertebrata* [London: Dulau, 1890], xxv–xxix; Agassiz, *An Essay on Classification* [London: Longmans, 1859]).

The insights of modern intelligent design theory (ID) add plausibility to this view. As ID proponents have pointed out, the discontinuous origin of novel forms of life as attested in the fossil record would have required the production of new genetic and epigenetic forms of information. And since, as one of us (Meyer) has argued elsewhere, intelligent design best explains the origin of such infusions of functional information, it seems perfectly reasonable to expect that the arrangement of new forms of life over time would express a rational ordering—i.e., one reflecting the role of rational or intelligent causation in the origin and introduction of new forms of life into the biosphere (Meyer, *Darwin's Doubt,* 336–403).

does their existence square with the claim that the fossil record shows a pervasive discontinuity? And how would a polyphyletic view explain such intermediates?

Recall, first, the distinction we made above between morphological and temporal intermediates. The vast majority of all intermediates in the fossil record exemplify the morphological rather than the temporal kind. For a fossil to be demonstrably part of a temporal sequence, that intermediate fossil must lie between a plausible ancestor and its possible descendants in the sedimentary strata.

Consequently, when proponents of universal common descent assert that fossil intermediates are very common (see above), and doubters of descent claim that transitional fossil are mostly absent, neither side is strictly incorrect. Instead, both sides often talk past each other because they have different types of intermediates in mind.

When proponents of universal common descent talk about transitional fossils, they usually refer to fossils such as *Archaeopteryx* that exhibit a mosaic of characters wherein some but not all of the characters from a proposed putative ancestor group (such as reptiles) are present in the intermediate form, while at the same time some (but not all) of the characters of the putative descendant group (such as birds) are also present in the intermediate. As noted above, the theory of universal common descent would expect that many such morphologically intermediate forms would be present in the fossil record—and, indeed, they are. Thus, UCD can offer a ready explanation for the presence of many such intermediates in the record, especially the many forms that lie morphologically in between different higher taxa (i.e., orders and families). It must be noted, though, that most of such transitional fossils also exhibit specialized anatomical features that exclude them from the direct ancestral lineage and place them on side branches of the tree close to the alleged descendants. They are not putative ancestors.

Nevertheless, a polyphyletic view of the history of life can account for such morphologically intermediate forms as well. Given the otherwise pervasive discontinuity and absence of genuine transitional sequences (i.e., temporal intermediates) between major groups of organisms discussed above, proponents of a polyphyletic view do not regard fossils such as *Archaeopteryx* as representatives of a temporally transitional sequence leading from ancestor to descendant (nor need they do so), but instead as precisely a "mosaic" of traits produced by an intelligent designer who, like human engineers or artists of our acquaintance, may choose to combine different traits into unique combinations exemplifying a distinctive form with elements or parts in common with two or more other products of his creation (see also note 60).

The Polyphyletic View, Discontinuity, and Alleged Transitional Intermediates

For this reason, to decide whether a polyphyletic or monophyletic view of the history of life best fits the data, we think the most important class of evidence to consider remains the pervasive pattern of discontinuity and the abrupt appearance of major groups of organisms. As we noted earlier, the attempt to explain that pattern away as an "artifact" of incomplete sampling of, or incomplete preservation within, the fossil record has largely failed within paleontology. (Meyer explains more about why paleontologists increasingly reject the artifact hypothesis in chapter 3 of his book *Darwin's Doubt*). And yet, evidence of true *transitional sequences* (i.e., *temporal* intermediates, as we have called them) is extremely rare within the fossil record, especially between higher taxonomic groups. Even the most dramatic of the alleged transitional sequences, such as the mammal-like reptile sequence and the land mammal-to-whale sequences—both touted as proof positive of universal common descent—are: (1) at best, extremely rare exceptions to an otherwise pervasive pattern of discontinuity, or (2) at worst, not at all the evidence of a continuous transformation that proponents of universal common descent claim.

Consider the alleged sequence to the fully aquatic whales. Though often cited as an example of a smooth evolutionary transition, this alleged transitional sequence itself displays dramatic evidence of abrupt appearance.[61] In *The Walking Whales: From Land to Water in Eight*

---

61. John Gatesy et al., "A Phylogenetic Blueprint for a Modern Whale," *Molecular Phylogenetics and Evolution* 66 (2013): 479–506; Stuart Wolpert, "UCLA Biologists Report HOW Whales Have Changed over 35 Million Years," UCLA Newsroom, May 28, 2010, http://newsroom.ucla .edu/releases/ucla-biologists-report-how-whales-159231; Graham J. Slater et al., "Diversity versus Disparity and the Radiation of Modern Cetaceans," *Proceedings of the Royal Society B* 277 (2010): 3097–3104; http://www.sciencedirect.com/science/article/pii/S1055790312004186; http://rspb .royalsocietypublishing.org/content/277/1697/3097.

Million Years, leading cetacean paleontologist J. G. M. Thewissen admits that in a "dramatic transition" whales were "undergoing fast evolutionary change," with features that "change abruptly."[62] Thewissen likens the evolution of whales from land mammals to converting a bullet train into a nuclear submarine. "Whales," he notes, "started out with a . . . perfected body adapted to life on land. They changed it, in about eight million years, to a body perfectly tuned to the ocean."[63] More recent fossil evidence shows that the first fully aquatic whales, the basilosaurids, appeared even more abruptly than previously thought. Indeed, basilosaurids first appeared 49 million years ago, perhaps within only 4.5 million years after the earliest Pakicetidae, a family of terrestrial mammals that are supposedly ancestral to whales.[64] The basilosaurids even *predate* some of their supposed protocetid ancestors such as the 47.5-million-year-old "proto-whale" *Maiacetus*—a mammal that gave birth on land, had well-developed hind limbs, and lacked even rudimentary tail flukes.[65] Indeed, the phylogenetic tree based on cladistic analysis of fossils does not reveal a gradual origin of aquatic adaptations; instead, the *defining features* of true whales appear abruptly in the clade Pelagiceti.[66] (Similar, though arguably more acute, problems afflict the putative reptile-like mammal transitional sequence.[67])

---

62. J. G. M. "Hans" Thewissen, *The Walking Whales: From Land to Water in Eight Million Years* (Berkeley: University of California Press, 2014).

63. Ibid.

64. The best geological evidence indicates basilosaurids appear by 49 mya. See Mónica R. Buono et al., "Eocene Basilosaurid Whales from the La Meseta Formation, Marambio (Seymour) Island, Antarctica," *Ameghiniana* 53 (2016): 296–315; Evolution News, "An Unbearable Rush: Antarctic Whale Fossil Poses a Challenge to Evolution that Won't Go Away," *Evolution News and Views*, November 16, 2016, http://www.evolutionnews.org/2016/11/an_unbearable_r_1103292.html. The earliest Pakicetidae is *Himalayacetus*, about 53.5 mya. See M. D. Uhen, "The Origin(s) of Whales," *Annual Review of Earth and Planetary Sciences* 38 (2010): 189–219; Felix G. Marx et al., *Cetacean Paleobiology* (Chichester, UK: Wiley, 2016). In order to account for the origin of the defining features of truly aquatic whales, Thewissen has proposed that one or a few *macro*-mutations led to the modern Cetacea (Thewissen, *Walking Whales*).

65. Philip D. Gingerich et al., "New Protocetid Whale from the Middle Eocene of Pakistan: Birth on Land, Precocial Development, and Sexual Dimorphism," *PLoS ONE* 4 (2009): e4366.

66. Mark D. Uhen, "New Protocetid Whales from Alabama and Mississippi, and a New Cetacean Clade, Pelagiceti," *Journal of Vertebrate Paleontology* 28 (2008): 589–593; Uhen, "Origin(s) of Whales."

67. See Stephen C. Meyer et al., *Explore Evolution: The Arguments for and against Neo-Darwinism* (Melbourne and London: Hill House, 2007), 20–24 and 128–133. Even a seemingly well-ordered sequence of transitional intermediates may be equivocal at best as evidence of *continuous material descent* with modification. As noted in note 60, such a sequence may represent the rational ordering of a designing mind rather than an actual process of material descent—as occurs with, say, a series of similar but ever-changing models of the same kind of car year by year. Further, it is worth remembering that extant organisms can easily be arranged (by assessing degrees of

Thus, though common descent and its fully connected monophyletic picture of biological history can explain some of the fossil evidence—such as the progression of increasingly complex forms and the increasing similarity of fossil form to modern forms of life as observers ascend the stratigraphic column—the polyphyletic view can explain those same classes of evidence and can, in our judgment, explain other aspects of the fossil evidences (such as fossil discontinuity, a "top-down" pattern of appearance, and the pervasive absence of genuine temporal/transitional intermediates) more adequately and more simply than can a monophyletic view. Indeed, a polyphyletic view would seem to explain and describe more adequately the overall pattern of increasing complexity *and* abrupt appearance than would a monophyletic view.

V. Other Classes of Evidence and the Theory of Universal Common Descent

We have found that this same logical relationship obtains between other classes of biological evidences and these competing views of biological history. If only some facets of the evidence in question are considered, then a monophyletic view of the history of life explains the evidence as well as a polyphyletic view. But if other facets of that evidence are considered, then a polyphyletic view ends up providing a more adequate explanation of all the facets of that relevant class of evidence.

Consider, for example, molecular homology, the class of evidence that many evolutionary biologists think supports UCD most decisively. When biologists compare the amino acid sequences of proteins and

---

similarity and complexity) into a hypothetical series of transitional forms from bacteria to humans: starting with cyanobacteria, via archaebacteria, protists (Choanozoa), placozoans, flat worms (Platyhelminthes), arrow worms (Chaetognatha), lancelets (Cephalochordata), lampreys, lung fish, salamanders, tuataras, monotremes, opossums, shrews, tree shrews, lemurs, monkeys, apes, to humans. To consider such an arrangement indicative of a true historical sequence and, thus, evidence of common ancestry, conflates pattern (or sequence) and process, however. All that we observe in the present, *as well as in the fossil record*, is a pattern of discontinuous similarities that can be hierarchically ordered (by degree of similarity or complexity). Nevertheless, such a pattern or arrangement by itself does not tell us by what kind of a process (or cause) the pattern arose. Instead, that is a question of interpretation of the evidence that is not provided by the evidence itself. Common ancestry (material descent with modification) qualifies as a plausible explanation only if there is a viable process by which one form of life can be transformed into another. Neo-Darwinists, of course, affirm that random mutation and natural selection can accomplish such transformations, but critics of the creative power of the mutation/selection mechanism, and other more recently proposed evolutionary mechanisms, have offered compelling reasons to doubt such claims. (See chapters 1–9, and chapters 2 and 8 especially, for a summary of reasons to doubt the creative power of various evolutionary mechanisms).

genes in different species, they often find that they are quite similar in the "letter-by-letter" arrangement of their information-bearing subunits. Comparisons of the chimp and human genomes have indicated that the two are between 95 percent and 99 percent similar in sequence.[68] Proponents of UCD explain this similarity as the result of chimpanzees and humans having a common ancestor, one that possessed an ancestral genome that later evolved in two slightly different ways.

But that's only one possible explanation. The similarity between different genes and proteins in different organisms also might have arisen separately as the result of an intelligent designer choosing to provide similar molecular-level functional capabilities in different organisms. For example, on this view, hemoglobin proteins in chimps and humans should have similar amino acid sequences or structures (as they do)[69] since they perform the same function in each animal, namely, carrying oxygen in the blood stream. Thus, as with fossil progression, the evidence of sequence similarity admits more than one explanation.

Moreover, as was the case with the fossil evidence, an alternative picture (to the monophyletic view) of biological history better accounts for *other* aspects of the molecular evidence. Consider: if Darwin's tree of life picture is accurate, then we should expect different types of biological evidence to point to the same phylogenetic tree. Since life had only one history, then a "family history" of organisms based on comparative anatomy should match one based on comparisons of DNA, RNA, and proteins. Many studies have shown, however, that trees derived from analyses of anatomy often conflict with trees based on bio-macromolecules. Some recent examples for molecular and morphological data producing wildly different phylogenetic trees are grasses,[70] metazoan animals,[71] reptiles (i.e., the position of turtles),[72]

68. See, e.g., Stefan Lovgren, "Chimps, Humans 96 Percent the Same, Gene Study Finds," *National Geographic News*, August 31, 2005. See also chapter 15 in this book (on the human genome).

69. Susan Offner, "Using the NCBI Genome Databases to Compare the Genes for Human and Chimpanzee Beta Hemoglobin," *The American Biology Teacher* 72 (2010): 252–256.

70. Bryan K. Simon, "Grass Phylogeny and Classification: Conflict of Morphology and Molecules," *Aliso* 23 (2007): 259–266.

71. Ronald A. Jenner, "When Molecules and Morphology Clash: Reconciling Conflicting Phylogenies of the Metazoa by Considering Secondary Character Loss," *Evolution and Development* 6 (2004): 372–378.

72. Ylenia Chiari et al., "Phylogenomic Analyses Support the Position of Turtles as the Sister Group of Birds and Crocodiles (Archosauria)," *BMC Biology* 10 (2012): 65.

and lizards,[73] all of which contradict the result one would expect based on the theory of universal common descent.

Worse, various molecular analyses often generate widely different evolutionary trees.[74] As biologist Michael Lynch observes, "analyses based on different genes—and even different analyses based on the same genes" can yield "a diversity of phylogenetic trees."[75] More recently, genomics experts have found thousands of genes in different organisms with no known similarity to *any* other known gene.[76] The pervasiveness of these nonhomologous "orphan" genes is completely unexpected, given UCD. Yet, if different forms of life originated discontinuously and separately, then there would be no reason to expect that trees derived from different analyses would generate a single convergent tree. Moreover, if different forms of life were intelligently designed, with a mosaic of characteristics, some of which they share in common with some organisms and others of which they share in common with different organisms, then we would expect "phylogenetic" analyses to generate conflicting trees depending on which character was chosen. Indeed, phylogenetic analyses of different characters present in several different human-designed technological objects have been shown to generate precisely such conflicting trees.

Finally, there are instances where the evidence for UCD has simply crumbled. In the *Origin*, Darwin claimed that embryos of different classes of vertebrates progress through similar phases of development as they grow from embryos to adults. He thought this indicated that different vertebrate classes shared a common ancestor in which that common pattern of development first originated.[77] It turns out, however, that different classes of vertebrates do not progress through

73. Jonathan B. Losos et al., "Who Speaks with a Forked Tongue? State-of-the-Art Molecular and Morphological Phylogenies for Lizards Differ Fundamentally," *Science* 338 (2012): 1428–1429.

74. See, e.g., R. Christen et al., "An Analysis of the Origin of Metazoans, Using Comparisons of Partial Sequences of the 28S RNA, Reveals an Early Emergence of Triploblasts," *EMBO Journal* 10 (1991): 499–503.

75. Michael Lynch, "The Age and Relationships of the Major Animal Phyla," *Evolution* 53 (1999): 319–325.

76. Richard Buggs, "The Evolutionary Mystery of Orphan Genes," Nature.com, December 28, 2016, https://natureecoevocommunity.nature.com/users/24561-richard-buggs/posts/14227-the-unsolved-evolutionary-conundrum-of-orphan-genes.

77. Charles Darwin, "Chapter 13: Mutual Affinities of Organic Beings," in Darwin, *On the Origin of Species by Means of Natural Selection*, facsimile of the first ed. (London: John Murray, 1859; repr., Cambridge, MA: Harvard University Press, 1964), 442, 449.

similar phases of embryological development.[78] Yet, Darwin regarded alleged similarities in vertebrate development as "the strongest single class of facts in favor of" common descent.

VI. Conclusion

In summary, the case for UCD rests in part upon: (1) factual claims that have evaporated, (2) circumstantial evidence that admits alternative explanation, and (3) evidence (such as fossil discontinuity and conflicting phylogenetic trees) that is better explained by a polyphyletic view of biological history.[79] For that reason, we have both become skeptical about the theory of universal common descent and versions of theistic evolution that affirm this second meaning of evolution—as described in the "Scientific and Philosophical Introduction" to this volume.

78. Stephen J. Gould, "Abscheulich! Atrocious!" *Natural History* 190 (2000): 42–49; Adam Sedgwick, "On the Law of Development Commonly Known as von Baer's Law; and on the Significance of Ancestral Rudiments in Embryonic Development," *Quarterly Journal of Microscopical Science* 36 (1894): 35–52.

79. For more complete documentation of these claims, see Meyer et al., *Explore Evolution*; Meyer, *Darwin's Doubt*, 114–135.

11

Universal Common Descent: A Comprehensive Critique

CASEY LUSKIN

SUMMARY

Some theistic evolutionists will occasionally acknowledge problems with the mechanism of mutation and natural selection, but almost all theistic evolutionists claim that the historical part of Darwinian theory—universal common descent—is beyond dispute. Since Darwin's time, the theory of universal common descent has rested upon a number of independent lines of evidence and argument: biogeography, fossils, anatomical homology, and embryological similarity. In recent decades, molecular homology has been added to that list. This chapter will show that each of these separate lines of evidence is equivocal at best and that, instead, many new lines of evidence cast serious doubt upon the supposed "congruence" of these lines of evidence, challenging the case for universal common descent.

· · · · ·

Some theistic evolutionists will occasionally acknowledge problems with the mechanism of mutation and natural selection (or at least will decline to defend its creative power). Nevertheless, almost all theistic evolutionists claim that the historical part of Darwinian theory—universal common descent—is beyond dispute. Prominent theistic evolutionists treat universal common descent as almost an axiom of all biological science, and ridicule skeptics through comparisons to geocentrists or flat-earthers. Since Darwin's time, the theory of universal common descent has rested upon a number of independent lines of evidence and argument: biogeography, fossils, anatomical homology, and embryological similarity. In recent decades, molecular homology has been added to that list. This chapter will show that each of these separate lines of evidence is equivocal at best and that, instead, many new lines of evidence cast serious doubt upon the supposed "congruence" of these lines of evidence, challenging the case for universal common descent.

As other chapters have discussed, theistic evolution essentially takes a fully materialistic evolutionary view of biological history and says, "By the way, this is how God did it." But the term "evolution" can have different meanings, some of which are controversial and some of which are not.

For many, "evolution" simply means "change over time." Both theistic evolutionists and Darwin skeptics affirm that this definition of evolution is uncontroversial and correct.

A second definition is universal common ancestry, the hypothesis that all living organisms are genetically related through descent with modification. Under this view, not only are all living humans related to one another, but we also share a common ancestor with apes, and going back farther, we're related to everything from horses to tuna fish to broccoli to foot fungus and bacteria. This definition of evolution is controversial among many (though not all) Darwin skeptics, and is increasingly controversial among evolutionary biologists.

The third definition of evolution claims that natural selection acting upon random mutations was the driving mechanism behind the history of life. This definition is the most controversial among scientists both inside and outside of the evolutionary community, and it holds that the mechanisms producing change over time (definition one) and common ancestry (definition two) were apparently blind and undirected.

Other chapters in Section I, Part 1 of this book have amply addressed the inadequacy of evolution's mechanism (the third definition).

The purpose of this chapter is to examine *only* the second definition—universal common ancestry.

At first glance, common ancestry may not seem crucial to addressing theistic evolution. After all, the third definition is the one that addresses whether the history of life was unguided—a central question in the debate over theistic evolution. Moreover, common ancestry is compatible with intelligent design. For example, one possible way to view intelligent design is that God actively guided the history of life, but did so in a manner such that organisms share a common ancestry. Such a view supports both intelligent design and common ancestry yet avoids many of the logical, philosophical, and scientific difficulties that theistic evolution encounters when claiming that the entire history of life appears unguided (even though it really wasn't).

Nonetheless, for a variety of reasons, common ancestry is an important part of this conversation.

First, the pursuit of truth is of the utmost importance. If universal common ancestry is true, we should want to know about that. If it isn't, we should modify our views accordingly.

Second, theistic evolutionists devote much energy to arguing for common ancestry. They often mistakenly cite evidence for common ancestry as evidence for the full-blown Darwinian story and an apparently naturalistic history of life, conflating the second and third definitions of evolution. While this rhetorical strategy is logically flawed (evidence for common ancestry is not necessarily evidence for blind natural selection), if the evidence for universal common ancestry is weak then their argument faces not just a logical problem but also a factual one.

Moreover, in practice common ancestry sometimes (though not always) serves as a "gateway belief," taking people away from an intelligent design–based view to a full-throated theistic evolutionary view—and for some, then on to an atheistic view. The importance of common ancestry to this conversation is seen in that theistic evolutionists *commonly* argue for their view *not* by citing evidence for natural selection but rather by focusing on the evidence for common ancestry—and they often do so using the strongest of language.

Finally, once the mechanism of evolution (definition three) comes under scrutiny, and life's history no longer appears unguided, then evolutionary scientists lose an important rationale for claiming that all life is genetically related. If life evolved through an apparently unguided process like natural selection, then it follows that all life must be related. But if all life is not related, this challenges standard neo-Darwinian accounts of biological history. *Thus, another important reason to discuss common ancestry is that if life is not universally related, this undercuts a core problematic tenet of theistic evolution.*[1]

For these reasons, it is appropriate to devote some space to scientifically examining common ancestry. Most of the other chapters in this section of the book (Section I, Part 2) will focus on specific claims of human/ape common ancestry. This chapter, however, will focus more broadly on universal common ancestry—the idea that all living organisms are related.

I. Theistic Evolutionists Strongly Endorse Common Ancestry

The importance of common ancestry to theistic evolution is witnessed in the extremely strong language that theistic evolutionists use when defending the concept.

Francis Collins argues in *The Language of God* that "the conclusion of a common ancestor for humans and mice is virtually inescapable."[2] In *Coming to Peace with Science*, biologist and former BioLogos president Darrel Falk writes regarding mammals that "*virtually all* geneticists are convinced . . . they share common ancestors."[3] Another frequent BioLogos author, Dennis Venema, a biologist at Trinity Western University, argues that "[n]umerous independent lines of genomics evidence strongly support the hypothesis that our species shares a common ancestor with other primates."[4]

---

1. This is not to say that affirming universal common ancestry requires belief in a thoroughly Darwinian history of life. Rather, because neo-Darwinism requires common ancestry to be true, if common ancestry is false, then so is the dominant evolutionary paradigm of biological origins.
2. Francis Collins, *The Language of God: A Scientist Presents Evidence for Belief* (New York: Free Press, 2006), 136–137.
3. Darrel Falk, *Coming to Peace with Science* (Downers Grove, IL: IVP Academic, 2004), 192, emphasis added.
4. Dennis R. Venema, "Genesis and the Genome: Genomics Evidence for Human-Ape Common Ancestry and Ancestral Hominid Population Sizes," *Perspectives on Science and Christian Faith* 62 (September 2010): 166–178.

Robert Asher, a paleontologist at Cambridge University, writes in *Evolution and Belief: Confessions of a Religious Paleontologist*, that "the idea that the natural world around us does not teem with evidence in support of Darwin's theory of evolution, that humanity does not share common ancestry with other forms of life on Earth via the mechanism of descent with modification, is profoundly mistaken."[5] He further charges that "creationists" are incapable of a "fair, honest" evaluation of the data regarding common ancestry.[6]

In a 2011 InterVarsity Press book, Francis Collins and physicist Karl Giberson compare those who doubt common ancestry to geocentrists, writing, "virtually all geneticists consider that the evidence proves common ancestry with a level of certainty comparable to the evidence that the earth goes around the sun."[7] Elsewhere Giberson employed similar rhetoric, stating, "biologists today consider the common ancestry of all life a fact on par with the sphericity of the earth"[8]—unsubtly implying that those who doubt common ancestry are no better than flat-earthers.

Proponents of universal common ancestry may distastefully aim to use ridicule to bully skeptics into submission—but that in itself doesn't mean common descent is therefore wrong. Despite the outlandish rhetoric, the evidence is worth carefully considering.

Before we investigate the evidence, it's important to note that it is theoretically possible that common ancestry might be true, or false, at multiple levels of the taxonomic hierarchy. For example, universal common ancestry hypothesizes that all living organisms are related. Thus, *universal* common ancestry might be false, but common ancestry could still be true at lower taxonomic levels, such as among all animals, or all vertebrates, all mammals, or all primates, etc. Indeed, even if we question common ancestry among those various groups, everyone would probably agree that all humans share a common ancestor. Ultimately, common ancestry must be evaluated on a case-by-case basis depending on the evidence within the particular group being studied.

---

5. Robert J. Asher, *Evolution and Belief: Confessions of a Religious Paleontologist* (Cambridge: Cambridge University Press, 2012), 1.

6. Ibid., xv.

7. Karl Giberson and Francis Collins, *The Language of Science and Faith* (Downers Grove, IL: InterVarsity Press, 2011), 49.

8. Karl W. Giberson, *Saving Darwin: How to Be a Christian and Believe in Evolution* (New York: HarperOne, 2008), 53.

Evaluating the case for common ancestry among every single high and low taxonomic grouping is far beyond the scope of this chapter, and probably would entail an impossibly lengthy inquiry. This chapter will thus evaluate the case for universal common ancestry as it is commonly advocated in textbooks and in popular books by theistic evolutionists and evolution advocates. This approach will afford an analysis of the typical arguments for common ancestry, and allow the reader to critically evaluate whether those arguments hold up.

The case for universal common ancestry is often said to be "cumulative," based on multiple lines of evidence including biogeography, fossils, DNA and anatomical similarities, and embryology.[9] Because common descent is said to be demonstrated by multiple, independent lines of congruent evidence, those categories of evidence should be evaluated independently. This chapter will examine whether the evidence supports common ancestry in those different areas, starting with biogeography.

II. Does the Evidence Support Common Ancestry?

A. Biogeography

Biogeography is the study of the distribution of organisms in both time and space over the history of the earth. Defenders of neo-Darwinism commonly contend that biogeography strongly supports their viewpoint. For example, the National Center for Science Education (NCSE), a pro-Darwin advocacy group, cites a "consistency between biogeographic and evolutionary patterns" and argues, "[t]his continuity is what would be expected of a pattern of common descent."[10]

Much biogeographical data, however, has little to do with Darwinian evolution, and does not provide special evidence for com-

---

9. E.g., see Douglas L. Theobald, "A Formal Test of the Theory of Universal Common Ancestry," *Nature* 465 (May 13, 2010): 219–222, where he says, "UCA is now supported by a wealth of evidence from many independent sources, including: (1) the agreement between phylogeny and biogeography; (2) the correspondence between phylogeny and the palaeontological record; (3) the existence of numerous predicted transitional fossils; (4) the hierarchical classification of morphological characteristics; (5) the marked similarities of biological structures with different functions (that is, homologies); and (6) the congruence of morphological and molecular phylogenies."

10. National Center for Science Education, "Evolution on Islands," accessed October 13, 2016, https://ncse.com/book/export/html/5528. For a rebuttal, see Casey Luskin, "The NCSE's Biogeographic Conundrums: A Defense of Explore Evolution's Treatment of Biogeography," *ExploreEvolution.com*, January 19, 2010, accessed October 13, 2016, http://www.exploreevolution.com/exploreEvolutionFurtherDebate/2010/01/the_ncses_biogeographic_conund.php.

mon ancestry. It can be easily explained as the result of migration and continental drift—two conventional ideas accepted by virtually everyone in this debate. However, the NCSE's arguments ignore the many biogeographical puzzles that have vexed evolutionary biologists because they show a marked *dis*continuity between biogeography and common ancestry.

Evolutionary explanations of biogeography fail when terrestrial or freshwater organisms appear in a location (such as an isolated island or continent) at which no standard migratory mechanism can explain how those species arrived from their proposed evolutionary ancestors. In other words, take any two populations of organisms, and theistic evolution claims that if we go back far enough, they must be linked in space and time by common descent. But sometimes it is virtually impossible to explain how two particular populations arrived at their current geographical locations from some common ancestral population.

For example, a severe biogeographical puzzle for common ancestry is the origin of South American monkeys, called "platyrrhines." Based on molecular and morphological evidence, New World platyrrhine monkeys are thought to be descended from African "Old World" or "catarrhine" monkeys.

The fossil record shows that monkeys have lived in South America for about 30 million years.[11] But plate tectonics shows that Africa and South America separated around 100–120 million years ago (mya), and South America was an isolated island continent from about 80 to 3.5 mya.[12] If South American monkeys split from African monkeys around 30 mya, neo-Darwinism must somehow explain how monkeys crossed hundreds, if not thousands, of kilometers of open ocean to end up in South America.

This poses a major problem for common ancestry—one recognized by multiple experts. A HarperCollins textbook on human evolution

11. Alfred L Rosenberger and Walter Carl Hartwig, "New World Monkeys," *Encyclopedia of Life Sciences* (Nature Publishing Group, 2001), doi:10.1038/npg.els.0001562.

12. Carlos G. Schrago and Claudia A. M. Russo, "Timing the Origin of New World Monkeys," *Molecular Biology and Evolution* 20 (2003): 1620–1625; John J. Flynn and A. R. Wyss, "Recent Advances in South American Mammalian Paleontology," *Trends in Ecology and Evolution* 13 (November 1998): 449–454; C. Barry Cox and Peter D. Moore, *Biogeography: An Ecological and Evolutionary Approach* (Oxford, UK: Blackwell Science, 1993), 185.

states, "The origin of platyrrhine monkeys puzzled paleontologists for decades. . . . When and how did the monkeys get to South America?"[13] Primatologists John Fleagle and Christopher Gilbert explain,

> The most biogeographically challenging aspect of platyrrhine evolution concerns the origin of the entire clade. South America was an island continent throughout most of the Tertiary [66 to 2.5 million years ago] . . . and paleontologists have debated for much of this century how and where primates reached South America.[14]

For those unfamiliar with the explanations of evolutionary scientists, their responses to such puzzles can be almost too incredible to believe. They propose *not that common descent might be wrong*, but that monkeys must have rafted across the Atlantic Ocean, from Africa to South America, to colonize the New World. The HarperCollins textbook explains, "The 'rafting hypothesis' argues that monkeys evolved from prosimians once and only once in Africa, and . . . made the water-logged trip to South America."[15] Of course, there can't be just one seafaring monkey, or it will die, leaving no offspring. Thus, at least two monkeys (or perhaps a single pregnant monkey) must have made the rafting voyage.

Fleagle and Gilbert admit the rafting hypothesis "raises a difficult biogeographical issue" because "South America is separated from Africa by a distance of at least 2,600 km [~1,600 miles], making a phylogenetic and biogeographic link between the primate faunas of the two continents seem very *unlikely*."[16] But they are wedded to common ancestry, and are obligated to find such a "link," whether likely or not. Unwilling to consider non-evolutionary options, they conclude, "the rafting hypothesis is the most *likely* scenario for the biogeographic origin of platyrrines."[17] In other words, the "unlikely" monkey-rafting hypothesis is made "likely" only because they assume common descent *must* be true.

---

13. Adrienne L. Zihlman, *The Human Evolution Coloring Book* (Napa, CA: HarperCollins, 2000), 4–11.
14. John G. Fleagle and Christopher C. Gilbert, "The Biogeography of Primate Evolution: The Role of Plate Tectonics, Climate, and Chance," in *Primate Biogeography: Progress and Prospects*, ed. Shawn M. Lehman and John G. Fleagle (New York: Springer, 2006), 393–394.
15. Zihlman, *Human Evolution Coloring Book*, 4–11.
16. Fleagle and Gilbert, "Biogeography of Primate Evolution," 394.
17. Ibid., 394–395, emphasis added.

Needless to say, the rafting hypothesis itself faces serious difficulties. Mammals like monkeys have high metabolisms and require large amounts of food and water.[18] Fleagle and Gilbert thus concede that "over-water dispersal during primate evolution seems truly amazing for a mammalian order," and conclude, "[t]he reasons for the prevalence of rafting during the course of primate evolution remain to be explained."[19] Or, as another expert puts it, "the mechanical aspect of platyrrhine dispersal [is] virtually irresolvable" because evolutionary models "must invoke a transoceanic crossing mechanism that is implausible (rafting) or suspect . . . at best."[20] Fleagle and Gilbert compare the monkeys' voyage to winning the lottery: "by a stroke of good luck anthropoids were able to 'win' the sweepstakes."[21]

This is by no means the only case where evolutionary biologists are forced to invoke rafting or other speculative mechanisms of "oceanic dispersal" to explain away difficult problems. Other biogeographical conundra include the presence of lizards and large caviomorph rodents in South America,[22] the arrival of bees, lemurs, and other mammals in Madagascar,[23] the appearance of elephant fossils on various islands,[24] the appearance of freshwater frogs across isolated oceanic island chains,[25] and numerous other examples.[26]

---

18. Ibid., 404.

19. Ibid., 403–404.

20. Walter Carl Hartwig, "Patterns, Puzzles and Perspectives on Platyrrhine Origins," in *Integrative Paths to the Past: Paleoanthropological Advances in Honor of F. Clark Howell*, ed. Robert S. Corruccini and Russell L. Ciochon (Englewood Cliffs, NJ: Prentice Hall, 1994), 76, 84.

21. Fleagle and Gilbert, "Biogeography of Primate Evolution," 395.

22. John C. Briggs, *Global Biogeography* (Amsterdam: Elsevier Science, 1995), 93.

23. Susan Fuller, Michael Schwarz, and Simon Tierney, "Phylogenetics of the Allodapine Bee Genus *Braunsapis*: Historical Biogeography and Long-Range Dispersal Over Water," *Journal of Biogeography* 32 (2005): 2135–2144; Anne D. Yoder, Matt Cartmill, Maryellen Ruvolo, Kathleen Smith, and Rytas Vilgalys, "Ancient Single Origin of Malagasy Primates," *Proceedings of the National Academy of Sciences USA* 93 (May 1996): 5122–5126; Peter M. Kappeler, "Lemur Origins: Rafting by Groups of Hibernators?," *Folia Primatol* 71 (2000): 422–425; Christian Roos, Jürgen Schmitz, and Hans Zischler, "Primate Jumping Genes Elucidate Strepsirrhine Phylogeny," *Proceedings of the National Academy of Sciences USA* 101 (July 20, 2004): 10650–10654; Philip D. Rabinowitz and Stephen Woods, "The Africa-Madagascar Connection and Mammalian Migrations," *Journal of African Earth Sciences* 44 (2006): 270–276; Anne D. Yoder, Melissa M. Burns, Sarah Zehr, et al., "Single Origin of Malagasy Carnivora from an African Ancestor," *Nature* 421 (February 13, 2003): 734–737.

24. Richard John Huggett, *Fundamentals of Biogeography*, 2nd ed. (London: Routledge, 1998), 39.

25. G. John Measey, Miguel Vences, Robert C. Drewes, et al., "Freshwater Paths across the Ocean: Molecular Phylogeny of the Frog *Ptychadena newtoni* Gives Insights into Amphibian Colonization of Oceanic Islands," *Journal of Biogeography* 34 (2007): 7–20.

26. Alan de Queiroz, "The Resurrection of Oceanic Dispersal in Historical Biogeography," *Trends in Ecology and Evolution* 20 (February 2005): 68–73.

This problem exists for extinct species as well. A 2007 paper in *Annals of Geophysics* notes the "still unresolved problem of disjointed distribution of fossils on the opposite coasts of the Pacific."[27] However, this paper doesn't invoke rafting—instead it proposes something even more unlikely: populations became separated due to an "expanding earth"—a long-discarded geological hypothesis (different from well-accepted modern theories of plate tectonics) that could be taken seriously only when trying to save common descent from falsification.

A 2005 review in *Trends in Ecology and Evolution* explains the essence of the problem:

> A classic problem in biogeography is to explain why particular terrestrial and freshwater taxa have geographical distributions that are broken up by oceans. Why are southern beeches (*Nothofagus spp.*) found in Australia, New Zealand, New Guinea and southern South America? Why are there iguanas on the Fiji Islands, whereas all their close relatives are in the New World?[28]

After considering several "unexpected" biogeographical examples, the review concludes, "these cases reinforce a general message of the great evolutionist [Darwin]: given enough time, many things that seem unlikely can happen."[29]

Indeed, "unlikely" does appear to be the message here. If you're going to retain common ancestry, you must accept some extraordinary biogeographical claims. When evolutionary scientists are forced to resort to fantastical "expanding earth" hypotheses, or "unlikely" accounts of species rafting across oceans, common ancestry clearly faces a challenge.

B. The Fossil Record

A popular college-level biology textbook explains, "Fossils are the only direct record of the history of life."[30] This seems generally correct, making the fossil record an ideal place for testing universal common ancestry.

---

27. Giancarlo Scalera, "Fossils, Frogs, Floating Islands and Expanding Earth in Changing-Radius Cartography—A Comment to a Discussion on *Journal of Biogeography*," *Annals of Geophysics* 50 (December 2007): 789–798.
28. De Queiroz, "Resurrection of Oceanic Dispersal in Historical Biogeography."
29. Ibid.
30. Donald Prothero, *Bringing Fossils to Life* (Boston: McGraw-Hill, 1998), vii.

The textbook's author, geologist Donald Prothero, has elsewhere written that "The fossil record is an amazing testimony to the power of evolution, with documentation of transitions that Darwin could only have dreamed about."[31] If you feel otherwise, Prothero continues, then you're a "creationist," who shares "much in common with the Neo-Nazi Jew-hating Holocaust deniers."[32]

But what do fossils say about evolution? If all living organisms are related, as universal common ancestry predicts, then the fossil record should seemingly contain transitional forms that show the intermediate stages between life's various groups. But the history of life bears a repeated pattern of explosions, where new fossil types appear abruptly, without clear evolutionary precursors. Perhaps the most famous is the Cambrian explosion, where many of the major living animal groups (called "phyla") appear in the fossil record in a sudden geological eyeblink—lasting 5 to 10 million years, and possibly less.[33]

Before the Cambrian, very few fossils having anything to do with modern animal phyla are found in the record. As one invertebrate zoology textbook states,

> Most of the animal phyla that are represented in the fossil record first appear, "fully formed" and identifiable as to their phylum, in the Cambrian some 550 million years ago. . . . The fossil record is therefore of no help with respect to understanding the origin and early diversification of the various animal phyla . . . [34]

The diversity of complex animals that appear in the Cambrian explosion is impressive, ranging from worms to arthropods to mollusks to even vertebrate fish. But some familiar animals—like dinosaurs, parrots, or camels—don't appear until much later. Some evolutionists claim this progression is sufficient to demonstrate common ancestry. It isn't.

While the fact that life has "changed over time" doesn't bother

31. Donald Prothero, *Evolution: What the Fossils Say and Why It Matters* (New York: Columbia University Press, 2007), xx.

32. Ibid., 44.

33. See Casey Luskin, "How 'Sudden' Was the Cambrian Explosion," in *Debating Darwin's Doubt*, ed. David Klinghoffer (Seattle: Discovery Institute Press, 2015), 75–88.

34. R. S. K. Barnes, P. Calow, and P. J. W. Olive, *The Invertebrates: A New Synthesis*, 3rd ed. (London: Blackwell Scientific, 2001), 9–10.

intelligent design, the fact that reptiles, birds, and mammals don't appear until after the Cambrian period could be a major problem for neo-Darwinian evolution if, whenever these groups do appear, they do so in an abrupt fashion that betrays the predictions of neo-Darwinian common ancestry. For many of these subgroups of animals, again, they appear abruptly, in patterns of explosions.

"While during the Cambrian explosion numerous phyla and classes representing basic body plans originated," writes paleontologist Walter Etter, the post-Cambrian "Ordovician radiation was manifested by an unprecedented burst of diversification at lower taxonomic levels."[35] He continues, "The almost exponential increase in diversity was much more rapid during this Great Ordovician Biodiversification Event (GOBE) than at any other time [from the Cambrian to the present]," noting the increase was "for the most part abrupt."

Regarding the origin of major fish groups, Columbia University geoscientist Arthur Strahler wrote that "This is one count in the creationists' charge that can only evoke in unison from paleontologists a plea of *nolo contendere* [no contest]."[36] We also see an "explosive" and rapid appearance of other marine organisms such as ammonites,[37] other hard-shelled marine invertebrates,[38] and mosasaurs.[39]

As for plants, a paper in *Annual Review of Ecology and Systematics* explains that the origin of land plants "is the terrestrial equivalent of the much-debated Cambrian 'explosion' of marine faunas."[40] Regarding angiosperms (flowering plants), scientists refer to a "big bloom" or "explosion"[41] event. As one paper states, "[a]ngiosperms appear rather

35. Walter Etter, "Patterns of Diversification and Extinction," in *Handbook of Paleoanthropology: Principles, Methods, and Approaches*, ed. Winfried Henke and Ian Tattersall, 2nd ed. (Heidelberg: Springer, 2015), 351–415.

36. Arthur Strahler, *Science and Earth History: The Evolution/Creation Controversy* (Buffalo, NY: Prometheus, 1987), 408–409.

37. Steven M. Stanley, *Macroevolution: Pattern and Process* (Baltimore: Johns Hopkins University Press, 1998), 251.

38. Niles Eldredge, *Life Pulse: Episodes from the Story of the Fossil Record* (New York: Facts on File, 1987) 69, 81.

39. Michael J. Everhart, "Rapid Evolution, Diversification, and Distribution of Mosasaurs (Reptilia; Squamata) prior to the K-T Boundary," *Oceans of Kansas Paleontology*, June 11, 2010, accessed June 7, 2016, http://oceansofkansas.com/rapidmosa.html.

40. Richard M. Bateman, Peter R. Crane, William A. DiMichele, et al., "Early Evolution of Land Plants: Phylogeny, Physiology, and Ecology of the Primary Terrestrial Radiation," *Annual Review of Ecology and Systematics* 29 (1998): 263–292.

41. David Grimaldi and Michael S. Engel, *Evolution of the Insects* (Cambridge: Cambridge University Press, 2005), 302; Michael Krauss, "The Big Bloom—How Flowering Plants Changed the World," *National Geographic* (July 2002): 102–121, http://ngm.nationalgeographic.com/ngm

suddenly in the fossil record . . . with no obvious ancestors for a period of 80-90 million years before their appearance."[42]

Land animals show similar patterns. The fossil record shows an "explosion" of tetrapods when terrestrial vertebrates appear.[43] A 2011 article in *Science* admitted that tracing the evolutionary origin of major dinosaur groups "has been a major challenge for paleontologists."[44] A prominent ornithology textbook observes the "explosive evolution" of major living bird groups.[45]

Similarly, many authorities cite an "explosion" or "explosive diversification" of major mammal groups in the Tertiary.[46] Paleontologist Niles Eldredge notes that "there are all sorts of gaps: absence of gradationally intermediate 'transitional' forms between species, but also between larger groups—between, say, families of carnivores, or the orders of mammals."[47]

Eldredge and some others attempt to explain many of these abrupt appearances of major fossil groups through "punctuated equilibrium." This model accepts that major groups of organisms appear abruptly, but attempts to offer an evolutionary explanation where new species arise in small, short-lived populations that are unlikely to leave fossil remnants of transitions. This model has many problems,[48] and a lit-

/0207/feature6/ (accessed June 13, 2016); Stanley A. Rice, *Encyclopedia of Evolution* (New York: Checkmark, 2007), 70.

42. Stefanie De Bodt, Steven Maere, and Yves Van de Peer, "Genome Duplication and the Origin of Angiosperms," *Trends in Ecology and Evolution* 20 (2005): 591–597.

43. Jennifer A. Clack, *Gaining Ground: The Origin and Evolution of Tetrapods* (Bloomington: Indiana University Press), 278, 327; Thomas S. Kemp, *The Origin of Higher Taxa: Palaeobiological, Developmental, and Ecological Perspectives* (Chicago: Oxford University Press and University of Chicago Press, 2016), 157.

44. Michael Balter, "Pint-Sized Predator Rattles the Dinosaur Family Tree," *Science* 331 (January 14, 2011): 134.

45. Frank Gill, *Ornithology*, 3rd ed. (New York: W. H. Freeman, 2007), 42.

46. Peter D. Ward, *Out of Thin Air: Dinosaurs, Birds, and Earth's Ancient Atmosphere* (Washington, DC: Joseph Henry, 2006), 224; Grimaldi and Engel, *Evolution of the Insects*, 37; Rice, *Encyclopedia of Evolution*, 6; Edwin H. Colbert, *Evolution of the Vertebrates: A History of the Backboned Animals through Time* (New York: John Wiley & Sons, 1969), 123; Niles Eldredge, *Macroevolutionary Dynamics: Species, Niches, and Adaptive Peaks* (New York: McGraw-Hill, 1989), 44; Robert A. Martin, *Missing Links: Evolutionary Concepts and Transitions through Time* (Boston: Jones & Bartlett, 2004), 135, 139. 179; Marc Godinot, "Fossil Record of the Primates from the Paleocene to the Oligocene," in *Handbook of Paleoanthropology*, 1137–1259; Maureen A. O'Leary, Jonathan I. Bloch, John J. Flynn, Timothy J. Gaudin, Andres Giallombardo, et al., "The Placental Mammal Ancestor and the Post-K-Pg Radiation of Placentals," *Science*, 339 (February 8, 2013): 662–667.

47. Niles Eldredge, *The Monkey Business: A Scientist Looks at Creationism* (New York: Washington Square, 1982), 65.

48. See chapter 7 in Stephen C. Meyer, *Darwin's Doubt: The Explosive Origin of Animal Life and the Case for Intelligent Design* (New York: HarperOne, 2013), 136–152; Casey Luskin, "Punctuated Equilibrium," in *Dictionary of Christianity and Science*, ed. Paul Copan, Tremper Longman III, Christopher L. Reese, and Michael G. Strauss (Grand Rapids, MI: Zondervan, 2017), 549–550.

eral reading of the fossil record consistently shows a pattern of abrupt explosions of new types of organisms, which contradicts common descent—the opposite of what we would predict from a Darwinian process of small changes adding up to larger ones. As biologist Jeffrey Schwartz at the University of Pittsburgh explains,

> We are still in the dark about the origin of most major groups of organisms. They appear in the fossil record as Athena did from the head of Zeus—full-blown and raring to go, in contradiction to Darwin's depiction of evolution as resulting from the gradual accumulation of countless infinitesimally minute variations.[49]

Comparing those who recognize this non-Darwinian pattern to "Holocaust deniers" won't make it go away.

C. Molecular and Morphological Phylogenetic Trees

Perhaps the most common argument for universal common ancestry encountered by students in college-level biology textbooks is the universality of the genetic code—the claim that all life uses the same nucleotide triplets to encode the same amino acids.[50] However, the genetic code *is not* universal; many variants in the genetic code are known among various organisms.[51]

If the alleged universality of the genetic code provides evidence for universal common ancestry, should its nonuniversality count as evidence against it? Whatever the answer, despite the variants, it is true that the vast majority of organisms use the same "standard code," and all life forms employ similar types of biomolecules, such as, DNA, RNA,

---

49. Jeffrey H. Schwartz, *Sudden Origins: Fossils, Genes, and the Emergence of Species* (New York: John Wiley & Sons, 1999), 3.

50. E.g., see: Jane B. Reece, Lisa A. Urry, Michael L. Cain, et al., *Campbell Biology*, 9th ed (San Francisco: Person Education, 2011), 14; Mark Ridley, *The Problems of Evolution* (Oxford: Oxford University Press, 1985), 10–11; Benjamin Lewin, *Genes VII* (Oxford: Oxford University Press, 2000), 169; Nicholas H. Barton, Derek E. G. Briggs, Jonathan A. Eisen, David B. Goldstein, Nipam H. Patel, *Evolution* (Cold Spring Harbor, NY: Cold Spring Harbor Laboratory Press, 2007), 66; Scott Freeman and Jon C. Herron, *Evolutionary Analysis* (Upper Saddle River, NJ: Prentice Hall, 1998), 59; Mark Ridley, *Evolution*, 3rd ed. (Malden, MA: Blackwell, 2004), 66.

51. For a list of known variants to the standard genetic code, see Andrzej (Anjay) Elzanowski and Jim Ostell, "The Genetic Codes," *Taxonomy Browser*, National Center for Biotechnology Information (NCBI), accessed October 25, 2016, https://www.ncbi.nlm.nih.gov/Taxonomy /taxonomyhome.html/index.cgi?chapter=cgencodes. See also Robin D. Knight, Stephen J. Freeland and Laura F. Landweber, "Rewiring the Keyboard: Evolvability of the Genetic Code," *Nature Reviews Genetics* 2 (January 2001): 49–58.

nucleotides, and proteins. Are such widespread biomolecular similarities evidence for common ancestry? A 2010 paper in *Nature*, "A Formal Test of the Theory of Universal Common Ancestry," argued yes:

> [T]he 'universal' in universal common ancestry is primarily supported by two further lines of evidence: various key commonalities at the molecular level (including fundamental biological polymers, nucleic acid genetic material, L-amino acids, and core metabolism) and the near universality of the genetic code.[52]

The article's author, evolutionary biochemist Douglas Theobald, concluded that universal common ancestry is the "best" explanation for these widespread biomolecular similarities. But "best" compared to what? Theobald tested universal common ancestry against the exceedingly unlikely hypothesis that living organisms independently evolved the same biomolecules and sequences by sheer "chance." Universal common ancestry appeared compelling only because it was being compared to a preposterous null hypothesis. As critics writing in *Biology Direct* observed,

> Cogniscenti cringed when they saw the Theobald paper, knowing that "it is trivial". It is trivial because the straw man that Theobald attacks in a text largely formulated in convoluted legalese, is that significant sequence similarity might arise by chance as opposed to descent with modification.[53]

True, universal common ancestry is one possible explanation for many genetic similarities we observe between organisms—and probably better than chance—but are there other viable explanations? Indeed there are. Intelligent agents frequently reuse the same parts in different designs to meet functional requirements, such as reusing wheels on cars and airplanes, or reusing key computer codes in different versions of Microsoft Windows. As Paul Nelson and Jonathan Wells observe,

> An intelligent cause may reuse or redeploy the same module in different systems, without there necessarily being any material or

---

52. Theobald, "Formal Test of the Theory of Universal Common Ancestry."
53. Comments by William Martin in review of Eugene V. Koonin and Yuri I Wolf, "The Common Ancestry of Life," *Biology Direct* 5 (2010): 64.

physical connection between those systems. Even more simply, intelligent causes can generate identical patterns independently. . . . If
we suppose that an intelligent designer constructed organisms using
a common set of polyfunctional genetic modules—just as human
designers, for instance, may employ the same transistor or capacitor
in a car radio or a computer, devices that are not "homologous" as
artifacts—then we can explain why we find the "same" genes expressed in the development of what are very different organisms.[54]

Thus, common design—the intentional reuse of a common blueprint
or components—is a viable explanation for the widespread functional
similarities among the biomolecules found in different types of organisms. Universal common ancestry is not the only possible explanation.

(Indeed, contra Theobald's arguments for universal common ancestry, not all fundamental biomolecules are universal among organisms.
As the authors of one paper found, "several core components of the
bacterial [DNA] replication machinery are unrelated or only distantly
related to the functionally equivalent components of the archaeal/
eukaryotic replication apparatus," leading them to suggest, "DNA
replication likely evolved independently in the bacterial and archaeal/
eukaryotic lineages."[55] Even more striking, another paper compared
the genomes of 1,000 different prokaryotic organisms and found that
"of the 1000 genomes available, *not a single protein is conserved
across all genomes*."[56])

But it isn't mere similarity among biomolecules that evolutionary
biologists claim demonstrates universal common ancestry. They often
claim that *patterns* of similar nucleotide and amino acid sequences of
genes and proteins allow organisms to be organized into a phylogenetic "tree of life" (Fig. 11.1) showing the evolutionary relationships
between all living organisms.[57]

This "tree of life" was Darwin's only illustration in the *Origin of*

---

54. Paul Nelson and Jonathan Wells, "Homology in Biology," in *Darwinism, Design, and
Public Education*, ed. John Angus Campbell and Stephen C. Meyer (East Lansing: Michigan State
University Press, 2003), 316.

55. Detlef D. Leipe, L. Aravind and Eugene V. Koonin, "Did DNA Replication Evolve Twice
Independently?" *Nucleic Acids Research* 27 (1999): 3389–3401.

56. Karin Lagesen, Dave W. Ussery, and Trudy M. Wassenaar, "Genome Update: the 1000th
Genome—A Cautionary Tale," *Microbiology* 156 (March, 2010) 603–608, emphasis added.

57. E.g., see Carl Zimmer, *Evolution: The Triumph of an Idea* (New York: WGBH, 2001),
102–103.

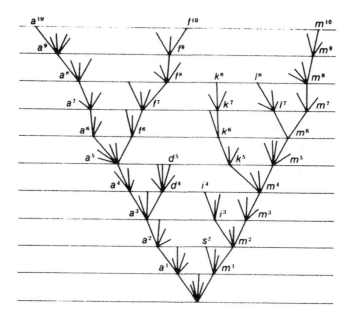

FIGURE 11.1 *Darwin's tree of life.*

Species, and it has become the most famous icon representing his theory. But does the tree of life exist?

In the 1960s, soon after the genetic code was uncovered, pioneering scientists Linus Pauling and Emile Zuckerkandl predicted that phylogenetic trees based on biomolecules would confirm expectations of common descent already held by evolutionary biologists who studied morphology (i.e., the physical traits of organisms). They declared that "If the two phylogenic trees are mostly in agreement with respect to the topology of branching, the best available single proof of the reality of macro-evolution would be furnished."[58] Presumably, then, if this prediction failed, and if there were sharp conflicts between trees built using different data sources, a compelling *disproof* of macroevolution would also be furnished.

Hoping to validate Pauling and Zuckerkandl's prediction, biologists

---

58. Emile Zuckerkandl and Linus Pauling, "Evolutionary Divergence and Convergence in Proteins," in *Evolving Genes and Proteins: A Symposium Held at the Institute of Microbiology of Rutgers, The State University,* ed. Vernon Bryson and Henry J. Vogel (New York: Academic Press, 1965), 101.

began sequencing genes from all manner of living organisms. In the 1990s, this led to a discovery that confounded evolutionary biologists: life falls into three basic domains which cannot be resolved into a neat, tree-like pattern. Thus, the prominent biochemist W. Ford Doolittle lamented,

> Molecular phylogenists will have failed to find the "true tree," not because their methods are inadequate or because they have chosen the wrong genes, but because the history of life cannot properly be represented as a tree.[59]

He explained that for many biologists, "It is as if we have failed at the task that Darwin set for us: delineating the unique structure of the tree of life."[60]

The basic problem is that one gene leads to one version of the "tree of life," but another gene leads to an entirely different tree. What seems to imply a closer evolutionary relationship in one case (i.e., two similar genes), doesn't in another. To put it another way, biological similarity is constantly appearing in places where it wasn't predicted by common descent, leading to conflicts between phylogenetic trees. When two trees conflict, at least one must be wrong. And if one tree must be wrong (i.e., in one case genetic similarity was not a good indicator of an evolutionary relationship), how do we know that both aren't wrong (i.e., in both cases genetic similarity is not indicating an evolutionary relationship)?

Numerous technical papers have noted the prevalence of contradictory phylogenetic trees among various taxonomic groups. In 1998, a study in *Genome Research* plainly observed that "different proteins generate different phylogenetic tree[s]."[61] A 2009 article in *Trends in Ecology and Evolution* acknowledged, "evolutionary trees from different genes often have conflicting branching patterns."[62] A 2013 paper

---

59. W. Ford Doolittle, "Phylogenetic Classification and the Universal Tree," *Science* 284 (June 25, 1999): 2124–2128.
60. W. Ford Doolittle, "Uprooting the Tree of Life," *Scientific American* (February 2000): 90–95.
61. Arcady R. Mushegian, James R. Garey, Jason Martin, and Leo X. Liu, "Large-Scale Taxonomic Profiling of Eukaryotic Model Organisms: A Comparison of Orthologous Proteins Encoded by the Human, Fly, Nematode, and Yeast Genomes," *Genome Research* 8 (1998): 590–598.
62. James H. Degnan and Noah A. Rosenberg, "Gene Tree Discordance, Phylogenetic Inference and the Multispecies Coalescent," *Trends in Ecology and Evolution* 24 (2009): 332–340.

in *Trends in Genetics* reported that "the more we learn about genomes the less tree-like we find their evolutionary history."[63]

Perhaps the most candid admissions came in a 2009 article in *New Scientist* titled "Why Darwin Was Wrong about the Tree of Life."[64] It quoted researcher Eric Bapteste admitting that "the holy grail was to build a tree of life," but "today that project lies in tatters, torn to pieces by an onslaught of negative evidence." According to the article, "[m]any biologists now argue that the tree concept is obsolete and needs to be discarded." The paper recounted the results of a study by Michael Syvanen, which compared two thousand genes across six animal phyla:

> In theory, he should have been able to use the gene sequences to construct an evolutionary tree showing the relationships between the six animals. He failed. The problem was that different genes told contradictory evolutionary stories.

Syvanen succinctly explained the problem: "We've just annihilated the tree of life. It's not a tree any more, it's a different topology entirely. What would Darwin have made of that?"

Clearly molecule-based trees often conflict with one another. But what about Pauling and Zuckerkandl's prediction that molecule-based phylogenetic trees should match those constructed by morphology? A review article in *Nature* titled "Bones, Molecules, or Both?" explained that "Evolutionary trees constructed by studying biological molecules often don't resemble those drawn up from morphology," admitting that "Battles between molecules and morphology are being fought across the entire tree of life."[65]

A classic example involves attempts to construct a phylogenetic tree of the animal phyla. Traditionally, many phyla were grouped according to whether they have a central body cavity, called a "coelom." But molecular data contradicted that grouping, and instead placed organisms that are morphologically very different, such as nematodes

---

63. Eric Bapteste, Leo van Iersel, Axel Janke, Scot Kelchner, Steven Kelk, et al., "Networks: Expanding Evolutionary Thinking," *Trends in Genetics* 29 (August 2013): 439–441.
64. Graham Lawton, "Why Darwin Was Wrong about the Tree of Life," *New Scientist* (January 21, 2009): 34–39.
65. Trisha Gura, "Bones, Molecules, or Both?" *Nature* 406 (July 20, 2000): 230–233.

and arthropods, very close. A *Nature* paper reported how unexpected this grouping was: "Considering the greatly differing morphologies, embryological features, and life histories of the molting animals, it was initially surprising that the ribosomal RNA tree should group them together."[66] Other fundamental animal characteristics, such as symmetry and early developmental processes, also yield a pattern of conflicting trees.[67]

Higher up the tree of life, conflicts persist. In 2014, the sequencing of various bird genomes led to the unexpected result that many types of birds that were previously thought to be closely related—water birds, birds of prey, and songbirds—evolved their groups' defining traits convergently.[68] As *Nature* put it, "the tree of life for birds has been redrawn."[69] The problem was, once again, after genomic data was sequenced and understood, many basic habits and lifestyles of birds no longer fit into a nested hierarchy.

As a final example, a 2013 paper acknowledged problems encountered when trying to reconcile conflicting versions of the mammalian tree:

> Untangling the root of the evolutionary tree of placental mammals has been nearly an impossible task. The good news is that only three possibilities are seriously considered. The bad news is that all three possibilities are seriously considered. Paleontologists favor a root anchored by Xenarthra (e.g., sloths and anteater), whereas

66. Anna Marie A. Aguinaldo, James M. Turbeville, Lawrence S. Linford, et al., "Evidence for a Clade of Nematodes, Arthropods, and Other Moulting Animals," *Nature* 387 (May 29, 1997): 489–493.

67. From the vantage of common ancestry, the animal tree ought to divide neatly according to whether organisms display bilateral symmetry (having a right half and a left half) or radial symmetry (circular symmetry around a central axis). But this is not what we find. Echinoderms, with radial symmetry, are placed much closer to vertebrates (which have bilateral symmetry) than they are to cnidarians and other radial phyla. Moreover, vertebrates place much closer to echinoderms than other bilaterian phyla. The vertebrate-echinoderm grouping is proposed on the basis of early developmental processes. Echinoderms and vertebrates are both deuterostomes, meaning that early in development the first opening in the blastopore becomes the anus rather than the mouth. The point is this: whether one compares the molecular data or morphological traits like animal symmetry or early developmental processes, they are not distributed in a tree-like pattern.

A critic might object that larval stages of echinoderms can have bilateral symmetry. But exactly the same can be said of some cnidarians, which are very far from echinoderms and vertebrates in the animal tree—showing, again, that symmetry is not distributed in a tree-like pattern. In any case, an evolutionary biologist could decide to group animal phyla according to early developmental processes, or according to symmetry, but either way you will get conflicting trees.

68. Erich D. Jarvis et al., "Whole-Genome Analyses Resolve Early Branches in the Tree of Life of Modern Birds," *Science* 346 (December 12, 2014): 1320–1331.

69. Ewen Callaway, "Flock of Geneticists Redraws Bird Family Tree," *Nature* 516 (December 11, 2014): 297.

molecular evolutionists have favored the two other possible roots: Afrotheria (e.g., elephants, hyraxes, and tenrecs) and Atlantogenata (Afrotheria + Xenarthra). Now, two groups of researchers have scrutinized the largest available genomic data sets bearing on the question and have come to opposite conclusions. . . . Needless to say, more research is needed.[70]

But is "more research" always solving these problems?[71] A 2012 paper noted that "phylogenetic conflict is common, and frequently the norm rather than the exception," since "Incongruence between phylogenies derived from morphological versus molecular analyses, and between trees based on different subsets of molecular sequences has become pervasive as data sets have expanded rapidly in both characters and species."[72]

In any case, these frequent discrepancies between molecular- and morphology-based trees, and between various molecule-based trees, have led some scientists to conclude that the prediction of Zuckerkandl and Pauling was fundamentally wrong. A paper in the journal *Biological Theory* explained:

[M]olecular systematics is (largely) based on the assumption, first clearly articulated by Zuckerkandl and Pauling, that degree of overall similarity reflects degree of relatedness. This assumption derives from interpreting molecular similarity (or dissimilarity) between taxa in the context of a Darwinian model of continual and gradual change. Review of the history of molecular systematics and its claims in the context of molecular biology reveals that *there is no basis for the 'molecular assumption.'*[73]

---

70. Emma C. Teeling and S. Blair Hedges, "Making the Impossible Possible: Rooting the Tree of Placental Mammals," *Molecular Biology and Evolution* (2013).

71. The authors of a 2016 paper using whole-genome phylogenetic analysis (a method that tends to ignore conflicts between individual gene-based trees) claimed to resolve the dispute between the different mammalian trees. However, their result was molecule-based and it still conflicted with the morphology-based tree preferred by paleontologists. See James E. Tarver, Mario dos Reis, Siavash Mirarab, Raymond J. Moran, Sean Parker, et al., "The Interrelationships of Placental Mammals and the Limits of Phylogenetic Inference," *Genome Biology and Evolution* 8 (2006): 330–344.

72. Liliana M. Dávalos, Andrea L. Cirranello, Jonathan H. Geisler, and Nancy B. Simmons, "Understanding Phylogenetic Incongruence: Lessons from Phyllostomid Bats," *Biological Reviews of the Cambridge Philosophical Society* 87 (2012): 991–1024.

73. Jeffrey H. Schwartz and Bruno Maresca, "Do Molecular Clocks Run at All? A Critique of Molecular Systematics," *Biological Theory* 1 (December 2006): 357–371, emphasis added.

To put it another way, conflicts between morphological and molecular trees seriously challenge common ancestry—and, as we will soon see, undermine the methods used to infer it. But what about those happy cases where molecule-based trees show some congruence with morphology-based trees? Does this provide some kind of special evidence for common descent? Not at all. Recall that morphological trees are based on comparing similarities in anatomical traits between different organisms. But if anatomical traits are generated by gene sequences in DNA, then it follows that organisms with more similar anatomy will typically have more similar DNA. Because of this gene-morphology linkage, one need not even consider common ancestry to predict that DNA-based trees (groupings of organisms with more similar DNA) might show some resemblance to morphology-based trees (groupings of organisms with more similar anatomy). *And both types of similarities—anatomical and DNA—can be explained by common design just as well as by common descent.*

1. Assumptions, Epicycles, and Ad Hoc Hypotheses

Centuries ago, when astronomers held to a geocentric model of the solar system, they would often encounter data that ran directly counter to that model. Sometimes planets would appear to temporarily move backwards, in "retrograde motion." Early scientists explained away the contrary data by invoking the "epicycle."

Epicycles didn't actually explain anything; such auxiliary hypotheses were adopted after the fact for the sole purpose of saving the flawed geocentric model from falsification. Eventually, scientists accepted that planets were not moving backwards and agreed that the geocentric model of the solar system was wrong. Planets orbited the sun, not the earth.

Today, evolutionary biology faces a similar dilemma. Biologists are constantly uncovering similarities between organisms that appear in patterns not predicted by universal common descent. Proponents of neo-Darwinian evolution thus adopt modern-day epicycles—ad hoc hypotheses invoked to explain why data run counter to the tree of life hypothesis. To appreciate how this works, we must examine some of the core assumptions that underlie evolutionary tree-building.

First and foremost, phylogenetic trees are based on the assumption that common ancestry is true. That assumption—*and it is merely an assumption*—is so deeply embedded in evolutionary thinking that theorists often forget it's there. In a rare example, Elliott Sober and Michael Steele acknowledge, "It is a central tenet of modern evolutionary theory that all living things now on earth trace back to a single common ancestor," and, "This proposition is central because it is presupposed so widely in evolutionary research." They acknowledge that phylogenetic methods assume that a tree exists and that common ancestry is correct:

> Whether one uses cladistic parsimony, distance measures, or maximum likelihood methods, *the typical question is which tree is the best one, not whether there is a tree in the first place.*[74]

A bioinformatics textbook concurs:

> The key assumption made when constructing a phylogenetic tree from a set of sequences is that they are all derived from a single ancestral sequence, i.e., they are homologous.[75]

These authorities affirm a crucial point: phylogenetic methods do not demonstrate common ancestry; they assume it. In other words, evolutionary biology doesn't test whether all organisms fit into a nested hierarchy (i.e., a phylogenetic tree) but rather *assumes* that common ancestry is true. If the data does not fit with preconceptions about common ancestry, then various methods are used to force-fit the data into a tree. Thus, Michael Syvanen notes the pro-tree biases of tree-building algorithms:

> Because tree analysis tools are used so widely, *they tend to introduce a bias into the interpretation of results.* Hence, one needs to be continually reminded that submitting multiple sequences (DNA,

---

74. Elliott Sober and Michael Steele, "Testing the Hypothesis of Common Ancestry," *Journal of Theoretical Biology* 218 (2002): 395–408, emphasis added. As another example, UC Berkeley Museum of Paleontology's introductory page on cladistics states:

What assumptions do cladists make?
There are three basic assumptions in cladistics:
1. Any group of organisms are related by descent from a common ancestor.

"An Introduction to Cladistics," accessed June 13, 2016, http://www.ucmp.berkeley.edu/clad /clad1.html.

75. Marketa Zvelebil and Jeremy O. Baum, *Understanding Bioinformatics* (New York: Garland Science, 2008), 239.

protein, or other character states) to *phylogenetic analysis produces trees because that is the nature of the algorithms used.*[76]

A more explicitly recognized assumption is that shared biological similarity between two species indicates inheritance from a common ancestor. This assumption is reflected in the statement quoted earlier from the journal *Biological Theory*: "degree of overall similarity reflects degree of relatedness." We'll call this the *main assumption*.

The main assumption sounds nice in theory, but in practice, it fails constantly. For instance, under the main assumption, the reason you have two eyes, and your dog has two eyes, is that you shared a common ancestor with two eyes. That is a possibility. But cephalopods (octopi and squid) also have two eyes, and according to standard evolutionary wisdom, there's no reason to think your most recent common ancestor with cephalopods had two eyes. We're not even sure if it had eyes.

"Perhaps," the defender of common ancestry replies, "both organisms independently evolved two eyes, just by chance." Perhaps. But human-cephalopod similarities go much deeper.

Cephalopods have a "camera eye" with a basic design that is almost identical to human eyes. Surely such similarities are taken to indicate common ancestry, right? Wrong.

According to evolutionary biologists, the extreme similarities between human and squid eyes result from "convergent evolution," where two different organisms independently stumbled upon almost the same complex biological designs.

"Convergence" can be found at some of the highest conceivable levels of complexity. For example, comb jellies have advanced nervous systems, but molecular studies suggest they branched off very close to the base of the animal tree—before such complexity evolved. However, sponges (which branch off later, according to molecular data) lack such structures. This means that either animal brains evolved convergently—i.e., they arose multiple times, independently—or important and complex nervous cells were lost in sponges.[77]

---

76. Michael Syvanen, "Evolutionary Implications of Horizontal Gene Transfer," *Annual Review of Genetics* 46 (2012): 339–356 (emphases added).

77. Maximilian J. Telford, "Fighting Over a Comb," *Nature* 529 (January 21, 2016): 286; Antonis Rokas; "My Oldest Sister Is a Sea Walnut?" *Science* 342 (December 13, 2013): 1327–1329; Benjamin J. Liebeskind, David M. Hillis, Harold H. Zakon, and Hans A. Hofmann, "Complex

Such extreme convergence is disconcerting to many evolutionary biologists, as Richard Dawkins acknowledges: "it is vanishingly improbable that exactly the same evolutionary pathway should ever be travelled twice." Yet he admits there are "numerous examples . . . in which independent lines of evolution appear to have converged, from very different starting points, on what looks very like the same endpoint." Not to worry, Dawkins tells us. Rather than facing the challenge of convergent evolution, he simply declares, "it is all the more striking a testimony to the power of natural selection."[78]

Beyond the fact that it is highly unlikely, extreme convergent evolution presents an even more serious problem for neo-Darwinian theory. It shows that the main assumption *has failed*—that biological similarity *does not* necessarily indicate inheritance from a common ancestor. This challenges the heart of the methodology used to infer common descent.

But why should that trouble us? After all, what assumption always holds true? It should trouble us because the main assumption (that biological similarity indicates a common ancestor) fails not occasionally, but frequently. Indeed, so often does the main assumption fail, and so quick are evolutionary biologists to tolerate its failure, that we cannot help but question the many instances where biologists believe the main assumption held true. The frequent failure of the main assumption calls into doubt the core assumptions and rational bases used to construct phylogenetic trees—the lifeblood of common ancestry.

One evolutionary systematist, Nicholas Matzke, maintains that these failures of methodology pose no problems for common descent, as he notes that we can statistically analyze the congruency of trees to assess whether the assumptions of tree-building are holding true.[79] In response to Darwin skeptics, he posted two phylogenetic trees (in this case, cladograms) and claimed that they demonstrated the common

---

Homology and the Evolution of Nervous Systems," *Trends in Ecology and Evolution* 31 (February 2016): 127–135; Amy Maxmen, "Evolution: You're Drunk: DNA Studies Topple the Ladder of Complexity," *Nautilus* 9 (January 30, 2014), accessed July 13, 2016, http://nautil.us/issue/9/time/evolution-youre-drunk.

78. Richard Dawkins, *The Blind Watchmaker: Why the Evidence of Evolution Reveals a Universe without Design* (New York: W. W. Norton, 1996), 94.

79. See Nicholas Matzke, "Meyer's Hopeless Monster, Part II," *Panda's Thumb*, June 19, 2013, accessed June 7, 2016, http://pandasthumb.org/archives/2013/06/meyers-hopeless-2.html.

388   The Case against Common Descent and for a Unique Human Origin

ancestry of arthropods. In reality, however, they demonstrated how the methods of phylogenetic reconstruction often fail to establish the assumptions that underlie common ancestry.

A main goal of tree-building is to construct a phylogenetic tree that minimizes the number of evolutionary events necessary to explain the observed distribution of traits. An "evolutionary event" is the gain or loss of a trait during the course of evolution. The fewer evolutionary events required, the "better" the data fits a tree. In the parlance of evolutionary biology, this is called maximizing parsimony.

One statistical method of determining the extent to which a data set fits a tree-like pattern is to calculate a tree's "consistency index" (CI). This is found by taking the minimum number of evolutionary events required by the overall data set, divided by the number of events required by the tree. A high CI (closer to one) indicates the data fits a tree-like pattern. A lower CI (closer to zero) usually indicates the data is inconsistent with a tree.[80]

The CI also measures the degree to which convergent evolution is required by a tree. In other words, a CI tells you how frequently the main assumption of tree-building has failed. But what happens when the "best" tree you can find (i.e., the tree with the highest CI) still has a low CI?

Consider the CIs for the arthropod trees posted by Matzke. One had CI of 0.565.[81] This means that 43.5 percent of the time, a given trait or character analyzed in the data set was *not* distributed in a tree-like pattern, meaning the main assumption—that biological similarity results from common ancestry—*failed*. If an assumption fails 43.5 percent of the time, can one justify making it in the first place?

Numerous similar examples could be given. A tree published in *Nature* purported to show the evolutionary relationships of many living mammals, but its CI was 0.43, meaning the main assumption

---

80. As one textbook puts it, "Measures of how tree-like the data are include the consistency index" (Susan P. Holmes, "Phylogenies: An Overview," in *Statistics in Genetics*, ed. M. Elizabeth Halloran and Seymour Geisser [New York: Springer, 1999], 104).

81. David A. Legg, Mark D. Sutton, Gregory D. Edgecombe, and Jean-Bernard Caron, "Cambrian Bivalved Arthropod Reveals Origin of Arthrodization," *Proceedings of the Royal Society B* 279 (2012): 4699–4704.

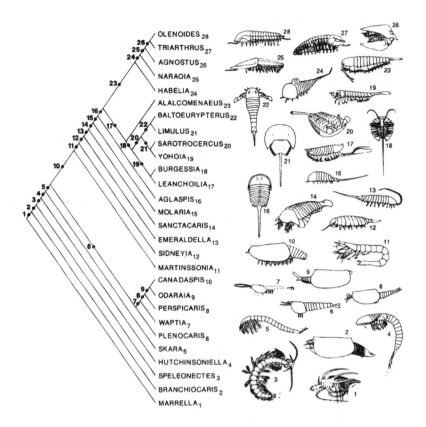

FIGURE 11.2. *Arthropod cladogram* cited by intelligent design critic Nicholas Matzke to purportedly demonstrate how common ancestry explains evolutionary relationships between various arthropods. In this cladogram, however, the main assumption of tree-building failed 61.6 percent of the time.

CREDIT: Derek Briggs and Richard Fortey, "The Early Radiation and Relationships of the Major Arthropod Groups," *Science* 246 (October 13, 1989): 241–243. Reprinted with permission from AAAS.

failed in 57 percent of cases.[82] Another *Nature* paper yielded a mammal tree with a CI of 0.34—a 66 percent failure rate.[83] A paper using DNA to study bird relationships produced a tree with a CI of 0.36, a 64 percent failure rate.[84] A 2007 paper in *Proceedings of the Royal*

82. Mark S. Springer, Gregory C. Cleven, Ole Madsen, et al., "Endemic African Mammals Shake the Phylogenetic Tree," *Nature* 388 (July 3, 1997): 61–64.

83. William J. Murphy, Eduardo Eizirik, Warren E. Johnson, et al., "Molecular Phylogenetics and the Origins of Placental Mammals," *Nature* 409 (February 1, 2001): 614–618.

84. F. Keith Barker, Alice Cibois, Peter Schikler, Julie Feinstein, and Joel Cracraft, "Phylogeny and Diversification of the Largest Avian Radiation," *Proceedings of the National Academy of Sciences USA* 101 (July 27, 2004): 11040–11045.

Society B produced a tree of early tertiary mammals with a CI of 0.35; the main assumption failed 65 percent of the time.[85] Likewise, consider the CI of the other cladogram Matzke posted (Fig. 11.2) which purports to show the relationships of various Cambrian arthropods. It has a CI of 0.384, which even the original authors admit was "rather low."[86] This means that in the cladogram Matzke referenced as a demonstration of common descent, the main assumption of tree-building failed 61.6 percent of the time. In such cases, *the main assumption failed more often than it held true.*

Perhaps the main assumption should be rewritten as: *biological similarities indicate inheritance from a common ancestor, except for when they don't.*

2. Is Common Descent Testable?

To be sure, plenty of trees enjoy much higher CIs. But even in those happy cases, how can we know whether the main assumption is valid, given how often it fails elsewhere? And if the main assumption hadn't held, would that have even mattered? Indeed, *why do evolutionary biologists tolerate the frequent failure of their field's core assumptions?*

They tolerate it because to do otherwise would be to abandon common ancestry. Thus, they build trees even when they aren't sure if the main assumption is true, or even worse, when they know the data doesn't fit very well into a tree-like pattern. The open secret of evolutionary phylogenetic reconstruction, therefore, is that, using the statistical methods of tree construction, you can force virtually any data set to fit a "tree," even if it strongly contradicts a tree-like pattern.

Sometimes, even data sets that *do* fit a tree and are well-supported by statistical analyses can sharply conflict. (As scientists commenting on a *Nature* paper stated, "trees produced by a number of well-supported studies have come to contradictory conclusions."[87]) Good

---

85. Rodolphe Tabuce, Laurent Marivaux, Mohammed Adaci, Mustapha Bensalah, Jean-Louis Hartenberger, et al., "Early Tertiary Mammals from North Africa Reinforce the Molecular Afrotheria Clade," *Proceedings of the Royal Society B* 274 (2007): 1159–1166.

86. Derek Briggs and Richard Fortey, "The Early Radiation and Relationships of the Major Arthropod Groups," *Science* 246 (October 13, 1989): 241–243.

87. "Untangling the Tree of Life," *ScienceDaily*, May 15, 2013, accessed June 13, 2016, http://www.sciencedaily.com/releases/2013/05/130515094809.htm. See also Leonidas Salichos and Antonis Rokas, "Inferring Ancient Divergences Requires Genes with Strong Phylogenetic Signals," *Nature* 497 (May 16, 2013): 327–331.

statistical support for a tree, apparently, doesn't always demonstrate common descent.

This demands the question: What possible pattern would refute common ancestry? Strongly supported tree-like patterns don't necessarily demonstrate common ancestry. And even when over half of the data is inconsistent with a tree, evolutionary biologists go ahead and impose a tree-like pattern. A 2010 paper reported trees with CIs under 0.1, meaning more than 90 percent of the data didn't fit a tree.[88] Predictably, the authors did not question common ancestry and had their own epicycles to try to explain the non–tree-like patterns. At what point can we falsify common descent? For evolutionary biologists, it seems we cannot, because common ancestry is not on the table for falsification.

Apparently no pattern is necessarily inconsistent with common ancestry because you can always invoke as much convergent evolution (or loss of traits) as needed to force the data into a tree. And when those explanations are unlikely, other epicycles—like horizontal gene transfer, incomplete lineage sorting or coalescence, and rapid evolution, to list a few—can be invoked to explain away data that doesn't fit a tree.

For example, one paper found that 23 percent of the human genome contradicts the standard human-ape tree, but unworriedly claimed the discrepancies simply result from incomplete lineage sorting.[89] Another paper found that 30 percent of the gorilla genome contradicts the conventional human-ape phylogeny, and explained away the data in the same manner.[90] Large percentages of whole genomes can contradict standard evolutionary trees, and that is never even seen as a possible challenge to common ancestry.

Indeed, modern genome sequencing has discovered thousands of "orphan genes"—unique genes that exhibit no homology (sequence similarity) to any other known gene.[91] These genes ought to refute com-

88. Shanan S. Tobe, Andrew C. Kitchener, Adrian M. T. Linacre, "Reconstructing Mammalian Phylogenies: A Detailed Comparison of the Cytochrome b and Cytochrome Oxidase Subunit I Mitochondrial Genes," *PLoS One* 5 (November 2010): e14156. This paper reported trees with the following CIs: 0.051612 and 0.065208.

89. Ingo Ebersberger, Petra Galgoczy, Stefan Taudien, et al., "Mapping Human Genetic Ancestry," *Molecular Biology and Evolution* 24 (2007): 2266–2276.

90. Aylwyn Scally et al., "Insights into Hominid Evolution from the Gorilla Genome Sequence," *Nature* 483 (March 8, 2012): 169–175.

91. Konstantin Khalturin, Georg Hemmrich, Sebastian Fraune, René Augustin, Thomas C. G. Bosch, "More than Just Orphans: Are Taxonomically Restricted Genes Important in Evolution?" *Trends in Genetics* 25 (2009): 404–413; Diethard Tautz and Tomislav Domazet-Lošo,

mon ancestry because they cannot be compared to genes from other species, and thus do not fit into any phylogenetic tree. The problem is usually ignored.[92]

Conversely, genome sequencing regularly uncovers genes that do bear homology to other known genes—but that homology should not be there because (according to common ancestry) the closest homologue is known only from very distantly related species. These cases, too, are not taken as evidence against common descent, but instead are said to indicate horizontal gene transfer (HGT, also called lateral gene transfer or LGT), where organisms obtain genes from neighboring organisms rather than from a parent.

Evolutionists sometimes reply that such phylogenetic oddities arise only when studying microorganisms like bacteria at the base of the tree of life—organisms that are known to readily swap genetic material through HGT. But this objection fails, since the tree of life faces incongruities among higher organisms where such gene-swapping is not prevalent. As Carl Woese, a pioneer of evolutionary molecular systematics, explains,

> Phylogenetic incongruities can be seen everywhere in the universal tree, from its root to the major branchings within and among the various taxa to the makeup of the primary groupings themselves.[93]

To explain away phylogenetic conflicts in higher branches, evolutionary biologists predictably argue that HGT must also be occurring in higher organisms, even if we don't directly observe it. One study found hundreds of genes in animals that were unexpected under common

---

"The Evolutionary Origin of Orphan Genes," *Nature Reviews Genetics* 12 (2011): 692–702; Robert G. Beiko, "Telling the Whole Story in a 10,000-Genome World," *Biology Direct* 6 (2011): 34.

92. A typical evolutionary response is that as more species' genomes are sequenced, homologues will eventually be uncovered and the number of orphan genes will drop. But biologists are finding the opposite: as more genomes are sequenced, the number of orphan genes is increasing. In some species, nearly half the genes appear to be orphan genes. See Garret Suen, Clotilde Teiling, Lewyn Li, Carson Holt, Ehab Abouheif, et al., "The Genome Sequence of the Leaf-Cutter Ant *Atta cephalotes* Reveals Insights into Its Obligate Symbiotic Lifestyle," *PLoS Genetics* 7 (2011): e1002007 ("We also found 9,361 proteins that are unique to *A. cephalotes*, representing over half of its predicted proteome."). See also Christopher D. Smith et al., "Draft Genome of the Globally Widespread and Invasive Argentine Ant (*Linepithema humile*)," *Proceedings of the National Academy of Sciences USA* 108 (2011): 5667–5672 ("A total of 7,184 genes [45%] were unique to *L. humile* relative to these three other species").

93. Carl Woese, "The Universal Ancestor," *Proceedings of the National Academy of Sciences USA* 95 (June 1998): 6854–6859.

ancestry, but simply explained them away by invoking HGT.[94] Another study found that the angiosperm *Amborella* is "rich" in "foreign" genes that don't fit the standard phylogeny; HGT came to the rescue and "explained" why they were there.[95] But HGT is not necessarily directly observed in these higher organisms—rather, it is inferred to occur based on the presence of so-called "foreign" genes.

Under this mind-set, genes that severely conflict with the standard phylogeny are not taken as evidence that the phylogeny might be wrong. Rather, they are taken as evidence *for* HGT. One paper admits this reasoning: "In the phylogenetic approach, each instance of topological discordance between a gene tree and a trusted reference tree is taken as a prima facie instance of LGT."[96]

When data that contradicts a paradigm *becomes evidence for* the epicycles rather than against the paradigm, it's clear that the paradigm is in crisis. This is exactly what we see taking place with regard to universal common ancestry.

D. Embryology

In a letter to the American botanist Asa Gray, Charles Darwin urged that embryology was "by far the strongest single class of facts in favor"[97] of his theory. Much has changed in the 150-plus years since Darwin penned those words, but embryology remains a favorite line of evidence cited by evolutionists to support common descent, particularly among the vertebrates.

Most modern biology textbooks will print some diagram depicting the early embryos of different vertebrate species as highly similar, then will claim that these similarities reflect common ancestry. *Life Science*, published by Holt, provides typical language: "Early in development, the human embryos and the embryos of all other vertebrates are simi-

---

94. Alastair Crisp, Chiara Boschetti, Malcolm Perry, Alan Tunnacliffe, and Gos Micklem, "Expression of Multiple Horizontally Acquired Genes Is a Hallmark of Both Vertebrate and Invertebrate Genomes," *Genome Biology*, 16, no. 1 (2015).

95. Danny W. Rice, Andrew J. Alverson, Aaron O. Richardson, Gregory J. Young, M. Virginia Sanchez-Puerta, et al., "Horizontal Transfer of Entire Genomes via Mitochondrial Fusion in the Angiosperm *Amborella*," *Science* 342 (December 20, 2013): 1468–1473.

96. Mark A. Ragan and Robert G. Beiko, "Lateral Genetic Transfer: Open Issues," *Philosophical Transactions of the Royal Society B* 364 (2009): 2241–2251 (internal citations omitted).

97. Charles Darwin, "To Asa Gray," *Darwin Correspondence Project*, September 10, 1860, accessed June 13, 2016, http://www.darwinproject.ac.uk/entry-2910.

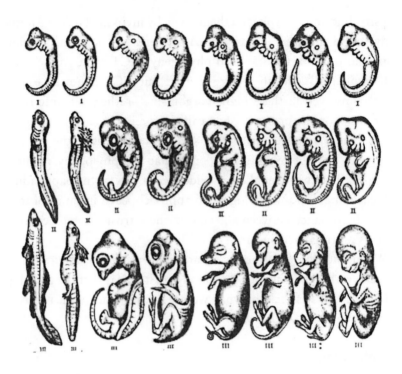

FIGURE 11.3. *Haeckel's embryo drawings* depicting (in this order): Fish, Salamander, Tortoise, Chicken, Hog, Calf, Rabbit, Human.

CREDIT: George Romane's 1892 book, *Darwinism Illustrated* (public domain), as used in figure 5-1, Jonathan Wells, *Icons of Evolution: Science or Myth?* (Washington, DC: Regnery, 2000).

lar. These early similarities are evidence that all vertebrates share a common ancestor."[98]

For decades, students were also taught that "ontogeny recapitulates phylogeny." Called recapitulation theory, this idea was promoted by the German biologist Ernst Haeckel, who believed that the development of an organism ("ontogeny") replays ("recapitulates") its evolutionary history ("phylogeny"). Since the standard evolutionary view holds that humans evolved from fish, recapitulation theory taught that at one point between conception and birth, we all went through a "fish stage."

98. Holt Science and Technology, *Life Science* (New York: Holt, Rinehart, & Winston, 2001), 183.

Biologists now know that vertebrate embryos do *not* replay their supposed earlier evolutionary stages, and firmly hold that recapitulation theory is false.[99] The concept has been removed from textbooks, but many textbooks still use inaccurate diagrams which overstate the degree of similarity between vertebrate embryos. Indeed, the journal *Science* observed that "[g]enerations of biology students may have been misled" by Haeckel's embryo drawings in textbooks.[100]

These drawings—commonly reprinted or adapted in textbooks[101]—overstate the degree of similarity between vertebrate embryos in their earliest stages. According to Stephen Jay Gould, Haeckel's methods "can only be called fraudulent" because he "simply copied the same figure over and over again"[102] when depicting the embryos of different species. This led embryologist Michael Richardson to call them "one of the most famous fakes in biology."[103]

In 2000, biologist Jonathan Wells published *Icons of Evolution*, which raised the public's consciousness about Haeckel's fraud, ultimately forcing many publishers to remove Haeckel's inaccurate drawings from most textbooks. Many textbooks, however, still claim that the early stages of vertebrate development are highly similar. But are those claims accurate?

No, they are not. Embryologists have found considerable differences among vertebrate embryos from their earliest stages onward, contradicting what we are told to expect from common ancestry.

Two of the earliest stages of vertebrate development are *cleavage* and *gastrulation*. During cleavage, a newly fertilized zygote undergoes rapid cell division until the embryo becomes a tiny ball of cells, laying out the basic axes that will define the body plan. Next, during gastrulation, the embryo increases in size while forming distinct germ layers which will later develop into individual

---

99. See "Early Evolution and Development: Ernst Haeckel," *Understanding Evolution*, accessed June 13, 2016, http://evolution.berkeley.edu/evolibrary/article/history_15.

100. Elizabeth Pennisi, "Haeckel's Embryos: Fraud Rediscovered," *Science* 277 (September 5, 1997): 1435.

101. See Casey Luskin, "Haeckel's Fraudulent Embryo Drawings Are Still Present in Biology Textbooks—Here's a List," *Evolution News and Views*, April 3, 2015, accessed June 13, 2016, http://www.evolutionnews.org/2015/04/haeckels_fraudu094971.html.

102. Stephen Jay Gould, "Abscheulich! (Atrocious!)," *Natural History* (March 2000): 42–49.

103. Quoted in Pennisi, "Haeckel's Embryos: Fraud Rediscovered."

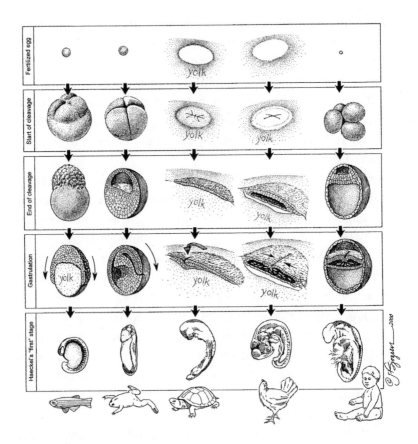

FIGURE 11.4. *Accurate drawings of the early stages of vertebrate embryo development.*

CREDIT: Copyright Jody F. Sjogren 2000, as used in figure 5-3, Jonathan Wells, *Icons of Evolution: Science or Myth?* (Washington, DC: Regnery, 2000). Used with permission.

organs. Yet a paper in *Systematic Biology* states, "such early stages as initial cleavages and gastrula[tion] can vary quite extensively across vertebrates."[104]

Likewise, a 2010 paper in *Nature* stated, "Counter to the expectations of early embryonic conservation [i.e., similarity], many studies have shown that there is often remarkable divergence between related

---

104. Andres Collazo, "Developmental Variation, Homology, and the Pharyngula Stage," *Systematic Biology* 49 (2000): 3–18.

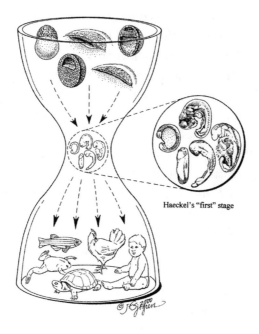

Haeckel's "first" stage

FIGURE 11.5. *The "hourglass" model of embryo development,* where vertebrate embryos start development differently, but are said to appear somewhat similar at a midpoint in development.

CREDIT: Copyright Jody F. Sjogren 2000, as used in figure 5-4, Jonathan Wells, *Icons of Evolution: Science or Myth?* (Washington, DC: Regnery, 2000). Used with permission.

species both early and late in development."[105] Or, as another article in *Trends in Ecology and Evolution* stated, "despite repeated assertions of the uniformity of early embryos within members of a phylum, development . . . [in those early stages] is very varied."[106]

Rather than looking highly similar in their early stages, vertebrate embryos look more like what we see in Figure 11.4.

To their credit, some evolutionary biologists acknowledge that vertebrate embryos begin development differently, but then they claim that embryos pass through a highly similar midpoint stage, called the "pharyngular" or "phylotypic" or "tailbud" stage. They propose an

105. Alex T. Kalinka, Karolina M. Varga, Dave T. Gerrard, Stephan Preibisch, David L. Corcoran, et al., "Gene Expression Divergence Recapitulates the Developmental Hourglass Model," *Nature* 468 (December 9, 2010): 811–816 (internal citations removed).

106. Brian Hall, "Phylotypic Stage or Phantom: Is There a Highly Conserved Embryonic Stage in Vertebrates?" *Trends in Ecology and Evolution* 12 (December 1997): 461–463.

"hourglass model," where this converging midpoint stage of development reveals common ancestry (Fig. 11.5).

Prominent atheist and developmental biologist P. Z. Myers named his popular blog "Pharyngula," where he has argued that "[v]ertebrate embryos at the phylotypic or pharyngula stage do show substantial similarities to one another that are evidence of common descent. That's simply a fact."[107] But does this pharyngula stage exist?

In a groundbreaking study published in *Anatomy and Embryology*, a team of embryologists investigated this question and noted, "It is almost as though the phylotypic stage is regarded as a biological concept for which no proof is needed."[108] After photographing vertebrate embryos during this purportedly similar stage, they found differences in major traits, including body size, body plan, growth patterns, and timing of development. They conclude the evidence is "[c]ontrary to the evolutionary hourglass model," because vertebrate embryos show "considerable variability" during "the purported phylotypic stage." In their view, this "wide variation in morphology among vertebrate embryos is difficult to reconcile with the idea of a phylogenetically-conserved tailbud stage."[109]

Likewise, a study in *Proceedings of the Royal Society of London B* found that embryological data is "counter to the predictions" of the phylotypic stage, since "phenotypic variation between species was highest in the middle of the developmental sequence." It noted that a "surprising degree of developmental character independence argues against the existence of a phylotypic stage in vertebrates."[110]

Even P. Z. Myers has conceded that early vertebrate embryos can "vary greatly"[111] and that "there is wide variation in the status of the embryo."[112] But, he tried to explain why these facts pose no challenge

107. P. Z. Myers, "Casey Luskin, Smirking Liar," *Pharyngula*, May 8, 2009, accessed June 13, 2016, http://scienceblogs.com/pharyngula/2009/05/08/casey-luskin-smirking-liar/.

108. Michael K. Richardson, James Hanken, Mayoni L. Gooneratne, et al., "There Is No Highly Conserved Embryonic Stage in the Vertebrates: Implications for Current Theories of Evolution and Development," *Anatomy and Embryology* 196 (1997): 91–106.

109. Ibid.

110. Olaf Bininda-Emonds, Jonathan Jeffery, and Michael Richardson, "Inverting the Hourglass: Quantitative Evidence against the Phylotypic Stage in Vertebrate Development," *Proceedings of the Royal Society of London, B* 270 (2003): 341–346.

111. P. Z. Myers, "Jonathan MacLatchie Collides with Reality Again," *Pharyngula*, June 17, 2011, accessed June 13, 2016, http://scienceblogs.com/pharyngula/2011/06/17/jonathan-maclatchie-collides-w/.

112. P. Z. Myers, "Jonathan MacLatchie Really Is Completely Ineducable," *Pharyngula*, June 25, 2011, accessed June 13, 2016, http://scienceblogs.com/pharyngula/2011/06/25/jonathan-maclatchie-really-is/.

to common ancestry: "I wish I could get that one thought into these guys' heads," he wrote. "[E]volutionary theory predicts differences as well as similarities."[113]

That's intriguing. Earlier, Myers cited the "substantial similarities" between vertebrate embryos as "evidence of common descent." But later, when forced to admit the "wide variation" among embryos, he argued that "evolutionary theory predicts differences" too. Perhaps so, but then how can he cite the "similarities" among embryos in the pharyngula stage as evidence for common ancestry?

In reality, Myers's comments reflect the fact that, in practice, evolutionary theory predicts whatever it finds. In other words, common ancestry predicts nothing. Myers's logic might help common descent avoid falsification, but it doesn't construct a robust model that makes testable predictions. It seems we're back to *common ancestry predicts similarities except for when it doesn't*. As the old adage says, "the theory which explains everything really explains nothing."

III. What's Left of the "Congruence" Argument for Universal Common Ancestry?

At the beginning of this chapter, we noted that the case for common descent is often said to be "cumulative," based on multiple lines of evidence including biogeography, fossils, DNA and anatomy, and embryology. How is the theory faring?

In biogeography, evolutionists resort to unlikely and speculative explanations where species must raft across vast oceans in order for common descent to account for their unexpected locations. Paleontology fails to reveal the continuous branching pattern predicted by common ancestry, and the fossil record is dominated by abrupt explosions of new life-forms.

Regarding molecular and morphology-based trees, conflicting phylogenies have left the "tree of life" in tatters. Phylogenetic methods are reduced to predicting that shared similarity indicates common inheritance, except for when it doesn't. Similar problems confound embryology, where evolutionary biologists predict similarities will exist

---

113. Myers, "Jonathan MacLatchie Collides with Reality Again."

between vertebrate embryos, except for when we find differences, and then it predicts those too.

Much data contradicts the sometimes-made predictions of common descent, but what, if anything, does evolutionary biology actually predict?

As P. Z. Myers has shown us, common descent seems to predict whatever is expedient. If there's any clear pattern here, it's this: the data often fails to fit the predictions of universal common descent, but when that happens, proponents of common descent simply change their predictions. This raises the question of the scientific status of common descent. At best, it's a scientific theory that is contradicted by much evidence. At worst, it's not even a scientific theory that makes concrete, testable predictions.

For these and many other reasons, even some mainstream evolutionary scientists are becoming increasingly skeptical of universal common ancestry and the "monophyly" of life.[114] A 2009 paper in *Trends in Genetics* noted that breakdowns in core neo-Darwinian tenets like the "traditional concept of the tree of life," or that "natural selection is the main driving force of evolution," indicate "the modern synthesis has crumbled, apparently, beyond repair."[115] A 2012 paper in *Annual Review of Genetics* explicitly doubted universal common ancestry, suggesting, "life might indeed have multiple origins."[116] Another paper in *Biology Direct* noted that the "sudden emergence" of new complex life forms contradicts a "tree pattern":

> Major transitions in biological evolution show the same pattern of sudden emergence of diverse forms at a new level of complexity.

---

114. See the discussion in Stephen C. Meyer, Paul A. Nelson, Jonathan Moneymaker, Ralph Seelke, and Scott Minnich, *Explore Evolution: The Arguments for and against Neo-Darwinism* (London: Hill House, 2007). See also Syvanen, "Evolutionary Implications of Horizontal Gene Transfer"; W. Ford Doolittle, "The Practice of Classification and the Theory of Evolution, and What the Demise of Charles Darwin's Tree of Life Hypothesis Means for Both of Them," *Philosophical Transactions of the Royal Society B* 364 (2009): 2221–2228; Malcolm S. Gordon, "The Concept of Monophyly: A Speculative Essay," *Biology and Philosophy* 14 (1999): 331–348; Eugene V. Koonin, "The Biological Big Bang Model for the Major Transitions in Evolution," *Biology Direct* 2 (2007): 21; Vicky Merhej and Didier Raoult, "Rhizome of Life, Catastrophes, Sequence Exchanges, Gene Creations, and Giant Viruses: How Microbial Genomics Challenges Darwin," *Frontiers in Cellular and Infection Microbiology* 2 (August 28, 2012): 113; Raoult, "The Post-Darwinist Rhizome of Life," *The Lancet* 375 (January 9, 2010): 104–105; Carl R. Woese, "On the Evolution of Cells," *Proceedings of the National Academy of Sciences USA* 99 (June 25, 2002): 8742–8747; Lawton, "Why Darwin Was Wrong about the Tree of Life."

115. Eugene V. Koonin, "The Origin at 150: Is a New Evolutionary Synthesis in Sight?" *Trends in Genetics* 25 (2009): 473–475.

116. Syvanen, "Evolutionary Implications of Horizontal Gene Transfer."

The relationships between major groups within an emergent new class of biological entities are hard to decipher and do not seem to fit the tree pattern that, following Darwin's original proposal, remains the dominant description of biological evolution.[117]

To be sure, these authors support some form of unguided materialistic evolution. But the precise reason that they are critiquing the classical evolutionary model is that much data contradicts universal common ancestry.

Twenty-first-century biology seems to be following the evidence beyond universal common ancestry and the neo-Darwinian "tree of life." Our friends in the theistic evolution community would be wise to follow suit—or at least to tone down their rhetoric against reasonable skeptics of universal common ancestry.

---

117. Eugene V. Koonin, "The Biological Big Bang Model for the Major Transitions in Evolution," *Biology Direct*, 2, no. 21 (August 20, 2007).

12

Five Questions Everyone Should Ask about Common Descent

PAUL A. NELSON

SUMMARY

According to the theory of universal common descent (UCD), all organisms on Earth have descended by modification from a common ancestor, dubbed the "last universal common ancestor" (LUCA). Within the past twenty years, however, a growing number of evolutionary biologists have expressed doubts that LUCA ever existed. Their skepticism of LUCA and hence of UCD rests on an important rule of biological inference known as the principle of continuity. The principle of continuity holds that every step in any evolutionary pathway must be biologically possible. This principle actually challenges UCD, or the tree of life, not only at its base but throughout its branches as well. Five key questions should be asked of any hypothesis of common descent, to make sure that the hypothesis answers the demands of the principle of continuity, and also to examine the larger context within which UCD lives as a biological and historical theory. UCD should not be maintained as an axiom, but should be vulnerable to evidential challenges, like any other scientific theory.

· · · · ·

Introduction: Is Common Descent Really a Theory That No Biologist Doubts?

Biology, a familiar aphorism tells us, is a science of exceptions. The protein hemoglobin binds oxygen molecules (O_2) with the iron atoms at its center, carrying O_2 in the bloodstream of animals—except when it doesn't. Hemocyanin carries O_2 in animals such as the octopus and horseshoe crab, binding the molecule with copper, not iron—making their blood appear blue, not red. Draw any generalization about life on Earth, and, from the back of the room, the exceptions will stand and take a bow.

A handful of biological propositions, however, seem truly exceptionless or universal in scope:

- All organisms are cells, or are made up of cells.
- All organisms have other organisms as parents.
- All organisms have descended with modification from a single common ancestor, itself an organism, designated the *last universal common ancestor* (abbreviated LUCA), at the root of the tree of life.

These propositions about life on Earth are seen by most biologists to hold so generally that each is thought to rise to the status of a theory, or even a law. Thus, we have, respectively,

- The Cell Theory
- The Law of Biogenesis
- The Theory of Common Descent

Here many biologists (including theistic evolutionists) would add, with some forcefulness, "And no well-respected biologist doubts any of these theories or laws."

Yet they do. Not the cell theory, or the law of biogenesis, however—today, it is the theory of common descent that is in trouble: possibly very serious trouble, from which it may never escape.

Thereupon hangs a tale, which I tell in this chapter. When the late National Academy of Sciences molecular evolutionist Carl Woese wrote, "The time has come for biology to go beyond the Doctrine of Common Descent," he was using "doctrine" to mean a scientific concept held dogmatically, standing in the way of biological under-standing.[1] Geneticist Craig Venter, whose company Celera Genomics independently sequenced the human genome in 2001, said that common descent was "counterintuitive" to him:

> I don't necessarily buy that there is a single ancestor. It's counter-intuitive to me. I think we may have thousands of recent common ancestors and they are not necessarily so common.[2]

Neither Woese nor Venter were motivated by creationism or intelligent design (ID), which they oppose, as do the growing number of evolution-ary biologists who openly express their doubts about common descent.

Rather, these biologists see the tree of life fracturing at its base, near where the thickest parts of the trunk—i.e., the major domains of Bac-teria, Archaea, and Eukarya—emerge from the prebiotic soil. LUCA, they contend, never existed as a discrete cell that was the unique an-cestor to these three domains: no single organism ever lived as the *ur*-parent to all life on this planet.

Nonetheless, while these biologists see common descent in this uni-versal sense as strictly false, they think that most groups of single-celled organisms, as well as fungi, plants, and animals, do share common ancestors higher up in the tree of life. Yet the same reasoning that leads skeptics of universal common descent to doubt the existence of LUCA can readily be extended to the supposed common ancestors of more recent branches in the tree of life.

Doubts about LUCA arise from its apparent biological impossi-bility, under an important rule of biological inference known as the *principle of continuity*.

As we shall see, the principle of continuity actually challenges the tree of life everywhere, not simply at its base. But common descent and continuity are themselves embedded in a wider scientific and philo-sophical context. How one evaluates the theory depends on the de-cisions one makes about that wider context—on questions such as the probability of the naturalistic origin of life (or abiogenesis), how

---

1. Carl Woese, "On the Evolution of Cells," *Proceedings of the National Academy of Sciences USA* 99 (2002): 8742–8747, at 8745.
2. J. Craig Venter, in *Life: What a Concept! An Edge Special Event*, ed. John Brockman (New York: Edge Foundation, 2008), 43.

many times abiogenesis occurred, and whether intelligent design is a live possibility. To paraphrase John Donne, no theory is an island, and common descent is no exception.

The relevance of common descent to the subject of this book hardly needs elaborating. BioLogos, the leading organization in the United States promoting theistic evolution, states that "evolution" means (among other things) that "all the life forms on earth share a common ancestor"[3]—i.e., common descent. To stress that no legitimate doubt exists about the theory, BioLogos adds,

> There is very little debate in the scientific community about this broad characterization of evolution (anyone who claims otherwise is either uninformed or deliberately trying to mislead). The observational evidence explained by common ancestry is overwhelming.[4]

But serious questions about common descent have existed since Darwin's time, and are even more significant today. Let's abbreviate common descent as "UCD" (i.e., "universal common descent"): this will stand for Darwin's idea that *all* organisms on Earth stemmed from a single common ancestor. We'll use CD for hypotheses about the shared ancestry of particular groups of organisms, where UCD may or may not be presupposed.

The scope of UCD includes all life on this planet, and even particular CD theories, such as the common ancestry of the animals, encompass enormous swaths of organismal diversity. Given this vast breadth, it is impossible in a single chapter, or even an entire book, to address every dimension of the problem (although, in chapter 11, Casey Luskin introduces some of the main controversies). Instead, this chapter analyzes how common descent hypotheses are constructed and how they are tested, setting these matters in the wider context of the origin of life and the possibility of intelligent design.

Five key questions capture the most important issues arising from UCD and CD. Think of these questions as a toolkit for evaluating any hypothesis of common ancestry.

---

3. "What Is Evolution?" *BioLogos*, accessed September 8, 2016, http://biologos.org/common
-questions/scientific-evidence/what-is-evolution.
    4. Ibid.

Before we consider the five questions, however, we should clear away some potential misunderstandings about the relationship between the concepts of "evolution," "common descent," "materialism" (or "naturalism"), and "intelligent design":

- **The terms "evolution" and "common descent" do not name the same idea.** When Darwin built his case for UCD in the *Origin of Species* (1859), "evolution"—meaning theories about the origin by natural processes of new groups of organisms—had already been in the air for many decades. Darwin's own grandfather Erasmus (1731–1802) speculated about the idea, and during the *Beagle* voyage (1831–1836), Darwin had absorbed Charles Lyell's critique of French zoologist Jean Baptiste de Lamarck's (1744–1829) theory of evolution. Thus, refuting UCD does not necessarily refute "evolution," because the latter idea allows for much more than common descent or shared ancestry.

- **The philosophies of materialism and naturalism do not entail UCD; for that reason, falsifying UCD would not necessarily threaten those worldviews.** Lamarck, for example, was a materialist with respect to biology, but he described evolution as occurring in multiple independent lineages, each spontaneously generated. Such a process yields separate trees of life, not a single tree (see Fig. 12.1).[5] The German materialist and embryologist Ernst Haeckel (1834–1919) also thought spontaneous generation occurred throughout the history of life. Hence, the single-celled organisms alive today did not descend from ancient cells, but originated recently, arising directly from nonliving materials.[6] Again, such an evolutionary scenario will generate multiple independent trees. Lastly, nearly all evolutionists who currently doubt UCD accept naturalism or materialism as their philosophy of science. Thus, falsifying UCD would not by itself threaten those philosophies.

- **Common descent may be false at one level of taxonomic inclusiveness, yet true at another level.** If that statement makes you

---

5. Peter Bowler, *Evolution: The History of an Idea*, 3rd ed. (Berkeley: University of California Press, 2003), 88–90.

6. Ernst Haeckel, *The History of Creation* (New York: D. Appleton, 1876), 348.

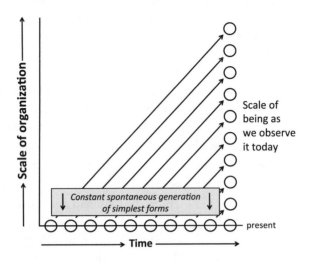

FIGURE 12.1. Following Peter Bowler (adapted by permission; see note 5), the figure shows one interpretation of the evolutionary ideas of Jean Baptiste de Lamarck. At the bottom, simple forms of life arise spontaneously as independent events, and then evolve into more complex forms along parallel lines of progressive change. Even though modification of species is continuous, all living things do not share a common ancestor.

scratch your head, look at Figures 12.2A and B. Notice that, in the hypothetical branching patterns of Figure 12.2A, the animals share common ancestry (CD), but UCD is false: multiple independent trees of life exist. In Figure 12.2B, by contrast, the animals don't share a common animal ancestor, but UCD is true: all organisms stem from LUCA. For this and other reasons, it is critical not to use the terms "common descent" or "common ancestry" without specifying which groups are included in the hypotheses of descent or ancestry. Every hypothesis of common descent needs to be weighed on its own merits, with respect to the evidence at hand.

- **Common descent and intelligent design are not mutually exclusive.** An ID colleague of mine, biochemist Michael Behe, argues vigorously for design while also accepting UCD. So did the Harvard botanist Asa Gray (1810–1887), a Christian who proposed God purposefully caused variations to occur,

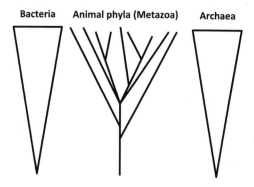

FIGURE 12.2A. In this hypothetical history of life, all *organisms* do not share a single common ancestor, but all *animals* are related by common descent.

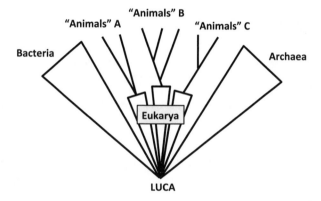

FIGURE 12.2B. In this contrasting history, LUCA existed, but the "animals" do not share a common ancestor (at the "animal" grade of organization).

a design hypothesis which Darwin rejected despite Gray's urging. Neither UCD nor CD restricts what one may infer about the causes of evolutionary change, meaning that, without additional philosophical assumptions, intelligent design remains a live possibility even if UCD or CD turned out to be the case.

Table 12.1 shows the historical diversity of opinion on UCD, in relation to intelligent design. Notice four positions are possible: every quadrant in the matrix is occupied by prominent biologists of the past or present.

	LUCA existed / Tree of Life	LUCA did not exist / no Tree of Life
No design	Charles Darwin (1809–1882) Ernst Mayr (1904–2005) Richard Lewontin (1929–) Richard Dawkins (1941–) Stephen Jay Gould (1942–2002) Jerry Coyne (1949–)	Jean Baptiste de Lamarck (1744–1829) Lev Berg (1876–1950) Gerald Kerkut (1927–2004) Carl Woese (1928–2012) W. Ford Doolittle (1941–) Didier Raoult (1952–)
Design	Asa Gray (1810–1887) Alfred Wallace (1823–1913) George Wright (1838–1921) Pierre Teilhard de Chardin (1881–1955) Michael Denton (1943–) Michael Behe (1952–)	Carl Linnaeus (1707–1778) Georges Cuvier (1769–1832) Louis Agassiz (1807–1873) Jonathan Wells (1942–) John Sanford (1950–) Günter Bechly (1963–)

TABLE 12.1. Matrix of opinion showing natural historians and biologists holding the four possible positions concerning universal common descent (UCD) and intelligent design. Left upper quadrant: the last universal common ancestor (LUCA) existed at the root of a single tree of life (TOL), and no intelligent design (ID) occurred. Right upper quadrant: LUCA did not exist, and no ID occurred. Left lower quadrant: LUCA and TOL existed and ID occurred. Right lower quadrant: LUCA and TOL did not exist and ID occurred.

Given these points, and the range of positions on offer, the reader may be wondering, "Well, if UCD is endorsed by some intelligent design theorists, and if UCD and materialism are independent of each other, why bother challenging UCD, or CD, at all? Wouldn't the wiser course be to withhold judgment about the theory, at least provisionally, since most biologists still accept UCD?"

Perhaps—but we think the wisest course is to pursue the truth. Here is the only question about UCD ultimately worth asking: *Is the theory true?* If UCD *is* true, then Christians—indeed, everyone—will have to make their peace with it. If UCD *isn't* true, however, then no one, Christians included, should hang on to the theory.

To begin, we should examine how evolutionary biologists normally infer that two or more species share a common ancestor. This will provide the terms and concepts we shall use throughout the remainder of the chapter.

The Anatomy of Inferences to Common Ancestry

Richard Dawkins says many things that are beautifully clear—wrong, maybe, but nonetheless clear and easy to follow. In *The Blind Watchmaker*, Dawkins explains why he thinks all organisms share a common ancestor:

> . . . it is a fact of great significance that every living thing, no matter how different from others in external appearance it may be, 'speaks' almost exactly the same language at the level of the genes. The genetic code is universal. I regard this as near-conclusive proof that all organisms are descended from a single common ancestor. The odds of the same dictionary of arbitrary 'meanings' arising twice are almost unimaginably small.[7]

We can use this excerpt from Dawkins as a model for showing how common descent hypotheses are constructed: every necessary element of any CD hypothesis is present and working within his argument. Dawkins is making a case for UCD; indeed, the "universal genetic code" argument for UCD is one of the most widespread in biology, occurring not only in popular books like *The Blind Watchmaker* but in textbooks and the technical literature as well. Chances are, you have seen this argument before. The terms highlighted with bold italics below will be the concepts we shall employ elsewhere.

Figure 12.3 depicts Dawkins's argument. Boxes P and Q could be any two species or *taxa* (singular *taxon*, meaning biological group): let's say taxon P is the domesticated dog (*Canis familiaris*) and taxon Q is portobello mushrooms (*Agaricus bisporus*). P and Q both exhibit *biological characters*—in this instance, the genetic code. (The genetic code comprises the 64-trinucleotide translation specifications by which information passes from nucleic acids, such as DNA and RNA, to amino acids, as proteins are assembled.) Biological characters include any observable features of organisms, ranging from their molecular details, such as the genetic code, up to complex behaviors, such as nest-building or speech. Dawkins asks us to decide which scenario is more likely: did the character "genetic code" arise *once*, in the unknown

---

7. Richard Dawkins, *The Blind Watchmaker: Why the Evidence of Evolution Reveals a Universe without Design* (New York: W. W. Norton, 1987), 270.

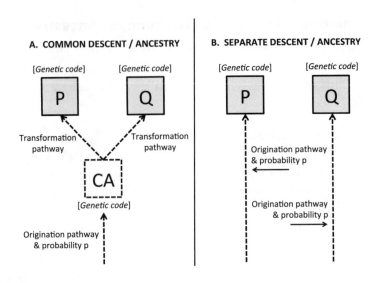

FIGURE 12.3. The argument for common descent based on the origin and evolution of the genetic code. Dotted lines indicate hypothetical (i.e., not directly observed) postulates and entities.

common ancestor for P and Q (Fig. 12.3A), or *twice independently*, as depicted in Figure 12.3B?

Now the single arrow in Figure 12.3A, leading to box CA (the unknown common ancestor where the code first appears), and the two separate arrows leading to P and Q in 12.3B, become important. In fact, these arrows, which we can call the *origination pathways and probabilities,* carry the weight of Dawkins's argument. Origination probabilities are estimated from the evolutionary processes and mechanisms that cause new biological characters to appear. "The odds of the same dictionary of arbitrary 'meanings' arising twice," argues Dawkins, "are almost unimaginably small."

Here is why. Let us suppose the origination probability for the first appearance of the genetic code occurring even once is far less than 1.0—and Dawkins estimates the probability, p, to be vanishingly small, much closer to 0.0 than to 1.0, because the code appears to him to be a chemically arbitrary "frozen accident." If so, then invoking *two* such frozen accidents, occurring independently of each other, as in 12.3B, the separate origins scenario, yet with those accidents somehow landing on the same apparently arbitrary molecular "meanings," will be the product, p^2, because the independent probabilities in 12.3B multiply by each other.

Originating the genetic code even once was hard enough. But twice? The *same* code? Thus, the separate origins scenario, 12.3B, will be much more improbable than the common descent scenario, 12.3A— that is, it will be exactly the square, p^2, of the origination probability, p, in 12.3A—if we consider only the character of the genetic code, and use Dawkins's assumption of a vanishingly small origination probability. Given the genetic code they share as an essential molecular character, therefore, dogs and portobello mushrooms *must* have stemmed from a common ancestor. (The mushrooms won't mind, but don't tell your dog.)

At this point, Dawkins's argument should make sense to the reader. We catch plagiarists by using the same probabilistic reasoning. If boxes P and Q in Figure 12.3B, for example, represented two texts supposedly written independently of each other, yet they contained whole paragraphs that were word-for-word identical, a scenario of "separate origins" would strike us as utterly unlikely.

Common Descent Is a Theory of Transformation, Not Similarity

Dawkins's argument for UCD may seem conclusive. But how could we test it? After all, UCD isn't supposed to be a deduction, or an axiom, but an empirical hypothesis, potentially vulnerable to contrary evidence.

The answer starts by thinking carefully about what any common descent hypothesis asserts, when compared to its logical opposite, separate origins. Notice the arrows leading from the common ancestor CA to taxa P and Q. These are the evolutionary *transformation pathways and probabilities*, and we need to know them, too, before we can decide if common descent or separate origins is more likely. We need to know these pathways and the underlying causal processes operating during the branching from CA, because if their associated probabilities turn out to be too small, or actually zero, common ancestry loses to separate origins.

And that is because common descent is *not* mainly a theory of *similarity*.[8] This is not the usual view, which takes the similarities that organisms exhibit to be both the principal evidence for UCD, and what the theory explains best. Notice, however, that similarity—i.e., pattern matching—exists in both the common descent and separate origins scenarios. (How we explain similarity under separate origins, we consider below.) Rather, common descent *is* mainly a theory of *transformation*.

The theory claims it is biologically possible to transform species, starting with a common ancestral form, and ending with very different descendant taxa. Taxa P and Q have different *names* because they exhibit different *characters*. If CD is true, those characters must arise as novel transformations on the branches from the common ancestor, CA. Common descent must explain the origin of *differences*—novel characters—and not simply similarities, along natural pathways or branching lineages starting with an ancestral form which did not possess those characters. (Logically, CA cannot exhibit the same characters that define its descendants, because if the same novel features distinguishing taxon P, for instance, also exist in CA, then the ancestral and descendant species would necessarily belong to the same taxon.)

This claim, namely, that species can be, and were, viably transformed over time *fundamentally distinguishes both UCD and CD from separate origins*. Similarity occurs in both scenarios. Transformation, however, does not. Therefore, finding and testing mechanisms and processes of species transformation represents the main explanatory challenge facing UCD and CD—as Darwin understood in 1859.

Darwin also understood that the challenge of explaining species transformations provided a way to test UCD and CD—which brings us to our first critical question:

---

8. One can see this with a simple thought experiment. Let us suppose that evolution as a process *maximizes similarities*. If so, then at the theoretical maximum, DNA sequences—in fact, every observable character—sampled from any two species should be identical (because identity = maximal similarity). If all the characters between any two species were identical, however, we would be able to distinguish or name only one taxon, and no "evolution," meaning the origin of novelty or differences, would have occurred. Thus, common descent must account for (i.e., explain) the origin of differences above all else. As similarity increases, differences must decrease, as a necessary or logical consequence, ultimately becoming identities—i.e., no observable change. Explaining the origin of *differences* is therefore the ontologically primary task for any theory of evolution.

Question 1: If species were not connected by common descent, how would we know it?

Many of the answers to this question in the biological literature may strike one as facetious. The author appears not to take the question seriously—after all, common descent is a fact, and who worries about testing facts?—and therefore offers what seems to be a flippant reply. Consider, for instance, evolutionary biologist John Maynard Smith's proposed test for neo-Darwinian evolution:

> [I]f someone discovers a deep-sea fish with varying numbers of luminous dots on its tail, the number at any one time having the property of . . . a prime number, I should regard this as rather strong evidence against neo-Darwinism. And if the dots took up in turn the exact configuration of the heavenly constellations, I should regard it as an adequate disproof.[9]

The apparent flippancy of this answer, however, conceals a deeper truth. If we ask *why* the hypothetical character of "constellations on deep-sea fish" would disprove common descent, we uncover a bona fide test first proposed by Darwin, and widely used by evolutionary biologists today.

UCD and CD claim species can be dramatically transformed over time, and, in the process, can give rise to the entirely novel characters which define new taxa. As Darwin himself realized, however, if those transformations cannot occur, UCD and CD "would absolutely break down":

> If it could be demonstrated that any complex organ existed, which could not possibly have been formed by numerous, successive, slight modifications, my theory would absolutely break down.[10]

This test, proposed by Darwin in the *Origin of Species*, has come to be known as the *principle of continuity*. The principle of continuity (hereafter, continuity) asserts that *every point in any hypothesized pathway of evolutionary transformation must be biologically possible.*

This may seem to be a truism. Since Darwin, however, continuity

---

9. John Maynard Smith, "The Status of Neo-Darwinism," in *Towards a Theoretical Biology*, ed. C. H. Waddington, vol. 2 (Edinburgh: Edinburgh University Press, 1969), 86.

10. Charles Darwin, *On the Origin of Species by Means of Natural Selection*, facsimile of the first ed. (London: John Murray, 1859; repr., Cambridge, MA: Harvard University Press, 1964), 189.

has been widely employed by biologists to test hypothesized evolutionary pathways. In 1968, for example, Francis Crick used continuity to rule out certain hypotheses about the evolution of the genetic code. Those hypotheses proposed that the size of codons (triplets of DNA nucleotides specifying amino acids in protein assembly) had changed from 1 to 2 to 3 nucleotides in length. "This seems highly unlikely," argued Crick, "since it violates the Principle of Continuity. A change in codon size necessarily makes nonsense of *all* previous messages and would almost certainly be lethal."[11]

Figure 12.4 illustrates Crick's argument. The hypothesized pathway from R, with one- or two-nucleotide-length codons, to S, with three-nucleotide codons, would necessarily pass through an inviable transitional phase, Crick argued, because the amino acid–specifying information carried by the shorter codons would be disrupted if their size increased— a state incompatible with protein assembly and hence cell function. Here is a natural language analogy: **herei san aturalla nguagean alogy.**

Continuity demands reproductive capability, because being able to reproduce is an absolutely necessary (i.e., essential) condition for the organisms in any evolutionary lineage. Just as "there is no crying in baseball," to quote Tom Hanks's character, manager Jimmy Duggan, from the movie *A League of Their Own*, there is—quite literally—no failing to leave offspring in common descent. If a hypothesized transformation pathway is biologically impossible—whether because of the lethality it would entail, or because of any lesser functional obstacle preventing reproduction—it could not and therefore did not happen.

Moreover, continuity also demands "no jumps" and "no foresight." In addition to no crying in baseball, there is also no hitting the ball and running straight to third base. A living system cannot leap to a distant novel functional or structural state in a single try, or in any series of increments larger than what undirected evolutionary processes will allow. Evolutionary processes cannot jump to distant destinations— i.e., to novel complex characters—because undirected processes, by definition, do not know where they are going. Moreover, the multiple coordinated changes required to specify novel functional characters

---

11. Francis Crick, "The Origin of the Genetic Code," *Journal of Molecular Biology* 38 (1968): 367–379, at 372.

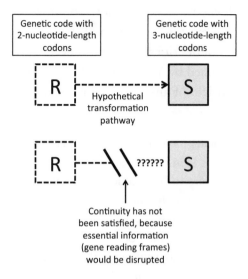

FIGURE 12.4. Francis Crick's argument, based on the requirements of the principle of continuity, against hypotheses that earlier forms of the genetic code used codons with a length of two nucleotides. Dotted lines indicate hypothetical postulates and entities.

map to very small probabilistic targets, lying within vastly larger *nonfunctional* spaces, where undirected processes are far likelier to land and wander irreversibly. For any long journey from A to B to C (and so on), it helps to know where you are supposed to be going.

Darwin understood the "no jumps" demand of continuity, because he put it front and center in the opening of the *Origin*. Someone might say, he noted, that

> after a certain unknown number of generations, some bird had given birth to a woodpecker . . . but this assumption seems to me to be no explanation, for it leaves the case of the coadaptations of organic beings to each other and to their physical conditions of life, untouched, and unexplained. It is, therefore, of the highest importance to gain a clear insight into the means of modification and coadaptation.[12]

We need to know the details of the pathways of transformation, or what Darwin calls "the means of modification," in order to decide if an

---

12. Darwin, *On the Origin of Species*, 3–4.

evolutionary pathway is possible or not. Continuity therefore obtains wherever organisms exist in lineages, and, accordingly, is deployed as an indispensable tool of critical analysis in every corner of evolutionary theory. As explained by Yuri Wolf and Eugene Koonin, continuity applies when the origin of any novel complex system is hypothesized to have occurred:

> When an evolutionary biologist strives to explain the origin of a truly novel system that is seen only in its elaborately complex state and, at face value, appears to be irreducibly complex, the task is much harder. Because evolution has no foresight, no system can evolve in anticipation of becoming useful once the requisite level of complexity is attained. . . . Darwin did not use a specific term for this crucial tenet of evolutionary biology; we will call it the ***Continuity Principle*** . . . evolution of complex systems still needs to be deconstructed into successive steps and explained in a Darwinian way.[13]

Anyone who studies evolutionary theory closely will see the sharp blade of continuity, whether explicitly by name, or implicitly, slicing through origination and transformation hypotheses everywhere. Evolutionary biologist David Penny, for instance, uses continuity to dismiss origination hypotheses for the ribosome invoking its current function, because those hypotheses violate continuity's "no foresight" rule:

> The ribosome is a huge macromolecular complex and there are many steps leading up to the synthesis of the peptide bond that joins amino acids. There is no way that a ribosome could have evolved *de novo* in a single step *and meet our **guidelines of continuity**. . . .* It is *impossible on an incremental model* that a very complex structure could evolve 'for' something that does not yet exist.[14]

Here is an easy way to remember the significance of continuity for testing UCD and CD: ***Continuity and common descent always travel together, everywhere.*** If a transformation hypothesis holds that taxa P

---

13. Yuri I. Wolf and Eugene V. Koonin, "On the Origin of the Translation System and the Genetic Code in the RNA World by Means of Natural Selection, Exaptation, and Subfunctionalization," *Biology Direct* 2 (2007): 14, emphasis added.

14. David Penny, "An Interpretive Review of the Origin of Life Research," *Biology and Philosophy* 20 (2005): 633–671, at 650, emphasis added.

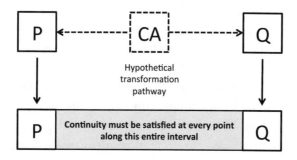

FIGURE 12.5. The entailment relationship between any hypothesis of common descent (ancestry) and the principle of continuity.

and Q stemmed from a common ancestor by an evolutionary pathway (see Fig. 12.5), then—because continuity is logically entailed whenever any such pathway is proposed—*the rule must be satisfied over the whole length of that pathway.*[15]

That brings us to the second key question:

Question 2: What were the actual transformation pathways, satisfying the continuity rule, which connect all organisms to LUCA?

For many leading evolutionary biologists, answering this question leads to a negative outcome for UCD. For them, continuity renders LUCA itself impossible, and thus, the associated transformation pathways to the three major domains were never traversed by species. In other words, UCD is false.

In 2002, in an article titled "On the Evolution of Cells," Carl Woese explained why he rejected the historical existence of LUCA—the last

---

15. A defender of common descent might object that refuting any *particular* transformation hypothesis for taxa P and Q does not refute *other possible* hypotheses—and therefore we would still be justified in holding that P and Q are related by descent from a common ancestor, even if we do not know exactly how the transformation occurred and how the continuity principle was satisfied. Indeed: refuting transformation hypothesis X (let's say) for P and Q says nothing about the merits of possible transformation hypotheses Y or Z. But then, of course, we need to *see and test* hypotheses Y and Z. If they stay in the shadows, unknown and unarticulated, they tell us nothing, and cannot satisfy the requirements of the continuity principle. Thus, we would *not* be justified in asserting that P and Q share a common ancestor, never mind the details of the transformation pathway, simply on the grounds that some other hypothesis might be constructed in the future. A possible but as-yet-unformulated and untested transformation hypothesis in evolutionary theory has the same standing as a possible, but yet-to-be-built bridge (for transporting vehicles over a river), or a possible, but still undiscovered, medicine (for curing a disease).

universal common ancestor—as an actual, identifiably unique cell, the progenitor of all organisms alive today. Woese argued that the characters making up the cellular architectures found in the three major domains of life, the Bacteria, Archaea, and Eukarya (architectures which Woese himself did much to discover), are too different to have evolved by descent from a single common ancestor. The transformation pathways from LUCA are therefore too improbable or—to put the same point another way—the dramatic transformations required make LUCA biologically impossible.

Take the essential processes of DNA replication, for instance—characters so basic they belong to the core set of vital functions within any cell. "Virtually no homology [similarity due to material descent]," Woese wrote, "exists between the bacterial genome replication mechanism and that basically common to the archaea and the eukaryotes. . . . Modern genome replication mechanisms seem to have evolved twice."[16] In other words, if LUCA existed, the similarity in these essential cellular characters which one would have expected to see, given the inescapable reproductive requirements of continuity, is not observed.

The same absence of fundamental similarity, Woese observes, exists in other basic cellular characters, to such a degree that

> what needs explaining is not why the major cell designs are so similar, but why they are so different. This apparent contradiction can be resolved by assuming that the highly diverse cell designs that exist today are the result of a common evolution in which each of them began under (significantly) different starting conditions.[17]

Continuity breaks apart the primary evolutionary lineages putatively stemming from LUCA, which, as a logical consequence, must itself vanish as a real organism. Because LUCA necessarily "associates physiologies that have not been observed together in any modern lineage and asks that all of this come about through vertical inheritance," Woese contends, "we are left with no consistent and satisfactory picture of the universal ancestor. It is time to question underlying assumptions."[18]

---

16. Woese, "On the Evolution of Cells," 8743.
17. Ibid., 8745.
18. Carl Woese, "The Universal Ancestor," *Proceedings of the National Academy of Sciences USA* 95 (1998): 6854–6859, at 6855.

And what is the result of that questioning? "The universal ancestor," says Woese, "is not an entity, not a thing."[19] When LUCA disappears as a real cell, therefore, we no longer expect to find a single tree of life, but a forest or a network, containing at least three separate (i.e., independent) cellular starting points: "Extant life on Earth," Woese concludes, "is descended not from one, but from three distinctly different cell types."[20]

Molecular evolutionist W. Ford Doolittle of Dalhousie University rejects LUCA on logically identical grounds: continuity cannot be satisfied. As in Woese's case, he focuses on the biological impossibilities raised by the transformation pathways needed to derive the enormous genetic diversity of life from a single ancestral cell. Calling LUCA "a profoundly problematic entity," Doolittle argues there could have been "no single common ancestral cell whose genome harboured a direct ancestor (either the last common ancestor or their lineal predecessors) of all the genes present in all genomes today."[21] As he explains, the rapidly increasing number of different genes and proteins (i.e., characters) that—if LUCA existed—must trace their ancestry via transformation pathways from that single organism, entail that LUCA instantly becomes a biologically unrealistic super-cell:

> In the end, [UCD] requires a last universal common ancestor with an enormous range of metabolic capabilities—essentially any gene that is now seen in at least one contemporary archaean, and one contemporary bacterium must find a home in that ancient cell. Such a 'genome of Eden' hypothesis seems, to us, unappealing.[22]

If LUCA did not exist, concludes Doolittle, then "Darwin arguably *was* wrong. For most of Life and most of its history, descent with modification is not the simple branching process he envisioned."[23]

---

19. Ibid., 6858.
20. Woese, "On the Evolution of Cells," 8746.
21. W. Ford Doolittle, "The Practice of Classification and the Theory of Evolution, and What the Demise of Charles Darwin's Tree of Life Hypothesis Means for Both of Them," *Philosophical Transactions of the Royal Society B* 364 (2009): 2221–2228, at 2224.
22. W. F. Doolittle, Y. Boucher, C. L. Nesbø, et al., "How Big Is the Iceberg of Which Organellar Genes in Nuclear Genomes Are But the Tip?" *Philosophical Transactions of the Royal Society B* 358 (2003): 39–58, at 46.
23. W. Ford Doolittle, "The Attempt on the Life of the Tree of Life: Science, Philosophy and Politics," *Biology and Philosophy* 25 (2010): 455–473, at 469.

Woese and Doolittle are not alone in rejecting the existence of LUCA and finding UCD false. University of California geneticist Michael Syvanen argues that "there is no reason to even postulate that a LUCA ever existed," because "the modern cell could have evolved in multiple parallel lineages. Earliest life could have been truly polyphyletic" [i.e., arising in several independent lineages].[24] French microbiologist Didier Raoult states flatly that "there is no such thing as a tree of life. The idea of a tree of life, which stringently follows Darwin['s] theory, is not pertinent in the genomic age."[25] National Center for Biotechnology Information lab director Eugene Koonin likewise waves LUCA and the tree of life aside: "a single, uninterrupted TOL *does not exist*," he contends.[26] For this growing cadre of evolutionary biologists, LUCA has disappeared under the scrutiny of continuity, and the base of the tree of life has splintered into pieces.

Continuity applies as a rule, of course, not just at the base of the tree of life, but upwards into its branches, such as at the origin of the animals. Evolutionary biologist and embryologist T. J. Horder explains how continuity applies to animal evolution, where the transformations in question necessitate the modification of developmental sequences. When considering such pathways, he writes, there exists

> an essential requirement which should be met by any hypothetical evolutionary sequence; a continuous sequence of morphogenetic events in an embryo is a repetition of a continuous sequence of morphological steps built up through the preceding evolving series of embryos, each stage of which must have been functionally advantageous in the transitional organism. *This will be referred to as the continuity principle.*[27]

Now, however, we run into a major complication—and the inescapable larger context mentioned in my "Introduction" to this chapter.

24. Michael Syvanen, "On the Occurrence of Horizontal Gene Transfer among an Arbitrarily Chosen Group of 26 Genes," *Journal of Molecular Evolution* 54 (2002): 258–266, at 265.

25. Didier Raoult, "There Is No Such Thing as a Tree of Life (And of Course Viruses Are Out!)" *Nature Reviews Microbiology* 7 (2009): 615, note numbers omitted.

26. Eugene V. Koonin, "The Biological Big Bang Model for the Major Transitions in Evolution," *Biology Direct* 2 (2007): 21.

27. T. J. Horder, "Embryological Bases of Evolution," in *Development and Evolution*, ed. B. C. Goodwin, N. Holder, and C. C. Wylie (Cambridge: Cambridge University Press, 1983), 315–352, at 339, emphasis added.

The Law of Biogenesis, the Origin
of Life, and UCD as Axiom

Thus far, we have been arguing that UCD and CD are tested by continuity, using *modus tollens*: *If* common descent is proposed for some taxa, via a transformation pathway, *then* continuity must be satisfied along the entire length of that pathway; *but* continuity has not been satisfied; *therefore*, that pathway did not occur, and common descent, in this instance at least, is false.

But common descent and continuity are not the only relevant considerations before us. As soon as we climb up into the tree of life, away from its earliest, simplest beginnings in a prebiotic milieu, we immediately collide with another of the genuinely universal propositions in biology, namely, the law of biogenesis: *all life comes from life.*

P. B. Medawar and J. S. Medawar call this proposition "arguably the most fundamental in biology":

> In its affirmative form, the Law of Biogenesis states that all living organisms are the progeny of living organisms that went before them. The familiar Latin tag is *Omne vivum ex vivo*—All that is alive came from something living; in other words, every organism has an unbroken genealogical pedigree extending back to the first living things. In its negative form, the law can be taken to deny the occurrence (or even the possibility) of spontaneous generation.[28]

The odd thing about the law of biogenesis is that no evolutionary biologist knows exactly when during Earth's history the law began to hold universally, as it surely does today, but *before which the law could not have been the case.* Under any naturalistic hypothesis for the origin of life, the law of biogenesis *must* be violated—spectacularly so, in fact—to get single-celled organisms up and running from nonliving starting materials. Once upon a time, there was no life on this planet; today there is. At some point in the past, therefore, the law of biogenesis could not have been true.

Nonetheless, evolutionary biologists today (unlike their nineteenth-century predecessors such as Lamarck and Haeckel) would say that

---

28. P. B. Medawar and J. S. Medawar, *Aristotle to Zoos: A Biological Dictionary* (Cambridge, MA: Harvard University Press, 1983), 39.

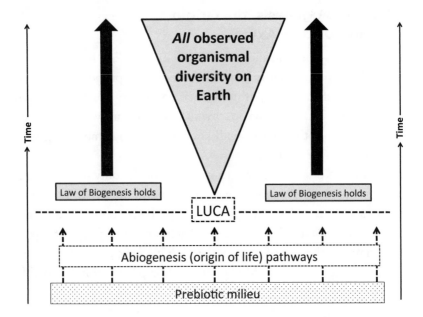

FIGURE 12.6. The law of biogenesis (all life comes from life) holds throughout Earth history, but under naturalistic theories of evolution it must be suspended during an indefinite period prior to the origin of life. If the law of biogenesis is in effect, however, and LUCA existed, universal common descent follows deductively. Dotted lines indicate hypothetical entities.

after life began in its simplest possible form, the possibility of abiogenesis ceased, irreversibly—and from that ill-defined interval to the present, any organism we observe must have descended from at least one parent that was itself an organism (see Fig. 12.6).

It requires little imagination to see how the law of biogenesis, when coupled with assumptions about the uniqueness of the origin of life on Earth, could yield UCD *as a deduction*—a deduction, moreover, that renders continuity powerless to test the theory. It simply wouldn't matter if we knew the transformation pathways from LUCA or not: UCD must be true. This explains, incidentally, why pervasive ignorance about the transformation pathways throughout the tree of life rarely counts against UCD: with a single occurrence of abiogenesis, there is literally nowhere else for organismal lineages to go, except back to LUCA. (This may also explain why—paradoxically, given their philosophical materialism—so many neo-Darwinian theorists are eager to assign a vanishingly small probability to the origin of life on Earth, so small in fact that the event could have occurred only once within the lifetime of the Solar System.) Indeed, if we buy the premise of a single origin of life, UCD achieves the status of a historical fact. As evolutionary biologist Keith Thomson explains,

> [UCD] can be derived from the twin premises that life arose only once on earth and that all life proceeds from existing life. Given these premises, and if the pattern of diversity among organisms has changed over time, then it must follow that any new forms have appeared as the result of a process of descent from preexisting forms. . . . descent from common ancestors is based upon such unassailable logic that we act as though it is a fact.[29]

Deductive or axiomatic formulations of UCD are surprisingly widespread in the biological literature.[30] Evolutionary biologist Kenneth Weiss, for instance, notes that "the assumption of a point source"— that is, an abiogenesis singularity, from which all life derives—"is important to the entire theory [i.e., UCD], so we insist upon spontaneous generation in the beginning, but must forbid it at any other time."[31] Postulate what one needs—namely, a first cell—climb up from the prebiotic milieu to that cell, once, and only once, and then kick away the ladder.[32]

Which brings us to our third key question:

Question 3: Have we genuinely tested UCD, or merely assumed its truth?

For evolutionary biologists, assuming a single origin of life is a classic good-news-bad-news move. The good news is that UCD follows as a

---

29. Keith Stewart Thomson, "The Meanings of Evolution," *American Scientist* 70 (1982): 529–531.

30. See, for instance, Otto Schindewolf, *Basic Questions in Paleontology* (Chicago: University of Chicago Press, 1993), 175–176; and Antoni Hoffman, *Arguments on Evolution* (Oxford: Oxford University Press, 1989), 8–9.

31. Kenneth Weiss, "We Hold These Truths to Be Self-Evident," *Evolutionary Anthropology* 10 (2001): 199–203, at 200.

32. Strictly speaking, UCD does not *require* a single origin of life. As many authors have pointed out, life could have begun many times—but, if UCD is to be maintained, only one of those abiogenesis events (logically) could have left any extant descendants, via the singularity of LUCA.

deductive consequence: all organisms *must* be related in one great tree of life. The status of UCD as historical fact is assured.

The bad news turns out to be exactly the same. By postulating the singularity of a unique (one-off) event of abiogenesis in Earth history, UCD follows as a deductive consequence—*but now UCD becomes untestable.* No biological evidence, no matter how compelling, could possibly challenge the theory. Assume a single origin-of-life event, and because of the law of biogenesis, LUCA must have existed, with countless pathways of transformation connecting that primordial cell to all other life—whatever we actually observe. Every organism, every species on this planet will necessarily lie within what might be called the "LUCA horizon."

Axiomatic formulations of UCD deductively channel all evolutionary inferences into a theoretical funnel running back to LUCA, outside of which no organism ever existed. Suppose one thinks, for example, that evidence indicates some animal group—say, the arthropods—did not share a common ancestor. Evolutionary biologist Geoffrey Fryer cites continuity as his reason for doubting the common ancestry of that group: "Those interested in tracing the course of evolution," he writes, "are concerned with mechanisms and how one mechanism or complex organism *might have been transformed* into another, *maintaining functional continuity throughout the transformation.*"[33] Under the scrutiny of continuity, he argues, "it is difficult to envisage a common ancestor even of crustaceans and tracheates."[34]

No worries—these lineages will still find their branching points and common ancestors *somewhere* within the tree of life. Under axiomatic UCD, all discontinuities or disparities in form and function among species can only be apparent, not true or aboriginal differences. The late Harvard paleontologist Stephen Jay Gould, who contended vigorously for the sudden origin of the remarkable disparities of animal form in events such as the Cambrian explosion, allayed the anxieties of his evolutionary critics by affirming the all-enveloping embrace of axiomatic UCD:

33. Geoffrey Fryer, "A Defense of Arthropod Polyphyly," in *Arthropod Relationships*, ed. R. A. Fortey and R. H. Thomas (London: Chapman & Hall, 1997), 22–33, at 22.
34. Ibid.

> Did any proponent of increased disparity ever doubt that a clado-
> gram [branching diagram of common descent] would root, if not in
> the Arthropoda at least at a more inclusive level? We are not, after
> all, creationists, and we do accept a monophyletic origin for life![35]

Axiomatic UCD robs biological evidence of its power to *test* the theory.
Now, if one wants UCD to be the case, come what may, testing against
evidence will only be a nuisance, but few biologists in my experience
are willing consciously to go there. They know that, throughout the
history of science, a widely accepted but erroneous theory may become
so deeply embedded within a community of thought that its influence
on scientific perception becomes all but invisible. When that occurs,
writes philosopher of biology Elliott Sober, the theory "guides scientific
inquiry without being vulnerable to the testimony of nature."[36]

So, should UCD be held axiomatically? The reader can see for herself how that happens—and can decide if she wants to place UCD
beyond ordinary testing, *or* to keep the theory "vulnerable to the testimony of nature."

Gould touched on another aspect of the larger context surrounding
UCD: "We are not, after all, creationists," he wrote. But why should
the issue of creationism have arisen in a technical discussion of arthropod evolution? Time to turn to our fourth key question:

Question 4: When explaining the history of life, have we assumed methodological naturalism only, or have we allowed for the possibility of intelligent design?

Gould brought up creationism because, in addition to his paleontological and evolutionary theory labors, he worked as a historian of
biology. Gould knew well the reasoning of the biologists and natural
historians in the yes-to-design and no-to-UCD quadrant, which occupies the lower right corner of Table 12.1 (above). Louis Agassiz,
for instance, whose name graces Harvard's Agassiz Museum of Comparative Zoology, where Gould kept his own office, resisted UCD for

---

35. Stephen Jay Gould, "The Disparity of the Burgess Shale Arthropod Fauna and the Limits of Cladistic Analysis: Why We Must Strive to Quantify Morphospace," *Paleobiology* 17 (1991): 411–432, at 415.

36. Elliott Sober, *Reconstructing the Past* (Cambridge, MA: MIT Press, 1988), 85.

evidential reasons, but also because Agassiz's scientific worldview included the possibility of intelligent design.[37] Gould understood from his study of Agassiz's work, not to mention the writings of other leading pre-Darwinian biologists, that for them, aboriginal or primary discontinuity (i.e., separate origins)—not UCD—was the main signal emerging from the fossil record, from comparative anatomy, and from the functional complexities of organisms. Once the possibility of intelligent design has entered the causal mix, of course, the range of explanations possible for any phenomenon grows accordingly.

Nowhere is this illustrated more vividly than when we consider the cause of similarities, overwhelmingly the principal line of evidence for UCD. "All living things have much in common," wrote Darwin in the summation of the *Origin*. "Therefore I should infer from analogy that probably all the organic beings which have ever lived on this earth have descended from some one primordial form"[38]—i.e., LUCA, the root of UCD. When living things are similar, they must be related by common descent, right? "Propinquity of descent," argued Darwin elsewhere in the *Origin*, is "the only known cause of the similarity of organic beings."[39]

Now, not only is this claim false—indeed, Darwin himself knew it was false[40]—but the whole record of comparative and historical biology since 1859 testifies to the incompetence of similarities to sort misleading resemblances from genuine family relationships.[41] Similarity does not entail common descent, which is only one of its many possible causes. Parentage, or begetting—i.e., genuine descent—is not a similarity relation.

The reader does not need to know the history of evolutionary the-

---

37. Louis Agassiz, *Essay on Classification*, ed. Edward Lurie (Mineola, NY: Dover, 2004).

38. Darwin, *On the Origin of Species*, 484.

39. Ibid., 413.

40. In the first edition of the *Origin*, only fourteen pages after this claim, Darwin writes that "animals, belonging to two most distinct lines of descent, may readily become adapted to similar conditions, and thus assume a close external resemblance; but such resemblance will not reveal—will rather tend to conceal their blood relationships to their proper lines of descent" (Darwin, *On the Origin of Species*, 427).

41. As Olivier Rieppel notes, "it is not genealogy [i.e., observed descent] but characters that give classification—and these characters may be equivocal or downright misleading. This only shows that there remains a gap to be bridged between the logical relation of homology (similarity) and the historically contingent process of phylogeny [evolutionary descent]" (Rieppel, "Things, Taxa, and Relationships," *Cladistics* 7 [1991]: 93–100, at 97).

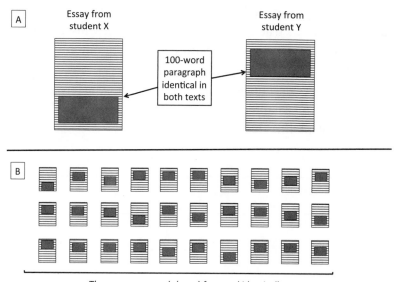

FIGURE 12.7. *Two essays, supposedly written independently of each other.*

ory, or comparative biology, or to be a biologist, to see that similarity may have multiple causes other than material descent. Consider a suggestive thought experiment. Let's go back to the plagiarism example, sketched above. Figure 12.7A shows two texts, written separately by two college students enrolled in a philosophy course, but each containing an entire paragraph (say, of 100 words length) word-for-word identical when compared across the two documents.

Plagiarism? Maybe.

But suppose we have *thirty such texts*, written by thirty different students—and each contains the same 100-word paragraph in question (see Fig. 12.7B). In fact, the philosophy class has thirty students enrolled, and they all submitted their essays on the same day.

Interestingly, the likelihood of plagiarism goes *down*, dramatically, as the number of texts including the same paragraph *goes up*, because as our sample grows, and we learn more, the probability increases that the cause of the paragraph matching was the professor's essay assignment: "Cite this paragraph from Descartes's *Discourse on Method* in your paper and analyze its argument." Raw similarity, in other words, underdetermines its true cause. To identify the true cause, we need to know the *full range* of possible causes, and ruling out any of them a priori can only hinder our search.

Consider an even simpler thought experiment, which requires your participation. This chapter was formatted to leave some white space, and the five blank lines below:

1. _____

2. _____

3. _____

4. _____

5. _____

Sign your name as you normally would on a legal form or bank check, five times. (If you experience moral qualms about writing in books, as I do, use a pencil so you can erase it later, or use a separate sheet of paper.) Do you observe any similarity in the five signatures? These patterns share no material descent. What they *do* share is *you*, a unique intelligent agent, as their true cause.

If we approach the phenomena of similarity in biology with the possibility of intelligent design in our explanatory toolkit, the gravitational pull of common descent as the only reasonable explanation is greatly weakened—as it should be.

Hence, our final key question:

Question 5. In the light of intelligent design as a causal possibility, what histories for life on Earth might be the case?

Answering *that* question opens before us a beautiful vista of fascinating research possibilities. The next step requires you, and your intellectual freedom. Get started.

13

The Battle over Human Origins (Introduction to Chapters 14–16)

ANN K. GAUGER

SUMMARY

The origin of humanity—where we came from—is an issue with many ramifications. It impacts our self-understanding in multiple ways. Did we evolve from a common ancestor shared with chimps, or might we have a unique origin? Mainstream science says that it is incontrovertible that we are the product of evolution. Is it therefore necessary to adapt our understanding of Scripture, or might the science be overstated? This short chapter, along with chapters 14–16, will argue that the question of our origin is far from settled, and that there are scientific arguments to be made in favor of a unique origin for humanity. There is no need to change traditional scriptural interpretations based on inconclusive science.

. . . . .

The intersection of evolutionary theory with Christian faith, in particular on the topic of human origins, leads immediately to one question: Are we descended from two first parents or not? This question raises a multitude of difficulties, both theologically and scientifically. Not surprisingly, the Christian church is divided on this issue, with some emphasizing the scientific arguments and some the biblical.

The standard scientific worldview accepts neo-Darwinism as the explanation for our origin. More specifically concerning human origins, the neo-Darwinian view is that we have a purely natural origin, fully explicable by unguided natural selection acting on random variation. According to this view, the fossil record shows that we evolved from an ape-like ancestor, we share common ancestry with chimps, and we evolved from a population of several thousand (at a minimum).

Theistic evolutionists operate from the perspective that this received view is accurate and trustworthy—in fact, more likely to be understood correctly than thousands of years of theological tradition. In their view, the scientific evidence against the possibility of a historical Adam and Eve is overwhelming. Our common descent from ape-like ancestors is obvious. Thus the first chapters of Genesis are viewed as nonhistorical.[1]

In this section of the book we are focusing on the *scientific* evidence relating to human origins. Nevertheless, we acknowledge that the debate over human origins is so consequential because it has implications that go beyond science. The difficulty for many Christians, as is pointed out in Wayne Grudem's "Biblical and Theological Introduction," is that discarding traditional readings of Genesis seems to vitiate the basis for essential doctrines of the Christian faith. Many of the theistic evolutionists who advocate for acceptance of the neo-Darwinian story themselves claim that the scientific evidence necessitates the loss of a historical first human couple, which in turn removes the idea of original sin and the fall, among other things.

It is important to stress that the Darwinian story in its unadulterated form is purely materialistic; it says that we are supposed to have evolved through an unguided process into the modern humanity we see today. The appearance of intelligence, language, and even morality and spirituality are attributed to undirected and incremental natural selection—either that or some highly improbable coincidence, of which we are the lucky recipients. There is no story of the infusion of a soul at any point, because in the materialistic worldview there are no souls. Intelligence, language, morality, and spirituality are all the product of

---

1. To be fair, it should be admitted that some theistic evolutionists try to reconcile the idea of an original pair with the "fact" of humanity's evolution, by saying that God chose to breathe his life into certain intelligent hominins, the ones called Adam and Eve.

happenstance and the gradual selection of more fit individuals. They derive not from any higher power but from the evolutionary process, which leads to increasingly complex social development. Darwin wrote quite clearly on this point: "The idea of a universal and beneficent Creator does not seem to arise in the mind of man until he has been elevated by long-continued culture."[2] In short, man is not made in God's image; God is made in man's image. It follows that our "moral sense," as Darwin called it, is the product of our "social instincts."[3] Even consciousness disappears in the naturalistic mind-set, which is ironic indeed. To paste the idea of a benevolent Creator onto this Darwinian story is like slapping a Band-Aid on a gaping wound. How is one to stanch the bleeding?

If the new Darwinian understanding of human origins has consequences this drastic, it is imperative that it be carefully examined for its rigor and veracity. Is it possible that, in the effort to accept the prevailing neo-Darwinian view, theistic evolutionists have lost sight of the truth? Might the story actually be wrong? Scientific consensus has been wrong *many* times—phlogiston, humoral pathology, luminiferous aether, astrology, globalism, spontaneous generation, eugenics; the list could go on—and it would be a shame, surely, to discard our Christian heritage for a mess of pottage.

Given our society's tendency to put science in the place of authority, we may be tempted to accept what we are told as proven established science. But we should be quite cautious about accepting any scientific theory with effects as far-reaching as neo-Darwinism has.

And there is good reason for doubt about the theory. Neo-Darwinism *fails to explain* many significant things in biology, as should be apparent from the previous chapters. It cannot account for the origin of information, the appearance of complex body plans in the Cambrian, or how an embryo develops into an adult. Even the idea of common descent, an idea that is essential for the neo-Darwinian story, is subject to challenge. Alternate theories such as those offered by the extended evolutionary synthesis also have problems. So just at a time when

---

2. Charles Darwin, *Descent of Man*, Princeton University Press photoreproduction ed. (London: J. Murray, 1871), chapter 21 (395).
3. Ibid., chapter 21 (394).

neo-Darwinism seems to be collapsing, why should Christians accept the story of our evolutionary origin from apes? Should we not investigate the merits of the case? Most especially, should we not examine the evidence that is offered in support of the theory of human evolution?

The Argument

Because of the "settled" science of today, theistic evolutionists (or evolutionary creationists) accept the idea of our common ancestry with chimps. To review, three dubious claims have been made concerning this:

- First, the fossil evidence reveals intermediates between us and our ape-like ancestors, apparently bridging the gap between us and them.
- Second, the fact that our DNA is nearly identical to chimp DNA is taken as evidence of our common ancestry.
- Third, population genetics says that the first steps on the way to humanity arose in a population of about ten thousand, and that no fewer than several thousand ancestors could have ever existed in the human lineage.

Now, are these claims true? How solid is the science behind them? That is what we examine in the next three chapters (14–16). These chapters will make the following key points:

- The actual evidence in the fossil record is starkly at odds with the narrative of human evolution. Realistic candidates for species transitional to humans are conspicuous by their absence.
- The alleged similarity between humans and chimpanzees at the genetic level is exaggerated. As our understanding of the complexity of the genome increases, so does the realization of the *differences* between humans and chimps.
- In particular, arguments relating to "junk" DNA have been vitiated by recent discoveries concerning the important (and often species-specific) functions of these elements of the genome.
- The time needed for humans to have evolved from an ancestor in common with chimps is orders of magnitude greater than the time available in conventional evolutionary models.

- Conventional population genetics models *assume* common descent of humans—that chimps and humans share a common ancestor. We propose an alternative model—one based on a unique origin of an original pair of humans with initial created diversity, giving four versions of each initial non-sex chromosome. This is consistent with the evidence of a block structure for a large percentage of human DNA, and is open to verification by means of computer simulation.

For all these reasons, the hypothesis of our shared ancestry with chimps—a hypothesis most contentious among Christians *and* vital to the theistic evolutionary position—is deeply flawed, and is a very unsound basis for revising the very foundations of Christian doctrine.

14

Missing Transitions: Human Origins and the Fossil Record

CASEY LUSKIN

SUMMARY

The standard evolutionary view of human origins—generally accepted by theistic evolutionists—holds that our species, *Homo sapiens*, evolved from ape-like species through apparently unguided evolutionary processes like natural selection and random mutation. Theistic evolutionists and other evolutionary scientists often claim the fossil evidence for this Darwinian evolution of humans from ape-like creatures is incontrovertible. But their viewpoint is not supported by the fossil evidence. Hominin fossils generally fall into one of two groups: ape-like species and human-like species, with a large, unbridged gap between them. Virtually the entire hominin fossil record is marked by fragmented fossils, especially the early hominins, which do not document precursors to humans. Around 3 to 4 million years ago, the australopithecines appear, but they were generally ape-like and also appear in an abrupt manner. When our genus *Homo* appears, it also does so in an abrupt fashion, without clear evidence of a transition from previous ape-like hominins. Major members of *Homo* are very similar to modern humans, and their differences amount to small-scale microevolutionary changes. The archaeological record shows an "explosion" of human creativity about thirty to forty thousand years ago. Despite the claims of evolutionary paleoanthropologists and the media hype surrounding many hominin fossils, the fragmented hominin fossil record does not document the evolution of humans from ape-like precursors, and the appearance of humans in the fossil record is anything but a gradual Darwinian evolutionary process. Theistic evolutionists should appreciate that Christians who doubt standard evolutionary accounts of human origins hold legitimate views that are backed by scientific evidence.

. . . . .

Evolutionists commonly tell the public that the fossil evidence for the Darwinian evolution of our species, *Homo sapiens*, from ape-like creatures is incontrovertible. Theistic evolutionists are no exception. In 2009, Southern Methodist University anthropology professor Ronald Wetherington testified before the Texas State Board of Education that human evolution has "arguably the most complete sequence of fossil succession of any mammal in the world. No gaps. No lack of transitional fossils. . . . So when people talk about the lack of transitional fossils or gaps in the fossil record, it absolutely is not true. And it is not true specifically for our own species."[1] According to Wetherington, human origins shows "a nice clean example of what Darwin thought was a gradualistic evolutionary change."[2]

Theistic evolutionists like Wetherington who teach at Christian universities are often adamant about the evidence for human evolution—sometimes more so than their counterparts at secular schools. But does the fossil record support their claims? Digging into the technical literature reveals a story starkly different from the one presented by Wetherington and other evolutionists.

Far from supplying "a nice clean example" of "gradualistic evolutionary change" that has "no gaps" or "no lack of transitional fossils," the record shows a dramatic discontinuity between ape-like and human-like forms. Human-like fossils appear abruptly in the record, without clear

---

1. Ronald Wetherington, testimony before Texas State Board of Education (January 21, 2009). Original recording on file with author, SBOECommtFullJan2109B5.mp3, Time Index 1:52:00–1:52:44.
2. Ibid.

evolutionary precursors, contradicting Darwinian expectations. The fossil record does not show that humans evolved from ape-like precursors.

I. The Fragmented Field of Paleoanthropology

The discipline of paleoanthropology studies the fossil remains of ancient hominins and hominids. Hominins and hominids may be defined differently, depending on which expert you consult, but this chapter will define "hominins" as humans and all of our extinct (supposed) ancestors and relatives tracing back to our (again, supposed) most recent common ancestor with chimpanzees.[3] The term "hominid" is often used in roughly the same manner, although officially it means any member of family Hominidae—including humans, great apes (chimpanzees, gorillas, and orangutans), and any extinct species descended from their proposed most recent common ancestor. (Thus, a hominin is a hominid, but a hominid is not necessarily a hominin.) Paleoanthropologists face many daunting challenges in their quest to explain human evolution from this hypothetical human/ape common ancestor. Their field is fragmented in multiple senses, making it difficult to bolster evolutionary accounts of human origins.

First, the fossil record is fragmented, and long periods of time exist for which there are few hominin fossils. *National Geographic* acknowledges, "Fossils attributed to *Homo* in the period two to three million years ago are exceedingly rare," and "You could put them all into a small shoe box and still have room for a good pair of shoes."[4] So "fragmentary and disconnected" is the data, according to Harvard zoologist Richard Lewontin, that "Despite the excited and optimistic claims that have been made by some paleontologists, no fossil hominid species can be established as our direct ancestor."[5]

A second challenge is the fragmented nature of the fossil specimens themselves. Typical hominid fossils consist of mere bone scraps, making

---

3. This definition of hominin thus includes only those species that lie on the human branch, and excludes species that sit on the branch that led to chimps.
4. Jamie Shreeve, "Oldest Human Fossil Found, Redrawing Family Tree," *National Geographic*, March 5, 2015, accessed July 10, 2016, http://news.nationalgeographic.com/news/2015/03/150304 -homo-habilis-evolution-fossil-jaw-ethiopia-olduvai-gorge/. See also Ann Gibbons, "Skeletons Present an Exquisite Paleo-Puzzle," *Science* 333 (September 9, 2011): 1370–1372 (noting "a significant gap in the fossil record 3 million to 2 million years ago").
5. Richard Lewontin, *Human Diversity* (New York: Scientific American Library, 1995), 163.

it difficult to form definitive conclusions about their morphology, behavior, and relationships. Primatologist Frans de Waal observes that the skeleton of the common chimpanzee is nearly identical to the bonobo, but they have great differences in behavior. "On the sole basis of a few bones and skulls," writes de Waal, "no one would have dared to propose the dramatic behavioral differences recognized today between the bonobo and the chimpanzee."[6] He issues "a warning for paleontologists who are reconstructing social life from fossilized remnants of long-extinct species"[7]—problems that intensify when fossil bones are missing.[8] Indeed this is often the case, as Stephen Jay Gould commented: "[m]ost hominid fossils, even though they serve as a basis for endless speculation and elaborate storytelling, are fragments of jaws and scraps of skulls."[9]

Flesh reconstructions of extinct hominins are likewise subjective. They often attempt to diminish the intellectual abilities of humans and overstate those of apes. One high school textbook[10] caricatures Neanderthals as intellectually primitive even though they exhibited intelligence and culture,[11] and casts *Homo erectus* as a bungling, stooped form—even though its skeleton is extremely similar to modern humans.[12] Conversely, the same textbook portrays an australopithecine (which in reality had a chimp-sized brain) with gleams of human-like intelligence and emotion—a common tactic in illustrated books on human origins.[13] University of North Carolina, Charlotte anthropologist Jonathan Marks warns against such "fallacies" of "humanizing

---

6. Frans B. M. de Waal, "Apes from Venus: Bonobos and Human Social Evolution," in *Tree of Origin: What Primate Behavior Can Tell Us about Human Social Evolution*, ed. Frans B. M. de Waal (Cambridge, MA: Harvard University Press, 2001), 68.

7. Ibid.

8. E.g., "A series of associated foot bones from Olduvai has been reconstructed into a form closely resembling the human foot today although a similarly incomplete foot of a chimpanzee may also be reconstructed in such a manner" (C. E. Oxnard, "The Place of the Australopithecines in Human Evolution: Grounds for Doubt?," *Nature* 258 [December 4, 1975]: 389–395, at 389).

9. Stephen Jay Gould, *The Panda's Thumb: More Reflections in Natural History* (New York: W. W. Norton, 1980), 126.

10. See Alton Biggs, Kathleen Gregg, Whitney Crispen Hagins, et al., National Geographic Society, *Biology: The Dynamics of Life* (New York: Glencoe/McGraw-Hill, 2000), 442–443.

11. See notes 169–177 below, and accompanying text.

12. See notes 153–162 below, and accompanying text.

13. E.g., see Biggs et al., *Biology: The Dynamics of Life*, 438; similarly, see Esteban E. Sarmiento, Gary J. Sawyer, and Richard Milner, *The Last Human: A Guide to Twenty-Two Species of Extinct Humans* (New Haven, CT: Yale University Press, 2007), 75, 83, 103, 127, 137; Donald Johanson and Blake Edgar, *From Lucy to Language* (New York: Simon & Schuster, 1996), 82; Richard Potts and Christopher Sloan, *What Does It Mean to Be Human?* (Washington, DC: National Geographic, 2010), 32–33, 36, 66, 92; Carl Zimmer, *Smithsonian Intimate Guide to Human Origins* (Toronto: Madison, 2005), 44, 50.

apes and ape-ifying humans."[14] The words of the famed physical anthropologist Earnest Hooton from Harvard University remain valid: "alleged restorations of ancient types of man have very little, if any, scientific value and are likely only to mislead the public."[15]

Third, the field itself is fragmented. The sparse nature of the data, combined with the desire to make confident assertions about human evolution, often betrays objectivity and leads to sharp disagreements.[16] An article in *Science* titled "The Politics of Paleoanthropology" compared the task of reconstructing human evolution "to that of reconstructing the plot of *War and Peace* with 13 randomly selected pages," leading to conflicts that make it "difficult to separate the personal from the scientific disputes raging in the field."[17] Similarly, Donald Johanson and Blake Edgar divulge that ambition and lifelong quests for recognition, funding, and fame can make it difficult for paleoanthropologists to admit when they are wrong:

> [H]uman evolutionary studies have been plagued by debate and controversy. The reasons for argument over a fragment of a jaw, a partial skull, a handful of teeth, or an uncertain geological date are not that difficult to understand. Often a scrappy fossil generates diverse interpretations. . . . The stakes are high. Hominid fossils are glamorous and bring scientific and popular success to those who find them. . . . The fossils themselves become revered and coveted. . . . The appearance of discordant evidence is sometimes met with a sturdy reiteration of our original views. . . . it takes time for us to give up pet theories and assimilate the new information. In the meantime, scientific credibility and funding for more fieldwork hang in the balance.[18]

14. Jonathan Marks, *What It Means to Be 98% Chimpanzee: Apes, People, and Their Genes* (Berkeley: University of California Press, 2003), xv.

15. Earnest Albert Hooton, *Up from the Ape*, rev. ed. (New York: McMillan, 1946), 329.

16. *The New Yorker* gave one paleoanthropologist's description of paleoanthropology: "'It's a competitive sport,' [Lee] Berger said in a recent lecture. 'There are very few players. And once your head is above the parapet—' He didn't finish the sentence" (Paige Williams, "Digging for Glory," *The New Yorker*, June 27, 2016, accessed July 10, 2016, http://www.newyorker.com/magazine /2016/06/27/lee-berger-digs-for-bones-and-glory). See also Lee R. Berger and Brett Hilton-Barber, *In the Footsteps of Eve: The Mystery of Human Origins* (Washington, DC: Adventure Press, National Geographic, 2000).

17. Constance Holden, "The Politics of Paleoanthropology," *Science* 213 (August 14, 1981): 737–740.

18. Johanson and Edgar, *From Lucy to Language*, 32.

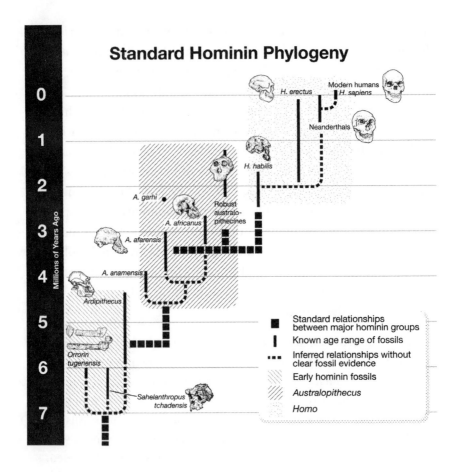

FIGURE 14.1. *Typical phylogeny of hominins.* *

CREDIT: Jonathan Jones.

* Phylogeny in Figure 14.1 based on information from multiple sources, including Carl Zimmer, *Smithsonian Intimate Guide to Human Origins* (Toronto: Madison, 2005), 41; Meave Leakey and Alan Walker, "Early Hominid Fossils from Africa," *Scientific American* (August 25, 2003), 16; Potts and Sloan, *What Does It Mean to Be Human?*, 32–33; Ann Gibbons, *The First Human: The Race to Discover Our Earliest Ancestors* (New York: Doubleday, 2006); Gibbons, "A New Kind of Ancestor: *Ardipithecus* Unveiled," *Science* 326 (October 2, 2009): 36–40; David Strait, Frederick E. Grine, and John G. Fleagle, "Analyzing Hominin Phylogeny: Cladistic Approach," in *Handbook of Paleoanthropology: Principles, Methods, and Approaches*, ed. Winfried Henke and Ian Tattersall, 2nd ed. (Heidelberg: Springer, 2015), 1989–2014.

The quest for recognition can inspire outright contempt toward other researchers. After interviewing paleoanthropologists for a documentary, PBS NOVA producer Mark Davis recounted that "[e]ach Neanderthal expert thought the last one I talked to was an idiot, if not an actual Neanderthal."[19]

Paleoanthropology is rife with dissent and has few universally accepted theories. Even the most established and confidently promoted evolutionary models of human origins are based on limited evidence. As *Nature* editor Henry Gee conceded, "[f]ossil evidence of human evolutionary history is fragmentary and open to various interpretations."[20]

II. The Standard Story of Human Evolution

Despite the disagreements, there is a standard story of human evolution which is retold in countless textbooks, news media articles, and coffee table books. Indeed, virtually all of the scientists cited in this chapter accept *some* evolutionary account of human origins. A representation of the most commonly believed hominin phylogeny is portrayed in Figure 14.1.

Starting with the early hominins, and moving through the australopithecines, and then into the genus *Homo*, this chapter will review the fossil evidence and assess whether it supports this standard account of human evolution. As we shall see, the evidence—or lack thereof—often contradicts this evolutionary story.

III. Early Hominins

In 2015, two leading paleoanthropologists reviewed the fossil evidence regarding human evolution in a prestigious scientific volume titled *Macroevolution*. They acknowledged the "dearth of unambiguous evidence for ancestor-descendant lineages," and admitted,

> [T]he evolutionary sequence for the majority of hominin lineages is unknown. Most hominin taxa, particularly early hominins, have no

---

19. Mark Davis, "Into the Fray: The Producer's Story," PBS NOVA Online, February 2002, accessed July 10, 2016, http://www.pbs.org/wgbh/nova/neanderthals/producer.html.
20. Henry Gee, "Return to the Planet of the Apes," *Nature* 412 (July 12, 2001): 131–132.

obvious ancestors, and in most cases ancestor-descendant sequences (fossil time series) cannot be reliably constructed.[21]

Nevertheless, numerous theories have been promoted about early hominins and their ancestral relationships to humans.

A. *Sahelanthropus tchadensis*: The Toumai Skull

Although *Sahelanthropus tchadensis* (also called the "Toumai skull") is known only from one skull and some jaw fragments, it has been called the oldest known hominin on the human line.

But not everyone agrees. Brigitte Senut, of the Natural History Museum in Paris, called Toumai "the skull of a female gorilla,"[22] and cowrote in *Nature* that "*Sahelanthropus* was an ape," not bipedal, and that "many . . . features . . . link the specimen with chimpanzees, gorillas or both, to the exclusion of hominids."[23] This debate has continued, but leading authorities caution that teeth and skull fragments alone are "probably not reliable for reconstructing the phylogenetic relationships of higher primate species and genera, including those among the hominins."[24] Unfortunately, for hominins like *Sahelanthropus*, craniodental fragments are all we have.

In his testimony at the 2009 Texas evolution hearings, Ronald Wetherington stated that "every fossil we find reinforces the sequence that we had previously supposed to exist rather than suggesting something different."[25] But *Sahelanthropus* provides a striking counterexample to that assertion. Commenting on Toumai, Bernard Wood of George Washington University observed, "A single fossil can fundamentally change the way we reconstruct the tree of life,"[26] and explained that if this advanced-looking skull belonged to our ancestor, "then it plays

---

21. Bernard Wood and Mark Grabowski, "Macroevolution in and around the Hominin Clade," in *Macroevolution: Explanation, Interpretation, and Evidence*, ed. Serrelli Emanuele and Nathalie Gontier (Heidelberg: Springer, 2015), 347–376 (365).

22. "Skull Find Sparks Controversy," *BBC News*, July 12, 2002, accessed July 10, 2016, http://news.bbc.co.uk/2/hi/science/nature/2125244.stm.

23. Milford H. Wolpoff, Brigitte Senut, Martin Pickford, and John Hawks, "*Sahelanthropus* or '*Sahelpithecus*'?," *Nature* 419 (October 10, 2002): 581–582.

24. Mark Collard and Bernard Wood, "How Reliable Are Human Phylogenetic Hypotheses?," *Proceedings of the National Academy of Sciences USA* 97 (April 25, 2000): 5003–5006.

25. Ronald Wetherington testimony, Time Index 2:06:00–2:06:08.

26. Bernard Wood, "Hominid Revelations from Chad," *Nature* 418 (July 11, 2002): 133–135.

havoc with the tidy model of human origins."[27] In other words, if *Sahelanthropus* was a human ancestor, then many later supposed human ancestors—including the australopithecines—are forced out of our family line.

B. Precious Little *Orrorin tugenensis*

Orrorin, which means "original man" in a Kenyan language, was a chimpanzee-sized primate known only from "an assortment of bone fragments,"[28] including pieces of the arm, thigh, lower jaw, and some teeth. When initially discovered, the *New York Times* declared, "Fossils May Be Earliest Human Link,"[29] and reported that *Orrorin* "may be the earliest known ancestor of the human family."[30] *Nature* responded to such hype by warning that the "excitement needs to be tempered with caution in assessing the claim of a six-million-year-old direct ancestor of modern humans."[31]

That seems like wise advice. Paleoanthropologists initially claimed *Orrorin*'s femur indicated bipedal locomotion "appropriate for a population standing at the dawn of the human lineage,"[32] but a later Yale University Press commentary admitted, "All in all, there is currently precious little evidence bearing on how *Orrorin* moved."[33]

If *Orrorin* did prove an upright-walking hominin from 6 million years ago (mya), would that qualify it as our ancestor? Not necessarily. Evolutionary paleoanthropologists often use bipedality as a litmus test for membership in the human lineage, but the fossil record has produced bipedal apes which even evolutionists recognize were far removed from human origins.[34] According to a *Nature* commentary,

---

27. Ibid.
28. Potts and Sloan, *What Does It Mean to Be Human?*, 38.
29. John Noble Wilford, "Fossils May Be Earliest Human Link," *New York Times*, July 12, 2001, accessed July 10, 2016, http://www.nytimes.com/2001/07/12/world/fossils-may-be-earliest-human-link.html.
30. John Noble Wilford, "On the Trail of a Few More Ancestors," *New York Times*, April 8, 2001, accessed July 10, 2016, http://www.nytimes.com/2001/04/08/world/on-the-trail-of-a-few-more-ancestors.html.
31. Leslie C. Aiello and Mark Collard, "Our Newest Oldest Ancestor?," *Nature* 410 (March 29, 2001): 526–527.
32. K. Galik, B. Senut, M. Pickford, D. Gommery, et al., "External and Internal Morphology of the BAR 1002'00 *Orrorin tugenensis* Femur," *Science* 305 (September 3, 2004): 1450–1453.
33. Sarmiento, Sawyer, and Milner, *Last Human*, 35.
34. *Oreopithecus bambolii*, e.g., was a bipedal ape that lived millions of years before the first hominins, had virtually nothing to do with human evolution, yet "acquired many 'humanlike' features in parallel" ("Fossils May Look Like Human Bones: Biological Anthropologists

one such ape, *Oreopithecus*, acquired bipedalism convergently with humans, and provides an "object lesson" that human-like features such as bipedalism don't necessarily indicate human ancestry.[35]

Much as the Toumai skull threatened to rewrite the hominin tree, if *Orrorin* were our ancestor it too would displace most australopithecines from our lineage.[36] Simply too little is known to determine its lifestyle, locomotion, or evolutionary relationships. As two critics argued in *Nature*, "*Orrorin* is not a hominin," and "we are a long way from a consensus on its role in human evolution."[37]

C. *Ardipithecus ramidus*: Irish Stew or Breakthrough of the Year?

In 2009, *Science* announced the long-awaited publication of *Ardipithecus ramidus*, a would-be hominin fossil that lived about 4.4 mya. Expectations mounted after its discoverer, UC Berkeley paleoanthropologist Tim White, promised a "phenomenal individual" that would be the "Rosetta stone for understanding bipedalism."[38] The media eagerly employed the hominin they affectionately dubbed "Ardi" to evangelize the public for Darwin.

Discovery Channel ran the headline "'Ardi,' Oldest Human Ancestor, Unveiled," and quoted White calling Ardi "as close as we have ever come to finding the last common ancestor of chimpanzees and humans."[39] The Associated Press declared, "World's Oldest Human-Linked Skeleton Found," and stated, "the new find provides evidence that chimps and humans evolved from some long-ago common ancestor."[40] *Science* named Ardi the "breakthrough of the year" for

Question Claims for Human Ancestry," *ScienceDaily*, February 16, 2011, accessed June 12, 2016, http://www.sciencedaily.com/releases/2011/02/110216132034.htm. See also Christopher Wills, *Children of Prometheus: The Accelerating Pace of Human Evolution* [Reading, MA: Basic Books, 1999], 156).

35. Bernard Wood and Terry Harrison, "The Evolutionary Context of the First Hominins," *Nature* 470 (February 17, 2011): 347–352.

36. Aiello and Collard, "Our Newest Oldest Ancestor?"

37. Ibid., 527.

38. Tim White, quoted in Ann Gibbons, "In Search of the First Hominids," *Science* 295 (February 15, 2002): 1214–1219, at 1216.

39. Jennifer Viegas, "'Ardi,' Oldest Human Ancestor, Unveiled," *Seeker*, October 1, 2009, accessed July 10, 2016, http://www.seeker.com/ardi-oldest-human-ancestor-unveiled-1766073270 .html. Note: This article was originally posted at Discovery News at http://news.discovery.com /history/ardi-human-ancestor.html.

40. Randolph E. Schmid, "World's Oldest Human-Linked Skeleton Found," NBC News, October 1, 2009, accessed July 10, 2016, http://www.nbcnews.com/id/33110809/ns/technology

2009,[41] and introduced her with the headline, "A New Kind of Ancestor: *Ardipithecus* Unveiled."[42]

Calling Ardi "new" may have been a poor word choice, since she was discovered in the early 1990s. Why did it take some fifteen years to publish the analyses? A 2002 article in *Science* explains the bones were so "soft," "crushed," "squished," and "chalky," that White reported, "when I clean an edge it erodes, so I have to mold every one of the broken pieces to reconstruct it."[43] Later reports similarly acknowledged that "portions of Ardi's skeleton were found crushed nearly to smithereens and needed extensive digital reconstruction," including the pelvis, which "looked like an Irish stew."[44] *National Geographic* similarly noted that Ardi's "trampled" remains were "badly crushed and distorted" and "so fragile they would turn to dust at a touch."[45]

Claims about bipedal locomotion require accurate measurements of the precise shapes of key bones (like the pelvis). Can one trust declarations of a "Rosetta stone for understanding bipedalism" when Ardi was "crushed to smithereens"? *Science* quoted various paleoanthropologists who were "skeptical that the crushed pelvis really shows the anatomical details needed to demonstrate bipedality."[46]

Even some who accepted Ardi's reconstructions weren't satisfied that she was a bipedal human ancestor. Primatologist Esteban Sarmiento concluded in *Science* that "All of the *Ar. ramidus* bipedal

---

_and_science-science/t/worlds-oldest-human-linked-skeleton-found/. Note: This article was originally published through MSNBC at http://www.msnbc.msn.com/id/33110809/ns/technology_and _science-science/t/worlds-oldest-human-linked-skeleton-found/.

41. Ann Gibbons, "Breakthrough of the Year: *Ardipithecus ramidus*," *Science* 326 (December 18, 2009): 1598–1599.

42. Gibbons, "New Kind of Ancestor," 36–40.

43. White, quoted in Gibbons, "In Search of the First Hominids," 1214–1219, at 1215–1216.

44. Michael D. Lemonick and Andrea Dorfman, "Ardi Is a New Piece for the Evolution Puzzle," *Time*, October 1, 2009, accessed July 10, 2016, http://www.time.com/time/printout/0,8816,1927289 ,00.html.

45. Jamie Shreeve, "Oldest Skeleton of Human Ancestor Found," *National Geographic*, October 1, 2009, accessed July 10, 2016, http://news.nationalgeographic.com/news/2009/10/091001 -oldest-human-skeleton-ardi-missing-link-chimps-ardipithecus-ramidus.html. See also Gibbons, "New Kind of Ancestor," 36–40 ("[T]he team's excitement was tempered by the skeleton's terrible condition. The bones literally crumbled when touched. White called it road kill. And parts of the skeleton had been trampled and scattered into more than a hundred fragments; the skull was crushed to 4 centimeters in height."); Gibbons, *First Human*, 15 ("The excitement was tempered, however, by the condition of the skeleton. The bone was so soft and crushed that White later described it as road-kill").

46. Gibbons, "New Kind of Ancestor," 36–40, at 39.

characters cited also serve the mechanical requisites of quadrupedal-ity, and in the case of *Ar. ramidus* foot-segment proportions, find their closest functional analog to those of gorillas, a terrestrial or semiter-restrial quadruped and not a facultative or habitual biped."[47] Bernard Wood questioned whether Ardi's postcranial skeleton qualified it as hominin,[48] and cowrote in *Nature* that, if "*Ardipithecus* is assumed to be a hominin," then it had "remarkably high levels of homoplasy [similarity] among extant great apes."[49] In other words, Ardi had ape-like characteristics which, if we set aside the preferences of Ardi's promoters, should imply a closer relationship to apes than to humans. An article in *Nature* stated that Ardi's "being a human ancestor is by no means the simplest, or most parsimonious explanation."[50] Stan-ford anthropologist Richard Klein agreed: "I frankly don't think Ardi was a hominid, or bipedal."[51] Sarmiento even observed that Ardi had characteristics different from both humans *and* African apes, such as its unfused jaw joint, which ought to remove her far from human ancestry.[52]

Whatever Ardi was, everyone agrees she was initially badly crushed and needed extensive reconstruction. No doubt this debate will con-tinue, but are we obligated to accept the "human ancestor" talking points promoted by Ardi's discoverers in the media? Sarmiento doesn't think so. According *Time* magazine, he "regards the hype around Ardi to have been overblown."[53]

IV. Later Hominins: The Australopithecines

Many paleoanthropologists believe the australopithecines were upright-walking hominins and ancestral to our genus *Homo*. Dig into the details, however, and ask basic questions like *Who*, *Where*, and *When*, and there is much controversy. As we'll discuss in parts V and

---

47. Esteban E. Sarmiento, "Comment on the Paleobiology and Classification of *Ardipithecus ramidus*," *Science* 328 (May 28, 2010): 1105b.
48. Gibbons, "New Kind of Ancestor," 36–40.
49. Wood and Harrison, "Evolutionary Context of the First Hominins," 347–352, at 348.
50. "Fossils May Look Like Human Bones."
51. Quoted in John Noble Wilford, "Scientists Challenge 'Breakthrough' on Fossil Skeleton," *New York Times*, May 27, 2010, accessed July 10, 2016, http://www.nytimes.com/2010/05/28/science/28fossil.html.
52. See Eben Harrell, "Ardi: The Human Ancestor Who Wasn't?," *Time*, May 27, 2010, ac-cessed July 10, 2016, http://content.time.com/time/health/article/0,8599,1992115,00.html.
53. Ibid.

VI of this chapter, one paper noted, "there is little consensus on which species of *Australopithecus* is the closest to *Homo*,"[54] if any. Even the origin of genus *Australopithecus* itself is unclear.

A. Retroactive Confessions of Ignorance

In 2006, *National Geographic* ran a story titled "Fossil Find Is Missing Link in Human Evolution, Scientists Say,"[55] reporting the discovery of what the Associated Press called "the most complete chain of human evolution so far."[56] The fossils, belonging to species *Australopithecus anamensis*, were said to link *Ardipithecus* to its supposed australopithecine descendants.

What exactly was found? According to the technical paper, the claims were based upon canine teeth of intermediate "masticatory robusticity."[57] If a few teeth[58] of intermediate size and shape make "the most complete chain of human evolution so far," then the evidence for human evolution must be indeed quite modest.

Besides learning to distrust media hype, there is another lesson here. Accompanying the praise of this "missing link" were retroactive confessions of ignorance, where evolutionists acknowledge a severe gap in their model *only after* thinking they have found evidence to plug that gap. Thus, the technical paper reporting these teeth admitted that "Until recently, the origins of *Australopithecus* were obscured by a sparse fossil record."[59] It continued,

---

54. Henry M. McHenry and Katherine Coffing, "*Australopithecus* to *Homo*: Transformations in Body and Mind," *Annual Review of Anthropology* 29 (2000): 125–146, at 126.

55. John Roach, "Fossil Find Is Missing Link in Human Evolution, Scientists Say," *National Geographic News*, April 13, 2006, accessed July 10, 2016, http://news.nationalgeographic.com/news/2006/04/0413_060413_evolution.html.

56. Seth Borenstein, "Fossil Discovery Fills Gap in Human Evolution," NBC News, April 12, 2006, accessed July 10, 2016, http://www.nbcnews.com/id/12286206/ns/technology_and_science-science/t/fossil-discovery-fills-gap-human-evolution/. Note: This article was originally posted at http://www.msnbc.msn.com/id/12286206/.

57. See Figure 4 in Tim D. White, Giday WoldeGabriel, Berhane Asfaw, Stan Ambrose, Yonas Beyene, et al., "Asa Issie, Aramis, and the Origin of *Australopithecus*," *Nature* 440 (April 13, 2006): 883–889.

58. This particular claim was based on the finding of just a few teeth. However, *Australopithecus anamensis* is known from additional specimens that include some postcranial bones. Nonetheless, known specimens attributed to *Australopithecus anamensis* are highly fragmented and a holotype is difficult to distinguish. The vast majority of known remains are craniodental. See table 1 in C. V. Ward, M. G. Leakey, and A. Walker, "Morphology of *Australopithecus anamensis* from Kanapoi and Allia Bay, Kenya," *Journal of Human Evolution* 41 (2001): 255–368.

59. White et al., "Asa Issie, Aramis, and the Origin of *Australopithecus*," 883.

The origin of *Australopithecus*, the genus widely interpreted as ancestral to *Homo*, is a central problem in human evolutionary studies. *Australopithecus* species differ markedly from extant African apes and candidate ancestral hominids such as *Ardipithecus*, *Orrorin* and *Sahelanthropus*.[60]

Evolutionists who retroactively confess ignorance about some previously unfilled "gap" risk falling into a situation where the new evidence which supposedly filled the gap may not prove very convincing. This seems to be the case here, where a couple of teeth were all that stood between an unsolved "central problem in human evolutionary studies"—the origin of australopithecines—and "the most complete chain of human evolution so far." Moreover, we're left with uncontested admissions that the australopithecines "differ markedly" from their supposed early hominin ancestors. Australopithecine origins, apparently, remain "obscure."

B. Australopithecines Are like Apes

While *Ardipithecus*, *Orrorin*, and *Sahelanthropus* are controversial due to their fragmentary remains, there are sufficient known australopithecine specimens to generally understand their morphology. *Australopithecus*, which literally means "southern ape," is a genus of extinct hominins that lived in Africa from about 5 to 1.2 mya. "Splitters" (paleoanthropologists who infer many different species) and "lumpers" (those who see fewer) have created a variety of taxonomic schemes for the australopithecines. The four most commonly accepted species are *afarensis*, *africanus*, *robustus*, and *boisei*. *Robustus* and *boisei* are larger-boned and more "robust," and are sometimes classified within genus *Paranthropus*.[61] They are thought to represent a later-living offshoot that went extinct without leaving any living descendants. The smaller "gracile" forms, *afarensis* and *africanus*, probably lived earlier, and are classified within the genus *Australopithecus*.[62]

---

60. Ibid.

61. See, e.g., Bernard A. Wood, "Evolution of the Australopithecines," in *The Cambridge Encyclopedia of Human Evolution*, ed. Steve Jones, Robert Martin, and David Pilbeam (Cambridge: Cambridge University Press, 1992), 231–240.

62. Some claim that another gracile species, *Australopithecus garhi*, lived about 2.5 mya and was a human ancestor. But this species is "not well documented" and its specimens may even belong to other species ("*Australopithecus garhi*," The Smithsonian Institution's Human Origins Program,

The most well-known australopithecine fossil is Lucy (which belonged to *afarensis*), one of the most complete known fossils among pre-*Homo* hominins. She is often described as a bipedal ape-like creature that is an ideal precursor to humans.

In 2009, I visited a traveling exhibit of Lucy's bones. In addition to the fact that Lucy did not look human-like (see Fig. 14.2), I was also struck by the incompleteness of her skeleton. Only 40 percent was found, and a large percentage is mere rib fragments. Very little useful material from Lucy's skull was recovered, and yet she is one of the most significant specimens ever found.

There are some possible reasons for skepticism over whether "Lucy" represents a single individual, or even a single species. In an exhibit video, Lucy's discoverer, Donald Johanson, admitted that her bones were found scattered across a hillside. His written account quotes Lucy-researcher Tim White further explaining how the bones were not found together: "[S]ince the fossil wasn't found *in situ*, it could have come from anywhere above. There's no matrix on any of the bones we've found either. All you can do is make probability statements [that Lucy was a single individual]."[63] Johanson admits that one more rainstorm might have washed Lucy's bones away, never to be found. What might have happened during prior storms to mix her up with who-knows-what? Could "Lucy" represent bones from multiple individuals or even multiple species?

The classic rejoinder notes that none of Lucy's bones appear duplicated, suggesting they represent a single individual. This is certainly possible, but given the fragmented and scattered nature of the skeleton, the rebuttal is far from conclusive. In particular, it's difficult to definitively say that key bones said to indicate her upright posture—the half-pelvis and half-femur—belonged to one individual. Indeed,

accessed July 10, 2016, http://humanorigins.si.edu/evidence/human-fossils/species/australopithecus-garhi. Due to morphological differences with *Homo*, one study concluded, "*A. garhi* is unlikely to be the direct ancestor of *Homo*" [Strait et al., "Analyzing Hominin Phylogeny: Cladistic Approach," 2003]. Other studies have also criticized claims that *A. garhi* was ancestral to *Homo*. See Berhane Asfaw, Tim White, Owen Lovejoy, et al., "*Australopithecus garhi*: A New Species of Early Hominid from Ethiopia," *Science* 284 [April 23, 1999]: 629–635; Brian Villmoare, William H. Kimbel, Chalachew Seyoum, et al., "Early *Homo* at 2.8 Ma from Ledi-Geraru, Afar, Ethiopia," *Science* 347 [March 20, 2015]: 1352–1355).

63. Tim White, quoted in Donald Johanson and James Shreeve, *Lucy's Child: The Discovery of a Human Ancestor* (New York: Early Man Publishing, 1989), 163.

in 2015 it was decided that one of Lucy's vertebrae probably came from a baboon.[64] The scientist who discovered the apparent anomaly explained it was "washed or was otherwise transported in the mix of Lucy's remains."[65] Could the same have happened with any of her other bones?

Regardless, the Lucy exhibit confidently asserted, "Lucy's species walked bipedally, in much the same way as we do," and her skeleton "approximate[s] a chimpanzee-like head perched atop a human-like body." Lucy *did* have a small, chimp-like head; as paleoanthropologist Lee Berger observes, "Lucy's face would have been prognathic, jutting out almost to the same degree as a modern chimpanzee."[66] But Bernard Wood refutes the misapprehension that she resembled some ape-human hybrid: "Australopithecines are often wrongly thought to have had a mosaic of modern human and modern ape features, or, worse, are regarded as a group of 'failed' humans. Australopithecines were neither of these."[67]

Others have questioned whether Lucy walked like humans or was significantly bipedal. Mark Collard and Leslie Aiello observe in *Nature* that much of her body was "quite ape-like," especially with respect to the "relatively long and curved fingers, relatively long arms, and funnel-shaped chest."[68] They report "good evidence" from Lucy's hand-bones that her species "'knuckle-walked', as chimps and gorillas do."[69] A *New Scientist* article adds that Lucy appears well-adapted for climbing, since "Everything about her skeleton, from fingertips to toes, suggests that Lucy and her sisters retain several traits that would be very suitable for climbing in trees."[70] Richard Leakey and Roger Lewin argue that *A. afarensis* and other australopithecines "almost certainly were not adapted to a striding gait and running, as humans

---

64. Colin Barras, "Baboon Bone Found in Famous Lucy Skeleton," *New Scientist*, April 10, 2015, accessed July 10, 2016, https://www.newscientist.com/article/dn27325-baboon-bone-found-in-famous-lucy-skeleton/.

65. Ibid.

66. Berger and Hilton-Barber, *In the Footsteps of Eve: The Mystery of Human Origins*, 114.

67. See, e.g., Wood, "Evolution of the Australopithecines," 232.

68. Mark Collard and Leslie C. Aiello, "From Forelimbs to Two Legs," *Nature* 404 (March 23, 2000): 339–340.

69. Ibid. See also Brian G. Richmond and David S. Strait, "Evidence that Humans Evolved from a Knuckle-Walking Ancestor," *Nature* 404 (March 23, 2000): 382–385.

70. Jeremy Cherfas, "Trees Have Made Man Upright," *New Scientist* 97 (January 20, 1983): 172–177.

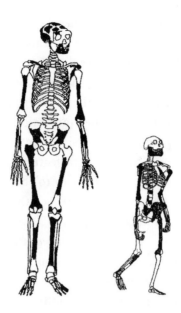

FIGURE 14.2. *Comparison of Lucy (right) to early Homo (left).* Black bones indicate those which have been discovered. The original caption states, "The first members of early *Homo sapiens* are really quite distinct from their australopithecine predecessors and contemporaries."

CREDIT: Figure 1, Hawks et al., "Population Bottlenecks and Pleistocene Human Evolution," *Molecular Biology and Evolution*, 17:2–22, copyright 2000 by Oxford University Press. Used with permission.

are."[71] They recount paleontologist Peter Schmid's striking surprise upon realizing Lucy's nonhuman qualities:

> Everyone had talked about Lucy as being very modern, very human, so I was surprised by what I saw. . . . What you see in *Australopithecus* is not what you'd want in an efficient bipedal running animal. . . . The shoulders were high, and, combined with the funnel-shaped chest, would have made arm swinging very improbable in the human sense. It wouldn't have been able to lift its thorax for the kind of deep breathing that we do when we run. The abdomen was potbellied, and there was no waist, so that would have restricted the flexibility that's essential to human running.[72]

71. Richard Leakey and Roger Lewin, *Origins Reconsidered: In Search of What Makes Us Human* (New York: Anchor, 1993), 195.
72. Peter Schmid, quoted in ibid., 193–194.

Other studies confirm australopithecine differences from humans, and similarities with apes. Their inner ear canals—responsible for balance and related to locomotion—are different from *Homo* but similar to great apes.[73] Traits like their ape-like developmental patterns[74] and ape-like ability for prehensile grasping by their toes[75] led a *Nature* reviewer to say that "ecologically they [australopithecines] may still be considered as apes."[76] Another analysis in *Nature* found the australopithecine skeleton shows "a mosaic of features unique to themselves and features bearing some resemblances to those of the orangutan," and concluded, "the possibility that any of the australopithecines is a direct part of human ancestry recedes."[77] A 2007 paper reported "[g]orilla-like anatomy on *Australopithecus afarensis* mandibles," which was "unexpected," and "cast[s] doubt on the role of *Au. afarensis* as a modern human ancestor."[78]

As for Lucy's pelvis, many claim it indicates bipedal locomotion, but Johanson and his team reported it was "badly crushed" with "distortion" and "cracking" when first discovered.[79] These problems led one commentator in the *Journal of Human Evolution* to propose that Lucy's pelvis is "so different from other australopithecines and so close to the human condition" due to "error in the reconstruction . . . creating a very 'human-like' sacral plane."[80] Another paper concluded that a lack of clear fossil data prevents paleoanthropologists from making firm conclusions about Lucy's mode of locomotion: "Prevailing views of Lucy's posture are almost impossible to reconcile. . . . To resolve such differences, more anatomical (fossil) evidence

---

73. Fred Spoor, Bernard Wood, and Frans Zonneveld, "Implications of Early Hominid Labyrinthine Morphology for Evolution of Human Bipedal Locomotion," *Nature* 369 (June 23, 1994): 645–648.

74. See Timothy G. Bromage and M. Christopher Dean, "Re-Evaluation of the Age at Death of Immature Fossil Hominids," *Nature* 317 (October 10, 1985): 525–527.

75. See Ronald J. Clarke and Phillip V. Tobias, "Sterkfontein Member 2 Foot Bones of the Oldest South African Hominid," *Science* 269 (July 28, 1995): 521–524.

76. Peter Andrews, "Ecological Apes and Ancestors," *Nature* 376 (August 17, 1995): 555–556.

77. Oxnard, "Place of the Australopithecines in Human Evolution."

78. Yoel Rak, Avishag Ginzburg, and Eli Geffen, "Gorilla-Like Anatomy on *Australopithecus afarensis* Mandibles Suggests *Au. afarensis* Link to Robust Australopiths," *Proceedings of the National Academy of Sciences USA* 104 (April 17, 2007): 6568–6572, at 6568.

79. Donald C. Johanson, C. Owen Lovejoy, William H. Kimbel, et al., "Morphology of the Pliocene Partial Hominid Skeleton (A.L. 288-1) From the Hadar Formation, Ethiopia," *American Journal of Physical Anthropology* 57 (1982): 403–451.

80. François Marchal, "A New Morphometric Analysis of the Hominid Pelvic Bone," *Journal of Human Evolution* 38 (March 2000): 347–365, at 359.

is needed. The available data at present are open to widely different interpretations."[81]

Paleoanthropologist Leslie Aiello states that when it comes to locomotion, "[a]ustralopithecines are like apes, and the *Homo* group are like humans. Something major occurred when *Homo* evolved, and it wasn't just in the brain."[82] The "something major" was the abrupt appearance of the human-like body plan—without direct evolutionary precursors in the fossil record.

V. Lacking Intermediates

If humans evolved from ape-like creatures, what were the transitional species between the ape-like hominins just discussed and the truly human-like members of the *Homo* genus found in the fossil record?

There aren't any good candidates.

A. The Demise of *Homo habilis*

Many have cited *Homo habilis* (literally "handy man") as a tool-using species that was a transitional "link" between the australopithecines and *Homo*.[83] But its association with tools is doubtful and appears driven mainly by evolutionary considerations.[84] Many questions remain about exactly which specimens belong to "*habilis*." Ian Tattersall, an anthropologist at the American Museum of Natural History, calls it "a wastebasket taxon, little more than a convenient recipient for a motley assortment of hominin fossils,"[85] and believes "more than one hominid species is represented."[86] Penn State paleoanthropologist

---

81. M. Maurice Abitbol, "Lateral View of *Australopithecus afarensis*: Primitive Aspects of Bipedal Positional Behavior in the Earliest Hominids," *Journal of Human Evolution* 28 (March 1995): 211–229 (internal citations removed).

82. Leslie Aiello, quoted in Leakey and Lewin, *Origins Reconsidered*, 196. See also Bernard Wood and Mark Collard, "The Human Genus," *Science* 284 (April 2, 1999): 65–71.

83. See Alan Walker and Pat Shipman, *Wisdom of the Bones: In Search of Human Origins* (New York: Alfred Knopf, 1996), 133 (expressing skepticism of *Homo habilis* as a "link," but stating, "if there is one attribute that has defined *habilis* from the very beginning, it is its intermediate position between australopithecines and *Homo erectus*.")

84. Jeffrey H. Schwartz and Ian Tattersall, "Defining the Genus *Homo*," *Science* 349 (August 28, 2015): 931–932.

85. Ian Tattersall, "The Many Faces of *Homo habilis*," *Evolutionary Anthropology* 1 (1992): 33–37.

86. Ian Tattersall and Jeffrey H. Schwartz, "Evolution of the Genus *Homo*," *Annual Review of Earth and Planetary Sciences* 37 (2009): 67–92. Another paper notes, "fossils attributed to *H. habilis* are poorly associated with inadequate and fragmentary postcrania" (Daniel E. Lieberman, David R. Pilbeam, and Richard W. Wrangham, "The Transition from *Australopithecus* to *Homo*,"

Alan Walker explains the severity of these disagreements: "[T]his is not a matter of some fragmentary fossils that are difficult to agree on. Whole crania are placed by different people in different species or even genera."[87] Even ignoring these difficulties and assuming *habilis* was a real species, chronology precludes it from being ancestral to *Homo*: habiline remains *postdate* the earliest fossil evidence of the genus *Homo*.[88]

Morphological analyses further confirm that *habilis* makes an unlikely "intermediate" between *Australopithecus* and *Homo*—and show *Homo habilis* doesn't even belong in *Homo*. An authoritative review in *Science*, by Bernard Wood and Mark Collard, found that *habilis* differs from *Homo* in terms of body size, shape, mode of locomotion, jaws and teeth, developmental patterns, and brain size, and should be reclassified within *Australopithecus*.[89] Another article in *Science* similarly notes that *habilis* "matured and moved less like a human and more like an australopithecine," and had a diet "more like Lucy's than that of *H. erectus*."[90] Another paper found "postcranial remains of *H. habilis* appear to reflect an australopith-like body plan."[91]

Like the australopithecines, many features of *habilis* indicate they were more similar to modern apes than to humans. According to Wood, habilines "grew their teeth rapidly, like an African ape, in contrast to the slow dental development of modern humans."[92] An analysis in *Nature* of *habilis* ear canals found its skull is most similar to baboons and suggested *habilis* "relied *less* on bipedal behaviour than the

in *Transitions in Prehistory: Essays in Honor of Ofer Bar-Yosef*, ed. John J. Shea and Daniel E. Lieberman [Cambridge: Oxbow, 2009], 1; see also Ann Gibbons, "Who Was *Homo habilis*—And Was It Really *Homo?*," *Science* 332 [June 17, 2011]: 1370–1371 ["researchers labeled a number of diverse, fragmentary fossils from East Africa and South Africa '*H. habilis*,' making the taxon a 'grab bag, . . . a *Homo* waste bin,' says paleoanthropologist Chris Ruff of Johns Hopkins University in Baltimore, Maryland"]).

87. Alan Walker, "The Origin of the Genus *Homo*," in *The Origin and Evolution of Humans and Humanness*, ed. D. Tab Rasmussen (Boston: Jones and Bartlett, 1993), 31.

88. See F. Spoor, M. G. Leakey, P. N. Gathogo, et al., "Implications of New Early *Homo* Fossils from Ileret, East of Lake Turkana, Kenya," *Nature* 448 (August 9, 2007): 688–691; Seth Borenstein, "Fossils Paint Messy Picture of Human Origins," NBC News, August 8, 2007, accessed July 10, 2016, http://www.nbcnews.com/id/20178936/ns/technology_and_science-science/t/fossils-paint -messy-picture-human-origins/.

89. Wood and Collard, "Human Genus"; see also Mark Collard and Bernard Wood, "Defining the Genus *Homo*," in *Handbook of Paleoanthropology*, 2107–2144.

90. Gibbons, "Who Was *Homo habilis*?"

91. Lee R. Berger, John Hawks, Darryl J. de Ruiter, Steven E. Churchill, Peter Schmid, et al., "*Homo naledi*, a New Species of the Genus *Homo* from the Dinaledi Chamber, South Africa," *eLife* 4 (2015): e09560.

92. Wood's views are described in Gibbons, "Who Was *Homo habilis*?" See also Wood and Collard, "Human Genus."

australopithecines."[93] The article concluded that "the unique labyrinth of [the *habilis* skull] represents an unlikely intermediate between the morphologies seen in the australopithecines and *H. erectus*."[94]

A study by Sigrid Hartwig-Scherer and Robert D. Martin in the *Journal of Human Evolution* found the skeleton of *habilis* was *more* similar to living apes than were other australopithecines like Lucy.[95] They conclude, "It is difficult to accept an evolutionary sequence in which *Homo habilis*, with less human-like locomotor adaptations, is intermediate between *Australopithecus afaren[s]is* . . . and fully bipedal *Homo erectus*."[96] Alan Walker and Pat Shipman similarly called *habilis* "more apelike than Lucy" and remarked, "Rather than representing an intermediate between Lucy and humans, [*habilis*] looked very much like an intermediate between the ancestral chimplike condition and Lucy."[97] Hartwig-Scherer explains that *habilis* "displays much stronger similarities to African ape limb proportions" than Lucy—results she calls "unexpected in view of previous accounts of *Homo habilis* as a link between australopithecines and humans."[98]

B. *Homo naledi* versus *Australopithecus sediba*: The Link Resurrected?

The news media might be heavily biased toward evolution, but at least it is predictable. Whenever a new hominin fossil is discovered, reporters seize the opportunity to push human evolution. Thus it was no surprise when news outlets buzzed about the latest "human ancestor" after a new species, *Homo naledi*, was unveiled in 2015.

CNN declared, "*Homo naledi*: New Species of Human Ancestor Discovered in South Africa."[99] *The Daily Mail* reported, "Scientists

---

93. Spoor et al., "Implications of Early Hominid Labyrinthine Morphology for Evolution of Human Bipedal Locomotion," emphasis added.

94. Ibid.

95. Sigrid Hartwig-Scherer and Robert D. Martin, "Was 'Lucy' More Human than Her 'Child'? Observations on Early Hominid Postcranial Skeletons," *Journal of Human Evolution* 21 (1991): 439–449.

96. Ibid.

97. Walker and Shipman, *Wisdom of the Bones*, 132, 130.

98. Sigrid Hartwig-Scherer, "Apes or Ancestors?" in *Mere Creation: Science, Faith, and Intelligent Design*, ed. William Dembski (Downers Grove, IL: InterVarsity Press, 1998), 226.

99. David McKenzie and Hamilton Wende, "*Homo naledi*: New Species of Human Ancestor Discovered in South Africa," CNN, September 10, 2015, June 12, 2016, http://www.cnn.com/2015/09/10/africa/homo-naledi-human-relative-species/.

Discover Skull of New Human Ancestor *Homo Naledi.*"[100] *PBS* pronounced, "Trove of Fossils from a Long Lost Human Ancestor."[101]
And so on.

To be sure, the find is striking because it represents probably the
largest cache of hominin bones—many hundreds—ever found. In a
field where a single scrap of jaw ignites the community, this is a big
deal. But do we know that *Homo naledi* is a "human ancestor," as
so many news outlets declared? As usual, dig into the details and the
answer is no.

The primary claim about *Homo naledi* is that it was a "transitional
form" or "mosaic"—a small-brained, upright-walking hominin with a
trunk similar to the australopithecines, but with human-like hands and
feet. But the technical material shows that even some of those supposedly human-like traits have unique features:

- The hands showed "a unique combination of anatomy"[102] including "unique first metacarpal morphology,"[103] and long,
  curved fingers which suggest *naledi* was, unlike humans, well-
  suited for "climbing and suspension."[104]
- Its foot "differs from modern humans in having more curved
  proximal pedal phalanges, and features suggestive of a reduced
  medial longitudinal arch," giving it an overall "unique locomotor repertoire."[105] The foot shows, again, that unlike humans, it
  was "likely comfortable climbing trees."[106]

The technical papers also reveal "unique features in the femur

100. Rachel Reilly, "Is This the First Human? Extraordinary Find in a South African Cave Suggests Man May Be up to 2.8 Million Years Old," *Daily Mail*, September 10, 2015, accessed July
10, 2016, http://www.dailymail.co.uk/sciencetech/article-3228991/New-species-ancient-human
-discovered-Fossilised-remains-15-bodies-unearthed-South-African-cave.html.

101. "Trove of Fossils from a Long-Lost Human Ancestor Is Greatest Find in Decades," PBS
Newshour, September 10, 2015, accessed July 10, 2016, http://www.pbs.org/newshour/bb/trove
-fossils-long-lost-human-ancestor-greatest-find-decades/.

102. "The Hand and Foot of *Homo naledi*," *ScienceDaily*, October 6, 2015, accessed July 10,
2016, http://www.sciencedaily.com/releases/2015/10/151006123631.htm.

103. Berger et al., "*Homo naledi*, a New Species of the Genus *Homo*."

104. Tracy L. Kivell, Andrew S. Deane, Matthew W. Tocheri, et al., "The Hand of *Homo naledi*," *Nature Communications* 6 (October 6, 2015): 8431.

105. W. E. H. Harcourt-Smith, Z. Throckmorton, K. A. Congdon, et al., "The Foot of *Homo
naledi*," *Nature Communications* 6 (October 6, 2015): 8432.

106. "Foot Fossils of Human Relative Illustrate Evolutionary 'Messiness' of Bipedal Walking,"
ScienceDaily, October 6, 2015, accessed June 12, 2016, http://www.sciencedaily.com/releases/2015
/10/151006131938.htm.

and tibia"—making a hindlimb which "differs from those of all other known hominins."[107] As for the head, "Cranial morphology of *H. naledi* is unique . . . "[108] Sound familiar? Whatever it was, overall *naledi* appears highly unique.

Indeed, the discoverers of *naledi* called it "a unique mosaic previously unknown in the human fossil record."[109] Such terminology should raise a red flag. In the parlance of evolutionary biology, "mosaic" usually means a fossil has a suite of traits that are difficult to fit into the standard evolutionary tree. This is the case here.

In 2010, some of the same scientists who discovered and promoted *naledi*—a team led by Lee Berger of the University of Witwatersrand— were promoting a *different* hominin species, *Australopithecus sediba*, as the intermediate *du jure* between the australopithecines and *Homo*. However, *sediba* and *naledi* differ in important ways that make them unlikely partners in an evolutionary lineage. Specifically, *sediba* (classified within *Australopithecus*) had an advanced "*Homo*-like pelvis,"[110] "surprisingly human teeth,"[111] and a "human-like" lower trunk,[112] whereas *naledi*—placed within *Homo*—bears an "australopith-like" and "primitive" pelvis,[113] "primitive" teeth, and a "primitive or australopith-like trunk."[114] An australopithecine with apparently advanced *Homo*-like features seems a poor candidate to evolve *into* a member of *Homo* with primitive australopith-like versions of those

---

107. Berger et al., "*Homo naledi*, a New Species of the Genus *Homo*."

108. Ibid.

109. Harcourt-Smith et al., "Foot of *Homo naledi*."

110. Kate Wong, "First of Our Kind," *Scientific American*, November 1, 2012, accessed July 10, 2016, http://www.scientificamerican.com/article/first-of-our-kind-2012-12-07/. See also Brandon Bryn, "*Australopithecus sediba* May Have Paved the Way for *Homo*," AAAS News, September 8, 2011, accessed July 10, 2016, http://www.aaas.org/news/science-australopithecus-sediba-may-have-paved-way-homo.

111. Ann Gibbons, "A Human Smile and Funny Walk for *Australopithecus sediba*," *Science* 340 (April 12, 2013): 132–133. See also Nadia Ramlagan, "Human Evolution Takes a Twist with *Australopithecus sediba*," AAAS News, April 11, 2013, accessed July 10, 2016, http://www.aaas.org/news/science-human-evolution-takes-twist-australopithecus-sediba.

112. Peter Schmid, Steven E. Churchill, Shahed Nalla, et al., "Mosaic Morphology in the Thorax of *Australopithecus sediba*," *Science* 340 (April 12, 2013): 1234598; Charles Q. Choi, "Humanity's Closest Ancestor Was Pigeon-Toed, Research Reveals," *LiveScience*, April 11, 2013, accessed July 10, 2011, http://www.livescience.com/28656-closest-human-ancestor-was-pigeon-toed.html.

113. Caroline Vansickle, Zachary D. Cofran, Daniel Garcia-Martinez, et al., "Primitive Pelvic Features in a New Species of *Homo*," The 85th Annual Meeting of the American Association of Physical Anthropologists, 2016, accessed July 10, 2016, http://meeting.physanth.org/program/2016/session39/vansickle-2016-primitive-pelvic-features-in-a-new-species-of-homo.html.

114. Berger et al., "*Homo naledi*, a New Species of the Genus *Homo*."

same features. If the goal is to elucidate a lineage ending with modern humans, key traits are evolving in the wrong direction. Thus, although both *sediba* and *naledi* have been called a "human ancestor"—by some of the same people, no less—evolutionarily speaking, both claims should not be true (unless you're willing to tolerate a very messy tree). As one news outlet put it, "Each [*sediba* and *naledi*] has different sets of australopith-like and human-like traits that can't be easily reconciled on the same family tree."[115]

(Paleoanthropologists have also criticized claims that *sediba* was our ancestor. One called it "way too primitive to be the ancestor of the human genus *Homo*" and warned the fossil "is surrounded by hype and over-interpretation."[116] Another thought it merely represents *Australopithecus africanus*.[117] Others have observed that *sediba* postdates *Homo*, and has the wrong traits.[118] Commenting on *sediba*, Harvard's Daniel Lieberman said, "The origins of the genus *Homo* remain as murky as ever,"[119] and Donald Johanson remarked, "The transition to *Homo* continues to be almost totally confusing."[120] Even Lee Berger acknowledged when publishing on *sediba* that "the ancestry of *Homo* and its relation to earlier australopithecines remain unresolved."[121])

Another dubious claim about *naledi* is that it intentionally buried

115. Ed Yong, "6 Tiny Cavers, 15 Odd Skeletons, and 1 Amazing New Species of Ancient Human," *The Atlantic*, September 10, 2015, accessed July 10, 2016, http://www.theatlantic.com/science/archive/2015/09/homo-naledi-rising-star-cave-hominin/404362/.

116. Hugh Macknight, "Experts Reject New Human Species Theory," *The Independent*, April 8, 2010, accessed July 10, 2016, http://www.independent.co.uk/news/science/experts-reject-new-human-species-theory-1939512.html.

117. See Michael Balter, "Candidate Human Ancestor from South Africa Sparks Praise and Debate," *Science* 328 (April 9, 2010): 154–155.

118. See Tim White, "Five's a Crowd in Our Family Tree," *Current Biology* 23 (February 4, 2013): R112–R115; William H. Kimbel, "Hesitation on Hominin History," *Nature* 497 (May 30, 2013): 573–574; Gibbons, "Human Smile and Funny Walk for *Australopithecus sediba*"; Gibbons, "Who Was *Homo habilis*?" *Science* 332 (June 17, 2011): 1370–1371; Nicholas Wade, "New Fossils May Redraw Human Ancestry," *New York Times*, September 8, 2011, accessed July 10, 2016, http://www.nytimes.com/2011/09/09/science/09fossils.html; John Noble Wilford, "Some Prehumans Feasted on Bark instead of Grasses," *New York Times*, June 27, 2012, accessed July 10, 2016, http://www.nytimes.com/2012/06/28/science/australopithecus-sediba-preferred-forest-foods-fossil-teeth-suggest.html.

119. Carl Zimmer, "Yet Another 'Missing Link'," *Slate*, April 8, 2010, accessed July 10, 2016, http://www.slate.com/articles/health_and_science/science/2010/04/yet_another_missing_link.single.html.

120. Balter, "Candidate Human Ancestor from South Africa."

121. Lee R. Berger, Darryl J. de Ruiter, Steven E. Churchill, et al., "*Australopithecus sediba*: A New Species of *Homo*-Like Australopith from South Africa," *Science* 328 (April 9, 2010): 195–204.

its dead—a testimony to its supposedly human-like intellect. Burying dead in the cave where it was found would require shimmying through a steep, narrow crevice while dragging a body a long distance in the dark—a physically challenging task for any hominin of any level of intelligence. For many reasons, multiple scientists—including two of Berger's colleagues at the University of Witwatersrand—dispute the intentional burial hypothesis.[122] Alison Brooks of George Washington University observed that claims of intentional burial are "so far out there that they really need a higher standard of proof."[123]

There are also controversies about whether *naledi* belongs within *Homo*. Biological classification is a subjective enterprise, but given the species's small brain and australopith-like pelvis and trunk, its placement within *Homo* has proven controversial. Even Berger predicted, "There may be debate over the *Homo* designation" as "the species is quite different from anything else we have seen."[124] Ian Tattersall writes that *naledi* "possesses an unusual combination of morphological attributes" which "seem to align more with the australopiths than with any *Homo*."[125] A 2016 study found that *naledi*'s place within *Homo* is "ambiguous," and concluded *naledi* doesn't appear intermediate between *Australopithecus* and *Homo*.[126]

A final deathblow to claims for *Homo naledi* as an ancestral or transitional fossil is its age. When first published, *naledi*'s promoters suggested, on the basis of evolutionary considerations rather than geological evidence, that it lived 2–3 mya. But at that time the fossils hadn't been dated geologically, leading Carol Ward of the University

122. See Kate Wong, "Debate Erupts over Strange New Human Species," *Scientific American*, April 8, 2016, accessed July 10, 2016, http://www.scientificamerican.com/article/debate-erupts-over-strange-new-human-species/; Tanya Farber, "Professor's Claims Rattle *Naledi*'s bones," *Sunday Times*, April 24, 2016, accessed July 10, 2016, http://www.timeslive.co.za/sundaytimes/stnews/2016/04/24/Professors-claims-rattle-Naledis-bones; Aurore Val, "Deliberate Body Disposal by Hominins in the Dinaledi Chamber, Cradle of Humankind, South Africa?," *Journal of Human Evolution* (2016), http://dx.doi.org/10.1016/j.jhevol.2016.02.004.
123. Kate Wong, "Mysterious New Human Species Emerges from Heap of Fossils," *Scientific American*, September 10, 2015, accessed July 10, 2016, http://www.scientificamerican.com/article/mysterious-new-human-species-emerges-from-heap-of-fossils/.
124. John Noble Wilford, "*Homo Naledi*, New Species in Human Lineage, Is Found in South African Cave," *New York Times*, September 10, 2015, accessed July 10, 2016, http://www.nytimes.com/2015/09/11/science/south-africa-fossils-new-species-human-ancestor-homo-naledi.html.
125. Ian Tattersall, "The Genus *Homo*," *Inference Review* 2 (2016), accessed July 10, 2016, http://inference-review.com/article/the-genus-homo.
126. Mana Dembo, Davorka Radovčić, Heather M. Garvin, Myra F. Laird, Lauren Schroeder, et al., "The Evolutionary Relationships and Age of *Homo naledi*: An Assessment Using Dated Bayesian Phylogenetic Methods," *Journal of Human Evolution* 97 (2016): 17–26.

of Missouri to warn, "Without dates, the fossils reveal almost nothing about hominin evolution."[127] This didn't stop paleoanthropologists from speculating about its evolutionary importance. They claimed *naledi* probably lived 2–3 mya and stated, "If these fossils are late Pliocene [~3–2.5 mya] or early Pleistocene [~2.5–2 mya], it is possible that this new species of small-brained, early *Homo* represents an intermediate between *Australopithecus* and *Homo erectus*."[128] In 2017 *Homo naledi*'s remains were "surprisingly" dated to the "startlingly young" age of between 236,000 and 335,000 years[129]—an order of magnitude younger than the age predicted by evolutionary considerations, and far too young to be related to the evolution of humans or ancestral to our species. Writing for BioLogos, anthropologist James Kidder candidly admitted, "Nearly everyone in the scientific community thought that the date of the *Homo naledi* fossils, when calculated, would fall within the same general time period as other primitive early *Homo* remains. We were wrong."[130]

Five years before the unveiling of *naledi*, the media touted *sediba* as the newest human ancestor. But cooler heads prevailed, and it was shown that *sediba* was not our ancestor. What will become of *Homo naledi*? Many have protested the "hype" over *naledi*,[131] and its trajectory resembles other hominins for which hyped claims of "transi-

127. Quoted in Yong, "6 Tiny Cavers."

128. University of Colorado Anschutz Medical Campus, "Ancient Ancestor of Humans with Tiny Brain Discovered," *ScienceDaily*, September 10, 2015, accessed July 3, 2017, https://www.sciencedaily.com/releases/2015/09/150910084610.htm; Pallab Ghosh, "New Human-Like Species Discovered in S Africa," *BBC News*, September 10, 2015, accessed July 3, 2017, http://www.bbc.com/news/science-environment-34192447; Paul Rincon, "Primitive Human 'Lived Much More Recently'," *BBC News*, April 25, 2017, accessed July 3, 2017, http://www.bbc.com/news/science-environment-39710315.

129. University of the Witwatersrand, "Homo Naledi's Surprisingly Young Age Opens Up More Questions on Where We Come From," *ScienceDaily*, May 9, 2017, accessed July 3, 2017; https://www.sciencedaily.com/releases/2017/05/170509083554.htm. See also Paul H. G. M. Dirks et al., "The Age of *Homo naledi* and Associated Sediments in the Rising Star Cave, South Africa," *eLife* 6 (2017): e24231.

130. James Kidder, "What Homo Naledi Means for the Study of Human Evolution," BioLogos, May 30, 2017, accessed July 3, 2017, http://biologos.org/blogs/guest/what-homo-naledi-means-for-the-study-of-human-evolution.

131. See Chris Stringer, "Human Evolution: The Many Mysteries of *Homo naledi*," *eLife* 4 (2015): e10627; Daniel Curnoe, "What about *Homo naledi*'s Geologic Age?," Phys.org, September 15, 2015, accessed July 13, 2016, http://phys.org/news/2015-09-opinion-homo-naledi-geologic-age.html; Michael Shermer, "Did This Extinct Human Species Commit Homicide?," *Scientific American*, January 1, 2016, accessed July 10, 2016, http://www.scientificamerican.com/article/did-this-extinct-human-species-commit-homicide1/; Michael Shermer, "*Homo naledi* and Human Nature," *Scientific American*, January 7, 2016, accessed July 10, 2016, http://blogs.scientificamerican.com/guest-blog/homo-naledi-and-human-nature/.

tional" or "ancestral" status eventually failed. When evaluating media claims of the newest "human ancestor," a dose of healthy skepticism is warranted.

VI. A Big Bang Origin of *Homo*

After realizing that *habilis* could not serve as a "link" between *Homo* and *Australopithecus*, two paleoanthropologists lamented, "this muddle leaves *Homo erectus* without a clear ancestor, without a past."[132] Indeed, with species like *habilis*, *sediba*, or *naledi* unable to serve as intermediates, it is difficult to find fossil hominins to serve as direct transitional forms between the ape-like australopithecines and the first human-like members of *Homo*. The fossil record shows abrupt changes which correspond to the appearance of our genus *Homo* about two mya.

From its first appearance, *Homo erectus* was very human-like, and differed markedly from prior hominins which were *not* human-like. Yet *Homo erectus* appears *abruptly*, without apparent evolutionary precursors. An article in *Nature* explains:

> The origins of the widespread, polymorphic, Early Pleistocene *H. erectus* lineage remain elusive. The marked contrasts between any potential ancestor (*Homo habilis* or other) and the earliest known *H. erectus* might signal an abrupt evolutionary emergence some time before its first known appearance in Africa at ~1.78 Myr [million years ago]. Uncertainties surrounding the taxon's appearance in Eurasia and southeast Asia make it impossible to establish accurately the time or place of origin for *H. erectus*. . . . Whatever its time and place of origin, and direction of spread, this species dispersed widely, and possibly abruptly, before 1.5 Myr.[133]

That article was written in 2002, but the problem remains. A 2016 paper admits, "Although the transition from *Australopithecus* to *Homo* is usually thought of as a momentous transformation, the fossil record bearing on the origin and earliest evolution of *Homo* is virtu-

---

132. Walker and Shipman, *Wisdom of the Bones*, 134.
133. Berhane Asfaw, W. Henry Gilbert, Yonas Beyene, et al., "Remains of *Homo erectus* from Bouri, Middle Awash, Ethiopia," *Nature* 416 (March 21, 2002): 317–320.

ally undocumented."[134] While that paper argues that the evolutionary distance between *Australopithecus* and *Homo* is small, it nonetheless concedes that "By almost all accounts, the earliest populations of the *Homo* lineage emerged from a still unknown ancestral species in Africa at some point between approximately 3 and approximately 2 million years ago."[135]

Early members of *Homo*, namely *Homo erectus*, show unique and previously unseen features that contributed to this "abrupt" appearance. The technical literature observes an "explosion,"[136] "rapid increase,"[137] and "approximate doubling"[138] in brain size associated with the appearance of *Homo*. Wood and Collard's major *Science* review found that *only one single trait of one hominin species qualified as "intermediate"* between *Australopithecus* and *Homo*: the brain size of *Homo erectus*.[139] However, this one trait does not necessarily indicate that humans evolved from less intelligent hominids. Intelligence is determined largely by internal brain organization, and is much more complex than the singular dimension of brain size.[140] Indeed, brain size is not always a good indicator of intelligence or evolutionary rela-

---

134. William H. Kimbel and Brian Villmoare, "From *Australopithecus* to *Homo*: The Transition that Wasn't," *Philosophical Transactions of the Royal Society B* 371 (2016): 20150248.

135. Ibid. The article maintains that "expanded brain size, human-like wrist and hand anatomy, dietary eclecticism and potential tool-making capabilities of 'generalized' australopiths root the *Homo* lineage in ancient hominin adaptive trends, suggesting that the 'transition' from *Australopithecus* to *Homo* may not have been that much of a transition at all." However, there are many reasons to dispute those claims. Many sources have noted the abrupt increase in brain size associated with the appearance of *Homo*. See below, notes 136–138 and accompanying text. Moreover, claims of australopith toolmaking are not established, and the paper's assertion of "dietary eclecticism" in *Australopithecus* does not account for the dramatic changes we see in *Homo erectus* versus *Australopithecus* regarding diet and foraging behavior. See below, notes 160–163 and accompanying text.

136. Stanley A. Rice, *Encyclopedia of Evolution* (New York: Checkmark, 2007), 241.

137. Franz M. Wuketits, "Charles Darwin, Paleoanthropology, and the Modern Synthesis," in *Handbook of Paleoanthropology*, 97–125, at 116. See also Susanne Shultz, Emma Nelson, and Robin I. M. Dunbar, "Hominin Cognitive Evolution: Identifying Patterns and Processes in the Fossil and Archaeological Record," *Philosophical Transactions of the Royal Society B* 367 (2012): 2130–2140. See also William R. Leonard, J. Josh Snodgrass, and Marcia L. Robertson, "Effects of Brain Evolution on Human Nutrition and Metabolism," *Annual Review of Nutrition* 27 (2007): 311–327.

138. Dean Falk, "Hominid Brain Evolution: Looks Can Be Deceiving," *Science* 280 (June 12, 1998): 1714 (diagram description omitted).

139. Specifically, *Homo erectus* is said to have intermediate brain size, and *Homo ergaster* is said to have a *Homo*-like postcranial skeleton with a smaller, more australopith-like brain size.

140. Terrance W. Deacon, "Problems of Ontogeny and Phylogeny in Brain-Size Evolution," *International Journal of Primatology* 11 (1990): 237–282. See also Terrence W. Deacon, "What Makes the Human Brain Different?," *Annual Review of Anthropology* 26 (1997): 337–357; Stephen Molnar, *Human Variation: Races, Types, and Ethnic Groups*, 5th ed. (Upper Saddle River, NJ: Prentice Hall, 2002), 189 ("The size of the brain is but one of the factors related to human intelligence").

tionships, as Wood and Collard observe: "Relative brain size does not group the fossil hominins in the same way as the other variables. This pattern suggests that the link between relative brain size and adaptive zone is a complex one."[141] Case in point: Neanderthals had an average skull size *larger* than modern humans. Given the range of modern human skull size variation (see Table 14.1), a progression of relatively small to very large skulls could easily be concocted using bones from living humans alone. Such a lineup might give the false impression of some evolutionary lineage when it is no such thing. Moreover, as seen in Table 14.1, *erectus* had an average brain size within the range of modern human variation. Finding a few skulls of "intermediate" size does little to demonstrate that humans evolved from primitive ancestors.

Much like the explosive increase in skull size, a study of the pelvis bones of australopithecines and *Homo* found "a period of very rapid evolution corresponding to the emergence of the genus *Homo*."[142] One *Nature* paper noted that early *Homo erectus* shows "such a radical departure from previous forms of *Homo* (such as *H. habilis*) in its height, reduced sexual dimorphism, long limbs and modern body proportions that it is hard at present to identify its immediate ancestry in east Africa"[143]—or anywhere else, for that matter. A paper in the *Journal of Molecular Biology and Evolution* found that *Homo* and *Australopithecus* differ significantly in brain size, dental function, increased cranial buttressing, expanded body height, vision, and respiration, and stated,

> We, like many others, interpret the anatomical evidence to show that early *H. sapiens* was significantly and dramatically different from . . . australopithecines in virtually every element of its skeleton and every remnant of its behavior.[144]

Noting these many differences, the study called the origin of humans "a real acceleration of evolutionary change from the more slowly chang-

---

141. Wood and Collard, "Human Genus," 70.
142. Marchal, "New Morphometric Analysis of the Hominid Pelvic Bone," 347, 362.
143. Robin Dennell and Wil Roebroeks, "An Asian Perspective on Early Human Dispersal from Africa," *Nature* 438 (Dec. 22/29, 2005): 1099–1104.
144. John Hawks, Keith Hunley, Sang-Hee Lee, and Milford Wolpoff, "Population Bottlenecks and Pleistocene Human Evolution," *Molecular Biology and Evolution* 17 (2000): 2–22, at 3.

ing pace of australopithecine evolution" and stated that such a transformation would have required radical changes:

> The anatomy of the earliest *H. sapiens* sample indicates significant modifications of the ancestral genome and is not simply an extension of evolutionary trends in an earlier australopithecine lineage throughout the Pliocene. In fact, its combination of features never appears earlier.[145]

These rapid and unique changes are termed "a genetic revolution" where "no australopithecine species is obviously transitional."[146]

For those not constrained by an evolutionary paradigm, it is not obvious that this transition took place at all. The stark lack of fossil evidence for this hypothesized transition is confirmed by three Harvard paleoanthropologists:

> Of the various transitions that occurred during human evolution, the transition from *Australopithecus* to *Homo* was undoubtedly one of the most critical in its magnitude and consequences. As with many key evolutionary events, there is both good and bad news. First, the bad news is that many details of this transition are obscure because of the paucity of the fossil and archaeological records.[147]

As for the "good news," they admit, "[A]lthough we lack many details about exactly how, when, and where the transition occurred from *Australopithecus* to *Homo*, we have sufficient data from before and after the transition to make some inferences about the overall nature of key changes that did occur."[148]

In other words, the fossil record shows ape-like australopithecines ("before"), and human-like *Homo* ("after"), but not fossils documenting a transition between them. In the absence of intermediates, we're left with inferences of a transition based strictly on the assumption of evolution—that an undocumented transition must have occurred somehow, sometime, and someplace. They assume this transition happened, even though we do not have fossils documenting it.

---

145. Ibid., 4.
146. Ibid.
147. Lieberman, Pilbeam, and Wrangham, "Transition from *Australopithecus* to *Homo*," 1.
148. Ibid.

Even *Science* admits, "Our genus *Homo* is thought to have evolved a little more than 2 million years ago from the earlier hominid *Australopithecus*. But there are few fossils that provide detailed information on this transition."[149] Likewise, William Kimbel of Arizona State University stated in *Nature*, "The evolutionary events that led to the origin of the *Homo* lineage are an enduring puzzle in palaeoanthropology."[150] Another review similarly notes the "seemingly abrupt appearance of *H. erectus*."[151] Similarly, the great evolutionary biologist Ernst Mayr recognized the abrupt appearance of our genus:

> The earliest fossils of *Homo*, *Homo rudolfensis* and *Homo erectus*, are separated from *Australopithecus* by a large, unbridged gap. How can we explain this seeming saltation? Not having any fossils that can serve as missing links, we have to fall back on the time-honored method of historical science, the construction of a historical narrative.[152]

Another commentator proposed that the evidence implies a "big bang theory" of the appearance of *Homo*.[153] This large, unbridged gap between the ape-like australopithecines and the abruptly appearing human-like members of genus *Homo* challenges evolutionary accounts of human origins.

VII. All in the Family

In contrast to the australopithecines, the major members of *Homo*— *erectus* and the Neanderthals (*Homo neanderthalensis*)—are very similar to us. Some paleoanthropologists have even classified *erectus* and *neanderthalensis* as members of our own species, *Homo sapiens*.[154]

---

149. Stella Hurtley, "From *Australopithecus* to *Homo*," *Science* 328 (April 9, 2010): 133.
150. Kimbel, "Hesitation on Hominin History."
151. Alan Turner and Hannah O'Regan, "Zoogeography: Primate and Early Hominin Distribution and Migration Patterns," in *Handbook of Paleoanthropology*, 623–642, at 630.
152. Ernst Mayr, *What Makes Biology Unique?: Considerations on the Autonomy of a Scientific Discipline* (Cambridge: Cambridge University Press, 2004), 198.
153. "New Study Suggests Big Bang Theory of Human Evolution," University of Michigan News Service, January 10, 2000, accessed July 10, 2016, http://www.umich.edu/~newsinfo/Releases/2000/Jan00/r011000b.html.
154. See, e.g., Eric Delson, "One Skull Does Not a Species Make," *Nature* 389 (October 2, 1997): 445–446; Hawks et al., "Population Bottlenecks and Pleistocene Human Evolution"; Emilio Aguirre, "*Homo erectus* and *Homo sapiens*: One or More Species?," in *100 Years of Pithecanthropus: The Homo erectus Problem 171 Courier Forschungsinstitut Senckenberg*, ed. Jens Lorenz (Frankfurt: Courier Forschungsinstitut Senckenberg, 1994), 333–339; Milford H. Wolpoff,

Homo erectus appears in the fossil record a little over two mya. Its name means "upright man," and unsurprisingly, below the neck they were extremely similar to us.[155] An Oxford University Press volume notes *erectus* was "humanlike in its stature, body mass, and body proportions."[156] An analysis of 1.5-million-year-old *Homo erectus* footprints[157] indicates "a modern human style of walking" and "human-like social behaviours."[158] Unlike the australopithecines and habilines, *erectus* is the "earliest species to demonstrate the modern human semicircular [ear] canal morphology."[159] Another study found that total energy expenditure (TEE), a complex character related to body size, diet, and food-gathering activity, "increased substantially in *Homo erectus* relative to the earlier australopithecines," approaching the high TEE value of modern humans.[160] Researchers believe the *earliest* representatives of *Homo erectus* were "*more similar* to modern humans than to the earlier *and contemporaneous* australopithecines," due to their "larger relative brain sizes, larger bodies, slower rates of growth and maturation, dedicated bipedal locomotion, and smaller teeth and jaws,"[161] and "major changes" in diet and foraging behavior.[162] These features reflect "a lifestyle that was more similar to that of modern humans than that inferred for earlier and contempo-

Alan G. Thorne, Jan Jelínek, and Zhang Yinyun, "The Case for Sinking *Homo erectus*: 100 Years of *Pithecanthropus* Is Enough!," in *100 Years of Pithecanthropus*, 341–361.

155. See Hartwig-Scherer and Martin, "Was 'Lucy' More Human than Her 'Child'?"

156. William R. Leonard, Marcia L. Robertson, and J. Josh Snodgrass, "Energetic Models of Human Nutritional Evolution," in *Evolution of the Human Diet: The Known, the Unknown, and the Unknowable*, ed. Peter S. Ungar (Oxford, UK: Oxford University Press, 2007), 344–359.

157. Kevin G. Hatala, Neil T. Roach, Kelly R. Ostrofsky, Roshna E. Wunderlich, Heather L. Dingwall, et al., "Footprints Reveal Direct Evidence of Group Behavior and Locomotion in *Homo erectus*," *Scientific Reports* 6 (2016): 28766, doi:10.1038/srep28766.

158. "*Homo erectus* walked as we do," *ScienceDaily*, July 12, 2016, accessed July 14, 2016, https://www.sciencedaily.com/releases/2016/07/160712110444.htm.

159. Spoor et al., "Implications of Early Hominid Labyrinthine Morphology for Evolution of Human Bipedal Locomotion," 645.

160. William R. Leonard and Marcia L. Robertson, "Comparative Primate Energetics and Hominid Evolution," *American Journal of Physical Anthropology* 102 (February 1997): 265–281, at 279. See also Leslie C. Aiello and Jonathan C. K. Wells, "Energetics and the Evolution of the Genus *Homo*," *Annual Review of Anthropology* 31 (2002): 323–338.

161. Aiello and Wells, "Energetics and the Evolution of the Genus *Homo*," 323, emphases added.

162. William R. Leonard, J. Josh Snodgrass, and Marcia L. Robertson, "Effects of Brain Evolution on Human Nutrition and Metabolism," *Annual Review of Nutrition* 27 (2007): 311–327; William R. Leonard, Size Counts: Evolutionary Perspectives on Physical Activity and Body Size from Early Hominids to Modern Humans," *Journal of Physical Activity and Health* 7 (2010): S284–S298; Leonard et al., "Energetics and the Evolution of Brain Size in Early Homo." See also Aiello and Wells, "Energetics and the Evolution of the Genus *Homo*."

raneous hominins."[163] While the average brain-size of *Homo erectus* is less than the modern human average, *erectus* cranial capacities are within the range of normal human variation (Table 14.1).[164]

TABLE 14.1. Cranial Capacities of Extant and Extinct Hominids.[165]

Taxon:	Cranial Capacities:	Taxon Resembles:
Gorilla (*Gorilla gorilla*)	340–752 cc	Modern Apes
Chimpanzee (*Pan troglodytes*)	275–500 cc	
Australopithecus	370–515 cc (Avg. 457 cc)	
Homo habilis	Avg. 552 cc	
Homo erectus	850–1250 cc (Avg. 1016 cc)	Modern Humans
Neanderthals	1100–1700 cc (Avg. 1450 cc)	
Homo sapiens	800–2200 cc (Avg. 1345 cc)	

Donald Johanson suggests that, were *erectus* alive today, it could mate with modern humans to produce fertile offspring.[166] In other words, were it not for our separation by time, we might be considered interbreeding members of the same species.[167]

The *Cambridge Encyclopedia of Human Evolution* observes, "It is very difficult judging whether a particular kind of early human had developed a language, society or art."[168] Nonetheless, *erectus* remains

---

163. Ibid.

164. Moreover, "Although the relative brain size of *Homo erectus* is smaller than the average for modern humans, it is outside of the range seen among other living primate species" (William R. Leonard, Marcia L. Robertson, and J. Josh Snodgrass, "Energetics and the Evolution of Brain Size in Early *Homo*," in *Guts and Brains: An Integrative Approach to the Hominin Record*, ed. Wil Roebroeks [Leiden University Press, 2007], 29–46).

165. References for cranial capacities cited in Table 14.1 are as follows: Gorilla and chimpanzee: Stephen Molnar, *Human Variation: Races, Types, and Ethnic Groups*, 4th ed. (Upper Saddle River, NJ: Prentice Hall, 1998), 203; *Australopithecus*: Glenn C. Conroy, Gerhard W. Weber, Horst Seidler, Phillip V. Tobias, Alex Kane, Barry Brunsden, "Endocranial Capacity in an Early Hominid Cranium from Sterkfontein, South Africa," *Science* 280 (June 12, 1998): 1730–1731; Wood and Collard, "Human Genus"; *Homo habilis*: Wood and Collard, "Human Genus"; *Homo erectus*: Molnar, *Human Variation*, 203; Wood and Collard, "The Human Genus"; Neanderthals: Molnar, *Human Variation: Races, Types, and Ethnic Groups*, 4th ed., 203; Molnar, *Human Variation: Races, Types, and Ethnic Groups*, 5th ed., 189; *Homo sapiens* (modern man): Molnar, *Human Variation*, 203; E. I. Odokuma, P. S. Igbigbi, F. C. Akpuaka and U. B. Esigbenu, "Craniometric Patterns of Three Nigerian Ethnic Groups," *International Journal of Medicine and Medical Sciences* 2 (February 2010): 34–37; Molnar, *Human Variation*, 5th ed., 189.

166. Donald C. Johanson and Maitland Edey, *Lucy: The Beginnings of Humankind* (New York: Simon & Schuster, 1981), 144.

167. Ibid.

168. C. B. Stringer, "Evolution of Early Humans," in *Cambridge Encyclopedia of Human Evolution*, 241.

have been found on islands, where the most reasonable explanation is that they arrived by boat. Karl Wegmann of North Carolina State University said, "We all have this idea that early man was not terribly smart. The findings show otherwise—our ancestors were smart enough to build boats and adventurous enough to want to use them."[169]

As for Neanderthals, though they have been stereotyped as bungling and primitive, if a Neanderthal walked down the street, you probably wouldn't notice. Wood and Collard note, "skeletons of *H. neanderthalensis* indicate that their body shape was within the range of variation seen in modern humans."[170] Washington University paleoanthropologist Erik Trinkaus maintains that Neanderthals were no less intelligent than contemporary humans,[171] and argues, "They may have had heavier brows or broader noses or stockier builds, but behaviorally, socially and reproductively they were all just people."[172] University of Bordeaux archaeologist Francesco d'Errico agrees: "Neanderthals were using technology as advanced as that of contemporary anatomically modern humans and were using symbolism in much the same way."[173]

Though controversial, hard evidence backs these claims. Anthropologist Stephen Molnar explains that "the estimated mean size of [Neanderthal] cranial capacity (1,450 cc) is actually higher than the mean for modern humans (1,345 cc)."[174] One paper in *Nature* suggested, "the morphological basis for human speech capability appears to have been fully developed" in Neanderthals.[175] Indeed, Neanderthal remains have been found associated with signs of culture including art, burial of their dead, and complex tools[176]—including musical instru-

169. Jørn Madsen, "Who Was *Homo erectus*," *Science Illustrated* (July/August 2012): 23. See also Heather Pringle, "Primitive Humans Conquered Sea, Surprising Finds Suggest," *National Geographic*, February 17, 2010, accessed July 10, 2016, http://news.nationalgeographic.com/news/2010/02/100217-crete-primitive-humans-mariners-seafarers-mediterranean-sea/.
170. See Wood and Collard, "Human Genus," 68.
171. Marc Kaufman, "Modern Man, Neanderthals Seen as Kindred Spirits," *Washington Post*, April 30, 2007, accessed July 10, 2016, http://www.washingtonpost.com/wp-dyn/content/article/2007/04/29/AR2007042901101_pf.html.
172. Michael D. Lemonick, "A Bit of Neanderthal in Us All?," *Time*, April 25, 1999, accessed July 10, 2016, http://www.time.com/time/magazine/article/0,9171,23543,00.html.
173. Joe Alper, "Rethinking Neanderthals," *Smithsonian magazine* (June 2003).
174. Molnar, *Human Variation: Races, Types, and Ethnic Groups*, 5th ed., 189.
175. B. Arensburg, A. M. Tillier, B. Vandermeersch, H. Duday, L. A. Schepartz, and Y. Rak, "A Middle Palaeolithic Human Hyoid Bone," *Nature* 338 (April 27, 1989): 758–760.
176. Alper, "Rethinking Neanderthals"; Kate Wong, "Who Were the Neanderthals?," *Scientific American* (August 2003): 28–37; Erik Trinkaus and Pat Shipman, "Neanderthals: Images of Ourselves," *Evolutionary Anthropology* 1 (1993): 194–201; Philip G. Chase and April Nowell, "Taphonomy of a Suggested Middle Paleolithic Bone Flute from Slovenia," *Current Anthropology*

ments like the flute.[177] While dated, a 1908 report in *Nature* reports a Neanderthal type skeleton wearing chain mail armor.[178] Archaeologist Metin Eren said, regarding toolmaking, "in many ways, Neanderthals were just as smart or just as good as us."[179] Morphological mosaics—skeletons showing a mix of modern human and Neanderthal traits—suggest "Neandertals and modern humans are members of the same species who interbred freely."[180] Indeed, scientists now report Neanderthal DNA markers in living humans,[181] supporting proposals that Neanderthals were a sub-race of our own species.[182] As Trinkaus says regarding ancient Europeans and Neanderthals, "[W]e would understand both to be human. There's good reason to think that they did as well."[183]

Darwin skeptics continue to debate whether we are related to Neanderthals and *Homo erectus*, and evidence can be mounted both ways.[184] The present point, however, is this: *Even if* we do share common ancestry with Neanderthals or *erectus*, this does *not* show that we share ancestry with any non–human-like hominins.

As noted, Leslie Aiello observes, "Australopithecines are like apes, and the *Homo* group are like humans."[185] According to Siegrid Hartwig-Scherer, the differences between human-like members of *Homo* such as *erectus*, Neanderthals, and us reflect mere microevolutionary effects of "size variation, climatic stress, genetic drift and differential expression of [common] genes."[186] Whether we are related

39 (August/October 1998): 549–553; Tim Folger and Shanti Menon, " . . . Or Much Like Us?," *Discover* magazine, January, 1997, accessed July 10, 2016, http://discovermagazine.com/1997/jan /ormuchlikeus1026; Stringer, "Evolution of Early Humans," 248.

177. Chase and Nowell, "Taphonomy of a Suggested Middle Paleolithic Bone Flute from Slovenia"; Folger and Menon, " . . . Or Much Like Us?"

178. Notes in *Nature* 77 (April 23, 1908): 587.

179. Metub Eren, quoted in Jessica Ruvinsky, "Cavemen: They're Just Like Us," *Discover* magazine, January, 2009, accessed July 10, 2016, http://discovermagazine.com/2009/jan/008.

180. Erik Trinkaus and Cidália Duarte, "The Hybrid Child from Portugal," *Scientific American* (August 2003): 32. It is worth noting that some paleoanthropologists disagree about the existence of human-Neanderthal hybrids.

181. Rex Dalton, "Neanderthals May Have Interbred with Humans," *Nature News*, April 20, 2010, accessed July 10, 2016, http://www.nature.com/news/2010/100420/full/news.2010.194 .html.

182. Delson, "One Skull Does Not a Species Make."

183. Erik Trinkaus, quoted in Kaufman, "Modern Man, Neanderthals Seen as Kindred Spirits."

184. See, e.g., Fazale Rana and Hugh Ross, *Who Was Adam: A Creation Model Approach to the Origin of Man* (Colorado Springs, CO: NavPress, 2005).

185. Leakey and Lewin, *Origins Reconsidered*, 196. See also Wood and Collard, "Human Genus."

186. Hartwig-Scherer, "Apes or Ancestors," 220.

to them or not, these small-scale differences do *not* show the evolution of humans from non–human-like or ape-like creatures.

IX. Conclusion.

Despite the claims of evolutionary paleoanthropologists and unceasing media hype, the fragmented hominin fossil record does not document the evolution of humans from ape-like precursors. While the hominin fossil record is marked by incomplete and fragmented fossils, known hominins fall into two separate groups: ape-like and human-like, with a distinct gap between them. The genus *Homo* appears in an abrupt, non-Darwinian fashion, without evidence of an evolutionary transition from ape-like hominins. Other members of *Homo* appear very similar to modern humans, and their differences amount to small-scale microevolutionary change—providing no evidence that we are related to non–human-like species.

But there's more evidence that contradicts an evolutionary model.

Many researchers have recognized an "explosion"[187] of modern human-like culture in the archaeological record about thirty-five to forty thousand years ago, showing the abrupt appearance of human creativity,[188] technology, art,[189] and even paintings[190]—showing the rapid emergence of self-awareness, group identity, and symbolic thought.[191] One review dubbed this the "Creative Explosion."[192] Indeed, a 2014 paper coauthored by leading paleoanthropologists admits we have "essentially no explanation of how and why our linguistic computations and representations evolved," since "nonhuman animals provide virtually no relevant parallels to human linguistic communication."[193]

187. Paul Mellars, "Neanderthals and the Modern Human Colonization of Europe," *Nature* 432 (November 25, 2004): 461–465; April Nowell, "From A Paleolithic Art to Pleistocene Visual Cultures (Introduction to Two Special Issues on 'Advances in the Study of Pleistocene Imagery and Symbol Use')," *Journal of Archaeological Method and Theory* 13 (2006): 239–249. Others call this abrupt appearance a "revolution." See Ofer Bar-Yosef, "The Upper Paleolithic Revolution," *Annual Review of Anthropology* 31 (2002): 363–393.

188. Randall White, *Prehistoric Art: The Symbolic Journey of Humankind* (New York: Harry N. Abrams, 2003), 11, 231.

189. Rice, *Encyclopedia of Evolution*, 104, 187, 194.

190. Robert L. Kelly and David Hurst Thomas, *Archaeology*, 5th ed. (Belmont: Wadsworth Cengage Learning, 2010), 303.

191. Bar-Yosef, "Upper Paleolithic Revolution."

192. Nicholas Toth and Kathy Schick, "Overview of Paleolithic Archaeology," in *Handbook of Paleoanthropology*, 2441–2464.

193. Marc Hauser, Charles Yang, Robert Berwick, Ian Tattersall, Michael J. Ryan, Jeffrey Watumull, Noam Chomsky, and Richard C. Lewontin, "The Mystery of Language Evolution,"

This abrupt appearance of modern human-like morphology, intellect, and culture contradicts evolutionary models, and may indicate design events in human history.

Of course there is room for civil disagreement among Christians on these questions. But theistic evolutionists who believe that humans evolved from ape-like species should—at the very least—temper their rhetoric in light of the sparse fossil evidence. They certainly should not demand that the church accept the evolutionary "consensus" on human origins. The fossil evidence simply isn't that clear. If anything, the fossil record contradicts the central evolutionary claim that humans evolved from ape-like creatures.

After all, as noted earlier, two top paleoanthropologists have admitted that "the evolutionary sequence for the majority of hominin lineages is unknown."[194] With the fossil evidence for human evolution so weak, why should our theistic evolutionist brothers and sisters insist that the church must adopt their viewpoint?

Frontiers in Psychology 5 (May 7, 2014): 401.
    194. Wood and Grabowski, "Macroevolution in and around the Hominin Clade," 365.

15

Evidence for Human Uniqueness

ANN K. GAUGER, OLA HÖSSJER,
AND COLIN R. REEVES

*In terms of what makes us human, it's not the things that
are the same, it is the things that are different that matter.*

Jonathan Marks[1]

SUMMARY

Scientists claim that our extreme genetic similarity with chimps
(on the order of 98.7 percent identity) indicates we share common ancestry. This statement neglects several facts. First, our
genetic differences are larger than that number represents. Common estimates of similarity are based on comparisons of the *single
nucleotide changes only*, while other kinds of genetic differences
are disregarded. In addition, noncoding regions of DNA—long
thought to be nonfunctional "junk"—contain many kinds of
genetic regulatory elements, some of which are species-specific.
These species-specific regulatory elements make up a very small
proportion of the total count of differences, but have a significant
effect on how our genome works. For example, many of these
regulatory elements are known to affect gene expression in the
brain. Taken together, these species-specific genetic differences

1. Jonathan Marks, "What Is the Viewpoint of Hemoglobin, and Does It Matter?" *History and
Philosophy of Life Sciences* 31 (2009): 241–262.

contribute to our anatomical and physiological differences with chimps. In addition, there is not enough evolutionary time for all these coordinated changes to have happened by the mutation/ selection process. Thus the evidences for common ancestry put forward by various scientists are not as solid as they might seem. The more we learn about our human genome, the more it seems to be brilliantly and uniquely designed.

. . . . .

I. Introduction

In 2007, *Science* magazine published an essay titled "Relative Differences: The Myth of 1%," by Jon Cohen.[2] The essay challenged the received knowledge of our culture that we are genetically nearly identical with chimpanzees. Cohen detailed how our genetic differences are significantly higher than 1 percent. But this news did not penetrate the culture—numerous articles, books, newspapers, and TV science shows still use the 1 percent figure. Even the major scientific journal *Science* used it as recently as 2012.[3]

The underlying concept that gives this figure its persistence is common descent. This concept is something that most biologists treat as axiomatic, untouchable, and completely self-evident, which is why the figure of 1 percent has such staying power. Even if they disagree with the neo-Darwinian account of evolution (and some scientists do; see chapter 8), most scientists (including most theistic evolutionists) still accept our common ancestry with chimpanzees.

The question at hand, then, concerns the steps that supposedly took us from being ape-like to being human. Are we fancy apes, with all the evolutionary baggage that comes along with that, or are we unique beings with capabilities far beyond the reach of animal species? Because we do not have access to much information about our supposed common ancestor with chimps, we will address this question by examining how we differ from chimps in our genetics, physiology, anatomy, and more.

---

2. Jon Cohen, "Relative Differences: The Myth of 1%," *Science* 316 (2007): 1836.
3. Ann Gibbons, "Bonobos Join Chimps as Closest Human Relatives," *Science*, June 13, 2012, http://www.sciencemag.org/news/2012/06/bonobos-join-chimps-closest-human-relatives.

FIGURE 15.1. *Very short segment of DNA, composed of two strands of nucleotides (left to right) with nucleotides paired together (top to bottom).*

II. Definitions

Before we begin, we need to define a few basic terms. Others will be defined as we go along:

> *DNA* is composed of two very long complementary strands of nucleotides (called A, C, T and G), with each nucleotide from one strand paired with one from the other strand. They always pair together in the same way, A with T and C with G. (See Fig. 15.1 for an illustration.)

> *Nucleotides.* Nucleotides are the chemical building blocks out of which DNA and RNA are made.

> *DNA expression.* When DNA is copied into RNA and used to make something, we say that it has been expressed, just as reading a text out loud can be said to be expressing the text.

> *Chromosomes.* Our DNA is segmented into separate chromosomes, which function as units of inheritance. We typically have forty-six chromosomes in each cell. (Eggs and sperm have twenty-three chromosomes each.)

> *SNPs.* When DNA is compared between two copies of a chromosome from different individuals, for example, differences are usually found. Often they are single nucleotide changes, as in Figure 15.2, and are called single nucleotide polymorphisms (SNPs). We can also compare a chimpanzee's chromosomes with ours—they are very similar, similar enough to know which chimpanzee chromosome matches each of ours. What differences there are between our chromosomes and theirs can be identified. The differences can be as small as an SNP, or they can be rearrangements, duplications, deletions, or insertions of DNA.

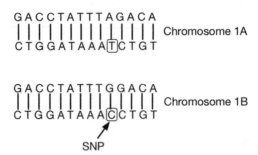

FIGURE 15.2. *Short sections of a chromosome pair with a single SNP between them.* Note that there is a nucleotide change in a single position on each strand. In this case the SNP refers to the change from T in chromosome 1A to C in chromosome 1B. Because nucleotides always pair together, A with T and G with C, the indicated change of T to C also changes the paired nucleotide on the other strand (changing an A to G.)

Gene. A gene is defined as DNA that carries information about how to make one or more proteins or RNAs.

RNA. RNAs are strings of nucleotides that are copied from genes and are used in a variety of ways by the cell. RNAs express the information in the DNA in order to carry out its function.

Amino acids. Amino acids are the molecular units that comprise a protein.

Proteins. Proteins are the building blocks from which the cell is primarily constructed, and they do the work of the cell, carrying out chemical reactions necessary for the cell to function. Each protein is made of a long string of amino acids whose sequence (order in the string) is specified by its corresponding coding sequence in the DNA.

Protein translation. DNA carries the information for how to make proteins, but the information carried in DNA needs to be interpreted by the cell: DNA is to be copied into RNA (DNA is *expressed*) and then translated into protein. Copying DNA into RNA and then translating it into protein is like translating the information in one language (the nucleotide sequence of the DNA) into another language (the amino acid sequence that makes a protein).

Genetic code. The genetic code determines how the DNA is turned into protein. Each set of three particular nucleotides, such as AAA, AAC, AAT, AAG, ATA, ATC, ATG, or ATT, for example, specifies one particular amino acid. There are roughly twenty amino acids, and sixty-four possible nucleotide triplets, called codons, that specifiy them. Because of this, most amino acids are specified by more than one codon. Said another way, a DNA string contains the information for making protein in the form of a digital code made up of triplet nucleotides. This code must be read and translated in order to make protein.

III. One Percent Similarity?

Sequencing the genome. Chimpanzees are our closest living relatives, according to standard evolutionary theory. It is assumed by the scientific establishment that we can look at their behavior, physiology, and genetics in order to learn both how we are the same and what makes us different. We can compare genomes (the whole complement of an organism's DNA) to find out which genes were crucial in making us who we are. We can identify differences in our DNA that perhaps make us prone to disease, or discover genes that may protect against disease. This was the rationale for sequencing the chimpanzee genome, and the project was begun in 2003, shortly after our own genome sequence was published.

Published in September of 2005, the chimpanzee genome sequence was primarily done using the human genome as a scaffold, a framework for piecing the chimpanzee genome together.[4] The chimpanzee DNA sequences, which had been deciphered in pieces, were ordered and assembled according to the arrangement of our human DNA in any places where the assembly was unclear. This means that the actual chimpanzee sequence could be different in order or sequence than has been reported and we might not know.

Because the sequencing process is prone to errors, each "read" of the sequence needed to be done multiple times. The preferred standard is at least twelvefold redundancy—each nucleotide must be read at least

---

4. The Chimpanzee Sequencing and Analysis Consortium, "Initial Sequence of the Chimpanzee Genome and Comparison with the Human Genome," *Nature* 437 (2005): 69–87.

twelve times. But the published chimpanzee genome has only a 3.6-fold sequence redundancy, which is problematic for determining which SNPs are genuine and which are errors in the sequencing process. Because of this low redundancy, the published chimpanzee genome sequence is generally referred to as a draft genome, not a definitive one.[5] (Even the canonical human genome sequence, which was "completed" in 2003, continues to be refined and annotated.) Nevertheless, the consortium that sequenced the chimpanzee genome claimed that the sequence reads were high quality and could be used for analysis. We must await another chimpanzee genome sequence assembled de novo (without a human scaffold) and with higher multiplicity to know for sure.

Comparing genomes. In the paper reporting that first sequence, the estimate for the percentage of SNPs in the human genome that differs when compared to the chimpanzee genome is 1.23 percent (1.08 percent when variation between humans is taken into account). This low percentage difference is one of the reasons it is claimed that we share common ancestry with chimpanzees. At this level we appear very similar. But there are other kinds of differences between chimpanzee and human DNA. Insertions and deletions add 2 to 4 percent (different studies use different samples and techniques, so this variation in numbers is not surprising).[6] Differences also exist between chimpanzee and human DNA in the number and location of repeating genetic elements. About 0.4 percent of the genome is comprised of repetitive genetic elements unique to humans, according to the Chimpanzee Sequencing Consortium.[7] In addition, the Y-chromosomes of chimpanzee and human males are very different from each other; the Y-chromosome represents 1.8 percent of the genome.[8]

---

5. Ibid.

6. Roy J. Britten, "Divergence between Samples of Chimpanzee and Human DNA Sequences Is 5%, Counting Indels," *Proceedings of the National Academy of Sciences USA* 99 (2002): 13633–13635; Anna Wetterbom, Marie Sevov, Lucia Cavelier, and Tomas F. Bergström, "Comparative Genomic Analysis of Human and Chimpanzee Indicates a Key Role for Indels in Primate Evolution," *Journal of Molecular Evolution* 63 (2006): 682–690; Chimpanzee Sequencing and Analysis Consortium, "Initial Sequence of the Chimpanzee Genome," 69–87; Julienne M. Mullaney, Ryan E. Mills, W. Stephen Pittard, and Scott E. Devine, "Small Insertions and Deletions (INDELs) in Human Genomes," *Human Molecular Genetics* 19 (2010): R131–R136.

7. Chimpanzee Sequencing and Analysis Consortium, "Initial Sequence of the Chimpanzee Genome," 73.

8. It is difficult to estimate the degree of difference in sequence or in location, based on the reported sequence comparisons (Human Reference Genome, from Genome Reference Consortium,

Among protein-coding genes, copy number variations represent a large number of differences. Human sequences may have two or more copies of particular genes, while chimpanzees have only one, for example. According to Demuth et al,

> Our results imply that humans and chimpanzees differ by at least 6% (1,418 of 22,000 genes) in their complement of genes, which stands in stark contrast to the oft-cited 1.5% difference between orthologous nucleotide sequences. This genomic "revolving door" of gene gain and loss represents a large number of genetic differences separating humans from our closest relatives.[9]

All told, based on current knowledge, there is *at least* a 5 percent difference in our DNA, and that does not count rearrangements in the DNA, where segments of the DNA appear flipped end to end in relation to chimp DNA, or where one segment of human DNA is in a different location than in chimpanzees.

In truth, though, counting raw difference is not the best way to calculate how different we are genetically speaking, and there are several reasons why it is not surprising that we share 95 percent of our DNA sequence with chimps. First, our basic building blocks, the proteins out of which our cells are made and the enzymes that carry out cellular metabolism, are very similar to those of chimpanzees, almost identical in many cases. One can think of our genes as being like the bricks and mortar, nails and wood, shingles and wires out of which houses are made. Two houses may look different but be composed of the same basic building blocks. By analogy, the building blocks out of which we are made, the genes, are very similar for chimps and humans, even if our bodily forms are different.

Second, the vast majority of our DNA does not code for protein but functions like an operating system, determining what files (genes) should be used when, and where. The routine processes of life are carried out by this operating system, and we share these basic rou-

"Human Genome Assembly GRCh38.p9," http://www.ncbi.nlm.nih.gov/projects/genome/assembly/grc/human/data/).

9. Jeffery P. Demuth, Tijl De Bie, Jason E. Stajich, Nello Cristianini, Matthew W. Hahn, "The Evolution of Mammalian Gene Families," *PLoS ONE* 1 (2006): e85, doi:10.1371/journal.pone.0000085.

tines with chimps. Thus in many respects our operating systems are the same as those of chimps.

Last, it is the things that are different that matter. As we will show, small sections of DNA can have a large effect on how things come together.

IV. Differences in How Our DNA Is Used

Back in the 1970s, when people were first beginning to get the idea that the human genome and chimpanzee genome were very similar, despite our obvious anatomic, physiological, and behavioral differences, Mary-Claire King and A. C. Wilson proposed that the differences that matter might not be in the sequence of the DNA but in how it is put to use.[10] At that time, there was not sufficient experimental precision to identify individual genes nor to detect the kinds of differences we will outline below. We now know that when, where, and how our DNA is used matters much more than an overall count of nucleotide differences. *Human-specific differences in gene regulation, as we will see, are what make us unique.*

Human-specific genes. We have twenty thousand or so genes—we now know that some are unique to us. Estimates vary as to how many—one report says there are about three hundred human-specific protein-coding genes, mainly due to new duplicates of existing genes.[11] Another paper reports over six hundred.[12] These new genes have been linked to disease, meaning their overexpression or underexpression can affect the progress of disease; they tend to be expressed in the brain and the testis.[13] As many as sixty de novo genes, not arising by duplication of existing genes but genuinely new, have also been reported. These genes may be disease-associated also,[14] meaning they are likely to have function.

10. Mary-Claire King and A. C. Wilson, "Evolution at Two Levels in Humans and Chimpanzees," *Science* 188 (1975): 107–116;

11. Yong E. Zhang and Manyuan Long, "New Genes Contribute to Genetic and Phenotypic Novelties in Human Evolution," *Current Opinion in Genetics and Development* 29 (2014): 90–96.

12. Matthew W. Hahn, Tijl De Bie, Jason E. Stajich, et al., "Estimating the Tempo and Mode of Gene Family Evolution from Comparative Genomic Data," *Genome Research* 15 (2005): 1153–1160.

13. Aida M. Andrés and Katja Nowick, "Editorial Overview: Genetics of Human Evolution: The Genetics of Human Origins," *Current Opinion in Genetics and Development* 29 (2014): v–vii; Yong E. Zhang, Patrick Landback, Maria D. Vibranovski, Manyuan Long, "Accelerated Recruitment of New Brain Development Genes into the Human Genome," *PLoS Biology* 9 (2011): e1001179.

14. D. G. Knowles and A. McLysaght, "Recent De Novo Origin of Human Protein-Coding Genes," *Genome Research* 19 (2009): 1752–1759, doi:10.1101/gr.095026.109; D. D. Wu, D. M.

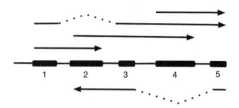

FIGURE 15.3. Alternative splicing of a single gene's RNA transcripts can generate many different gene products. Note that the DNA can be read (copied into RNA) in both directions.

It is worth noting that even one novel, functional gene is a remarkable thing from an evolutionary point of view. It used to be accepted that getting new genes was very hard, but now new genes are being found in every genome that is sequenced—genes that appear to be unique to that species. This was a surprise for evolutionary biologists. From a design point of view, however, the existence of new genes for each species makes sense.

Multipurpose genes. It was discovered in the late 1970s that protein-coding genes can be used to encode many different proteins. The genes are broken up into segments called exons, and after the genes have been transcribed into RNA, the RNA can be spliced into different arrangements of exons. Say a gene has exons 1–5. The RNA can be spliced to include exons 1, and 2; or 2, 3, 4; or 1, 3, 4; or 4, 5, for example (Fig. 15.3). There can also be genes expressed in the opposite direction, for example 5, 3, 2. So although we have only about 20,000 genes, we have potentially many thousands of different protein-coding RNAs made from those genes, with each unique RNA making a different protein.[15] There is "an important role for alternative splicing in establishing differences between humans and chimpanzees," one study reports.[16] In fact, *6 to 8 percent*

Irwin, and Y. P. Zhang, "De Novo Origin of Human Protein-Coding Genes," *PLoS Genetics* 7 (2011):e1002379, doi:10.1371/journal.pgen.1002379.

15. Yoseph Barash, John A. Calarco, Weijun Gao, Qun Pan, Xinchen Wang, Ofer Shai, Benjamin J. Blencowe, and Brendan J. Frey, "Deciphering the Splicing Code," *Nature* 465 (2010): 53–59.

16. John A. Calarco, Yi Xing, Mario Cáceres, Joseph P. Calarco, Xinshu Xiao, Qun Pan, Christopher Lee, Todd M. Preuss, and Benjamin J. Blencowe, "Global Analysis of Alternative Splicing Differences between Humans and Chimpanzees," *Genes and Development* 21 (2007): 2963–2975.

of genes that have been studied display splicing differences between chimps and humans. That means that our genes may be used to make different proteins, even though they appear to have the same DNA sequence.

Differential gene expression. Different tissues and organs in the body are made of specific cell types, and each cell type expresses its own set of *genes*. The pattern of expression of genes affects what kind of cell it becomes.[17] So where, when, and what genes are expressed all matter to the development of the body, and for its continued functioning. It follows that, in order for us to develop into humans and not chimpanzees, it is likely that differences in gene *expression* are involved. Significantly, there are substantial differences in gene expression between humans and chimpanzees, *particularly in the brain.*[18]

There are multiple kinds of elements involved in regulating differential gene expression. The most well known are protein *transcription factors* (roughly 1 to 3 percent of them human-specific).[19] The transcription factors recognize and bind to particular DNA binding sites, and influence the activity of their neighboring genes (Fig. 15.4). Some increase gene expression, some decrease it, some are tissue-specific, and some are general enhancers of gene expression. Some silence genes completely. *One to 3 percent of our transcription factors are unique to us.* This is significant because a single transcription factor can change the expression of multiple genes, thus having a greatly magnified effect. Those unique transcription factors can have a significant effect on how our genome is used, even though they account for very little of the total DNA themselves.

Noncoding DNA and its functions. Only about 2 percent of our genome carries the information to make protein—an astonishing

---

17. For a general introduction to cell and molecular biology, see Albert et al., *Molecular Biology of the Cell.*

18. Michael C. Oldham, Steve Horvath, and Daniel H. Geschwind, "Conservation and Evolution of Gene Coexpression Networks in Human and Chimpanzee Brains," *Proceedings of the National Academy of Sciences USA* 103 (2006): 17973–17978, doi:10.1073/pnas.0605938103; Ajit Varki, Daniel H. Geschwind, and Evan E. Eichler, "Explaining Human Uniqueness: Genome Interactions with Environment, Behaviour, and Culture," *Nature Review of Genetics* 9 (2008): 749–763, doi:10.1038/nrg2428.

19. Alvaro Perdomo-Sabogal, Sabina Kanton, Maria Beatriz C. Walter, and Katja Nowick, "The Role of Gene Regulatory Factors in the Evolutionary History of Humans," *Current Opinion in Genetics and Development* 29 (2014): 60–67.

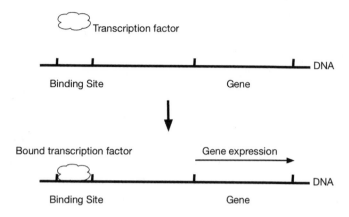

FIGURE 15.4. To activate gene expression, it is often necessary for a transcription factor (illustrated as a cloud-like shape) to bind to a particular site on the DNA, causing the nearby gene to be copied into RNA.

fact.[20] The remainder is noncoding (it does not specify how to make protein). Roughly half of that noncoding DNA is composed of repeating elements, sometimes called *mobile genetic elements.* This is another astonishing fact, that so much of our DNA should be composed of repeating DNA.[21] Many of these repeating elements resemble a certain kind of viral DNA that can copy itself and insert in new locations in the genome, though most of these "mobile genetic elements" are inactive.[22]

For a number of years, many scientists assumed that the non-protein-coding DNA was "junk," the detritus of evolution, like that junk drawer at home where bits of miscellany with no obvious purpose end up. This was based on the idea that mobile elements had copied and inserted themselves into new locations, accumulating over time, and elements that had become broken were inefficiently removed. Broken genes also accumulated. We now know that at least some of this "junk" DNA is involved in modulating the behavior and structure

20. International Human Genome Sequencing Consortium, "Finishing the Euchromatic Sequence of the Human Genome," *Nature* 431 (2004): 931–945.

21. International Human Genome Sequencing Consortium, "Initial Sequencing and Analysis of the Human Genome," *Nature* 409 (2001): 860–921; Haig H. Kazazian Jr., "Mobile Elements: Drivers of Genome Evolution," *Science* 303 (2004): 1626–1632.

22. Kazazian, "Mobile Elements."

of chromosomes, regulating the expression of genes, as well as perhaps providing ways for organisms to respond to their environments
genetically,[23] as will be discussed below.

The change in view is exemplified by the about-face on junk DNA
by Francis Collins, director of the National Institutes of Health. As
Marvin Olasky reports at *World* magazine,

> Collins claimed on page 136 [of his book *The Language of God*]
> that huge chunks of our genome are "littered" with ancient repeti-
> tive elements (AREs), so that "roughly 45 percent of the human
> genome [is] made up of such genetic flotsam and jetsam." In [a
> talk given in New York] he claimed the existence of "junk DNA"
> was proof that man and mice had a common ancestor, because
> God would not have created man with useless genes. Last year,
> though, speaking at the J.P. Morgan Healthcare Conference in San
> Francisco, Collins threw in the towel: "In terms of junk DNA, we
> don't use that term anymore because I think it was pretty much a
> case of hubris to imagine that we could dispense with any part of
> the genome, as if we knew enough to say it wasn't functional. . . .
> Most of the genome that we used to think was there for spacer turns
> out to be doing stuff."[24]

We should be clear, though. Collins has not given up his position
that chimps and humans have a common ancestor.

We focus below on specific kinds of "junk" DNA because they
make up a large portion of our genome, and have in many cases been
shown to have function.

SINEs and LINEs. Short interspersed nuclear elements (SINEs) are
a type of mobile genetic element that represents about *12 percent* of
the genome. Among other things, SINEs help to specify in which cells
genes should be expressed. *Seven thousand Alus (a kind of SINE) are
species-specific*, present in humans but not in chimpanzees.[25] SINEs
tend to be present near genes of particular functional types, and af-

---

23. James A. Shapiro, "Epigenetic Control of Mobile DNA as an Interface between Experience and Genome Change," *Frontiers in Genetics* 5 (2014): 1–16.

24. Marvin Olasky, "Admission of Function," *World* magazine, June 2016, accessed July 2, 2016 https://world.wng.org/2016/06/admission_of_function.

25. Varki, Geschwind, and Eichler, "Explaining Human Uniqueness," 749–763.

fect their expression, often in cell-type specific ways.[26] Human-specific Alu elements, as they are called, are also involved in RNA editing, a process by which RNA is changed after it has been copied from the DNA.[27] RNA editing can affect many aspects of RNA processing, such as splicing and stability.[28]

This SINE-induced RNA editing is most notable in the human brain, and is largely species-specific.[29] Of course the brain is one of the areas where we differ most from chimpanzees. But RNA editing is not just in the brain. It is essential for development, and improper editing results in diseases like cancer and psychiatric disorders.[30]

Other mobile genetic elements, called "long interspersed nuclear elements" (LINEs), are about 17 percent of the genome. *Many (about 1,800) are species-specific.*[31] They have a role in regulating the way chromosomes behave—where they cluster in the nucleus, how they are packed—and they inhibit gene expression.[32] Thus they play an important role in the organization of the nucleus. They also tend to flank groups of genes, so as to control the expression of RNAs from different strands of the DNA. In other words, they delineate units of gene expression.[33]

LINEs also help direct different kinds of cells to develop in the brain. LINEs move to new locations in the genome *of particular brain cells* as they develop, landing near different genes involved in neuronal

26. Aristotelis Tsirigos and Isidore Rigoutsos, "Alu and B1 Repeats Have Been Selectively Retained in the Upstream and Intronic Regions of Genes of Specific Functional Classes," *PLoS Computational Biology* 5 (2009): e10006; Nurit Paz-Yaacova, Erez Y. Levanonc, Eviatar Nevod, Yaron Kinare, Alon Harmelinf, et al., "Adenosine-to-Inosine RNA Editing Shapes Transcriptome Diversity in Primates," *Proceedings of the National Academy of Sciences USA* 107 (2010): 12174–12179.

27. Dennis D. Y. Kim, Thomas T. Y. Kim, Thomas Walsh, et al., "Widespread RNA Editing of Embedded Alu Elements in the Human Transcriptome," *Genome Research* 14 (2004): 1719–1725.

28. Alekos Athanasiadis, Alexander Rich, and Stefan Maas, "Widespread A-to-I RNA Editing of Alu-Containing mRNAs in the Human Transcriptome," *PLoS Biology* 2 (2004): 2144–2158.

29. Paz-Yaacova, "Adenosine-to-inosine RNA Editing."

30. Tim R. Mercer, Marcel E. Dinger, and John S. Mattick, "Long Non-Coding RNAs: Insights into Functions," *Nature Reviews: Genetics* 10 (2009): 155–159; Gilad Silberberg, Daniel Lundin, Ruth Navon, and Marie Öhman, "Deregulation of the A-to-I RNA Editing Mechanism in Psychiatric Disorders," *Human Molecular Genetics* 21 (2012): 311–321.

31. Jeffrey S. Han, Suzanne T. Szak, and Jef D. Boeke, "Transcriptional Disruption by the L1 Retrotransposon and Implications for Mammalian Transcriptomes," *Nature* 429 (2004): 268–274.

32. Ibid.; Laura Manuelidis and David C. Ward, "Chromosomal and Nuclear Distribution of the HindIII 1.9-kb Human DNA Repeat Segment," *Chromosoma* 91 (1984): 28–38.

33. Giorgio Bernardi, "Chromosome Architecture and Genome Organization," *PLoS ONE* 10, no. 11: e0143739.

development.[34] That means many of our brain cells literally *rewrite* their genetic instructions during the process of becoming mature neurons.[35] The same is true in other tissues of the body as well.

To reiterate, *many LINEs and SINEs are species-specific*, meaning we have a unique set of these elements in our genomes compared to chimpanzees. From all we have said it should be apparent that these species-specific elements can make a profound difference in our anatomy, physiology, and behavior. Not to mention our brains.

Long noncoding RNAs. Seventy to 90 percent of the genome is transcribed into RNA but does not produce any protein. Called long noncoding RNAs (lncRNAs), these RNAs can be nested within genes going in either direction, or they can come from DNA with no protein-coding genes.[36] They often originate from or contain SINEs and LINEs. Figure 15.5 illustrates the kinds of lncRNAs that are possible.[37]

These RNAs have been a matter of some controversy. They tend to be *species-specific* (the evolutionary biologists like to say they are not "conserved" across species), and so they have been called junk, the product of indiscriminate transcription like so much background noise. Yet when examined, they do have functions. They often act by changing the DNA architecture. Some link different stretches of DNA together, looping the DNA into functional domains, or causing changes in gene expression. Others tether the DNA to the nuclear periphery when it is not needed. Still others act as buffers to prevent gene expression from different segments of DNA from interfering with one another.[38]

This is important because overexpression can lead to diseases such as cancer.[39] Many of these lncRNAs are also tissue-specific. For example, there are human-specific lncRNAs expressed in the brain.[40]

HARs. Human accelerated regions are human DNA segments whose

---

34. Kyle R. Upton, Daniel J. Gerhardt, J. Samuel Jesuadian, Sandra R. Richardson, Francisco J. Sánchez-Luque, et al., "Ubiquitous L1 Mosaicism in Hippocampal Neurons," *Cell* 161 (2015): 228–239.

35. Ibid.

36. Mercer et al., "Long Non-Coding RNAs."

37. Johnny T. Y. Kung, David Colognori, and Jeannie T. Lee, "Long Noncoding RNAs: Past, Present, and Future," *Genetics* 193 (2013): 651–669.

38. Ibid.

39. Perdomo-Sabogal, "Gene Regulatory Factors."

40. Ibid.

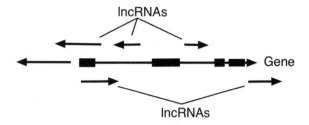

FIGURE 15.5. Long noncoding RNAs (lncRNAs) can come from just about any position in the DNA with respect to genes, or from outside of genes entirely. The black bars on the coding gene in this illustration represent the coding portions of the gene. The direction of transcription of the lncRNAs is indicated by arrows.

sequences differ substantially from related mammalian sequences. The mammalian sequences are conserved, meaning they differ very little among species. Yet the human HARs are quite different. The evolutionary interpretation is that there has been a burst of evolutionary change in these regions, after the separation of the chimpanzee and the human lineages. HARs could also be different by design. Interestingly, these HARs tend to be located near "developmental genes, transcription factors, and genes expressed in the central nervous system."[41]

More differences. All nonhuman primates, in fact most mammals, carry endemic infectious retroviruses, a kind of virus that integrates itself into the host genome in order to replicate itself. There are two kinds, simian foamy viruses (SFVs) and simian infectious retroviruses (SIVs) that are shared among most nonhuman primates. Among humans, we have only the newly introduced HIV and human T leukemia virus, and no others. If we were descended from a common ancestral population with chimpanzees, we should carry the SIV and SFVs viruses also, but we don't. Either we were purged of the viruses or we never had them.[42]

The organization of our DNA sequence differs considerably. We have different recombination hotspots than chimpanzees; these hotspots are

41. Melissa J. Hubisz and Katherine S. Pollard, "Exploring the Genesis and Functions of Human Accelerated Regions Sheds Light on Their Role in Human Evolution," *Current Opinion in Genetics and Development* 29 (2014): 15–21.
42. Varki, Geschwind, and Eichler, "Explaining Human Uniqueness."

places where homologous chromosomes recombine, shuffling segments of DNA into new combinations. As a result, our DNA is organized into different shuffled blocks. As for rearrangements of the DNA, stretches of DNA are inverted in humans compared to chimpanzees, contributing greatly to sequence divergence. Insertions of ten to fifteen thousand bases of DNA account for 32 million bases of human-specific DNA; insertions of greater than fifteen thousand bases contribute 8 million bases of human-specific DNA. Finally, our chromosome 2 differs from that of chimpanzees. See the section on chromosomal fusion near the end of this chapter for more on this.[43]

Genetic networks. Transcription factors, SINEs, LINEs, and lnc-RNAs all act to regulate genes in a sort of genetic network of interactions. Some genes interact with other genes, which in turn interact with still other genes. Within this network of gene interactions, some genes act as hubs of connectivity. If the expression of these hub genes is shifted, they affect the expression of many other genes.[44] Thus, changing the expression of a few genes can have a large effect. For example, an estimated *17 percent of the neural network in the cortex of the brain is unique to humans*, even though our total genomes may differ from chimpanzees by only 5 percent.[45] Other parts of the brain show other differences also. This means that small changes in gene regulatory elements like the ones mentioned above can have large effects on our gene networks, and thus on our physical and behavioral characteristics.

The genome as an operating system. If the genome sounds complicated, it is. It needs to be complicated in order to enable the timing and location of differential gene expression. Genes are grouped into folders, and then into superfolders. DNA is organized into loops, then mega folders; chromosomes are arrayed in the nucleus, each with its own territory, so that sets of genes can be expressed in a coordinated fashion. Genes in active folders take various inputs and combine them into a single output, functioning like logic gates. The output of all the

43. Hildegard Kehrer-Sawatzki, and David N. Cooper, "Understanding the Recent Evolution of the Human Genome: Insights from Human–Chimpanzee Genome Comparisons," *Human Mutation* 28 (2007): 99–130.

44. Miles Fontenot and Genevieve Konopka, "Molecular Networks and the Evolution of Human Cognitive Specializations," *Current Opinion in Genetics and Development* 29 (2014): 52–59.

45. Oldham, Horvath, and Geschwind, "Conservation and Evolution of Gene Coexpression Networks in Human and Chimpanzee Brains," 17973–17978.

cellular logic gates combines, and the outcome is carefully regulated cellular behavior, and ultimately, a functioning human being. We may share 95 percent or even 99 percent of our DNA sequence with chimpanzees, but it's how the DNA is used that matters.[46]

Thus, one can say that our genome functions like a very complex operating system, more complex than anything we have ever built. Our genome and its coordinated expression are a wonder of intricacy, responsiveness, and beauty—far, far more sophisticated than anything we have dreamed of. Looking down into the depths of that complexity is truly dizzying, leaving one with a sense of awe.

V. Physiological and Anatomical Differences

Given all the genetic differences and regulatory complexity described above, it should come as no surprise that our physiology and anatomy is different from that of chimpanzees. We do not have the same reproductive biology. Our teeth develop more slowly after birth than chimpanzees' teeth do, and our young are born profoundly helpless and require prolonged maternal care. Our brains are larger and continue to develop long after birth, forming neurons and connections at a rapid rate. In fact, new neurons continue to form even into adulthood. Our musculature is weaker, with smaller bone insertion points. Our thyroid hormone metabolism differs. We get AIDs and malaria and chimpanzees don't. Our immune systems differ. Our diets differ, and our intestines reflect that difference. We shed tears; chimpanzees don't. We can swim and have a diving reflex, but chimpanzees can't swim. We have chins; chimpanzees do not.[47]

We walk and run upright. Our feet are different—ours are designed for walking and chimpanzees' for climbing. Our necks are longer, and the skull is set on top of the spine for balance and to be able to look forward. Our rib cages move freely from side to side to accommodate our gait, and expand to allow deep breathing during running.[48] Our

---

46. Richard Sternberg and James A. Shapiro, "How Repeated Retroelements Format Genome Function," *Cytogenetic and Genome Research*, 110 (2005): 108–116.
47. Ajit Varki and Tasha K. Altheide, "Comparing the Human and Chimpanzee Genomes: Searching for Needles in a Haystack," *Genome Research* 15 (2005): 1746–1758.
48. Dennis M. Bramble and Daniel E. Lieberman, "Endurance Running and the Evolution of Homo," *Nature* 432 (2004): 345–352.

shoulders are designed for throwing, while chimpanzees' are designed for climbing.[49] Our pelvis and hips are oriented so as to permit upright walking. Our legs angle in so that our feet are underneath us. Our inner ear canals are oriented differently to increase our sense of balance. Our hands are designed for tool use, not knuckle walking. We have a poorer sense of smell but a greater tactile sensitivity in our fingertips. We have greater fine motor control, and our thumbs can touch the far side of our hands.[50]

Finally, there are all the cultural and behavioral differences. We plan. We think about the past and the future. We make intentional decisions. We can delay gratification for long periods. We engage in long-range trade. Adults play. We dance. We make music. We have language and communicate symbolically,[51] and we write novels and poetry. We have mathematics and art. We domesticate animals and engage in agriculture. We wear clothing. We engage in hospitality. We control fire and we measure time. We practice religion, and bury the dead. We have empathy for others, and altruism on a scale unknown in the animal world. We care for the infirm and the elderly.[52]

Some may say that these traits are inherited from our common ancestors, that they are all honed by natural selection to help the individual compete. But we see nothing like the human scale of behavior in chimpanzees. Our culture is exceptional, even unique, by any standard of the animal kingdom. It is orders of magnitude more sophisticated than anything chimpanzees do.

A paper titled "Comparing the Human and Chimpanzee Genomes: Searching for Needles in a Haystack," by Ajit Varki and Tasha Altheide, describes literally a hundred or more physiological and behavioral differences, some of which we have cited here.[53] Bramble and Lieberman, in the journal *Nature*, list the changes necessary for long-distance running—they include twenty-six anatomical and physiological innovations.[54]

---

49. Neil T. Roach, Madhusudhan Venkadesan, Michael J. Rainbow and Daniel E. Lieberman, "Elastic Energy Storage in the Shoulder and the Evolution of High-Speed Throwing in *Homo*," *Nature* 498 (2013): 483–487.

50. Varki and Altheide, "Comparing the Human and Chimpanzee Genomes."

51. Marc D. Hauser, Charles Yang, Robert C. Berwick, et al., "The Mystery of Language Evolution," *Frontiers in Psychology* 5 (2014): 401.

52. Bramble and Lieberman, "Endurance Running."

53. Varki and Altheide, "Comparing the Human and Chimpanzee Genomes."

54. Bramble and Lieberman, "Endurance Running."

The most striking trait that distinguishes us from chimpanzees is our intellect. There is no evolutionary explanation for its appearance. Varki et al. state,

> [I]t is difficult to explain how conventional natural selection could have selected ahead of time for the remarkable capabilities of the human mind, which we are still continuing to explore today. An example is writing, which was invented long after the human mind evolved and continues to be modified and utilized in myriad ways. Explanations based on exaptation [the adaptation of a trait originally used for some other purpose] seem inadequate, as most of what the human mind routinely does today did not even exist at the time it was originally evolving. Experts in human evolution or cognition have yet to provide a truly satisfactory explanation.[55]

One can find simplistic accounts of our evolution on the Internet and in museums. Favorite genes are listed as causal agents for our evolution from ape-like ancestors. But in order for our common descent from an ape-like ancestor by purely natural means to be true, many of these features had to arise at the same time in a coordinated fashion, meaning some number of mutations also had to happen at the same time. For example, an enlarged brain would require changes to the jaw and teeth as well as to the brain case. This significant and defining anatomical change would have needed multiple mutations to occur. In this regard, an article from the Associated Press discussed a scenario where a single genetic mutation, found in humans, was proposed to have reduced the size of our ancestors' jaw muscles, thereby reducing jaw size, and permitting large brain cases and large brains to evolve. Critics disagreed, saying evolution does not work so neatly:

> The first early humans with the mutation probably would have had weaker mouths, but still had large teeth and jaws. Many additional mutations would have been needed.
>
> "The mutation would have reduced the Darwinian fitness of those individuals," said anthropologist Bernard Wood of George Washington University. "It only would've become fixed if it

---

55. Varki, Geschwind, and Eichler, "Explaining Human Uniqueness."

coincided with mutations that reduced tooth size, jaw size and increased brain size. What are the chances of that?"[56]

Clearly, many mutations would have had to occur together, simultaneously, to accomplish the kind of coordinated change necessary for our evolution. They could not have been just any mutations, for by themselves or in the wrong combinations they would have been deleterious or even fatal, thereby wiping out any progress.

VI. Time Enough for Change?

Let's ask the question, then: how long would it take to acquire a specific mutation, or even two mutations, to accomplish a particular anatomical change?

The general assumption by population geneticists is that mutations arise at a regular rate (though this may not be true!). Once a mutation has occurred in one individual, it must spread through the population over succeeding generations to make a lasting change in the species. When the mutation is finally the only version of a particular gene in the population, we say the mutation has become "fixed" in the population.

How long this process takes depends on several factors. The first is whether the mutation is beneficial by itself or not. Second, the size of the population matters. Third, the generation time also is important. Finally, of course, the mutation rate itself has an important effect. When these factors are taken into account, it is possible to build mathematical models to estimate how long it would take a particular kind of mutation to appear.

The estimates of these factors most commonly given by population geneticists are that we supposedly came from a population of about ten thousand, with a generation time of ten years (apes have shorter generation times than we do) and a mutation rate of 10^{-8} mutations (that is, 1 in 100 million) per base per generation, at the time we last shared common ancestry with chimpanzees. A number of mathematicians and biologists have used these or similar estimates to calculate the length of time it would take to obtain a binding site in

---

56. Joseph B. Verrengia, "Scientists Debate Suggestion Jaw Mutation Led to Evolution," Associated Press, *USA Today*, March 24, 2004.

the DNA within one thousand bases of some gene, in order to change its gene expression. The reason for this calculation? It is assumed that changing a binding site in the DNA would change gene expression, and thus change that individual's behavior or anatomy in some way. The mutation would then need to spread through the population and become fixed.

Here's the problem: To get a single mutation in a DNA binding site and have it become fixed would take anywhere from 1.5 million years[57] to 6 million years,[58] depending on whose calculations are used. If two mutations are needed to get a change in behavior or anatomy, it would take approximately between 84 and 216 million years—once again, depending on whose calculations are used.[59] Other research using different methods merely confirms the problem.[60]

Yet we have only 6 million years since we supposedly diverged from chimpanzees. One proposed solution is to allow the search space to include one thousand bases near *any* gene in the genome. That means that for a five-base binding site there are a maximum of 20,000 x 200 five-base nonoverlapping sequences or 4 million places available for a new binding site to appear. That reduces the waiting time considerably, to 7,500 years on average for a five-base binding site.[61]

The problem is that very few binding site mutations are likely to be beneficial. Not just any old binding site will do. And most beneficial traits will require more mutations than just one. *If even one essential trait required two specific coordinated mutations, the evolutionary process would stall completely,* because 216 million years is too long to wait. The neo-Darwinian process cannot accomplish what is needed to explain our origin in the time available.

57. John Sanford, Wesley Brewer, Franzine Smith, and John Baumgardner, "The Waiting Time Problem in a Model Hominin Population," *Theoretical Biology and Medical Modelling* 12 (2015): 18.

58. Richard Durrett and Deena Schmidt, "Waiting for Regulatory Sequences to Appear," *The Annals of Applied Probability* 17 (2007): 1–32, doi:10.1214/105051606000000619.

59. Richard Durrett and Deena Schmidt, "Waiting for Two Mutations: With Applications to Regulatory Sequence Evolution and the Limits of Darwinian Evolution," *Genetics* 180 (2008): 1501–1509, doi:10.1534/genetics.107.082610.

60. Winston Ewert, "Overabundant Mutations Help Potentiate Evolution: The Effect of Biologically Realistic Mutation Rates on Computer Models of Evolution," *BIO-Complexity* 2015, no. 1 (2015): 1–11.

61. Sarah Behrens and Martin Vingron, "Studying the Evolution of Promoter Sequences: A Waiting Time Problem," *Journal of Computational Biology* 17 (2010): 1591–1606.

VII. Does Similarity Indicate Common Descent?

We have ruled out the Darwinian mechanism as being sufficient to account for our origin, but we have not addressed the question of common descent—namely, could a designer have used the evolutionary process to make human beings? We already know that it would have to be a guided process, because of the problem of the amount of time required to accumulate all the necessary coordinated mutations. So now the question is, do we indeed share common ancestry with chimpanzees? Are our bodies the product of guided evolution from an ape-like ancestor? Or do we have a unique created origin as human beings? In this section we will examine several arguments that are typically made by evolutionary biologists in support of common descent, and consider the responses of design biologists.

Assumptions. Before we examine the evidence, though, it should be mentioned that there are some basic differences between the way evidence is approached by evolutionary biologists and design biologists. The chief assumption made by evolutionary biologists is that the genetic changes responsible for evolutionary change are random, and therefore, if a group of species share a trait in common that is not found in other related species, it is presumed that the common ancestor of the group developed that trait, and they all share it because of common descent. On the other hand, if genetic change is directed rather than random, the trait is most likely shared because the organisms use similar solutions to a physiological need. This beautifully explains convergent evolution, where unrelated organisms share a trait in common.

It should also be noted that many arguments about common descent are circular, in particular those concerned with pseudogenes (supposedly broken genes of no use to the organism but still in the DNA). If organisms are *not* thought to be closely related, then the existence of a particular pseudogene is claimed to be due to functional requirements;[62] on the other hand, if organisms *are* thought to be closely related, that pseudogene is taken to indicate common descent.[63] To say that pseudogenes prove common descent when the organisms

---

62. Evgeniy S. Balakirev and Francisco J. Ayala, "Pseudogenes: Are They 'Junk' or Functional DNA?" *Annual Review of Genetics* 37 (2003): 123–151.

63. Jonathan Wells, *The Myth of Junk DNA* (Seattle: Discovery Institute Press, 2011), 113–114.

involved are closely related, but prove a functional constraint when the organisms in question are unrelated is to assume common descent from the very beginning, not to prove it. Logicians know this as the fallacy of begging the question.

Evolutionary biologists tend to assume randomness and attribute any similarity to common descent; design biologists tend to assume order and purpose and assume that any similarity is functional, not *necessarily* due to common descent. Darwinian evolutionists tend to assume that many poorly understood aspects of our genomes (e.g., pseudogenes, synonymous codons, or junk DNA—see below) do not have important functions and are the product of random mutations and common descent. In contrast, proponents of intelligent design predict that, if our genomes were designed, then many of these mysterious features will turn out to have important functions. The problem is to distinguish between the two viewpoints.

VIII. Arguments Used to Support Common Descent

Pseudogenes. Because pseudogenes appear to make defective protein, or none at all, they have been thought to be "junk," remnants of the evolutionary process. Because they tend to be located in the same place and have the same "errors" in humans and in chimpanzees, they are taken as evidence for common descent, for example by Francis Collins and Denis Alexander.

Pseudogenes have not received much attention in the scientific literature because they are assumed to be "junk." But that is changing rapidly. Where pseudogenes have been carefully studied, they are often found to be functional, and in some nonstandard ways.[64] Part of the problem is that a pseudogene may be active in specific tissues only during particular stages of development, making identification of their functions difficult. Nonetheless, researchers in the field are confident that continued research will yield more evidence of functionality. As one group states, "We believe that more and more functional pseudogenes will be discovered as novel biological technologies are developed in the future. . . . definitely, the so-called pseudogenes are really

---

64. Balakirev and Ayala, "Pseudogenes: Are They 'Junk'?"

functional, not to be considered any more as just 'junk' or 'fossil' DNA. Surely, many functional pseudogenes and novel regulatory mechanisms remain to be discovered and explored in diverse organisms."[65]

There are several ways in which pseudogenes have been found to work so far. They can fuse with adjacent genes to form "chimeras" that produce either coding or noncoding RNAs, and they can form RNA–RNA duplexes with their "parental" gene and prevent its expression or signal its degradation.[66]

One sign pointing toward their likely functionality is that their sequence is very similar in many different species. There are more than eight thousand processed pseudogenes in the human genome; 60 percent are very similar in mouse and human. The fact that their sequences are so similar means that they are likely to have a sequence-dependent essential function, so that their sequence cannot be changed without harm.[67] That degree of similarity is not something that would be expected if pseudogenes served no biological function.

If they *do have* a function in both chimpanzees and humans that is highly dependent on their precise sequences, the similarity between chimpanzee and human sequences would not be surprising. They could be performing the same function, requiring the same sequence in both genomes. As an example, a pseudogene in the beta-globin cluster of genes in humans shows evidence of sequence similarity within and between the human and chimpanzee populations. The similarity is not due to protein coding but appears to involve regulation of developmental changes via chromosomal interactions.[68]

Synteny refers to how well chromosomal sequences from different species align with one another—how similar the arrangement of genes along their chromosomes is. If they align well, it is assumed to indicate they came from a common ancestor. But there is a possible functional explanation: chromosomal structure has a profound effect

---

65. Y. Z. Wen et al., "Pseudogenes Are Not Pseudo Any More," *RNA Biology* 9, no. 1 (January 2012): 27–32.

66. Deyou Zheng and Mark B. Gerstein, "The Ambiguous Boundary between Genes and Pseudogenes: The Dead Rise Up, or Do They?" *Trends in Genetics* 23 (2007): 219–224.

67. Wen et al., "Pseudogenes Are Not Pseudo Any More."

68. Ana Moleirinho, Susana Seixas, Alexandra M. Lopes, Celeste Bento, Maria J. Prata, and António Amorim, "Evolutionary Constraints in the β-Globin Cluster: The Signature of Purifying Selection at the δ-Globin (HBD) Locus and Its Role in Developmental Gene Regulation," *Genome Biology and Evolution* 5 (2013): 559–571.

on gene regulation, and where genes are located in the nucleus affects their expression.[69]

Long- and short-range interactions between genes, the way the DNA loops, whether genes are sequestered or not—all these things are affected by chromosomal order. Rodley et al. say, "[t]he association of chromosomes with each other and other nuclear components plays a critical role in nuclear organization and genome function. . . . Genomes are highly ordered yet dynamic entities in which chromosomal positions, structures and interactions are controlled in order to regulate nuclear processes."[70] This sophistication is a strong argument for design.

Thus, it is possible that any similarity in gene order might be a function both chimps and humans need. If the sequence similarity is due to function, then it *need not* indicate common ancestry.

Synonymous codon use. One of the evidences offered in favor of common descent is the "reuse" of synonymous codons. Some codons—triplet nucleotide sequences in DNA—specify the same amino acid. For example, lysine may be encoded by four different codons in RNA—CUU, CUC, CUA, or CUG. The assumption has been that these codons truly are synonymous and ought to be able to be used interchangeably. Yet when there is a choice among possible codons, chimpanzee and human genomes almost always use the same codon. It is therefore argued that this is because the sequences share a common ancestor.

However, it has since been discovered that codons are used for multiple purposes—which codons are used changes the DNA sequence, which in turn can affect gene expression,[71] protein degradation (the

---

69. Joanna W. Jachowicz, Angèle Santenard, Ambre Bender, Julius Muller, and Maria-Elena Torres-Padilla, "Heterochromatin Establishment at Pericentromeres Depends on Nuclear Position." *Genes and Development* 27 (2013): 2427–2432; Jolien Suzanne Verdaasdonk, Paula Andrea Vasquez, Raymond Mario Barry, et al., "Centromere Tethering Confines Chromosome Domains," *Molecular Cell* 52 (2013): 6819–6831; Dirar Homouz and Andrzej S. Kudlicki, "The 3D Organization of the Yeast Genome Correlates with Co-Expression and Reflects Functional Relations between Genes," *PLoS One* 8 (2013): e54699; Stephen A. Hoang and Stefan Bekiranov, "The Network Architecture of the *Saccharomyces cerevisiae* Genome," *PLoS One* 8 (2013): e81972.

70. C. D. M. Rodley, F. Bertels, B. Jones, and J. M. O'Sullivan, "Global Identification of Yeast Chromosome Interactions Using Genome Conformation Capture," *Fungal Genetics and Biology* 46 (2009): 879–886.

71. A. B. Stergachis, E. Haugen, A. Shafer, W. Fu, B. Vernot, et al., "Exonic Transcription Factor Binding Directs Codon Choice and Affects Protein Evolution," *Science* 342 (2013): 1367–1372.

controlled destruction of proteins by the cell), or how proteins fold into three-dimensional shapes.[72]

Codons may therefore be identical because they have to perform multiple jobs that are specific to one codon—none of the others will do. The fact that both humans and chimpanzees use the same codons may be due to this rather than to their ancestry. In addition, this is a strong argument for design: the sophistication required to have codes within codes would not arise by simple mutation and natural selection.

Chromosomal fusion. When chimpanzee and human genomes are compared, our chromosome 2 appears to be a fusion of two chimpanzee chromosomes. The argument is made that this demonstrates our common ancestry with chimpanzees. However, the junction where the supposed fusion took place is not made of typical telomeric sequences. (Telomeres are special sequences found at the end of chromosomes.) Instead, degenerate sequences are found, sequences found elsewhere in the genome but not associated with breaks or fusions.[73]

The human chromosome 2 may have always been as it appears now. There is no particular reason to propose there was a fusion event except under the assumption of common descent. Therefore it cannot be used as an argument *for* common descent.[74]

The designer as a deceiver. This argument goes something like this: "If there is an intelligent designer, then why did he make it look like things evolve? That makes him a deceiver."

There is a logical flaw here as well: it is stated as fact that things look like they evolved by natural processes. But things do *not* look like they evolved. As has been shown, many good reasons to believe things were designed are found in molecular biology. There are also

72. F. Zhang, S. Saha, S. A. Shabalina, A. Kashina, "Differential Arginylation of Actin Isoforms Is Regulated by Coding Sequence-Dependent Degradation," *Science* 329 (2010): 1534–1537; I. Weygand-Durasevic, and M. Ibba, "New Roles for Codon Usage," *Science* (*Washington*) 329 (2010): 1473–1474; G. W. Li, E. Oh, J. S. Weissman, "The Anti-Shine-Dalgarno Sequence Drives Translational Pausing and Codon Choice in Bacteria," *Nature* 484 (2012): 538–541; Gina Cannarozzi, Nicol N. Schraudolph, Mahamadou Faty, et al., "A Role for Codon Order in Translation Dynamics," *Cell* 141 (2010): 355–367.

73. Yuxin Fan, Elena Linardopoulou, Cynthia Friedman, Eleanor Williams, and Barbara J. Trask, "Genomic Structure and Evolution of the Ancestral Chromosome Fusion Site in 2q13-2q14.1 and Paralogous Regions on Other Human Chromosomes," *Genome Research* 12 (2002): 1651–1662.

74. Ann K. Gauger, Douglas Axe, and Casey Luskin, *Science and Human Origins* (Seattle: Discovery Institute Press, 2012).

many examples from the design of larger-scale structures like the eye or a bird's wing; even the complementary and interlocking nature of the biosphere all give evidence of design.[75] In fact, biologists are continually told that they must remember that things only *look* designed—they really aren't.[76] That clearly means the designer is not a deceiver. He has made it so that everyone can detect his design.

IX. Population Genetics and Adam and Eve

In recent years there has been much discussion about whether the genetic data indicates that humans could not have descended from an initial couple. Evolutionary biologists often cite population genetics models in this regard. Based on these models, current estimates are that there were about ten thousand individuals in the population when we first split from chimpanzees. Ten thousand individuals are too many to allow for a unique origin with Adam and Eve. However, the basic assumptions used in population genetics may be flawed, and there is good reason to think that an alternate model for our origin is possible. This argument is presented in the next chapter.

X. Conclusions

The preponderance of the evidence says that we humans have a unique origin. First, arguments from chapters 1 through 14 show that neo-Darwinism cannot explain the information-bearing, complex, and specified nature of life, and that common descent is a flawed hypothesis. Then in this chapter we have demonstrated that neo-Darwinism cannot account for the specific patterns we see in *our* genomes, and that the common ancestry of chimps and humans is questionable. The amount and kinds of differences in our DNA cannot be accounted for in the proposed evolutionary time available. The apparently purposeful placement of repeated elements like SINEs and LINEs, plus their important roles in species-specific differences, argue against an unguided process of common descent. The sheer, amazing complexity of gene

---

75. Stephen C. Meyer, *Signature in the Cell: DNA and the Evidence for Intelligent Design* (New York: HarperCollins, 2009); Michael J. Denton, *Evolution: A Theory in Crisis* (Maryland: Adler & Adler, 1986; M. Leisola, O. Pastinen, D. D. Axe, "Lignin—Designed Randomness," *BIO-Complexity* 2012, no. 3 (2012): 1–11.

76. Richard Dawkins, *The God Delusion* (New York: Random House, 2009).

regulation and chromosome interactions argue for brilliant design. Our anatomical and physiological differences would require many specific coordinated changes, changes that could not happen without guidance. But more importantly, if things like synteny, shared codon usage, and pseudogenes can be explained functionally, the argument for common descent deteriorates, and a unique origin becomes more likely.

The chief question asked about human evolution is this: are we descended from an ape-like ancestor, or are we unique, with a distinct origin? In the context of this book, of course, this question is paramount. One of the reasons people tend to become theistic evolutionists is precisely because they consider the evidence based on genetic similarity for our descent from an ape-like ancestor to be incontrovertible. We have presented arguments here that indicate the evidence for chimp and human common ancestry may not be so incontrovertible after all, and that in light of our basic ignorance of the way our genome functions, and in light of the increasing evidence for human-specific design, the rewriting of theology is a bad idea.

Let us now review the overall argument we are making and where we are so far, in brief:

- Chapter 14 shows that the fossil record does not support the idea of a continuous evolution between a chimpanzee-like ancestor and us.
- This chapter shows that our genetic differences are far greater than have been commonly reported, and that they reveal many functionally significant, uniquely human changes. There are too many such changes to have happened by random mutation and selection.
- In the next chapter we will examine whether the claim that we had to come from a starting population of at least several thousand is necessarily true. We will report ways to distinguish between that idea and the possibility that we may have come from a single pair, Adam and Eve, and we will describe a new population genetics model that may allow us to test the two possibilities, to see which best corresponds with the actual genetic data we have.

16

An Alternative Population Genetics Model[1]

OLA HÖSSJER, ANN K. GAUGER, AND COLIN R. REEVES

SUMMARY

What can be said about human history from DNA variation among us today? Population genetics is used in academia to infer that we share a common ancestry with apes; that most of our human ancestors emigrated from Africa fifty thousand years ago; that they possibly had some mixing with Neanderthals, Denisovans, and other archaic populations; and that the early Homo population was never smaller than a few thousand individuals. It uses mathematical principles for how the genetic composition of a population changes over time through mutation, natural selection, genetic drift, and other forces of change. In this chapter we investigate the assumptions about this theory and conclude that it is full of gaps and weaknesses. We argue that a unique origin model, where humanity arose from one single couple,[2] seems to explain data at least as well, if not

---

1. A longer version of this chapter, with a more detailed argument, can be found in Ola Hössjer, Ann Gauger, and Colin Reeves, "Genetic Modeling of Human History Part 1: Comparison of Common Descent and Unique Origin Approaches," *BIO-Complexity* 2016, no. 3 (2016): 1–15.

2. The use of the term "first couple" will undoubtedly raise the issue of Adam and Eve in the reader's mind. We the authors each have our own views on the reading of Genesis. Our goal here is to show that the argument against a historical Adam and Eve made by some scientists is not justified by the scientific evidence, and that there is a real possibility of a founding first pair.

better. We finally propose an alternative simulation approach that could be used in order to validate such a model.

· · · · ·

We all have a genetic fingerprint. The more closely related we are, the more similar our fingerprints. Genetic data can be used for a number of purposes: to find out whether we carry a risk gene of an inheritable disease; to ascertain that a young man is the father of a newborn child; to find evidence against a suspect of a crime; or to retrieve our ethnic mix at ancestry.com. In this chapter we will investigate what human genetic data has to say about common ancestry. In academia, the prevailing view is that human beings are descendants of ape-like ancestors, whose numbers were never less than a few thousand individuals at any time in history.

There is another possible scenario, though, that of an original first pair. This scenario has never been adequately tested scientifically using the methods of population genetics. Given the importance of this subject, it is imperative to rigorously examine both scenarios. In this chapter we describe a method to test them against each other.

1. Population Genetics

Population genetics[3] is a discipline that describes how the genetic makeup of a group of people changes over time. It has numerous applications, but here we will use it as a tool for comparing different scenarios of human history. Before doing so, we will first review some basic principles of genetics.[4]

Genetic information is stored in all of our cells as forty-six chromosomes, twenty-three of which are inherited from our father and twenty-three from our mother. Forty-four of these are non-sex (autosomal) chromosomes and come in almost identical (homologous) pairs. The remaining two chromosomes determine our sex. Females have two

---

3. An introduction to population genetics can be found, for instance, in Daniel L. Hartl, *A Primer of Population Genetics*, 3rd ed. (Sunderland, MA: Sinauer, 2000).

4. A comprehensive introduction to genetics is *Approaches to Gene Mapping in Complex Human Diseases*, ed. Jonathan L. Haines and Margaret A. Pericak Vance (New York: Wiley-Liss, 1998).

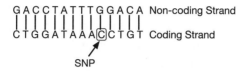

FIGURE 16.1. *Illustrating SNPs.* Two copies of a small part of a DNA molecule, showing fourteen base pairs. In the lower DNA molecule the 10th base pair is C-G rather than T-A. This position is a single nucleotide polymorphism (SNP), with two possible alleles T and C on the coding strand.

copies of an X-chromosome, one from each parent, whereas males have one Y-chromosome from the father, and one X-chromosome from the mother. There is also genetic information in the mitochondria (organelles in our cells, inherited from our mothers).

The forty-six chromosomes of the cell nucleus and the mitochondria of the cell cytoplasm are molecules. The genetic information is stored in these molecules as nucleotides of A, C, T, and G, linked together to form the double-stranded DNA helix. Each nucleotide, or base, pairs with another in a stereotypical fashion: A with T and C with G (see Fig. 16.1). The sum total of the DNA in our cells—our genome—can be thought of as a book with 3 billion base pairs of DNA. Most parts of DNA are the same for all humans, but those that vary are called polymorphisms. They are the ones that make us genetically unique. A Single Nucleotide Polymorphism (SNP) is the most common kind of variation.[5] For each base pair of the DNA molecule, the convention is to refer to only one of its two nucleotides, the one located on the coding strand.[6] This nucleotide usually exists in two variants at an SNP, for

---

5. Other types of polymorphisms include, for instance, indels, short tandem repeats, copy number variation of larger genomic regions, and Alu insertions. Statistics for their relative occurrence in human DNA can be found in The 1000 Genomes Project Consortium, "A Global Reference for Human Genetic Variation," *Nature* 526, no. 7571 (2015): 68–87.

6. This is the strand involved in protein coding. Less than 2 percent of the coding strand of human DNA actually codes for proteins. This coding part consists of a number of exons that are first transcribed into mRNA and then translated into proteins.

instance C or T, also referred to as the two alleles of the SNP. A typical genome differs from the human reference sequence (which has the most common SNP at all positions) at about 4 to 5 million nucleotides, slightly more than 0.1 percent of the human genome.[7]

Since our genomes are not identical, population genetics can tell us something about human variation and history. We can study how big the genetic differences in the worldwide human population are, and indirectly how these differences have changed in the past. We can also compare the genetic makeup of individuals from different regions like Europe, Africa, Middle East, or East Asia, or study smaller groups of people, like the inhabitants of Sardinia, Iceland, or Polynesia. Population genetics is a discipline that uses mathematical methods to quantify how genetic differences vary among individuals, between geographic regions, and over time. Starting in the 1920s, much of its theory was built by prominent mathematicians and geneticists like Ronald Fisher, Sewell Wright, John Haldane, Motoo Kimura, and Samuel Karlin.[8] Its theory is built on the principle of small stepwise changes, and as such is a good tool for describing microevolution within species, and some limited degree of speciation. This has many applications, for instance animal and plant breeding, and also wildlife management and conservation biology, where the viability of species, their adaptation to environmental changes, and inbreeding can be quantified and estimated over time.[9] However, population genetics was also intended as a method to explain how small changes could lead to big ones. In other words, it was largely founded to support macroevolution and common descent, based on the idea that macroevolution was merely microevolution writ large. But today it is possible to use it for the opposite purpose, to show how unlikely macroevolution is.[10] In the following sections, we will describe this in more detail.

---

7. 1000 Genomes Project Consortium, "Global Reference for Human Genetic Variation," 68–74.

8. A comprehensive treatment of the mathematics of population genetics can be found, for instance, in James F. Crow and Motoo Kimura, *An Introduction to Population Genetics Theory* (Caldwell, NJ: Blackburn, 1970); and Warren J. Ewens, *Mathematical Population Genetics*, 2nd ed. (New York: Springer, 2004).

9. Fred W. Allendorf and Gordon H. Luikart, *Conservation and the Genetics of Populations* (Malden, MA: Blackwell, 2007).

10. In fact, many researchers who adhere to common descent of humans and chimpanzees have recently suggested explanations other than macroevolution-driven genetic mechanisms of population change (see section 2 of this chapter, which immediately follows, and chapter 8).

2. Mechanisms of Population Change

Our genomes are scrambled images of our ancestors' genomes. In order to understand how history has scrambled our ancestral DNA, we first need to describe mechanisms that cause the genetic composition of a population to change over time. These mechanisms reflect population behavior (demography) as well as genetic inheritance, and thus can tell us something about a population's history. They can be summarized as follows:

Mutations are changes to DNA. These mutations are typically copying errors. The ones of interest in population genetics are those that occur when germ cells are formed during a special type of cell division called meiosis, which halves the genetic material of ordinary cells and reduces the number of chromosomes from forty-six to twenty-three. These mutations are important since they spread to all cells of the offspring after fertilization. Suppose, for instance, that a single nucleotide of a non-sex chromosome is changed from an A to a G in a sperm cell, which fertilizes an egg. (The probability of mutation occurring is very small, about 10^{-8} per nucleotide per generation in nuclear DNA.) As the resulting embryo develops, all the cells inherit that mutated allele G from the father, as well the mother's version, say, A. The two versions of the inherited DNA form a pair, AG, of alleles[11] in the new individual. That individual will in turn pass on either the A or the G to each of its offspring, at random usually. Mutations also occur in sex chromosomes and mitochondrial DNA.

Genetic drift means that alleles will change in their frequency from one generation to the next simply by chance. Some alleles may be passed more often to the next generation, and some less often. Say, for example, a certain SNP has alleles A and T. If a woman with two copies of A (allele pair AA) has no children, then neither of the two copies will be passed on to the next generation. If many other individuals with allele pair AA happen to have fewer children (by chance) than those with allele pair TT, or those parents with allele pair AT happen to pass on T to their children more often than A, the overall effect is that the frequency of A decreases and that of T increases.

---

11. Such a pair is called a genotype.

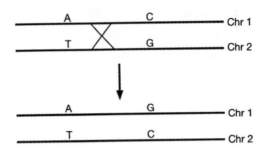

FIGURE 16.2. *Illustrating recombination.* Consider two SNPs at the same non-sex chromosome, and suppose there are only AC and TG copies of this chromosome in a population. This means that allele A is associated with C, and T with G. Recombinations will gradually break up this association, so that chromosomes with all four allele pairs AC, AG, TG, and GC are formed. The reason is that a recombination between a parent's two homologous copies of the chromosome (at the top) results in shuffling of alleles when either two sperm cells or two ova cells (at the bottom) are formed. In the figure, the A and C alleles on the parent's chromosome copy 1 are recombined, so that the new chromosome copy 1 carries A and G, and the new chromosome copy 2 carries T and C.

Natural selection is similar to genetic drift. Some parents have higher fitness and produce more offspring than others, due to differences in their ability to have children, or differences in the survival of their children to the next generation. If parents with more copies of a certain allele (say, A) at an SNP tend to be more fit than those that have more copies of the other allele (say, T), the frequency of A will increase in the next generation, and eventually T may disappear in the whole population.[12] On the other hand, if individuals with one copy each of A and T (allele pair AT) are more fit, the frequency of both alleles will tend to stabilize over time.[13]

Recombination is a way of generating more diversity between chromosomes, by shuffling the arrangement of alleles along the chromosomes. No novel DNA is produced, but existing DNA is combined in new ways (see Fig. 16.2).

Recombinations make variation at different parts of the chromosome more independent, as they gradually break up association be-

---

12. This kind of natural selection is called directional selection (alleles with higher fitness take over the population) or purifying selection (deleterious alleles are lost). See, for instance, Richard Durrett, *Probability Models for DNA Sequence Evolution*, 2nd ed. (New York: Springer Science, 2008).

13. This type of natural selection is called balancing selection.

tween alleles. This happens, for example, in Figure 16.2 between A at the first SNP on chromosome 1 and C at the second SNP. Since recombinations occur more often if the SNPs are far apart, the association between a distant SNP pair will tend to be smaller.

Colonization, isolation, and migration. Especially in the past, humans have been more or less isolated by distance, with mating couples living nearby. Sometimes new subpopulations are formed (colonization), and occasionally men or women migrate over longer distances to find their spouses. It is evident that migration will decrease the differences between subpopulations, whereas isolation will increase them.

3. Statistics Describing Genetic Variation in a Population

There are certain statistics that describe the current genetic variation of the human population. Nucleotide (or allelic) diversity roughly says how many SNPs there are in the overall population. Allele frequency spectra show how many rare and common alleles there are in the population. Linkage Disequilibrium (LD) plots give a description of how recombination has affected the variation we see along chromosomes today. The more recombination events there were in the past, the shorter are the chunks of DNA that have been inherited together. There are also other statistics that can be used to describe the degree of differentiation between subpopulations.

When population geneticists try to reconstruct human history from genetic data, they combine different demographic scenarios (population size changes, colonization, and migration, for example) with the genetic mechanisms of mutations, recombinations, genetic drift, and selection, to see how well these scenarios reconstruct the statistics mentioned above. There are highly sophisticated mathematical methods for doing this, but it is still very difficult to reconstruct human history. The main reason for this is lack of data from the past. It is indeed possible to sequence DNA from ancient people such as Neanderthals, and in recent years this line of research has exploded.[14] In

---

14. Marc Haber, Massimo Mezzavilla, Yali Xue, and Chris Tyler-Smith, "Ancient DNA and the Rewriting of Human History: Be Sparing with Occam's Razor," *Genome Biology* 17, article 1 (2016): 1–8.

spite of these advances, ancient DNA is still so sparse that, to a large extent, genetic analyses of human history will continue to rely on DNA samples from the most recent generations. With little historical data, any reconstructed genealogy is an estimate only, with assumptions embedded in it.

In order to illustrate how the past has shaped the genetic variation of today, let us consider allelic diversity. It is a balance between genetic drift, mutations, recombinations, selection, and migration. Genetic drift will first of all decrease diversity, since some alleles are lost by chance, and this happens much more quickly the smaller a population is. Mutations and recombinations, on the other hand, will increase diversity, since either new alleles enter the population, or existing ones are combined in new ways. Natural selection may either increase or decrease allelic diversity. Diversity will decrease if alleles with higher fitness take over, or if deleterious alleles are lost, whereas diversity increases if coexisting alleles have a selective advantage. Migration and colonization shuffles around existing alleles between subpopulations. The more isolated subpopulations are, and the less migration there is between them, the larger is the diversity in the whole population, since different alleles tend to take over in different subpopulations, whereas the diversity in each subpopulation decreases due to the isolation.

4. Alternate Human Histories

There are two important, controversial, and interwoven aspects of human history: the age of our initial population, and its size.

Age. How can we use allelic diversity to say something about age? Because of the balance between genetic drift on one hand, and mutations and recombinations on the other, population geneticists argue that the younger a population is, or the more recently in the past its size was drastically reduced (a so-called bottleneck), the less variation we see among the members of the population alive today, since there has been less time for mutations to produce new variants. A small amount of diversity therefore indicates a young population, or an old population that recently went through a severe bottleneck. More refined conclusions can be drawn if we also take the other statistics (allele frequency spectra, LD plots, and subpopulation differentiation) into account. For instance, the LD plot of an older population reveals that shorter segments of DNA have been inherited together, since there has been more time for recombinations to shuffle around chromosome segments.

Size. Based on genetic diversity and these other statistics, population geneticists estimate that our population never contained less than several thousand individuals to account for current diversity, and that it probably contained about ten thousand at the time of our last common ancestor with chimps, which they estimate to be about 6 million years ago. The rationale of this argument is that the diversity we see in human DNA today is not only too large to be explained by a single founding couple. It is also too large to be explained by an old population that more recently went through a bottleneck much smaller than a few thousand individuals.

It is possible, however, that a first founding couple were created with initial diversity, each individual with twenty-two pairs of autosomal chromosomes and either an XX for the female or an XY for the male. Thus there would have been four total copies of each non-sex chromosome (two from each). Those four copies could each have been created unique, giving rise to a very large number of SNPs, all of which were present in the first generation. This could be true for the all of the twenty-two sets of four homologous chromosomes. In the same way, the three X-chromosomes copies (two for the female and one for the male) could have been created with diversity. Some diversity from the first generation is also possible for mitochondrial DNA. Since the female carried hundreds of mitochondria that could have been diverse, she may have passed some of that diversity on to her daughters.

So we now have two competing hypotheses: *common descent* of humans with other species, or a *unique origin* for a first founding couple with created diversity. In the next section we will juxtapose these two models of human history: the standard model that assumes common descent, and the other model that assumes we came from two first parents (unique origin). The two models have different starting assumptions, but follow the same rules of inheritance and population genetics in their working out.

5. The Competing Models

A. Common Descent Model

The most widely accepted common descent theory of humanity currently holds that our ancestors diverged from chimps about 6 million years ago. Then a hominid species *Homo erectus* evolved in Africa. It spread to Europe and Asia about 2 million years ago. Various archaic species are believed to have evolved from *Homo erectus* over the past 500,000–800,000 years, including Neanderthals in Europe and Denisovans in Asia. (See chapter 14 for more on this subject.) There are two main variants within this framework for how *Homo sapiens*, our species, came about:

1. **Out of Africa replacement model:**[15] According to this theory, modern humans evolved from *Homo erectus* in Africa 100,000 to 200,000 years ago. Then they went through a bottleneck that reduced the population size to an order of 10,000 individuals or smaller. A large part of this group emigrated from Africa about 50,000 years ago to the Middle East, Europe, East Asia, and America, gradually replacing existing archaic species. After leaving Africa, all non-African populations have experienced much more recent and long-lasting bottlenecks before they started to grow.[16]

2. **Multiregional evolution**[17] posits that our ancestors evolved in parallel from archaic species in several parts of the world, possibly with an African dominance. As a consequence, we have to trace human lineages up to 2 million years before they all end up in Africa.

The replacement model has been the most popular common descent model of human history for several decades, but there is no distinct boundary between it and multiregional evolution. An Out of Africa scenario with some interbreeding with archaic populations is not too

---

15. Paul Mellars, "Going East: New Genetic and Archaeological Perspectives on the Modern Human Colonization of Eurasia," *Science* 313 (2006): 796–800.

16. According to the 1000 Genomes Project (2015), these bottlenecks reduced effective population sizes to less than 1,500 individuals, lasted at least ten thousand years, and may have ended as recently as 15,000–20,000 years ago.

17. M. H. Wolpoff, J. Hawks, and R. Caspari, "Multiregional, Not Multiple Origins," *American Journal of Physical Anthropology* 112 (2000): 129–136.

different from a multiregional model with an African dominance. Over the past few years, ancient DNA has been retrieved from Neanderthal and Denisovan bones in different parts of the world[18] and compared with that of present-day humans. These studies reveal that all human populations except sub-Saharan Africans have about 1 to 2 percent of Neanderthal DNA. In fact, it seems that as much as 40 percent of Neanderthal DNA is found in at least some individuals alive today.[19] Lower levels (fractions of 1 percent) of Denisovan ancestry can be found mainly in Southeast Asia, Oceania, and among Native Americans. This has caused many researchers to adopt a hybrid of the replacement and multiregional models, according to which our ancestors originated from Africa but still had some interbreeding with archaic populations.[20]

B. Unique Origin Model

By a "unique origin" model we mean one in which humanity originates from a single couple. There is still the question of geographic origin. There are at least two versions of the unique origin model, with different geographic ancestry:

1. **African ancestry.** This is a scenario by which the first couple lived in Africa. It has many similarities with the Out of Africa model, except for the unique origin assumption. The subsequent migration scenario out of Africa could be similar for both models. In the next section we will argue that a unique origin with an African ancestry typically gives old estimates for the age of humanity.

2. **Middle East ancestry** posits that the most recent common ancestors (MRCA) of all humans lived in the Middle East. The

---

18. Four of the first papers on sequencing of archaic DNA are: R. E. Green, I. Krause, A. W. Biggs, T. Maricic, U. Stenzel, M. Kircher, et al, "A Draft Sequence of the Neandertal Genome," *Science* 328 (2010): 710–722; D. Reich, R. E. Green, M. Kircher, I. Krause, N. Patterson, E. Y. Durand, et al., "Genetic History of an Archaic Hominin Group from Denisova Cave in Siberia," *Nature* 468 (2010): 1053–1060; K. Prufer, F. Racimo, N. Patterson, F. Jay, S. Sankararaman, S. Sawyer, et al, "The Complete Sequence of a Neanderthal from the Altai Mountains," *Nature* 505, no. 43 (2014): 9; and M. Meyer, M. Kircher, M-T Gansauge, et al., "A High Coverage Genome Sequence from an Archaic Denisovan Individual," *Science* 338 (2012): 212–216.

19. Svante Pääbo, "The Contribution of Ancient Hominin Genomes from Siberia to Our Understanding of Human Evolution," *Herald of the Russian Academy of Sciences* 85, no. 5 (2015): 392–396.

20. Haber et al., "Ancient DNA."

subsequent migration from Middle East to Europe, Asia, America, and Oceania could be similar to that of the Out of Africa and the African Unique Origin models discussed earlier, in that the migration is in the same general direction. However, this model differs from the African ancestry model and Out of Africa models by proposing that Africa was colonized from the Middle East rather than the opposite. In the next section we will argue that, in light of genetics, this gives a much younger age of humanity.

6. Comparison of the Models

The crucial question is which of the different scenarios of common descent or unique origin in section 5 the actual genetic data supports the most. We will consider the evidence in several parts.

Differences with other species. A major drawback of the common descent model(s) is the difficulty with handling the significant genetic differences between humans and other species. This is treated in detail in chapter 14. There are indeed research papers that try to estimate a common genealogy of humans, chimps, and gorillas, using those parts of their genomes that show more similarity, but comparisons of this kind have limited scope, since they focus too little on the regions where the species differ.[21] Models that compare human DNA with that of other species should incorporate the difficulty for mutations and other genome arrangements to build up such genomic interspecies divergence, as well as anatomical and physiological differences. Other studies that take this into account typically reveal that the time it takes for these mutations to appear and be fixed in the population is much longer than what macroevolution requires.[22]

Variability in human genetic data. The main argument against a unique origin is that the nucleotide diversity within the human population seems too high to make a single founding couple possible. But this is not a problem for non-sex and X-chromosome DNA if there was

---

21. Hildegard Kehrer-Sawatzki and David Cooper, "Understanding the Recent Evolution of the Human Genome: Insights from Human-Chimpanzee Genome Comparisons," *Human Mutation* 28, no. 2 (2007): 99–130.

22. John Sanford, Wesley Brewer, Franzine Smith, and John Baumgardner. "The Waiting Time Problem in a Model Hominin Population," *Theoretical Biology and Medical Modelling* 12, article 18 (2015): 1–28.

initial created diversity. Although it is not possible to invoke created diversity for Y-chromosomes, recent studies have shown that its diversity is in fact a lot smaller than for other types of DNA.[23]

Genetic data also indicates that all non-African populations are quite closely related. According to the Out of Africa model, this is explained by a severe and very recent bottleneck (of the order 10,000 to 50,000 years ago) that the non-African ancestors supposedly experienced. This is perhaps the main reason why this model is more popular today than multiregional evolution. African populations, on the other hand, look older, at least at first sight. There are also considerable genetic differences between African groups, indicating that their ancestors lived in small and relatively isolated tribes.[24] Out of Africa model adherents interpret the bottleneck that the ancestors of all non-Africans supposedly experienced as descendants of a few thousand people that migrated out of Africa. For a long time the non-African populations stayed very small,[25] but then they quickly expanded and diverged. These arguments for the Out of Africa model seem convincing at first. But they could also be used for a unique origin model with an old African ancestry. The only difference is that the ancestral population of all people alive today, supposed to have lived in Africa before the migration and expansion to other continents took place, is a single couple with created diversity.

But what about a founding couple from the Middle East? Is this unique origin version incompatible with data? Not necessarily. This model requires that the age of humanity is much more recent. The reason is that the originating pair replaces the long-lasting bottleneck that supposedly occurred after immigration to the Middle East from Africa.[26] And the genetic diversity that remains after this bottleneck population is replaced by created diversity in the first pair. This would explain the relatively large genetic variability we find among humans

23. M. A. Wilson Sayres, K. E. Lohmuller and R. Nielsen, "Natural Selection Reduced Diversity on Human Y Chromosomes," *PLoS Genetics* 10 (2014): e1004064.

24. See, for instance, S. F. Schaffner, C. Foo, S. Gabriel, D. Reich, M. J. Daly, and D. Altshuler, "Calibrating Coalescent Simulation of Human Genome Simulation," *Genome Research* 15 (2005): 1576–1583; and H. Li, and R. Durbin, "Inference of Human Population History from Individual Whole-Genome Sequences," *Nature* 475 (2011): 493–496.

25. 1000 Genomes Project Consortium, "Global Reference for Human Genetic Variation," 68–74.

26. Ibid.

of today for non-sex and X-chromosome DNA (recall that the diversity of Y-chromosomes is much smaller). A recent paper that compared sequences among Y-chromosomes found that a large group of Africans are in fact more related to non-Africans than to all other Africans.[27] A possible explanation for this is several migration events into Africa from the Middle East. There are also tentative explanations within the Middle East unique origin framework for the observation that African populations look older than non-African ones for non-sex and sex-chromosome DNA. Future research will tell how credible these explanations are.[28]

Block structure of DNA. A large part of our autosomal and X-chromosomes have apparently been recombined into blocks of varying length.[29] Many of them are on the order of ten thousand nucleotides long,[30] but the variation in length is large. But even though the blocks are long, there is still very little variation within them. Each block comes in just a few variants—four, for many parts of the genome. Our chromosomes are different mosaics of these block variants.

This DNA block structure is remarkably consistent with a unique origin hypothesis. If the first couple originated with DNA diversity, there would have been four different copies of each autosomal chromosome—two for each individual. Their four chromosomes have since been scrambled by ancestral recombinations, and today each of us has one mosaic of the four founder chromosomes inherited from our father, and another one from our mother.

Inbreeding depression and genetic entropy. It is well known that many alleles will be lost due to genetic drift when a population experiences a severe bottleneck. The long-term consequence is a decreased

---

27. G. David Poznik, Yali Xue, Fernando L. Mendez, Thomas F. Willems, Andrea Massaia, Melissa A. Wilson Sayres, Qasim Ayub, et al. "Punctuated Bursts in Human Male Demography Inferred from 1,244 Worldwide Y-Chromosome Sequences," *Nature Genetics* 48, no. 6 (2016): 593–599.

28. For a more detailed argument, see Ola Hössjer, Ann Gauger, and Colin Reeves, "Genetic Modeling of Human History Part 1: Comparison of Common Descent and Unique Origin Approaches," *BIO-Complexity* 2016, no. 3 (2016): 1–15.

29. Two of the first published papers on the existence of haplotype block structure along the human genome are M. J. Daly, J. D. Rioux, S. F. Schaffner, T. F. Hudson, and E. L. Lander, "High-Resolution Haplotype Structure in the Human Genome," *Nature Genetics* 29 (2001): 229–232; and S. B. Gabriel et al., "The Structure of Haplotype Blocks in the Human Genome," *Science* 296 (2002): 2225–2229.

30. S. Myers et al., "A Fine-Scale Map of Recombination Rates and Hotspots across the Human Genome," *Science* 310 (2005): 321–324.

ability for long-term adjustment to environmental changes, but there is also a more acute risk of inbreeding depression when the frequency of recessive disorders increases, as more offspring receive from both of their parents a harmful variant of a disease-causing gene. The smaller the population is during the bottleneck, and the longer time it takes before its size starts to increase, the more severe are the consequences for the population's viability, so that ultimately it may die out.[31] Conservation biologists have devised rules for minimal population sizes in order to ensure short- and long-term protection of animal species.[32] For humans there are several well-known examples of the drastic effects of continued inbreeding, such as the extinction of the Spanish Habsburg dynasty around 1700[33] and the high occurrence of a severe form of color blindness on the Micronesian atoll of Pingelap, after a typhoon hit the island in 1775 and 90 percent of the inhabitants died. All present-day inhabitants can trace their ancestry to one of the survivors that carried the harmful variant of the gene that codes for this type of color blindness.[34]

Inbreeding depression is potentially a difficulty for the common descent model. Recent calculations reveal that the model predicts a very small bottleneck, of the order a few thousand individuals, and that it lasted for at least a thousand generations.[35] In spite of this, the survivors of the bottleneck are believed to have expanded, to conquer the rest of the world.

A unique origin model avoids, to some extent, the problem of inbreeding depression, if the created diversity of the first pair had only neutral variants, whereas the harmful ones occurred later through germline mutations. The younger the population is, the shorter is the time for such germline mutations to occur, and the smaller is the risk of inbreeding depression. For a similar reason, a model with a young

31. M. Lynch, J. Conery, and R. Burger, "Mutation Accumulation and Extinction of Natural Populations," *American Naturalist* 146 (1995): 489–518.

32. Fred. W. Allendorf, and Nils Ryman, "The Role of Genetics in Population Viability Analysis," in *Population Viability Analysis*, ed. S. R. Bessinger and D. R. McCullough (Chicago: University of Chicago Press, 2002).

33. Gonzalo Alvarez, Francesco C. Ceballos, and Celsa Quinteiro, "The Role of Inbreeding in the Extinction of a Royal Dynasty," *PLoS ONE* 4, no. 4 (2009): e5175.

34. N. E. Norton, R. Lew, I. E. Hussels, and G. F. Little, "Pingelap and Mokil Atolls: Historical Genetics," *American Journal of Human Genetics* 24 (1972): 277–289.

35. 1000 Genomes Project Consortium, "Global Reference for Human Genetic Variation," 68–74.

518 *The Case against Common Descent and for a Unique Human Origin*

age of humanity has another advantage: It can handle the problem that the slightly deleterious mutations are so many that natural selection cannot remove them all. For an old population, as the mutations accumulate over time (the technical term for this is that the genetic entropy increases), they can have potentially very damaging effects.[36] But if the pair lived recently, and if all present-day harmful variants arrived only through mutations in their descendants, there has not been enough time to accumulate them into large numbers. In contrast, any model with an old age of humanity faces a problem, since either the number of slightly deleterious or deleterious alleles increases, or a bottleneck occurred that removed some of these harmful variants, but at the cost of spreading others that could initiate inbreeding depression.[37]

Archaic populations, humans or not? As mentioned in section 5 of this chapter, significant fragments of Neanderthal and Denisovan DNA have been found among present-day humans, so researchers suggested that some interbreeding took place between archaic populations and the ancient humans that supposedly emigrated out of Africa. This admixture is believed to have happened at least 50,000 years ago, and probably later on as well. It is in fact well known that gene flow between closely related populations is helpful in order to increase genetic variability and to avoid inbreeding, and indeed, the archaic introgression is believed to have had positive effects, like helping the Tibetans to adapt to high altitudes, and the non-Africans in general to adapt to colder temperature[38] and to ward off infections.[39] But the common descent model predicts a split between humans and archaic hominins more than 500,000 years ago.[40] It would therefore be remarkable if two populations, after such a long time of separation, were still able

36. John Sanford, *Genetic Entropy and the Mystery of the Genome*, 3rd ed. (Waterloo, NY: FMS, 2008).

37. See Sanford, *Genetic Entropy*, and references therein, for estimates of the fractions of mutations that are neutral, slightly deleterious, or deleterious. If the total number of slightly deleterious alleles is large, their cumulative effect may be large as well.

38. Haber et al., "Ancient DNA"; S. Sankararaman et al., "The Genomic Landscape of Neanderthal Ancestry in Present-Day Humans," *Nature* 505 (2014): 43–49.

39. Matthieu Deschamps et al., "Genetic Signatures of Selective Pressures and Introgression from Archaic Hominins at Human Innate Immunity Genes," *American Journal of Human Genetics* 98 (2016): 5, doi:10.1016/j.ajhg.2015.11.014; and Michael Danneman et al. "Introgression of Neanderthal- and Denisovan-Like Haplotypes Contributes to Adaptive Variation in Human Toll-Like Receptors," *American Journal of Human Genetics* 98 (2016): 22, doi:10.1016/j.ajhg.2015.11.015.

40. Haber et al., "Ancient DNA."

to have fertile offspring.[41] But even if this were possible, because of the long separation, it is reasonable to believe that the offspring had low fitness, since our archaic ancestors had, most likely, accumulated many alleles which were deleterious for humans, before the admixture took place.

In view of this, it seems that the large fraction of archaic DNA among present-day humans is more reconcilable with a unique origin model, in which Neanderthals and Denisovans are descendants of the originating pair and hence are our fully human relatives.

Conclusions. We have argued that a unique origin model (with either a young or an old age of humanity) with created diversity should have at least the same explanatory power for human genetic data as the most popular common descent scenario of today. Any model must be able to explain the big genetic differences between humans and other species, solve the problem of inbreeding depression, support the viability of human and archaic population admixtures, and give reasons why our DNA resembles a mosaic of about four founder genomes. The conclusion is that the unique origin model seems more plausible.

7. Testing of the Models

The qualitative arguments of section 5 lead us to conclude that the unique origin scenario of human history seems plausible. It is of interest to follow this up in a more formal way. The basic idea is to simulate genetic data from each proposed model many times, and then compare how well the simulated output fits real data. This comparison should include nucleotide diversity, allele frequency spectra, LD plots, and other statistics. There are at least two different ways to proceed with these simulations.

Forward simulation. The most straightforward way of simulating genetic data is to start at the founder generation and then proceed forward in time.[42] For each simulation round, one first assigns genomes to the first pair of humans. Demographic and genetic data are then

41. P. S. Burgoyne, S. K. Mehadevala., and J. M. A. Turner, "The Consequences of Asynapsis for Mammalian Meiosis," *Nature Review Genetics* 10 (2009): 207–216.

42. J. C. Sanford, J. Baumgardner, W. Brewer, P. Gibson, and W. ReMine, "Mendel's Accountant: A Biologically Reasonable Forward-Time Population Genetics Program," *Scalable Computing: Practice and Experience* 8, no. 2 (2007): 147–165.

simulated one generation at a time, using the hereditary principles of section 2.

The main advantage of forward simulation is its great flexibility. Virtually any type of model for human history can be simulated and validated with real data. But the method requires that DNA of all humans is simulated. In view of the size of the worldwide human population, this is computationally very demanding, and requires long execution times.

Backward simulation. There is another much faster simulation algorithm. A more detailed description of it can be found elsewhere.[43] In each simulation round, only a small subset of genetic data is generated. The main idea is first to select a small sample of humans alive today (for instance, a few thousand individuals), then simulate their genealogy backwards in time (using a method called coalescence theory[44]) until the founder generation is reached. When the genealogy has been generated, DNA is assigned, first to the founders, and then forward in time to all their descendants along the branches of the simulated genealogy. The genealogy will be only a small subset of the ancestral human population. We refer to this method as backward simulation since the genealogy is simulated backwards in time.

We are currently working on implementing a model based on backward simulation. The intent is to validate it with real data. This is a long-term project, whose outcome we hope to publish elsewhere. Using this approach, our intent is to demonstrate that a unique origin model is able to replicate current human diversity as well as or better than the common descent model.[45] That is the purpose of the model—to test this possibility. Therefore, if more than one plausible account of human origins can explain the data, the common descent model of our origin from ape-like ancestors can no longer be claimed as conclusive proof that there could not have been a single first pair.

Here we complete our one long argument for a unique origin for

---

43. See Ola Hössjer, Ann Gauger, and Colin Reeves, "Genetic Modeling of Human History Part 2: A Unique Origin Algorithm," *BIO-Complexity* 2016, no. 4 (2016): 1–36.
44. Durrett, *Probability Models.*
45. We may also be able to test more detailed scenarios, such as the time of the first couple, or from what area geographically their progeny spread. Updates on the progress of the work are available at uniqueoriginresearch.org.

humanity begun in chapter 13 with an outline of the importance of the question. In chapters 14 through 16 we have shown that,

- The fossil evidence shows an absence of intermediates between ape-like fossils and human ones, indicating that the story told by evolutionists of a well-documented continuous bridge between the two is false.
- The genetic evidence shows there are many more uniquely human elements in our genome than are commonly ascribed to it, significantly more than the oft-quoted 1 percent genetic difference between chimpanzees and us.
- Many of these elements come from what used to be called junk DNA, but are now thought to be functionally significant.
- There isn't enough time for all these differences to have been selected and fixed in the ancestral human population by purely natural means.
- Population genetics models that say we had to come from an original population of thousands rather than two are subject to question, and can be tested against an alternative model starting with just two first parents.

Taken together, our argument leads to the conclusion that it is unwarranted to discard traditional interpretations of our origin.

17

Pressure to Conform Leads to Bias in Science

CHRISTOPHER SHAW

SUMMARY

Science has become all-pervasive in modern society and is regarded by many as the means to solve all of our major problems. For many, science has become a new religion, endowed with an infallibility extending even to answering the fundamental questions about our origins and the purpose of our existence—questions that once were the subject matter of philosophers and religious scholars. As a consequence of this new role, the scientific process has been increasingly departing from its objective basis to one of crass subjectivity, with regular highly speculative claims being made by renowned scientists in the popular media and even in the scientific press. Phrases such as "I/We believe that . . . " have become common among some scientists, particularly in the fields of evolutionary biology and cosmology. The "high priests" of this new religion—we'll call it "scientism"—are the worst offenders, and many have achieved international celebrity status. But there is also a largely unknown dark side to this new religion: control of the freedom of thought. As acknowledged by the majority of scientists, the allocation of research funding and the peer-review system of scientific publication are both seriously flawed and serve to maintain the *status quo* within the establishment by filtering out perceived intellectual heretics. New thoughts, ideas, and insights are often viewed with suspicion and require evaluation not only of their worth but also, increasingly, of their potential to challenge widely accepted dogma. Indeed, this has been an almost universal experience in the early, ridicule-fraught careers of most Nobel laureates in the sciences. New recruits to the system must obey the rules if they wish to obtain training positions, tenure, and career progression.

. . . . .

I. Scientism: The New Religion

Scientific advances in the past two hundred years have been instrumental in producing rapid changes in virtually every aspect of life, particularly with regard to the global environmental changes associated with expanding human agriculture and industry required to feed and maintain a burgeoning human population. Science has produced numerous benefits for humanity in terms of technological innovations that have generated unprecedented advances in healthcare, nutrition, and telecommunications. The apparent solutions to many of life's problems and the relatively cozy lives of people in developed nations has led to the demise of traditional Christian beliefs and their replacement by the new religion of scientism. The rationale for this is simple: why feel obliged to abide by the often inconvenient and lifestyle-intruding rules of a superior being, a Creator God, when science is solving all of our problems? The church of scientism has its anti-theist prophets and priesthood who pervade almost all aspects of modern life, and who pursue this new religion with an almost unequaled evangelistic zeal, beginning in our schools and continuing into higher education. Those who do not convert but maintain their biblical beliefs are often subjected to name-calling, usually with an implication of low intelligence. Interestingly, as we shall see, the same strategy is used for scientists who challenge the accepted scientific dogma of the establishment.

Basically, the catechism of scientism states that the universe and life arose through cosmic accidents over vast periods of time, and that therefore our human existence has no defined purpose. Individuals are free to do as they please, as there is no rational scientific basis for moral concepts such as good and bad. We are told that we are not alone in the universe and that, indeed, many universes may exist, of which ours is only one. These dogmas are not, as one would expect, based on scientific proof in the form of reproducible experimental evidence, but rather are based on speculation or individual beliefs. Stephen Hawking, quoted in the *Mail Online* in an article titled "New Hunt for Alien Life," said,

> We *believe* that life arose spontaneously on Earth. So in an Infinite Universe, there *must be* other occurrences of life. Somewhere in the cosmos, *perhaps*, intelligent life *may be* watching these lights of ours, aware of what they mean. Or do our lights wander a lifeless cosmos—unseen beacons, announcing that here, on one rock, the Universe discovered its existence. Either way, there is no bigger question. . . . *We must know.*[1]

Such statements would not be considered scientific, and are more consistent with a religious belief system, but, being uttered by one of the most high-profile scientists of our time, they are taken by the general public as factual and true. Such subjective commentaries from eminent scientists are now commonplace, and many, especially the young, are being subconsciously initiated into the new religion. Evolutionary theory was one of the first areas of science to travel this path, and any alternative explanations or beliefs concerning life's origins or diversity are treated as heresies in the vast majority of schools; deviation from this establishment dogma by teachers can result—and indeed has resulted—in litigation or dismissal from employment.

Among his great scientific achievements, Craig Venter, an entrepreneurial molecular biologist, succeeded in making the first synthetic bacterial cell, which he named Synthia.[2] Many scientists and nonscientists claimed that Venter was "playing God"—a claim that Venter denied, saying that he could not be modeling himself on someone he did not believe in. When an interviewer pointed out that some scientists did not

---

1. Stephen Hawking, as quoted by Richard Gray, "New Hunt for Alien Life: Professor Stephen Hawking and Russian Billionaire Back $100 million Quest to Find ET by 2025," *Daily Mail*, July 20, 2015, accessed October 25, 2016, http://www.dailymail.co.uk/sciencetech/article-3168066/New-hunt-alien-life-launched-Professor-Stephen-Hawking-backs-100-million-search-extraterrestrial-signals.html (emphasis added).

2. Richard Alleyne, "Scientist Craig Venter Creates Life for First Time in Laboratory Sparking Debate about 'Playing God,'" *The Telegraph*, May 20, 2010, accessed October 25, 2016, http://www.telegraph.co.uk/news/science/7745868/Scientist-Craig-Venter-creates-life-for-first-time-in-laboratory-sparking-debate-about-playing-god.html.

rule out belief in God, Venter replied that it was their issue to reconcile, not his, and that for him, it was either faith or science—one could not have both.[3] Of course, many scientists have had long and distinguished careers while maintaining their belief in God and, indeed, many of the fundamentals of a variety of scientific disciplines were put in place by just such people. (I often smile when discussing Venter's creation of Synthia, as I see this as a great example of intelligent design, albeit a much less complex derivative of the original version.)

In an interview for the *Kings Review* magazine, the eminent scientist Sydney Brenner commented about his experience as a scientist in the early days in the mid-twentieth century, a time of unparalleled fundamental biological discovery as he worked at Cambridge with pioneering innovators such as Max Perutz, Francis Crick, and Fred Sanger, all of whom became Nobel laureates:

> What people don't realise is that at the beginning, it was just a handful of people who saw the light, if I can put it that way. So it was like belonging to an evangelical sect, because there were so few of us, and all the others sort of thought that there was something wrong with us.
>
> They weren't willing to believe. Of course they just said, well, what you're trying to do is impossible. . . .
>
> I remember when going to London to talk at meetings, people used to ask me what I am going to do in London, and I used to tell them I'm going to preach to the heathens.[4]

So the message of true scientific innovation is often treated with ridicule by one's peers, and it takes a special type of person to persevere and ultimately win the day. Without this unified and determined focus, the discipline of molecular biology would not have been born when it was. Brenner went on in this interview to say, "I think that being in science is the most incredible experience to have, and I now spend quite

---

3. Craig Venter in "SPIEGEL Interview with Craig Venter: 'We Have Learned Nothing from the Genome,'" *SPIEGEL Online*, July 29, 2010, accessed October 25, 2016, http://www.spiegel .de/international/world/spiegel-interview-with-craig-venter-we-have-learned-nothing-from-the -genome-a-709174-3.html.

4. Quoted in Elizabeth Dzeng, "How Academia and Publishing Are Destroying Scientific Innovation: A Conversation with Sydney Brenner, *King's Review*, February 24, 2015, http://kingsreview .co.uk/articles/how-academia-and-publishing-are-destroying-scientific-innovation-a-conversation -with-sydney-brenner/.

a lot of my time trying to help the younger people in science to enjoy it and not to feel that they are part of some gigantic machine, which a lot of people feel today." In the following sections, we will consider some of the reasons[5] why young scientists feel that way.

II. The Typical Paths Followed by a Career Scientist

After graduating from high school, a young person wishing to pursue a career in science will carefully choose an undergraduate degree course in their area of interest, usually in a university with a good reputation in that discipline.

After a number of years, usually between three and five, they will emerge with an undergraduate degree in their chosen subject. The potential career pathways that can be followed at this stage are varied. Graduates may leave university at this point and enter the job market directly, especially if their qualification is vocational. Those who aspire to be high school teachers will usually then obtain a postgraduate teaching qualification and enter that venerable career. Those who develop an interest in scientific research, however, are really just at the beginning of a period of intense postgraduate study which may involve one to three years of study in a more specialized Master's program with both classroom and research project elements, followed by a PhD program of even more specialized research of three to seven years' duration. Many industries require scientists seeking positions in research and development to be qualified to the PhD level, and a considerable number of those who achieve this level of education will avail themselves of such jobs at this stage. These relatively well-paying jobs are favored by many who are worried by the often sizeable debts incurred to reach this point. By now, they may be nearing thirty years of age.

For those who remain, who have a passion to pursue a career in academic scientific research, a series of postdoctoral research fellow positions now have to be obtained in order to acquire relevant experience in even more specialized techniques in increasingly specialized areas of research.[5] The competition for these positions is even more

---

5. Cynthia N. Fuhrmann, Philip S. Clifford, Jennifer A. Hobin, Bill Lindstaedt, "Narrowing Choices, What Career Path Is Right for You?" *Science*, September 24, 2013, http://www.sciencemag .org/careers/2013/09/narrowing-choices-what-career-path-right-you; Kendall Powell, "The Future of the Postdoc," *Nature* 520, no. 7546 (April 7, 2015), http://www.nature.com/news/the-future

intense than for those already described. To obtain the requisite positions, candidates may have to travel extensively, with associated costs of relocation, etc. After successful completion of an average of two such positions, with associated appropriate academic outputs, the aspiring research scientists, now in their mid-thirties, will be in a position to apply for the even rarer tenured or tenure-track academic jobs, for which competition is fierce. At this career stage, the candidates will have been studying or working on small incomes for an average of fifteen years, and this takes its toll on many of them, not least in their social and personal lives. For the few who obtain tenured or tenure-track positions, while many battles have been fought and won, the war is not yet over. These positions invariably have periods of probation of sometimes three-years duration, after which the relative security of tenure will be achieved subject to a satisfactory performance as judged by faculty and/or university administration. Such performance indicators may include quantity of research grant income, number and quality of research publications, and assessments by the undergraduate students they have taught. In fact, in many institutions, established academics are subjected to regular performance assessments, the results of which may determine salary increments, progression to higher grades, and, in some instances, maintaining positions per se.

It is thus not surprising that, after undergoing such stringent selection procedures, those who emerge at the end of the process are highly talented, highly motivated, determined individuals. However, they are thus, for the most part, highly unlikely to do anything that would serve to create dissent or engender disfavor within their respective university or scientific establishments—for the not unreasonable fear of losing all that they have strived to obtain. The common view that scientists are free thinkers who are open to all new ideas and can pursue such without hindrance is not what occurs in reality, and the following sections give some insights into how controls occur in internal university appraisal processes, the obtaining of external income for research, the

-of-the-postdoc-1.17253; Julie Gould, "The Elephant in the Lab," *Nature Jobs*, Nature, February 17, 2015, http://blogs.nature.com/naturejobs/2015/02/17/the-elephant-in-the-lab/; Tyler J. Ford, "What the Heck Do You Do with a Ph.D. in the Biomedical Sciences?" *Science in the News*, Harvard University, February 2, 2015, http://sitn.hms.harvard.edu/flash/2015/What-the-heck-do-you-do-with-a-ph-d-in-the-biomedical-sciences/.

peer-reviewed publication of results, and how these factors relate to one another.

III. The Financing of Research through Externally Acquired Income

A colleague of mine once said, in response to a question from the dean as to why he was considerably more successful than his peers in obtaining external research income, that he "only wrote an application for funding when he had a good and novel idea." This would probably be the general impression of the public, but it is apparent rather than real. It may come as a surprise to many that the topics of scientific research are actually not chosen by the applying scientists but rather by the funders themselves. These research themes and special initiatives are driven largely by economic and political agendas and are not curiosity-driven by the scientists themselves—hence the drive toward applied research and away from individual curiosity-inspired questions. While this situation could be deemed a logical path in the maximizing of research efforts for economic benefits, especially considering that much of the research depends on public funds, it actually serves to prevent innovators from pursuing projects that would be considered unconventional, and this is exactly where true innovative discoveries most often arise.

External income for university research comes from a multitude of sources, including federal or other government funding, charities devoted to specific issues, industry, philanthropy, and bequests. Income can be defined in several ways, such as that for specific projects addressing specific research questions, for major equipment, and for new infrastructure. While each source of income can be approached for all of these uses, the major sources of external income for specific research projects tends to be government, charities, and industry.

Each source works in different ways, with different agendas. The funding from government sources is divided across organizations of broad research focus, which are subdivided into panels of discrete interests or themes, which may in turn be subdivided from time to time into special initiative groups. Applications are usually externally peer-reviewed, by reviewers who are chosen either from those nominated by the applicant or from those nominated by the panel, or a mixture of both. Final funding decisions are made by the specific panel, taking external peer reviews and ratings into account, and often after supplying the applicants with questions or comments arising from this process, for reply, prior to the final decision. It is not uncommon for these questions/comments to be highly subjective and to clearly show that the reviewers have either not carefully read and/or have not understood the application.

Charities tend to have scientific advisory boards consisting of specialists in their areas of focus, such as in a particular disease, and they often employ external peer review as well in their decision making processes. Industry will, for reasons of intellectual security, review grants internally by specialist consultants and team leaders and usually will fund areas of specific commercial interest to their company but may also fund more fundamental research if deemed to be of strategic importance.

While various sources of external research income are very important to the research machine, the most favored and predominant are those from government sources. There are several reasons for this, including the fact that it is the most highly competitive source, but also that such grants often cover full economic costs of the research for the university administration. The highly competitive nature of acquiring such funding (often no more than 10 percent of applications are successful) is commonly used by administrators as an index of the quality of the applicant's research, which can have promotion implications. And, of course, these grants oil the bureaucratic machine. For these reasons, scientists are encouraged to apply to such sources as a top priority. A well-written application may take several months to write and, with a low level of potential success, it places a considerable burden on researchers. Can one imagine a recently established researcher writing an application which challenges accepted dogma or which proposes a new idea, bearing in mind that those who make the final decisions on funding have built careers on established dogma and may even be the authors of such? When one takes into account everything that is at stake in this process, it is not surprising that the vast majority of applicants decide not to be too critical of what has gone before but rather to describe an incremental study based on what has been previously published. The names and affiliations of panel members on national research funding bodies are usually published, and it would be foolish not to avail oneself of information about them through examination of their own publications. Since many universities have representatives on the panels of national research bodies, it is often useful to have a chat with such persons prior to submission of applications. There is a lot at stake in this process, and of all that is expected of a university academic, it is probably the area that causes the most stress, due to the enormous uncertainty of success.

An eminent colleague of mine, with a good track record in research funding, while addressing a group of newly recruited scientists was asked what the difference is between a successful and an unsuccessful application. He replied that he could not answer that question as, in his opinion, he had written superb applications that had not been funded and others that he thought less highly of that *were* funded. In essence, all things being equal, funding is largely no more than a lottery, perhaps being decided by no more than one reviewer having a bad day before writing his or her report or by someone who is not familiar with the science producing an erroneous assessment.

Sir Harry Kroto, 1996 Nobel Prize winner in Chemistry for the discovery of carbon-60, in an interview with the *Guardian* newspaper, recalled,

> "You hear through the grapevine that you're in the running [for the Prize], but on the day I forgot all about it and went to the pub for lunch."
>
> The timing had a nice irony, for only hours before—causing huge embarrassment for the Engineering and Physical Science Research Council (UK)—he had been refused a £100,000 grant for research into exactly the same subject.[6]

Sydney Brenner describes the current situation in obtaining research funding in his own inimitable style:

---

6. Harry Kroto, as quoted by John Crace, "Clever Move," *The Guardian*, September 27, 2004, https://www.theguardian.com/education/2004/sep/28/careers.highereducationprofile.

> Even God wouldn't get a grant today because somebody on the committee would say, oh those were very interesting experiments (creating the universe), but they've never been repeated. And then someone else would say, yes and he did it a long time ago, what's he done recently? And a third would say, to top it all, he published it all in an un-refereed journal (The Bible).[7]

So, to summarize, the system of training and employing young scientists requires many years (as many as fifteen) of hard work and monetary investment in a highly competitive environment. The end point of this effort is a tenured or tenure-track position as a university academic, but the selection process does not end here. The acquisition of external research income is a major factor in establishing tenure and is used by administrators in deciding on career progression, often through rigorous annual appraisal procedures. Achieving success in this arena largely precludes the high risk of proposing new ideas in applications, and most scientists adopt the incremental approach to research which does not attack or question established thinking. So much for the popular public view that academic research scientists are unrestrained free thinkers.

IV. The Peer-Reviewed Publication Process

The peer-reviewed publication process can be defined as the review of a scientific manuscript by a small number of scientists working in the same field as the subject matter of the submitted work, objectively assessing its quality. Most scientists would question the objectivity of this process, but the general feeling is that it is the best we have in the absence of an alternative. But is it really good enough, in the twenty-first century, to have a subjective system which has endemic bias and which can effectively undermine the dissemination of new information and ideas, and can influence the careers of academics in an unfair and unregulated manner?[8]

In a tribute to his colleague Fred Sanger (Nobel Prizes in Chemistry, 1958 and 1980), published in *Science*, Sydney Brenner wrote,

---

7. Sydney Brenner, quoted in "How Academia and Publishing Are Destroying Scientific Innovation."
8. Richard Smith, "Peer Review: A Flawed Process at the Heart of Science and Journals," *Journal of the Royal Society of Medicine* 99 (2006): 178–182.

A Fred Sanger would not survive today's world of science. With continuous reporting and appraisals, some committee would note that he published little of import between insulin in 1952 and his first paper on RNA sequencing in 1967 with another long gap until DNA sequencing in 1977. He would be labeled as unproductive, and his modest personal support would be denied. We no longer have a culture that allows individuals to embark on long-term—and what would be considered today extremely risky—projects.[9]

Interestingly, and in a similar vein, Peter Higgs, who won a Nobel Prize more recently for prediction of the boson which bears his name, said in an interview in the *Guardian* newspaper that he doubts a similar breakthrough could be achieved in today's academic culture, because of the expectations on academics to collaborate and keep churning out papers. He went on to say that "it's difficult to imagine how I would ever have enough peace and quiet in the present sort of climate to do what I did in 1964."[10] Such immense figures in science are not wrong in their assertions, and there are few career scientists in the academic world today who would disagree with these sentiments. Maybe one of the reasons why so many Nobel Prize–winning scientists are critical of the subjectivity of the peer-review system is that, in their early careers, papers describing their initial award-winning discoveries were rejected by their peers.[11]

These "rejected laureates" include Arne Wilhelm Kaurin Tiselius (1948, Chemistry), Hideki Yukawa (1949, Physics), Hans Adolf Krebs (1953, Physiology/Medicine), John Bardeen (1956, Physics), Pavel Alekseyevich, Ilya Mikhailovich Frank and Igor Yevgenyevich Tamm (1958, Physics), Arthur Kornberg and Severo Ochoa (1959, Physiology/Medicine), Frank Macfarlane Burnet (1960, Physiology/Medicine), Eugene Paul Wigner (1963, Physics), Murray Gell-Mann (1969, Physics), John Bardeen (1972, Physics), Baruch Samuel

9. Sydney Brenner, "Frederick Sanger (1918-2013)," *Science* 343 (2014): 262.
10. Peter Higgs, quoted in Decca Aitkenhead, "Peter Higgs Interview: 'I Have This Kind of Underlying Incompetence,'" *The Guardian*, December 6, 2013, https://www.theguardian.com/science/2013/dec/06/peter-higgs-interview-underlying-incompetence.
11. Juan R. Gonzalez-Alvarez, "Science in the 21st Century: Social, Political and Economic Issues," *Canonical Science Reports* (2008): 20082v1.

Blumberg (1976, Physiology/Medicine), William Nunn Lipscomb (1976, Chemistry), Rosalyn Yalow (1977, Physiology/Medicine), Herbert Charles Brown (1979, Chemistry), Henry Taube (1983, Chemistry), John Charles Polanyi (1986, Chemistry), Gerd Binnig and Heinrich Rohrer (1986, Physics), Stanley Cohen (1986, Physiology/Medicine), Harbut Michel (1988, Chemistry), Richard Robert Ernst (1991, Chemistry), Michael Smith and Kary Banks Mullis (1993, Chemistry), Martin Rodbell (1994, Physiology/Medicine), David Morris Lee, Douglas Dean Osheroff, Robert Coleman Richardson (1996, Physics), Paul Delos Boyer (1997, Chemistry), Robert Francis Furchgott and Louis J. Ignarro (1998, Physiology/Medicine), Gunther Blobel (1999, Physiology/Medicine), Herbert Kroemer (2000, Physics). Journals rejecting their papers included *Nature, Physical Review, Journal of Biological Chemistry, Journal of the American Chemical Society, Journal of Organic Chemistry, Chemical Reviews, Physical Review Letters, Journal of Chemical Physics, Science, Analytical Biochemistry, Applied Physics Letters,* and *Journal of Clinical Investigation.*

As can be seen from that list, the rejection of papers by well-known and highly respected scientific journals is not discipline-specific.

There has thus been a most fundamental and dramatic "climate change" in academic science over the past decades—one of such a magnitude and severity that the innovators in our global society are finding it hard to flourish or even just survive. How has this happened, and why have we let it happen?

One of the most obvious reasons for this lies in the commercialization of academic institutions. Few academics would deny that institutions cannot run at a loss, but the drive today is to maximize profits. To this end, the bureaucracy within universities has mushroomed, and the old view of administrators as support staff for academics has now been effectively reversed. Many academics now regard themselves as no more than cash cows for a burgeoning administration who top-slice research grants for their own needs and who, having been given the powers to do so, set the agendas for academic appraisals, including sums to be obtained externally for each academic grade, numbers of postgraduate students to be supervised,[12] and number and quality of peer-reviewed articles to be published. Actually, in some academic systems, such as that of the UK, the number of quality publications is not an important aspect of academic assessment as long as each tenured academic has published the minimum number required (usually three to five) in periodic (five-year) central government assessments of research productivity. Failure to produce the requisite number of such publications can have detrimental effects on an academic's ability to pursue their chosen research, or much worse. The fact that peer review is a fundamental aspect of both publishing articles and obtaining external research income necessitates a more detailed analysis.

Sydney Brenner said of peer review,

> And of course all academics say we've got to have peer review. But I don't believe in peer review because I think it's very distorted and as I've said, it's simply a regression to the mean. I think peer review is hindering science. In fact, I think it has become a completely corrupt system. It's corrupt in many ways, in that scientists and academics have handed over to the editors of these journals the ability to make judgment on science and scientists. There are universities in America, and I've heard from many committees, that won't consider people's publications in low impact factor journals. Now I mean, people are trying to do something, but I think it's not publish or perish, it's publish in the okay places [or perish]. And this has assembled a most ridiculous group of people. I wrote a column for many years in the nineties, in a journal called Current Biology. In one article, "Hard Cases," I campaigned against this [culture] because I think it is not only bad, it's corrupt. In other words, it puts the judgment in the hands of people who really have no reason to exercise judgment at all. And that's all been done in the aid of commerce, because they are now giant organisations making money out of it.[13]

There are various descriptors used when discussing scientific

---

12. Allocation of research students to a given researcher is often dependent on their level of external research income.

13. Sydney Brenner, in "How Academia and Publishing Are Destroying Scientific Innovation."

publication, and it would be useful to look at the meaning of these in more detail.

High Impact Factor Journals

"Impact factors" for scientific journals are a relatively recent arrival on the publishing scene and provide the administrators in academic institutions with a numeric score for the quality of a given publication—or do they?[14] Such factors result from assessing a range of parameters such as number of citations and the "time decay rates" of citations, but they are mean values given for journals, not for individual articles in the journals. So two papers published in the same journal may have radically different individual scores. The scenario has indeed occurred, where an individual paper in a high impact journal may have a lower impact score than a paper published in a lower impact journal. Some journals have lower impact scores due to their highly specialized discipline focus, while others have higher impact scores due to their more generalized nature. It has been noted that some high impact factor journals that become more selective of the papers they accept actually force contributors to send their papers to lower impact factor journals. Ironically, over relatively short time periods (impact factors are reviewed annually), some of the former journals become lower in impact factor, while the latter ones increase. Thus impact factors are not in reality an indicator of the quality of individual papers, and such factors can change over short periods of time. Unfortunately, impact factors are now widely used by university bureaucracies as a metric of the worth and reputation of the academic output of individual scientists, which brings an observation of Albert Einstein to mind: "Not everything that can be counted counts, and not everything that counts can be counted." A mentor of mine who was a senior professor in the National Institutes of Health and a member of the National Academy of Sciences in the United States was most dismissive of impact factors as a measure of publication quality. As a distinguished chemist and pharmacologist, he often said that, for most

---

14. M. Rosner, H. V. Epps, E. Hill, "Show Me the Data," *Journal of Cell Biology* 179 (2007): 1091–1092; S. Saha, S. Saint, D. A. Christakis, "Impact Factor: A Valid Measure of Journal Quality," *Journal of the Medical Library Association* 91 (2003): 42–46.

of his career, he published in the most appropriate journals for his work to be read by the most appropriate people—his research peers. These were also the most appropriate people to gauge the relative impact and importance of his work.

Peer Review

The definition of peer review previously given would seem quite reasonable to most people: review of a scientific manuscript by a small number of scientists working in the same field as the subject matter of the submitted work, objectively assessing its quality. However, for some journals this does not happen, as decisions on whether to publish are often made by an editor or a subeditor, with rejection letters usually containing phrases referring to their large numbers of submissions, lack of space in their journal, and a suggestion that one send the manuscript to a more specialized journal. Most often, however, upon submission, authors are requested to name several potential reviewers, and sometimes to name individuals that one would *not* wish to review the paper, and then the editor reserves the right to use some or all of the suggested reviewers or to choose their own. Most commonly, editors will use a minimum of three reviewers for each submission. In the world of professional scientists, just as in any other sphere of life, there are people one can get along with and others one cannot, so authors would tend to choose their friendly colleagues as reviewers and not their known professional rivals. However, sometimes most of one's peers in a given area of scientific research are one's rivals, especially if they are within the same academic system/country and are competing for the same funds for similar research. Can such "peers" really be totally objective in assessing a rival's application? Over many years of publishing scientific papers, a productive author can develop skills in identifying the sources of reviews by use of a number of clues in writing style and word usage. Sometimes such reviews contain clearly subjective statements in the equally clear absence of objective points, indicating a reviewer's obvious reluctance to see the submission published.

Editorial decisions to accept or reject a submitted paper, following review, will take into account the consensus among the three reviewers used or, when contentious, the editor may use additional reviewers or make a decision personally. However, one often sees reviews written by individuals who obviously are not familiar with the subject matter or who make statements that are factually incorrect. In the past, most editors afforded a right of reply for such anomalies, but this has become increasingly rare in today's publication climate. The peer-review system for academic publication, as currently constituted, thus rejects some papers that are scientifically valid and, conversely, accepts some that are not. Some, but not all, of the latter may subsequently be retracted, and some of the former may never appear on the printed page. Critics of nonmainstream robust scientific findings often cite the fact that these have not been subjected to peer-reviewed publication, but surely it is clear that this argument is facile. Many of the so-called modern gurus of science disseminate their often outrageous and untested pseudoscientific dogma in the popular press, and it is becoming increasingly obvious that the public are unwittingly influenced by such, believing this to be authentic scientific fact. On the other hand, the current system of peer review both in funding for research and in publication of papers is highly focused on maintaining the *status quo* and is often highly dismissive of genuine ideas and novel findings. This has been and continues to be the experience of many innovative scientists, including most Nobel laureates (note, again, our long list of "rejected laureates").

Although it is clear that the peer-review process is highly subjective in many aspects, many authors have wondered whether actual bias exists in the process. The answer is yes, with elements of both sexism and nepotism having been found. There is strong evidence of bias against women applicants in the awarding of research grants, as well as a bias toward favorable outcomes for submissions based on well-known authors in the author list and/or the level of prestige of the institutions in which the research was performed. There may also be bias depending on the country in which the research has been performed and on whether the paper contains negative results which either relate to a new study or demonstrate a failure to replicate a study that has been previously published—especially in the same journal. The more sinister side to the process is that reviewers may steal the submitting author's ideas to present them as their own at a later date and/or may delay publication if their own research group is working on the same or similar questions.

Editors and editorial boards (reviewers) are constituted either by members of specific learned societies and/or by scientists working in the same or related discipline, and, by inference, these individuals are working and competing in similar if not identical areas. Traditionally, research journals were managed by specific learned societies, and latterly by publishing houses, and in both cases, funding to produce these journals, and sometimes associated profits, were made through subscriptions for access by university libraries, less often by individuals. However, in more recent years, the trend in scientific publishing has gravitated toward so-called "open access," driven initially by a desire for public-purse funding agencies to see the results of their funded research being made available to the general public. This aspiration, on the face of it, is good, but it comes at a substantial cost. Most such funding agencies provide finance for open access publishing, or if not, this is supplied by special funds in universities. The costs of this process to funding donors/university hosts, and the profits to be made by publishers, are not trivial, and there has thus been a veritable explosion in the numbers of open access journals and of established journals who now offer such an alternative service. While some open access journals began their lives as high impact factor, highly selective, quality journals, many have now become repositories for the mundane, as the huge profits to be made have been realized. The peer-review process occurs much as before, but the approach to this has become somewhat softhanded, with the academic reviewers often not being specialists in the subject matter but still receiving little remuneration for their professional input.

A second alarming factor arising from softhanded review procedures is an increase in the likelihood of publication of fraudulent, misinterpreted, or selective data, which cannot be replicated by the interested reader. Replication of published data by other research groups is a fundamental aspect of validation in research and often uncovers such malpractices. To the surprise of many outside the field of scientific research, such errant behaviors are not unusual. In a featured article in the *New Scientist*, Sonia van Gilder Cooke wrote,

"Listening to *When I'm Sixty-Four* by the Beatles," can make you younger. This miraculous effect, dubbed "chronological rejuvenation," was revealed in the journal *Psychological Science* in 2011. It wasn't a hoax but you'd be right to be suspicious. The aim was to show how easy it is to generate statistical evidence for pretty much anything, simply by picking and choosing methods and data in ways that researchers do every day. The paper caused a stir among psychologists, and has become the most cited in the journal's history. The following year, Nobel prizewinning psychologist, Daniel Kahneman, stoked the fire with an open email to social psychologists warning of a "train wreck" if they didn't clean up their act.[15] But things only came to a head last year with the publication of a paper in *Science*. It described a major effort to replicate 100 psychology experiments published in top journals. The success rate was little more than a third. People began to talk of a "crisis" in psychology. In fact, the problem extends far beyond psychology— dubious results are alarmingly common in many fields of science. Worryingly, they seem to be especially shaky in areas that have a direct bearing on human well-being—the science underpinning everyday political, economic and healthcare decisions. No wonder the whistle-blowers are urgently trying to investigate why it's happening, how big the problem is and what can be done to fix it.[16]

Fiona Godlee concluded, in a study of peer review, that it "does not do well at detecting innovative research or filtering out fraudulent, plagiarized, or redundant publication."[17] Perhaps the most disturbing conclusion was that the process often fails in detecting the innovative. In his conclusion to an article titled "Peer Review: A Flawed Process at the Heart of Science and Journals,"published in the *Journal of the Royal Society of Medicine*, Richard Smith, chief executive of UnitedHealth Europe, stated, "So peer review is a flawed process, full of

15. For more information, see Ed Yong, "Nobel Laureate Challenges Psychologists to Clean Up Their Act," *Nature*, October 3, 2012, http://www.nature.com/news/nobel-laureate-challenges -psychologists-to-clean-up-their-act-1.11535.

16. Sonia van Gilder Cooke, "Why So Much Science Research Is Flawed—And What to Do about It," *New Scientist*–featured investigation, April 13, 2016, https://www.newscientist.com /article/mg23030690-500-why-so-much-science-research-is-flawed-and-what-to-do-about-it/ [internal citations removed].

17. Fiona Godlee, "The Ethics of Peer Review," in *Ethical Issues in Biomedical Publication* (Baltimore: Johns Hopkins University Press, 2000), 59–84.

easily identified defects with little evidence that it works. Nevertheless, it is likely to remain central to science and journals because there is no obvious alternative, and scientists and editors have a continuing belief in peer review. How odd that science should be rooted in belief."[18]

V. Summary and Closing Thoughts

Science is widely regarded as a totally objective means of establishing a contemporary worldview as an alternative to the faith-based worldview described in the Bible. Put simply, science often claims that so-called scientific facts produce a superior interpretation of the reasons for the existence of the universe and its component subatomic particles, and for the appearance of life and its component biomolecules and its gradual evolution into multiple and diverse forms. However, science is not omniscient, and it is subject to regular and often dramatic revelations that concepts once regarded as absolute truth are not. The origins of the universe and of life itself have not been proven scientifically, and still today represent major unanswered questions, although this reality is often not stated in open debate or indeed in school textbooks. So many of the fundamental dogmas associated with scientism are held by faith or, to use a more appropriate scientific term, speculation. The so-called scientific dogma pertaining to the origins of the universe and of life do not in themselves fulfill one of the essential attributes of the scientific process—that is, having firm and testable evidence. Anything less is thus a faith-based system, which may come as a revelation to many.

A second revelation we have seen is that science itself, and virtually all of its component machinery, is subject to bias. Young aspiring research scientists have to undergo a long period of study and training and may, if fortunate, secure a tenured or tenure-track position in their early to mid-thirties, having invested much time and financial resources and often having personal and social commitments that can affect the objectivity of their work. Under such circumstances, they may have little interest in challenging the scientific establishment. In times past, once a tenured position was secured, the researcher was essentially free to pursue new ideas that would challenge accepted dogma without fear

---

18. Smith, "Peer Review."

of dismissal, but in more recent times this contractual provision has all but vanished from academia. In many institutions, academics are now subjected to regular appraisals by the administration to evaluate their progress through analysis of key performance indicators, and failure to meet such arbitrary criteria can result in failure to progress through salary scales and obtain promotions, and can ultimately result in dismissal from employment in one's chosen field.

A research scientist's performance is often defined by things such as quantity and source of external research funding, number and quality of peer-reviewed publications, and number of postgraduate research students under his or her supervision. For some researchers with significant undergraduate teaching time, there will also be assessment of student feedback. The academic thus has to spend much time writing funding applications and publications, supervising research students, and preparing and delivering lectures.

Career research scientists thus have to abide by certain "rules of engagement" if they wish to be successful in this highly competitive environment, and challenging establishment dogma or practices in their respective chosen fields would be detrimental to smooth and rapid advancement. This is one of the main reasons why many of them remain silent or guarded in their speech and writing during their employment, choosing to "toe the party line." However, upon retirement and/or after a major award such as a Nobel Prize, many scientists are free to speak openly about the state of bias and the problems in science—as is the case with some of the authors cited in this chapter.

Perhaps this chapter can best be summarized by an article written by Lee Smolin, published in *Physics Today* and titled "Why No 'New Einstein'," in which he analyzes the position of innovative and independent-thinking scientists in what he calls the "hostile environment" which they currently inhabit. He writes,

> Those who follow large well-supported research programs have lots of powerful senior scientists to promote their careers. Those who invent their own research programs usually lack such support and hence are often undervalued and underappreciated. People with the uncanny ability to ask new questions or recognize unexamined assumptions, or who are able to take ideas from one field and apply

them to another, are often at a disadvantage when the goal is to hire the best person in a given well-established area. In the present system, scientists feel lots of pressure to follow established research programs led by powerful senior scientists. Those who choose to follow their own programs understand that their career prospects will be harmed. That there are still those with the courage to go their own way is underappreciated. It is easy to write many papers when you continue to apply well-understood techniques. People who develop their own ideas have to work harder for each result, because they are simultaneously developing new ideas and the techniques to explore them. Hence they often publish fewer papers, and their papers are cited less frequently than those that contribute to something hundreds of people are doing.[19]

It is thus evident that the current system of funding, review, and publication of scientific research, rather than facilitating those with brilliant, innovative, and questioning minds, serves to make their work more difficult and demanding than that of their compliant peers. Perhaps this is one of the reasons why the current research literature is composed predominantly of incremental studies on previously revolutionary scientific discoveries and not with those of a game-changing nature. In view of the fact that scientific research currently receives considerably more funding than at any time in human history, the scientific establishment urgently requires a revolution in its operational practices to eliminate the numerous points in its procedures at which bias in all its forms takes place. It is not good enough for the establishment to say that the systems of academic appointments, promotions, evaluation, and peer review of grants and publications are flawed but are the best that we have. It is also unacceptable that research themes and funding initiatives should be set by politicians and administrators, and that what appears in published form should be the final decision of journal editors. Science agendas need to be set by scientists themselves, and freedom of thought and the generation of diverse ideas should be the main drivers in these processes.

To paraphrase Albert Einstein, "The problems we face today cannot be solved by the minds that created them."

19. Lee Smolin, "Why No 'New Einstein'," *Physics Today* 58 (2005): 56–57. S-0031-9228 -0506-230-7.

SECTION II:

THE PHILOSOPHICAL CRITIQUE OF THEISTIC EVOLUTION

18

Why Science Needs Philosophy

J. P. MORELAND

SUMMARY

We shall explore two philosophical theses from philosopher George Bealer that illuminate ways in which philosophy is relevant to science, especially to the debate about theistic evolution versus intelligent design:

(1) The *autonomy of philosophy:* Among the central questions of philosophy that can be answered by one standard theoretical means or another, most can in principle be answered by philosophical investigation and argument without relying substantively on the sciences.

(2) The *authority of philosophy:* Insofar as science and philosophy purport to answer the same central philosophical questions, in most cases the support that science could in principle provide for those answers is not as strong as that which philosophy could in principle provide for its answers. So, should there be conflicts, the authority of philosophy in most cases can be greater in principle. (See below for attribution.)

The "autonomy of philosophy" refers to areas of philosophical investigation that lie completely outside the competence of science. The "authority of philosophy" refers to areas which both science and philosophy investigate, where the philosophical factors carry more weight than and trump those of science. I list key examples of both that are relevant to setting the intellectual context for debating the relative merits of theistic evolution versus intelligent design.

. . . . .

People sometimes ask, "What does Athens (reason) have to do with Jerusalem (faith)?" The implied answer is usually "nothing." In my view, the correct answer is "plenty," but I cannot defend that claim here. Similarly, many people, especially many—maybe most—scientists ask, "What does philosophy (idle speculation) have to do with science (which secures hard facts about reality)?" Again, the usual answer is "nothing." But nothing could be further from the truth. Science and philosophy have interacted and do interact with each other in a number of ways, ways that, in the normal course of science education and practice, are sadly not made available to scientists themselves.

In this introduction to Section II ("The Philosophical Critique of Theistic Evolution"), I shall focus on two philosophical theses that illuminate ways in which philosophy is relevant to science, especially to the debate about theistic evolution versus intelligent design. Here are the two theses, stated clearly by philosopher George Bealer:

> I wish to recommend two theses. (1) The *Autonomy of Philosophy:* Among the central questions of philosophy that can be answered by one standard theoretical means or another, most can in principle be answered by philosophical investigation and argument without relying substantively on the sciences. (2) The *Authority of Philosophy:* Insofar as science and philosophy purport to answer the same central philosophical questions, in most cases the support that science could in principle provide for those answers is not as strong as that which philosophy could in principle provide for its answers. So, should there be conflicts, the authority of philosophy in most cases can be greater in principle.[1]

To illustrate briefly, the "autonomy of philosophy" refers to areas

---

1. George Bealer, "On the Possibility of Philosophical Knowledge," in *Philosophical Perspectives 10: Metaphysics, 1996,* ed. James E. Tomberlin (Cambridge, MA: Blackwell, 1996), 1.

of philosophical investigation—e.g., debates about abstract objects, different interpretations of modal logic, the relative merits of utilitarian versus virtue ethics—that lie completely outside the competence of science. The "authority of philosophy" refers to areas which both science and philosophy investigate— e.g., the nature of time, the question of whether unobservable theoretical entities of scientific theories exist or are useful fictions—where the philosophical factors carry more weight than and trump those of science. In what follows, I shall list key examples of both that are relevant to setting the intellectual context for debating the relative merits of theistic evolution versus intelligent design, starting with the principle of authority.

I. Examples of the Principle of Authority

Example 1: Stephen Hawking on the beginning of the universe. In the past few decades, there has been a stunning revival of an argument for God's existence from the fact that the universe had a beginning. The argument—called the "kalam" cosmological argument—is, in fact, many centuries old, but it has been given new strength and clarity in recent times. For our purposes, there are four arguments for the universe's having a beginning: the impossibility of an actual infinite set of concrete entities such as events; the impossibility of traversing an actual infinite series of events by successive addition; the Standard Big Bang model; and the Second Law of Thermodynamics. Most of those who say that the universe did have a beginning hold the first two (philosophical) arguments to carry more weight than the last two (scientific) arguments and, thus, on the assumption that arguments for and against this claim are themselves philosophical, this seems to be a clear example of the authority thesis—that philosophy carries more weight than science.

In his book *A Brief History of Time*,[2] Hawking develops a "no boundary" model of the "beginning of the universe," and he uses imaginary time (e.g., multiples of the square root of -1) to avoid a cosmological singularity (an absolute beginning), to retain a finite past, and to depict the initial segment of space-time as rounded off very much like

---

2. Stephen Hawking, *A Brief History of Time* (New York: Bantam, 1988).

the South Pole being the "beginning" of the earth and various circles of latitude playing the role of time itself. Just as you cannot ask what is south of the South Pole, you cannot ask what was before the rounded off section of the initial segment of space-time. So there is no need for a beginning, yet the past is finite.

Philosophers, especially philosophers of science, have responded to Hawking in two ways. First, the philosophical support for the kalam cosmological argument's first premise (the universe had a beginning) is stronger than the support for Hawking's model, so one should still believe in a beginning. Second, because Hawking's model employs imaginary time—a notion that is literally conceptually unintelligible if taken to depict reality as it really is—the model should be understood in an anti-realist way (e.g., in an instrumentalist or positivist way, e.g., as a useful fiction) rather than in a realist way (as an actual depiction of the real world). Hawking admits that his model is nothing but a useful fiction, and that he himself is an anti-realist, a positivist, and an instrumentalist. But these notions are not scientific ones and, in fact, cannot be found in purely scientific writings. Thus, for Hawking to know the meaning of these notions and explicitly identify his views with them, he had to do some reading in the *philosophy* of science. Why? Because these viewpoints and labels are philosophical in nature, and the field that has developed and debated them is philosophy, not science. So in order for Hawking to express the real implications of his model, he had to turn to philosophy, not to science. As a result, this nicely illustrates the authority of philosophy. This is an odd result, since Hawking claims that philosophy is dead yet he must turn to philosophy in a foundational way to express how he understands his own model![3]

Thus, it was the discipline of philosophy that both placed Hawking's model in the classification to which it belongs, and continued to show that his model did nothing whatsoever to undermine belief in the universe's beginning.

Example 2: Stephen Hawking on the universe coming to be from nothing. In *The Grand Design*, Hawking and his coauthor, Leonard Mlodi-

---

3. Stephen Hawking and Roger Penrose, *The Nature of Space and Time* (Princeton, NJ: Princeton University Press, 1996), 3–4, 53–55, 121.

now, claim that quantum physics has made the need for a creator and designer superfluous.[4] This is because the universe can "create itself," that is, it came into existence out of nothing.

This claim upset the faith of a number of believers, because it was the considered judgment of a scientist, indeed, one of the top living scientists. But alas, Hawking and Mlodinow may well be great scientists, but they are very poor philosophers. Why? Because their concept of "nothing" is not the same as the philosophical one, and the philosophical notion is the relevant one in deciding on the "need" for a creator. For Hawking and Mlodinow, "nothing" means a quantum vacuum, which contains energy and is itself located in space. The universe comes into being spontaneously as a fluctuation of the energy in the vacuum.

Unfortunately, this is hardly a case of the universe coming into being from nothing! The philosophical notion of nothing is just that— the complete and total lack of any being whatsoever, including the absence of particles, causal powers, fields, properties, and so on. Given this notion of nothing, it becomes self-evident that, necessarily, something cannot come *from* nothing without a cause, because there is nothing to come from! The Hawking/Mlodinow claim reminds me of a joke: A group of scientists come up to God and tell him that they don't need him anymore because they can now create life. So God asks them to show him their new discovery. The scientists bend down, scope up some dirt, but before they can go farther, God interrupts them and says, "If you don't mind, get your own dirt!" Similarly, if we say that we don't need God anymore because the universe can come from "nothing" (that is, a quantum vacuum), then the proper response from God would be, "If you don't mind, get your own quantum vacuum!"

In this example, the philosophical considerations carry more weight than do the scientific claims.

Example 3: The origin of life. There has been a long-running debate as to whether or not we can discover a reasonable, natural-scientific explanation for the origin of life without the need for divine intervention or even the discovery of characteristics of life that are best explained by an intelligent designer. And that debate has, for quite some time,

---

4. Stephen Hawking and Leonard Mlodinow, *The Grand Design* (New York: Bantam, 2010).

centered on scientific considerations, e.g., the high improbability of chance and natural law doing the job.

But some philosophers have resisted the notion of a purely naturalistic, physicalistic account of life's origin. To begin with, it has been very difficult for biologists to define life. As origin-of-life researcher Antonio Lazcano notes, "Life is like music; you can describe it but not define it."[5] According to Fazale Rana, biologists have collected a list of around a hundred different definitions of life.[6] According to biologists, some of the essential characteristics of life include biological stability, permanence, and coherence; being made of atoms, molecules, and cells that obey the laws of chemistry and physics; being composed of a highly structured homeostatic nature; being able to ingest nutrition, expel waste, and reproduce.

But scientific or biological attempts to define or provide essential characteristics of life flounder because, as many philosophers have pointed out, "life" is a univocal, projectable predicate. What does this mean? First, the term "life" is something we predicate of certain things and not others. Second, "life" is univocal and not equivocal; that is, it means the same thing whenever we employ it. Thus, to say a dog or a human or a fish is alive is to use the term "life" in the same way. Different living things may live in different ways and sustain their lives by employing different factors, but they are all "living." We don't have one definition of "life" for a dog, one for a human, and one for a fish. If we did, "life" would be an unwieldy predicate of which we would have no understanding when we applied it to a newly discovered creature.

Finally, "life" is projectable. While we start out by using the term "life" for living things with which we are acquainted, we can also use the term for yet to be discovered actual or possible living things (e.g., life in outer space, unicorns).

But now a problem arises for biological attempts to define or essentially characterize life. "Life" is univocally predicable of disembodied souls after death, of angels, and of God himself. Even if none of these things exist, their existence is coherent and intelligible, and the projec-

---

5. Antonio Lazcano, "The Transition from Nonliving to Living," in *Early Life on Earth*, ed. Stefan Bengston (New York: Columbia University Press, 1994), 61.

6. Fazale Rana, *Creating Life in the Lab* (Grand Rapids, MI: Baker, 2011), 24.

tion of "life" into possibly living things should be univocal. But none of these entities satisfy physical/biological characteristics for life. Thus, life itself cannot be physical, so the argument goes, and there will never be a strictly scientific account of life or its origin. To get life from rearranging matter is to get something (life, which is not physical) from nothing (brute matter that does not have life).

Interestingly, many philosophers have provided new evidence for this argument by claiming, following biologists, that living things are constituted by information. But apart from a few exceptions, many, perhaps most philosophers who work in this area have claimed that information is immaterial, more fundamental to reality than matter, and, given its nature, there can be no material explanation for the origin of (immaterial) information and, thus, for the origin of life.[7]

II. Examples of the Principle of Autonomy

Example 1: The nature and existence of consciousness and the soul.
I doubt that any list of the proper issues within a sub-branch of philosophy would be complete. Still, it is possible to provide a reasonably adequate characterization of the central first-order topics that are ubiquitous in the literature in philosophy of mind. Those topics tend to revolve around four interrelated families of issues, constituted by the following kinds of representative questions:

(1) **Ontological questions.** To what is a mental or physical property identical? To what is a mental or physical event identical? To what is the owner of mental properties/events identical? What is a human person? How are mental properties related to mental events (e.g., do the latter exemplify or realize the former?)? Are there (Aristotelian or Leibnizian) essences and, if so, what is the essence of a mental event or of a human person?

(2) **Epistemological questions.** How do we come to have knowledge or justified beliefs about other minds and about our own minds? Is there a proper "epistemic order" to first-person knowledge of one's own mind and third-person knowledge of other minds? That

---

7. See William Dembski, *Being as Communion* (Burlington, Vermont: Ashgate, 2014), iv, xii, xiv, 75, 77.

is, does the information we gain from our own first-person perspective about our own conscious states and our own self have rational authority over third-person attempts by others to gain such knowledge, or is it the other way around? How reliable is first-person introspection, and what is its nature (e.g., is it an experiential seeming, or a disposition to believe)? If the former, then experience of one's mental state, e.g., an awareness of the hurtfulness of a pain, is prior to the tendency to believe that a pain hurts. In this case, one has to admit that experiential states of consciousness (seeming states) are real and cannot be reduced to a belief (which can be reduced further to linguistic behavior, e.g., the ability to use the word "pain" correctly, an ability that an unconscious computer could possess). If first-person introspection *is* reliable, should it be limited to providing knowledge of consciousness, or should it also include knowledge about one's own ego?

Why worry about such issues? The answer is this: When we are trying to gain authoritative knowledge about consciousness, if the first-person perspective is of primary importance, then one will take consciousness to be what one experiences in introspection, and this supports the nonphysical nature of consciousness. However, if one takes the third-person perspective to have priority, then scientific claims about the brain will have more authority than introspective claims offered from the first-person point of view, and this pecking order will support physicalist reductions of consciousness to brain states.

(3) **Semantic questions.** What is a meaning? What is a linguistic entity, and how is it related to a meaning? Is thought reducible to or a necessary condition for language use? How do the terms in our commonsense psychological vocabulary get their meaning?

The main second-order topics in philosophy of mind revolve around a fourth set of representative questions:

(4) **Methodological questions.** How should one proceed in analyzing and resolving the first-order issues that constitute the philosophy of mind? What is the proper order between philosophy and science? Should we adopt some form of philosophical naturalism, set aside so-called first philosophy, and engage topics in philoso-

phy of mind within a framework of our empirically best-attested theories relevant to those topics? What is the role of thought experiments in philosophy of mind, and how does the "first-person point of view" factor into generating the materials for formulating those thought experiments?

These are the sorts of questions that form the warp and woof of philosophy of mind. Please read the list carefully. It becomes evident that these are in no way scientific questions; they are philosophical to the core and nicely illustrate the autonomy thesis. But, you may respond, as Nancey Murphy has, "[S]cience has provided a massive amount of evidence suggesting that we need not postulate the existence of an entity such as a soul or mind in order to explain life and consciousness."[8] This evidence consists of the fact that "biology, neuroscience, and cognitive science have provided accounts of the dependence on physical processes of *specific* faculties once attributed to the soul."[9]

I offer two responses, the first stated nicely by Steve Evans regarding the findings of localization studies:

> What, exactly, is it about these findings that are supposed to create problems for dualism? . . . Is it a problem that the causal effects should be the product of specific regions of the brain? Why should the fact that the source of the effects are localized regions of the brain, rather than the brain as a whole, be a problem for the dualist? It is hard for me to see why dualism should be thought to entail that the causal dependence of the mind on the brain should only stem from holistic states of the brain rather than more localized happenings.[10]

Second, all neuroscience can do is establish precise, brute correlations, causal relations, or dependency relations between mental and physical states. It can tell us nothing about the intrinsic nature of consciousness or whether or not there is a soul. These are philosophical

---

8. Nancey Murphy, "Human Nature: Historical, Scientific and Religious Issues," in *Whatever Happened to the Soul?*, ed. Warren S. Brown, Nancey Murphy, and H. Newton Malony (Minneapolis: Fortress, 1998). 18.

9. Ibid., 17, cf. 13, 27.

10. C. Stephen Evans, "Separable Souls: Dualism, Selfhood, and the Possibility of Life after Death," *Christian Scholar's Review* 34 (2005): 333–334.

questions. To see this, consider the discovery that if one's mirror neurons are damaged, then one cannot feel empathy for another. How are we to explain this? Three empirically equivalent solutions (solutions consistent with all and only the same set of observations) come to mind: (1) strict physicalism (a feeling of empathy is identical to the firings of mirror neurons); (2) mere property dualism (a feeling of empathy is an irreducible state of consciousness in the brain whose obtaining depends on the firing of mirror neurons); (3) substance dualism (a feeling of empathy is an irreducible state of consciousness in the soul whose obtaining depends [while embodied] on the firing of mirror neurons).

No empirical datum can pick out which of these three is correct, nor does an appeal to epistemic simplicity help. Epistemic simplicity is a tie-breaker, and the substance dualist will insist that the arguments and evidence for substance dualism are better than those for the other two options mentioned above.

Example 2: Methodological naturalism, agent causation, and the nature of science. When it comes to the task of defining or giving the essential characteristics of science, that task belongs to philosophers and historians of science, and not to scientists themselves.

Perhaps the main philosophical issue in the theistic evolution/intelligent design dialogue involves the appropriateness of using science to warrant the inference to an intelligent cause for some phenomenon. Central to this dialogue is the question of whether or not science must adopt methodological naturalism, roughly the idea that, while doing science, one must seek only natural causes/explanations for scientific data.

There has been some controversy as to which field is the proper place to turn to in order to seek professional expertise in resolving this debate. Nor is the question of professional expertise merely an academic matter of turf protection, because, currently, it is largely scientists and science educators who are the gatekeepers for the public schools in this area. That there is a controversy can be seen from this statement by J. W. Haas Jr., former editor of the influential *Perspectives on Science and Christian Faith*: "The place of the philosopher in the practice of science has long been controversial. Whether philosophers should (can?) be the arbiters of what constitutes science remains problematic for the working scientist."[11] Along similar lines, scientist Karl Giberson rejects "the traditional viewpoint that practicing scientists find so annoying, namely that philosophers are the relevant, competent and final authorities to determine the rules of science."[12]

Actually, the issue here is not controversial at all, since the central topics do not involve how to *practice* science (which requires familiarity with instrumentation, procedures, etc.), but how to *define* science and *distinguish* it from nonscience or pseudoscience. To understand this debate and the proper field of study for resolving it, we must first make a distinction between a first- and a second-order issue. A first-order issue is a topic *of* science *about* some phenomenon, e.g., how to predict earthquakes or manipulate chemical reaction rates. A second-order issue is a topic *of* philosophy *about* science itself, e.g., its methods, its nature, its differences from other fields. Now the question of how to define science is clearly a topic for philosophers and historians of science. This is not to say that scientists and others cannot be a part of this discussion; it is merely to affirm that when they participate, they will be largely dealing with philosophical issues for which they are not professionally trained.

The fact that these issues are philosophical and not primarily scientific can be seen from the following: Read the relevant debates and discussions and ask what scientific experiment, what scientific procedure one would use to resolve the dispute about the nature, proper definition, and limits of science. Or get any college catalog and look at the course descriptions in different branches of science. You will discover that almost nowhere in an undergraduate or graduate program in any branch of science are the relevant topics discussed, except perhaps in the first week of freshman chemistry. By contrast, entire graduate study programs in the history or philosophy of science are devoted to definitions of science and to drawing lines of demarcation between science and other fields.

---

11. J. W. Haas Jr., "Putting Things into Perspective," *Perspectives on Science and Christian Faith* 46 (March 1994): 1.

12. Karl Giberson, "Intelligent Design on Trial—A Review Essay," *Christian Scholar's Review* 24 (May 1995): 460.

What is the relevance of the authority of philosophy and autonomy of philosophy theses and the illustrations of both in this introduction and in the chapters in this section to follow? The answer is at least two-fold. First, a very well-known Christian philosopher recently noted that when scientists make claims that seem to conflict with biblical teaching and solid theology, with notable exceptions (including the biblical scholars and theologians who contribute to this volume!), theologians and biblical scholars start ducking into foxholes, hoist the white flag of surrender, and trip over each other in the race to see who can be first to come up with a revision of biblical teaching that placates the scientists. Thus, the "dialogue" between science and theology or biblical exegesis is really a monologue, with theologians asking scientists what the latest discoveries allow them to teach. Homosexuality is caused by our DNA? No problem. The Bible doesn't teach the immorality of homosexuality anyway; we have misread it for two thousand years. Neuroscience shows there is no soul? No problem. Dualism and the soul are Greek ideas not found in the Bible, which is more Hebraic and holistic. A completely naturalistic story of evolution is adequate to explain the origin and development of all life? No problem. After all, the Bible isn't a science text. Adam and Eve? Do we really need them literally to be historical figures? No. And on and on it goes.

Lest you think I exaggerate, listen to the views of the late theologian Arthur Peacocke:

> [T]here is a strong prima facie case for re-examining the claimed cognitive content of Christian theology in the light of the new knowledge derivable from the sciences. . . . If such an exercise is not continually undertaken theology will operate in a cultural ghetto quite cut off from most of those in Western cultures who have good grounds for thinking that science describes what is going on in the processes of the world at all levels. The turbulent history of the relation of science and theology bears witness to the impossibility of theology seeking a peaceful haven, protected from the sciences of its times, if it is going to be believable.[13]

Wow! What robust and vibrant confidence in the Bible! The truth is,

---

13. Arthur Peacocke, *Theology for a Scientific Age* (Minneapolis: Fortress, 1993), 6–7.

when Peacocke, Giberson, and others make statements like this, for the statements to be credible they need to be expressions of a fairly thorough acquaintance with epistemology. After all, if one is going to claim that one field (science) is cognitively superior to another field (biblical studies, theology), one should have a pretty good idea of what knowledge is and how one can tell the difference between weakly and strongly justified beliefs.

This leads me to my second observation about the relevance of the authority and autonomy theses for this book. Scientists are usually ill-equipped to draw metaphysical, epistemological, or moral conclusions from scientific data. And the reason is that drawing those conclusions is largely a philosophical matter, as I have tried to illustrate above. If this is correct, then an issue arises: If some alleged scientific discovery seems to contradict a time-tested understanding of the Bible, and if it contradicts historically embraced and epistemically justified theological models, then why jump immediately to a revisionist view of the Bible and theology?

Instead, folks like those involved in BioLogos should slow down, take a deep breath, and form integrative teams with philosophers, theologians, and scientists who can present rigorous defenses of the tradition Christian positions. This approach is especially incumbent on scientists when they realize that (1) formulating models of things like the existence of Adam and Eve or the adequacy of naturalistic mechanisms to explain life and its diversity is an integrative affair that should include philosophers and theologians who are able to defend the traditional view; and (2) there is at least a small (or large!) but robust group of significant, intellectually rigorous scientists, philosophers, and theologians who are quite competent to defend the traditional view. Such a group exists, though it is far from small, and it is the intelligent design movement. If these two admonitions are followed, then it will become evident that philosophy, especially the authority and autonomy theses, are at the very heart of the issues. In one way or another, all the chapters in this section illustrate the centrality of philosophical issues in the intelligent design/theistic evolution debate. And after reading these chapters, I believe it will become clear that the crucial philosophical issues and arguments to follow show beyond a reasonable doubt that intelligent design theory is far more reasonable than theistic evolution.

19

Should Theistic Evolution Depend on Methodological Naturalism?[1]

STEPHEN C. MEYER AND
PAUL A. NELSON

SUMMARY

Nearly all theistic evolutionists say that some naturalistic process will eventually explain the origin of novel forms of life. They do so because they accept a philosophical rule known as *methodological naturalism*. Methodological naturalism asserts that, to qualify as scientific, a theory must explain by strictly physical or material— that is, non-intelligent or non-purposive—causes. This chapter shows that, as a supposedly neutral rule for how science *should* function, methodological naturalism fails. Nor can one rely on "demarcation criteria" devised to define science normatively. These criteria, which purport to distinguish science from pseudoscience or religion, die by a thousand counterexamples. The history of science includes many theories violating one or another allegedly necessary demarcation criterion (such as observability, explanation by natural law, or falsifiability), yet such theories have figured centrally in the development of their respective sciences. Moreover, demarcation

---

1. This chapter draws on material previously published as Stephen C. Meyer, "The Methodological Equivalence of Design and Descent: Can There Be a Scientific 'Theory of Creation,'" in *The Creation Hypothesis*, ed. J. P. Moreland (Downers Grove, IL: InterVarsity Press, 1994), 67–112; and Meyer, "Sauce for the Goose: Intelligent Design, Scientific Methodology, and the Demarcation Problem," in *The Nature of Nature*, ed. Bruce L. Gordon and William A. Dembski (Wilmington, DE: ISI Books, 2014), and is used with kind permission.

criteria cannot justify methodological naturalism itself. Naturalistic evolutionary theories and competing theories of intelligent design or creation either equivalently satisfy demarcation criteria, or fail to do so. The truth about the history of life on Earth cannot be decided by philosophical definitions. Given that no sound justification exists for holding methodological naturalism as a science-defining rule, Christians should not use it as a reason for adopting theistic evolution, or excluding other theories.

. . . . .

I. Introduction: Making the Rules and Playing the Game

A young basketball fan today—say, a ten-year-old boy growing up in San Jose, California, who religiously follows the Golden State Warriors and their star Stephen Curry—might be astonished to learn that the three-point shot wasn't always allowed in the NBA. It simply did not exist. But older basketball fans, such as the authors of this chapter, remember the game before 1979, when the three-point shot was first introduced. No three-pointers back then. A field goal from anywhere on the court yielded two points.

Imagine yourself as an NBA executive in 1979, the rookie season for both Magic Johnson and Larry Bird. You are seated in a conference room, discussing the rule change that will allow three-point shots. You cannot envision that an entire strategy will develop around what happens when an arc is placed on the court, twenty-three feet and nine inches from the hoop, at or beyond which three points will be awarded to a successful shooter. You just want to make the game more interesting—so you raise your hand to endorse the new rule.

Now, were you playing basketball when you voted for the three-point shot? Of course not: the games themselves will take place in wholly different venues, under circumstances that bear no resemblance to discussing rule changes in an executive suite. But your rule-making decisions will affect the future of basketball, and indeed, its very nature—namely, how the game will be played, what skills will be valued, how teams will construct their strategies, and so forth.

Let us draw a parallel. While making the rules of science is not the same thing as playing the game of science (that is, actually conducting research), rule-making influences the practice and content of science, shaping what it will be as an enterprise and a body of knowledge—*including what kinds of hypotheses its practitioners will permit themselves to consider.* Science is something we humans invent and do—it has not been delivered to us—and we devise its rules, methods, and conventions. Moreover, the rules of science *can* change, because over the course of history, they *have* changed.

But when might a rule need to be changed? In sports, rule changes usually occur when the quality of competition has stagnated or declined. Science is not a game in that exact sense, of course, but metrics of the success or failure of scientific theories exist, and we can ask the same questions, at a deeper level, about scientific methodology itself. "Science should be interested in determining the *truth*," writes Caltech physicist Sean Carroll, "whatever that truth may be—natural, supernatural, or otherwise."[2] If truth is the ultimate goal of scientific investigation, then any rule that may keep us from reaching that goal needs the closest critical scrutiny.

In this chapter, we shall argue that historical biology—the science concerned with explaining how living things came to be—is long overdue for just such a rule change. More than 150 years after the publication of the *Origin of Species*, evolutionary theory has stalled out. As the preceding section of this book demonstrates, neither standard neo-Darwinian theory, nor any of the other strictly materialistic theories of evolution recently proposed to supplement (or replace) it, can explain the origin of novel biological form. And yet that was supposed to be evolutionary theory's main job.

Many theistic evolutionists readily admit this. Biologist Darrell Falk, for example, the past president and currently senior scholar at BioLogos (a group promoting theistic evolution), acknowledges that neo-Darwinian mechanisms cannot explain the major changes and innovations in the history of life. In his review of a book (*Darwin's Doubt*) written by one of us (Stephen Meyer), Falk wrote that the book identified "one of the great mysteries in evolutionary biology today," namely, the origin of animal form. He observed that this problem has

---

2. Sean Carroll, *The Big Picture: On the Origins of Life, Meaning, and the Universe Itself* (New York: Dutton, 2016), 133.

never been addressed by neo-Darwinian theory, and he reflected on his own experiences as a college teacher of evolution, discovering the shortcomings of textbook theory when confronted with explaining the origin of, for example, the first animals. He added that the process of natural selection, important as it may be in certain contexts, is not the "driving mechanism" of macroevolutionary change, and thus, the mystery of the origin of animal life still awaits a solution. Calling the Cambrian explosion of animal life a "big mystery," he also acknowledged that none of the newer evolutionary mechanisms or models adequately explain the origin of novel animal form either. Referring specifically to these post–neo-Darwinian mechanisms, Falk admitted, "Stephen [Meyer] is right, that none of the other models fit the bill in a fully satisfactory manner yet."[3]

Yet, despite these candid admissions, Falk remains fully committed to some form of theistic evolution. Why?

II. Methodological Naturalism as the Ground Rule of Science

Clearly, Falk's reason for remaining committed to theistic evolution cannot be strictly empirical. Given the currently available scientific evidence, evolutionary theory doesn't work, as Falk concedes. Rather, he remains committed to theistic evolution because of how he understands *the rules of science* to operate. Like nearly all theistic evolutionists, Falk accepts the rule of *methodological naturalism*. Methodological naturalism asserts that, to qualify as scientific, a theory must explain all phenomena by reference to purely physical or material—that is, non-intelligent—causes or processes. Or as the National Academy of Sciences explains, methodological naturalism holds that "the statements of science must invoke only natural things and processes."[4] The key terms here, of course, are *natural* (meaning the matter and energy of the physical world, but excluding *intelligent* causes or conscious mind) and *only*, a logical modifier that *restricts* scientific explanation

3. Darrell Falk, "Further Thoughts on 'Darwin's Doubt' after Reading Bishop's Review," *Bio-Logos*, September 11, 2014, accessed July 25, 2016, http://biologos.org/blogs/archive/thoughts-on-darwins-doubt-reviewing-darwins-doubt-darrel-falk-part-2.
4. Working Group on Teaching Evolution, National Academy of Sciences, *Teaching about Evolution and the Nature of Science* (Washington, DC: National Academy Press, 1998), 42.

to whatever is "natural." As Fuller Seminary philosopher and theistic evolutionist Nancey Murphy observes, methodological naturalism *forbids* referring "to creative intelligence" in scientific theories.[5]

Because of his commitment to methodological naturalism, Darrell Falk will not consider any theory (such as intelligent design) that invokes "creative intelligence." Instead, he waits—into the indefinite future—for the formulation of an adequate, strictly naturalistic evolutionary theory. As he explains,

> I see no scientific, biblical, or theological reason to expect that [an intelligent agent might have acted discretely or discernibly in the history of life]. Natural processes are a manifestation of God's ongoing presence in the universe. The Intelligence in which I as a Christian believe, has been built into the system from the beginning, and it is realized through God's ongoing activity which is manifest through the natural laws. Those laws are a description of that which emerges, that which is a result of, God's ongoing presence and activity in the universe. I see no biblical, theological, or scientific reason to extend that to extra supernatural "boosts" along the way . . . [6]

Falk's description of his philosophy and theology of nature is admirably clear. It amounts to the a priori conviction that, during natural history, God acted exclusively through naturalistic or materialistic causes. Hence, we are justified in seeking only such causes to explain all phenomena—including the *origin* of fundamentally new forms of life, and the information necessary to produce them. His philosophy of nature commits Falk to explaining all of natural history via what philosophers and theologians call "secondary causes." But that is just another way of expressing a commitment—perhaps a distinctively Christian commitment—to methodological naturalism.

Thus, for Falk and other theistic evolutionists, methodological naturalism compensates for the glaring evidential defects in the scientific case for materialistic evolution—not by demonstrating the creative

5. Nancey Murphy, "Phillip Johnson on Trial: A Critique of His Critique of Darwin," *Perspectives on Science and Christian Faith (PSCF)* 45, no. 1 (1993): 33.

6. Darrell Falk, "Thoughts on *Darwin's Doubt*, Part 1," *BioLogos*, September 9, 2014, accessed July 25, 2016, http://biologos.org/blogs/archive/thoughts-on-darwin's-doubt-reviewing-darwin's-doubt-darrel-falk-part-1.

power of a previously unknown evolutionary mechanism, but simply by ruling out competing ideas such as the theory of intelligent design, or even a divinely guided evolutionary process (where such guidance is empirically detectable). Under methodological naturalism, these theories fall outside what the received norms of scientific inference allow. In that case, a version of theistic evolution that does not involve God actively or discernibly guiding the evolutionary process remains as the only scientifically acceptable theory for theistically minded scientists.

In this chapter, we evaluate methodological naturalism, both as a normative rule for doing science and as an extra-evidential philosophical principle justifying theistic evolution. If methodological naturalism turns out to be a well-supported rule for governing the practice of science, then *some* fully natural process must explain the origin of life, plants, animals, and humans, and no other possibilities need— or should—be considered. Indeed, if methodological naturalism turns out to be sound, then theistic evolutionists may well be justified in holding the view that some fully materialistic mechanism of evolution *must* have caused new forms of life, even if evidence for the necessary creative power of known evolutionary mechanisms is currently lacking.

If methodological naturalism is unsound, however, theistic evolution as a theory will need to stand on its own two feet, without any philosophical buttressing. Then, as we evaluate evolutionary theory without the protective philosophical armature of methodological naturalism, we may have to accept that there is no evidence showing that undirected evolutionary mechanisms have the creative power to produce new forms of life (as, in fact, we saw in chapters 1–9). In that case, scientists may wish to consider the possibility that a designing or creative intelligence played a discernible and causal role in the history of life—and that such a theory may provide a better explanation than materialistic theories for the origin of biological form and information. After all, shouldn't the *evidence*, rather than an abstract rule like methodological naturalism, decide the outcome of a scientific investigation?

III. Why Methodological Naturalism?

So why have so many scientists, including many Christians, accepted that scientific explanations "must invoke only natural things and processes"? Perhaps they are merely following the established conventions of their disciplines, out of respect for the customary rules and practices of science, as those rules have come down to them throughout history. As Nancey Murphy explains, most scientists accept methodological naturalism as an unobjectionable convention because seeking natural causes is just what science *does*:

> Science *qua* [as] science seeks naturalistic explanations for all natural processes. Christians and atheists alike must pursue scientific questions in our era without invoking a Creator. . . . Anyone who attributes the characteristics of living things to creative intelligence has by definition stepped into the arena of either metaphysics or theology.[7]

Yet what determined the placement of the boundary line? For Murphy, the boundary we have today (which, as she notes, excludes "creative intelligence" or intelligent causation) is just the boundary that we were given by history: "*For better or worse*, we have *inherited* a view of science as methodologically atheistic."[8]

Historical inertia, however—to give the "inherited rules" view a name—hardly justifies methodological naturalism, if we recall that the goal of science is *truth*, rather than dutifully following whatever our immediate predecessors did, because they followed whatever *their* predecessors did. If methodological naturalism were only this type of historically contingent convention, scientists seeking true explanations could ignore the rule, especially if they believe the evidence is best explained by intelligent, rather than strictly material, causes. The search for truth should override any custom or convention.

Most defenders of methodological naturalism, however, insist that the rule is more than merely an arbitrary convention or the product of historical inertia. Instead, they insist that methodological naturalism is supported by sound methodological principles—by independent and objective criteria of proper scientific methodology, or what are known as "demarcation criteria." Demarcation criteria—such as the idea that scientific theories (1) must be based on observable data and/or (2) must

---

7. Murphy, "Phillip Johnson on Trial," 33.
8. Ibid., emphasis added.

be testable or falsifiable and/or (3) must offer explanations based on natural law—purport to distinguish genuine science from pseudoscience, metaphysics, or religion. Defenders of methodological naturalism assert that only a fully naturalistic or materialistic approach to scientific inquiry and explanation allows scientists to meet these standards of good scientific practice. Conversely, they argue that nonmaterialistic or design-based theories (that do invoke creative intelligence) do not meet these criteria or standards of method and thus do not qualify as genuine scientific theories or explanations.

So let us look closely at these demarcation criteria. Do they provide what is needed—namely, a principled philosophical or methodological reason for supporting methodological naturalism? Do the criteria enable scientists or philosophers to define the practice of science in a normative way? Do the criteria justifiably exclude, a priori, some theories as unscientific or pseudoscientific (that is, irrespective of what the evidence may show)? If so, then it may be perfectly justifiable to exclude from scientific consideration theories of the origin and development of life that invoke creative intelligence, and it may also be justifiable to require that theories refer only to materialistic causes or natural processes, just as many theistic evolutionists assume. If methodological naturalism is not well-grounded, however, then the rule may be damaging science, and limiting the freedom of scientists (indeed, anyone) to seek the truth (about how life actually originated, for example).

IV. A Conversation about Methodological Naturalism—And What *Wasn't* Said

On rare occasions in the life of a student, something so significant happens—in conversation with an older mentor or scholar—that the episode determines the future thinking of that student. Such a conversation happened to one of us (Paul Nelson) in October 1983, when he was still an undergraduate, studying the philosophy of science and evolutionary biology at the University of Pittsburgh. The episode, a discussion about methodological naturalism with the distinguished historian of science Ronald Numbers, is worth recounting, as it illuminates the central problem with methodological naturalism—in particular, with methodological naturalism's putatively objective standing as a ground rule for science.

Numbers is a professor of the history of science at the University of Wisconsin and one of the world's leading scholars on the relationship of science and religion. In 1983, he received a fellowship from the Guggenheim Foundation to write a history of American creationism. He had learned that Paul possessed some historically valuable correspondence and papers belonging to his grandfather, Byron C. Nelson (1893–1972), an influential early-twentieth-century creationist, so Numbers made an appointment to visit Pittsburgh and review the materials.[9] On October 18, 1983, after a morning of reading the letters, Numbers took Paul out to lunch at a local restaurant.

At the time, Paul was preparing to write his senior thesis in the philosophy of science, on the topic of intelligent design in biology.[10] He was troubled by a pervasive incongruity in how the empirical possibility of design (i.e., causation by an intelligent agent) had been treated in biology since Darwin's time. For Darwin, design was not only a live possibility but represented the central target of his "one long argument" in the *Origin of Species* (1859).[11] In other words, design *might* have been true. Darwin thought it *was* true, in fact, when he set sail on the *Beagle* in 1831, though he later concluded the evidence spoke against it. "I can entertain no doubt," wrote Darwin, " . . . that the view which most naturalists entertain, and which I formerly entertained—namely, that each species has been independently created—is erroneous."[12]

But whatever *can* be false ("erroneous," in Darwin's words) could by logical symmetry also be true. The evidence should decide—except that methodological naturalism says otherwise. Never mind the evidence; design categorically may not be considered as an empirical possibility. "The statements of science," says the National Academy, "must invoke only natural things and processes."

Over lunch, Paul presented this philosophical incongruity to Num-

---

9. Ronald Numbers, *The Creationists: From Scientific Creationism to Intelligent Design* (Cambridge, MA: Harvard University Press, 2006).
10. Paul A. Nelson, "The Possibility of Design" (BA thesis, Independent Study Term, University of Pittsburgh Department of Philosophy, 1984; supervisor, Nicholas Rescher).
11. Charles Darwin, *On the Origin of Species by Means of Natural Selection*, facsimile of the first ed. (London: John Murray, 1859; repr., Cambridge, MA: Harvard University Press, 1964), 459.
12. Ibid., 6.

bers. Methodological naturalism seemed arbitrary at best, Paul said. If design can be false, as Darwin argued, then it might also be true. Whatever philosophy of science we adopt, therefore, should allow for both possibilities, letting the evidence determine the outcome—right?

Without looking up from his food, Numbers nodded his agreement—but only with the *possibility* of intelligent design. Of course intelligent design is *possible*, he replied. But that isn't the issue. Look, he went on, why is it that in baseball, when one hits the ball outside the first or third base lines (i.e., a foul ball), one cannot run to first base?

Baseball has its rules, he said, answering his own question. So does science. Since the rise to dominance of scientific materialism in the nineteenth century, the rules of science have included methodological naturalism. Not every empirical possibility is going to be able to get into the game. That may strike you as unfair, Numbers acknowledged, but that is how the game of science has been played for a long time now, and it's not going to change. If you want to participate, follow the rules—particularly methodological naturalism—or find another game.[13]

Well, rules *are* rules, Paul thought to himself, and if everyone accepts them, one can hardly make a fuss about those rules, at least if one wants to join the game as it is currently being played. But what struck Paul most powerfully at that moment, and what has influenced his thinking ever since, was what Numbers did *not* say at the lunch table that afternoon.

V. Demarcation Criteria Work, Except when They Don't

Numbers did not support methodological naturalism by appealing to any of the familiar and supposedly neutral methodological criteria used

---

13. UCLA biochemist Richard Dickerson expresses the "game" metaphor vividly: "Science, fundamentally, is a game. It is a game with one overriding and defining rule: Rule No. 1: Let us see how far and to what extent we can explain the behavior of the physical and material universe in terms of purely physical and material causes, without invoking the supernatural" (Dickerson, "The Game of Science," *PSCF* 44 [June 1992]: 137–138). More recently, in a 2013 lecture to the Ogilvie Institute at Fuller Theological Seminary, Numbers has described methodological naturalism as having been fostered in large measure by theists, to assure themselves a place within a neutral scientific enterprise where "everybody could play the game of science," because parochial or divisive religious opinions had been excluded. In any case, according to Numbers, methodological naturalism is now "the cardinal methodological principle of science" and uppermost among "the long-established rules for doing science." See his lecture "Talk of Science without Talk of God," Ogilvie Institute, YouTube, August 11, 2013, https://www.youtube.com/watch?v=bzNVB-RCgTY.

to define or "demarcate" science, such as observability, testability, falsifiability, or explanation by reference to natural law. He didn't even try.

And there are good reasons for that.

Historians and philosophers of science have long known that attempts to define science by reference to abstract demarcation criteria have failed. In particular, the attempt to define science normatively by such criteria has inevitably died by a thousand counterexamples. Many highly esteemed theories lack some of the allegedly necessary features of science. Demarcation criteria typically either exclude too much already established science—for instance, forcing one to disqualify as unscientific major works in the development of physics (e.g., Newton's *Principia* and his *Optics*, both of which carry significant theological content and fail to meet specific demarcation criteria; see below)—or inadvertently to cut the legs out from under current research fields generally regarded as "scientific," such as cosmology, theoretical physics, historical geology, psychology, or even evolutionary biology itself. Theories in these fields often refer to unobservables (thus running afoul of the widely cited requirement that proper theories refer only to observable entities) *or* fail to make testable or falsifiable predictions *or* do not explain via natural laws. Or all of the above.

The failure of demarcation criteria became a public issue in the immediate wake of a famous court trial that was decided shortly before Nelson's conversation with Numbers. In January 1982, federal judge William Overton overturned an Arkansas law requiring the teaching of creationism alongside evolution in the Arkansas public schools. To justify his ruling in the *McLean v. Arkansas* case, Overton cited demarcation criteria by which he claimed science could be defined normatively—and against which creationism could be measured to determine whether it qualified as a scientific theory. Overton ruled, basing his judgment on the plaintiffs' expert witnesses, that creationism did not qualify as a scientific theory (but was instead an establishment of religion) because it failed to exhibit distinguishing characteristics of a scientific theory, such as: (1) being guided by natural law; (2) explaining by reference to natural law;

572   The Philosophical Critique of Theistic Evolution

(3) being testable against the empirical world, (4) being falsifiable; and others.[14]

Within months of the ruling, the adequacy of the *McLean* criteria, and Overton's use of demarcation criteria generally, had come under blistering attack from philosophers of science (with no sympathies for creationism, incidentally). They explained that many theories throughout the history of science simply could not be described by the *McLean* criteria—yet those theories were unquestionably scientific, in the critical sense of advancing the growth of empirical knowledge about the natural world. Nor could the criteria be justified philosophically, as defining the norms of science. The philosophers who critiqued the *McLean* ruling understood firsthand that the demarcation program, a central preoccupation of twentieth-century philosophy of science, had failed to find adequate criteria to define scientific theories normatively. In other words, no criteria comprehensively captured the features of science (to the exclusion of metaphysics, theology, or other knowledge claims) such that scientists, philosophers—or federal judges, for that matter—could decide if any theory was "scientific" *without ever examining the relevant empirical evidence.*[15]

To illustrate the problems associated with using demarcation criteria to judge the scientific status of a theory, consider the second of Judge Overton's criteria, "explanation by natural law." Thanks to the expert testimony of philosopher of science Michael Ruse, this criterion featured prominently among the *McLean* demarcation standards. Nevertheless, writing after the trial, philosopher of science Larry Laudan, an expert on the demarcation problem, could barely restrain his contempt for the dismal inadequacy of the natural law rule:

> [T]o suggest, as the McLean Opinion does repeatedly, that an existence claim . . . is unscientific until we have found the laws on which the alleged phenomenon depends is simply outrageous. Galileo and Newton took themselves to have established the existence of gravitational phe-

---

14. McLean v. Arkansas Board of Education, 529 F. Supp. 1255, 50 U.S. Law Week 2412 (1982) Decision by U.S. District Court Judge William R. Overton.

15. The *locus classicus* explaining the failure of the demarcation program is Larry Laudan's essay, "The Demise of the Demarcation Problem," reprinted in *But Is It Science? The Philosophical Question in the Creation/Evolution Controversy*, ed. R. T. Pennock and M. Ruse, updated ed. (Amherst, NY: Prometheus, 2009), 312–330.

nomena, long before anyone was able to give a causal or explanatory account of gravitation. Darwin took himself to have established the existence of natural selection almost a half-century before geneticists were able to lay out the laws of heredity on which natural selection depended. If we took the McLean Opinion criterion seriously, we should have to say that Newton and Darwin were unscientific; and, to take an example from our own time, it would follow that plate tectonics is unscientific because we have not yet identified the laws of physics and chemistry which account for the dynamics of crustal motion.[16]

Laudan's observations are telling and insightful. A glance at a historical timeline—for the development of any science, such as geology—shows that the original publication of its laws, such as Nicholas Steno's articulation in 1669 of the laws of original horizontality and superposition of strata,[17] requires that those laws first *be discovered* by someone. Paradoxically, however, the "explanation by natural law" criterion entails that any research or reasoning activity conducted *before* geology's laws were discovered and published would *ipso facto* be "unscientific." One cannot explain via a natural law until one knows what that law might be. The criterion thus renders "unscientific" the many decades or even centuries of unquestionably essential empirical work as sciences have developed and matured.

In any case, natural laws are often used to *describe*, but not to *explain*, natural phenomena. Newton famously declared that he did not know the cause of universal gravitation: *"hypotheses non fingo,"* as he said in Latin.[18] He freely admitted he could not *explain* what caused gravitational attraction, but instead could only describe the phenomenon mathematically with his law.[19] Thus, a strict applica-

---

16. Larry Laudan, "Science at the Bar—Causes for Concern," in *But Is It Science?*, 334–335.

17. "Original horizontality" asserts that sedimentary strata are first deposited in a horizontal orientation by gravity; "superposition" asserts that, in any undisturbed vertical sequence of strata, the oldest strata occur at the bottom, and youngest at the top. See Nicholas Steno, *The Prodromus of Nicolaus Steno's Dissertation Concerning a Solid Body Enclosed by Process of Nature within a Solid*, trans., ed. John Garrett Winter, an English version with an introduction and explanatory notes (New York: Macmillan, 1916), available at https://archive.org/details/cu31924012131458.

18. "I frame no hypotheses" (Isaac Newton, "General Scholium" in *Philosophiae Naturalis Principia Mathematica*, 3rd ed., trans. I. Bernard Cohen and Anne Whitman [Berkeley: University of California Press, 1999], 943).

19. Imre Lakatos, "Falsification and the Methodology of Scientific Research Programmes," in *Criticism and the Growth of Knowledge*, ed. I. Lakatos and A. Musgrave (Cambridge: Cambridge University Press, 1970), 189–195.

tion of Judge Overton's second demarcation criterion would, again, imply that Newton's Universal Law of Gravitation, and many other fundamental laws of physics, are "unscientific" because they do not offer *causal* explanations for the fundamental physical phenomena they describe.

Conversely, many other sciences do offer causal explanations, but they do so, not primarily by citing general laws, but instead by citing past events. Historical sciences, including evolutionary biology,[20] for example, typically explain particular events in the past by citing prior *events and conditions* that played a causal role in producing the events in question. For example, if a historical geologist seeks to explain what caused the unusual height of the Himalayas, he or she will cite particular events or factors that were present in the case of the Himalayan mountain-building episode that were not present in other such episodes. Knowing the laws of physics that describe the forces at work in all mountain-building events will not greatly aid the geologist in accounting for the contrast between the height of the Himalayas and all other mountain ranges. To explain what caused the Himalayas to rise to such heights, the geologist does not need to cite a general law but instead needs to give evidence of a distinctive set of past events or conditions.[21]

Or consider testability, another key *McLean* demarcation criterion. Judge Overton's ruling stated that "creationism" was "not testable," and thus could not be considered scientific. Ironically, just as the criterion of "must explain by natural law" can be applied in such a way as to render both Newtonian physics and Darwinian biology *un*scientific, the criterion of testability can be rendered in such a way as to show creationism as a completely *scientific* research program—quite in opposition to what those using these criteria wanted to show. As Laudan pointed out after the trial, "Creationists make a wide range of testable

20. Michael Scriven, "Explanation and Prediction in Evolutionary Theory," *Science* 130 (1959): 477–482; Stephen C. Meyer, "Of Clues and Causes: A Methodological Interpretation of Origin of Life Studies" (PhD thesis, Department of History and Philosophy of Science, Cambridge University, 1990), 40–76.

21. Michael Scriven, "Causation as Explanation," *Nous* 9 (1975): 3–15, 14; W. P. Alston, "The Place of the Explanation of Particular Facts in Science," *Philosophy of Science* 38 (1971): 13–34; Peter Lipton, *Inference to the Best Explanation* (London and New York: Routledge, 1991), 47–81.

assertions about empirical matters of fact."[22] Indeed, in the *Origin of Species*, Darwin built an *evidential* case *against* special creation precisely by *testing* and finding wanting the special creationist theories of his time. As Ernst Mayr (a leading neo-Darwinian theorist) observed in his 1964 introduction to the *Origin of Species*, "again and again, [Darwin] describes phenomena that do not fit the creation theory."[23] Consequently, that theory must have been testable and—by the criteria employed by Judge Overton—must be considered scientific. Moreover, the expert witnesses who testified against the Arkansas law in November 1981 (including Michael Ruse and Stephen Gould, among others) clearly thought that geological and biological evidence contradicted the claims of the modern young earth version of creationism discussed at the trial. That version must, therefore, have been testable—and, thus, by the testability criterion, must be scientific. Consequently, by Overton's own rationale, creationism could legitimately be taught in public school science classrooms—*contra* his ruling.

VI. One Measuring Stick for Everyone: The Methodological Equivalence of Materialistic and Nonmaterialistic (I.e., Design-Based) Theories

Moreover, the failure of demarcation criteria to distinguish scientific from nonscientific theories applies in spades when considering materialistic versus nonmaterialistic (design-based) origins theories. Hence these criteria cannot justify methodological naturalism, since that principle is used precisely to eliminate nonmaterialistic theories—i.e., those that invoke creative intelligence as a cause.

While researching the demarcation problem, one of us (Stephen Meyer) discovered an unexpected equivalence between materialistic and design-based theories with respect to their ability to meet a whole range of demarcation criteria.[24] He has found that, invariably, if the

22. Laudan, "Science at the Bar," 332.

23. Ernst Mayr, Introduction to the facsimile reprint of the *Origin of Species* (London: John Murray, 1859; repr., Cambridge, MA: Harvard University Press, 1964), xii.

24. Meyer, "Methodological Equivalence of Design and Descent"; Meyer, "Laws, Causes, and Facts: A Response to Professor Ruse," in *Darwinism: Science or Philosophy*, ed. J. Buell and G. Hearn (Dallas: Foundation for Thought and Ethics, 1994) 29–40; Meyer, "The Nature of Historical Science and the Demarcation of Design and Descent," in *Facets of Faith and Science*, vol. 4 (Lanham, MD: University Press of America, 1996), 91–130; Meyer, "The Demarcation of Science and Religion," in *The History of Science and Religion in the Western Tradition: An Encyclopedia*,

critics of nonmaterialistic theories such as intelligent design apply definitional criteria—such as observability, testability, or law-like explanation—in a strict way, then these criteria not only disqualify the design hypotheses from consideration as science, they also disqualify their chief materialistic rivals—other historical scientific theories—that invoke only undirected evolutionary processes.

Conversely, if definitional or demarcation criteria are applied in a less restrictive way—perhaps one that takes into account the distinctive historical aspects of inquiry into biological origins—then these criteria not only establish the scientific bona fides of various fully materialistic theories (i.e., rivals of intelligent design); they also confirm the scientific status of the design hypothesis (and other nonmaterialistic theories) as well. We saw this already in the case of creationism's ability to meet the criterion of testability. In no case that we have studied, however, has the demarcation criterion successfully differentiated the scientific status of nonmaterialistic theories (such as intelligent design) and competing materialistic theories of evolution. Either science gets defined so narrowly (in the way these criteria are applied) that the criteria disqualify both types of theory, or science is defined so broadly in the way the criteria are applied that the initial reasons for excluding intelligent design (or its competitors) evaporate. If one type of theory meets a specific criterion, then so does the other; if one type of theory fails to do so, then its rivals also fail—provided the criteria are applied in an evenhanded and non–question-begging way.

Theories invoking creative intelligence and their strictly materialistic rivals are *equivalent* in their ability to meet various demarcation criteria or methodological norms. Given this equivalence, and given that materialistic evolutionary theories are already widely regarded as scientific, there does not seem to be any reason to classify theories invoking creative intelligence as inherently unscientific by definition. Consequently, there seems to be no reason to think that scientists must limit themselves to affirming some form of undirected evolutionary process as the sole possible type of explanation for the origin and de-

ed. G. Ferngren (Garland, NY: Routledge, 2000), 12–23. Meyer, "The Scientific Status of Intelligent Design: The Methodological Equivalence of Naturalistic and Non-Naturalistic Origins Theories," in: *Science and Evidence for Design in the Universe*, vol. 9, Proceedings of the Wethersfield Institute (San Francisco: St. Ignatius, 2002), 151–211. Meyer, "Sauce for the Goose," 95–131.

velopment of life on Earth—and also no reason that theists working in the sciences should have to affirm such theories (or affirm versions of theistic evolution that deny that God played an active discernible causal role in the process of creation).

To illustrate this equivalence in the case of theories of biological origins, let's look at two widely cited demarcation criteria, one of which was used in the Arkansas trial and another that has been used by opponents of the theory of intelligent design (which was not yet on trial, in Arkansas).

Lawful Explanation

We saw already that many scientific theories do not explain by citing natural law. Some do not offer explanations at all—they describe, but do not explain, using laws of nature. Other sciences *do* offer explanations, but they do so by reference to causal *events* rather than general laws of nature.[25] Consequently, it turns out that this demarcation criteria ("must explain by natural law") offers little support for those who wish to use it to exclude design-based origins theories and, at the same time, use it to validate materialistic theories.

Many historical scientific theories do not explain primarily *by natural law.*[26] Instead, they postulate past events (or patterns of events) to explain other past events as well as presently observable evidence. Evolutionary theories, also, often emphasize the importance of past events—specific mutational events of various kinds, or the postulated existence of transitional forms, for example—in their explanations.[27] Aleksandr Oparin's chemical evolutionary theory, for example, postulated a series of events (a scenario), not a general law, in order to explain how the first living cells arose.[28] Similarly, in *On the Origin of Species*, Darwin proposed both a mechanism (natural selection) and

25. Meyer, "Of Clues and Causes," 11–113, 125, 174–179, 194–198, 211–212; Meyer, "Laws, Causes, and Facts," 29–40.

26. Gordon Graham, *Historical Explanation Reconsidered* (Aberdeen: Aberdeen University Press, 1983), 17–28; W. P. Alston, "The Place of the Explanation of Particular Facts in Science," *Philosophy of Science* 38 (1971): 13–34; Michael Scriven, "Truisms as the Grounds for Historical Explanations," in *Theories of History*, ed. P. Gardiner (Glencoe, Ill.: Free Press, 1959), 443–475; Scriven, "Causes, Connections and Conditions in History," in *Philosophical Analysis and History*, ed. W. Dray (New York: Harper & Row, 1966), 238–264.

27. Scriven, "Explanation and Prediction in Evolutionary Theory," 477–482.

28. A. I. Oparin, *The Origin of Life* (New York: Dover, 1952 [first translation published in 1938]); Meyer, "Of Clues and Causes."

a historical theory—the theory of universal common descent. Evolutionary biologists debate whether the mechanism of natural selection can be formulated as a general law. But within Darwin's argument, the theory of common descent had its own explanatory power.[29] Yet it did not explain by reference to a law of nature. Instead, common descent explained a range of present-day biological and paleontological evidence by postulating a hypothetical pattern of *events* (as depicted in Darwin's famous tree of life). Common descent makes a claim about what happened in the past—namely, that a series of unobserved transitional organisms existed, forming a genealogical bridge between presently existing life-forms—to account for a variety of presently observed evidence (such as the similarity of anatomical structures in different organisms, or the pattern of fossil progression). Darwin himself referred to common descent as the *vera causa*[30] (i.e., the actual cause) of a diverse set of biological observations. But the theory of common descent represented a pattern of events, not a law, and yet it also clearly provided an explanation of a diverse "class of facts," as Darwin put it.[31]

Of course, past events and historical scenarios are assumed to have taken place in a way that obeys the laws of nature. Moreover, our knowledge of cause-and-effect relationships (which we can sometimes formulate as laws) will often guide the inferences that scientists make about what happened in the past and will influence their assessment of the plausibility of competing historical scenarios and explanations. Even so, many historical scientific theories make *no* mention of laws at all. Laws at best play only a secondary role in historical scientific theories. Instead, *events* play the primary explanatory role. Ironically, as if to underscore this point, Michael Ruse, who offered the "must explain by natural law" criterion at the Arkansas trial, himself has noted that "it is probably a mistake to think of modern evolutionists as seeking universal laws at work in every situation."[32]

---

29. Ernst Mayr, "Darwin's Five Theories of Evolution," in *The Darwinian Heritage*, ed. David Kohn (Princeton NJ: Princeton University Press, 1985), 755–772; Meyer, "Of Clues and Causes," 11–113, 125, 174–179.

30. Darwin, *On the Origin of Species*, 159.

31. Charles Darwin, "To Asa Gray," *Darwin Correspondence Project*, September 10, 1860, http://www.darwinproject.ac.uk/entry-2910.

32. Michael Ruse, *Darwinism Defended* (New York: Addison-Wesley, 1982), 59.

The theory of intelligent design, and other such theories of origins, exemplify the same style of scientific explanation as other historical scientific theories. Intelligent design invokes a past event—albeit a mental event—rather than a law to explain the origin of information necessary to produce various novel forms of life as well as the complexity of the cell. As in other historical scientific theories, our knowledge of cause and effect ("information habitually arises from conscious activity") supports the inference to design. A law (the law of conservation of information) also helps to justify the inference of an intelligent cause as the best explanation. Advocates of intelligent design use a law ("since there is no informational 'free lunch,' the origin of complex specified information always requires intelligent input") to justify their inference to a past causal event, namely, the act of a designing mind. But that act or causal *event* explains the evidence in question. Though laws play a subsidiary role in the theory of intelligent design, a past causal event (or events) explains the ultimate origin of biological information.

Nevertheless, if explaining events primarily by reference to prior events, rather than laws, does not disqualify other historical scientific theories, including materialistic evolutionary theories, from consideration as science, then by the same logic it should not disqualify the theory of intelligent design either. Similarly, if laws can play no role or only a subsidiary role in other historical theories, then why is it "inappropriate" for a law to play only a supportive role in the theory of intelligent design?

Conversely, if invoking a past event, rather than a law, makes intelligent design unscientific, then by the same token it should make materialistic evolutionary theories unscientific as well. Either way, the demarcation criterion "must explain by natural law" does not discriminate the scientific status of the two types of theories. Provided the demarcation criterion is applied with the same degree of rigidity or liberality, both materialistic and nonmaterialistic theories of origin are *equivalent* in their capacity to meet the definitional standard advanced in the Arkansas trial (and are, thus, either equally scientific or equally unscientific, depending on how rigidly that standard is applied).

Observability

We have discovered a similar equivalence with respect to every other demarcation criterion that we have examined. Consider, for example, the oft-cited criterion of "observability."

According to critics of intelligent design, the unobservable character of a designing intelligence renders it inaccessible to empirical investigation and, therefore, makes it unscientific. For example, in 1993 biophysicist Dean Kenyon was removed from teaching his introductory biology class at San Francisco State University after he discussed his reasons for supporting intelligent design with his students. His department colleagues believed their actions against him were justified because they believed that he had been discussing an unscientific theory with his class. Some of Kenyon's colleagues argued that the theory of intelligent design did not qualify as a scientific theory because it invoked an *unobservable* entity, in particular, an unseen designing intelligence.[33] In making this argument, Kenyon's colleagues assumed that scientific theories must invoke only *observable* entities. Since Kenyon discussed a theory that violated this convention, they insisted that neither the theory he discussed, nor he himself, belonged in the biology classroom. Others who defended the action of the biology department, such as Eugenie Scott of the National Center for Science Education, used a similar rationale. She insisted that the theory of intelligent design violated the rules of science because "you can't put an omnipotent deity in a test tube (or keep it out of one)."[34] Molecular biologist Fred Grinnell has similarly argued that intelligent design cannot be a scientific concept, because if something "can't be measured, or counted, or photographed, it can't be science."[35]

But is that true? Does referring to unobservable entities or events render a theory unscientific?

The answer depends, again, on how science is defined. If scientists

---

33. Stephen C. Meyer, "A Scopes Trial for the '90s," *The Wall Street Journal*, December 6, 1993, A14; see also Meyer, "The Harmony of Natural Law," *Wall Street Journal*, January 17, 1993, letters section, A9; Meyer, "Scientist Stifled from Teaching Life's Origins," *Oregonian*, January 4, 1994, B7; Meyer, "Open Debate on Life's Origins," *Insight*, February 21, 1994, 27–29. See also "Letters-to-the-Editor," *Insight*, April 4, 1994, 4.

34. Eugenie Scott, "Keep Science Free from Creationism," *Insight*, February 21, 1994, 30.

35. Fred Grinnell, "Radical Intersubjectivity: Why Naturalism Is an Assumption Necessary for Doing Science," in *Darwinism: Science or Philosophy?*, ed. J. Buell and V. Hearn (Richardson, TX: Foundation for Thought and Ethics, 1994), 99–105.

(and all other relevant parties) decide to define science as an enterprise in which scientists can posit only observable entities or events in their theories, then clearly the theory of intelligent design would not qualify as a scientific theory. Advocates of intelligent design infer, rather than directly observe, the activity of the designing intelligence responsible for the digital information in DNA, for example.

But this definition of science would render many other scientific theories, including many evolutionary theories of biological origins, unscientific by definition as well. Many scientific theories infer or postulate unobservable entities, causes, and events. Instead, scientists often infer the existence of unobservable entities in order to explain observable events, evidence, or phenomena. Physical forces, electromagnetic or gravitational fields, atoms, quarks, past events, subsurface geological features, biomolecular structures—*all* are unobservable entities inferred from observable evidence.

Materialistic evolutionary theories also infer or postulate past unobservable events. Theories of chemical evolution invoke past events as part of the scenarios they use to explain how the first living cell arose.[36] Insofar as these events occurred millions of years ago, they are clearly not observable today. Neo-Darwinian biologists, for their part, have long defended the putatively unfalsifiable nature of their claims by reminding critics that many of the creative processes to which they refer occur at rates too slow to observe in the present and too fast to have been recorded in the fossil record. Furthermore, the existence of many transitional intermediate forms of life, the forms represented by the nodes on Darwin's famous branching tree diagram, are also unobservable. Instead, as noted, unobservable transitional forms of life are *postulated* to explain the pattern of observable biological evidence—as Darwin himself explained. But how is this different in principle from postulating the past activity of an unobservable designing intelligence to explain observable features of the living cell or the pattern of appearance in the fossil record?[37] Neither Darwinian transitional forms, neo-Darwinian mutational

---

36. Meyer, "Of Clues and Causes."
37. Stephen Meyer, *Darwin's Doubt: The Explosive Origin of Animal Life and the Case for Intelligent Design* (New York: HarperOne, 2014); Meyer, *Signature in the Cell: DNA and the Evidence for Intelligent Design* (New York: HarperOne, 2010).

events, the "rapid branching" events of Stephen Jay Gould's theory of punctuated equilibria, the events comprising chemical evolutionary scenarios, nor the past action of a designing intelligence are directly observable. With respect to direct observability, each of these theories is equivalent.

Thus, if the standard of observability is applied in a strict way, neither intelligent design nor any other theory of biological origins qualifies as a scientific theory. But if the standard of observability is applied in a more flexible and, perhaps, realistic way, then both materialistic and nonmaterialistic theories (those that invoke unobservable actions of a creative intelligence) should be considered equally scientific. Indeed, both types of theories are equivalent in their ability to meet the demarcation criterion of "observability" and every other criterion that we have examined.

It has been said that "behind every double standard lies a single hidden agenda." It takes only a smattering of philosophical training, and even less historical sophistication, to see that the flawed demarcation criteria cited in *McLean* had been specially contrived by the ACLU to try to discredit creationism.[38] But if we take the criteria seriously, and apply them dispassionately with an unabridged history of science in hand, the methodological equivalence of theories of materialistic evolution and intelligent design (or other nonmaterialistic theories invoking creative intelligence) emerges quite naturally—almost as if philosophy of science herself had refused to take the role of referee in our scientific disputes. Proponents of competing scientific theories must fight it out, however messy that may be—i.e., their theories must compete for the standing of best explanation—with the *evidence* as the final arbiter. There is no *philosophical* shortcut to empirical truth; indeed, if abstract methodological criteria could perform that task, why bother with examining the evidence?

---

38. "Philosophically, these criteria may have been acceptable sixty or eighty years ago, but they are not rigorous, they are redundant, and they take no account of many distinctions nor of historical cases. The opinion does not state whether they are singly necessary or jointly sufficient. One would not recommend to graduate school a student who could do no better than this. Fortunately, Judge Overton and the litigators were not applying to graduate school. They were in a court of law. . . . In this forum, confronted with Creationism . . . are these criteria so far off the mark? . . . Are they not sufficient to refute Creationism?" See Barry Gross, "Commentary: Philosophers at the Bar—Some Reasons for Restraint," *Science, Technology, and Human Values* 8 (1983): 30–38.

VII. The Permitted versus the Possible: Science as Open-Ended Quest

Thus far, none of the arguments advanced in support of a naturalistic definition of science has provided a justification for methodological naturalism. Nevertheless, perhaps such arguments are irrelevant. Perhaps scientists should just accept the definition of science that has come down to them. After all, the search for natural causes or materialistic processes has served science well. What compelling reasons can be offered for overturning the prohibition against design-based explanations in science? What harm can come from continuing with the status quo?

In fact, methodological naturalism damages science—and for several interrelated reasons.

First, with respect to origins, defining science as a strictly materialistic enterprise limits the ability of scientists to determine the truth—to find out what actually happened to cause life to arise on Earth. Consider: it is at least logically possible that a personal agent or a creative intelligence existed before the appearance of the first life on Earth, and that such an agent played a causal role in the origin and development of life. Further, proponents of intelligent design have shown in other places[39] that we do live in the sort of world where knowledge of such an agent could possibly be known or inferred from empirical data. This suggests that it is logically and empirically possible that such an agent designed or influenced the origins of living forms on Earth in an empirically detectable (to us) way. To insist that postulations of creative intelligence are inherently unscientific in the historical sciences (where the express purpose of such inquiry is to determine what happened in the past) simply excludes by assumption a logically and empirically possible answer to the question motivating historical biology: what actually happened to cause life to arise on Earth? Indeed, the (historical) question that must be asked about biological origins is not "Which materialistic scenario will prove most adequate?" but "How did life as we know it actually arise on Earth?" Since one of the logically possible answers to this later question is "Life was designed

---

39. William A. Dembski, "The Very Possibility of Intelligent Design," paper presented at Science and Belief, First International Conference of the Pascal Centre, Ancaster, Ontario, August 11–15, 1992.

by an intelligent agent that existed before the advent of humans," it seems contrary to the truth-seeking function of the natural sciences to exclude the design hypothesis without a consideration of all the evidence, including the most current evidence, that might support it.

This conclusion has been reinforced by recent developments in the philosophy of science. Recent accounts of scientific rationality in the philosophy of science suggest that scientific theory evaluation is an inherently comparative enterprise. Notions such as consilience[40] and Peter Lipton's inference to the best explanation[41] imply the need to compare the explanatory power of competing hypotheses or theories. If this process is subverted by philosophical gerrymandering, the rationality of scientific practice is vitiated. Theories that gain acceptance in artificially constrained competitions can claim to be neither "most probably true" nor "most empirically adequate." Instead, such theories can only be considered "most probable or adequate among an artificially limited set of options."

We illustrate the way in which methodological naturalism impedes the truth-seeking function of science visually with Figure 19.1, a Venn diagram depicting the logical relationship between what is empirically possible *versus* what our scientific methods, under the rule of methodological naturalism, have permitted us to infer. Notice that the space of what is possible—that is, the space of what might be true, should the evidence turn up—extends far beyond, and *encloses*, the space of what has been permitted under methodological naturalism.

This asymmetry, between what is possible and what has been permitted, will not necessarily trouble the philosophical materialist or naturalist who simply assumes that there cannot have been creative intelligence at work in the production of life or the universe. Thus, for them the boundary line of what might be true empirically is coextensive precisely with what the methods of science, as defined by methodological naturalism, allow as possibilities.

But the asymmetry between the possible and the permitted should

---

40. Paul Thagard, "The Best Explanation: Criteria for Theory Choice," *Journal of Philosophy* 75 (1978): 79; Meyer, "Of Clues and Causes," 99–109; William Whewell, *The Philosophy of the Inductive Sciences*, vol. 2 (London: Parker, 1840), 109, 242; L. Laudan, "William Whewell on the Consilience of Induction," *The Monist* 55 (1971): 371–379.

41. Lipton, *Inference to the Best Explanation*.

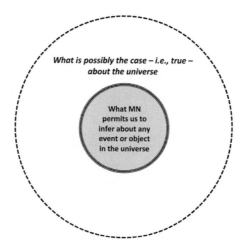

FIGURE 19.1. *The domain of methodological naturalism (MN) enclosed within the domain of the possible.*

bother everyone else, starting with intellectually curious naturalists, atheists, and agnostics who want to know whether the evidence from the natural world actually supports their scientific philosophy, worldview, and preferred origins theories. Those who cherish their intellectual independence do not like to be told what they can or cannot know about the universe. Methodological naturalism doesn't open up explanatory options and possibilities; it can only take them away.

The asymmetry between the possible and the permitted, as imposed on science by methodological naturalism, should bother theists and Christians most of all—including theistic evolutionists who have accepted methodological naturalism as defining science. Figure 19.1 gives the reason: for *theistic* evolutionists, the whole of reality is not, and never could be, coextensive with the physical or material universe—if the adjective "theistic" has any content, that is. Thus, not only is it *possible* that a personal agent existed before the first appearance of life on Earth, and before the universe itself came to be; rather, *this is what theistic evolutionists take to be the case.* After all, all Christian theists, including theistic evolutionists, affirm that "In the beginning was the Word."

VIII. An Explanatory Palette for Science, without Limit

Ironically, many atheistic scientists and philosophers of science now themselves reject methodological naturalism precisely because they see that it impedes an open-ended search for the truth about the universe, life, and reality. As the Caltech physicist (and atheist) Sean Carroll, whom we quoted earlier, has explained,

> Science should be interested in determining the *truth*, whatever that truth may be—natural, supernatural, or otherwise. The stance known as methodological naturalism, while deployed with the best of intentions by supporters of science, amounts to assuming part of the answer ahead of time. If finding truth is our goal, that is just about the biggest mistake we can make.[42]

Other atheists or committed scientific materialists now agree. Mathematician Jason Rosenhouse of James Madison University also objects to methodological naturalism as a nonnegotiable first principle. "Viewed as a fundamental ground rule to which science must always and everywhere adhere," he writes, "MN [methodological naturalism] seems dogmatic and unnecessary."[43] University of Texas philosopher and biologist Sahotra Sarkar, himself a philosophical naturalist, worries that trying to rule out intelligent design "in terms of demarcation criteria or on the basis of [methodological] naturalism is both unnecessary and, it seems to me, a tactical mistake . . . "[44] Lastly, Belgian philosopher of science and atheist Maarten Boudry, evaluating the status of methodological naturalism, argues that "The most widespread view, which conceives of methodological naturalism as an intrinsic or self-imposed limitation of science, is philosophically indefensible."[45]

---

42. Carroll, *Big Picture*, 133.

43. Jason Rosenhouse, *Among the Creationists* (New York: Oxford University Press, 2012), 123.

44. Sahotra Sarkar, "The Science Question in Intelligent Design," *Synthese* 178 (2011): 291–305, 302–303.

45. Maarten Boudry, Stefaan Blancke, and Johan Braeckman, "How Not to Attack Intelligent Design Creationism: Philosophical Misconceptions about Methodological Naturalism," *Foundations of Science* 15 (2010): 227–244, at 228. Many philosophical naturalists such as Carroll, Rosenhouse, and the others still insist, of course, that science works best by assuming naturalism (meaning the causal primacy of the physical/non-intelligent), and that methodological naturalism packaged in a more modest, pragmatic, or provisional flavor merely represents the successful track record of the naturalistic premise. But these commentators allow that evidence might turn up requiring us to suspend methodological naturalism, although in their judgment such evidence has yet to appear. Provisional or pragmatic methodological naturalism, however,

But why would atheists and philosophical naturalists worry about methodological naturalism? It is clear from their writings that Carroll et al. want materialistic theories of evolution to have prevailed in a fair competition—winning their place in science because those theories explained the data better than any design-based competitors. They see an openness to empirical arguments for intelligent design, and against the adequacy of undirected materialistic evolution, as a necessary condition of a fully rational historical biology—one that is committed to following the evidence wherever it leads, and one where the evidence might have shown their favored theories to be wrong. As Sarkar stresses, naturalism as a philosophy (as well as naturalistic theories of evolution) should be "defeasible," i.e., possibly *wrong*. "Most importantly," he writes, "since naturalism is derived from experience, it, as well as any other philosophical position, is fallible, just like the claims of science."[46]

Methodological naturalism, however, when delivered as an a priori *diktat* armored by "must" and "only," renders the proposition "life arose via undirected materialistic or naturalistic evolutionary processes" anything but defeasible. As Rosenhouse worries,

> To say that science "requires this ground rule," or that "one denies God a role in the creation" while doing science, certainly makes it sound as though, no matter how strongly the evidence pointed to design, scientists, in their professional work, would simply be forced to disregard it.[47]

---

is not really methodological naturalism at all. Recall the succinct formulation of the National Academy: "The statements of science must invoke only natural things and processes." Now consider a provisional formulation of methodological naturalism, which we have synthesized from various statements by Carroll et al.:

> The statements of science should invoke natural things and processes, because that is what has worked in the past—unless compelling evidence turns up to the contrary, in which event we may need to enlarge our explanatory resources beyond the strictly natural.

Whatever this might be, it isn't a rule that excludes consideration of creative intelligence or the theory of intelligent design. Methodological naturalism supports undirected materialistic evolution as the only possible type of origins theory—that is, to the necessary exclusion of other theories— only if the imperative "must" and the logical modifier "only" raise an impenetrable logical wall around "materialistic causes" or "natural things and processes." Anything less would be ordinary scientific disputation, contending about the best explanation for the phenomena in the light of every causal possibility, with the normal hurly-burly of empirical debate to follow—a competition modern proponents of the theory of intelligent design, for example, eagerly welcome.

46. Sahotra Sarkar, *Doubting Darwin* (Malden, MA: Blackwell, 2007), 145.
47. Rosenhouse, *Among the Creationists*, 120.

And that, again, damages the truth-seeking goal of science—which is, in fact, the most compelling reason to reject methodological naturalism.

IX. Objection: Do Non-Naturalistic Theories Commit the God-of-the-Gaps Fallacy?

Defenders of methodological naturalism frequently justify its prohibition against nonmaterialistic explanations by claiming that any such explanation for the origin of new forms of life—such as intelligent design or special creation—would necessarily commit a God-of-the-gaps fallacy. According to those who raise this objection, a God-of-the-gaps fallacy occurs when proponents of design or creation invoke the activity of a designing intelligence or Creator to explain some unexplained phenomenon or feature of the natural world. Doing this, they argue, necessarily invokes the action of a designing intelligence to fill a "gap" in our knowledge of the true cause(s) of a given phenomenon or feature and, consequently, hinders or stalls scientific inquiry. By searching for naturalistic or materialistic causes only, the objection continues, we avoid inserting "God" (or mind or intelligence) into the gap in our understanding—a gap that will inevitably be filled by genuine knowledge of a physical, material, or natural mechanism or process.

But to what does the word "gaps" in this objection refer?

Imagine someone who mistakenly enters an art gallery, expecting to find croissants on sale—that is, someone who thinks the gallery is a fancy bakery where pastries and rolls are sold. Such a person may think that he has encountered a puzzle about the wares provided by the business. He may even think that he has a gap in his knowledge of what must definitely be present *somewhere* in the museum. *I cannot see the baked goods, so they must keep them in the back room—clever minimalism!* Based on his assumptions, the visitor may then stubbornly cling to his perception of a gap, insisting it is real and badgering the gallery staff to "bring out the croissants already," until with exasperation they show him to the exit.

The moral of our little story? The gallery visitor sees an unsolved puzzle, or perceives a gap in his knowledge about the location of the baked goods. Both the puzzle and the gap, however, derive from his false assumption that he has walked into a bakery.

In a similar way, *perceived gaps* in our knowledge of natural processes responsible for given phenomena or features of the world *are based on our background assumption about the kind of processes or entities that ought to be present in nature.* In the debate about biological origins, theistic evolutionists and mainstream evolutionary biologists assume that all living systems necessarily were produced by some naturalistic process, and that their origin will, thus, ultimately have a completely naturalistic or materialistic explanation. The background assumption implicit in, for instance, the question "How did life first arise via materialistic chemical evolutionary processes or pathways?" implies a gap in our scientific knowledge when it becomes apparent (as it has; see chapter 3) that no satisfactory materialistic chemical evolutionary process has been discovered that can generate living cells from simpler nonliving molecules. But our present lack of knowledge of any such chemical process entails a "gap" in knowledge of the actual process by which life arose *only if* such a materialistic chemical evolutionary process *actually did* produce the first life.

Yet if life did *not* arise via a strictly materialistic chemical evolutionary process, but was, for example, intelligently designed or specially created, then our absence of knowledge of a strictly materialistic process responsible for life does not represent a gap in knowledge of an actual process—i.e., one that actually exists and/or was acting in the past. In that case, the perceived gap in our knowledge would merely reflect a false assumption about what *must have* happened, or a false assumption about the existence of a certain kind of process—namely, a materialist one with the creative power to generate life.

But what if such a materialistic process did not produce either the first life or fundamentally new forms of life?

Theistic evolutionists use the God-of-the-gaps objection to justify the claim that scientists should consider only *materialistic* evolutionary theories to explain the origin of new living forms (i.e., they use it to justify methodological naturalism). Yet, their use of the God-of-the-gaps objection to justify methodological naturalism ultimately begs the question. Why? Because the claim that "gaps" in our knowledge of materialistic evolutionary processes constitutes an actual gap in knowledge of how life forms came to be *assumes* that materialistic evolutionary mechanisms *must* have produced new forms of life (and, thus, *must* explain the origin of those forms). *But that is simply the assumption of materialism (metaphysical and methodological) in another form.* Yet, methodological materialism or naturalism is precisely what theistic evolutionists invoke fear of the God-of-the-gaps fallacy to justify.

We can unpack the circularity of this reasoning still further. Theistic evolutionists justify protecting *materialistic evolutionary theories* (despite their empirical shortcomings) from theoretical competition from nonmaterialistic origins theories by invoking *methodological naturalism*. They justify *methodological naturalism* by invoking fear of the *God-of-the-gaps* fallacy. But the gaps to which they refer in warning against this alleged fallacy are only gaps if evidence shows that there are materialistic evolutionary mechanisms capable of generating biological novelty—that is, if there is an adequate, fully *materialistic evolutionary theory.* But since many theistic evolutionists admit that there isn't such a theory, they justify their exclusionary commitment to some form of fully *materialistic evolutionary theory* by invoking none other than . . . *methodological naturalism*, which they justify by invoking the *God-of-the-gaps fallacy.* And around and around they go.

Thus, using fear of the God-of-the-gaps fallacy to justify methodological naturalism subtly assumes a materialistic answer to the central question at issue, namely, How did life actually arise? Yet, again, rather than assuming that life *must have* arisen by strictly materialistic processes, scientists interested in finding out what caused life to arise would do better to ask a more open-ended question of nature, such as, What *actually happened* to cause new forms of life on earth to come into existence?

Seen in this light, the God-of-the-gaps objection fades into insignificance. To have force, theistic evolutionists must first show that we have genuine gaps in our knowledge of materialistic causes of the origin of new forms of life—i.e., that we have grounds for thinking that present "gaps" will ultimately be filled with knowledge of an actual natural process or mechanism capable of biological innovation. But this (as we showed in chapters 1–9) is exactly what evolutionary biologists (and theistic evolutionists) have failed to do. Indeed, if theistic evolutionists had discovered materialistic processes with demonstrated creative power, or if they had empirical grounds for thinking that such processes do exist, they would not need to invoke methodological naturalism or justify methodological naturalism by warning of the God-of-the-gaps fallacy. Nor would they need to declare their commitment to waiting indefinitely for an adequate materialistic evolutionary explanation for the origin of biological novelty to emerge. Instead, the fact that they cannot justify their confidence that some materialist evolutionary process will ultimately prove sufficient to explain the origin of novelty, means that they don't know that there is a gap in our knowledge of such a process—that is, of an actual process at work in nature, either now or in the past. Indeed, they have no grounds for believing in the existence and causal powers of such a hypothetical process apart from their prior commitment to methodological naturalism—which is the very principle they seek to justify by invoking the specter of the God-of-the-gaps objection.

X. Conclusion

We have seen that there are no neutral methodological criteria by which we can define science normatively and exhaustively. But fruitful science does not need definitions: it needs creativity, hard work, and evidence most of all. We have also seen that specific demarcation criteria fail to distinguish the scientific status of materialistic and design-based theories of biological origins—i.e., the proposed justifications *in support* of methodological naturalism fail. In addition, we have seen that there is a strong affirmative reason *to reject* methodological naturalism; namely, that it hinders the truth-seeking function of science by forcing scientists to reject the possibility that a creative intelligence played a discernible role in the origin and history of life—even before experience can freely testify. Methodological naturalism gives nothing to scientists but intellectual bondage and limited options. Even if the authors of this chapter were atheists, we would not want to work with the chains of methodological naturalism around our ankles.

Nor should theistic evolutionists. They will lose nothing by letting go of this wretchedly bad rule, erasing a philosophical boundary that never should have been drawn in the first place. But whether they do so or not, it should now be clear that there is no compelling reason to accept methodological naturalism and every good reason to reject it. Consequently, there is no reason to continue holding to theistic evolution in the face of the mounting evidential difficulties that now confront all theories of unguided evolution. It may well be time to consider alternative types of causal explanations for the origin and development of life—to consider, for example, the possibility, at least, of intelligent design and its explanatory power.

And, why not? Basketball is *better* with the three-point shot! More fun to play, more fun to watch.

20

How to Lose a Battleship: Why Methodological Naturalism Sinks Theistic Evolution

STEPHEN DILLEY

SUMMARY

Theistic evolutionists should reject methodological naturalism. Among other reasons, methodological naturalism prohibits both (1) the use of theology-laden claims within scientific discourse and (2) scientific engagement with so-called "nonscientific" theories, like creationism and intelligent design. And yet, key scientific arguments for evolutionary theory—from the *Origin* to the present—either rely on theology-laden claims or engage creationist (or intelligent design) theories in a scientific manner. Under methodological naturalism, however, this dynamic is not acceptable. Accordingly, if theistic evolutionists accept methodological naturalism, they forfeit significant justification for their favored theory. Insofar as theistic evolutionists wish to retain this justification, they ought to set methodological naturalism aside.

. . . . .

The year 1866 was conspicuous for Charles Darwin. Scientific consensus was at last leaning toward common ancestry and away from special creation. Darwin keenly monitored this development. In the fourth edition of the *Origin*, published that year, he inserted a new claim—namely, that special creation's account of homology was "not a scientific explanation."[1] In the first three editions, Darwin's general strategy had been to attack special creation as empirically false and explanatorily empty. But in the fourth edition, he flatly characterized special creation as beyond the pale of science. He went on to reiterate this claim in the fifth edition and, by the sixth and final edition, added three more claims to similar effect.[2]

Yet through all six editions, Darwin also continued to give *scientific* arguments as to why evolutionary theory was empirically superior to special creation. Moreover, Darwin also deployed an array of partisan theological claims as part of his positive argument for evolutionary theory.[3] In effect, he adopted a dual strategy: assail special creation using scientific arguments *and*, when useful, declare that special creationism is not scientific. This tactic enabled Darwin to maximize his empirical argument as well as capitalize on the scientific community's shifting allegiance toward common ancestry. The move gave the *Origin* considerable rhetorical power. But it also came at an epistemic cost: Darwin's dual strategy was intellectually incoherent. Two mutually exclusive options were on the table, and Darwin took both.

A similar dilemma persists to the present day. As we will see, contemporary theistic evolutionists cannot coherently accept scientific arguments that support evolutionary theory over creationism *and* also accept methodological naturalism, which bars creationism from scientific analysis. My core thesis in this chapter is that theistic evolutionists should reject methodological naturalism. Doing so allows them to retain a central justification for evolutionary theory—the apparently "overwhelming" evidence that supports it over all rivals.

My argument falls into four parts. In part 1, I set the stage by defining relevant terms, noting clarifications, and the like. In part 2, I move

---

1. Charles Darwin, *On the Origin of Species*, 4th ed. (London: John Murray, 1866), 513.

2. Stephen Dilley, "The Evolution of Methodological Naturalism in the Origin of Species," *HOPOS: The Journal of the International Society for the History of Philosophy of Science* 3, no. 1 (Spring 2013): 20–58.

3. Stephen Dilley, "Charles Darwin's Use of Theology in the Origin of Species," *British Journal for the History of Science* 44, no. 1 (2012): 29–56.

to the body of my argument, contending that theistic evolutionists must choose one of the two mutually exclusive routes outlined above. In part 3, I argue against methodological naturalism by exploring several ways in which evolutionary thinking involves theology. As we will see, for example, many evolutionary biologists routinely treat creationism as a scientifically testable theory, marshaling empirical evidence to refute it. More strikingly, a wide range of scientific arguments *for* evolutionary theory actually depend on theological claims. Collectively, these ways of supporting evolutionary theory involve "God-talk" and thus run contrary to methodological naturalism.

In part 4, I turn to the other strategy available to theistic evolutionists: accept methodological naturalism and treat creationism as outside of science. I argue that this approach fails. The reasons for methodological naturalism are weak, while reasons against it are strong. Among other things, I contend that acceptance of methodological naturalism greatly harms the case for evolutionary theory, rendering scientific evidence impotent to support evolutionary theory over creationism.

All told, if theistic evolutionists wish to retain maximum support for evolution—if they wish to keep their battleship—they ought to discard methodological naturalism.

Part 1: Setting the Stage

Definitions

Before turning to the main argument, a few definitions are necessary. First, what is methodological naturalism? There are a number of conceptions afoot, yet the mainstream version holds that, like all domains of human inquiry, science has a particular scope, context, and purpose—namely, to focus solely on the properties and processes of nature. As such, the only permissible explanations *within* scientific research, articulation, and argument are those that appeal to natural entities, causes, processes, laws, and the like. While theological explanations for natural phenomena may be legitimate in their own right, they fall outside the purview of science proper. In short, natural explanations, rather than theological ones, belong in science.

A brief exposition of this conception of methodological naturalism is in order. First, methodological naturalists offer an array of reasons for the convention that draw upon theological, historical, empirical, conceptual, and pragmatic grounds. I will turn to these in due course. For now, it's important to note that, according to methodological naturalists, the convention is not an arbitrary rule imposed upon science but a thoughtful conclusion based on reflection about the nature, context, and purposes of science.

Second, methodological naturalism does not imply that natural causes, laws, etc., are in contrast to God's governance of the cosmos. In fact, Christian methodological naturalists typically regard natural causes and laws as *secondary* causes and laws—that is, as God's ordinary way of ruling the universe. God ontologically sustains creation, upholding all things "by the word of his power" (Heb. 1:3). From this vantage, methodological naturalism allows a rich dialogue between science and theology. Even if science and theology are distinct disciplines with their own contexts and purposes, the prohibition of God-talk within science in no way suggests that theology and science have nothing vital to say to each other in conversation. For example, theology can play a meta-level role in motivating, inspiring, and sanctioning scientific work and discourse.[4] In particular, many methodological naturalists believe theological perspectives offer accounts that are complementary to scientific explanations. A scientist can gaze at a sunset and describe how the atmosphere scatters blue and violet light away from his vision, making the sky appear more red and pink. A theologian can behold these colors and say, with equal truthfulness,

> The heavens declare the glory of God;
>   the skies proclaim the work of his hands. (Ps. 19:1 NIV)

Under methodological naturalism, both accounts can be correct. And, just as important, both can be essential for a comprehensive and textured understanding of the natural world.

In addition, with methodological naturalism, science and theology can be (or ought to be) integrated in one's life and thought. While science and theology are different disciplines, nonetheless *individuals*

---

4. E.g., John Brooke, *Science and Religion* (Cambridge: Cambridge University Press, 1991), 19–33.

arguably ought to partake of both areas, melding each complementary account into their personal unified experience. The scientist who describes the properties of light in a sunset can be the same person who also discerns God's reflected glory. In fact, a Christian who is a scientist can affirm that scientific inquiry reveals possible means through which God has created the world and continues to work in nature. On this view, a believer who studies nature as a scientist is engaged in profound worship of the Almighty. For Christian methodological naturalists, science and theology embrace in deep accord.

Having noted that methodological naturalism allows a complementary relationship between science and theology, especially in the life of believing scientists, I now wish to focus on what methodological naturalism implies *within science itself*—the central focus of this chapter. As mentioned, methodological naturalism runs contrary to the incursion of theological explanations within scientific research and discourse.[5] At a deeper level, methodological naturalism also prohibits *any* substantive theological propositions within science. All things being equal, it would be arbitrary to bar theological explanations but allow other theological propositions, especially if these propositions were neither shared by all scientists nor necessary for particular (or general) types of scientific reasoning or research. If methodological naturalism means anything at all, it means that God-talk is barred within science in toto. As theistic evolutionists Denis Alexander, Holmes Rolston III, and Jeffery Schloss note, "the very purpose of science . . . is to explain the workings of nature without recourse to religious language."[6] Or as Michael Ruse observes, "the methodological naturalist insists that, inasmuch as one is doing science, one avoid all theological or other religious references."[7] And the National Academy of Science says simply, "The statements of science must invoke only natural things and

---

5. By "scientific discourse," I mean "scientific articulation, argument, and explanation."

6. Holmes Rolston III, Denis Alexander, Jeff Schloss, et al., "The Concept of 'Intelligent Design,'" *The International Society for Science and Religion*, 2011, accessed March 28, 2017, http://www.issr.org.uk/issr-statements/concept-intelligent-design/. See also Patrick McDonald, "Naturalism," in *A Science and Religion Primer*, ed. H. A. Campbell and H. Looy (Grand Rapids, MI: Baker Academic, 2009), 149–151: inter alia, methodological naturalism holds that "within science, theological assumptions are not appropriate elements in the evaluation of arguments, observations, models, hypotheses, and so on" (149).

7. Michael Ruse, "Methodological Naturalism Under Attack," in *Intelligent Design Creationism and Its Critics*, ed. R. Pennock (Cambridge, MA: MIT Press, 2001), 365.

processes."[8] Consequently, a straightforward implication of methodological naturalism is that scientific investigation, articulation, argument, and explanation ought to remain free of theological claims.[9]

In sum, from the point of view of Christian methodological naturalists, science is simply one tool for understanding the physical world. A complete understanding of creation requires a broader Trinitarian framework. On this view, the scientific enterprise ultimately rests on religious moorings, and the deliverances of science are held to be insights into God's work in and through creation. Yet *science itself* is regarded as a limited endeavor. It has a circumscribed domain that focuses exclusively on natural (or secondary) phenomena. Claims about God's actions, nature, or purposes are not permitted, even if these are necessary for a full (theological) understanding of creation. From this perspective, when scientists engage in scientific work *as* scientific work, they are to avoid religious language.

Having clarified the heart of methodological naturalism, I note that the convention comes in two flavors: intrinsic and pragmatic. The former treats methodological naturalism as an inviolable rule that governs science. Theological claims are never allowed within scientific discourse or research, even in principle. The latter is more modest. On this view, the default practice of scientists within the context of their field should be to explain natural phenomena by reference only to natural (or secondary) causes, laws, and the like. But scientists can be open to supernatural explanations (or claims) within science proper, should the need arise. In this chapter, I use the term "methodological naturalism" to refer to the intrinsic version; I will address the pragmatic version separately in part 4.

What is theistic evolution?[10] In general, the view holds that God planned or guided the evolutionary process. There are variations and exceptions to this main theme, yet most versions have in common the claim that God's design of biological phenomena (or history) is *not*

---

8. National Academy of Science, *Teaching about Evolution and the Nature of Science* (Washington, DC: National Academy Press, 1998), 42.

9. Strictly speaking, I can make my argument in this chapter *even if* methodological naturalism, properly understood, allows some kinds of theological claims within science. My argument only requires that, within science, methodological naturalism (1) prohibits conditionals about supernatural beings (e.g., "If the God of the Bible exists, then he would have created life on Earth about ten thousand years ago") and (2) disallows scientific evidence to either critique supernatural hypotheses (e.g., "The features of the vertebrate eye count as evidence against divine design") or to favor evolutionary hypotheses over supernatural ones (e.g., "The panda's suboptimal thumb supports evolutionary theory over divine design").

10. My characterization of theistic evolution equally applies to "evolutionary creation."

empirically detectable using the rigorous methods of science. God signs his handiwork "using invisible ink," as they say.[11]

A few other definitions will round out matters. By "evolutionary theory" (or just plain "evolution"), I mean standard neo-Darwinism, although my argument applies equally well to any other (naturalistic) theory that explains the origin of biological complexity without reference to God's empirically detectable design.

I use the term "theological theory" in a stipulated way. I mean a claim (or set of claims) about a supernatural agent's action, vis-à-vis biological phenomena (or history), in a manner that purports to be scientifically confirmable or falsifiable, in principle. Because this is precisely the type of theory that methodological naturalism rejects within science, it is directly relevant to assessing the viability of methodological naturalism.[12] For stylistic variety, I will sometimes use instead the terms "supernatural theories" or "God hypotheses."

By "creationism," I mean a theological theory in which the deity in question is the God of the Bible, who is said to have created in a manner that accords with a more or less literal reading of Genesis 1. Finally, just to be clear, by "theology," I mean propositions about any supernatural being.

Clarifications

Several key items remain to be clarified. First, the crucial difference between "theological theories" and "theistic evolution," as I've characterized them, turns on whether there is scientific evidence of God's design in biological phenomena or history. The former affirms this, while the latter denies it.

The difference between the two is *not* about the following:

1. Whether God ontologically sustains creation, including its causal properties and events. Many "theological theories" are

---

11. Robert Bishop and Robert O'Connor, "Doubting the Signature," *Books and Culture* (November–December 2014): 21.

12. My argument does not deny the importance (or truth) per se of theological accounts that are complementary to scientific natural (or secondary) explanations. I simply focus on "theological theories"—which *purport* to compete with, or substitute for, *specific* natural explanations in science—in order to analyze the viability of methodological naturalism. From a Christian perspective, God is ontologically involved in all causes, whether unmediated or secondary.

      compatible with a robust view of God's ongoing ontological involvement in all of creation.

2. Whether God created a given biological phenomenon by a direct miracle or, alternatively, indirectly through secondary (or natural) means. Some "theological theories" are perfectly compatible with either option.

3. Whether common ancestry is true. As with the previous point, some theological theories are perfectly compatible with this thesis.

4. At what time in history God designed organisms or their features. For present purposes, it matters little whether God acted during biological history or instead "front-end loaded" the cosmos at its initial creation so that it expressed marks of design later in biological history.

5. Whether God designed anything at all in organic history or, if he did, how many things.

None of these points mark the salient difference between theistic evolution and theological theories. Instead, what separates them is epistemological: whether there is empirically detectable scientific evidence of God's design in biological phenomena or history.

    Crucially, the line that separates theistic evolution from theological theories does not hinge on the acceptance (or rejection) of methodological naturalism. Both approaches are compatible with either this convention or its denial. In particular, theistic evolutionists are free to discard methodological naturalism. That is, they can allow religious language, including "theological theories," into science proper while also accepting that evolutionary theory provides a true physical explanation of organic history. In this approach, theological theories are regarded as false but not necessarily as unscientific. (A false theory may still be a scientific one; in fact, the history of science is littered with such theories.) The rejection of methodological naturalism simply means that God-talk is *permissible* within scientific research and discourse; it does not imply any judgment regarding the truth or falsity of this God-talk. Methodological naturalism itself concerns what counts as scientific, not what counts as correct per se. As such, theistic evolution is fully compatible with the rejection of this convention.

A third clarification focuses on intelligent design theory (ID). Is it a theological theory? Opinions vary. For now I grant that ID is a theological theory—given that many theistic evolutionists regard it as such—but my argument does not hinge upon the matter one way or the other. I should note in passing that if ID is not a theological theory, then methodological naturalism, which prohibits theology, poses no barrier to regarding ID as fully scientific.[13]

Fourth, I want to be clear that this chapter does not dispute the truth of evolutionary theory or of theistic evolution. The truth or falsity of these positions is the subject of other chapters in this volume. Instead, my concern is simply whether theistic evolutionists ought to embrace methodological naturalism.

Finally, although I suspect that most theistic evolutionists hold or apply methodological naturalism in an inconsistent way, my purpose here is not to argue for this claim. Instead, my central thesis is that, regardless of any alleged inconsistency, theistic evolutionists ought to reject methodological naturalism.

Theistic Evolution and Methodological Naturalism: Compatible Companions?

As it happens, the overwhelming majority of theistic evolutionists accept methodological naturalism in one form or another. Although some thinkers are not totally clear, the list of those who accept it apparently includes Denis Alexander, Ian Barbour, Ernan McMullin, Keith B. Miller, Francis Collins, Ard Louis, Darrel Falk, Mark Sprinkle, Mark Mann, Robert Bishop, Robert O'Connor, Edward Davis, Richard Wright, Kathryn Applegate, Denis Lamoureux, Conor Cunningham, Jeff Hardin, Karl Giberson, Jeffrey Schloss, Holmes Rolston III, Kenneth Miller, and others.[14]

---

13. Some versions of methodological naturalism prohibit appeal to *any* agent-based explanations within science, not just supernatural agents. Curiously, advocates of these versions of methodological naturalism rarely insist that archeologists and forensic scientists step up their game.

14. E.g., Francis Collins, *The Language of God* (New York: Free Press, 2006), 165–166; Robert Bishop, "Meyer's Inference to Intelligent Design as the Best Explanation (Reviewing *Darwin's Doubt*: Robert Bishop, Part 3)," *BioLogos*, September 8, 2014, accessed June 3, 2015, http://biologos.org/blog/meyers-inference-to-intelligent-design-as-the-best-explanation-reviewing-da#footnote-return-1; Robert O'Connor, "Science on Trial: Exploring the Rationality of Methodological Naturalism," *Perspectives on Science and Christian Faith* 49 (March 1997): 15–30. Edward Davis, "Edward Davis Replies," *National Center for Science Education* (1999), available at http://ncse.com/rncse/19/4/edward-davis-replies; John Polkinghorne, as described in Ted

At an organizational level, one of the leading groups of theistic evolutionists in the United States, BioLogos, also accepts methodological naturalism: "At BioLogos, we believe that our intelligent God designed the universe, but we do not see scientific or biblical reasons to give up on pursuing natural explanations for how God governs natural phenomena."[15] BioLogos's allegiance to methodological naturalism is part of its overall mission to persuade Christians, especially evangelicals, to accept evolutionary theory as irenic to robust faith. Many other national or international organizations likewise adhere to methodological naturalism. Indeed, a strong majority of scientists, whether theistic or otherwise, regard methodological naturalism as canonical for biological research and discourse.

Part 2: Mutually Exclusive Routes

Having set out the initial groundwork, I now turn to the body of the chapter. Theistic evolutionists have two primary routes by which to

---

Davis, "Searching for Motivated Belief: Understanding John Polkinghorne, Part 2," *BioLogos*, March 14, 2013, accessed August 30, 2016, http://biologos.org/blogs/ted-davis-reading-the-book -of-nature/searching-for-motivated-belief-understanding-john-polkinghorne-part-2; Darrel Falk, *Coming to Peace with Science* (Downers Grove, IL: InterVarsity Press, 2004), 39; Ard Louis, "Southern Baptist Voices: A Response to James Dew, Part 2," *BioLogos*, May 30, 2012, accessed June 3, 2015 http://biologos.org/blog/southern-baptist-voices-a-biologos-response-to-james-dew -part-ii; Mark Sprinkle, "Teaching the Whole Controversy," *BioLogos*, April 22, 2012, accessed June 3, 2015, http://biologos.org/blog/teaching-the-whole-controversy; Mark Mann, "Let's Not Surrender Science to the Secular World! Part 5," *BioLogos*, February 6, 2012, accessed April 4, 2016, http://biologos.org/blogs/archive/lets-not-surrender-science-to-the-secular-world-part-5; Kathryn Applegate, "A Defense of Methodological Naturalism" *PSCF* 65, no 1 (March 2013): 37–45; Keith B. Miller, "An Evolving Creation: Oxymoron or Fruitful Insight?" *Perspectives on Evolving Creation*, ed. Keith B. Miller (Grand Rapids, MI: Eerdmans, 2003), 7; Denis Lamoureux, personal correspondence; although Deborah Haarsma is inconsistent in this area, see Haarsma, "Are Scientists Biased by Their Worldviews?" *BioLogos*, April 2, 2013, accessed April 9, 2015, http://biologos.org/blog/cultural-influences-on-science; Conor Cunningham, *Darwin's Pious Idea* (Grand Rapids, MI: Eerdmans, 2010), 265; Denis Alexander, *Creation or Evolution: Do We Have to Choose?*, rev. and expanded ed. (Grand Rapids, MI: Monarch, 2014), 216–218; Jeff Hardin, "Christianity and Science: Current Disputes among the Faithful," at The Faith Angle Forum, South Beach, Florida, November 18, 2014, available at http://eppc.org/publications/jeff-hardin-faith -angle-forum-science-disputes-evolution-creationism/; Rolston, Alexander, Schloss, et al., "Concept of 'Intelligent Design,'"; Kenneth Miller, *Finding Darwin's God* (New York: HarperCollins, 1999), 167–169, 218–219, 239–243; Miller, *Only a Theory* (New York: Viking, 2008), 185–187; Ernan McMullin, "Plantinga's Defense of Special Creation," *Intelligent Design Creationism and Its Critics*, 165–168; Roy Clouser, "Is Theism Compatible with Evolution?" *Intelligent Design Creationism and Its Critics*, 513–536, esp. 536; Ian Barbour, "Science and Scientism in *Why Religion Matters*," ed. Huston Smith, *Zygon* 36, no. 2 (June 2001): 207–214, esp. 209–210; Richard T. Wright, *Biology through the Eyes of Faith*, rev. and updated ed. (New York: HarperCollins, 2003), 31–51, 74–75; Karl Giberson, *Saving Darwin* (New York: HarperCollins, 2008), 159–160.

15. See "How Is BioLogos Different from Evolutionism, Intelligent Design, and Creationism?" *BioLogos*, accessed June 3, 2014, http://biologos.org/questions/biologos-id-creationism. The language here is not precise, but seems to be an endorsement of methodological naturalism.

support evolutionary theory and counter rival theological theories. These routes are mutually exclusive; choosing one means forgoing the other.

The first route is to adopt methodological naturalism. On this path, theistic evolutionists can claim that there are good grounds to exclude God hypotheses from biology. These grounds are generally theological, historical, conceptual, empirical, or pragmatic. Yet because methodological naturalism bars supernatural theories from science proper, it follows that methodological naturalism also prohibits scientific analysis of such theories. Consequently, theistic evolutionists can neither use scientific arguments to critique these theories nor to favor evolutionary theory over them. Of course, biologists who take this route can draw on scientific evidence to support evolutionary theory over other naturalistic (or secondary) theories, but they cannot do so to support evolutionary theory over God hypotheses. I will examine this "methodological naturalism only" route for theistic evolutionists in part 4.

By contrast, an alternative route rejects methodological naturalism. In this approach, theistic evolutionists can bolster evolutionary theory and critique supernatural rivals by placing them in head-to-head competition within science. On this basis, theistic evolutionists can argue that evolutionary theory is empirically superior to its theological counterparts. I will examine this route in part 3.

As noted, the two routes described here are mutually exclusive. If theistic evolutionists adopt methodological naturalism, which prohibits theology within biology, then they cannot make a scientific argument against God hypotheses, nor can they utilize theology in their positive scientific case for evolution. If "you pays your money," as the old saw goes, "you takes your choice."

The landscape looks as shown in Table 20.1.

A critic might disagree with this way of carving up the territory. He might contend that, even while holding methodological naturalism, theistic evolutionists can still make extensive empirical evaluation of God hypotheses, yet do so under the rubric of a nonscientific discipline such as "natural theology" (or something similar). Alternatively, a critic might contend that theology-based views can be scientifically evaluated without any God-talk (and so without violating methodological

TABLE 20.1. Two Mutually Exclusive Routes to Support Evolutionary Theory and Counter Theological Theories

Route 1: *The Methodological Naturalism Approach*	Route 2: *The Non-Methodological Naturalism Approach*
Permitted • Demarcation arguments that God hypotheses are not "scientific" • Scientific arguments that favor evolutionary theory over other naturalistic (or secondary) theories only **Prohibited** • Scientific criticisms of God hypotheses • Scientific arguments that favor evolutionary theory over God hypotheses • Theological claims used in the scientific case for evolutionary theory	**Permitted** • Scientific criticisms of God hypotheses • Scientific arguments that favor evolutionary theory over God hypotheses • Theological claims used in the scientific case for evolutionary theory **Prohibited** • Demarcation arguments that God hypotheses are not "scientific"

naturalism). Suppose, for example, a paleontologist wished to evaluate the scientific credentials of young earth creationism. Suppose further that young earth creationism predicts that humans and dinosaurs lived during overlapping geological eras. Can't a paleontologist scientifically assess this claim without using any theological statements? After all, he would mainly analyze fossils and wouldn't rely on propositions about God per se. Accordingly, since theology is not present, no violation of methodological naturalism occurs.

In response to this last objection, the matter is surely complex. In a sense, much of my chapter functions as a reply to this objection. For now, I note that theology is actually quite relevant to the young earth case (as it is to other cases discussed in this chapter). The proximate claim under assessment is that humans and dinosaurs lived during overlapping geological eras. While assessing this claim in isolation requires no theological language, the claim in context is part of a broader conditional: *If young earth creationism is true*, then humans and dinosaurs lived during overlapping geological eras. The very reason to analyze the consequent in the first place arises from the crucial presence of the antecedent. And the antecedent is simply shorthand for a set of specific claims about the God of the Bible. Moreover, if the consequent turns out to be false, then, in light of the conditional about young earth creationism, *modus tollens* mandates that young earth creationism is likewise false. Thus, in this context, empirical observations and logical implications inevitably touch theology. God-talk is clearly present, in direct violation of methodological naturalism.

I turn now to the first criticism, which held that God hypotheses can undergo extensive empirical evaluation under a nonscientific heading (such as "natural theology"). This possibility amounts to little more than superficial relabeling. As a de facto matter, this evaluation *is* scientific. While other disciplines make use of empirical data, the hallmark of science is extensive empirical analysis. Thus, all things being equal, any such examination of a supernatural theory ought to be regarded as a scientific one. Accordingly, unless one wants to play word games, theistic evolutionists must choose one of two mutually exclusive routes: adopt methodological naturalism and so be silent about the empirical credentials of God hypotheses, *or* attack these hypotheses and establish evolutionary theory in head-to-head empirical competition.

Part 3: God-Talk in Evolutionary Reasoning
Theology Alive and Well

Evolutionists have a long history of both engaging God hypotheses on scientific grounds and using theology in the scientific case for evolutionary theory. Darwin's theory, after all, originally arose in response to a theological counterpart. As historian Abigail Lustig observes,

> Modern evolutionary biology traces its descent (with modifications) from Charles Darwin, and most particularly from the *Origin of Species* of 1859. . . . The *Origin* . . . was itself created as a response to one of the greatest conundrums of natural history—the order

and diversity of life—and to one of its most convincing answers—the theological argument from design.[16]

Evolutionary theory was, in short, "born in theology."[17] As other scholars have observed, in the *Origin*, Darwin borrowed from natural theology similar research problems, presuppositions, patterns of argumentation, metaphors, concepts, and content.[18] More poignantly, Darwin plainly stated in the introduction to the *Origin* that one of his chief goals was to argue that special creation is "erroneous."[19] Throughout the *Origin*, his "one long argument" for evolution repeatedly engaged in an empirical combat with this theological rival.[20]

But Darwin didn't simply critique a theological counterpart in the *Origin*, he actually deployed theology-laden claims as part of his extended argument. These theological claims were not mere rhetorical flourish designed to persuade a Victorian audience; they were crucial elements of several of his epistemic arguments for evolution. These theology-laden claims include:

1. Human beings are not justified in believing that God creates in ways analogous to the intellectual powers of the human mind.
2. A God who is free to create as he wishes would create new biological limbs de novo rather than from a common pattern.

---

16. Abigail Lustig, "Natural Atheology," *Darwinian Heresies*, ed. A. Lustig et al. (Cambridge: Cambridge University Press, 2004), 69–83, esp. 70.

17. Ibid., 70.

18. John Brooke, "The Relations between Darwin's Science and His Religion," *Darwinism and Divinity*, ed. John Durant (New York: Oxford University Press, 1985), 40–75, esp. 48–49. See also Neal Gillespie, *Charles Darwin and the Problem of Creation* (Chicago: Chicago University Press, 1979); Dilley, "Charles Darwin's Use of Theology," 29–56; Richard England, "Natural Selection, Teleology, and the Logos," *Osiris* 16 (2001): 270–287, esp. 274–275; Dov Ospovat, "God and Natural Selection," *Journal of the History of Biology* 13, no. 2 (September 1980): 169–194; Ospovat, "Darwin's Theology," Review of Neal Gillespie's Charles Darwin and the Problem of Creation," *Science* 207, no. 4430 (February 1, 1980): 520; Ospovat, *The Development of Darwin's Theory* (Cambridge: Cambridge University Press, 1981), 223–224; Momme von Sydow, "Charles Darwin: A Christian Undermining Christianity?" in *Science and Beliefs: From Natural Philosophy to Natural Science, 1700–1900*, ed. D. M. Knight and M. D. Eddy (Burlington, VT: Ashgate, 2005), 141–156; John Cornell, "God's Magnificent Law: The Bad Influence of Theistic Metaphysics on Darwin's Estimation of Natural Selection," *Journal of the History of Biology* 20, no. 3 (Fall 1987): 381–412; John Cornell, "Newton of the Grassblade? Darwin and the Problem of Organic Teleology," *Isis* 77, no. 3 (September 1986): 405–421; James Moore, *The Post-Darwinian Controversies* (New York: Cambridge University Press, 1979), 318; Robert J. Richards, "Theological Foundations of Darwin's Theory of Evolution," in *Experiencing Nature*, ed. P. H. Theerman and K. H. Parshall (Dordrecht: Kluwer Academic, 1997), 61–79.

19. Charles Darwin, *On the Origin of Species*, 1st ed. (London: John Murray, 1859), 6.

20. E.g., Darwin, *On the Origin of Species*, 1st ed., 55–56, 185–186, 242–243, 275–276, 354–355, 372, 393–398, 453–454.

3. A respectable deity would create biological structures in accord with a human conception of the "simplest mode" to accomplish the functions of these structures.

4. God would create only the minimum structure required for a given part's function.

5. God does not provide false empirical information about the origins of organisms.

6. God impressed the laws of nature on matter.

7. God directly created the first "primordial" life.

8. God did not perform miracles within organic history subsequent to the creation of the first life.

9. A "distant" God is not morally culpable for natural pain and suffering.

10. The God of special creation, who allegedly performed miracles in organic history, is not plausible given the presence of natural pain and suffering.[21]

None of this ought to be surprising. Cornelius Hunter has noted that evolutionary theory's pedigree includes centuries of engagement with design theories:

> [C]ontrastive thinking is pervasive in evolutionary thought. . . .
> The alternative model, against which evolution is compared, is independent creation. Since the seventeenth century, scientists, philosophers, and theologians have elucidated a wide spectrum of refutations of design and creation. With Darwin these refutations were applied to the origin of species.[22]

In fact, the contest between natural and supernatural explanations of the physical world has been intertwined with the Western tradition from its inception. Classicist David Sedley points out that the matter was considered "fundamental" by ancient thinkers like Socrates, Plato, Aristotle, Anaxagoras, Empedocles, Democritus, the Epicureans, and the Stoics.[23]

---

21. Dilley, "Charles Darwin's Use of Theology," 29–56, esp. 52.

22. Cornelius Hunter, "Darwin's Principle: The Use of Contrastive Reasoning in the Confirmation of Evolution," *HOPOS* 4 (Spring 2014): 106–149, esp. 136.

23. David Sedley, *Creationism and Its Critics in Antiquity* (Berkeley: University of California Press, 2007), xvi.

Little wonder that this pattern extends into the twenty-first century. Many contemporary biologists—both theistic evolutionists and others—rely on claims about God's nature and ways in their scientific case for evolution. These luminaries include Francis Collins, Kenneth Miller, Denis Alexander, Theodosius Dobzhansky, Ian Barbour, Karl Giberson, Francisco Ayala, Niles Eldredge, Douglas Futuyma, John Avise, Neil Shubin, Jerry Coyne, Richard Dawkins, George Williams, Stephen Jay Gould, and many others.[24]

24. R. Diogo and J. Molnar, "Links between Evolution, Development, Human Anatomy, Pathology, and Medicine, with a Proposition of a Re-Defined Anatomical Position and Notes on Constraints and Morphological 'Imperfections,'" *Journal of Experimental Zoology* 326, no. 4 (2016): 1–10; Patrick Forterre and Daniele Gadelle, "Phylogenomics of DNA Topoisomerases: Their Origin and Putative Roles in the Emergence of Modern Organisms," *Nucleic Acids Research* 37, no. 3 (2009): 679–692, esp. 679; Ulrich Kutschera, "Photosynthesis Research on Yellowtops: Macroevolution In Progress," *Theory in Biosciences* 125 (2007): 81–92, esp. 90–91; Émile Zuckerkandl, "Intelligent Design and Biological Complexity," *Gene* 315 (2006): 2–18, esp. 10; Donald Prothero, *Evolution* (New York: Columbia University Press, 2007), 30–49, esp. 37–39; Theodosius Dobzhansky, "Nothing in Biology Makes Sense Except in the Light of Evolution," *The American Biology Teacher* (March 1973): 125–129; Stephen Jay Gould, *Ever Since Darwin* (New York: W. W. Norton, 1977), 91–96; Gould, *The Panda's Thumb* (New York: W. W. Norton, 1980), 20–21, 24, 28–29, 248; Gould, *Hen's Teeth and Horse's Toes* (New York: W. W. Norton, 1983), 258–259, 384; Gould, *The Structure of Evolutionary Theory* (Cambridge, MA: Harvard University Press, 2002), 104; Gould, "Evolution and the Triumph of Homology, Or Why History Matters," *American Scientist* 74, no. 1 (1986): 60–69, esp. 63; Douglas Futuyma, *Science on Trial: The Case for Evolution* (Sunderland, MA: Sinauer, 1995), 46–50, 121–131, 197–201, 205; Niles Eldredge, *The Triumph of Evolution . . . And the Failure of Creationism* (New York: W. H. Freeman, 2000), 99–100, 144–146; Francisco Ayala, *Darwin and Intelligent Design* (Minneapolis: Fortress, 2006), 25–42, 85–89, esp. 34–36; Ayala, *Darwin's Gift to Science and Religion* (Washington, DC: Joseph Henry, 2007), x–xi, 1–6, 22–23, 76, 88–92, 154–160; Jerry A. Coyne, *Why Evolution Is True* (New York: Penguin, 2009), 12, 13, 18, 26–58, 64, 71–72, 81–85, 96, 101, 108, 121, 148, 161; Richard Dawkins, *The Blind Watchmaker: Why the Evidence of Evolution Reveals a Universe without Design* (New York: W. W. Norton, 1986), 93; Dawkins, *River out of Eden: A Darwinian View of Life* (New York: Basic Books, 1995), 95–133, esp. 105; Dawkins, *The Greatest Show on Earth: The Evidence for Evolution* (New York: Free Press, 2009), 270, 296–297, 315, 321–322, 332, 341, 351, 354, 356, 362, 364, 369, 371, 375, 388–389, 390–396 (I thank Colin Zwirko and Caitlin Maples for their fine research on Coyne and Dawkins); George C. Williams, *The Pony Fish's Glow* (New York: Basic Books, 1997), 2, 4, 6–10, 104, 132–160; John C. Avise, *Inside the Human Genome: A Case for Non-Intelligent Design* (New York: Oxford University Press, 2010); Neil Shubin, *Your Inner Fish* (New York: Pantheon, 2008), 173–198; Ian Barbour, *When Science Meets Religion* (New York: HarperCollins, 2000), 111–114; Denis Alexander, *Creation or Evolution*, 234–251; Collins, *Language of God*, 130, 134–137, 139, see also 176–177, 191, 193–194; Karl Giberson and Francis Collins, *The Language of Science and Faith* (London: SPCK, 2011), 34, 38, 55, 101–108, 161; Kenneth Miller, *Finding Darwin's God*, 80, 100–103, 267–269; see also Stephen Dilley, "Nothing in Biology Makes Sense Except in Light of Theology?" *Studies in History and Philosophy of Biological and Biomedical Sciences* 44 (2013): 774–786; Lustig, "Natural Atheology," 69–83; Jonathan Wells, "Darwin's Straw God Argument," *Journal of Interdisciplinary Studies* 22 (2010): 67–88; Gregory Radick, "Deviance, Darwinian-style," *Metascience* 14 (2005): 453–457, esp. 455; Cornelius Hunter, *Science's Blind Spot* (Grand Rapids, MI: Brazos, 2007); Paul Nelson, "Methodological Naturalism: A Rule No One Needs or Obeys," *Evolution News and Views*, September 22, 2014, accessed June 28, 2016, http://www.evolutionnews.org/2014/09/methodological_1089971.html. The seminal work on this topic is Paul Nelson, "The Role of Theology in Current Evolutionary Reasoning," *Biology and Philosophy* 11 (1996): 493–517 (in addition, this article originally brought to my attention the tension between methodological naturalism and theology-laden arguments for evolutionary theory). Of course, I do not claim that

Theology-laden arguments appear in major areas of biology, including genetics, embryology, biogeography, paleontology, physiology, organic diversity, genomics, and the like. Biologists who make these arguments overwhelmingly view them as scientific—no doubt because they draw on scientific data, inferences, patterns of reasoning, and peer-reviewed research. Moreover, careful analysis shows that these theological claims are typically indispensable to the arguments in which they appear.[25] Without God-talk, the arguments do not support evolutionary theory. More poignantly, these arguments are often central to a given thinker's overall scientific case for evolution. Indeed, some of these thinkers' self-reported *best* arguments for evolution depend upon God talk.[26] Things below, it seems, rest upon things above.

Just to be clear, my claim is not that evolutionary theory itself contains theological propositions. Instead, my claim is that self-reported scientific justifications for this theory often include theological claims. Moreover, my claim is not that every biologist who utilizes theology in his case for evolution is a religious believer. In fact, some atheists and agnostics have the strongest opinions about what God would have done in organic history, were he to exist.[27] And while some of these theological claims are entailed by creationism, a number of them are foreign to creationism and ID. That is, evolutionists often import their own partisan theology into their scientific case for evolution and against creationism or ID. They bring their own God-talk to the table.[28]

Notably, the widespread use of theology occurs not just in debates with creationists or intelligent design theorists but even in "neutral" or "purely scientific" contexts such as encyclopedia entries or textbooks.[29]

---

the evolutionists among those listed above have *only* theology-laden arguments for evolution. For more examples of theology-laden arguments for evolution, see note 29.

25. E.g., Dilley, "Nothing in Biology"; Nelson, "Role of Theology."

26. Among others, Coyne, *Why Evolution Is True*, 26–54, 79; Dawkins, *Greatest Show on Earth*, 296–297, 315, 321–322; Gould, *Structure of Evolutionary Theory*, 104; Dobzhansky, "Nothing in Biology," 126–128; see note 24.

27. E.g., see the work of Gould, Coyne, Dawkins, and Futuyma cited in note 24.

28. E.g., Dilley, "Nothing in Biology," 775, 782–783.

29. Nelson, "Role of Theology," 497; Dilley, "Nothing in Biology," 784; e.g., Kenneth Mason et al., *Biology*, 10th ed. (New York: McGraw-Hill, 2014), 9, 428–433; Scott Freeman et al. *Biological Science*, 5th ed. (San Francisco: Pearson, 2014), 449–450; Jay Phelan, *What Is Life?*, 2nd ed. (New York: W. H. Freeman, 2013), 334–336; Colleen Belk and Virginia Borden Maier, *Biology: Science for Life*, 3rd ed. (San Francisco: Pearson/Benjamin Cummings, 2010), 224–253, esp. 235, 238, 247; Jon C. Herron and Scott Freeman, *Evolutionary Analysis*, 5th ed. (San Francisco: Pearson, 2014), 42, 56, 66–67; Douglas Futuyma, *Evolution*, 3rd ed. (Sunderland, MA: Sinauer, 2013), 53–54, 631–656, esp. 636–641; Nicholas H. Barton et al., *Evolution* (New York: Cold Spring

That is, even when the rhetorical setting is a straightforward description of the reasons for evolution, theological claims often surface—including in sections explicitly marked, "The Evidence for Evolution."

This entrenched pattern clearly runs contrary to methodological naturalism. If religious language ought to be cordoned from biological science, then much of the case for evolutionary theory, past and present, remains curiously off limits to biology proper. To paraphrase a familiar saying, theistic evolutionists cannot serve both God and methodological naturalism: they must choose between a full-blooded scientific case for evolution on the one hand *or* their naturalistic method on the other.

Two Examples of Theological Involvement in Evolutionary Reasoning

Having noted the pattern of theological involvement in the case for evolutionary theory, I now turn to two extended examples. They capture two complementary ways that evolutionists typically use to support their favored theory. First, evolutionists sometimes deploy explicit theological claims as part of their scientific case for evolution or as part of their scientific case against supernatural theories. At other times, evolutionists use only nontheological claims but employ them in arguments directly against God hypotheses. Both approaches violate methodological naturalism.

Example One: God and the Eye

Francis Collins is perhaps the most prominent theistic evolutionist in North America. His resume includes pioneering the groundbreaking Human Genome Project, garnering both the National Medal of Science and the Presidential Medal of Freedom, and receiving an appointment as director of the National Institutes of Health, including management

---

Harbor Laboratory Press, 2007), 65–83, esp. 70, 75, 81; Teresa Audesirk et al., *Biology: Life on Earth*, 10th ed. (Upper River Saddle, NJ: Prentice Hall, 2014), 258–264; Brian Hall and Benedikt Hallgrímsson, *Strickberger's Evolution*, 4th ed. (Burlington, MA: Jones & Bartlett, 2007), 672; Jane Reece et al., *Campbell Biology*, 9th ed. (San Francisco: Pearson, 2011), 460–468, esp. 463; John Relethford, *The Human Species: An Introduction to Biological Anthropology*, 7th ed. (New York: McGraw-Hill, 2008), 22–23; Carl T. Bergstrom and Lee Alan Dugatkin, *Evolution* (New York: W. W. Norton, 2012), 52, 107; David M. Hillis et al., *Principles of Life* (Sunderland, MA: Sinauer, 2012), 281; Mark Ridley, *Evolution*, 3rd ed. (Oxford: Blackwell Science, 2004), 52–68, 263–264; David Sadava et al., *Life: The Science of Biology*, 10th ed. (New York: W. H. Freeman, 2012), 432, 444; Stanley A. Rice, *Encyclopedia of Evolution* (New York: Facts on File, 2007), 2.

of its modest $26 billion budget. In his best-selling *The Language of God*, Collins contends that the imperfection of the vertebrate eye confirms evolutionary accounts but poses a grave problem for intelligent design. He notes that, while Darwin recognized the challenge the eye presented to his theory, nonetheless Darwin "proposed 150 years ago a series of steps in the evolution of this complex organ, which modern molecular biology is rapidly confirming."[30] By contrast,

> . . . the design of the eye does not appear on close inspection to be completely ideal. The rods and cones that sense light are the bottom layer of the retina, and light has to pass through the nerves and blood vessels to reach them. Similar imperfections of the human [body] . . . defy the existence of truly intelligent planning of the human form.[31]

As Collins makes clear here and elsewhere in his book, imperfections are expected given evolution but unexpected given intelligent design.[32] Whereas evolution is a tinkering process that often produces suboptimal organisms, matters are different for an intelligent designer. Collins believes ID advocates have in mind a benevolent God who creates by direct supernatural fiat.[33] Such a being would create a perfect eye, Collins thinks. In fact, Collins's line of reasoning implies that, if scientists discover that the eye is suboptimal for vision *in the present*, then they can rightly conclude that God did not miraculously create the eye *in the past*. That is, God would ensure the optimality of the eye in (or to) the present day. So, if we discover a suboptimal eye, this fact favors evolution over direct divine design. More precisely,

1. If evolution had produced the eye in the past, it would not necessarily be "completely ideal" for vision in the present.
2. If God had created the eye by direct miracle in the past, he would have ensured that it is "completely ideal" for vision in the present.
3. The vertebrate eye "does not appear to be completely ideal" for vision in the present.

---

30. Collins, *Language of God*, 191.
31. Ibid.
32. Ibid., 109–142, 190–194.
33. Ibid., 183, 186–188, 193–195.

4. If the evidence is predicted by one hypothesis but contrary to the prediction of another, then the evidence supports the former hypothesis over the latter.

5. Thus, a less than "completely ideal" vertebrate eye supports the evolutionary hypothesis over the divine miracle hypothesis.

A few observations about the argument as a whole are in order. First, it's a scientific argument. Collins includes it under the heading "Scientific Objections to ID."[34] More importantly, the evidence cited in the argument arises from a scientific analysis of the structure and function of the rods, cones, and retina of the eye. Second, this polemic is a positive argument for evolution, not just a critique of ID or creationism. Despite Collins's heading, which treats the matter as merely an objection to ID, it's clear from the internal logic of the argument itself that the whole point is to show that the vertebrate eye counts as evidence for evolution over ID.

I now shift to a few observations about individual premises of the argument. First, it's worth noting that recent research raises serious questions about premise 3, which claims that the eye is suboptimal.[35] Collins's key empirical claim may be flawed.

In any case, the theological claim in premise 2 is of primary interest. In it, Collins says that if God had created the eye by direct miracle in the past, he would have ensured that it is completely ideal for vision in the present. Note that the premise is in the subjunctive mood—it states what God *would* have done in the present if he had performed a miracle in the past. In addition, the claim is indispensable for Collins's argument. If premise 2 is removed, then the argument is no longer logically valid, and the conclusion literally does not follow from the premises. In fact, like many other theistic

---

34. Ibid., 186.

35. Amichai M. Labin and Erez N. Ribak, "Retinal Glial Cells Enhance Human Vision Acuity," *Physical Review Letters* 104 (2010): 158102; Kristian Franze et al., "Müller Cells Are Living Optical Fibers in the Vertebrate Retina," *Proceedings of the National Academy of Sciences USA* 104 (2007): 8287–8292; Amichai M. Labin et al., "Müller Cells Separate between Wavelengths to Improve Day Vision with Minimal Effect upon Night Vision," *Nature Communications* 5 (2014): 4319; Jonathan N. Tinsley et al., "Direct Detection of a Single Photon by Humans," *Nature Communications* 7 (2016): 12172; Erez Ribak, "The Purpose of Our Eyes' Strange Wiring Is Unveiled," *Scientific American*, March 18, 2015, available at http://www.scientificamerican.com/article/the-purpose-of-our-eyes-strange-wiring-is-unveiled/.

evolutionists, Collins strongly emphasizes biological imperfections as important evidence for evolutionary theory over creationism or ID. All such arguments depend on "suboptimality theology" similar to that of premise 2.

Collectively, my observations about premise 2, as well as the argument as a whole, can be summarized thus: Collins's scientific argument for evolution, based on the vertebrate eye, relies on an indispensable subjunctive claim about what God would have done in organic history had it been the case that he miraculously created the eye.

A few concerns now surface. Importantly, while I focus on Collins's particular argument, similar observations apply to virtually all other theology-laden arguments given by theistic evolutionists (and others) for evolutionary theory. First, Collins provides no justification for his theological premise. He asserts it without any argument or citation from the Bible, creeds, theological texts, or nonreligious sources. This is especially troubling given that, as noted above, premise 2 is a subjunctive claim. It asserts what God would have done in the past, contrary to what he actually did. On what basis does Collins know this bold counterfactual?

Second, Collins does not borrow premise 2 from his rivals. Neither ID nor creationism entail (or make probable) this theological claim. Instead, Collins inserts his own sectarian theology into the discussion.

Third, Collins's partisan claim ignores relevant biblical doctrines like the fall, in which, according to some scholars, the created order itself experiences decay and disorder.[36] On this interpretation, a degree of suboptimality in creation is actually expected.

A wide array of theology-laden arguments for evolutionary theory share similar features. These arguments frequently rely on partisan, subjunctive theological assertions as a crucial part of the scientific justification for evolutionary theory. God-talk is indeed alive and well in evolutionary biology. Yet such discourse clearly violates methodological naturalism.

---

36. According to New Testament scholar Douglas Moo, the majority of modern commentators believe Saint Paul spoke directly about the adverse effects of the fall on creation in Romans 8:19–22 (Moo, *The Epistle to the Romans* [Grand Rapids, MI: Eerdmans, 1996], 513–514).

Example Two: God and Flagella

Theistic evolutionists have more in their arsenal than just arguments that rely on theological claims, of course. Indeed, in light of the last section, some theistic evolutionists might contend that they can set aside theology-laden arguments for evolution and still make a strong empirical case for evolutionary theory over its supernatural rivals. All they need to do is use theology-free statements to attack God hypotheses and to bolster evolutionary theory.

But this objection, even if correct, is irrelevant. Methodological naturalism prohibits any assessment of theological theories within science, even when this assessment uses only theology-free statements. Consider, for example, Kenneth Miller's widely praised critique of Michael Behe's irreducible complexity argument. Miller, a theistic evolutionist, uses scientific methods, sources, and data to establish nontheological claims, which he then deploys both to undermine Behe's intelligent design view and to support evolutionary theory.

To understand Miller's argument, we ought to recall Behe's position. Using the famed bacterial flagellum as an example, Behe's argument can be represented as follows:

1. Intelligent agency, rather than unguided natural processes, is the best explanation of irreducibly complex biological entities.
2. The bacterial flagellum is an irreducibly complex biological entity.

3. Thus, intelligent agency, rather than unguided natural processes, is the best explanation of the bacterial flagellum.

Miller attacks both premises. Consider premise 2 first, which holds that the bacterial flagellum is irreducibly complex. Miller says this claim "can be put to the test in a very direct way":

> If we are able to find contained within the flagellum an example of a machine with fewer protein parts that serves a purpose distinct from motility, the claim of irreducible complexity is refuted. . . . The flagellum does indeed contain such a machine, a protein-secreting apparatus that carries out an important function even in species that lack the flagellum altogether. A scientific idea rises or falls on

the weight of the evidence, and the evidence in the case of the bacterial flagellum is abundantly clear. . . . The very existence of the type III secretory system shows that the bacterial flagellum is not irreducibly complex.[37]

In other words, Miller argues something like this:

1. If the bacterial flagellum is an irreducibly complex biological entity, then we should *not* find that the bacterial flagellum contains a machine with fewer protein parts (than the flagellum) and which serves a purpose distinct from motility.
2. But we do find that the bacterial flagellum contains a machine with fewer protein parts (than the flagellum) and which serves a purpose distinct from motility.

3. Thus, the bacterial flagellum is not an irreducibly complex biological entity.

Pretty clearly, Miller's argument presupposes the empirical testability of Behe's intelligent design hypothesis. Behe's hypothesis predicts the absence of the type III secretory system. But such a system has been discovered. So, the bacterial flagellum is not irreducibly complex. As a result, premise 2 of Behe's ID argument, which claimed otherwise, is false, and thus his ID hypothesis is empirically refuted.

Notice that, in attacking premise 2, Miller uses only nontheological statements (about protein parts, the type III system, etc.). But he appropriates these statements to attack Behe's ID perspective. Miller clearly engages ID using scientific data and analysis. Unsurprisingly, Miller characterizes ID as a "scientific position."[38] This enables him to coherently conclude that ID views are "rejected by science because they do not fit the facts."[39] Of course, whether or not Miller's critique is successful is a matter for another time.[40] For now, the key point is that

---

37. Kenneth Miller, "The Flagellum Unspun," in *Debating Design*, ed. M. Ruse and W. Dembski (Cambridge: Cambridge University Press, 2004), 81–97, esp. 95.

38. Ibid., 95.

39. Ibid. Although Miller claims Behe's argument is an "argument from ignorance," Miller's own analysis shows that Behe's argument is amenable to scientific evaluation.

40. For Behe's response, see "Irreducible Complexity: Obstacle to Darwinian Evolution," in *Debating Design*, 352–370; Behe, *Darwin's Black Box*, 10th anniversary ed. (New York: Free Press, 2006), 259–262.

Miller clearly provides a scientific evaluation of ID—in direct contrast to methodological naturalism, which prohibits the consideration of God hypotheses in scientific contexts.[41]

Yet Miller does not simply attack ID, he also makes a comparative argument, which claims that evolution, rather than ID, best explains complex biochemical machines. That is, Miller tries to reverse premise 1 of Behe's ID argument, which favors intelligent agency over unguided natural processes as the best explanation of irreducibly complex biological entities. Miller writes,

> Michael Behe's purported biochemical challenge to evolution rests on the assertion that Darwinian mechanisms are simply not adequate to explain the existence of complex biochemical machines. Not only is he wrong, he's wrong in a most spectacular way. The biochemical machines . . . actually provide us with powerful and compelling examples of evolution in action. When we go to the trouble to open that black box, we find out once again that Darwin got it right.[42]

Miller plainly believes that empirical data about biochemical machines support evolutionary theory over intelligent design theory. Indeed, he thinks the data "provide us with powerful and compelling examples of evolution in action." Rather than claiming the supernatural hypotheses cannot be considered within science, Miller provides a careful scientific analysis of ID and evolution, and concludes that the latter prevails.[43] So, in contrast to methodological naturalism, Miller engages a supernatural hypothesis within a scientific context as part of his positive case for evolutionary theory.

Miller's approach is hardly novel among theistic evolutionists. One does not have to look far to see that they engage various God hypotheses using scientific evidence and methods, often as part of their positive case for evolution.[44] Doing so is, of course, plainly contrary to methodological naturalism.

---

41. Recall that, for the sake of argument, I assume that ID theory is a God hypothesis, just as a number of theistic evolutionists argue. On the other hand, if ID is *not* a theological theory, then methodological naturalism poses no barrier to regarding ID as fully scientific. See also note 13.
42. Miller, *Finding Darwin's God*, 160.
43. Ibid., 129–164.
44. Note 24 includes examples.

Part 4: "Methodological Naturalism Only" Strategy

Recall that theistic evolutionists can choose one of two mutually exclusive strategies to bolster evolution and counter supernatural rivals: (1) adopt methodological naturalism *or* (2) establish evolutionary theory as scientifically superior to God hypotheses. I have explored the latter strategy above; I now turn to the former. In what follows, I raise two arguments against the "methodological naturalism only" approach.

Argument 1: The Irrelevance of Scientific Evidence

Liabilities abound with a "methodological naturalism only" tactic. First, by exclusively adopting methodological naturalism, theistic evolutionists are left with arguments that attempt to cast God hypotheses as "unscientific" or as otherwise unacceptable. Such arguments are familiar: creationism and ID are God-of-the-gaps explanations; they also demean God's ontological preeminence, lessen his explanatory uniqueness, misconstrue the doctrine of creation, fail to be empirically testable, and so on. While I will address some of these arguments shortly, it is important to note that they have already been under intense fire for quite some time.[45]

Second, adhering to methodological naturalism yields no epistemic gains for theistic evolution. That is, barring creationism and ID from science does nothing *in itself* to make theistic evolution more plausible. Theistic evolution simply accepts a biological theory that bears the title "scientific" whereas its supernatural rivals are "nonscientific." But a scientific designation does not itself make a claim (or set of claims) more likely to be true (or justified) than nonscientific claims.[46] For example, some moral claims, such as the golden rule, are not scientific and yet their designation as "outside" of science does not mean they are any less likely to be true or justified. Likewise,

---

45. Among the many examples, see Errki Vesa Rope Kojonen, *The Intelligent Design Debate and the Temptation of Scientism* (New York: Routledge, 2016), 73–87; Del Ratzsch, *Nature, Design, and Science* (Albany, NY: SUNY Press, 2001); Stephen Meyer, *Signature in the Cell* (New York: HarperOne, 2009), 373–438; J. P. Moreland, "Theistic Science and Methodological Naturalism," in *The Creation Hypothesis*, ed. J. P. Moreland (Downers Grove, IL: InterVarsity Press, 1994), 44–66; Alvin Plantinga, "Methodological Naturalism?" *Origins and Design* 18, no. 1–2 (1997); see also chapters 19, 22, and 24 of the present volume.

46. Strictly speaking, claims are not justified but rather *people* are justified in believing claims. For ease of style, I leave aside this nuance in the main text.

some other views, such as the caloric theory of heat, are rightly regarded as scientific yet are also clearly false. In fact, history is littered with thousands of false scientific claims. The mere label "scientific" does not itself make a claim true or false, well justified or poorly justified. Of course, designating a claim "scientific" can be rhetorically powerful. But the key point is that such a designation does nothing to affect the claim's epistemic features—which are the crucial attributes relevant to its truth and justification. So, while methodological naturalism may lend the patina of plausibility to evolutionary theory, it actually grants no more intellectual credibility to that theory than to supernatural rivals. Methodological naturalism yields no epistemic advantage.

Third, and more important, with methodological naturalism in play, theistic evolutionists cannot draw upon scientific evidence to critique any God hypothesis. Evidence is off limits from paleontology, molecular homology, comparative anatomy, embryology, genomics, biogeography, and all the rest. For example, empirical data about radiometric dating, which ostensibly suggest an ancient earth, cannot be utilized at all to offer a scientific critique of the claim that God created the universe about ten thousand years ago. It is difficult to imagine theistic evolutionists giving up such evidence. Yet under methodological naturalism, all scientific evidence is irrelevant to evaluation of God hypotheses.

Fourth, with methodological naturalism in play, scientific evidence is impotent to support evolutionary theory *over* its supernatural rivals. No quantity or quality of scientific data has any bearing whatsoever on the superiority of evolution over creationism or ID. At best, theistic evolutionists can argue that scientific data favor evolutionary theory over other naturalistic (or secondary) theories. But evolution enjoys no such superiority over supernatural theories. Not only are theology-laden arguments for evolution flatly prohibited, but so are theology-free arguments that support evolution over any God hypothesis (as with Miller's critique of Behe). Theistic evolutionists who take methodological naturalism seriously ought to march through every subdiscipline of biology—from biochemistry to paleobiology to genomics—and systematically reject all scientific arguments that purportedly favor evolution over creationism or ID. Surely, this is an exacting price to pay.

Finally, by adhering to methodological naturalism, theistic evolutionists arguably have to surrender their most important grounds for evolutionary theory itself. As I have noted, the history of evolutionary theory—past and present—is rife with contrastive arguments against ID or creationism (in one form or another).[47] As mentioned, some of the self-reported best arguments for evolutionary theory by leading biologists entail a comparison to creationism or ID. Arguably, these are the best grounds for belief in evolution. Yet under methodological naturalism, all such arguments are prohibited within science. If some of the top biologists' arguments are *verboten*, then what befalls the case for evolutionary theory?[48]

Of course, the temptation still exists for theistic evolutionists to retain these arguments but file them under a different rubric—for example, by calling them "natural theology" rather than "science." But as I have already pointed out, this is merely superficial relabeling of arguments that draw on scientific data, methods, inferences, articles, and patterns of thinking. If something looks like a duck, quacks like a duck, and walks like a duck, then it's best to call it a duck.

Put simply, theistic evolutionists who adhere to methodological naturalism do so at great empirical cost to the justification of their own theory. Surely this ought to give them pause. A navy that has lost its mightiest battleship cannot easily declare victory.

Argument 2: Critique of Reasons for Methodological Naturalism

Despite strong reasons against a "methodological naturalism only" approach, it is possible that justifications for methodological naturalism are so powerful that theistic evolutionists ought to retain the convention. To assess this possibility, I now turn to these justifications.

---

47. This dynamic squares with the conventional view among philosophers of science that scientific testing is inherently contrastive, at least when a hypothesis does not entail an observation, or vice versa.

48. The problem runs even deeper. For example, in some modes of reasoning, such as Bayesianism, any empirical confirmation of evolutionary theory may be impossible without also engaging theological rivals (Dilley, "Nothing in Biology," 784).

Broadly speaking, they fall into five categories: conceptual, theological, pragmatic, historical, and empirical. The final two typically dovetail together, so I will refer to both under the "empirical" rubric. In what follows, I critique what I take to be the best representative of each category.

A Preliminary

An initial comment will help prepare the ground. Earlier in the chapter, I mentioned two versions of methodological naturalism: intrinsic and pragmatic. To this point, this chapter has focused on intrinsic methodological naturalism, which holds that methodological naturalism is a necessary condition of science. By contrast, pragmatic methodological naturalism is a working version in which methodological naturalism is not a necessary condition of science but rather a general default. On this view, biologists should try to explain natural phenomena by reference only to natural (or secondary) causes, laws, and the like, but they can be open to God hypotheses in principle should empirical evidence or other considerations warrant doing so.

By way of brief assessment, this version is not a meaningful type of methodological naturalism. If biologists are open to God hypotheses in principle, then the only way they can know whether, say, a *new* God hypothesis has scientific merit is to analyze it. Of course, many biologists may be justifiably suspicious about a new supernatural theory; and all biologists are certainly justified in dismissing claims about the divine that are *not* empirically testable. But God hypotheses, as I've defined them, hold that there is detectable empirical evidence of a divine being. If biologists are to be open to God hypotheses in principle, as pragmatic methodological naturalism allows, then they cannot make a judgment about a (new) God hypothesis until they examine its conceptual and empirical credentials. But careful empirical scrutiny, in particular, just *is* a de facto scientific analysis, all things being equal. In these cases, the God hypothesis has been treated as amenable to scientific testing. So, the working version of methodological naturalism really isn't methodological naturalism at all. While it recommends sticking to purely natural factors as a matter of general routine, it also permits a given biologist to consider any supernatural theory he deems worthy of scientific analysis, refutation, or (possible) confirmation. This opens the door for scientists who accept supernatural theories, or who are against them, to examine, develop, apply, test, vindicate, or falsify these theories. Critics of methodological naturalism will hardly protest.

Conceptual Justifications of Methodological Naturalism

Having cleared the ground, I now turn to conceptual justifications for (intrinsic) methodological naturalism. This justification typically secures methodological naturalism by analyzing the conceptual properties of supernatural hypotheses and contending that such hypotheses lack at least one necessary feature of scientific hypotheses.

Elliott Sober, perhaps the top philosopher of biology in North America, has articulated a nuanced objection to creationism and ID that can be parlayed into a conceptual justification of methodological naturalism.[49] (Sober himself actually defends methodological naturalism based on the widespread success of naturalistic theories, an approach I address below.[50] Even so, his critique of the design argument provides a basis for a topflight conceptual defense of methodological naturalism.) Sober's view is quite sophisticated, yet the basic idea is that the most promising way to formulate the design argument is as a likelihood argument, according to which, in this case, the empirical data are said to favor the design hypothesis over the evolutionary hypothesis. But to make this argument, Sober points out that one must know how likely it is that an intelligent designer would create the phenomena in question. This requires knowing the designer's powers and plans. For example, in order to say that it is more likely that a designer would create, say, the vertebrate eye than would evolutionary processes, we must have some grounds for saying that a designer *can* make the eye and *wants* to do so. In particular, we must be able to say that it's more likely a designer would make the eye than it is that evolutionary processes would do so. But aside from self-serving *prior* beliefs about a designer, Sober thinks we don't have any *independent* basis for the

49. Elliott Sober, *Evidence and Evolution* (Cambridge: Cambridge University Press, 2008), 109–188.

50. Elliott Sober, *Did Darwin Write the Origin Backwards?* (Amherst, NY: Prometheus, 2011), 121–152.

required claims about a designer's plans or powers.[51] Put bluntly, we have no idea what a designer would do. This lack of knowledge means that we cannot predict a designer's actions. Without the ability to generate a prediction, we cannot evaluate a design hypothesis against an evolutionary hypothesis. This means we cannot say that the empirical data favor design over evolution. In effect, we cannot empirically test the design hypothesis when formulated as a likelihood argument.

An advocate of methodological naturalism can appropriate this line of reasoning. He can claim that the best formulation of the design argument is a likelihood version, but that this version posits God hypotheses that cannot be empirically tested in the proper way. Unfortunately, God hypotheses, as I use the term, *do* purport to be scientifically testable. Given that they are intended to be testable yet cannot actually be tested, they arguably fail to qualify as scientific. Thus, the best type of design argument falls outside the pale.

There is a lot to be said for this justification for methodological naturalism; it ranks as perhaps the best conceptual apologetic for the convention. Yet it falls prey to a fatal counterexample. Consider the logical (although outlandish) possibility that biologists discover an ancient line of cells with an inscribed message: "Elliott Sober's view of the design argument is suspect. Moreover, the Los Angeles Rams will win the 2030 Super Bowl. And, yes, John 3:16 is true." Suppose it comes to pass that, against all odds, the Rams not only win a regular-season game but actually make the playoffs and triumph in the 2030 Super Bowl. Wouldn't biologists be scientifically justified to at least consider divine design as a *possible* explanation?

This counterexample holds even if we accept the likelihood framework of the design argument.[52] On this view, we need independent information about a designer's plans and powers. Fair enough. Yet even if it is difficult to articulate what these plans and powers are, or

---

51. As Sober says, "we must be careful not to beg the question. We can't reason that since the eye was made by God, that God must have wanted human beings to have eyes with the features we observe. What is needed is evidence about what God would have wanted the human eye to be like, where the evidence does not require a prior commitment to the assumption that there is a God and also does not depend on looking at the eye to determine its features" (Sober, *Evidence and Evolution*, 146).

52. Notably, Stephen Meyer's *Signature in the Cell* and *Darwin's Doubt* are perhaps the best biology-based design arguments available, yet they both utilize inference to the best explanation rather than a likelihood formulation.

how we know them, in this case surely we *do* know them. After all, it is patently obvious that the message about Sober, the Rams, and John 3:16 is the product of design rather than evolutionary processes.

A critic might protest that biologists need not concern themselves with unlikely possibilities, including mere logical possibilities like the whimsical message about Sober, the Rams, and John 3:16. Instead, biologists need only focus on pragmatic and empirical realities. Yet this criticism misses the point. The "conceptual" justification for methodological naturalism is the matter before us; and this justification holds that the best design arguments (rendered in a likelihood formulation) articulate design hypotheses that rely on concepts or information that are unattainable. (In this case, design hypotheses require independent information about a divine agent's plans and powers, yet we have no such information.) This justification is neither empirical nor pragmatic: it does not claim that empirical data fail to confirm design hypotheses, nor does it claim that, as a practical matter, design hypotheses hamper fruitful research. Instead, it claims that likelihood arguments are the most promising way to argue for design, yet such arguments posit design hypotheses that are untestable. Pragmatic or empirical factors of the type in question do not alter this deep flaw. Accordingly, this "conceptual justification" for methodological naturalism ought to hold even in cases as pragmatically and empirically outlandish as the Sober, Rams, and John 3:16 message.

Yet it would be absurd to retain methodological naturalism in the face of this message. Surely the message should compel us, at the least, to put design on the table as a scientific possibility. But methodological naturalism excludes even this modest consideration. The convention implies that *no possible empirical data can ever* provide good grounds to consider a design hypothesis within science. Such a view is a tad extreme.

Theological Justifications of Methodological Naturalism

I now turn to theological justifications for methodological naturalism. These justifications typically contend that the Scriptures support methodological naturalism, or that methodological naturalism preserves important doctrines of the faith. For example, Denis Alexander argues that methodological naturalism protects God's ontological preeminence and explanatory uniqueness, ensuring that he is not treated simply as another explanatory element within creation or as less involved in certain aspects of the natural world than in others.[53] Other theistic evolutionists, like Robert Bishop, believe that the Christian doctrine of creation, when applied to scientific inquiry, naturally favors methodological naturalism.[54] These and other thinkers hold that methodological naturalism suitably maintains the Creator/creature distinction, affirms God's gift of creational freedom, preserves Scripture's emphasis on God's normal "mediated" way of relating to creation, and the like.

By way of reply, it would be quite a task to address all of these justifications in detail. Fortunately, much of the relevant exegetical and theological work has already been done. In particular, C. John Collins has convincingly argued that the Scriptures affirm (1) God's "ordinary providence" of ontologically sustaining created things and of concurring in their effects, and also (2) God's "extraordinary" providence in which he acts in (or on) creation in ways that go beyond the "natural" powers of creation (which are themselves gifted and sustained by his ordinary providence). In short, God sometimes treats domains of creation differently than he normally does. Moreover, Collins contends that the Bible regards God's extraordinary actions as sometimes resulting in empirically detectable states of affairs. God's special actions can leave traces. Examples include creation ex nihilo, the virgin conception of Jesus, transformation of water into wine, raising of Lazarus and others, the resurrection of Jesus, conversion of sinners, and so on.[55]

These considerations hobble many of the theological justifications for methodological naturalism noted above. To illustrate, suppose God acted in an extraordinary way to raise Jesus from the dead. This event reportedly resulted in states of affairs—an empty tomb and resurrection appearances, for example—which were said to be empirically detected by multiple people (John 20–21; Luke 24; Matthew 28; 1 Cor. 15:1–8). If this occurred as reported in the New Testament, should

---

53. Alexander, *Creation or Evolution*, 216–127.
54. E.g., Robert Bishop, *Understanding Scientific Theories of Origins* (Downers Grove, IL: InterVarsity Press, in press), chapters 2–4.
55. C. John Collins, *The God of Miracles* (Wheaton, IL: Crossway, 2000), 25, 51–140. In the present volume, see also the general introduction by Wayne Grudem as well as chapters 21–22, 24, 27–30.

Christian theistic evolutionists worry about the theological problems raised above? For example, was God somehow less involved in the rest of creation when he was busy raising Jesus from the dead? Or, by raising Jesus, is God's explanatory status reduced to that of a creature? Has God violated creation's alleged freedom, say, to keep dead people as they are? Has God violated his own alleged commitment to mediated actions? Clearly, the answer to these questions is no. An extraordinary act of God that leaves empirically detectable effects can avoid all such quandaries.

Likewise, suppose God acted in an extraordinary way prior to the advent of humans, say, by creating the first life on Earth. In this case, do the theological problems noted above suddenly arise? It is exceedingly hard to see how. Moreover, suppose this extraordinary divine action was such that humans could eventually detect it using careful observation, orderly analysis, established patterns of reasoning, and other tools of science.[56] Do untoward theological problems now rear their heads? Again, it's hard to see how. All that's happened is that God has treated one part of creation differently than he ordinarily does, and has done so in a way amenable to systematic human investigation. If the good Lord chose to sign his handiwork, Christians need not demur.

As far as I can tell, the biblical data do not favor the adoption of methodological naturalism in biology. Yet suppose it turns out that exegetical and theological evidence are underdeterminative with respect to the question of methodological naturalism in biology. In this case, why not simply go to creation to decide the matter? Given that Christians have long regarded creation as radically contingent—God could have made it any way he chose—perhaps it's best simply to investigate as carefully as we can.[57] If the glory of God is to conceal a matter, as a proverb intimates (Prov. 25:2), then perhaps the glory of scientists is to investigate. Of course, to scientifically examine whether biological phenomena (or history) manifest God's extraordinary action just *is* to set methodological naturalism aside. If one is genuinely open to both

---

56. Of course, there might be *scientific* worries about how to confirm an alleged divinely produced event, but that's another matter entirely. (The sources in note 45 address this concern.) Instead, my main point is that the event I describe avoids the *theological* problems raised by some theistic evolutionists.

57. More precisely, the mainstream Christian view of creation's radical contingency is that God could have made it in any logically possible way he desired.

possibilities—either God acted in a scientifically detectable way or he did not—then methodological naturalism has already been discarded. If the book of Scripture turns out to be unclear on the matter, why not simply try to read the book of nature?

Pragmatic Justification of Methodological Naturalism

Perhaps more promise lies with a pragmatic justification for methodological naturalism. At a practical level, God hypotheses are said to inhibit scientific progress whereas naturalistic hypotheses enable the progress of science, in both the past and the present.

A response to this objection hinges upon what constitutes the "progress of science." If "progress" is understood in nonrealist terms, then methodological naturalism is allegedly justified because, whether naturalistic hypotheses are true or false, they uniquely generate fruitful lines of investigation. In my view, Del Ratzsch has already successfully critiqued this view.[58] In particular, a reasonable argument can be made that, at times, naturalistic approaches have inhibited research whereas some theological approaches have been quite fruitful.[59]

On the other hand, if "progress" is construed in a realist fashion, so that progress is measured in terms of the qualitative and/or quantitative increase in (naturalistic) hypotheses that are true, then the objection is a version of the empirical (and historical) justification for methodological naturalism, which I address next.

Empirical (and Historical) Justification
for Methodological Naturalism

We are led, then, to the empirical (and historical) justification for methodological naturalism. On this view, the pattern of scientific discovery over hundreds of years is marked by the growing explanatory power of naturalistic (or secondary) theories and also the diminished explanatory power of their (testable) theistic rivals. On realist grounds, this pattern suggests that, as a category, naturalistic hypotheses are true, approximately true, or at least significantly more likely to be true than

---

58. Ratzsch, *Nature, Design, and Science*, 127–136.
59. E.g., ibid., 137–141; Stephen Jay Gould, *Hen's Teeth and Horse's Toes*, 79–106; Jonathan Wells, *The Myth of Junk DNA* (Seattle: Discovery Institute Press, 2011).

their supernatural counterparts. Accordingly, there is epistemic reason to block the incursion of hypotheses into science that have a track record of being empirically substandard.[60]

I have addressed this view in detail elsewhere;[61] here, I'll mention just a few points. First, this justification for methodological naturalism implies that what separates "science" from "nonscience" is truth, approximate truth, or the property of being more likely to be true than a rival. But demarcation along these lines is tenuous. Surely truth (or its cousins) is not a necessary condition of science. Such a demarcation plainly leads to absurdities: any past or present hypothesis, no matter how fruitful or significant, can no longer be deemed scientific if it is no longer considered true, approximately true, or much more likely true than its rivals. Thus false hypotheses like Darwin's pangenesis view of heredity and Copernicus's model of the solar system (with its perfectly circular orbits) are decidedly nonscientific. On this view, naturalistic origin-of-life research has fallen on hard times. At present there is no consensus in the field, but only a number of hypotheses on offer. Insofar as these hypotheses are mutually exclusive, at most only one of them can be true. Does that mean the rest are literally nonscientific?

The empirical justification for methodological naturalism fails for two additional, related reasons. First, recall that it draws on a historical pattern of naturalistic theories' success. Yet even if, for the sake of argument, past supernatural theories have a poor track record whereas naturalistic theories have a strong one, it hardly follows that a forthcoming *new* supernatural theory—based on updated evidence and methods—ought to be excluded from science automatically. A basketball program with a weak legacy can still field a good team now and again.

Second, it remains unclear whether naturalistic (or secondary) theories actually do enjoy a relevant pattern of explanatory success in the history of science. It is true that naturalistic theories have increased in number and explanatory power since the scientific revolution. But the relevant question is whether this increase manifests a historical

---

60. E.g., Patrick McDonald and Nivaldo J. Tro, "In Defense of Methodological Naturalism," *Christian Scholar's Review* 38, no. 2 (Winter 2009): 201–229.

61. Stephen Dilley, "Philosophical Naturalism and Methodological Naturalism: Strange Bedfellows?" *Philosophia Christi* 12, no. 1 (Summer 2010): 118–141, esp. 133–136.

pattern sufficient to warrant barring God hypotheses altogether from biology. Much of the success of naturalistic explanations have occurred in "bench" sciences, like physics and chemistry, which focus on the day-to-day workings of natural objects, events, and properties. Yet in the Judeo-Christian tradition, God hypotheses typically have not been invoked in these areas. Instead, these hypotheses have been (and are) generally posited to explain the *origin of novelty* in the history of the cosmos, such as the origin of the universe, planetary systems, geological features, life, biological complexity, consciousness, and the human mind.[62] Strikingly, in these areas naturalistic theories have had mixed success. There have been *some* successes to be sure—theistic evolutionists would point to Darwinian evolution has the best explanation of biological complexity, for example.[63] Yet even granting this (and other) alleged successes, naturalistic approaches have arguably failed to explain the origin of the universe, life, consciousness, and the human mind. And these failures have persisted from the ancient Milesians to the present day—over two thousand years of intellectual miscarriage. The upshot is that reconstructing the historical pattern of naturalistic (or secondary) success is not so simple. Many complexities are close at hand, and these complexities are part of the point. The alleged historical pattern may not be as clear as one might think.[64]

---

62. There are many theological traditions besides the Judeo-Christian one. These traditions conceptualize supernatural hypotheses in a great variety of ways and invoke these hypotheses to different degrees, with different frequency, and in different contexts, respectively. Each tradition ought to be taken on its own terms vis-à-vis the "historical pattern" justification of methodological naturalism.

63. As I will argue below, the attempt to use the alleged success of Darwinian theory as a justification for methodological naturalism in biology turns out to be question begging.

64. For a contrary view of methodological naturalism and its historical function, see Robert Bishop, "God and Methodological Naturalism in the Scientific Revolution and Beyond," *PSCF* 65, no. 1 (March 2013): 10–23. Bishop's article includes a number of fine points, yet also has serious flaws. In particular, Bishop presents Robert Boyle and Isaac Newton as his prime examples of early modern scientists who accepted methodological naturalism. Yet Bishop is wrong on both counts. In endnote 36, Bishop admits as much about Boyle: "for Boyle, MN [methodological naturalism] did not extend to the origin of matter, or living creatures" (22). Thus, according to Bishop, Boyle rejected methodological naturalism in cosmogony and biology. In the present day, biology (in particular) stands as the crucial field entangled in the debate about methodological naturalism. As such, Boyle actually sides with today's *critics* of methodological naturalism. Moreover, Bishop's characterization of Isaac Newton is flawed for similar reasons. Newton also rejected methodological naturalism; in fact, he made design arguments in both *Opticks* and *Principia*. In the former work, Newton's design argument centered on the eye, a *biological* phenomenon. And, in the latter work Newton flatly stated, "And thus much concerning God; to discourse of whom from the appearances of things, does certainly belong to Natural Philosophy" (Newton, *Principia*, ed. Stephen Hawking [Philadelphia: Running Press, 2002], 425–429, esp. 428). Given that the vast majority of scientists and philosophers of science regard the *Principia* as a work of science (rather than of

Of course, a critic might counter that the pattern in question is not just about past naturalistic and supernatural theories but also about present ones. In this case, the "empirical" justification for methodological naturalism also draws upon contemporary scientific data, methods, and inferences to argue that naturalistic theories enjoy explanatory success whereas supernatural theories flounder in explanatory failure. In the context of biology, this means that the scientific success of current evolutionary theory, juxtaposed to the failure of contemporary creationism and ID, justifies barring the latter duo from biology.

But wait. Methodological naturalism holds that supernatural theories cannot be considered within biology. Science is silent about them. Yet, this justification of methodological naturalism depends upon the scientific superiority of evolutionary theory over its theology-laden opponents. It *uses* the very grounds it *excludes*. The empirical justification for methodological naturalism quietly draws upon the alleged scientific superiority of evolutionary theory over its supernatural rivals as the basis for declaring that these very rivals are not worthy of scientific scrutiny. Rivals cannot be tested and yet have failed all tests. This is incoherent, like saying that the Duke basketball team failed to make the NCAA tournament because they lost in the first round. The empirical justification for methodological naturalism undermines itself.

Moreover, this justification begs the question. Arguably, the fundamental contest between evolution and its theological rivals centers on which approach best explains biological complexity. Yet the "empirical" justification of methodological naturalism *assumes* the explanatory superiority of evolutionary theory over its supernatural counterparts. That is, this justification grounds the credibility of methodological naturalism on the assumption that evolution successfully explains biological complexity whereas creationism and ID do not. Yet this is the very point at issue. Is evolutionary theory explanatorily superior? Or is a given supernatural theory superior? These are precisely the questions that creationists and intelligent design theorists try to answer. The "empirical" justification of methodological naturalism bars their

mere "Natural Philosophy"), Newton's God hypothesis and other theological claims in this work run directly counter to methodological naturalism. See also chapter 19 of the present volume as well as Paul Nelson, "Methodological Naturalism" (cited in note 24).

answers from science because it has *already* decided that evolutionary theory is superior. It presupposes a self-serving point of view, and so begs the question at hand.

Stepping back for a moment, there is much more to be said about methodological naturalism, both for and against. For now, in light of the apparent weaknesses of some of the best justifications for methodological naturalism, coupled with the liabilities of methodological naturalism noted above, theistic evolutionists may wish to consider a more open approach to science.

No doubt some theistic evolutionists will demur, however. They will choose to retain methodological naturalism. In one sense, I welcome their persistence: *if they preserve the convention, then they ought to systematically repudiate all theology-laden arguments for evolutionary theory and also abandon all scientific engagement with creationism and ID.* Once they have done so, they should articulate whatever grounds remain for evolutionary theory. My suspicion is that their case will be thin indeed.

Part 5: Final Thoughts

Regardless of whether methodological naturalism is intellectually justifiable, the convention itself retains enormous rhetorical power. It allows theistic evolutionists to designate their favored theory as "scientific" while deeming theological rivals as "nonscientific." Doing so boosts the perceived intellectual credibility of evolutionary theory.

This dynamic is nothing new. Similar maneuvers that purport to distinguish science from nonscience have been part of the Western tradition for a long time. In ancient times, Aristotle distinguished between scientific and technical knowledge as a way to embarrass rival Hippocratic physicians. In the early seventeenth century, Galileo lobbied for the title "natural philosopher," rather than mere "mathematician," in order to increase the credibility of his views. In the late seventeenth and early eighteenth centuries, Cartesian natural philosophers attacked Newton's account of universal gravitation as unscientific because it lacked a proper mechanism. In the nineteenth century, Darwin claimed special creation was "not a scientific explanation" just when the tide turned in favor of common ancestry.[65] And in the twentieth century, German scientist Walther Nernst shunned the Big Bang theory on the grounds that science, by definition, requires an infinite cosmos.[66]

The melee continues. Philosopher Larry Laudan aptly characterizes this pattern: "No one can look at the history of debates between scientists and 'pseudo-scientists' without realizing that demarcation criteria are typically used as *machines de guerre* in a polemical battle between rival camps."[67] Methodological naturalism, like all such maneuvers, often relies on the prestige of science as a substitute for careful analysis of competing theories. It exchanges real engagement for the veneer of respectability.

In the end, theistic evolutionists must make their choice. The case for evolutionary theory time and again involves theological claims or comparisons with theology-laden rivals, in direct violation of methodological naturalism. If theistic evolutionists wish to retain a maximally strong case for evolution—if they wish to keep their battleship—they should reject methodological naturalism. It matters little whether natural or supernatural theories have titles like "scientific" or "nonscientific." What matters is the empirical and conceptual credentials of each theory; what matters is which one best explains biological complexity. What matters, in short, is which one is *true*.[68]

65. Larry Laudan, "The Demise of the Demarcation Problem," in *But Is It Science?*, ed. Michael Ruse (Amherst, NY: Prometheus, 1996), 344. Dilley, "Philosophical Naturalism," 138–141 (see also note 2).

66. C. F. von Weizsäcker, *The Relevance of Science* (New York: Harper and Row, 1964), 151.

67. Laudan, "Demise of the Demarcation Problem," 344.

68. For perceptive suggestions, criticisms, and other forms of support, I wish to thank Robert Bishop, Jeff Cregg, Andrea Palpant Dilley, Bob Jefferis, J. P. Moreland, Paul Nelson, Elliott Sober, Nicholas Tafacory, Colin Zwirko, Caitlin Maples, and Michael White.

21

How Theistic Evolution Kicks Christianity Out of the Plausibility Structure and Robs Christians of Confidence that the Bible Is a Source of Knowledge

J. P. MORELAND

SUMMARY

We can have knowledge (that is, justified true belief) of a wide range of things: logic, mathematics, the truth of Christianity, various biblical doctrines, ethical truths, and so forth. While important, science is only one of the many ways humans know things. However, given the widespread scientism—the view that the hard sciences are the only or the vastly superior way to know things, especially in comparison to theology and ethics—in our culture, theistic evolutionists reinforce this view by constantly revising biblical teachings and interpretations because science says so. Thus, by adopting this unbiblical epistemological outlook, theistic evolutionists weaken the rational authority of biblical teaching among Christians and non-Christians. As a result, the Bible is no longer regarded by many as a genuine source of knowledge, and fewer and fewer people take the Bible seriously. In this way, perhaps unintentionally, those who adopt theistic evolution marginalize Christian truth claims in the church and the public square.

. . . . .

In 1941, Harvard sociologist Pitirim A. Sorokin wrote a book titled *The Crisis of Our Age*. Sorokin divided cultures into three major types, two of which are relevant to this chapter: *sensate* and *integral*. A *sensate* culture is one in which people believe only in the reality of the physical universe capable of being experienced with the five senses. A sensate culture is secular, this-worldly, and empirical. Knowledge is limited to the sense perceptible world.

By contrast, an *integral* culture embraces the sensory world but goes on to accept the notion that an extra-empirical, immaterial reality can be known as well, a reality consisting of God, the soul, immaterial beings, values, purposes, and various abstract objects such as numbers and propositions. Sorokin noted that a sensate culture eventually disintegrates because it lacks the intellectual resources necessary to sustain a public and private life conducive to corporate and individual human flourishing. After all, if we can't know anything about values, life after death, God, and so forth, how can we receive solid guidance to lead a life of wisdom and character?

As we move through the early portion of the twenty-first century, it is obvious that the culture of the West, including the United States, is *sensate* rather than *integral*.[1] To see this, consider the following: In 1989, the state of California issued a new Science Framework to provide guidance for the state's public school science classrooms. In that document, advice is given to teachers about how to handle students who approach them with reservations about the theory of evolution:

> At times some students may insist that certain conclusions of science cannot be true because of certain religious or philosophical beliefs they hold. . . . It is appropriate for the teacher to express in this regard, "I understand that you may have personal reservations

---

1. Julie Reuben, *The Making of the Modern University* (Chicago: University of Chicago Press, 1996).

about accepting this scientific evidence, but it is scientific knowledge about which there is no reasonable doubt among scientists in their field, and it is my responsibility to teach it because it is part of our common intellectual heritage."[2]

The real importance of this statement lies not in its promotion of evolution over creation, though that is no small matter in its own right. No, the real danger in the Framework's advice resides in the picture of knowledge it presupposes: The only knowledge we can have about reality—and, thus, the only claims that deserve the backing of public institutions—is empirical knowledge gained by the hard sciences.

Nonempirical claims (those that cannot be tested with the five senses) outside of the hard sciences, such as those at the core of ethics, political theory, and religion are not items of knowledge but, rather, matters of private feeling. Note carefully the words associated with science: *conclusions, evidence, knowledge, no reasonable doubt, intellectual heritage.* These deeply cognitive terms express the view that science and science alone exercises the intellectual right (and responsibility) of defining reality. By contrast, religious claims are described in distinctively noncognitive language: *beliefs, personal reservations.*

In such a culture we now live and move and have our being. Currently, a three-way worldview struggle rages in our culture between ethical monotheism (especially Christianity), postmodernism (roughly, a cultural form of relativism about truth, reality, and value), and scientific naturalism. I cannot undertake here a detailed characterization of scientific naturalism, but I want to say a word about its role in shaping the crisis of the West.

Scientific naturalism takes the view that the physical cosmos studied by science is all there is. Scientific naturalism has two central components: a view of reality, and a view of how we know things. Regarding reality, scientific naturalism implies that everything that exists is composed of matter or emerges out of matter when it achieves a suitable complexity. There is no spiritual world, no God, no angels or demons, no life after death, no moral absolutes, no objective purpose to life, no such thing as the kingdom of God. And scientific naturalism (strong

---

2. See Mark Hartwig, Paul A. Nelson, *Invitation to Conflict: A Retrospective Look at the California Science Framework* (Colorado Springs: Access Research Network, 1992), 20.

scientism) suggests that physical science is the only, or (weak scientism) at the very least a vastly superior way of gaining knowledge. Since competence in life depends on knowledge (you can't be competent at selling insurance if you don't know anything about it!), this implies that there just is no such thing as learning to live life competently in the kingdom of God. Spiritual competence is a silly idea, since spiritual knowledge, as science has repeatedly shown, does not exist. And the same claim would be made and is being made regarding ethical assertions and moral behavior. Since there is no known spiritual knowledge or competence, Oprah Winfrey feels free to pontificate about matters religious (after all, she is, indeed, an authority about her own private feelings and subjective beliefs), but she would never do this if the topic were a scientific one. Why? Because there are experts she would call in to her show. What is an expert? It is someone with the relevant knowledge. Since there are no experts in ethics or religion, Oprah is free to say what she wants in those areas of discourse without fear of censure.

In the early 1960s, naturalist Wilfrid Sellars announced that "in the dimension of describing and explaining the world, science is the measure of all things, of what is that it is, and of what is not that it is not."[3] Scientific knowledge is taken to be so vastly superior that its claims always trump the claims made by other disciplines. The key component of naturalism, then, is the belief either that scientific knowledge is the only kind of knowledge there is, or that it is an immeasurably superior kind of knowledge. As we shall see in more detail later, combined with postmodernism, scientism raises this central challenge to the Christian church at this time in history: The central issue is not whether Christianity is true (one could claim Christianity is true and is based on blind faith and emotion, and would probably be tolerated by European and North American elites); the central issue is whether Christianity *can be known to be true*. Is or is not Christianity a knowledge tradition, a set of ideas that through history provide us, in its key claims, with truths about reality that can be known to be true?

Years ago I was invited to speak at an evangelistic dessert and I was put on notice by one believer that he was bringing his boss, a

---

3. Wilfrid Sellars, *Science, Perception, and Reality* (London: Routledge & Kegan Paul, 1963), 173.

man who had been a chief engineer for decades, who was finishing a belated PhD in physics from Johns Hopkins, and who went out of his way to attack and ridicule Christians. Upon being introduced to me at the dessert table, he wasted no time launching into me: "I understand you are a philosopher and theologian," he said in an amused manner. Before I had a chance to respond, he said, "I used to be interested in those things when I was a teenager. But I have outgrown those interests. I know now that the only sort of knowledge of reality is that which can be and has been quantified and tested in the laboratory. If you can measure it and test it scientifically, you can know it. If not, the topic is nothing but private opinion and idle speculation!" This is what I mean by scientism. It never occurred to the gentleman that his claim was self-refuting, since the claim could not itself be "quantified and tested in the laboratory."

Scientism accords the right to define reality and speak with knowledge and authority to scientists and scientists alone. And this posture is, sadly, pervasive throughout our culture. In the June 25, 2001, issue of *Time* magazine, the cover story was titled "How the Universe Will End?" The universe is winding down, the story said, and it will eventually go out with a cold, dark whimper. It never occurred to the writer that if something is winding down, it must have been wound up, and if something is wound up, there has to be a winder-upper! But for those with eyes to see, the article's claim about the fate of the universe is not the main issue of concern. It is the article's implicit epistemology (theory of knowledge). It claims that, for centuries, humans have wanted to know how all this will end, but because they could only use religion and philosophy, solid answers were unavailable. But now that science has moved into this area of inquiry, for the first time in human history we have firm answers to our questions, answers that will force religion and philosophy to rethink their views. This same attitude is currently pervasive about the origin and nature of human beings and the ethical views—especially those about sexual ethics—we have inherited from Christianity.

This is scientism, and *Time* magazine employed the naturalist epistemology without batting an eye or, indeed, without knowing it was doing so. In the same issue, *Time* featured an article defending stem-cell

research on human embryos: "These [embryos] are microscopic groupings of a few differentiated cells. There is nothing human about them,
except potential—and, if you choose to believe it, a soul."[4] Note the
presupposed scientism. We *know* scientific facts about embryos, but
nonscientific issues like the reality of the soul are not items of knowledge. When it comes to belief in the soul, you're on your own. There is
no evidence one way or another. You must choose arbitrarily or, perhaps, on the basis of private feelings, what you believe about the soul.
In a scientistic culture, belief in the soul is like belief in ghosts—an issue
best left to the pages of the *National Enquirer*. No wonder people in
our churches increasingly fail to take Christianity seriously!

It is on the basis of knowledge (or perceived knowledge)—not faith,
mere truth, commitment, or sincerity—that people are given the right
to lead, act in public, and accomplish important tasks. We give certain
people the right to fix our cars, pull our teeth, write our contracts,
counsel our souls, and so on, because we take those people to be in possession of the relevant body of knowledge. Moreover, it is the possession of knowledge (and, more specifically, the knowledge that one has
knowledge), and not mere truth alone, that gives people confidence and
courage to lead, act, and risk. Accordingly, it is of crucial importance
that we promote the central teachings of Christianity in general as a
body of knowledge and not as a set of faith-practices to be accepted
on the basis of mere belief or a shared narrative alone. To fail at this
point is to risk being marginalized and disregarded as those promoting a privatized set of feelings or desires that fall short of knowledge.

In 1983, Os Guinness wrote a book in which he claimed that the
church had become its own gravedigger.[5] The upshot of Guinness's
claim was that the very things that were bringing short-term growth
in the Christian community were also, unintentionally and impercep-
tibly, sowing the very sorts of ideas that would eventually undercut
the church's distinctive power and authority. The so-called gravedigger
does not hurt the church on purpose. Usually well-intentioned, he or
she simply adopts views or practices that are counterproductive to and
undermining of a vibrant, attractive Christian community. In my view,

---

4. Michael Kinsley, "If You Believe Embryos Are Human," *Time*, June 25, 2001, 80.
5. Os Guinness, *The Gravedigger File* (Downers Grove, IL: InterVarsity Press, 1983).

there are certain contemporary currents of thought that risk undercutting Christianity as a source of knowledge, and I shall argue that by its very nature, theistic evolution is the prime culprit. It is one of the church's leading gravediggers. For instance, we may think that not encouraging potential converts to reject theistic evolution will cause more to come to Christ. In the short run, it may. But in the long run, the price to be paid by such an approach is the de-cognitivizing of Christianity—making Christianity a religion that has nothing at all to do with the mind or reason—with the result that, over the long haul, most people will simply ignore Christianity as a silly superstition whose practitioners caved in to the prevailing contemporary currents of ideas, instead of holding their ground and eventually winning the argument due to hard-hitting scholarship and confidence in the Bible.

In what follows I shall first clarify the nature of knowledge; second, identify the nature of a plausibility structure along with the central plausibility structure constituting our contemporary milieu; and third, identify three intellectual areas that, if embraced, run the risk of turning us into our own gravediggers. As I hope to show, these three areas are natural results of embracing theistic evolution.

The Nature of Knowledge

Here's a simple definition of knowledge: It is *to represent reality in thought or experience the way it really is, on the basis of adequate grounds. Knowledge is true belief based on adequate grounds.* To know something (e.g., the nature of cancer, forgiveness, or God) is to think of or experience it as it really is, on a solid basis of evidence, experience, intuition, and so forth. Little can be said in general about what counts as "adequate grounds." The best one can do is to start with specific cases of knowledge or its absence in, e.g., art, chemistry, memory, Scripture, or logic, and formulate helpful descriptions of "adequate grounds" accordingly.

Please note that *knowledge has nothing to do with epistemological certainty—the logical impossibility of being wrong—or an anxious quest for it.* One can *know* something without being epistemologically *certain* about it (psychological certainty is different; it is a sense of complete confidence and rest in an idea: I have psychological, but not epistemological, certainty that God exists; as a result, e.g., I do not pray, "Our Father who probably art in heaven"!); and one can know in the presence of doubt or the admission that one might be wrong.

Recently, I know that God spoke to me about a specific matter but I admit it is possible I am wrong about this (though, so far, I have no good reason to think I am wrong). When Paul says, "This you know with certainty" (Eph. 5:5 NASB), he clearly implies that one can know *without* certainty; otherwise, the statement would be redundant. Why? If I say, "Give me a burger with pickles on it," I imply that it is possible to have a burger without pickles. If, contrary to fact, pickles were simply essential ingredients of burgers, it would be redundant to ask for burgers with pickles. The parallel to "knowledge with certainty" should be easy to see. When Christians claim to have knowledge of this or that—for example, that God is real, that Jesus rose from the dead, that the Bible is the word of God—they are not saying that there is no possibility that they could be wrong, that they have no doubts, or that they have answers to every question raised against them. They are simply saying that these and other claims satisfy the definition given at the beginning of this section.

The deepest issue facing the church today is this: Are its main creeds and central teachings items of knowledge or mere matters of blind faith, privatized personal beliefs, issues of feeling to be accepted or set aside according to the individual or cultural pressures that come and go? Do these teachings have cognitive and behavioral authority that set a worldview framework for approaching science, art, ethics—indeed, all of life? Or are cognitive and behavioral authority set by what scientists, evolutionary biologists, or the members of BioLogos say, or by what Gallup polls tell us is embraced by cultural and intellectual elites? Do we turn to these sources and then set aside or revise two thousand years of Christian thinking and doctrinal/creedal expressions in order to make Christian teaching acceptable to the neuroscience department at UCLA or the paleontologists at Cambridge?

The question of whether or not Christianity provides its followers with a range of knowledge is no small matter. It is a question of authority for life and death, and the church is watching Christian thinkers and leaders to see how we approach this matter. And, in my view, as theistic

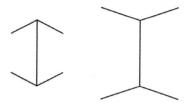

FIGURE 21.1

evolutionists continue to revise the Bible over and over again, they inexorably give off a message about knowledge: science gives us hard knowledge based on evidence and with which we can be confident, and while theology and biblical teaching do not give us knowledge, they provide personal meaning and values for those with the faith to embrace them.

The Importance of a Plausibility Structure

Take a look at Figure 21.1 and notice what you see. Notice that the vertical line on the right looks longer than the one on the left, even though their lengths are the same. Why? Because we see these shapes hundreds of times a day (the right diagram is the inside corner of a room; the left is the outside corner of a building), we are unconsciously used to seeing them as three-dimensional objects, and so we unconsciously try to adjust to the two-dimensionality of the figures on the page. In this case, our habits of perception and thought shape (note: they don't completely determine, they just shape) what we see. When this diagram is shown to people in primitive cultures with no square or rectangular buildings, they have no such subconscious habits and they see the horizontal lines accurately as being of equal length.

There's an important lesson in this. A culture has a set of background assumptions—we can call it a plausibility structure—that sets a tone, a framework, for what people think, what they are willing to listen to and evaluate, how they feel, and how they act. This plausibility structure is so widespread and subtle that people usually don't even know it is there, even though it hugely impacts their perspective on the world. The plausibility structure can be composed of thoughts (scientists are smart;

religious people are gullible and dumb), symbols (a person in a white lab coat), music, and so forth. For example, a book published by Oxford University Press will be taken by a reader to be more credible and to exhibit greater scholarship than a book by an evangelical publisher, even though this assumption is clearly false in certain cases.

Here's the problem this raises for trust in God: Without even knowing it, we all carry with us this cultural map, this background set of assumptions, and our "self talk," the things that form our default beliefs (ones we naturally accept without argument), the things we are embarrassed to believe (if they run contrary to the authorities in our map), and related matters create a natural set of doubts about Christianity. Most of these factors are things of which people are not even aware. In fact, if they are brought to one's attention, one would most likely disown them even though, in fact, they are the internalized ideas that actually shape what people do and don't believe.

Our current Western cultural plausibility structure elevates science and scorns and mocks religion, especially Christian teaching. And it has been the acceptance of theistic evolution by many Christians that has contributed most significantly to this situation. Why? There are at least three reasons. First, theistic evolution reinforces scientism because it exemplifies the view that, when science and biblical/theological teaching are in conflict, we have to revise the Bible. We don't ever revise the science, because scientific truth claims exhibit solid knowledge based on facts.

Second, this sort of revisionism—changing biblical interpretations that have held steady for two thousand years at just the time when there is politically correct pressure to do so, especially when that pressure comes from science—gives off the message that biblical teaching is pretty tentative. We shouldn't hold to it with strong conviction because, if we do, we may become embarrassed when we have to revise that teaching in years to come. According to advocates of scientism—and virtually all theistic evolutionists embrace some form of scientism—biblical/theological ideas, ethical positions, and other claims that fail to have the backing of science are simply personal feelings and blind-faith commitments.

Third, the most pervasive definition of theistic evolution is that the general, naturalistic theory of evolution is true, and God is allowed somehow or another to be involved in the process as long as there is no way to detect his involvement. Design in biology must be unknowable and undetectable! For a thinking unbeliever (or a believer, for that matter), the question surfaces as to why anyone should think God had anything to do with the development of life. What, exactly, did God do, and how could we know the answer to this question? If he was "involved," no one could know it, so God begins to take on some of the characteristics of the tooth fairy.

As a result, the attitude seems to be that, for intelligent, well-educated people, commitment to Christianity should not rise above the level of a hobby. And thus we see that believers in Western cultures do not as readily believe the supernatural worldview of the Bible in comparison with their Third World brothers and sisters. As Christian anthropologist Charles Kraft observes,

> In comparison to other societies, Americans and other North Atlantic peoples are *naturalistic*. Non-Western peoples are frequently concerned about the activities of supernatural beings. Though many Westerners retain a vague belief in God, most deny that other supernatural beings even exist. The wide-ranging supernaturalism of most of the societies of the world is absent for most of our people. . . . Our focus is on the natural world, with little or no attention paid to the supernatural world.[6]

There is a straightforward application here for evangelism and church growth. A person's plausibility structure is the set of ideas the person either is or is not willing to entertain as possibly true. For example, no one would come to a lecture defending a flat earth because this idea is just not part of our plausibility structure. We cannot even entertain the idea. Moreover, a person's plausibility structure is a function of the beliefs he or she already has. Applied to evangelism, J. Gresham Machen got it right when he said,

> God usually exerts that [regenerative] power in connection with certain prior conditions of the human mind, and it should be ours

---

6. Charles Kraft, *Christianity with Power* (Ann Arbor, MI: Servant, 1989), 27.

to create, so far as we can, with the help of God, those favorable conditions for the reception of the gospel. False ideas are the greatest obstacles to the reception of the gospel. We may preach with all the fervor of a reformer and yet succeed only in winning a straggler here and there, if we permit the whole collective thought of the nation or of the world to be controlled by ideas which, by the resistless force of logic, prevent Christianity from being regarded as anything more than a harmless delusion.[7]

The simple truth is that ideas have consequences. If a culture reaches the point where Christian claims are not even part of its plausibility structure, fewer and fewer people will be able to entertain the possibility that such claims might be true. Whatever stragglers do come to faith in such a context would do so on the basis of felt needs alone, and the genuineness of such conversions would be questionable to say the least. And theistic evolution has helped to place Christianity outside our culture's plausibility structure.

To see this, consider the following example. A few years ago when I picked up the morning paper, I found a two-page feature story in section one titled "Intelligent Design Debate Heats Up."[8] The article cites John F. Haught, a lay Catholic theologian at Georgetown University, as opposing intelligent design (ID) theory as bad science and bad theology. According to Haught, just as different explanations can be proffered for why water is boiling (as evidence that the kinetic energy of water molecules are responding to heat, or as evidence that someone wants tea), so evolution can be seen both as the result of natural selection and as part of God's purposes.

I disagree with Haught about the scientific and theological merits of ID theory, but he is entitled to his opinion. If ID theory is bad theology and bad science, then so be it. What troubles me, however, is that Haught and others who opt for theistic evolution seem to do so with little appreciation for the emergence of scientism in our culture and its impact on people's perception of the availability of theological, ethical, and political knowledge. Theistic evolution is intellectual pacifism that

---

7. J. Gresham Machen, *What Is Christianity?* (Grand Rapids, MI: Eerdmans, 1951), 162.
8. Richard N. Ostling, "Intelligent Design Debate Heats Up," *The Orange County Register*, August 20, 2005, 14–15.

lulls people to sleep while the barbarians are at the gates. In my experience, theistic evolutionists are usually trying to create a safe truce with science so that Christians can be left alone to practice their privatized religion while retaining the respect of the dominant intellectual culture.

And while this may not be true of all theistic evolutionists, the majority of the ones I have met have a view of theology and faith as exhibiting very low cognitive value, while science is the most cognitively excellent approach to knowledge we have. For example, theistic evolutionist, physicist, and active member of BioLogos Karl Giberson has said of science, " . . . I would argue that it is the most epistemologically secure perspective we have."[9] By contrast, as I have said elsewhere of Giberson,

> He also seems to regard theology as a degenerate program forever mired in Kuhnian periods of crisis when no one can agree on the best paradigm, when no progress is evident and when theologians do more to impede the search for scientific knowledge . . . than to contribute to its progress. It is hard to see how such a view could countenance theological knowledge. In fact, Giberson's understanding of faith seems to include the notion that as rational justification for a particular belief increases, the possibility of faith decreases. This is seen, for example, in his contrast between the "limited faith" involved in the inference of water in the bottom of a well from the observation of a splash and the so-called "profound" faith of the theist. For Giberson, such a faith is profound, I suppose, in light of the low epistemological value of theology as a discipline.[10]

Giberson's theistic evolution is rooted in (weak) scientism, which inevitably results in placing biblical teaching and theology outside the plausibility structure and depicting them as largely noncognitive fields based on a blind "profound" faith. And I maintain that, however unintentional it may be, this is the posture and result of most theistic evolutionists.

I am not interested in that posture. I don't want to play merely

---

9. Karl Giberson, "Intelligent Design on Trial—A Review Essay," *Christian Scholar's Review*, May, 1995, 469.

10. J. P. Moreland, "Theistic Science and the Christian Scholar: A Response to Giberson," *Christian Scholar's Review*, May, 1995, 447.

not to lose; I want to play to win. I want to win people to Christ and to "destroy strongholds" that undermine knowledge of God (2 Cor. 10:3–5), to penetrate culture with a Christian worldview—to undermine our culture's plausibility structure which, as things stand now, does not include objective theological claims. While there are exceptions, many theistic evolutionists simply fail to provide a convincing response to the question of why one should adopt a theological layer of explanation for the origin and development of life in the first place. Francis Schaeffer made an important distinction that is relevant here. He contrasted the "lower story"—the realm of fact, evidence, knowledge, reason and truth—with the "upper story"—the realm of meaning, blind faith, emotion, and privatized belief. Given scientism, theistic evolution greases the skids toward placing nonscientific claims in a privatized "upper story" in which their factual, cognitive status is undermined. Thus, inadvertently, Haught and those of his persuasion contribute to the marginalization of a Christian worldview.

This is why apologetics, especially scientific apologetics precisely like what we find in the intelligent design movement, is so crucial to evangelism and church growth. It seeks to create a plausibility structure in a person's mind—"favorable conditions," as Machen put it—so that the gospel can be considered. To plant a seed in someone's mind in pre-evangelism is to present a person with an idea that will work on his or her plausibility structure to create a space in which Christianity can be entertained seriously. If this is important to evangelism, it is strategically crucial that local churches think about how they can address those aspects of the contemporary worldview that place Christianity outside the plausibility structures of so many. And I believe we will need to rethink the message we are giving to the culture when we constantly fail to have confidence in the knowledge claims of Scripture and repeatedly revise the Bible, as theistic evolutionists do, when "scientists" tell us we must.

When science appears to conflict with Scripture, we shouldn't immediately lay our intellectual arms down and wait for scientists to tell us what we can allow the Bible to say and how we need to revise Scripture. No, we should be patient, acknowledge the problem, and press into service Christian intellectuals who are highly qualified academically, who have respect for the fact that Scripture presents us with knowledge, not just truth to be accepted by blind faith, and who want to work to preserve the traditional interpretation of Scripture and avoid revisionism. These intellectuals should be encouraged to develop rigorous models that preserve historical Christian teaching (except, of course, in cases where our interpretation of Scripture has been wrong). These intellectuals are heroes, because they value loyalty to historic understandings of Scripture over the desire to fit in with what scientists are currently claiming. The intelligent design movement is just such a set of intellectuals.

Adolfo Lopez-Otero, a professor of materials science and engineering at Stanford and an atheist, was once asked what an unbelieving intellectual expects from a Christian thinker. Lopez-Otero said that the Christian should be daring and humble (try not to act like you are superior) in approaching other professors and secular thinkers: "Be as daring as politeness and civilized behavior allows. But, as I implied before, do not be shy to deconstruct the pretentiousness of his [the atheist's] world in the same way that he is not shy to point out the 'triumphs' of science, the Enlightenment, and rationalism over the 'superstitions' of religion."[11] Lopez-Otero goes on to say that Christian thinkers cannot afford to give excuses for their faith; that is the price they must pay for having declared themselves Christians.

In my opinion, advocates of the intelligent design movement are doing exactly what Lopez-Otero correctly describes. Rather than tucking their tails between their legs at the first sign of a conflict between the Bible and science, and standing ready, even eager, to let the scientists tell them what they must revise, the members of the ID movement have the intellectual courage and confidence in biblical teaching not to back down. Rather, ID advocates "deconstruct the pretentiousness" of truth claims that go against biblical assertions. They don't make excuses for the Bible; they advance arguments in its support.

It should be clear that naturalism is not consistent with biblical Christianity. If that's true, then the church should do all it can to undermine the worldview of naturalism and to promote, among other things,

---

11. Adolfo Lopez-Otero, "Be Humble, Be Daring," *The Real Issue*, September–October, 1997, 10–11.

the cognitive, alethic nature of theology, biblical teaching, and ethics. This means that when Christians consider adopting certain views widely accepted in the culture, they must factor into their consideration whether or not such adoption would enhance naturalism's hegemony and help dig the church's own grave by contributing to a hostile, undermining plausibility structure.

Consider as an example the abandonment of belief in the historical reality of Adam and Eve. Now, if someone does not believe Adam and Eve were real historical individuals, then so be it. My present concern is not with the truth or falsity of the historical view, though that issue matters greatly. Rather, my concern is the readiness, sometimes eagerness, of some to set aside the traditional view, the ease with which the "real estate" of historical Christian commitments is abandoned, and the unintended consequences of jettisoning such a belief. Given the current plausibility structure set by scientific naturalism, rejecting the historical Adam and Eve contributes to the marginalization of Christian teaching in the public square and in the church, and thereby those who reject Adam and Eve unintentionally undermine the church. How so?

First, the rejection reinforces the idea that science and science alone is competent to get at the real truth of reality; theology and biblical teaching are not up to the task. If historically consistent understandings of biblical teaching conflict with what most scientists claim, then so much the worst for those understandings.

Second, the rejection of historical Adam and Eve reinforces the privatized, noncognitive status of biblical doctrine, ethics, and practices—especially supernatural ones that need to be construed as knowledge if they are to be passed on to others with integrity and care. If the church has been mistaken about one of its central teachings for two thousand years, why should we trust the church regarding its teaching about extramarital sex, homosexuality, or the role of women in the church? Admittedly, the church is not infallible in its teachings; still, to the degree that its central teachings through the ages are revised, to that degree the non-revised teachings are also undermined in their cognitive and religious authority. The non-revised teachings become more tentative.

Finally, the rejection of such key Christian beliefs reinforces the modernist notion that we are individuals, cut off from our church community, and that we are free to adopt new beliefs and practices in disregard of that community and our impact on it.

If I am right about the broader issues, then the rejection of a historical Adam and Eve has far more troubling implications than those that surface in trying to reinterpret certain biblical texts. The very status of biblical, theological, and ethical teachings as knowledge is at stake in the current cultural milieu, as is the church's cognitive marginalization to a place outside the culture's plausibility structure. Those who reject a historical Adam and Eve inadvertently harm the church and become its gravedigger.

Three Things to Avoid If You Don't Want to Become a Gravedigger

I suspect that most Christians still accept a historical Adam and Eve (though the same scientism and methodological naturalism that leads to embracing theistic evolution also leads most naturally to—though it does not entail—rejection of a historical Adam and Eve). But there are three revisionist views that may be more acceptable to Christians but that, in my view, seriously undermine the plausibility of Christian teaching in general and that therefore undermine a growing, vibrant church. As we shall see, the adoption of theistic evolution leads to the other two areas of revision.

Theistic evolution. It is widely acknowledged that evolutionary theory, to be clarified in more detail shortly, has "made the world safe for atheists" (to paraphrase Richard Dawkins[12]). Whether theistic or atheistic, when properly understood, evolutionary theory entails the denial of a scientifically detectable Christian God, and as a result, places the detection of divine design outside of science. Given widespread cultural scientism, this is tantamount to saying that the proposition "God designed the world" belongs in an Alice in Wonderland novel. In this way, evolutionary theory has funded the growth of an increasingly aggressive form of atheism. Thus, former Cornell biologist William Provine proclaimed,

---

12. See Richard Dawkins, *The Blind Watchmaker: Why the Evidence of Evolution Reveals a Universe without Design* (New York: W. W. Norton, 1986), 6.

Let me summarize my views on what modern evolutionary biology tells us loud and clear. . . . There are no gods, no purposes, no goal-directed forces of any kind. There is no life after death. . . . There is no ultimate foundation for ethics, no ultimate meaning, and no free will for humans, either.[13]

It can hardly be doubted that the greatest impact of evolutionary theory is its significant contribution to the secularization of culture, a shift that places a supernatural God who makes himself known through creation, intervened or made his actions detectable at various times in the creation of life, and who still intervenes today in answered prayer, miraculous healing, and so on, outside the plausibility structure of Western society. In light of that, why would any Christian want to flirt with theistic evolution?

There are three general understandings of evolution: change within limits (microevolution), the thesis of common descent, and the "blind watchmaker" thesis. The first is accepted by everyone, the second is not yet established, and the third seems to me to be wildly implausible, especially given Christian theism as a background belief. Why? Because the blind watchmaker thesis is the idea that solely blind, mechanical, efficient causal processes are sufficient to produce all the life we see without any need or room for a god to be involved in the process, and there are good reasons (e.g., probability considerations) to reject this thesis.

Recently, even the atheist philosopher Thomas Nagel has weighed in on the matter and claimed that this Darwinian thesis is implausible.[14] Theistic evolution is the view that the blind watchmaker thesis is true, that there is no scientifically detectable evidence for God being involved in the process of evolution (remember: theistic evolutionists are committed to methodological naturalism), and that we are free to reject *metaphysical* or *philosophical* naturalism—by blind faith, I suppose—even though we accept *methodological* naturalism while doing science.

But theistic evolutionists fail to provide sufficient reasons for rejecting metaphysical naturalism. Why be a theist in the first place? After

---

13. William Provine, quoted in Dallas Willard, *Knowing Christ Today* (New York: HarperCollins, 2009), 4.

14. Thomas Nagel, *Mind and Cosmos* (Oxford: Oxford University Press, 2012); cf. J. P. Moreland, "A Reluctant Traveler's Guide for Slouching towards Theism," *Philosophia Christi* 14, no. 2 (2012).

all, while evolution is logically consistent with theism, there is nothing in evolution that would lead one *to* theism; and if the "God hypothesis" isn't needed until humans appear, it is less credible to think it is needed subsequently. Given (1) the presence of a very vibrant, intellectually sophisticated interdisciplinary intelligent design movement, (2) the atheistic implications that most naturally follow from accepting general evolutionary theory (and many, perhaps most, draw those implications), and (3) the fact that the blind watchmaker thesis is far from being justified, why would a believer want to embrace something that undermines the plausibility of Christianity?

Sometimes theistic evolutionists claim that, by embracing evolution, they are actually contributing to the plausibility of Christianity by removing an unnecessary stumbling block—the rejection of evolution—before one can be a well-informed Christian. In my experience, nothing could be further from the truth. I believe and have seen that revisionist interpretations of Scripture—especially in the area of theistic evolution—weaken people's confidence in Scripture and can easily dampen the vibrancy of their faith. Ideas have consequences, and if one has had to revise the early chapters of Genesis, it will weaken his confidence in the rest of the Bible.

More on that later. But more importantly, by adopting theistic evolution, people become the church's gravedigger: their strategy may bring short-term success by keeping a handful of scientists from leaving the faith, but over the long haul, it will contribute to the secularization of culture with its scientistic epistemology, and to the marginalization of the church. After all, if we have to provide naturalistic revisions of the Bible over and over again, why take the yet-to-be-revised portions of Scripture seriously? This approach significantly weakens the cognitive authority of the Bible as a source of knowledge of reality.

If science has shown that, since the Big Bang until the emergence of *Homo sapiens*, there is no good reason to believe in God, isn't it special pleading to embrace this deity when it comes to biblical miracles? Surely history, archeology, and related disciplines have, under the same methodological naturalist constraints, "shown" that biblical miracles are legendary myths that helped Israel and the early church make sense of their subjective religious experiences. And surely there are naturalistic accounts of the Big Bang, the universe's fine-tuning, the origin of life, etc. If theistic evolution applies methodological naturalism to evolution, why not also apply it to cosmological issues and biblical miracles? It seems to me that the naturalization of biblical teaching and miracles is much more consistent with theistic evolution (e.g., they both adopt methodological naturalism; they both place religion in a noncognitive upper story of faith) than with intelligent design.

If we want to be consistent and to contend that core biblical teachings provide us with items of knowledge, it seems to me that we should not let the naturalist camel's nose under the tent from the Big Bang up to the appearance of human life. Clearly, if we need to postulate an active God to explain the origin and development of life, as intelligent design advocates claim, then before we step into the door of a church we are already warranted in believing biblical supernaturalism, and biblical teaching fits easily in our worldview. But if we come to church as theistic evolutionists, a supernatural, intervening God and a knowledge-based Bible are less at home in our worldview and, indeed, may fairly be called ad hoc.

Neuroscience and the soul. The great Presbyterian scholar J. Gresham Machen once observed, "I think we ought to hold not only that man has a soul, but that it is important that he should know that he has a soul."[15] From a Christian perspective, this is a "trustworthy saying." Christianity is a dualist, interactionist religion in this sense: God, angels/demons, and the souls of human persons are immaterial substances that can causally interact with the world. Specifically, human persons are (or have) souls that are spiritual substances that ground personal identity in a disembodied intermediate state between death and final resurrection.[16] Clearly, this was the Pharisees' view in Intertestamental Judaism, and Jesus (Matt. 22:23–33; cf. Matt. 10:28) and Paul (Acts 23:6–10; cf. 2 Cor. 12:1–4) sided with the Pharisees on this issue over against the Sadducees.[17] "Physicalism," by contrast, is the view that the universe is all there is and that everything that exists in it is entirely physical. Some, today, advocate "Christian physical-

---

15. Machen, *The Christian View of Man* (New York: Macmillan, 1937), 159.
16. See John Cooper, *Body, Soul, and Life Everlasting* (Grand Rapids, MI: Eerdmans, 2000).
17. See N. T. Wright, *The Resurrection of the Son of God* (Minneapolis: Fortress, 2003).

ism," which accepts the existence of the Christian God but implies that virtually everything within the universe is entirely physical. There is no soul or substantial mind, though some Christian physicalists will admit that consciousness (sensations, thoughts, beliefs, desires) is a range of nonphysical mental states that depend on and belong to the brain. Thus, upon death, there is no disembodied intermediate state between death and the final resurrection when people receive new resurrected bodies. In my view, Christian physicalism involves a politically correct revision of the biblical text that fails to be convincing.[18]

Nevertheless, today, many hold that, while broadly logically possible, dualism is no longer plausible in light of advances in modern science. This attitude is becoming increasingly prominent in Christian circles. Thus, Christian philosopher Nancey Murphy claims that physicalism is not primarily a philosophical thesis but the hard core of a scientific research program for which there is ample evidence. This evidence consists in the fact that "biology, neuroscience, and cognitive science have provided accounts of the dependence on physical processes of *specific* faculties once attributed to the soul."[19] Dualism cannot be *proven* false—a dualist can always appeal to correlations or functional relations between soul and brain/body—but advances in science make it a view with little justification. According to Murphy, "science has provided a massive amount of evidence suggesting that we need not postulate the existence of an entity such as a soul or mind in order to explain life and consciousness."[20]

One of these pieces of "evidence" is evolution. It is widely agreed that if evolution is the story of how we got here, then we are creatures of matter—consciousness and the self (if such a notion is still used) are entirely physical. I repeat: It is well known that one of the driving forces behind physicalism is evolutionary theory. Evolutionist Paul Churchland makes this claim:

---

18. See Joel Green, *Body, Soul, and Human Life* (Grand Rapids, MI: Baker, 2008); cf. John Cooper, "The Bible and Dualism Once Again," *Philosophia Christi* 9 (2007); Cooper, "The Current Body-Soul Debate: A Case for Holistic Dualism," *Southern Baptist Journal of Theology* 13 (2009); Cooper, "Exaggerated Rumors of Dualism's Demise," *Philosophia Christi* 11 (2009).

19. Nancey Murphy, "Human Nature: Historical, Scientific, and Religious Issues," in *Whatever Happened to the Soul?*, ed. Warren S. Brown, Nancey Murphy, and H. Newton Malony (Minneapolis: Fortress, 1998), 17.

20. Ibid., 18.

> . . . the important point about the standard evolutionary story is that the human species and all of its features are the wholly physical outcome of a purely physical process. . . . If this is the correct account of our origins, then there seems neither need, nor room, to fit any nonphysical substances or properties into our theoretical account of ourselves. We are creatures of matter. And we should learn to live with that fact.[21]

One might think that theistic evolution has the resources to solve this problem, because God could add consciousness or a soul at any place in the evolutionary process. But it must be remembered that, according to theistic evolution, God is allowed to "act" in the natural realm only as long as God's actions are not detectable and we don't need to postulate God's action as the correct explanation of some phenomenon that resulted from his act.

As I have already pointed out, it is almost universally acknowledged that naturalistic evolution cannot explain the origin of consciousness or a soul. Since humans are merely the result of an entirely physical process (the processes of evolutionary theory) working on wholly physical materials, then humans are wholly physical beings. Something does not come into existence from nothing, and if a purely physical process is applied to wholly physical materials, the result will be a wholly physical thing, even if it is a more complicated arrangement of physical materials! And claiming that consciousness is "emergent"[22] is just a name for the problem, not a solution. Thus, if God were to insert consciousness or souls into the evolutionary process, we no longer have evolution, strictly speaking.

I cannot undertake here a comprehensive critique of physicalism and a defense of dualism.[23] Suffice it to say that, contrary to what some may think, dualism is a widely accepted, vibrant intellectual position. I suspect that the majority of Christian philosophers are dualists (consciousness and the soul are immaterial and not physical). And it is important to mention that neuroscience really has nothing to do

---

21. Paul Churchland, *Matter and Consciousness* (Cambridge, MA: MIT Press, 2013), 35.

22. I.e., when matter reaches a certain level of complexity, totally new kinds of properties like consciousness appear and depend on and belong to that complex material structure—e.g., the brain.

23. J. P. Moreland and Scott Rae, *Body and Soul* (Downers Grove, IL: InterVarsity Press, 2000); Moreland, *The Soul: How We Know It's Real and Why It Matters* (Chicago: Moody, 2014).

with which view is most plausible. Without getting into details, this becomes evident when we observe that many leading neuroscientists— e.g., Nobel Prize winner John Eccles,[24] UCLA neuroscientist Jeffrey Schwartz,[25] and Mario Beauregard[26] —are dualists, and they know the neuroscience. Their dualism, and the central intellectual issues involved in the debate, are quite independent of neuroscientific data.

The irrelevance of neuroscience also becomes evident when we consider the recent best-seller *Proof of Heaven*, by Eben Alexander.[27] Regardless of one's view of the credibility of near-death experiences in general, or of Alexander's in particular, one thing is clear: Before whatever it was that happened to him, Alexander believed the (allegedly) standard neuroscientific view that specific regions of the brain generate and possess specific states of consciousness. But after his near-death experience, Alexander came to believe that it is the soul that possesses consciousness, not the brain, and the various mental states of the soul are in two-way causal interaction with specific regions of the brain. Here's the point: Alexander's change in viewpoint was a change in metaphysics that did not require him to reject or alter a single neuroscientific fact. Dualism and physicalism are empirically equivalent views consistent with all and with only the same scientific data. Thus, the authority of empirical data in science cannot be claimed on either side.

For example, the overstatement of neuroscience's authority is increasingly recognized from various sources, including some neuroscientists. As Alissa Quart's op-ed in the *New York Times* observes, "Writing in the journal *Neuron*, the researchers concluded that 'logically irrelevant neuroscience information imbues an argument with authoritative, scientific credibility.' Another way of saying this is that bogus science gives vague, undisciplined thinking the look of seriousness and truth."[28]

Given this, and given the fact that Jesus believed in a soul, as did

---

24. Karl Popper and John Eccles, *The Self and Its Brain: An Argument for Interactionism* (London: Springer, 1977).

25. Jeffrey Schwartz and Sharon Begley, *The Mind and the Brain* (New York: HarperCollins, 2002).

26. Mario Beauregard and Denyse O'Leary, *The Spiritual Brain* (New York: HarperCollins, 2007).

27. Eben Alexander, *Proof of Heaven* (New York: Simon & Schuster, 2012).

28. Alissa Quart, "Neuroscience Under Attack," *New York Times*, November 23, 2012, http://www.nytimes.com/2012/11/25/opinion/sunday/neuroscience-under-attack.html?_r=5&.

the other biblical writers, it is hard to see why believers would reject dualism in favor of some form of Christian physicalism. Moreover, loss of belief in the soul has contributed to a loss of belief in life after death. As John Hick pointed out, "This considerable decline within society as a whole, accompanied by a lesser decline within the churches, of the belief in personal immortality clearly reflects the assumption within our culture that we should only believe in what we experience, plus what the accredited sciences certify to us."[29]

What is the motive, the reasoning here for those believers who reject dualism? The answer: evolution entails or strongly underwrites anthropological physicalism. But if the church's teaching on this has been wrong for two thousand years, why should we believe her teaching when it comes to various doctrinal and ethical claims? As with theistic evolution's accomodationism, physicalism accedes to science a hegemony it does not deserve.

Here's the important takeaway: acceptance of theistic evolution (which entails or strongly supports physicalism), along with irrelevant appeals to neuroscientific authority, undermines the view that theology, biblical teaching, and commonsense views of the mind and so on can stand on their own without the need for scientific backing. Such appeals (that we have to accept theistic evolution and the physicalism that comes along with it) reinforce the relegation of theology and biblical teaching to the noncognitive realm, and they contribute to the placement of biblical teaching outside the culture's plausibility structure. It seems inconsistent and ad hoc to allow science to revise theological anthropology while not allowing it to do the same regarding such things as demonization and religious experience.

Doctrine and ethics. Finally, the adoption of theistic evolution has undermined the cognitive authority of biblical doctrine and ethical teaching and, thus, has contributed to a revisionist approach to them. How so?

The late Harvard paleontologist and atheist Stephen Jay Gould proposed a way of integrating science and religion called the nonoverlapping magisterium. On this view, religion and science had different, noninteracting spheres of teaching authority. The magisterium of

---

29. John Hick, *Death and Eternal Life* (San Francisco: Harper & Row, 1980), 92.

science is the domain of hard, empirically verifiable facts that tell us how things got here, what they are made of, and how they work. The magisterium of religion deals with morals, privatized religious teaching, and spirituality, all of which must be accepted by simple faith and personal feeling.

For decades now, theistic evolutionists have adopted the basic idea of the nonoverlapping magisterium, but they have called it the "complementarity" view.[30] According to this view, science and religion approach the world from different standpoints, different perspectives, different levels of explanation such that science focuses on *what* things are and how they got here and religion focuses on *who* made things and the ethical significance of things. In a scientistic culture, it didn't take long for the complementarity view to treat science as a cognitive enterprise that provides us with truth and knowledge, while religion is a private-feelings approach that gives us a noncognitivist, relativist set of feelings and personal beliefs about meaning and value.

The complementarity view, and the theistic evolution that supports it, is a chief gravedigger of the contemporary church in Western culture. After all, if the areas of the Bible that can be tested require that we revise its teachings and adopt theistic evolution, why should we continue to embrace culturally embarrassing doctrinal views (e.g., that hell is real and some people will go there) or ethical positions (e.g., that homosexual practice is deeply immoral) that, according to complementarians, can be neither empirically tested nor understood in any way other than as subjective, private feelings about "meaning" and "values."

As I have admitted earlier, the church's teaching is not infallible. Still, we should be very careful and reluctant to revise what the church has held for centuries, especially when two factors are present: (1) there is available an intellectually robust defense of the traditional view; (2) there is politically correct pressure suddenly to "find" that the Bible all along taught what our secular friends and peers tell us it *should* teach if we are going to be culturally and academically respectable. There is

---

30. For one of the founders of this approach to the integration of science and religion, see Donald MacKay, *The Clock Work Image* (Downers Grove, IL: InterVarsity Press, 1974), 90–92; MacKay, *Human Science and Human Dignity* (Downers Grove, IL: InterVarsity Press, 1979), 25–34.

a sober-mindedness that should characterize any self-identifying Christian scholar or pastor regarding these matters, since our laity often look to us or consider us as representative spokespersons of the Christian tradition. To many laypeople, it seems hardly a coincidence that just when the naturalistically informed culture puts pressure on us to believe a certain thing, even though the history of biblical interpretation supports the exact opposite, we conveniently discover that we have misunderstood the Scriptures all along!

I think the Christian community expects more courage out of its leaders, and we run the risk of making our own desired views of biblical interpretation more authoritative than the text itself. It is as though some exegetes have a desired view they want to sustain, and they fiddle with the Bible until they get it to turn out the "right" way. Revisions of the church's teaching about homosexuality seem suspicious in just this way. I am not arguing that the current revisionist views are false, though I believe that to be the case. What I am urging us to consider is the unintended consequences of embracing revisionist positions: the marginalization of Christian doctrine and ethics (after all, if we "find" the church was wrong for two thousand years at just the time when it is convenient to make such a discovery, what does this say about the epistemic [i.e., rational] and alethic [i.e., truth] status of the views we just happened not to have revised at present), and the placement of Christianity outside the plausibility structure. And when we do consider this, we should come to the conclusion that the revisionist position of theistic evolution has made it much easier to revise other biblical teachings when there is cultural pressure on us to do so.

22

How to Think about God's Action in the World[1]

C. JOHN COLLINS

SUMMARY

Christians have traditionally thought of God's works of "providence" as including what we call "natural" and "supernatural," and both are equally "God's action." They have also thought that at least some of the supernatural actions are in principle discernible as special by humans. This provides a robust tool for reading the Bible, for living wisely, and for doing science. A fully evolutionary perspective that seeks to be traditionally Christian affirms that God "acts" through the "natural" events of the evolutionary process, and still allows for "miracles" outside this process, such as the death of the Egyptian first-born. However, whatever processes of descent with modification God might have used, its "natural" functioning is not enough to account for the origin of the world, of life, and of human reason—nor does recognizing this involve us in a "God-of-the-gaps" fallacy. In fact, for good critical thinking, we should be careful *both* about appealing to miracle to cover our ignorance *and* about excluding, before we even begin our study, the possibility of extra help from outside the natural process.

· · · · ·

1. This chapter develops material from my books *The God of Miracles: An Exegetical Examination of God's Action in the World* (Wheaton, IL: Crossway, 2000); and *Science and Faith: Friends or Foes?* (Wheaton, IL: Crossway, 2003), and from my article, "Miracles, Intelligent Design, and God-of-the-Gaps," *Perspectives on Science and Christian Faith* 55, no. 1 (March 2003): 22–29.

My goal in this chapter is to explain how the traditional Christian way of talking about God's action in the world—which accounts well for the biblical materials—provides us with an intellectually robust way of thinking about how "miracles" and "design" relate to "science."

1. Introduction: The Issues

One way to begin our discussion is to see how people want either to assert or to deny the credibility of what we call "miracles" in the Bible, thinking them to be incompatible with a modern scientific outlook. A classic denial comes from the German New Testament scholar Rudolph Bultmann (1884–1976):

> It is impossible to use electric light and the wireless and to avail ourselves of modern medical and surgical discoveries, and at the same time to believe in the New Testament world of spirits and miracles. We may think we can manage it in our own lives, but to expect others to do so is to make the Christian faith unintelligible and unacceptable to the modern world.[2]

Christians have sought various ways of countering this denial, whether by clarifying how the traditional understanding meets it (as will I), or else by reframing their description of how to think about God's action. One common way of reframing is to employ a notion of God's action in which "miracles" are not metaphysically different from "natural" events; the difference is rather in their noticeability to the human observer. This can go in one of two ways: "providentialism," in which every event is in principle the product of created natural forces that God providentially sustains;[3] and "occasionalism," in which created things have no actual causal power, and every event is

---

2. Rudolph Bultmann, "New Testament and Mythology," in *Kerygma and Myth*, ed. H. W. Bartsch (London: SPCK, 1964), 5. The original German essay appeared in 1951; a slightly different rendering appears in Bultmann, *The New Testament and Mythology and Other Basic Writings* (Philadelphia: Fortress, 1984), 4–5.

3. E.g., R. J. Berry, a providentialist: "Probably all miracles are susceptible to an explanation other than the supernatural"; see *Science and Christian Belief* 9, no. 1 (1997): 77 (a response to P. Addinall's reply to Berry's previous article on "The Virgin Birth of Christ," *Science and Christian Belief* 8, no. 2 (1996): 101–110); Berry, "Divine Action: Expected and Unexpected," *Zygon* 37, no. 3 (2002): 717–727. The term "providentialism" is my own coinage: see Collins, *God of Miracles*, 26–29; Robert Larmer, "Miracles, Divine Agency, and the Laws of Nature," *Toronto Journal of Theology* 27, no. 2 (2011): 267–290, uses "theistic complementarianism" with the same meaning.

"supernatural."[4] These two alternative views often share similar notions of what "miracles" are, namely events that are subjectively important without being metaphysically different from any other event.

A challenge to sorting these matters out comes from the fact that the Bible writers rarely, if ever, give what we can call a "technical" or "metaphysical" discussion of the mechanics of the events they record. For example, an ordinary pregnancy is God's action (see Ps. 139:13–15; Jer. 1:5), as is Elizabeth's pregnancy with John, and Mary's with Jesus (Luke 1:35–37).

In the sections that follow, I will lay out the traditional way of describing God's actions, which suits the biblical presentations better than the alternatives. I will also show why using this traditional understanding, together with literary sensitivity, can help us steer clear of the kinds of difficulties that Bultmann found. Finally, I will mention briefly how this discussion also helps us think about the controversial notion of "design" as we find it (or *think* we do) in the world of nature.

2. Traditional Notions of Natural and Supernatural

We ought first to define what we are speaking of: what is "ordinary" or "natural," and what is a "miracle"? Straightaway we face difficulties, since there is no technical biblical discussion of either of these notions. That, of course, is hardly evidence that the *concepts* themselves are foreign to the Bible. Rather than rely on etymologies,[5] or on the various definitions of miracle that have been offered (often for polemical purposes, and often representing varied metaphysics),[6] I shall content myself with stating the standard scholastic metaphysic of ordinary and

---

4. The occasionalist G. C. Berkouwer, *The Providence of God* (Grand Rapids, MI: Eerdmans, 1952), 196, asserted that a miracle "means nothing more than that God at a given moment wills a certain thing to occur differently than it had up to that moment been willed by Him to occur."

5. The English word "miracle" derives from Latin *miraculum*, which in turn comes from the verb *miror*, "to wonder." That is, it contains the notion of the subjective response of amazement on the part of the onlookers; but this notion is not uniformly present in the biblical passages which are held to describe miracles.

6. E.g., David Hume (1711–1776), *Enquiries concerning the Human Understanding and concerning the Principles of Morals*, ed. L. A. Selby-Bigge (Oxford: Oxford University Press, 1902), 114 (section x.1), defined a "miracle" as "a *violation* of the laws of nature," while others have preferred to speak of a *suspension* of those laws. Still others, such as providentialists and occasionalists, think of an event that is personally significant but not necessarily metaphysically distinct from ordinary events (for examples, see Collins, *God of Miracles*, 36–39).

miraculous events, and citing a few biblical texts that clearly support this position.[7]

The Lutheran theologian Heinrich Schmid (1811–1885) gives a representative description of divine providence as having three elements: *preservation, concurrence,* and *governance*:[8]

> I. *Preservation* is the act of Divine Providence whereby God sustains all things created by Him, so that they continue in being with the properties implanted in their nature and the powers received in creation. . . . Created things have no power of subsistence in themselves. . . . Therefore *preservation* is also designated as *continued creation*.[9]
>
> II. *Concurrence.* . . . Concurrence, or the co-operation of God, is the act of Divine Providence whereby God, by a general and immediate influence, proportioned to the need and capacity of every creature, graciously takes part with second causes in their actions and effects.[10]
>
> III. *Government* is the act of Divine Providence by which God most excellently orders, regulates, and directs the affairs and actions of

---

7. A full exegetical and theological discussion of the options in traditional Christianity appears in Collins, *God of Miracles*, where I conclude that the scholastic metaphysic has the advantages both of being exegetically sound and of being robust in the face of modernism and postmodernism. Support for this analysis from an exegete comes in Craig Keener, *Miracles: The Credibility of the New Testament Accounts* (Grand Rapids, MI: Baker, 2011), and from philosophical theologians in Lydia Jaeger, "Against Physicalism-Plus-God: How Creation Accounts for Divine Action in the World," *Faith and Philosophy* 29 (2012): 295–312; Robert Larmer, "Miracles, Divine Agency, and the Laws of Nature."

8. Heinrich Schmid, *Doctrinal Theology of the Evangelical Lutheran Church*, trans. Charles Hay and Henry Jacobs (Minneapolis: Augsburg, 1961 [1875]), 170–194. For the same position from other branches of Western Christianity, cf. Heinrich Heppe (1820–1879), *Reformed Dogmatics*, trans. G. T. Thomson (Grand Rapids, MI: Baker, 1978 [1950]), 251–280; and Alfred Freddoso (Roman Catholic), "God's General Concurrence with Secondary Causes: Why Conservation Is Not Enough," *Philosophical Perspectives* 5 (1991): 553–585. Some theologians dispute whether *concurrence* should be included, but Freddoso's essay is, I believe, proof that it must be. The Presbyterian theologian William G. T. Shedd, *Dogmatic Theology*, 3 vols. (Nashville: Nelson, 1980 [1888–1894]), 1:527–530, speaks only of preservation and government, but from his exposition it is clear that his definition of preservation *includes* concurrence.

9. The term "continued creation" can cause some confusion, since different writers may mean different things by it. Heppe's Reformed compendium uses similar language about "continued creation," but adds a clarification: "*conservatio* is to be conceived as a *continuata creatio*, resting upon the same command of God as creation. . . . At the same time preservation must not be conceived as a continued creation, as though by preservation the essential identity of the once created world were abolished" (Heppe, *Reformed Dogmatics*, 257–258).

10. The expression "graciously takes part" is somewhat vague; it refers to God's confirming the interactions of the causal properties. Heppe, *Reformed Dogmatics*, 258, cites the Swiss theologian J. H. Heidegger (ca. 1700) for a definition: "concurrence or co-operation is the operation of God by which he co-operates directly with the second causes as depending upon him alike in their essence as in their operation, so as to urge or move them to action and to operate along with them in a manner suitable to a first cause and adjusted to the nature of the second causes."

creatures according to His own wisdom, justice, and goodness, for the glory of His name and the welfare of men. . . .

The Providence of God ordinarily employs second causes, and thus accomplishes its designs; but God is by no means restricted to the use of those second causes, for He often exercises His Providence without regard to them, and operates thus contrary to what we call the course of nature, and hence arises the difference between *ordinary* and *extraordinary* providence.[11]

There is no doubt here that both ordinary and extraordinary (miraculous) providence are expressions of God's *active* power: it is never correct to refer to the miraculous as having God more "directly" or "immediately" involved. However, the mode of that expression of power is different, and, at least in principle, some of those differences are discernible by human observers.[12] God's activity in maintaining the creation is not *physically* detectable, since it is not part of the order of the world we experience with our senses.[13]

Some sample texts show that this is a good inference from the biblical material:[14] e.g., James 3:11–12 supports the idea of "natural powers" by which a fig tree *cannot* yield olives; Hebrews 1:3 speaks of all things depending on Christ's active power of upholding;[15] Exodus 14:21 shows an extraordinary (miraculous) event that uses a means (the east wind); and Luke 1:34–35 describes the mechanism of a

---

11. "The form of divine *gubernatio* in which God is active without second causes or uses them in a manner deviating from their orderly appointment and activity is God's performance of miracle" (Heppe, *Reformed Dogmatics*, 263).

12. Cf. Stephen T. Davis, "God's Actions," in *In Defense of Miracles*, ed. R. D. Geivett and G. R. Habermas (Downers Grove, IL: InterVarsity Press, 1997), 163–177, at 166. I say "at least in principle" and "some of those differences" because it is conceivable that a given special divine action is not distinguishable *to us* from a "natural event." Some which are clearly distinguishable, under the supernaturalist scheme, are the initial creation ex nihilo event; the virgin conception of Jesus; the turning of water into wine; and the resurrection of Jesus.

13. Cf. Paul Helm, *The Providence of God* (Downers Grove, IL: InterVarsity Press, 1994), 82, who helpfully says, "the exact sense in which objects which are distinct from God are yet upheld by him is difficult to get clear"; and 89, "it should be stressed that this upholding, being metaphysical or ontological in character, is physically undetectable." Other writers have referred to the hiddenness of what Austin Farrer called the "causal joint" between God and the creation: see Farrer, *Faith and Speculation* (London: A&C Black, 1967), 142.

14. These and many other texts are discussed at length in Collins, *God of Miracles*, chapters 5–7. This conclusion is stronger than that of Paul Gwynne, *Special Divine Action* (Rome: Gregorian University Press, 1996), 65, who supposes that the biblical material is not decisive.

15. It is common to include Colossians 1:17 along with Hebrews 1:3. However, its focus is more on the way everything works together coherently: see discussion in Collins, "Colossians 1,17 'hold together': A Co-opted Term," *Biblica* 95, no. 1 (2014): 64–87.

supernatural event (the conception of Jesus) as being due to the special agency of the Holy Spirit.[16]

Let's use this approach to God's providence to analyze an example, the deliverance of Jerusalem from the forces of Sennacherib (2 Kings 19:35; Isa. 37:36; 2 Chron. 32:21).[17] The biblical texts say that an angel of the Lord slew a large number of Assyrian soldiers, which caused the surviving army to flee. Herodotus (*Histories*, 2.141.5) records an incident in which, during the night, "an army of field mice swarmed through [the Assyrian] camp and chewed up their quivers, bowstrings, and even the handles of their shields." As a result the army woke up and, defenseless, fled, after many fell. Let us suppose, for the sake of this discussion alone, that these two accounts deal with the same events: are they competing alternatives? Certainly not: a "supernatural" event can use means (the mice), and, if the mice were a "natural" occurrence, it is still, to the eye of faith, God's act. Indeed, it remains possible that Herodotus's telling missed out on the possible function of the mice as symbolic of pestilence, in which case the event had more complexity than Herodotus told.[18]

With this traditional metaphysic we can speak of the "natural properties" of created things and their interactions in place of the more common "laws of nature."[19] This leads to the following definitions:

Natural: God made the universe from nothing and endowed the things that exist with natural properties; he preserves those properties, and he also confirms their interactions in a web of cause-and-effect relations.

Supernatural: God is also free to "infuse" special operations of his power into this web at any time, e.g., by adding objects, directly causing events, enabling an agent to do what its own natural properties would never have made it capable of, and by imposing organization, according to his purposes.[20]

---

16. See also Matthew 1:18, 20. Of course God is represented as active in the formation of *every* embryo (cf. Ps. 139:13); the question is the *mode* of his involvement.

17. See further A. R. Millard, "The Old Testament and History: Some Considerations," *Faith and Thought* 110 (1983): 34–53; Millard, "Sennacherib's Attack on Hezekiah," *Tyndale Bulletin* 36 (1985): 61–77.

18. See Robert Strassler, ed., *The Landmark Herodotus: The Histories* (New York: Anchor, 2007), 184 (note 2.141.5a).

19. For a similar approach, see Stephen S. Bilynskyj, *God, Nature, and the Concept of Miracle* (PhD diss., University of Notre Dame, 1982), 104–105, who speaks of "natural powers."

20. Compare this with Blaise Pascal's similar definition of "miracle," as "an effect which exceeds the natural power of the means which are employed for it; and what is not a miracle is an effect

Some object to the very idea of distinguishing "natural" and "supernatural" in the Bible. The Old Testament scholar John Walton insists,

> People in the ancient world had no category for what we call *natural laws*. When they thought in terms of cause and effect, even though they could make all the observations that we make . . . , they were more inclined to see the world's operation in terms of divine cause.[21]

This, however, is a *mistaken reading of the rhetoric* of passages like Psalm 104. A text like that does *not* give the ordinary view; rather, it cultivates the perspective of faith (which includes natural causality, as we saw), which corrects the default views. John Rogerson had a better sense of the rhetoric when he observed,

> These passages [that express pervasive divine activity] do not represent what the average Israelite felt; they are religious texts, containing a religious interpretation of the natural world, a religious interpretation that was certainly not 'given' along with ordinary perception of the world, and which was by no means self-evident to anyone who reflected on the processes of the natural world. . . . The attempt of the Old Testament writers to claim the sovereignty of God over nature and its workings was not something easily attained with the help of thought processes or an 'outlook' that readily saw the divine in everything. It was rather a courageous act of faith, persisted in when there was often much in personal experience and competing religions and outlooks, that suggested that such a conviction was false.[22]

(See also Joseph's professions of faith in Gen. 45:7–8; 50:20.)

---

which does not exceed the natural power of the means which are employed for it" (*"Miracle. C'est un effet qui excède la force naturelle des moyens qu'on y emploie; et non-miracle est un effet qui n'excède pas la force naturelle des moyens qu'on y emploie"*), in *Pensées* (Paris: Garnier Frères, 1964), no. 804 (no. 891 in Krailsheimer's system). See also Gwynne's definition of "special divine action" in *Special Divine Action*, 24: "God brings it about that some particular outcome is different from what it would have been had only natural, created factors been operative."

21. John H. Walton, *The Lost World of Adam and Eve: Genesis 2–3 and the Human Origins Debate* (Downers Grove, IL: InterVarsity Press, 2015), 18.

22. John Rogerson, "The Old Testament View of Nature: Some Preliminary Questions," in *Instruction and Interpretation*, ed. H. A. Brongers et al., Oudtestamentische Studiën 20 (Leiden: Brill, 1977), 67–84, at 79, 84.

3. What Role Do Miracles Play In Biblical Faith?

It is inherent in the traditional Christian metaphysic that "miracles"—
or better, "supernatural events"—are possible. Under what conditions
they may be expected is another question; Christian theologians commonly add provisos about miracles not being capricious but related to
God's pursuit of relationship with human beings. That is to say, they
mark key phases in the unfolding story of God's development of his
people, and this is particularly the case with the miracles in the Bible.[23]

This puts us in a position to evaluate Bultmann's objection, to see
that it is the combination of *both* a faulty reading of the biblical materials *and* the imposition of a worldview preference (naturalism: the
universe as closed system), which is not itself inherent in the scientific
outlook. Of course, within the biblical worldview we can use the electric lights and the wireless, not to mention modern medicine. These
are all technologies that exploit the natural properties of the things
God made; they are part of our exercising dominion. And the "spirits
and miracles" in the Bible do not come willy-nilly or capriciously; nor
do they undermine the functioning of the natural properties. Some
people mistakenly suppose that because we have *so many* occasions of
miracles, therefore the Bible leads us to expect them all the time. But,
as a matter of fact, the speech act theory idea of "tellability" helps us
here:[24] the authors select what events to record, precisely because they
are worth telling about—probably because they rarely occur!

These provisos are quite appropriate; at the same time, Christian
theism resists the notion that supernatural events are in some way
unworthy of God. It is quite true that a doctrine of creation posits a
created world that has all its necessary capacities built into it, needing
no tinkering. But those capacities are the ones *necessary for the world's
assigned purpose*: namely, of being the background for the lives and
choices of rational agents, with whom God intends to interact.[25]

---

23. The role of miracles *outside* of the Bible is controversial, and I am not entering into that
discussion here.

24. See Mary Louise Pratt, *Toward a Speech Act Theory of Literary Discourse* (Bloomington:
Indiana University Press, 1977), 136–147.

25. Cf. Helm, *Providence*, 106–107. The objection that miracles are unworthy of a fully fitted
creation seems frequently to rely on a metaphor for the world as a machine or artifact: it would be
a reproach on the Craftsman if it needed "tinkering." But suppose we change the metaphor, and
picture the world as a musical instrument, and its history as the tune (as Athanasius, *Contra Gentes*
§38, did). It is no shame to the Craftsman if his instrument does not have the tune within itself!

While these special events often address crises of human need, they play two main roles: first, they authenticate divinely approved messengers (prophets and apostles: e.g., Deut. 18:21–22; Acts 2:22; 2 Cor. 12:12), and second, they make God's interest in the corporate well-being of his people (Israel and the church) especially clear (e.g., Ex. 14:30–31). An additional role is that of testifying about God's interest, to those outside his own people, with a view toward leading them to faith (e.g., Ex. 15:14–16).

4. Miracles, Science, and God-of-the-Gaps

To claim to have discerned a miracle renders one liable to the charge of committing the "God-of-the-gaps" fallacy. That is to say, suppose we come upon some object or event for which we do not have a naturalistic explanation, and then say, "See, God must have done that," and then proceed to base either our own belief or our apologetic for belief on such an instance. This involves us in a risk: suppose the sciences eventually provide a natural-process–based explanation; then where does that leave God's involvement in the matter? Are what were once grounds for believing in God thereby made an argument for disbelief?[26]

A serious theological problem is also involved (at least within traditional theism) if we think that it is possible to say of some events or objects, "God made this," and of the natural ones, "God did *not* make this."[27] The doctrine of providence cited above affirms that the products of second causes are every bit as much direct divine action as the miraculous events.

What, then, does it mean to declare that a "supernatural event" has taken place? How is it discernible, and to whom may we legitimately argue that we have discerned such an event—that is, is the explanation

---

26. Fundamentalists are not the only ones to commit this blunder. I have heard religious speakers on the BBC, who would best be described as left-wing Anglican, celebrate ignorance on the causes, say, of lightning strikes or the 1987 hurricane in the south of England, because that leaves room for God's mysterious action in his world.

27. For example, the subtitle of Geivett and Habermas, *In Defense of Miracles*, is "A Comprehensive Case for *God's Action in History*" (emphasis added to subtitle). Although some of the authors in the collection try to provide a more careful nuancing to this, it nevertheless shows the problem in popular parlance. A Scripture text such as Psalm 119:126, "It is time for the LORD *to act*," must be taken as analogical—that is, it speaks *as if* God were doing nothing about the wicked, rather than asserting that he *actually is* doing nothing.

"supernatural" credible only to those who already believe, or is it more publicly accessible?

Normally, we consider an event "special" when it is more than simply unusual—after all, lots of things are unusual! Rather, we have some notion that the result was both contingent (that is, it could have happened otherwise) and against our expectations, and that it served some important need. Sometimes that notion of ours is intuitive, in which case we do not assess our expectations of the outcome too strictly for their reasonableness.

In other cases we may apply more rigorous assessment of our expectations, and if they were reasonable, we feel a kind of wonder.

In a few cases we go even further: we conclude that the result *should* have been otherwise, and we base this on our knowledge of the factors involved. For us to declare an event "supernatural," it must meet this most stringent requirement. But this leads to our difficulty: Are we not simply appealing to gaps in our understanding of the natural course of things? Further, if our sense of its specialness *depended on* the event being "miraculous," then a "scientific" (or "natural") explanation diminishes the specialness.

It will help us to recall the two domains of scientific explanation, the *nomothetic* and the *historical*.[28] In nomothetic explanations we consider what normally happens, and explain its causation. We are looking for regularities or "laws," hence the name. This domain predominates in most common definitions of science. In historical explanations we are asking what specific chain of cause-and-effect produced the item we are studying. Obviously the two are related, but they are also distinguishable: e.g., how animals interact in an ecosystem (nomothetic) versus why a particular species went extinct (historical). Of course our historical explanations make use of our nomothetic ones.

Now the biblical theist ought not appeal to special divine action in a nomothetic context, because in these situations, the ordinary function of God's creation, we recognize that God's activity is that of maintaining the order of what he made. In a context like that, to invoke supernatural causation would involve the God-of-the-gaps fallacy. Further, many historical events, such as the 1980 Mount St. Helens eruption, may in

---

28. Ian Barbour, *Religion in an Age of Science* (New York: HarperSanFrancisco, 1990), 66–71.

fact be explicable by appeal to natural factors. To attribute these to supernatural action would also be improper (at least, without plenty of further research!). On the other hand, there can be unique events that *do* involve special divine activity (e.g., creation, exodus, virgin birth, resurrection of Jesus). In such cases it would be incorrect and misleading to insist that only natural factors are valid for describing what happened in those events; it would also be empirically inadequate.

That is, there are gaps and then there are gaps. First, there are *gaps due to ignorance* (Latin: *lacunae ignorantiae causā*), which are simply gaps in our knowledge, which may eventually be filled. But there are also *gaps due to the nature* (Latin: *lacunae naturae causā*) of the things involved: the result goes beyond what these natural properties would have brought about.[29]

We should exercise caution in declaring that we have discovered a *lacuna naturae causā*, since we do not know everything there is to know about the relevant natural properties. For example, we might speak of a medical miracle when someone recovers from cancer, when all we really have a right to say is that we do not understand the process. (Again, however, it is still God's work of healing: see Sir. 38:1–15.)

On the other hand, we know enough about some things that we can have confidence when speaking of them. As C. S. Lewis pointed out, "No doubt a modern gynaecologist knows several things about birth and begetting which St. Joseph did not know. But those things do not concern the main point—that a virgin birth is contrary to the course of nature. And St. Joseph obviously knew *that*."[30]

5. What about "Design"?

To say that God created, maintains, and governs the world is to claim that his purposes are at work; and this raises the question of what has been called "design," and the discernibility of design. This further impinges on our notions of God's action in his world.

---

29. John Polkinghorne employs a similar dichotomy of gaps in *Quarks, Chaos, and Christianity* (New York: Crossroad, 1994), 71–72: he describes gaps that are "patches of contemporary ignorance" and "*intrinsic* gaps in the bottom-up description alone in order to leave room for top-down action." This is especially interesting because Polkinghorne does not favor the scholastic metaphysic given above.

30. C. S. Lewis, *Miracles: A Preliminary Study* (New York: Macmillan, 1960), chapter 7, paragraph 5.

The notion of "design" in the world of nature has had varied emphases, which we must keep distinct. It goes beyond this essay to rehearse all the history of notions of "design," worthy as that effort would be;[31] I will focus on a few points that come into play in contemporary discussions. Generally speaking, when people have seen "design" in the world, they interpreted it as a signpost to the Deity, who has fashioned the world as such a suitable place for humankind. For example, in Thomas Aquinas's "five ways" (five variations on one way of establishing the grounds for believing in God), we have the fifth, Thomas's "argument from design" (*Summa Theologiae*, I.2.3):

> The fifth way is taken from the governance of the world. We see that things which lack intelligence, such as natural bodies, act for an end, and this is evident from their acting always, or nearly always, in the same way, so as to obtain the best result. Hence it is plain that *not fortuitously, but designedly* [*non a casū sed ex intentione*], do they achieve their end. Now whatever lacks intelligence cannot move towards an end, unless it be directed by some being endowed with knowledge and intelligence; as the arrow is shot to its mark by the archer. Therefore some intelligent being exists by whom all natural things are directed to their end; and this being we call God.[32]

The "design" in view here is, as Francis Beckwith noted, "the universe's design as a *whole*, appealing to those scientific laws that make motion possible."[33] We may call this large-scale, or system design. We can further see that the system design has at least two aspects: there is the design of properties (say, to sustain our lives here), and the design that orchestrates events (so that the whole process produces the results God intends).

William Paley (1743–1805) paid more attention to instances of

---

31. For a brief overview with bibliography, see my *Science and Faith: Friends or Foes?*, chapter 18; see also David Sedley, *Creationism and Its Critics in Antiquity* (Berkeley: University of California Press, 2007); and *Design in the Bible and the Early Church Fathers* (e-book from Discovery Institute, 2009).

32. Latin: P. Caramello, *Summa Theologiae* (Taurini: Marietti, 1950). For discussion see Peter Kreeft, *A Summa of the Summa* (San Francisco: Ignatius, 1990), 69.

33. Francis J. Beckwith, "How to Be an Anti-Intelligent Design Advocate," *University of St. Thomas Journal of Law and Public Policy* 4, no. 1 (2010): 35–65, at 46 (a condensed version of this article appears as a scholarly essay on BioLogos.org).

"contrivance" that make up the larger system, that is, places where he inferred that design had been imposed on smaller systems.[34] The title of Paley's book, *Natural Theology, Or, the Evidence and Attributes of the Deity, Collected from the Appearances of Nature*,[35] makes clear his theological and apologetic purpose.[36]

Many say that Darwin's theory (*The Origin of Species*, [1]1859, [6]1872) undermined the Paleyesque argument from design. According to that reading, Paley had put forward many instances in the biological world that were impossible to account for except by divine imposition of design. Then, however, Darwin's theory of natural selection provided a natural-process–based explanation of the features and interactions of organisms.[37] The most that design could claim, by this understanding, was that God had designed the properties and the laws governing the process, along the lines of the "system design" discussed above (as Darwin himself allowed).[38]

Darwinism, or, more properly today, neo-Darwinism, has been

---

34. It is likely that Paley, writing a quarter of a century after David Hume's *Dialogues concerning Natural Religion* (New York: Hafner, 1948 [1779]), intended to overwhelm Hume's case with examples; and some think he was at least partially successful: cf. D. L. LeMahieu, *The Mind of William Paley* (Lincoln: University of Nebraska Press, 1976), 29–54, 67–68; David Burbridge, "William Paley confronts Erasmus Darwin: Natural Theology and Evolutionism in the Eighteenth Century," *Science and Christian Belief* 10 (1998): 49–71. For the purposes of this chapter, I accept Elliott Sober's assessment of Hume's objections to the design argument, in *Philosophy of Biology* (Boulder, CO: Westview, 1993), 34–35, namely that they do not defeat Paley's form of it. (Sober thinks that Darwin's case does defeat Paley.)

35. Originally published in 1802. In 2006 Oxford University Press brought out a new edition, with introduction and notes (ed. Matthew Eddy and David Knight).

36. From within the perspective of traditional Christian theology, there are many possible critiques of Paley's argument, and I will give only three. First, he overreaches: he apparently thought that ascertaining design involved discerning the purpose for a large part of the creation, and potentially for the whole of it. The book of Ecclesiastes (as I read it, following J. Stafford Wright, "The Interpretation of Ecclesiastes," *Evangelical Quarterly* 18 [1946]: 18–34), explicitly denies that such is possible. Second, he apparently assumed a static view of the creation, i.e., that what one observes today is just what came forth from the special design of the Creator. This makes no allowance for development under natural (and possibly supernatural) factors; nor does it allow for the reality of human evil. And finally, Paley apparently assumed that a fairly full range of divine attributes, including benevolence, could be discerned from the created order. Paul simply referred to "his eternal power and divine nature" (Rom. 1:20).

37. Strictly speaking, the situation is actually more complex than that: many of Paley's examples seem to be to the effect, "I cannot imagine a natural scenario that could have produced such phenomena," while Darwin replied, "But I can." Darwin described variation plus natural selection as a mechanism that *could have* produced these structures; he never supported the modality shift from *imaginable* to *possible*, much less to *plausible* or *probable*. Instead he argued, "I cannot see why it could not," shifting the burden of proof; and he offered no empirical tests for the proposed possibility.

38. In the final chapter of Darwin's *Origin* (6th ed.), he insists that he does not see that his views "should shock the religious feelings of any one," and he speaks of the evolutionary process in terms of "the laws impressed on matter by the Creator."

given a naturalistic and anti-theistic spin among many science popularizers. In this context, it is no surprise that critiques of Darwinism
would arise: and many (but certainly not all) of these critiques were
made in support of theism. The leading critiques are associated with
intelligent design, which "holds that certain features of the universe
and of living things are best explained by an intelligent cause, not an
undirected process such as natural selection."[39] The controversial claim
is that we can find instances of design in the world of nature not only
at the larger scale, but also at the smaller, and that we can have good
grounds for calling these instances "design." Examples from the larger
scale include the fine-tuning of the universe; while from the smaller
scale we have the origin of life, and the origin of the human mind.
Although many intelligent design proponents are theists of some sort,
and many of those will use their findings for apologetic purposes, that
use is not inherent in the project—hence to say, as some critics do, that
intelligent design is simply Paley's project brought up to date, is highly
mistaken.

Because I must limit the scope of this essay, I will address two main
criticisms directed against the idea of intelligent design. I have chosen
some leading and representative critics of intelligent design within the
orthodox Christian world: Francis Beckwith, Alister McGrath, and
Simon Conway Morris. These authors share the view that we may see
the evolutionary process as the outworking of characteristics that God
built into the world; by this perspective, it is God's means of creating,
and is no less God's activity for being "natural." Conway Morris has
even argued that the process is not strictly random or contingent; the
number of possible outcomes is highly restricted.[40]

The first criticism that I shall address is that intelligent design falls
into the "God-of-the-gaps" fallacy: Since (the critique goes) we cannot
think of a natural process that could produce this structure or subsystem, therefore we conclude God must have made it directly. Oftentimes
this criticism is coupled with the expectation that all gaps are simply

---

39. From the Center for Science and Culture, "Frequently Asked Questions," Discovery Institute, accessed August 31, 2016, www.discovery.org/id/faqs/.
40. Beckwith, "How to Be an Anti-Intelligent Design Advocate"; Alister McGrath, *A Fine-
Tuned Universe* (Louisville: WJK, 2009); Simon Conway Morris, "The Boyle Lecture 2005: Darwin's Compass: How Evolution Discovers the Song of Creation," *Science and Christian Belief* 18
(2006): 5–22.

gaps in our knowledge (*lacunae ignorantiae causā*).[41] Some have even suggested that it insults the Creator if we think there is any other kind of gap than this one.

A second theological criticism is related; it is the interpretation of intelligent design that declares that God "designed" some things, while he did *not* design others. Francis Beckwith states this objection clearly:

> the ID advocate tries to detect instances of design in nature by eliminating chance and necessity (or scientific law). This implies that one has no warrant to say that the latter two are the result of an intelligence that brought into being a whole universe whose parts, including its laws and those events that are apparently random, seem to work in concert to achieve a variety of ends.[42]

Let us grant for the sake of argument that there are indeed people who make these fallacious arguments—who confuse the acknowledgment "we do not know how this happened" with "there is no way this could have happened on its own," or who think "*this* is designed" therefore means "*that* is not designed." The real question is not whether some do this; the issue is whether such follies are inherent in the position. The Latin phrase to invoke is *abusus usum non tollit*: "abuse does not take away proper use." To use a biological analogy, to find a problem with one *species* does not prove that the entire *genus* (or even *family*) has the same problem; and I will argue that the genus manifestly does not.[43]

First, in asking whether we can identify what we can call "small-scale" design, one is not logically denying the large-scale, system design. It would be entirely reasonable for, say, Beckwith or McGrath

---

41. Examples of the charge are easy to multiply: e.g., Michael Roberts's review of Behe's *Darwin's Black Box* in *Science and Christian Belief* 9, no. 2 (1997): 191–192, and his reply to a response to that review, *Science and Christian Belief* 10, no. 2 (1998): 189–195; Richard Bube, "Seven Patterns for Relating Science and Theology," in *Man and Creation: Perspectives on Science and Theology*, ed. Michael Bauman (Hillsdale, MI: Hillsdale College Press, 1993), 75–103, at 83–86; Robert Pennock, *Tower of Babel: The Evidence against the New Creationism* (Cambridge, MA: MIT Press, 1999), 163–172.

42. Beckwith, "How to Be an Anti-Intelligent Design Advocate," 47. See also Conway Morris, "Darwin's Compass," 9: "ID is surely the deist's option." Neither offers any actual instances of an informed intelligent design advocate who commits this blunder.

43. Beckwith really ought to begin by addressing a more basic question, namely whether the version he objects to is a *malformed* instantiation of the species. Unfortunately, he omits this, probably because he failed to account for the different levels on which "design" might be a factor.

or Conway Morris to propose that God could make a world that he designed to produce all manner of creatures by way of evolution; these would still be his creatures, the products of his action. Indeed, I quite agree that the passages in Genesis about the "kinds" do not speak to the issue of evolution one way or the other: if the kinds arise through some kind of evolutionary process (with or without extra help from God), that is still God's process.[44]

At the same time, there may be places in which the designed process does not of itself have the capacity to produce the desired results: say, at the origin of life (which involves instituting an information processing system),[45] and at the origin of the human mind (which participates in transcendence).[46] These are not likely to be *lacunae ignorantiae causā*, since there is a principle that shows why the natures of the things involved are not enough. This means that the arguments for finding *lacunae naturae causā* in these places are worthy of discussion: if they are mistaken, the mistake is not self-evident, and the arguments deserve more than the brush-off they often receive.

Further, this openness to finding *lacunae naturae causā* within the overall process is no insult to the Creator's omnipotence. As C. S. Lewis observed,

> Omnipotence means power to do all that is intrinsically possible, not to do the intrinsically impossible. . . . Meaningless combinations of words do not suddenly acquire meaning simply because we prefix to them the two other words 'God can.' It remains true that all *things* are possible with God: the intrinsic impossibilities are not things but nonentities.[47]

---

44. I have explained this point in my comments on Denis Lamoureux's essay, in *Four Views on the Historical Adam*, ed. Michael Barrett and Ardel B. Caneday (Grand Rapids, MI: Zondervan, 2103), 73–74.

45. This is a major theme of Stephen Meyer in many places, e.g., *Signature in the Cell: DNA and the Evidence for Intelligent Design* (New York: HarperCollins, 2009).

46. Lewis argued this in many places; see my exploration in "A Peculiar Clarity: How C. S. Lewis Can Help Us Think about Faith and Science," in *The Magician's Twin: C. S. Lewis on Science, Scientism, and Society*, ed. John West (Seattle: Discovery Institute Press, 2012), 69–106. Lewis drew on Arthur James Balfour, *Theism and Humanism* (New York: Hodder & Stoughton, 1915); important figures who agree with Lewis include Alvin Plantinga, *Warrant and Proper Function* (New York: Oxford University Press, 1993); Thomas Nagel, *Mind and Cosmos: Why the Materialist Neo-Darwinian Conception of Nature Is Almost Certainly False* (New York: Oxford University Press, 2012). Concisely and trenchantly, Robert Larmer, "Theistic Complementarianism and Ockham's Razor," *Philosophia Christi* 7, no. 2 (2005): 503–514.

47. Lewis, *The Problem of Pain* (New York: Macmillan, 1962), chapter 2.

Let us turn it around. Intelligent design is not the same as Aquinas's argument from design;[48] nor is it the same as Paley's overreaching apologetic. It might or might not be "science," depending on how we define that term. But surely the better question is whether it is a true account of the world we encounter. In the three points that G. K. Chesterton pointed to, it certainly seems to be:

> No philosopher denies that a mystery still attaches to the two great transitions: the origin of the universe itself and the origin of the principle of life itself. Most philosophers have the enlightenment to add that a third mystery attaches to the origin of man himself. In other words, a third bridge was built across a third abyss of the unthinkable when there came into the world what we call reason and what we call will.[49]

Those who insist before all investigation that all gaps are *lacunae ignorantiae causā* are themselves committing a theological fallacy; as Paul Helm noted,

> It is not appropriate to argue, *a priori*, what God will and will not do with and in the physical creation, but—as with any contingent matter of fact—it is necessary to investigate what God has done.[50]

Perhaps, though, one may acknowledge the *possibility* of such *lacunae naturae causā*, but nevertheless expect that they are invisible to the human observer. There is certainly a strand of Christian thought that denies that the creation offers much testimony to its Creator—but that strand is not the main stream; nor does it speak for the critics of intelligent design that I have interacted with here, as they happily use "scientific" arguments for their natural theology.[51]

---

48. Some Thomistic critics of intelligent design make much of this point, as if it were a decisive blow. For incisive critique of such arguments, see Robert C. Koons and Logan Paul Gage, "St. Thomas Aquinas on Intelligent Design," *Proceedings of the American Catholic Philosophical Association* 85 (2012): 79–97. In further critique, we should note that Athanasius's version of a design argument, looking at the coherence of the otherwise disparate elements that make up the world, appeals to this as an unexpected outcome unless an intelligence had imposed this coherence (see his *Contra Gentes*, §37.1–3). Thus the two kinds of design we might discern, on the large scale and on the small scale, are not as far apart as Beckwith has implied!

49. G. K. Chesterton, *The Everlasting Man* (Garden City, NY: Doubleday, 1955 [1925]), 27.

50. Helm, *Providence*, 76.

51. For an example of such denial, see Neil MacDonald, *Metaphysics and the God of Israel: Systematic Theology of the Old and New Testaments* (Grand Rapids, MI: Baker, 2006), 36 (drawing on Karl Barth).

Nevertheless, there is a pastoral reason for an interest in such "design," that leaves the apologetic issue aside. Recall the various ways in which we infer that some event is "special." The stronger the confidence we legitimately have, that the outcome should have been different, the more clearly we are entitled to ponder what purpose may be behind the event—even when we do not know whose purpose, or what purpose, it might be.

This matters to daily living, because we live our lives against a backdrop of seeming arbitrariness, or even meaninglessness, as controlling the things that befall us. As Helm noted,

> Often there is a sharp disjunction between the view that God is in control, and the seeming chaos and meaninglessness of human lives, and human affairs in general. Is not this chaos a *disproof* of the Christian claim that God rules the universe providentially? It *would* be a disproof if the idea of divine providence were an empirical hypothesis, if it were built up only out of a person's direct experience and based wholly upon it. . . . Rather, for Christians, reliance upon the providence of God, and an understanding of the character of that providence, is based upon what God has revealed in Scripture, and is confirmed in their own and others' experience.[52]

There is nothing wrong with wanting confirmation—to reassure us that the purpose we profess is real, and is not simply our fanciful projection!

For example, a curious combination of coincidences and human misunderstandings led a young woman from Seattle to come to MIT, where she joined a Bible Study that was "just right" for her—led by the young graduate student whom she eventually married (me!). I would not call that a "miracle," though I am grateful, and count it God's generosity. I am content to account for it in terms of "orchestration" (with God foreknowing contingencies, choices, and even mistakes).[53] But once during my teenage years, I was looking for snakes with fellow herpetologists, and foolishly sat as the spotter on the passenger-side

52. Helm, *Providence*, 223.
53. All Christians profess such foreknowledge, though they disagree on just how to describe it in relation to God's sovereignty; I am not adjudicating that here. A deist might quarrel with the implication that God takes an interest in all of the details of each life, but Christians gladly insist on it.

hood of a car moving on a gravel road. I signaled the driver that I saw a snake; he braked, and I went sliding forward, off of the hood and right into the path of the oncoming front tire. My ordinary inclination would have been to roll counter-clockwise; for reasons I still do not grasp, I rolled clockwise instead, into the ditch on the right; the wheel stopped a little past my head. I should have been killed, or at least paralyzed. Was it an interference, a rescue by a guardian angel, something more than an orchestration? I cannot say—though I have my suspicions—but it is surprising nonetheless, and moving. A skeptic can always dismiss these as "luck"; the epistemic situation is analogous to that of answered prayer.[54]

The key point in all cases, though, is that the unexpected outcome impels us to question whether an overarching *purpose* was at work. As Gandalf says to Frodo about Bilbo's "lucky" discovery of the ring,

> Behind that there was something else at work, beyond any design of the Ring-maker. I can put it no plainer than by saying that Bilbo was *meant* to find the Ring, and not by its Maker. In which case you also were *meant* to have it. And that may be an encouraging thought.[55]

I conclude, then, that those who insist that all events are in principle "natural" have taken a position that is inadequate in all the relevant dimensions—theological, empirical, and pastoral. By contrast, the traditional Christian metaphysic gives us a sound way of thinking about God's activity *in every event*. That is, we have no right to declare a priori that we may expect to find created natural factors alone to be adequate for everything; Christians certainly have the theological resources to be happy should we find, a posteriori, that they are sufficient for most things.

The problem becomes acute when we consider that our discernment of large-scale design can yield a weaker confirmation than what we hope for. Finding design in the universe's properties, commonly called fine-tuning, is helpful, though it is hard to know just how contingent

---

54. I offer a brief discussion of that issue in Collins, *God of Miracles*, chapter 9.
55. J. R. R. Tolkien, *The Fellowship of the Ring* (Boston: Houghton-Mifflin, 1982), 65 (book 1, chapter 2).

the physical properties of the universe are.[56] To appeal to the design of orchestrated events in the world's history is very indecisive; as C. S. Lewis observed, we know far too little to offer anything remotely resembling a reliable reading of these events.[57]

Mind you, these arguments may be weaker than we would like, but they are not pastorally useless, *if we are already theists*. For example, my children, who are Christians, can properly take the stories of my narrow escape from death, and of how their mother came to MIT, as pointers to God's purposeful provision for their own lives.[58]

6. God's Action, Worldviews, and the Public Square

I mentioned above that it is controversial whether the notion of design belongs to the sciences or to some other discipline. That is an important question, but it matters more whether such notions can be seen as a true account of the world. Theists debate the degree to which instances of design should factor in to their apologetic arguments to those outside the faith. But I want to narrow in on the matter of how we function in our larger culture, working daily with people who do not share our beliefs. Should we insist that they acknowledge design anyhow? Might we at least ask them not to describe the sciences in such a way that these considerations are ruled out of court at the very outset?

For example, two leading affiliations for science teachers in the United States, the National Science Teachers Association (NSTA) and the National Association of Biology Teachers (NABT), have issued statements on teaching biological evolution.

The NSTA statement (2003 edition, reaffirmed in 2013) declares,

> Evolution in the broadest sense leads to an understanding that the natural world has a history and that cumulative change through

---

56. As Conway Morris, "Darwin's Compass," 8, said of fine-tuning, "All this smacks of design: physicists are rightly wary and the invisible host of multiverses is ever popular."

57. C. S. Lewis, "Historicism," in *Christian Reflections*, ed. Walter Hooper (Grand Rapids, MI: Eerdmans, 1967), 100–113, while noting that Christianity sees history as "a story with a well-defined plot" (103), shows how unreasonable it is to suppose that one who is not a prophet can interpret how any individual event fits into that story.

58. Thus it was not necessarily wrong of the pious James Murray, the major figure in editing the Oxford English Dictionary, to see his whole life as God's preparation for his work on the Dictionary—though one may disagree on his estimate of the importance of the task (philologist that I am, I do not disagree!). See Simon Winchester, *The Meaning of Everything: The Story of the Oxford English Dictionary* (Oxford: Oxford University Press, 2003), 134.

time has occurred and continues to occur. . . . Biological evolution refers to the scientific theory that living things share ancestors from which they have diverged; it is sometimes called "descent with modification." Biological evolution also encompasses a range of mechanisms that cause populations to change and diverge over time, and include natural selection, migration, and genetic drift. . . .

There is no longer a debate among scientists about whether evolution has and is occurring. There is debate, however, about how evolution has taken place . . . [59]

In principle, this leaves open the question of where the changes come from, and thus represents a healthy open-minded approach to science.

On the other hand, the NABT statement (2011 edition) is more decidedly naturalistic:

Evolutionary biology rests on the same scientific methodologies the rest of science uses, appealing only to natural events and processes to describe and explain phenomena in the natural world.[60]

In effect they are saying that, in order for you to be scientific and rational, you must agree beforehand that "All explanatory gaps are *lacunae ignorantiae causā* only."

It is unwise to construct, a priori, unrealistic requirements for what constitutes rationality. It makes more sense to identify actions and judgments that we know to be rational, and to discern from them what characteristics they have.[61] We know that the judgment that Stonehenge is an instance of (small-scale) *imposed design* is rational; and any philosophy that would call the rationality of this judgment into question is itself undermined by the clash between the philosophy and our intuitive recognition. We have experience of rocks, wind, and water,

59. National Science Teachers Association, "NSTA Position Statement: The Teaching of Evolution," 2003, accessed January 2016, http://www.nsta.org/about/positions/evolution.aspx.

60. National Association of Biology Teachers, "NABT Position Statement on Teaching Evolution," adopted in 1995 and modified in 1997, 2000, 2004, 2008, and 2011, accessed January 2016, http://www.nabt.org/websites/institution/?p=92. Earlier versions held that "natural selection . . . has no specific direction or goal," but this has been removed—so at least a teleological reading of the whole process is allowed for.

61. I profess the influence of Mikael Stenmark, *Rationality in Science, Religion, and Everyday Life* (Notre Dame, IN: University of Notre Dame Press, 1995), who stresses that our criteria of rationality ought to describe something it is possible for real people to achieve.

and the kinds of arrangements they produce. We recognize in Stonehenge, however, something that is beyond those natural capacities; we see that a pattern has been imposed on the components. Or consider William Clark's signature on the stone formation called Pompey's Pillar in Montana: we have no problem being confident that either Clark himself wrote it, or someone forged it. It simply cannot be a product of the stone, because a linguistic message is not a product of the properties of its medium. The key to identifying *lacunae naturae causā*, then, is to identify the principle that separates the design from the natural properties.

This approach to detecting small-scale *imposed design* is, to be sure, an intuitive one, and perhaps some people will find this to be a shortcoming. We may also feel cautious about using it, since we do not know everything there is to know about the relevant natural properties. On the other hand, we know enough about some things that we can have confidence when speaking of them. Further, to notice this kind of imposed design is not the same as knowing how or when the design was infused.

The claim that *all* appeals to special divine action lead to the God-of-the-gaps fallacy, amounts to a claim that *all gaps are gaps due to ignorance*—namely, that behind every gap lies a completely natural explanation. Now on the face of it, this is not an empirical claim: instead it sets limits on what kinds of explanations are allowed for what we meet empirically. Suppose, though, that we want to make that approach the rule in science: The only way this could be rational is if we knew beforehand that there are no such gaps; but that is beyond the bounds of the natural sciences. No scientist who disavows small-scale design should be required to say that these gaps have a supernatural cause; but it is only honest to acknowledge the gaps' existence, say, with a form of words:

> This object or event *looks like* it has an agent as its cause. I do not know of a non-purposive process that could have produced this effect. I do not wish to attribute the effect to an agent.

For better or for worse, the sciences do occupy a de facto authoritative role in our culture's public discourse, at least to the point of influencing what people will count as plausible.[62] This is because the sciences offer a story of where we came from and how we got to where we are; they also make promises about how we can proceed from here. The "new atheists" recognize this, and have hijacked the sciences to support a naturalistic story of origins. The biological providentialists recognize this as well, and put a teleological cast on natural evolution.

Stephen Barr, a biological providentialist, acknowledges, "We would all be better off if more scientists simply admitted that there are things we don't understand about the hows and whys of evolution."[63]

Now, I am not interested in laying the blame solely at the feet of these scientists.[64] All I really ask for is a suitable approach to the sciences, such as the NSTA statement offers, informed by good critical thinking. That is, a geneticist is an expert in the genome, and a paleontologist in the fossil record. Then, when they want to integrate their findings into the larger story of what it means to be human, their reasoning is open to review by all kinds of people; their expertise does not mean that their integrations automatically trump every critique.[65]

Under such an arrangement, I am sure that both the sciences and Christian faith will thrive.

---

62. It needs to be said that the definition of *science* given in the NABT statement looks more like an exercise in wielding social power than it looks like anything a philologist like me would recognize as historical and empirical lexicography.

63. Stephen Barr, "The Miracle of Evolution," *First Things* 160 (February 2006): 30–33.

64. Colin A. Russell, "The Conflict Metaphor and Its Social Origins," *Science and Christian Belief* 1, no. 1 (1989): 3–26, documents the way in which Thomas Huxley et al. waged a war to wrest cultural supremacy from the clergy. It would be wrong to blame biologists in general for this.

65. Compare the remark of C. S. Lewis, "Is Progress Possible?" in Lewis, *God in the Dock*, ed. Walter Hooper (Grand Rapids, MI: Eerdmans, 1970), 315: "I dread specialists in power because they are specialists speaking outside their special subjects. Let scientists tell us about sciences. But government involves questions about the good for man and justice, and what things are worth having at what price; and on these a scientific training gives a man's opinion no added value."

23

Theistic Evolution and the Problem of Natural Evil

GARRETT J. DEWEESE

SUMMARY

"Natural evil" refers to the pain and suffering caused by natural processes, in contrast to "moral evil," the wicked acts of morally responsible persons. The amount of suffering due to natural causes seems to show that the existence of an omnipotent, omniscient, omnibenevolent God is impossible, or at least highly improbable. Thus, until recently, Christian theologians, philosophers, and apologists had thought it was important to show that God was not directly responsible for the suffering and death caused by natural evil. However, conservative Christians who have embraced theistic evolution have *not* thought it necessary to "insulate" God from direct responsibility for natural evil. If natural evil is of necessity a part of evolutionary history, and if evolution is the process instituted by God, then it follows that God is the direct cause of natural evil—it is part of his plan. We will see, however, that opponents of theistic evolution have much better explanations of natural evil—explanations that do not make God the direct cause of the resultant pain and death.

. . . . .

"Natural evil" refers to the pain and suffering caused by natural processes, in contrast to "moral evil," the wicked acts of morally responsible persons. Surely natural evil exists, as a representative sampling of recent news shows:

- December 26, 2004, Sumatra, Indonesia. A magnitude 9.3 undersea earthquake and tsunami killed more than 230,000 in fourteen countries.
- January 12, 2010, Léogâne, Haiti. A magnitude 7.0 earthquake left more than 310,000 dead, 300,000 injured, and 1,000,000 homeless.
- AIDS: An estimated 25 million dead, with 14 million orphaned in southern Africa alone.

The tragic litany could continue, but the list wouldn't begin to communicate the grief, the suffering, the fear, the horror caused by such events. The theist—especially the Christian—faces a severe challenge: How is it that God, the Creator of the universe, is not directly responsible for evil? How is it that so much suffering due to natural causes doesn't show that the existence of an omnipotent, omniscient, omnibenevolent God is impossible, or at least highly improbable? This, in a nutshell, is the problem of natural evil.[1]

I. Preliminaries

Why should we call the sorts of events described above "evil"? Doesn't the term itself imply moral agents? I think the answer, technically speaking, is yes. However, I'll continue to use the term "natural evil." The terminology is traditional, and the problem it introduces is meaningful. So let me stipulate that by "natural evil" I'll understand any event that meets the following three conditions: (1) the event causes serious physical or mental injury to a sentient creature, resulting in severe pain or death; (2) it is not caused directly by a moral agent, and (3) it is not a case of "useful pain," that is, pain which is a positive indicator to a sentient creature of a possibly harmful condition. On this understanding,

---

1. Portions of this chapter are adapted from Garry DeWeese, "Natural Evil: A Free Process Defense," in *God and Evil*, ed. Chad Meister and James K. Dew Jr. (Downers Grove, IL: InterVarsity Press, 2012), used with permission.

then, natural evil would include not only natural disasters such as those mentioned above, but also animal suffering, such as a fawn being seriously burned in a lightning-caused forest fire and suffering great pain before dying.[2] It would also include events such as a tornado blowing down a tree, resulting in the death of a person, even if the tree should have been removed because of obvious rot. Contributory negligence of a human does not remove this event from the category of natural evil as I'm taking it here. And, clearly, pain can serve as a warning to humans and animals of a condition of potential harm, either internal to the organism or in the external environment. The pain response may be very unpleasant, but since it is part of properly functioning physiology, I won't count such "useful pain" as natural evil.

Until recently, except when the problem was stuffed in a box labeled "mystery," Christian theologians, philosophers, and apologists had taken one of two strategies, both designed to show that God was not directly responsible for the suffering and death caused by natural evil. A *theodicy* seeks to explain what God's reasons for allowing evil actually are, while a *defense* is more modest, seeking only to offer a logically possible reason for why God might have allowed evil.[3] However, an increasing number of conservative Christians have embraced theistic evolution, and have not thought it necessary to "insulate" God from direct responsibility for natural evil. If natural evil is of necessity a part of evolutionary history, and if evolution is the process instituted by God to, in the end, result in creatures on Earth with whom he could have a relationship, then it follows that God is the direct cause of natural evil—it is part of his plan.

My purpose in this chapter is threefold. First, I will survey the response of theistic evolution to the problem of natural evil, and suggest that the response is seriously inadequate since it leaves God directly responsible for natural evil. Second, after briefly touching on two creationist[4] responses, I will go into some detail on a third response, a "free process defense." I conceive of the free process defense as a *de-*

---

2. The example is from William L. Rowe, "The Problem of Evil and Some Varieties of Atheism," reprinted in *The Problem of Evil*, ed. Marilyn McCord Adams and Robert Merrihew Adams (New York: Oxford University Press, 1990), 129–130.

3. See Alvin Plantinga, *God, Freedom, and Evil* (Grand Rapids, MI: Eerdmans, 1974), 24–26.

4. I will use the term "creationism" (and "creationist") neutrally between young earth creationism and old earth creationism (or progressive creationism), making the distinction where necessary.

fense (hence its name), not a theodicy. But I'll stop short of claiming it is precisely *the* (or the *only*) reason God may have for allowing natural evil. Rather, I will claim more modestly that it offers creationists a defense that is not only logically possible but also quite plausible, with considerable empirical support. Third, my ultimate claim will be that creationists have *much better* explanations of natural evil than does theistic evolution, explanations according to which God is not directly responsible for evil. For this reason alone, creationism should be preferred to theistic evolution.

II. Theistic Evolution and Natural Evil

Advocates of theistic evolution are generally committed to several significant theses:

1. *There were no individuals, Adam and Eve, who were the progenitors of the whole human race.* George Murphy claims that "Genetic evidence now points very strongly to a minimum human population of at least 5,000 individuals at any time in history."[5] Dennis Lamoureux maintains (in a classic non sequitur), "The *de novo* creation of Adam and Eve is based on ancient science, and consequently the first man and woman in Scripture never existed."[6] R. J. Berry is unequivocal: "Science excludes a single progenitor (or pair) for humankind, beyond a reasonable doubt."[7] This thesis is a corollary of common descent, and leads directly to the next thesis.

2. *There was no "fall" of humanity, at a point in time, from a state of innocence into sin.* Murphy writes that

[S]ince the first humans were the product of a long evolutionary history that in some ways would have encouraged competitive and selfish behaviors, the idea of an initial state of "original righteousness" is implausible. Thus modification of the idea of a historically

---

5. George L. Murphy, "Necessary Natural Evil and Inevitable Moral Evil," *Perspectives on Science and Christian Faith* (*PSCF*) 68, no. 2 (June 2016): 112. Murphy's is one of four theme articles in this significant issue of *Perspectives* devoted to addressing the problem of natural evil from the perspective of theistic evolution.

6. Denis O. Lamoureux, *Evolutionary Creation: A Christian Approach to Evolution* (Eugene, OR: Wipf & Stock, 2008), 330.

7. R. J. (Sam) Berry, "Natural Evil: Genesis, Romans, and Modern Science," *PSCF* 68, no. 2 (June 2016): 95.

first sin ("original sin originating") is needed, and the traditional explanation for moral evil needs revision.[8]

Lamoureux eschews nuance:

> First, Adam never existed. . . . Second, Adam never actually sinned because he never existed. Consequently, sin did not enter the world on account of Adam. Third, Adam was never judged by God to suffer and die. Again, he lacks existence, and as a result the ability to sin, so he was never condemned for his transgression.[9]

The implications of this view for the origins of human moral evil (sin) are profound, especially in light of passages such as Romans 5:12–21, but they are the subject of other chapters in this volume.[10] What concerns us here, though, is that proponents of theistic evolution, by denying a space-time fall, cannot (and do not) use the fall in an explanation, defense, or theodicy of natural evil. This is the third thesis.

3. *The "evil" in our world cannot ultimately be attributed to a "fall." Natural evil cannot be a consequence of God's "curse" on creation after a "fall."* Lamoureux insists, "To conclude, there is no sin-death problem. Adam never existed, and therefore suffering and death did not enter the world in divine judgment for his transgression."[11] He argues elsewhere that

> [S]cience has made remarkable advances in understanding the natural world since the sixteenth century and Calvin's belief in a cosmic fall. The fossil record offers overwhelming evidence that predation, suffering, and death have been on Earth for hundreds of millions of years prior to the appearance of humans and their sins. Geology also provides indisputable evidence that floods, droughts, and ice ages have occurred throughout Earth history, indicating that

---

8. Murphy, "Necessary Natural Evil," 112.

9. Lamoureux, *Evolutionary Creation*, 319. Not all proponents of theistic evolution are quite so dogmatic. Denis Alexander, e.g., considers several "models" which differ in their commitment to a historical Adam and a historical fall. See chapter 12, "Evolution and the Fall," in Denis Alexander, *Creation or Evolution: Do We Have to Choose?* (Grand Rapids, MI: Monarch, 2008), 254–276. My personal belief is that there was indeed an original pair of humans, Adam and Eve, whose sin—the fall—affected all subsequent humans. Moral evil is the result.

10. See the discussions of Romans 5 by Wayne Grudem on pages 805–810 and by Guy Waters on page 885. See also Garrett J. DeWeese, "Paul, Second Adam, and Theistic Evolution," *Christian Research Journal* 37 (2014).

11. Lamoureux, *Evolutionary Creation*, 329.

they are not 'fruits of sin.' And environmental science reveals that 'noxious insects' play an essential role in maintaining ecological balance.[12]

Again, there are serious implications here for the interpretation of texts such as Romans 8:18–28, which are dealt with in another chapter.[13] It is clear, though, that, according to theistic evolution, the fall cannot explain natural evil. In fact, it seems that evolution demands that natural evils occur—the fourth thesis.

4. *During the 4.55-billion-year history of planet Earth, and the 3.8-billion-year history of life on Earth, natural cataclysmic events, predation, pain, and death, have necessarily accompanied (and in some cases have driven) the evolution of life.* Bethany Sollereder notes,

> Evolutionary history has shown how the devastations of the past—such as the great extinction events and the development of predator-prey relations—have generated immense amounts of biodiversity and physical values. In the poetic words of Holmes Rolston, the "cougar's fang has carved the limbs of the fleet-footed deer."[14]

John R. Wood, in an engaging article concerning the ecological function of organic death, asks, "Can we conceive any functioning ecosystem, under any of the range of suggested time frames (days to millennia to billions of years), functioning without organisms dying? Not under any ecological conditions that we have experienced or theorized."[15]

5. *In light of the above theses, natural evil is seen as inherent in the way God chose to create; no theodicy or defense is necessary.* Sollereder says, "God, it seems, has chosen to use an evolutionary process to create the world even though it is replete with suffering, death, and extinction," and then asks, "Why?"[16] Her answer assumes the truth of

---

12. Denis O. Lamoureux, "Beyond the Cosmic Fall and Natural Evil," *PSCF* 68, no. 1 (March 2016): 45–46. In this article, Lamoureux ascribes the doctrine of a "cosmic fall" to the redaction of an "optimistic Priestly" source and a "pessimistic Jahwist" source, both imbedded in a false prescientific mind-set. This of course assumes the validity of a literary-critical methodology of Old Testament interpretation.

13. See the references in note 10 above.

14. Bethany Sollereder, "Evolution, Suffering, and the Creative Love of God," *PSCF* 68, no. 2 (June 2016): 102.

15. John R. Wood, "An Ecological Perspective on the Role of Death in Creation," *PSCF* 68, no. 2 (June 2016): 81.

16. Sollereder, "Evolution," 103.

theistic evolution. Referring to the work of Christopher Southgate,[17] she imagines that "evolution is not only the sole available option to fill the earth, but perhaps it is also the only way to give rise to beings that will one day populate heaven."[18] Keith Miller concludes, "Creation is good, and the death and pain embedded within it are part of God's will and purpose for it. Creation is not a fallen thing to be conquered and controlled, but a divine gift we are to serve and rule and enjoy as God's stewards."[19]

William Dembski summarizes, "By letting Darwinian natural selection serve as a designer substitute, theistic evolutionists can refer all those botched and malevolent designs to evolution. This, in their view, is supposed to resolve the problem of natural evil."[20] Dembski concludes, "Bottom line: Evolution, with or without God, does nothing to mitigate the problem of evil."[21]

III. Creationist Responses

My claim, as stated, is that creationists have *better* explanations of natural evil, and so have a theodicy or defense against the charge that God is directly responsible for evil.[22]

Young earth creationists have a ready response. Since the universe, and so the earth, are much younger than the scientific consensus, somewhere around ten thousand years old, clearly evolution is impossible. So there necessarily was a first human pair, Adam and Eve. Also, young earth creationists hold tightly to a literal reading of Genesis 1–3, including a space-time fall which introduced evil to God's "very good" creation. Human sin, rather than processes of planetary or biological evolution, is responsible for the suffering and death in the natural world.[23]

---

17. Christopher Southgate, *The Groaning of Creation: God, Evolution, and the Problem of Evil* (Louisville: Westminster John Knox, 2008), 29.

18. Sollereder, "Evolution," 103.

19. Keith B. Miller, "'And God Saw that It Was Good': Death and Pain in the Created Order," *PSCF*, 63, no. 2 (June 2011), 92.

20. William Dembski, "Evil, Creation, and Intelligent Design," in *God and Evil*, 262.

21. Ibid., 269.

22. Keith Miller offers an excellent survey of different serious attempts to deal with the problem of natural evil; his preferred solution, though, rests on his commitment to theistic evolution (Keith B. Miller, "'And God Saw That It Was Good': Death and Pain in the Created Order," *PSCF*, 63, no. 2 [June 2011]).

23. William Dembski sees all natural evil, even animal suffering in the world before the arrival of humans, as retroactively due to human sin (William A. Dembski, *The End of Christianity:*

Many conservative Christians, however, believe the scientific evidence strongly favors an old universe (some 13.8 billion years) and an old earth (4.55 billion years), see no theological doctrine entailing a young earth, and claim a consistent hermeneutic that does not require that Genesis 1 portrays literal, consecutive, twenty-four-hour days.[24] My account below is from an old earth creationist perspective.

IV. A "Free Process" Defense

One standard defense deployed against the problem of moral evil is the free will defense.[25] Theologian and scientist John Polkinghorne suggests a similar strategy to address natural evil:

> The moral and physical evils of the world result from the freedom granted by God to humankind, and to the whole developing physical process, respectively. [The] free will defence, relating to moral evil, needs augmentation by a free process defence, relating to physical evil.[26]

In this chapter I'll take up Polkinghorne's suggestion and attempt to show how such a free process defense might be possible.[27] I'll develop a free process defense in three stages. I'll begin with the claim that chaos systems in our world make natural evil possible. I'll then argue that God might well have good reasons to create such a world, even with the possibility of natural evil. And I'll claim that even God cannot make such a world where natural evil never occurs. Finally, I'll reflect on some implications of the argument.

1. Free Processes

Stage one of the free process defense goes like this:

Finding a Good God in an Evil World [Nashville: B&H, 2009]). While interesting, I won't pursue this line of argument here.

24. See, e.g., Henri Blocher, *In the Beginning: The Opening Chapters of Genesis* (Downers Grove, IL: InterVarsity Press, 1984); Victor P. Hamilton, *The Book of Genesis: Chapters 1–17*, New International Commentary on the Old Testament, ed. R. K. Harrison (Grand Rapids, MI: Eerdmans, 1990); John C. Lennox, *Seven Days That Divide the World: The Beginning According to Genesis and Science* (Grand Rapids, MI: Zondervan, 2011).

25. Plantinga, *God, Freedom, and Evil*; John S. Feinberg, *The Many Faces of Evil* (Wheaton, IL: Crossway, 2004), chapter 4.

26. John Polkinghorne, *Science and Providence* (Boston: Shambala, 1989), 3.

27. Polkinghorne is a theistic evolutionist. My development of a free process defense, though, is from a creationist perspective.

(1) The natural world is a dynamic world composed of a vast number of interacting nonlinear dissipative dynamical systems that are sensitively dependent on initial conditions.

(2) Nonlinear dissipative dynamical systems may, given a very slight disturbance in initial conditions, lose equilibrium and behave in wildly erratic ways.

(3) Wildly erratic systems in the natural world cause natural evil.

Unpacking the Concepts

First, by "dynamic world" I mean simply one that can change over time. A "nonlinear dissipative dynamical system," more precisely, is a mathematical concept that picks out a system that changes over time (dynamical), which is open, exchanging energy with its environment (dissipative), and in which the evolving elements are not linked in a regular, direct, proportional manner (nonlinear). The key idea, though, is that a dynamical system is *sensitively dependent on initial conditions*. Such systems exhibit the phenomenon of *deterministic chaos*: very small differences in initial conditions result in widely diverging outcomes.[28] Dynamical systems that are in this way sensitively dependent on initial conditions are called "chaos systems." In what follows, I'll often say simply "dynamic world" for a world that contains this sort of system. And I'll refer to such systems as "free processes."

Here's an example. At one time or another, probably all of us have tried to balance an inverted broom in the palm of our hand. At first it's easy to keep the broom fairly stable, but sooner or later, the initial conditions of the system will be altered by varying air currents or slight tremors in our hand or arm, and we will have to make larger and larger corrections until finally equilibrium is completely lost and the broom falls.

In 1972, the meteorologist Edward Lorenz gave a famous speech to the American Association for the Advancement of Science titled "Predictability: Does the Flap of a Butterfly's Wings in Brazil Set Off a Tornado in Texas?"[29] The idea is simple, but the implications are

---

28. James Gleick, *Chaos: Making a New Science* (New York: Penguin, 1987), 230–239; 280–283; Celso Grebogi, Edward Ott, and James A. Yorke, "Chaos, Strange Attractors, and Fractal Basin Boundaries in Nonlinear Dynamics," *Science* 238 (1987): 585–718.

29. The paper is widely available on the Internet.

startling. Imagine that we could divide the lower atmosphere into one-square-foot cubes, and at each corner of each cube of air we could locate a sensor. Each sensor would relay to a massive supercomputer all relevant meteorological data: atmospheric pressure, temperature, humidity, wind velocity, and so on. With the earth covered by this enormous web of sensors, with such an accurate "map" of the atmosphere, couldn't we precisely predict the weather anywhere on Earth? No, comes the answer: the flap of a butterfly's wings within one cube in, say, Brazil, could disturb the initial conditions in the surrounding cubes, with wildly unanticipated results elsewhere. As a result of Lorenz's thought experiment, the name "butterfly effect" was given to chaos systems.[30]

It's important to understand that chaos systems are not random. Such free processes are quite often capable of being described by differential equations. However, the class of differential equations which can be solved is quite small. Nonlinear differential equations—those that describe the behavior of nonlinear dynamical systems—are in general unsolvable. In practice, numerical methods are employed to approximate a solution to a sufficient degree of accuracy, given specified initial conditions and other theoretical constraints. The study of chaos, along with the development of powerful computers, has opened a large class of previously intractable differential equations to new mathematical techniques. However, the degree of dependence on initial conditions often lies below the sensitivity of our most accurate instruments. In numerical calculations of the evolution of the system over time (e.g., in a computer program), round-off errors at the smallest decimal value will dramatically affect the final result. And it turns out that no matter how closely the initial states of two nonlinear dynamical systems resemble each other, there will always be a third state between the other two which will evolve in a wildly divergent way. So although chaos systems are not random, they are, from the human standpoint, unpredictable.

And one more important note about chaos systems: They may behave in a quite orderly way for periods of time, but quite dramatically

---

30. For an entertaining and readable history of the study of chaos systems, see Gleick, *Chaos*; or Roger Lewin, *Complexity: Life at the Edge of Chaos* (New York: Macmillan, 1992).

become disorderly, exhibiting the characteristics commonly associated with the ordinary language use of "chaos." A graphical plot of the behavior of chaos systems typically shows regions of order and regions of disorder.[31] So the presence of a vast number of interacting chaos systems in the world does not entail that chaos, understood as disordered, out-of-whack behavior, will always prevail. In other words, chaos systems are not *necessarily* chaotic; rather, chaos systems entail the *possibility* of chaotic behavior.

Defending the Premises

Premise (1) claims that our world is made up of a vast number of interacting chaos systems. But is it? The answer is clearly yes. Chaos systems abound. The past five or so decades have seen tremendous progress in discovering, analyzing, and understanding chaos systems. Weather patterns, of course, but also many other phenomena in the world, are chaos systems. The behavior of automobile independent suspension systems; the propagation of electrical impulses through heart muscles; the fluctuations of the stock market; the firing patterns of neurons in the brain; the balance of species populations in ecosystems; patterns of turbulence generated by an aircraft's wing; the allocation of sales versus production staffs in industries; superposition of waveforms, as in broadcast interference patterns—all these meet the classical definition of a chaos system: all are sensitively dependent on initial conditions. Both ordinary and scientific investigation shows that we do indeed inhabit a dynamic world, filled with innumerable free processes.

Premise (2) claims that such systems may go out of control, and premise (3) says that the result of such systems going chaotic is often natural evil. For example, unpredictable long-range weather patterns affect crops, and in turn disturb patterns of supply and demand, change the logistics of getting food to markets, induce unexpected economic fluctuations, and even cause large-scale migrations of animal or even human populations. Changing environmental factors affect the mutation and transmission of diseases, leading to drug-resistant bacteria and the possibility of pandemics. Plate tectonics causes earthquakes

---

31. The graphical depiction of the behavior of chaos systems will be a plot in "phase space." The regions of orderly behavior are called "strange attractors." The details need not concern us here.

and tsunamis, and unleashes volcanic fury, destroying forests and cities. And so on and on.

Our world of interacting chaos systems is a much wilder, more disorderly place than was once thought.

2. The Goodness of Free Processes

The second part of the argument goes like this:

(4) A dynamic world in which free creatures can exercise genuine creativity, thereby bringing about truly novel effects, is better than a static world.

(5) God would want to create a dynamic world.

It's easy to see that a world composed of interacting free processes will be a world where natural evil is possible. But premise (4) claims that such a world is better than a world in which natural evil is not possible, and (5) says God would want to create such a world. How might premises (4) and (5) be defended?

Biological Considerations

Several lines of argument support the claim that a dynamic world is better than a static world; we'll look at just two. The first has to do with neurophysiology. In mammals, the propagation of electrical impulses across cardiac muscles is sensitively dependent on initial conditions—it is a chaos system. And in all animals of a certain brain complexity, the pattern of neural activity is also a chaos system. Strong empirical evidence points to the conclusion that it is beneficial to life—perhaps even essential—that these are chaos systems. Take the neuromuscular activity of the heart, a complex three-dimensional propagation of electrical signals. Chaotic behavior here allows the organism to cope with heart disease and minor heart attacks. If the neuroelectrical propagation were linear, any interruption or perturbation in heart physiology, such as that caused by any one of many varieties of arrhythmia, would be fatal. However, since the propagation pattern is chaotic, a small change in the initial conditions will produce a significantly different pattern, thus allowing for many minor abnormal cardiac events to occur without serious heart damage or death.[32]

Similar considerations apply to neural firing patterns in the complex brains of higher mammals and humans. The astronomical number of possible pathways through the brain would make thought, sensation, and especially memory, extremely problematic if neuron firing were a linear phenomenon, even using a complex tree structure analogous to algorithms used in many computer applications.[33] If the neural network of the brain were a linear or orderly tree structure, it is doubtful that much of the brain's activity in the affected area could be recovered after even a minor brain injury. Nonlinear pathways, however, offer hope of reestablishing proper brain function. Empirical evidence shows that recovery of both heart and brain from trauma is accelerated, if not made possible in the first place, by the nonlinear dynamical structure of the respective neural pathways.[34] Indeed, life itself—or at least life of the complexity as we know it in higher mammals and humans—depends on physiological chaos systems.

A second line of reasoning that free processes are desirable in our world is an aesthetic argument having to do with novelty and creativity. If the natural world were static, or even linearly mechanistic, rather than nonlinearly dynamic, natural processes presumably could not produce novel outcomes. Trees and ferns, snowflakes and clouds, shorelines and faces would all be predictable, with perhaps only a small number of variations within well-defined limits. But nonlinear systems which are sensitively dependent on initial conditions allow for infinite variety. Surely our world is much more interesting and beautiful as a result.

But we may wonder whether novelty and beauty are sufficient to justify God's creating nonlinear systems with the possibility of horrendous natural evil. But it is also true that the presence of chaos systems makes possible invention of novel processes and products by human agents. A mechanistic world, where natural processes would "snap back" to their original orientation, would not allow for genuine

---

32. Gleick, *Chaos*, 280–284.

33. Martin Carrier and Jurgen Mittelstrass, *Mind, Brain, Behavior: The Mind-Body Problem and the Philosophy of Psychology* (Berlin: Walter de Gruyter, 1991), 261 and passim.

34. Gleick, *Chaos*, 298–299 and references cited there.

696   The Philosophical Critique of Theistic Evolution

creativity in science, technology, and engineering. Certainly not all of humanity's creativity is for the good, but it's difficult to imagine how impoverished the world and our individual lives would be without the possibility of bringing about truly novel effects in the world. Indeed, as creatures made in God's image, the exercise of reasoned creativity seems essential to a meaningful and flourishing life. And that creativity depends on both the unpredictable patterns of brain activity and the flexibility of nature inherent in nonlinear systems and thus capable of quite unexpected and entirely new results. Human creativity depends on the possibility of a nonlinear dynamical world.[35]

Theological Considerations

Premise (5) claims that God desires a dynamical world. Within a Christian worldview, we see, in Genesis 1, God bringing order out of the chaos of verse 2, and then in Genesis 1:28 and 2:15 assigning to humanity the duty to exercise responsible stewardship of the earth. Those commands imply that humans can indeed affect the natural world, so the world must be a dynamical one that will respond to human activity.

We can see why God might well have regarded complex organisms made possible by nonlinear dynamical systems as a good which would outweigh the possibility of natural evil inherent in those systems, and that he might well have regarded the openness and creative potential of such a world as of higher intrinsic value than a linear, deterministic world.

But I think we can say even more in support of (5). I'll introduce this line of argument with examples of moral evil, and then make the application to natural evil. A critic might claim that it would be possible for God to create a world where the laws of nature are as they are in the actual world—with solid material objects that can strike living creatures with enough force to cause significant damage, even death; and with genuinely free moral agents who sometimes go wrong. It would be possible in such a world for an evil agent, Al, acting in rage, to clobber his neighbor, Bo, with a baseball bat, killing him. But, asks the critic, why can't God act in that world so that no actual damage would be

---

35. Roger Penrose, *The Emperor's New Mind* (New York: Oxford University Press, 1992), 11, 79–102.

done? Why couldn't God simply dematerialize the baseball bat when it approached poor Bo's head and rematerialize the bat afterwards? Al would still be free to act in anger, but no damage would be done.

Only brief reflection, however, shows that such a world certainly would not be a world in which any science or technology or even learning would occur, since the laws of nature would be so apparently random.[36] But it gets worse. For we could invoke the plausible principle that God would allow actions that otherwise would be evil, if doing so would prevent an equal or greater evil. So if Al takes his automatic rifle to the mall and fires blindly into the crowd, the bullets would dematerialize so no innocent people would be harmed. But if God foreknew that Cal would become a mass murderer sometime in the future, then God could allow Al's bullets to kill Cal, thereby preventing greater harm. Now here's why that world would be greatly impoverished: the denizens of that world would have no reason to live responsibly and act morally, since they would have learned from history or experience that they could never do anything really evil. Consequently, morality and responsibility would be undermined. That world might contain freedom of thought, but not of action; it would not, then, contain genuine moral good.[37]

Now if natural evil were not possible in that world, it also would be a world in which natural science, engineering, even education would be vacuous. Courage and excitement would be absent, since no real harm would occur. Careful structural design would be meaningless, since no earthquake or tornado would destroy homes or buildings. Medical arts would be nonexistent, since disease would not harm or kill. It would not be a world worthy of rational, creative agents, even if it was a world that was livable.

But note carefully: the claim is that natural evil is *possible*, not that it is *necessary*. However, for advocates of theistic evolution such as Murphy, Lamoureux, Sollereder, and others, the fact of evolution entails the necessity of natural evil (where the necessity modality is physical, that is, according to the laws of nature).

---

36. A similar point is made by Sollereder, "Evolution," 100; and Murphy, "Necessary Natural Evil," 116.

37. Several philosophers have offered arguments along these lines; e.g., David O'Connor, "A Variation on the Free Will Defense," *Faith and Philosophy* 4 (1987): 160–167.

3. What God Cannot Do

A very obvious objection clamors for attention at this juncture. Very simply, why *couldn't* God have made a dynamic world that never goes out of whack? For the free process defense to go through, I need to defend one more premise:

> (6) Even God cannot make a dynamic world in which natural evil could not occur.

It may seem clearly false to suggest that there is something God cannot do, but a little reflection shows differently. First, God cannot do something contrary to his perfect nature. He cannot commit suicide, or break his promises, or decide that torturing philosophers for fun is good. And we should be very thankful that God's nature is perfect and he *cannot* do such things. Beyond those sorts of things, we also understand that God cannot do what is logically impossible. He cannot make a square circle, or a married bachelor, or make 5+7 = green chocolate middle-C.

So the question is this: Is it possible for God to make a dynamic world where natural evil is not a possibility? I suggest that there are several reasons for thinking it is not. We can begin to make progress here by distinguishing the *possibility* for evil from the *actuality* or *necessity* of evil. The free will defense against moral evil claims that by creating genuinely free creatures, God only created the *possibility* for moral evil, not the *actuality* (and surely then, not the *necessity*) of such evil; similarly, the free process defense claims that by creating a dynamic world, God merely created the *possibility* for natural evil, not its *actuality* (and certainly not its *necessity*).

It is certainly logically possible that any world containing as many interacting nonlinear dynamical systems as the actual world would be one in which the systems themselves, behaving in a dissipative non-linear fashion, would eventually impact other systems, altering the conditions and knocking them out of equilibrium. And as soon as the world was populated with even minimally free creatures who could move about in the environment, perturbations would be introduced and equilibrium would be lost (recall the butterfly effect).

If this line of reasoning is correct, then although God surely knew (given his omniscience) that natural evil would occur, he had overriding reasons to create such a world anyway. Putting it a bit differently, God created the world as an open system of cause and effect, granting a qualified self-sufficiency to nature to operate according to the laws that he designed. In this world, then, the wind could blow a tree down, causing injury or death, and God would not be the direct cause.

4. Reflections

In this final section I want to reflect briefly on the possible connection between natural and moral evil. Working from within the Christian tradition, I want to suggest that both human and demonic agents can cause natural free processes to become chaotic in behavior. To the degree that this is so, the resultant "natural" evil would be moral evil after all.

Demons and Natural Evil

Following Augustine and a number of subsequent theologians, C. S. Lewis invokes satanic forces as the direct cause of natural evils:

> It seems to me, therefore, a reasonable supposition, that some mighty created power had already been at work for ill on the material universe, or the solar system, or, at least, the planet Earth, before ever man came on the scene: and that when man fell, someone had, indeed, tempted him. . . . If there is such a power, as I myself believe, it may well have corrupted the animal creation before man appeared.[38]

Alvin Plantinga writes in the same vein:

> Satan, so the traditional doctrine goes, is a mighty nonhuman spirit who, along with many other angels, was created long before God created man. Unlike most of his colleagues, Satan rebelled against God and has since been wreaking whatever havoc he can. The result is natural evil. So the natural evil we find is due to free actions of nonhuman spirits.[39]

---

38. C. S. Lewis, *The Problem of Pain*, in *The Complete C. S. Lewis Signature Classics* (New York: HarperOne, 2002), 632.

39. Alvin Plantinga, *God, Freedom, and Evil* (Grand Rapids, MI: Eerdmans, 1974), 58.

Plantinga emphasizes that this suggestion need not be true for a defense (as opposed to a theodicy) to succeed; it need only be logically possible and consistent with the hypotheses of God's omnipotence and omnibenevolence.

No reader of the Bible can doubt that the authors of the Bible, as well as most of the people and cultures portrayed in its pages, believed in the existence of a created spiritual being, Satan, who rebelled against God and gained the allegiance of a myriad of other spiritual beings.[40] Some commentators have seen figurative depictions of Satan's rebellion and judgment in passages such as Isaiah 14:3–23 and Ezekiel 28:11–19.[41]

Now, whatever a modern reader makes of these passages, unless she wishes to dismiss totally the worldview of both the Old and the New Testaments, and indeed of Jesus himself, she must allow for some sort of prehistoric cataclysmic judgment of the Devil. And she must allow for some sort of interaction between the material realm and the immaterial. The Gospels especially abound with accounts of physical effects caused directly by demonic activity: dumbness (Matt. 9:32–33); blindness (Matt. 12:22–23); epileptic seizures (Matt. 17:14–18); supernatural strength (Mark 5:1–10); physical deformity (Luke 13:10–13); and even a mass drowning of pigs (Mark 5:11–13).

If this is indeed the case, and Christian theology informed by the authoritative Word of God accepts that it is, then it is entirely plausible that the spiritual "fall" of Satan could have occasioned physical effects on Earth. It is logically possible that this was the event that introduced the initial perturbations into the dynamical systems that God had created in equilibrium. And continued activity of the demonic horde could, over the history of the world, continue to perturb chaos systems as part of their ongoing campaign against the establishment of the kingdom of God.

Seen in this light, there is added significance in God's command to Adam and Eve to "subdue" the earth (Gen. 1:28): the activity of Satanic hordes aimed at disruption, creating devastating chaotic conditions,

---

40. Millard J. Erickson, *Christian Theology*, 2nd ed. (Grand Rapids, MI: Baker, 1998), 470–475.
41. Ibid., 604; Charles Lee Feinberg, *The Prophecy of Ezekiel* (Chicago: Moody, 1969), 161–164.

needs to be restrained. Adam was charged to work and watch over the relative perfection of the garden of Eden. Moral evil was already present in the garden (the serpent surely represents Satan; Gen. 3:1–7), and—if my argument to this point holds—natural evil was also present in the world. A part of humanity's task is to work to correct natural evil, realizing all the while that the ultimate elimination of both moral and natural evil awaits the eschaton—a view endorsed by the apostle Paul in Romans 8:19–25.[42]

Thus it is plausible that at least some natural evil is the result of the activity of Satan and his hordes. Consider just one example, the movement of tectonic plates. Plate subduction recycles greenhouse gases, and contributes to the relative stability of the earth's surface temperature by conducting away the heat generated in the earth's radioactive core.[43] While it seems to us today that such activity inevitably produces volcanism and earthquakes, it is certainly possible that, as God created the earth, the process of subduction was smooth, only later being subjected to forces, produced or directed with malevolent intent by Satan's hordes, that made the movement chaotic. It is also possible that such reasoning could apply to ecosystemic interactions such as predation, to weather events, and so on.

Humans and Natural Evil

While I have just suggested that some natural evil is due to malicious demonic activity, surely human activity can also be responsible. If immaterial evil beings—demons—can plausibly affect the free processes of the natural world, surely human persons can do so as well. Whether out of ignorance, inattention, arrogance, or outright evil intent, humans can on a small scale affect the natural world, and small effects can bring about grave ill. Deforestation, overgrazing, and poor land management, for example, have contributed to severe famine and population dislocation in the Sahel region of sub-Saharan Africa. Overuse of antibiotics has led to the rise of drug resistant bacteria such as MRSA (Methicillin-resistant *Staphylococcus aureus*), with the incidence of

---

42. This is to suggest that science, medicine, engineering, and technology partake, in part, of spiritual warfare.

43. Sollereder, "Evolution," 100.

serious infections and deaths significantly rising. Overfishing of Atlantic cod led to a collapse of the cod population in the North Atlantic in the 1990s, and in a time without readily available replacement sources of food could have caused starvation of coastal populations.

Other examples of serious natural effects of human actions could be given; all stem from ignorance, inattention, arrogance, or evil intentions such as greed. The failure of humans to act wisely as God's stewards of the natural world can lead to natural evil—which, as in the case of demons, would be ultimately caused by moral evil. All of these cases can be analyzed as instances of nonlinear dynamical systems that had been significantly disturbed out of a generally stable equilibrium, with harmful consequences.

Finally, it is at least logically possible, and (apparently depending on your politics) likely, that thoughtless, ignorant, or selfish human behaviors are leading to global warming conditions that will bring profound suffering to the poorest of the poor. Climate change might after all be a purely natural phenomenon, and the suffering it possibly causes would be natural evil, the result of free processes pushed to disequilibrium. But it might, perhaps after it is too late to ameliorate the negative effects, be recognized as a result of moral evil.

V. Conclusion

I have attempted to show how a world, composed of a vast array of interacting nonlinear dynamical dissipative systems—chaos systems— makes natural evil *possible* but not *necessary*. And I have suggested that God might well have good reasons to have created such a world. I've concluded by suggesting that at least some (and perhaps much) natural evil is due to the actions of moral agents, demonic and human.

Consequently, old earth creationists have at hand an explanation according to which the natural processes in the world today that result in natural evil are perturbations of systems originally created by God in a "very good" state of equilibrium. God is not directly responsible for natural evil, as he must be in a theistic evolution model. This conclusion is in concert with the consistent views of theologians and philosophers throughout the history of the church.

Since, then, we have a significantly better explanation of God's relation to natural evil, we have yet another reason to prefer creationism to theistic evolution.

But in all our theologizing and philosophizing, we must not forget the suffering and grief caused by natural evil. And we must also remember that there is still much in the world that is good and lovely and worthy of admiration. Even while mirroring the suffering of the Cross,[44] the world still reflects the glory of the Creator.

---

44. A point developed nicely by Murphy, "Necessary Natural Evil."

24

Bringing Home the Bacon: The Interaction of Science and Scripture Today

COLIN R. REEVES

SUMMARY

Recent years have seen several examples where apparent scientific "truth" has been used to cast doubt on traditional biblical doctrines. Principally, this has concerned the reinterpretation of the early chapters of Genesis in order to question the need for a historical Adam, and for a fall that entailed physical death. This chapter addresses not so much the biblical evidence for these doctrines, which has been forcefully defended elsewhere, but the underlying methodology of those who question them. Their approach can be traced back to Francis Bacon's works of the early seventeenth century, which argued that God has spoken in "Two Books," where the "book of nature" (for which, today, read science) is the key to interpreting the Bible. It is commonly asserted that (contrary to writers such as Richard Dawkins) there is no conflict between science and Scripture: these two books are "complementary" and not opposed to each other. In this chapter we shall see that, like Bacon, those who promote this view most assiduously do not in fact so regard the interaction between science and the Bible. "Science" (that is, science assumed to be an *autonomous* source of truth) *in practice* always trumps Scripture. This has consequences, not only for particular doctrines such as the fall or the atonement, but for a whole way of doing theology. The Bible is no longer inerrant, authoritative, sufficient, or even perspicuous. The "scientific" approach to biblical interpretation really follows closely the lines of classical liberalism. Thus, there is indeed a conflict between "Science" and Scripture, a conflict that is dangerous not only for theology but also for true science itself.

. . . . .

Introduction

Advocates of "theistic evolution" are increasingly urging us to modify or even abandon historic biblical doctrines. That Adam and Eve were the ancestors of the whole human race; that the fall was an event in space-time history that introduced sin and death to the world; that Christ died as a substitutionary atonement for the sins of his people— all these need revision.

Atheists have long contended that this logically follows from a belief in evolution. One atheist argues as follows:

> . . . evolution destroys utterly and finally the very reason Jesus' earthly life was supposedly made necessary. Destroy Adam and Eve and the original sin, and in the rubble you will find the sorry remains of the son of god. . . . If Jesus was not the redeemer who died for our sins, and this is what evolution means, then Christianity is nothing![1]

For too long the church has refused to face up to this argument, preferring to pretend that we can accept the claims of evolution and still adhere to historical Christianity. But recent books such as those by Francis Collins[2] and Denis Alexander[3] have raised important issues for the Christian church, as has the advent of the BioLogos[4] website. Several authors have pointed out[5] that theistic evolution has serious implications for the integrity of the gospel of Jesus Christ.

---

1. G. Richard Bozarth, "The Meaning of Evolution," *The American Atheist* (February 1978): 30.
2. Francis Collins, *The Language of God* (London: Simon & Schuster, 2007).
3. Denis Alexander, *Creation or Evolution: Do We Have to Choose?* (Oxford: Monarch, 2008).
4. BioLogos is a term invented by Francis Collins.
5. Norman Nevin, ed., *Should Christians Embrace Evolution?* (Leicester, UK: Inter-Varsity Press, 2009).

Many who disagree with adherents of theistic evolution may previously have supposed, in all charity, that theistic evolutionists had not thought through these implications, especially the soteriological ones, but supporters of theistic evolution are starting to break cover. Joseph Bankard, for example, argues (with commendable honesty) on the Bio-Logos website that "substitutionary atonement does not fit well with the theory of evolution." He explains,

> If evolution is true, then the universe is very old, humans evolved from primates . . . [and] . . . the Fall is not a historical event. . . . However, if denying the historical Fall calls into question the doctrine of original sin, then it also calls into question the role of the cross of Christ within substitutionary atonement. If Jesus didn't die in order to overcome humanity's original sin, then why *did* Jesus die? What is Jesus, the second Adam, attempting to restore with the cross, if not the sin of the first Adam? Substitutionary atonement sees original sin as a major reason for Christ's death. But macroevolution calls the Fall and the doctrine of original sin into question. Thus, evolution poses a significant challenge to substitutionary atonement.[6]

Part 2 of Bankard's article explains that, in his alternative view of the cross, "Christ's death was *not part of God's divine plan*" (emphasis added). Could anyone more blatantly contradict Acts 2:23? But this follows from the theistic evolution approach to Scripture, a typical example of which is articulated by Alexander in an article on the Faraday Institute website.[7] A common view today, the stock thesis of the "new atheists," is that science and religion are intrinsically in conflict. In fact, science has "won." This is not new, of course—as T. H. Huxley put it, "whenever science and orthodoxy have been fairly opposed, the latter has been forced to retire from the lists, bleeding and crushed if not annihilated."[8] Alexander rejects the conflict thesis, as well as the

---

6. Joseph Bankard, "Substitutionary Atonement and Evolution, Part 1," June 9, 2015, accessed September 15, 2016, *BioLogos*, https://biologos.org/blogs/archive/substitutionary-atonement-and-evolution-part-1 (emphasis added).

7. Denis Alexander, "Models for Relating Science and Religion," Faraday Institute for Science and Religion, April 2007, available online at https://www.faraday.st-edmunds.cam.ac.uk/resources/Faraday%20Papers/Faraday%20Paper%203%20Alexander_EN.pdf. The Faraday Institute is functionally the British equivalent of BioLogos.

8. Quoted in G. Himmelfarb, *Darwin and the Darwinian Revolution* (New York: Norton, 1962), 263.

ideas of the late Stephen Jay Gould, who regarded science and religion as "nonoverlapping magisteria." On balance, Alexander prefers what is generally called a "complementary" or "Two Books" model, one popular with many theistic evolution writers.

Francis Bacon and the Two Books

David Tyler[9] has helpfully surveyed the "Two Books" model of scientific and theological interaction in medieval Catholicism. Within Protestantism,[10] it received greater development, notably by Francis Bacon:

> For our Saviour saith, "You err, not knowing the Scriptures, nor the power of God;" laying before us two books or volumes to study, if we will be secured from error: first the Scriptures, revealing the will of God, and then the creatures expressing His power; whereof the latter is a key unto the former. . . . [11]

Bacon's contention was that traditional philosophy, exemplified by Aristotle, had mistakenly proceeded from basic axioms to deduce necessary consequences about the world. In contrast, he strongly urged an *inductive* methodology, proceeding from facts about the natural world in order to discover generalized descriptions or laws. His later *Novum Organum Scientiarum* (patterned on Aristotle's *Organon*, but offering a radically different direction) developed his ideas more extensively. In the earlier work, he sums up as follows:

> To conclude, therefore, let no man . . . think or maintain that a man can search too far, or be too well studied in the book of God's word, or in the book of God's works, divinity or philosophy; but rather let men endeavour an endless progress or proficience [*sic*] in both; only let men beware . . . that they do not unwisely mingle or confound these learnings together.[12]

This quotation, significantly, was used by Darwin in the *Origin of*

---

9. David Tyler, "The 'Double Revelation' Approach to Knowledge," *Origins* 23 (1997): 2–6.
10. The Reformers used the metaphor, but primarily in relation to our knowledge of God (e.g., the Belgic Confession, Art. 2, describes the universe as a "beautiful book"). Bacon's focus was different.
11. Francis Bacon, *Works: The Advancement of Learning*, book 1, section 6, 16, available online at http://www.gutenberg.org/ebooks/author/296.
12. Bacon, *Advancement*, book 1, section 1, 3.

Species. Already we see that Bacon's idea of the interaction of science and Scripture leans toward an autonomous model. Moody Prior's seminal article[13] argued that Bacon believed "that nothing can be known except in a certain way," and this way entailed separating "completely the realms of religion and of natural knowledge." These "learnings" must not be mingled together; indeed, Bacon goes further—science is the key to Scripture, certainly not the reverse. As Prior shows, when Bacon did write on specific biblical passages (the fall; Cain and Abel) he interpreted them in terms of his "favorite notions." One important notion was Bacon's "chronic optimism" that science is a pathway to cumulative knowledge and progressive enlightenment. Positively, this advanced philanthropy and humanitarian action, but negatively it produced the concept of the scientist as Superman. Bacon assumed that "religion" is merely a means of limiting the abuse of the power that the scientist gains.

This is a very condensed survey, but some brief comments are in order. Bacon's main target was Aristotelian thought, which had stifled scientific enquiry by relying on speculative metaphysics rather than empirical data. Bacon argued that we should have our minds "washed clean from opinions" and let the facts speak for themselves. This empirical approach was a factor in the growth of science in the seventeenth century.[14] But it was not the only factor: for example, Peter Harrison stresses the particular role played by the Reformers' approach to biblical interpretation:

> Whereas the accounts of creation in the book of Genesis had previously provided scope for the imaginations of exegetes given to allegory, now the significance of these stories was seen to lie in their *literal truth* as depicting past events.[15]

Actually, the primary impulse for scientific investigations was not Baconian empiricism but a conviction that scientific investigation was a religious duty, so that " . . . legitimate meanings of the book of nature

---

13. Moody E. Prior, "Bacon's Man of Science," *Journal of History of Ideas* 15 (1954): 348–370.
14. See Reijer Hooykaas, *Religion and the Rise of Modern Science* (Edinburgh: Scottish Academic Press, 1972); Peter Harrison, *The Bible, Protestantism, and the Rise of Natural Science* (Cambridge: Cambridge University Press, 2001); Rodney Stark, *For the Glory of God* (Princeton, NJ: Princeton University Press, 2003).
15. Harrison, *Bible, Protestantism*, 122, emphasis added.

were sought in the purposes for which God had *designed* its living contents."[16]

Indeed, what became known as "physico-theology"—which Harrison summarizes as "a detailed elaboration of the design argument"—was seen as "the key to the interpretation of the book of nature."[17] Of this teleological approach, to be developed most clearly by Robert Boyle and John Ray, Bacon was rather scornful—as noted above, he would reverse the roles of key and lock. In modern parlance, Harrison's analysis makes a compelling case that science was founded on the presupposition of "intelligent design."

Bacon did assert that the scientific enterprise should be carried out to God's glory and mankind's benefit, but his concept of how science works has serious flaws.[18] Moreover, its application as a philosophical paradigm to other spheres has dire consequences for theology in particular. In a critique of relevance to the theistic evolution position, Nancy Pearcey argues that it has led to a "two-story" view of the relationship between Scripture and the world around us.[19]

Finally, we should not miss the irony underlying the "Two Books" approach: how do we truly know that creation is "a book of God's works" apart from the fact that the Scriptures tell us so (Psalm 19; Rom. 1:19–21; etc.)? If the Bible is not what it declares itself to be, the infallible and inerrant Word of God, why should we expect a second "book" at all?

Complementarity

In his Faraday Institute article, Alexander concludes that the two realms are not autonomous, but *complementary*. Two accounts may be given of some physical phenomenon without being in conflict: both can be true, if they focus on different aspects, or operate at different levels. This modified Baconian view is widespread within the organization Christians in Science, as evidenced by frequent comments in their newsletters and articles in the journal *Science and Christian Belief*.

---

16. Ibid., 169, emphasis added.
17. Ibid., 171, 203.
18. See Del Ratzsch, *Science and Its Limits: The Natural Sciences in Christian Perspective* (Downers Grove, IL: IVP Academic, 2000), esp. chapter 2.
19. Nancy Pearcey, *Total Truth* (Wheaton, IL: Crossway, 2004), 298–311.

A generation ago, Gareth Jones stated the view as follows:

> Biblical knowledge and scientific knowledge represent different levels of appreciating reality. At best these two levels are complementary; at the worst they *may be contradictory*.[20]

This is echoed more recently by Melvin Tinker:

> ... while a description of a phenomenon may be given by a scientist which might be complete in its own terms of reference, this does not rule out other levels of description which are logically 'higher' and complementary.[21]

Thus Derek Burke contends that Genesis 1 is a "why" account, but not a "how" account, so it need not be seen as historical.[22] This is an example of *false dichotomy*: insisting that because something is X, it is therefore not Y, without establishing that X and Y are mutually exclusive. That the Bible is not a scientific textbook is a truism, but prima facie, early Genesis does appear to be a record of literal historical events. And, according to Harrison, that presumption—rather than Baconian autonomy—was the foundation on which science began in the seventeenth century.

The "complementary" view leads to different conclusions from those of the early scientists. For example, Tinker quotes the scientist Donald MacKay:

> It is impossible for a scientific discovery given by God to contradict a Word given by God. If therefore a scientific discovery, as distinct from a scientific speculation, contradicts what we have believed by the Bible, it is not a question of error in God's Word, but of error in our way of interpreting it.[23]

But this begs the question. What is in dispute is precisely whether Darwinism *is* a scientific discovery given by God, rather than a

---

20. D. Gareth Jones, "Our Fragile Brains: A Christian Perspective on Brain Research," in *Creation and Evolution*, ed. Derek Burke (Leicester, UK: Inter-Varsity Press, 1985), 211, emphasis added.

21. Melvin Tinker, *Evangelical Concerns* (Fearn, UK: Christian Focus, 2001), 55.

22. Burke, *Creation and Evolution*, 165.

23. In Melvin Tinker, ed., *The Open Mind and Other Essays* (Leicester, UK: Inter-Varsity Press, 1988, 150.

projection onto science of an anti-theistic naturalism. And at least part of the answer must consider its implications for Christian doctrine.

In biblical hermeneutics (principles of interpretation) we sometimes encounter the "language of appearances," as in Psalm 19's description of the sun's progress through the sky. As Calvin phrased it, there is an "accommodation" of biblical language to the observations of the reader—thus, he says, Genesis 1 calls the moon a "great light," although it is smaller than the planets. Nor is it contentious that genre is important, although in considering such questions, one must always beware a false dichotomy. Thus, even if we suppose, *arguendo*, that Genesis 1–3 is a poetic account, it is not therefore excluded from being history as well.

Regardless, the questions surrounding Darwinism go beyond such considerations in that they affect a whole theological tradition. Granted, tradition is not an autonomous authority either, but as J. I. Packer argues, it is not unimportant:

> . . . [tradition] yields much valuable help in understanding what Scripture teaches. . . . The history of the Church's labour to understand the Bible forms a commentary on the Bible which we cannot despise or ignore without dishonouring the Holy Ghost.[24]

As Alexander's book demonstrates, theistic evolution has a serious problem in attempting to reconcile Darwinism with classical Reformed doctrines concerning the nature of mankind and the fall. And the doctrine of Scripture that it presupposes is the key.

A Question of Priority

Alexander believes that those who think Genesis has evidence of relevance to science exemplify a model that presents "religious convictions as if they were science, seeking to fuse scientific and religious knowledge by assigning priority to religious beliefs."[25] He is correct about the need to prioritize, although *he* clearly thinks science ranks higher than "religious convictions."

---

24. J. I. Packer, *"Fundamentalism" and the Word of God* (Leicester, UK: Inter-Varsity Press, 1958), 48.
25. Alexander, "Models for Relating Science and Religion," 3.

Herein lies the fundamental problem with the complementarian position. A model that creationists would accept was outlined forty years ago by Francis Schaeffer.[26] Agreed, Schaeffer says, the Bible is not a scientific textbook, but it does create *boundaries* for our scientific theories. Within the circle so defined, science is free to consider questions that Scripture does not deal with directly. Under God's common grace, truth about the world can be found by believer and unbeliever alike, provided they operate within the circle.

But what if our interpretation of the Bible seems at variance with a "scientific discovery"? According to John Frame, " . . . if, after reflection, I determine that my original interpretation of Scripture was correct, and that still conflicts with the apparent results of science, then I must follow Scripture."[27] Creationists do not have all the answers, but they agree with Frame: if a fundamental Christian doctrine is negated by a scientific hypothesis, we should consider alternative hypotheses.

It is particularly ironic that an alternative to Darwinism exists today in the work of the intelligent design (ID) movement. ID is essentially consistent with biblical doctrine, and is supported by many scientists and theologians whose views cannot lightly be dismissed. Yet proponents of theistic evolution regularly do so, either ignoring ID altogether or treating it with lofty disdain. In this regard, R. J. Berry's "review" of Norman Nevin's book[28] is a classic of *its* genre. Even less intemperate theistic evolution proponents continue to privilege modern science above the Bible. Tinker, for instance, states that "the facts of science, as distinct from speculation, provide us with a check or corrective to ensure that we are looking at the passage from the right angle."[29] An aroma of Bacon?

And still the question is begged, for how do we distinguish facts from speculation? Elsewhere, Tinker appears to suggest that the criterion for a "fact" is its acceptance by the "international scientific community."[30] This can surely not be definitive for the Christian believer. After all, it

---

26. Francis Schaeffer, *No Final Conflict* (London: Hodder & Stoughton, 1975).
27. John Frame, *The Doctrine of the Knowledge of God* (Phillipsburg, NJ: Presbyterian & Reformed, 1987), 136.
28. R. J. Berry, *Science and Christian Belief* 22 (2009): 207–208 (reviewing Nevin's *Should Christians Embrace Evolution?*; see note 5, above).
29. Tinker, *Evangelical Concerns*, 58.
30. Melvin Tinker, "No Conflict," *Evangelicals Now*, February 2009, 19.

is not unknown for the international scientific community to be wrong. Moreover, theistic evolution literature is prone to ignore the distinction between facts and speculation. Consider this from Ernest Lucas, for example, writing on the Genesis "kinds":

> The statement about animals reproducing 'according to their kind' probably expresses nothing more than the fact we all observe that dogs have puppies, not kittens. It should not be taken to rule out the possibility that major changes might occur over many generations.[31]

Lucas clearly does not confine himself to facts ("dogs have puppies"), but explicitly speculates ("major changes might occur").

Furthermore, while "Science"[32] is seen as a corrective for biblical hermeneutics, the notion that Scripture might correct our scientific notions is never entertained for a moment. Graeme Finlay and Stephen Pattemore want us to "adopt a stance of humility towards our current understanding of Scripture."[33] Well, we are not infallible, and shouldn't confuse what Scripture teaches with what *we think* it teaches—but we do have two millennia of Christian theology to inform us. Moreover, there is no suggestion of an equivalent stance of humility toward our current understanding of science! This is especially strange in the light of history, which contains many examples of scientific "facts" (on the consensus criterion) that turned out to be incorrect.[34] (The "self-correcting" potential of science may be raised here, but the basis for that argument is precisely the provisional status of scientific theories.)

Francis Collins and Denis Alexander clearly take this position: Christian theology is presumed to be corrigible in a way that science is not. Scripture, far from being complementary, actually becomes subordinate to "Science." Berry, whose article[35] appears to have served

---

31. Ernest Lucas, *Can We Believe Genesis Today? The Bible and the Questions of Science* (Leicester, UK: Inter-Varsity Press, 2005), 55–56.

32. By "Science," I mean what Schaeffer used to call "modern modern science": science as an autonomous source of knowledge.

33. Graeme Finlay, Stephen Lloyd, Stephen Pattemore, and David Swift, *Debating Darwin* (Bletchley, UK: Paternoster, 2009), 36.

34. A recent case is the discovery of quasi-crystals; their discoverer, Dan Shechtman, was ridiculed and abused as a "quasi-scientist," and was told to "go and read the textbook," merely because his work did not fit the current consensus.

35. R. J. Berry, "This Cursed Earth: Is 'the Fall' Credible?" *Science and Christian Belief* 11 (1999): 29–49.

as a rehearsal for parts of Alexander's book, is actually "horrified" at Frame's suggestion that Scripture might serve to modify scientific ideas! In contrast, Vern Poythress affirms this as a natural part of Christian reflection on Scripture:

> Biblical interpretation affects science at the very least by leading us to reassess whether all the conclusions drawn from a scientific theory are warranted, or in some cases to ask whether the theory as a whole is suspect.[36]

In summary, there is sufficient evidence that theistic evolution is only too happy to prioritize, provided "Science" has the priority. Modifying Alexander's formula, we might conclude that theistic evolution "fuses scientific and religious knowledge by assigning priority to *scientific* beliefs." The nature of the interaction between "Science" and Scripture is such that the complementary model is unstable.

The Noetic Effect of the Fall

While biblical interpretation may occasionally need revision, and such revision may perhaps be suggested by scientific discoveries, anyone who claims to stand on the same ground as the Reformers should be wary of overconfidence in our rational faculties. Packer stated it well more than fifty years ago:

> We may not look to reason to tell us whether Scripture is right in what it says . . . ; instead, we must look to Scripture to tell us whether reason is right in what it thinks on the subjects with which Scripture deals.[37]

Herman Bavinck concurs:

> If Christianity . . . seeks to redeem human beings from all sin, from errors of the mind as well as the impurity of the heart . . . , [Scripture] in the nature of the case cannot subject itself to the criticism of human beings but must subject them to its criticism.[38]

---

36. Vern S. Poythress, *Science and Hermeneutics* (Grand Rapids, MI: Zondervan, 1988), esp. chapter 2.
37. Packer, *"Fundamentalism,"* 48. Packer's remark is interesting, as he has endorsed Alexander's book. If he still holds to what he wrote in 1958, he has not given the book due attention.
38. Herman Bavinck, *Reformed Dogmatics*, vol. 1 (Grand Rapids, MI: Baker, 2003), 505.

These quotations focus on the "noetic" effect of sin: its effect on the intellect. The fall was a radical and comprehensive transformation of human nature; mankind's rebellion against God touches every faculty, including our minds. To assume that human reason can sit in judgment on the "correctness" of Scripture is thus an error. Reason is not a neutral and dispassionate umpire; indeed, the unregenerate mind is bent on *suppressing* the truth about God that it sees in creation (Rom. 1:18–20).

Prior to the Reformation this doctrine was somewhat attenuated— Aquinas, for example, saw the fall as producing a "wound of ignorance" to the mind. But Calvin in particular (following Augustine) saw the effect as more serious than mere ignorance: mankind is not merely deprived, but depraved. The subsequent development of this theme for a Christian epistemology has been most prominent in the work of Reformed theologians such as Abraham Kuyper and Cornelius van Til.

For Kuyper, in science there are two sorts of thinking—and thinkers. *Abnormalists* assume that the present condition of the cosmos is different from what it was in the beginning. *Normalists*, on the other hand, disregard the Bible's evidence and presuppose that everything results from an unbroken naturalistic chain of cause and effect; moreover, these two schools are locked in deadly combat. Kuyper made some exceptions, and acknowledged that the effect of Normalist thinking is restrained and ameliorated by common grace.[39] It is also clear that the Bible has nothing to say on (for example) how I should apply statistical methods to investigate the adsorption characteristics of squaraine particles.[40] But were I to apply such methods to derive a phylogenetic tree linking humans to an ape-like "common ancestor," I would be ignoring what the Bible says about human ancestry. Thus, in at least some cases, the *antithesis* (one of Kuyper's favorite words) not only exists but is manifest in scientific practice.

So asking "Can We Believe Genesis Today?" (Lucas) or "Is the Fall Credible?" (Berry) presupposes that autonomous human reason has

---

39. For a more comprehensive discussion see Abraham Kuyper, *Lectures on Calvinism* (Grand Rapids, MI: Eerdmans, 1931), 130; Cornelius van Til, *A Christian Theory of Knowledge* (Nutley, NJ: Presbyterian & Reformed, 1977). The latter would go further in his estimation of the (lack of) capabilities of the fallen human mind. The *fact* of the antithesis is however the same for both, as it is also in the works of Francis Schaeffer.

40. A recent project in which I was involved. The details are unimportant.

the authority to answer these questions, and so to judge the Scriptures. If fallen man is competent to judge the credibility of the fall, should we be surprised at the answer?

Clarity of Scripture

Another key doctrine of the Reformation was that the Bible is *perspicuous*.[41] Against medieval church dogma—that Scripture could only truly be understood through officially sanctioned church teaching, mediated by the clergy—Luther insisted on *claritas scripturae* (the clarity of Scripture). Hence the importance of translating the Bible into ordinary language, as in Tyndale's affirmation that the ploughboy with a Bible would know more than the pope.

The Reformers did not despise hermeneutics: they knew that some Scriptures are hard to understand (2 Pet. 3:16), and provided extensive expository material for the edification of the church. Nor did they denigrate the preaching and teaching offices of the church in favor of "private interpretation," as became fashionable later with post-Enlightenment individualism.[42] There is a tension inherent in *claritas scripturae* (one helpfully explored by James Callahan[43] and Larry Pettegrew[44]), but perspicuity does mean that Scripture needs no *external* source of validation, whether the Roman church or, latterly, the "arbitrary authority of academic elitism" (Callahan) arising from "higher criticism." Essentially, perspicuity emphasizes, in the words of the Westminster Confession, that "the infallible rule of interpretation of Scripture is the Scripture itself."[45]

This is where theistic evolution diverges from historic Reformed doctrine. Its exponents frequently state that Scripture is authoritative; perhaps many affirm its inerrancy. But they do not seem to believe it is *clear*, in the sense indicated above. Sadly, as Douglas Kelly points out,[46]

---

41. See D. A. Carson, *Collected Writings on Scripture* (Wheaton, IL: Crossway, 2010), 179–193. Carson shows that the doctrine was not unknown in Patristic writings; Scripture's alleged "obscurity" came later.
42. See K. A. Mathison, *The Shape of Sola Scriptura* (Moscow, ID: Canon, 2001), esp. chapter 4.
43. James Patrick Callahan, "*Claritas Scripturae*: The Role of Perspicuity in Protestant Hermeneutics," *Journal of the Evangelical Theological Society* 39, no. 3 (1996): 353–372.
44. Larry D. Pettegrew, "The Perspicuity of Scripture," *The Master's Seminary Journal* 15 (2004): 209–225.
45. To see how this works in practice, see Wayne Grudem, "The Perspicuity of Scripture," *Themelios* 34, no. 3 (2009): 288–308.
46. Douglas F. Kelly, *Creation and Change* (Fearn, UK: Christian Focus, 2004), 48–52.

liberal exegetes have no problem in seeing Genesis 1–3 as intended to be history (although they dismiss it as primitive); it is evangelicals who doubt its clarity,[47] imposing an external *scientific* framework that entails a variety of tortured exegetical speculations.[48]

Thus Alexander seeks to make Genesis 1–3 cohere with current ideas of human evolution. Adam becomes just one of many Neolithic farmers, and the account of his "creation," temptation, and fall is adjusted to fit this framework. Far from being an account of historical events, the narrative is a polemic against ancient Near Eastern (predominantly Babylonian) ideologies. According to Alexander, it is against this background that we must consider the early chapters of Genesis.

Similarly, John H. Walton writes, "If we accept Genesis 1 as ancient cosmology, then we need to interpret it as ancient cosmology" and "we need to read [the text] as . . . the ancient audience would have heard it."[49] Question-begging, once more. Why accept that Genesis is "ancient cosmology"? How do we know what the "ancient audience" heard? Yet Alexander, Walton, and many others all assume that early Genesis cannot be properly interpreted without the "insights" gained from ancient Near Eastern (ANE) texts.

According to Noel Weeks,[50] however, Genesis is distinguished from much of the Old Testament by its *lack* of polemic against polytheistic idolatry. The Pentateuch's concern with idolatry becomes very obvious in Exodus, but assuming equal prominence in Genesis is imposing an interpretation on the text. Moreover, on the basis of Mosaic responsibility for the Pentateuch, we might expect any polemic to focus on Egypt and its gods, not Babylon. In any case, where is the evidence that Israel based its foundational narrative on Near Eastern myths? It is surely equally plausible that the ANE texts are a polemic against

---

47. Ironically, statistical methods show that the Genesis creation account shares the linguistic characteristics of Old Testament historical narrative. To conclude that it is poetry is perverse—and unscientific! (Steven W. Boyd, "Statistical Determination of Genre in Biblical Hebrew: Evidence for an Historical Reading of Genesis 1:1-2-3," in *Rate II*, ed. Larry Vardiman, Andrew A. Snelling, and Eugene F. Chaffin [El Cajon, CA: Institute for Creation Research, 2005], chapter 9, available online at http://www.icr.org/i/pdf/technical/Statistical-Determination-of-Genre-in-Biblical-Hebrew.pdf.)

48. As statisticians say, if you torture the data enough, you will always get a confession.

49. John H. Walton, *The Lost World of Genesis One* (Downers Grove, IL: IVP Academic, 2009), 17, 103. See also Walton, *The Lost World of Adam and Eve: Genesis 2–3 and the Human Origins Debate* (Downers Grove, IL: IVP Academic, 2015).

50. Noel Weeks, "More than History," *Australian Presbyterian* 633 (2011): 4–9.

the true account, being a corrupted version of an oral tradition dating from the scattering at Babel. Finally, even if, *arguendo*, Genesis 1–11 is a polemic, it would only gain in force were the events described truly historical, compared to Babylonian myths.

When faced with hermeneutical issues, the proper context for interpreting a particular passage of Scripture is Scripture itself. What chapters 1–3 of Genesis "mean" cannot be isolated from the larger context of chapters 1–11, nor from Genesis as a whole, nor the Pentateuch, and so on. Above all, we cannot safely ignore the New Testament, which gives no hint that the apostles or Jesus himself regarded Genesis as an anti-Babylonian polemic. Rather, they treat the early chapters of the Bible as describing historical events—moreover, events of crucial soteriological significance.

In contrast Walton, in a revealing radio debate[51] about his second book (*The Lost World of Adam and Eve*), insists that we cannot possibly interpret Genesis properly from the New Testament; rather, we "start with what the author intended to say." And we can discern this intent today much better than the apostles could,[52] as they were part of a "Hellenistic world." What of Tyndale's ploughboy, in this scenario? Walton allows that the "ordinary Christian" may understand the general outline, but otherwise must just rely on expert scholarship.

Walton himself called in an "expert" to help make his case in *The Lost World of Adam and Eve*. Apparently feeling unqualified fully to evaluate what the New Testament says about Adam (how unclear it must be!), Walton invited New Testament scholar N. T. Wright to add his own thoughts, in an excursus in chapter 19. The title of this chapter ("Paul's Use of Adam Is More Interested in the Effect of Sin on the Cosmos than in the Effect of Sin on Humanity and Has Nothing to Say about Human Origins") is also revealing in the light of Wright's own controversial views on justification. Apparently, the accumulated theology of the last two millennia has promulgated an "inadequate and misleading" reading of pretty much everything that Paul wrote,

---

51. Walton, in "Unbelievable? Have We Misread the Adam and Eve Story? John Walton vs Stephen Lloyd," *Premier Christian Radio*, March 28, 2015, available at http://www.premierchristian radio.com/Shows/Saturday/Unbelievable/Episodes/Unbelievable-Have-we-misread-the-Adam-and -Eve-story-John-Walton-vs-Stephen-Lloyd. The passages cited lie between 50 and 62 minutes in.

52. Walton seems to have given no thought at all to the question of what the Holy Spirit might have intended.

so Wright is happy to endorse twenty-first-century science as a hermeneutic for Genesis.[53]

From the viewpoint of perspicuity, the theistic evolution approach
also raises further problems: was a true interpretation of Genesis 1–11
even *possible* prior to the discovery of *Enuma Elish* and other ANE
stories? Did a "correct" understanding of Adam and the fall await the
advent of Charles Darwin? Even from a practical viewpoint, giving
science the final word in this way is dubious: when Darwinism is sup-
planted by something else, we will need to adjust our theology again!
In the nineteenth century, the great James Clerk Maxwell pointed out
the folly of this approach, gently chiding Bishop Ellicott, who was
overexcited by another piece of speculative science:

> The rate of change of scientific hypotheses is naturally much more
> rapid than that of biblical interpretations, so that if an interpreta-
> tion is founded on such an hypothesis, it may help to keep the
> hypothesis above ground long after it ought to have been buried
> and forgotten.[54]

Rather more caustically, the historian and theologian Carl Trueman
recently observed,

> . . . how come some people, with little or no scientific training, and
> who spend their lives telling us how difficult it is to understand
> messy, written texts—texts designed to, ahem, communicate in a
> relatively direct fashion—seem to think that scientific data is univo-
> cal, unequivocal, and perspicuous on [evolution]?[55]

This echoes the view of Martyn Lloyd-Jones over fifty years ago. Of
the relationship of science to Scripture, he wrote,

> If you study the history of science you will have much less respect
> for its supposed supreme authority than you had when you began.

---

53. Unfortunately, Walton and Wright exemplify what C. S. Lewis called "chronological snob-
bery": discerning ancient cultural influences on earlier authors, while oblivious of modern influences on their own thinking.

54. James Clerk Maxwell, "Reply to Letter from the Bishop of Gloucester and Bristol," in
The Life of James Clerk Maxwell, ed. L. Campbell and W. Garnett (London: Macmillan, 1882),
393–395.

55. Carl Trueman, "Life on the Cultic Fringe," *Reformation21*, 2010, accessed on September 1,
2016, online at http://www.reformation21.org/articles/life-on-the-cultic-fringe.php.

. . . Without arguing in detail about scientific matters . . . it is not only lacking in faith and un-scriptural, but it is ignorant to accord 'Science,' 'Modern Knowledge' or 'Learning' an authority which they really do not possess.[56]

Since the Bible of theistic evolution is obscure, so is its *theology*— descending into incoherence when it attempts to reconstruct what salvation means, for example. Alexander's article on the purpose of the Incarnation merely states that Christ "opens up the way back to friendship with God through his sacrifice for sin on the cross."[57] Traditional words, but the content is not. In fact, according to Alexander, physical death is not a penalty for sin, nor is sin inherited; Adam is "Everyman"; all people sin; Christ died for the sins of us all. But what does "Everyman" mean? And why the cross? If physical death is normal, what did this death accomplish? Is "friendship" an adequate summary of our relationship to God? As was said of the Victorian liberal preacher F. W. Robertson, Denis Alexander's soteriology reduces to "Christ did something or other, which, somehow or other, has some connection or other with salvation."

Theological Liberalism

Earlier generations saw the denial of scriptural priority as typical of old-style "liberal Christianity." Packer described this "subjectivist" view of Scripture as one in which "reason and conscience must judge Scripture and tradition, . . . re-fashioning the whole to bring it into line with the accepted philosophy of the time."[58] That this led to a wholesale reinterpretation of Genesis in particular is a simple matter of record. Nigel Cameron has documented several examples of this phenomenon in the nineteenth century.[59]

Packer's reasoned answer to liberal methodology is very relevant: Scripture's authority is (a) established by the teaching of Christ

---

56. D. Martyn Lloyd-Jones, *Authority* (London: Inter-Varsity Press, 1958), 40.
57. Denis Alexander, "Evolution, Christmas, and the Atonement," *The Guardian* (December 23, 2011), online at http://www.theguardian.com/commentisfree/belief/2011/dec/23/evolution-christmas-and-the-atonement.
58. Packer, *"Fundamentalism,"* 50.
59. Nigel M. de S. Cameron, *Evolution and the Authority of the Bible* (Exeter: Paternoster, 1983).

concerning the Old Testament, (b) confirmed by the teaching of the apostles, and (c) recognized in the attitude of the early church. Therefore, "The Bible . . . does not need to be revised and corrected by reason. Instead it demands to sit in judgment on [reason's] dictates."[60]

The motivations of proponents of theistic evolution also resemble those of yesteryear's liberals. The liberals wanted people to become Christians, but thought this required the "demythologization" of Christianity. Similarly, Alexander argues that, as Darwinism is undeniable, any reading of Scripture that assumes the historical nature of early Genesis must be revised. Those who maintain the historical view are "embarrassing, and bring the gospel into disrepute."[61]

A recent symposium in the online *9Marks* journal on the history of liberalism is very relevant to theistic evolution. Al Mohler observes that Alexander's preoccupation is precisely where problems begin: "The lesson of theological liberalism is clear—embarrassment is the gateway drug for theological accommodation and denial." In a similar vein, Gregory Wills points out that "[Evangelicals] proposing new ways of accepting evolution without rejecting the Bible [sense that] the church's message is no longer credible to the educated, intelligent, and cultured classes."[62]

This is no misrepresentation. Daniel Harlow, for example, argues explicitly that "for Christianity to remain intellectually credible and culturally relevant, it must be willing to revise—and thereby enrich—its formulation of classic doctrines if the secure findings of science call for revision."[63] (Isn't that "thereby" interesting? Does revision *necessarily* entail enrichment? And note the question-begging "secure.") Or hear Alexander again: "The public promotion of creationism and ID . . . continues to create intellectual barriers for scientists, significantly diminishing the likelihood of their taking the gospel seriously."[64] But according to Paul (1 Cor. 1:22–23), so does the preaching of the cross!

---

60. Packer, *"Fundamentalism,"* 48.
61. Alexander, *Creation or Evolution*, 352.
62. Gregory A. Wills, "What Lessons Can We Learn from the History of Liberalism?" *9Marks eJournal*, 7, no. 1 (2010). Online at http://9marks.org/journal/new-evangelical-liberalism/. The whole issue makes sobering reading.
63. Daniel C. Harlow, "After Adam: Reading Genesis in an Age of Evolutionary Science," *PSCF* 62, no. 3 (2010): 192.
64. Alexander, *Creation or Evolution*, 352.

Moreover, as the 9*Marks* authors show, historically the effect of the liberal project was the opposite of its intention. Far from making Christianity more acceptable to the "educated, intelligent, and cultured," it provided them with excuses to ignore its claims. Without doubting the sincerity of the liberal theologians, it is clear that their project was disastrous for the church. As the historic Western "mainline" denominations slip beneath the waves of contemporary thought, like Debussy's *cathédrale engloutie*, only an occasional muffled chime recalls that once a church was there. Will theistic evolution fare any better?

Theodicy

Darwinism conflicts radically with orthodox Christian doctrine in relation to the existence of evil. Cameron's survey is a good starting point. In his view, rather than an anti-ANE polemic, Genesis 1–3 is the "Great Theodicy."[65] Without the "goodness of the original world and man's responsibility for its fall," to believe in God's goodness is "wholly irrational."[66] As Kuyper argued, science has to reckon with the truth that the world is *abnormal*—it is *not* as God originally created it. Evolutionary thinking must deny this. Yet, without the discontinuity of the fall and the subsequent curse, there is a problem that, ironically, *non*-Christian thinkers understand very well. Here is the philosopher David Hull:

> The God implied by evolutionary theory . . . is . . . not a loving God who cares about His productions. . . . [He] is careless, wasteful, indifferent, almost diabolical . . . not the sort of God to whom anyone would be inclined to pray.[67]

Hull's solution is simple—jettison God altogether. But theists can't follow suit, so the theologian Christopher Southgate, for example, ponders at length the problems delineated by Hull. Since he accepts Darwinism, Southgate has difficulty finding a solution. Pain, suffering, and death are intrinsic to evolution, so evolution is in need of "redemption." But how? After laboring manfully for pages, he settles for the

---

65. The term "theodicy," coined by the philosopher Gottfried Leibniz, denotes a defense of God's goodness.
66. Cameron, *Evolution and Authority*, 63.
67. David Hull, "The God of the Galápagos," *Nature* 352, no. 6335 (1991): 485–486.

rather underwhelming notion of a "pelican heaven," symbolizing the hope that everything will be fine in the end.[68] Alexander is similarly unable to find answers; it seems that "God created a tough world . . . [one] in which there is pain and death."[69] Although expressed in rather more scholarly terms, this is also the message of John Schneider.[70] It seems we must just shrug our shoulders and stop worrying.

That would be unfortunate. This question is serious, as Howard van Till demonstrated very clearly. For many years, van Till—a faculty member at Calvin College, Michigan—espoused a theistic evolutionary position, defending it tirelessly in the journal edited by Alexander, *Science and Christian Belief*, or in its American counterpart, *Perspectives on Science and Christian Faith*. Eventually, however, his reflections on evolution and theodicy led him to renounce belief in a supernatural God altogether.[71]

Although, thankfully, many do not take the view to its logical conclusion, van Till's position demonstrates that theistic evolution is an uneasy compromise, and its theodical implications are potentially faith-destroying. Darwinism does have significant implications for the Christian, and theistic evolution challenges historic Christianity at many points. Once the Reformed doctrine of Scripture is revised, anything can happen—and probably will.

No Conflict?

What then of the "no-conflict" thesis? Try as we might to keep the two realms apart, they stubbornly refused to stay independent. As Gareth Jones acknowledges,[72] there *are* contradictions, and when conflict arises, "Science" insists on being top dog. Complementarians will say that this is "scientism," not science—but the commentator Bryan Appleyard regards this as a distinction without a difference. Science *as currently practiced* has a profound tendency toward totalitarianism:

---

68. Christopher Southgate, "God and Evolutionary Evil: Theodicy in the Light of Darwinism," *Zygon* 37, no. 4 (2002): 803–824, at 820.

69. Alexander, *Creation or Evolution*, 288.

70. John R. Schneider, "Recent Genetic Science and Christian Theology on Human Origins: An 'Aesthetic Supralapsarianism'," *PSCF* 62, no. 3 (2010): 196–212.

71. In an Internet exchange with a clergyman; there is a transcript at http://stmatthews.org.nz /nav.php?sid=53&id=321&print.

72. Note 20 above.

Science possesses an intrinsically domineering quality. This kind of triumphant scientism is *built into* all science. Opposition tends to be subdued and demoralized to the point where we can no longer identify the damage done . . .

If there is another realm, Appleyard continues, science will attempt to "colonize" it:

Science is not a neutral or innocent commodity which can be employed as a convenience. . . . Rather it is spiritually corrosive. . . . It cannot really coexist with anything. Scientists inevitably take on the mantle of the wizards, sorcerers and witch-doctors.[73]

Richard Dawkins is perhaps the most famous exemplar of this attitude, but he is not alone; consider comments from the American physicist Bob Park: "Science is, in fact, the only way of knowing. Anything else is just religion, which is all about authority"; and the British neuroscientist Sir Colin Blakemore writes, "Science is the only way of moving beyond anecdote and ideology towards the truth."[74] In contrast, the Christian scientist Maxwell was an object lesson in modesty and candor; in discussing the nature and limits of scientific hypotheses, he warned that "we see the phenomena only through a medium, and are liable to . . . blindness to facts and rashness in assumption," and are thus prone to being "carried *beyond* the truth."[75]

Appleyard's book caused controversy and dissension on its first publication, but his conclusions are carefully argued. Western societies, particularly, have an uneasy relationship with science. Frequently, we look to it for answers: "Science now answers questions *as if* it were a religion, . . . and these answers are believed to be the Truth—again *as if* it were a religion[76] On the other hand, Appleyard notes, we maintain a suspicious distance, because we don't always like the answers science provides. We recognize that science is incomplete and provisional, yet

---

73. Bryan Appleyard, *Understanding the Present: An Alternative History of Science*, 2nd ed. (London: Tauris Parke, 2004), 2, 9, emphasis added.

74. Bob Park, "Watch Out for the UFOs," *New Scientist* (December 9, 2006), 49; Colin Blakemore, *The Times* (November 5, 2012), 26. Note that such statements are incoherent: there is no scientific way of proving them to be true!

75. W. D. Niven, ed., *The Scientific Papers of James Clerk Maxwell* (Dover, NY, 1965), 155–156, emphasis added.

76. Appleyard, *Understanding*, 228, emphasis original.

paradoxically we also believe it to be uniquely authoritative. (Bacon's "chronic optimism" is alive and well!) The American philosopher Richard Weaver also pondered the relationship of science (especially Darwinism) and religion in the modern world. This was his conclusion, shortly before his death more than fifty years ago:

> We hear smooth words to the effect that there is no real conflict between [Darwinian] science and religion. . . . There is no real conflict anywhere when one side gives up. The question still at issue is whether the facts and the logic dictate so complete a surrender as has been urged on one party.[77]

Can we really entertain the thesis of "no conflict" between science and religion? There is a sense in which the thesis may be granted, but its reflex universal assertion is clearly inadequate; it really depends on how these concepts are defined. Does "complementarity" save the day? Appleyard is skeptical:

> Liberally redefining the faith to embrace or co-exist with science is unconvincing because it is too obviously trying to make the best of a bad job. There is no certainty of where such definitions should stop. . . . It merely attempts to pretend it is not a problem.[78]

So, no *real* conflict? Hmm. Can scientists keep science and scientism apart? Is science as understood by Ray and Newton, Faraday and Maxwell, really the same animal as the "Science" of Dawkins, Park, and Blakemore?

Two Ways

Appleyard's arguments are weighty, yet they fail to get to the root of the problem. He describes a science that has become too big for its boots, but he can see only its continuation into the chaos and tyranny of absolute relativism. (This oxymoron is not explicitly his, but it gets close to the sense of desperation in what he describes.) For Appleyard, modern scientists conceive of science as self-attesting, autonomous, re-

---

77. Quoted in David Klinghoffer, "No Real Conflict when One Side Gives Up," *Evolution News and Views*, 2010, available online at http://www.evolutionnews.org/2010/05/there_is_no _real_conflict_anyw035061.html.
78. Appleyard, *Understanding*, 229.

morseless, untrammeled by notions of morality or transcendence—the only limits are those of feasibility. "Science" certainly needs no ties to any ancient book. How did scientific advance, the roots of which grew in Christian soil,[79] arrive at a place where it threatens to destroy the human condition? Largely, because it has forgotten those roots. Kirsten Birkett, a Christian historian of science, agrees:

> We are still trying to [build the tower of Babel]. Instead of seeing science as the noble pursuit that it is . . . we try to make it our means of becoming God ourselves.[80]

As strenuously as we may affirm the complementary nature of science and Christian doctrine, there is ample empirical evidence that it doesn't really work. A colleague of mine used to have a slogan on his office door:

> *In theory, there is no difference between theory and practice. In practice, there is.*[81]

Precisely! While some theistic scientists proclaim the gospel of complementarian orthodoxy, their bolder colleagues are tearing up the script. And it is a very hard position to maintain, because there *are* points of conflict. Today's "Science" has—*in practice*—become an autonomous source of knowledge. Even if it doesn't actually rule out God a priori, it assumes that it can apply rationalistic thinking to interpret his revealed Word, and thus find a god that is suitably subservient to the higher knowledge of "Science." As Schaeffer says, there is "no *final* conflict" between science and Scripture, but a science that refuses to recognize that it is dealing with a fallen world cannot fail to be in conflict. How then should Christians relate to science?

A recent book on this topic by Vern Poythress[82] is helpful. His approach is to start with God. After all, he says, scientists—despite their denials—really do presuppose God, as otherwise the whole concept of

---

79. See note 14, above.
80. Kirsten Birkett, *Unnatural Enemies* (Sydney: Matthias Media, 1997), 136.
81. Web searches are not unanimous on its origin. Some attribute it to the late Yogi Berra, source of many wonderful lines (e.g., "if you don't know where you're going, you might end up some place else," which could be a motto for theistic evolution).
82. Vern Poythress, *Redeeming Science* (Wheaton, IL: Crossway, 2008).

scientific law has no basis. His book is an outworking of the principle that the Bible is what it claims to be, with an authority above that of un-inspired natural reason. It should also be affirmed, of course, that human *interpretations* of what the Bible means for science are not infallible. We might debate some of the particular conclusions that Poythress reaches, but there is no issue with his methodology.

The theistic evolution approach, on the other hand—and despite its ostensible concern for complementarity—really starts from "Science." In practice, it brings home Bacon's view, quoted at the outset, that science is the key to the Bible, "opening our understanding to conceive the true sense of the Scriptures by the general notions of reason." John Calvin believed the relationship was quite different. In a famous passage, he likens Scripture to spectacles that correct our defective sight, so that in "considering the works of God" we should be "confined within due bounds by listening to the Word [and not] exult in our own vanity."[83]

Bacon wrote another book, *The New Atlantis*. This describes the utopian kingdom of Bensalem, whose preeminent organ of state is "Salomon's House," a society of scientists run by a caste of "Fellows," complete with twelve "Merchants of Light" and twenty-four others carrying out a structured scientific program.[84] Bensalem had converted to Christianity following a strange supernatural event—the preaching of the gospel is absent. They also received the Scriptures—oddly, at a time when the New Testament had not even been written! But the Bible seems here to function as a magic book; certainly something very different from the idea of Bacon's Puritan contemporaries. In Salomon's House, "Science" really calls all the shots—somewhat prophetic, perhaps, of today's "Scientocracy." As one commentator says, scientists are now presumed to be supremely authoritative on any subject, a "priestly class" using the "magical attributes" of science "to counsel our politicians, judges, financiers and military leaders."[85] The

83. John Calvin, *Institutes*, book 1, chapter 6.
84. Some see this as foreshadowing the Royal Society, but it may have sprung from Bacon's connections with the occult Rosicrucian movement. See Frances Yates, *The Occult Philosophy in the Elizabethan Age* (London: Routledge & Kegan Paul, 1979).
85. Bernard Boudreau, "Pursuit of Science: New Social Factors," *Canadian Family Physician*, 45 (2010): 1134–1136. Science as magic, and its use as an instrument of power were important

unorthodox scientist Rupert Sheldrake provides a similar tongue-in-cheek analysis:

> Scientists constitute a priesthood superior to the priesthoods of religions . . . [standing] in the vanguard of human progress, leading humanity onwards and upwards to a better and brighter world.[86]

This is where today's disciples of Bacon have arrived. We now have a Bible that has lost its authority, is marked by obscurity rather than clarity, and is certainly insufficient for a true understanding of the world. From these methodological flaws spring the other theological problems arising from theistic evolution.

Furthermore, an autonomous science sitting over Scripture actually ends up destroying its own foundations, which ultimately derive from God's revelation *in Scripture* as to his own character and the nature of his creation. Science arose because the Reformers and their heirs rejected the primacy of a figurative, allegorical hermeneutic for Scripture, but the theistic evolution approach to Genesis would turn the clock back[87] in the name of science! The problems Appleyard describes—an exaltation of speculation over evidence and a reliance on ideologically driven and politically motivated programs—are then inevitable. There is a pervasive corruption of scientific ideals, so that scientific objectivity is now often illusory.[88] It is no surprise also that a large proportion of scientific work is now subject to governmental funding, and thus control.

On the other hand, by operating within "Schaeffer's circle," science would be restored to its proper place as a revelation of God's glory and an instrument for the good of humanity. Thoughtful secular commentators like Appleyard are deeply pessimistic, expecting only doom and disaster. But they do not know God, nor the truth of his Word, nor the power of his Spirit, who can release science from its Babylonian captivity.

---

themes in C. S. Lewis's relatively neglected book *The Abolition of Man* (Grand Rapids, MI: Zondervan, 2001).

86. Rupert Sheldrake, *The Science Delusion* (London: Hodder & Stoughton, 2012), 291.

87. E.g., Denis Alexander prefers Philo and Origen to the Reformers—see *Creation or Evolution*, 155–156.

88. Sheldrake, *Delusion*, chapter 11. See also chapter 17 of this volume.

25

The Origin of Moral Conscience: Theistic Evolution versus Intelligent Design[1]

TAPIO PUOLIMATKA

SUMMARY

Theistic evolutionists generally agree that Darwinian evolution is not able to establish the origin of actual moral obligations. All that the evolutionary story can possibly do is to explain how we acquired moral beliefs and emotions. The problem for theistic evolutionists is, however, that current evolutionary accounts fail even in the latter task: they fail to explain the origin of moral conscience. The human capacity to discern moral truths cannot be reduced to a product of the kind of combinatorial processes that are available to a Darwinian account of evolution. Although theistic evolutionists assume that the idea of moral conscience as an expression of God's design for humans is fully compatible with various naturalistic explanations of the origin of moral conscience, they fail to specify a natural process that could plausibly do the job. In this respect theistic evolutionism amounts to little more than the statement that they do not see a logical problem in assuming that God could have used a natural process.

· · · · ·

---

1. I was helped by comments by Michael Beauty, C. Stephen Evans, Rope Kojonen, J. P. Moreland, and Julie Yonker.

Although theistic evolutionists usually adhere to the theories prevalent in evolutionary science and claim that God used evolutionary mechanisms to attain his purposes, the origin of morality presents a special problem. Morality is generally experienced as involving a transcendent source of obligation, which seems to assume a divine Lawgiver. As C. Stephen Evans argues in detail, moral obligations are "objective, motivating, binary in nature, universal, overriding, and allow us to bring deliberation to closure."[2] To see moral obligations as originating in the commands of a good, wise God provides an adequate explanation for all these features. It provides an ontological foundation for moral obligations and it "fits well with the idea that God has endowed humans with conscience, an ability to grasp moral truths."[3] Thus it allows for the view that even atheists are generally conscious of the obligating force of moral rules and in that sense have knowledge of God: "They are aware of God's claim on their lives, even if they are not aware of that claim as God's claim on their lives."[4] In that sense, as Kierkegaard points out, there "has never been an atheist, even though there certainly have been many who have been unwilling to let what they know (that the God exists) get control over their minds."[5] This experience is confirmed from the atheistic side by Jesse Bering: "As a way of thinking, God is an inherent part of our natural cognitive systems, and ridding ourselves of Him—really, thoroughly, permanently removing Him from our heads—would require a neurosurgeon, not a science teacher."[6]

Theistic evolutionists generally agree that evolutionary theory cannot explain or account for actual moral obligations. The moral sources available within the context of Darwinian evolution are not able to establish the origin of overriding moral obligations and provide the foundation for universal benevolence and human rights. So theistic evolutionists would reject what Angus Menuge[7] calls strong evolu-

---

2. C. Stephen Evans, *God and Moral Obligation* (Oxford: Oxford University Press, 2013), 181.
3. Ibid.
4. Ibid., 183.
5. Quoted in ibid., 183.
6. Jesse Bering, *The Belief Instinct: The Psychology of Souls, Destiny, and the Meaning of Life* (New York: Norton, 2011), 200.
7. Angus J. L. Menuge, "Why Human Rights Cannot Be Naturalized: The Contingency Problem," in *Legitimizing Human Rights: Secular and Religious Perspectives* (London: Ashgate 2013), 57–78.

tionary ethics (Strong EE), which argues that what counts as a moral value itself depends on biological history. As theists, they would reject this ontological thesis and instead adhere to a weaker thesis (Weak EE) about moral psychology which states that moral sensibilities have developed through an evolutionary process. In this view, all that the evolutionary story can possibly do is explain how we acquired moral beliefs and emotions.

Theistic evolutionists thus believe that current evolutionary accounts can explain the emergence of the human capacity to discern moral values. My aim in this chapter is to argue, on the contrary, that current evolutionary accounts fail to explain the origin of moral conscience: the human capacity to discern the morally right and good cannot be reduced to a product of the kind of combinatorial processes that are available to a Darwinian account of evolution.[8] Although theistic evolutionists assume that the idea of moral conscience as an expression of God's design plan for humans "is fully compatible with various naturalistic causal stories about how humans might have acquired such a faculty,"[9] they fail to specify a natural process that could plausibly do the job. In this respect, theistic evolutionism amounts to little more than the statement, on a very abstract and metaphorical plane, that they do not see a logical problem in assuming that God could have used a natural process.

I. Naturalistic Attempts at Explaining the Origin of Moral Sensibilities

Various naturalistic evolutionary theories acknowledge that human beings generally experience moral obligations as commands by a godlike being. Thus attempts have been made to account for these features within a naturalistic context. For example, the supernatural punishment theory of Dominic Johnson and Oliver Kruger suggests that belief in supernatural punishment has brought evolutionary advantage as it serves to promote cooperation: individuals are dissuaded from freeriding because they fear supernatural retribution as a consequence of

---

8. Cf. J. P. Moreland, *The Recalcitrant Imago Dei: Human Persons and the Failure of Naturalism* (London: SCM, 2009).

9. Evans, *God and Moral Obligation*, 42.

their actions.[10] Combined with the assumption that human cognition is an "evolutionary novel canvas for the workings of natural selection,"[11] it leads to a naturalistic theory that the expectation and fear of supernatural punishment serves to promote cooperation. "If supernatural punishment is held as *a belief*, then this threat becomes a deterrent *in reality*, so the mechanism can work regardless of whether the threat is genuine or not."[12]

These naturalists assume that some of the cognitive faculties conducive to survival produce a tendency to believe in a God to whom people feel morally accountable. However, the process of natural selection does not select beliefs on the basis of their truth but on the basis of their value for survival. Thus the natural tendency to believe in a God does not provide a reason to believe that God actually exists or that morality is objective, since there is a wholly natural explanation for this religious tendency. The belief in God and objective morality can therefore be regarded as an illusion.[13]

Even though primitive hominids, according to this theory, developed the automatic tendency to fear a supercreator that holds them morally responsible, such instinctive moral convictions are illusions without any truth value. Morality is merely an instinct that has become a universal feature of the human species because of its value for survival. Once people's critical capacities develop and they become aware of the instinctive nature of moral obligations, they will see them as illusions.

Many naturalists claim that scientific knowledge about the evolutionary origin of "the God instinct" implies knowledge of its illusionary nature. The more enlightened members of culture will use this new knowledge to get rid of religious and moral illusions. This naturalistic approach appeals to the so-called dual-process theory, according to which human beings reason on two levels: on an automatic, fast, and

---

10. Dominic Johnson and Oliver Kruger, "The Good Wrath: Supernatural Punishment and the Evolution of Cooperation," *Political Theology*, 5 (2004): 159–176.

11. Jesse Bering and Todd Shackelford, "The Causal Role of Consciousness: A Conceptual Addendum to Human Evolutionary Psychology," *Review of General Psychology* 8 (2004): 227–248.

12. Dominic Johnson and Jesse Bering, "Hand of God, Mind of Man: Punishment and Cognition in the Evolution of Cooperation," in *The Believing Primate: Scientific, Philosophical and Theological Reflections on the Origin of religion,* ed. Jeffrey Schloss and Michael Murray (Oxford: Oxford University Press, 2010), 30–31.

13. Bering, *Belief Instinct,* 200.

intuitive system 1 level, and on a reflective, slow, and analytic system 2 level. The automatic tendency to believe in a godlike being to whom human beings feel morally responsible remains, even if a person reflectively rejects it on the basis of advanced scientific knowledge, because it has been programmed into the human cognitive functioning by the processes of evolution.

The dual-process approach has been subjected to some criticism, however: not all conscious, deliberate, system 2 activity is properly called analytic.[14]

Naturalists thus assume that, the more people rely on their automatic reasoning and follow their immediately arising spontaneous intuitions, the more they tend to believe in God or exhibit intrinsic religiosity. On the other hand, the more people are ready to evaluate arguments objectively and critically consider alternatives, the more they show religious disbelief.[15] As the force of the God instinct fades, its embedded moral sense of being responsible to the supercreator will vanish as well.

This line of reasoning is a more refined version of the rough idea of the "new atheists" that religious beliefs are childish everyday beliefs that some people never grow out of. Several empirical studies claim to find a correlation between analytic thought, reflective reasoning, critical evaluation of arguments, and religious disbelief.[16]

However, an empirical study by Julie Yonker and others obtained opposite results: analytic thought does not necessarily influence intrinsic religiosity, but if there is such an influence, it goes toward more religiosity.[17]

Certain naturalistic theories thus acknowledge that morality is experienced as divine commands. But they argue that once people develop in their critical thinking, they become aware of the illusionary nature of morality as commanded by God.

---

14. Julie E. Yonker, Laird R. O. Edman, James Cresswell, and Justin L. Barrett, "Primed Analytic Thought and Religiosity: The Importance of Individual Characteristics," *Psychology of Religion and Spirituality* 8, no. 4 (November 2016): 298–308.

15. Elisa Järnefelt, *Created by Some Being: Theoretical and Empirical Exploration of Adults' Automatic and Reflective Beliefs about the Origin of Natural Phenomena* (academic dissertation, University of Helsinki, 2013), 41.

16. E.g., W. Gervais and A. Norenzayan, "Analytic Thinking Promotes Religious Disbelief," *Science* 336 (2012): 493–496.

17. Yonker et al, "Primed Analytic Thought and Religiosity."

These naturalistic theories can be challenged by pointing out that many people with critical minds and extensive knowledge end up with the rational conviction that morality actually originates in God's commands, and that without this theistic foundation morality would lose much of its significance.

II. The Approach of Theistic Evolutionism

While intelligent design supporters focus their main attack on the scientific claim that moral and religious sentiments evolved through the combinatorial processes involved in Darwinian evolution, theistic evolutionists regard that as a wrong strategy. A major strategy of theistic evolutionism is to attack the uncritical ways in which naturalistic theories often mix philosophical assumptions with scientific results:

> The scientific fields of sociobiology and evolutionary psychology are young. Because these fields presently have theories running well in advance of empirical data, this [attack on the scientific claim that human moral and religious sentiments evolved] might seem an attractive strategy. Nevertheless, I believe it is the wrong strategy. The problem does not lie in the scientific claim. The problem lies in the philosophical claim that if our moral and religious sentiments evolved, then moral and religious beliefs cannot have objective status or truth content.[18]

Loren Haarsma suggests that we need not dispute the current scientific hypotheses about how morality evolved. We need only dispute the naturalistic philosophical extrapolation as to why morality exists. One such naturalistic fallacy is "the fallacy of nothing but-tery." This is the claim that a complete evolutionary description of the existence of morality does invalidate the truth, utility, or significance of other levels of description of morality.[19]

So a major difference between intelligent design theory and theistic evolutionism is a difference in strategy. Theistic evolutionists like Haarsma admit that current naturalistic theories are vulnerable to

---

18. Loren Haarsma, "Evolution and Divine Revelation," in *Evolution and Ethics, Human Morality in Biological and Religious Perspective*, ed. Philip Clayton and Jeffrey Schloss (Grand Rapids, MI: Eerdmans), 154.
19. Ibid., 157.

attack as scientific theories. But they assume that, given time, a well-founded naturalistic theory will emerge to explain the way moral and religious sentiments have evolved. Therefore, they think it wiser to focus on the philosophical weaknesses of naturalistic theories and their inadequate separation of philosophical assumptions and scientific results.

The intelligent design strategy is of course more risky in the sense that, once you attack a specific scientific theory, you risk being proved wrong. But many intelligent design supporters see such grave problems in current evolutionary theories that they feel justified in criticizing them instead of merely trying to reconcile the Christian faith with the evolutionary story. To some extent theistic evolutionists do this as well.

A. Various Interpretations of Theistic Evolution

There are at least two major approaches that a theistic evolutionist may take with regard to the origin of moral conscience.

(1) She may argue that the evolutionary account is valid insofar as it deals with topics that belong to the field of natural science. The standard evolutionary account can explain the development of human beings as biological beings. But we may need to rely on other sources of information to gain insight about the origin of the spiritual and moral aspects of the human nature. For example, God may create human beings by conferring an immaterial soul on what was formerly a wholly material primate. In such a view, God creates "human life" within the processes of common biological ancestry, although humans are constituted by more than biology.

(2) A theistic evolutionist may think that the scientific account of the origin of moral conscience explains the development of the affective and cognitive capacities to make moral judgments and recognize the difference between good and evil, right and wrong. Once evolutionary mechanisms have developed the human capacities to discern the difference between good and evil, right and wrong, human beings may then use these capacities to recognize the moral law, which has a transcendent origin. In order for human beings to acquire adequate knowledge of moral principles, "at some points in human history, the

evolutionary development of morality must be augmented with divine personal revelation."[20]

A theistic evolutionist of this sort may argue that God has pre-ordained or guided natural processes to create human beings in his image and has provided them with a genuine sense of morality. God may design initial conditions conducive to the development of human beings with a moral conscience, or he may exert influence on the genetic material of a primate gamete "by directly causing a mutation or by influencing the outcome of probabilistic events like recombination or chromosomal assortment in ways that would present no evidence of intervention."[21] This view would not be in obvious conflict with naturalistic accounts, since God's intervention could not be discerned by science.

The crucial problem with evolutionary theory in regard to moral development can be highlighted with the following questions: (1) If human moral sensibilities have gradually developed from animal forms of co-operation based on individual or group advantage, how can we account for the qualitative jump from mere instinctual drives and prudential considerations to genuine moral considerations that trump self-interest and make human beings aware of their obligation to follow the commands of an absolutely good and loving God? (2) Can we claim a qualitative difference between human beings and animals and establish a foundation for the human capacity to discern human dignity and fundamental human rights if we suppose that human beings have gradually developed from their animal ancestors through Darwinian mechanisms?

B. Human Morality as a Result of God's Special Intervention

The first approach common among theistic evolutionists is represented by Francis Collins, who rejects the evolutionary account of the origin of moral conscience. Collins thinks that the validity of the evolutionary account is limited to the biological nature of human beings. He regards morality as part of man's spiritual nature that has been directly created by God.

---

20. Ibid., 154–155.
21. Jeff Schloss and Michael Murray, "Evolution," in *The Routledge Companion to Theism*, ed. Charles Taliaferro, Victoria S. Harrison, and Stewart Goetz (New York and London: Routledge, 2013), 227.

Although there are many subtle variants of this form of theistic evolutionism, Collins argues that a typical version rests on six premises.[22] I will quote here the last three, which are relevant to our topic:

4. Once evolution got under way, no special supernatural intervention was required.
5. Humans are part of this process, sharing a common ancestor with the great apes.
6. But humans are also unique in ways that defy evolutionary explanation and point to our spiritual nature. This includes the existence of the Moral Law (the knowledge of right and wrong) and the search for God that characterizes all human cultures throughout history.

Collins argues that human moral conscience and the sense of the divine are essential to the spiritual nature of human beings. He assumes that they transcend evolutionary explanations, while he otherwise argues that human beings were produced by the same evolutionary mechanisms as nonhuman animals: "God intentionally chose the same mechanism to give rise to special creatures who would have intelligence, a knowledge of right and wrong, free will, and a desire to seek fellowship with him."[23]

Collins does not feel any tension between his premises 4 and 6. Collins probably thinks that, as far as the biological evolution of human beings is concerned, no special supernatural intervention was required once God had created the initial conditions and the mechanisms of evolution. But he seems to assume such an intervention with regard to the origin of the spiritual nature of human beings.

I think that Collins is right in his assumption that human moral conscience cannot be explained by referring to animal affections and their forms of cooperation. Animal forms of cooperation consist of instinctual drives and automatic cognitive tendencies to feel and react in certain ways, and these fall within the scope of a causal account. A failure to act according to an instinctive solidarity felt toward members of one's own herd is not a moral failure but only a malfunction of the

---

22. Francis Collins, *The Language of God* (New York: Free Press), 200.
23. Ibid., 200–201.

biological-psychological instinct. The malfunction of an instinct hardly makes one morally guilty.

C. Moral Conscience as an Evolutionary Product

Collins's approach can be seen as a deviation from the more general theistic evolutionary approach—to accept evolutionary explanations wholesale and to argue that God has used evolutionary processes for his purposes. Thus a more prevalent approach within the theistic evolutionist camp is to assume that evolutionary theories about the origin of morality explain the origin of human moral conscience, even though these evolutionary accounts might need supplementing and enriching by theological accounts.

One representative of this approach is Karl Giberson. He suggests that human morality has developed through an evolutionary process that favors animals controlled by selfish desires:

> Selfishness, in fact, drives the evolutionary process. Unselfish creatures died, and their unselfish genes perished with them. Selfish creatures, who attended to their own needs for food, power, and sex, flourished and passed on these genes to their offspring. After many generations selfishness was so fully programmed in our genomes that it was a significant part of what we now call human nature.[24]

Giberson denies that the fall into sin is a specific historical event. He interprets the fallenness of human nature as inherent selfishness produced by the evolutionary struggle for survival. Thus no human being is morally responsible for the fall. Rather, human selfishness is coded into our genes.

While pointing out the role of selfish desires in the processes of evolutionary development, Giberson argues that human beings also have an innate tendency to altruism, a readiness to make sacrifices for others, which Giberson admits is "scientifically harder to understand than selfishness."[25]

But Giberson still thinks that the origin of these altruistic affections

---

24. Karl W. Giberson, *Saving Darwin* (New York: HarperOne, 2009), 12.
25. Ibid.

can be explained by evolutionary science. He argues that "animals, especially the higher primates" have "a moral sense that is only quantitatively different from that of humans."[26] He recounts the story by Frans de Waal about a bonobo who saw a starling hit a glass wall and fall to the ground. The bonobo picked up the bird and tried to help it fly again. When its attempts failed, it watched the bird until it flew away on its own. Giberson argues that "This story is close enough to that of the Good Samaritan to make it hard to treat morality as a purely human attribute. And we have records of countless other examples of similar animal behaviors."[27]

Giberson does not consider the possibility that this kind of animal behavior could be controlled by instincts, in which case it would have nothing to do with morality. He points out that there are "countless other examples of similar animal behaviors" and they seem to resemble the story of the Good Samaritan.

Giberson thereby rejects the idea of "a great qualitative distinction between humans and the higher primates."[28] He assumes that his rejection is based on incontrovertible evidence and seems to be oblivious to the fact that his rejection may be a priori, and may be reflected in his conceptualization of the evidence. His evolutionary scheme assumes that human beings are not unique, and that there is only a gradual difference between humans and the higher animals.

Giberson's extreme interpretation of the historical fall into sin in completely biological terms is rejected even by many theistic evolutionists. Loren Haarsma criticizes the idea that an action should be labeled "selfish" merely because it provides long-term benefit to one's reproductive chances. It is misleading to follow popular literature on sociobiology and evolutionary psychology, which employs "a linguistic maneuver in which every action that improves one's reproductive chances is labeled 'selfish,'" because to be prudential doesn't mean being inherently selfish.[29]

Theistic evolutionists like Giberson follow naturalists in minimizing the differences between humans and their closest evolutionary

---

26. Ibid., 13.
27. Ibid., 13–14.
28. Ibid., 14.
29. Haarsma, "Evolution and Divine Revelation," 158.

links. They appeal to the kind of evidence presented by the primatologist Frans de Waal, who claims that human moral sentiments and
intuitions show remarkable continuity with other primates, and that
the roots of moral sensibilities can be found in the social behavior of
monkeys and apes. De Waal does not suggest that apes or even chimpanzees possess morality. But he argues that human morality presupposes certain emotional building blocks that are at work in chimp
and monkey societies. Sociality is based on four kinds of behavior:
empathy, the ability to learn and follow social rules, reciprocity, and
peacemaking.[30]

De Waal acknowledges one inherent problem in the evolutionary
account of the origin of moral sensibilities: human morality has evolved
as a way of banding together against adversaries: "The profound irony
is that our noblest achievement—morality—has evolutionary ties to
our basest behavior—warfare," he writes. "The sense of community
required by the former was provided by the latter."[31]

De Waal recognizes that the basic idea of morality is contrary to
the logic of evolutionary struggle for survival. However, he does not
seem to recognize that this discrepancy is a serious problem for the
evolutionary account: the evolutionary struggle for survival, where
each creature tries to destroy its competitors, involves a perspective
contrary to that of the universal ethic of love. Mere prudential concern
for one's own tribe is qualitatively different from a universal ethic of
love, which involves an altruistic concern for objective justice inspired
by universal benevolence.

De Waal admits that the endeavor to derive human moral sensibilities from their supposed animal precursors leads to an understanding
of morality as an instinctive tendency rather than as something controlled by rational deliberation and conscious choice. "Human behavior derives above all from fast, automated, emotional judgments, and
only secondarily from slower conscious processes," de Waal writes.[32]
This is due to the fact that morality evolved at a time when hominids
lived in small foraging societies and had to make instant life-or-death

---

30. Frans de Waal, *Primates and Philosophers: How Morality Evolved*, ed. Stephen Macedo
and Josiah Ober (Princeton, NJ: Princeton University Press, 2013).
31. Ibid., 55.
32. Ibid., 6.

decisions without time for conscious moral deliberation. Reasoning comes afterwards, as a justification.

Once the emphasis is put on fast, automated, largely unconscious processes, moral responsibility is downplayed. The effect is similar to that of Giberson's assumption that human selfishness is not really a moral choice but a result of genetic coding in the process of natural selection. Selfishness may be a fault, but not one for which we are morally responsible.

1. Theology and Biology in Cooperation

Jeffrey Schloss, another representative of the second approach within theistic evolutionism, defends the following main theses: (1) The naturalistic account of evolution can be reconciled with theism mainly because (a) God may have set the initial conditions so that the evolutionary process eventually produces human beings created in the image of God, (b) God may have influenced the causal processes of evolution in ways that cannot be detected by natural science, (c) God has influenced the contents of human morality through direct encounters with human beings. (2) Although the naturalistic account of evolution is right in giving a correct outline of the evolutionary process, the naturalistic description can be enriched by theological considerations. (3) Although the evolutionary process is often described as completely contingent (completely the result of chance), it actually shows a planned progress toward higher forms of life.

Schloss argues that theistic evolutionism will have a healthy impact on the discussion about the evolutionary origin of humans as it will bring theological considerations into the discussion. It will thereby mitigate the reductionistic tendency of evolutionary science and enrich the scientific accounts of the evolutionary origin of morality. In order to have such a positive effect, theology must be ready to listen to science on the issues of ethics—it may actually gain fresh spiritual understanding by learning from contemporary evolutionary accounts. For example, scientific accounts of kin selection and reciprocal altruism may advance our understanding of the central tendency of moral affections, which may be "theologically regarded as expressions of common grace."[33]

In Schloss's view, at least the human capacity to recognize the difference between right and wrong, good and evil, is the result of a long evolutionary process. But Schloss assumes that God's active engagement with human beings has influenced their moral convictions, not only by clarifying the right moral commands but also by offering forgiveness, which then makes it possible for human beings to recognize their faults and sharpen their understanding of the moral law.

In this view, God has a twofold role in the development of human morality. He has guided those evolutionary processes that led to the development of human moral capacities and he has personally engaged with human beings, thereby influencing their moral perceptions, affections, and prescriptions. In this way Schloss wants to account for the human capacity to sense moral obligations as God's commands: God has directly intervened in human history and has had personal encounters with human beings.[34]

But can Schloss account for the fact that this sense of moral obligation is built into human nature? In this respect he doesn't want to appeal to God's direct intervention—he regards the development of moral capacities as a result of natural evolutionary processes. Thus he has to appeal to a naturalistic theory that explains the qualitative change from animal instincts to genuine morality through Darwinian mechanisms.

Schloss compares the evolutionary development of moral capacities to the development of human babies into morally conscious human beings: "Just as toddlers start out as premoral creatures, still of great worth, but not morally responsible, in the same way the moral sense itself may have emerged over a long evolutionary history. What the Christian as opposed to the nontheist would believe is that this process ultimately reflects the sculpting and the design of a wise and ultimately moral being, so that you and I have ultimately developed a moral

---

33. Jeffrey Schloss, "Introduction: Evolutionary Ethics and Christian Morality," in *Evolution and Ethics: Human Morality in Biological and Religious Perspective*, ed. Philip Clayton and Jeffrey Schloss (Grand Rapids, MI: Eerdmans), 18–19.

34. Jeffrey Schloss, Veritas Forum, "Altruism in Evolution" (discussion with John Tooby, 2011).

sense that is capable of recognizing morality as God intended it to be recognized."[35]

His comparison of the moral maturation of a toddler with the evolutionary development of prehuman hominids into morally responsible human beings is misleading, however, as these two processes are qualitatively different. Schloss is right in claiming that toddlers are not yet morally responsible for their behavior, but that is due to their deficient conception about the consequences of their actions. The research conducted by Paul Bloom and others indicates that not only toddlers, but even babies, have a moral sense, "the capacity to make certain types of judgments—to distinguish between good and bad, kindness and cruelty."[36]

Thus the comparison with toddlers doesn't help here, because toddlers already have the moral sense built into their human nature, and their moral maturation involves the opening up of this potential. Evolutionary theory assumes that primitive hominids had only the ruthless mechanisms of survival of the fittest to guide them in their development from instinctual animals into morally conscious human beings. The assumption that human morality can develop out of nonmoral origins assumes a qualitative jump. I will later argue that such a qualitative jump cannot be explained by Darwinian mechanisms.

2. The Contingency Problem

In order to maintain the idea of God's ultimate control of the evolutionary processes, theistic evolutionists have to challenge the extreme contingency view defended by naturalists like Stephen Jay Gould. The evolutionary approach assumes that an instinctual morality has developed because of its survival value in the processes of evolution, or as a by-product of evolved capacities. There is nothing *necessary* in such moral convictions, however.

This kind of a naturalistic evolutionary process cannot account for moral knowledge, because the Darwinian evolutionary story regards human beings as one contingent occurrence among many possibilities. The natural history that led to human beings consists of contingent

---

35. Ibid.
36. Paul Bloom, *Just Babies: The Origins of Good and Evil* (New York: Broadway Books, 2013), 31.

events which could have led to another kind of being. Stephen Jay Gould argues that the history of life is a reduction of initial possibilities to just a few surviving groups: "the reduction of 100 initial possibilities to ten or so was the analogue of a bingo game, a grand-scale lottery. In fact any ten of the 100 could have made it. If you could rewind the tape of life, erasing what actually happened and let it run again, you'd get a different set of ten each time."[37]

Charles Darwin argues that this has radical implications for our understanding of morality; moral sensibilities could have acquired completely different characteristics had the contingent evolutionary processes taken alternative routes:

> If, for instance, to take an extreme case, men were reared under precisely the same conditions as hive-bees, there can hardly be a doubt that our unmarried females would, like the worker-bees, think it a sacred duty to kill their brother, and mothers would strive to kill their fertile daughters; and no one would think of interfering.[38]

In the same vein, Michael Ruse argues that our moral convictions are ultimately contingent: "Or take the termites. . . . They have to eat each other's feces. . . . Had humans come along a similar trail, our highest ethical imperatives would have been very strange indeed."[39]

Jeffrey Schloss and Michael Murray, however, challenge this interpretation. They argue that evolutionary history displays "a more complicated interplay of contingency and necessity than the radical contingency view entails." It is not clear that the evolutionary trajectory was "massively improbable." And even if the outcome of evolution were contingent on chance events, it does not exclude divine providence: "Even if an event that is necessary for a particular outcome appears to be highly improbable, this does not mean that an omniscient God could not know it would happen, or an omnipotent God could not guarantee it would happen."[40]

---

37. Stephen Jay Gould, "Interview: Stephen Jay Gould, Evolutionary Biologist and Paleontologist," *Academy of Achievement*, June 28, 1991, accessed November 25, 2015, http://www.achievement.org/autodoc/page/gou0int-1.
38. Charles Darwin, *The Descent of Man* (Amherst, NY: Prometheus, 1998), 102.
39. Michael Ruse, "Evolutionary Theory and Christian Ethics," Zygon, *Journal of Religion and Science* 29 (March 2013).
40. Schloss and Murray, "Evolution," 238.

As mentioned at the beginning of this chapter, the contingency problem receives a different form depending on whether we understand evolutionary ethics as a weak thesis about moral sensibility (Weak EE) or as a stronger thesis about the origin of morality itself (Strong EE).[41] Theistic evolutionists usually adhere to Weak EE, which faces the problem of accounting for adequate moral knowledge.

As Menuge points out, if weak evolutionary ethics is affirmed in its ambitious form (Ambitious Weak EE), then "although beings raised like a hive bee would not make fratricide a duty, our moral sense would tell us that it was." If so, our moral beliefs do not provide reliable access to moral reality. So, "even if our actual moral beliefs about fratricide happen to be true, this is a lucky coincidence." It no more constitutes knowledge than does the belief of someone lucky enough to learn the right time from a broken clock.[42]

Theistic evolutionists might then appeal to Modest Weak EE, "which admits the unreliability of humanity's moral sense but claims that evolution has provided other faculties such as reason and intuition that allow access to moral truth."[43] One problem with this approach is that we do not have an adequate evolutionary explanation for the emergence of reason and rational intuition, as Peter van Inwagen points out:

> If I may judge by some unguarded remarks I've heard, I think that some adherents of philosophical naturalism are a bit uneasy about the time span in which the gulf between non-rationality and rationality was bridged—but, unlike us theists, they have no alternative to supposing that the gulf was bridged by purely natural mechanisms within the time span, and, in one way or another, they have made their peace with it.[44]

A further problem is that mere principles of reason like the principle of universalizability do not guarantee moral truth without a properly functioning moral sense. So the basic dilemma of evolutionary ethics is that, if that belief system is true, moral truths are unknowable.

---

41. Menuge, "Why Human Rights Cannot Be Naturalized," 57–78.
42. Ibid., 59.
43. Ibid., 76.
44. Peter van Inwagen, *The Problem of Evil* (Oxford, Clarendon, 2006), 128–129.

Theistic evolutionists try to escape these epistemological problems by appealing to God's guidance: God has guided the evolutionary processes so that our cognitive faculties can reliably recognize moral truths. Schloss and Murray argue that evolutionary history displays a trajectory that is progressive and in some sense suggestive of purpose. There are sustained directional trends across evolutionary history: "characteristics such as body size, sensory acuity, homeostatic precision, cellular differentiation, and parental investment all increase over evolutionary history." Furthermore, there are coherent themes underlying these increases: functional specialization and cooperative interdependence:

> Thus it does appear that there is a thematically consistent directionality to the series of transitions that have reformulated the scale and function of living organisms according to which formerly independent units evolve into dependent parts of a whole.

Furthermore, such trends constitute progress:

> If there is a loving God whose purposes include the creation of beings capable of receiving and transmitting love, evolutionary history seems to entail an escalating series of organic innovations that are concordant with and necessary for—but not sufficient for—the attainment of such purpose.[45]

The problem, however, is that Schloss and Murray can hold on to this idea only on the metaphorical level, because the Darwinian combinatorial processes do not allow a qualitative change from instinctive morality to the cognitive capacity to discern moral truths. So they either have to presuppose God's miraculous intervention or assume that we still function at the instinctual level in our moral behavior: we are not actually free to make moral choices or to recognize moral truths.

3. The Moral Gap

Theistic evolutionists usually assume that the human capacity to discern moral obligations developed from instinctual forms of cooperation

---

45. Schloss and Murray, "Evolution," 236–238.

among animals. The difficulty then is to find a mechanism to explain how these instinctual drives have developed into genuine moral cognitions capable of discerning the requirements of universal benevolence, transcendent justice, overriding moral obligation, and absolute human dignity.

The theistic evolutionist has only the resources available in the Darwinian mechanisms to explain the transition from an instinctual habit to moral conscience as a source of genuine moral knowledge, guidance, and sentiment. As Moreland points out, the basic problem both for naturalists and for theistic evolutionists is that "he/she must employ combinatorial processes constitutive of the Grand Story according to which all change is the rearrangement of separable parts into various external, spatio-temporal, causal relations to form differently structured relational wholes."[46]

Moreland argues that genuinely new kinds of properties cannot, in principle, be explained by the atomic theory of matter or by Darwinian evolution, because these theories only employ combinatorial explanations: they explain things by appealing to a new combination of the atoms and molecules. Thus, they are not suited for the appearance of new simple properties such as consciousness and the cognitive capacity to discern intrinsic, normative value properties.

Moreland argues in detail that there is no naturalistic, combinatorial explanation of the appearance of simple properties of consciousness. This would then be true for simple value cognitions as well. The naturalistic claim that these properties are "emergent"[47] is not a solution: rather, it just provides a place-holder or a name to the problem. Insofar as theistic evolutionists agree that we really have irreducible consciousness and the capacity to discern intrinsic value, they presuppose that human beings have features that cannot be explained by naturalistic evolution. If they do not want to accept a genuine theistic explanation for these features, they have to assume some form of panpsychism (with both latent consciousness and value). Panpsychism is similar to naturalism in denying the existence of a personal God, but as David Skrbina[48] points out, panpsychism has always been a rival to

---

46. Moreland, *Recalcitrant Imago Dei*, 68.
47. See chapter 21 of this volume, note 22.
48. David Skrbina, *Panpsychism in the West* (Cambridge, MA: Bradford Books [MIT Press], 2007).

naturalism because it denies that atomism and mechanistic explanations are adequate. The best explanation for the existence of consciousness and the capacity to discern intrinsic value is God's special creative act. But this implies rejecting theistic evolution. Therefore, theistic evolutionists must take some sort of physicalist view of consciousness, which makes it then difficult to account for genuine moral conscience.[49]

A major problem for theistic evolutionism is that naturalistic evolution undermines our ability to claim that we can have knowledge of objective values. Thomas Nagel, among others, makes this claim.[50] He begins by asserting a fairly obvious epistemic principle, that if a belief is formed by a process that is not counterfactually sensitive, then we have a defeater for the belief and should reject it even if it might be true. Insofar as our faculties are not counterfactually sensitive, we could believe in the existence of an object even if it was not there. Even if there is an objective moral order out there (a sort of Plato's heaven), and my moral beliefs (racism is wrong) and my moral actions (I am kind to the elderly) are actually true and correspond to the objective moral order, given that my moral beliefs/actions were formed by evolution because of their survival value and not their truth value, then I would believe and act in this way whether or not they corresponded to an objective moral order, since my cognitive faculties are not counterfactually sensitive. Thus, naturalistic evolution provides strong evidence that we can never trust our moral judgments even if, miracle of miracles, they happen to be true. If a theistic evolutionist ascribes to human faculties capabilities that cannot be explained by naturalistic evolution, they are attributing something to us that theism can explain but which cannot be explained by naturalistic evolution. Thereby they would be rejecting the basic principle of theistic evolutionism.[51]

Thus, the theistic evolutionist faces the problem of explaining how these originally instinctual drives were transformed into a consciousness of genuine moral obligations and a capacity to discern moral truth. A theistic evolutionist would have to find a way of explaining the transition from herd instincts of primitive hominids to a consciousness of

---

49. J. P. Moreland, *Consciousness and the Existence of God: A Theistic Argument* (New York: Routledge, 2008).

50. Thomas Nagel, *The Last Word* (New York: Oxford University Press, 1997).

51. Moreland, *Recalcitrant Imago Dei*, appendix.

good and evil with a high success rate for tracking the moral truth. An instinct to help and support the members of the herd is not genuine morality. How do theistic evolutionists think that genuine moral conscience was developed through the mechanisms of Darwinian evolution?

John Hare suggests that any evolutionary account of the origin of morality faces the problem of the "moral gap" in its two aspects. "First, there is what I will call the 'affection gap' between those animals who have only the affection for advantage and humans who have also the affection for justice. Second, there is the 'performance gap' within our own lives between the demands to be moral and our actual performance."[52]

The theories of kin selection, reciprocal altruism, and social control proposed as precursors of human moral conscience fall victim to the affection gap. These forms of animal cooperation show only complicated forms of the affection for advantage—none of them shows animals having the affection for justice. Since animals lack the affection for justice, they also lack the freedom that is a necessary precondition for morality. Thus "there is something crucial about human morality that is not found in nonhuman animals."[53]

Thus evolutionary accounts about the origin of human moral sensibilities face the affective moral gap: How can basically selfish affections directed at group or individual advantage be changed into genuine affections for justice that do not make any difference between one's group and others and are ready for self-sacrifice.

The second argument that evolutionary ethicists make concerns the performance gap. "Even if they cannot appeal to common origin to explain human moral capacity, they can appeal to evolutionary pressure during early periods of human history. . . . the fundamental explanation is in terms of natural selection or adaptation, and hence reproductive advantage." But Hare argues that "there is something crucial about human morality that cannot be explained by locating its source in natural selection."[54]

---

52. John Hare, "Is There an Evolutionary Foundation for Human Morality?," in *Evolution and Ethics: Human Morality in Biological and Religious Perspective*, ed. Philip Clayton and Jeffrey Schloss (Grand Rapids, MI: Eerdmans, 2004), 190.
53. Ibid., 191.
54. Ibid., 191–192.

The qualitative difference between animal forms of cooperation and human morality provides one reason to assume that the creation of human beings involves God's intervention in history. Human beings and their moral sense are not the result of an evolutionary process, whether guided or unguided, but a result of a unique act of creation. On this view, the general human capacity to believe in God and his moral order that are built into the human mind constitute one of the highest human capacities: the capacity to discern between good and evil. We don't only discern the difference; we feel a moral obligation to follow the good and the right.

Not only are naturalistic explanations unable to account for the emergence of moral conscience, but as J. P. Moreland has shown, naturalism isn't able to account for human consciousness, free will, universal rationality, or substantial soul either.[55] Without these human capacities, morality would lose its significance.

III. Conclusion

Theistic evolutionists have the commendable goal of helping theistic students keep their faith under secular educational systems that indoctrinate them with the naturalistic worldview. The problem with their accommodating approach is that they eventually end up modifying the contents of the theistic faith and the nature of morality to fit in the evolutionary account. They hide the problems in the evolutionary account by vague metaphors and create the impression that Darwinian mechanisms are able to produce qualitatively new forms of consciousness. The vague idea that God has used evolutionary processes to attain his goals may ease the tension that believers feel between their faith and the current consensus in evolutionary science. Eventually, however, the problems inherent in such vague metaphors could undermine our trust in the human capacity for moral knowledge.

While theistic students may be helped in the short term because they are relieved of the pressure either to reject their theistic faith or be labeled bigoted representatives of an anti-science and anti-knowledge superstition, the foundations of their faith may be undermined in the

---

55. Moreland, *Recalcitrant Imago Dei*.

long term because of the widespread accommodation of the Christian faith and the nature of morality into the presuppositions of the naturalistic worldview.

The weak point in the reasoning of theistic evolutionists is their inadequate analysis of the qualitative difference between nonmoral forms of cooperation and genuine moral considerations. What is lacking is an adequate philosophical analysis of the unique nature of moral conscience and its difference from mere prudential or other nonmoral considerations.

26

Darwin in the Dock:
C. S. Lewis on Evolution

JOHN G. WEST

SUMMARY

Few twentieth-century writers are as beloved by modern Christians as C. S. Lewis. In recent years, there has been considerable discussion about the views of Lewis on evolution, with some claiming that he is best described as a proponent of theistic evolution. This chapter, drawing on Lewis's public and private writings, shows that Lewis in fact expressed deep and growing concerns about major aspects of modern evolutionary theory. Lewis did not object in principle to the evolutionary idea of common descent, but he sharply limited its application in a way that mainstream proponents of evolution would find unacceptable. More importantly, Lewis was a thoroughgoing skeptic of the creative power of unguided Darwinian natural selection, and he sharply criticized the application of what he called "evolutionism" to morality and society. Finally, Lewis validated raising questions about Darwinian evolution by showing how science itself depends on many nonscientific assumptions.

. . . . .

Few twentieth-century writers are as beloved by modern Christians as C. S. Lewis.[1] Through his works of fiction like the Chronicles of Narnia and nonfiction books like *Mere Christianity*, Lewis continues to shape in profound ways the faith of millions of people around the globe. Given his prominence, it is understandable why so many Christians want to know about Lewis's views on evolution.

Lewis has been treated in recent years as a virtual patron saint by certain proponents of theistic evolution. In his best-selling book *The Language of God* (2006), biologist Francis Collins invoked Lewis to defend the idea that Christians should accept the animal ancestry of humans.[2] In the journal *Perspectives on Science and Christian Faith*, Michael Peterson of Asbury Theological Seminary went considerably further. According to Peterson, Lewis not only embraced "both cosmic and biological evolution as highly confirmed scientific theories," but he would have rejected out-of-hand arguments offered by modern proponents of intelligent design.[3] Peterson's article on Lewis and evolution was serialized online by the pro–theistic evolution group BioLogos.[4]

There is little doubt that Lewis was interested in the topic of evolution. He discussed it repeatedly in his books and essays. He wrote about it in his private letters. And his personal library contained more than a dozen books and pamphlets focused on evolution, some of which were marked up with extensive underlining and annotations, including his personal copy of Charles Darwin's *Autobiography*.[5]

---

1. This chapter was condensed and reworked from my chapter 6 in John G. West, ed., *The Magician's Twin: C. S. Lewis on Science, Scientism, and Society* (Seattle: Discovery Institute Press, 2012). Anyone desiring an even more detailed discussion of Lewis's views on evolution, as well as an exploration of his views on scientism and intelligent design, should consult my chapters 1, 6, and 7 in that book. I gratefully acknowledge the research of Jake Akins at the Wade Center Collection, Wheaton College, which contributed to an earlier version of this essay, and the permission of both the Wade Center and the C. S. Lewis Company to quote from some of Lewis's unpublished writings deposited at the Wade Center. Finally, I would like to thank Jay Richards, Sonja West, and Cameron Wybrow for their thoughtful comments on an earlier version of this essay. Any faults, of course, are entirely my own.

2. Francis Collins, *The Language of God* (New York: Free Press, 2006), 21–31, 208–209, 222–225.

3. Michael L. Peterson, "C. S. Lewis on Evolution and Intelligent Design," *Perspectives on Science and Christian Faith (PSCF)* 62, no. 4 (December 2010): 253–266.

4. Michael L. Peterson, "C. S. Lewis on Evolution and Intelligent Design," *The American Scientific Affiliation* (April 2011), accessed December 15, 2016, http://www.asa3.org/ASA/PSCF/2010/PSCF12-10Peterson.pdf.

5. Some of these books and pamphlets with a significant focus on evolution in Lewis's library include Bernard Acworth, *The Cuckoo*; Alfred Balfour, *Theism and Humanism*; Henri Bergson, *L'Evolution Creatrice*; Charles Darwin, *Autobiography*; L. M. Davies, *BBC Abuses Its Monopoly*; L. M. Davies, *Evolutionists Under Fire*; Douglas Dewar, *The Man from Monkey Myth*; Douglas

However, to accurately determine Lewis's real views on evolution, we first need to untangle the distinct ways in which Lewis employed the term. One of the most challenging things about discussing "evolution" today is that the term is so elastic, covering everything from mere "change over time" to the development of all living things from one-celled organisms to man through an unguided process of natural selection acting on random variations.[6]

Lewis addressed at least three different kinds of evolution in his writings: (1) evolution as a theory of common descent; (2) evolution as a theory of unguided natural selection acting on random variations (a.k.a. Darwinism); and (3) evolution as a cosmic philosophy ("evolutionism").

Lewis did not object in principle to evolution in the first sense (common descent), although he sharply limited its application in a way that mainstream proponents of evolution would find unacceptable. The case for Lewis as a supporter of evolution in the second sense (Darwinism) is almost nonexistent. Lewis was a thoroughgoing skeptic of the creative power of unguided natural selection. As for evolution in the third sense—evolutionism—Lewis respected the poetry and grandeur of what he sometimes called the "myth" of evolution, but he certainly regarded it as untrue.

Lewis's Limited Acceptance of Common Descent

Common descent is the claim that all organisms currently living have descended from one or a few original ancestors through a process Darwin called "descent with modification." According to this idea, not only humans and apes share an ancestor, but so do humans, clams, and fungi. Common descent is a hallowed dogma among today's evolution proponents, held with quasi-religious fervor.

Dewar, *Science and the BBC*; Evolution Protest Movement, *Evolution: How the Doctrine Is Propagated in Our Schools*; C. W. Formby, *The Unveiling of the Fall*; E. O. James, *Evolution and the Fall*; Edmund Sinnott, *Biology of the Spirit*; Joseph Solomon, *Bergson*; Pierre Teilhard de Chardin, *The Phenomenon of Man*. Much of Lewis's personal library is currently housed at the Wade Center, Wheaton College. For a listing of the extant books from Lewis's personal library, consult the description in "C. S. Lewis Library" (Wade Center, 2010), Wheaton College, accessed December 15, 2016, http://www.wheaton.edu/wadecenter/Authors/CS-Lewis.

6. On the different meanings of evolution, see the helpful discussion by Jay Richards, ed., *God and Evolution: Protestants, Catholics, and Jews Explore Darwin's Challenge to Faith* (Seattle: Discovery Institute Press, 2010), 18–25.

Lewis clearly believed that Christians can accept evolution as com-mon descent without doing violence to their faith. This is what Lewis was getting at when he wrote to evolution critic Bernard Acworth, "I believe that Christianity can still be believed, even if Evolution is true."[7] In Lewis's view, whether God used common descent to create the first human beings was irrelevant to the truth of Christianity. As he wrote to one correspondent late in his life, "I don't mind whether God made man out of earth or whether 'earth' merely means 'previous millennia of ancestral organisms.' If the fossils make it probable that man's physical ancestors 'evolved,' no matter."[8]

In *The Problem of Pain* (1940), Lewis even offers a possible evo-lutionary account of the development of human beings, although he makes clear he is offering speculation, not history: "[I]f it is legitimate to guess," he writes, "I offer the following picture—a 'myth' in the Socratic sense," which he defines as "a not unlikely tale," or "an ac-count of what *may have been* the historical fact" (emphasis original). Lewis then suggests that "[f]or long centuries God perfected the animal form which was to become the vehicle of humanity and the image of Himself. . . . The creature may have existed for ages . . . before it be-came man."[9]

Nevertheless, Lewis did not go out of his way to champion the animal ancestry of humans. When pressed on the subject by evolution critic Bernard Acworth in the 1940s, Lewis backpedaled, replying that his "belief that Men in general have immortal & rational souls does not oblige or qualify me to hold a theory of their prehuman organic history—if they have one."[10] A few years later, Lewis relished the ex-posure of "Piltdown Man" as a hoax. Originally touted as evidence for the long-sought "missing link" between apes and humans, the Piltdown Man's skull was discovered in the 1950s to be a fake forged from the skull of a modern human, the jawbone of an orangutan, and the teeth

7. C. S. Lewis to Bernard Acworth, December 9, 1944, in *C. S. Lewis: Collected Letters*, ed. Walter Hooper, 3 vols. (London: HarperCollins, 2000), 2:633.
8. C. S. Lewis to Joseph Canfield, February 28, 1955, unpublished letter, Wade Center Collec-tion, Wheaton College.
9. C. S. Lewis, *The Problem of Pain* (New York: Macmillan, 1962), 76–77.
10. C. S. Lewis to Bernard Acworth, September 23, 1944, reprinted in Gary B. Ferngren and Ronald L. Numbers, "C. S. Lewis on Creation and Evolution: The Acworth Letters, 1944–1960," *PSCF* 48 (March 1996), accessed December 15, 2016, http://www.asa3.org/ASA/PSCF/1996/PSCF3-96Ferngren.html.

of a chimpanzee.[11] Lewis wrote to Bernard Acworth that although he didn't think the scandal should be exploited, "I can't help sharing a sort of glee with you about the explosion of poor old Piltdown . . . one inevitably feels what fun it wd. be if this were only the beginning of a landslide."[12]

Whatever Lewis's final position on the animal ancestry of the human race, it would be wrong to conclude that his acceptance of some kind of human evolution placed him in the camp of mainstream evolutionary biology, or even of mainstream theistic evolution. In fact, Lewis insisted on three huge exceptions to evolutionary explanations of humanity that placed him well outside evolutionary orthodoxy, both then and now.

A Historic Fall

Lewis's first exception to human evolution was his insistence on an actual fall of mankind from an original state of innocence. In Christian theology, God originally created human beings morally innocent. These first humans then freely rejected God's will for them, resulting in a fall from innocence and harmony into the sinful condition of the human race as we currently find it. According to historic Christian teaching, not only human beings but the entire creation was tainted by man's initial act of wrongdoing. It was to reverse the impact of the fall that God became incarnate to save us from our sins. Thus, the fall provides the necessary "back story" for Jesus Christ and his death on the cross.

Leading theistic evolutionists, no less than secular evolutionists, insist that a historic fall is incompatible with mainstream evolutionary theory. In the words of Episcopalian Bishop John Shelby Spong, "Darwin . . . destroyed the primary myth by which we had told the Jesus story for centuries." Post-Darwin, "there was no perfect human life which then corrupted itself and fell into sin. . . . And so the story of Jesus who comes to rescue us from the fall becomes a nonsensical story."[13]

---

11. For more information about the Piltdown hoax, see Frank Spencer, *Piltdown: A Scientific Forgery* (New York: Oxford University Press, 1990).

12. C. S. Lewis to Bernard Acworth, December 16, 1953, reprinted in Ferngren and Numbers, "C. S. Lewis on Creation and Evolution."

13. Interview with Bishop John Shelby Spong, *Compass* [television program on ABC network in Australia], July 8, 2001, accessed December 15, 2016, http://www.abc.net.au/compass/intervs /spong2001.htm.

Spong is well known for his theological liberalism, but similar views have gained support among evangelical Christian proponents of evolution. In his book *Saving Darwin*, Karl Giberson included a section titled "Dissolving the Fall" where he basically argued that, since human beings were created through Darwinian evolution, they were sinful from the very start because the evolutionary process is based on selfishness.[14] Evangelical Christian Francis Collins wrote an enthusiastic foreword to Giberson's book, and Giberson helped Collins found BioLogos.

Lewis observed that it was "not yet obvious" to him "that all theories of evolution do contradict" the fall. But he was emphatic that any evolutionary theory that *does* deny a real fall is unacceptable: "I believe that Man has fallen from the state of innocence in which he was created: I therefore disbelieve in any theory wh. contradicts this."[15] Accordingly, Lewis was careful in *The Problem of Pain* to preserve a historical fall as part of his hypothetical account of human evolution. Indeed, he titled the chapter in which his evolutionary account appears, "The Fall of Man," and at the end of that chapter he declared that "the thesis of this chapter is simply that man, as a species, spoiled himself."[16] Following traditional Christian teaching, Lewis emphasized that the first humans prior to the fall were morally good, had unimpeded fellowship with God, and lived in a Paradise.[17]

Lewis had little patience for those evolutionists (theistic or otherwise) who asserted that modern science made it impossible to believe in man's original Paradisal state and subsequent fall. At the heart of their assertions, in Lewis's view, was what he called "the idolatry of artefacts"[18]—the assumption that we can discern the morality or intelligence of ancient peoples from their material products. Lewis pointed out that pottery shards or spearheads might expose the primitive state of a prehistoric people's technology, but they do not reveal the state of the people's morality or even their native intelligence.[19]

If Lewis dismissed claims that science refuted the fall, he was equally skeptical of efforts to reinterpret the fall to make it part of evolutionary

14. Karl Giberson, *Saving Darwin* (New York: HarperOne, 2008), 11–13.
15. C. S. Lewis to Bernard Acworth, September 23, 1944.
16. Lewis, *Problem of Pain*, 88.
17. Ibid., 78–79.
18. Ibid., 74.
19. Ibid.

history. In the standard evolutionary picture (popularized by Darwin himself in *The Descent of Man*), human beings started out as brutes and gained morality and religion only after a long struggle for survival.[20] Given this view of the development of human beings, it is hardly surprising that some theistic evolutionists have concluded that if there was a "fall" in evolutionary history, it must have been a "fall upward" into greater maturity and responsibility of the sort advocated by liberal theologians since Hegel and Kant. For example, contemporary Christian thinker Brian McLaren argues that the fall is best understood not as a fall from a higher state of innocence and goodness, but as a "compassionate coming of age story" that represents "the first stage of ascent as human beings progress from the life of hunter-gatherers to the life of agriculturalists and beyond."[21] McLaren does acknowledge that the ascent of man is marked by struggles with sin. But he seems to believe that human wrongdoing is a natural part of God's plan to bring about human maturity. Lewis spent much of his novel *Perelandra* (1943) critiquing this kind of thinking, arguing that God intended for human beings to progress to self-knowledge and maturity by obedience, not rebellion.[22] Four years later, in his book *Miracles* (1947), Lewis ridiculed those who "say that the story of the Fall in *Genesis* is not literal; and then go on to say (I have heard them myself) that it was really a fall upwards—which is like saying that because 'My heart is broken' contains a metaphor, it therefore means 'I feel very cheerful'. This mode of interpretation I regard, frankly, as nonsense."[23]

Lewis continued to defend the reality of the fall to those who corresponded with him. To one correspondent who questioned the grounds of Lewis's belief that the earliest humans lived unfallen in a paradise-like state, Lewis replied tartly, "[Y]ou *do* know very well what grounds I have for assuming the existence of *Paradisal Man*—namely that it is part of orthodox Christianity."[24]

20. See discussion of Darwin's account of morality in John G. West, *Darwin Day in America: How Our Politics and Culture Have Been Dehumanized in the Name of Science* (Wilmington, DE: ISI Books, 2007), 29–37.

21. Brian D. McLaren, *A New Kind of Christianity: Ten Questions That Are Transforming the Faith*, Kindle ed. (HarperCollins E-Books, 2010), 49–50.

22. C. S. Lewis, *Perelandra* (New York: Macmillan, 1965).

23. C. S. Lewis, *Miracles: A Preliminary Study* (New York: Macmillan, 1947), 95.

24. C. S. Lewis to Miss Jacob, July 3, 1951, unpublished letter, Wade Center Collection, Wheaton College. See also C. S. Lewis to Joseph Canfield, February 28, 1955.

A Literal Adam

Lewis not only believed in a historic fall; he also embraced the literal existence of Adam and Eve, which was another important exception to his acquiescence to human evolution. Lewis's acceptance of a historical Adam and Eve is widely unrecognized today. Popular Christian pastor Tim Keller, for example, writes that "C. S. Lewis . . . did not believe in a literal Adam and Eve."[25] Keller is misinformed, at least when it comes to Lewis's beliefs after he became a Christian. While Lewis was still a young atheist in the 1920s, he certainly disbelieved in Adam and Eve, although he was simultaneously skeptical of orthodox Darwinism.[26] By the 1940s, however, he was publicly noncommittal, writing in *The Problem of Pain* that "we do not know how many of these [unfallen] creatures God made, nor how long they continued in the Paradisal state."[27] In private, he was not so reticent. In a discussion at his home attended by Oxford colleague Helen Gardner, Lewis stated that the person from history he would most like to meet in heaven was Adam. When Gardner protested that "if there really were, historically, someone whom we could name as 'the first man', he would be a Neanderthal ape-like figure, whose conversation she could not conceive of finding interesting," Lewis is said to have responded with disdain: "I see we have a Darwinian in our midst."[28]

It is worth noting that throughout Lewis's imaginative works, Adam and Eve are typically treated as real figures from history, not as allegories or myths, even when the characters in Lewis's stories are seeking to explain truths about the "real" world. In the Narnian Chronicles, human beings are repeatedly referred to as "Sons of Adam" and "Daughters of Eve," and during Lewis's telling of a temptation story on another planet in *Perelandra*, the hero repeatedly affirms the teachings of traditional theology to the planet's equivalent of Eve, including a traditional account of Adam and Eve.[29]

25. Tim Keller, "Creation, Evolution, and Christian Laypeople," www.biologos.org (February 2011): 7, accessed December 15, 2016, http://biologos.org/uploads/projects/Keller_white_paper .pdf.

26. In his diary for August 18, 1925, Lewis relates that Maureen Moore asked him how Adam and Eve related to evolutionary theory, and he replied that "the Biblical and scientific accounts were alternatives. She asked me which I believed. I said the scientific" (*All My Road before Me: The Diary of C. S. Lewis, 1922–1927*, ed. Walter Hooper [San Diego: Harcourt Brace Jovanovich, 1991], 361).

27. Lewis, *Problem of Pain*, 79.

28. A. N. Wilson, *C. S. Lewis: A Biography* (New York: W. W. Norton, 1990), 210.

29. Lewis, *Perelandra*, 120.

Additionally, Lewis treated Adam as a real person in history in his private correspondence. To his friend St. Giovanni Calabria, an Italian priest, he wrote about the "necessary doctrine that we are most closely joined together alike with the sinner Adam and with the Just One, Jesus,"[30] while to another correspondent he described his novel *Perelandra* as the working out of the "supposition" that what happened to Adam and Eve on Earth could happen to another first couple elsewhere: "Suppose, even now, in some other planet there were a first couple undergoing the same [temptation] that Adam and Eve underwent here, but successfully."[31]

A Mindless Process Could Not Produce Man

Lewis's final exception to human evolution was his insistence that the development of human beings required far more than a mindless material process. In his own words, his speculations about human evolution "had pictured Adam as being, physically, the son of two anthropoids, on whom, after birth, God worked the miracle which made him Man."[32] In Lewis's view, Darwinian evolution might possibly explain man's physical form; but it could not explain man's mind, his morality, or his eternal soul. That is because the driving force of modern Darwinism was supposed to be the mindless mechanism of natural selection acting on random variation, and Lewis was deeply skeptical about what such a mindless mechanism could actually achieve.

Lewis's Doubts about the Creative Power of Natural Selection

Lewis knew that the truly momentous feature of modern evolutionary theory is its insistence that life is the product of an unguided process. This claim that evolution is the product of chance and necessity forms the core of orthodox Darwinian theory, which asserts that the primary driver of evolution is an unguided process of natural selection (or "survival of the fittest") operating on random variations in nature (random mutations, according to modern evolutionists).

---

30. C. S. Lewis to Don Giovanni Calabria, March 17, 1953, *Collected Letters*, 3:306.
31. C. S. Lewis to Mrs. Hook, December 29, 1958, *Collected Letters*, 3:1004.
32. C. S. Lewis to Sister Penelope, January 10, 1952.

Darwin himself repeatedly made clear that evolution by natural selection neither required nor involved intelligent guidance. Indeed, according to Darwin, his theory of natural selection provided a definitive refutation of the idea that the features of the natural world reflected a preconceived design:

> The old argument of design in nature, as given by Paley, which formerly seemed to me so conclusive, fails, now that the law of natural selection has been discovered. We can no longer argue that, for instance, the beautiful hinge of a bivalve shell must have been made by an intelligent being, like the hinge of a door by man. There seems to be no more design in the variability of organic beings and in the action of natural selection, than in the course which the wind blows.[33]

The dominant view of evolution today in the scientific community remains essentially Darwinian. In the words of thirty-eight Nobel laureates who issued a statement defending Darwin's theory in 2005, evolution is "the result of an *unguided, unplanned* process of random variation and natural selection."[34]

One certainly can conceive of a theory of guided evolution, but mainstream Darwinian theory is not it. *Darwinian* evolution by definition is an unguided process. But can such a fundamentally mindless and undirected process create the exquisite form and function seen throughout the natural world? Lewis didn't seem to think so.

He did affirm that "[w]ith Darwinianism as a theorem in Biology I do not think a Christian need have any quarrel."[35] But for Lewis "Darwinianism as a theorem in Biology" was a pretty modest affair. Contra leading evolutionists, Lewis thought Darwinism "does not in itself explain the origin of organic life, nor of the variations, nor does it discuss the origin and validity of reason." So what *can* the Darwinian mechanism explain, according to Lewis? "Granted that we now have

---

33. Charles Darwin, *The Autobiography of Charles Darwin and Selected Letters*, ed. F. Darwin (New York: Dover, 1958), 63.

34. Letter from Nobel Laureates to Kansas State Board of Education, September 9, 2005, accessed May 18, 2012, formerly available at http://media.ljworld.com/pdf/2005/09/15/nobel_letter.pdf, can be accessed via Archive.org Wayback Machine at https://web.archive.org/web/20061209120655/http://media.ljworld.com/pdf/2005/09/15/nobel_letter.pdf.

35. C. S. Lewis, "Modern Man and His Categories of Thought," *Present Concerns*, ed. Walter Hooper (New York: Harcourt Brace Jovanovich, 1986), 63.

minds we can trust, granted that organic life came to exist, it tries to explain, say, how a species that once had wings came to lose them. It explains this by the negative effect of environment operating on small variations."[36] In other words, Darwin's theory explains how a species can change over time by losing functional features it already has. Suffice it to say, this is not the key thing the modern biological theory of evolution purports to explain. Noticeably absent from Lewis's description is any confidence that Darwin's unguided mechanism can account for the formation of fundamentally new forms and features in biology. Natural selection can knock out a wing, but can it build a wing in the first place? Lewis didn't seem to think so.

A further indication of Lewis's skepticism about the creative power of natural selection appears in a talk he delivered to the Oxford University Socratic Society in 1944. There Lewis stated that "[t]he Bergsonian critique of orthodox Darwinism is not easy to answer."[37] Lewis was referring to Henri Bergson (1859–1941), a French natural philosopher and Nobel laureate who offered a decidedly non-Darwinian account of evolution in his book *L'Evolution Creatice* (*Creative Evolution*).[38]

Lewis first read Bergson in France during World War I while recovering from shrapnel wounds from the front lines, and the experience on Lewis was profound.[39] Lewis continued to reread Bergson in the years that followed as he continued his studies at Oxford.[40] The impact of Bergson on Lewis is indicated in Lewis's 1917 copy of *L'Evolution Creatice*, which is filled with careful annotations and underlining on most of its nearly four hundred pages.[41]

Bergson was an unsparing critic of the creative power of Darwinian natural selection. Granting that "[t]he Darwinian idea of adaptation by automatic elimination of the unadapted is a simple and clear idea," he argued that precisely "because it attributes to the outer cause which controls evolution a merely negative influence, it has great difficulty in

---

36. C. S. Lewis, "The Funeral of a Great Myth," in *Christian Reflections*, ed. Walter Hooper (Grand Rapids, MI: Eerdmans, 1967), 86.
37. C. S. Lewis, "Is Theology Poetry?" in *The Weight of Glory and Other Addresses*, rev. and expanded ed., ed. Walter Hooper (New York: Macmillan, 1980), 89.
38. Henri Bergson, *Creative Evolution*, trans. Arthur Mitchell (London: Macmillan, 1920).
39. C. S. Lewis, *Surprised by Joy* (New York: Harcourt Brace Jovanovich 1955), 198.
40. C. S. Lewis to Arthur Greeves, June 19, 1920, *Collected Letters*, 1:494.
41. Lewis's annotated copy of *L'Evolution Creatice* resides in the Wade Center Collection, Wheaton College.

accounting for the progressive and, so to say, rectilinear development of [a] complex apparatus" like the vertebrate eye.[42] Bergson stressed that Darwinism's reliance on accidental variations as the raw material for evolution made the development of highly coordinated and complex features found in biology nothing short of incredible.

From the extensive annotations Lewis made in his personal copy of *L'Evolution Creatice*, it is clear that he understood and appreciated Bergson's critique of natural selection. Lewis aptly summarized the Darwinian mechanism of adaptation according to Bergson as the "[e]limination of the unfit" and noted that it "plainly cannot account for complicated similarities on divergent lines of evolution."[43] Lewis also noted Bergson's view that "pure Darwinism has to lean on a marvellous series of accidents" and how Darwinists try to "escape" this truth "by a bad metaphor."[44] Lewis paid particular attention to Bergson's critique of Darwinian accounts of eye evolution in mollusks and vertebrates, concluding that "[n]atural selection . . . fails to explain these Eyes."[45] Bergson's critique of natural selection likely paved the way for Lewis's doubts about Darwin, and may help explain a comment he wrote to his father in 1925 that "Darwin and Spencer. . . . stand themselves on a foundation of sand."[46]

Lewis's skepticism toward natural selection also drew inspiration from G. K. Chesterton's *The Everlasting Man* (1922), which Lewis read for the first time in the mid-1920s. Near the end of his life, Lewis placed *The Everlasting Man* on a list of ten books that "did [the] most to shape" his "vocational attitude and . . . philosophy of life."[47] In chapter 2 of *The Everlasting Man* ("Professors and Prehistoric Men"), Chesterton skewered the pretensions of anthropologists who spun detailed theories about the culture and capabilities of primitive man based on a few flints and bones, likely inspiring Lewis's discussion of "the idolatry of artefacts" in *The Problem of Pain*. Chesterton also

---

42. Bergson, *Creative Evolution*, 59.
43. C. S. Lewis, annotation to copy of Henri Bergson, *L'Evolution Creatice* (Paris, 1917), 60; Wade Center Collection, Wheaton College.
44. Ibid., 61.
45. Ibid., 74.
46. C. S. Lewis to his father, August 14, 1925, *Collected Letters*, 1:649.
47. Lewis's list was in answer to a query from *The Christian Century* magazine, and was published in the June 6, 1962 edition of the magazine. See "Top Ten Books that Influenced C. S. Lewis," http://www.cslewisweb.com/2012/08/top-ten-books-that-influenced-c-s-lewis/.

provided in his book a full-throttled argument as to why Darwinism cannot explain the higher capabilities of human beings. In Chesterton's words, "Man is not merely an evolution but rather a revolution," whose rational faculties far outstrip those seen in the other animals.[48]

Chesterton's book prepared the ground for Lewis's own eventual critique of natural selection with regard to humans—as did a lesser-known volume, *Theism and Humanism* (1915), by Sir Arthur Balfour. Best remembered today as the British prime minister who issued the Balfour Declaration, Balfour adapted *Theism and Humanism* from the Gifford Lectures he had presented at the University of Glasgow in 1914. Balfour's goal was to show his audience "that if we would maintain the value of our highest beliefs and emotions, we must find for them a congruous origin. Beauty must be more than accident. The source of morality must be moral. The source of knowledge must be rational." Balfour thought that once this argument "be granted, you rule out Mechanism, you rule out Naturalism, you rule out Agnosticism; and a lofty form of Theism becomes, as I think, inevitable."[49] With regard to the human mind, Balfour argued that any effort to explain mind in terms of blind material causes was self-refuting: "all creeds which refuse to see an intelligent purpose behind the unthinking powers of material nature are intrinsically incoherent. In the order of causation they base reason upon unreason. In the order of logic they involve conclusions which discredit their own premises."[50] Balfour offered a similar critique of materialistic accounts of human morality, which he thought destroyed morality by depicting it as the product of processes that are essentially nonmoral. Balfour took special aim throughout his book at Darwinian explanations of mind and morals.

It is not known when exactly Lewis first came across *Theism and Humanism*. His father, Albert, owned a copy of a previous Balfour book, *The Foundations of Belief* (1895), but Lewis's first known mention of *Theism and Humanism* was in a lecture in the 1940s.[51] He later included it on the list of books that influenced his philosophy of life

---

48. G. K. Chesterton, *The Everlasting Man* (San Francisco: Ignatius, 1993), 42.
49. Arthur J. Balfour, *Theism and Humanism*, ed. Michael W. Perry (Seattle: Inkling, 2000), 138.
50. Ibid., 141.
51. C. S. Lewis, "Is Theology Poetry?" 77–78. Albert Lewis's copy of *Theism and Humanism* currently resides in the Wade Center Collection, Wheaton College.

the most,[52] and its basic arguments are on prominent view in Lewis's *Miracles: A Preliminary Study* (1947). As Paul Ford points out, "[T]he thesis and even the language of Balfour's first Gifford lectures permeates the first five chapters of *Miracles*."[53]

The revised 1960 edition of *Miracles* is generally recognized as presenting Lewis's most mature critique of the ability of naturalism/materialism to account for man's rational faculties. What is less noticed is the challenge Lewis's book raises for Darwinian evolution in particular.

In the words of Lewis, naturalists argue that "[t]he type of mental behavior we now call rational thinking or inference must . . . have been 'evolved' by natural selection, by the gradual weeding out of types less fitted to survive."[54] Lewis flatly denied that such a Darwinian process could have produced human rationality: "[N]atural selection could operate only by eliminating responses that were biologically hurtful and multiplying those which tended to survival. But it is not conceivable that any improvement of responses could ever turn them into acts of insight, or even remotely tend to do so." This is because "[t]he relation between response and stimulus is utterly different from that between knowledge and the truth known."[55] Natural selection could improve our responses to stimuli from the standpoint of physical survival without ever turning them into *reasoned* responses. Following Balfour, Lewis went on to argue that attributing the development of human reason to a nonrational process like natural selection ends up undermining our confidence in reason itself. After all, if reason is merely an unintended by-product of a fundamentally nonrational process, what grounds do we have left for regarding its conclusions as objectively true?

Lewis knew that the corrosive impact of a Darwinian account of the mind was not merely theoretical. In his personal copy of Darwin's *Autobiography*, he highlighted two passages where Darwin himself questioned whether the conclusions of a mind produced by a Darwinian process could in fact be trusted. In the second passage, Lewis un-

---

52. "Top Ten Books that Influenced C. S. Lewis."
53. Paul F. Ford, "Arthur James Balfour," in *The C. S. Lewis Readers' Encyclopedia*, ed. Jeffrey D. Schultz and John G. West (Grand Rapids, MI: Zondervan, 1998), 92.
54. C. S. Lewis, *Miracles: A Preliminary Study*, 1960 ed. (New York: Macmillan, 1978), 18.
55. Ibid., 18–19.

derlined the following stark admission by Darwin: "But then with me the <u>horrid doubt always arises whether the convictions of man's mind, which has been developed from the mind of the lower animals, are of any value or at all trustworthy. Would any one trust in the convictions of a monkey's mind, if there are any convictions in such a mind?</u>"[56]

Lewis argued that the theist need not suffer such paralyzing doubts because "[h]e is not committed to the view that reason is a comparatively recent development moulded by a process of selection which can select only the biologically useful. For him, reason—the reason of God—is older than Nature, and from it the orderliness of Nature, which alone enables us to know her, is derived." Thus, "the preliminary processes within Nature which led up to" the human mind—"if there were any"—"were designed to do so."[57] In short, if an evolutionary process did produce the human mind, it was not Darwinian evolution. It was evolution by intelligent design.

Just as Lewis, in *Miracles*, rejected a Darwinian explanation for the human mind because it undermined the validity of reason, he rejected a Darwinian account of morality because it would undermine the authority of morality by attributing it to an essentially amoral process of survival of the fittest. As a practical matter, Lewis questioned whether Darwinism could actually explain the development of key human moral traits such as friendship or romantic love.[58] But in *Miracles* he made a more fundamental point: A Darwinian process "may (or may not) explain why men do in fact make moral judgments. It does not explain how they could be right in making them. It excludes, indeed, the very possibility of their being right."[59] According to Lewis, by attributing our moral beliefs and practices completely to mindless and nonmoral causes, Darwinists undermined the belief that moral standards are something objectively true or even the belief that some moral beliefs are objectively preferable over others.

After all, if human behaviors and beliefs are ultimately the products of natural selection, then all such behaviors and beliefs must be equally

---

56. C. S. Lewis's copy of Charles Darwin, *Autobiography of Charles Darwin*, *The Thinker's Library* No. 7 (London: Watts & Co. for the Rationalist Press, 1929), 153. Wade Center Collection, Wheaton College (underlining original).

57. Lewis, *Miracles* (1960 ed.), 22–23.

58. C. S. Lewis, *The Four Loves* (New York: Harcourt Brace Jovanovich, 1960), 90.

59. Lewis, *Miracles* (1960 ed.), 36.

preferable. The same Darwinian process that produces the maternal instinct also produces infanticide. The same Darwinian process that generates love also brings forth sadism. Hence, the logical result of a Darwinian account of morality is not so much immorality as relativism. According to Lewis, the person who offers such an account of morality should honestly admit that "there is no such thing as wrong and right . . . no moral judgment can be 'true' or 'correct' and, consequently . . . no one system of morality can be better or worse than another."[60]

Whether it be man's intellect or his morals, the cardinal difficulty with Darwinian natural selection according to Lewis is that it is mindless, and a mindless process should not be expected to produce either minds or genuine morals.

This shows why it would be so misleading to classify Lewis as a theistic evolutionist, at least according to how that term is typically used today. Theistic evolution can mean many things, including a form of guided evolution, but many contemporary proponents of theistic evolution are more accurately described as theistic *Darwinists*. That is, they do not merely advocate a guided form of common descent, but they are attempting to combine evolution as an undirected Darwinian process with Christian theism. Although they believe in God, they strenuously want to avoid stating that God actually guided biological development. For example, Anglican John Polkinghorne writes that "an evolutionary universe is theologically understood as a creation allowed to make itself."[61] Former Vatican astronomer George Coyne claims that because evolution is unguided, "not even God could know . . . with certainty" that "human life would come to be."[62] And Christian biologist Kenneth Miller of Brown University, author of the popular book *Finding Darwin's God* (which is used in many Christian colleges), insists that evolution is an undirected process, flatly denying that God guided the evolutionary process to achieve any particular result—including the development of us. Indeed, Miller insists that "mankind's appearance on this planet was not preordained, that we are here . . . as an after-

---

60. Ibid.

61. John Polkinghorne, *Quarks, Chaos, and Christianity* (New York: Crossroad, 2005), 113.

62. George V. Coyne, SJ, "The Dance of the Fertile Universe" (2005): 7, formerly available at http://www.aei.org/docLib/20051027_HandoutCoyne.pdf, can be accessed via Archive.org Wayback Machine at https://web.archive.org/web/20110201010024/http://www.aei.org/docLib/20051027_HandoutCoyne.pdf.

thought, a minor detail, a happenstance in a history that might just as well have left us out."[63]

In short, many modern theistic evolutionists want to retain a belief in a Creator without actually affirming the guidance of that Creator in the history of life. In their view, the Creator delegated the development of life to a self-contained mindless process from which genuinely new things like mind and morals emerged over time. Modern theistic evolution's attempt to strike a third way between materialism and intelligent design with a kind of emergent evolution has all the logical coherence of a square circle.

Lewis was familiar with attempts in his own day to imbue blind evolution with some sort of purposiveness while still denying the operation of a guiding intelligence.[64] In *Mere Christianity*, Lewis dissected this supposed third way between outright materialism and a history of life guided by design, and found it wanting:

> People who hold this view say that the small variations by which life on this planet 'evolved' from the lowest forms to Man were not due to chance but to the 'striving' or 'purposiveness' of a Life-Force. When people say this we must ask them whether by Life-Force they mean something with a mind or not. If they do, then 'a mind bringing life into existence and leading it to perfection' is really a God, and their view is thus identical with the Religious. If they do not, then what is the sense in saying that something without a mind 'strives' or has 'purposes'? This seems to me fatal to their view.[65]

In his novel *Perelandra*, Lewis satirized the incoherence of the emergent evolution view, which he assigned to the villain of the story, Professor E. R. Weston, a scientist run mad. Lewis gave Weston a speech of non sequiturs and mumbo jumbo where he solemnly appealed to "the unconsciously purposive dynamism" and "[t]he majestic spectacle of this blind, inarticulate purposiveness thrusting its way . . . ever upward in an endless unity of differentiated achievements toward an

---

63. Kenneth Miller, *Finding Darwin's God* (New York: HarperCollins, 1999), 272.
64. See Lewis, *Mere Christianity*, 35; C. S. Lewis to Bernard Acworth, March 5, 1960, *Collected Letters*, 3:137; Lewis, *Four Loves*, 152–153; C. S. Lewis, *Studies in Words* (Cambridge: Cambridge University Press, 1960), 300–301.
65. Lewis, *Mere Christianity*, 35.

ever-increasing complexity of organization, towards spontaneity and spirituality." Weston ultimately identified this blind and unconscious purposiveness with what he called "the religious view of life" and even with "the Holy Spirit."[66]

The hero of the story, Dr. Elwin Ransom, was not impressed. "I don't know much about what people call the religious view of life," he replied. "You see, I'm a Christian. And what we mean by the Holy Ghost is not a blind, inarticulate purposiveness."[67]

Near the end of his life, Lewis read prominent theistic evolutionist Pierre Teilhard de Chardin's posthumously published book *The Phenomenon of Man*, which proposed yet another kind of emergent evolution. Lewis filled his copy of the book with critical annotations such as "Yes, he is quite ignorant," and "a radically bad book."[68] In letters to others, Lewis called Teilhard de Chardin's book "both commonplace and horrifying,"[69] and he derided Teilhard de Chardin's position as "pantheistic-biolatrous waffle"[70] and "evolution run mad."[71]

Lewis knew that ultimately there is no third way, no halfway house, no magical hybrid: Biological development is either the result of an unintelligent material process or a process guided by a mind, a.k.a. intelligent design. That being the case, Lewis thought that a mind-driven process is a far more plausible option than a mindless one.

Lewis's Critique of Evolutionism

In addition to limiting his acceptance of common descent and critiquing the power of unguided natural selection, Lewis throughout his life attacked what he called "evolutionism" or the "Myth" of "Evolution." This was evolution as a materialistic creation story that provides a competing narrative to traditional monotheism. Purporting to embody the discoveries of modern science, this "Myth" teaches that the cosmos was preceded by "the infinite void and matter endlessly, aimlessly mov-

---

66. Lewis, *Perelandra*, 90–91.
67. Ibid., 91.
68. C. S. Lewis, annotations to Pierre Teilhard de Chardin, *The Phenomenon of Man*, with an introduction by Sir Julian Huxley (London: Collins, 1959), 217, cover page, 227. Wade Center Collection, Wheaton College.
69. C. S. Lewis to Dan Tucker, December 8, 1959, *Collected Letters*, 3:1105.
70. C. S. Lewis to Father Frederick Joseph Adelmann, SJ, September 21, 1960, *Collected Letters*, 3:1186.
71. C. S. Lewis to Bernard Acworth, March 5, 1960, *Collection Letters*, 3:1137.

ing to bring forth it knows not what. Then by some millionth, millionth chance—what tragic irony!—the conditions at one point of space and time bubble up into that tiny fermentation which we call organic life." Against the hostility of Nature and without purposeful direction or design, life "spreads, it breeds, it complicates itself . . . from the amoeba up to the reptile, up to the mammal." Finally, "there comes forth a little, naked, shivering, cowering biped, shuffling, not yet fully erect, promising nothing: the product of another millionth, millionth chance. His name in this Myth is Man." Eventually "he has become true Man. He learns to master Nature. Science arises and dissipates the superstitions of his infancy. More and more he becomes the controller of his own fate."[72] Finally, mankind becomes "a race of demi-gods" with the assistance of Darwinian eugenics, psychoanalysis, and economics. Then "the old enemy" Nature returns with a vengeance. The Sun cools, and life is "banished without hope of return from every cubic inch of infinite space. All ends in nothingness."[73]

"I grew up believing in this Myth and I have felt—I still feel—its almost perfect grandeur," observed Lewis rather wistfully. "Let no one say we are an unimaginative age: neither the Greeks nor the Norsemen ever invented a better story."[74] For Lewis, the problem with this "Myth" is not that it does not appeal to the imagination, but that it is all imagination and no logic. In fact, it contradicts the very foundation of the scientific worldview it claims to espouse.

The scientific method is premised on the idea that "rational inferences are valid," but the Myth undercuts human reason by depicting it as "simply the unforeseen and unintended by-product of a mindless process at one stage of its endless and aimless becoming. The content of the Myth thus knocks from under me the only ground on which I could possibly believe the Myth to be true." Darwin's own gnawing doubt rears its head yet again: "If my own mind is a product of the irrational . . . how shall I trust my mind when it tells me about Evolution?"[75]

Lewis distinguished cosmic evolutionism from the "science" of evolution, and he initially attributed it to the distortions of popularizers

---

72. Lewis, "Funeral of a Great Myth," 87.
73. Ibid., 88.
74. Ibid.
75. Ibid., 89.

and journalists rather than scientists themselves. However, Lewis eventually came to better understand just how intertwined evolution as a scientific theory was with what he had called evolutionism. Much of his growing awareness was likely due to his sixteen-year correspondence with Bernard Acworth, a leader in Britain's Evolution Protest Movement. Starting in the mid-1940s, Acworth began sending Lewis books and essays critical of Darwin's theory, materials which Lewis read and retained for his private library.[76]

Soon after coming into contact with Acworth, Lewis drew attention to a comment made by evolutionary zoologist David Watson that seemed to expose the dogmatism driving the beliefs of prominent evolutionary scientists. "Evolution," declared Watson, " . . . is accepted by zoologists not because it has been observed to occur or . . . can be proved by logically coherent evidence to be true, but because the only alternative, special creation, is clearly incredible."[77] Lewis drew this quote from an article written by two of Acworth's colleagues in the Evolution Protest Movement. Lewis found Watson's comment "disquieting."[78] Nevertheless, he still trusted that "[m]ost biologists have a more robust belief in Evolution than Professor Watson." Otherwise it "would mean that the sole ground for believing [evolution] . . . is not empirical but metaphysical—the dogma of an amateur metaphysician who finds 'special creation' incredible. But I do not think it has really come to that."[79]

By 1951, Lewis was not so sure. Acworth sent him a lengthy manuscript critical of evolution, and Lewis wrote back that he had "read nearly the whole" of it. Acworth's manuscript hit home. "I must confess it has shaken me," Lewis wrote, "not in my belief in evolution, which was of the vaguest and most intermittent kind, but in my belief that the question was wholly unimportant." Lewis added that the most telling point for him was the dogmatism of the evolutionary scientists

---

76. These materials included Bernard Acworth, *The Cuckoo*; L. M. Davies, *BBC Abuses Its Monopoly*; L. M. Davies, *Evolutionists Under Fire*; Douglas Dewar, *The Man from Monkey Myth*; Douglas Dewar, *Science and the BBC*; and Evolution Protest Movement, *Evolution: How the Doctrine Is Propagated in Our Schools*. All of these materials reside in the Wade Center Collection, Wheaton College.

77. David Watson, quoted in C. S. Lewis, "Is Theology Poetry?" 89; and "Funeral of a Great Myth," 85.

78. Lewis, "Is Theology Poetry?" 89.

79. Lewis, "Funeral of a Great Myth," 85.

cited by Acworth: "What inclines me now to think that you may be right in regarding it [evolution] as the central and radical lie in the whole web of falsehood that now governs our lives is not so much your arguments against it as the fanatical and twisted attitudes of its defenders."[80] Lewis could no longer easily maintain that evolutionism was simply something foisted on evolutionary science by outsiders. He was appalled by the growing dogmatism and intolerance he saw among evolutionists, who seemed to treat any criticism of their views as an attack upon science itself.

Lewis had a sharply different vision of what science should be like, and he made clear that knee-jerk orthodoxy was not part of it. In Lewis's view, there was nothing anti-science about questioning dogmatic claims made in the name of science. As he came to appreciate even more deeply in the final years of his life, the scientific enterprise requires humility and an open mind in order to prosper. Those two qualities often seem sadly lacking in discussions of evolution today.

Lewis's Most Important Legacy for the Evolution Debate

At the root of Lewis's willingness to question evolutionary claims was a healthy skepticism of the scientific enterprise itself. Lewis respected modern science, and he respected modern scientists. But unlike many contemporary champions of evolution, he did not embrace a simple-minded view of natural science as fundamentally more authoritative or less prone to error than all other fields of human endeavor.

One of the last books about science Lewis read before he died was *The Open Society and Its Enemies*, by philosopher Karl Popper. Near the end of that book, Popper frankly admits the lack of objectivity to be found even in experimental science. Lewis underlined the passage:

> For even our experimental and observational experience does not consist of 'data'. Rather, it consists of a web of guesses— of conjectures, expectations, hypotheses with which there are interwoven accepted, traditional, scientific, and unscientific, lore and prejudice. There simply is no such thing as pure experimental

---

80. C. S. Lewis to Bernard Acworth, September 13, 1951, *Collected Letters*, 3:138.

and observational experience—experience untainted by expectation and theory.[81]

Lewis's growing awareness of the human fallibility of science was
expressed powerfully in his final book, *The Discarded Image* (1964).[82]
Published after his death, the book is ostensibly about the medieval
worldview. But the nature of science is one of the underlying themes.
Lewis argues in the book that scientific theories are "supposals" and
should not be confused with "facts." Properly speaking, scientific theories try to account for as many facts as possible with as few assumptions as possible. But according to Lewis, we must always recognize
that such explanations can be wrong: "In every age it will be apparent
to accurate thinkers that scientific theories, being arrived at in the way
I have described, are never statements of fact."[83] They "can never be
more than provisional," and they "have to be abandoned" if someone
thinks of a "supposal" that can account for "observed phenomena
with still fewer assumptions, or if we discover new phenomena" that
the previous theory cannot account for "at all."[84]

The truly radical part of Lewis's critique of modern science was still
to come. In his epilogue to *The Discarded Image*, Lewis discusses at
length the shift from the medieval to the modern model of biology. It
soon becomes evident that he does not think empirical evidence drives
scientific revolutions. Lewis declares that the Darwinian revolution in
particular "was certainly not brought about by the discovery of new
facts."[85]

Lewis recalled that when he was young he "believed that 'Darwin discovered evolution' and that the far more general, radical, and
even cosmic developmentalism . . . was a superstructure raised on
the biological theorem. This view has been sufficiently disproved."
What really happened according to Lewis was that "[t]he demand for
a developing world—a demand obviously in harmony both with the

81. C. S. Lewis's copy of K. R. Popper, *The Open Society and Its Enemies, The High Tide of Prophecy: Hegel, Marx, and the Aftermath* (London: Routledge & Kegan Paul), vol. 2, 388. Wade Center Collection, Wheaton College.
82. C. S. Lewis, *The Discarded Image* (Cambridge: Cambridge University Press, 1964).
83. Ibid., 15–16.
84. Ibid.
85. Ibid., 220.

revolutionary and the romantic temper" had developed first, and when it was "full grown" the scientists went "to work and discover[ed] the evidence on which our belief in that sort of universe would now be held to rest."[86]

Lewis's view has momentous implications for how we view the reigning paradigms in science at any given time—including Darwinian evolution. "We can no longer dismiss the change of Models [in science] as a simple progress from error to truth," argued Lewis. "No Model is a catalogue of ultimate realities, and none is a mere fantasy. . . . But . . . each reflects the prevalent psychology of an age almost as much as it reflects the state of that age's knowledge." Lewis added that he did "not at all mean that these new phenomena are illusory. . . . But nature gives most of her evidence in answer to the questions we ask her."[87]

So the answers we receive from nature are dictated by the questions we ask, and the questions we ask are shaped by the assumptions and expectations of the scientific theories we embrace—assumptions and expectations likely borrowed from larger cultural attitudes that pre-dated the scientific evidence they seek to interpret. Hence, the potential for even good scientific theories to blind us to key aspects of reality is huge.

Nowhere is this more true than in the field of Darwinian evolution itself, which is based on the inviolable assumption that everything in biology must be the result of unguided material processes. Over the past century, this assumption has undoubtedly inspired many interest-ing research questions and scientific advances. At the same time, it also has undoubtedly discouraged and delayed many *other* important research questions. Witness the unhelpful Darwinian preoccupation with "vestigial" organs over the past century. Time and again, bio-logical features we do not fully understand have been dismissed by advocates of Darwinian evolution as nonfunctional leftovers from a blind evolutionary process. Time and again, researchers who even-tually bothered to look discovered that such supposedly "vestigial" features—the appendix and tonsils, to name two—actually perform

---

86. Ibid., 220–221.
87. Ibid., 222–223.

important biological functions.[88] The evidence of function was there all along, but scientists were discouraged by the existing paradigm from asking the questions that would elicit the evidence.

More recently, one of the biggest mistakes in the history of modern biology may turn out to have been the belief that the human genome is riddled with "junk DNA." Random mutations in protein-coding DNA are supposed to drive Darwinian evolution, and so when it was discovered that the vast majority of DNA does not code for proteins, some leading Darwinists jumped to the conclusion that non-protein-coding DNA must be mere "junk" leftover from the evolutionary process just like some vestigial organs. Not only that, leading evolutionists ranging from atheist Richard Dawkins to Christian Francis Collins championed "junk DNA" as proof that human beings were the result of a Darwinian process rather than intentional design.[89]

However, when scientists finally started to look more closely at noncoding DNA, they were shocked to learn that reality did not correspond to their ideological assumptions. Indeed, over the past decade science journals have been flooded with new research showing the rich and varied functionality of so-called "junk DNA." In the words of biologist Jonathan Wells, "Far from consisting mainly of junk that provides evidence against intelligent design, our genome is increasingly revealing itself to be a multidimensional, integrated system in which non-protein-coding DNA performs a wide variety of functions."[90] Again, the evidence of functionality in non-protein-coding DNA was always there to find, but the evidence was not forthcoming because few people were asking the right questions. As Lewis pointed out so perceptively, treating reigning paradigms in science as all-encompassing dogmas will blind us to how much about nature we may be missing. Such dogmatism also breeds a kind of scientific authoritarianism that

---

88. See Casey Luskin, "Vestigial Arguments about Vestigial Organs Appear in Proposed Texas Teaching Materials," *Evolution News and Views*, June 20, 2011, accessed December 15, 2016, http://www.evolutionnews.org/2011/06/vestigial_arguments_about_vest047341.html; David Klinghoffer, "Looks like the Appendix Isn't a 'Junk Body Part' after All," *Evolution News and Views*, Jan. 4, 2012, accessed December 15, 2016, http://www.evolutionnews.org/2012/01/now_its_the_app054761.html.

89. Jonathan Wells, *The Myth of Junk DNA* (Seattle: Discovery Institute Press, 2011), 19–20, 23–24, 98–100. In more recent years, Collins has seemed to abandon or at least diminish his support for the junk DNA paradigm. See ibid., 98–100.

90. Ibid., 9.

is incompatible with a free society, which Lewis eloquently rebuked in books such as *The Abolition of Man* and *That Hideous Strength*.[91]

By highlighting the all-too-human frailties of modern science, Lewis made his most important contribution to the evolution debate. In essence, he legitimized the right to dissent from Darwin. By stressing the nonscientific underpinnings of scientific revolutions, Lewis showed that Darwinian evolution should not be privileged as some special form of knowledge that is immune from critical scrutiny. By exposing just how limited a window on reality a given scientific theory can provide, he did not merely validate the questioning of Darwinian evolution. He showed why such questioning was essential for the continued progress of science.

---

91. C. S. Lewis, *The Abolition of Man* (New York: Macmillan, 1955); *That Hideous Strength* (New York: Macmillan, 1965).

SECTION III

THE BIBLICAL AND
THEOLOGICAL CRITIQUE
OF THEISTIC EVOLUTION

27

Theistic Evolution Undermines Twelve Creation Events and Several Crucial Christian Doctrines

WAYNE GRUDEM

SUMMARY

This chapter provides an overview of the issues raised by theistic evolution in relationship to the truthfulness of the Bible and several historic Christian doctrines. First, it enumerates twelve specific affirmations about the origin of human beings and other living creatures that are held by the most prominent advocates of theistic evolution today. It then seeks to show that these affirmations are in direct conflict with multiple passages of Scripture, including passages not only from the Old Testament but also from ten books in the New Testament. It concludes that belief in theistic evolution is inconsistent with belief in the truthfulness of the Bible. In addition, it shows how theistic evolution undermines eleven significant Christian doctrines. (This chapter relies heavily on the detailed exegetical work of John Currid and Guy Waters in chapters 28 and 29.)

· · · · ·

A. Summary of Introductory Chapter

This chapter must be read in connection with my "Biblical and Theological Introduction" (pages 61–77), for there I explained that this book is not concerned with the age of the earth, or whether Genesis 1–3 should be interpreted "literally," or whether people who support theistic evolution are genuine Christians or are sincere in their beliefs. Instead, the question from the standpoint of the Bible and theology is *whether Genesis 1–3 should be understood as a truthful historical narrative, reporting events that actually happened.*

I defined theistic evolution as follows:

> God created matter and after that did not guide or intervene or act directly to cause any empirically detectable change in the natural behavior of matter until all living things had evolved by purely natural processes.[1]

My introductory chapter also quoted several prominent advocates of theistic evolution to show that, in order to make their viewpoint consistent with modern evolutionary theory, they have concluded that God was the initial Creator of matter, but not of individual living creatures; that the human race has descended not from merely two original parents but from something like ten thousand ancestors; and that God selected one man and one woman from the many thousands of human beings on the earth and designated them as "Adam" and "Eve," to represent the human race. But this "Adam" and "Eve" were not the first human beings, nor did human sin or human death originate with them. Because of these conclusions, advocates of theistic evolution argue that Genesis 1–3 should not be understood as historical narrative but as figurative or allegorical literature.

B. An Enumeration of Twelve Theistic Evolution Beliefs That Conflict with the Creation Account in Genesis 1–3

I concluded my introductory essay with an enumeration of twelve points at which theistic evolution (as currently promoted by its prominent supporters) differs from the biblical creation account if it is taken as a historical narrative. According to theistic evolution:

---

1. This definition of theistic evolution was written by the editors of this book as a concise summary of the view we are opposing. In my "Introduction," I provided several quotations from authors who support theistic evolution in this sense (pages 67–68), and those quotations give more detailed explanations of what the viewpoint involves.

1. Adam and Eve were not the first human beings (and perhaps they never even existed).

2. Adam and Eve were born from human parents.

3. God did not act directly or specially to create Adam out of dust[2] from the ground.

4. God did not directly create Eve from a rib[3] taken from Adam's side.

5. Adam and Eve were never sinless human beings.

6. Adam and Eve did not commit the first human sins, for human beings were doing morally evil things[4] long before Adam and Eve.

7. Human death did not begin as a result of Adam's sin, for human beings existed long before Adam and Eve and they were always subject to death.

8. Not all human beings have descended from Adam and Eve, for there were thousands of other human beings on Earth at the time that God chose two of them as Adam and Eve.

9. God did not directly act in the natural world to create different "kinds" of fish, birds, and land animals.

10. God did not "rest" from his work of creation or stop any special creative activity after plants, animals, and human beings appeared on the earth.

11. God never created an originally "very good" natural world in the sense of a world that was a safe environment, free of thorns and thistles and similar harmful things.

12. After Adam and Eve sinned, God did not place any curse on the world that changed the workings of the natural world and made it more hostile to mankind.

In the remainder of this chapter, I will attempt to establish the following four points as a response to theistic evolution:

---

2. It is possible that "dust" in Genesis 2:7 refers to a collection of different kinds of nonliving materials from the earth. My argument in this chapter does not depend on that interpretative detail. See further discussion of the Hebrew word for "dust" by John Currid on pages 868–869.

3. It is possible that the "rib" was accompanied by other material substances taken from Adam's body, for Adam himself says, "This at last is bone of my bones *and flesh of my flesh*" (Gen. 2:23). My overall argument is not affected by that difference. See further discussion of the Hebrew word for "rib" on pages 802–803 and 859–860.

4. Some advocates of theistic evolution may claim that human beings prior to Adam and Eve did not have a human moral conscience, but they would still admit that these human beings were doing selfish and violent things, and worshiping various deities, things that from a biblical moral standard would be considered morally evil.

1. A nonhistorical reading of Genesis 1–3 does not arise from factors in the text itself but rather depends upon a prior commitment to an evolutionary framework of interpretation, a framework which the science and philosophy chapters in this volume show to be unjustifiable.

2. Several literary factors within Genesis itself give strong evidence that Genesis 1–3 is intended to be understood as historical narrative, claiming to report events that actually happened.

3. Both Jesus and the New Testament authors, in ten separate New Testament books, affirm the historicity of several events in Genesis 1–3 that are inconsistent with the theory of theistic evolution.

4. If the historicity of several of these events in Genesis 1–3 is denied, a number of crucial Christian doctrines that depend on these events will be undermined or lost.

Even if some readers differ with one or another of the details in my analysis of the twelve points listed above,[5] the remaining points should still be sufficient to demonstrate that theistic evolution is incompatible with Genesis 1–3 when understood as historical narrative. That is because my argument is a cumulative one based on the accumulated weight of these twelve historical differences and, also very significantly, on the eleven threatened doctrines that I will discuss at the end of this chapter.

Four other chapters on biblical and theological topics follow this chapter and provide more detailed support for it:

In chapter 28, John Currid analyzes in further detail specific Old Testament passages that are incompatible with theistic evolution.

In chapter 29, Guy Waters similarly analyzes specific New Testament passages that are incompatible with theistic evolution.

In chapter 30, Gregg Allison argues that, throughout the history of the church, those who were recognized as leaders and teachers in the church were required to affirm the belief that God is the "Maker of heaven and earth, and of *all things visible* and invisible" (Nicene

---

5. Some of the authors in the science and philosophy sections of this book may not agree with my specific understanding of all of the biblical passages I cite as contradicting these twelve points, for example, but they would still agree that Genesis 1–3 presents a historical narrative that is incompatible with theistic evolution at many points.

Creed; emphasis added), an affirmation incompatible with theistic evolution.

In chapter 31, Fred Zaspel concludes that the eminent nineteenth-century Princeton theologian B. B. Warfield, though often cited as a supporter of theistic evolution, would not have agreed with theistic evolution as it is understood today.

I must emphasize that what I have written in this chapter depends substantially on the detailed analyses by Currid and Waters in those later chapters. Although I will interact to some extent with alternative interpretations of key passages by authors who advocate theistic evolution, much more extensive and more fully documented interaction with other views has been carried out with substantial expertise in the chapters by Currid and Waters. My purpose in this chapter is simply to lay out the biblical evidence in order to give a clear overview of what is at issue in this debate.

C. Genesis 1–3 Is Both Similar to and Different from Other Historical Narratives in Scripture

Anyone who reads Genesis 1–3 immediately realizes that in some ways these chapters are different from other historical chapters in the Bible. The subject matter is different, for these chapters do not talk about kings and armies and battles but about the origins of the universe before any human beings existed. The method of collecting the information also had to be different, for there were no human observers when God created light and darkness, the sun, moon, and stars, and plants and animals. And the setting is different, because Genesis 2 portrays the garden of Eden, an idyllic place with no sin or shame, no suffering or death.

In addition, the style in Genesis 1 is distinctive, because it is written with an elegant six-day structure with majestic repetitive phrases such as "And God said. . . . And it was so," and, "God saw that it was good." C. John Collins appropriately refers to Genesis 1 as "exalted prose narrative."[6]

But these distinctives do not nullify the fundamentally historical

---

6. C. John Collins, "Response from the Old-Earth View," in *Four Views on the Historical Adam,* ed. Matthew Barrett and Ardel B. Caneday (Grand Rapids, MI: Zondervan, 2013), 74; also 248.

nature of Genesis 1–3. As I will argue in the following discussion, many specific details in the text of Genesis 1–3, the connection of these chapters with the rest of Genesis, the way in which ten New Testament books refer to details in these chapters as historical events, and the significant foundation that these chapters provide for several important Christian doctrines, all provide an overwhelming amount of evidence demonstrating that these chapters must be understood as historical narrative, claiming to report events that actually happened.

D. Analysis of Twelve Theistic Evolution Beliefs That Conflict with Teachings of the Bible

1. Adam and Eve Were Not the First Human Beings (and Perhaps They Never Even Existed)

As I indicated in my "Introduction" (see pages 61–77), some Christians who support theistic evolution believe that the early chapters of Genesis are merely symbolic stories, and that *Adam and Eve never existed.* Others believe that *Adam and Eve were actual historical persons,* but that they were just one man and one woman out of many thousands of human beings on Earth, and God chose to relate to them personally and designate them as representatives of the entire human race. Both of these groups claim that Adam and Eve were not the first human beings on Earth.

a. The Evidence from Genesis

The claim that Adam and Eve were not the first human beings creates tension with specific statements in Genesis 1 and 2, chapters that present Adam as the first human being and Eve as a woman specially created to be his wife. The initial evidence is seen in Genesis 1:

> Then God said, "Let us make man in our image, after our likeness. And let them have dominion over the fish of the sea and over the birds of the heavens and over the livestock and over all the earth and over every creeping thing that creeps on the earth."
>
> *So God created man in his own image,*
> *in the image of God he created him;*
> *male and female he created them.*

And God blessed them. And God said to them, "Be fruitful and multiply and fill the earth and subdue it, and have dominion over the fish of the sea and over the birds of the heavens and over every living thing that moves on the earth." (***Gen. 1:26–28***)[7]

Is this passage intended to be understood as historical narrative? The larger literary context is important here. The passage occurs in the first chapter of the first book in the entire Bible, a chapter that tells how all things in the universe began. The subject matter is an explanation of how things originally came into being—which is a historical question. The chapter speaks sequentially of the original creation—*the beginnings*—of light, land and sea, plants, the heavenly bodies, fish and birds, animals, and finally human beings. Such a report of the beginning of each type of thing in the creation leads us to think that this is not just a story about choosing one man and one woman to represent thousands of human beings who were already living, but is a story of the *beginning* of the human race—the creation of the *first* man and first woman.

There is in fact nothing in this passage that would cause us to think that it is nonhistorical literature. Only a prior commitment to an evolutionary framework of interpretation would cause a reader to search for a way to understand this as figurative or poetic literature rather than historical narrative. But the science and philosophy chapters in this book have provided abundant evidence that such a prior commitment to evolution is unjustified, and therefore Genesis 1–3 should be approached with an open mind rather than with a prior commitment to consider only materialistic explanations for the origin of human beings and a prior commitment to consider only those explanations of Genesis that are consistent with evolutionary theory.

In addition, Genesis 1 does not stand alone in the biblical text. Genesis 2 is closely tied to Genesis 1 and provides a more detailed

---

7. In this chapter I have used boldface italic font in the reference for each biblical text that affirms the historicity of the specific detail of the Genesis 1–3 account that is under discussion. I have done this in order to provide at a glance a quick overview of the extensiveness of the biblical testimony regarding these chapters in Genesis. It is not just the truthfulness of one or two verses that is at stake (though that itself would be significant), but the reliability of numerous verses that affirm several themes that are woven through the entire texture of biblical history.

account of the initial creation of a man and a woman in God's image.[8] In Genesis 2 we read,

> the LORD God formed the man of dust from the ground and breathed into his nostrils the breath of life, and the man became a living creature. (**Gen. 2:7**)

This passage asks us to believe that there was no other human being on Earth at this time, for the narrative goes on to say that the man was alone when he was created: "Then the LORD God said, 'It is not good that the man should be *alone*; I will make him a helper fit for him'" (**Gen. 2:18**).[9] After that, God brought the animals to Adam, so that he could name them (vv. 19–20), but "for Adam there was not found a helper fit for him" (**Gen. 2:20**; here the first man is named as "Adam").[10] This again affirms that there was no other human being on Earth at that time.

Finally, God "caused a deep sleep to fall upon the man, and while he slept took one of his ribs and closed up its place with flesh. And the rib that the LORD God had taken from the man he made into a woman and brought her to the man" (Gen. 2:21–22). The narrative in this way presents Eve as the second human being on the earth, and the first woman.

We find these ideas reaffirmed in later Old Testament passages. Genesis 5 reinforces the idea that Adam was the first human being:

> This is the book of the generations of *Adam. When God created man, he made him in the likeness of God. Male and female he created them*, and he blessed them and named them Man [Hebrew

---

8. See pages 863–870 for John Currid's detailed argument that Genesis 2 must be understood as a detailed recapitulation of Genesis 1, not as a contradictory account and not as an account of some later events.

9. Someone might object that the verse only means that Adam was alone *in the garden*, but that there were thousands of other human beings outside the garden (cf. John H. Walton, *The Lost World of Adam and Eve: Genesis 2–3 and the Human Origins Debate* [Downers Grove, IL: InterVarsity Press, 2015], 109). However, that is an unlikely proposal because then no special creation of Eve would have been necessary, for God could simply have taken a woman from outside the garden and brought her into the garden.

10. Walton, *Lost World of Adam and Eve*, 60–61, prefers to translate this verse, "But for *the man*" instead of "but for *Adam*," which would support his view of the man in Genesis 1–2 as an "archetype," but he admits that he has to repoint the Masoretic text (changing indefinite *le-* to definite *lā-*) in order to translate it this way. Most translations (including ESV, NASB, NIV, NET, KJV, NKJV) prefer "Adam" at this verse, following the Masoretic text. Walton also prefers to translate "the man" instead of "Adam" in Genesis 3:17 and 21, but the Masoretic text and most translations read "Adam" in those places as well.

'ādām] when they were created. When *Adam* had lived 130 years, he fathered a son in his own likeness, after his image, and named him Seth. The days of Adam after he fathered Seth were 800 years; and he had other sons and daughters. (*Gen. 5:1–5*)

This passage links the specific man "Adam" to the initial creation account in Genesis 1 with the words "When God created man" and with the clear echoes of Genesis 1 in "he made him in the likeness of God" and "Male and female he created them."[11] Therefore Adam is viewed as the specific man created by God in Genesis 1:27, the very first man, and a man who had a son named Seth. Then, almost as if he wants to reinforce to his readers that this is a report of specific historical events, the writer immediately specifies a whole line of descendants leading from Seth directly to Noah and Noah's three sons (Gen. 5:6–32).[12] Adam and Eve are directly connected to historical persons in this subsequent historical narrative.

A later genealogy traces the beginning of the human race back to Adam: "Adam, Seth, Enosh" (*1 Chron. 1:1*). Following this verse we find nine chapters of genealogies—names of specific people who descended from Adam, bringing us into the families of David and Solomon (1 Chronicles 3) and even into the exile (1 Chronicles 9). In this genealogy, Adam is again viewed as a historical person who stands at the beginning of the human race.

b. Is This Poetic, Figurative, or Allegorical Literature?

Francis Collins says Genesis 1–3 should be understood as "poetry and allegory."[13] But what is the evidence for this? No Bible translation known to me presents the entirety of Genesis 1–3 as Hebrew poetry, which uses relatively short lines, one after another, and shows evident parallelism in succeeding sets of balanced lines.

---

11. C. John Collins provides a longer argument showing that "Genesis 1–11 Is a Unity on the Literary Level"; see C. John Collins, "A Historical Adam: Old-Earth Creation View," in Barrett and Caneday, *Four Views on the Historical Adam*, 155–157.

12. Even if there are gaps in the genealogies, so that only certain individuals are mentioned, they are still intended to be accurate historical records that name actual people. Regarding Genesis 5:1–2, C. John Collins notes, "that Adam and Eve are presented as a particular pair, the first parents of all humanity, is pretty widespread in the exegetical literature" (C. John Collins, *Did Adam and Eve Really Exist?: Who They Were and Why You Should Care* (Wheaton, IL: Crossway, 2011), 57.

13. Francis Collins, *The Language of God* (New York: Free Press, 2006), 206; also 150, 151, 175, 207.

Notice how translation committees present the Psalms, for example:

The LORD is my shepherd; I shall not want.
   He makes me lie down in green pastures.
He leads me beside still waters.
   He restores my soul. (Ps. 23:1–3)

This is poetry. It contains successive short lines that reemphasize similar or related ideas, typical of Hebrew parallelism. But Genesis 1–3 is not written in this way, and Genesis 1–3 is not poetry.[14] It is written as a narrative of historical events. That is why the New Testament authors uniformly treat it as truthful history.

In chapter 28 of this book, John Currid points to several additional features in the Hebrew linguistic structure and in the interconnectedness of the narrative that demonstrate that these chapters must be taken as historical narrative, not as poetic, figurative, or allegorical literature. He concludes, "If we remove the profoundly historical nature of Genesis 1–3, we will remove the historical foundation on which all the remainder of the Bible rests."[15]

Nor is Genesis 1–3 an extended *metaphor*. We do find metaphorical language in Scripture, but we recognize it as metaphor because it cannot be literally true. When Jesus says, "I am the light of the world" (John 8:12), or "I am the true vine, and my Father is the vinedresser" (John 15:1), we know that he is not literally the sun or a grapevine, and so we understand it as a metaphor. But there are no such features in Genesis 1–3. For thousands of years, interpreters have readily understood the details in Genesis 1–3 to be actual historical events.

Nor is Genesis 1–3 an extended *allegory*. Essential to allegorical stories is that they have a continuous second level of meaning.[16] For example, in the book of Judges, Jotham told an allegorical story:

---

14. There are some poetic verses, such as Genesis 1:27, 2:23, and 3:14–19, but even these recount historical facts using a poetic form of expression, as here:

So God created man in his own image,
   in the image of God he created him;
      male and female he created them. (Gen. 1:27)

15. See page 862.

16. I am grateful to my friend Leland Ryken (professor of English emeritus at Wheaton College) for a telephone conversation in which he explained this characteristic of allegories.

[Jotham] went and stood on top of Mount Gerizim and cried aloud and said to them, "Listen to me, you leaders of Shechem, that God may listen to you. *The trees once went out to anoint a king over them*, and they said to the olive tree, 'Reign over us.' But the olive tree said to them, 'Shall I leave my abundance, by which gods and men are honored, and go hold sway over the trees?' And the trees said to the fig tree, 'You come and reign over us.' But the fig tree said to them, 'Shall I leave my sweetness and my good fruit and go hold sway over the trees?'" (Judg. 9:7–11)

Readers realize at once that this is an allegory, both because trees don't actually talk to each other or go out "to anoint a king over them," and because they recognize that the reactions of the different kinds of trees are specific details that carry a continuous second level of meaning (describing, in this case, various men who had refused to lead the people).

But Genesis 1–3 is not like this, and it is not an extended allegory. It is not possible to link together the details in a coherent second level of meaning, with each part corresponding to something else in the reader's experience, as in Jotham's allegory. To label a narrative passage in a historical book as an allegory when nothing in the context demands that it be taken as an allegory is not proper interpretation; it is "allegorizing." Genesis 1–3 should rather be understood as historical narrative.

Scot McKnight has recently proposed that Genesis 1–3 does not present a "historical Adam" but rather a "literary Adam" who is later viewed as a "genealogical Adam" in Jewish literature.[17] But in order to argue this, McKnight over-specifies what is meant by a "historical Adam" so that he makes it include not only what is explicitly recorded in Genesis 1–2 but also elements that would not be clearly taught until the New Testament (that Adam and Eve "passed on their sin natures . . . to all human beings"), some theological conclusions that are implied but not explicitly affirmed by the New Testament (e.g., "if one denies the historical Adam, one denies the gospel of salvation"), and one factor that would not be understood until modern genetics ("their DNA is our DNA").

17. Dennis R. Venema and Scot McKnight, *Adam and the Genome: Reading Scripture after Genetic Science* (Grand Rapids, MI: Brazos, 2017), 107–108, 118, 145–146.

McKnight then denies that this kind of a "historical Adam" can be found in Genesis 1–2: "I have major doubts that when Genesis 1–2 was written, any of that or at least most of that was what was meant by 'Adam and Eve.'"[18] But to argue that Genesis 1–2 is not "historical" because it does not explicitly contain doctrinal material found in Romans 5 and 1 Corinthians 15 is surely not what "historical" means in ordinary English.

A better understanding is found in the statement of C. John Collins that I quoted earlier: "In ordinary English a story is 'historical' if the author wants his audience to believe the events really happened" (see page 64, note 4). In that sense of "historical," McKnight has not disproved that Genesis 1–2 presents Adam and Eve as historical persons.

McKnight also explores various discussions of Adam in extrabiblical Jewish literature, showing that different authors used the Genesis story of Adam and Eve as a platform for *expanding on* the Genesis narrative with various kinds of moral lessons, philosophical allegories, and creative elaborations on the Genesis story,[19] but his extensive survey turns up no Jewish authors who *deny* the historical reality of the events that are recorded in Genesis 1–2. Even McKnight admits that "Paul, *like the Jews of his day*, would have thought that the *literary* Adam and Eve were also the *genealogical* Adam and Eve, and that as such they were persons in the history of Israel."[20]

Therefore, while McKnight claims that we should not view Adam and Eve in Genesis as "*historical*" but rather as "*literary* Adam and Eve," his claim fails to be persuasive. The fact that Adam and Eve are viewed as actual historical persons elsewhere in the Old Testament, in later Jewish literature, and also in Paul, argues for, not against, their historicity. In addition, McKnight fails to even discuss several other New Testament books that also affirm the historicity of Adam and Eve (see evidence below).

c. The Larger Structure of Genesis

After Genesis 1 gives an overview of the entire process of creation, Genesis 2 begins a long, continuous historical narrative that carries all

---

18. Ibid., 108, cf. 158, 169.
19. Ibid., 147–169.
20. Ibid., 189, emphasis added for "*like the Jews of his day*."

the way through until the death of Joseph in Genesis 50:26, the end of the book.

The entire book of Genesis is connected together as a single historical document in two ways:

(1) The genealogies in later chapters (see Genesis 5, 10, 11) explicitly tie all of the later historical persons and events back to their direct descent from Adam and Eve in Genesis 1–3, showing that the entire story of Genesis from the beginning is intended to be understood as one historical narrative, reporting people who actually existed and events that actually happened. Abraham, Isaac, and Jacob are presented as real historical persons who descended from Adam and Eve, and therefore Adam and Eve are also viewed as real historical persons.

(2) The introductory phrase "These are the generations of . . ."[21] (or a similar expression) occurs eleven times in Genesis (see Gen. 2:4, 5:1; 6:9; 10:1; 11:10, 27; 25:12, 19; 36:1, 9; 37:2). This literary device begins with the first link in the chain at Genesis 2:4, *"These are the generations of* the heavens and the earth when they were created." This phrase is the introductory heading for Genesis 2:4 to 4:26, a section that includes the details of the creation of Adam and Eve, the fall, and the stories about Cain, Abel, and Seth. The second link in the chain is Genesis 5:1, "This is the book of the generations of Adam," and it introduces a long list of Adam's descendants including Enoch, Methuselah, and Noah.

The eleventh and last link in this connected literary chain is the story of Jacob and his twelve sons, beginning with the introduction in Genesis 37:2, "These are the generations of Jacob," and ending with the death of Joseph in Genesis 50:26, the end of the book.

Therefore this literary device links together the story of Adam and Eve with the stories about the lives of Abraham, Isaac, Jacob, and Jacob's twelve sons, stories that are unquestionably intended as factual historical narratives. Therefore the entire book is intended to be understood as historical narrative. This significant literary feature is analyzed in more detail by John Currid and Guy Waters in chapters 28 and 29.[22]

---

21. Some translations render this as, "This is the account of . . . " (so NASB, NIV, NET, NLT).

22. See pages 869–870 and 893–894. As Waters points out, it seems that Matthew is connecting his gospel to the stories in Genesis when he begins the gospel with *"The book of the genealogy of Jesus Christ, the son of David, the son of Abraham"* (Matt. 1:1).

The interconnectedness of the whole of Genesis because of the unbroken links of genealogy from Genesis 1–3 all the way to the stories of the patriarchs in Genesis 12–50 must not be minimized. Gordon Wenham, professor emeritus of Old Testament at the University of Gloucestershire and author of a highly respected two-volume commentary on Genesis, writes,

> If the later figures in the genealogies are real people—and they certainly behave in very human fashion—then *the earlier characters, the ancestors of Abraham, must also be viewed as real persons.* . . .
> As an interim conclusion we may say that Gen 1–11 is a genealogy, which has been expanded with stories from ancient times to produce an account of the development of the human race from its origin to the time of Abraham. . . . The backbone of Gen 1–11 is an expanded linear genealogy: ten generations from Adam to Noah and ten generations from Noah to Abram.[23]

James Hoffmeier, professor of Old Testament and Near Eastern Archaeology at Trinity Evangelical Divinity School, similarly affirms that Genesis 1–11 must be understood as historical:

> Genealogical texts in the ancient Near East, by their very nature, are treated seriously by scholars and not cavalierly dismissed as made-up or fictitious, even if such lists are truncated or selective. . . . The "family history" structuring of the book [of Genesis] indicates that *the narratives should be understood as historical*, focusing on the origins of Israel back to Adam and Eve, the first human couple and parents of all humanity. . . . *The narratives are dealing with real events involving historical figures*—and this includes Genesis 1–11. . . . The author of the narrative goes to great lengths to place Eden within the known geography of the ancient near East, not some made-up mythological, Narnia-like wonderland.[24]

---

23. Gordon Wenham, "Genesis 1–11 as Protohistory," in *Genesis: History, Fiction, or Neither? Three Views on the Bible's Earliest Chapters*, ed. Charles Halton (Grand Rapids, MI: Zondervan, 2015), 85, 95, emphasis added. Wenham was the author of *Genesis 1–15* and *Genesis 16–50*, the two-volume Word Biblical Commentary on Genesis (Waco, TX: Word, 1987, 1994).

24. James Hoffmeier, "Genesis 1–11 as History and Theology," in Charles Halton, ed., *Genesis: History, Fiction, or Neither?* (Grand Rapids, MI: Zondervan, 2015), 30, 32, emphasis added.

d. The Evidence from the New Testament

In the New Testament, Jesus reinforces the idea of Adam as the first human being, for he says,

> [He] who created them from the beginning made them male and female, and said, "Therefore a man shall leave his father and his mother and hold fast to his wife, and the two shall become one flesh" (*Matt. 19:4–5*).[25]

Jesus must be referring to the narrative about Adam and Eve in Genesis 2, because "a man shall leave his father and his mother" is taken directly from Genesis 2:24. But Jesus also ties this Adam and Eve narrative *in Genesis 2* to the first creation of man on the earth *in Genesis 1*, for "from the beginning" echoes "In the beginning" in Genesis 1:1. Moreover, Jesus quotes Genesis 1:27 with the words *"made them male and female."*[26] Jesus thus affirms the historicity of both Genesis 1 and Genesis 2, and thus affirms Adam and Eve as the first human beings on the earth, not (as theistic evolution would have it) as two among thousands of other human beings on the earth.

Luke's gospel traces the genealogy of Jesus all the way back to Adam, at the beginning of the human race: "the son of Enos, the son of Seth, *the son of Adam, the son of God*" (*Luke 3:38*).[27] Luke considers Adam the very first human being, the one directly created by God as specified in the narrative in Genesis 1–2.

When Paul is speaking to Greek philosophers on the Areopagus, he says,

> And he made from *one man* every nation of mankind to live on all the face of the earth. (*Acts 17:26*)

Paul says that "one man" was the first human being on the earth (for all were "made" from him), and in Paul's understanding, this one man is Adam (for Paul repeatedly calls Adam the "one man" in

---

25. See pages 894–895 for Guy Waters's discussion of the necessary historical nature of the basis of marriage as Jesus affirms it in this passage.

26. Jesus's words in Matthew 19:4, ἄρσεν καὶ θῆλυ ἐποίησεν αὐτούς, are an exact word-for-word citation of the Septuagint translation of Genesis 1:27.

27. See pages 882–884 for Guy Waters's discussion of this genealogy in Luke.

referring to the beginning of the human race in Romans 5:12, 14, 15, 16, 17, 19).[28]

In 1 Corinthians, Paul explicitly calls Adam the "first man":

> Thus it is written, "The *first man* Adam became a living being"; the last Adam became a life-giving spirit. (*1 Cor. 15:45*)

Therefore, the literary setting and content of the whole of Genesis 1–2 indicate that the author intends these chapters to be understood as a historical narrative of the *beginnings* of everything in creation, including the creation of Adam as the first human being. In addition, later Old Testament records in Genesis 5 and 1 Chronicles 1 place Adam first in long lists of people descended from Adam, people whom they understand to be historical persons in subsequent generations. In the New Testament, Luke, Jesus, and Paul all affirm the historicity of the Genesis account of Adam as the first human being.

But advocates of theistic evolution all deny that Adam and Eve were the first human beings, and some deny that Adam and Eve even existed.[29]

2. Adam and Eve Were Born from Human Parents

This idea is the second point of tension between theistic evolution and Genesis 1–3. Our friends who hold to theistic evolution maintain that Adam and Eve (if they even existed) were ordinary human beings with human parents, but this presents a conflict with the text of Genesis, which affirms that God directly *"formed the man of dust from the ground* and breathed into his nostrils the breath of life, and the man became a living creature" (*Gen. 2:7*). If this is understood as historical

---

28. See the more detailed discussion of Acts 17:26 by Guy Waters on pages 884–885, demonstrating that the "one man" must be Adam.

29. Denis Lamoureux writes, in an article posted on the BioLogos website, "Did the apostle Paul believe that Adam was a real person? Yes, well of course he did. Paul was a first-century-AD Jew and like every Jewish person around him, he accepted the historicity of Adam. . . . It is understandable why most Christians believe that Adam was a real historical person. This is exactly what Scripture states in both the Old and New Testaments" (Denis Lamoureux, "Was Adam a Real Person? Part 3," *BioLogos*, September 17, 2010, http://biologos.org/blogs/archive/was-adam -a-real-person-part-3).

But in spite of the fact that he thinks the Bible says this, Lamoureux himself does not believe that Adam ever existed: "My central conclusion in this book is clear: Adam never existed, and this fact has no impact whatsoever on the foundational beliefs of Christianity" (Denis Lamoureux, "Was Adam a Real Person, Part 2," *BioLogos*, September 11, 2010, http://biologos.org/blogs/archive /was-adam-a-real-person-part-2, citing Lamoureux's summary statement from his 2008 book, *Evolutionary Creation* [Eugene, OR: Wipf & Stock]).

narrative, Adam had no human parents but was formed directly from the earth.[30]

Eve is also portrayed as having no human parents, for we read that she was created from a rib taken from Adam's body: "and the rib that the LORD God had taken from the man he made into a woman and brought her to the man" (*Gen. 2:22*).

Luke's gospel similarly portrays Adam as having no human parent, for his genealogy leads backward from Jesus ultimately to "Seth, the son of Adam, the son of God" (*Luke 3:38*).

Paul also affirms that Adam had no human parent, for he calls him "the first man Adam" (*1 Cor. 15:45; also verse 47*). But if Adam had had a human father, he would not be the first man.

This is another point of tension with theistic evolution, which requires that Adam and Eve were born from human parents, and that they were only two out of many thousands of human beings on Earth at that time.

3. God Did Not Act Directly or Specially to Create Adam out of Dust from the Ground

This point is the counterpart to the previous point about Adam and Eve having human parents. Theistic evolution requires that "Adam" (if there was an Adam) descended from a long line of previously existing human beings, but the account in Genesis 2 claims that God made the first man from the dust:

> then the LORD God *formed the man of dust from the ground* and breathed into his nostrils the breath of life, and the man became a living creature. (*Gen. 2:7*)

As John Currid demonstrates in chapter 28, the expression "formed the man of dust from the ground" specifies the material from which God made the man, because "verbs of forming often require two accusatives, an object accusative (the thing made) followed by a material accusative (the material from which the thing is made)."[31] The material

---

30. For a discussion of John Walton's alternative interpretations of this verse and the verse about Eve's creation from Adam's rib, see the following two sections of this chapter.

31. See page 868. Vern Poythress rightly notes that "dust from the ground" simply "hints at the common material stuff making up his body" (Poythress, *Did Adam Exist?* Christian Answers to Hard Questions [Phillipsburg, NJ: P&R, 2014], 16).

is "dust," that is, "the dry, fine crumbs of the earth"[32]—specifying that God directly created man from the ground, not from a line of previously existing human beings and nearly human animals.

However, in defending the possibility of theistic evolution, John Walton argues that "the LORD God formed the man of dust from the ground" simply means that Adam was mortal, subject to death. He argues that the verb for "formed" need not refer to forming a material object.[33] He also argues that "formed . . . of dust" simply means that human beings are subject to death because "dust refers to mortality."[34] He quotes Psalm 103:14: "For he knows how we are formed, he remembers that we are dust" (NIV), where the Hebrew words for "formed" and "dust" are the same or similar, and the Psalm is speaking about our mortality.

But Walton does not give sufficient attention to the decisive differences in the contexts of Genesis 2 and Psalm 103. Psalm 103 is poetic literature that speaks elegantly about the fleeting nature of human life (the next verse says, "As for man, his days are like grass"). When David says, "He remembers that we are dust," it is an evident allusion to God's punishment in Genesis 3:19: "You are dust, and to dust you shall return."

The context of Genesis 2:7 is different. Genesis 2 is closely tied to Genesis 1 as a more detailed explanation of how God created human beings.[35] Walton makes a verse about the *creation* of man into a verse predicting man's death!

---

32. Ludwig Koehler, Walter Baumgartner, and Johann J. Stamm, *The Hebrew and Aramaic Lexicon of the Old Testament*, trans. and ed. under the supervision of Mervyn E. J. Richardson, 5 vols. (Leiden: Brill, 1994–2000), 723.

33. As evidence he points to other verses where the Hebrew verb for "formed" (Hebrew *yātsar*) "is used in a variety of nonmaterial ways," such as forming days and forming events to happen (Walton, *Lost World of Adam and Eve*, 71). But this is simply an exegetical mistake on Walton's part, because he fails to give sufficient attention to this specific context: when the verb is used *in contexts that specify the material that is used and the object that is formed* (as in Gen. 2:7), and when those are both physical items, then it evidently is speaking about a material creation.
C. John Collins says, "Walton's treatment of the verb in Genesis 2:7 ('form') lacks appropriate lexical rigor. No doubt other things can be formed (as in Zech. 12:1); but the specific syntactical structure in Genesis 2:7 employs what some call a double accusative, which is common for verbs that denote making or preparing: the first accusative ('the man') is the object of the verb, the thing made; the second accusative ('dust from the ground') is the stuff out of which the thing is made" (Collins, "Response from the Old-Earth View," in Barrett and Caneday, *Four Views on the Historical Adam*, 129).

34. Walton, *Lost World of Adam and Eve*, 73.

35. See the arguments of John Currid showing the close ties between Genesis 1 and Genesis 2 (pages 863–870).

Here is what Genesis 2:7 says:

> then the LORD God formed the man *of dust from the ground* and breathed into his nostrils the breath of life, and the man became a living creature. (Gen 2:7)

But according to Walton's interpretation, "formed from dust" means that man is mortal. If we insert that idea back into the verse, this is what Genesis 2:7 would mean:

> then the LORD God formed the man *so that he would die* and breathed into his nostrils the breath of life, and the man became a living creature.

On this reading, the text tells us that man would die *before* man even began to live (by receiving the breath of life). The very passage that proclaims to us that God amazingly made *nonliving* "dust" into a *living* human being now becomes a passage that tells us that God made a man who would die. But death is continually seen as a flaw, an enemy (1 Cor. 15:26), a tragedy that according to Genesis 3 came only as a judgment for Adam's sin, not at the very beginning of creation.

Therefore Walton's proposed interpretation is unpersuasive, both because of the specific linguistic construction in Genesis 2:7 and because of the Bible's consistent claim that death was not part of the way God originally created man but was a horrible punishment that came later because of sin.

The next chapter of Genesis also affirms Adam's creation directly from the earth:

> By the sweat of your face
>   you shall eat bread,
> till you return to the ground,
>   *for out of it you were taken;*
> *for you are dust,*
>   *and to dust you shall return.* (**Gen. 3:19**)

Then the narrative continues, "therefore the LORD God sent him out from the garden of Eden to work *the ground from which he was taken*" (**Gen. 3:23**).

In the New Testament, Paul reaffirms Adam's creation from the dust of the earth as reported in Genesis 2 when he says, "the first man was from the earth, *a man of dust*" (*1 Cor. 15:47*).

4. God Did Not Directly Create Eve from a Rib Taken from Adam's Side

Theistic evolution requires that "Eve" (if there was an Eve) had human parents, but the narrative in Genesis 2 gives a different explanation of how God created Eve:

> The man gave names to all livestock and to the birds of the heavens and to every beast of the field. But for Adam there was not found a helper fit for him. So the LORD God caused a deep sleep to fall upon the man, and while he slept *took one of his ribs* and closed up its place with flesh. *And the rib that the Lord God had taken from the man he made into a woman* and brought her to the man. Then the man said,
>
> > "This at last is bone of my bones
> > and flesh of my flesh;
> > she shall be called Woman,
> > because she was taken out of Man."
>
> Therefore a man shall leave his father and his mother and hold fast to his wife, and they shall become one flesh. And the man and his wife were both naked and were not ashamed. (*Gen. 2:20–25*)

The text does not present the creation of Eve from Adam's rib[36] as a minor detail, for it is immediately presented as an explanation for the institution of marriage in the human race and for sexual union within marriage as a reuniting of two halves that were originally one ("*Therefore* a man shall . . . hold fast to his wife, and they shall become one flesh"; v. 24).

---

36. Christopher Shaw, one of the science editors of the present volume, pointed out to me the interesting fact that a rib is one of the few bones in the human body that can be removed without significant loss of function. In addition, he called my attention to a 2011 letter to the editor published in *American Journal of Hematology*, which noted that "The rib, in particular, represents an anatomic type of long bone with a wide, spongious component rich in hematopoietic bone marrow, containing multipotent, pluripotent, and unipotent stem cells" (Francesco Callea and Michelle Callea, "Adam's Rib and the Origin of Stem Cells," *American Journal of Hematology* 86, no. 6 (2011): 529; http://onlinelibrary.wiley.com/doi/10.1002/ajh.22005/full).

God's forming of Eve from Adam's body also demonstrates that Eve is not an inferior creature but one who is of the *same substance* as Adam, and therefore someone who is fully human, of equal value to Adam in God's sight. In addition, it provides the historical basis for affirming that all human beings, including Eve, have descended from Adam, something that is more explicitly affirmed in the New Testament (see Acts 17:26; 1 Cor. 15:22).

John Walton argues that God did not create Eve from Adam's rib, but Adam had a "visionary experience" where he saw "himself being cut in half[37] and the woman being built from the other half." This was "something he saw in a vision."[38] But once again Walton has offered an implausible interpretation that does not fit with the actual wording of the text. Elsewhere in Genesis, when someone sees a vision or has a dream, the text makes this clear:

The word of the LORD came to Abram *in a vision.* (Gen. 15:1)

But God came to Abimelech *in a dream* by night. (Gen. 20:3)

And [Jacob] *dreamed,* and behold, there was a ladder set up on the earth, and the top of it reached to heaven. (Gen. 28:12)

Now Joseph had a *dream,* and when he told it to his brothers they hated him even more. (Genesis 37:5; also "He said to them, '*Hear this dream* that I have dreamed'"; Gen. 37:6)

Then [Joseph] he dreamed another dream and told it to his brothers and said, "Behold, *I have dreamed another dream.* Behold, the sun, the moon, and eleven stars were bowing down to me." (Gen. 37:9)

---

37. Walton argues for the translation, "he took one of Adam's sides" instead of "one of his ribs," and thus the text means that God "cut Adam in half" (Walton, *Lost World of Adam and Eve,* 78–79). The Hebrew word *tsēlāʿ* can mean either "rib" or "side," depending on the context, but "closed up its place with flesh" suggests removal of a smaller part of Adam, not his entire side, and this idea is more suitable in a context in which Adam immediately afterward is able to function normally (not as a half-person) and welcome God's gift of Eve. The same Hebrew word *tsēlāʿ* is used elsewhere to refer to the wooden bars that support the fabric of the tabernacle (Ex. 26:26; 36:31) or the boards of wood that Solomon used to line the inside of the temple (1 Kings 6:15). This same word is used to mean "rib" in rabbinic literature: see Marcus Jastrow, *A Dictionary of the Targumim, the Talmud Babli and Yerushalmi, and the Midrashic Literature* (New York: Judaica Press, 1971), 1285. In the phrase "took one of his ribs," the translation "ribs" is found in ESV, RSV, NRSV, NASB, NIV, NLT, CSB, NKJV, KJV (I found no translation with "sides").

38. Walton, *Lost World of Adam and Eve,* 80.

Pharaoh *dreamed* that he was standing by the Nile. (Gen. 41:1)

There are no such contextual indicators of a dream or vision in Genesis 2. It is presented as straightforward narrative in which God causes a deep sleep to fall on Adam (presumably to anesthetize him), then removes one of his ribs, then closes up the place where the rib was removed, and then creates Eve and brings her to Adam, and Adam welcomes her. The passage does not say that Adam had a dream or saw a vision.

Jesus also affirms the historicity of Genesis 2 when he says,

> Have you not read that he who created them from the beginning made them male and female, and said, "*Therefore* a man shall leave his father and his mother and hold fast to his wife, and the two shall become one flesh"? (*Matt. 19:4–5*)

His words "Have you not read" indicate that he is relying on the narrative in Genesis 1–2, and his report in Matthew 19:5 of what God "said" is a direct quotation from Genesis 2:24. It is significant that Jesus includes the word "Therefore" in his quotation, for this word in the text of Genesis 2:24 links it explicitly to the story of how God created Eve from a rib from Adam's side in the immediately preceding verses (vv. 21–23).

The reasoning is, "Eve was taken out of Adam's side, and *therefore* a man shall hold fast to his wife, and the two shall become one flesh, and what was separated will be reunited." This "therefore" statement cannot work unless the reader believes that Eve was created from the rib taken from Adam's side as reported in Genesis 2:21–23. Jesus is relying on and affirming the historical accuracy of the record in Genesis—that Eve was created from a rib from Adam's side.

Paul affirms the historicity of Eve's creation from Adam's body when he says, "For man was not made from woman, *but woman from man*" (*1 Cor. 11:8*).[39] Paul is not saying that Adam dreamed this, but that it actually happened.

Paul also affirms the accuracy of the history of Eve's creation in Genesis 2 in another epistle when he writes, "For Adam was formed

---

39. See the further discussion of this passage by Guy Waters on pages 885–886.

first, then Eve" (*1 Tim. 2:13*). He could not have known this from Genesis 1, where no details are given about the sequence of the creation of man and woman, but he could only have known it from Genesis 2.[40] Once again he is affirming the historicity of the creation of Eve from Adam's side.

Therefore both Paul and Jesus understand Genesis 2 as a historical narrative, and they claim that the specific details of Genesis 2 are factually true—they actually happened. But theistic evolution must say that Eve was not created from Adam's rib—or from any part of Adam's body at all. Are we willing to say that both Paul and Jesus were wrong?

5. Adam and Eve Were Never Sinless Human Beings

Our friends who hold to theistic evolution maintain that Adam and Eve were ordinary human beings, doing sinful deeds for their entire lives just as all other human beings do. By contrast, the entire story of the creation of Adam and Eve as recorded in Genesis 1–2 indicates only blessing and favor from God, and gives no hint of the existence of any human sin or God's judgment on sin.

God created them, and "God blessed them" (Gen. 1:28), and then,

God saw everything that he had made, and behold, *it was very good.* (*Gen. 1:31*)

"Very good" in the eyes of a holy God implies there was no sin present in the world.[41]

Where there is no sin or guilt, there also is no shame, and so the picture of a sinless world is confirmed by this statement that closes the narrative in Genesis 2: "And the man and his wife were both naked and were not ashamed" (*Gen. 2:25*).

---

40. Paul's statement that "Adam was formed first" uses the Greek verb *plassō*, "to form, mold," which is the same verb used in the Septuagint of Genesis 2:7, "the Lord God *formed* the man of dust from the ground."

41. John Walton argues that "good" (Hebrew *tôb*) in Genesis 1:31 does not imply freedom from sin or suffering, because "in reality the word never carries this sense of unadulterated, pristine perfection" (*Lost World of Adam and Eve*, 53). But his argument is unpersuasive because (1) this is a unique, pre-fall context, unlike the post-fall contexts in which the word later occurs; (2) this verse gives an evaluation of what is "very good" in the eyes of an infinitely holy God, not in the eyes of sinful human beings; (3) Walton inexplicably considers only the word *tôb*, "good," not the emphatic expression *tôb me'od*, "very good" which occurs in this verse. It is unthinkable that God would look at a world filled with moral evil and declare it to be "very good."

But then sin, and the guilt and shame that accompany sin, begin with Adam and Eve eating the forbidden fruit in Genesis 3, and it is only then that "the man and his wife hid themselves from the presence of the LORD God among the trees of the garden" (*Gen. 3:8*).

This perspective on a sinless creation followed by the fall is also seen in Ecclesiastes: "See, this alone I found, that *God made man upright*, but they have sought out many schemes" (*Eccles. 7:29*).

In the New Testament, the first entrance of sin into the world through the disobedience of Adam is affirmed when Paul says, "sin came into the world through one man" (*Rom. 5:12*).[42]

If sin "came into the world through one man," and specifically through that "one man's trespass" (Rom. 5:15), then Paul is affirming that there was no sin in the world before Adam's sin. This means that God created Adam and Eve as sinless human beings, as the narrative in Genesis 1–2 indicates.

But theistic evolution argues that Adam and Eve (if they existed at all) were never sinless human beings. Therefore theistic evolution once again implies that Paul himself was wrong.

6. Adam and Eve Did Not Commit the First Human Sins, for Human Beings Were Doing Morally Evil Things Long before Adam and Eve

This is the counterpart to the previous point about God not creating Adam and Eve as sinless people. According to theistic evolution, human beings have always committed morally evil deeds, and therefore human beings were sinning for thousands of years before Adam and Eve.[43]

But this claim is again in tension with the biblical witness, for just as the Genesis narrative shows that God created Adam and Eve as sinless human beings (see previous section), it also shows that Adam and Eve committed the *first* human sins in a world that was perfect and free from human sin. God had commanded Adam not to eat of the fruit of the tree of the knowledge of good and evil (Gen. 2:17), but the

---

42. See the extensive discussion of this passage by Guy Waters on pages 907–926 of this volume, especially its implications for the origin of human sin.

43. John Walton says, "Anthropological evidence for violence in the earliest populations deemed human would indicate that there was never a time when sinful (= at least personal evil) behavior was not present" (*Lost World of Adam and Eve*, 154).

serpent tempted Eve (Gen. 3:1–6), and she ate of the fruit, and then Adam also ate:

> So when the woman saw that the tree was good for food, and that it was a delight to the eyes, and that the tree was to be desired to make one wise, she took of its fruit and ate, and she also gave some to her husband who was with her, and he ate. (*Gen. 3:6*)

After that, sin quickly proliferates as the narrative unfolds. God drives Adam and Eve out of the garden (Gen. 3:16–24), and then Cain murders Abel (Gen. 4:8), Lamech murders a man in vengeance (Gen. 4:23), and eventually, "the LORD saw that the wickedness of man was great in the earth, and that every intention of the thoughts of his heart was only evil continually" (Gen. 6:5). All this is pictured in Genesis as something that began with the initial sin of Adam and Eve.

A reference to the sin of Adam is also the most likely interpretation of a passage in Hosea:

> But *like Adam* they transgressed the covenant (*Hos. 6:7*).[44]

Paul reaffirms that sin began with Adam and Eve[45] in an extensive discussion in Romans 5:

> Therefore, just as *sin came into the world through one man*. . . .
>   For if many died through *one man's trespass*, much more have the grace of God and the free gift by the grace of that one man Jesus Christ abounded for many. And the free gift is not like the result of that *one man's sin*. For the judgment following *one trespass* brought condemnation, but the free gift following many trespasses

---

44. Denis Alexander says, "Most scholars maintain that the 'Adam' referred to in Hosea 6:7 refers to a place not a person" (Denis Alexander, *Creation or Evolution: Do We Have to Choose?*, 2nd ed. (Oxford: Monarch, 2014), 475n164). He gives no basis for this assertion. The translation "like Adam" (referring to Adam as a person) is found in ESV, NASB, NLT, and CSB, while the translation "at Adam" is found in NIV, NET, RSV, and NRSV.

The *ESV Study Bible* note says, "to whom or to what does 'Adam' refer? Many commentators suggest a geographical locality. The difficulty is that there is no record of covenant breaking at a place called Adam. . . . And it requires a questionable taking of the preposition 'like' (Heb. *ke-*) to mean 'at' or 'in'. . . . It is best to understand 'Adam' as the name of the first man" (*ESV Study Bible* [Wheaton, IL: Crossway, 2008], 1631).

45. Although Eve sinned first in the narrative in Genesis 3, Paul focuses on the sin of Adam, apparently because Adam alone had a representative role with respect to the entire human race, a role in which Eve did not share. Similarly, Paul elsewhere says, "For as in Adam all die, so also in Christ shall all be made alive" (1 Cor. 15:22).

brought justification. For if, because of *one man's trespass*, death reigned through that one man, much more will those who receive the abundance of grace and the free gift of righteousness reign in life through the one man Jesus Christ.

Therefore, as *one trespass led to condemnation for all men*, so one act of righteousness leads to justification and life for all men. For as *by the one man's disobedience the many were made sinners*, so by the one man's obedience the many will be made righteous (*Rom. 5:12, 15–19*).[46]

Paul also affirms the historicity of the account of the sin of Adam and Eve with reference to a specific detail in Genesis 2: "But I am afraid that as *the serpent deceived Eve by his cunning*, your thoughts will be led astray from a sincere and pure devotion to Christ (*2 Cor. 11:3*).[47]

Paul returns to this theme in a later epistle: "and Adam was not deceived, but the woman was deceived and became a transgressor" (*1 Tim. 2:14*).[48]

Therefore the theistic evolution claim that thousands of human beings were committing sinful acts long before the time of Adam and Eve would require us again to say that Paul was wrong in what he wrote.

7. Human Death Did Not Begin as a Result of Adam's Sin, for Human Beings Existed Long before Adam and Eve and They Were Always Subject to Death

All living things known to evolutionary science, including human beings, eventually die, and therefore theistic evolution requires that human beings have always been subject to death, and that human beings were dying long before Adam and Eve existed.

But according to the biblical narrative, when God first created Adam and Eve, they were not subject to death (as I argued in section 3 above, in response to John Walton's view of "formed the man of dust from the ground"). The absence of death when Adam and Eve were created is implied by the summary statement at the end of the sixth

---

46. See pages 917–920 for Guy Waters's answer to Walton's claim that Romans 5 simply means that people were not accountable for their sin before Adam.

47. Guy Waters discusses this passage more fully on pages 886–888.

48. See the discussion of this passage by Guy Waters, pages 888–891.

day of creation, "and God saw everything that he had made, and behold, *it was very good*" (**Gen. 1:31**). In light of later biblical teachings that death is the "last enemy to be destroyed" (1 Cor. 15:26), and the prediction that in the age to come, "death shall be no more" (Rev. 21:4), the initial "very good" creation should be understood to imply that Adam and Eve were not subject to death when they were first created.

In addition, in the next chapter, God said to Adam, "But of the tree of the knowledge of good and evil you shall not eat, for in the day that you eat of it *you shall surely die*" (**Gen. 2:17**). This implies that death would be the *penalty for disobedience*, not something to which they were initially subject. (Nothing is implied in Genesis 2 about animal death, for God's statement directed to Adam implies only human death: "*you* shall surely die.") After Adam sinned, God pronounced the promised judgment, which would be carried out over time through a life filled with painful toil, culminating in death:

> By the sweat of your face
>   you shall eat bread,
> *till you return to the ground*,
>   for out of it you were taken;
> for you are dust,
>   and to dust you shall return" (**Gen. 3:19**).

In the New Testament, Paul states explicitly that human death came into the world through Adam's sin, for he says,

> Therefore, just as sin came into the world through one man, *and death through sin*, and so death spread to all men because all sinned— (*Rom. 5:12*)[49]

Once again, the emphasis is on human death, for Paul's statement, "and so death spread to all *men*" uses a plural form of the Greek term *anthrōpos*, a term that refers only to human beings, not to animals. (The entire Bible says nothing one way or another about the death of animals before the fall.)

---

49. See Guy Waters's discussion of this passage and its implications for human death, pages 907–910.

810   *The Biblical and Theological Critique of Theistic Evolution*

In 1 Corinthians, Paul affirms again that death came through Adam's sin:

> For as *by a man came death*, by a man has come also the resurrection of the dead. For as *in Adam all die*, so also in Christ shall all be made alive (*1 Cor. 15:21–22*).[50]

But theistic evolution requires us to deny that human death began as a result of Adam's sin,[51] and this once again requires us to say that the Genesis account is not a trustworthy historical narrative, and that Paul was wrong.

8. Not All Human Beings Have Descended from Adam and Eve, for There Were Thousands of Other Human Beings on Earth at the Time That God Chose Two of Them as Adam and Eve

The "Adam and Eve" advocated by theistic evolution were just two individuals among many thousands on the earth at that time, and therefore not all human beings have descended from Adam and Eve.

But Genesis portrays Adam and Eve as the first human beings (see section 1 above), and that is why God then says to them, "Be fruitful and multiply and fill the earth and subdue it" (Gen. 1:28). The earth had no human beings, so Adam and Eve were to begin to fill it.

Later in Genesis, "The man called his wife's name Eve, because *she was the mother of all living*" (*Gen. 3:20*). The sentence cannot mean "all living things," because plants and animals existed before Adam or Eve (Gen. 1:11–25), and so the intended sense must be "all living human beings." All human beings have descended from Adam as the male progenitor, and from Eve, his wife, as the female progenitor.

By contrast, several theistic evolution authors claim that there must have been many other human beings on the earth at the time of Adam and Eve. The evidence they give is that Cain's wife (Gen. 4:17) had to come from somewhere, and Cain expected that there were other people who would want to kill him (Gen. 4:14). Genesis even says that Cain

---

50. See Guy Waters's discussion of this passage and its implications for human death, pages 911–916.
51. See, e.g., Walton, *Lost World of Adam and Eve*, 144; also 72–77 and 159.

built a "city," which had to be a place populated by numerous people (Gen. 4:17).

But are we to think that the author of Genesis (whom I believe to be Moses) was unaware of this difficulty? The text of Genesis itself provides an obvious solution to this problem, because it says that Adam lived 930 years, "*and he had other sons and daughters*" (Gen. 5:4–5). How many? The text does not say, but Adam and Eve, created as full-grown adults, could have begun to have children in their very first year. Adam was 130 years old when Seth was born (Gen. 5:3), but he and Eve could well have had many dozens of children both prior to that time and after that time—the text does not tell us.

Yes, this requires that Cain and Seth and others would have married their sisters in the first generation, but that was necessary in order to have the entire human race descend from Adam and Eve, and the prohibitions against incest were not given by God until much later (see Lev. 18:6–18; 20:11–20; Deut. 22:30).

In the New Testament, Paul said that God "made *from one man* every nation of mankind to live on all the face of the earth" (*Acts 17:26*). This implies that all human beings descended from Adam.

Such a descent of the entire human race from Adam is important (a) because it shows the actual physical unity of the human race, thus precluding any ideas of racial superiority or inferiority. It is also important (b) because it explains how *the guilt of Adam's sin* could be justly imputed to all his descendants, and it also provides the mechanism by which a *sinful nature* (or disposition toward sin) has been transmitted from generation to generation throughout the entire human race. Finally, it is important (c) because it provides a category of people who are "in Adam" in such a way that Adam's sentence of death also applied to all who descended from Adam: "For as *in Adam all die*, so also in Christ shall all be made alive" (*1 Cor. 15:22*).

But theistic evolution denies that all human beings have descended from Adam, and so the actual physical unity of the entire human race is denied, and Adam's role as representative head of the entire human race is nullified, because it is inextricably tied to the physical descent of every human being from Adam. As Guy Waters argues in a detailed analysis of 1 Corinthians 15 in chapter 29, "Were there a human being not descended from Adam, he would not be eligible for redemption. Only those who have borne Adam's image may bear Christ's image."[52]

9. God Did Not Directly Act in the Natural World to Create Different "Kinds" of Fish, Birds, and Land Animals

Theistic evolution claims that God created matter and after that did not guide or intervene to cause any empirically detectable change in the natural behavior of matter until all living things had evolved by purely natural processes.

But this proposal is in tension with the picture presented in Genesis, where God carries out *distinct and separate actions* to directly create different specific parts of creation, and then, in further distinct actions, creates specific kinds (or types) of animals.

For example,

> And God said, "Let the earth sprout vegetation." . . . And it was so. (*Gen. 1:11*)

That was on day 3. Then in a separate act on day 5,

> And God said, "Let the waters swarm with swarms of living creatures, and let birds fly above the earth across the expanse of the heavens." (*Gen. 1:20*)

Then on day 6 there is more creative activity:

> And *God made the beasts of the earth* according to their kinds *and the livestock* according to their kinds, *and everything that creeps on the ground* according to its kind. And God saw that it was good. (*Gen. 1:25*)

The Hebrew text includes the direct object marker ['*eth*] three times in this verse, showing that there are three distinct direct objects of the verb "made" (Hebrew '*āsāh*): the verse says that God specifically made (1) the beasts of the earth, and also (2) the livestock, and also (3) everything that creeps on the ground. In addition, within each of

---

52. See pages 903–926. Waters maintains that theistic evolution supporters fail to adequately explain, in a way consistent with New Testament teaching, just how Adam could represent the entire human race if not all human beings have descended from him.

these groups he made creatures "according to their kinds," indicating a number of different specific types of animals within each group (though Scripture gives us no indication of the size of each category that is called a "kind"). This verse pictures a direct, active involvement of God in making different kinds of animals, which is far different from the "hands-off" allowing of matter to evolve following its own properties that we find in theistic evolution.

Later, in a separate action on this same day, God said, "Let us *make* (once again, another distinct action designated by Hebrew *'āsāh*) man in our image. . . . So God created man in his own image, in the image of God he created him; male and female he created them" (***Gen. 1:26–27***).

Finally, at the end of the sixth day, "God saw everything *that he had made*, and behold, it was very good" (***Gen. 1:31***). The scope of "everything that he had made" (once again, Hebrew *'āsāh*) must include both the separate kinds of animals (from day 6) and also man himself (from day 6) which have just been specified as things that God "made."

The picture given in Genesis, therefore, is that God *directly made* various kinds of animals and also made human beings in distinct, separate acts. But theistic evolution says that God did not "make" these things in any sense that the Hebrew reader of these verses would understand from the verb "made" (Hebrew *'āsāh*), but only in the sense that inanimate matter that God had created billions of years earlier at the beginning of the universe evolved by virtue of its own properties, with no additional creative action from God, into all these animals and human beings.[53]

The Psalms also speak about God's *specific acts* of creating individual parts of nature. David says to God that "the moon and the stars" are things that "you have set in place" (***Ps. 8:3***). Then he says to

---

53. Theistic evolution advocates frequently affirm that they believe in God's ongoing providential involvement in all of creation, but by this they do not mean that God intervened in, or in any way directed, the actions of the material universe, but rather that God *sustained* the materials of the universe so that they continually acted according to the physical properties with which they were initially created. Denis Alexander speaks about "the precious materials God has so carefully brought into being in the dying moments of exploding stars" and says it is wrong to deny that they have the "potentiality to bring about life" (*Creation or Evolution*, 436). But if matter merely acting according to its own created properties can create life, then there would have been no need for God to repeatedly *act* in the natural world, in a way different from ordinary providence, to create different kinds of living things, as Genesis 1 portrays him.

God that many different kinds of animals fall in the category of "the works of your hands":

> What is man that you are mindful of him. . . .
>
> You have given him dominion over *the works of your hands*;
>   you have put all things under his feet,
> all *sheep* and *oxen*,
>   and also the *beasts* of the field
> the *birds* of the heavens, and the *fish* of the sea,
>   whatever passes along the paths of the seas.
>
> O Lord, our Lord,
>   how majestic is your name in all the earth! (*Ps. 8:4–9*)

These creatures are nowhere said to be the product of "materials that assembled themselves" (the theistic evolution view); they are specifically the *works of God's hands*.

A similar understanding is found in Psalm 104, which views various creatures as specific indications of God's wisdom:

> O Lord, how manifold are your works!
>   *In wisdom have you made them all*;
>   the earth is full of *your creatures*.
> Here is the sea, great and wide,
>   which teems with creatures innumerable,
>   living things both small and great. (*Ps. 104:24–25*)

In the New Testament, Paul speaks of "the God who made the world *and everything in it*" (*Acts 17:24*). In this statement, "everything in it" must refer to something different from "the world" itself, and therefore it is best understood to include all the varieties of plants and animals that exist on the earth. Paul does not say that God made the raw materials of the universe and these materials made themselves into living creatures, but that God himself made "everything" that exists in the world (see also John 1:3: "all things were made through him"—showing that the Son of God, the eternal second person of the Trinity, was the active personal agent in bringing all things into existence, a view far different from the idea that matter itself brought all things into existence).

In a similar way, Paul says that God's "invisible attributes, namely, his eternal power and divine nature" have been "clearly perceived, ever since the creation of the world, *in the things that have been made*" (*Rom. 1:20*). Created things, especially plants and animals and human beings in their complexity, bear witness to God's power and divine nature—a fact that has been evident to all generations of human beings who instinctively realize, "Only God could create something as amazing as this flower or this hummingbird." But on a theistic evolution account, complex living things only bear witness to *the amazing properties of matter* that God made billions of years earlier, and bear no direct witness to God's wisdom or power in their specific creation.

When Paul writes, "by him *all things* were created, in heaven *and on earth*, visible and invisible" (*Col. 1:16*), he surely intends to include all living creatures. He says *Christ* specifically created them, not inanimate matter. Similarly, when Paul says that "everything created by God is good" (*1 Tim. 4:4*), he is speaking specifically about "foods that God created to be received with thanksgiving" (1 Tim. 4:3), foods which are made from living plants and animals. These things have not evolved by random mutation, for Paul says they have been "created by God."

The book of Revelation includes two additional references affirming that God himself, not inanimate matter, created all things that exist in the world, including specifically all the creatures of the sea:

> Worthy are you, our Lord and God,
>> to receive glory and honor and power,
> for you *created all things*,
>> and by your will they existed and were created. (*Rev. 4:11*)

> . . . him who lives forever and ever, *who created* heaven and what is in it, *the earth and what is in it*, and *the sea and what is in it*. (*Rev. 10:6*)

None of the original readers of Genesis or of these New Testament writings would have understood these verses to mean that God originally created nonliving matter and that *this matter then created all living things* over the course of billions of years, without any additional intervention from God. Nor could this have been the intended meaning of any of the authors of these New Testament books. Rather, the intent of the human authors (and of the divine author), as rightly understood by the original readers, would be to affirm that God directly acted in the natural world to create all the different kinds of plants and animals that exist on the earth today.

But theistic evolution requires us to believe that these passages from Genesis, Psalms, Acts, Romans, Colossians, 1 Timothy, and Revelation are all mistaken in the way they tell us of God's direct and specific creation of all things in heaven and on Earth.

10. God Did Not "Rest" from His Work of Creation or Stop Any Special Creative Activity after Plants, Animals, and Human Beings Appeared on the Earth

Theistic evolution holds that, after the initial creation of matter, God did not intervene in the world to create any living things. Karl Giberson and Francis Collins say, "The model for divinely guided evolution that we are proposing here thus requires no 'intrusions from outside' for its account of God's creative process, except for the origins of the natural laws guiding the process."[54]

But this also means that, according to theistic evolution, there was no special activity of God from which he could have "rested" after the six days of creation recorded in Genesis 1. The biblical record, however, is incompatible with this theistic evolution viewpoint, for after narrating the events of God's six days of creative work, it says,

> Thus the heavens and the earth were finished, and all the host of them. And on the seventh day *God finished his work* that he had done, and *he rested on the seventh day from all his work that he had done.* So God blessed the seventh day and made it holy, because on it *God rested from all his work* that he had done in creation. (*Gen. 2:1–3*)

---

54. Karl Giberson and Francis Collins, *The Language of Science and Faith* (Downers Grove, IL: InterVarsity, 2011), 115.

Oxford mathematics professor John Lennox explains why these verses cannot be reconciled with theistic evolution:

> According to Genesis, then, creation involved not just one, but a sequence of several discrete creation acts, after which God rested. This surely implies that those acts involved processes that are not going on at the moment. . . . In both Old and New Testaments, the Bible clearly distinguishes between God's initial acts of creation on the one hand and his subsequent upholding of the universe on the other. This distinction is also apparent in Genesis 1: it records a sequence of creation acts followed by God's resting. I also think, by contrast with my theistic evolutionary friends, that science supports this distinction.[55]

Two additional passages in Scripture also view this Genesis account of God's resting as an actual historical event—something that really happened. First, in the Ten Commandments, God himself says,

> For in six days the LORD made heaven and earth, the sea, and all that is in them, *and rested on the seventh day*. Therefore the LORD blessed the Sabbath day and made it holy. (*Ex. 20:11*)

Then the author of Hebrews also affirms that God rested from his work of creation:

> For he has somewhere spoken of the seventh day in this way: "And *God rested* on the seventh day from all his works." . . . for whoever has entered God's rest has also rested from his works as God did from his. (*Heb. 4:4, 10*)

Yet according to a theistic evolution viewpoint, there was no special kind of work that God did during these six days of creation, because the *providential* work of God in sustaining the materials of the universe while evolution was happening was no different from the ongoing *providential* work of God in sustaining the materials of the universe even today. *There was no particular creative work of God from which he could "rest."* This is another event in the history of the universe

---

55. John Lennox, *Seven Days That Divide the World: The Beginning according to Genesis and Science* (Grand Rapids, MI: Zondervan, 2011), 161, 170–171.

which the Bible claims to have happened but which theistic evolution says didn't happen.

11. God Never Created an Originally "Very Good" Natural World in the Sense of a Safe Environment That Was Free of Thorns and Thistles and Similar Harmful Things

Theistic evolution requires that all plants and animals living today resulted from an unbroken line of evolutionary change, and therefore there never was a different kind of natural order from what we know today.

By contrast, for many centuries interpreters have understood Genesis 1–2 to speak of an idyllic garden of Eden, an earth in which there were no "thorns and thistles" (*Gen. 3:18*), no curse on the ground because of sin (*Gen. 3:17*), and, by implication, no weeds hindering beneficial crops, and no natural disasters such as hurricanes, tornadoes, earthquakes, floods, or droughts. It was also thought to be an earth where no animals were hostile to human beings, because of the prophetic predictions of God's future restoration of an earth where, "The nursing child shall play over the hole of the cobra, and the weaned child shall put his hand on the adder's den," and, "They shall not hurt or destroy in all my holy mountain" (*Isa. 11:8–9*).

This was understood (I think rightly) to be the kind of earth implied by the summary statement at the end of the sixth day of creation, "and God saw everything that he had made, and behold, *it was very good*" (*Gen. 1:31*). Indeed, the kind of earth we have today, with frequent earthquakes, hurricanes, floods, droughts, poisonous snakes and venomous scorpions, malaria-spreading mosquitoes, and man-eating sharks and lions, can hardly be thought to be the best kind of creation that God could make, a creation that would cause God to say, "and behold, *it was very good*."

This idea of an originally idyllic creation is reaffirmed by the passage where God pronounces judgment on Adam after he sinned, telling him that now the ground would be "cursed" and would bring forth "thorns and thistles." (See further discussion of this idea in the next section.)

But theistic evolution cannot affirm such an originally idyllic creation, because it holds that all living things *as they exist today*, including all the things that are hostile to human beings, are the results of a fully natural evolutionary process. Therefore the earth has always been the way it is today. Therefore the picture of an idyllic creation given in Genesis is not a historically reliable narrative.

12. After Adam and Eve Sinned, God Did Not Place Any Curse on the World That Changed the Working of the Natural World and Made It More Hostile to Mankind

This belief of theistic evolution advocates is the counterpart of the previous point. They do not believe in an original idyllic creation, and so they also do not believe that God placed a curse on the ground as judgment for Adam's sin, or that God altered the operation of nature in any way to make the world more hostile to human beings.

But the biblical text, if understood as a historical record of actual events, shows that God did indeed alter the workings of the natural world when he spoke to Adam in words of judgment:

And to Adam he said,

> "Because you have listened to the voice of your wife
>   and have eaten of the tree
> of which I commanded you,
>   'You shall not eat of it,'
> *cursed is the ground because of you*;
>   in pain you shall eat of it all the days of your life;
> *thorns and thistles* it shall bring forth for you;
>   and you shall eat the plants of the field.
> By the sweat of your face
>   you shall eat bread,
> till you return to the ground,
>   for out of it you were taken;
> for you are dust,
>   and to dust you shall return." (*Gen. 3:17–19*)

Adam's life would eventually end in death ("to dust you shall return"), but even while he continued alive, his life would consist of painful toil to provide enough food from the ground that had now become hostile ("cursed is the ground. . . . By the sweat of your face you shall eat bread").

God's statement that the ground would now produce "thorns and thistles" is best understood as a synecdoche, a common feature in biblical speech by which two or three concrete examples represent an entire category of things. Taken in this way, God's words of judgment mean that the earth would not only produce thorns and thistles, but would also harbor insects that would destroy crops (such as locusts, Deut. 28:38; Amos 7:1), diseases that would consume them (see Deut. 28:22), foraging animals that would eat crops before they could be harvested, and floods and droughts, tornadoes and hurricanes that would make farming difficult and life precarious (see Eccles. 11:4).

Paul affirms in the New Testament that the present operation of the natural world is not the way God originally created it to work, but is a result of God's judgment. He pictures nature as longing to be freed from its bondage in much the same way as we long to be freed from our dying physical bodies and obtain new resurrection bodies:

> For I consider that the sufferings of this present time are not worth comparing with the glory that is to be revealed to us. For *the creation waits with eager longing* for the revealing of the sons of God. For *the creation was subjected to futility*, not willingly, but because of him who subjected it, in hope that *the creation itself will be set free from its bondage to corruption* and obtain the freedom of the glory of the children of God. For we know that *the whole creation has been groaning together* in the pains of childbirth until now. And not only the creation, but we ourselves, who have the firstfruits of the Spirit, groan inwardly *as we wait eagerly for* adoption as sons, *the redemption of our bodies*. For in this hope we were saved. (Rom. 8:18–24)[56]

Paul does not say that the creation will suddenly be raised to a brand-new, wonderful state of operation that it had never known before. Instead, he says that the creation will be "*set free* from its bondage," the bondage to which it was previously "subjected." Surely he is here referring to God's curse on the ground and his alteration of the

---

56. See the further discussion of this passage by Guy Waters, pages 896–897.

functioning of nature because of sin in Genesis 3. But theistic evolution requires us to affirm that Paul was also wrong at this point.

E. Significant Christian Doctrines That Are Undermined or Denied by Theistic Evolution

Why is this entire issue of theistic evolution important? Ideas often have consequences in our lives, and theistic evolution, as an overarching explanation for the origin of all living things, leads to several destructive consequences for a number of Christian doctrines. Theistic evolution is not at all a harmless "alternative opinion" about creation, but will lead to progressive erosion and often even a denial of at least the following eleven Christian doctrines:

1. The Truthfulness of the Bible

As I have argued in the pages above, proponents of theistic evolution must deny that Genesis 1–3 should be understood as historical narrative in the sense of literature that intends to report events that actually happened. But, in contrast to theistic evolution, these chapters are understood as truthful historical narrative by later chapters in Genesis, as well as by later Old Testament passages in Exodus, 1 Chronicles, Psalms, and Hosea.

In addition, theistic evolution requires us to believe that both Jesus and the New Testament authors were wrong in their affirmations of the historical reliability of many details in Genesis 1–3. More specifically, theistic evolution requires us to believe that passages in Matthew, Luke, Acts, Romans, 1 Corinthians, 2 Corinthians, Colossians, 1 Timothy, Hebrews, and Revelation were all in error in what they affirmed about Genesis 1–3. This is much deeper than a challenge to the historicity of one verse or another. This is a challenge to the truthfulness of the three foundational chapters of the entire Bible, and to the truthfulness of ten of the twenty-seven books of the New Testament.[57]

Even if there were no other harmful consequences from this theory,

---

57. The "Chicago Statement on Biblical Hermeneutics," adopted at the Summit II conference sponsored by the International Council on Biblical Inerrancy, which was held November 10–13, 1982, appropriately included the following statement: "WE DENY that generic categories which negate historicity may rightly be imposed on biblical narratives which present themselves

this alone would be sufficient to conclude that theistic evolution is not a viewpoint that Christians should accept. In addition, when significant historical records in Scripture are explained away as not being truthful records of actual events, then eventually other passages of Scripture—usually those unpopular in modern culture at the moment—will eventually also be explained away as untrustworthy, for they will be seen simply as the result of God accommodating his words to the beliefs of the ancient world in order to communicate his larger saving message to his people.[58] By this process, many of the second- and third-generation followers of those who hold to theistic evolution today will abandon belief in the Bible altogether, and will abandon the Christian faith.

Several years ago the respected evangelical leader Francis Schaeffer used the example of a watershed in the Swiss Alps to illustrate what happens when some Christians begin to abandon the complete truthfulness of the Bible in places where it speaks to matters of history and science. When spring comes, two bits of snow that are only an inch apart in the high mountains of Switzerland will melt on two sides of a ridge in the rock, and the drop of water from one side of the watershed will eventually flow into the Rhine River and then into the cold waters of the North Sea, while the drop of water on the other side of the watershed will eventually flow into the Rhône River and finally into the Mediterranean Sea. In the same way, Christians who seem so close together on many issues, if they differ on the watershed issue of biblical inerrancy, will in the next generation or two train up disciples who will be a thousand miles apart from each other on many of the most central matters taught in the Bible.[59]

---

as factual" (Article XIII), quoted from *Hermeneutics, Inerrancy, and the Bible: Papers from ICBI Summit II*, ed. Earl Radmacher and Robert Preus (Grand Rapids, MI: Zondervan, 1984), 884.

58. Theistic evolution literature frequently appeals to the idea that God "accommodated" his words to the scientific knowledge of the day in order to communicate well. See Denis Lamoureux, "No Historical Adam: Evolutionary Creation View," in *Four Views on the Historical Adam*, Barrett and Caneday, 54, 57; Alexander, *Creation or Evolution*, 55–56. Whether or not this idea is consistent with belief in the complete truthfulness of the Bible depends on what is meant by "accommodation." If it means that God, through human authors, used language and concepts that would be *understood* by the original readers, this does not negate the truthfulness of what is said in Scripture. But if it means that God in Scripture *affirmed ancient ideas that were in fact false* (such as that the sky is a solid dome), then this concept is not consistent with the truthfulness of the entire Bible.

59. See Francis Schaeffer, *The Great Evangelical Disaster* (Westchester, IL: Crossway, 1984), 43–51.

I disagree, therefore, with the emphasis of Denis Alexander, who says, "Least of all should supporting one model [about creation] over another become a bone of contention among Christians, as if it were some central point of doctrine on a par with the death and resurrection of Jesus for our sin. . . . this is a secondary issue, which is not essential for salvation."[60]

But if the real issue here is the truthfulness of the Bible, then it *is* a central point of doctrine and it is not at all a secondary issue. I would not say that this issue is "essential for salvation," for people can be saved by simple faith in Jesus even while refusing to believe a number of important Christian doctrines.[61] But that does not mean this is a secondary issue—not at all. Once the truthfulness of Scripture is lost, the entire Christian faith begins to unravel.

It is important to recognize what is actually happening here. Proponents of theistic evolution are claiming, in essence, that there are whole areas of human knowledge about which they will not allow the Bible to speak with authority. They will allow the Bible to speak to us about salvation, but not about the origin of all living things on the earth, the origin of human beings, the origin of moral evil in the human race, the origin of human death, the origin of natural evil in the world, the perfection of the natural world as God originally created it, and even the nature of Christ's own personal involvement as the Creator of "all things . . . in heaven and on earth, visible and invisible" (Col. 1:16). These are massive areas of human knowledge, affecting our outlook on our entire lives. Yet theistic evolution has decreed that the Bible cannot authoritatively speak to us about these areas of human knowledge. Those topics are the exclusive domain of modern naturalistic science, off-limits for God to speak to us about.

But do Christians today really want to accept a theory that decrees that God is not allowed to speak to us about these vast areas of human

---

60. Alexander, *Creation or Evolution*, 287. Later he adds, "Launching attacks on evolution is divisive and splits the Christian community" (462).

61. Denis Lamoureux, e.g., says, "I simply want evangelicals to be aware that there are born-again Christians who love the Lord Jesus and who do not believe there ever was a first man named 'Adam'" (Lamoureux, "No Historical Adam," 38). I have no reason to doubt Lamoureux's statement, but that does not make this a secondary issue. The question is not whether many people who hold to theistic evolution are themselves born-again Christians, but rather whether this belief undermines confidence in the truthfulness of the Bible and brings significant harmful consequences to the church.

knowledge? The appropriate response to such a claim would seem to be God's challenge to Job:

> "Where were you when I laid the foundation of the earth?
>   Tell me, if you have understanding.
> Who determined its measurements—surely you know! . . .
> On what were its bases sunk,
>   or who laid its cornerstone,
> when the morning stars sang together
>   and all the sons of God shouted for joy?

> "Or who shut in the sea with doors
>   when it burst out from the womb,
> when I made clouds its garment
>   and thick darkness its swaddling band. . . .

> "Have you commanded the morning since your days began,
>   and caused the dawn to know its place? . . .

> "Do you give the horse his might?
>   Do you clothe his neck with a mane? . . .

> "Is it by your understanding that the hawk soars
> and spreads his wings toward the south?
> Is it at your command that the eagle mounts up
>   and makes his nest on high?" . . .

And the LORD said to Job:

> "Shall a faultfinder contend with the Almighty?
>   He who argues with God, let him answer it." (Job 38:4–9,
>   12; 39:19, 26–27; 40:1–2)

Theistic evolution supporters often claim that "the Bible doesn't teach science." Karl Giberson and Francis Collins write, "The Bible is not even trying to teach science. Nowhere in the entire Bible do we read anything that even hints that the writer is trying to teach science."[62] And John Walton writes, "There is not a single incidence of new information being offered by God to the Israelites about the regular

---

62. Giberson and Collins, *Language of Science and Faith*, 108.

operation of the world (what we would call natural science)."[63] These statements are offered as justification for the idea that the Bible cannot speak authoritatively to questions about the origin of life on Earth.

But the question is not whether the Bible "teaches science" (whatever that might mean). The question is *whether the Bible is truthful in all that it affirms*, on whatever topic it wishes to speak about.[64]

If the Bible tells us that God said, "Let the earth bring forth living creatures according to their kinds" (Gen. 1:24), is that statement historically true, or not? Did God speak these words and thereby cause living creatures to appear on the earth, or not? If the Bible tells us that "the rib that the LORD God had taken from the man he made into a woman and brought her to the man" (Gen. 2:22), is that a truthful report of a historical event, or not? And so it goes with every detail that Genesis 1–3 tells us about the earliest history of the earth and the human race. The most important issue at stake here is the truthfulness of the Bible as the Word of God.

In some theistic evolution literature, the authors double down on their denial of the historical truthfulness of the creation accounts and argue that the Bible affirms other scientifically false ideas as well—thus adding more examples to shore up their denial of the truthfulness of Scripture. Denis Lamoureux tells us that the Bible affirms a three-tiered universe with a solid sky overhead that holds back large reservoirs of water,[65] and that Jesus affirmed a scientific falsehood when he said

---

63. Walton, *Lost World of Adam and Eve*, 21; see also 188. To ask whether the Bible reveals new information about the operation of the natural world is to ask the wrong question. The question is *whether the Bible is truthful in all that it affirms about the natural world*. The astounding fact is that there is no statement in the Bible about the natural world that is scientifically false (when interpreted according to sound principles of grammatical-historical exegesis). Even though the Bible was written by multiple authors in diverse ancient cultures over a period of 1,500 years (approximately 1400 BC–AD 90), nothing that it affirms as true has ever been shown to be false by modern standards of archaeology, history, and scientific inquiry—as is evident from multiple evangelical books that thoughtfully defend the inerrancy of the Bible. In its astounding freedom from falsehood, the Bible stands in stark contrast to all other ancient literature.

64. Some of our friends who support theistic evolution object that they do not want to affirm a "God-of-the-gaps" argument, a kind of argument that calls upon belief in God's activity as an explanation for events that scientists currently cannot explain. Francis Collins says, "Faith that places God in the gaps of current understanding about the natural world may be headed for crisis if advances in science subsequently fill those gaps" (Collins, *Language of God*, 93; see also 95, 193–195). But my argument throughout this chapter has not claimed that we need God as an explanation for events that science cannot currently explain. My argument instead has been that we should believe the Bible on whatever topic it speaks about, including the origin of living things, the origin of human beings, and the earliest history of the earth and human beings on the earth.

65. Lamoureux, "No Historical Adam," 49, 51, 61.

that the mustard seed was "the smallest of all seeds on earth" (Mark 4:31).[66] John Walton says that the ancient writers "believed that the heart was the center of intellect and emotion, and the text affirms that belief."[67] Karl Giberson and Francis Collins say that the opening chapters of Genesis have "*two* stories of creation, not one," and "only an unreasonable interpretation that mutilates the text can resolve the differences."[68] Apparently the purpose for bringing up these additional affirmations of falsehood in other statements of Scripture is to demonstrate that the Bible cannot speak accurately to scientific issues, because it makes so many mistakes. But these challenges have been known for centuries, and the standard evangelical commentaries contain reasonable, textually sensitive explanations that do not require us to conclude that the Bible anywhere affirms false statements about the natural world.[69]

John Walton claims that belief in theistic evolution does not entail a denial of biblical inerrancy, because no theological point is lost. He says, "Historical Adam is only tied to inerrancy to the extent that it can be demonstrated not just that the biblical authors considered him historical but that the biblical teaching incorporated that understanding into its authoritative message. . . . I do affirm the historicity of Adam. But I do not consider interpreters who are trying to be faithful to Scripture to be denying inerrancy if they arrive at a different conclusion."[70]

But Walton clearly misunderstands the doctrine of inerrancy. The inerrancy of Scripture does not apply merely to those details that the biblical writers "incorporated" into some "authoritative message" that is somehow less than what the Bible actually affirms as truthful. Rather, inerrancy applies to *everything* that the biblical text affirms to be true,

---

66. Ibid., 60.

67. Walton, *Lost World of Adam and Eve*, 201. He fails to consider the obvious possibility that the biblical authors were using "heart" in a metaphorical way to refer to the center of our deepest emotions and convictions, rather than referring to a literal physical heart.

68. Giberson and Collins, *Language of Science and Faith*, 101; see also 208.

69. I will not discuss these passages in detail at this point, but interested readers could consult a standard reference work such as the *ESV Study Bible* (Wheaton, IL: Crossway, 2008), or the *NIV Zondervan Study Bible*, ed. D. A. Carson (Grand Rapids, MI: Zondervan, 2015), as well as any of a number of widely used commentaries.

70. Walton, *Lost World of Adam and Eve*, 201–202. Walton elsewhere says that someone who denied that Adam and Eve were the first human beings and the ancestors of all humanity, and also denied that there was material discontinuity between Adam and other species, still "could not be accused of rejecting the Bible or the faith" (John H. Walton, "A Historical Adam: Archetypal Creation View," in *Four Views on the Historical Adam*, Barrett and Caneday, 113.

for its "authoritative message," understood rightly, includes everything that it affirms: "*All Scripture* [not just some parts of it] is breathed out by God and profitable for teaching, for reproof, for correction, and for training in righteousness" (2 Tim. 3:16).

In a brief definition that is consistent with what many evangelicals have affirmed for generations, "The inerrancy of Scripture means that Scripture in the original manuscripts does not affirm anything that is contrary to fact."[71] The widely used Chicago Statement on Biblical Inerrancy (1978) gives a fuller explanation:

> We affirm that inspiration, though not conferring omniscience, guaranteed true and trustworthy utterance *on all matters of which the Bible authors were moved to speak and write.* We deny that the finitude or fallenness of these writers, by necessity or otherwise, introduced distortion or falsehood into God's Word. (Article IX).

> We affirm that Scripture . . . is true and reliable *in all matters it addresses.* (Article XI).

> We affirm that *Scripture in its entirety is inerrant,* being free from all falsehood, fraud, or deceit. We deny that biblical infallibility and inerrancy are limited to spiritual, religious, or redemptive themes, exclusive of assertions in the fields of history and science. We further deny that scientific hypotheses about earth history may properly be used to overturn the teaching of Scripture on creation and the flood. (Article XII).[72]

These explicit explanations of inerrancy clearly differ from the much weaker understanding of biblical inerrancy advocated by John Walton.

While I consider the denial of the complete truthfulness of the Bible to be the most significant harmful consequence of theistic evolution,

---

71. Wayne Grudem, *Systematic Theology* (Leicester, UK, and Grand Rapids, MI: Zondervan, 1994), 91. Although these are my words, such an understanding of inerrancy did not originate with me but is consistent with what evangelical Christians have believed for centuries about the truthfulness of the Bible.

72. "The Chicago Statement of Biblical Inerrancy," available at *Alliance of Confessing Evangelicals*, http://www.alliancenet.org/the-chicago-statement-on-biblical-inerrancy. The Evangelical Theological Society bylaws refer members to the Chicago Statement on Biblical Inerrancy to understand "the intent and meaning of the reference to biblical inerrancy in the ETS Doctrinal Basis" ("Bylaws," *The Evangelical Theological Society*, see item 12, available at http://www.etsjets.org/about/bylaws).

I must also mention several other harmful doctrinal consequences in the following points.

2. Direct Creation by God's Powerful Words

According to theistic evolution, there was no special action of God or intervention by God in the created order after the initial creation of matter. But the biblical picture is far different. It shows God speaking living things into existence by his powerful creative words, and the picture it gives is that those powerful words of God bring immediate response:

> And God said, "Let the earth sprout vegetation, plants yielding seed, and fruit trees bearing fruit in which is their seed, each according to its kind, on the earth." *And it was so.* (Gen. 1:11)

> And God said, "Let the earth bring forth living creatures according to their kinds—livestock and creeping things and beasts of the earth according to their kinds." *And it was so.* (Gen. 1:24)

Several other passages of Scripture also emphasize that God's powerful words brought into existence various aspects of creation:

> By the word of the LORD the heavens were made,
>   and by the breath of his mouth all their host. . . .

> For he spoke, and it came to be;
>   he commanded, and it stood firm (Psalm 33:6, 9; see also
>   Psalm 148:5–6; Rom. 4:17; Heb. 11:3; 2 Pet. 3:5).

By contrast, the picture given by theistic evolution denies that there were any such powerful words of God, or any other direct intervention of God into the creation, that caused plants and animals to exist. Instead of appearing immediately in obedience to God's powerful creative words, these things evolved over billions of years, and new forms of life are the result of random mutations, not God's commands. The driving force that brings about mutations in living things is randomness, not God's command.[73] The Bible's emphasis on the wonder of God's direct activity in creation, and the power of God's creative words, is lost.

---

73. Theistic evolution supporters insist that the process is "not a random process." Giberson and Collins say, "We emphasize that there is nothing random about an organism that is better

3. Overwhelming Evidence in Nature for God's Existence

The Bible claims that nature gives abundant evidence of God's existence.[74] Paul writes,

> For what can be known about God is plain to them, because God has shown it to them. For *his invisible attributes*, namely, his eternal power and divine nature, *have been clearly perceived*, ever since the creation of the world, *in the things that have been made*. So they are without excuse. (Rom. 1:19–20)

Paul's phrase "the things that have been made" certainly includes plants, animals, and human beings, all of which give clear *evidence* of God's power and other attributes (such as wisdom, knowledge, creativity, love, goodness, and faithfulness). This evidence is so strong that God's attributes are "clearly perceived" in the natural world. Therefore people who rebel against God are *"without excuse." The evidence from creation for God's existence is so overwhelming that God holds people morally accountable for denying it.*

This means that when people ponder the astounding complexity of the human eye, or a bird's wing, or a single living cell, the evidence for God's existence is so strong that people have no good excuse for unbelief. Only an infinitely wise and powerful God could create things as wonderful as these. An old hymn put it this way:

> This is my Father's world, the birds their carols raise,
> The morning light, the lily white, declare their Maker's praise.
> This is my Father's world: He shines in all that's fair;
> In the rustling grass I hear Him pass;
> He speaks to me everywhere.[75]

---

adapted to its environment having greater reproductive success. This is an orderly and predictable trajectory in the direction of better adaptation" (*Language of Science and Faith*, 38).

But that is not the point I'm making here. No one is claiming that it is a "random" process by which those creatures that survive are those that are best able to survive. The claim of randomness has to do not with which animals *survive* but with the driving force behind the beneficial *mutations* that (according to evolution) cause the development of a new type of animal. The fact remains that, according to evolutionary theory, these mutations are random. Giberson and Collins themselves say later in this same book, "*The process of evolution is driven in large part by random mutations*, so it certainly seems possible that earth could have been home to an entirely different assortment of creatures" (198, emphasis added).

74. I wish to thank Casey Luskin of the Discovery Institute for his suggestions that led to a significant strengthening of this section.

75. "This Is My Father's World," by Maltbie D. Babcock, 1901.

But theistic evolution *takes away that evidence for God completely.* While the Bible says that "the things that have been made" give clear evidence of God's "eternal power and divine nature" (Rom. 1:20), theistic evolution says that the living creatures give no such evidence, for the existence of all living things can be explained solely from the properties of matter itself.[76]

The contrast is clear. While the Bible says that *everything* in nature bears witness to God, theistic evolution says that *no living creature* in nature bears witness to God. When an unbeliever is confronted with the wondrous complexity of living things, theistic evolution allows him just to think that random mutations produce surprising results, and therefore he has no need for any thought of God. Evolutionary science has given him (so he thinks) a complete explanation for why life exists. Theistic evolution completely nullifies the evidence for God's existence in living things, and therefore significantly hinders evangelism.[77]

Now, sometimes scientists who support theistic evolution suggest that *maybe* God was working behind the scenes in an invisible way. Giberson and Collins say,

> Another way to think about God's relationship to evolution is to view God guiding the evolutionary process, working *within* the randomness. . . . Mutations appear to be genuinely random occurrences that can be initiated by quantum mechanical events. . . . There is no reason why God could not work within such processes, shaping evolutionary history. What appear to be genuinely random events might actually be the subtle influence of God working within the system of natural law.[78]

But according to this viewpoint, there is still no visible or detect-

---

76. Some supporters of theistic evolution will say that the fine-tuning of the universe to make it suitable to support human life is evidence of God's existence, and we agree, but that kind of evidence from modern physics and chemistry, evidence which was unknown to ancient readers, would not have been Paul's intention in speaking of "the things that have been made" in Romans 1:20. He surely would have thought of all living creatures as included in "the things that have been made," an evident allusion to Genesis 1:31, "And God saw everything that he had made [LXX *poieō*, a verb cognate to *poiēma* in Rom. 1:20], and behold, it was very good."

77. Notice Paul's appeal to people's ordinary experience of "rains from heaven and fruitful seasons" in the natural world as a testimony to "a living God, who made the heaven and the earth and the sea and all that is in them" (Acts 14:15–17). Psalm 104:24 proclaims that the "creatures" who fill the earth are evidence for God's wisdom: "In wisdom you have made them all."

78. Giberson and Collins, *Language of Science and Faith*, 199–200, emphasis original.

able evidence of God's working in the natural world. It is a proposal that says, essentially, "*Maybe* God was working secretly in a way that we cannot detect." In other words, even though science has shown us that *nothing* in nature bears witness to God's power and wisdom, *maybe* God was working in it anyway, but it must have been only in a way that cannot be detected.

This is the complete opposite of the perspective of Scripture, in which everything in nature gives undeniable, overwhelming testimony to God's existence. "For his invisible attributes, namely, his eternal power and divine nature, have been *clearly perceived*, ever since the creation of the world, *in the things that have been made*. So they are *without excuse*" (Rom. 1:20). But according to theistic evolution, unbelievers have a gigantic excuse, for they could say that all living things can be explained as a result of the properties of matter without any special creative action by God.

4. Evidence in Nature for Moral Accountability to God

In a society where a traditional belief in God as the Creator of all living things is prominent, the wonder of creation leads people to think of their moral accountability to God. When people (even many unbelievers) observe the wonder of tiny seeds growing into large trees or a mother robin caring for her chicks, they often have an instinctive sense of moral accountability to their Creator: "Only an infinitely powerful and wise God could have made such amazing creatures, and that means that I will one day be accountable for my actions to this very God."

The apostle Paul himself reasoned in a similar manner, beginning with God's actions in creation and then going on to speak about moral accountability to this same God, when he spoke to pagan Greek philosophers in Athens: "*The God who made the world and everything in it*, . . . made from one man every nation of mankind. . . . now he commands all people everywhere to *repent*, because he has fixed a day on which *he will judge the world* in righteousness by a man whom he has appointed" (Acts 17:24, 26, 30, 31). This is similar to Paul's words in Romans 1:20, mentioned in the previous section, where Paul says that people are "without excuse"—and therefore are accountable to God—because of the evidence in nature for God's existence.

But theistic evolution severs the cord of connection between observing the creatures and fearing accountability to the Creator, because theistic evolution allows an unbeliever to think, not, "There must be an all-powerful God who made such amazing creatures," but rather, "*Matter* is so wonderful that it produced these amazing living creatures *all by itself.* Wow!" The next thought will often be, "I don't see any evidence for a Creator who will hold me accountable for my actions. Wow!" And in this way, within the theistic evolution system, the complexity of living things no longer leaves unbelievers "without excuse" (Rom. 1:20).

5. The Wisdom of God

Theistic evolution undermines the glory given to God for his unfathomable wisdom in the creation of all living things, because in theistic evolution no divine intelligence or wisdom beyond the properties present in inanimate matter is required for matter to evolve into all forms of life.

In addition, in theistic evolution God does not *wisely* create various kinds of animals on his first attempt, but clumsily, by his providence, brings about millions of failed mutations in each creature before he finds a beneficial change.

According to a traditional Christian view of creation, when we contemplate the beauty and complexity of a sunflower or hummingbird or rainbow trout, we are struck with a sense of awe at the wisdom and skill of the Creator. "God is an amazingly wise Creator!" But when we look at the same creatures through the eyes of theistic evolution, we first have to think, "*Matter* is really an amazing thing!" Then, perhaps later, a Christian believer might think, "God built remarkable properties into the matter that makes up the universe." But the connection between the original creation of matter and the existence of living creatures is so distant that it will lead to scant praise for God's wisdom.

That is so different from the perspective of the Bible, which repeatedly praises God for his great wisdom that is evident in the amazing creatures he has made:

Is it by your understanding that the hawk soars
>   and spreads his wings toward the south? (Job 39:26)

Behold, Behemoth,
>   which I made as I made you;
>   he eats grass like an ox. (Job 40:15)

Denis Alexander does not think that theistic evolution robs glory
from God by attributing such amazing potentialities to the materials
of creation. He says, regarding the objection that life could not emerge
out of chemicals by "blind, materialistic, naturalistic forces,"

> But wait a minute: these are God's chemicals, God's materials, that
> are being talked about here. . . . Is this God's world or isn't it? Imag-
> ine going into an artist's studio, seeing the tubes of paint arranged
> in neat rows on one side and then telling the artist, 'You've chosen
> the wrong type of paints, they're really hopeless!' I think we would
> all agree that would be insulting. But to confidently proclaim that
> the precious materials God has so carefully brought into being in
> the dying moments of exploding stars do not have the potentiality
> to bring about life seems to me equally insulting.[79]

John Lennox quotes this paragraph from Alexander and then effectively replies as follows:

> This argument is fatally flawed, since the analogy does not corre-
> spond to the application. No one is suggesting that the Creator's ma-
> terials are "the wrong type" or "hopeless." What is being suggested
> is that the Creator's good materials cannot bring life into existence
> without the additional direct intelligent input of the Creator. This is
> no more an insult to the Creator that it would be an insult to the art-
> ist to suggest that his paints are incapable of producing a masterpiece
> without his direct input. It is rather the (ludicrous) suggestion that
> the paints could do it on their own without him that would be an
> insult to the painter![80]

Lennox is correct in his criticism. If inanimate matter, by itself,

---

79. Alexander, *Creation or Evolution*, 436.
80. Lennox, *Seven Days*, 176.

without any additional input from God, is responsible for all living things, then we ought to praise this remarkable matter that could accomplish such wonders without God's direction. Theistic evolution robs God of the glory he deserves for the infinite wisdom he exhibited in the creation of all living things. If God's providential control of nature is limited to maintaining the properties of matter, then created things do not give evidence of anything greater than matter. The properties of matter only give evidence of the properties of matter.

How different from theistic evolution is the perspective of Scripture, which sees evidence of God's wisdom in every created thing. Psalm 104 views all the creatures of the earth and the sea as evidence of God's wisdom in creation:

> O Lord, how manifold are your works!
> *In wisdom have you made them all;*
>   the earth is full of your creatures.
> Here is the sea, great and wide,
>   which teems with creatures innumerable,
>   living things both small and great. (Ps. 104:24–25)

6. The Goodness of God

Theistic evolution also undermines belief in the goodness of God, because according to this view God is responsible for (somehow) creating a world filled with deadly diseases, dangerous animals, and natural disasters that have brought suffering and destruction to human beings for the entire duration of the human race on the earth. (By contrast, on a traditional view of Genesis 1–3, the blame for evil in the world belongs to Adam and Eve, and not to God.)

7. The Moral Justice of God

According to theistic evolution, the earliest human beings that were somehow "created" by God's use of evolution were sinful human beings, committing morally evil deeds from their earliest existence on Earth. But if that is the case, it is hard to escape the conclusion that God himself is responsible for human sin, for he never created sinless human beings who were able to obey him and not to sin.

8. Human Equality

According to theistic evolution, some human beings have evolved primarily from one group of early humans, while others have evolved primarily from another group of early humans. But that means there is no foundational physical unity to the human race, and it opens the possibility that some human beings (or even some racial groups) are superior to others—perhaps they are the recipients of more beneficial random mutations—and other human beings are therefore inferior.

The biblical picture of the unity of all human beings is a far different picture, because it teaches that we have all descended from the same man, Adam. The conviction that God "made *from one man* every nation of mankind to live on all the face of the earth" (Acts 17:26) leads to an affirmation of human equality.

9. The Atonement

Paul links the historicity of the sin of one man, Adam, and the unity of the human race as represented by Adam, to the effectiveness of the atonement worked by Christ for those whom he represented. Paul writes,

> Sin came into the world through one man, and death through sin, and so death spread to all men because all sinned. . . . For as by the one man's disobedience the many were made sinners, so by the one man's obedience the many will be made righteous. (Rom. 5:12, 19)

However, as Guy Waters explains more fully in chapter 29,[81] if we deny that sin came into the world through Adam, and if we deny that all human beings have descended from Adam, then Paul's argument about the unity of the human race as represented by Adam does not work. And then the parallel with the unity of the redeemed who are represented by Christ does not work. In this way, theistic evolution significantly undermines the doctrine of the atonement.

In this regard, it is not surprising that Scot McKnight, in denying a historical Adam, also denies the historic Christian doctrine of "original sin" (or "inherited sin"); that is, the idea that Adam in the garden of Eden represented the entire human race, with the result that, (1) when Adam

---

81. See pages 903–926.

sinned, God counted the entire human race as guilty (Rom. 5:12–19), and also that (2) all human beings are born with a sinful nature, a disposition to sin against God (Ps. 51:5; 58:3; Eph. 2:3). But McKnight does not think we have all descended from Adam and Eve.[82] Therefore he denies the doctrine of original sin and says instead that "each human being stands condemned before God as a sinner because each human being sins as did Adam (and Eve)."[83] He wants to keep Christ as our representative in his obedience,[84] but he denies a similar representation by Adam in Adam's disobedience ("by one man's disobedience many were made sinners"; Rom. 5:19), and so undercuts Paul's argument about the atonement.

10. The Resurrection

Paul also links the unity of the human race in Adam, and the reality of death coming to the entire human race through the sin of Adam, to the efficacy of the resurrection of Christ to bring new life to all who are represented by him:

> For as by a man came death, by a man has come also the resurrection of the dead. For as in Adam all die, so also in Christ shall all be made alive. (1 Cor. 15:21–22)

However, if we deny that death came into the world through Adam, and if we deny the unity of the human race as descending from Adam, then once again the parallel between Adam and Christ does not work. In this way, theistic evolution undermines the effectiveness of the resurrection to give new life to all who are saved by Christ. Guy Waters also explains this parallel more fully in chapter 29.[85]

11. The Value of Improving on Nature

According to a traditional Christian understanding of creation, the natural world is not the best it could be, because it is still under the curse that God placed on it as a result of the sin of Adam in Genesis 3:17–19. But God's plan in the history of redemption is that nature

---

82. Scot McKnight, in Venema and McKnight, *Adam and the Genome*, 93, 100, 145–146.
83. Ibid., 187.
84. Ibid., 186.
85. See pages 903–926.

will one day "be set free from its bondage to corruption and obtain the freedom of the glory of the children of God" (Rom. 8:21).

Therefore, Christians have historically thought it was pleasing to God to work to overcome the "thorns and thistles" and other hostile forces in creation, because this is his ultimate goal for the end of history, and the ongoing advance of the kingdom of God properly manifests that final redemptive result *in partial form* even in this current age. As a result, Christians have worked "as for the Lord" (Col. 3:23) to develop improved, disease-resistant crops, hybrid plants that produce more food in the same acreage, healthier chickens and cattle and pigs, and more pleasant products such as seedless oranges and watermelons.

But according to theistic evolution, there never was a "better" form of the natural world. In fact, nature as it exists today is apparently the best natural world that God could have brought about through the millions of years of theistic evolution. In this view, the natural world is not currently under a curse from God as a result of human sin. Yet this conviction tends to undermine the value of seeking to improve on nature, and tends to discourage people from thinking that any part of the natural world might itself be evil, that is, something we should seek to change. Perhaps nature is already the best it can be?

F. Conclusion

Theistic evolution, as defined by its most respected defenders today, implies a denial of twelve specific events that are recorded in Genesis 1–3. The placement of these chapters at the beginning of Genesis, the absence of literary markers in these passages signaling to readers that they should be understood in a figurative way, and the matter-of-fact way in which subsequent chapters in Genesis assume that Genesis 1–3 is reliable historical narrative, provide convincing evidence that Genesis 1–3 is intended to be taken as a historical record of events that actually happened. In addition, all of these twelve events are affirmed or implied in various places in four other books in the Old Testament and ten books in the New Testament.

Because theistic evolution denies the historicity of these twelve events, it also denies or undermines eleven significant Christian doctrines. In sum, belief in theistic evolution is incompatible with the truthfulness of the Bible and with several crucial doctrines of the Christian faith.

28

Theistic Evolution Is Incompatible with the Teachings of the Old Testament

JOHN D. CURRID

"There is nothing new under the sun."

Ecclesiastes 1:9

SUMMARY

This chapter explores ways in which theistic evolution is incompatible with the teachings of the Old Testament. It closely examines Genesis 1–3 and responds to the five most common alternative explanations proposed by advocates of theistic evolution: (1) the "functional model" of Genesis 1–3; (2) the view that Genesis 1–3 is "myth"; (3) the view that Genesis 1–3 should be understood as "figurative and theological literature"; (4) the "sequential scheme" interpretation, which argues that the events of Genesis 2 occurred long after Genesis 1; and (5) the "etiology as methodology" interpretation, which claims that Genesis 1–3 was written not as factual history but as an explanation for certain features that we see in the world (though the explanation need not record actual historical events). Multiple features in the text of Genesis 1–3 show these alternative explanations to be unpersuasive.

. . . . .

In 1884, Dr. James Woodrow, who held the Perkins Professorship of Natural Science in Its Relation to Revealed Religion at Columbia Seminary in Columbia, South Carolina, was asked by the seminary trustees to deliver a lecture on the issue of evolution and the Bible.[1] He had been teaching at Columbia Seminary since 1861, and his views regarding the issues of creation had evolved over his twenty-plus years at the school. He had simply become more convinced of what he believed to be the scientific evidence in favor of evolutionary theory. Woodrow had made the following statement in 1883:

> The Bible teaches nothing as to God's method of creation, and therefore it is not teaching anything contradicting God's word to say that he may have formed the higher beings from the lower by successive differentiations; and as several series of facts, more or less independent of each other, seem to point this out as the method which he chose.[2]

In his lecture, Woodrow admitted that he had changed his position from one in which evolution was not true to one in which it likely was true. He concluded the following: "I am inclined to believe that it pleased God, the Almighty Creator, to create present and intermediate past organic forms not immediately but mediately."[3]

In regard to humanity, Woodrow alleged that only the soul of man was of immediate creation. His body, on the other hand, came from the "dust" (Gen. 2:7). He argued that this creative act is open to varying interpretations, and perhaps "dust" refers merely to preexisting material. Therefore, mankind may have descended from some type of animal ancestor.

This lecture by Woodrow created a firestorm, and it produced a division in the Southern Presbyterian Church. The board of Columbia Seminary, who had called for Woodrow's lecture, met to consider his position on origins. Frank Smith comments that the board concluded

---

1. A summary of the lecture and the ensuing controversy is found in D. B. Calhoun, *The Glory of the Lord Risen upon It: First Presbyterian Church, Columbia, South Carolina 1795–1995* (Columbia, SC: First Presbyterian Church, 1994), 147–149.

2. Quoted in E. T. Thompson, *Presbyterians in the South*, vol. 2 (Richmond: John Knox Press, 1963, 1973), 461.

3. James Woodrow, *Evolution: An Address Delivered May 7th, 1884 before the Alumni Association of the Columbia Theological Seminary* (Columbia, SC: Presbyterian Publishing House, 1884), 28.

that, while not agreeing with his belief regarding the probable way in which Adam's body was created, there was nothing with his carefully-delineated views on evolution that was incompatible with the faith.[4]

The courts of the Presbyterian Church were not quite as forgiving. After a complicated and detailed debate and controversy at the synod levels, the issue came to the General Assembly of 1886. The Assembly debated the question for five days. At the end it overwhelmingly voted, 137 to 13, that "Adam and Eve were created, body and soul, by immediate acts of God's power" and that Adam's body was made "without any human parentage of any kind."[5]

The General Assembly took further action by recommending to the four synods in charge of Columbia Seminary that Dr. Woodrow be dismissed from his teaching position (the vote was 65 to 25).[6] Eventually he was dismissed from the seminary. However, he was allowed to remain an ordained Presbyterian minister in good standing because when he came under trial in 1886 by the Augusta (Georgia) Presbytery, he was acquitted of heresy by a vast majority of presbyters.

The evangelical church today is facing increasing controversies over the relationship of science and the Bible and, in particular, over the view of theistic evolution.[7] But as we can see from what happened with Dr. Woodrow more than 130 years ago, this debate at its core is nothing new. The relationship between the Bible and science, especially in regard to origins, has been at the forefront of discussion since the mid-nineteenth century. Perhaps the arguments today are more nuanced, but the basic issues are the same. The difference today, as I see it, is that there is an increasing acceptance of theistic evolution (or "evolutionary creation," as it is often called) in evangelicalism, and that acceptance is growing by the day.

Some evangelical scholars have joined the ranks that advocate theistic

---

4. F. J. Smith, "Presbyterians and Evolution in the 19th Century: The Case of James Woodrow," *Contra Mundum* 6 (1993): 7.

5. Calhoun, *Glory of the Lord Risen upon It*, 149.

6. Smith, "Presbyterians and Evolution," 17.

7. See, e.g., Denis Alexander, *Creation or Evolution: Do We Have to Choose?* 2nd ed., rev. and updated (Oxford: Monarch, 2014 ed.); Francis S. Collins, *The Language of God: A Scientist Presents Evidence for Belief* (New York: Free Press, 2006); and, H. J. Van Till, D. A. Young, and C. Menninga, *Science Held Hostage* (Downers Grove, IL: InterVarsity Press, 1988).

evolution. Bruce Waltke, currently distinguished professor emeritus of Old Testament at Knox Theological Seminary, made a video for Bio-Logos in which he argued that evolution is compatible with evangelical, orthodox Christianity. In the video, titled, "Why Must the Church Come to Accept Evolution?," Waltke gives warning that if the church does not accept evolution then it risks becoming "a cult," "an odd group," "not credible," and "marginalized."[8] Peter Enns and John Walton, both highly respected Old Testament scholars, have made significant contributions in favor of evolutionary creation on the BioLogos website and in other writings. These men are accomplished Old Testament exegetes, and their work must be taken seriously and discussed. Tremper Longman, Robert H. Gundry Professor of Biblical Studies at Westmont College, fits squarely into this camp.[9] In a 2014 blog post, Longman concluded the following: "But it seems to me that there is a good case, especially on genetic evidence, that God used evolution. So I find myself affirming an evolutionary creationist perspective."[10] Longman also serves on the Advisory Council of BioLogos.

Others who are not Old Testament scholars but have great influence in evangelicalism have come out in favor of evolutionary creation. For example, Presbyterian Church in America pastor Tim Keller authored an article for BioLogos titled "Creation, Evolution, and Christian Lay People," in which, at the very least, he shows sympathy to the theistic evolution viewpoint.[11] New Testament scholar N. T. Wright is clear in his support of evolutionary creation.[12] My point here is not simply to name names, but rather to show that the evolutionary creation

---

8. The video was originally posted on March 24, 2010, on the BioLogos website biologos.org, but it created a significant controversy. Waltke subsequently asked BioLogos to remove the video, which they did. But then on April 6, 2010, Reformed Theological Seminary accepted Waltke's resignation, an action that was widely understood as directly related to Waltke's endorsement of theistic evolution. See "OT Scholar Bruce Waltke Resigns following Evolution Comments," *Christianity Today*, April 9, 2010, http://www.christianitytoday.com/gleanings/2010/april/ot-scholar-bruce-waltke-resigns-following-evolution.html.

9. See, e.g., his most recent commentary: Tremper Longman, *Genesis* (Grand Rapids, MI: Zondervan, 2015).

10. See Jonathan Watson, "Temper Longman Responds to Justin Taylor on the Historicity of Adam," *Academic*, March 24, 2014, accessed August 25, 2016, https://academic.logos.com/2014/03/25/tremper-longman-responds-to-justin-taylor-on-the-historicity-of-adam/.

11. See Tim Keller, "Creation, Evolution, and Christian Laypeople," *BioLogos*, 2006, https://biologos.org/uploads/projects/Keller_white_paper.pdf.

12. See his "Excursus on Paul's Use of Adam," in John H. Walton, *The Lost World of Adam and Eve: Genesis 2-3 and the Human Origins Debate* (Downers Grove, IL: InterVarsity Press, 2015), 170–180.

movement is stronger than it has ever been and is making inroads into evangelical thought today.[13]

In this chapter, I would like to consider some of the more recent developments in the debate over the early chapters of Genesis, and especially human origins, in Old Testament studies. I will examine five models that advocates of theistic evolution have proposed to explain how Genesis 1–3 can be interpreted as consistent with theistic evolution:

    I. The Functional Model
    II. Genesis 1–3 as Myth
    III. Genesis 1–3 as Figurative and Theological Literature
    IV. The Sequential Scheme
    V. Etiology as Methodology

I. The Functional Model: Genesis 1–3 Is about Functions, Not Origins

Perhaps the most prominent advocate of theistic evolution among evangelical Old Testament scholars is John Walton, professor of Old Testament at Wheaton College. Walton has written extensively on the nature of the Hebrew creation account in Genesis 1–3.[14] In general, he proposes that these chapters are about the assigning of *roles and functions* to the various elements of the universe and not about the historical origins of the universe.[15]

Walton does some excellent work in highlighting the presence of

---

13. Some would argue that this position has had long-standing acceptance in evangelicalism, and rarely is the name of the Princeton theologian B. B. Warfield not raised in support of that contention. See, e.g., B. B. Warfield, *Evolution, Science, and Scripture: Selected Writings*, ed. D. N. Livingstone and M. A. Noll (Grand Rapids, MI: Baker, 2000). However, see the response of Fred Zaspel elsewhere in this volume (pages 953–972); see also Fred G. Zaspel, "B. B. Warfield on Creation and Evolution," *Themelios* 35, no. 2 (2010): 198–211. Zaspel argues that, while Warfield entertained the *possibility* that God used an evolutionary process as part of his creative work, he never affirmed evolutionary theories as true, and he explicitly denied that someone could hold to the teachings of the Bible and affirm several of the key concepts of modern theistic evolution proponents, such as there being sinful humans prior to Adam and Eve, or human death before Adam and Eve, or that Adam and Eve were not created sinless.

14. Among his many works, I would point the reader to the following ones that get at the heart of his position on Genesis 1–3: John H. Walton, *Genesis*, NIV Application Commentary (Grand Rapids, MI: Zondervan, 2011); Walton, *Genesis 1 as Ancient Cosmology* (Winona Lake, IN: Eisenbrauns, 2011); Walton, *Lost World of Adam and Eve*; and Walton, *The Lost World of Genesis One: Ancient Cosmology and the Origins Debate* (Downers Grove, IL: InterVarsity Press, 2009).

15. Walton's position is making its way into recent literature in regard to the interpretation of Genesis 1–3. See, for example, Scot McKnight's acceptance of it—hook, line, and sinker—in Dennis R. Venema and Scot McKnight, *Adam and the Genome* (Grand Rapids, MI: Baker, 2017), 124–125. My critique in this section thus applies not only to Walton but to McKnight as well.

concern for functions in Genesis 1–3, and I am in agreement with him that such a concern is present in the text. However, where I take exception to his writings is the claim that Genesis 1–3 has nothing to do with *material origins*, and that it is merely about establishing *functions* alone. I want to focus on one critical, foundational aspect of his model.[16]

One linchpin of Walton's design is the proposition that Genesis 1–3 is an ancient Near Eastern text, and, as such, is similar to other creation accounts of antiquity. He believes that ancient Near Eastern creation documents are primarily interested in function and not material origins. Therefore, Genesis 1, like those texts, is merely about the function and role of the various elements of the cosmos. This understanding extends into Genesis 2, which, he claims, *does not teach the material creation of humankind* but deals with the nature of humanity's function and purpose in the world.

In relation to our discussion in this book, Walton's argument has an important consequence: if the opening chapters of Genesis have nothing to do with material beginnings of the universe, including the origin of humanity, then the historical clash between science and the Bible regarding the nature of physical origins is a moot point. In other words, the early chapters of Genesis are really not interested in material origins and, therefore, there is no conflict between them and science.

It is my intention to test Walton's view of the design and purpose of ancient Near Eastern creation documents, and to see if his position stands on firm ground or not. The question simply put is, do the creation accounts of the ancient Near East have a concern not only for functions but also for the *material origins* of the cosmos and, in particular, of mankind? Or, to put it another way, are the ancient Near Eastern creation documents *solely* interested in functions and roles of the various elements of the cosmos?

A. Egyptian Creation Texts

The first thing one must realize when dealing with ancient Egyptian creation accounts is that there are many of them, and some of them are antithetical to one another.[17] The Egyptologist John Wilson gives expres-

---

16. For an extensive and perceptive review of Walton's most recent work, see R. E. Averbeck, "The Lost World of Adam and Eve: A Review Essay," *Themelios* 40, no. 2 (2015): 226–239.

17. I give a more extensive discussion of these Egyptian texts in my book *Ancient Egypt and the Old Testament* (Grand Rapids, MI: Baker, 1997). For other studies on Egyptian creation accounts,

sion to this reality when he says, "It is significant that a plural should be necessary, that we cannot settle down to a single codified account of beginnings. The Egyptians accepted various myths and discarded none of them."[18] Henri Frankfort calls this the mythopoeic mind, which admits "the validity of several avenues of approach at one and the same time."[19] In addition, one must be aware that many of the references in Egyptian literature to the origin of the universe appear sporadically in various contexts, such as in the Coffin Texts, the Pyramid Texts, and elsewhere. So, for example, there is no single documented account of the creation of mankind, but the subject of human origins is found in various places in a wide array of texts. Siegfried Morenz properly concludes that there is "an abundance of more or less scanty references in the most varied texts which give us some very disjointed information about Egyptian notions concerning God the creator and the evolution of the world (and life on it)."[20] It is important to keep these thoughts in mind as we consider the views of the ancient Egyptians regarding creation.

After an extensive investigation of these Egyptian texts, my conclusion is this: while it is true that Egyptian creation texts do, in fact, have a focus on how the universe operates and how mankind functions within it, this is not at the exclusion of concerns about the origins of the material creation. It is clear, at least to me, that material origins were of utmost importance to the ancient Egyptians in their literature. The beginning of physical objects in the universe is a distinct aspect of the various creation accounts.

1. Self-Creation of a Creator-God

A number of texts not only describe the creation of the universe, but even picture the creator-god materializing in an act of self-creation. Utterance 587 of the Pyramid Texts states,

> Praise to you, Atum!
> Praise to you, Kheprer, *who created himself!*

---

see, e.g., J. P. Allen, *Genesis in Egypt: The Philosophy of Ancient Egyptian Creation Accounts* (New Haven, CT: Yale Egyptological Seminar, 1988); and J. K. Hoffmeier, "Some Thoughts on Genesis 1 and 2 and Egyptian Cosmology," *Journal of Ancient Near Eastern Studies* 15 (1983): 39–49.

18. Quoted in Henri Frankfort et al., *Before Philosophy* (repr., Baltimore: Penguin, 1973), 59.

19. Ibid., 29.

20. Siegfried Morenz, *Egyptian Religion* (Ithaca, NY: Cornell University Press, 1973), 160.

You became high in this your name High Ground.
You created yourself in this your name Kheprer.[21]

That is an early text that dates to the end of the third millennium (c. 2400–2200) BC.

Later Egyptian creation texts echo this belief that the creator-god was a product of self-creation. Coffin Text 714 says,

I [am] Nu the one with no equal.
I came into being on the
Great Occasion of the inundation, when I came into being.
I am he who flew, who became Dbnn
Who is in his egg.
I am he who began there [in] Nu.
See, the chaos-god came forth from me.
See, I am prosperous.
I created my body in my glory.
I am he who made myself;
I formed myself according to my will and according to my heart.[22]

This idea that the creator-god brought himself into being is a common element of Egyptian creation texts, including The Sun Hymn of Haremhab, Spell 601 of the Coffin Texts, and Spell 85 of the Book of the Dead.[23] The ancient Egyptians were interested in where the creator-god came from and when he began his existence.

2. Creation of Other Gods

Numerous texts then describe the acts of the creator-god in bringing into existence the lesser gods of the cosmos that are personified in the various physical elements of the universe. These acts are pictured in a variety of ways. In some texts, the creator-god is portrayed as creating the elements of the cosmos by expectoration or spitting out of the

---

21. This is my own translation. Italics added for emphasis. For various other renderings, see R. O. Faulkner, *The Ancient Egyptian Pyramid Texts* (New York: Oxford University Press, 1969), 238–241; and R. T. Rundle Clark, *Myth and Symbol in Ancient Egypt* (London: Thames and Hudson, 1959), 37–38. For original texts, see K. Sethe, *Die Altaegyptischen Pyramidentexte* (Leipzig: J. C. Hinrichs, 1908–1922).

22. My own translation, emphasis added. For Coffin Texts, see *Oriental Institute Publications*, 8 vols. (Chicago: University of Chicago Press, 1935–2006).

23. For the Book of the Dead, see R. O. Faulkner and C. Andrews, *The Ancient Egyptian Book of the Dead* (Austin: University of Texas Press, 1972).

lesser gods.[24] Other creation texts describe the creator-god exhaling or sneezing the lesser gods from his nostrils, such as in Coffin Texts 75, 80, and 81. A third method spelled out in the Pyramid Texts is creation by an act of onanism (masturbation) by the creator (see Utterance 527). Spell 245 of the Coffin Texts alludes to that earlier text when the god Shu says to the creator-god Atum, "This was the manner of your engendering: you conceived with your mouth and you gave birth from your hand in the pleasure of emission. I am the star that came forth from the two."[25] One further description of creation is the Memphite theology of the Old Kingdom found on the Shabaka Stone. It tells of the god Ptah, "who made all and brought the gods into being."[26] Ptah is glorified in this text because he formed the universe by speech, that is, by mere verbal fiat. He spoke, and the gods burst forth.

These stories are frankly and directly concerned with explaining the details of the history of the physical universe as it comes into being. Ancient Egyptian theogony is cosmogonic (it explains the origin of the universe) because each of the gods fashioned by the creator-god is a personification of an element of nature. As I have written elsewhere,

> Thus in some of the myths the creator-god produces four children who correspond to the basic structure of the universe: Shu (= air), Tefnut (= atmosphere), Geb (= earth), and Nut (= heavens). They in turn breed another generation of gods who represent elements of nature (e.g., Seth = storm). So we must in no way think that the Egyptian creation myths describe merely a metaphysical or spiritual creation.[27]

3. Creation of Mankind

The same is true of the creation of mankind in Egyptian literature. Many texts refer to that event and to the fact that humanity was specially formed by a creator-god. Some texts portray the creator-god as a potter who creates mankind by molding it on a potter's wheel or

---

24. See, e.g., Utterance 600 of the Pyramid Texts, trans. J. A. Wilson, in J. B. Pritchard, ed., *Ancient Near Eastern Texts relating to the Old Testament* (*ANET*) (Princeton, NJ: Princeton University Press, 1955); and, Spell 76 of the Coffin Texts, trans. J. Zandee, "Sargtexte Spruch 76," *Zeitschrift für ägyptische Sprache und Altertumskunde* 100 (1973): 60–71.

25. Translation in Clark, *Myth and Symbol*, 44.

26. *ANET*, 5.

27. Currid, *Ancient Egypt and the Old Testament*, 60.

table. For instance, the creator-god Khnum is pictured as "modeling people on his wheel. He has fashioned men."[28] The creator-god Ptah is similarly represented as a potter crafting mankind out of a lump of clay.[29] "Man is clay and straw, and God is his potter" is a pronouncement in the Instruction of Amenemope.[30]

Thus, in contrast to Walton's contention that Genesis 1–3, like other ancient Near Eastern texts, is primarily interested in function rather than origins, in Egyptian texts there is a substantial focus on the origins of the universe. The purpose and function of mankind in creation are not central ideas. The Egyptian texts have much more to do with humanity's origins than with humanity's utility and capacity.

B. A Significant Mesopotamian Creation Text

Among the cosmological texts of Mesopotamia, perhaps the most important is the Babylonian epic called *Enuma Elish*.[31] This document does spend a lot of time describing the order, function, and purpose of the various elements of creation. For instance, the purpose of mankind in the universe is stated directly:

> He shall be charged with the service of the gods,
> That they might be at ease![32]

However, such descriptions are not at the exclusion of acts of descriptions of material creation. Thus, the passage just quoted begins with the following words by the creator-god Marduk:

> Blood I will mass and cause bones to be,
> I will establish a savage, "man" shall be his name.
> Verily, savage-man I will create.

---

28. From *The Great Hymn to Khnum*, in Miriam Lichtheim, *Ancient Egyptian Literature*, 3 vols. (Berkeley: University of California Press, 1975–1980), 3:114.

29. A. H. Sayce, *The Religions of Ancient Egypt and Babylonia* (Edinburgh: T&T Clark, 1903), 138.

30. W. K. Simpson, ed., *The Literature of Ancient Egypt* (New Haven, CT: Yale University Press, 1973), 262.

31. This title derives from the opening words of the account, which are "When on high" or "When . . . above." The literature on this text is vast; see, e.g., A. Heidel, *The Babylonian Genesis*, 2nd ed. (Chicago: University of Chicago Press, 1951); and W. G. Lambert, *Babylonian Creation Myths* (Winona Lake, IN: Eisenbrauns, 2013).

32. For a study of this idea, see W. R. Mayer, "Ein Mythos von der Erschaffung des Menschen und des Königs," *Orientalia* 56 (1987): 55–68.

A rift between origins (the act of creation of mankind) and function (man's place in the order of creation) is not evident here. Both are present.

The same holds true for the rest of the universe as described in the *Enuma Elish*. While Walton and others are certainly correct that a good part of the text deals with the creator-god's ordering of the universe and the assigning of functions to its various parts, this text certainly does not omit attention to material origins. For example, central to the story is a cosmic battle between the gods of order and the gods of chaos, and this supports Walton's claim that there is a concern for function. Yet, the beginning of the text describes a situation in which material things did not exist and then tells how they were brought into being through divine agency:

> When the heavens above did not exist,
> And earth beneath had not come into being—
> There was Apsu, the first in order, their begetter,
> And the demiurge Tiamat, who gave birth to them all;
> They mingled their waters together
> Before meadow-land had coalesced and reed-bed was to be
>   found—
> When not one of the gods had been formed
> Or had come into being, when no destinies had been decreed,
> The gods were created in them.[33]

The watery chaos pictured in this text consists of two gods, Apsu and Tiamat, who create other deities through sexual procreation. The created gods each represent a vital element of the universe, such as sky, water, and earth. This second generation desires order rather than the chaotic status quo of Apsu and Tiamat. Order wins the day in a great cosmic battle. The point is, again, that the text is concerned about both the ordering of the universe and its material origins. Averbeck puts it well when he concludes, "Driving a wedge between material creation as over against giving order to the cosmos by assigning functions or roles is a false dichotomy that cannot bear the weight of the text."[34]

33. Quoted in Lambert, *Babylonian Creation Myths*, 50–51.
34. Averbeck, "Lost World," 235.

It is interesting that Walton comments, "Our first proposition is that Genesis 1 is ancient cosmology. . . . In these ways, and many others, they thought about the cosmos in much the same way that anyone in the ancient world thought . . . "[35] I agree that Genesis 1 is similar to other ancient cosmology in several important ways. But since it is evident that ancient Near Eastern creation accounts had great concern for *both function and material origins*, we would expect the biblical creation account to have the same focus and interests. Consequently, the idea that the origins debate can be swept away because Genesis 1–3 is not paying attention to physical, material beginnings is simply mistaken.

C. Functions and Origins in Genesis 1–3

The Hebrew creation account begins with the words "In the beginning, God created . . . " In ancient Hebrew there are a variety of words meaning to make or to form something; and these words have various subjects, that is, either men or God. The verb used in Genesis 1:1 for "create" is only and always used for the work of God when it appears in the qal stem as it does here. In the qal stem, it is not used for the action of mankind. Simply put, it is God who is at work in Genesis 1; this is his creation. Verse 1 then describes the object of God's creative activity: it was "the heavens and the earth"; here we see a figure of speech called a "merism," which is a set of opposites that are all-inclusive (see, e.g., Ps. 139:8; Rev. 22:13). It is a designation for all that exists. God has simply created all things.

In verse 2 the universe and, in particular, the earth is pictured in the process of creation. It is described as *tohu*, that is, "without form." This is a Hebrew word that commonly reflects a state of wildness and wilderness; it indicates a circumstance of chaos and what is unordered. The earth is also described as *bohu*, which is often translated as "void" (ESV). It denotes "emptiness." So at this point in the account, the earth is wild and empty. It is *tohu* and *bohu*. These two words are important because they serve as headings for the remainder of the creation account in Genesis 1. In days 1–3, God

---

35. Walton, *Lost World of Genesis 1*, 16.

brings order out of the *tohu* by putting things in their right places. That is followed by days 4–6, in which God takes care of the *bohu* by filling the universe with celestial bodies and filling the earth with plants, animals, and humans.

The account does report the various roles and functions of various elements of the creation. For example, he placed the lights in the heavens "to separate the day from the night" (v. 14) and "to give light upon the earth" (v. 15). Mankind, as well, was created for a purpose and that was to "have dominion over the fish of the sea and over the birds of the heavens and over the livestock . . . " (v. 26) and to "be fruitful and multiply and fill the earth and subdue it . . . " (v. 28) We certainly do not want to underappreciate this aspect of the creation account. God made things for specific roles, functions, and purposes.

The problem with Walton's functional model is that it highlights the roles of the elements of the universe at the expense of their actual creation. The reality is that God was not only ordering the cosmos and assigning roles to the different parts of nature, but he was filling the universe as well. In other words, he created light (v. 3), oceans (v. 9), land (v. 9), plants (v. 11), celestial bodies (v. 14), animals (v. 24), and humans (v. 26). To interpret Genesis 1 as merely about functions and not about origins is a failure to account for some of the very prominent features of the narrative.

II. Genesis 1–3 as Myth

Another way that supporters of theistic evolution attempt to resolve the conflict between the Bible and evolution is by claiming that Genesis 1–3 is not factual history but is an ancient Near Eastern "myth." They are using the word "myth" in the sense of a legendary story without determinable basis in fact or history. In regard to creation, they see myth as a symbolic tale of primordial times that deals principally with the realm of the gods. It is a "narrative only in the sense that the stories have a linear forward movement, but they are simply ahistorical. Their purpose is to explain the order and meaning of the universe as it stands."[36]

---

36. See J. D. Currid, *Against the Gods: The Polemical Theology of the Old Testament* (Wheaton, IL: Crossway, 2013), 43. Cf. P. Veyne, *Did the Greeks Believe in Their Myths? An Essay on Constitutive Imagination*, trans. P. Wissing (Chicago: University of Chicago Press, 1988).

Theistic evolution advocate Peter Enns argues for the "Genesis 1–3 as myth" position with his claim that " . . . the opening chapters of Genesis participate in a worldview that the earliest Israelites shared with their Mesopotamian neighbors. . . . the stories of Genesis had a context within which they were first understood. And that context was not a modern scientific one *but an ancient mythic one.*"[37]

The belief that the Hebrew creation account is based on the Babylonian creation myth, and is itself mythic, has been standard fare for a long time among liberal Old Testament scholars. A dominant early advocate of this position was the German professor Hermann Gunkel (1862–1932).[38] He states that the biblical creation narrative "is only the Jewish elaboration of far older material, which must have been originally much more mythological."[39] More modern critical scholars continue to hold this core belief, but with a few more twists and turns.[40] Joseph Blenkinsopp, for example, comments on the nature of Genesis 1–11, saying, "For its basic structure and major themes it has drawn on a well-established literary tradition best represented by the Mesopotamian *Atrahasis* text, and in this limited respect it is comparable with the work of early Greek mythographers."[41]

But this approach raises a question: Why does Genesis 1–3 contain so many elements that appear to be literal history if in fact it was borrowed from an ancient Near Eastern myth? Many liberal scholars answer that the writer of Genesis borrowed ancient Near Eastern myths of creation, and then stripped them of their mythological elements and made them look like historical records. The author thus employed a

---

37. Peter Enns, *Inspiration and Incarnation: Evangelicals and the Problem of the Old Testament* (Grand Rapids, MI: Baker, 2005), 55, emphasis added.

38. See, in particular, Hermann Gunkel, *Schöpfung und Chaos in Urzeit und Endzeit* (Gottingen: Vandenhoeck & Ruprecht, 1895); and Gunkel, *Die Sagen der Genesis* (Gottingen: Vandenhoeck & Ruprecht, 1901).

39. Quoted in J. Niehaus, *Ancient Near Eastern Themes in Biblical Theology* (Grand Rapids, MI: Kregel, 2008), 23–24.

40. See the recent contribution of K. L. Sparks, "Genesis 1–11 as Ancient Historiography," in C. Halton, ed., *Genesis: History, Fiction, or Neither? Three Views on the Bible's Earliest Chapters* (Grand Rapids, MI: Zondervan, 2015). He argues that the various parts of Genesis 1–11 are "myth, legend, and tale" (109).

41. Joseph Blenkinsopp, *The Pentateuch: An Introduction to the First Five Books of the Bible* (New York: Doubleday, 1992), 93–94.

form of *demythologization* to rid the creation story of myth and then replaced it with a monotheistic, non-mythic orthodoxy.

But then how can they be so sure it originated with a myth? These same commentators believe that through a close reading of Genesis 1–3 they can still see some of the original mythic character. And this is important for our study, for if Genesis 1–3 is merely a sanitized text that is really mythic at its core, then the question of origins, including human beginnings, is a moot one—myths are never intended to be taken as real history in the first place. Those who embrace a mythic interpretation simply have no trouble accepting evolution as a means of material and human origins; there is no tension between the Genesis myth and science in this regard.

No doubt there are many parallels between the Hebrew creation account and the myths of the ancient Near East.[42] The question is, is the position of *demythologization* the best explanation for the relationship between the two literatures? This interpretation clearly highlights the close association of Genesis 1–3 and other ancient Near Eastern texts, while it undervalues the uniqueness and originality of the Hebrew account. But are the early chapters of Genesis in their original form merely another myth that is later partially cleansed, or are they unique and distinct in their own right?

There are compelling reasons for rejecting the "Genesis as myth" view. The mythic explanation underestimates the deep, fervent resistance of the Hebrews to anything that even smacks of the mythological. Again, many modern commentators view any reticence to myth as a very late aspect of the compositional process of the early chapters of Genesis. To the contrary, I would argue that Genesis 1–3 is at its very core anti-mythological, and this can be seen in its polemical quality and disposition.[43] Since I have dealt elsewhere with the polemical nature of the Hebrew creation account, I will not take time to restate my entire case in detail, but will give some specific examples of polemic at work in the general account of the creation and of human origins in particular.[44]

---

42. See Heidel, *Babylonian Genesis.*
43. Consider the ground-breaking work of G. F. Hasel, "The Polemic Nature of the Genesis Cosmology," *Evangelical Quarterly* 46 (1974): 81–102. The strength of this article is his sound argument that a primary purpose of the Genesis account is anti-mythological.
44. See Currid, *Against the Gods,* 33–46.

A. Anti-Mythic Polemic in the Creation of Humanity

In the Mesopotamian creation myth, the gods created mankind for the specific purpose of easing the work load of the deities. The *Atrahasis* text says,

> The gods' load was too great,
> The work too hard, the trouble too much . . .
> The gods dug out the Tigris river
> And then dug out the Euphrates . . .
> For 3,600 years they bore the excess,
> Hard work, night and day,
> They groaned and blamed each other.[45]

Mankind's function was to be a slave to the gods so that "they might be at ease." After their creation, humans multiply quickly and they become a thorn in the sides of the gods. People are tumultuous and they disturb the sleep of the gods, in particular, Enlil the head of the pantheon:

> And the country was as noisy as a bellowing bull.
> The god grew restless at their racket . . .
> He addressed the great gods,
> "The noise of mankind has become too much,
> I am losing sleep over their racket.
> Give the order that *suruppu*-disease shall break out."

Enlil's attempt to destroy humanity with a plague is a failure. He then tries to inflict them with a famine, but that fails as well. Finally, he orders a flood to consume them all. It is clear that the deluge in the *Atrahasis* epic contains several similarities and has parallels with the biblical account of the flood.[46]

But there are far greater differences. Israel's account of mankind's creation and the subsequent flood is opposed at its very heart to the worldview conceptions of the rest of the ancient Near East. Humanity's creation is not for the purpose of being slaves to the gods and to carry

---

45. Trans. S. Dalley, *Myths from Mesopotamia* (Oxford: Oxford University Press, 1997).
46. For a good study of the Mesopotamian flood account, see W. G. Lambert and A. R. Millard, *Atrahasis: The Babylonian Story of the Flood* (Winona Lake, IN: Eisenbrauns, 1999).

their workload, but rather mankind is created in the image of God (Gen. 1:27), as the "crown of creation," and as God's co-regent, ruling over the created order. Humanity's very purpose and dignity arise from this special, sovereign act of the Creator.

The flood in Scripture is not a consequence of mankind's not caring for the ease of the gods or awakening the gods from their slumber (these gods have all the foibles of human character); rather, it is due to mankind's unholiness in contrast to a holy God (Gen. 6:5). Such major distinctions cannot be accounted for by a simple cleansing of myth from the text.

B. Anti-Mythic Polemic in the Creation of the Luminaries

In ancient Near Eastern creation texts, a dominant feature is theogony, which refers to the creation of the gods who are personified in the elements of the universe. The forming of astral bodies of the sun, moon, and stars is theogonic. So, in the Mesopotamian *Enuma Elish*, the creator-god Marduk made the gods and then "constructed stations for the great gods, fixing their astral likenesses as constellations."[47]

The biblical author, in contrast, presents God as creating the luminaries, but there is no interest in theogony. He is rigidly monotheistic and sanctions no deification of the heavenly bodies. Heidel comments, "The opening chapters of Genesis, as well as the Old Testament in general, refer to only one Creator and Maintainer of all things, one God who created and transcends all cosmic matter. In the entire Old Testament, there is not a trace of theogony, such as we find, for example, in *Enuma Elish* and Hesiod."[48]

It is significant that the luminaries are not given names in the Genesis 1 account. They are merely called "the two great lights," one being "the greater light" and the other being "the lesser light" and "the stars" (1:16). While some commentators believe this fact has no significance or that it is simply "the rhetorically high style of the narrative,"[49] it clearly distinguishes the Israelite worldview from the other ancient

---

47. *ANET*, 67.
48. Heidel, *Babylonian Genesis*, 97.
49. C. John Collins, *Genesis 1–4* (Phillipsburg, NJ: P&R, 2006), 82–83.

Near Eastern theogonic views. The creation texts from the ancient Near East believe the luminaries to be gods, and they bear deific names. To the contrary, Hebrew religion conceives of the luminaries as mere material objects that are not to be worshiped. Hasel correctly comments, "They share in the creatureliness of all creation and have no autonomous divine quality."[50]

Other examples could easily be cited of Hebrew polemic in the Genesis creation account against common ancient Near Eastern creation documents.[51] The conclusion is obvious. Ancient Near Eastern creation texts are myth, and they bear all the identifying marks of myth—things such as polytheism, theogony, magic, and fertility.[52] But Genesis 1–3 is zealously anti-mythological. It is monotheistic to its very core, and it in no way sanctions the existence of other gods or the creation of other gods. It also promotes a high view of mankind and its creation over against the man-as-a-slave morality of other religions. These are issues that are central to the Hebrew world and life view, and they are not attained by some sort of mythological cleansing. Contrary to some supporters of theistic evolution, Genesis 1–3 is not dark mythological polytheism but stands in stark contrast to it and is in fact a sustained polemic against it.

III. Figurative and Theological Literature

One of the most common and popular ways to deal with the issue of origins in Genesis 1–3 is to argue that the account is figurative. In other words, it is not the biblical author's intention to present his material in a historical and scientific manner. His aim is really theological; that is, the account exalts the Lord as the Creator of the universe, but the writer is not interested in the manner of creation. As Denis Alexander says, "The purpose of Genesis 2, like Genesis 1, is to teach theology."[53] Thus, a wedge is driven between what some call "theological history" (i.e., Genesis 1–3) and modern scientific inquiry (geology, geography, physics, etc.) and modern social sciences

---

50. Hasel, "Polemic Nature," 89.
51. See, again, Currid, *Against the Gods*, 33–46.
52. See my article, "Cosmologies of Myth," in W. A. Hoffecker, ed., *Building a Christian World View*, vol. 2 (Phillipsburg, NJ: P&R, 1988), 9–20.
53. Alexander, *Creation or Evolution*, 196.

(history, anthropology, and other fields of research). The end-all, of course, is a sweeping dismissal of Genesis 1–3 having any concern about the methods and manners of creation. Modern scientific re-search provides the answers to the issue of the mechanics of origins, and the Bible does not.

The approach of Francis Collins also falls into this general category. He classifies Genesis 1–3 as "poetry and allegory"[54] and therefore not intended to be understood as factually true historical narrative.

John Walton is a third author to adopt this "figurative literature" approach, although his descriptive label is "archetypal literature." By "archetype" he means a kind of Everyman allegorical story in which what happens to Adam and Eve is a kind of allegory (an archetype) to tell us what happens to every person. For example, after discussing Genesis 2:7, in which "the LORD God formed the man of dust from the ground and breathed into his nostrils the breath of life, and the man became a living creature," Walton writes,

> . . . the next question to consider is whether this statement about Adam pertains to him uniquely or to all of us. The core proposal of this book is that the forming accounts of Adam and Eve should be understood archetypally rather than as accounts of how those two individuals were uniquely formed. When I use the word *archetype* . . . I am referring to the simple concept that an archetype embodies all others in the group.[55]

Another commentator, New Testament scholar Scot McKnight, calls Adam and Eve in Genesis 1–3 "literary," and certainly what he means is that in the text there is "no sign of a historical or biological or genetic Adam and Eve."[56]

The end result is the same from the approaches of Denis Alexander, Francis Collins, John Walton, and Scot McKnight: Genesis 1–3 should not be understood as historical narrative reporting actual events that

---

54. Francis Collins, *The Language of God* (New York: Free Press, 2006), 206; see also 150–151, 175, 207.

55. Walton, *Lost World of Adam and Eve*, 74. Walton goes on to explain that an "archetype" will sometimes be a historical figure and sometimes not (74–75, 96). He decides that Adam and Eve were "real people who existed in a real past" (96) with regard to the account of Genesis 3 of their fall into sin (101–103), but the accounts of how they were initially created in Genesis 2 are not historical, and we do not need to consider them to be the first human beings (75–77, 101, 103).

56. Scot McKnight, in Venema and McKnight, *Adam and the Genome*, 136.

happened in the past, but instead we should understand these chapters as "figurative" or "allegorical" or "archetypal" or "literary" literature. My objections here will apply to all four of these approaches, because my contention is that Genesis 1–3 should be understood as historical narrative.

Alexander supplies a number of examples to demonstrate why Genesis 1–3 should be understood figuratively and theologically, but not historically or scientifically. For instance, he states the following:

> For myself I have never met a Christian who, upon reading Genesis 3:8—"the man and his wife heard the sound of the Lord God as he was walking in the garden in the cool of the day"—imagines that God was physically walking around in the garden with two legs. No Hebrew reading this would have imagined that the God of Israel, of whom no form was seen when he spoke out of the fire (Deuteronomy 4:15), was clattering round the garden in noisy footwear. In reality, this is a rather vivid and heart-aching picture of the results of sin . . . [57]

Actually, the Hebrew reader would have no trouble understanding that what is being described in this incident is a *theophany*, that is, a temporary appearance of God in physical form.[58] At times, the Lord even takes on a theophanic form as a human being. In Genesis 18:1–2, for example, the text tells us that "Yahweh appear[ed]" before Abraham at the tent-door when three men stand before the patriarch. Two of the "men" are designated as angels later in the story (18:22; 19:1), and the third figure is the Lord himself (see 18:13, 17). Thus we see the Lord appearing in human form, accompanied by two of his angels. There is nothing figurative about this account or the Lord's appearance in physical form.

The warning that the proponents of this position give is that the primary purpose of the early chapters of Genesis is theological, and, therefore, one should not expect these chapters to be scientific in regard to the how God made the universe or the biological intricacies of existence. Again, Alexander presents this position well when he says,

---

57. Alexander, *Creation or Evolution*, 198.
58. See J. Niehaus, "In the Wind of the Storm: Another Look at Genesis III 8," *Vetus Testamentum* 44 (1994): 263–267.

These chapters represent the opening manifesto of the Bible, setting its parameters and its priorities, and the danger is that if we start interpreting the text as if it were scientific literature, or was intended to tell us how God created biological diversity, then we run the risk of missing the central theological messages.[59]

This argument, of course, is a non sequitur. The mere fact that one views the text as historical literature, and not as some type of figurative manifesto, certainly does not mean that one will miss the main theological points of the text. In reality, the reverse is true: the person who views the early chapters of Genesis as figurative will miss some of the principal teachings of the account. Let us turn to consider this point.

Walton's argument for taking Genesis 2 as "archetypal literature" is based on a simple test. Walton comments,

In order to determine whether the treatment of Adam in the text focuses on him primarily as an archetype or as an individual, we can ask a simple question: is the text describing something that is uniquely true of Adam, or is it describing something that is true of all of us? If only Adam is formed from dust, then it is treating him as a discrete and unique individual. . . . If Eve's formation conveys a truth about her that is true of her alone, then it is the history of an individual.[60]

But then, in order to demonstrate that Genesis 2 is not describing the unique creation of Adam and Eve but is in fact "describing something that is true of all of us," Walton has to do violence to the actual words of the text. In the midst of an entire chapter that speaks repeatedly of numerous specific actions that the Lord God carried out (Gen. 2:2, 3, 7, 8, 9, 15, 16, 19, 21, 22), Walton tells us that verse 7, "then the Lord God formed man of dust from the ground," does not mean that the Lord God formed man of dust from the ground. It means, rather, that all people are created mortal, subject to death.[61] He says that "the LORD God caused a deep sleep to fall upon the man, and while he slept took one of his ribs and closed up its place with flesh

---

59. Ibid., 196–197.
60. Walton, *Lost World of Adam and Eve*, 75.
61. Ibid., 72–74.

... the rib that the Lord God had taken from the man he made into a woman" (Gen. 2:21–22) does not mean that God created Eve from a rib that he took from Adam's side. It simply implies something that is true of all human beings generally, and that is that a man's wife "is his ally, his other half."[62]

However, several decisive considerations in Genesis 1–3 show that these chapters are rightly understood not as poetry or allegory or figurative literature, but as historical narrative.

A. Genre of Genesis 1–3

Genesis 1–3 bears all the markings of Hebrew historical narrative. One common grammatical device that reflects a historical genre is the Hebrew verbal construction of the vav-consecutive with an imperfective verb.[63] This construction appears frequently in the first three chapters of Genesis: for instance, this device of historical sequence occurs fifty-one times in Genesis 1 alone ("And God said," v. 3; "And God saw," v. 4; etc.). Another indicator of prose narrative is the use of the small Hebrew word *'eth* as the sign of the direct object.[64] The early chapters of Genesis actually contain little indication of figurative language. There are few tropes, symbols, or metaphors. The dearth of figurative language is quite striking. A question thus arises: if the text was not meant to be taken historically and sequentially, why did the biblical author employ narrative devices so freely?

Yes, Genesis 1, in particular, is highly structured. Elements like the repetition of "evening and morning" throughout the passage reflect its compositional grid. However, repetitive formulas do not necessarily signify nonhistorical, figurative accounts. For example, the entire book of Genesis is structured according to the repeated formula "This is the book of the generations of . . . " (2:4; 5:1; 6:9; 10:1; 11:10, 27; 25:12, 19; 36:1, 9; 37:2),[65] but that in no way indicates that the entire book is figurative in what it relays to its readers. Genesis 1 has an elevated

---

62. Ibid., 81.
63. B. T. Arnold and J. H. Choi, *A Guide to Biblical Hebrew Syntax* (Cambridge: Cambridge University Press, 2003), 84–87. This function is quite rare in Hebrew poetry.
64. R. J. Williams, *Hebrew Syntax: An Outline*, 2nd ed. (Toronto: University of Toronto Press, 1976), 78, comments that this accusative marker "is rare in poetry but normal in prose."
65. See my discussion of this formula below, in the section "C. *Toledoth* Formula ("These Are the Generations of . . . ")."

style, yet it is still historical narrative. C. John Collins perhaps has
the best genre definition of Genesis 1 when he calls it "exalted prose
narrative."[66] As I conclude elsewhere, "This description properly reflects the sequence, chronology, and historicity of the account, while at
the same time underscoring its exceptional quality."[67]

The historical nature of the Hebrew creation account underscores
the reality that God invented time and history. And the history that
God created in Genesis 1 is one that is moving and unfolding: it is a
linear history that moves from inception to consummation. The universe had a beginning, and it is moving toward an end. This truth distinguishes the biblical creation account from the cosmogonical texts of
the ancient Near East. The non-Israelite accounts are legendary stories
that have no determinable basis in fact or history. They are symbolic
sagas of primordial times that describe the realm and activities of deities. They are what can be called "mythic narrative," that is, the stories
have linear forward movement, but they are simply ahistorical. Models
such as the figurative approach simply de-historicize the Hebrew creation account and, therefore, minimize this important "theological"
aspect of the text.

The deeply historical nature of Genesis 1–3 is profoundly important to the entire Bible because these chapters stand at the beginning
of the Bible, whose overall structure is historical. The Bible shows the
great scope of the work of God from the beginning of time to a final
judgment and a new heavens and a new earth. The first three chapters
of Genesis do not stand alone in the Bible as isolated chapters but are
structurally tied to the narrative in Genesis 4 about Adam and Eve and
their children Cain, Abel, and Seth, and to the genealogies of human
beings found in Genesis 5, and to the historical record in Genesis 6–9
of Noah's family and the flood, and to the historical narrative in Genesis 10 of the nations that descended from Noah's sons, and to the tower
of Babel and to the descendants of Shem in Genesis 11, and to Abraham and the patriarchs in Genesis 12–50. Genesis 1–3 does not stand
alone but is closely linked to the rest of this entire historical narrative.

The macro-structure of the Bible is a historical account of God's

---

66. C. John Collins, *Genesis 1–4*, 44.
67. Currid, *Against the Gods*, 44.

actions from beginning to end. If we remove the profoundly historical nature of Genesis 1–3, we will remove the historical foundation on which all the remainder of the Bible rests.

B. Context of Genesis 1–3

The most basic premise of hermeneutics from the time of the Reformation is that when one faces a difficult text, one must proceed on the assumption that Scripture interprets Scripture. The Westminster Confession of Faith (1646) puts it well: "The infallible rule of interpretation of Scripture is the Scripture itself: and therefore, when there is a question about the true and full sense of any Scripture (which is not manifold, but one), it must be searched and known by other places that speak more clearly."[68] I am certain that few would disagree that the early chapters of Genesis are difficult. The obvious question, then, is how does the remainder of Scripture handle the Genesis creation account? I know of no text in the Bible that suggests that Genesis 1–3 is a figurative passage or that would counter the basic chronological/sequential structure of the account. In fact, whenever the creation texts are referred to in the rest of Scripture, chronology and history predominate. So, for example, Exodus 20:8–11 reflects the reality that mankind's earthly seven-day week has a set and solid foundation in God's activity in the creation week. Psalm 104, which reviews the creative work of God at the beginning of time, confirms the sequence and history of the early chapters of Genesis. While it is true that not every jot and tittle of the creation account is dealt with in the rest of the Bible, yet when it is considered, it is not understood as figurative in any way but as a report of actual historical events.

Often those who promote a figurative view of Genesis 1, in particular, use Genesis 2:5 as evidence: the claim is that this verse cannot be harmonized with the progression of the week in Genesis 1.[69] This is an important issue, and I will deal with it in the next section of this essay.

More could be added regarding the sequential and historical nature of the early chapters of Genesis, but space and time do not allow us

---

68. Westminster Confession of Faith, 1.9.
69. See, in particular, M. G. Kline, "Because It Had Not Rained," *Westminster Theological Journal* (*WTJ*) 20 (1958): 146–157; and M. Futato, "Because It Had Rained: A Study of Gen. 2:5-7 with Implications for Gen. 2:4-25 and Gen. 1:1-2:3," *WTJ* 60 (1998): 1–21.

to go into much greater detail.[70] In any event, although some authors merely dismiss the Hebrew account as figurative and not historical, some by a mere flick of the wrist, the nature of the text is much more complicated and complex than they suppose. They do not do proper justice to the chronological reality of Genesis 1–3, and to the fact that God is the God of history. Surely the intention of the author cannot be merely to theologize and to divorce history from the account?

IV. The Sequential Scheme

For many decades, the question of the relationship between the account of Genesis 1:1–2:3 and Genesis 2:4–3:24 has been a dominant issue in Old Testament studies. The liberal higher critics, with few exceptions, argue that the two accounts are from different sources, and they are therefore not complementary but competing narratives of creation.[71] They are "two excerpts from two separate compositions, which a later editor arranged consecutively by pure chance."[72]

Others dismiss that claim. Brandeis professor Nahum Sarna, for example, simply concludes that "Chapter 2 is not another creation story."[73] More traditional and conservative commentators take the position that the two texts harmonize, and the second narrative is a more detailed exposition focused especially on Adam and Eve and events of the sixth day of creation.

More recently, John Walton has proposed a third alternative.[74] He says that perhaps "the second account might be considered a sequel to the first. . . . the second account is not detailing the sixth day, but identifying a sequel scenario, that is, recounting events that potentially and arguably could have occurred long after the first account."[75]

But here are some of the key verses in Genesis 2 that have long

---

70. For further study, see my response to the "Framework View of Gen. 1:1-2:3" in John Currid, *Genesis*, vol. 1, EP Study Commentary (Darlington, UK: Evangelical Press, 2003), 34–42.

71. See E. A. Speiser, *Genesis*, vol. 1 (Garden City, NY: Doubleday, 1964), 18–20.

72. Umberto Cassuto, *A Commentary on the Book of Genesis, Part One: From Adam to Noah* (Jerusalem: Magnes, 1989 ed.), 85.

73. N. M. Sarna, *The JPS Torah Commentary: Genesis* (Philadelphia: Jewish Publication Society, 1989), 16.

74. John H. Walton, "A Historical Adam: Archetypal Creation View," in *Four Views on the Historical Adam*, ed. Matthew Barrett and Ardel B. Caneday (Grand Rapids, MI: Zondervan, 2013), 89–118.

75. Ibid., 109.

been understood to give a more detailed explanation of the creation of Adam and Eve that is just mentioned briefly in Genesis 1:

> Then the LORD God formed the man of dust from the ground and breathed into his nostrils the breath of life, and the man became a living creature. (Gen. 2:7)

> So the LORD God caused a deep sleep to fall upon the man, and while he slept took one of his ribs and closed up its place with flesh. And the rib that the LORD God had taken from the man he made into a woman and brought her to the man. (Gen. 2:21–22)

Making these verses talk about something other than the creation of Adam and Eve as the first human beings would provide a convenient solution for theistic evolutionists. This is because, if Genesis 2 is a more detailed explanation of the creation events of Genesis 1 (as Christians have historically held), then the statements "formed the man of dust from the ground" and "the rib that the LORD God had taken from the man he made into a woman" simply cannot be reconciled with the theistic evolution view that Adam and Eve were born from previously existing human beings.

So Walton's sequential scheme has weighty consequences for the issue of the origin of humanity in Scripture. Walton recognizes the significance of this when, after proposing his "sequel scenario," he goes on to say,

> In such a case, Adam and Eve would not necessarily be envisioned as the first human beings, but would be elect individuals drawn out of the human population and given a particular representative role in sacred space.[76]

If, as Walton suggests, Genesis 2–3 is not representing Adam and Eve as the first humans created, then the issue of human origins is thrown wide open. Walton himself recognizes this reality when he comments on the idea that Adam and Eve were not the first humans: "If the Bible makes no such claims, then the Bible will not stand opposed to

---

76. Ibid.

any views that science might offer (e.g., evolutionary models or population genetics), as long as God is not eliminated from the picture."[77]

In other words, Walton is proposing that God created humanity as a species in Genesis 1, but at a later time or stage he chose Adam and Eve "out of the human population" to serve as an archetype of humankind. This allows Walton to affirm that he believes in Adam and Eve as historical personages. However, he also contends that perhaps they were not the first humans nor were they the parents of the entire human species. Those conclusions certainly make his position controversial.

But Walton's proposal faces several decisive objections.

A. Clear Indicators of Historical Narrative in Genesis 2

On Walton's proposal, key portions of Genesis 2 must be understood not as straightforward narrative history but as some kind of poetic or figurative descriptions of God's activity. For example, there are explicit statements about God forming Adam and Eve from the dust of the ground and making Eve from a rib taken from Adam's side. But in Walton's view these become part of a description of the time, perhaps "tens of thousands of years" after human beings first appeared on the earth, when "individuals whom the Bible designates as Adam and Eve are chosen by God as representative priests in sacred space."[78]

This means that if we follow Walton's view, "the LORD God formed the man of dust from the ground" does not really mean that the Lord God formed man from the dust of the ground. Rather, it has something to do with God choosing a specific human being as a representative of the human race. And "the rib that the LORD God had taken from the man he made into a woman and brought her to the man" does not mean that the rib that the Lord God had taken from the man he made into a woman. Rather, it has something to do with God choosing a specific female human being as a representative priest with Adam.

Several factors in Genesis 1–2 stand in clear opposition to Walton's position. The two accounts of Genesis 1–2 are both of the genre of historical narrative, not poetic or allegorical literature, and they bear the markings of it (see discussion above, under "A. Genre of Genesis 1–3").

---

77. Ibid., 112–113.
78. Ibid., 114–115.

However, although both chapters are presented as historical prose narrative, they are stylistically different. As noted above, Genesis 1 is what C. John Collins appropriately calls "exalted prose narrative."[79] It is exceptional narrative that is highly structured, with much repetitive material. The text that begins in Genesis 2:4 is also unusual material, but it employs the common historical prose narrative normally used in Old Testament literature.

Corresponding to the stylistic differences, the nature of the content of the two accounts is distinct. Whereas Genesis 1:1–2:3 provides a broad sweep in its description of the creation of the universe, Genesis 2:4ff. is a pointed, localized record of events in the garden of Eden. In the opening narrative, God is the sole actor; in the second one, there are other participants working in the story besides God. This latter difference is reflected in the distinct names for God in the two narrations. In Genesis 1:1–2:3 the only name for God used in Hebrew is Elohim (translated as "God"); it appears thirty-six times in those thirty-four verses. The use of only this name perhaps carries a universal sense for the original audience, in which the transcendence of God is being emphasized. But in Genesis 2:4–24, the Hebrew name used for God is Yahweh Elohim (eleven times, translated "the LORD God"), and the addition of Yahweh to Elohim may be for the purpose of defining the universal Creator God as none other than the covenant God of Israel, Yahweh. The idea is to see the movement from the general to the particular: the transcendent God of Genesis 1 is the same as the immanent God of Genesis 2.[80]

The distinctiveness of the two narratives is also highlighted by the closing words of Genesis 2:4, which reads, "in the day Yahweh Elohim made *the earth and the heavens.*" This expression echoes the phrase "heavens and earth" of Genesis 1:1, but the order is reversed. This is probably because the heavens are at center stage in the opening account as God displays his mighty acts to produce the universe, while the second episode focuses on the earth and, in particular, the garden of Eden with mankind in it.

Therefore, the two episodes are historical narrative and they are

---

79. C. John Collins, *Genesis 1–4*, 44.
80. The compounding of the two divine names occurs twenty times in Genesis 2–3, but on only one other occasion in the entire Pentateuch (Ex. 9:30).

not diametrically opposed; rather, they highlight different aspects of God's creative activity. Again, this appears to be a stylistic move from the general to the particular: a change of focus from the larger universal picture to a telescopic view of one part of the universal picture. This means that Genesis 2 does not describe events perhaps "tens of thousands of years" after the creation of Genesis 1, but gives a more particular description of the original creation of Adam and Eve.

Such a movement from the general to the particular in Hebrew narrative is a common rhetorical device. For example, we read in Joshua 14:6–14 about the episode of Caleb requesting an inheritance of land that had been promised to him. At the close of the passage the text says that Joshua "gave Hebron to Caleb. . . . [and] Hebron became the inheritance of Caleb the son of Jephunneh the Kenizzite to this day. . . . And the land had rest from war" (vv. 13–15). Later, in Joshua 15:13–17, we read the particulars of Caleb's capture of the Hebron region that helped to lead to peace in the land. Although this passage occurs later in the text, it is not sequential to 14:6–14 but is homing in on some specifics and particulars of the earlier passage.

B. Genesis 2:5

> When no bush of the field was yet in the land and no small plant of the field had yet sprung up—for the LORD God had not caused it to rain on the land, and there was no man to work the ground . . .

This verse is commonly used by commentators to deny that Genesis 2:4ff. is a particularization of day 6 of Genesis 1. The reason is simple: the verse provides a different picture of the circumstances at the beginning of day 6. As Meredith Kline comments, "Verse 5 itself describes a time when the earth was without vegetation."[81] Since, according to Genesis 1:11–12, vegetation was created on day 3, then there is discord between the two accounts. Consequently, some scholars conclude that Genesis 1 is not sequential but topical, and Genesis 2, by contrast, is the historical, chronological account of the creation of mankind, vegetation, and animals.[82]

---

81. Kline, "Because It Had Not Rained," 149.
82. Futato, "Because It Had Rained," 1–21, goes as far as to argue that neither chapter 1 nor chapter 2 are to be understood as chronological.

But the incongruity between Genesis 1 and Genesis 2:5 is not as sharp as some commentators would have us believe. First, the text does not say there was no vegetation on the earth at this time; it declares that every plant (*'eseb*) of the field simply had not yet sprouted (*yitsmakh*). In other words, plants were there, but they simply had not blossomed or budded.[83] The verb *tsamach* ("to sprout") is not used of the vegetation in Genesis 1:11–12. Second, this verse refers to only two categories of plant life, and not to all vegetation.[84] As a result, a preferable explanation is that some plant life existed on the earth prior to the description of Genesis 2:5 and, therefore, this verse is not an insurmountable obstacle to the generalization-particularization view.

The reason the plants had not sprouted yet is twofold: the Lord had not brought rain, and there was "no man" to cultivate the ground. The Hebrew negative particle *'eyn* employed in the last clause of verse 5 ("there was no man to work the ground") is a particle of nonexistence.[85] The use of this particle indicates that no human beings yet existed, and thus argues against a sequential understanding of Genesis 1–2, in which mankind was created in Genesis 1:26–27 and then Adam and Eve were elected out of the existing human population to be representatives in the garden. We need to be careful here because, while the Hebrew particle of nonexistence can be used to negate the existence of something completely, it can also negate the presence of something in a particular location. This text, however, does not seem to localize the nonexistence to the garden, because verse 5 precedes God's planting of a garden in Eden (2:8) and, therefore, it likely refers to the circumstances of the entire earth: "There was no man."

Genesis 2:7 also affirms the nonsequential nature of Genesis 1–2. The text declares that Yahweh "formed the man, dust from the ground." Verbs of forming often require two accusatives, an object accusative (the thing made) followed by a material accusative (the ma-

---

83. Ludwig Koehler, Walter Baumgartner, and Johann J. Stamm, *The Hebrew and Aramaic Lexicon of the Old Testament*, trans. and ed. under the supervision of Mervyn E. J. Richardson, 5 vols. (HALOT) (Leiden: Brill, 1994–2000), 807.

84. Futato, "Because It Had Rained," 4–5; and Cassuto, *Commentary on the Book of Genesis*, 101–103.

85. See the discussion of this particle in Paul Joüon, *A Grammar of Biblical Hebrew*, vol. 2 (Rome: Pontifical Biblical Institute, 2005), 576, 604–605.

terial from which the thing is made).[86] This signifies that the material composition of the man Adam was dust; the Hebrew term for "dust" (*'aphar*) simply means "the dry, fine crumbs of the earth."[87] The man who is placed in the garden did not descend from previous humans, but was formed directly from the material earth.

C. *Toledoth* Formula ("These Are the Generations of . . . ")

The clause "These are the generations of . . . " is a repetitive formula that is a structural device for the entire book of Genesis. It appears eleven times in the book (2:4; 5:1; 6:9; 10:1; 11:10, 27; 25:12, 19; 36:1, 9; 37:2). Many interpreters understand this expression as a caption or heading for the section that is to follow. In fact, this understanding is so prevalent that several translations do not translate the Hebrew phrase as "These are the generations of," but as "This is the account of," showing it to be a heading for what follows (this is the translation of Genesis 2:4 used in the NIV, NASB, NET, NLT, and CSB, for example).

But John Walton claims that sometimes this *toledoth* formula "functions as an introduction to the next sequential time period."[88] He concludes that *toledoth* in Genesis 2:4 is just such an introduction, and there it is transitional and conjunctive. The verse, therefore, transitions one narrative to another, and the second narrative would be later in time than the first. Based on this literary analysis, Walton suggests "that the text is not making an overt claim that Adam and Eve should be identified as the people of the first account if it presents the second account as sequential to the first."[89]

But the evidence that *toledoth* serves as a transitional marker between two narratives in sequence is quite thin. The only instance of the eleven appearances of the formula that Walton cites as bridging two narratives in this way is Genesis 6:9, "These are the generations of Noah. Noah was a righteous man, blameless in his generation. Noah walked with God." However, a close reading of that verse indicates it is introductory to a concise genealogy in the next verse: "And Noah

---

86. Arnold and Choi, *Guide to Biblical Hebrew Syntax*, 21; and, B. K. Waltke and M. O'Connor, *An Introduction to Biblical Hebrew Syntax* (Winona Lake, IN: Eisenbrauns, 1990), 174.
87. HALOT, 723.
88. Walton, "Historical Adam: Archetypal Creation View," 109.
89. Ibid., 110.

had three sons, Shem, Ham, and Japheth" (Gen. 6:10). Therefore, this verse fits into a pattern in which the formula frequently introduces genealogies in Genesis, but these cases do not require that the following passage is historically sequential to the previous one.

In fact, the preponderance of the usages of the *toledoth* formula is disjunctive, indicating that a new topic is being discussed, not that the next material will be a sequence that follows from the previous material. It introduces a new topic in two ways: first, the formula regularly introduces a genealogy in Genesis and elsewhere in the Old Testament (see Gen. 10:1; 11:10, 27; 25:12; 36:1, 9; Num. 3:1; Ruth 4:18; 1 Chron. 1:29). Genealogies by nature are disjunctive, and they disrupt the flow of sequential narrative. Second, *toledoth* is a common heading in the book of Genesis announcing a new block of significant writing (see Gen. 2:4; 5:1; 25:19; 37:2). The term itself, *toledoth* ("generations"), derives from the Hebrew root *yld*, and it means "beginnings, births." The *toledoth* formula is, therefore, a caption or heading of what is to come and not a sequential bridge from what went before.[90]

For several reasons, then, Walton's proposal that Genesis 2 reports events long after Genesis 1 is not persuasive as a legitimate interpretation of what is actually in the text.

V. Etiology as Methodology

One of the ways in which some scholars today view the account of creation is through the lens of etiology. "Etiology" in Old Testament studies means claiming that a biblical story was written for the purpose of explaining the existence of some feature in the known world—even if the explanatory story itself does not record any true historical facts. The etymology of the Greek word "etiology" indicates that it means simply "to give a reason for something."[91] The interpretive method of etiology has been practiced in the field of biblical studies for a long time.[92] M. P. Nilsson provides a classic definition of etiological narra-

---

90. Some commentators have argued that Genesis 2:4 is a summation of Genesis 1 rather than a caption to Genesis 2. In response, see J. Brinktrine, "Gn 2, 4a, Überschrift oder Unterschrift?" *Biblische Zeitschrift* 9 (1965): 277.

91. It derives from the Greek *aitia*, "cause, reason."

92. The champions of the etiological perspective were German scholars of the first half of the twentieth century. Classic examples are: Albrecht Alt, *Kleine Schriften*, I (Munich: Beck, 1953);

tive in Greek mythology: " . . . a narrative which seeks to explain why something has come to be, or why it has become such and such."[93]

Critical Old Testament scholars have commonly used etiology as a means to interpret a biblical text and to define why a certain narrative may have been written. I will first provide a couple of examples from other parts of the Old Testament for clarity.

A. Etiology Used to Deny the Historicity of Some Old Testament Events

1. Genesis 19: The Destruction of Sodom and Gomorrah

The Dead Sea region plays a prominent geographical role in parts of the Abrahamic narratives (Genesis 13–14 and 18–19). This area is barren and largely devoid of flora and fauna. The Dead Sea itself lies 1,300 feet below sea level, and its salt concentration is seven times as dense as seawater. No fish are able to live in it. Now, according to some biblical commentators, the writer(s) of Genesis sought to explain the saltiness and barrenness of the Dead Sea area in his(their) day by spinning a tale about the destruction of Sodom and Gomorrah (Gen. 19:24–25). Then, for literary emphasis, the author(s) added a yarn of Lot's wife turning into a pillar of salt (Gen. 19:26). Gerhard Von Rad comments that "it is quite probable that an old aetiological motif is present in the strange death of Lot's wife, i.e., that a bizarre rock formation was the reason for this narrative."[94]

2. Joshua 8:28–29: The Conquest of Ai as an Explanation for a Pile of Rubble

Another example appears in Joshua 8:28–29, and it is what can be called a "double etiology." At the close of the story of Israel's conquest of the city of Ai, two monuments are mentioned in the text. The first memorial is the city of Ai itself in its post-destruction state. Israel has burned it down and it has become "forever a heap of ruins" (v. 28). The

---

Hermann Gunkel, *Die Sagen der Genesis*; and M. Noth, *Das Buch Josua* (Tubingen: J. C. B. Mohr, 1938).

93. M. P. Nilsson, *Geschichte der griechischen Religion*, vol. 1 (Munich: Beck, 1941), 25. Quoted in B. O. Long, *The Problem of Etiological Narrative in the Old Testament*, BZAW 108 (Berlin: de Gruyter, 1968), 1.

94. Gerhard Von Rad, *Genesis* (Göttingen: Vandenhoeck & Ruprecht, 1949), 221.

biblical writer then comments that this heap remains "to this day"—
a reference to the time of the composition of the story. At face value,
the ruins of Ai attest to the victory of Israel over the city of Ai during
the time of Joshua. However, numerous commentators believe that
the biblical author was, in fact, trying to explain why a large, ruined
mound existed in the central highlands, and so he created a fictitious
account (with perhaps a kernel of historical validity).[95] Such stories,
written by Israelites living in the land of Canaan, were purposefully
written to provide justification and explanation for their presence in
the land. This reconstruction is common thought in modern biblical
scholarship.

The second monument at Ai, in addition to the city itself, is a large,
distinctive pile of stones. This is described as "a great heap of stones"
that the people of Israel placed over the body of Ai's king at the gate
of the city. This memorial serves as a warning, and it also remains "to
this day" (Josh. 8:29). Again, many biblical interpreters argue that the
heap of stones preceded the narrative and that it (not any real historical
event) was the reason that the narrative was composed. Thus, rather
than the heap reflecting a prior historical incident, the narrative was
invented to give meaning to the heap.

B. Etiology Used to Deny the Events of the Creation Account

Etiological methodology in biblical studies has also had a recent, strong
impact on the interpretation of the Hebrew creation account. Notre
Dame professor Joseph Blenkinsopp, in his major work on the Pentateuch, makes a case that a parallel exists between Adam and Eve in
the garden and the history of Israel as a nation.[96] He claims that the
story of Adam and Eve was not intended to recount actual historical
events but was created sometime after Israel's exile (after 586 BC) as
an etiological explanation for the exile. He understands that Israel,
like mankind in Genesis 2–3, was placed in a favorable environment,
namely, the Land of Promise that was a veritable garden of Eden. In
this "paradise," Israel is required to obey God's law, and if Israel fails

---

95. See, e.g., the comments of Carolyn Pressler, *Joshua, Judges, and Ruth* (Philadelphia: West-
minster/John Knox, 2002), 63; and Hartmut Rosel, *Joshua* (Louvain: Peeters, 2011), 130–131.

96. Blenkinsopp, *Pentateuch*.

then a curse will descend upon them. This sanction comes to pass when Israel is thrown out of the land into exile, in much the same way as Adam and Eve are expulsed from the garden. Blenkinsopp's argument extends beyond a mere general similarity between the accounts. For instance, he argues that Canaanite cult practices that lure Israel to fall may be compared to the serpent in the garden who tempts Eve. He says, "Behind the figure of the seductive serpent we also detect the cults practiced by the native inhabitants of the land, and behind the words he utters the promises which they hold out for their practitioners."[97] He goes so far as to suggest that the role of Eve in the temptation account may parallel women as a catalyst for adopting pagan cults in the history of Israel (e.g., as in the time of Solomon; 1 Kings 11:1–8).[98]

Blenkinsopp's conclusion is clear and pointed: "One would therefore think that the pattern of events in the history has generated a reflective recapitulation, recasting the national experience in universal terms by the learned use of familiar mythic themes and structures, and placing it at the beginning as a foreshadowing of what was to follow."[99] In other words, the Eden episode is to be "read as a sapiential reflection in narrative form on the historical experience of Israel."[100]

But now at least one Old Testament scholar from the evangelical world has adopted Blenkinsopp's position on the Edenic episode, and his position is promoted as a legitimate view on the BioLogos website. In a white paper hosted by the BioLogos Foundation, Eastern University professor Peter Enns writes, "Israel's history happened first, and the Adam story was written to reflect that history. In other words, the Adam story is really an Israel story placed in primeval time."[101] Consequently, the Adam and Eve episode is to be viewed as etiology. It is a symbolic, even a mythic, account used to explain the origin of Israel. Adam is, therefore, "proto-Israel."[102]

---

97. Ibid., 66.

98. For further parallels, see Martin Emmrich, "The Temptation Narrative of Genesis 3:1–6: A Prelude to the Pentateuch and the History of Israel," *Evangelical Quarterly* 73, no. 1 (2001): 3–20.

99. Blenkinsopp, *Pentateuch*, 66.

100. Ibid., 67; in Old Testament studies, "sapiential" literature is writing that gives wise insight into some aspect of life.

101. Available at Peter Enns, "Understanding Adam," *BioLogos*, https://biologos.org/uploads/projects/enns_adam_white_paper.pdf.

102. Scot McKnight, in Venema and McKnight, *Adam and the Genome*, uncritically accepts Enns's interpretation, and then concludes that Genesis 1–3 "is far more about *Adam and Eve as Israel* than about the historical, biological, and genetic Adam and Eve" (144, emphasis original).

The consequences of this etiological position in respect to the Hebrew creation account are enormous and far-reaching. Enns gets at the heart of it when he says in the BioLogos white paper that the Adam story "is not a story of human origins but of Israel's origins." In other words, the Adamic episode is not an account of the creation of mankind but is "really an Israel story placed in primeval time." If that be the case, then what follows is astounding: according to Enns, "if the Adam story is not about absolute human origins, then the conflict between the Bible and evolution cannot be found there."[103]

Thus, in one full etiological swoop, the ages-long tension between science and the Bible in regard to human origins is solved. Genesis 2–3 is, therefore, a backward projection of Israel's history that is to be read symbolically, and certainly not as a historical account that gives true insight into human origins. Blenkinsopp sums up this kind of position well when he comments, "The impulse to trace the course of history backward to human origins arose not only from a natural curiosity about the remote past, but also a need to validate the present social and political order."[104]

C. Response to Etiological Interpretations

1. The Assumption that Genesis 2–3 Was Written after Israel's Exile

When one considers the validity of an interpretation, it is critical to uncover the various presuppositions that are foundational to the position. No one comes to the biblical material without such presuppositions. At the heart of the etiological interpretation of Genesis 2–3 is the belief that these chapters were composed after the written history of Israel that appears in the historical literature of Judges through 2 Chronicles. This is a critical point. The exile of Judah in 586 BC, for example, must have occurred before the writing of Genesis 2–3 because, according to this view, the content of these two chapters is dependent on the exile already having taken place: Adam's exile from the garden is written as a retroactive reflection of Judah's exile from the Promised Land. This etiological chronology, however, is a titanic assumption that is far from certain.

---

103. Ibid.
104. Blenkinsopp, *Pentateuch*, 54.

The assumption of such a late date of composition for Genesis 2–3 has been foundational to higher critical theories of the Old Testament for many decades.[105] However, there is little agreement among scholars regarding the specific century in which they think this material was written. The early source critics believed that Genesis 2–3 was part of what they called the "J" (Jehovist) source that dated to the time of the United Monarchy (tenth century BC), and this position is held by some more recent commentators as well.[106] Others, to the contrary, argue that this postulated "J" source was a person living in the exilic period (that is, that it was written after 586 BC).[107] R. N. Whybray correctly judges the current state of affairs when he says,

> There is at the present moment no consensus whatever about when, why, how, and through whom the Pentateuch reached its present form, and opinions about the date of composition of its various parts differ by more than five hundred years.[108]

The reality is that an etiological explanation for the Genesis account of human origins is on shaky chronological footing. The assumption that all of Israel's history until the exile occurred prior to the composition of Genesis 2–3, and that the description of human origins is merely a reflective echo, is exactly that . . . merely an assumption.

2. The Assumption that Earlier Events Were Fabricated

A second major presupposition of the etiological method is that the connection between the given phenomenon and its explanation must be artificial and nonhistorical.[109] In other words, a story is fabricated in order to explain, describe, and give meaning to an existing phenomenon. Albrecht Alt and others conclude that etiology is a creative force. The present incident or scene is the causal antecedent of the story/tale.

One problem with this presupposition is the reality that, in Israel's

---

105. See, for instance, John Van Seters, *Abraham in History and Tradition* (New Haven, CT: Yale University Press, 1975); and T. L. Thompson, *Historicity of the Patriarchal Narratives: The Quest for the Historical Abraham* (Berlin: de Gruyter, 1974).

106. See, e.g., T. E. Fretheim, *Creation, Fall, and Flood* (Minneapolis: Augsburg, 1969).

107. Van Seters, *Abraham in History*, 125–153; and R. N. Whybray, *Introduction to the Pentateuch* (Grand Rapids, MI: Eerdmans, 1995).

108. Whybray, *Introduction to the Pentateuch*, 12–13.

109. Brevard S. Childs, "The Etiological Tale Re-Examined," *Vetus Testamentum* 24 (1974): 387–397.

writings, an actual historical event can be the reason for something like the name of a city or location, and thus a "genuinely historical tradition might assume an etiological form."[110] So, for instance, after the Israelites cross into the Land of Promise, Joshua commands that the people be circumcised. It is done at the site of Gibeath-haaraloth: "So Joshua made flint knives and circumcised the sons of Israel at Gibeath-haaraloth" (Josh. 5:3). The Hebrew name Gibeath-haaraloth significantly means "the hill of the foreskins." Its name is an example of a genuine historical etiology, in which the site receives a name based on the incident that occurred there.[111]

Another example from the book of Joshua is the common expression "until this day," or "to this day," as in the story of the death of Achan: "And they raised over him a great heap of stones that remains to this day. Then the LORD turned from his burning anger. Therefore, to this day the name of that place is called the Valley of Achor" (Josh. 7:26). The phrase "to this day" occurs several other times (e.g., Josh. 4:9; 5:9; 8:28, 29; 9:27), and it always is a reference by the biblical writer to the time of the composition of that particular story and not to the time of the episode's occurrence. Many critical scholars believe the phrase "to this day" reflects a nonhistorical etiology in which the author has formulated a story in order to account for a natural phenomenon. But Yale professor Brevard Childs, to the contrary, has demonstrated that the expression "seldom has an etiological function of justifying an existing phenomenon, but in the great majority of cases is a formula of personal testimony added to, and confirming, a received tradition."[112] And, therefore, it is true that biblical writers employ etiology, but much of it is their attempt to explain a real and genuine chronology of events.

In regard to the etiological explanation for Genesis 2–3, Blenkinsopp argues that the biblical writers recast Israel's national experience "in universal terms by the learned use of familiar mythic themes and

---

110. Brevard S. Childs, "A Study of the Formula 'Until This Day'," *Journal of Biblical Literature* 82 (1963): 279–292.

111. The Midrash Rabbah agrees by saying that Gibeath-haaraloth is named this because, "It was the place, said R. Levi, which they had made into a hill by means of foreskins." See H. Freedman and M. Simon, *The Midrash Rabbah*, vol. 3 (London: Soncino, 1977), 422.

112. Childs, "Study of the Formula," 292.

structures."[113] This judgment assumes that Israel's writers accepted the use of nonfactual myth to tell the story of the people and the nation. However, it ignores Israel's deep resistance to anything mythological. In regard to Genesis 1, the immediately preceding chapter, critical scholars have argued for a long time that the biblical writer demythologized the account. In other words, the Hebrew creation account is essentially an ancient Near Eastern myth that has been "cleansed" of its myth by a biblical author. But surely it would be paradoxical if the biblical writer would employ a familiar ancient Near Eastern myth to describe creation and then proceed to demythologize the account. Consequently, the foundational point of the etiological position when it comes to the Hebrew creation account is an "unwarranted mythologizing of Israel's historical tradition."[114]

3. Adam as an Actual Historical Prototype of Israel

Certainly there are thematic parallels between the history of Israel and the Edenic episode of Genesis 2–3. But the most natural way to read the material is *chronologically* and not in a reversal of the sequence of the two events. Adam serves as a genuine historical person who also serves as an archetype or prototype of Israel, and not vice versa.

Therein is the great theological lesson: as Adam was exiled from the garden for not obeying God's word, so Israel, a second Adam, is expelled from the Land of Promise for its failure to keep God's commands. There is, therefore, a need for a true second Adam to come (see 1 Cor. 15:45), to obey God's word, and to secure an inheritance—a true Promised Land (see Heb. 11:15–16)—for the people of God. When understood in this historical, sequential framework, then the question of human origins cannot be swept away by the mere brushstroke of etiology.

VI. Conclusion

As can be seen in these various approaches to the issue of origins, and human origins in particular, the landscape in the field of biblical studies has changed dramatically in recent years. In evangelical Old Testament

---

113. Blenkinsopp, *Pentateuch*, 66.
114. Childs, "Etiological Tale," 396.

scholarship especially, several scholars who confess to orthodox, historic, evangelical Christianity also support evolutionary creation.[115] At the forefront of this movement is the BioLogos Foundation, whose mission is to invite "the church and the world to see the harmony between science and biblical faith as we present an evolutionary understanding of God's creation."[116] At a recent national meeting of the Evangelical Theological Society (Atlanta, 2015), the BioLogos Foundation maintained a booth to promote its evolutionary creation views.

The shape of the debate on origins, and on human origins in particular, will no doubt continue to change. This will happen on both sides of the issue, with science and biblical interpretation. Science, of course, is a continuing process, and new data and theories will emerge. I further suppose that new interpretations of Scripture will appear, but I also think it is likely that the more traditional interpretations will increasingly prevail in the church. At base level, the issue is the same as it has been for more than a hundred and fifty years: does one hold to the complete truthfulness of the facts reported for us in Genesis 1 and 2, and especially in the immediate creation of Adam and Eve as the first humans, or not? This is the question that thundered during the time of the James Woodrow controversy, and it still thunders today.

At least for Presbyterians who affirm the Westminster standards, and I would hope for countless others who believe the Bible, the Westminster Larger Catechism, question 17, satisfactorily summarizes the correct position:

> How did God create man? After God had made all other creatures, he created man male and female; formed the body of the man of the dust of the ground, and the woman of the rib of the man, endued them with living, reasonable, and immortal souls; made them after his own image, in knowledge, righteousness, and holiness; having the law of God written in their hearts, and power to fulfill it, and dominion over the creatures; yet subject to fall.

---

115. The acceptance of evolutionary creation *and* the view that Adam and Eve were not individual, historical, genetic persons from whom all humanity descended has some possible grave, sorrowful consequences. One of these is evident in the recent publication of Venema and McKnight, *Adam and the Genome*, in which McKnight clearly and brazenly denies the historic doctrine of original sin (see, in particular, 139, 145, 183–187). Pelagianism is almost an inevitable result of the denial of the historical Adam and Eve.

116. This mission statement appears on the website biologos.com.

29

Theistic Evolution Is Incompatible with the Teachings of the New Testament

GUY PRENTISS WATERS

SUMMARY

This chapter claims that theistic evolution is incompatible with the teachings of the New Testament. It surveys the passages in the New Testament that address Adam and Eve (as reported in Genesis 1–3) and also passages that reflect on the period of history covered in Genesis 4–11. It shows that the New Testament writers regarded the entirety of Genesis 1–11 in fully historical terms. The chapter also gives closer attention to two of the most extended New Testament expositions of Adam: 1 Corinthians 15:20–22, 44–49; and Romans 5:12–21. Paul understands Adam to be as historical a figure as Jesus of Nazareth, and the biological parent of the entire human race. He also attributes the entrance of sin and death into the human race to the first sin of Adam, and shows that Adam's one sin is imputed to his natural posterity. The chapter finally shows the ways in which leading proponents of theistic evolution depart from the New Testament writers' testimony to Adam and Eve, thereby calling into question the historical underpinnings of the gospel.

. . . . .

Introduction

At first glance, it might appear that the testimony of the New Testament lies at the periphery of discussions concerning the detailed historicity of Adam. The New Testament, after all, makes sparing explicit mention of Adam (Luke 3:38; Rom. 5:14; 1 Cor. 15:22, 45; 1 Tim. 2:13–14; Jude 14; cf. Acts 17:26; 1 Cor. 11:8). These passages, furthermore, add little by way of historical detail to the narratives of Genesis 1–2.

The New Testament's witness to Adam, however, must sit at the very center of these discussions for at least two reasons. First, Christians properly recognize the New Testament as the final and climactic installment of God's inscripturated revelation to his people (Heb. 1:1–2). As such, New Testament revelation is possessed of a clarity and fullness that, relatively speaking, is lacking in Old Testament revelation. This progressive character of special revelation requires that "the Old Testament . . . be read in light of the New" and not vice versa.[1]

Special revelation is also organic in character.[2] One implication of Scripture's organic character is that the New Testament writers' statements about Old Testament people, events, or texts are true to the intention of the original Old Testament authors.[3] We are therefore not in a position to dismiss the statements of Jesus or the apostles concerning the early chapters of Genesis. On the contrary, such statements are faithful expositions of the meaning of those earlier passages. Therefore, when the New Testament authors speak to the historicity or theological significance of Adam, that speech is regulative of our readings of Old Testament passages that speak about Adam.

A second reason for the importance of the New Testament's witness to Adam concerns the content of that witness. The apostle Paul offers two extended reflections on the person and work of Adam in relation to the person and work of Christ (1 Cor. 15:20–22, 44–49;

---

1. Richard B. Gaffin Jr., *No Adam, No Gospel: Adam and the History of Redemption* (Phillipsburg, NJ: P&R, 2015), 9.

2. The organic character of Scripture has been likened to the growth of a tree, from seed to mature plant: "the organic progression is from seed-form to the attainment of full growth; yet we do not say that in the qualitative sense the seed is less perfect than the tree" (Geerhardus Vos, *Biblical Theology: Old and New Testaments* [Edinburgh: Banner of Truth, 1975], 7).

3. The subject of the New Testament's use of the Old Testament is a complex and debated one in contemporary scholarship. For a helpful overview in relation to recent discussions, see G. K. Beale, *The Erosion of Inerrancy in Evangelicalism: Responding to New Challenges to Biblical Authority* (Wheaton, IL: Crossway, 2008).

Rom. 5:12–21). As we will see, the ways in which Paul tethers Adam to Christ has necessary implications for how we are to understand Adam's historicity and the relationship of Adam to the human race. Paul's reflections, furthermore, reveal a macrostructure not only to the history of redemption (Rom. 5:12–21), but also to the whole of human history itself (1 Cor. 15:20–22, 44–49). One is therefore not in a position to relegate Adam to the periphery of the apostle's theology. Furthermore, one is not able to extract Adam's historicity, his relationship with the human race, or his historical work from Paul's teaching without destroying the fundamental integrity of that teaching.

In this chapter, we will first survey the passages in the New Testament that address Adam (and Eve). In addition, in response to attempts to understand much or all of Genesis 1–11 in nonhistorical or semi-historical terms, we will also consider some of the New Testament's reflections on the period of history covered in Genesis 4–11.

Second, we will look at the two most extended expositions of Adam in the New Testament—1 Corinthians 15:20–22, 44–49, and Romans 5:12–21. Here we will see that the apostle Paul understood Adam to be a figure as historical as Jesus of Nazareth, and to be the biological parent of the entire human race. We will also see that Paul attributes the entrance of sin and death to the human race to the first sin of Adam, and that Adam's one sin is imputed to his natural posterity. These New Testament teachings are incompatible with the views of contemporary advocates of theistic evolution.

Third, we will survey the way in which some proponents of theistic evolution have read these New Testament passages, especially Paul's statements concerning Adam in 1 Corinthians and Romans. We will conclude that these readings fail to satisfy the demands of the text. We will also see that these readings effectively undermine the apostle Paul's authority as an apostle of Jesus Christ, and call into question the historical underpinnings of the gospel that Paul preached.

I. Adam and Eve in the New Testament

What is the testimony of the New Testament to Adam and Eve? We will first consider what the New Testament writers explicitly say about

Adam and Eve. We will then broaden our horizon of study to explore the New Testament's testimony to the events recorded in Genesis 4–11.

A. Adam and Eve in the New Testament

1. Luke 3:38

In one of the two New Testament genealogies of Jesus, Luke identifies Jesus as "the son (as was supposed) of Joseph, the son of Heli" (Luke 3:23). Luke proceeds to trace Jesus's descent back to "Adam, the son of God":

> Jesus, when he began his ministry, was about thirty years of age, being the son (as was supposed) of Joseph, the son of Heli, the son of Matthat, the son of Levi, the son of Melchi, the son of Jannai, the son of Joseph. . . . the son of Jacob, the son of Isaac, the son of Abraham, the son of Terah, the son of Nahor, . . . the son of Cainan, the son of Arphaxad, the son of Shem, the son of Noah, the son of Lamech, the son of Methuselah, the son of Enoch, the son of Jared, the son of Mahalaleel, the son of Cainan, the son of Enos, the son of Seth, the son of Adam, the son of God. (Luke 3:23–38)

Setting aside the exegetical questions attending this passage, and the challenges of harmonizing this genealogy with that of Matthew, we may draw a few observations about the way in which Luke presents Adam in this genealogy.[4]

First, Adam appears among dozens of figures whom the biblical writers regard as fully historical ("Jacob . . . Isaac . . . Abraham . . . Noah . . . Seth . . . Adam . . . God"). There is no basis for exempting Adam from this grouping as a nonhistorical or semihistorical figure.[5]

Second, Adam is placed at the head of a linear genealogical sequence.

---

4. For a recent and brief survey of the interpretative issues attending the genealogies in Matthew and Luke, see James R. Edwards, *The Gospel according to Luke*, Pillar New Testament Commentary (PNTC) (Grand Rapids, MI: Eerdmans, 2015), 123–124; and D. R. Bauer, "Genealogy," *Dictionary of Jesus and the Gospels*, ed. Joel B. Green, Jeannine K. Brown, and Nicholas Perrin, 2nd ed. (Downers Grove, IL: InterVarsity Press, 2013), 299–302. A venerable and satisfying harmonization understands Matthew's genealogy to document Jesus's legal line of descent and Luke's genealogy to document Jesus's biological line of descent.

5. "The name of Adam is on a line with all other names. Given the character of the genealogies and the accuracy with which they are attended, it is inconceivable that Luke would have thought about Adam other than as a historical person" (J. P. Versteeg, *Adam in the New Testament: Mere Teaching Model or First Historical Man*, trans. Richard B. Gaffin Jr., 2nd ed. [Phillipsburg, NJ: P&R, 2012], 33).

Each of the human beings in Luke 3:23c–38a traces his descent from Adam. Part of Luke's objective in presenting this genealogy is to show that Jesus, who traces his descent from Adam, is thereby qualified to be the Redeemer of all kinds of people.[6] Back of this message is Luke's conviction that all human beings trace their descent from Adam.[7]

Third, Adam, as a historical person and genealogical progenitor, is the first man. Luke recognizes no progenitor of Adam and thereby exempts him from the normal sequence of biological parentage that follows Adam. The reason for this unique circumstance is that Adam is descended from no man. Adam is, rather, "the son of God," a reference to his special creation in Genesis 1–2. All human beings trace their descent from Adam, while Adam traces his descent from no human.

In view of these observations, it is surprising to see Old Testament professor Peter Enns, an advocate of theistic evolution, claim that "the issues raised by these genealogies (i.e., Luke 3:38 and Jude 14) add little to the conversation" about the historicity of Adam.[8]

Wheaton College professor John H. Walton, on the other hand, acknowledges the theological significance of Luke's genealogy, but dismisses it as a testimony either to the historicity of Adam or to Adam as progenitor of the entire human race.[9] He says that we are simply meant to understand Adam as "the first *significant* human," who, by virtue of his "very particular role" as "federal head" and "priest," had a special "connection to God."[10] He admits that Luke may well have understood Adam to be "the first human being," but says that God merely "use[d] [Luke's] contemporary concepts as a framework for communication."[11]

---

6. Darrell L. Bock, *Luke 1:1–9:50*, Baker Exegetical Commentary on the New Testament (BECNT) (Grand Rapids, MI: Eerdmans, 1994), 359–60; Edwards, *Gospel according to Luke*, 124. The Greek word translated "as was supposed" likely is intended to exempt Jesus from biological descent from Joseph (Robert W. Yarbrough, "Adam in the New Testament," in *Adam, the Fall, and Original Sin: Theological, Biblical, and Scientific Perspectives*, ed. Hans Madueme and Michael Reeves [Grand Rapids, MI: Baker, 2014], 40); Edwards, *Gospel according to Luke*, 122. As Bock notes, "the genealogical line is Joseph's, despite the virgin birth. It is merely a legal line" (*Luke 1:1–9:50*, 352).

7. In view of this conviction, which Luke states at the outset of his gospel, we may concur with Yarbrough's assessment that "Adam is a dominant if unspoken presence in the redemptive narrations of the Gospels and Acts" ("Adam in the New Testament," 41).

8. Peter Enns, *The Evolution of Adam: What the Bible Does and Doesn't Say about Human Origins* (Grand Rapids, MI: Baker, 2012), 150n9.

9. John H. Walton, *The Lost World of Adam and Eve: Genesis 2–3 and the Human Origins Debate* (Downers Grove, IL: InterVarsity Press, 2015), 188.

10. Walton, *Lost World of Adam and Eve*, 188–189, emphasis added.

11. Ibid., 188.

This viewpoint, that Adam was not the first human but the first *significant* human, allows Walton to avoid any conflict with current evolutionary theory, which affirms that the current genetic diversity in the human race does not go back to just one or two human beings but can best be explained by descent from a very early population of approximately ten thousand genetically diverse humans.[12]

The problem with Walton's analysis is that Luke is founding a theological claim upon a historical foundation. If Adam is merely the first *significant* human and not the first human being and the progenitor of all human beings, then Luke's claim that Jesus, by virtue of his genealogy, is qualified to be the Redeemer of all human beings is void. To separate the historical and the theological in Luke's genealogy is to forfeit them both.[13]

2. Acts 17:26

A second reference to Adam in Luke's writings appears in his account of Paul's address to the Areopagus in Athens (Acts 17:26):

> And he made from one man every nation of mankind to live on all the face of the earth, having determined allotted periods and the boundaries of their dwelling place.

Although Paul does not mention Adam by name, he testifies to the universal descent of humanity from a single man, whom Paul knew to be "Adam" (Rom. 5:12–21; 1 Cor. 15:20–22, 44–49).[14]

The Greek text underlying this translation does not explicitly use the word "man." It reads literally "from one" (*ex henos*), but since the Greek word *henos* is a masculine singular form, the translation "from one man" is legitimate. Some proponents of theistic evolution have argued that Paul is not referring to Adam in this expression. Walton argues that the refer-

---

12. See Francis Collins, *The Language of God* (New York: Free Press, 2006), 126; see also 207.

13. G. B. Caird has articulated the point positively: "By calling Adam son of God [Luke] makes a link between the baptism and God's purpose in creation. Man was designed for that close filial relationship to God which was exemplified in Jesus, and which Jesus was to share with those who became his disciples" (*Saint Luke*, PNTC [Middlesex: Penguin 1963], 77–78, cited at Edwards, *Gospel according to Luke*, 124n86).

14. F. F. Bruce, *The Acts of the Apostles: The Greek Text with Introduction and Commentary*, 3rd ed. (Grand Rapids, MI: Eerdmans, 1990), 382; C. K. Barrett, *The Acts of the Apostles*, International Critical Commentaries (ICC), vol. 2 (Edinburgh: T&T Clark, 1998), 842; David Peterson, *The Acts of the Apostles*, PNTC (Grand Rapids, MI: Eerdmans, 2009), 497.

ent is Noah.[15] He concludes that Paul's concern in this speech is "national origins" not "biology or human origins."[16] Paul is therefore said to be referencing the Septuagint translation of Genesis 10:32, in which "the nations" of the earth are said to originate from the three sons of Noah.

Paul, however, must be referring to Adam. David Peterson rightly concludes that the phrase "on all the face of the earth" "echoes the teaching of Genesis 1:28–29," thereby identifying the "one man" as Adam.[17] Furthermore, the conclusion of Paul's speech centers upon the "man" whom God raised and who will judge "the world" at the end of the age (Acts 17:31). The one man, Adam, is a natural and expected counterpoint to the one man, Christ Jesus.[18] As from a man the world has been populated, so by a man the world will be judged. The "one" of Acts 17:26, then, must refer to Adam, the ancestor of every human being. Walton's proposal about Noah is simply not persuasive.

3. Romans 5:12–21

This significant passage begins by saying,

> Therefore, just as sin came into the world through one man, and death through sin, and so death spread to all men because all sinned . . . (Rom. 5:12)

Paul then continues with an extended discussion of the parallels between Adam and Christ. I will treat this passage in more detail in the second section of this chapter.

4. 1 Corinthians 11:8–9

> For man was not made from woman, but woman from man. Neither was man created for woman, but woman for man.

15. John H. Walton, "A Historical Adam: Archetypal Creation View," in *Four Views on the Historical Adam*, ed. Matthew Barrett and Ardel B. Caneday (Grand Rapids, MI: Zondervan, 2013), 105; Walton, *Lost World of Adam and Eve*, 186–187. In addition to Walton, see Denis Alexander, *Creation or Evolution: Do We Have to Choose?*, 2nd ed. (Oxford: Monarch, 2014), 234.

16. Walton, *Lost World of Adam and Eve*, 186.

17. Peterson, *Acts of the Apostles*, 497. In Genesis 1:28–29, God gives to Adam and Eve dominion "over every living thing that moves on the earth" and every plant yielding seed "on the face of all the earth."

18. So rightly E. Jerome Van Kuiken, "John Walton's *Lost Worlds* and God's Loosed Word: Implications for Inerrancy, Canon, and Creation," *Journal of the Evangelical Theological Society* 58, no. 4 (2015): 687. Van Kuiken has also suggestively proposed that "one man" (Acts 17:26) may echo Deuteronomy 4:32 (ibid.).

Although Paul does not mention Adam and Eve by name in 1 Corinthians 11:8–9, these verses summarize the biblical account of the
creation of Adam and Eve in Genesis 1–2.[19] Specifically, Paul recounts
the special creation of Eve from Adam (1 Cor. 11:8; cf. Gen. 2:21–23).
Paul furthermore observes that Eve was created "for man," that is, in
the words of Genesis, to be "a helper fit for him" (1 Cor. 11:9; Gen.
2:18). On the basis of the creation account, Paul issues a command
concerning the deportment in public worship of the wives in the Corinthian church (1 Cor. 11:10).

This passage sheds light on Paul's understanding of Adam and Eve
in at least two respects. First, Paul regards Adam and Eve to have been
historical persons, and the account of Genesis 1–2 to be a historical
account. Second, Paul understands, with Genesis, Eve to have been specially created by God from Adam. Paul's words exclude any scenario
in which Eve may be said to have descended from a previously existing
human being or humanoid.

5. 1 Corinthians 15:20–22 and 44–49

This long discussion about the resurrection includes significant parallels and differences between Adam and Christ, such as this:

> For as by a man came death, by a man has come also the resurrec-
> tion of the dead. For as in Adam all die, so also in Christ shall all
> be made alive. (1 Cor. 15:21–22)

I will treat this passage, as well, more extensively in section 2 of this
chapter.

6. 2 Corinthians 11:3

> But I am afraid that as the serpent deceived Eve by his cunning,
> your thoughts will be led astray from a sincere and pure devo-
> tion to Christ.

---

19. David Garland has observed that "Paul interprets Gen. 1:27 . . . through the creation account in Gen. 2" (*1 Corinthians*, BECNT [Grand Rapids, MI: Eerdmans, 2003], 522). Gordon
Fee sees Genesis 2:23, 18–20 as the verses that Paul especially has in view (*The First Epistle to the
Corinthians*, rev. ed. [Grand Rapids, MI: Eerdmans, 2014], 572). In particular, Fee notes a verbal
reference to the Septuagint translation of Genesis 2:23 in 1 Corinthians 11:8, 12 ("from man")
(ibid., 572n106).

In this passage, Paul is concerned about the spiritually destructive influences of false teachers in Corinth. These teachers are "false apostles, deceitful workmen, disguising themselves as apostles of Christ" (2 Cor. 11:13). Paul likens their strategies to those of Satan. Just as "Satan disguises himself as an angel of light," so these false teachers "disguise themselves as servants of righteousness" (2 Cor. 11:14, 15). Paul assures the Corinthians that the false teachers' "end will correspond to their deeds" (2 Cor. 11:15). That is to say, they will fall under the judgment of God.[20] Just as Satan fell under God's judgment for his role in enticing Eve to sin, so also these false teachers will be held to account for their Satan-like activities.

In 2 Corinthians 11:3, Paul draws a more direct connection between these false teachers and Satan. Paul likens the church in Corinth to Eve. He fears that, just as "the serpent deceived Eve by his cunning," these teachers will lead the Corinthians' thoughts "astray from a sincere and pure devotion to Christ." In the words of Murray Harris, "just as Eve was deceived in her thinking (Gen. 3:1–6) and so lost her innocence (Gen. 3:7), so too the Corinthian church was at risk of being deluded in thought . . . and so losing her virginity."[21]

This extended analogy in 2 Corinthians 11 assumes readers' awareness of the account in Genesis 3. There are verbal echoes of Genesis 3 in 2 Corinthians 11:3, namely "deceived" and "cunning."[22] Moreover, Paul regards this account to be a thoroughly historical account. Satan is a historical personage who poses no less a threat to the Corinthians than he did to Eve.[23] Furthermore, Eve is no less a historical person than the Corinthians are historical people—Paul's warning, in fact, requires the full historicity of Eve.

Not only does Paul understand the narrative of Genesis 3 to be historical, but his argument in 2 Corinthians 11 also assumes the historicity of the previous two chapters of Genesis. Paul's analogy predicates the uprightness and sinlessness of Eve when Satan approached her to

---

20. Paul Barnett, *The Second Epistle to the Corinthians*, New International Commentary on the New Testament (NICNT) (Grand Rapids, MI: Eerdmans, 1997), 527n22.

21. Murray J. Harris, *The Second Epistle to the Corinthians*, New International Greek Testament Commentary (NIGTC) (Grand Rapids, MI: Eerdmans, 2005), 740.

22. See Genesis 3:13; 3:1 ("crafty") (ibid., 740, 741–742).

23. Understanding Satan to be the "cause of any enticement toward disloyalty among the Corinthians" (so, rightly, ibid., 741).

tempt her to sin (see 2 Cor. 11:2–3). Eve's moral rectitude, according to the testimony of Genesis 1:26–31, was concreated. That is to say, God created her a righteous person. That Paul should assume the historicity of this one detail in Genesis 1 confirms his confidence in the historicity of the whole of Genesis 1–2.

7. 1 Timothy 2:11-14

> Let a woman learn quietly with all submissiveness. [12] I do not permit a woman to teach or to exercise authority over a man; rather, she is to remain quiet. [13] For Adam was formed first, then Eve;[14] and Adam was not deceived, but the woman was deceived and became a transgressor.

Paul speaks explicitly about Adam and Eve in 1 Timothy 2:11–14. In the larger context (1 Tim. 2:1–15), Paul is giving the church instructions about public worship. In the course of these instructions, Paul says that he does not permit "a woman to teach or to exercise authority over a man; rather, she is to remain quiet" (1 Tim. 2:12). The ground for this command follows in verse 13: "For Adam was formed first, then Eve."[24] To this ground, Paul appends the observation in verse 14, "and Adam was not deceived, but the woman was deceived and became a transgressor."[25] Both statements treat very specific details of Genesis 2–3 as historical fact, not as parts of a myth or a parable or an allegorical or figurative story.

It is outside the scope of this chapter to address precisely how these statements explicate the command that precedes, or the way in which these verses apply to the church[26] but we may specifically address what

---

24. For an extended, syntactical defense of our saying that verse 13 supplies grounds for verse 12 and is not merely an illustration of verse 12, see William D. Mounce, *The Pastoral Epistles*, Word Biblical Commentary (WBC), vol. 46 (Nashville: Thomas Nelson, 2000), 131–133.

25. Commentators debate the place of 1 Timothy 2:14 in Paul's argument of 1 Timothy 2:11–15, on which see I. H. Marshall, *The Pastoral Epistles*, ICC (Edinburgh: T&T Clark, 1999), 460–461. George W. Knight has argued that "Paul argues not from creation and fall but from creation, and then illustrates this argument, albeit negatively, from the fall . . . " (Knight, *The Pastoral Epistles: A Commentary on the Greek Text*, NIGTC [Grand Rapids, MI: Eerdmans, 1992], 144). While Knight may put matters too strongly here, he is surely correct to highlight the primacy of creation for Paul's argument in 1 Timothy 2:11–15.

26. For detailed exegetical treatments of this text, see especially Douglas Moo, "What Does It Mean Not to Teach or Have Authority over Men?" in *Recovering Biblical Manhood and Womanhood*, ed. John Piper and Wayne Grudem (Wheaton, IL: Crossway, 1991), 179–193; Thomas R. Schreiner, "An Interpretation of 1 Timothy 2:9–15: A Dialogue with Scholarship," in *Women in the Church: An Analysis and Application of 1 Timothy 2:9–15*, ed. Andreas J. Köstenberger and

Paul says here about Adam and Eve. In verse 13, Paul appeals to the creation of Adam and Eve, observing the sequence in which each was formed: "Adam was formed first, then Eve," referring to Genesis 2:7, 22: "then the LORD God formed the man of dust from the ground. . . . And the rib that the LORD God had taken from the man he made into a woman and brought her to the man."[27]

In verse 14, Paul reflects upon the deception and transgression of Eve when he says, "and Adam was not deceived, but the woman was deceived and became a transgressor." This statement is based on Genesis 3:13: "The woman said, 'The serpent deceived me, and I ate.'" Paul cited these specific details in the life of Adam and Eve only because he took Genesis 2–3 as literal history, not as mythological, figurative, or allegorical stories.

In addition, Paul understands the creation of Adam prior to Eve to ground his command to the church in Ephesus. What follows in verse 14 is "by a negative example the importance of heeding the respective roles established by God in the creation of Eve from Adam."[28] Paul is treating the accounts of the creation and the fall as historical accounts that serve as the norm for the way in which human beings subsequent to Adam and Eve are to relate to one another.[29] The historical details of the creation, including the creation of Adam and Eve, provide the basis upon which Paul expects all Christians to order their lives.

Walton has argued that Paul "is using Adam and Eve as illustrations for the Ephesians," and nothing more.[30] He dismisses an "ontological" understanding of Paul's words on the basis that such an understanding would require Paul to say not only "that man by his created nature is first," but also that "woman by her created nature is deceivable."[31] Since, however, "that vulnerability [i.e., "susceptibility to deception"]

Thomas R. Schreiner, 2nd ed. (Grand Rapids, MI: Baker, 2005), 85–120; and Wayne Grudem, *Evangelical Feminism and Biblical Truth* (Sisters, OR: Multnomah, 2004), 279–328.

27. Note the expressly temporal language that Paul uses: "first," "then" (so Moo, "What Does It Mean?," 190). For a fuller statement of the ways in which Genesis 2 lies behind Paul's claim in verse 13, see Mounce, *Pastoral Epistles*, 130–131.

28. Knight, *Pastoral Epistles*, 144. As Schreiner rightly observes, "the appeal to Genesis 3 serves as a reminder of what happens when God's ordained pattern is undermined" ("An Interpretation of 1 Timothy 2:9–15," 115).

29. Knight, *Pastoral Epistles*, 142, 143.

30. Walton, *Lost World of Adam and Eve*, 95.

31. Ibid.

is not ontological to only one gender," Paul's words cannot be onto-logically referential.[32]

But Paul does not say here or elsewhere that women are inherently gullible.[33] Having affirmed that Eve, like Adam, was created (1 Tim. 2:13), Paul proceeds to rehearse the historical account of the deception of Eve, and the subsequent transgression of both Eve and Adam (2:14). Paul recognizes that Eve's deception was subsequent to her creation, but he nowhere ascribes Eve's deception *to* her creation, much less her creation as a woman.[34] What undergirds Paul's injunction in verse 12 is the historical fact that Eve, on this particular occasion, was deceived, not that Eve was created as a gullible person. This circumstance, Paul reasons, served to upend the order that God had established for human beings at the creation (2:13).[35]

Paul, then, is treating the account of Genesis 1–3 as fully histori-cal narrative. He regards Adam and Eve as specially created by God. He regards Eve's deception as a historical event with implications for the way in which, after the fall, her descendants are to relate to one another.[36] Paul's argument in 1 Timothy 2:13–14 requires that Adam and Eve are the first man and woman and, as such, are the parents of every human being. This is why the command of 1 Timothy 2:12 is not provisional but universal.[37] It is not restricted to time, circumstance, or geography, but is for all kinds of people.[38] Were Paul to have regarded

---

32. Ibid.

33. For a partial listing of commentators who have read Paul to say that women are more prone to deception than men, see Schreiner, "An Interpretation of 1 Timothy 2:9-15," 225n210. For fuller discussion, see Daniel Doriani, "Appendix 2: History of the Interpretation of 1 Timothy 2," in *Women in the Church*, ed. A. J. Köstenberger, T. R. Schreiner, and H. S. Baldwin (Grand Rapids, MI: Baker, 1995), 215–269.

34. Furthermore, to say that women are ontologically more gullible than men counters Paul's earlier affirmation of the ontologically equality of men and women (1 Cor. 11:11–12).

35. For support of this view, see Moo, "What Does It Mean?," 190.

36. As Philip Towner has observed, to women in Ephesus who were "influenced to think that they were free from the constraints and limitations brought on by the fall, [Paul] reminds women of their role in the fall and of the present unfinished nature of Christian existence" ("1–2 Timothy and Titus," in *Commentary on the New Testament Use of the Old Testament*, ed. G. K. Beale and D. A. Carson [Grand Rapids, MI: Baker, 2007], 897, as cited in Yarbrough, "Adam in the New Testament," 50). In this respect, as Towner also notes, Paul's argument in 1 Timothy 2 is of a piece with his broader argument in this letter that Christians live within the callings, norms, and boundaries established by God for all humanity at creation (ibid.).

37. See further Moo, "What Does It Mean?," 188ff.; Grudem, *Evangelical Feminism and Bibli-cal Truth*, 280–288, 296–302.

38. This is not to say, of course, that local circumstances or conditions did not occasion Paul's teaching in these verses. As Moo argues, "local or cultural issues may have provided the *context* of the issue, [but] they do not provide the *reason* for his advice" ("What Does It Mean?," 190). The reason that Paul gives, rather, "is the created role relationship of man and woman" (ibid.).

"Adam and Eve" as "mere mythological symbols of the timeless truth that men pre-exist women," then "Paul's argument would collapse into nonsense."[39]

8. Jude 14

In the midst of a warning (Jude 3–16) about false teachers who are threatening the churches of which Jude's readers are a part, Jude reminds his audience that these false teachers were the concern of earlier prophecy. Specifically,

> Enoch, the seventh from Adam, prophesied, saying, "Behold, the Lord came with ten thousands of his holy ones . . . " (Jude 14)

Jude here identifies "Enoch" as descended from Adam, in the seventh generation from Adam. He treats Enoch as a historical personage, who utters the prophesies documented in verses 14–15. The fact that Enoch is identified as "the seventh from Adam" not only confirms Enoch's historicity but also assumes Adam's historicity.

The citation in verses 14–15 has been the subject of considerable academic attention.[40] Many scholars have observed the similarities between the words that Jude records here and *1 Enoch* 1:9, a pseudepigraphical book, authored between the third and first centuries BC, that has a complicated literary history.[41] Scholars have differed over how to account for these similarities.[42] Most now agree that Jude has quoted from some version of *1 Enoch* available to him.[43] Some have argued that Jude quotes from a book that his opponents regarded as authoritative, but that Jude did not. Others more plausibly have suggested that Jude regarded these words as a historically accurate, authentic utterance of the prophet

---

39. Michael Reeves, "Adam and Eve," in *Should Christians Embrace Evolution? Biblical and Scientific Responses*, ed. Norman C. Nevin (Phillipsburg, NJ: P&R, 2009), 44.

40. For overviews, see representatively Richard J. Bauckham, *Jude, 2 Peter*, WBC, vol. 50 (Waco, TX: Word, 1983), 93–101; Thomas R. Schreiner, *1, 2 Peter, Jude*, New American Commentary, vol. 37 (Nashville: B&H, 2003), 468–473; Peter H. Davids, *The Letters of 2 Peter and Jude*, PNTC (Grand Rapids, MI: Eerdmans, 2006), 75–80.

41. On which, see Davids, *Letters of 2 Peter and Jude*, 77.

42. For what follows, see D. A. Carson, "Jude," in *Commentary on the New Testament Use of the Old Testament*, 1078.

43. On the particular text that Jude used, see the discussion at Bauckham, *Jude, 2 Peter*, 94–96. Bauckham concludes that Jude "*knew* the Greek version, but made his own translation from the Aramaic" (96, emphasis original).

Enoch, an utterance that, in the providence of God, was preserved in *1 Enoch*.[44]

Walton has characterized the words of Jude 14–15 as a "*literary* factuality (yes, this is how the familiar story goes)" rather than a "*historical* factual[ity] (yes, this is what really happened in time and space)."[45] Jude, then, is quoting a myth or story that is part of the common cultural vocabulary of his audience. To take Jude as historically factual, Walton reasons, requires one to conclude that the (historical) Enoch was the "author of the intertestamental book of *Enoch*."[46]

But this is surely an unnecessary inference. One may cogently argue that *1 Enoch* preserves some authentic statements of the historical Enoch, the seventh from Adam, without attributing the whole of *1 Enoch* to the historical Enoch. That Jude identifies Enoch with a precise genealogical marker and quotes him in the train of a host of historical Old Testament references (Jude 5–11) indicates Jude's understanding of Enoch in Jude 14–15 as a historical person.[47] That Enoch is said to be "the seventh from Adam" furthermore requires the conclusion that Jude understood Adam to be no less a historical person than Enoch. Versteeg rightly notes, "When [Jude] calls Enoch 'the seventh from Adam,' he sees a specific historical distance between Enoch and Adam."[48] Jude makes this statement because he regards the narratives about both Adam and Enoch in Genesis 1–5 as historically accurate.

Jude's identification of Enoch as "the seventh from Adam" points to an important but distinct strand of the New Testament's testimony to the historicity of Adam. It is that the New Testament writers do not separate the events of the first two chapters of Genesis from conventional space-time history. The creation of Adam and Eve is as qualitatively historical as any other event documented in biblical history. It is neither mythological nor semihistorical. For this reason, then, Jude

---

44. Schreiner, *1, 2 Peter, Jude*, 469. This observation need not commit one to the conclusion that the entirety of *1 Enoch* is genuine prophecy, or that *1 Enoch* has a warranted claim to belong to the canon of Scripture; see Schreiner, ibid., and Carson, "Jude," 1078.

45. Walton, *Lost World of Adam and Eve*, 100, emphasis added.

46. Ibid.

47. The Old Testament references include "disobedient Israelites (v. 5); rebellious angels (v. 6); residents of Sodom and Gomorrah (v. 7); and an unholy trio consisting of Cain, Balaam, and Korah (v. 11)" (Yarbrough, "Adam in the New Testament," 35).

48. Versteeg, *Adam in the New Testament*, 43.

without qualification or defense yokes Enoch to Adam. Both men are fully and equally historical persons.

Both Adam and Enoch, furthermore, occupy the same historical space as other events that Jude mentions from the Pentateuch—the exodus (Jude 5, "Jesus who saved a people out of the land of Egypt . . . "); the destruction of Sodom and Gomorrah (Jude 7, "just as Sodom and Gomorrah and the surrounding cities, which likewise indulged in sexual immorality and pursued unnatural desire, serve as an example by undergoing a punishment of eternal fire"); Cain's murder of Abel, the prophetic activity of Balaam, and Korah's rebellion (Jude 11, "Woe to them! For they walked in the way of Cain and abandoned themselves for the sake of gain to Balaam's error and perished in Korah's rebellion"). This conjunction of events in the letter indicates that Jude did not understand the events of Genesis 1–11 as a semihistorical or mythological prologue to the events documented in Genesis 12ff. He understood Genesis 1–11 to be fully historical.

B. Other Texts about Genesis 1–11 in the New Testament

1. Matthew 1:1

> The book of the genealogy of Jesus Christ, the son of David, the son of Abraham . . .

Many commentators have observed how the opening line of Matthew's Gospel intentionally echoes portions of the book of Genesis. Specifically, Matthew's opening words ("the book of the genealogy") are identical with the Septuagint translation of Genesis 2:4 ("These are the generations of the heavens and the earth when they were created, in the day that the LORD God made the earth and the heavens") and of Genesis 5:1 ("This is the book of the generations of Adam"). Since, as R. T. France has observed, "the phrase occurs nowhere else in the [Septuagint]," Matthew must be intentionally connecting the opening of his Gospel with "the opening chapters of Genesis."[49]

What is the significance of this Matthean literary connection with Genesis? First, Matthew intends for his readers to understand his historical account of the birth, life, death, and resurrection of

---

49. R. T. France, *The Gospel of Matthew*, NICNT (Grand Rapids, MI: Eerdmans, 2007), 26n1.

Jesus Christ in light of the biblical narrative of Genesis. Matthew's genealogy explicitly situates the life and ministry of Jesus within the larger "history of the people of God from its very beginning with Abraham, the ancestor of Israel."[50] Matthew's phrase "the book of the genealogy" furthermore compels readers to place the life and ministry of Jesus in the wider history narrated in the first chapters of Genesis.

Second, this connection shows that Matthew understands the narrative of Genesis to be as fully historical as the narrative of Jesus Christ that follows Matthew 1:1–17. Matthew thus regards Adam and Eve to be fully historical persons. He regards the details of their creation in Genesis 2:4b–25 to be fully historical. He does not situate either the persons or the origins of Adam and Eve in a mythological or prehistorical past. For Matthew, history is a seamless garment running from creation through Abraham and Jesus Christ to "the end of the age" (Matt. 28:20).[51]

2. Matthew 19:4–6

> He answered, "Have you not read that he who created them from the beginning made them male and female, and said, 'Therefore a man shall leave his father and his mother and hold fast to his wife, and the two shall become one flesh'? So they are no longer two but one flesh. What therefore God has joined together, let not man separate."

Jesus addresses the institution of marriage at the creation at Matthew 19:4–6 (citing Gen. 2:24). We are not at liberty to say, with Denis O. Lamoureux, that Jesus "was accommodating to the Jewish belief of the day that Adam was a real person."[52] The distinction that Jesus draws between the grant of the certificate of divorce through Moses and "the beginning" (Matt. 19:8) is a fundamentally historical one. Jesus therefore understands the institution of marriage (Gen. 2:24) and the subsequent giving of the law through Moses to exist on a single

---

50. Ibid., 29.
51. On Matthew's word "end" (28:20) as an echo of Matthew's word "genealogy" (1:1), see John Nolland, *The Gospel of Matthew*, NIGTC (Grand Rapids, MI: Eerdmans, 2005),71.
52. Denis O. Lamoureux, "No Historical Adam: Evolutionary Creation View," in Barrett and Caneday, *Four Views on the Historical Adam*, 60.

historical continuum. Furthermore, Jesus's statement, "but from the beginning it was not so," independently testifies to the fall of humanity in Adam as marking a decisive shift in the human experience of marriage.[53] Jesus's words assume the universal ramifications of Adam's one sin for the entire human race.[54]

3–4. Matthew 23:35 and Luke 11:51

> ... so that on you may come all the righteous blood shed on earth, from the blood of righteous Abel to the blood of Zechariah the son of Barachiah, whom you murdered between the sanctuary and the altar. (Matt. 23:35)

> ... from the blood of Abel to the blood of Zechariah, who perished between the altar and the sanctuary. Yes, I tell you, it will be required of this generation. (Luke 11:51)

In this statement, Jesus references Cain's murder of Abel (Genesis 4). He places that event on the same historical continuum as the martyrdom of "Zechariah the son of Barachiah" (Matt. 23:35), recorded at 2 Chronicles 24:21. Scholars dispute the precise identification of "Zechariah the son of Barachiah," but many have plausibly identified him with the prophet Zechariah mentioned in 2 Chronicles 24:20–22.[55] On this identification, Jesus is speaking about the range of martyred prophets across the Old Testament Canon (Genesis–Chronicles).[56] Jesus's words are not only a testimony to the historicity of Abel but also a testimony to the historicity of the entirety of Genesis.[57] We have no reason to doubt, then, that Jesus regarded the entirety of the events of Genesis to be fully historical. But if someone claims that the early chapters of Genesis are mythological or merely

---

53. France, *Gospel of Matthew*, 720.

54. Yarbrough, "Adam in the New Testament," 41; C. John Collins, *Did Adam and Eve Really Exist?: Who They Were and Why You Should Care* (Wheaton, IL: Crossway, 2011), 77.

55. See the discussion at Nolland, *Gospel of Matthew*, 946–947.

56. As France has observed, "the death of Zechariah in the late ninth century BC was of course not the last martyrdom in historical sequence, but because it is recorded toward the end of 2 Chronicles, the last book of the Hebrew canon, it suitably rounds off the biblical record of God's servants killed for their loyalty" (France, *Gospel of Matthew*, 880). "The scope is mapped," Nolland argues, "by the choice of the first and last pertinent murders in the Hebrew Bible" (Nolland, *Gospel of Matthew*, 947).

57. That is to say, had there been a martyred prophet prior to Abel in Genesis, we fully expect that Jesus would have mentioned him, and mentioned him as a historical person.

allegorical fiction, does this claim not imply that Jesus was mistaken in his belief?

5–6. Matthew 24:37–38 and Luke 17:26–27

> For as were the days of Noah, so will be the coming of the Son of Man. For as in those days before the flood they were eating and drinking, marrying and giving in marriage, until the day when Noah entered the ark, . . . (Matt. 24:37–38)

> Just as it was in the days of Noah, so will it be in the days of the Son of Man. They were eating and drinking and marrying and being given in marriage, until the day when Noah entered the ark, and the flood came and destroyed them all. (Luke 17:26–27)

Jesus here predicts the sudden character of his return in glory to judge the world. Unbelievers will not be prepared for his return and will be taken by surprise when it happens. Jesus likens this state of affairs to "the days of Noah." People went about their daily activities until they were overtaken by the divine judgment of the flood. Noah escaped this judgment because he heeded God's Word and "made advance preparation."[58] The same principle applies to humanity in anticipation of the return of Christ—those who heed Christ's Word and prepare will be spared the judgment that will fall upon human beings. Jesus's warning employs an analogy that requires Jesus's acceptance of the historicity of Noah and of the biblical narrative about Noah (Genesis 6–9). It is further indication that Jesus regarded the opening chapters of Genesis as fully historical.

7. Romans 8:18–23

> For I consider that the sufferings of this present time are not worth comparing with the glory that is to be revealed to us. For the creation waits with eager longing for the revealing of the sons of God. For the creation was subjected to futility, not willingly, but because of him who subjected it, in hope that the creation itself will be set free from its bondage to corruption and obtain the freedom of the glory of the children of God. For we know that the whole creation

---

58. France, *Gospel of Matthew*, 940.

has been groaning together in the pains of childbirth until now. And not only the creation, but we ourselves, who have the firstfruits of the Spirit, groan inwardly as we wait eagerly for adoption as sons, the redemption of our bodies.

In these verses, Paul contrasts the "sufferings of this present time" with "the glory that is to be revealed to us." The revelation of this glory is something that even the creation eagerly anticipates. The creation does so because it "was subjected to futility," is presently in "bondage to corruption," and now "groan[s] together in the pains of childbirth until now." That creation "was subjected to futility" means two things. First, the present state of affairs here described by Paul did not characterize creation at its inception. Second, creation did not choose, as it were, its present condition. God has consigned the creation to its present condition.[59] We have, then, an "obvious reference to the Gen. 3 narrative," and a "commentary on Genesis 3:17, 18."[60] The "hope" appended to this subjection, then, must refer to the hope offered in the divine promise of Genesis 3:15—"the very decree of subjection was given in the context of hope."[61] Paul, then, regards the opening chapters of Genesis to be fully historical. The world that God created has, in light of the fall of Adam into sin, been subjected to the curse of God. This subjection, however, was attended by a promise that the creation would become at the consummation a fit and glorious habitation for the children of God. This state of affairs constitutes no small part of the hope that the gospel holds out to suffering Christians in the present. Were the opening chapters of Genesis anything less than fully historical, then the hope that Paul sets before Christians in these verses would be illusory.

8. Hebrews 11:1–7

Now faith is the assurance of things hoped for, the conviction of things not seen. [2] For by it the people of old received their commendation. [3] By faith we understand that the universe was created by

---

59. Taking "God" as the implied agent of the passive verb, "was subjected," on which see Douglas J. Moo, *The Epistle to the Romans*, NICNT (Grand Rapids, MI: Eerdmans, 1996), 516.
60. Moo, *Epistle to the Romans*, 515; John Murray, *Epistle to the Romans*, cited at ibid.
61. Ibid., 516.

the word of God, so that what is seen was not made out of things that are visible.

⁴ By faith Abel offered to God a more acceptable sacrifice than Cain, through which he was commended as righteous, God commending him by accepting his gifts. And through his faith, though he died, he still speaks. ⁵ By faith Enoch was taken up so that he should not see death, and he was not found, because God had taken him. Now before he was taken he was commended as having pleased God. ⁶ And without faith it is impossible to please him, for whoever would draw near to God must believe that he exists and that he rewards those who seek him. ⁷ By faith Noah, being warned by God concerning events as yet unseen, in reverent fear constructed an ark for the saving of his household. By this he condemned the world and became an heir of the righteousness that comes by faith.

The writer to the Hebrews presents a table of examples of persevering faith (Heb. 10:39) in Hebrews 11:1–40. Beginning with the creation (Heb. 11:1–3), the writer draws examples of faith from Abel (11:4, "by faith Abel offered to God a more acceptable sacrifice than Cain, through which he was commended as righteous, God commending him by accepting his gifts"; cf. Genesis 4); Enoch (11:5, "by faith Enoch was taken up so that he should not see death, and he was not found, because God had taken him"; cf. Genesis 5); Noah (11:7, "by faith Noah, being warned by God concerning events as yet unseen, in reverent fear constructed an ark for the saving of his household"; cf. Genesis 6); Abraham (11:8–19); Isaac (11:20); Jacob (11:21); Joseph (11:22); Moses (11:23–29); and multiple judges and prophets, some named and some unnamed (11:32–38). While the writer has clear exhortatory purposes in this catalog (11:39–12:1), the very nature of the writer's exhortations to persevere in faith requires that each of the individuals named be flesh and blood human beings.⁶² Nonhistorical figures could not persuasively model persever-

---

62. There are other considerations, noted by C. John Collins, including Hebrews's reference to the individuals of Hebrews 11 as "the people of old" (Heb. 11:2); the fact that "the list begins with an affirmation about the creation of the universe, which is taken to be an actual event"; and the fact that "these people [will] be 'made perfect' along with himself and his audience (v. 40) . . ." (*Did Adam and Eve Really Exist?*, 91). F. F. Bruce argues that the "catalog of spiritual heroism" of Hebrews 11 falls in a "literary genre" attested elsewhere in Jewish literature (Sir. 44:1–50:21;

ing faith for historical people. The writer evidences no categorical distinction of historicity between, for example, the account of Abel and the account of Moses. Each person occupies the same historical space. The very way in which the writer crafts his argument in this chapter, then, indicates his understanding of the entirety of biblical narrative, extending back to its earliest beginnings, as fully and conventionally historical.[63]

9. Hebrews 12:24

> . . . and to Jesus, the mediator of a new covenant, and to the sprinkled blood that speaks a better word than the blood of Abel.

In the previous chapter, the writer to the Hebrews references Abel as a historical person. In this chapter, the writer once again references Abel in the same fashion. Here, Abel is brought into relation with Jesus Christ. Abel is in view as the righteous sufferer, martyred by his brother, Cain. The writer likely references God's words to Cain in Genesis 4:10 that "the voice of your brother's blood is crying to me from the ground." The blood of Abel called for "vengeance against Cain," but Christ's blood brings salvation to sinners.[64] In placing Abel and Jesus in the relation that he does, the writer understands Abel to be as historical a figure as he understands Jesus to be. That is to say, the writer understands Genesis 4 to be a record of fully historical persons and events.

10. 1 Peter 3:20

> . . . because they formerly did not obey, when God's patience waited in the days of Noah, while the ark was being prepared, in which a few, that is, eight persons, were brought safely through water.

---

1 Macc. 2:51–60; cf. 4 Macc. 16:20ff., 18:11ff.) (*The Epistle to the Hebrews*, NICNT [Grand Rapids, MI: Eerdmans, 1990], 278). The Jewish catalogs that Bruce mentions all commend *historical* figures to readers' attention. See the fuller listings at Paul Ellingworth, *The Epistle to the Hebrews: A Commentary on the Greek Text*, NIGTC (Grand Rapids, MI: Eerdmans, 1993), 560–561; and Peter T. O'Brien, *The Letter to the Hebrews*, PNTC (Grand Rapids, MI: Eerdmans, 2010), 395. O'Brien also notes that Hebrews sets the historical exemplars of this chapter in their historical, narratival sequence: "our author's examples, like many Jewish lists, create a sustained account of Israel's history" (ibid.).

63. As C. John Collins has rightly observed, "if . . . the author of Hebrews assumes the historicity of these characters from Genesis 4–5, there is no reason to exclude Adam and Eve from the same assumption" (*Did Adam and Eve Really Exist?*, 91).

64. Ellingworth, *Hebrews*, 682.

In this verse, Peter crisply summarizes the events narrated in Genesis 6–9. Noah prepared the ark that he, his wife, his three sons, and their wives entered. God stayed his hand of judgment until Noah had finished building the ark. Having entered the ark, these eight persons were delivered from that judgment, having been "brought safely through water." Peter proceeds to draw a comparison between these events and the experience of Christians with the sacrament of baptism (1 Pet. 3:21). Peter understands the waters of judgment in Genesis 6–9 to be typological of the judgment that Christ has undergone for his people.[65] It is of this eschatological judgment that Christian baptism is a sign. Like Noah, believers, united with Christ in his death and resurrection, have been delivered through judgment. In these verses, Peter treats the narrative of Genesis 6–9 as fully historical in character. The comparison that Peter draws between Noah and the new covenant community, furthermore, assumes that God's dealings with Noah are as fully and as truly historical as his dealings with Christ in Christ's death and resurrection.

11. 2 Peter 2:5

> . . . if he did not spare the ancient world, but preserved Noah, a
> herald of righteousness, with seven others, when he brought a flood
> upon the world of the ungodly; . . .

Peter again appeals to Noah with reference to the judgment of the flood of Genesis 6–9. God spared Noah "with seven others" from the "flood" that he "brought . . . upon the world of the ungodly," that is, "the ancient world." He infers from God's actions in the distant past God's ability "to rescue the godly from trials . . . " (2 Pet. 2:9). The "trials" that are facing Peter's readership are occasioned by the presence and activity of false teachers in their midst (2:1–3). Peter encourages his readers by appealing to God's preservation of his people in times past. If God was willing to preserve his people then, Peter reasons, he is no less willing to preserve his people now. That Peter makes such an argument indicates his conviction that the events of Genesis 6–9 are fully historical in nature.

---

65. Schreiner, *1, 2 Peter, Jude*, 193. Schreiner further notes, "The waters of baptism, like the waters of the flood, demonstrate that destruction is at hand, but believers are rescued from these waters in that they are baptized with Christ . . . " (194).

12. 1 John 3:12

We should not be like Cain, who was of the evil one and murdered his brother. And why did he murder him? Because his own deeds were evil and his brother's righteous.

This reference to Cain constitutes the sole explicit "reference to the [Old Testament] in 1 John."[66] Cain here is said to be "of the evil one," that is, one who is spiritually allied to Satan. He shows his allegiance to Satan by his heinous act of fratricide, his murder of Abel. John further specifies what motivated Cain to do this "evil" deed. It was that his brother's "deeds" were "righteous." John proceeds to broaden his concern from Cain specifically to "the world" generally.[67] As righteous Abel, allied with God against Satan, was hated by Cain, so those who have been "born of God" will be hated by the world (3:9, 13). On the other hand, John warns believers not to "be like Cain," who hated his brother (3:12, 15). John's argument treats the account of Cain and Abel in Genesis 4 as relating fully historical events. The nature of the analogy that John draws between Cain and the "world," and the warning in verse 15 (" . . . you know that no murderer has eternal life abiding in him") undergirded by that analogy require, furthermore, that Cain be a fully historical personage.

13. Jude 11

Woe to them! For they walked in the way of Cain and abandoned themselves for the sake of gain to Balaam's error and perished in Korah's rebellion.

Jude warns his readers at length about false teachers who "pervert the grace of our God into sensuality and deny our only Master and Lord Jesus Christ" (Jude 4). Here Jude pronounces a word of judgment ("Woe to them!") upon these false teachers and proceeds to offer reasons ("for") why they are subject to this judgment. Jude first says that "they walked in the way of Cain," that is, "they have followed in Cain's footsteps by imitating his sin."[68] In saying this, Jude

---

66. Stephen S. Smalley, *1, 2, 3 John*, WBC, vol. 51 (Waco, TX: Word, 1984), 183.
67. Ibid., 185.
68. Richard Bauckham, *Jude, 2 Peter*, WBC, vol. 50 (Waco, TX: Word, 1983), 80.

"hint[s] that to follow in Cain's path will lead to Cain's fate."[69] Jude immediately follows this comparison with Cain with two further comparisons, Balaam (Numbers 22–24) and Korah (Numbers 16). As we have observed above, the fact that Jude conjoins these three persons indicates his belief that they are equally and fully historical. One is not in a position, then, to understand Cain in mythological or subhistorical terms. Furthermore, Scripture records that each of these three persons came under the judgment of God for his sin. Jude is able to pronounce a word of judgment on false teachers in his own generation because God brought his own opponents under judgment in past generations. Jude's word of woe, in other words, requires that all three men (Cain, Balaam, and Korah) be fully historical persons.

II. The Significance of Adam in the New Testament

We have surveyed the testimony of multiple New Testament authors to the historicity of Adam and Eve. And they affirm much more than the mere fact that there once existed two individuals named Adam and Eve. Without exception, the New Testament writers uphold the full historicity of both Adam and Eve, affirming many specific details about their lives as recorded in Genesis 1–3. They clearly regard Adam and Eve to be the first human beings, having been specially created by God. They affirm both the order in which they were created (Adam, then Eve) and the fact that Eve was specially created from Adam. They understand every human being to be descended from Adam. They recognize that Eve was deceived by Satan. They confess Adam to be the man through whom sin entered into the world, and the occasion of the creation's subjection to futility.

The New Testament writers' affirmations about Adam and Eve occur in the context of an unswerving and uncompromising commitment to the full historicity of the events recorded in Genesis 1–11, and the full trustworthiness of the record of those events, that is, the Old Testament Scripture. We should furthermore appreciate the wide range of the New Testament authors who testify to the historicity of Adam and Eve. Matthew, Luke, John, Paul, the author of Hebrews, Peter,

---

69. Ibid., 81.

and Jude all concur in their testimony to the historicity of the events recorded in the opening chapters of Genesis. We should finally register the fact that no New Testament author mounts an apologetic for the historicity of the events under review.[70] The reason that they mount no apologetic is that none was needed in the first-century church. We have no record from the New Testament of any early Christian denying the historicity of Adam, Eve, or any person or event from the opening chapters of Genesis. In light of these considerations, we must pause to ask, were the New Testament authors incorrect in these beliefs?

The apostle Paul offers two extended reflections on Adam, in 1 Corinthians and in Romans, and I will now consider these passages in more detail. In these passages, Paul not only affirms the historicity of Adam but also reflects at length on the significance of Adam's person and work. In both places, Paul tethers Adam's person and work to the person and work of Christ. In light of this conjunction, we will consider what implications questioning the historicity of the details from Genesis 1–3 about the life of Adam may have for the historical integrity of the gospel that Paul preached.

A. 1 Corinthians 15:20–22, 44–49

Paul's argument in 1 Corinthians 15 is in three parts. In 1 Corinthians 15:1–11, Paul defends the bodily resurrection as an essential part of "the gospel I preached to you" (15:1, cf. v. 2, "the word I preached to you"); in verses 12–34 he addresses the "that" of the bodily resurrection; and in verses 35–58 he addresses the "how" of the bodily resurrection.[71]

Paul addresses "Adam" in the latter two sections of the argument of the chapter. The section that is most relevant for our purposes is this:

> But in fact Christ has been raised from the dead, the firstfruits of those who have fallen asleep. For as by a man came death, by a man has come also the resurrection of the dead. For as in Adam all die, so also in Christ shall all be made alive. (1 Cor. 15:20–22)

---

70. In fact, Peter appeals both to the fact of the creation of the world and to the judgment of the world by the flood to prove an event that false teachers in his day were denying—the future and glorious return of Christ in judgment (see 2 Pet. 3:1–7).

71. Herman Ridderbos, *Paul: An Outline of His Theology*, trans. John Richard de Witt (Grand Rapids, MI: Eerdmans, 1975), 540.

In verse 22, Paul sets in antithetical parallel "Adam" and "Christ": "for as in Adam all die, so also in Christ shall all be made alive." Adam is the "man" of the previous verse—"for as by *a man* came death, by *a man* has come also the resurrection of the dead" (v. 21). The two men are similar in that they are representative persons. Death comes to "all" those who are "in Adam"; resurrection life comes to "all" those who are "in Christ."[72] Each is "a man" whose actions come into the possession of those human beings whom they represent. The two men are different with respect to their actions as representative persons. Adam has brought "death," so that "in Adam all die" (vv. 21, 22). Christ has brought the "resurrection of the dead," so that "in Christ . . . all [are] made alive" (vv. 21, 22). The phrase "of the dead" (v. 21) has reference to the "death" of verse 21 and "die" of verse 22. Christ, by his resurrection, reverses and overcomes for his people the death that is theirs in Adam. The death that Christ has overcome, we should note, is not merely spiritual death. Christ has also overcome the physical death that came to human beings because of Adam's sin.

We may draw two important implications from Paul's statements in these verses. First, the parallel that Paul establishes between Adam and Christ not only requires that each be a representative figure, but also that each be a representative *man* (v. 21). To question or to compromise the humanity of the one is necessarily to question or to compromise the humanity of the other. Second, Paul's claims about Adam and Christ in these verses lie not on the periphery but at the heart of his gospel. The resurrection is among the matters "of first importance" that Paul delineates at verses 3–4. Since Paul explicates the resurrection of the man Christ in terms of the death that the man Adam has brought to the human race, Paul inseparably yokes the historicity of each man to the resurrection of Christ. The historicity of Adam, then, is not a disposable element of Paul's teaching concerning the resurrection of Christ.

Paul continues his comparison of Adam and Christ in verses 44b–49:

---

72. That these respective outcomes belong to those and only those who are "in" each respective person suffices to eliminate universalism as a legitimate reading of this verse. Paul is not saying that every human being will be saved, that is, receive resurrection life in Christ. He is saying that all those who are united with Christ will receive the resurrection life that he has won on their behalf (Gordon Fee, *The First Epistle to the Corinthians*, rev. ed., NICNT [Grand Rapids, MI: Eerdmans, 2014], 832).

If there is a natural body, there is also a spiritual body. Thus it is written, "The first man Adam became a living being"; the last Adam became a life-giving spirit. But it is not the spiritual that is first but the natural, and then the spiritual. The first man was from the earth, a man of dust; the second man is from heaven. As was the man of dust, so also are those who are of the dust, and as is the man of heaven, so also are those who are of heaven. Just as we have borne the image of the man of dust, we shall also bear the image of the man of heaven.

In 1 Corinthians 15:44–49, Paul maintains his focus on the two men, Adam and Christ, but he broadens that horizon beyond the scope of verses 21–22. As Richard B. Gaffin Jr. has observed, "in 1 Corinthians 15:44b–49 [Paul's] perspective is the most comprehensive possible, covering nothing less than the whole of human history from its beginning to its end, from the original creation to its consummation."[73] In 1 Corinthians 15:44–49, both Adam and Christ are representative persons.[74] Adam is "the first man Adam" (v. 45) and "the first man" (v. 47). Christ is "the last Adam" (v. 45) and "the second man" (v. 47).

One difference from Paul's argument earlier in the chapter is that the apostle here enumerates each man. Adam is "first"; Jesus is "second" and "last." This enumeration conveys how sweeping the reach of the work of each man is. That Christ is the "second man" indicates that there is no representative person that stands between Adam and Christ. That Christ is the "last Adam" indicates that there is no representative person or age that will follow Christ. That Adam is "first" indicates that there is no representative person who precedes Adam. The "contrast between Adam and Christ" here "is not only pointed but also comprehensive and exclusive."[75]

There is another difference between Paul's presentation of Adam in 1 Corinthians 15:21–22 and his presentation of Adam in verses 44–49. In the earlier verses, Adam is the one through whom "death" comes to

---

73. Gaffin, *No Adam, No Gospel*, 9. See further Richard B. Gaffin Jr., *Resurrection and Redemption: A Study in Paul's Soteriology*, 2nd ed. (Phillipsburg, NJ: P&R, 1987), 78–92.

74. I have drawn the material that follows from my "1–2 Corinthians," in *A Biblical-Theological Introduction to the New Testament*, ed. Michael Kruger (Wheaton, IL: Crossway, 2016), 212–214.

75. Gaffin, *Resurrection and Redemption*, 85.

his posterity. In view is the sin of Adam and its consequences for himself and for humanity. In the latter verses, however, Paul's perspective on Adam is decidedly on Adam before he sinned. That is to say, Adam is in view as created but not (yet) fallen. The citation of Genesis 2:7 at 1 Corinthians 15:45a ("The first man Adam became a living being") confirms Paul's interest in Adam prior to his fall into sin.

When Paul speaks of Adam as "the man of dust" (15:48), then, this description has reference to Adam-as-created. When Paul goes on to speak of human beings as "of the dust" and as those who "have borne the image of the man of dust," he has in view humanity, outside of Jesus Christ, represented by Adam.[76] The sole alternative to being "of the dust" is to be "of heaven," to "bear the image of the man of heaven" (vv. 48, 49). This descriptor is true of those who have been brought from union with Adam to union with Christ, who is "the man of heaven" (vv. 48, 49).

We are now in a position to draw some implications from these observations for the historicity of several important details about Adam. First, the comprehensiveness of Paul's discussion of Adam precludes any human ancestry that does not trace its ultimate biological origin to Adam, "the first man." Adam is not "the 10,000th man on the earth" (as a proponent of theistic evolution might claim); he is "the first man." That is to say, for Paul, Adam is not simply one historical man among 10,000 human beings who existed at the same time. Adam, rather, is the ancestor of *every* human being. Every human being, according to Paul, bears, as one naturally descended from Adam, the image of the man of dust. The sole alternative, for Paul, is the Christian who, by grace, "shall also bear the image of the man of heaven" (v. 49). As far as Paul is concerned, there is no alternative. Every human being in every time and place falls into one or the other of these two categories.

Second, for Paul, those who "shall also bear the image of the man of heaven" are those who once "have borne the image of the man of dust" (v. 49). The Christian is one who has been transferred from Adam to Christ. Gaffin rightly notes, "It is quite foreign to this passage, especially given its comprehensive outlook . . . , to suppose that

---

76. Even though human beings continue to bear the Adamic image (James 3:9), it has been profoundly defaced, although not completely effaced, in consequence of the fall.

some not in the image of Adam will bear the glory-image of Christ."[77] Were there a human being not descended from Adam, he would not be eligible for redemption. Only those who have borne Adam's image may bear Christ's image. In light of the fact that the New Testament writers insist that the gospel is to be proclaimed to every human being without exception, we are thereby bound to conclude that every human being in every time and place of the world traces his genealogical descent from Adam.

Third, Paul presents the ministry of Christ in a particular light. Christ's work of death and resurrection was not designed to destroy or eliminate our humanity. Neither was it designed so that we might transcend our humanity. It was designed to perfect and to advance our humanity. For this reason Paul repeatedly refers to Adam and to Christ, in parallel, as "man" (1 Cor. 15:47, 48, 49). If the omega point of our redemption is an eschatologically consummate humanity, then Paul's alpha point in this chapter is the pre-eschatological humanity of Adam (v. 45, citing Gen. 2:7). To call into question the humanity of Adam or to challenge the universal descent of humans from Adam therefore has dire implications for the gospel as Paul outlines it in this chapter. Absent either a historical Adam or the universal descent of humanity from Adam, Paul's gospel is incoherent.

B. Romans 5:12–21

The other place in Paul's correspondence where he offers an extended reflection on Adam and Christ is Romans 5:12–21. These verses raise many issues that range widely across Paul's theology.[78] We will confine our attention to the implications of what Paul says here for Adam's historicity.

As in 1 Corinthians 15, Paul sets Adam and Christ in parallel. On the one hand, there is "Adam" (Rom. 5:14, twice), or, as Paul prefers to refer to him in this passage, the "one man" (vv. 12, 15, 16, 17 [twice], 19). On the other hand, there is "Jesus Christ" (vv. 15, 17, 21), who is also referred to as "one man" (vv. 15, 17, 19). Each is a representative

---

77. Gaffin, *No Adam, No Gospel*, 12.

78. For helpful exegetical and theological overviews of Paul's teaching in these verses, see John Murray, *The Imputation of Adam's Sin* (Phillipsburg, NJ: P&R, 1992); and Thomas R. Schreiner, "Original Sin and Original Death," in *Adam, the Fall, and Original Sin*, 271–288.

person. The destinies of many hang upon the actions of Adam and Christ. For this reason, Paul says, "many died through one man's trespass," while "the free gift by the grace of that one man Jesus Christ abounded for many" (v. 15).

The parallel between Adam and Jesus, as in 1 Corinthians 15, is an *antithetical* parallel. This antithesis emerges as Paul details both the work that each representative has done on behalf of the represented, and the consequences or results of that work for the represented.[79] By the one trespass (Rom. 5:16, 18; cf. v. 14) of Adam has come "condemnation" (vv. 16, 18) and "death" (vv. 17, 21). But by the "one act of righteousness" or "obedience" (vv. 18–19) of Jesus has come "justification" vv. 16, 18) and "life" (vv. 17–18, 21).[80] Adam and Christ differ, then, in the nature and outcome of their respective actions. Their work also differs with respect to scope ("much more," v. 17; "all the more," v. 20). The "life" that Christ has won far surpasses the reign of death inaugurated by Adam's sin (v. 17).[81] Because it is Christ's righteousness alone that has secured "life" for his people, they may be assured that they will "reign in life through the one man Jesus Christ" (v. 17; cf. v. 21).

How does Paul's argument inform our understanding of Adam? First, Paul identifies Adam in verse 14 as "a type (Greek *typos*) of the one who was to come," that is, Jesus. Adam, then, is a "type" of Jesus. At the very least, the word "type" denotes correspondence. As a representative man whose action is imputed to those whom he represents, Adam corresponds to Jesus as his "prefiguration."[82] But this prefigurative correspondence is *fundamentally historical* in nature.[83] As Versteeg aptly summarizes the denotation of this word, "a type always stands

---

79. Material in this paragraph has been drawn from my "Romans," in *Biblical-Theological Introduction to the New Testament*, ed. Michael Kruger (Wheaton, IL: Crossway, 2016), 186–187.

80. The mode of the transfer of the work of the representative to the represented is rightly termed "imputation," on which see further Murray, *Imputation of Adam's Sin*.

81. "Adam's transgression introduced death as the king of human beings, but the grace of God brooks no rivals, conquering both sin and death" (Schreiner, "Original Sin and Original Death," 284).

82. Versteeg, *Adam in the New Testament*, 10.

83. Ibid., citing H. N. Ridderbos, *Aan de Romeinen* (Kampen: J. H. Kok, 1959), 116, "in a previously established redemptive-historical correlation" (in *een tevoren vastgestelde heilshistorische correlatie*); and L. Goppelt, *Typos: The Typological Interpretation of the Old Testament in the New* (Grand Rapids, MI: Eerdmans, 1982), 130, "Adam is not only an illustrative figure. [Paul] views Adam through Christ as a type in redemptive history, as a prophetic personality placed in Scripture by God."

at a particular moment in the history of redemption and points away to another (later) moment in the same history."[84] That is to say, "type" denotes a *fundamentally historical relationship*. Paul's application of this term to the correspondence between Adam and Christ confirms the essentially historical relationship between these two men. Adam and Christ are historical men who occupy the same plane of history. This historical plane, furthermore, finds its meaning and integration in the "redemptive plan of God."[85] The relationship that Paul expresses between Adam and Christ therefore carries necessary implications for our understanding of Adam's person. Adam is a historical person, no less a historical person than Jesus Christ. One is not free to maintain, then, that Adam is a mythical or semihistorical figure while Jesus Christ is a fully historical figure. Affirming the historicity of Jesus Christ requires affirming the historicity of Adam. It bears reiterating that this Adam, for Paul, is the Adam of whom Genesis 1–3 speaks in detail, the first human being, whom God specially created and from whom the entirety of the human race is biologically descended.

Second, Paul represents Adam as a historical person in yet another way. In Romans 5:13–14, Paul speaks of a bounded period in human history "before the law was given" (v. 13), that is, "from Adam to Moses" (v. 14). This historical window ranges from Adam to the giving of the Mosaic law at Sinai (Exodus 19ff.). As Versteeg has rightly observed, "as surely as a historical terminus is in view in the case of Moses, a historical starting point is in view in the case of Adam."[86] Adam can be no less historical a person than Moses.

Third, Paul argues in this passage that sin and death are not perennial features of the human experience. They are not essential to human nature. They have a particular point of entry into humanity. This alpha point is the "one man's trespass" (Rom. 5:15)—not the lifetime of Adam's sinning, but the single sin of disobeying God's command not to eat of the fruit of the tree of knowledge of good and evil.[87] Death is not a given of human life, but the judicial consequence

---

84. Versteeg, *Adam in the New Testament*, 11.
85. Ibid., 13.
86. Ibid., 24.
87. Note how in the following verse Paul contrasts the "one trespass" with the "many trespasses" (Rom. 5:16).

of the one sin of the one man (5:12; cf. Eccles. 7:29, "See, this alone I found, that God made man upright, but they have sought out many schemes"). Because Adam's one sin has been transferred to all those whom he represents, death is the universal penalty that they justly bear in consequence of that one sin (Rom. 5:12). Therefore Paul attributes the reign of "death" to "the one man's trespass" (v. 17), and can speak of "sin reign[ing] in death" (v. 21). For Paul, "death" in the experience of those who are "in Adam" is inescapably judicial or penal in character.

Fourth, Paul's statements about Adam, the work of Adam, and the conveyance of Adam's work to those whom Adam represents provide the framework for the gospel of Jesus Christ. Jesus Christ is a *representative* man. His obedience and death were undertaken on behalf of his people (v. 19; cf. vv. 6–11). That obedience and death are so transferred or imputed to his people that they are now justified or declared righteous through faith in him (vv. 16–19). Because of the work of Christ, they have passed from "death" to nothing less than "eternal life through Jesus Christ our Lord" (v. 21). Each of these propositions about Jesus parallels a comparable proposition about Adam in verses 12–21. To compromise or to deny the historicity of the person and work of Adam, therefore, is not without consequence for the gospel. Paul does not give us the liberty of extracting the gospel from the redemptive-historical framework within which the gospel exists and has its meaning.

Fifth, and similarly to his argument in 1 Corinthians 15:20–22, 44–49, Paul understands the gospel solution to correspond to the Adamic plight. For Paul, as "all" human beings share in the Adamic plight, so "all" human beings who are represented by Christ receive the salvation that Christ has won for his people (Rom. 5:18).[88] This plight-solution framework is comprehensive of all humanity. Paul recognizes no individual person or group of persons that is exempt from this framework.

---

88. In Romans 5:18, Paul is not teaching universalism, that is, the salvation of all human beings. The "all" in the latter part of 5:18 refers to all people who are represented by the one man, Jesus Christ, just as the "all" in the former part of verse 18 refers to all people who are represented by Adam. That this is Paul's understanding of these two uses of the term translated "all" is in part confirmed by his use of the term "many" twice in the following verse (v. 19).

III. Theistic Evolutionary Readings of Paul
(1 Cor. 15:20-22, 44-49; Rom. 5:12-21)

How have proponents of theistic evolution approached and understood
the apostle Paul's two extended reflections on the person and work of
Adam (1 Cor. 15:20–22, 44–49 and Rom. 5:12–21)? We may answer
that question by exploring what three proponents, Denis Alexander,
John H. Walton, and Peter Enns, have argued from these passages.
Because Alexander, Walton, and Enns are not altogether agreed upon
these passages' meaning, we will address each separately.

A. Denis Alexander on Paul's Understanding of Adam

Denis Alexander has argued that the biblical writers speak of "three
types of death: physical death; spiritual death here and now; and eternal spiritual death."[89] According to Alexander, the Old Testament writers do not view "death per se [as] caused by sin."[90] He says that the
New Testament writers, by contrast, conceived "physical death" as "an
enemy to be overcome," which in fact has happened in the resurrection
of Jesus from the dead.[91] The difference between the Testaments with
respect to physical death, then, is that the Old Testament sees physical
death "as the normal lot of humankind," whereas the New Testament
"transforms [physical death] into something that has no place in the
future kingdom of God."[92]

Spiritual death refers to "alienation from God caused by sin."[93] In
the New Testament, spiritual death and physical death are so closely
related that it is difficult to "distinguish" the two in many instances.[94]
Eternal, spiritual death is "the spiritual death that continues on after
this life" and is "permanent."[95]

This understanding of death informs Alexander's readings of Romans 5 and 1 Corinthians 15. Paul's concern in Romans 5 is said to be
spiritual death, brought about by sin.[96] Paul understood Adam to be "a

---

89. Alexander, *Creation or Evolution*, 306.
90. Ibid., 310.
91. Ibid., 311.
92. Ibid., 312.
93. Ibid.
94. Ibid., 313.
95. Ibid., 315.
96. Ibid., 329.

real person," a "historical figure," no less than Jesus himself was.[97] Paul also sees Adam in "corporate solidarity" and "federal headship" with the people who follow him. Adam's sin has somehow resulted in the humans after him having "a propensity to sin," even as "each person is responsible for his or her own sin."[98]

Alexander is unwilling to say from Romans 5 that physical death originated with Adam. He makes this point explicit in his exposition of 1 Corinthians 15.[99] According to Alexander, Paul sees "physical death" in 1 Corinthians 15 as " . . . the normal state of humankind and always has been. This is the status of earthly men (v. 48); it's what you expect."[100] The cross and the resurrection, however, have conquered not only spiritual death but also physical death. With death so comprehensively nullified, we are therefore qualified to enter the kingdom (vv. 48–49).

What, then, may be said of Adam's disobedience and its implications for humanity? Alexander denies that Adam and Eve are the "genetic progenitors of the entire human race."[101] We do not inherit *guilt* from Adam, "but *a propensity to sin,* so that . . . everyone does in a sense repeat the sin of Adam."[102] Part of Alexander's reticence in affirming that we inherit the sin of Adam is that the idea "implies some kind of genetic transmission."[103] In some fashion, which Alexander acknowledges he is unable satisfactorily to articulate, every human has a "propensity to sin" and "repeats the sin of Adam" but does not "inherit" sin from his "parents in any genetic sense."[104]

What may be said of the person of Adam himself? Adam and Eve were "real historical people . . . the progenitors of God's new family on earth, comprising all those who would enter into a personal relationship with God by faith."[105] These two people were "a couple of Neolithic farmers in the Near East" or even a "community of farmers,

---

97. Ibid., 330.
98. Ibid., 331.
99. "1 Corinthians 15 does not actually address the question as to whether physical death began with Adam's sin—nowhere is this mentioned" (ibid., 332).
100. Ibid., 333.
101. Ibid., 343.
102. Ibid., 344, emphasis added.
103. Ibid., 345.
104. Ibid. Alexander, on the following page, wishes to set his view apart from that of Pelagius, even as he sets his view apart from that of Augustine.
105. Ibid., 317–318.

to whom [God] chose to reveal himself in a special way."[106] This call of God did not render them human, for they were already human. Prior to this call, people, presumably including Adam and Eve, "sought after God or gods in different parts of the world, offering their own explanations for the meaning of their lives."[107] What the call did was to bring them to spiritual life "in fellowship with God."[108] Adam and Eve furthermore stood in "federal headship in relation to the rest of humanity."[109] By virtue of the divine choice, Adam and Eve come to represent, then, presumably all human beings, even those who are "not descended genetically" from them.[110]

How are we to assess Alexander's understanding of Adam from the perspective of Paul's writings? First, the distinction that Alexander presses between physical and spiritual death is alien to Paul's thought. For Paul, death is not a given of human nature. It is an intruder. Its entrance into human experience came with the first sin of the first man, Adam.[111] Paul cannot conceive of death, furthermore, apart from its penal character (cf. 1 Cor. 15:54–57). Believers, who continue to experience the evil of death, do not experience death as the penalty for their sin only because Christ, in his death, bore that penalty for them.

Second, Alexander's proposal that Adam and Eve were selected from an existing group of human beings and appointed as federal representatives over all human beings, whether descended from them or not, runs counter to the testimony of Paul. Paul affirms that all human beings, Christ excepted, by nature bear the "image" of Adam (1 Cor. 15:49). They do so as they are naturally descended from Adam, the "first man" (v. 45). As Gaffin has observed, *"image bearers of Adam* is hardly an apt, much less valid or even intelligible, description of human beings who are held either to have existed before Adam or subsequently not to have descended from him."[112] Paul knows no mode

---

106. Ibid., 290.
107. Ibid.
108. Ibid.
109. Ibid., 291.
110. Ibid., 292.
111. For a perceptive critique of Alexander's allowance for pre-Adamic "sin," see Michael Reeves, "Adam and Eve," 48–49.
112. Gaffin, *No Adam, No Gospel*, 12, emphasis original.

of Adamic representation that is not conjoined to and predicated upon genetic descent from Adam.

Third, Alexander acknowledges a difficulty in affirming two propositions. On the one hand, all human beings have a universal propensity to sin that is traceable to the first sin of Adam. On the other hand, we may not use the language of "inheritance" to explain this state of affairs, nor may we explain any process of transmission in terms of or in light of a genetic relationship between Adam and his posterity. One may appreciate Alexander's stated insistence to distance himself from the Pelagian denial of the transmission of Adam's sin to his posterity. The question remains, however, in what precise sense Alexander has affirmed Adamic representation. We are said to derive from Adam not guilt but a "propensity to sin," but we are not told how that propensity comes into our possession.[113] A person's guilt is said to commence when he or she personally commits sin.[114] Alexander's statements do not adequately safeguard Paul from the "personal self-determination" that characterizes Pelagian readings of Paul.[115] If, for Alexander, Adam is more than a bad exemplar for the human beings who followed him, it is difficult to discern just in what sense that is so.

The liabilities attending this position advocated by Alexander are illuminated in a recent publication by another proponent of theistic evolution, Scot McKnight.[116] McKnight has argued that "the Adam of Paul was not the historical Adam."[117] For Paul, McKnight insists, Adam is "literary" and "genealogical," that is, "the entire history of Israel is built" upon Adam in the Old Testament.[118] In company with other Second Temple Jewish writers, Paul is said to conceive Adam as an "archetypal" and "moral" figure.[119]

---

113. "It is not guilt that is inherited from Adam but a propensity to sin, so that as a matter of fact everyone does in a sense repeat the sin of Adam. Exactly how that propensity is transmitted is a moot point and a matter of much theological speculation. . . . [T]he propensity is part of that dark theological cloud of sin, which affects the whole of humanity. But irrespective of how we precisely define that propensity, we can agree that people become guilty when they then proceed to sin . . ." (Alexander, *Creation or Evolution*, 344).

114. See the quote in the previous note.

115. Reeves, "Adam and Eve," 52.

116. Dennis R. Venema and Scot McKnight, *Adam and the Genome: Reading Scripture After Genetic Science* (Grand Rapids, MI: Brazos, 2017).

117. Ibid., 191.

118. Ibid., 176.

119. Ibid., 180.

In the course of making this argument, McKnight advances some troubling claims regarding the relationship between the sin of Adam and the sinful condition of human beings. He claims that "original sin and damnation for all humans by birth is not found in Paul."[120] No one sins "in Adam"; rather, "each person is *Adamic in that each person sins in the way Adam sinned.*"[121] To be sure, each person sins in the wake of the "cosmic death" that Adam "unleash[ed]" by his own sin, but, for Paul, "each of us [is] an Adam or Eve generating our own death."[122] "Humans have been impacted by Adam's sin, but individuals are not accountable until they sin themselves."[123]

This understanding of Adam and human beings has implications for the way that McKnight understands the relationship between Christ and his people. McKnight explains Romans 5:18–19 in these terms: "*just as one must act—believe—in order to benefit from the one act of Christ's obedience in order to inherit eternal life, so we need to act—sin or disobey—in order to accrue to ourselves death.*"[124] Adam "is the paradigmatic human who failed to live according to God's demand and so becomes the paradigmatic moral (or immoral) man, leaving the haunting question that runs right through the whole Bible: Will we follow Adam or will we follow Christ?"[125]

This understanding of sin and redemption is indisputably semi-Pelagian and arguably Pelagian (the unorthodox view that we are not born with a sinful nature, but are able to choose by our own moral strength to obey God). These formulations follow directly on McKnight's denial of the full historicity of Adam. They confirm that one's understanding of the historicity of Adam has serious implications for the integrity of the biblical gospel.

To conclude our discussion of the way in which Alexander understands Adam in Paul, Alexander's proposal conflicts in fundamental ways with Scripture's testimony about Adam, sin, death, and the work of Christ. Alexander not only denies that all human beings are biologically descended from Adam, but also fails to offer a clear and coherent

---

120. Ibid., 183.
121. Ibid., 183, 184, emphasis original.
122. Ibid., 184.
123. Ibid., 186.
124. Ibid., emphasis original.
125. Ibid., 188.

account of the relationship between Adam's sin and his posterity. Alexander, furthermore, fails adequately to account for Scripture's understanding of death, on the one hand, and of the work of Christ to deliver sinners from death, on the other. In an attempt to accommodate Scripture to evolutionary theory, Alexander's proposal, at best, dilutes the testimony of Scripture concerning matters that lie at the heart of Scripture's teaching about sin and salvation.

B. John H. Walton on Paul's Understanding of Adam

Although Wheaton Old Testament professor John H. Walton has concentrated his attention on the Old Testament witness to Adam, he has also addressed what Paul had to say about Adam in 1 Corinthians 15 and Romans 5. Walton argues that in both Testaments Adam appears as an *archetype*. An archetype, as Walton has recently defined the term, "refers to *a representative of a group* in whom all others in the group are embodied. As a result, all members of the group are included and participate with their representative."[126]

Walton distinguishes the *historical existence* of such a figure as Adam from his *archetypal significance* in the biblical literature. The recognition that "the New Testament authors believe Adam and Eve to be real individuals in a real past (as do I)" is distinct from the "theological" or "archetypal" "use that is made of them."[127] It is as an archetype that the New Testament writers are said to have interest in Adam.

What implications does Walton's distinction have for the way in which he approaches the Pauline material? Romans 5:12–21 is said to represent Adam archetypally in two ways: "first, he is seen as a pattern of Christ; second, Adam represents all people in Paul's treatment (through him all sinned)."[128] Paul is not interested in committing his readers to the proposition that "Adam was the first human being or that we all must be related biologically or genetically to Adam"; or that "sin [is] passed through biological relationship."[129] Paul does

---

126. Walton, *Lost World of Adam and Eve*, 240, emphasis added.
127. Walton, "Historical Adam: Archetypal Creation View," 105.
128. Ibid., 106.
129. Ibid. "Here [i.e., Rom. 5:12–21] the archetypal use is connected to the fall, not to his forming" (*Lost World of Adam and Eve*, 93).

commit us, however, to "the reality of sin and death entering human experience in an event," with the implication that there is "a historical Adam."[130]

Walton draws similar conclusions from 1 Corinthians 15:22, 45. Although Adam is the "first" man, he cannot be the "first biological specimen" because "Christ was not the last biological specimen."[131] Furthermore, since Paul terms Jesus both "second" and "last," these two terms must be the "same" and must "not focus on actual numeration value."[132] Paul's interest in the two men is as archetypes, "contrast[ing] and compar[ing] Adam to Jesus and our relationship to both." Paul has no interest in "genetic relationships" of human beings with Adam or "material origins" other than saying that "we share the 'dust' nature of the archetype."[133]

What, then, may be positively affirmed of Adam and his work in relation to humanity? Walton argues that Adam and Eve were drawn from a larger human population (all of whom, as human beings, were in the "image of God") and these two were appointed "representative priests for humanity."[134] Adam and Eve are not "de novo creations." They are, rather, "positioned as fountainheads of humanity even if we are not all their direct descendants."[135]

Walton states, furthermore, that in the pre-Adamic "earliest populations" . . . "there was never a time when sinful (= at least personal evil) behavior was not present."[136] Appealing to Romans 5:13, Walton argues that, prior to Adam and Eve, when "law or revelation" was first given, "there was no sin (no consciousness of relationship, no immorality)."[137] They were behaving badly and committing evil, but they were not morally accountable to God for their actions, nor were they in "a personal, conscious relationship" with God.[138]

130. Walton, "Historical Adam: Archetypal Creation View," 106.
131. Ibid., 107.
132. Walton, *Lost World of Adam and Eve*, 93.
133. Walton, "Historical Adam: Archetypal Creation View," 107. Elsewhere, Walton concludes "that all of Paul's treatment of Adam pertains to the issues of sin, death and the theological archetypal roles of both Adam and Jesus. His patently theological comments do not address the issues of science" (*Lost World of Adam and Eve*, 168).
134. Walton, *Lost World of Adam and Eve*, 159.
135. Ibid., 206.
136. Ibid., 154.
137. Ibid., 155.
138. Ibid.

This state of affairs changed when Adam and Eve sinned. They brought "sin to the entire human race by bringing accountability."[139] Furthermore, their sin "made the antidote to death inaccessible." How particularly does Adam's sin reach subsequent generations of human beings? Walton suggests that "the world . . . got polluted because of that first act (disorder let loose and run amok)," and that we are thereby "infected" from this world.[140] We are "born into [a] toxic environment," and "suffer the consequences both universally and particularly." And we are not only "victims" of this state of affairs, but "we all contribute to it."[141] It was this "disorder" that "brought the need for resolution through the work of Christ," who alone brings order into disorder.[142] The "historicity of Adam," Walton concludes, "finds its primary significance in the discussion of the origins of sin rather than in the origins of humanity."[143]

How may we assess Walton's reading of Paul? First, Walton insists that Paul's interest is not the "forming accounts" of the Old Testament but "the accounts of the fall."[144] But we have argued from 1 Corinthians 15:20–22, 44–49, that Paul evidences sustained interest in Adam *prior to any sin*. His identification of Adam as the "first man" and of human beings as bearing his "image" shows that, for Paul, Adam is both the first human being and the genetic ancestor of all human beings. Adam's representative role in 1 Corinthians 15 and Romans 5 is therefore tethered to his historical place as the first man and the ancestor of the human race. Paul has so woven these two strands together that we may not retain the former while jettisoning the latter.

Second, Walton's formulations on sin and accountability part ways with the way in which Paul understands sin and accountability. Walton identifies pre-Adamite human beings as image-bearers, and describes their behavior as "evil." Even so, appealing to Romans 5:13, he refrains from characterizing this behavior as "sin." He does so because "sin" is said to require the moral accountability that commenced in human history only with Adam and Eve. Paul's words in

---

139. Ibid.
140. Ibid., 157.
141. Ibid., 158.
142. Ibid., 159.
143. Ibid., 203, emphasis removed.
144. Ibid., 95. He notes 1 Corinthians 15:47–48 as "one exception" (ibid.).

Romans 5:13–14, however, are far removed from Walton's construction, for Paul says,

> . . . for sin indeed was in the world before the law was given, but sin is not counted where there is no law. Yet death reigned from Adam to Moses, even over those whose sinning was not like the transgression of Adam, who was a type of the one who was to come. (Rom. 5:13–14)

Paul's words concern the narrow historical window between the sin of Adam and the giving of the Mosaic law; Paul predicates the prevalence of sin in humanity even before the Mosaic law. For all of the complexities of Paul's argument in Romans 5:13–14, there is no reason to think that, at any point in human history, Paul conceived of human beings who were "engaged in activity that would be considered sin [but who were] not . . . held accountable for it."[145]

One may also fairly ask by what standard Walton characterizes pre-Adamite human beings' behavior as "evil"? Is their behavior intrinsically evil or is this a judgment after the fact? If such behavior merits the wrath of God presently (see Rom. 1:18–32), would one say that pre-Adamite humans did not suffer divine displeasure for their own evil actions? These questions underscore the impossibility of Walton's position and return us to Paul's contention that sin commenced with the one act of disobedience of the first man and progenitor of the entire human race, Adam.

Third, Walton employs the metaphor of pollution to explain how Adam and Eve's sin affected subsequent humanity. The metaphor, however, is imprecise and fails to explain exactly how it is that Adam and Eve's sin is passed along to other human beings. Walton does not exonerate these other human beings—they are said to be both victims of and contributors to the toxic environment in which people find themselves. At the same time, it remains unclear exactly *how* or even *if* human beings enter the world guilty of sin or merely disposed to commit sin.

Such a view of man's nature, to put it mildly, is considerably less

---

145. Ibid., 155. We are not saying that Walton understands Paul to be speaking of pre-Adamite human beings in Romans 5:13. We are saying, rather, that the principle he articulates is not founded in Romans 5:13 and, therefore, may not legitimately be applied to any segment of the human population.

pessimistic than that of the apostle Paul. It fails to reckon with the specificity with which Paul speaks of the imputation of Adam's sin to his posterity and the radical universality of the "reign" of "sin . . . in death" in Romans 5:12–21.

Walton's proposal counters Scripture's testimony to the person and work of Adam, to the nature of sin, and to the way in which Adam's sin was passed on to his posterity. It denies the universal, biological descent of humanity from Adam. It fails to adequately account for the Bible's understanding of sin, of moral accountability, and of the origin and transmission of sin among human beings. In the interest of reconciling Scripture with evolutionary theory, Walton's proposal stands against the teaching of Scripture in matters that are central to that teaching, namely, sin and redemption.

C. Peter Enns on Paul's Understanding of Adam

Old Testament professor Peter Enns, who is now at Eastern University and also is a Senior Fellow in Biblical Studies with the BioLogos Foundation, argues that previous generations have not adequately reckoned with Paul as a first-century reader of Old Testament Scripture. When we do so, we will necessarily have to adjust our "understanding of Adam."[146] Decisive for Paul's reading of the Old Testament was "his experience of the risen Christ."[147] This experience "drive[s] . . . his reading of the Old Testament in general," a reading that is "creative."[148]

What, then, were the contours of this reading? Paul had a "high view of Christ," which required his "recast[ing]" of "Israel's story, specifically Adam . . . to account for Christ." For this reason, Paul "invests Adam with capital he does not have either in the Genesis story, the Old Testament as a whole, or the interpretations of his contemporary Jews."[149] "Paul's understanding of Adam is shaped by Jesus, not the other way around."[150]

Critical for Enns's readings of 1 Corinthians 15 and Romans 5,

---

146. Peter Enns, *Evolution of Adam: What the Bible Does and Doesn't Say about Human Origins* (Grand Rapids, MI: Baker, 2012), xiii.
147. Ibid., 135. "Paul's reading of the Adam story was conditioned by his experience of the risen Christ" (142).
148. Ibid., 135.
149. Ibid.
150. Ibid., 122.

then, is that Paul's statements about Adam are reflective of his experience of Christ. Therefore, Paul gives us "not a plain reading of Genesis but a transformation of Genesis." Paul's statements about Adam do not "settle what Adam means in Genesis itself, and most certainly not the question of human origins as debated in the modern world."[151]

What, then, does Paul say about Adam, and how are these statements said to stem from his prior experience of the risen Christ? Adam is both a "theological and *historical* figure for Paul."[152] Paul assumed that Adam was "the first man created by God . . . from whom the human race descended and from whom all inherited sin and death."[153] Not only does Paul affirm the historicity of Adam as the first man and as the progenitor of every human being, but these realities, for Paul, are what "makes [Adam] such a vital theological figure."[154] In other words, these historical convictions were integral, as far as Paul was concerned, to Adam's theological importance in 1 Corinthians 15 and Romans 5.

And yet, Paul did not come to these convictions about Adam independently. His point of entry to them was his experience of the crucified and risen Christ. In light of "the cross and resurrection of Christ," Paul and other Christians saw "grace."[155] No longer did Gentiles have to become Jews in order to be part of God's people. "The resurrection of the Son of God is a game changer: gentiles can now be part of the family of God as gentiles."[156] Jew and Gentile are "on an even footing" now. It is in light of this solution ("Jesus's death and resurrection") that Paul came to the conclusion that Jew and Gentile "are both saved from the same plight (sin and death)."[157]

Paul's handling of Adam in Romans 5:12–21 is in service of advancing a solution to the human plight. Because the solution had "such earth-shattering significance, there must have been a corresponding

---

151. Ibid., 117.
152. Ibid., 120.
153. Ibid. Enns mentions efforts "to preserve an 'Adam' who is not the first human as Paul has it but is the first 'spiritual' hominid (or group of hominids) endowed with a soul and so forth, who acts as a 'representative head' of humanity," but he concludes that "any such creature is as foreign to Paul as any other solution that is trying to bring Paul and evolution into conversation" (*Evolution of Adam*, 123).
154. Ibid., 120.
155. Ibid., 129.
156. Ibid., 130.
157. Ibid.

'problem' it was designed to address."[158] This plight is not failure to "keep the law," but "death."[159] Paul "trace[d]" the "cause of death . . . to the trespass of Adam, understood as the first man."[160] Adam was responsible for bringing "sin and death . . . into the world," antecedently to "the law."[161] Not only did Adam introduce sin into the world, but his "trespass somehow is responsible for putting all of humanity under the power of sin."[162] Therefore, Adam's first sin, "the cause of death, was handed on . . . [to] *all* humans . . . somehow."[163]

For Paul, Enns continues, Adam has the effect of displacing the Mosaic law as the solution to the human plight. The Adamic plight (sin and death) was "at work before the law," therefore, "Christ's resurrection—death's reversal—was clearly a solution to a much deeper problem than the law."[164] The plight of the first Adam required for its solution not the law but the work of the second Adam.[165]

Enns insists that if we "take Paul's *theology* with utmost seriousness [we] are not also bound to accept Paul's view of Adam *historically*."[166] Why is this? All that is essential to the gospel is that we accept "the reality of the human plight of sin and death" and "of God's unexpected, universal solution."[167] The "universal and self-evident problem[s]" of "death" and "sin" (along with "the historical event of the death and resurrection of Christ") are what are said to be the three "core elements of the gospel."[168] Paul's explanations of sin and death are not necessary to the retention of the plight that makes up a core element of the gospel. For Enns's part, we are free to say that "Adam is not the historical first man" and thereby "leav[e] behind Paul's understanding of the *cause* of the universal plight of sin and death."[169] "The need for a Savior does not require a historical Adam."[170]

---

158. Ibid., 131.
159. Ibid.
160. Ibid.
161. Ibid., 133.
162. Ibid.
163. Ibid., 134.
164. Ibid., 135.
165. Ibid.
166. Ibid., emphasis original.
167. Ibid.
168. Ibid., 123.
169. Ibid.
170. Ibid., 143.

What are we to make of Enns's proposals concerning Paul and Adam? We may, as a preliminary observation, note an important difference between Enns, on the one hand, and Alexander and Walton, on the other. Alexander and Walton claim a shared belief with the apostle Paul concerning the existence and activity of a historical Adam. Their conception of Adam, however, is markedly different from that of most Christians and, we have argued, from that of Paul himself. Enns, however, argues for a *Pauline* understanding of Adam that more closely approximates classical understandings of the person of Adam. Unlike Alexander and Walton, however, Enns senses a freedom explicitly to disagree with and to shed that Pauline understanding of Adam.

Critical for Enns's proposal is that the person and activity of Adam do not constitute a core element of the gospel. That is to say, we are free to shed Paul's statements about Adam without jeopardizing the integrity of the gospel that Paul preached. What Paul has done is to "appropriat[e] an ancient way to address pressing concerns of the moment. That has no bearing whatsoever on the truth of the gospel."[171]

In point of fact, however, Paul places his testimony to the historicity of Adam at the core of his gospel. For Paul, Adam and Christ stand or fall together as historical persons occupying the same plane of history. Adam is a "type" of Christ (Rom. 5:14). Adam is the "first man," while Christ is the "second man" and "last Adam" (1 Cor. 15:47, 45).[172] Christ's work *in history* remedies the work of Adam *in history*. The sins for which Christ has died (vv. 3–4) are sins that follow in the train of our Adamic plight—the imputation of his sin to us, and the transmission of his corrupt nature to his posterity by natural generation. To jettison the historicity of Adam's person or actions necessarily calls into question the historicity and effectiveness of the saving work of Christ and, therefore, of the gospel that proclaims that saving work.

But what of Enns's contention that one may hold on to the universal plight of sin and death without holding on to Paul's Adamic explanation of that plight? May we not set to the side "original sin" while

---

171. Ibid., 102.
172. We are therefore not free to say, with Enns, that Paul's statements about Adam are "a *cultural* assumption that Paul makes about *primordial* time," while his statements about the resurrection reflect "*present*-time reality, an actual *historical event*," even as Enns acknowledges that Paul understood the "historical Adam" to be "an unquestioned historical reality *for him*" (*Evolution of Adam*, 126, emphasis original).

maintaining "sin of origin," that is, the "absolute inevitability of sin that affects every human being from *their* beginnings, from birth"?[173] May we not be content to say "*that* all humans are born in sin (sin of origin)" while "remain[ing] open on the ultimate origins of *why* all humans are born in sin (original sin)"?[174]

Decisively against this distinction, as Enns employs it, is its refusal to affirm, in the words of Gaffin, "that sin entered human history at a point subsequent to its beginnings." As Gaffin goes on to explain, Enns's view would have us believe that sin "is not a matter of human *fallenness* but of human *givenness*. Whatever else being human may mean, it entails being sinful or at least being naturally and inalterably disposed to sin."[175]

The gospel, however, does not treat sin as a constituent part of our humanity. It is something that has entered human experience after the creation of humanity. It is, therefore, something that may be removed from human experience by divine grace. Apart from this understanding of sin, redemption, at least on any biblical terms, is meaningless. Paul's gospel simply has nothing to say to the kind of human condition that Enns describes.

Enns's explanation of sin and, correspondingly, redemption stands at odds with the testimony of Scripture. In an effort to reconcile Scripture's teaching about Adam, sin, and salvation with evolutionary theory, Enns effectively dehistoricizes a core element of the biblical gospel, namely, its testimony about sin. To undertake such a project, we have seen, not only parts ways with the Bible's understanding of sin but also renders meaningless the Bible's teaching about redemption. Enns's proposal raises serious and foundational questions about the integrity of the biblical gospel.

IV. Conclusion

The New Testament authors speak with one voice about the person and work of Adam. Adam is a historical man, not mythological or semihistorical. Adam is the first man, specially created by God. Adam

---

173. Ibid., 124, emphasis original. Enns has drawn this distinction from Lutheran theologian George L. Murphy.
174. Ibid., 125, emphasis original.
175. Gaffin, *No Adam, No Gospel*, 16, emphasis original.

is the progenitor of the human race. All people (except for Jesus Christ) descend from Adam by natural generation. Adam is, furthermore, a representative man. His first sin has been imputed to his natural posterity. As a result, we are all guilty of Adam's first sin. We are all justly subject to death, and sin now reigns in death. The reigning depravity and corruption of sin and the consequence of sin, death, are the norm for all those who are "in Adam."

Some proponents of theistic evolution have attempted to reconcile modern evolutionary theory with the teaching of the New Testament. These efforts are not uniform, but we have observed certain patterns emerging. First, what we have summarized as the united testimony of the New Testament concerning Adam is rejected. Some see Adam as a human being, chosen from among other already existing human beings to undertake a special calling from God. Enns sees Adam, for Paul at least, as a culturally appropriate way of articulating the depth of the human plight in light of his experience of Christ and his corresponding conviction that the death and resurrection of Christ provided the solution to that plight. Each proponent surveyed refuses to affirm the biological descent of all human beings from a common and first ancestor, Adam. Each refuses to affirm that the transgression of Adam marked the alpha point of sin and evil into humanity. Each functionally understands sin and evil to be a given of human existence. Each declines to understand death on the judicial and penal terms that the New Testament writers, and especially the apostle Paul, understand death.

Second, the proponents whom we have surveyed advance understandings of sin and death that strike at the integrity of the biblical gospel. All agree that sin pervades present human experience, and some will find ways to trace the universality of human sin to Adam. Such explanations, however, are invariably vague and imprecise. We are left wondering how and under what circumstances a person becomes a sinner. Furthermore, death is presumed to be a standing and perennial part of the human experience. At the very least, the biblical connection between sin and death is left without adequate explanation.

Such imprecision concerning sin and death cannot bode well for the gospel. The gospel, we have observed, comes to us in a particular redemptive-historical framework. The work of Christ is set forth and explicated in light of the work of the representative man, Adam. Christ presents the solution to our Adamic plight. But if our plight is other than what the New Testament writers represent it to be, then how can the gospel solution proffered by the New Testament writers be a solution to our genuine plight? On what basis can the church proclaim to the world a gospel that poses a solution to a nonexistent problem?

These questions underscore the fact that the New Testament writings cannot be accommodated to theistic evolution apart from transforming their teachings in a fundamental fashion. This observation in no way militates against Christians undertaking the hard and necessary work of participating in and engaging the broader scientific community. It is simply to say that underlying this engagement is a deep and perennial hermeneutical question: Will the regnant scientific consensus determine what the Bible may or may not say, or will the Bible be permitted to speak for itself?[176] We may be grateful that on the important matters before us—human origins, sin, death, and salvation—the Bible is not silent, and it speaks with clarity a message that is truly good news to the perishing.

---

176. See here the brief but perceptive hermeneutical reflections, to which I am indebted, of Gaffin, *No Adam, No Gospel*, 8–9.

30

Theistic Evolution Is Incompatible with Historical Christian Doctrine

GREGG R. ALLISON

SUMMARY

Church leaders have historically been called upon to embrace and guard the orthodox position of the church on creation. This chapter develops the specific components of sound doctrine in the area of creation. It articulates the church's historical perspective and demonstrates how theistic evolution is incompatible with the consensus viewpoint. It briefly discusses the views of several more recent evangelical writers.

. . . . .

The thesis of this chapter is that theistic evolution is incompatible with doctrinal standards that have been required for church leadership, as those doctrinal standards have been developed throughout church history. At the heart of this matter is the conviction that church leaders are required to embrace sound doctrine, in accordance with Paul's insistence for an elder: "He must hold firm to the trustworthy word as taught, so that he may be able to give instruction in sound doctrine and also to rebuke those who contradict it" (Titus 1:9). Church leaders must steadfastly cherish sound doctrine for themselves, be competent to communicate sound doctrine to others through preaching and teaching (1 Tim. 3:2; 5:17), and be able to expose and refute false doctrine and silence its purveyors. While it is certainly true that all Christians bear the responsibility "to contend for the faith that was once for all delivered to the saints" (Jude 3), that grave duty falls especially on the shoulders of church leaders. Furthermore, as Jude notes, the sound doctrine that is enjoined on leaders today comports well with the historical faith of the church.[1]

Held to doctrinal standards and responsible for the teaching and defense of those sound doctrines, church leaders are called upon to embrace and guard the orthodox position on creation. This chapter will develop the identity of that sound doctrine by articulating the church's historical perspective on creation and by demonstrating how theistic evolution is incompatible with this consensus viewpoint.

A. The Doctrinal Standard on Creation in the Early Church

The particular doctrinal standard that is at stake with regard to theistic evolution is the creedal affirmation or confessional statement in the first sentence of what is now commonly known as the Nicene Creed:

> I/We believe in one God, the Father Almighty, *maker of heaven and earth, and of all things visible and invisible.*[2]

Explicit in this credo is monotheism, divine omnipotence, and creation of all that exists (outside of God, of course), specifically the present world but not limited to it, including all that is seen (e.g., dry land, seas, vegetation and trees of all kinds, the sun and the moon, fish and sea creatures and birds, amphibians and reptiles and land mammals, and human beings; Gen. 1:3–31) and all that is unseen (e.g., angels). It is this belief that the church from its earliest days has confessed as

---

1. Indeed, as argued elsewhere, such theological consensus should enjoy presumptive authority in the church (Gregg R. Allison, "The *Corpus Theologicum* of the Church and Presumptive Authority," in *Revisioning, Renewing, and Rediscovering the Triune Center: Essays in Honor of Stanley J. Grenz*, ed. Derek J. Tidball, Brian S. Harris, and Jason S. Sexton (Eugene, OR: Wipf & Stock, 2014), 319–342.

2. More precisely this is identified as the Nicene-Constantinopolitan Creed (381). This formulation combined into one affirmation the two affirmations of the Creed of Nicaea (325). This earlier creed had affirmed that God the Father is "maker of all things *visible and invisible.*" It had further affirmed that the Son is the one "*by whom all things were made*, both which be in *heaven* and in *earth*" (emphases added).

being the truth in regard to creation. The phrase "maker of heaven and earth" is a clear echo of Genesis 1:1, "In the beginning, God created the heavens and the earth," and the added specification that God is the "maker" of "all things visible" was uniformly understood in the early church to affirm God's direct creation of all the varieties of plants and animals on the earth. Yet this creedal affirmation contradicts the claim of theistic evolution that God was the "maker" only of the initial inanimate matter in the universe and that that matter, apart from divine guidance or intervention, eventually developed by purely natural processes into "all things visible."

Certainly, this early creed did not specifically address the issue of evolution in general or theistic evolution in particular. At the same time, it was not articulated in a vacuum. Indeed, it was formulated within a biblical-theological framework and against philosophical theories that challenged the belief.

Theologically, creation ex nihilo was affirmed over against the Platonic idea of the eternality of matter. Tatian underscored, "Matter is not, like God, without beginning, nor, as having no beginning, is of equal power with God; rather, it is begotten, and not produced by any other being, but brought into existence by the Framer of all things alone."[3] Theophilus reasoned,

> If God is uncreated and matter is uncreated, God is no longer, according to the Platonists' own thinking, the Creator of all things, nor, so far as their opinions hold, is the monarchy [God is the first and only principle] established. And what great thing is it if God made the world out of existing materials? For even a human artist, when he gets material from someone, makes out of it whatever he pleases. But the power of God is manifested in this, that out of things that are not, he makes whatever he pleases.[4]

Irenaeus expressed the church's belief in creation ex nihilo, explaining that God "himself called into being the substance of creation, when previously it had no existence."[5] Undergirding this belief was the divine

---

3. Tatian, *Address to the Greeks* 5, in *Ante-Nicene Fathers* (ANF) 2:67.
4. Theophilus, *Theophilus to Autolycus* 2.4, in ANF 2:95.
5. Irenaeus, *Against Heresies* 2.10.4, in ANF 1:370; cf. Tertullian, *The Prescription against Heretics*, 13, in ANF 3:249.

character: God is self-sufficient; therefore "It cannot be said that God made the world for his own sake, since he can exist without the world, as he did before it was made."[6] Furthermore, he is omnipotent and wise; indeed, "The God of hosts . . . by his invisible and mighty power and by his great wisdom created the world."[7] And God is sovereign; thus, "he created all things not influenced by anyone but according to his own free will."[8] The early church thus appealed to divine aseity (God's self-sufficiency or independence), omnipotence, wisdom, and sovereignty in its affirmation of creation ex nihilo.

Biblically, the silence of Scripture on how God created the heavens and the earth implied creation ex nihilo. Noting that in Genesis 1, "whenever anything is made out of anything, [the Holy Spirit] mentions both the thing that is made and the thing of which it is made,"[9] Tertullian concluded,

> God, when producing other things out of things which had been already made, indicates them by the prophet [Moses], and tells us what he has produced from such and such a source. . . . If the Holy Spirit took upon himself so great a concern for our instruction, that we might know from what everything was produced, would he not in like manner have kept us well informed about both the heaven and the earth, by indicating for us what it was that he made them of, if their original consisted of any material substance? . . . He confirms (by that silence our assertion) that they were produced out of nothing. "In the beginning," then, "God made the heaven and the earth."[10]

Furthermore, Christian writers often affirmed (though never put into creedal confession) that this creation out of nothing took place in six literal days in the not too distant past. For example, Methodius affirmed that God created "heaven and earth, and the things which are in

---

6. Lactantius, *Divine Institutes* 7.4, in ANF 7:198.

7. Shepherd of Hermas, *Vision* 1.3 (3.4), in ANF 1:10.

8. Irenaeus, *Against Heresies* 2.1.1, in ANF 1:359. Cf. Clement's "the sheer exercise of his [God's] will" (Clement of Alexandria, *Exhortation to the Heathen* 4, in ANF 2:189–190).

9. Examples include Genesis 1:11–12 (the land brought forth vegetation, plants, and fruit trees after their own kinds), Genesis 1:20–21 (the seas brought forth living creatures and the sky brought forth living creatures according to their own kinds), and Genesis 1:24 (the earth brought forth living creatures according to their own kinds).

10. Tertullian, *Against Hermogenes* 22, in ANF 3:490.

them, in six days," and that "the creation of the world in six days was still recent."[11] Though not all early Christians interpreted Genesis 1 literally (Origen, for example, did not[12]), most did, taking the six days of creation as also indicative of how long the created world would exist. Relying on the biblical phrase "a day with the Lord is like a thousand years" (2 Pet. 3:8), Irenaeus calculated, "In as many days as this world was made, in so many thousand years it shall be concluded. . . . For the day of the Lord is as a thousand years; and in six days created things were completed. It is evident, therefore, that they will come to an end at the sixth thousand year [mark]."[13] From this reasoning, many in the early church considered the creation to be not very old, having taken place in the not too distant past.[14]

This doctrine of creation, formulated within this biblical-theological framework, was set in opposition to several prevailing philosophical theories that challenged the belief.[15] Important for our discussion

---

11. Methodius, *The Banquet of the Ten Virgins* 8.11 and 7.5, in *ANF* 6:339 and 6:333. Basil the Great understood the days of creation as twenty-four-hour periods (Basil the Great, *The Hexaemeron*, Homily 2.8, in *Nicene and Post-Nicene Father*, Series 2 [*NPNF*²] 8:64).

12. Origen, *First Principles* 4.1.16, in *ANF* 4:365. Rather than embracing a literal interpretation of Genesis 1, Origen spiritualized the creation account (as he did the rest of Scripture) and promoted the strange idea that God originally created an invisible spiritual world (Gen. 1:1). Following the fall of rational creatures that inhabited this spiritual world, God created the material, visible world (Gen. 1:2–31).

13. Irenaeus, *Against Heresies* 5.28.3, in *ANF* 1:557. Cf. *Letter of Barnabas* 15, in *ANF* 1:146–147; Hippolytus, *Fragments from Daniel* 2.4–5, in *ANF* 5:179. Some early Christians tacked on the Sabbath day to these calculations, resulting in the conviction that the span of the world's existence was seven thousand years (Cyprian, *Treatise* 11.11, in *ANF* 5:503).

14. This literal, historical reading of Genesis 1 stands at odds with Denis Alexander's position: "Figurative and theological understandings of Genesis 1 were the dominant approach to the text among both Jewish and Christian commentators until at least into the fourteenth century" (Denis Alexander, *Creation or Evolution: Do We Have to Choose?*, 2nd ed. (Oxford and Grand Rapids, MI: Monarch, 2014), 185. In support of his view, Alexander appeals to Origen and Augustine. Certainly, Origen applied an allegorical hermeneutic to Genesis 1, but this approach also led him to postulate the creation of an invisible, spiritual world prior to the creation of this present spatio-temporal world, a position that no one in the church's history has embraced. Augustine also used a figurative hermeneutic in interpreting Genesis 1, but again, Alexander's appeal to this approach neglects another important matter. Like (nearly?) all the pastors and theologians of the early church, Augustine "believed in a fairly recent creation and explicitly warned against accepting the view that the world is old": "They are deceived, too, by those highly untrue documents that profess to give the history of many thousand years. If we calculate by the sacred writers, however, we find that not six thousand years have already passed" (Augustine, *The City of God*, 12.10, in *Nicene and Post-Nicene Father*, Series 1, 2:210; cited in Gregg R. Allison, *Historical Theology: An Introduction to Christian Doctrine* (Grand Rapids, MI: Zondervan, 2011), 259). In other words, while adopting figurative and spiritual applications for the early chapters of Genesis, Augustine did not deny that the events recorded in Genesis actually happened. He simply added figurative and spiritual applications to the historical record.

15. The Platonic idea of the eternality of the universe has already been discussed above. Another false theory involved the idea of a demiurge, an emanation from God that possessed sufficient spiritual nature to bring something into existence and sufficient material nature to create a material

was the challenge of the atomic theory: This was the view that all life had originated by the chance collision of atoms in the unlimited void of the universe.[16] Origen described Celsus's version of this theory as affirming that

> a certain fortuitous concurrence [an accidental collision] of atoms gave birth to qualities so diverse that it was owing [due] to chance that so many kinds of plants, trees, and herbs resemble one another, that no disposing reason [the infinite mind of God] gave existence to them, and that they do not derive their origin from an understanding that is beyond all admiration.[17]

This atomic theory postulated that the accidental collision of small elements resulted in the world as it is today, completely apart from the infinite mind of God directing those atoms. The early church stood firmly against this theory: "We Christians, however, who are devoted to the worship of the only God, who created these things, feel grateful for them to him who made them."[18] This atomic theory that the church rejected bears striking similarities to some aspects of contemporary theistic evolution theories.

From this brief survey of the early church's development of its doctrine of creation, several themes stand out:

1. There is only one God who alone is eternal, self-sufficient, omnipotent, wise, and sovereign. This affirmation contradicts the idea of the eternality of matter.

2. This God created the universe and everything in it out of nothing. Scripture at least implies creation ex nihilo. The extensive-

---

world. By means of this demiurge, the supreme deity, being spiritual and thus good, was able to create the world, which is material and thus evil (Irenaeus, *Against Heresies* 2.1.5, in *ANF* 1:360).

16. The concept of "atoms" as used in these theories was not the scientifically developed idea—the smallest unit of a chemical element, consisting of neutrons, protons, and electrons—common today. Rather, "atoms," as the basic elements of life, were the smallest, solid, distinct, indivisible, and invisible entities that existed.

17. Origen, *Against Celsus* 4.75, in *ANF* 4:531.

18. Ibid. Cf. Minucius Felix, who considered the atomic theory to be rationally absurd: "they who deny that this furniture [existing reality] of the whole world was perfected by the divine reason, and assert that it was heaped together by certain fragments casually adhering to each other, seem to me not to have either mind or sense, or, in fact, even sight itself. For what can possibly be so manifest, so confessed, and so evident, when you lift your eyes up to heaven, and look into the things which are below and around, than that there is some deity of most excellent intelligence, by whom all nature is inspired, is moved, is nourished, is governed?" (Minucius Felix, *The Octavius* 17, in *ANF* 4:182).

ness of divine creation is all-encompassing: all visible things, including the sun, moon, stars, land, seas, trees, fish, birds, animals, and human beings; and all invisible things, like the angelic realm.

3. Divine creation took place in six literal days in the not too distant past.

4. The notion of an undirected process—a random collision of already existing elements—fortuitously resulting in the origin and development of the vast diversity of living beings currently in existence was strongly denounced and considered absurd.

This was the doctrine of creation that the early Christians embraced and defended. It was enshrined in the first article of one of its earliest and most widely influential creeds, popularly known as the Nicene Creed: "maker of heaven and earth, and of all things visible and invisible."

But there is more.

Another important aspect of this creed is what its second article affirms. It expresses belief in the

Lord Jesus Christ, the only begotten Son of God . . . *by whom all things were made*; who for us men and for our salvation came down from heaven and was incarnate of the Holy Spirit and of the Virgin Mary and made man; was crucified . . . suffered and was buried . . . rose again . . . and ascended into heaven . . . and shall come again . . .

Formulated against the Arian heresy, which denied the divinity of the second person of the Trinity, this article offered compelling evidence for the Son's deity: his role as agent in the creation of the world. As Creator along with the Father, the Son is fully God, as is the Father. Moreover, the Son's work of creation and his work of salvation go hand in hand. As Creator of the universe and Savior of humanity, the Son is fully God. The Creator-Savior link is crucial: "The one who became incarnate to save the world was none other than the one who had created the world in the first place."[19] Thus, the church warned, "A man is altogether irreligious and a stranger to the truth if he does

---

19. Allison, *Historical Theology*, 259.

not say that Christ the Savior is also the Maker of all things."[20] Accordingly, to the above summary of the early church's doctrine of creation is added,

> 5. The creation of the world and "all things" in it is evidence for the deity of the Son of God, whose work of creation and work of salvation are linked together. The Creator is also the Savior, and vice versa.

Thus, the early church affirmed that God the Father created, out of nothing, the heavens and the earth and all that is visible and invisible, through God the Son, in six days, a few thousand years ago.[21]

In addition to the doctrine of creation, the early church affirmed its belief in divine providence, or God's continuous operation to sustain in existence and direct everything that he created. Divine providence applies to the physical universe, as Clement of Rome affirmed:

> The heavens move at God's direction and obey him in peace. Day and night complete the course assigned by him, neither hindering the other. The sun and the moon and the choirs of stars circle in harmony within the courses assigned to them, according to his direction, without any deviation at all. . . . The seasons, spring and summer and autumn and winter, give way in succession, one to the other, in peace.[22]

The same providence applies to the angelic and human realms.[23] Such control means, according to Origen,

> Of those events that happen to men, none occur by accident or chance, but in accordance with a plan so carefully considered, and so stupendous, that it does not overlook even the number of hairs on a person's head. . . . And the plan of this providential govern-

20. Amphilochius, *Fragment* 16, cited in Jaroslav Pelikan, *The Christian Tradition: A History of the Development of Doctrine*, 5 vols. (Chicago and London: University of Chicago Press, 1971–1991), 1:204–205.
21. As for the relative silence of Scripture on the role of the Holy Spirit in creation, see Gregory of Nyssa, *On the Holy Spirit against the Followers of Macedonius*, NPNF² 5:319–320.
22. Clement of Rome, *Letter of the Romans to the Corinthians* 20, cited in Michael Holmes, *The Apostolic Fathers: Greek Texts and English Translations* (Grand Rapids, MI: Baker, 1999), 53; cf. ANF 1:10.
23. Irenaeus, *Against Heresies*, 5.22.2, in ANF 1:551.

ment extends even to caring for the sale of two sparrows for a penny.[24]

Thus, the early church affirmed both God's creation of "all things visible and invisible" and his providential sustaining and ordering of the creation. But it never collapsed or confused these two divine works, as in the case of some contemporary versions of theistic evolution.

B. The Later Catholic and Protestant Developments of the Doctrinal Standards on Creation

This doctrine of creation (along with the doctrine of providence) continued to be the belief of the church in the medieval era and in the Reformation and post-Reformation periods.

Additions to this basic framework included the role of the Holy Spirit in the work of creation,[25] continuing rejection of theories that creation came about by chance,[26] ongoing affirmation of exhaustive divine providence,[27] strengthening the biblical basis for creation ex nihilo,[28] and application of the doctrine in terms of the proper human use of created things.[29] For example, influential Catholic theologian Thomas Aquinas affirmed that God alone creates, and he rejected the idea that the creation itself possesses the ability to create or develop other living realities:

> [S]ome have supposed that although creation is the proper act of the universal cause [God], still some inferior cause acting by the power of the first cause, can create. And thus [the philosopher] Avicenna asserted that the first separate substance created by God created another after itself, and the substance of the world and its soul; and that the substance of the world creates the matter of inferior

---

24. Origen, *First Principles*, 2.11.5, in *ANF* 4:299. The text has been changed to make it clearer. His biblical allusions are to Matthew 10:29–30.

25. Thomas Aquinas, *Summa Theologica*, pt. 1, q. 45, art. 6; Martin Luther, *Lectures on Genesis: Chapters 1–5*, in *Luther's Works*, ed. Jaroslav Pelikan, Hilton C. Oswald, and Helmut T. Lehmann, 55 vols. (St. Louis: Concordia, 1955–1986), 1:1–9.

26. Thomas Aquinas, *Summa Theologica*, pt. 1, q. 1, art. 2. For Aquinas, if the world came about by chance, the existence of God could not be proven by the cosmological argument, which demonstrates God's existence by cause (God) and effect (the world).

27. Ibid., pt. 1, q. 22; q. 103; q. 104.

28. John Calvin, *Commentaries on the First Book of Moses Called Genesis*, vol. 1, trans. John King (repr., Grand Rapids, MI: Baker, 2005), 70.

29. John Calvin, *Institutes of the Christian Religion*, 3.10.1–2, in *LCC* 20:719–721.

bodies [creatures]. And in the same manner [Peter Lombard] says
. . . that God can communicate to a creature the power of creating,
so that the latter can create ministerially, not by its own power.[30]

Aquinas rejected this idea because only the first cause, God, as absolute being, possesses the power of creating, which is impossible for created things. His position stands against theistic evolution views that attribute creative power to matter and its development by purely natural processes.

In the Protestant churches after the Reformation, while the confessions of faith and catechisms carefully articulated the many differences between Protestant doctrines and Roman Catholic doctrines (e.g., Scripture and Tradition, justification, Mary), the doctrine of creation (and providence) was not one of those fault lines. The Augsburg Confession of Faith,[31] the Heidelberg Catechism,[32] and the Second Helvetic Confession,[33] for example, briefly restate the traditional view, which was not a matter of controversy.

At the same time, these Protestant confessions and catechisms expanded to include specific affirmations not previously incorporated into the church's doctrinal standards. These detailed confessional elements included angels, Adam and Eve, the fall, original sin, death, and more about divine providence.

1. The Creation of Angelic and Human Beings

To the general profession of divine creation of all things, Protestant doctrinal standards added details about the types of created beings. The Belgic Confession of Faith, for example, affirmed,

> We believe that the Father, by the Word, that is, by his Son, has
> created of nothing, the heaven, the earth, *and all creatures*, as it

---

30. Thomas Aquinas, *Summa Theologica*, pt. 1, q. 45, art. 5. Aquinas's reference to Peter Lombard is *Sentences* 4.D.5.

31. Augsburg Confession, pt. 1, art. 1: God is "the creator and preserver of all things, visible and invisible."

32. Heidelberg Catechism, q. 26: The confession "I believe in God the Father, Almighty, Maker of heaven and earth" means "the eternal Father of our Lord Jesus Christ . . . of nothing made heaven and earth, *with all that is in them* . . . [and] likewise upholds and governs the same by his eternal counsel and providence."

33. Second Helvetic Confession, 7: "GOD CREATED ALL THINGS. This good and almighty God created *all things*, both *visible* and *invisible*, by his co-eternal Word, and preserves them by his co-eternal Spirit."

seemed good unto him, *giving unto every creature its being, shape, form*, and several offices to serve its Creator. . . . He also created the angels good. . . . We believe that God *created man out of the dust of the earth*, and made and formed him after his own image and likeness, *good, righteous, and holy*, capable in all things to will, agreeably to the will of God.[34]

Though the church had always believed that "all things in heaven and earth, visible and invisible" were created by God, this belief was specified as including the angels, all of whom were originally created good, and the first man, Adam, who was created out of the dust of the ground (Gen. 2:7) in the divine image and likeness (Gen. 1:26–27) and endowed with uprightness. Similarly, the Westminster Confession of Faith expressed the historical doctrine: "It pleased God the Father, Son, and Holy Spirit, . . . in the beginning, to create, or make of nothing, the world, *and all things therein* whether visible or invisible, in the space of six days; and all very good."[35] It continued,

> After God had made all other creatures, he created man, male and female, with reasonable and immortal souls, endued with knowledge, *righteousness, and true holiness*, after his own image; having the law of God written in their hearts, and power to fulfill it: and yet under a possibility of transgressing, being left to the liberty their own will, which was subject unto change. Beside this law written in their hearts, they received a command, not to eat of the tree of the knowledge of good and evil; which while they kept, they were happy in their communion with God, and had dominion over the creatures.[36]

This doctrinal standard specified belief in God's creation of Adam and Eve in the divine image as complex moral beings (consisting of both body and soul, and endowed with a sense of right and wrong) who were created righteous and holy and given the responsibility to obey

---

34. Belgic Confession of Faith, 12, 14. Italics added to emphasize differences with theistic evolution.

35. Westminster Confession of Faith, 4.1. Italics added to emphasize differences with theistic evolution.

36. Ibid., 4.2. Italics added to emphasize differences with theistic evolution. Cf. Second Helvetic Confession, 7.

the Edenic command. Many advocates of theistic evolution do not affirm these beliefs about Adam and Eve.

2. The Creation of Adam and Eve versus the Pre-Adamite Theory

The post-Reformers were even more specific about the beginning of the human race as a divine act, affirming the creation of Adam and Eve as the first human beings and as the progenitors of the entire human race. This declaration was necessary as a response to the "pre-Adamite" theory, first articulated in 1655–1656 by Isaac Le Peyrère in his *Prae-Adamitae* and *Men before Adam*.[37] His theory asserted that Adam was not the first human being created by God, but the first person of the Jewish people. Indeed, he claimed that the Gentiles existed long before Adam and the Jewish race:

> The Gentiles are diverse from the Jews in race and origin; the Jews were formed by God in Adam, the Gentiles were created before, on the same day as other animate beings. The origin of the latter [the Gentiles] is described in Gen. 1, that of the former [the Jews] in Gen. 2. . . . Gentiles are many ages before the Jewish nation and, by race and nature, diverse from the same, and survivors of the Noachian flood of the Jews. . . . [Accordingly], the epoch of the creation of the world should not be dated from that beginning which is commonly imagined in Adam, but must be sought for still further back, and from ages very remote in the past.[38]

In this way, Isaac Le Peyrère challenged the historical view that Adam and Eve were the precursors of the entire human race.

The post-Reformers vigorously refuted this pre-Adamite theory. Positively, the influential Lutheran theologian John Quenstedt explained, "Adam, framed by God on the sixth day of the first hexa-

---

37. Isaac Le Peyrère, *Prae-Adamitae sive exercitatio . . . capitis quinti Epistolae D. Pauli ad Romanos* (Latin, 1655) and *A Theological Systeme upon That Presupposition that Men Were before Adam* (English, 1656).

38. John Andrew Quenstedt, *Theologia Didactico-Polemica*, 2 vols. (1685), 1:543; in Schmid, *Doctrinal Theology of the Evangelical Lutheran Church*, 165. Quenstedt cites a section of Le Peyrère's *Prae-Adamitae*. Quenstedt underscores this point over against the antithesis of Le Peyrère's position.

hemeron [six-day creation], is the first of all men, and the parent of the entire human race, throughout the whole globe."[39] Biblical support included Genesis 2:7; Luke 3:23–38; Acts 17:26; Romans 5:12; and 1 Corinthians 15:22, 45–48. Further support was the "constant opinion thus far not only among Christians, but also among the Jews (yea even among the Mohammedans [Muslims] themselves) . . . that Adam was created in the beginning of the world and was the first man, the father not only of the Jews, but also of all men universally."[40]

Negatively, the pre-Adamite theory was critiqued from several angles: First, Reformed theologian Francis Turretin argued,

> if innumerable men had been created before Adam, there would have been no need of a repeated creation of men from the dust (since ordinary generation would have been abundantly sufficient). And it cannot be said that there could not have been found for man a helpmeet [helper, i.e., Eve] similar to himself, if myriads of women already existed; nor would man have been alone, as is said in Gen. 2:18.[41]

Second, the theory failed in regard to the first woman created, Eve (Gen. 2:18–25), "so named because she was 'the mother of all living' (Gen. 3:20), which would be untrue if only the Jewish nation sprang from her."[42]

Thus, the leading theologians of the church had a ready answer to Le Peyrère's pre-Adamite theory, and they defended the traditional view that Adam and Eve were the parents of the entire human race.[43] This dismissed pre-Adamite theory bears similarities to the view of theistic evolutionists today that there were human beings on Earth for thousands of years before Adam and Eve.

---

39. Ibid.

40. Francis Turretin, *Institutes of Elenctic Theology*, ed. James T. Dennison Jr., trans. George Musgrave Giger, 3 vols. (Phillipsburg, NJ: P&R, 1997), 1:457.

41. Ibid., 1:460.

42. Ibid., 1:458. Cf. Caspar Brochmann, *Universae Theologiae Systema* (1633), 239; in Schmid, *Doctrinal Theology of the Evangelical Lutheran Church*, 165.

43. To take a contemporary example, the Reformation rejection of the pre-Adamite theory is still reflected in Wheaton College's Statement of Faith: "WE BELIEVE that God directly created Adam and Eve, the historical parents of the entire human race." Available at "Statement of Faith and Educational Purpose," *Wheaton College*, accessed September 12, 2016, http://www.wheaton .edu/About-Wheaton/Statement-of-Faith-and-Educational-Purpose.

3. The Relationship between Creation, Death, and the Fall

In its wrestling with this wrong view, the church also had to face another issue regarding natural death before Adam and Eve's fall into sin. Le Peyrère had made a distinction between natural sin and death, on the one hand, and legal sin and death, on the other hand. The former existed among "the Gentile Preadamites who were liable to sin and natural death from their innate corruptible and mortal nature."[44] The latter was introduced only after Adam and Eve, to whom God had given the prohibition in the garden of Eden, disobeyed that law, thus falling into legal sin and death.

Turretin roundly denounced Le Peyrère's novel idea:

> [S]in cannot be called natural without impinging upon God himself the author of nature; nor ought death to be called natural, as if man was necessarily to die even if he had not sinned. . . . False also is the pretense that there can be any sin which is not against law, since it is nothing else than lawlessness (*anomia*). It is also false that there can be a death which is not legal, since from no other source than from the power of the law and by its sanction was it ordained that man should die once.[45]

Accordingly, the Reformers and post-Reformers emphasized the origination of the human race with Adam and Eve and their tragic fall into sin.

To this was added the belief that original sin is passed down from Adam and Eve to their posterity, the entirety of the human race. Not only were Adam and Eve the first human beings; they were also those whose disobedience wreaked havoc for all human beings after them.

The Belgic Confession exemplifies this doctrinal standard. It first treats Adam's disobedience to the Edenic law:

> [T]he commandment of life, which he had received, he transgressed; and by sin separated himself from God, who was his true life, having corrupted his whole nature; whereby he made himself liable to corporal and spiritual death. And being thus become

---

44. Turretin, *Institutes of Elenctic Theology*, 1:459–460.
45. Ibid., 1:460.

wicked, perverse, and corrupt in all his ways, he has lost all his excellent gifts.[46]

It then addresses original sin:

Through the disobedience of Adam, original sin is extended to all mankind; which is a corruption of the whole nature, and a hereditary disease, wherewith infants themselves are infected even in their mother's womb, and which produces in man all sorts of sin, being in him as a root thereof; and therefore is so vile and abominable in the sight of God, that it is sufficient to condemn all mankind."[47]

Similarly, the Westminster Confession of Faith addressed the originating sin of Adam and Eve—"our first parents, being seduced by the subtlety and temptations of Satan, sinned, in eating the forbidden fruit"—and the original sin that devastates their progeny, the human race:

By this sin they fell from their original righteousness and communion with God, and so became dead in sin, and wholly defiled in all the parts and faculties of soul and body. They being the root of all mankind, the guilt of this sin was imputed; and the same death in sin, and corrupted nature, conveyed to all their posterity descending from them by ordinary generation.[48]

The Lutheran theologians concurred, with David Friedrich Hollaz representing their view:

Adam and Eve were substitutes for the whole human race, inasmuch as they ought to be regarded as both the *natural* (i.e., *seminal*) and also the *moral* source of the human race, namely, of the entire progeny in nature and grace. . . . For our first parents were then considered not only as the first individuals of the human race, but also as the true root, stock, and source of the whole human race, which in them could both stand and fall.[49]

---

46. Belgic Confession of Faith, 14.
47. Ibid., 15.
48. Westminster Confession of Faith, 6.2–3. Cf. New Hampshire Confession of Faith, 3.
49. Quenstedt, *Theologia Didactico-Polemica*, 2.53; in Schmid, *Doctrinal Theology of the Evangelical Lutheran Church*, 240, emphasis original.

Accordingly, the post-Reformation Protestant church insisted on the introduction of both sin and death into the originally good creation through Adam and Eve, and the transmission of original sin from them to their progeny, all subsequent human beings. This position refutes a view similar to the theistic evolution proposal by John Walton that, prior to Adam and Eve, human beings were committing sinful deeds and were dying but "they were not being held accountable" for their sin.[50]

4. The Creation and Divine Providence

Like the early church and the medieval church, Protestant churches continued to affirm God's ongoing providential care of all that he created, yet the acts of initial creation and subsequent providential care were continually distinguished. Thomas Aquinas earlier had formulated the basic idea of divine government, or God's rulership and direction of the creation in accordance with his eternal purpose:

> In government there are two things to be considered; the design of government, which is providence itself; and the execution of the design. As to the design of government, God governs all things immediately; whereas in its execution, he governs some things by means of others.[51]

The Westminster Confession of Faith continued this idea. Specifically, it linked God's meticulous, exhaustive providence to his wisdom, holiness, omniscience, and sovereign decree ("the free and immutable counsel of his own will"; Eph. 1:11) while acknowledging that such divine direction and government occurs "according to the nature of second causes." Thus, God uses means (e.g., the laws of physics and genetic codes) to carry out his providential care of all things. Still, one of the effects of divine providence is that God's image-bearers praise his glorious "wisdom, power, justice, goodness, and mercy"; that is, the character of God is revealed and recognized from his creative handiwork.[52] The Belgic Confession emphasized the comfort supplied by such providence:

---

50. John H. Walton, *The Lost World of Adam and Eve: Genesis 2–3 and the Human Origins Debate* (Downers Grove, IL: InterVarsity, 2015), 155.
51. Thomas Aquinas, *Summa Theologica*, pt. 1, q. 103, art. 6.
52. Westminster Confession of Faith, 5.1–3.

We believe that the same God, after he had created all things, did not forsake them, or give them up to fortune or chance, but that he rules and governs them according to his holy will, so that nothing happens in this world without his appointment. . . . This doctrine affords us unspeakable consolation, since we are taught thereby that nothing can befall us by chance, but by the direction of our most gracious and heavenly Father; who watches over us with a paternal care, keeping all creatures so under his power, that not a hair of our head (for they are all numbered), nor a sparrow, can fall to the ground, without the will of our Father, in whom we do entirely trust; being persuaded, that he so restrains the devil and all our enemies, that without his will and permission, they cannot hurt us. And therefore we reject that damnable error of the Epicureans, who say that God regards nothing, but leaves all things to chance.[53]

In this way, divine providence, by which God sustains in existence everything that he created and directs all things toward his eternal goal, was given detailed attention in the Reformation and post-Reformation period. But, in contrast to contemporary theories of theistic evolution, this providential work of God, by which he maintains the properties of all created things, was never confused with or used as the explanation for the initial work of God in creating all things.

With these details spelled out, it is now possible to summarize the Protestant doctrinal standards as specifying belief in the following tenets:

1. God created ex nihilo all things in heaven and earth, both visible and invisible, including human beings in the divine image and angels.
2. Adam and Eve were created as the first human beings and as the progenitors of the entire human race.
3. As originally created, Adam and Eve were upright moral beings governed by the Edenic command and charged with the responsibility to exercise dominion over the rest of the created order.
4. By disobeying this Edenic command, they fell into sin. Adam and Eve became guilty before God and thoroughly corrupted in nature, and their punishment included both spiritual and

---

53. Belgic Confession of Faith, 13. The biblical allusions are to Matthew 10:29–30.

physical death, the first incidence of such death in the human race.

5. Because of solidarity with Adam and Eve, their progeny—each and every member of the human race—enters into life loaded down with guilt and characterized by corruption of nature. This is the state of original sin.

6. Not only did God initially create all things in heaven and earth, both visible and invisible; he also exercises providential care and control over all created things. Such meticulous, exhaustive providence does not allow for randomness, accident, chance, fortune, luck, and fate. On the contrary, while using secondary means to accomplish his eternal purpose, God directs all created things teleologically, ruling out all notions of undirected processes at work in this world.

C. Contemporary Doctrinal Standards on Creation

Ever since the outset of the modern period, the doctrinal standards that have been widely, if not unanimously, held by churches have come under fierce attack. The doctrine of creation is no exception; indeed, it can be argued that this belief has been the target of extreme criticism. Moreover, many churches/denominations that have formulated or reformulated their doctrinal standards in the modern period have expressed their beliefs without great detail. Again, the doctrine of creation exemplifies this trend. It means that the doctrinal standards about creation of many contemporary churches/denominations are very basic affirmations, if they even appear.

For example, the Baptist Faith and Message of the Southern Baptist Convention, which states that God is "the Creator, [Redeemer], Preserver, and Ruler of the universe," expresses its belief about God the Father: "God as Father reigns with providential care over His universe, His creatures, and the flow of the stream of human history according to the purposes of His grace."[54] This doctrinal statement also affirms a basic belief in the special creation of human beings as divine image-bearers and their fall into sin.[55] The foundational documents

---

54. The Baptist Faith and Message, II and IIA. The title "Redeemer," and the statement titled "God the Father," are not found in the 1925 version of the Baptist Faith and Message.

55. The Baptist Faith and Message, III.

of the United Methodist Church (with the Evangelical United Brethren Church) are similarly brief: The Articles of Religion acknowledge
that God is "the maker and preserver of all things, both visible and
invisible."[56] The Confession of Faith states that God is "the Creator,
Sovereign and Preserver of all things visible and invisible."[57] The Statement of Fundamental Truths of the General Council of the Assemblies
of God affirms belief in God as "the Creator of heaven and earth."[58]
It makes no affirmation about divine providence, and has only a brief
statement about the fall into sin.[59] The Evangelical Free Church Statement of Faith affirms that God is the "Creator of all things" and that
he "created Adam and Eve in His image."[60] In some statements of faith,
the issue does not even appear. For example, the Evangelical Covenant
Church does not address the doctrine of creation; nor does the United
Church of Christ.

Exceptions to this trend are found. For example, the Lutheran
Church Missouri Synod has an explicit statement affirming the traditional doctrinal standard on creation and repudiating evolutionary
theory:

> We teach that God has created heaven and earth, and that in the
> manner and in the space of time recorded in the Holy Scriptures,
> especially Gen. 1 and 2, namely, by His almighty creative word,
> and in six days. We reject every doctrine which denies or limits the
> work of creation as taught in Scripture. In our days it is denied or
> limited by those who assert, ostensibly in deference to science, that
> the world came into existence through a process of evolution; that
> is, that it has, in immense periods of time, developed more or less of
> itself. Since no man was present when it pleased God to create the
> world, we must look for a reliable account of creation to God's own
> record, found in God's own book, the Bible. We accept God's own
> record with full confidence and confess with Luther's *Catechism*, "I
> believe that God has made me and all creatures."[61]

56. The Articles of Religion of the Methodist Church, article 1.
57. Confession of Faith of the Evangelical United Brethren Church, article 1.
58. Statement of Fundamental Truths of the General Council of the Assemblies of God, 2.
59. Ibid., 4.
60. Evangelical Free Church Statement of Faith, 1, 3.
61. A Brief Statement of the Doctrinal Position of the Missouri Synod (1932), 5. The citation
is from Martin Luther's Small Catechism, II. The Creed; The First Article, Of Creation; Answer.

This Lutheran statement continues with a denial of an evolutionary development of human beings—"We teach that the first man was not brutelike nor merely capable of intellectual development"—and an affirmation of God's creation of human beings in his image and of their tragic fall into sin.[62]

Another exception is the Presbyterian Church of America, which has the Westminster Confession of Faith for its doctrinal standards on creation, providence, Adam and Eve, the fall, and sin.[63]

With this amount of variation among churches and denominations, it is difficult to generalize about the compatibility or incompatibility of theistic evolution with doctrinal standards throughout Protestant churches, or even evangelical Protestant churches. This chapter's approach, however, which considers this matter from the historical position of the church, finds that *theistic evolution is incompatible with all the historical doctrinal standards that address these specific questions.*[64]

D. The Incompatibility of Theistic Evolution with the Church's Doctrinal Standards

The incompatibility of these doctrinal standards and theistic evolution, the view that God created matter and after that did not guide or intervene to cause any empirically detectable change in the natural behavior of matter until all living things had evolved by purely natural processes, can be demonstrated in three points: (1) Theistic evolution's affirmation that God created matter is, in itself, neither wrong nor controversial, but it does not go far enough. Such a view falls short of affirming, as the church has historically believed, that God created not only inanimate matter but also all visible things, including the sun, moon, stars, land, seas, trees, fish, birds, animals, and human beings; and all invisible things, like the angelic realm. God's creation, therefore, was not a creation of generic material but of specific kinds and varieties of creatures.

---

62. A Brief Statement of the Doctrinal Position of the Missouri Synod (1932), 6, 7.

63. Westminster Confession of Faith, 4–6.

64. Theistic evolution also encounters problems with the doctrine of the inerrancy of Scripture, as emphasized in the Chicago Statement on Biblical Inerrancy: Article 12: "**We affirm** that Scripture in its entirety is inerrant, being free from all falsehood, fraud or deceit. **We deny** that Biblical infallibility and inerrancy are limited to spiritual, religious or redemptive themes, exclusive of assertions in the fields of history and science. We further deny that scientific hypotheses about earth history may properly be used to overturn the teaching of Scripture on creation and the flood." The last two sentences oppose theistic evolution (but make no claim about the age of the earth).

(2) Theistic evolution's view that, after creating matter, God did not guide or intervene to cause any empirically detectable changes in the natural behavior of matter, is in clear conflict with the church's historical position. It must be noted that only some varieties of theistic evolution deny that the process was directed.[65] Other types of theistic evolution, like that of Francis Collins, do not specify the nature of the evolutionary process, whether it is undirected or directed.[66] In both cases, however, the idea of an undirected evolutionary process that produces no detectable change in what exists, encounters three problems with the church's doctrinal standards.[67]

First, the early church clearly denounced the idea of an undirected process by which the universe and everything in it came into existence. The church has traditionally considered as absurd the notion that random collisions of existing elements fortuitously resulted in the development of what currently exists. Though the atomic theory against which the early church argued and the contemporary theory of theistic evolution are not the same theory, the basic tenet that some type of natural process acted on random variation to unexpectedly produce what exists today is at the heart of both theories. The church's denunciation of the basic tenet of the earlier theory would seem to carry over to the contemporary theory.

Second, the concept of the universe developing by means of an undirected process like natural selection acting on random mutations does not provide support for the deity of Jesus Christ, as proved by

---

65. As Stephen Meyer underscores in this volume's opening essay ("Scientific and Philosophical Introduction"), "Some proponents of theistic evolution openly affirm that the evolutionary process is an unguided, undirected process. Kenneth Miller, a leading theistic evolutionist and author of *Finding Darwin's God*, has repeatedly stated in editions of his popular textbook [*Biology*] that 'evolution works without either plan or purpose. . . . Evolution is random and undirected'" The passage cited by Meyer is from Kenneth R. Miller and Joseph S. Levine, *Biology* (Upper Saddle River, NJ: Prentice Hall, 1991, 1993, 1995, 1998, 2000), 658. In *Finding Darwin's God*, Miller further describes the process of evolution in these terms: random, undirected, and blind. (Kenneth R. Miller, *Finding Darwin's God: A Scientist's Search for Common Ground between God and Evolution* [New York: HarperCollins, 1999], 51, 102, 137, 145, 244).

66. Again, as Meyer notes in his opening essay ("Scientific and Philosophical Introduction"), "Nevertheless, most theistic evolutionists, including geneticist Francis Collins, perhaps the world's best-known proponent of the position, have been reluctant to clarify what they think about this important issue. In his book *The Language of God*, Collins makes clear his support for universal common descent. He also seems to assume the adequacy of standard evolutionary mechanisms but does not clearly say whether he thinks those mechanisms are directed or undirected—only that they 'could be' directed." See Francis Collins, *The Language of God* (New York: Free Press, 2006), 205.

67. The lack of affirmation of a directed process would face similar objections from those who hold to the historic doctrinal standards of the church.

his creation of all things visible and invisible, whom the church has historically proclaimed to be both Savior and Creator. The church has repeatedly affirmed that Christ's work of creation furnishes proof of his divine nature.

Third, the concept of the universe developing by means of an undirected process that does not give evidence of divine activity contradicts the church's historical position, based on Scripture (e.g., Rom. 1:18–25), that God's creative handiwork reveals and prompts praise for his power, divinity, care, omniscience, sovereignty, wisdom, goodness, and kindness.

(3) Theistic evolution's view that, after creating matter, God did not guide or intervene in the development of that matter until all living things had evolved by purely natural processes, is at odds with the church's doctrinal standards, for several reasons. First, this view introduces an internal inconsistency in the church's historical position that God created not only the visible realm but the invisible realm as well. The church has always affirmed that God created angels, who were originally morally good. But this was a direct supernatural act of God. It could possibly be postulated that God used two very different processes in creating visible things (through an evolutionary process) and in creating invisible things (through some type of supernatural process). But such a divergent approach does not accord well with the church's doctrinal standards, which at least imply a similarity of processes (neither of which was natural) by which God (supernaturally) created these two distinct realms of creatures.

Second, and more significantly, the view of the evolution of the world by purely natural processes stands in contrast with the church's doctrinal standard that God created Adam and Eve as the first human beings and the progenitors of the whole human race. Theistic evolution holds to some theory of pre-Adamite human beings who preceded Adam and Eve. The church has historically denounced this view.

One problem that any pre-Adamite view faces is its conflict with Scripture (Gen. 2:7, 18–25; 3:20; Hosea 6:7; Luke 3:23–38; Acts 17:26; Rom. 5:12–21; 1 Cor. 15:22, 45–48; 1 Tim. 2:13–14). Another problem is that the viewpoint diverges from the church's affirmation of God's creation of Adam and Eve in his image as complex (material and immaterial), originally sinless, moral beings.

Still another problem is that any pre-Adamite position entails natural death in the human realm. In this case, natural death would be the demise of pre-Adamite humans, with legal death—the penalty for the violation of a divine command—being first introduced with Adam and Eve's sin. The church has historically denounced this view.

A final problem encountered by any pre-Adamite theory is explaining the relationship between the originating sin of Adam and Eve—their fall from original uprightness through disobedience to the divine command—and the original sin passed on to all their progeny.[68] Purely natural processes and the existence of thousands (and, through eventual multiplication, millions or billions) of human beings who are not descended from Adam and Eve do not result in moral accountability, universal guilt before God, corruption of human nature passed down from generation to generation, liability to suffer divine punishment, enmity with God, enslavement to sin, depravity and inability, and so forth.[69]

E. What about Evangelical Leaders Who Affirm Theistic Evolution?

What, then, should we make of pastors and other Christian leaders who embrace(d) theistic evolution? The following citations from several leaders are representative: (1) John Stott sought to wed belief in a literal Adam and Eve with some form of theistic evolution:

---

68. All these problems with the pre-Adamite theory present similar problems for the viewpoint espoused by Dennis R. Venema and Scot McKnight in their recent book, *Adam and the Genome: Reading Scripture after Genetic Science* (Grand Rapids, MI: Brazos, 2017). As the church has historically refuted the pre-Adamite theory of human origins, it should be troubled by the stance promoted by that book. It goes against the doctrinal standards historically required for church leadership.

69. Attention may be drawn to a controversial aspect of the doctrinal standards: the church has historically affirmed creation in six literal days in the not too distant past, while many church leaders today hold to a day-age theory, intermittent day theory, a framework (literary) hypothesis theory, or gap theory. They deny, therefore, a recent creation in six literal days. Without entering into the debate between young earth creationists and old earth creationists (a debate on which this book takes no position), the following points underscore that this intramural contest is in a different category than the position of theistic evolutionists:

(1) Both the young earth position and the old earth position affirm divine creation and deny theistic evolution as it is defined in this volume. Both are creationist positions, not evolutionist positions, and therefore accord well with the church's doctrinal affirmation of creation.

(2) The disagreement over the meaning of the Hebrew word *yom* (day) in Genesis 1 is a debate about the meaning of only one word in Scripture and does not involve extrabiblical considerations like random mutations, natural selection, and the like, or a denial of major Christian doctrines such as the specific creation of "all things visible and invisible," the special creation of Adam and Eve as the first human beings, Adam and Eve as initially sinless, the entrance of human death into the world through Adam's sin, and the initial goodness of God's entire creation.

(3) Although some historic creeds affirmed that God created all things in six days, none of them included a specification that these were literal twenty-four-hour days.

But my acceptance of Adam and Eve as historical is not incompatible with my belief that several forms of pre-Adamic 'hominid' may
have existed for thousands of years previously. These hominids
began to advance culturally. They made their cave drawings and
buried their dead. It is conceivable that God created Adam out of
one of them. You may call them *Homo erectus*. I think you may
even call some of them *Homo sapiens*, for these are arbitrary scientific names. But Adam was the first *Homo divinus*, if I may coin a
phrase, the first man to whom may be given the biblical designation
'made in the image of God.'[70]

(2) Tim Keller thinks "God guided some kind of process of natural
selection," yet he also "reject[s] the concept of evolution as an All-
encompassing Theory."[71] (3) Keller relies to a great degree on Derek
Kidner's *Genesis*, a commentary in the Tyndale Old Testament Commentaries series.[72]

(4) C. S. Lewis is claimed by evolutionists and creationists alike,
depending on whether appeal is made to Lewis's embrace of evolution in the *Problem of Pain* (1940) or to the letter he wrote in
1951 to Bernard Acworth, author of *This Progress: The Tragedy of
Evolution*:

I have read nearly the whole of *Evolution* and am glad you sent it. I
must confess it has shaken me: not in my belief in evolution, which
was of the vaguest and most intermittent kind, but in my belief that
the question was wholly unimportant. I wish I was younger. What
inclines me now to think that you may be right in regarding it as
the central and radical lie in the whole web of falsehood that now
governs our lives, is not so much your arguments against it as the
fanatical and twisted attitudes of its defenders.[73]

(5) Princeton theologian B. B. Warfield (1851–1921) is often claimed

---

70. John Stott, *Understanding the Bible*, expanded ed. (Grand Rapids, MI: Zondervan, 1999),
55–56.
71. Tim Keller, *The Reason for God: Belief in an Age of Skepticism* (New York: Penguin,
2008), 94.
72. Derek Kidner, *Genesis*, Tyndale Old Testament Commentaries (Downers Grove, IL: Inter-
Varsity Press, 1967), 26–31.
73. *The Collected Letters of C. S. Lewis*, ed. Walter Hooper, 3 vols. (San Francisco: Harper-
SanFrancisco, 2007), 3:138. See the detailed discussion of Lewis by Lewis scholar John G. West in
this volume's chapter 26, "Darwin in the Dock: C. S. Lewis on Evolution."

as a supporter of evolution.[74] However, while Warfield allowed that it was possible that God used some kind of evolutionary process for parts of creation, he never explicitly affirmed this as his personal belief. In addition, he did not allow for the possibility of human sin or death before Adam and Eve, or the possibility that Adam and Eve were not created as sinless human beings.[75]

What is to be made of the views of these Christian pastors and leaders? None of them explicitly embraced theistic evolution as this book defines it: the view that God created matter and after that did not guide or intervene to cause any empirically detectable change in the natural behavior of matter until all living things had evolved by purely natural processes. Indeed, at least some of them gave evidence of confusion over the nature of theistic evolution and/or expressed hesitation about it. Additionally, none of them denied that Adam and Eve were created in the image of God, that Adam and Eve were originally sinless, that all human beings have descended from Adam and Eve,[76] and that human death began as a result of Adam's sin.

Though in many respects the church looks up to pastors and leaders like these men, the overwhelming consensus of church history still argues against following their lead in embracing some form of theistic evolution.[77]

F. Conclusion

In summary, theistic evolution encounters numerous obstacles. The previous chapters in this book have enumerated those problems: logical contradictions, convoluted and scientifically vacuous explanations, biblical misinterpretations, and the like. The focus of this chapter has

---

74. See B. B. Warfield, *Evolution, Science, and Scripture: Selected Writings*, ed. D. N. Livingstone and M. A. Noll (Grand Rapids, MI: Baker, 2000). For a detailed response, see Fred G. Zaspel, "B. B. Warfield on Creation and Evolution," *Themelios* 35, no. 2 (2010): 198–211.

75. See the detailed discussion of Warfield by Warfield expert Fred Zaspel in this volume's final chapter, "Additional Note: B. B. Warfield Did Not Endorse Theistic Evolution as It Is Understood Today."

76. An exception is Kidner, who allows for the possibility that prior to Adam there were many nearly human creatures, and that, after conferring his image on Adam, and after specially creating Eve (an action that "clinched the fact that there is no natural bridge from animal to man"), God may have "conferred His image on Adam's collaterals, to bring them into the same realm of being" (*Genesis*, 29).

77. In this regard, see the recent events related to senior Old Testament scholar Bruce Waltke as presented in John Currid's chapter in this volume (chapter 28, "Theistic Evolution Is Incompatible with the Teachings of the Old Testament").

been on theistic evolution being incompatible with doctrinal standards required for church leadership, as those doctrinal standards have been developed throughout church history. Please note what this chapter does not do: it does not demonstrate or imply that Christian leaders who embrace theistic evolution are not or cannot be true disciples of Jesus Christ. But this chapter does show that Christian leaders who hold to theistic evolution stand outside the church's historical position.[78]

---

78. Many evangelical pastors and leaders would add that, by reason of holding similar responsibilities, leaders of parachurch organizations should also adhere to these doctrinal standards of the church and thus should not embrace theistic evolution.

31

Additional Note: B. B. Warfield Did Not Endorse Theistic Evolution as It Is Understood Today

FRED G. ZASPEL

SUMMARY

This chapter quotes extensively from published and unpublished writings of Princeton theologian B. B. Warfield on creation and evolution, demonstrating that Warfield did not endorse theistic evolution as it is understood and advocated today.

. . . . .

Despite the claims of some recent authors,[1] renowned Princeton theology professor Benjamin Breckinridge Warfield (1851–1921) was not a theistic evolutionist. In fact, those on both sides of the evolution question who might like to claim him will find him somewhat of a disappointment, for different reasons. That is, he spoke with obvious openness to the possibility of evolution *if* it could be established with a reasonable degree of scientific certainty; however, throughout his

---

1. See especially David N. Livingstone, "B. B. Warfield, the Theory of Evolution, and Early Fundamentalism," *Evangelical Quarterly* 58, no. 1 (January 1986): 78; David N. Livingstone and Mark A. Noll "B. B. Warfield (1851–1921): A Biblical Inerrantist as Evolutionist," *Journal of Presbyterian History* 80, no. 3 (Fall 2002): 153–171; see also B. B. Warfield, *Evolution, Science, and Scripture: Selected Writings* (hereafter *ESS*), ed. Mark A. Noll and David N. Livingstone (Grand Rapids, MI: Baker, 2000).

career he remained skeptical on exactly this score, often even mocking the theory's speculative nature and lack of supporting evidence. Warfield maintained an obvious interest in the subject throughout his life, and through to the end his writings reflect both his openness and his critical suspicion regarding the theory. At the end of it all we must conclude that, although Warfield allowed for the possibility of evolution, he himself remained uncommitted to it, and he clearly rejected most of the main components of theistic evolution as it is understood today.

A. Warfield on Evolution in Summary

Warfield makes it a point to affirm the complete truthfulness of both "volumes" of divine revelation—Scripture and the created order—and that there can be no conflict between the two. He is therefore very willing to allow the established facts of the one to check our interpretations of the other. He recognizes that biblical interpreters, no less than interpreters of physical science, can err, so he is willing to adjust even his own understanding of Scripture to the established facts of scientific findings *once and if* those facts are established. However, he does not view both volumes of revelation as equal in clarity, so he argues that due weight of consideration must be granted accordingly: interpretations of general revelation must give way to the clearer statements of special revelation. Remarks in his review of Luther Townsend's *Evolution or Creation* illustrate his thinking well:

> Rejecting not merely the naturalistic but also the timidly supernaturalistic answers, he insists that man came into the world just as the Bible says he did. Prof. Townsend has his feet planted here on the rock. When it is a question of scriptural declaration versus human conjecture dignified by any name, whether that of philosophy or that of science, the Christian man will know where his belief is due. . . . [Professor Townsend's] trust in the affirmations of the Word of God as the end of all strife will commend itself to every Christian heart.[2]

---

2. (1897) *ESS* 177–178. See also (1895) *ESS* 153–154, where Warfield complains about the view that in "modern thinking . . . it is to science that we must go for the final test of truth." Also (1888) *ESS* 130, where Warfield insists that biblical pronouncement is "the test point" in the discussion and that an evolutionary theory that would "reverse" clear biblical teaching is unacceptable. See also (1896) *The Works of Benjamin B. Warfield*, vol. 9 (Grand Rapids, MI: Baker, 1991), 60–61,

Here Warfield is clear in his conviction that, where physical scientists' claims contradict the plain written Word, they must be rejected. Scripture alone is the final test of truth.

It must be emphasized that Warfield continually reflected a willingness to consider the evolutionists' scientific claims. Throughout his life he very clearly kept abreast of their writings and seems very much at home distinguishing the arguments of one scientist over against another, and of one evolutionary theory over another. And often he reflects striking openness to the idea. For example, in his lecture titled "Evolution or Development," prepared in 1888, he writes,

> The upshot of the whole matter is that there is no *necessary* antagonism of Christianity to evolution, *provided that* we do not hold to too extreme a form of evolution. To adopt any form that does not permit God freely to work apart from law and that does not allow *miraculous* intervention (in the giving of the soul, in creating Eve, etc.) will entail a great reconstruction of Christian doctrine, and a very great lowering of the detailed authority of the Bible. But if we condition the theory by allowing the constant oversight of God in the whole process, and his occasional supernatural interference for the production of *new* beginnings by an actual output of creative force, producing something *new*, i.e., something not included even *in posse* [potentially] in preceding conditions, we may hold to the modified theory of evolution and be Christians in the ordinary orthodox sense.
>
> I say we may do this. Whether we ought to accept evolution, even in this modified sense, is another matter, and I leave it purposely an open question.[3]

This kind of openness on the question is common in Warfield. Throughout his many reviews of evolutionary literature he routinely speaks of evolution as impossible apart from divine intrusion and purpose ("mediate creation"), and he can even assume evolution as a given[4]—until, that is, particular arguments are taken up for dispute.

---

where Warfield argues pointedly for the superiority of written over natural revelation. (Note that I am including, in parentheses, the year for each Warfield citation.)

  3. *ESS*, 130–131, emphasis original.

  4. E.g., (1899) *ESS* 189.

And in these same pieces he can often express his skepticism and doubt also.

It is also important to note that in addressing the question of evolution—as in the sample above—Warfield makes careful distinction between theism and Christianity. That is, he argues on the one hand that the upward progress of evolution is impossible apart from teleology (purpose)—a fact which he comments would necessarily define evolution as a theistic concept. But he further argues that to acknowledge evolution as theoretically possible within a theistic worldview is one thing; affirming that it is a specifically Christian option is quite another.[5] Again, by this he means to say that Scripture just may not allow what a broader theistic view perhaps could.

It must be noted additionally that, within his openness to the possibility of evolution thus considered, Warfield makes a pointed argument that evolution cannot by itself explain the world as it is. Here he makes careful distinction between creation, mediate creation, and evolution. Only creation can explain origins, he insists. And if God has providentially directed various developments of his created order (evolution), this process can never account for factors such as life, personality, consciousness, the human soul, Christ, and so on. Such realities as these require divine, creative "intrusions" (mediate creation). Providence is not creation:

> What he [the Christian] needs to insist on is that providence cannot do the work of creation and is not to be permitted to intrude itself into the sphere of creation, much less to crowd creation out of the recognition of man, merely because it puts itself forward under the new name of evolution.[6]

Warfield was very insistent on this point. He specifically denied that evolution could account for *everything* after Genesis 1:1. Whatever evolution there might have been, it cannot account for the arrival of anything specifically *new*. It cannot explain the original "stuff" of the created order, and it cannot account for other subsequent realities that depend for their existence on divinely creative acts. Thus, for example,

---

5. (1901) *ESS*, 202.
6. (1901) *ESS*, 210; cf. 100.

Warfield could never accept abiogenesis (spontaneous generation of life), and he explicitly denied that evolution could account for life, the origin of the human soul, the human sense of morality, the continued existence of the soul ("immortality") in the afterlife, or the incarnate Christ.

Yet this careful distinction still leaves open the possibility of a theistic evolution carefully defined, and so it becomes necessary to address specific questions that are determinative of Warfield's understanding. The short answer here is that Warfield remained both open to some kind of evolution, within prescribed limits, and yet very skeptical of it.

In agreement with his theological mentor, Charles Hodge, Warfield condemns Darwinian evolution as atheistic, and he complains often of the naturalistic (and anti-supernaturalistic) bias that drives so much of the evolutionists' agenda—and that has rubbed off on the church.[7] He understands the distinction between Darwinian evolution and other theories (although at times, as was increasingly the case generally, Warfield can use the terms "Darwinism" and "evolution" interchangeably), but even so he judges the evolutionary notion itself as essentially atheistic[8] and comments that "the whole body of these evolutionary theories" is "highly speculative," even "hyperspeculative." "None" of them, he insists, "have much obvious claim to be scientific. . . . The whole body of evolutionary constructions prevalent today impresses us simply as a vast mass of speculation which may or may not prove to have a kernel of truth in it."[9]

Warfield insists that any claim that evolution has been proven betrays an overly zealous enthusiasm that exceeds the evidence.[10] And despite his frequent open tone regarding evolution, when he addresses the proffered evidence for it he consistently speaks in a skeptical—and often even mocking—tone. Evolutionary theories, he insists, cry out with questions they cannot answer and rest on faulty logic even of the most elementary sort:[11]

---

7. (1897) *ESS*, 177.
8. (1901) *ESS*, 196.
9. (1907) *ESS*, 244–245; cf. (1908) *ESS*, 255–256.
10. Cf. his 1888 review of James McCosh's *The Religious Aspect of Evolution* (Cornell University Library, 1890); *ESS*, 67.
11. (1891) *ESS*, 143; (1898) *ESS*, 184–187, etc.

The lay reader [speaking inclusively of himself, it seems] is left with strong suspicion that, if their writers did not put evolution into their premises they would hardly find so much of it in their conclusions. . . . The time has already fully come when the adherents of evolution should do something to make it clear to the lay mind that a full accumulation of facts to prove their case can never come—or else abate a little of the confidence of their primary assumption.[12]

Warfield finds no evidence for abiogenesis (that is, the spontaneous generation of life from nonliving matter), as I've already mentioned. He also criticizes evolution on grounds of the geological record, which, "when taken in its whole scope and in its mass of details is confessed as yet irreconcilable with the theory of development by descent." Likewise he finds the appeal to embryology unable to account for the fact that supposed later stages of development retain a transcript of previous stages. So also the evolutionist faces difficulty, he says, with the "limits to the amount of variation to which any organism is liable."[13]

Similarly, Warfield makes much over the seemingly limitless and impossible demands the evolutionary theory makes on time. This, he notes, is becoming more a problem recognized within the evolutionary-scientific community itself. "The matter of time that was a menace to Darwinism at the beginning thus bids fair to become its Waterloo."[14] Warfield allows that the age of the earth—and the age of humanity, for that matter—are not questions of biblical or theological interest. Warfield is willing to allow an "immense" age of the earth, and he is open to a great age of humanity also, but he notes the general consensus of his day that the age of man is probably not more than twenty thousand years.[15] And he contends often that science has not demonstrated the time it demands for the theory.

Warfield speaks often along these lines in criticism of evolutionary theories, insisting throughout his career that evolution remains an unproven hypothesis. But is it not likely that it will be proven? "Is it not at least *probable*?" he asks rhetorically. Cannot prescient minds expect

12. (1898) *ESS*, 184, 187.
13. (1888) *ESS*, 122–124.
14. (1888) *ESS*, 124 (emphasis original).
15. (1911) *ESS*, 272–279.

that proof will be forthcoming? He responds, "Many think so; many more would like to think so; but for myself, I am bound to confess that I have not such prescience. Evolution has not yet made the first step" toward explaining many things. "In an unprejudiced way, looking over the proofs evolution has offered, I am bound to say that none of them is at all, to my mind, stringent."[16]

Warfield insists that laymen have the right to affirm with confidence that the evolutionary hypothesis remains "far from justified by the reasoning with which it has been supported." If the facts are with the evolutionist, they "have themselves to thank for the impression of unreality and fancifulness which they make on the earnest inquirer."[17] In another place he cautions, "We would not willingly drag behind the evidence, indeed—nor would we willingly run ahead of it."[18] Again, "Most men today know the evolutionary construction of the origin of man; there are many of us who would like to be better instructed as to its proofs."[19] Similarly, he writes in 1908,

> What most impresses the layman as he surveys the whole body of these evolutionary theories in the mass is their highly speculative character. If what is called science means careful observation and collection of facts and strict induction from them of the principles governing them, none of these theories have much obvious claim to be scientific. They are speculative hypotheses set forth as possible or conceivable explanations of the facts. . . . For ourselves we confess frankly that the whole body of evolutionary constructions prevalent today impresses us simply as a vast mass of speculation which may or may not prove to have a kernel of truth in it. . . . This looks amazingly like basing facts on theory rather than theory on facts.[20]

In a 1916 review Warfield speaks optimistically of evolution as demonstrating teleology (design): "Imbedded in the very conception of evolution, therefore, is the conception of end." Here he seems to be more open to evolution. But later in this same review he writes more critically of the woeful lack of proof for it:

16. (1888) *ESS*, 121–122.
17. (1891) *ESS*, 143.
18. (1893) *ESS*, 153.
19. (1896) *ESS*, 171.
20. (1908) *ESS*, 244–246.

The discrediting of [Darwin's] doctrine of natural selection as the sufficient cause of evolution leaves the idea of evolution without proof, so far as he is concerned—leaves it, in a word, just where it was before he took the matter up. And there, speaking broadly, it remains until the present day. . . . Evolution is, then, if a fact, not a triumph of the scientist but one of his toughest problems. He does not know how it has taken place; every guess he makes as to how it has taken place proves inadequate to account for it. His main theories have to be supported by subsidiary theories to make them work at all, and these subsidiary theories by yet more far-reaching subsidiary theories of the second rank—until the whole chart is, like the Ptolemaic chart of the heavens, written over with cycle and epicycle and appears ready to break down by its own weight.[21]

So although Warfield can speak of evolution as theistically allowable, his skepticism remains, as do the biblical hurdles as he understands them.

Of the specifically biblical problems, he sees God's creation of Eve as the most obvious, the account of which in Genesis 2 would seem impossible to reconcile with any evolutionary theory. But there are further problems he sees also, such as the origin of the human soul, the human sense of morality, the continued existence of the soul ("immortality") and the afterlife, and the incarnate Christ, none of which can be accounted for on evolutionary grounds.

It is common to hear it said that Warfield understood the creation "days" of Genesis 1 in terms of ages, and this in order to allow time for evolutionary development. This rumor may have arisen from Warfield's openness to a very old earth, if such could be scientifically demonstrated, and his affirmation (with Henry Green) of gaps in the genealogies of Genesis 5 and 11. But it is in fact something Warfield nowhere affirms. Indeed, he explicitly rejects the view that the days represent geological ages and the view that understands them as literal but representative days that stand at the end of a long process of development.[22] And more generally he comments in agreement with another author that "the necessity for indefinitely protracted time does not arise from

---

21. (1916) *ESS*, 319–320.
22. (1892) *ESS*, 145–146.

the facts, but from the attempt to explain the facts without any adequate cause."[23] Warfield speaks similarly in 1908.[24] That is, Warfield was very skeptical even of the time required for evolution. And as will be shown below, he tended to understand the age of humanity in terms of thousands, not millions, of years. At any rate, beyond this, Warfield nowhere specifies his own understanding of the days of Genesis.

B. Elements of Theistic Evolution That Warfield Would Not Accept as Consistent with the Christian Faith

Warfield argues that there are observable gaps in the genealogies of Genesis 5 and 11 and, thus, that Scripture does not speak to the age of earth or of man. He insists that this is not a theological question. Yet he seems to think—presumably on scientific grounds—that humanity cannot be more than ten thousand or perhaps twenty thousand years old.[25] This observation alone seems to rule out most any evolutionary theory of human origins.

More to the point, in his discussion of the evidence available to evolutionists, Warfield seems clearly to rule out the notion of a progressive rise of human forms, asserting that "the earliest human remains differ in type in no respect from the men of our day."[26] He scorns the evolutionary idea of "primitive man," and he expresses agreement with John Laidlaw that "to propound schemes of conciliation between the Mosaic account of creation and the Darwinian pedigree of the lower animals and man would be to repeat an old and, now, an unpardonable blunder."[27] Even so, he also writes that the creation of man by the direct act of God need not "exclude the recognition of the interaction of other forces in the process of his formation." Again, he speaks with allowance, but he goes to pains to emphasize that, in the creation of man, God made something specifically "new," and that the Genesis narrative itself makes this plain. "He was formed, indeed, from the dust of the ground, but he was not so left; rather, God also breathed into his nostrils a breath of life," making him something distinct from

---

23. (1903) *ESS*, 228–229.
24. *ESS*, 242–243.
25. (1911) *Works of Benjamin B. Warfield*, vol. 9, 235–245; . *ESS*, 272–279.
26. (1888) *ESS*, 124.
27. (1895) *ESS*, 165.

all other creation. Thus, he concludes, a "properly limited evolution" is not excluded by the Genesis text *if*—and as always he emphasizes the "if"—an evolutionary process was, in fact, involved. That is to say, he allows for some kind evolution, carefully defined, but he does not commit to it.[28]

In Warfield's 1906 review of James Orr's *The Image of God in Man* he notes Orr's argument that disparate development of mind and body is impossible, that it would be absurd to suggest an evolutionary development of the human body from a brutish source and a sudden creation of the soul by divine fiat. Warfield commends Orr's grasp of man as body and soul in unity and refers to this as "the hinge of the biblical anthropology." Warfield seems in obvious agreement, but in terms of the argument against evolution, he characterizes this as a "minor point"; that is, he does not think this argument will be effective given that it could be answered with a theory of evolution *per saltum* (macroevolution).

Two factors in context militate against taking this as a statement of Warfield's own belief, however. First, earlier in the same review, Warfield praises Orr for his "courage to recognize and assert the irreconcilable-ness of the two views and the impossibility of a compromise between them" and that "the Christian view is the only tenable one in the forum of science itself." Second, Warfield commends Orr's thesis explicitly:

> That he accomplishes this task with distinguished success is the significance of the volume. . . . The book is a distinct contribution to the settlement of the questions with which it deals, and to their settlement in a sane and stable manner. It will come as a boon to many who are oppressed by the persistent pressure upon them of the modern point of view. It cannot help producing in the mind of its readers a notable clearing of the air.[29]

It may be helpful to recall here Warfield's 1897 affirmation, cited above, that "man came into the world just as the Bible says he did," and his understanding of the creation of Eve as the leading obstacle to believing in evolution.

---

28. (1903) *ESS*, 214–216.
29. *ESS*, 230–236.

We find this same tone in a student's (N. W. Harkness) extensive 1898 class notes from Warfield's lectures on the origin of man. Here Warfield makes repeated references to Adam's creation from the dust by God, in his image, God having breathed into him the breath of life, so to make him a living being. Never is the plain understanding of the Genesis narrative questioned; it is always taken at face value and treated as both theology and historic fact. Several times Warfield is quoted as speaking of evolution as "modern speculation" that "runs athwart" the biblical record. Warfield concedes—as throughout his writings—that evolution and creation are not necessarily mutually exclusive, so long as evolution is not understood in reference to origins.[30] "Man is not improved organic matter, but was created new out of nothing, the intrusion of divine power for something entirely new," Harkness records his professor as saying. At this point evolution cannot be reconciled to Scripture. "To agree with us," Warfield argues, the evolutionist "must admit that the chain was broken at one or more points by intrusion of divine power." We must insist, he says, that man was created.

Warfield further instructed his students that Adam was "created perfect" and that this perfection must be understood in physical as well as moral terms. Adam, the first man, was created "mature and without defect." Warfield also debunks the evolutionary idea of "primitive man" and insists that "there is no proof of progressive stages in man." Indeed, sin, having entered, debased and degenerated humanity. Adam was created in God's image, in righteousness and holiness—"an intellectual, moral, voluntary being" who is "like God" and "different from the beasts." Warfield is reported to affirm in summary, "We hold that God made Adam well and good."[31]

This material from the student's lecture notes is in keeping with

---

30. Note that Warfield can speak of creation and evolution as mutually exclusive at times and as *not* mutually exclusive at other times, but the contradiction is only apparent. His point is that creation speaks of origins while evolution can only speak of modification. In this sense they are mutually exclusive: evolution cannot account for origins. But a modification (evolution) of previously created matter is possible, and in this sense the two are *not* mutually exclusive. This is the sense here.

31. Unpublished class notes of N. W. Harkness Jr., from Warfield's Princeton Seminary course on Systematic Theology (1898), 1–5; Princeton Theological Seminary Archives. For more reflections on the original perfection of man, see also Warfield's (1903) *The Power of God unto Salvation* (Grand Rapids, MI: Eerdmans, 1930), 1–9.

what we find in Warfield's lecture itself, prepared originally in 1888, in which he explicitly affirms that Adam is the "first man," that Adam and Eve were created with "a fully developed moral sense" and in "moral perfection," that in Adam the human race stood on probation and fell into sin, and that an evolutionary model would seem to reverse the biblical order of original perfection followed by sinfulness.[32]

All of this from Warfield's lectures is in keeping with what we have of his published writings. Every reference in Warfield to Adam and Eve and to human origins asserts or presumes the historicity of that original pair as the first humans from whom all the race has descended and by whom sin entered the race—a traditional reading of the Genesis narrative. And often the references, always unqualified, are so brief that the reader is left with the impression that this was for Warfield "assumed" ground scarcely in need of defense or further explication.

Warfield touches on the question of the origin of human death only briefly in his review of James Orr's *God's Image in Man*, and he expresses surprise at Orr's ambivalence on this question:

> The problem of the reign of death in that creation which was cursed for man's sake and which is to be with man delivered from the bondage of corruption, presses on some with a somewhat greater weight than seems here to be recognized.[33]

Warfield does not here state this explicitly as his own belief (he says the problem "presses on some," which of course might include himself), and in fact he never failed to point out a better argument for either side in this discussion. But he clearly considers this a strong argument for Orr's position that he should have employed. And given his strong endorsement of Orr's defense of Adam's creation, along with our previously mentioned considerations, it seems that this affirmation, stated in his conclusion, does reflect Warfield's own thinking. The implications of this are telling: Warfield does not seem to allow any room for previous generations of humanity who lived and died prior to Adam.

It is also significant that Warfield here (in his 1906 Orr review) de-

---

32. *ESS*, 128–130.
33. (1906) *ESS*, 236.

scribes the fallenness and hostility of this present world as "the reign of death in that creation which was cursed for man's sake." That is, he seems to indicate that not just human death but also the general fallenness of the larger created order came about as a result of Adam's sin.[34] Warfield reflects this condition elsewhere. First, in 1902 Warfield reviews an essay that treats *4 Esdras*, where the author laments the suffering that is in the world and of Israel in particular. Warfield characterizes this problem as, "the sin and misery of the whole world, plunged by the fall of Adam into every kind of evil."[35] And in his brief 1908 participation in "A Symposium on the Problem of Natural Evils," Warfield again traces all calamity to Adam's sin. Commenting on Luke 13:1ff., he says,

> On the other hand, your questioner in the Bible class argues apparently on the assumption that there is no necessary relation between sin and calamity. He seems to suppose that calamity can fall when there is no sin. In other words he has forgotten (as many forget nowadays) the Fall. Given the Fall, and there is a place for the use of calamity in the moral government of the world. God may then visit or withhold the suffering which is due to all, as best suits his ends. . . . If there had been no Fall, however, there would be no such use made of calamity.[36]

Warfield speaks only in passing to the question of God's direct intervention in the creation of animals "after their kind." He held that God created all this "lower creation," but he nowhere exactly specifies it as *immediate* creation. He can allow only the possibility of "mediate creation," and he remarks that "let the sea/earth bring forth" can be so understood. But at the same time he argues vigorously that even a divinely guided developmental process (providence) cannot do the work of creation. He simply affirms God's creation of the animals "after their kinds."[37]

Moreover, given (1) Warfield's general assessment of evolution as

---

34. (1906) *ESS*, 236.
35. *The Bible Student*, September 1902, 177.
36. *The Biblical World* 31:2 (February 1908), 124. Cf. (1916) B. B. Warfield, *Faith and Life* (Carlisle, PA: Banner of Truth, 1974), 330–332.
37. (1903) *ESS* 211–215. Cf. Harkness class notes.

speculative, (2) his expressed acceptance of the Genesis record elsewhere, (3) his criticism of abiogenesis and his insistence that life is a divinely creative act (something specifically "new" that evolution cannot accomplish), and (4) his observations that the fossil records provide no indication of transitional forms,[38] it is safe to assume that he held to God's direct intervention in the creation of animal "kinds."

Warfield's thinking on these defining issues is rather traditional. We may say in summary that Warfield held the following:

- the creation of Adam from the dust of the ground
- the creation of Eve from Adam
- that Adam and Eve were the original pair
- that Adam and Eve were not highly developed animals
- that all humanity has descended from Adam and Eve
- that humanity was created in moral and physical perfection
- that sin entered humanity by Adam
- that humanity has not progressed from primitive man upward but has fallen because of sin
- that human death entered by Adam
- that the created order itself is in disarray because of Adam's sin
- that the arrival of the animal world, as it is, also required divine, creative intervention

In his "Biblical and Theological Introduction" to this book, Wayne Grudem has enumerated twelve points at which theistic evolution as currently endorsed differs from the biblical account.[39] We can review these twelve points and describe Warfield's understanding regarding each:

1. Adam and Eve were not the first human beings (and perhaps they never even existed).
Warfield would deny this. He affirmed that Adam and Eve were historic persons and were the original human pair.

2. Adam and Eve were born from human parents.
Warfield would deny this. He affirmed repeatedly that Adam and Eve were created by God as the first human pair.

---

38. (1908) *ESS* 253.
39. See pages 72–73.

3. God did not act directly or specially to create Adam out of dust from the ground.
Warfield would deny this. He affirmed Adam's creation by God from the ground as per the Genesis narrative.

4. God did not directly create Eve from a rib taken from Adam's side.
Warfield would deny this. He affirmed that Eve's creation from Adam was the leading obstacle to a Christian's embracing of evolution.

5. Adam and Eve were never sinless human beings.
Warfield would deny this. He affirmed the original perfection of Adam and Eve and their fall from that perfect state.

6. Adam and Eve did not commit the first human sins, for human beings were doing morally evil things long before Adam and Eve.
Warfield would deny this. He affirmed that sin entered humanity by Adam.

7. Human death did not begin as a result of Adam's sin, for human beings existed long before Adam and Eve and they were always subject to death.
Warfield seemed to deny this. He seemed to affirm that death came to humanity and to the created order by Adam's sin.

8. Not all human beings have descended from Adam and Eve, for there were thousands of other human beings on Earth at the time that God chose two of them as Adam and Eve.
Warfield would deny this. He affirmed that Adam and Eve were the original humans and that all humanity descended from them and is united in them.

9. God did not directly act in the natural world to create different "kinds" of fish, birds, and land animals.
Warfield would deny this. Although he spoke to this issue only in passing, he spoke to it and the related discussion sufficiently to affirm God's intervention in the creation of animal "kinds."

10. God did not "rest" from his work of creation or stop any special creative activity after plants, animals, and human beings appeared on the earth.

Warfield would deny this. He affirmed God's rest on the seventh day:

> He who needed no rest, in the greatness of his condescension, rested from the work which he had creatively made, that by his example he might woo man to his needed rest. The Sabbath, then, is not an invention of man's, but a creation of God's. . . . God rested, not because he was weary, or needed an intermission in his labors; but because he had completed the task he had set for himself (we speak as a man) and had completed it well. "And God *finished* his work which he had made"; and God saw everything that he had made, and behold it was *very good*."[40]

11. God never created an originally "very good" natural world in the sense of a world that was a safe environment, free of thorns and thistles and similar harmful things.
Warfield would deny this. He affirmed the fallenness of the perfect created order in Adam.

12. After Adam and Eve sinned, God did not place any curse on the world that changed the workings of the natural world and made it more hostile to mankind.
Warfield would deny this. He affirmed the fallenness of the created order as a result of Adam's sin.

C. Warfield in Transition?

One question remains: Did Warfield change his position later in life? The notion that Warfield was a theistic evolutionist is common, fueled especially by various works by David Livingstone and Mark Noll, most notably their collection of Warfield's writings in *Evolution, Science, and Scripture: Selected Writings.*[41] Livingstone and Noll argue that Warfield's position on this question changed—that late in his career he came again to embrace an evolutionary theory of origins. I have addressed this point at greater length elsewhere,[42] but I can make a few summary remarks here.

---

40. (1915) "The Foundations of the Sabbath in the Word of God," *Selected Shorter Writings of Benjamin B. Warfield*, vol. 1, John E. Meeter, ed. (Philipsburg: Presbyterian & Reformed, 1980), 309, 318.
41. This is the work cited in note 1 above and cited thereafter as *ESS*.
42. See my "B. B. Warfield on Creation and Evolution" *Themelios* 35, no. 2 (2010): 198–211. Also chapter 9 in my *The Theology of B. B. Warfield: A Systematic Summary* (Wheaton, IL: Crossway, 2010).

First, all sides acknowledge that Warfield's lecture, "Evolution or Development," prepared in 1888, reflects his clear skepticism regarding the theory. At least six observations are worthy of note here.

1. It would be possible to trace sentiments of Warfield's skepticism expressed here throughout his later writings also.

2. Warfield's later "positive" statements about evolution are substantively no more positive or open than some found in his 1888 lecture. If we agree that in 1888 he was also skeptical of evolution, then his later allowances can scarcely indicate anything more. This observation is especially relevant given Warfield's continued expressions of skepticism. *Both* his openness to evolution and his skepticism regarding it continued to the last.

3. It appears that Warfield continued to use this 1888 lecture, with various emendations, at least through 1902 (when he began to share the teaching load with C. W. Hodge Jr., who eventually succeeded him, and whose lectures, interestingly, followed Warfield's closely).

4. Some of the emendations Warfield added to the lecture along the way seem in fact to reflect a strengthening of his convictions against evolution, not a weakening.

5. We have no later or replacement lecture from Warfield on this topic—this was the last he used, and he preserved it along with his other works to be examined by those coming after him.

6. For a theologian the stature of Warfield to change course after passing the age of 50 on an issue so well studied and on which he had pronounced so often and so clearly, would be remarkable indeed. I don't see any evidence for it.

One major factor lending confusion to the question of Warfield's later commitments regarding evolution is a 1915 essay on Calvin's doctrine of creation in which Warfield argued that Calvin understood the work of the creation week (Genesis 1) in evolutionary terms. On the face of it, this may seem to reflect Warfield's own persuasion—why else would he make such an unprecedented claim regarding the Reformer?

But there is more to the story. In this essay, Warfield points out that Calvin held to a literal six-day creation week and a young earth of less than six thousand years, so we must at least say that, in his famous (notorious?) claim that Calvin's doctrine of creation was "an evolutionary one," Warfield makes no connection to any evolutionary theory current in his own day. There is not enough time allowed.

More substantively, what Warfield refers to as "evolution" in this essay is nothing more than "second causes" which God employed in forming the world. (Of course, Calvin would have had no idea of Darwin's theory of evolution, which was published nearly three hundred years after Calvin's death.) Warfield argues that, for Calvin, "creation" proper refers only to the original fiat of Genesis 1:1 (and to the origin of each human soul). God "created" the original world stuff (Gen. 1:1), and it is from this that the rest of the created order was brought forth and formed.[43] This is what Warfield refers to as Calvin's "evolutionary" view. And he acknowledges that Calvin makes no indication as to just how the rest of the created order thus "evolved." Clearly, Warfield uses the term "evolution" somewhat loosely here. He certainly does not refer to any particular *theory* of evolution. Indeed, he notes that Calvin held no such "theory" but simply believed that the Creator employed "second causes" in the development of the world in six days from the original world-stuff. Moreover, Warfield judges this "evolutionary" teaching of Calvin to be "inadequate." All considered, whatever Warfield's motivations were in describing Calvin's teaching as evolutionary, there just is not enough evidence to attribute any evolutionary theory to Warfield himself.

Indeed, one year later Warfield insists that evolution necessarily entails teleology, purpose, mind, intelligence, and therefore a Designer. He argues that, given the current rejection of natural selection, evolution is left without explanation. Then he offers his latest (final) assessment of the various evolutionary theories:

> The discrediting of [Darwin's] doctrine of natural selection as the sufficient cause of evolution leaves the idea of evolution without proof. . . . And there, speaking broadly, it remains until the present day. . . . Evolution is, then, if a fact, not a triumph of the scientist but one of his toughest problems.[44]

43. *The Works of Benjamin B. Warfield*, vol. 5 (Grand Rapids, MI: Baker, 1991), 304–305.
44. (1916) *ESS*, 319–320. For the larger quote see page 960 above.

Finally, we must note that in a 1916 piece written for the college newspaper, Warfield reminisces on his time as an undergraduate student in Princeton. Here Warfield affirms that he was a convinced (theistic) evolutionist in his teenage years when he entered the College of New Jersey (Princeton), but he also affirms that he had abandoned the theory by the time he was thirty years old (1881). That is, although theistic evolution was championed by his revered professor and college president James McCosh, Warfield says that he had outgrown it himself early on, and the clear implication is that as he was writing now at age 67, just four years before his death, his evolutionary beliefs remained a thing of the past.[45]

D. Conclusion

The claim that Warfield held to theistic evolution goes beyond the evidence. Throughout the years of his writing on the subject, Warfield spoke with marked openness and even allowance of evolution. Many of these statements were obviously made simply for the sake of argument, and many are not so obvious. But it must be recognized that all along, at the very same time and through to the end, Warfield spoke very critically of evolution, pointing out the obstacles to accepting it, characterizing it as mere speculation, and commending refutations of it (such as Orr's). He spoke with evidently genuine openness to the idea, and this is doubtless the source of the confusion on the question; in fact, it may be said that the confusion is Warfield's own fault. But his openness to evolution is only half the picture, for all along he also spoke critically of its purely "speculative" character. And in fact he said late in life that he had left it in his youth.

Moreover, he very clearly held that Adam and Eve (created from Adam) were historical persons, that they were created perfect, that the entire human race is descended from them, that theirs was the first human sin, and that the human race and all creation with it is fallen in Adam. This would seem to rule out theistic evolution as we understand it today, and in fact it must be admitted that it would be impossible to identify any theory of evolution that Warfield himself held. Again, the

---

45. "Personal Recollections of Princeton Undergraduate Life IV—The Coming of Dr. McCosh," *Princeton Alumni Weekly* 16:28 (April 19, 1916): 652.

claim that Warfield held to theistic evolution goes beyond the evidence. Indeed, the claim seems to go *against* the evidence.

We may say this in summary:

- Warfield seemed very open to evolution and spoke allowingly of it.
- Warfield at the same time was very critical of evolution, questioned its scientific grounding, mocked its speculative character and logical fallacies, and recognized the biblical obstacles to it. Indeed, his last assessment of evolutionary theories is sharply critical.
- It would be impossible to identify any specific evolutionary theory that Warfield allegedly held.
- Warfield did not hold to the essentials of any theistic evolutionary theory held today (as enumerated in Grudem's twelve points above).
- Warfield asserted in 1916 that he had left theistic evolution behind him years earlier.

There, it seems, we must leave it also.

General Index

Scripture Index